(continued from front page)

" I just wanted to thank you for helping me get a great score
on the AP U.S. History exam... Thank you for making great test preps! "
Student, Los Angeles, CA

" Your *Fundamentals of Engineering Exam* book was the absolute best
preparation I could have had for the exam, and it is one of the major
reasons I did so well and passed the FE on my first try. "
Student, Sweetwater, TN

" I used your book to prepare for the test and found that the advice and the sample tests were highly relevant... Without using any other material, I earned very
high scores and will be going to the graduate school of my choice. "
Student, New Orleans, LA

" What I found in your book was a wealth of information sufficient to shore up
my basic skills in math and verbal... The section on analytical ability was
excellent. The practice tests were challenging and the answer explanations most
helpful. It certainly is the *Best Test Prep for the GRE*! "
Student, Pullman, WA

" I really appreciate the help from your excellent book. Please keep up
the great work. "
Student, Albuquerque, NM

" I am writing to thank you for your test preparation... your book helped me
immeasurably and I have nothing but praise for your *GRE* preparation."
Student, Benton Harbor, MI

The Best Test Preparation for the

AP
Human
Geography Exam

With REA's TESTware® on CD-ROM

Christian L. Sawyer
AP Human Geography Instructor
Hillsboro High School
Nashville, Tennessee

Research & Education Association
Visit our website at
www.rea.com

Research & Education Association
61 Ethel Road West
Piscataway, New Jersey 08854
E-mail: info@rea.com

The Best Test Preparation for the
AP HUMAN GEOGRAPHY EXAM
With TEST*ware* on CD-ROM

Printed in the United States of America

Library of Congress Control Number 2007941759

ISBN 13: 978-0-7386-0371-1
ISBN 10: 0-7386-0371-6

Windows® is a registered trademark of Microsoft Corporation.

A08-0101

CONTENTS

About Our Author

Christian Sawyer has implemented and taught AP Human Geography and other Advanced Placement and standard-level social studies courses at Hillsboro High School in Nashville, Tennessee, and Assumption High School in Louisville, Kentucky. Additionally, he has been an adjunct instructor at Vanderbilt University, a guest instructor in Taiwan, an instructor of geopolitics at the Johns Hopkins Center for Talented Youth, and an Atlantik-Brücke Fellow studying German-American relations with the Tennessee Department of Education. Mr. Sawyer's work in advocating for broader geographic studies led to his being named the 2006 National Outstanding Secondary Social Studies Teacher of the Year by the National Council for the Social Studies, the 2006 Tennessee Outstanding Social Studies Teacher of the Year by the Tennessee Council for the Social Studies, a White House Fellows Regional Finalist, and a "Local Hero" by Vanderbilt University's Peabody School of Education. In addition to his teaching, Mr. Sawyer has written and edited curriculum for the Modern Red Schoolhouse Institute and other publishers. In his spare time, Mr. Sawyer serves on statewide committees, is a community volunteer, and enjoys working in community theater. A native of Louisville, Kentucky, Mr. Sawyer graduated with highest distinction, Phi Beta Kappa, from the Honors Program at the University of North Carolina at Chapel Hill. Awarded a fellowship at Vanderbilt's Peabody School of Education, Mr. Sawyer earned a master's degree in education and was inducted into the nation's oldest education honor society, Kappa Delta Pi.

About Our Expert Reviewer

Daryl Wenner is a doctoral candidate in geography at the University of Tennessee, where he is specializing in cultural and urban geography. He earned his master's degree in geography at South Dakota State University and his bachelor's degree at Pennsylvania State University. He is currently an instructor at South College in Knoxville, Tennessee. Mr. Wenner is a volunteer with the Tennessee Geographic Bee and the Tennessee Geographic Alliance and has taught more than a thousand elementary and middle school students about geography.

A Note from the Author

Dear AP Human Geography Student,

Have you ever wondered how many McDonald's restaurants there are in the world? Why have the Israelis and Palestinians been in conflict for so long? What is Hinduism, and where did it start? Is English the most widely spoken language on the earth? How has the spread of Wal-Mart stores changed rural landscapes?

You have? Then you are in the right place, in perhaps one of the most powerful and useful courses you will ever take. Because human geography will help you answer these types of questions and give you a new understanding of your world. Studying human geography will push you to develop a new set of tools to use in analyzing the patterns and processes that define the earth's geographic realities—its people and places. It is a course about the map and the fascinating patterns of people behind the map.

In your human geography studies, you will probably investigate interesting questions and issues related to this advanced cultural analysis. Why has India faced a population expansion crisis, while some European countries have declining birth rates? How did current economic patterns develop? For example, why is eastern Europe less well developed than western Europe? And how has colonialism continued to have an impact on newly independent states? How does the South American city structure and layout compare with the North American pattern? How does gentrification of urban areas affect the low-income residents of those areas?

In searching for solutions to these fascinating questions, you should take pride in your studies but also realize that you have a duty to learn about the world and its people with the aim of sharing that information with others. You will probably come to see the world as beautifully diverse, but often quite cruelly unequal. Take what you learn and try to improve the world in your own way. Join the efforts of an organization that you think is bettering the world—Invisible Children, Doctors Without Borders, Save Darfur, or any other program you feel is trying to improve the human condition.

You will likely feel empowered after having completed this introductory course in human geography. But remember, this is only the beginning of your geographic journey. Many students have commented that once they completed their AP Human Geography course, they were unable to look at the world in quite the same way as before. This course will change your paradigm of thought. You will develop "geographic eyes," opening your mind to finding reasons for patterns that you see in the landscapes all around.

With your new set of skills and knowledge, travel to new places, search for innovative solutions, build new bridges. After all, learning about the world is ultimately learning more about yourself. I remember a student in one of my AP human geography classes telling me, after touring a glorious Hindu temple in our region, "Mr. Sawyer, before your class, I had no idea this temple or Hindus even existed in Nashville." I smiled and thought of the words of T.S. Eliot:, "At the end of all exploring will be to arrive where we started and know the place for the first time."

Best of luck to you in your studies,

Christian L. Sawyer

Author Acknowledgments

I am sincerely thankful for my supportive colleagues, friends, and family (especially my dear mother, father, and brothers) for their belief in me. I am especially appreciative of the insightful additions made by Daryl Wenner, who generously opened his test files to contribute several multiple-choice questions to this project. I also want to thank my "Geo Scholar," Roger Diehl, for his helpful reviews from a student's perspective, and Diane Goldschmidt for her motivational leadership as my editor. I would like to dedicate this project both to my brilliant "Geo Scholars" and to my beloved grandmother, MJ.

MJ, my book is on your nightstand.

—Christian Sawyer

About Research & Education Association

Founded in 1959, Research & Education Association is dedicated to publishing the finest and most effective educational materials—including software, study guides, and test preps—for students in middle school, high school, college, graduate school, and beyond. Today, REA's wide-ranging catalog is a leading resource for teachers, students, and professionals. We invite you to visit us at *www.rea.com* to find out how "REA is making the world smarter."

Acknowledgments

In addition to our author, we would like to thank Larry B. Kling, Vice President, Editorial, for supervising development; Pam Weston, Vice President, Publishing, for setting the quality standards for production integrity and managing the publication to completion; John Cording, Vice President, Technology, for coordinating the design and development of REA's TEST*ware*®; Diane Goldschmidt, Senior Editor, for preflight editorial review; Jeff LoBalbo, Senior Graphic Artist, for his graphic arts contributions and post-production file mapping; Heena Patel, Technology Project Manager, for design contributions and software testing efforts; Christine Saul, Senior Graphic Artist, for cover design; and Kathy Caratozzolo of Caragraphics for typesetting the manuscript. We also extend special thanks to Mapping Specialists, Inc., for rendering many of the maps contained in the book.

AP Human Geography Study Schedule

This study schedule allows for thorough preparation for the AP Human Geography exam. Although it is designed for eight weeks, it can be condensed into a four-week course by collapsing each two-week period into a single week. Be sure to set aside at least two hours each day to study. Bear in mind that the more time you spend studying, the more prepared and relaxed you will feel on the day of the exam.

Week	Activity
1	Acquaint yourself with the AP Human Geography exam by reading Chapter 1, "Excelling on the AP Human Geography Exam." You will be introduced to key aspects of the exam and be given tips for success on the exam. Take Practice Exam 1 on CD-ROM and score the exam.
2	Carefully read and study Chapter 2, "Geography: Its Nature and Perspectives." Use the Chapter Review and Pre-Exam Practice sections to be certain that you understand the content of the chapter.
3	Read and study Chapter 3, "Population." Assess your knowledge by using the Chapter Review and Pre-Exam Practice sections included at the end of the chapter.
4	Carefully read and study Chapter 4, "Cultural Patterns and Processes." Use the Chapter Review and Pre-Exam Practice sections to be certain that you understand the content of the chapter.
5	Read and study Chapter 5, "Political Organization of Space." Use the Chapter Review and Pre-Exam Practice sections to assess your knowledge of the chapter's content.
6	Carefully read and study Chapter 6, "Agricultural and Rural Land Use." Assess your knowledge by using the Chapter Review and Pre-Exam Practice sections included at the end of the chapter.
7	Read and study Chapter 7, "Industrialization and Economic Development." Use the Chapter Review and Pre-Exam Practice sections to be certain that you understand the content of the chapter.
8	Read and study Chapter 8, "Cities and Urban Land Use." Take Practice Exam 2 on CD-ROM. Use the diagnostic table included with the exam to identify areas where you may need more review. Study any areas in which you consider yourself to be weak by using the Human Geography Review in this book and any other reliable sources you have on hand. If time allows, and you would like to enhance your feel for the rhythm and flow of the exam, take the printed version of our practice exams found in this book.

CHAPTER 1

Excelling on the
AP Human Geography Exam

Excelling on the AP Human Geography Exam

About This Book and TESTware®

This book, along with our companion TESTware® software, provides an accurate and complete representation of the Advanced Placement Examination in Human Geography. REA's practice exams are based on the format of the most recently administered AP Human Geography exam and each includes every type of question that you can expect to encounter on the real test. Following each of our practice tests is an answer key, complete with detailed explanations designed to clarify the material for you. By using the subject reviews, completing both practice tests, and studying the explanations that follow, you will put yourself in the best possible position to do well on the actual test.

The two practice exams are also included on the enclosed TESTware® CD-ROM. The software provides timed conditions and instant, accurate scoring, which makes it all the easier to pinpoint your strengths and weaknesses.

About the Exam

The Advanced Placement Human Geography examination is offered each May at participating schools and multi-school centers throughout the world.

The Advanced Placement Program is designed to allow high school students to pursue college-level studies while attending high school. The participating colleges, in turn, grant credit and/or advanced placement to students who do well on the examinations.

The Advanced Placement Human Geography course is designed to be the equivalent of a college introductory Human Geography course.

AP Human Geography Exam Format and Content

The AP Human Geography exam is approximately two hours and fifteen minutes long. Each section of the exam is completed separately and each counts for half of the student's score.

The exam is divided into two sections:

Section I: The multiple-choice section of the exam is 60 minutes long and contains 75 questions. The approximate breakdown of topics covered includes the following:

Topic	Approximate Percentage
Geography: Its Nature and Perspectives	5–10%
Population	13–17%
Cultural Patterns and Processes	13–17%
Political Organization of Space	13–17%
Agriculture and Rural Land Use	13–17%
Industrialization and Economic Development	13–17%
Cities and Urban Land Use	13–17%

Each question in the multiple-choice section has five possible answer choices. Each correct answer is worth one point, and 1/4 point is deducted for each incorrect answer.

Section II: This is the free-response section of the exam. Students are asked to answer three constructed-response questions in the allotted 75 minutes. Questions may be based on stimulus material such as maps, graphs, photographs, diagrams and verbal descriptions. Students are expected to use their analytical and organizational skills in writing their responses. While a formal essay is not required, a simple listing of facts will not receive a high score. All three questions are required to be answered and are weighted equally.

For more information about what to include on the essays, how to manage the time allotted, and how they are scored, please visit the AP Human Geography outline provided by the College Board at *www.collegeboard.com*.

You may find the AP Human Geography exam considerably more difficult than many classroom exams. In order to measure the full range of your ability in Human Geography, the AP exams are designed to produce average scores of approximately 50% of the maximum possible score for the multiple-choice and essay sections. Therefore, you should not expect to attain a perfect or even near-perfect score.

How to Use This Book and TEST*ware*®

What do I study first?

To begin your studies, read over the introduction and the suggestions for test taking. Take Practice Exam 1 on CD-ROM to determine your strengths and weaknesses, and then study the course review material, focusing on your specific problem areas. Studying the review material thoroughly will reinforce the basic skills you will need to do well on the exam. Make sure to follow up your diagnostic work by taking Practice Exam 2 on CD-ROM to become familiar with the format and feel of the AP Human Geography exam.

To best utilize your study time, follow our Study Schedule, which you will find in the front of this book. The schedule is based on an eight-week program, but if necessary can be condensed to four weeks by combining each two-week period into one week.

When should I start studying?

It is never too early to start studying for the AP Human Geography examination. The earlier you begin, the more time you will have to sharpen your skills. Do not procrastinate! Cramming is *not* an effective way to study, since it does not allow you the time needed to learn the test material. The sooner you learn the format of the exam, the more time you will have to familiarize yourself with it.

SSD accommodations for students with disabilities

Many students qualify for extra time to take the AP Human Geography exam and our TEST*ware*® can be adapted to accommodate your time extension. This allows you to practice under the same extended-time accommodations that you will receive on the actual test day. To customize your TEST*ware*® to suit the most common extensions, visit our website at *http://www.rea.com/ssd.*

About Our Review Section

This book contains an AP Human Geography Course Review that can be used as both a primer and as a quick reference while taking the practice exams. Our course review is meant to complement your AP Human Geography textbook and is by no means exhaustive. By studying our review along with your text, you will be well prepared for the exam.

Scoring the Official Exams

The College Board creates a formula (which changes slightly every year) to convert raw scores into composite scores grouped into broad AP grade categories. The weights for the multiple-choice sections are determined by the Chief Reader, who uses a process called *equating*. This process compares the current year's exam performance on selected multiple-choice questions to that of a previous year, establishing a level of achievement for the current year's group and a degree of difficulty for the current exam. This data is combined with historical trends and the reader's professional evaluation to determine the weights and tables.

The AP free-response is graded by teacher volunteers, grouped at scoring tables, and led by a chief faculty consultant. The consultant sets the grading scale that translates the raw score into the composite score. Past grading illustrations are available to teachers from the College Board, and may be ordered using the contact information given in this chapter. These actual examples of student responses and a grade analysis can be of great assistance to both the student and the teacher as a learning or review tool.

When will I know my score?

In July, a grade report will be sent to you, your high school, and the college you chose to notify. The report will include scores for all the AP exams you have taken up to that point and will show a grade of between 1 and 5. Normally, colleges participating in the Advanced Placement Program will recognize grades of 3 or better.

Your grade will be used by your college of choice to determine placement in its Human Geography program. This grade will vary in significance from college to college, and is used with other academic information to determine placement. Contact your college admissions office for more information regarding its use of AP grades.

Tips for Success on the AP Human Geography Exam

- Invent your own "review system." Get a new binder and label it "AP Human Geo Review Binder." Place all review sheets and other pertinent material in this binder for cumulative reviewing.

- Make flashcards for each key term in the content review and cumulatively review the terms each night. Define the term in your own words, rather than copying the definition from the glossary. Write related notes and ideas to each flashcard.

- Review cumulatively. For example, during the week you are studying Chapter 3, review the flashcards and notes for the chapters you previously studied.

- Throw your flashcards in the air and stack them into related groups. Quiz yourself and others. Make a pact with yourself that if you get one key term wrong in a stack, you have to start the stack over again. Keep going until you get the entire stack correct!

- As you study each review chapter in this book, review your textbook's corresponding chapter and your class notes.

- Save magazine and newspaper articles that relate to what you learn in your AP Human Geography course. Put them in a folder to read later.

- Keep a chart of the geographic models that you encounter throughout your review. Make a flashcard for each model. Analyze each model's strengths and weaknesses.

- As you review, keep a list of questions for which you need answers. Seek the help of your teacher in getting the answers. Your questions can lead to important new ideas and further discussions.

- Form a study group with other trustworthy students studying AP Human Geography. (Remember, friends don't always make the best study partners.) Find a quiet place where the group can meet regularly to study and keep the group focused. Put one person in charge of "re-teaching" each section in the course and designing a "crash study guide" for the rest of the group.

- As you prepare for the free-response section, try writing your own free-response questions and sharing them with other students.

- As an alternative to the suggested study schedule provided in this book, try taking one of the practice exams *before* you study the content review chapters. By doing this, you can be aware of your strengths and weaknesses before you start preparing for the exam.

- If multiple-choice questions are not your strongest skill, carefully analyze your answers in each of the review chapters in this book and on the practice tests. Be sure to read the answer explanations to see why the selected choice is correct and the others are wrong. Also, remember that you do *not* have to get 100% of the multiple-choice questions correct! A student can earn a good passing score by answering less than 50% of the multiple-choice questions correctly, if he/she does well on the Free Response Section.

- When you take the practice tests in this book, simulate real testing conditions. Find a quiet place and time yourself. Ask your teacher to administer a "mock" AP exam.

- Trust in your ability! If you prepare in advance, apply your intelligence, and tap into what AP Human Geography is really about, then you will succeed on the exam. However, the course should be more important to you than your test score. Recent research by test-makers shows that even students who do not earn a passing score on the AP exam are <u>more</u> successful in college than their peers who did not attempt an AP course. You will be a more powerful thinker, a better-prepared college student, and a more enriched person for having applied your time and talents to learning about the world and its people. You're in a win-win situation—there is no way to lose!

Tips for Success on the Free-Response Section of the Exam

After the multiple-choice section of the exam, you will have a short break. Afterwards, you will move on to Section II, the free-response section. This section requires that you answer three free-response questions (called FRQs) in 75 minutes. A pen is required for this section, so bring three of your favorite black or blue-ink pens with you (no markers or jelly pens, please!). You must answer all three questions and each question usually has multiple parts. It is recommended that you spend about 25 minutes on each one. The best way to approach this section is to spend a few minutes previewing all of the questions. After you have read through all of them, choose one and jump right in!

Begin by taking three to five minutes to outline your response to the FRQ or "free-writing" your initial thoughts. Then spend about 20 minutes on that question, formulating your official response in the answer booklet. Your proctor will not stop you until the end of the 75 minutes, so pace yourself to answer each of the three FRQs in the allotted time. Be sure to write the number of the question you are answering at the top of each answer-booklet page. Start each of your free-response answers on a new page in your answer booklet—in other words, don't cram your response to question 1 on the same page as your response to question 2.

Historically, the free-response questions have been a mix of recall and critical thinking questions. Often, the FRQs ask you to define a key term from the course and then calls upon you to apply that concept to a map, figure, or analysis. For example, a recent FRQ asked the students to define "distance decay." Then, the students applied that term to a map of migration streams provided with the exam. In the past, the three FRQs on the exam have been a well-balanced mix of concepts from across the AP Human Geography curriculum.

If you have taken AP History or English courses or exams, it's highly likely that you were instructed to write a formal essay in response to the free-response questions. AP Human Geography is different—a formal essay is NOT required! Hooray! Think of the FRQs as short-answer questions. Don't bother with a thesis statement or a conclusion. Jump right into your response. The graders do not give you points for a thesis or a conclusion statement; rather, they grade the *content* that you include in your response. Look through the review chapters and the practice exams in this book to find sample AP-like scoring rubrics that are similar to the rubrics the actual AP graders are likely to use in scoring your FRQ responses. Use these to score your own responses.

In previous years, the official AP exam instructions recommend that you label and number each part of your response in the margins of your answer booklet to keep your reader aware of where you are in your response to the FRQ. For example, if you are answering FRQ 1, part A, label your response in the margin "1A." When you move to part B, write "1B" in the margin. Continue for each subsequent part. Also, as previously mentioned, remember to put the FRQ number at the top of the each answer booklet page. If you're answering FRQ 1, write "1" in the box at the top of the answer-booklet page and label each subpart of your response in the margin.

While a formal essay is not required (and not really wanted), simply listing facts is NOT enough. Write complete sentences with coherent, supporting thoughts (like a short answer). You should also support your responses with accurate geographic examples whenever possible. If the FRQ calls for examples from a particular region, be certain you use examples from that region and link your examples to the question's prompt. AP readers have commented that students often confuse geographic regions. Therefore, while studying for the exam, take time to review geographic regions: East Asia, Southwest Asia, Western Europe, Eastern Europe, North America, etc. Familiarize yourself with examples and situations in each region that you could use in your responses.

An AP reader, who is either a college professor or an experienced AP teacher, will score your answers. Teams of graders will be formed and each team will specialize in grading one of the questions. Each grader will use a scoring rubric that spells out *exactly* how to give points while grading the FRQ. Therefore, the graders don't have much flexibility in scoring your responses. They have to follow the rubric created. Remember also that they *award* points; they don't take points off. Thus, while reading FRQ 1, part A, the grader will look for specific elements in your response to give you points. If you don't have those specific parts in your response, you will not get the points. It's that simple.

So how can you make sure you get the points in each part of the FRQ? First, **make sure you answer the question being asked**. Carefully study the language used in the questions. Circle the key words in the FRQ. If it says "define," write a definition. If it says "evaluate," analyze the different parts of the issue.

Second, **make sure you answer all parts of the question**. If the question asks you to define a term and then offer an example, be sure you address both parts of that multi-part question.

Third, **check to see if the FRQ calls for a specific type of example**. The question might ask you for an example from a particular historical era or a particular region on the map. The FRQ may ask you to give an example of a *country* or it may call for you to cite a *region*—so be careful to use the appropriate example. Don't use an example that doesn't fit. Choose your example carefully and integrate it into your response.

Fourth, **be geographically analytical in your response.** Avoid injecting personal opinions and side-comments that distract from your direct response to the question. Try to draw together appropriate relationships from different parts of the course. For example, if the question asks you to discuss how globalization is threatening linguistic diversity, you might include treatment of time-space compression and the friction of distance. You might address assimilation, cultural diffusion, or other related concepts. The more you can support your response with substantive geographic examples, the better your response will be viewed. However, you should not write in random and unrelated ideas just to impress the reader with your geographic vocabulary! Instead, only integrate concepts directly tied to the FRQ's focus. Again, the object is to get right to the point and to support your point. No need for flowery language or Shakespearean prose.

Fifth, **if there is a "stimulus" in the FRQ, such as a chart, map, or graph, be sure that you integrate this into your response.** Use specifics from the "stimulus" in formulating your response. It's there for a reason—so use it! Take time to analyze what the stimulus shows you and how it relates to the FRQ. Feel free to draw on it and mark it up!

Here are some commonly asked questions and responses:

Can I include a diagram or a sketch in my FRQ?

Yes, you can include a diagram or a sketch in your FRQ. It is highly recommended that you do not include this as the only piece in your response. If you choose to use a diagram or sketch, link it to your overall response and be sure to describe what it means and how it relates to your response.

What if I have no idea how to respond to the question?

This could happen, but do not panic if it does. More than likely, you can offer some geographic analysis of the issue, even if you are truly stumped. Start writing something related to the course and an issue you think might be tied to the FRQ. In a past administration of the exam, some students were stumped by an FRQ calling for an analysis of the distribution of chicken farming in the U.S. Several stumped students started writing about agricultural changes in the U.S., the movement towards agribusiness and the decline of the family-owned farm in the U.S. They were successful because they offered a related idea. Above all else, do *not* leave a free-response question blank. Many well-prepared students find that one of the FRQs is their "challenge FRQ," meaning the one that really gave them a run for their money.

How long should my FRQ response be?

There is no right or wrong length for your FRQ answer. If your response fully answers the FRQ, then it is the right length. There is no word count or set limit. Make sure you do not spend too long on one FRQ and lose time to address the other two FRQs adequately.

Will I have enough time to write my answers?

Students generally have just enough time to write their responses to the free-response questions. Remember, though, that it is your responsibility to keep an eye on your own time and progress.

How can I prepare for the FRQs?

One of the strongest ways to prepare for these questions is to pay close attention to key terms throughout the course. Define the key terms in your own words. Look at the maps and diagrams in your book and think about how they apply to the chapter's focus. Keep a list of current events, controversies, and issues in each region of the world. If you do all this, you will have an arsenal of geographic concepts to draw from on exam day. Lastly, practice, practice, and practice! Use the practice FRQs in this book and given by your teacher to prepare for the big day.

The Day of the Exam

Before the exam

On the day of the test, you should wake up early (preferably after a good night's rest) and have a good breakfast. Make sure to dress comfortably, so that you are not distracted by being too hot or too cold while taking the test. Also plan to arrive at the test center early. This will allow you to collect your thoughts and relax before the test, and will also spare you the anxiety that comes with being late.

Before you leave for the test center, make sure that you have your admission form, social security number, and another form of identification, which must contain a recent photograph, your name, and signature (i.e., driver's license, student identification card, or current alien registration card). You will not be allowed to take the test if you do not have proper identification. You will also need to bring your school code. Also, bring several sharpened No. 2 pencils with erasers for the multiple-choice questions and black or blue pens for the free-response questions.

You may wear a watch, but only one without a beep or alarm. No dictionaries, textbooks, notebooks, compasses, correction fluid, highlighters, rulers, computers, cell phones, beepers, PDAs, scratch paper, listening and recording devices, briefcases, or packages will be permitted and drinking, smoking, and eating are prohibited while taking the test.

During the exam

Once you enter the test center, follow all of the rules and instructions given by the test supervisor. If you do not, you risk being dismissed from the test and having your scores canceled.

After the exam

You may immediately register when taking the exam to have your score sent to the college of your choice; you may also wait and later request to have your AP score reported to the college of your choice.

Contacting the AP Program

For registration bulletins or more information about the AP Human Geography exam, contact:

AP Services
Educational Testing Service
P.O. Box 6671
Princeton, NJ 08541-6671
Phone: (609) 771-7300 or (888) 225-5427
E-mail: apexams@ets.org
Website: *www.collegeboard.com*

COURSE REVIEW

AP Human Geography

Chapter 2

Geography: Its Nature and Perspectives

Introduction

Driving through Nashville, Tennessee, the country music capital of the world, you would expect to pass numerous tourist attractions and shops devoted to that music genre, but you would likely be surprised to see a large Hindu temple built on the city's west side. The study of human geography is related to such an observation. A human geographer would be interested in studying how Hinduism spread to the United States and why this temple was built in a southern city.

Figure 2.1. Sri Ganesh Hindu Temple, Nashville, Tennessee

Or perhaps you are strolling down a crowded city street in Beijing, China, and come across a Kentucky Fried Chicken restaurant. Human geographers would be interested in analyzing the spread of KFC to China and its impact on local culture.

What is particularly interesting about human geography is its approach to studying the world by looking at the interaction between humans and the lands

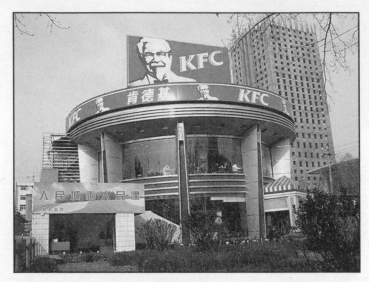

Figure 2.2. Kentucky Fried Chicken restaurant in Beijing, China

they inhabit. While most *world* geography classes teach students about the earth from a regional perspective—for instance, starting with North America and moving towards Asia—*human* geography takes a *thematic* approach, looking at the earth and its many different peoples in the context of many different patterns. That is the essence of human geography: defining and explaining patterns in human interactions with the earth.

Key Questions

- *What is human geography, and how is it related to the geographic perspective?*

- *How is geography a field of inquiry?*

- *How is spatial analysis embedded in the geographic perspective?*

- *How are humans and their landscapes related?*

- *What is geographic scale, and how does it affect geographic inquiry?*

- *What is regionalization, and how is it related to human geography?*

- *What effect do globalization and spatial interconnection have on people and places?*

- *How are various map forms and spatial data used?*

- *How does technology impact our understanding of geographic patterns and processes?*

PART 1 Geographical Concepts, the Geographical Perspective, and Key Skills

Geography as a Field of Inquiry

Geography is an exciting field of investigation that focuses on understanding the world and its patterns. One geographer compared geography to a quest for the answer to a strange question: "Why of where?" Yes, geographers study the patterns that appear on a map of the earth when they chart the locations of rivers, mountains, poverty, religions, and other aspects of life. But geographers are also fundamentally concerned with trying to find the *reasons* for the patterns. For example, not only do geographers design maps that show large concentrations of Hindus in India, but they also search to understand *why* most Hindus congregate in India.

Just as an archeologist digs into the earth, geographers search through the layers of patterns in the earth's physical and human landscapes to "write about earth" (which is what *geography* means when translated literally from its Greek roots).

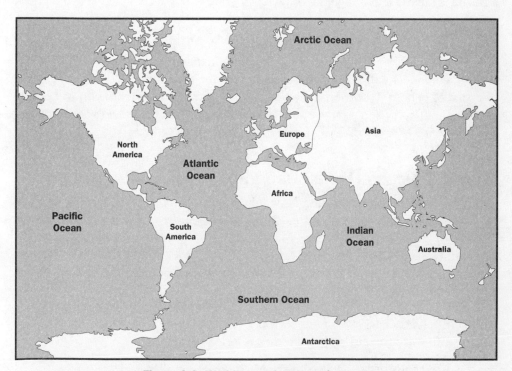

Figure 2.3. World's continents and oceans

The Spatial Perspective

At the very base of the geographer's craft is an obsession with space. No, not just outer space, where ET roams, but space in general: rooms, countries, parks, continents, cyberspace, rivers—all types of space. Geographers have a special eye for looking into space and investigating the patterns within it. For example, a geographer might look at the space of your bedroom and ask several questions: How are things distributed? What movements are occurring? What processes operate in that space? How does this space relate to other nearby spaces?

Such a way of identifying, explaining, and predicting the human and physical patterns in space and the interconnectedness of various spaces is known to geographers as the **spatial perspective**.

Often geographers create and use **geographic models** to explain and predict spatial patterns in the earth's human and physical landscapes. Geographic models are simplified versions of what exists on the earth and what might exist in the future. Models help geographers search for answers to why patterns exist the way they do—why, for example, India's population growth rate is different from South Africa's. One geographer created a model to explain rural land use patterns in his town. Then other geographers could use that model to explain and predict the patterns of farmland they saw in their towns.

You will study several models in human geography—the demographic transition model, the concentric zone model, and the von Thünen model, to name just a few—and each one will help you understand why patterns exist as they do on the earth. Each model will also give a sense of what the future might look like in terms of a spatial pattern. However, as you study each model, consider the drawbacks to applying it to every situation. Be sure to take into account the model's assumptions and where it was created.

Physical Versus Human Geography

Although all geographers are obsessed with the spatial perspective, the particular type of space they focus on varies. **Physical geography** is concerned with spatial analysis of the structures, processes, and locations of the earth's natural phenomena, like soil, climate, plants, and topography. **Human geography**, on the other hand, is primarily concerned with analyzing the structures, processes, and locations of the earth's human creations and their interactions. In essence, both fields of geography analyze the central "why of where" question, but each field approaches the question from a different focus.

The Five Themes of the Spatial Perspective

To understand the spatial perspective even more precisely, we must look into its five central themes: location, human–environment interaction, region, place, and movement. The five themes of geography are like five lenses through which

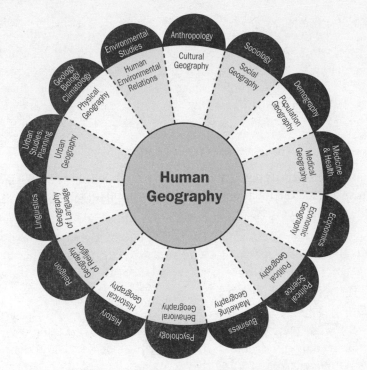

Figure 2.4. Fields of human geography

geographers look at a space, each lens giving the geographer a different sense of the patterns in that space.

Location

The theme of location is concerned with analyzing where something is on the earth and the effects that position has on human life. A location can be either absolute or relative.

Absolute Location

Absolute location refers to a position on the global grid. Technically, a location is absolute when it has only one possible reference point. That is why latitude and longitude work; only one place is 85 degrees north, 37 degrees west on the planet. Your home address is another absolute location. There is only one 28 North Main Street in Williamsport, Pennsylvania.

The U.S. Postal Service is the second-largest employer in the United States and processes more than 8,000 pieces of mail each second.

The global grid is an invisible map of latitude and longitude lines. **Lines of latitude** are measured in degrees north and south from the equator, which is 0 degrees latitude. The North Pole is 90 degrees north latitude, while the South Pole is 90 degrees south latitude. Interestingly, lines of latitude never intersect, so geographers often call lines of latitude *parallels*. Because lines of latitude encircle the earth and never intersect, the circumferences of lines of latitude decrease as they move away from the equator in both directions. Therefore, the equator has the largest circumference of all the lines of latitude.

Lines of longitude are measured in degrees east and west of one line of longitude known as the prime meridian, which runs through Greenwich, England, and is located at 0 degrees longitude. The line of longitude on the opposite side of the prime meridian is known as the international date line. The international date line is aligned with the 180-degree longitude line for some latitudes but not for others. This reflects the political influence on time zones. For example, the international date line was moved to put all of Russia ahead of Greenwich mean time (which is discussed later in this section).

Interestingly, the prime meridian was selected by a group of politicians and geographers, but any line of longitude could technically be named prime if the world wanted to change it. In fact, some geographers argue that the current prime meridian is **Anglocentric**, meaning that it orients the global grid around English (western European) culture. Critics ask why a line of longitude that runs through Asia, for example, was not selected as the prime meridian.

Thus, the absolute location of anything on the global grid—be it a city, person, boat, or Coke machine—is given as its latitude and longitude. To get more precise readings, each line of latitude and longitude can be broken down into minutes and seconds. There are 60 minutes (′) per degree (°) and 60 seconds (″) per minute.

For instance, a coordinate might be written as 75°45′32″ E, which would be a line of longitude read as "75 degrees, 45 minutes, and 32 seconds east (of the prime meridian)." Locations can be pinpointed within inches on the global grid. A degree of latitude is nearly 69 miles; a minute, nearly 1.1 miles; and a second, about 100 feet. Because lines of longitude all meet at the North and South poles, lines of longitude get closer and closer together moving toward the poles.

The earth's equatorial diameter is longer than its polar diameter, making the earth slightly "fatter" than it is tall.

Time zones revolve around the prime meridian, which establishes **Greenwich mean time (GMT)**, or **Universal time**, as the baseline for time throughout the

Figure 2.5. World's 24 time zones, each representing 15 degrees of longitude

world. The sun "rises in the east and sets in the west" because the earth rotates about its axis in an eastward direction. Taiwan, for example, is nearly 12 hours ahead of Louisville, Kentucky. When it is 6 p.m. on Monday in Louisville, it is 6 a.m. on Tuesday in Taiwan.

Earth's time is divided into 24 standard time zones. With each 15-degree-longitude move you make away from the prime meridian (or GMT), you go ahead or fall back by one hour and one standard time zone. For example, if you move 15 degrees east of the prime meridian, you go one hour ahead of GMT. So when it is 6 p.m. in London (GMT), it is 7 p.m. in countries 15 degrees of longitude east, and it is 8 p.m. in countries 30 degrees of longitude east. The reverse is true if you move in a westward direction from GMT. Interestingly, politics influence time zones, too. China, for example, has instituted one time zone for its entire country, even though its provinces fall into nearly three different standard time zones. The Chinese government believed that one time zone would help unify its vast country.

Related to latitude and longitude are **great circles**, which are circles formed on the earth's surface by a plane that passes through the center of the earth. The equator and every line of longitude paired with its twin on the opposite side of the earth form great circles. Any arc of a great circle shows the shortest distance between two points on the earth's surface; thus, airplanes often fly great-circle routes to save gas.

Relative Location

In addition to absolute location, anything can have a **relative location**, or its location as described in relation to places around it. The relative location of Nashville, Tennessee, could be described as being "south of Louisville, Kentucky," for example. "Hillsboro High School is located 9 miles southwest of McGavock High School" is another example of a relative location.

While the absolute location of a place remains the same (as long as the place does not move on the global grid), a description of a place's relative location can change if the place's surroundings change. For example, Kroger Grocery's relative location of being 2 miles south of Jane's Deli might change if Jane's Deli relocates to another location or goes out of business. Therefore, relative location is contextual and subject to change.

Site and *situation* are two more terms that describe a place's location. **Site** refers to a place's *internal* physical and cultural characteristics, such as its terrain and dominant religions. For example, the site of Sarasota, Florida, contains sandy beaches, Catholic churches, and humid equatorial climates, among other internal characteristics. On the other hand, **situation** refers to the location (or context) of a place relative to the physical and cultural characteristics around it. The more interconnected a place is to other powerful places, the better is its situation. A strong situation implies a place having a high degree of connectivity and accessibility, which allow for higher levels of spatial interaction. Moreover, modes of connectivity and

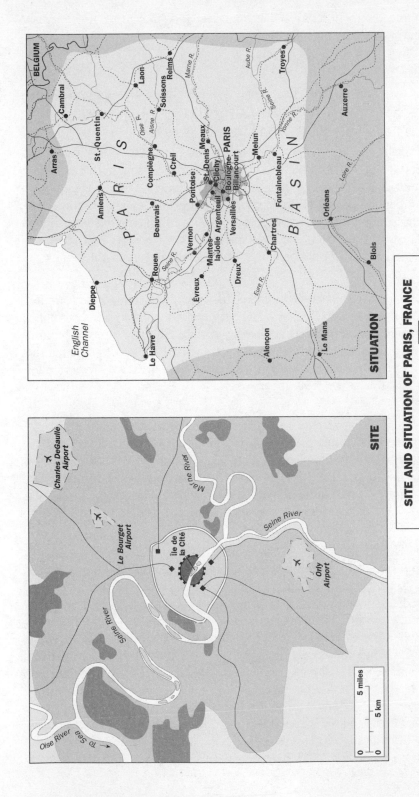

Figure 2.6. Site (left) and situation (right) of Paris, France

accessibility are becoming multilayered as land, sea, and air access points increase and communication technologies like the Internet become increasingly complex.

Human–Environment Interaction

The second major theme in the geographer's toolbox is analyzing **human–environment interaction**, the study of which is referred to as **cultural ecology**. Geographers analyze both directions of this type of interaction: how human activities affect their environment and how environmental changes impact human life. Geographers also analyze the positive and negative effects of human–environment interaction.

Region

The third geographic theme is the region, a way of classifying information about places. Just as historians classify their content by epochs and centuries, geographers classify their information by **regions**, which are spatial units that share some similar characteristics.

Geographers create regions to help them classify and understand the complexity of the earth. Every region consists of an area and a location and is contained by boundaries, which are sometimes not evident. There are three types of regions: formal, functional, and perceptual. However, each region links places together that share something. The physical and cultural character of an area and people's interconnections in that area allow geographers to create and define it as a region.

Formal Regions

Formal regions (sometimes referred to as uniform regions) are areas that have common (or uniform) cultural or physical features. A country is a formal region, or an area of places linked by a shared government. A climate region is a formal region because it links places that share a climate. A map showing where Christianity is practiced is showing a formal region, or a group of places sharing that religion.

Functional Regions

A **functional region** (sometimes referred to as a nodal region) is a group of places linked together by some function's influence on them. Often the influencing function diffused, or spread, from a central **node**, or originating point. Functional regions are created through the movement of some phenomenon, like a disease, or a perceived interaction among places, like pizza delivery routes. For example, a functional region might appear on a map of Delta Airlines' flights from Atlanta, Georgia. A mapmaker would plot all the places to which Delta travels from its hub in Atlanta—the node. Then the mapmaker would draw a boundary enclosing all those places into one functional region. The area affected by the spread of a flu epidemic is a functional region. A functional region could even show the transmission of a rumor from its source to all the people who hear it. Remember, functional regions are defined by the places affected by the movement of some phenomenon from its source (or node) to other places.

Perceptual Regions

The third type of region is a **perceptual (or vernacular) region**. The boundaries of a perceptual region are determined by people's beliefs, not a scientifically measurable process. For example, the space in which the "cool kids" sit at lunch would be a perceptual region because its boundaries are totally determined by the region maker's perception of who is cool and who is not—something that could be debated by any other person in the room. Another example of a perceptual region is the South in the United States. People differ in their perceptions of which places are considered part of the South.

Formal regions based on dominant crop types.

Functional regions tied to a central node. These could be banks serving their branches, diary farms providing milk to suppliers, etc.

Perceptual regions of a city.

Figure 2.7. Three types of regions: formal regions based on crop types, functional regions linked to a central node, and perceptual regions in a city

Place

The fourth geographic theme is **place**, which is a unique combination of physical and cultural attributes that give each location on the earth its individual "stamp." Human components of place include religion, language, politics, and artwork, whereas the physical attributes include climate, terrain, and natural resources. The combination of these two parts of place, the human and physical, are what differentiate each location from another, almost like a fingerprints.

Humans also develop a **sense of place**, which is a person's perception of the human and physical attributes of a location that give it a unique identity in our minds. For example, you probably remember a set of smells, sounds, and images from your ninth-grade English classroom. Think of how that sense of place differs from the total set of memories you have of your childhood bedroom or a favorite vacation spot. People can even develop a sense of place for a location they have never visited—through movies, television, and interactions with others who have traveled or heard of the places. You probably have never been to Siberia, but I bet you think it is a place you never want to visit because of its harsh climate!

Movement

The fifth theme is that of **movement**. Geographers analyze the movement occurring in a space—movement of information, people, goods, and other phenomena. Geographers also evaluate how places interact through movement, a process known as **spatial interaction**. Although everything is theoretically linked to everything else, nearer things are usually related more to each other than to faraway things. Thus, the extent of spatial interaction often depends on distance.

In evaluating movement and spatial interaction, geographers often evaluate the **friction of distance**, which is the degree to which distance interferes with some interaction. For example, the friction of distance for a working-class Ohio man wanting to visit a dentist in Ethiopia is quite high, meaning that the distance gets in the way of this interaction occurring. However, the friction of distance has been reduced in many aspects of life with improved transportation and communication infrastructures.

Today, the friction of distance is not as much of a problem for a business in Kentucky to sell something to a business in Taiwan, for example. Businesses can now communicate over the Internet, buying and selling their goods in transactions that would have taken months to complete just 30 years ago. This increasing sense of accessibility and connectivity seems to bring humans in distance places closer together, a phenomenon known as **space–time compression**. Note that space–time compression is reducing perceived distance, which is the friction of distance thought by humans, not the actual distance on the land.

Related to space–time compression is the effect of **distance decay**, in which the interaction between two places declines as the distance between the two places increases. Imagine putting a magnet on your desk and putting an iron nail on it. The farther you pull the iron nail away from the magnet, the less of a pull effect the

**Figure 2.8. Distance decay curve showing that
as distance increases, the level of interaction decreases**

magnet has on the nail, right? It is the same with distance decay; as the distance between two entities increases, the effect of their interaction decreases.

However, improved transportation and communication technologies have reduced the effect of distance decay on most human interactions. In 1850 on any given day, a person living in Atlanta probably never interacted with someone from 30 miles outside the city. Now a person in Atlanta can interact with people from all over the world via the Internet and improved transportation.

Mapmaking

A **map** is a two-dimensional model of the earth or a portion of its surface. The process of mapmaking is called **cartography**. All maps include a somewhat simplified view of the earth's surface. **Simplification** is when a cartographer gets rid of unnecessary details and focuses on the information needing to be displayed on the map. When designing a map of Europe for high school students to use to help them memorize the names of countries and capitals, a mapmaker would present a simplified map of Europe's political states and boundaries, eliminating details such as vegetation or climate. Another example of simplification involves a cartographer designing a map of London's underground subway for tourists. Such a cartographer might eliminate unnecessary details such as unrelated buildings and streets from their maps because tourists do not need these details to understand London's subway tracks. Tourists are simply interested in getting on and off the correct subway stops.

Distortion and Map Properties

It is impossible to take the earth's round surface and put it onto a flat surface without some form of **distortion**, or error resulting from the "flattening" process. Think of distortion as caused by a process similar to trying to flatten an orange peel. Sorry to inform you of this, but all the maps you have memorized are wrong. As it is often said, "All maps lie flat, and all flat maps lie." Yes, that's right; every map is, in some way, wrong. The globe is the most accurate representation of the earth.

Each map has **four main map properties**: shape, size (area), distance, and direction. *Shape* refers to the geometric shapes of the objects on the map. *Size* (area) refers to the relative amount of space taken up on the map by the landforms or objects on the map. *Distance* refers to the represented distance between objects on the map. *Direction* refers to the degree of accuracy representing the **cardinal directions**—north, south, east, and west—and their **intermediate directions**—northwest, northeast, southwest, and southeast. Less accurate are the **relative directions** that people commonly use to describe a location, such as *right, left, up,* and *down,* among many others.

All four properties cannot be accurately represented, so a cartographer must choose which of the properties to distort. Cartographers make this decision by considering the map's purpose. When designing a map for navigational purposes, the cartographer would keep direction and distance accurate; size (area) and shape are not as important.

The Process of Mapmaking: Projection

In making a flat map of the round earth, geographers use geometric shapes. They can choose a cylinder, cone, or flat plane to touch to the earth and construct a map. To visualize this process, imagine that the globe has a light in it and is in a dark room. When the chosen geometric shape, such as a flat plane, is placed on the globe, the globe reflects onto this geometric shape, forming a flat image, or projection, of the round earth. The resulting projection reflects the geometric surface used in constructing it.

The projection is distorted in some way, however, depending on the geometric shape used to make the map. Geographers have different labels for maps that reflect the different properties distorted by the maps:

- **Equal-area (or equivalent) projections:** maps that maintain area but distort other properties

- **Conformal (or orthomorphic) projections:** maps that maintain shape but distort other properties (it is impossible to have a projection that is both conformal and equal area)

- **Azimuthal projections:** maps that maintain direction but distort other properties

- **Equidistant projections:** maps that maintain distance but distort other properties

The Mercator projection, described in more detail in the next section, is a conformal projection created using a cylindrical surface, and the Albers projection was created using a conic surface. Azimuthal projections are flat-plane-constructed maps of each hemisphere. Great-circle routes are apparent on azimuthal projections.

Uses of Projections

Consider the different maps you have seen in your lifetime. You probably have used a **Robinson projection** in your social studies class to memorize points on the world map because the Robinson projection shows the world according to slight distortion of all four properties, rather than getting just one correct and drastically distorting others. Before the Robinson projection was invented, social studies teachers often used the **Mercator projection**. Though the Mercator projection shows the shapes of the continents and landforms accurately, it drastically distorts the size (area) of the continents. For example, Greenland is almost as large as Africa on the Mercator. Moreover, schools in the former Soviet Union used the Mercator projection to teach its children because the map made the USSR look larger than its enemies. A geographer created the **Peter projection** to show relative sizes of

RELATIVE LOCATION: EUROPE IN THE LAND HEMISPHERE

Figure 2.9. Azimuthal projection centered on Hamburg, Germany

the earth's continents accurately (equal area), but because it distorts shape, it is not conformal.

A Brief History of Mapmaking

Just as a painting is a reflection of the artist holding the brush, a map reflects the biases, experiences, and objectives of the cartographer who creates it. An evaluation of Inuit maps of Alaska shows extreme detail in the shapes of inland waterways, because the Inuit people navigated those passageways every day to fish and travel to different villages. Before the Greco-Roman civilizations, maps were largely cognitive and created for spiritual and immediate travel needs.

Because the Greeks and Romans were empire builders, scholars developed an interest in mapping landholdings and charting new places. Thus during the height

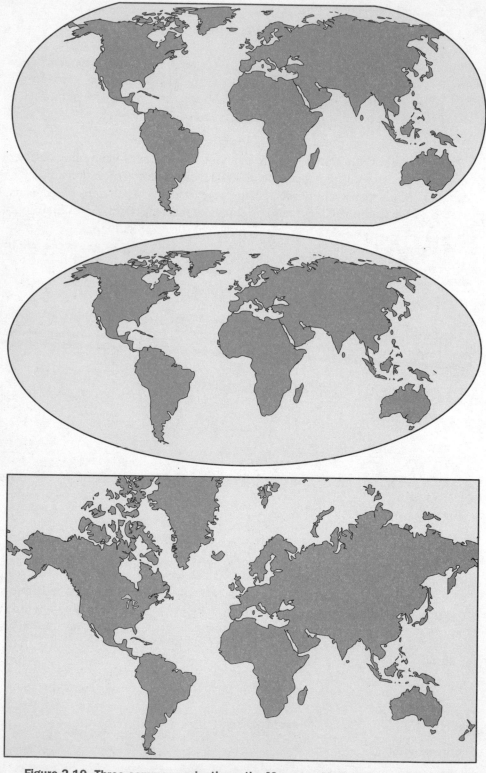

Figure 2.10. Three common projections: the Mercator, Mollweide, and Robinson

of those empires, from 1000 BCE to 500 CE, the discipline of geography was born. The Greeks and Romans had great interest in geographic inquiry. The Greek philosopher Aristotle was the first to show that the earth was spherical. Eratosthenes calculated the circumference of the earth and coined the word *geography* to mean "to write about the earth." He also created one of the earliest maps of the world and its climatic zones. Ptolemy wrote his eight-volume *Guide to Geography*, the first text to define the basic principles of geographic study and show examples of detailed maps.

After the fall of the Roman Empire in about 500 CE, maps were often oriented around religious and spiritual themes and less developed for exploration and scientific inquiry. Many medieval European maps were products of religious propaganda, chartered by the Catholic Church and oriented around Jerusalem for religious purposes. In the same way, Islamic maps often used Mecca (in Saudi Arabia, the holiest site to Muslims) as the focal point. However, cartographic progress continued outside Europe, in places like China and Southwest Asia. In the 15th century, as feudalism started to decline and western European empires were starting to search for colonies, interest in mapmaking and geographic inquiry grew. The Mercator projection, created in the 16th century, shows the influence of knowledge gained through exploration in its high degree of directional and shape accuracy. Today maps of the earth are less concerned with charting new territories and more concerned with analyzing the lands on the maps. Geographic focus has shifted away from merely asking "where" to asking the "why of where."

Cognitive Maps

Cognitive (or mental) maps are drawn from memory. A geographer can peer into the human mind by evaluating a cognitive map because it provides a glance into environmental perception. Children often draw maps with a gigantic United States surrounded by tiny neighboring countries, or all by itself. This shows children's view that their home is the center of the world.

The emphasis of a cognitive map is also useful to a geographer trying to understand a culture. While early water-based cultures produced mental maps that often emphasized fishing streams, the map your father drew on a napkin to show you how to get to the maritime museum in a nearby city probably emphasized streets and key landmarks that have been important to him (and others in the community) in navigating your region. In studying cognitive maps, it is essential to evaluate not only what you can see but also what you cannot see. The items left out of a cognitive map are a geographer's clues to both the purpose of the map and the focus (and degree of knowledge) of the individual who drew it.

Scale

Scale, another prominent feature in geographic analysis, can refer to the scope of geographic inquiry or discussion—that is, whether you are studying or discussing a topic affecting the entire world or just a village. In cartography (mapmaking), scale refers to the relationship between a distance on the map and the actual measurement in the real world. In other words, **map (or cartographic) scale** is the degree to which a map "zooms in" on the area it is representing. Scale tells you to what extent the portion of the earth represented on the map has been reduced from its original size to fit on the map.

For example, 1 inch on a map may equal 10 miles in the real world (on the portion of the earth being represented in the map). That scale might be written as "1 inch = 10 miles." Sometimes, the scale is indicated as a fraction, known as a representative fraction. For example, a scale written as "1/40 miles" (or "1:40 miles") means 1 inch on the map equals 40 miles in the real world.

One counterintuitive part of mapping is describing map scale as "large" or "small." Think of it this way: *the larger the area of space being represented on the map, the smaller its scale.* For example, a map of Africa would have a smaller scale than a map of just one country in Africa. A map of the world has a smaller scale than the map of a village. A map of a street has a larger scale than a map of its city. That is, the more "zoomed in" the map is on an area, the larger is its map scale. A large-scale map depicts a smaller area with more detail than does a small-scale map, which represents a larger area with less detail. A small-scale map is less "zoomed in."

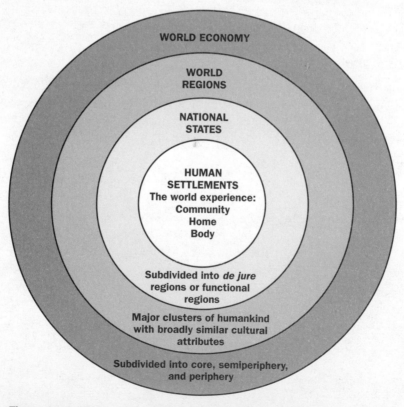

Figure 2.11. Diagram of scales commonly used in geographic research

Categories of Maps

Like a graphic designer choosing the best way to represent an image, geographers can choose from many different types of maps to use in representing different spaces. **Reference maps** show common features such as boundaries, roads, highways, mountains, and cities. A **thematic map**, however, zeroes in on one feature, such as climate, city size, or number of alligators.

Thematic maps come in various forms. **Isoline thematic maps** display the lines that connect points of equal value, as in showing elevation levels. A **choropleth thematic map** shows a pattern of some variable, such as population density or voting patterns, by using various colors or degrees of shading. A now-famous example of a choropleth thematic map is the one displaying the 2004 election results by shading conservative-voting states in red and liberal-voting states in blue. A **proportional-symbol thematic map** uses some symbol (whether it is a circle, star, triangle, or

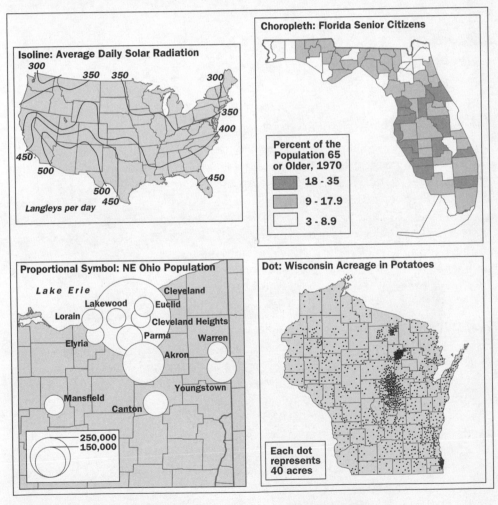

Figure 2.12. Four types of thematic maps

even a Mickey Mouse ear) to display the frequency of a variable. The larger the symbol on the map, the higher is the frequency of the variable found in that region. For example, a proportional symbol of population density in the United States would have larger circles in New York City than in Bagdad, Kentucky (which really exists). **Dot density maps** are thematic maps that simply use dots to represent the frequency of a variable in a given area, such as the number of college graduates living in counties within a state. A dot density map specifies what each dot represents. In the college graduates map, for example, each dot might equal 100 graduates.

A **cartogram** is another type of map that uses proportionality to show a particular variable. In other words, cartograms use space on the map to show a particular variable. For example, a cartogram showing the frequency of factory labor throughout the world would show a large space taken up by China and a much smaller space taken up by the United States. Cartograms manage to maintain some degree of geographic accuracy in the relative positions of geographic entities.

PART 2 **New Geographical Technologies and Geographical Data**

Obtaining Geographic Data

Mapmakers use data to construct thematic maps. They obtain data from various sources. **A geographic information system (GIS)** is a computer program that stores geographic data and produces maps to show those data. The city government of Nashville, Tennessee, has an entire department devoted to geographic information collection. Geographers in that department collect and manage geographic data and generate maps for the government using a GIS. For example, the city's GIS can produce a map showing property values throughout Nashville. Then it can layer another spatial characteristic such as population density on top of property values to show the relationship between the two variables.

Often geographic data are collected using **remote sensing**, which is the collection of information from satellites and distant collection systems. In other words, remote sensing is the technique of obtaining information about objects through the study of data collected by special instruments that are not in physical contact with the objects being analyzed. **A global positioning system (GPS)** uses satellites to determine exact locations on the global grid. Data directly collected by the geographer making the map or conducting the study are called **primary data**. On the other hand, **secondary data** are collected by a source that previously conducted a study and made data available for future use. For example, to make maps of the frequency of people aged 65 years and older in various cities, cartographers can use the U.S. Census Bureau's website to gather the necessary data. In doing so, the mapmakers would be using secondary data, which saves them time and eliminates the hassle of conducting their own count. However, in using secondary data, cartographers must carefully evaluate sources that gathered the data to ensure the accuracy and authenticity of the information. Be careful of what you find on the Web!

Figure 2.13. Layers of data compiled in a geographic information system

Data Aggregation

Another issue in cartography is the level of **data aggregation**, which is the size of geographic units being represented on a map. The larger the area that is being represented in a study, such as a country or continent, the "coarser" is the study's (or map's) level of data aggregation. The smaller the area that is being represented, such as a county or neighborhood, the "finer" the study's (or map's) level of data aggregation. That is, "coarser" studies show less detail than "finer" studies.

**PART
3**   **Chapter Review**

Terms Review

Absolute location—Position of an object on the global grid; latitude and longitude.

Anglocentric—Focused on the English culture.

Azimuthal projection—Map that maintains direction but distorts other properties; flat-plane-constructed map of each hemisphere; direction is accurate, and great-circle routes are apparent.

Cardinal directions—North, south, east, and west.

Cartogram—Map that uses proportionality (i.e., space on the map) to show a particular variable.

Cartography—Process of mapmaking.

Choropleth thematic map—Map that shows a pattern of a variable, such as population density or voting patterns, by using various colors or degrees of shading.

Cognitive (or mental) map—Map drawn from memory.

Conformal (or orthomorphic) projection—Map that maintains shape but distorts other properties.

Cultural ecology—Study of human–environment interaction.

Data aggregation—Size of geographic units being represented on a map.

Distance decay—Pattern in which the interaction between two places declines as the distance between the two places increases.

Distortion—Necessary error resulting from trying to represent the round, nearly spherical earth on a flat plane, or map.

Dot density map—Thematic map that uses dots to represent the frequency of a variable in a given area.

Equal-area (or equivalent) projection—Map that maintains area but distorts other properties.

Equidistant projection—Map that maintains distance but distorts other properties.

Formal region—Region composed of areas that have a common (or uniform) cultural or physical feature; sometimes referred to as uniform regions.

Four main properties of a map—Shape, size (area), distance, and direction. Shape refers to the geometric shapes of the objects on the map. Size (area) refers to the relative amount of space taken up on the map by the landforms or objects on the map. Distance refers to the represented distance between objects on the map. Direction refers to the degree of accuracy representing the cardinal and intermediate directions.

Friction of distance—Degree to which distance interferes with some interaction.

Functional region—Group of places linked together by some function's influence on them after diffusing from a central node; sometimes referred to as a nodal region.

Geographic information system (GIS)—Computer program that stores geographic data and produces maps to show the data.

Geographic model—Simplified version of what exists on the earth or what might exist in the future; helps a geographer search for answers to why patterns exist on the earth as they do.

Global positioning system (GPS)—System of satellites used to determine an exact location on the global grid.

Great circles—Circles formed on the surface of the earth by a plane that passes through the center of the earth. The equator and every line of longitude paired with its twin on the opposite side of the earth form great circles. Any arc of a great circle shows the shortest distance between two points on the earth's surface.

Greenwich mean time (GMT)—Baseline for time zones around the world, centered on the prime meridian; sometimes called Universal time.

Human–environment interaction—One theme of geography through which geographers analyze humans' impact on their environment and their environment's impact on them.

Human geography—Branch of geography primarily concerned with analyzing the structures, processes, and location of human creations and interactions with the earth.

Intermediate directions—Northwest, southwest, northeast, and southeast.

Isoline thematic map—Map displaying lines that connect points of equal value; for example, a map showing elevation levels.

Lines of latitude—Measured in degrees north and south from the equator, which is 0 degrees latitude. The North Pole is 90 degrees north latitude, and the South Pole is 90 degrees South latitude. Lines of latitude never intersect, so geographers often call lines of latitude parallels.

Lines of longitude—Measured in degrees east and west of one line of longitude known as the prime meridian, the line of longitude that runs through England's Greenwich Observatory. The prime meridian represents 0 degrees longitude.

Map—Two-dimensional model of the earth or a portion of its surface.

Map (or cartographic) scale—Relationship between distance on the map and the actual measurement in the real world.

Mercator projection—Map showing the shapes of the continents and landforms accurately but drastically distorting the size (area) of the continents. For example, Greenland appears almost as large as Africa.

Movement—Theme in geography involving the movement occurring in a space: movement of information, people, goods, and other phenomena.

Node—Place from which a diffusing phenomenon spreads to other places (its originating point).

Perceptual (or vernacular) region—Region whose boundaries are determined by people's beliefs, not a scientifically measurable process.

Gall-Peters projection—Map created by a geographer to show the relative sizes of the earth's continents accurately (equal area). However, it distorts shape, so it is not conformal.

Physical geography—Branch of geography concerned with spatial analysis of the structures, processes, and locations of the earth's natural phenomena, like soil, climate, plants, and topography.

Place—Theme in geography that involves the unique combination of physical and cultural attributes that give each location on the earth its individual "stamp."

Primary data—Data directly collected by the geographer making the map or conducting the study.

Proportional-symbol thematic map—Map that uses some symbol to display the frequency of a variable. The larger the symbol on the map, the higher the frequency of the variable found in that region.

Reference map—Map showing common features like boundaries, roads, highways, mountains, and cities.

Region—Theme in geography involving a spatial unit that has many places sharing similar characteristics.

Relative directions—Directions commonly given by people, such as *right, left, up,* and *down*, among many others.

Relative location—Location of a place or object described in relation to places or objects around it.

Remote sensing—Technique of obtaining information about objects through the study of data collected by special instruments that are not in physical contact with the objects being analyzed.

Robinson projection—Map showing the world with slight distortions to all four properties, rather than having one property correct and the other three drastically distorted.

Secondary data—Data used by a geographer but collected by another source that previously conducted a study and made the data available for future use.

Sense of place—Person's perception of the human and physical attributes of a location that give it a unique identity in that person's mind.

Simplification—Cartographer's process of eliminating unnecessary details and focusing on the information that needs to be displayed in the map.

Site—Internal physical and cultural characteristics of a place, such as its terrain and dominant religions, among others.

Situation—Location (or context) of a place relative to the physical and cultural characteristics around it. The more interconnected a place is to other powerful places, the better its situation.

Space–time compression—Increasing sense of accessibility and connectivity that seems to be bringing humans in distance places closer together.

Spatial interaction—Process in which goods, ideas, information, and people move among places.

Spatial perspective—Outlook through which geographers identify, explain, and predict the human and physical patterns in space and the interconnectedness of different spaces.

Thematic map—Map that zeroes in on one feature such as climate, city, or size.

PART 4   **Some Suggested Web Resources for Further Exploration**

Association of American Geographers (AAG): http://www.aag.org/

With many of America's professional geographers among its membership, the AAG is a tremendous resource for researching a career in geography, reading about political issues in geography, and finding reviews of geography-related books and other publications.

National Council for Geographic Education (NCGE): http://www.ncge.org/

The NCGE website contains ample resources for educators looking for information on national teaching standards and lesson plans in geography.

National Geographic Society: http://www.nationalgeographic.com/

One of the most fascinating websites, National Geographic has catalogued articles and images from all over the world on virtually every interesting geographic topic.

Gallery of Map Projections: http://www.galleryofmapprojections.com/

This site displays hundreds of map projections in all forms and types and explains each kind.

Buckminster Fuller Institute: http://www.bfi.org/

Check out this site on Buckminster Fuller, one of the most intriguing minds of the 20th century, who created one of the most unique map projections known to man, based on the geodesic dome.

GIS Software: http://www.esri.com/

This is the site of a leading GIS software producer, ESRI. You can download the company's free product and explore the wonders of GIS technology.

PART 5 Pre-Exam Practice

Terms Review Quiz

Use the Terms Review list or your own memory to determine the extent of your knowledge of key terms and concepts. Remember, the AP exam does not include this kind of exercise, but it is included here as a review tool.

1. *formal regions* — Region composed of areas that have a common (or uniform) cultural or physical feature; sometimes referred to as uniform regions.

2. *Globalization* — Outlook through which geographers identify, explain, and predict the human and physical patterns in space and the interconnectedness of various spaces.

3. *relative location* — Location (or context) of a place relative to the physical and cultural characteristics around it.

4. *perceptual region* — Region whose boundaries are determined by people's beliefs, not a scientifically measurable process.

5. *Directions* — Southeast, southwest, northeast, and northwest.

6. *Human Geography* — Branch of geography primarily concerned with analyzing the structures, processes, and location of human creations and interactions with the earth.

7. *GPS* — System of satellites used to determine an exact location on the global grid.

8. *Longitude* — Baseline for time zones around the world, centered on the prime meridian.

9. _____ — Directions commonly given by people, such as *right, left, up,* and *down,* among many others.

10. ___Distortion___ Necessary error resulting from trying to represent a round, nearly spherical earth on a flat plane, or map.

11. ___Absolute Location___ Position of an object on the global grid: latitude and longitude.

12. _____ Circles formed on the surface of the earth by a plane that passes through the center of the earth. The equator and every line of longitude paired with its twin on the opposite side of the earth form great circles.

13. ___Cartography___ Process of mapmaking.

14. _____ Degree to which distance interferes with some interaction.

15. _____ Map that maintains distance but distorts other properties.

16. _____ Simplified version of what exists on the earth or what might exist in the future; helps a geographer search for answers to why patterns exist on the earth as they do.

17. _____ Two-dimensional model of the earth or a portion of its surface.

18. _____ Person's perception of the human and physical attributes of a location that give it a unique identity in that person's mind.

19. _____ Study of human–environment interaction.

20. _____ Map created by a geographer to show the relative sizes of the earth's continents accurately (equal area). However, it distorts shape, so it is not conformal.

21. _____ Map that shows a pattern of some variable, such as population density or voting patterns, by using various colors or degrees of shading.

22. _____ Internal physical and cultural characteristics of a place, such as its terrain and dominant religions, among others.

23. _____ Map showing the world with slight distortions to all four properties, rather than having one property correct and the others drastically distorted.

24. _____ Cartographer's process of eliminating unnecessary details and focusing on the information that needs to be displayed in the map.

25. _____ Map displaying lines that connect points of equal value; for example, a map showing elevation levels.

Multiple-Choice Review Questions

1. Which of the following would have the smallest map scale?

   (A) Map of Asia

   (B) Map of Kentucky

   (C) Map of the world

   (D) Map of Nashville, Tennessee

   (E) Map of 6th Avenue, New York City

2. Which of the following maps would be most useful for demonstrating varying levels of oceanic elevation?

   (A) Dot density   (D) Proportional symbol

   (B) Isoline topographic   (E) Azimuthal

   (C) Cartogram

3. Which of the following would be most important to a human geographer?

   (A) Ethnicity   (D) Space

   (B) Gender   (E) Density

   (C) Diversity

4. If two cities are three inches apart on a map with a scale of 1:60,200, how far apart are they on the surface of the earth?

(A) 2.85 miles   (D) 100 miles

(B) 4 miles   (E) 250 miles

(C) 6 miles

5. Which of the following has the coarsest level of data aggregation?

(A) Analysis of Asian birthrates

(B) Analysis of lead in a classroom

(C) Analysis of gender ratios in Kentucky

(D) Analysis of literacy rates in Afghanistan

(E) Analysis of copyright violations in Germany

6. If you were measuring the concentration of white Americans using a dot density map, which threshold would put the most visual emphasis on those whites living in rural areas?

(A) One dot per 3,000 white Americans

(B) One dot per 50,000 white Americans

(C) One dot per 100,000 white Americans

(D) One dot per 150,000 white Americans

(E) The proportion is insignificant to the visual emphasis

7. Louisville, Kentucky, is located in a valley and is built on the Ohio River. Its street patterns follow the orientation of the river. These features refer most directly to Louisville's

(A) situation   (D) site

(B) relative distance   (E) absolute location

(C) gentrification

8. If it is 2 p.m. in your city and it is 12 p.m. in Greenwich, England, what is your city's approximate longitude?

    (A)   15 degrees west   (D)   30 degrees east

    (B)   15 degrees east   (E)   30 degrees west

    (C)   45 degrees west

9. Europe and Asia are primarily divided along the line that extends along the

    (A)   Alps, Black Sea, and Indian Ocean

    (B)   Himalayas and Indian Ocean

    (C)   Ural Mountains, Black Sea, and Caspian Sea

    (D)   Transylvanian Alps and Danube River

    (E)   Volga River and Dinaric Alps

10. In approximately 365¼ days, the earth completes

    (A)   one revolution   (D)   one leap year

    (B)   one rotation   (E)   one eclipse

    (C)   one solstice

11. Distortion can be defined as

    (A)   the error in accuracy that occurs in all maps

    (B)   a technique for giving each location on the earth a corresponding place on a flat surface

    (C)   a mathematical formula for translating cultural understandings of rivers

    (D)   a spherical, scaled model of the earth

    (E)   the process of calculating map scale

12. Human geography is best defined as the study of

    (A)   where and why human activities are located where they are

    (B)   where and why natural forces occur as they do

    (C)   populations and birth rates

    (D)   human conflicts

    (E)   the earth's impacts on humans

13. Saying "Louisville, Kentucky, is located at 38 degrees north, 85 degrees west" is giving Louisville's

   (A) relative location   (D) functional region

   (B) region   (E) cognitive map

   (C) absolute location

14. Kentucky, Canada, the Ohio River Valley, a German-speaking region, and Northern Ireland are all classified as

   (A) functional regions   (D) heterogeneous cultures

   (B) formal regions   (E) shatter belts

   (C) perceptual regions

15. Which of the following is NOT used by geographers to determine absolute location?

   (A) Equator   (D) Prime meridian

   (B) Distance from the ocean   (E) Longitude

   (C) Latitude

16. Which of the following map projections shows the relative sizes of earth's landmasses most accurately?

   (A) Gall-Peters projection   (D) Molleweide projection

   (B) Robinson projection   (E) Buckminster Fuller projection

   (C) Mercator projection

17. Which of the following is an absolute location?

   (A) 18 degrees north

   (B) 3 miles west of Denver

   (C) the equator

   (D) 123 Main Street, Beverly Hills, CA 90210

   (E) Athens

18.   Which of the following is NOT one of the five themes of geography?

    (A)   Region   (D)   Location

    (B)   Place   (E)   Movement

    (C)   Maps

19.   Conformal maps maintain

    (A)   area   (D)   distance

    (B)   direction   (E)   size

    (C)   shape

20.   Verbal, representative fraction, and graphic are all forms of

    (A)   maps   (D)   cardinal directions

    (B)   scales   (E)   intermediate directions

    (C)   geographic themes

21.   A map that uses a symbol to display frequency (the larger the symbol the higher the frequency) is a(n)

    (A)   isoline thematic map

    (B)   choropleth thematic map

    (C)   proportional-symbol thematic map

    (D)   dot density map

    (E)   cartogram

Free-Response Question

Of great interest to geographers are the cultural and political implications of technological innovations that affect human interaction.

(A)   Define *space–time compression*, relating it to technological innovations. Give an example of its impact on human interaction.

(B)   Describe the impact of space–time compression on the friction of distance.

(C)   Explain one positive and one negative effect of space–time compression on one of the following regions:

   • Southeast Asia

   • Southwest Asia

   • Eastern Europe

PART 6

Pre-Exam Practice Answers

Terms Review Answers

1. Formal regions
2. Spatial perspective
3. Situation
4. Perceptual (or vernacular) region
5. Intermediate directions
6. Human geography
7. Global positioning system
8. Greenwich mean time
9. Relative direction
10. Distortion
11. Absolute location
12. Great circles
13. Cartography
14. Friction of distance
15. Equidistant (or azimuthal) map
16. Geographic model
17. Map
18. Sense of place
19. Cultural ecology
20. Gall-Peters projection (or equal-area projection)
21. Choropleth map
22. Site
23. Robinson projection (or average projection)
24. Simplification
25. Isoline thematic map

Multiple-Choice Answers

1. **(C)**

   The smaller the map scale, the larger the area being represented on the map. The largest area from the list of choices is a map of the world.

2. **(B)**

   An isoline map uses lines (isolines) to connect areas of equal elevation. Therefore, such a map would be useful for showing varying elevations. Dot density maps are used for showing density; cartograms show some unit of analysis in a proportional, geometric pattern that is geographically accurate; proportional-symbol maps use some symbol, such as a star or circle, to represent a pattern of some measured statistic across a map; and azimuthal maps show great-circle routes.

3. **(D)**

   Just as time is essential to a historian, space is the quintessential tool to geographers. You might argue that it depends on the study, but in all geographic studies, spatial patterns are the basis of analysis.

4. **(A)**

   If 1 unit on the map represents 60,200 units in real life, then 3 inches on the map represents 180,800 inches in real life. There are 5,280 feet in a mile, which equals 63,360 inches. 180,800 / 63,360 = 2.85 miles.

5. **(A)**

   The larger the area being studied, the coarser the study's level of data aggregation. The smaller the area being studied, the finer the study's level of data aggregation. In this question, the largest spatial area listed is the level of Asian birthrates, because Asia is the largest space of the listed options.

6. **(A)**

   The threshold is the number of units represented by a dot. In this question, the threshold that would give most attention to rural white Americans would be the threshold that creates the most dots in rural areas. One dot per 3,000 whites would create the most dots on the map, rather than some of the higher thresholds.

7. **(D)**

   A city's internal characteristics make up its site, whereas its connection to other cities is its situation. Gentrification is the remodeling and revamping of urban areas by returning suburbanites who consider the areas "underdeveloped" and in need of repair and resettling.

8. **(D)**

For every hour difference from the prime meridian and Greenwich mean time (GMT), 15 degrees of longitude separate the time zones. In this question, because 2 hours separate your city from GMT, 30 degrees of longitude separate it from Greenwich. If your city's time is <u>ahead</u> of GMT, then it is <u>east</u> of Greenwich. If it is <u>behind</u> GMT, then it is <u>west</u> of GMT.

9. **(C)**

Although some geographers see Europe and Asia undivided as a continental Eurasian landmass, the two continents are typically divided along a line extending from the Ural Mountains to the Caspian and Black Seas. Places east of this boundary are considered to be part of Asia, and those west are considered to be part of Europe.

10. **(A)**

It takes one year for the earth to make a complete revolution around the sun. Interestingly, the extra one-fourth of a day is accumulated over four years for the 366th day in a leap year. The earth makes one rotation about its axis in 24 hours.

11. **(A)**

Distortion occurs on all flat maps because it is impossible to take the round earth and represent it on a flat surface. An analogy is peeling an orange peel in one piece and then trying to flatten the peel; it would crack.

12. **(A)**

Human geography is the study of people's patterns and their processes in relation to the earth's patterns and processes. (B) is too narrow in that it does not include human processes. (C), (D), and (E) are also too narrow, although all are a part of human geography.

13. **(C)**

Latitude and longitude together represent a place's absolute location on the global grid. (A) would be its relative position in relation to other places; (B) would be a group of places in which Louisville shares some commonality; (D) would be a group of places sharing some form of a movement (or function) with Louisville, perhaps an airliner's destination route; and (E) would be a map drawn from memory or recollection.

14. **(B)**

Formal regions are groups of places sharing internal uniformity, whether sharing a political affiliation, religious characteristic, topographic similarity, or language usage. All the answer choices include places linked through such a characteristic—not based on a moving function or diffusion route (functional region) and not based on people's perceptions or opinions (perceptual regions). Shatter belts are countries or areas existing in the fall-out range of larger, competing countries.

15. **(B)**

Distance from the ocean is not a part of pinpointing an absolute location on the global grid, whereas the other answer choices are all components in the determination of latitudinal–longitudinal intersection.

16. **(A)**

The Gall-Peters projection was created to more accurately portray the relative sizes of the landmasses, so that areas such as Africa are not understated on maps in relation to size, as they were on earlier maps such as the Mercator and Robinson projections.

17. **(D)**

The address in (D) is the only one of its kind; therefore, it is an absolute location. (A) and (C) are lines that run around the earth with multiple places along them. (B) changes depending on what part of Denver you leave from. (E) is the name of cities in Greece, Georgia, Tennessee and many other places.

18. **(C)**

Maps are a tool geographers use to study the earth. The other choices, along with human–environment interactions, make up the five basic themes geographers use to conduct research.

19. **(C)**

Conformal maps maintain shape. Equal-area projections (A) maintain area, azimuthal projections (B) maintain direction, and (D) equidistant projections maintain distance. Only a globe (E) can maintain all four properties.

20. **(B)**

Verbal scales state the map scale in linguistic terms (e.g., 1 inch equals 10 miles). Representative fractions give a mathematical representation of the scale (e.g., 1:24,000 or 1/24,000). A graphic scale is a pictorial representation of the scale—for example:

miles

0 ——————— 1

would mean the length of the dashes above equals 1 mile on the map.

21. **(C)**

Proportional-symbol thematic maps use a symbol (e.g., a circle) to show some feature on a map (e.g., population). The larger the circle, the larger the population. Isoline thematic maps (A) display lines that connect points of equal value. A choropleth thematic map (B) shows a pattern of some variable, such as population density or voting patterns, by using various colors or degrees of shading. A dot density map (D) uses dots to represent the frequency of a variable in a given area. A cartogram (E) uses space to show a particular variable.

Free-Response Answers

The following is a list of suggested main points for each part of the question.

Part A

- Space–time compression is the process that seems to bring places and people closer together, in terms of communicational distance, through the improvement of communication and transportation technology.

- Although the absolute distance remains the same between two places, the relative distance decreases as the places become increasingly interconnected through technological and transportation conduits.

- The distance between Taiwan and Kentucky remains the same as it was 80 years ago, but people in Kentucky and Taiwan are relatively closer because they can communicate quickly via e-mail and airline travel.

Part B

- Space–time compression is reducing the friction of distance, the degree that distance is a barrier to communication and travel.

- With improved telephone and Internet connections on top of more available and affordable air travel, the degree that distance inhibits travel and communications is diminishing. This simplifies the transmission or trade of ideas, information, and goods among individuals or groups.

Part C

- Possible topics to discuss:

  - *Southeast Asia*—movement of multinational corporations into countries and employing citizens in factories; growth of sweatshops and unchecked free trade at workers' expense

  - *Southwest Asia*—involvement of foreign powers in local political conflicts, increased media coverage of inter-religious wars, and globalization of local conflicts among Jews and Arabs; improved travel to and knowledge of Mecca and Jerusalem; improved oil-based transport and trade; perceived cultural imperialism and invasion of Arab culture by Western cultural forces (e.g., MTV)

  - *Eastern Europe*—increased advertisement and knowledge of foreign opportunities to locals, causing increased emigration from the economically depressed East; fall of communism in the East linked to knowledge of democracy; increased sex slavery/trade

Chapter 3

Population

Introduction

An essential part of human geography is the study of the earth's population, particularly the trends in population growth and change. Over the last 12,000 years, human population has been growing at rates faster than ever seen in history. The earth's population has increased 10 times in just 2,000 years. The fastest rates have been seen in the past 200 years; in fact, the global population has more than doubled in just the last 50 years.

Key Questions

- *Will the earth's population increase to a level that could lead to a global crisis?*

- *What patterns exist in the earth's population densities and distributions?*

- *Why are populations growing faster in some areas of the world than in others?*

- *How have governments and religions attempted to influence population growth trends?*

- *How do geographers measure and study human population patterns?*

PART 1 Geographical Analysis of Population

Basics of Demography

Demography is the study of human populations. Currently, nearly 6.5 billion people live on the earth. Geographers use demographic analysis to study the spatial distributions of humans and their movements. Demographers are experts in demography.

The size, composition, and growth of a country's population affect its well-being. Rapid increases in population in areas like the Middle East (Southwest Asia) and sub-Saharan Africa strain their **infrastructures**, or support systems, including housing, food supplies, education, and health care.

Population Equation

Scale of inquiry, or the size of a geographic investigation (e.g., global, regional, or local) is important to demographic analysis. At the global level, demographers are looking at where the earth's populations are growing the fastest and where they are expanding more slowly. Present trends show that populations are growing fastest in poor areas with the least amount of stability and little access to and control of resources, as in parts of Africa and Asia.

The critical issue is not so much that children are being born at faster rates and in higher numbers. It is more important that populations are growing the fastest in less-developed regions that cannot support vast numbers of people.

At the subglobal level, demographers analyze population trends within regions, like continents, countries, or states. They are interested in discovering facts that only closer analysis can provide. Where are populations growing the fastest in North America? How does Africa's growth rate compare to Asia's? Locally, demographers may look at different neighborhoods or towns to get a clearer picture of what is happening to a region's population.

Two, key **demographic accounting equations** relate to scale of inquiry. Population change at the global level is calculated using the following formula:

Global Population Accounting Equation
P_0 = Size of population at *start* of interval of measurement
P_1 = Size of population at *end* of interval of measurement
B = Number of births during interval of measurement
D = Number of deaths during interval of measurement

$$P_1 = P_0 + B - D$$

This formula simply means that the new size of the population, P_1, is the original population, P_0, plus the number of people born into the population, B, minus the number of people in the population who died during the interval of measurement, D.

The formula for population change at the regional level is very similar, but it adds two important features: immigration and emigration. **Immigration** refers to people coming into a country (or region), whereas **emigration** refers to people exiting, or leaving, a country (or region). Remember that *immigration* starts with an *i* for coming "into," whereas *emigration* starts with an *e* for "exiting."

Subglobal Population Accounting Equation
P_0 = size of population at *start* of interval of measurement
P_1 = Size of population at *end* of interval of measurement
B = Number of births during interval of measurement
D = Number of deaths during interval of measurement
I = Number of immigrants moving *into* region during interval of measurement
E = Number of emigrants moving *out* of region during interval of measurement

$$P_1 = P_0 + B - D + I - E$$

Geo Factoid

Why are I and E not factors in the global population accounting equation? Because humans do not immigrate and emigrate from the earth to other planets enough to be included. Technically, we could petition to add astronauts to the global equation, but it is not practical.

Here is a short example to demonstrate how the subglobal population accounting equation works: Country A has 1 million people in 1990. Over the next 10 years 75,000 babies are born; 50,000 people die; 10,000 people move into the country; and 5,000 people exit. In 2000, the population would be

$$P_1 = 1,000,000 + 75,000 - 50,000 + 10,000 - 5,000 = 1,030,000 \text{ people}$$

Population Distribution

Distribution of population is the pattern of people across the earth's surface—where they live. Throughout human history, people have been *unevenly* concentrated, clustering around sustaining resources, such as bodies of water, and in regions where people can farm.

Where people live is heavily influenced by physical conditions. Fewer people live in deserts and tundra, for example. Approximately three-fourths of the people in the world live on only 5 percent of the earth's surface. The part of the earth on which people *can* live is termed the **ecumene**. About 50 percent of people on the earth live in cities, while the other half lives in rural areas.

Global Population Distribution

Here are some interesting population statistics:

- Approximately 81 percent of the earth's population lives in poorer, less-developed countries in Latin America, Africa, and Asia.

Figure 3.1. A dot density map representing world population distribution

World Population
Distribution
One dot represents
100,000 people

2000 miles
2000 km

- The only two countries to have more than 1 billion people are India (1.1 billion) and China (1.3 billion).

- One in three of the earth's people lives in either India or China. Combined with the rest of Asia, nearly one in two of the earth's people is Asian.

- Nearly 3 of every 5 people in the world live in Asia and Europe.

- The largest concentration of people on the earth is found in East Asia (China, Japan, Taiwan, and North and South Korea). Nearly 25 percent of all people live in this region. Most of China's population lives on the North China Plain to take advantage of the land that the Yellow River (Huang He) has made **arable**, or fit for growing crops. Most East Asians are subsistence farmers.

- The second-largest concentration of humans is in South Asia (India, Bangladesh, Sri Lanka, and Pakistan). Currently, India's rate of natural increase is higher than China's; thus, India is projected to overtake China by nearly 2030 as the world's most heavily populated country. Most South Asians are subsistence farmers living on the arable land surrounding the Indus and Ganges rivers.

- The third-largest concentration of people is in Europe, from the Atlantic to the Ural Mountains (in Russia). This is highly related to Europe's climate and the coal deposits that largely facilitated a population explosion during the Industrial Revolution of the 1800s. In contrast to Asians, most Europeans are **urban** dwellers, living in cities.

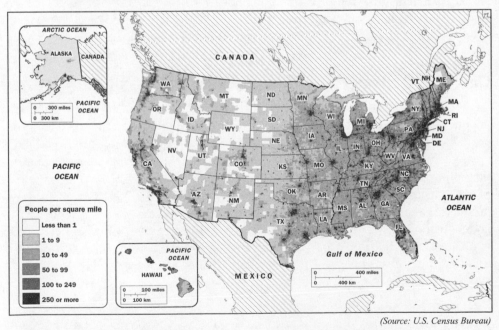

(Source: U.S. Census Bureau)

Figure 3.2. Population density map of the continental United States illustrating population per square mile in 2000

Population Density

Density is another tool geographers use to study population distributions. Density is simply the number of people in a particular land area. Demographers use several types of density to analyze population trends:

- **Arithmetic density** (also called population density) is the total number of people divided by the total land area. For example, 4.4 million people live in Minnesota, the area of which is 84,000 square miles. Therefore, Minnesota has an arithmetic density of 52 people per square mile. Arithmetic density can be deceptive because it does not show concentration patterns effectively. Egypt, for example, has an arithmetic density of 177 people per square mile. But 98 percent of Egyptians live on only 3 percent of the land nearest the Nile River.

- **Physiological density** is the number of people per unit of arable land. In other words, it is the population divided by the number of square miles of farmland in the region. This measurement can be helpful in analyzing the amount of farmland available to the population. The physiological density of the United States is 340 people per square mile, whereas that of Japan is 7,000 people per square mile. While Egypt's arithmetic density is only 177 people per square mile, its physiological density is greater than 3,000. In fact, the fertile land surrounding the Nile River in Egypt has a density of nearly 8,000 Egyptians per square mile.

- **Agricultural density** is the number of farmers per unit of arable land. A very high agricultural density means that many farmers are on each piece of farmland. A low agricultural density suggests the presence of larger farms.

Carrying Capacity and Overpopulation

Related to density is a region's or country's **carrying capacity**, the number of people the area can sustain or support. This number varies depending on a region's available technology, wealth, climate, and ability to bring in resources from other areas to support its people. For example, Japan is a classic example of a country that imports (or brings in) needed food and supplies to sustain its large population in exchange for its exportation of technologically advanced products, such as Sony products. Israel, in its largely arid (dry) environment, has developed advanced irrigation methods to create more arable lands for farming. Saudi Arabia has developed innovative **desalination** plants to remove salt from ocean water and turn it into drinking water for its people. These innovative tactics have increased these regions' carrying capacities.

Overpopulation occurs when a region's population outgrows its carrying capacity, but that carrying capacity can be increased through global trade and communication. It is not always simply a reflection of the natural resources available in that particular country or region. For example, Japan increased its carrying

Figure 3.3. Arithmetic density throughout the world, 2007

capacity by developing extensive trade relationships with other countries so Japan could import food for its people in exchange for trading technology. Japan is not overpopulated, although it has a high population density. Therefore, a large population can be thought of as a problem when the number of people in the area is larger than the resources available to sustain that population and keep the people living at a decent standard.

Keep in mind, though, that some places are capable of producing more resources than they are able to harvest. This is the case in some less-developed countries with infrastructures and agricultural processes that are not sufficiently productive because of the lack of advanced technology (among other factors). A region's carrying capacity can be increased through improved farming practices and economic development.

Population Pyramids

Demographers use **population pyramids**, also known as age-sex structures, to evaluate the distribution of ages and genders in a given population. A group of people of the same age is known as a **cohort**. Each cohort is split between men and women on the pyramid. The wider the base of the pyramid, the higher the percentage of young people exists in the community. The more top-heavy the pyramid, the higher the percentage of elderly people. A population pyramid can also help predict future growth of populations. Because a woman typically has a baby when she is between the ages of 15 and 45, the more women in that age range, the higher the world's birth rates will be. Let's practice with population pyramids by analyzing Algeria's population pyramid for 2000 and comparing it with Italy's pyramid for that year. Then we will look at projected 2025 pyramids for both countries.

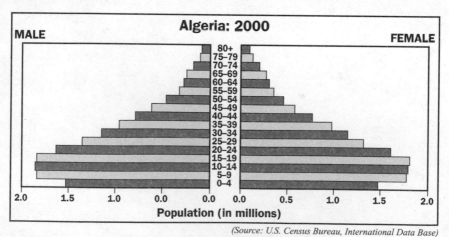

(Source: U.S. Census Bureau, International Data Base)

Figure 3.4. Algeria's 2000 population pyramid

Check to see if you can use the Algerian pyramid:

- How many males are there in the 0–4 cohort in 2000? (About 1.6 million.)

- How many females are there in the 55–59 cohort in 2000? (About 0.4 million.)

- Algeria's pyramid has a wide base and a flattened top. What does that mean? (More young people than old people live in Algeria.)

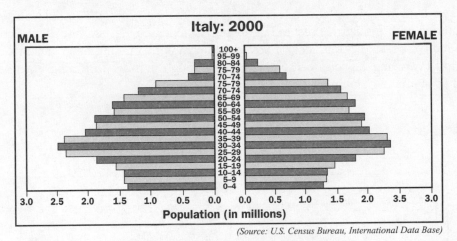

(Source: U.S. Census Bureau, International Data Base)

Figure 3.5. Italy's 2000 population pyramid

Check to see if you can use the Italian pyramid:

- How many males are there in the 0–4 cohort in 2000? (About 1.4 million.)

- How many females are there in the 55–59 cohort in 2000? (About 1.6 million.)

- Italy's pyramid is wider in the middle than at the base. What does that mean? (The population growth rate is slowing because the women in the childbearing ages of 15 to 45 are not having as many babies as their parents did.)

Before we look at each country's 2025 pyramids, let's consider what we would expect them to show:

- Because Algeria had a larger population of 0–4-year-olds in 2000, we would expect a larger population in 2025 for the 25–29-year-olds.

- We would expect Italy to have larger number of elderly people than younger people in 2025, because in 2000 women were not reproducing enough to replace the generations. In other words, we would expect Italy's pyramid to be more top-heavy than Algeria's. Another factor to consider is that Italians typically live longer than Algerians because of better health care and higher average wealth.

Now let's look at the 2025 pyramids for both countries to check our predictions.

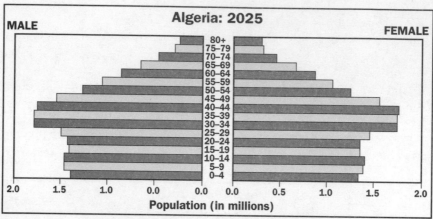

(Source: U.S. Census Bureau, International Data Base)

Figure 3.6. Algeria's 2025 population pyramid

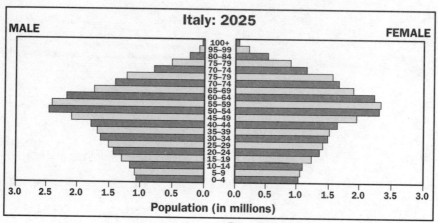

(Source: U.S. Census Bureau, International Data Base)

Figure 3.7. Italy's 2025 population pyramid

How do the pyramids compare?

- Algeria's growth rate did decrease, because the base of the pyramid is thinner than the middle section. That means the parents in the childbearing cohorts (ages 15 to 45) are not having enough babies to sustain their numbers (or the babies are not surviving).

- Italy has a more dramatic decrease in population growth rates, as indicated by the top-heavy pyramid with a thinner base. That is a sign of a **graying population,** or a population that has more middle-aged and older people than young people.

About 20 percent of western Europe's population is over the age of 60 years. By 2030 about 36 percent of its population is projected to be over 60 (Population Reference Bureau).

Let's do one more quick analysis, looking at the 2007 population pyramid for the United States.

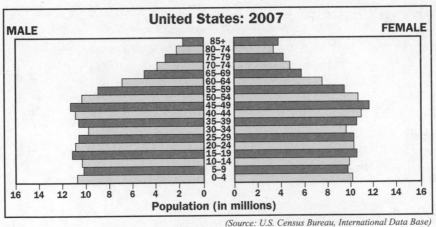

(Source: U.S. Census Bureau, International Data Base)

Figure 3.8. 2007 U.S. population pyramid

Notice the bulge in the U.S. population pyramid? It occurs in the 45–49 and 50–54 cohorts. People in those cohorts were born between 1953 and 1962 and are members of what has been called the baby boom generation, born in the years immediately following World War II, when the troops returned home and started families. History is important to analyzing population pyramids.

Graying Population

The **dependency ratio** is a helpful tool in analyzing the workforce and age distribution in a country. People in a country aged 15 through 64 are considered *nondependent* because they can support themselves (usually) through work. *Dependents* are usually people who are older or younger than the working group; they depend on the workers (nondependents) for their survival. Dependents are usually the elderly and children. The dependency ratio shows the relationship between the dependents and the nondependents.

A high dependency ratio means that there are more people who are dependent than are working. This can lead to problems because there are fewer workers able to pay taxes to support health care and Social Security programs for the dependents. The dependency ratio is growing in western Europe and the United States as the baby boomers age. A graying population is related to an increasing dependency ratio. Rapid growth also increases the dependency ratio and is the reason dependency ratios in Africa are fairly high.

Geo Factoid

The year 2000 marked the first time in human history that people under 14 years of age were outnumbered by people over 60 (Population Reference Bureau).

PART 2 — Population Growth and Decline Over Time and Space

Population Explosion

Over the last three centuries, the earth has experience a **population explosion**, a dramatic population increase. Currently, the global human population of nearly 6.5 billion is growing at an **exponential growth rate**, which means that the more people that are added, the faster the population is growing. Exponential growth is different from **linear (or arithmetic) growth**, which is a constant of fixed rate of growth. For example, if you trace the human population over time, in 1750, the population was at about 700 *million* people. However, in just over 200 years, the population has growth to 6 *billion* (one billion equals one thousand million).

Historical Trends in Population Change

Approximately 10,000 to 12,000 years ago, the **first agricultural revolution** empowered humans with the ability to domesticate crops and build stationary settlements through farming, rather than always hunting and gathering on the move. Thereafter, cities began to develop and the population began to grow at faster speeds. IR spurred 2nd ag. rev.

In the 1700s, the **Industrial Revolution,** diffusing from England, facilitated the growth of new technologies and industry. Alongside the Industrial Revolution was the **second agricultural revolution**, in which improved fertilization and food storage technology was invented. This improved and increased the food supply,

1st: domestication
2nd: technology

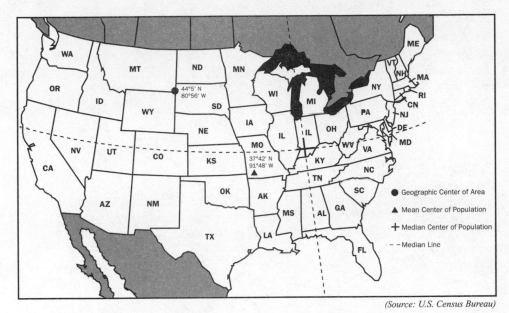

(Source: U.S. Census Bureau)

Figure 3.9. Map of the center of the U.S. population

fostering population growth to meet the demands of the Industrial Revolution for more workers. Cities rapidly became overcrowded as people moved from the farms to get factory jobs; urban populations boomed.

Malthus: population-exponential
food-linear

Theories of Population Growth

In response to the fast-growing urban areas and an increasing population, British theorist **Thomas Malthus** wrote in his 1798 publication *An Essay on the Principle of Population* that the world's population growth would outpace its carrying capacity. He argued that the global population was growing geometrically, while its food supply was only growing arithmetically. That is, the population was growing faster than the food supply. He advocated for birth control and celibacy, which he called positive checks. He also warned of negative checks, such as war, starvation, and disease.

Critics of Malthusian theory point to the unpredictability of the future as the theory's major flaw. Malthus could not have envisioned innovations in agriculture, such as genetic modification and improved fertilization techniques, that improved output. Nor could he have foreseen modern farming equipment, which enabled farmers to cover more ground than in Malthus's time, leading to greater food production. **Karl Marx** wrote that the problem was not population growth rates but the unequal distribution of resources and wages. **Ester Boserup** wrote another theory that contrasted with both Malthus and Marx. He believed that the overpopulation problem could be solved by increasing the number of subsistence farmers.

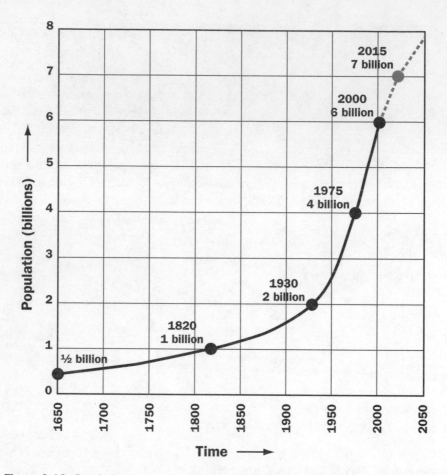

Figure 3.10. Graph demonstrating exponential global population growth over time

Neo-Malthusians apply some of ideas in the Malthusian theory. The neo-Malthusian idea of sustainable development hinges on the Malthusian idea that human population growth must reach a "sustainable" level within carrying capacity. These arguments are more regional rather than global in that, for economic and technological reasons, different regions can support different levels of population. As mentioned earlier, many of the highest population growth rates are occurring in poorer regions with lower carrying capacities.

Population Projections for the Future

By the 1820s, the human population reached 1 billion. The **United Nations** devised **growth scenarios** to predict population growth. In its low-growth scenario, the United Nations predicts that the earth's population will begin declining, reach 7.5 billion in 2050 and 5.1 billion in 2100. In contrast, its high-growth scenario predicts a global population of 11 billion in 2050 and 16 billion in 2100. The United Nations' medium-growth scenario, the one most accepted by demographers, predicts 9.0 billion in 2050 and 9.5 billion in 2100.

Among the negative checks on population growth that have occurred throughout world history are the Black Plague of the 1300s in Europe, which decimated 40 percent of the European population and killed 13 million Chinese; the Irish potato famine, which killed nearly one in two Irish people and caused massive emigration from Ireland; and HIV/AIDS, which since the 1980s has risen to be a **pandemic,** a disease affecting very large amounts of area and people, often at a global scale (in contrast with an **epidemic**, which affects a more local group).

HIV/AIDS

The number of people living with HIV/AIDS in the Middle East and North Africa rose 75 percent between 2003 and 2005 (Population Reference Bureau).

In 2005, nearly 39 million people were living with HIV and nearly 3 million people died from AIDS. Overall the global infection rate is believed to have peaked in the 1990s, but the number of people with HIV is growing because of popula-

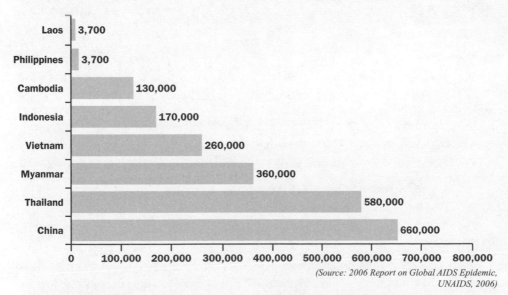

(Source: 2006 Report on Global AIDS Epidemic, UNAIDS, 2006)

Figure 3.11. Number of adults and children infected with HIV in some Asian countries

tion growth and increased life expectancy resulting from better medicine for AIDS patients. In sub-Saharan Africa, the area most acutely affected by AIDS, some epidemics are still expanding; nearly 19 percent of all adults there are infected. Africa is the global **epicenter**, or region at the center of impact, of the AIDS pandemic. China, also facing an AIDS epidemic, is projected to see nearly 11 million infections by 2010. Death rates in sub-Saharan African countries are higher because of AIDS-related deaths.

A Demographer's Toolbox: Key Measurements

Demographers use key terms to analyze population patterns. Here is a list of the primary measurement tools:

- **Crude birth rate (CBR)**: number of live births per 1,000 people in a year.

- **Crude death rate (CDR)**: number of deaths per 1,000 people in a year. One interesting aberration exists in some more-developed (richer) countries in western Europe that have higher death rates than less-developed (poorer) countries. This occurs because more-developed countries have a higher percentage of elderly people as a result of longer life expectancies and decreased birth rates.

The CBR and CDR are considered "crude" not because they are rude but because they are general statistics and do not look specifically at the age groups most likely to either give birth or die. They are calculated based on entire populations, making them general statistics.

- **Infant mortality rate (IMR)**: number of infant deaths per 1,000 live births. Infants who die before their first birthdays are counted in the IMR.

- **Life expectancy**: average number of years to be lived by a person.

- **Fecundity**: the ability of a woman to conceive. The fecund years are generally 15 to 45, but this range is believed to be expanding.

- **General fertility rate (GFR)**: number of births per 1,000 women in the fecund years. This measure of fertility is more specific than the CBR.

- **Total fertility rate (TFR)**: predicted number of births a woman will have as she passes through the fecund years. The 2006 global TFR was greater than 3.0, which means that a woman is likely to have three children as she ages from 15 to 45. Importantly, a TFR of 3.2 does not mean that a woman is likely to have 3 kids and two-tenths of a child. It is a statistical average, so you round to the nearest whole number. The TFRs of most developed

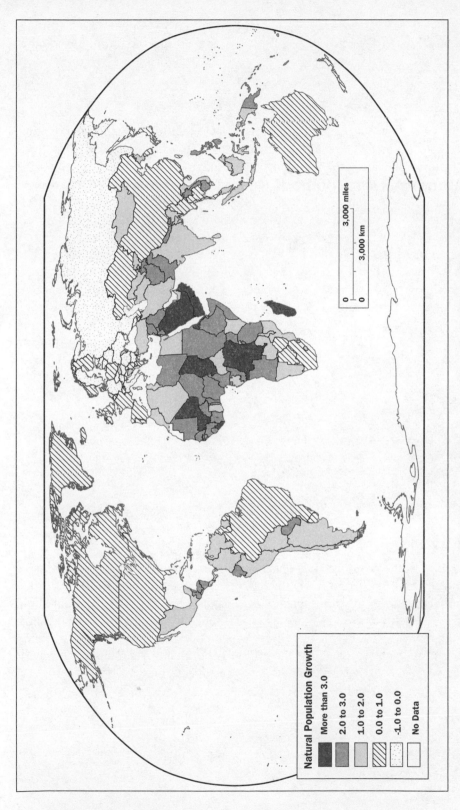

Natural Population Growth

More than 3.0

2.0 to 3.0

1.0 to 2.0

0.0 to 1.0

-1.0 to 0.0

No Data

3,000 miles

3,000 km

0

0

Figure 3.12. Rate of natural increase (annual percentage)

countries (western Europe and North America) and China were 2.1 or less in 2006. However, the U.S. TFR is still higher than the birth rates in other industrialized countries.

Replacement-Level Fertility

A TFR of 2.1 is considered **replacement-level fertility**, meaning that parents will produce the number of children needed to replace themselves. This leads to **zero population growth (ZPG)**, when the population size remains the same from year to year. For this to happen, the number of births minus the number of deaths must equal 0. Such a situation results in a **rate of natural increase (RNI)** of zero. The RNI is the growth rate of a population calculated using the formula CBR – CDR/10. An RNI equal to zero means that the population will neither grow nor decline. The global 2006 RNI was roughly 1.2 percent. In more-developed countries, it was only 0.1 percent, nearly ZPG. In the less-developed countries, it was 1.5 percent; in Africa, it was 2.3 percent. The RNI is called "natural" because it does not include migration—people moving in and out of the country. Therefore, a country may have a low RNI, but it might have immigration—people moving into the country. The RNI affects the country's **doubling time**, or the number of years it will take for the country to double in population size.

At the current RNI of around 1.2 percent, the global population will double in approximately 50 years (Population Reference Bureau).

Fertility and Mortality

Fertility is the reproductive behavior of a population, whereas **mortality** is death-related behavior. Fertility is affected by several key factors. Biologically, the most important factor affecting fertility is the age of the reproductive population. Obviously, the fertility rate in a nursing home is much lower than that in a neighborhood with many 20- to 30-year-olds. For a woman, fecundity usually begins around 15 years of age and terminates in the mid-40s. For males, reproductive behavior peaks at about age 20, but the termination age is undetermined.

Studies indicate that women with lower levels of body fat tend to be less fecund than others.

A population's diet and nutritional intake also has an impact on fertility. Famine reduces fertility rates. Economic factors also play a role in shaping fertility. Industrialization tends to reduce fertility rates because families move from being rural farmers to city dwellers. Children are needed on the farms to help, but they are expensive in the cities.

Sociocultural factors, such as when men and women can marry, also affect fertility patterns. If a culture believes men and women should marry young, it is encouraging higher fertility rates. The simple fact is that the couple that is together longer has more time to have babies. Such **pronatalist population policies** encourage families to have more children.

Population Policies

Pronatalist policies promote reproduction and bigger families; they are often called expansive policies. Policies such as tax breaks for families with children and antiabortion laws are considered pronatalist. Adolf Hitler was trying to encourage the growth of his country's "Aryan" population when he established pronatalist policies to reward Aryan women with public recognition for having many babies. Hitler's racist policies were also considered **eugenic population policies** because they encouraged the reproduction of only certain groups of people and discouraged or terminated the growth of others. In the 1950s, Chairman Mao Zedong encouraged Chinese families to reproduce by rewarding families with medals and cash prizes for having many children. Currently, former East Germany is engaging in advertisements and promotions to encourage higher birth rates in an attempt to reverse the approaching **underpopulation**, when not enough people would be available to fill the jobs and fulfill the responsibilities necessary to sustain the society.

In contrast, **antinatalist population policies** encourage a reduction in fertility rates. They are often called restrictive policies because they limit population growth. India has adopted antinatalist approaches to try to reduce its fertility rates. Abortion is readily accessible, as are contraceptive measures. In fact, the government has been accused of forcing women to be sterilized, a procedure that terminates a human's ability to reproduce.

In the 1980s, China adopted the antinatalist **one-child policy**, which punished families for having more than one child in many regions of China. This policy was created under Deng Xiaoping's administration in response to the pronatalist approach of his predecessor, Mao, which created overpopulation problems in China. Allowed to have just one child, many families preferred to have only boys to carry on the family name and be able to earn more money, since men have more earning power in Chinese society. This led to **female infanticide** problems, with some families aborting or killing their female newborns so they could try to have male children instead. It also led to gender imbalances because some regions had more men than women. This is measured by the **sex ratio**, the number of males per 100 females. Some demographers link these gender imbalances to China's HIV/AIDS rates, a result of men being unable to find wives and thus hiring prostitutes, who are more likely to be HIV positive.

For every two births in the world, at least one pregnancy is aborted. Only about half of the 60 million abortions throughout the world are legal. Abortions actually outnumber deaths on a worldwide scale (Population Reference Bureau).

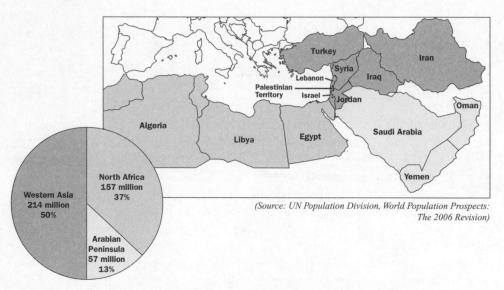

(Source: UN Population Division, World Population Prospects: The 2006 Revision)

Figure 3.13. 2007 population in the Middle East and North Africa

Global Population Conferences

The United Nations has held several conferences on controlling population growth. The **1974 UN population conference** in Romania was burdened by cold-war tensions. The Soviets (Russians) felt that population control was a conspiracy by the United States to stop the growth of communist countries, such as the Soviet Union and China. The **1984 conference** held in Mexico was colored by the advent of the Green Revolution's new technologies to increase global food production in the neediest countries. China had also enacted its one-child policy. The **1994 conference** in Egypt proposed the "Cairo Strategy" to teach contraception uses in schools in poorer countries. However, conservative elements, such as the Roman Catholic Church and Muslim countries, vehemently disagreed with the strategy and blocked its implementation. The **2004 conference** declared that the key to reducing the global RNI is to empower women throughout the world by improving women's educational and economic parity (equality) with that of men. In other words, if women have increased economic and educational opportunities, they can make career choices beyond just having children.

Worldwide, women who have completed their high school education have an average of three children; without it, the average is seven (Population Reference Bureau).

Demographic Transition Model

As described in Chapter 2, geographic models help explain and predict human patterns. The model developed to explain and predict changes in population growth is called the **demographic transition model (DTM)**, which predicts changes in birth, death, and natural increase rates in countries as they "transition" or mature. It is based on the assumptions that economics drive demographic change and that all countries will pass through four stages of demographic transition or change. The three measurements in the model are crude birth rate, crude death rate, and rate of natural increase. Let's look at each of the stages.

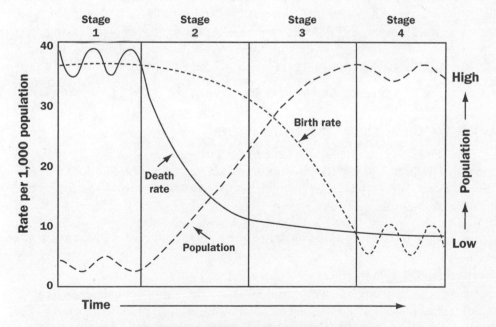

Figure 3.14. Demographic transition model

Stage 1: Low Growth (High Stationary Stage)

- High CBR and CDR, leading to low RNI.

- Fluctuation in CBR and CDR because of disease, famine, and war.

- This stage usually characterizes a subsistence farming country without an industrialized economy.

Stage 2: High Growth (Expanding Stage)

- High CBR: children are still needed on the farms to help.

- Declining CDR: the crude death rate starts to drop as new health care systems arrive, such as better medicine. Industrialization has begun, but the birth rate has not fallen because families are still living in the subsistence agriculture mode that requires lots of children, many of whom did not survive before the arrival of the new medicine and technology. It takes time for families to realize the changes in society.

- The RNI increases because the same high number of births is occurring with fewer deaths to match the high birth numbers. Therefore, population expansion is at a high rate.

Stage 3: Moderate Growth (Expanding Stage)

- Declining CBR: the crude birth rate begins to drop because of families' decisions to lower the number of children they are having. As families move to live in cities growing as a result of industrialization, they have fewer children (raising children is expensive in cities). They also realize that their children will live longer with the new health care technology available. Women have more options in the newly industrialized economy.

- The RNI is decreasing but still greater than zero, so the population is still expanding in size.

Stage 4: Low Growth (Low Stationary Stage)

- The CBR and CDR meet at equal levels (equilibrium), but this time they are at low levels (rather than the high levels seen in stage 1).

- The RNI is low.

- This stage is seen as the modern-society stage with zero population growth.

Criticisms of the DTM

Critics of the demographic transition model point to its being based on England's transition from a subsistence economy to an industrialized society. They believe not all countries will pass through the same demographic transition pattern. For example, some African countries benefited from the diffusion of medicine and food supplies from more-developed countries, a pattern not seen in England's case. Further, demographic growth in 19th-century England occurred in the millions, not the billions of people seen in today's transitions. England progressed from stage 2 to stage 3 over the course of 100 years, but today's stage-2 countries are being pushed to enter stage 3 at a much faster pace.

Some demographers propose adding a fifth stage to the DTM. This new stage would show a continuing decline in the CBR, as seen in many more-developed countries such as France and Germany. This would show the graying-population patterns noticed throughout some wealthier countries.

Demographic Momentum

Demographic momentum, sometimes called **hidden momentum**, occurs in many developing countries when the population continues to grow even after replacement-level fertility is reached. How could this happen if the TFR is 2.1 to 2.5 and parents are producing only enough children to replace themselves? Remember that the rate of natural increase is CBR – CDR. Many developing countries have population pyramids that are wide at the bottom and very thin at the top because life expectancy is not high. Therefore, when the huge number of young people start having babies, even if only two per couple, that new generation of births far surpasses the number of old people dying. Thus, you have population growth even when people are practicing replacement-level TFRs. This makes reaching zero population growth very difficult for countries with wide-based population pyramids.

Global Variations in Demographic Transition

Importantly, the DTM demonstrates that the CDR is a function of technological innovation and improvements in health care, whereas the CBR is more a function of cultural choice and individual decisions by people. The CBR often takes longer to change, unless it is forcibly changed at a governmental level, as in China's one-child policy.

Different countries are in different DTM stages. These varying stages reflect, to some degree, their economic and demographic development. All countries have progressed beyond stage 1, largely through the diffusion of medical technology from more-developed countries in the late 20th century during the **medical revolution**. With improved medicine, people in these poorer regions began having longer life expectancies, which, coupled with the already high birth rates, led to higher population growth rates.

Many of the poorest countries were pushed into stage 2. Most Latin American and Asian countries remain in stage 3 at moderate growth, while most African countries remain at high growth in stage 2. Many western European countries are at the end of stage 4's zero population growth equilibrium and pushing toward a potential stage 5, if it exists. Japan is also facing the fifth stage, or the graying-population problem.

Instead of encouraging immigration to fill jobs once occupied by the growing number of elderly people, Japan is trying to increase the age of its workers.

Africa's share of the world population rose from 9 percent to 14 percent between 1950 and 2005 (Population Reference Bureau).

Epidemiologic Transition Model

One other model to mention is the **epidemiologic transition model**, which focuses on the causes of death in each of the stages of the DTM. For example, pandemics like the Black Plague affect the CDR in stage 1, while diseases (such as cholera) associated with overcrowding during massive movement into cities affect the CDR during stage 2. The CDR is most affected in stages 3 and 4 by diseases associated with the growing numbers of elderly people. Some demographers call for a fifth stage in the epidemiologic model, one showing the reemergence of infectious and parasitic diseases that were once thought to be eradicated during stage 3, such as bubonic plague and smallpox. This is speculated to occur because of improved transportation and space–time compression, allowing human contact to occur more rapidly. This was seen recently in the SARS epidemic and the avian flue outbreaks of the early 21st century.

PART 3 Population Movement

Spatial Interaction and Friction of Distance

Have you noticed that the interconnectedness of the world is increasing? It seems that we are getting closer together, even though our real distance is not decreasing. For example, communicating with someone in Taiwan today is not as big of an ordeal as it was 20 or even 10 years ago. It takes just seconds to log onto a computer and send an instant message to a person as far away as East Asia. It seems as if the difficulty of distance, known as the **friction of distance**, has been reduced. In other words, distance is not the barrier to communication and travel that it once was.

This process of coming closer together and more in contact with each other, even though the real distance remains the same, is called **space–time compression**. The friction of distance is being reduced through space–time compression, and consequently spatial interaction is increasing. **Spatial interaction** is simply the interaction between two places, whether through communication, economic transaction, or migration and travel.

Migration Defined

As we become more linked together, our ability to move across the earth's surface is increasingly more accessible. This is affecting **migration**, the process of *permanently* moving from your home region and crossing an administrative boundary, such as between counties, states, or countries. Perhaps someday it will include planets. Today more than 174 million people have moved outside the country in which they were born.

The number of migrants has more than doubled since 1975, with most living in Europe, Asia, and North America. The United States attracts the most migrants of all countries in the world.

Migration Streams

Why do people migrate? Migration patterns often give clues to what is happening in various parts of the world. A **migration stream** is a pathway from a place of origin to a destination. If hordes of people are emigrating from a place, perhaps something is pushing those masses of people out. Places attracting lots of migrants must have high **place desirability**—possession of positive features making people want to move there. If a place has more immigrants (moving into it) than emigrants (leaving it), it has a **net in-migration**. Places with more emigrants than immigrants have a **net out-migration**. A net in-migration usually indicates that an area has high place desirability; net out-migration usually indicates the opposite.

Migration streams often develop because of information exchange. People in the place of origin may hear of great opportunities in the new place, may have family members in the new community, or may be seeing advertisements for the new place. Usually, where there is a migration stream there is a **migration counterstream** of people moving back to the place of origin from the new place.

Push and Pull Factors

Migration is usually not a random act but is based on thoughtful consideration. Often migration decisions are based on a combination of push and pull factors influencing a person's movement. **Push factors** are the negative influences that make a person want to move away, such as high taxes, high crime rates, and abusive governments, among others. **Pull factors** are the positive influences that pull a person toward a particular place, such as affordable real estate, good schools, and clean parks. The assignment of what is a push and what is a pull factor is highly personal. For example, being near family members may be a positive pull factor to some people but a negative push factor to others.

Voluntary Versus Forced Migration

Voluntary migration occurs when migrants have an option of whether or not to move. However, **involuntary (or forced) migration** is when migrants are pushed from their land. The largest forced migration occurred with the North Atlantic slave trade, forcing nearly 30 million Africans from their homes to migrate to the Americas. **Refugees** are migrants fleeing some form of persecution or abuse. **International refugees** flee their country and move to another country, while *intra*national refugees abandon their homes but remain in their country to escape persecution. Intranational refugees are also known as **internally displaced peoples**.

In 2005, an estimated 23.7 million people were internally displaced, roughly 1.6 million fewer than in 2004 (Internal Displacement Monitoring Centre).

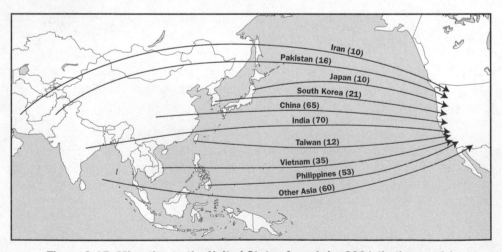

Figure 3.15. Migration to the United States from Asia, 2001 (in thousands).

Some Major Regions of Dislocation and Refugees

The following is a list of some regions of dislocation, or places where people are being forced to migrate as refugees because they are being persecuted:

- **Sub-Saharan Africa** is one area of the world with the largest refugee crisis. Millions of people fled from Rwanda and the Congo in response to tribal or ethnic conflicts. In the Darfur region of northeastern Sudan, religious and ethnic tensions between the North and the South, Muslims and animists, and the government and rebels have led to massive dislocation. Zaire, Tanzania, Uganda, Liberia, Sierra Leone, Angola, and Burundi are also seeing large numbers of war-related refugees.

- **The Middle East** (which many argue includes North Africa): A major migration stream in the Middle East includes emigration (or dislocation) of Palestinians after the formation of the Israeli state to neighboring Southwest Asian countries such as Jordan, Syria, and Egypt. Additional dislocations include the Kurdish people from the former Iraq and Afghanistan's citizens during Soviet occupation in the 1980s.

- **Europe:** The fall of Yugoslavia in the Balkans led to the largest refugee crisis in Europe since World War II. Nearly 7 million refugees fled their homes during this conflict.

- **Southeast Asia:** The Vietnam War created nearly 2 million refugees, Cambodia's violent governmental transition uprooted nearly 300,000 refugees, and the dictatorial government of Burma (now Myanmar) has dislocated thousands.

- **South Asia:** In addition to Afghani refugees fleeing to neighboring Pakistan, Sri Lanka has seen nearly 1 million of its citizens dislocated by a feud with the Sinhalese government.

More Major Migrations at Different Scales

About 3 percent of the world's people have migrated from their countries of origin. North America, Oceania, and Europe have net in-migration, while Asia, Africa, and Latin America have net out-migration. About 50 percent of Southwest Asia's population are immigrants, making it the region with the highest percentage in the world.

The United States has seen three major waves of immigration, and each wave originated from a different region. In the colonial era, from 1607 until 1776, Europe and Africa were the primary sources of migrants, both voluntary and involuntary, to the United States. Many Europeans were escaping political and religious persecution in Europe, while many Africans were forced to come to the Americas as slaves.

Country of asylum/ Leading countries of origin	Number of refugees	Country of asylum/ Leading countries of origin	Number of refugees
MENA-Western Asia		**North Africa**	
Iran	994,000	Algeria	94,500
Afghanistan	940,000	Morocco	890,000
Iraq	54,000	Former Palestine	4,000
Iraq	63,400	Egypt	86,700
Former Palestine	34,000	Former Palestine	57,000
Iran	14,300	Sudan	23,600
Turkey	13,600	Somalia	4,200
Jordan	609,500	Libya	12,000
Iraq	450,000	Former Palestine	8,700
Former Palestine	558,200	Somalia	2,900
Palestinian Territory	1,685,800	Morocco	2,300
Gaza Strip	986,000		
West Bank	699,800	**Countries outside MENA**	
Lebanon	296,800	Germany	
Former Palestine	256,800	Turkey	7,200
Iraq	9,200	Iraq	4,900
Sudan	8,300	Iran	4,400
Syria	866,300	Greece	
Former Palestine	512,100	Iraq	2,100
Iraq	351,000	Mauritania	
Turkey	7,300	Morocco	26,700
Iran	3,600	United States	2,800
Iraq	2,300	Iran	
Arabian Peninsula			
Kuwait	14,300		
Former Palestine	13,500		
Saudi Arabia	240,800		
Former Palestine	240,000		
Yemen	82,700		
Somalia	78,600		

(Source: U.S. Committee for Refugees and Immigrants, World Refugee Survey 2006)

Figure 3.16. 2005 Refugee populations in the Middle East and North Africa (MENA)

The 19th century saw continued migration from Europe. Before 1840, most immigrants in America originated in England, but in the 1840s and 1850s, massive numbers of Irish and Germans made the trip across the Atlantic in search of

Source	Destination
Europe	North America
Africa	Americas (slavery)
Southern Europe	South and Middle America
Britain and Ireland	Africa and Australia
India	Eastern Africa, Southeast Asia, and Caribbean America
China	Southeast Asia
Eastern United States	Western United States
Western Russia	Eastward

Figure 3.17. Major migration streams before 1950

opportunity. More than 4.2 million people migrated in the 1840s and 1850s, more than twice that seen since the New World had been colonized.

Many early immigrants to the New World were second sons who did not inherit land from their fathers because the land went to the first-born male. These second sons were in search of opportunity in America to build wealth.

Immigration to the United States slumped during the Civil War but surged again in the early 20th century, fueled by the Industrial Revolution. This wave, starting around 1907, came not just from northern and western Europe but also from areas like Italy, Austria-Hungary, and Russia. European migration never reached such heights after World War I.

During the Great Depression and World War II (1930s through 1940s), immigration to the United States dropped dramatically, but it picked up again thereafter and reached new heights in the 1980s and 1990s. During the 1970s and 1980s, Asia was the leading source of immigrants to the United States. By the late 1980s, Latin America was the chief source of immigrants to the United States. Many U.S. immigrants send money home to their family members in their home countries, a transaction known as a **remittance**. Many immigrants are **guest workers**, temporarily allowed in the United States on work permits.

In 1921, unrestricted immigration to the United States was halted by the **Quota Act of 1921**, which allowed the highest numbers of immigrants from European countries and discriminated against Asians and other regions.

Figure 3.18. Migration streams of guest workers into Europe, 2001

Internal Migration

Internal migration is movement within a country, as opposed to international or external migration, which is movement outside a country. The two types of internal migration are interregional and intraregional. **Interregional migration** is moving from one region in the country to another region, whereas **intraregional migration** is moving within a region, such as from a city to a suburb. As industrialization built up cities in America, more and more Americans migrated from farms to cities in a pattern of **urban migration**, a form of interregional migration. A counterstream soon developed as people left crowded cities for suburbs (intraregional migration). Recently, an increasing number of U.S. city dwellers have been moving back to the solace of rural areas in a trend known as counterurbanization.

The U.S. migration pattern has shifted its center of population consistently westward and in a southerly direction. During the Great Migration, which occurred while the nation was fighting World War I, many southern African-Americans moved north in search of industrial jobs not being filled by immigrants because of the war. By the 1970s, however, more African-Americans were returning to the South than were moving north. This pattern is part of the trend by northerners, especially baby boomers, moving south for better weather and increased job opportunities as U.S. factory jobs decrease in number. This aging of industrial-era factories in the United States is forming a **Rustbelt** in the Northeast and a **Sunbelt** in the South.

The following is a list of other prominent external (or international) migrations after World War II:

- Jewish immigrants to Israel in the Middle East from countries all over the world, including large sources such as Germany and Russia

- Emigration by East Germans to other countries during transition to Soviet control

- From Asia to the United States, with the largest sources being the Philippines, Vietnam, and India

- From North Africa and Turkey to Europe—namely France, Germany, and England

Migration Selectivity

The decision to migrate often fits into a predictable pattern based on age, income, and other socioeconomic factors. This is called **migration selectivity**, the evaluation of how likely someone is to migrate based on personal, social, and economic factors. Age is the most influential factor in migration selectivity. People are most likely to move between the ages of 18 and 30, the time in which they leave their parents' homes, find employment, attend college, go to war, and so on.

Most individuals move 12 times in their lives, and half of those moves occur before age 25.

Brain Drain

Education is also a factor in migration selectivity. Typically, the more educated people are, the more likely they are to make long distance moves because of their increased knowledge of more-distant opportunities and greater job qualifications. Some places experiencing net out-migration suffer from **brain drain**, when the most educated workers leave for more-attractive destinations. The Appalachian region in Kentucky often loses its most talented cohort, causing it to suffer from brain drain. Often governments will try to create programs to try to keep the most educated in their workforce. The Kentucky Governor's Scholars Program was one such program to try to persuade the state's most talented high school students to go to college in Kentucky and stay in Kentucky's workforce.

Gravity Model

Geographers use the **gravity model** to estimate spatial interaction and movement between two places. It is known as the gravity model because it resembles Isaac Newton's theory of gravitational pull. Essentially, it says that larger places attract more migrants, just as larger planets have more gravitational pull. However, the model also asserts that closer places attract more migrants than more distant places. Therefore, migration between two places is directly proportionate to population size and inversely proportionate to the distance between the two places. In all, the gravity model proposes an equation that balances distance and size in trying to predict spatial interactions. For example, the model could be used to predict higher numbers of Mexicans choosing to migrate to the United States than to England because of distance decay factors; the United States is simply closer to Mexico. Thus, the model can be a helpful tool in predicting migration patterns, but it has some limitations: It does not factor in migration selectivity factors, such as age and educational level, and human behavior does not always fit into predicted patterns.

Ravenstein's Migration "Laws"

In the late 1800s, British geographer **Ernst Ravenstein** identified 11 generalizations about migration, some of which still apply today. Here are some of the most important generalizations:

- **The majority of migrants travel short distances.** Migration occurs step by step. A migrant moving from Massachusetts to Florida might stop in North Carolina first and then move on to his final destination of Florida. This is called **step migration**, when a person has a long distance goal in mind and achieves it in a series of small steps. Related to this idea is the rule of short-distance migration, which states that most people never move a long distance. For example, you and your wife can't stand living with your parents so you want to move, but you still want to be close enough so your parents can watch the kids. Therefore, you only move 5 miles away.

  Often, in the process of making a long journey to a final destination, migrants will find an opportunity they like so much that they just stop their journey and stay in the new place they found along the way. This is called an **intervening opportunity**. Suppose, for instance, that on a migration to Florida you stop in Chapel Hill, North Carolina, and decide to stay there instead of proceeding on to Florida; you will have experienced the intervening opportunity of Chapel Hill. **Intervening obstacles** are barriers in a migratory journey. Financial problems, roadblocks, immigration requirements, and wars are just a few of the forms of intervening obstacles that can prevent migrants from reaching their planned final destinations.

- **Migrants who are traveling a long way tend to move to larger cities than smaller cities.** Ravenstein's idea was that the large city, with all its jobs and opportunities, has an almost magnetic pull that makes the long journey worthwhile. Keep in mind that during Ravenstein's lifetime in the 1800s, the Industrial Revolution was pulling people to big cities like Manchester and London. Today this is somewhat true, but modern technology, such as the Internet, makes many "big city" amenities and jobs available in smaller towns.

- **Rural residents are more likely to migrate than are urban residents.** This was true in Ravenstein's time, again because of the Industrial Revolution and its pull of rural dwellers to the cities in search of job opportunities. It is still true in many developing countries, such as China, because many rural folks in these developing countries are moving into large cities within their countries, such as Shanghai, Beijing, Mexico City, Brasilia, and others.

- **Families are less likely to migrate across national borders than are young adults.** Ravenstein based this generalization on the observation that it is simply easier for single people to migrate than it is for whole families. For example, it is difficult for a family to move children and all their belongings over a border. In many cases, single people are less encumbered with responsibilities and are thus more mobile.

- **Every migration stream creates a counterstream.** Therefore, net migration is the number of people in the original flow minus the number of people in the opposite flow (or counterstream). A counterstream can be caused by many factors, sometimes economic, legal, or personal. Even the out-migration of Jews from Nazi Germany had a small counterstream back into Germany because of their capture and forced return by border officials in other countries refusing fleeing Jews shelter from Nazi oppression. A less tragic example might be counterstreams of young Chinese men who originally left their rural villages for new horizons in Chinese cities only to return back to their rural villages after giving city life a try.

Chain Migration

Chain migration occurs when people migrate to be with other people who migrated before them and with whom they feel some tie—be it familial, religious, ethnic, cultural, or some other type of connection. Many immigrants to the United States move in this pattern, following their relatives or friends to destinations that have been the arrival points for generations. For example, the author's grandparents moved from Hamburg, Germany, to the small town of Lebanon, Ohio, because their German relatives had already moved to Lebanon in previous years.

Model of Migration Transition

Wilber Zelinsky constructed a model known as the **migration transition model** to explain and predict migration changes in a country, much like the demographic transition model explains population changes. In Zelinsky's model, people from stage-1 countries are searching on a local basis for necessities but only moving on a temporary basis in their search for food and shelter materials. Stage-2 countries are experiencing such high rates of natural increase that overtaxing of resources and limited opportunities push people to migrate to the more-developed countries in stages 3 and 4. Many North Africans are currently emigrating from their stage-2 countries for new horizons in more-developed western European countries, where jobs and opportunities are often thought to be available. In stage-4 countries, most migration is intraregional, with people moving from cities to suburbs and back.

Short-Term Local Movements and Activity Space

In addition to studying migration, geographers analyze people's daily movements that do not classify as migration. The area in which you travel on a daily basis is known as your activity space. In some more technologically advanced societies, people's activity spaces are wide and vast because they have planes, trains, and automobiles to move them around each day. For example, a United States senator may have an activity space that involves several states each day, as they fly back and forth for political meetings. However, an average citizen in South Africa, for example, may have a much smaller activity space consisting of only a few miles. There are various classifications of this shorter-term, impermanent movement:

- **Cyclic movement** is movement during your daily routine from your home and back. Commuting is a form of cyclic movement.

- **Seasonal movement** is a form of cyclic movement that involves leaving your home region for a short time in response to a change in season. Leaving New England and going to Florida for the winter is a form of seasonal movement. Nomadism, following animal herds for subsistence, is another form, with people moving their herds seasonally to better pastures.

- **Transhumance**, a pastoral farming practice of moving animals from hillsides to pastures, is periodic, seasonal movement.

- **Periodic movement** involves longer periods of stay, as for serving in the military or attending college.

PART 4	Chapter Review

Models Review

Demographic Transition Model (DTM)

In four stages of transition from an agricultural subsistence economy to an industrialized country, demographic patterns move from extremely high birth and death rates to low birth and death rates. In the process, population growth rates skyrocket and then fall again. The crude death rate first falls because of the influx of better health technology, and then the birth rate gradually falls to match the new social structure.

Epidemiologic Transition Model

Disease vulnerability shifts in patterns similar to the DTM. In the early stages, plague and pestilence spread as a result of poor medical technology. As industrialization proceeds, diseases related to urban life spread. In later stages, diseases once thought eradicated reappear as more-developed societies come into easier contact with less-developed regions struggling with the more primitive diseases, such as smallpox and the bubonic plague.

Gravity Model of Spatial Interaction

When applied to migration, larger places attract more migrants than do smaller places. Additionally, destinations that are more distant have a weaker pull effect than do closer opportunities of the same caliber.

Zelinsky Model of Migration Transition

Migration trends follow demographic transition stages. People become increasingly mobile as industrialization develops. More international migration is seen in stage 2 as migrants search for more space and opportunities in countries in stages 3 and 4. Stage-4 countries show less emigration and more intraregional migration.

Terms Review

Agricultural density—Number of farmers per area of farmland.

Antinatalist population policy—Restrictive policy that discourages people from having babies.

Arable land—Land that can be used for agriculture.

Arithmetic density—Number of people per area.

Brain drain—Net out-migration of the most educated individuals from a region.

Carrying capacity—Maximum number of people a region can reasonably sustain.

Chain migration—When migrants move to a new place based on information they received from family or community members who made the same journey earlier.

Cohort—Group of people usually classified by age.

Crude birth rate (CBR)—Number of live births per 1,000 people over a year.

Crude death rate (CDR)—Number of deaths per 1,000 people over a year.

Cyclic movement—Movement made on a daily basis that involves a very short move to and from one's home.

Demographic accounting equation—Equation used for evaluating population change on global and subglobal levels. At the global level, the CBR and CDR are the only two factors in the equation of change. At the subglobal level, immigration and emigration are taken into account.

Demographic momentum (hidden momentum)—Phenomenon of a growing population size even after replacement-level fertility has been reached. This occurs when the base of the population pyramid is so wide that the generation of parents will take time to cycle out before zero growth occurs.

Demography—Study of population characteristics, transitions, and projections.

Dependency ratio—Measurement in which the number of people unable to work because of age is compared with the number of workers in a society.

Desalination—Removal of salt from saltwater to make potable drinking water.

Distribution—Spread of a particular phenomenon across a given space.

Doubling time—Number of years it will take for a population to double in size.

Ecumene—Portion of the earth's surface that is habitable for humans.

Emigration—Movement out of a country or region.

Epicenter—Center, or most intensely affected region, of an outbreak or disaster.

Epidemic—Disease spread acutely over a localized area.

Ernst Ravenstein—Nineteenth-century geographer who wrote essays outlining 11 generalizations of migration, some of which still apply today, whereas others have changed since he wrote them during the Industrial Revolution in England.

Ester Boserup—Principal critic of Malthusian theory who argued that overpopulation could be solved by increasing the number of subsistence farmers.

Eugenic population policy—Policy that encourages some groups of people to have babies and discriminates against other groups, discouraging their reproduction.

Exponential growth—Growth that is compounded, like interest in a bank account; contrasts with linear (arithmetic, or regular) growth, which does not increase in rate.

Fecundity—Ability to conceive a child.

Female infanticide—In response to restrictive population policies, families kill their female infants so they can try to have male babies.

Fertility—Reproductive behavior in a population leading to births.

First agricultural revolution—Occurred 10,000 to 12,000 years ago when humans first developed the ability to remain in a settlement and domesticate crops and animals. Led to the development of cities.

Friction of distance—Negative impact that distance has on spatial interaction, including communication and travel.

General fertility rate (GFR)—Number of births per 1,000 women in the fecund range over a year.

Graying population—Evidenced by a population pyramid showing a higher number of older, or elderly, people in its projection than younger, working-age people. The pyramid is top-heavy.

Guest worker—Migrant who is temporarily permitted to stay in a country only to work.

HIV/AIDS—Human immunodeficiency virus is the onset of what turns into the acquired immunodeficiency syndrome. A global pandemic, outbreaks are most acute in Africa and Asia.

Immigration—Movement into a country or region.

Industrial Revolution—Began in England around the 1700s and later diffused eastward in Europe and to the United States. Saw the development of factory-based economies and urban migration at a large scale. Coincided with the second agricultural revolution and high population growth rates.

Infant mortality rate (IMR)—Number of deaths of children under 1 year of age per 1,000 births over a year.

Infrastructure— "Backbone" of a society, including communication, transportation, and other such maintenance structures.

Internally displaced person—Another name for an intranational refugee, someone who is forced from home but remains within the country.

International refugees—Refugees who flees their country and move to another country.

Interregional migration—Internal migration among particular regions in a country.

Intervening obstacle—Barrier encountered on a journey that prevents or interferes with getting to the planned, final destination.

Intervening opportunity—New opportunity that arises along a journey that is more attractive to the person making the journey and diminishes the attractiveness of the final destination.

Intranational refugees—Refugees who abandon their homes but remain in their country to escape persecution.

Intraregional migration—Internal migration within a particular region, such as from a suburb to an inner city.

Involuntary (or forced) migration—Occurs when a migrant is forced to move because of abuse, war, or similar negative circumstances against their will.

Karl Marx—Principal critic of Malthusian theory who argued that overpopulation was the fault of unchecked capitalism and unequal distribution of resources, leaving some places unable to care for their populations.

Life expectancy—Average number of years a person is expected to live.

Linear (or arithmetic) growth—Growth that is regular and not compounded over time. The growth remains at a steady pace, rather than increasing in pace over time (exponential).

Medical revolution—Period in stage 2 of the demographic transition model when lifesaving medical technology drastically reduces the CDR, leading to longer life expectancies and higher rates of natural increase.

Migration—Movement of a person across an administrative border. The move is intended to be permanent.

Migration selectivity—Combination of factors that predict a person's likelihood to migrate based on factors like age, gender, and education.

Migration streams and counterstreams—In a migration stream migrants are moving from a place of origin to a destination. When the original flow of migrants produces an opposite flow of returning migrants, a counterstream results.

Mortality—Death-related activity in a population.

Neo-Malthusians—Contemporary believers in Thomas Malthus's original ideas. They call for sustainable population growth to be achieved through birth control teachings and regional attention to birth patterns.

Net in-migration—Occurs when the number of immigrants is larger than the number of emigrants.

Net out-migration—Occurs when the number of emigrants exceeds the number of immigrants.

One-child policy—Restrictive, antinatalist policy in China that aimed at immediately reducing China's birth rate to replacement level and below.

Overpopulation—Occurs when a region exceeds its carrying capacity. This is difficult to measure because of changing technology and environmental issues that continually alter the carrying capacity.

Pandemic—Disease spread acutely over a large area or worldwide.

Physiological density—Number of people per area of farmland.

Place desirability—Degree of attractiveness of a place to a migrant.

Population explosion—Exponential, unprecedented growth in human population size over the last three centuries.

Population pyramid—Often called age-sex pyramids, a population pyramid shows the distribution of ages and genders in a particular year.

Pronatalist population policy—Expansive policy that encourages more live births in a population.

Pull factor—Factor that attracts a migrant to a region, such as good schools or nice weather.

Push factor—Factor that causes a migrant to move out of a region, such as high taxes or poor schools.

Rate of natural increase (RNI)—Natural growth rate of a population, which is CBR minus CDR expressed as a percentage. A positive RNI indicates a growing population, whereas a negative RNI indicates a population reducing in size. An RNI equal to zero indicates a stabilizing population.

Refugee—Migrant forced from his or her home by threat, real persecution, or abuse.

Remittance—Sum of money sent by a migrant to his or her family back home.

Replacement-level fertility—When the number of births equals the number of deaths. Usually reached at a TFR between 2.1 and 2.5.

Rustbelt—Decay of the once bustling factory-based economy regions of the northeastern United States

Scale of inquiry—Level of geographic area being investigated. At a very large scale, a neighborhood may be the focus. At a very small scale, the entire earth may be the focus.

Seasonal movement—Form of cyclic movement when a person moves temporarily because of a change in season.

Second agricultural revolution—Coincided with the Industrial Revolution in England and a higher population growth rate, and saw the development of improved sanitation, storage, and fertilization techniques, allowing for greater food output.

Sex ratio—Number of males compared to 100 females in a population.

Space–time compression—Reduction of the friction of distance and distance decay effects because of improved transportation and communication technology. Often space–time compression is seen as the increasing links among people of the earth so that real distance remains the same but perceived distance decreases.

Spatial interaction—Exchange of ideas, people, money, and products among various places.

Step migration—Long migration that occurs as a journey of smaller steps from one place to another until the destination is reached.

Sunbelt—Growth of the economy in the sunny regions of the southern United States that developed as the dominance of the factory-based economy in the northeastern United States decreased.

Thomas Malthus—Malthus's *An Essay on the Principles of Population* was an alarming report during the British Industrial Revolution that predicted that food production would be outpaced by population growth rates. He warned of negative checks, such as famine, and called for positive checks, such as birth control.

Total fertility rate (TFR)—Number of children predicted to be born to a woman as she passes through the fecund years.

Transhumance—Form of pastoral nomadism in which people herd their animals from higher altitudes, such as mountains, to lower places, such as pastures.

Underpopulation—Measure that is difficult to pinpoint; occurs when a population size is below its carrying capacity and cannot sustain the economic development it has reached.

United Nations growth scenarios—Predictions by the United Nations that yield high, medium, and low population growth forecasts for the earth's future.

United Nations population conferences—United Nations conferences held in 1974, 1984, 1994, and 2004 to address population. International controversies and tensions beside population drove the approaches taken at each conference, with the most recent focusing on empowering women as a primary approach to reducing global population growth.

Urban—Pertaining to the city, as opposed to rural, pertaining to the farmlands.

Urban migration—Migration into cities from rural areas.

U.S. Quota Act of 1921—Immigration legislation that limited the number of people from any one country and discriminated against Asians and favored European migrants.

Voluntary migration—Move made by a migrant because he or she wants to move.

Zero population growth—Occurs when births equal deaths, leading to a stationary population level.

PART 5	Some Suggested Web Resources for Further Exploration

Population Reference Bureau (PRB): http://www.prb.org/

This is an excellent, reliable, and user-friendly resource of demographic data and analyses. The PRB compiles an annual analysis of demographic data for the world and its countries.

Population Council: http://www.popcouncil.org/

According to its website, "The Population Council, an international, non-profit, nongovernmental organization, seeks to improve the well-being and reproductive health of current and future generations around the world and to help achieve a humane, equitable, and sustainable balance between people and resources."

United States Census Bureau: http://www.census.gov/

The Census Bureau's website contains U.S. demographic data, analyses, and helpful charts and graphs. It also has a fun population clock that estimates the U.S. population by the minute.

United Nations Population Fund (UNFPA): http://www.unfpa.org/

According to its website, "UNFPA, the United Nations Population Fund, is an international development agency that promotes the right of every woman, man and child to enjoy a life of health and equal opportunity. UNFPA supports countries in using population data for policies and programs to reduce poverty and to ensure that every pregnancy is wanted, every birth is safe, every young person is free of HIV/AIDS, and every girl and woman is treated with dignity and respect."

United Nations Statistics Division: http://unstats.un.org/unsd/

This is the UN's primary engine for distribution of demographic data and analyses. A subscription is required for retrieving much of the information on the site.

U.S. Committee for Refugees and Immigrants: http://www.refugees.org/

According to its website, the mission of the program is, "to address the needs and rights of persons in forced or voluntary migration worldwide by advancing fair and humane public policy, facilitating and providing direct professional services, and promoting the full participation of migrants in community life."

The site contains useful information on refugees, their origins, migrations, and treatment.

U.S. Citizenship and Immigration Services: http://www.uscis.gov/

This site contains data on immigration to the United States, both legal and illegal, as far back as the early 1800s.

Statue of Liberty–Ellis Island Foundation: http://www.ellisisland.org/

On this website, you can look up anyone you know that may have immigrated to the United States through Ellis Island. According to the foundation, "From 1892 to 1924, more than 22 million immigrants, passengers, and crew members came through Ellis Island and the Port of New York. The ship companies that transported these passengers kept detailed passenger lists, called 'ship manifests.' Now, thanks to the generous efforts of volunteers of The Church of Jesus Christ of Latter-day Saints, these manifests have been transcribed into a vast electronic archive, which you can easily search to find an individual passenger."

Internal Displacement Monitoring Center: www.internal-displacement.org/

Affiliated with the United Nations, The Internal Displacement Monitoring Centre (IDMC), is the preeminent international body monitoring conflict-induced internal displacement worldwide. It is an advocacy and educational agency whose site contains data, solutions, and coverage of the world's displaced peoples.

PART 6 Pre-Exam Practice

Terms Review Quiz

Use the Terms Review list or your own memory to determine the extent of your knowledge of key terms and concepts. Remember, the AP exam does not include this kind of exercise, but it is included here as a review tool.

1. _____ Exchange of ideas, people, money, and products among various places.

2. _____ Sum of money sent by a migrant to his or her family back home.

3. _____ Measure that is difficult to pinpoint; occurs when a population size is below its carrying capacity and cannot sustain the economic development it has reached.

4. _____ Form of pastoral nomadism in which people herd their animals from higher altitudes, such as mountains, to lower places, such as pastures.

5. _____ He predicted that the population growth rate would outpace the food supply and called for positive checks on population growth to prevent (or reduce) negative checks.

6. _____ Long migration that occurs as a journey of smaller steps from one place to another until the destination is reached.

7. _____ Number of children predicted to be born to a woman as she passes through the fecund years.

8. _____ Coincided with the Industrial Revolution in England and a higher population growth rate, and saw the development of improved sanitation, storage, and fertilization techniques, allowing for greater food output.

9. _____ Form of cyclic movement when a person moves temporarily because of a change in season.

10. _____ Reduction of the friction of distance and distance decay effects because of improved transportation and communication technology.

11. _____ Exponential, unprecedented growth in human population size over the last three centuries.

12. _____ When the number of births equals the number of deaths. Usually reached at a TFR between 2.1 and 2.5.

13. _____ Factor that attracts a migrant to a region, such as good schools or nice weather.

14. _____ Movement of a person across an administrative border. The move is intended to be permanent.

15. _____ Natural growth rate of a population, which is CBR minus CDR expressed as a percentage.

16. _____ Degree of attractiveness of a place to a migrant.

17. _____ Evidenced by a population pyramid showing a higher number of older, or elderly, people in its projection than younger, working-age people. The pyramid is top-heavy.

18. _____ Restrictive, antinatalist policy in China that aimed at immediately reducing China's birth rate to replacement level and below.

19. _____ Number of people per area of farmland.

20. _____ Occurs when the number of immigrants is larger than the number of emigrants.

21. _____ Occurs when a migrant is forced to move because of abuse, war, or similar negative circumstances against their will.

22. _____ Occurred 10,000 to 12,000 years ago when humans first developed the ability to remain in a settlement and domesticate crops and animals. Led to the development of cities.

23. _____ Barrier encountered on a journey that prevents or interferes with getting to the planned, final destination.

24. _____ Disease spread acutely over a large area or worldwide.

25. _____ "Backbone" of a society, including communication, transportation, and other such maintenance structures.

Multiple-Choice Review Questions

1. Which of the following is most clearly a pronatalist policy?

    (A) Awarding tax breaks to families with three or more children
    (B) Giving families cash rewards for not having more than three children
    (C) Forced sterilization programs
    (D) A law similar to China's one-child policy
    (E) Hospitals offering parenting classes to new parents

2. In which of the following countries is life expectancy projected to drop the most by the year 2015?

    (A) Luxembourg   (D) Japan
    (B) Namibia   (E) Mongolia
    (C) Russia

3. Which of the following countries most likely has the highest agricultural density?

    (A) Germany   (D) England
    (B) United States   (E) Egypt
    (C) Brazil

4. The number of people a region can reasonably support, given its landscape, resources, and trading ability, is known as

    (A)   infrastructure

    (B)   overpopulation

    (C)   physiological density

    (D)   carrying capacity

    (E)   age-sex pyramid

5. Why does the rate of natural increase (RNI) not accurately demonstrate population change for subglobal regions?

    (A)   RNI data do not include immigration and emigration.

    (B)   RNI data are not specific enough to focus on fecund women.

    (C)   The RNI does not change in a region without a cultural decision to change the birth rate.

    (D)   HIV/AIDS has dramatically altered RNI data.

    (E)   Mortality is increasing because of decreased fertility rates in more-developed regions.

6. Country X's demographic transition is depicted in the following table:

Year	CBR	CDR
1975	45	12
1980	46	13
1985	40	12
1990	35	11

    Based on this information, which stage of the demographic transition model best fits Country X in 1990?

    (A)   Stage 1

    (B)   Stage 2

    (C)   Stage 3

    (D)   Stage 4

    (E)   Stage 5

7. Karl Marx would most likely have agreed with which of the following statements?

   (A) Overpopulation results from exponential population growth and arithmetic growth of food supply.

   (B) The unequal distribution of resources creates surplus population.

   (C) Overpopulation is a direct result of not having enough subsistence farmers in an economy.

   (D) Surplus population is impossible.

   (E) Death rates must exceed birth rates.

8. Italy's demographic data differ from Algeria's in that Italy has

   (A) a much higher percentage of women

   (B) a larger percentage of people considered dependents

   (C) a lower average life expectancy

   (D) more people who are rural dwellers

   (E) a population growing at a faster rate

9. Which of the following measurements would give a demographer the closest prediction of reproductive behavior in a fecund woman in a country?

   (A) crude birth rate   (D) total fertility rate

   (B) rate of natural increase   (E) life expectancy

   (C) infant mortality rate

10. By 2050, which country is projected to have the highest population in the world?

   (A) China   (D) India

   (B) Japan   (E) United States

   (C) Russia

11. In the 1990s, which factor was identified at the United Nations population conference as the key to controlling population growth?

    (A) health care
    (B) political ideology
    (C) farming methods
    (D) HIV/AIDS
    (E) the status of women

12. Margaret embarked on her move to California. En route to San Diego from her home of Louisville, Kentucky, she stopped in Santa Fe, New Mexico. While in Santa Fe, she fell in love with the city and decided to stay there. In Margaret's migration, Santa Fe represents a(n)

    (A) intervening opportunity
    (B) intervening obstacle
    (C) remittance
    (D) push factor
    (E) pandemic

13. Which country is in the region with the highest concentration of people?

    (A) Brazil
    (B) Nigeria
    (C) United States
    (D) Czech Republic
    (E) South Korea

14. Which of the following trends matches the urban migration pattern of the 1880s noted by Ernst Ravenstein?

    (A) The majority of migrants move long distances.
    (B) Most migrants are young children following their young parents
    (C) Countercurrents of migration tend to be larger than their original streams.
    (D) Migrants who move long distances tend to move to large cities
    (E) Rural dwellers tend to be less migratory than urban dwellers.

15. Which of the following regions produced the largest migration stream into Germany in the period 1999–2005?

    (A) Latin America
    (B) China
    (C) North Africa
    (D) United States
    (E) Australia

16. Which of the following is NOT a variable in the subglobal population accounting equation?

   (A) Number of births during the interval of measurement

   (B) Number of deaths during the interval of measurement

   (C) Number of people moving into the region during the interval of measurement

   (D) Number of people moving out of the region during the interval of measurement

   (E) Number of children predicted to be born to a woman

17. In which stage of the demographic transition model does the medical revolution take place?

   (A) Stage 1   (D) Stage 4

   (B) Stage 2   (E) Stage 5

   (C) Stage 3

18. Approximately 81 percent of the earth's population lives in poorer, less-developed countries in which three regions?

   (A) Africa, Australia and Asia

   (B) Latin America, Africa, and Asia

   (C) North American, Asia, South America

   (D) Europe, Africa, Pacific Rim

   (E) North America, Europe, Africa

19. Overpopulation in a country occurs when

   (A) total population reaches 10 billion

   (B) there is more of one sex than the other

   (C) the country's population outgrows its carrying capacity

   (D) the country imports food

   (E) large parts of a country are desert

20. Population pyramids are used to show

    (A) the age of a country's population

    (B) the sex ratio of a country's population

    (C) the average income of a country's population

    (D) disease rates

    (E) both A and B

Free-Response Question

Germany is currently experiencing net in-migration.

(A) Define *net in-migration*, and describe the stream identified in the map above.

(B) Define *push factors* and *pull factors*. Give an example of and explain one push and one pull factor that a migrant in the stream shown in the map above may have experienced.

(C) Relate the immigration pattern noted on the map to Germany's negative rate of natural increase.

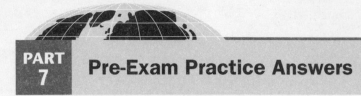

Terms Review Answers

1. Spatial interaction
2. Remittance
3. Underpopulation
4. Transhumance
5. Thomas Malthus
6. Step migration
7. Total fertility rate
8. Second agricultural revolution
9. Seasonal movement
10. Space–time compression
11. Population explosion
12. Replacement-level fertility
13. Pull factor
14. Migration
15. Rate of natural increase
16. Place desirability
17. Graying population
18. One-child policy
19. Physiological density
20. Net in-migration
21. Involuntary (or forced) migration
22. First agricultural revolution
23. Intervening obstacle
24. Pandemic
25. Infrastructure

Multiple-Choice Answers

1. **(A)**

    Pronatalist laws encourage people to have babies, whereas antinatalist policies discourage people from having babies. Cash rewards in the form of tax breaks would encourage people to have more children. (B), (C), and (D) are antinatalist policies discouraging families from having babies, whereas (E) is neither. Some might argue that (E) promotes child birth, but (A) is more clearly encouraging higher birth rates, while (E) is simply supporting new parents.

2. **(B)**

    In sub-Saharan Africa, life expectancy is projected to drop nearly 10 years, on average. Namibia alone is projected to lose 26 years. These drops are primarily attributed to HIV/AIDS infections. (C) would have been the next-best choice because of Russia's struggling economy and rising HIV/AIDS rates, but sub-Saharan Africa has higher loss of life expectancy years. (A) and (D) are both in more-developed regions, and (E) is improving as a result of improved health technology.

3. **(E)**

    Agricultural density is the number of farmers per unit area of farmland. (E) is the best choice because Egypt has a limited amount of farmland near the fertile Nile River; the rest of the country is desertlike. All of Egypt's many farmers crowd near the Nile, packing it densely. (A), (B), and (D) have lower agricultural densities because their farms are more technologically well developed, allowing fewer farmers to farm larger areas and thus decreasing the number of farmers in their economies. (C) has more farmland per person than does Egypt, thereby reducing its agricultural density.

4. **(D)**

    Carrying capacity is like the fire capacity of a theater, which indicates the number of people who can safely sit in the theater and exit in an emergency. Carrying capacity is the number of people who can be sustained in a given region, such as a country. When a country exceeds its carrying capacity, it is considered overpopulated (B). (A) is an integral part of a region's carrying capacity, because the infrastructure is its support network of transportation, health care, communication, and so forth. (C) is the number of people divided by the amount of farmland in a region, and (E) is a demographic tool showing the size of cohorts (age groups) divided by gender in a given country or region.

5. **(A)**

RNI data only include fertility and mortality rates and therefore do not give a complete picture for a region. Although U.S. fertility rates may be moving toward replacement level, the amount of immigration to the U.S. is increasing the size of the overall U.S. population. However, immigration is not accounted for in the RNI. (B) is more applicable to the CBR rather than the RNI. (C) refers to the birth rate, not the RNI. (D) is true in regions acutely hit by HIV/AIDS, but that does not make the RNI less comprehensive in its use. (E) is also a true statement but is not a cause of the RNI's limited picture.

6. **(C)**

Stage 3 depicts a country with a birth rate that begins a substantial decline to match the already low death rate. In Country X, the crude birth rate begins to fall almost 10 points to reach the already-low (or developed-level) death rate. (B) is characterized by a plummeting death rate and a high birth rate; (D) shows a country at low birth and death rates that are at equilibrium. (E) is a suggested addition to the DTM that shows a higher death rate than birth rate, caused by graying populations.

7. **(B)**

Karl Marx argued that a "surplus population," when there are unemployed workers, is only a manifestation of the unequal distribution of resources causing some economic classes and areas to have more resources than others. (A) is the philosophy of Thomas Malthus, who believed that overpopulation results when the birth rate grows faster than the food supply, which leads to famine and chaos. (C) was a belief held by Ester Boserup in the 1960s. Marx would not have agreed with (D) because he did see surplus populations occurring in capitalistic societies. (E) would indicate population reduction, which Marx would not have advocated in by any instance.

8. **(B)**

Italy is experiencing a graying population with its lower birth rates and increasing death rates (because the older generation is larger than the younger generation). Algeria, on the other hand, has not yet moved into stage 4 of demographic transition model and is still experiencing natural population growth. (A) is not true because the percentages of men and women are nearly equal in both countries. (C) is untrue because life expectancy is higher in Italy as a result of its more equally distributed and more well-developed health care practices. (D) is untrue and reversed, because more people are subsistence, rural farmers in Algeria than in Italy. (E) is false for the same reason (B) is true.

9.   **(D)**

The total fertility rate is the number of babies a woman is likely to have as she passes through her fecund (fertile) years, usually from 15 to 45 years of age. It is a predictive measure of the number of children a woman will have. (A) is a general statistic not specific to fecund women, (B) refers to the overall difference between fertility and mortality, (C) refers to the death rates of infants, and (E) is the average number of years a person is expected to live.

10.   **(D)**

China's growth rate was drastically controlled through its one-child policy in the 1980s, forcing its population to reach (or very nearly reach) replacement-level fertility. However, India's drastic growth was not as forcibly controlled, in part because India is a democracy and not a totalitarian state. Therefore, India's growth rate continues to increase, and through hidden momentum, its population will continue to grow for many years to come.

11.   **(E)**

The status of women was first identified at the 1994 U.N. conference in Cairo. Leaders discussed the crucial relationship between opportunities for women beyond reproductive roles and global population control. (A) is related but recognized at earlier conferences; (B) was on focus in the 1970s during the cold war; (C) was a focus in the 1980s, during the Green Revolution; and (D), though a factor discussed at the 1994 conference, has not been considered critical to controlling growth because it reduces population growth.

12.   **(A)**

An intervening opportunity is a place a migrant comes to on her journey and, because of its high place desirability, decides to stay there rather than continue on to her planned destination. (B) is a blockage or barrier that prevents the migrant from reaching her planned destination, (C) is money an immigrant sends back home, (D) is a factor that causes a migrant to move away from a place, and (E) is a very widespread disease.

13.   **(E)**

East Asia has the highest concentration of people. South Korea is in East Asia, as is China, Taiwan, North Korea, and Japan, to name a few. The second-largest concentration on the earth is found in South Asia, composed of India, Sri Lanka, Pakistan, and Bangladesh.

14. **(D)**

In Ravenstein's time, England was industrializing, and most migrants moved only small distances. However, those who went long distances moved to cities in search of opportunities, making (D) correct and (A) incorrect. (B) is incorrect because most migrants were young adults. (C) is incorrect because most migration streams tend to produce smaller counterstreams in the opposite direction. (E) is incorrect because Ravenstein noticed the opposite trend, that rural dwellers were more migratory than urban dwellers because rural dwellers were moving into cities.

15. **(C)**

North Africans are streaming into many western European countries to fill the job vacancies created by the graying population and shrinking birth rates. Although China (B) may be a tempting choice because of its size, the country limits its emigration. A large number of immigrants into the United States come from Latin America (A), but migration to Europe is too long and difficult for many in Latin America compared with the nearer opportunity offered by the United States.

16. **(E)**

The subglobal population accounting equation only uses the actual number of births, deaths, in-migrations, and out-migrations. It does not use predicted values.

17. **(B)**

The medical revolution occurs in stage 2 and is the cause of lowering death rates. At that point, birth rates remain high, which accounts for the rapidly increasing population. (A) is a time of high birth and death rates, (C) is a time of low death rates and falling birth rates, (D) is the time of low birth and death rates, and (E) is the theoretical time when deaths overtake births because of an aging population.

18. **(B)**

Containing India and China, Asia is the world's most populated region. Africa and Latin America are also both experiencing high population growth rates.

19. **(C)**

Carrying capacity is based on the resources and technology of a people. Increasing agricultural output and international trade are two methods of increasing the sustainability levels of a country. (A) is incorrect because there is no set number for overpopulation. If you can only feed 10 people, 11 is overpopulated. Likewise if you can feed 10 billion then a population of 9 billion is not a problem. (B) defines the sex ratio and is not related to overpopulation in this sense. (D) is a way of preventing overpopulation by increasing resources, and (E) is not a limiting factor for food production if technology can make other areas produce sufficient food.

20. **(E)**

Population pyramids show the age and sex ratios of a population. They can be useful to geographers in identifying trends in a country's population as well as pointing to potential future problems, such as a growing dependency ratio. (C) is incorrect because population pyramids do not consider income. (D) Although population pyramids can show the effects of disease on a population, they cannot specifically prove a cause. Loss of population through war, disease, migration, or famine would all appear the same on a pyramid.

Free-Response Answers

The following is a list of suggested main points for each part of the question.

Part A

- Net in-migration occurs when a region has more immigrants than emigrants. In other words, there are more people moving in than moving out of a region.

- The migration stream on the map shows a thick in-migration into Germany from North Africa.

Part B

- A push factor affects a migrant's decision by making him or her want to leave a region, such as high taxes and poor schools, among others. A pull factor affects a migrant's decision by making her or him want to move to a particular location, like a magnetic force.

- Possible pull factors in Germany include better health care, better quality of life, more job opportunities, increased stability of life, and less fighting and warfare.

- Possible push factors in North Africa include civil insurrection and warfare, poor economic conditions, few job opportunities, and poor educational opportunities.

Part C

•   Germany's negative rate of natural increase has created a situation in which more deaths than births occur each year. Therefore, the Germans are not able to fill the number of jobs once held by the larger, older generations that are dying out. This opens up jobs for potential migrants, who hear about the opportunities and move to find jobs once filled by German-born citizens. This relates to the net in-migration of North Africans to Germany seeking to fill the jobs as demanded by the German economy and its graying population.

Chapter 4

Cultural Patterns and Processes

Introduction

When you walk into a shop in a small German town, you are bombarded by elements of culture, just as you are when you go to the movie theater with friends. Even a study of McDonald's restaurants throughout the world leads to interesting questions about cultural differences. Visit a McDonald's in Sweden and you are seated at a candlelit table and served by a waiter. Across the world in Taiwan, McDonald's is considered a place for a quick snack rather than a restaurant. How about ordering a McBeer in Germany? It's on the menu.

Cultural geography is the study of people's lifestyles, their creations, and their relationships to the earth and the supernatural. It is a wide-ranging concept that involves the study of humans' tangible creations, like architecture, languages, and clothing, and their intangible creations, such as their religions and morals. For example, when you visit a Muslim mosque, you are not likely to find pictures of humans. You are much more likely to see geometric patterns on the walls because many Muslims believe that displaying the human image is a form of idolatry. The painting is a human creation, but the image depicted in the painting and where it is displayed are aspects of the Islamic belief system.

> ### Key Questions
>
> - *How do geographers define culture?*
>
> - *How do geographers look at spatial and place aspects of culture in the form of language, religion, race, ethnicity, and gender?*
>
> - *How are cultural patterns represented at different scales, from local to global?*
>
> - *How do cultural traits move through space and time?*
>
> - *What are key aspects to the geography of language and religion?*
>
> - *How does culture shape human–environment relationships?*
>
> - *How is culture expressed in landscapes, and how do different land-scapes reflect different cultural identities?*

PART 1 · Concepts of Culture

The Basics of Culture

Culture is seen by human geographers to be a people's way of life, their behavior, and their shared understanding of life. It is a learned system of meaning that has both material and nonmaterial components. **Material components of culture** include tangible artifacts that can be physically left behind, such as clothing and architecture. **Nonmaterial components of culture** include the thoughts and ideas of a people—for example, their religions or morals—that help define a culture. Cultural geography is a field of study within human geography that looks at how and why culture is expressed in different ways in different places.

Cultural geography analyzes not just religion and language but all aspects of cultural expression, including governments, economies, urban structures, and much more. It is an area of geographic study largely linked to the 20th-century geographer **Carl Sauer**, who championed the study of the **cultural landscape**, sometimes referred to as the **built environment.** The cultural landscape comprises the physical implications of human culture. In other words, wherever a human culture exists, a cultural landscape exists as that culture's unique imprint on their space on the earth.

When you look at your school, for example, the buildings, lawns, flagpoles, and sports fields are all a part of the cultural landscape of that space. Interestingly, when you look at a classroom in your school, you might see remnants of earlier generations of students. For example, on the wall of a certain high school classroom in Nashville, Tennessee, is a map painted by a class of students and their teacher who occupied that space 30 years ago. This might be considered an example of **sequent occupance**, the succession of different cultures. You could argue, however, that both classes were part of American culture. A better example of sequent occupance might be what happened when the Romans, Saxons, Vikings, and others conquered England over a period of 3,000 years, taking over the same space, changing it to fit their needs, and in the process leaving an imprint for future occupiers. The systematic study of this human–environment interaction is called **cultural ecology**.

Environmental Determinism Versus Possibilism

In studying human–environment interactions, cultural geographers encounter the question, "Does the earth make humans take the actions they do?" They also wonder why certain regions thrive and others do not. **Environmental determinism**, a school of thought developed as early as the Greeks, posits that human behavior is controlled (or determined) by the physical environment. "Ideal" climates lead to productive civilizations, as in Egypt near the Nile River. Harsher climates, as in

Siberia, do not foster productivity. Environmental determinists would argue that people are friendlier and more outgoing in Florida but more introverted and reclusive in Minnesota because of the climate.

Possibilism developed as a counterargument to environmental determinism. Possibilists argue that the natural environment places limits on the set of choices (or possibilities) available to people. For example, people living in Florida are not likely to choose to build an igloo park. Not only are Floridians choices limited by the state's climate, but those limitations also drive Floridians constructions and actions. According to possibilists, therefore, it is people, not the environment, that propel human cultural development, although the environment limits the set of choices available to them.

Recently, many geographers have discounted possibilism in favor of a concept known as **cultural determinism**. These geographers argue that the environment places no restrictions on humans whatsoever. The only restrictions we face are the ones we place on ourselves. For example, golf courses require grass, water, and fertile soil. None of these is found naturally in a desert; therefore, it seems impossible for a group of people to build a golf course in the desert. But what about Arizona? If you truck in the dirt, pipe in the water, and hire a grass expert who can manage the seeds, you can have a world-class golf course in a world-class desert. So what is possible, and what is not? Cultural determinists argue that humans create everything from their cultural perspective.

Even more ideas have developed around this central question of human–environment interaction. Both environmental determinism and possibilism start with the environment. Adding to the debate is **political ecology**, a school of thought that argues the government of a region affects the environment, which in turn affects the choices (and possibilities) available to the people in the region.

The Jigsaw of Culture

Like a jigsaw puzzle, culture can be broken down into various pieces, or layers. The simplest component of culture is a **culture trait**, a single attribute of a culture, such as the trait of bowing out of respect. Although we think of this culture trait as being Japanese, bowing to show respect is also shared by other cultures outside Japan. Culture traits are not necessarily unique to one group of people. However, the combination of all culture traits creates a unique set of traits called a **culture complex**. For example, all the things Americans do makes up the American culture complex. No other culture group in the world has the exact same combination of traits in its culture complex. When many complexes share particular traits, such as bowing out of respect, those complexes can merge together to form **culture systems**. For example, people living in the northern region of Germany speak with a different accent than Germans living in the southern region. But these two complexes share many other traits and can therefore be fused into the German culture system.

Figure 4.1. Perceptual (or vernacular) regions of North America defined by names of businesses listed in telephone books

Culture Regions and Realms

Chapter 2 introduced three types of regions: formal, functional, and perceptual. Another type of region is the culture region. **Culture regions** are drawn around places and peoples with similarities in their culture systems. Interestingly, people often share a sense of common culture and **regional identity,** or emotional attachment, to the group of people and places associated with a particular culture region. Such regional identity leads to the existence of **perceptual regions** (often called vernacular regions), regions whose boundaries are defined by people's emotions and feelings about an area, rather than objective means. It is difficult to cite examples of culture regions because they become whatever people want them to be. While some Tennesseans might argue they are "southern," some Alabamans would argue Tennesseans are not. On the other hand, a Pennsylvanian might argue that both Tennessee and Alabama are "southern" states.

Thus, the definition of culture regions often comes down to a question of perspective. The perceptual region of "the South" in the United States is a culture region defined through people's beliefs and attitudes about Civil War, grits, and many other cultural symbols, or items through which people express their cultural

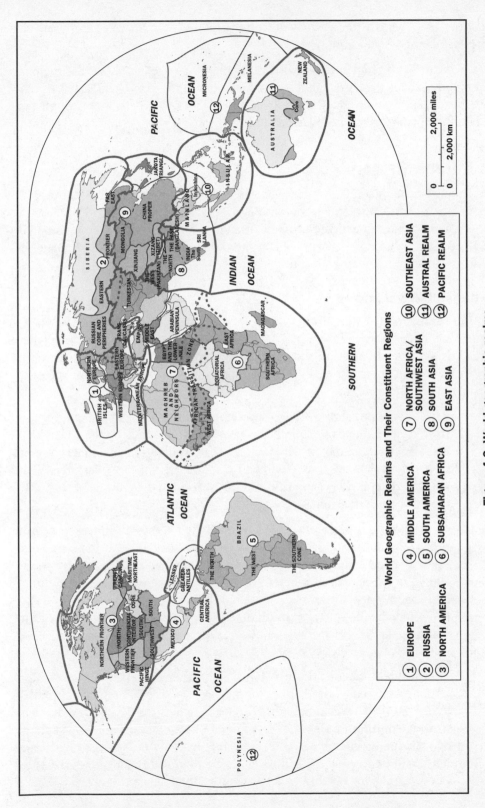

Figure 4.2. World geographic realms

identities. For example, the cowboy is seen as a cultural symbol most expressive of a western United States culture region.

A **culture (or geographic) realm** is the merging together of culture regions. Commonly accepted geographic realms include the Anglo-American, Latin American, European, Islamic, sub-Saharan African, Slavic, Sino-Japanese, Southeast Asian, Indic, and Austral-European realms.

Cultural Diffusion

People's material and nonmaterial creations spread across space and time, moving to new places and being carried through generations. The spread of people's culture across space is called **cultural diffusion**. The spread of any phenomenon (such as a disease) across space is called **spatial diffusion**. There are two categories of diffusion: expansion and relocation.

Expansion Diffusion

In **expansion diffusion**, the cultural component spreads outward to new places while remaining strong in its original hearth, or place of origin. For example, Islam spread from its hearth area in Saudi Arabia to other areas around and outside of its hearth while remaining strong in Mecca and Medina. There are several forms of expansion diffusion:

- **Stimulus expansion diffusion** occurs when the innovative idea diffuses from its hearth outward, but the original idea is changed by the new adopters. For example, the diffusion of iced tea throughout the southern region of the United States was modified by southerners into "Sweet Tea." The general concept (iced tea) diffused but was altered by the adopters to fit their sweet-toothed needs.

- **Contagious expansion diffusion** occurs when numerous places or people near the point of origin become adopters (or infected, in the case of a disease). A good example of the effects of contagious expansion diffusion is shown in the spread of tuberculosis from its point of origin (or node) to surrounding people. Another, more cultural example of contagious diffusion might be the spread outward of the Green Hills Grille restaurant from where it started in Nashville to other cities and towns around its point of origin.

- **Hierarchical expansion diffusion** occurs when the diffusion innovation or concept spreads from a place or person of power or high susceptibility to another in a leveled pattern. Hip-hop music diffused in a hierarchical pattern, spreading from a few large inner cities to other large inner cities, and then to smaller inner cities, and finally to more-suburban and rural places. Information often diffuses in a hierarchical pattern. For example, knowledge of the identity of the terrorists behind the September 11 attacks in 2001 first traveled through the higher levels of the U.S. government to the media and then to the general public.

A. Contagious Diffusion   **B. Hierarchical Diffusion**

LEGEND
● Hearth   ● Early diffusion   ○ Later diffusion
○ Important person or place   ○ No diffusion

Figure 4.3. Contagious versus hierarchical diffusion

Relocation Diffusion

Relocation diffusion involves the actual movement of the original adopters from their point of origin, or hearth, to a new place. This movement of the adopters facilitates diffusion. Whereas in expansion diffusion it is the innovation or disease that does the moving, in relocation diffusion the people pick up and move, carrying the innovation or disease (or whatever is spreading) with them to a new place. When the capital of Russia was moved from Saint Petersburg to Moscow after the revolution, the power and prestige of the Russian government moved, through relocation diffusion, to the city of Moscow, leaving Saint Petersburg vacant of that power and prestige. The spread of HIV/AIDS in the 1980s and 1990s shows the effects of relocation diffusion, as infected individuals moved, perhaps unknowingly, with the virus to a new city and got others sick in their new cities. One form of relocation diffusion is **migrant diffusion**, in which the innovation spreads and lasts only a brief time in the newly adopting place. The flu often shows migrant patterns of diffusion, spreading to a new place and weakening in that place after already spreading to a new place of infection. Therefore, the original hearth of the innovation (or node of the disease) is sometimes difficult to find because of the fading nature of the diffusing phenomenon's presence in any one place.

Mix of Diffusion Patterns

What you have probably noticed, however, is that many diffusing phenomena spread through a mix of diffusion patterns. For example, HIV/AIDS may have first spread through relocation diffusion, as infected individuals traveled to a new city, carried the virus with them (obviously), and unknowingly infected others in that city. Then those newly infected individuals spread the virus in a more hierarchical pattern, infected others in their most susceptible groups, such as homosexual men, before spreading in larger numbers into the heterosexual communities.

Acculturation, Assimilation, and Transculturation

Diffusion involves two (or more) cultures coming into contact with each other. This can lead to the exchange and/or adoption of ideas. The process of two cultures adopting each other's traits and becoming more alike is called **cultural convergence**.

Often when two cultures come into contact with one another, one culture is more dominant than another, possessing either more power or more attractiveness, making its traits more likely to be adopted or maintained than the traits of the less dominant culture. **Acculturation** occurs when the "weaker" of the two cultures adopts traits from the more dominant culture. Sometimes acculturation leads to **assimilation**, when the original traits of the weaker culture are completely erased and replaced by the traits of the more dominant culture. For example, immigrants to the United States might adopt elements of U.S. culture through acculturation while maintaining some traits from their original culture. However, if assimilated, the immigrants lose most (if not all) of the original traits they brought with them from their homeland.

A heated debate surrounds the "English as the official language" controversy in America, with many people arguing that forcing immigrants to adopt the English language is a necessary step in creating a unified country and many others arguing that forced acculturation is culturally biased and erosive to the "melting pot" concept of the United States as a "nation of immigrants." **Transculturation** occurs when two cultures of just about equal power or influence meet and exchange ideas or traits without the domination seen in acculturation and assimilation.

Diffusion often follows an **S curve** adoption pattern. For example, cell phones were originally purchased by only a small number of people who knew about them and could afford their initially expensive prices. Those people were known as the "early adopters," or innovators. Once more people learned about them and the price met the demand, a much faster rate of adoption developed (the "majority adopter"

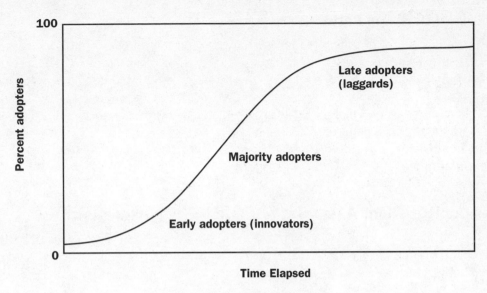

Figure 4.4. Diffusion S curve

stage). During this phase, most of the people who were susceptible (or likely) to be affected by the diffusing phenomenon became adopters.

In the last stage, most people who were likely to buy cell phones bought them (and thus became adopters). The rate of adoption therefore slowed down (note the flattening curve) in the "late adopters" stage. Only the stragglers, the "laggards," who had not yet bought cell phones purchased them in this final stage. Notice that the adoption rate does not reach 100 percent in the S curve graph. A 100 percent adoption rate would mean, for example, that everyone who could, adopted a cell phone; but surely some people have chosen not to adopt a cell phone, even though they might be able to afford one. A diffusing phenomenon (or disease) rarely reaches 100 percent adoption.

Culture Hearth

Culture hearths are areas where innovations in culture began, such as where agriculture, government, and urbanization originated. Culture hearths were the sources of human civilization. Many hearths invent similar innovations without knowing about each other, a process called **independent innovation (or invention)**. When agricultural innovation occurred in both East Asia and Mesopotamia, it did so without interaction through independent innovation. Ancient culture hearths are believed to have developed in places with the capability of innovation, all near water sources and arable land.

Figure 4.5. Hypothesized culture hearths and early diffusion routes

Hypothesized Ancient Hearth	Direction of Diffusion of Civilization from Ancient Hearth
Andean America (near Andes Mountains in South America)	Eastward direction throughout South America
Mesoamerica	Eastern and western North America
West Africa	Throughout Africa
Nile River valley	Throughout Africa and Southwest Asia
Mesopotamia	Throughout Southwest Asia, Europe, Central and East Asia, West Africa
Indus River valley	Throughout Southwest, Central, and East Asia
Ganges River delta	Throughout South, Southeast, and Southwest Asia
Wei and Huang rivers (China)	Throughout East and Southeast Asia

Figure 4.6. Hypothesized locations of ancient hearths and the diffusion paths of culture from those hearths

PART 2 Cultural Identities and Landscapes

Why do many people in Croatia practice Roman Catholicism, whereas most of their neighbors in Serbia practice Eastern Orthodox Christianity? Why do people in South Africa speak Afrikaans? Why are there differences in the way Christians worship? Between Muslims and Jews? Hindus and Sikhs? Why are there so many dialects of Chinese? These questions relate to the origin, diffusion, and blending of cultures. In seeking answers, cultural geographers analyze where cultures began and why they changed to understand the tapestry of human culture in the world today.

Religion

A fundamental part of human culture is **religion**, a set of beliefs and activities that are created to help humans celebrate and understand their place in the world. Religions help humans define right and wrong, good and bad. Religion can have a profound effect on human interaction with their environment and other cultures, thereby shaping the development of a people's cultural landscape.

There are two classifications of religions: universalizing and ethnic. **Universalizing religions** try to have a universal appeal and attract all people to their beliefs, whereas **ethnic religions** attempt to appeal not to all people but to only one group, perhaps in one place or of one ethnicity. Additionally, religions can be **monotheistic**, believing in one supreme being, or **polytheistic**, believing in more than one supreme being.

Figure 4.7. Map of world religions

Figure 4.8. Countries with the highest numbers of atheists and agnostics*

Country	Atheists, Agnostics, or Nonbelievers (%)
Sweden	46–85
Vietnam	81
Denmark	43–80
Norway	31–72
Japan	64–65
Czech Republic	54–61
Finland	28–60
France	43–54
South Korea	30–52
Estonia	49
Germany	41–49
Russia	24–48

(Source: Adherents.com)

* Many people surveyed indicated that they were nonbelievers but did not identify as atheists.

Universalizing Religions

About 60 percent of the world's people follow the universalizing religions. Universalizing religions can be broken down into branches, denominations, and sects. **Branches** are large, fundamental divisions within a religion. **Denominations** are groups of common congregations within a branch. **Sects** are smaller groups that have broken away from a recognized denomination within a branch.

Buddhism

Origins: Buddhism was the world's first universalizing religion. An outgrowth of Hinduism, Buddhism was founded in India near the **Indo-Gangetic Hearth**, the area between the Indus and Ganges rivers, by Prince Siddhartha Gautama, born in 644 BCE (before the Common Era).

Diffusion Route: After spreading throughout India, Buddhism spread to China, Korea, Japan, Tibet, Mongolia, and Southeast Asia along the Silk Road. Buddhism is now practically extinct in India where it was founded. Nearly 350 million people world-wide are Buddhist.

Primary Branches: Theravada and Mahayana Buddhism are the primary branches in the following list:

Figure 4.9. Map of origins and diffusion routes for selected religions

- *Theravada Buddhism* is monastic, meaning its followers are monks and nuns. It is practiced by nearly 55 percent of all Buddhists, mainly in Southeast Asian countries such as Sri Lanka, Myanmar (Burma), Thailand, Laos, and Cambodia.

- *Mahayana Buddhists* do not spend time as monks but find salvation through meditation and prayer. It is practiced by nearly 40 percent of all Buddhists and is found primarily in Korea, Vietnam, Japan, and China.

- *Lamaism in Tibet* (now part of China) combines the monasticism of Theravada with local images of deities and demons. It is practiced by only about 5 percent of all Buddhists. The Chinese government is seen by many to be trying to suppress this branch of Buddhism because the government sees it as a threat to its total control over the region. The Dalai Lama is a prominent adherent of this sect of Buddhism but has been exiled from Tibet by the Chinese government.

- *Zen Buddhism* exists primarily in Japan.

Cultural Landscape Features: Buddhism is most famous structure is the pagoda, which is derived from ancient burial mound shapes. According to Buddhism, Gautama (Buddha) reached enlightenment under the Bodhi tree in India, which is the site of many pilgrimages.

(Photo by: Ryuch)

Figure 4.10. A pagoda structure, typical of Buddhist architecture

Christianity

Origins: Christianity, the second universalizing religion to develop, began about 600 years after Buddhism and is an offshoot of Judaism. It originated in the **Semitic Hearth**, which is near modern-day Israel. It originated when its prophet, Jesus Christ, was seen as the expected messiah by disciples. A monotheistic religion, Christianity's main holy book is the Bible.

Diffusion Route: Christianity diffused through expansion and relocation diffusion from its hearth in Palestine. It currently contains the largest number of adherents, nearly 2 billion. The expanse of its spread was widened and accelerated in 312 CE when the Roman Empire adopted Christianity as its official religion. The European colonial efforts starting in the 15th century also carried Christianity throughout the world to new places. Nearly 90 percent of people in the Western Hemisphere are Christians.

Primary Branches: Christianity has three major branches:

- *Roman Catholics* make up the largest and original piece of Christianity, with nearly 830 million adherents (believers). It is considered a hierarchical religion because of its well-defined, organized, territorial governance structure, with the pope at its helm and cardinals, archbishops, and priests at its lower organizational levels. Unlike Protestantism, there are no prominent divisions, or denominations, within the Roman Catholic branch of Christianity. The Roman Catholic Church's headquarters is in Vatican City, an autonomous region in Italy.

- *Protestant Christians* total nearly 503 million adherents throughout the world, about 25 percent of all Christians. The Protestant branch is broken into denominations, of which the Baptist, Methodist, Pentecostal, and Lutheran are the largest. Protestantism has its origins in the Reformation, which occurred around the 15th century.

- *Eastern Orthodox Christianity* developed in 1054, when the Roman Catholic Church split (notice this was long before Protestantism began). It is a collection of 14 self-governing churches, the largest of which is the Russian Orthodox Church. The Eastern Orthodox branch, with nearly 192 million adherents, is dominant in eastern Europe and Russia (which is considered a part of eastern Europe). It has its roots in Constantinople, modern day Istanbul.

Cultural Landscape Features: The varied nature of Christian-influenced cultural landscapes reflects the changes that have occurred in the religion throughout its history. Prominent cathedrals in the cityscape tower above feudal villages as symbols of the leading influence in medieval life, the Roman Catholic Church. Defiantly simple, wooden, plain churches define Protestant communities and outposts in what was the "New World," a haven for Protestants from England before the Revolutionary War in "America." Baroque cathedrals with ornate sculptures and domes were

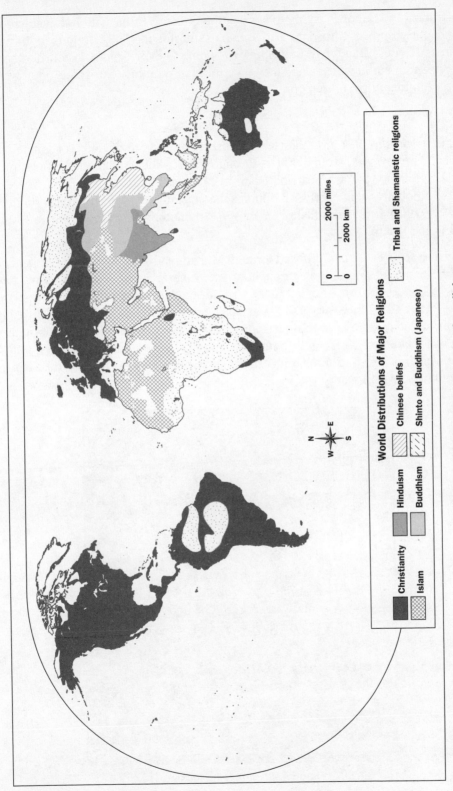

Figure 4.11. Global distribution of major religions

constructed by Catholics trying to combat the growing Reformation movement in 17th century Europe. Christians also use up the most land of all religions for burial, whereas Hindus, Buddhists, and Shintoists cremate their dead. Class differences are evident in burial yards where the gravestones of wealthier Christians often were more prominent than those poorer adherents.

Islam

Origins: Islam, the third major universalizing religion to develop, originated in Mecca, Saudi Arabia, around 600 CE through its prophet, Muhammad (sometimes spelled Mohammed), who carried Islam to Medina, Saudi Arabia, from where it diffused globally. With nearly 1.2 billion adherents, it is the second-largest religion on the earth, but it is the fastest growing. A monotheistic religion, Islam's holy book is the Koran.

Diffusion Route: Islam diffused through Muhammad's followers, who organized armies to spread the religion throughout extensive areas of Africa, Europe, and Asia. Its successful diffusion led to the Crusades, which were efforts by Christians in the 11th and 12th centuries to "take back" and "save" lands from the diffusing Muslims. Today there is ongoing tension in parts of Africa between the missionary forces of Islam and Christianity, both competing to convert Africans to their faiths. Most Muslims are concentrated in Asia (note that much of the Middle East is part of Southwest Asia).

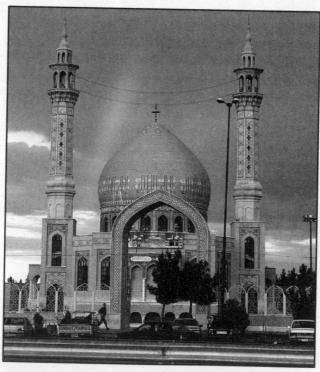

Figure 4.12. A Muslim mosque

Primary Branches: There are two principal branches of Islam:

- **Sunni Muslims** (*Sunni* means "orthodox") account for about 85 percent of Muslims. Sunnis dominate in the Arabic-speaking areas of Bangladesh and Pakistan. Whereas Shiites (or Shia) believe that only decendents of Ali, and therefore Muhammad, should be the head of Islam, Sunni caliphs, or religious emperors, in the Umayyad Dynasty were not descendants of Muhammad, nor were Ottoman emperors.

- **Shiite Muslims** are the majority in Iran and Iraq, though the Sunnis controlled the government of Iraq's former president, Saddam Hussein. They account for nearly 15 percent of all Muslims. As stated previously, in contrast to Sunnis, Shiites believe that descendants of Ali were acceptable authorities in Islam.

Cultural Landscape Features: Most prominent in the Islamic religion is the mosque, the center of Muslim worship. The mosque is often the center of a Muslim town's focus; it often has four minarets, or towers used to call worshippers, surrounding it. Islam's prohibition of depicting human form in architecture is the primary reason so many mosques are ornately designed with geometric patterns. One of the Five Pillars of Islam, which are analogous to the Ten Commandments to Christians and Jews, requires most Muslims to make a pilgrimage to Mecca, the holiest site to Muslims where Muhammad was born. The second-holiest site is Medina, where Muhammad moved with his knowledge of the religion. Third holiest is the Dome of the Rock in Jerusalem, where Muslims believe Muhammad ascended into heaven and returned to the earth with divine inspiration.

Sikhism

With nearly 22 million adherents, Sikhism is one of the smaller universalizing religions but is larger than the ethnic religion of Judaism. Founded in the late 15th century in present-day Pakistan, Sikhism is seen by many to be a **syncretic religion**, or a blend of the beliefs and practices of Hinduism and Islam. It follows the teachings of Guru Nanak and has its holiest site at the Golden Temple in Amritsar, India. In India, there are continuing tensions between the Sikhs and Hindus, and a high concentration of Sikhs live in the Punjab region, which straddles northwestern India and northern Pakistan. Sikhism is a monotheistic religion, and its holy book, known as the Guru Granth Sahib, contains the teachings of its prophets, called gurus.

Ethnic Religions

The major ethnic religions developed before the major universalizing religions. The largest ethnic religions are Hinduism and Judaism.

Hinduism

Origins: Hinduism claims more than 900 million adherents, most living in India. It evolved in the Indo-Gangetic Hearth in about 2000 BCE. Hinduism was the first

Figure 4.13. Distribution of Sunni and Shiite Muslims

AREAS WITH MUSLIM POPULATION

Sunni

Shia

major religion to originate in this area, before Buddhism. Instead of one holy book, Hinduism has a collection of ancient scriptures called the Veda.

Diffusion Route: Hinduism spread from its Indo-Gangetic Hearth eastward via the Ganges and south through India. As it spread, Hinduism blended with other faiths. Though it diffused to places beyond India, it never developed a dominant presence elsewhere. It is considered an ethnic religion because of its close identity with its Indian origins.

Primary Branches: There are no formal branches in Hinduism, although among its believers there are definite variations in practices. Hinduism is believed to be a polytheistic religion by some but a monotheistic religion by others. Some Hindus say there is only one supernatural being reflected in Hinduism's hundreds of deities.

Cultural Landscape Features: One of Hinduism's principal beliefs is reincarnation, or the rebirth of souls from one generation of life to another. Alongside reincarnation is Hinduism's link to India's tradition of a **caste system**, or a social hierarchy into which people are born. According to the caste system, some people are born into power, others into destitution. In recent years, India's caste system has been lessening in influence because of political pressure. Perhaps the most famous Hindu was Mahatma Gandhi, who worked to free India from England's colonial rule in the 20th century. Because Hindus believe temple builders receive divine reward, the Hindu landscape is dotted with countless shrines and temples to Hindu gods, often adorned by food offerings from local believers. Further, because Hindus believe in cremating their dead, corpses are often burning along the streets and beside rivers in Hindu areas. It is considered a very holy act to bathe in the Ganges River in India, so many Hindus make a pilgrimage to the river's banks to bathe.

Judaism

Origins: The oldest monotheistic religion on the earth, Judaism originated around 2000 BCE in its Semitic Hearth. Judaism grew out of the belief system of a tribe in Southwest Asia known as the Jews, whose headquarters became Jerusalem. The roots of the faith exist in the teachings of Abraham, who is believed to have united his people. Interestingly, Christianity's Jesus Christ and Islam's Muhammad both trace their ancestry through Abraham. Jesus Christ even considered himself a Jew. A monotheistic religion, Judaism's holiest books are the Torah, which consists of Old Testament teachings, and the Talmud, the collection of rabbinical and historical teachings passed down from one generation to the next.

Diffusion Route: After the Roman Empire destroyed their holy city of Jerusalem, the Jews were scattered throughout the world. A scattering of any ethnic group is known as a **diaspora**. The Jewish people scattered north into central Europe and toward the Iberian Peninsula. Currently, there are about 18 million Jews worldwide, with about 7 million in North America and 5 million in Europe and Russia. A heavy concentration of Jews is in Israel, the only country in which Judaism is not a minority religion, one practiced by less than half of the people. Sixty-six percent of all Jews live in the United States and Israel. In 1948, Israel was declared the official Jewish homeland, much to the disagreement of some of its Arab neighbors.

Primary Branches: Judaism has three primary branches: Orthodox Judaism, which seeks to retain the original traditions of the faith; Reform Judaism, which developed in the 1800s as a branch attempting to adjust the religion to fit more modern times; and Conservative Judaism, which is the most recent of the branches and is a more moderate approach to the religion than either the Reform or Orthodox branches.

Cultural Landscape Features: Perhaps the most prominent feature in the Jewish-influenced cultural landscape is the synagogue, or Jewish house of worship and community gathering. Though architecturally varied, all synagogues have an ark housing their sacred book, the Torah, written in Hebrew. An important symbol in Judaism is the six-pointed star. Perhaps the holiest site to Jews is Jerusalem's Western Wall, which is believed by Jews to be the western side of the holy Temple Mount complex that once housed two holy temples destroyed by invaders. Many Jews try to make pilgrimages to the Temple Mount to see the Western Wall and offer prayers and mourn the destruction of their holy temples. Importantly, the Muslims' holy Dome of the Rock is only feet from the Jews' holy Western Wall. This intersection of religions in Jerusalem's cultural landscape has led to a centuries-long conflict over control of this sacred space.

East Asian Ethnic Religions

Shintoism is a syncretic, ethnic religion blending principles of Buddhism with a local religion of Japan. From the 1800s until after World War II, Shintoism was the state religion of Japan. There are about 118 million worshippers, by some estimates.

Taoism (or Daoism) and **Confucianism** both have had a profound impact on Chinese life. Taoism is linked to the philosopher Laozi, who lived around the 6th century BCE, the same time as another philosopher, Confucius. In his writings, Laozi taught that people should live in harmony with nature in all aspects of their lives. This created feng shui, the practice of organizing living spaces in harmonious ways. Geomancers are considered truth-knowing, wise advisers in the Taoist faith.

Confucius built a system of morals and a way of life for Chinese in areas such as government, education, religion, and philosophy. Confucianism focuses more on the worldly life rather than the ideas of a heaven and a hell. Confucius rejected the Chinese aristocrats' claim that they were divine and the poor were not.

Both Taoism and Confucianism have spread beyond China to the Korean Peninsula, Japan, Southeast Asia, North America, and Europe. There has been some conflict between China's communist government and these faiths. Collectively, there are an estimated 263 million followers of these faiths. Many adherents of East Asian ethnic religions are also Buddhists.

Shamanism and Animism

Shamanism is a term given to any ethnic religion in which a community follows its shaman, or religious leader, healer, and truth knower. It has strongest presence in Africa, but shamanism has historically existed in North America, Southeast Asia, and East Asia. Some shamans teach **animism**, a belief that objects such as trees, mountains, and rivers have divine spirits in them.

Figure 4.14. Top-10 largest international religious bodies*

Religious Body	Number of Adherents
Catholic Church	1,100,000,000
Sunni Islam	875,000,000
Eastern Orthodox Church	225,000,000
Anglican Communion**	77,000,000
Assemblies of God	50,000,000
Seventh-day Adventists	16,811,519
Jehovah's Witnesses	16,500,000
Church of Jesus Christ of Latter-day Saints	12,275,822
New Apostolic Church	10,260,000
Ahmadiyya	10,000,000
Bahai World Faith	6,000,000

(Source: Adherents.com)

* These are religious bodies in which at least 30% of their world membership lives outside the core country (the country with the largest number of members).

** This figure represents the Anglican Church, Episcopal Church, and other derivatives throughout the world.

Secularism and Theocracy

Worldwide, there are more than 4 billion believers in some religion or faith. However, millions of people, called secularists, have rejected or are indifferent to religion. **Secularism** is the movement away from control of life by a religion. On the other hand, a **theocracy** is a government run by a religion. For example, a theocracy existed in the former government of Afghanistan, in which the Taliban, a group of fundamentalist Muslims, controlled all aspects of life for the Afghani people. Currently, Iran is another example of a theocracy.

Religion and Conflict

Humans have consistently warred over land, particularly when it involves sacred space. They have also warred for their right to practice their religions or to terminate others' rights to do so. If history is our teacher, then humans will forever war over similar issues. **Interfaith boundaries** divide space between two or more religions. **Intrafaith boundaries** divide space within one religion, often among denominations.

Such boundaries can lead to conflicts, often very passionate in nature. Figures 4.15 and 4.16 list some recent conflicts that have occurred in each category.

Figure 4.15. Examples of interfaith boundary conflicts

Place	Interfaith Boundary	Conflict
China (Tibet)	Tibetan Buddhism and Atheism	The atheist Chinese government is allegedly destroying Tibetan Buddhist monasteries and arresting and exiling its adherents to suppress religion in the area and assimilate the region to Chinese control.
Nigeria	Islam and Christianity	Islam prevails in the northern region, while Christianity and local religions prevail in the south. Such division causes power-based tensions for control of the one government.
India	Hinduism and Sikhism	Sikhs in the northwestern state of Punjab demand autonomy from the Hindu-controlled government of India.
India and Pakistan	Hinduism and Islam	Pakistan, once a part of India, was established in 1947 as a Muslim state. Pakistan and India are raging over control of the northern territory known as Jammu and Kashmir.
Former Yugoslavia	Christianity and Islam	In the Yugoslavian civil wars of the 1990s, Serb leader Slobodan Milosevic (an Eastern Orthodox Christian) tried to kill or evict the Muslim population in Bosnia and other Serb-controlled lands in the region.
Palestine (modern-day Israel)	Judaism and Islam	For centuries, Jews and Muslims have warred for control of Palestine. This fight intensified after the creation of Israel following World War II.

Language

Language and religion are fundamental components in cultural identity; they define human culture. Language is a cultural trait, learned from one generation to another. It is speculated that nearly 2.5 million years ago language first developed to organize human activity. All original speakers communicated in the prototongue, or original language. Once those speakers diffused to various places on the earth, language divergence occurred, and new languages and dialects were spawned from

Figure 4.16. Examples of intrafaith boundary conflicts

Place	Intrafaith Boundary	Conflict
Iraq	Sunni Islam and Shiite Islam	After the fall of the largely Sunni government controlled by Saddam Hussein, both Sunnis and Shiites are warring for control of the newly forming political landscape.
United States	Christian fundamentalism and moderate, liberal Christianity	Christians have conflicted not just in the U.S. but worldwide over political-cultural issues such as homosexuality, evolution, and abortion. In some cases, violent tactics have been used.
Northern Ireland	Protestant Christians and Roman Catholics	British colonialism deposited large numbers of Protestants in traditionally Catholic Northern Ireland. This intrafaith boundary has caused violent conflicts between the two groups in the region.

the original source. **Language divergence** occurs when speakers of the same language scatter and develop variations of that original form of the language to meet their needs in the new surroundings. For example, the original language may not have had words for concepts such as a *snake* or *iceberg*. Once the human group came into contact with these new concepts, they created new words for them.

Nearly 50 million Americans spoke a language at home other than English in 2004 (Population Reference Bureau).

A blending of two or more languages can take place when speakers come into contact with other languages. **Language replacement** occurs when invaders replace the language of those places they conquer. This can lead to **language extinction**, when a language is no longer used by people in the world.

Geographers can trace diffusion paths of language through **reverse reconstruction**. For example,

- if two languages share a common word for an extinct animal that no longer exists and

- that animal only existed in one of the many places where the two languages are now spoken,

- then one possible conclusion is that the language diffused from the place where the extinct animal once existed, and the speakers carried with them the word for the hearth's extinct animal.

Geographers have organized languages into a language tree. The tree is subdivided into the following hierarchy:

19 language families

    Each family has its own branches

        Each branch has its own groups

            Each group has its own language

                Each language has its own dialects

Figure 4.17. Some major language families

Language Family	Approximate Number of Languages	Percentage of World's Speakers	Approximate Number of Speakers (in millions)
Indo-European	430	44.78%	5,960 (5.9 billion)
Sino-Tibetan	399	22.28%	1,275 (1.2 billion)
Niger-Congo	1,495	6.26%	358
Afro-Asiatic	353	5.93%	339
Austronesian	1,246	5.45%	311
Dravidian	73	3.87%	221

(Source. ethnologue.com)

Indo-European Hearth

About 50 percent of all people speak an Indo-European language, most prominently, English. English is part of the Germanic branch of the Indo-European language family. Other major branches include the Balto-Slavic, Romance, and Indo-Iranian branches. The original Indo-European language is referred to as **Proto-Indo-European**. New languages developed through language diversification as a result of migration of Proto-Indo-European speakers from the hearth of this language family.

The location of the hearth of the Proto-Indo-European language is the subject of speculation. The **conquest theory** argues that it began in the empire-building Kurgan culture located in the steppe region of Russia, north of the Caspian Sea. The **agriculture theory** argues that Proto-Indo-European started in a farming community in the Europe's Danube River region. Because modern Indo-European languages share words for *snow* but not *sea*, the hearth is believed to have been somewhere with snow but distant from the sea. Geographers estimate its origin to have been between 6000 and 4500 BCE. As the Proto-Indo-European speakers diffused using the horse and wheel, the language evolved into various forms.

Figure 4.18. Distribution of language families

Monolingual and Multilingual States

Language often defines national identity and is linked to territorial claims. A common language makes communication possible among a people. It can also be used to declare "sameness" or unity. However, linguistic boundaries are often hard to define. **Multilingual states** are countries in which more than one language is spoken. Multilingual states contain linguistic minorities, or groups of speakers who are outnumbered by another language in the country. This can lead to conflict over language and its ties to national identity and power.

Monolingual states, on the other hand, contain speakers of only one language. Because of the increasing pace of spatial–cultural interaction globally, monolingual countries no longer exist. One might argue that Japan, for example, is relatively monolingual with its stringent immigration laws. Countries like France have fought to preserve their monolingual heritage. For example, French politicians called for laws to keep French pure and prohibit the infusion of English words into their vocabulary.

Figure 4.19 lists some recent conflicts related to multilingualism. Keep in mind that the conflicts highlighted in the table reflect multi-faceted conflicts, not singularly related to language. Instead, language is an important symbol of the ethnocultural divisions at the root of the conflicts in these regions.

Figure 4.19. Some conflicts related to multilingualism

Place	Languages	Conflict
Canada	English and French	French speakers, concentrated in Quebec, have fought for increased recognition and power against the English-speaking Canadian majority. Some Quebec citizens have even called for secession from Canada.
Belgium	Dutch and French	The Dutch-speaking north and French-speaking south compete for power and control. The nation's capital city, Brussels, is located in the Dutch-speaking south, but most inhabitants are French speakers.
Cyprus	Greek and Turkish	The Greek majority and Turkish minority compete for control of this island-country. Cyprus is divided by a "Green-Line" partition separating the two cultures.
Nigeria	Hausa, Yoruba, Ibo and nearly 230 other languages	Hausa speakers in the north, Yoruba in the southwest, and Ibo in the southeast paint a divided Nigeria in which some 230 other languages complicate Nigeria's unification. English was declared the official language as an attempt to create a tool of common communication.

Official and Standard Languages

Often countries declare official languages to define and declare national identity. An **official language** is declared by the leaders of a country to be the language used in legal and governmental proceedings. It often is the language of the powerful, linguistic majority. In 2006, the United States engaged in a national debate surrounding the longstanding call for a declaration of English as its official language. Declaration of an official language in multilingual states is often very controversial. In Nigeria, for example, English was chosen as a neutral choice, rather than one of the three largest languages in the country, to prevent calls of dominance by one group over another. Canada declared both French and English to please both culture groups within the state.

Figure 4.20. Top 10 native languages

Language	Speakers
Mandarin Chinese	885,000,000
Spanish	332,000,000
English	322,000,000
Bengali	189,000,000
Hindi	182,000,000
Portuguese	170,000,000
Russian	170,000,000
Japanese	125,000,000
German (Standard)	98,000,000
Wu Chinese	77,175,000

(Source: ethnologue.com)

Related to the concept of *official language* is the concept of *standard language*. **Standard language** is the acceptable form of a given language as declared by political or societal leaders. For example, the British government declared British Received Pronunciation (BRP) English as the standard form of the language to be taught in all schools, rather than American English. German schools teach High German (Hoch Deutsch), the form of German originally spoken by the powerful in the upper Rhine region of Germany.

Lingua Franca, Pidgin, and Creole Languages

When many languages are spoken in one region, people living in the region will often use one language when speaking with one another and conducting trade, almost like a bridge between two cultures. A **lingua franca** is a language used to facilitate trade among groups speaking different languages. For example, in the very multilingual East Africa, where hundreds of native languages are spoken in villages and cities, people turn to Swahili as their lingua franca to communicate with speakers of other languages.

When regions are invaded or economically dominated by a particular foreign-language-speaking group, the people being dominated are forced to pick up on the language of the dominators in order to trade with them and conduct business. When the dominated culture picks up on the new language, they usually speak a simplified version of it known as a **pidgin** of the dominators' language. For example, when the French dominated the Caribbean region, the native people began speaking a simplified version of French, known as pidgin French. Eventually, the speakers of this simplified pidgin language taught their children to speak the pidgin. Once a pidgin becomes part of a culture and is even written, it is known as a **creole** (or creolized) language, a pidgin language that becomes the main language of a group of people. In the Caribbean, pidgin French became such a part of life that it became the mother language of the dominated people, thus becoming a creole.

Toponyms

Toponyms are place names that reflect cultural identity and impact the cultural landscape. Just as parents take pride in naming their child, a people take pride in naming their place, often a controversial task. Determining a toponym indicates ownership and control over space. For example, controversy erupted in India when the government announced it would rename the city of Bombay. The Indian government wanted to rid the city of the name its English colonizers had given the city and replace it with a name that reflected Indian culture and ownership. However, the new toponym of Mumbai reflects Hindu dominance because it relates to a Hindu god. Non-Hindus were angered that their cultures were not being reflected in the new toponym for the city.

Toponyms can also give geographers clues into the origins and aspirations of the related cultures. Saint Petersburg, Russia, was named by Czar Peter the Great, perhaps conveniently, after his patron saint, Peter. Toponyms can also indicate the dreams of a people for their place, such as Paradise, California; Hope, Arkansas; and even Hell, Michigan. The toponym Santa Barbara in California reflects the Spanish-Portuguese language and Catholic religious influences on the region. Santa (Spanish for *Saint*) Barbara was a Catholic martyr.

Ethnicity

Cultural identity also includes ethnicity. **Ethnicity** relates to sets of rules that people create to define their group through actual or perceived shared culture traits, such as language, religion, and nationality. It is a much-debated term because different groups express ethnicity in different ways. Territory is often a unifying trait for ethnicities, such as Albanians' attachment to Albania. Ethnic groups may be spatially divided, as were the Jews who were forcibly segregated from non-Jews in Nazi Germany into a Jewish ghetto. A **ghetto** is a region in which an ethnic minority is forced to live by economic, legal, or governmental pressures. An **ethnic enclave** is a place in which an ethnic minority is concentrated, sometimes in the form of a ghetto. The term **enclave** can indicate a place in which a minority group is concentrated and surrounded by a hostile or unwelcoming majority. An ethnic *neighborhood* tends to be a place in which an ethnic minority is concentrated but is not surrounded by a majority as unwelcoming as that in an enclave. However, an enclave is just a group that is surrounded by another group; it does not have to be hostile. The only real difference is that neighborhoods do not have to be surrounded, whereas enclaves do. A **barrio** is a Spanish-speaking ethnic neighborhood (or enclave) in a city, although the term is often used with negative racial connotations.

Within ethnic landscapes, ethnicities often use space to celebrate their group, such as through parades and festivals. Ethnic enclaves indicate social segregation in space. In addition to the often-present discriminatory pressures, chain migration processes can foster the development of an ethnic enclave. As discussed in Chapter 3, chain migration occurs when family members and associates migrate to the same places because they have heard from others who have made the journey that the region is "safe" or "welcoming" to them. Often migrants move into these ethnic enclaves because they have relatives or friends there.

Race

Race is another factor that can influence ethnic definition. **Race** refers to a classification system of humans based on skin color and other physical characteristics. Race has been used to separate people within a territory, such as its use by South Africa's **apartheid** government, which separated whites and blacks by racial categories. In that example and others, race affects humans' use and division of space. What differentiates race and ethnicity is unclear, but ethnicity is usually seen to incorporate more than just race. For example, Puerto Rican ethnicity includes more than a "Hispanic race," because it includes a national, territorially based cultural identity. Your ethnicity is made up of the cultural traits you acquire while attached to some national group. So people from Armenia living in Germany may consider themselves ethnically Armenian. After living in Germany for five generations, their children would probably have picked up enough German cultural traits that they might consider themselves ethnic Germans, even if they still looked like their great-great-grandparents.

Social Distance

Tensions often arise when ethnicities and races compete for political and territorial control. **Social distance** is a measurement of how "distant" two ethnicities or social groups are from each other. Often groups perceived as very different from the majority or powerful group are cast into the marginalized social periphery. Such marginalized groups are often the targets of discrimination and hatred by the more powerful social group. **Ethnocentrism**, or one group's use of its cultural identity as the superior standard by which to judge others, often causes such discriminatory behavior.

Ethnic Conflict

In their divisive powers, race and ethnicity have been used by leaders to motivate warfare and forced expulsion of people perceived as being "different" from the majority's classification. **Ethnic cleansing** is a process in which a racial or ethnic group attempts to expel from a territory another racial or ethnic group. An extension of ethnic cleansing is **genocide**, when a racial or ethnic group tries to kill another racial or ethnic group. Slobodan Milosevic, the Serb leader of former Yugoslavia, led a genocide campaign against ethnic Albanians living in Kosovo, a region in Serbia. Adolf Hitler targeted the Jews and other minority ethnic groups; and Sudan's government is accused of attempting to eliminate ethnic groups in Darfur, a region in northwestern Sudan.

Gender

Gender is another category of classifying humans reflecting not just biological but also social differences between men and women. Social concepts of what is "masculine" and what is "feminine" vary across space and time. For example, having long hair is considered masculine for men in some East Asian cultures but considered feminine in others. Globally, women do not have the opportunities men do; male dominance economically, politically, and socially remains the pattern, a situation referred to as the **gender gap**. Following are some problems related to gender:

- High **maternal mortality rates**, or death rates among women giving birth, indicate that women in poorer regions are 100 to 600 times more likely to die giving birth that are women in wealthier regions.

- High **female infanticide** rates, or the murder of female infants, exist in regions where families want male children to carry on the family name or be able to earn more money for the family. Population control policies, such as the one-child policy in China, can cause higher female infanticide rates. In places like India, for example, the female bride's family must pay a sum of money, called a dowry, to the male groom's family. Therefore, some families may try to abort female children in favor of profit-creating male children.

- Dowry deaths in India were rising in the 1980s but have been statistically declining. A **dowry death** occurs when a bride is murdered by her husband's family because her father failed to pay the dowry.

- Women were not given the right to vote, called **enfranchisement**, until the 20th century in most places. Although high in northern Europe and most industrialized countries, on average the election of females to legislative bodies remains much lower than men's.

- **Gender imbalances** also exist in places like India and China, where men outnumber women. This can lead to higher rates of male depression as a result of their inability to find female mates. It can also lead to more men employing prostitutes and thus higher rates of HIV infection.

Despite these discriminations, women typically live longer than men, a fact described as the **longevity gap**.

A global average of life expectancies shows women live about four years longer than men. This varies according to place, however. (Population Reference Bureau)

Folk and Popular Culture

Culture traits may be defined as being either folk or popular culture. **Folk culture** is limited to a smaller region and a smaller number of people than popular culture. Folk cultures are usually isolated groups that have had long-lasting culture traits that have not changed substantially over long periods. **Popular culture** is mass culture that diffuses rapidly (the reason it is called popular). Folk cultures either have not been exposed to more common, or popular, culture or they have chosen not to adopt popular culture.

A well-known example of folk culture is the Amish use of horse-drawn carriages in their communities instead of the popular culture trait of using cars. Folk culture is evident in its people's cultural landscape, in housing styles that are found only in the region of their origin, and even in the artistic and musical components of the folk culture's landscape. Usually, folk culture spreads through relocation diffusion, when the original group moves to another location and takes their folk traits with them. Country music originated as a folk music in various places in the Appalachian region, each with its own sound and set of instruments. As the various strains of what became known as country music diffused, they started to popularize and become more uniform in sound to please the masses of listeners.

Maladaptive Diffusion

Popular culture diffuses rapidly, primarily through expansion diffusion, across space and varied cultures. Popular culture does not necessarily reflect its original environment. Wearing blue jeans, for example, is a popular culture trait that has diffused across space and cultures. Listening to the Beatles and Snoop Dogg are examples of pop(ular) music that diffused globally. Sometimes this can lead to **maladaptive diffusion**, the adoption of a diffusing trait that is impractical for a region or culture. The diffusion of blue jeans has popularized wearing them even in very warm months, even though jeans can be quite hot (in terms of temperature, that is).

Cultural Imperialism

The diffusion of popular culture can create cultural conflict, when a part of a culture group may protest the arrival of a type of popular culture in its region. For example, when McDonald's arrived in one African city, protesters attacked the restaurant, claiming McDonald's represented **cultural imperialism**—the invasion of a culture into another with the intent of dominating the invaded culture politically, economically, and/or socially. Many Middle Eastern cultures resent the influx of Western popular culture into their cultures. Even in the United States, some people resent the arrival of Starbucks, for example, which is argued to cause the demise of local coffee shops that represent their local people. **Cultural nationalism** is the rise of anticultural imperialism forces; it is the fight by regions and cultures to resist cultural convergence and imperialism and remain distinct.

Geo Factoid

McDonald's on average opened two new restaurants a day in 2006. Nearly 31,000 McDonald's restaurants are operating worldwide. (www.McDonalds.com)

Cultural Homogeneity

With increasing access to the Internet, efficient transportation tools, and other communication technology, the diffusion of popular culture is increasing in speed and scope. One of the concerns about the increasing dominance of popular culture is that it is threatening regional and cultural diversity, because the diffusion of popular culture makes everyone look, sound, act, and believe more of the same rather than in unique, local ways. When cultures become more similar, the result is **cultural homogeneity**, or cultural sameness. However, the arrival of popular culture can also be perceived as increasing opportunities and access.

Popular Culture and Consumption

Another related concern about popular culture is its impact on the environment. Many popular culture traits lead to increased consumption of the earth's limited natural resources and increases waste production. For example, whereas people once carpooled or rode public transportation, the popularizing of every individual owning and driving a car has led to increased fuel consumption and pollution.

Americans' consumption of resources grew faster than its population, which doubled between 1950 and 2005 (Population Reference Bureau).

Landfills are stockpiled with people's plastic water bottles, a fad that has recently developed instead of drinking tap water. In fact, one city government in California recently banned selling bottled water in government offices to try to reduce this waste.

| PART 3 | Chapter Review |

Major Religions Review Chart

The following chart includes an overview of some of the world's largest religions.

Religion	Hearth	Prophet or a Founding Thinker	Sacred Text and Worship Center	Significant and/or Holy Places (list contains only a select few, in some cases)	Classification	Major Branches or Divisions
Buddhism	Indo-Gangetic	Siddhartha Gautama	Tipitaka; temple	Bodh Gaya in India	Universalizing; neither monotheistic or polytheistic	Theravada, Mahayana, Lamaism, Zen
Christianity	Semitic	Jesus	Holy Bible; church	Jerusalem, Vatican City, Constantinople	Universalizing, monotheistic	Roman Catholic, Protestant, Eastern Orthodox
Hinduism	Indo-Gangetic	Unknown	Veda; temple	Ganges river, many sites in India	Ethnic, debatable whether monotheistic or polytheistic	No formal major branches, though various local forms exist
Islam	Arabian peninsula	Muhammad	Koran; mosque	Mecca, Medina, Jerusalem	Universalizing, monotheistic	Sunni, Shiite
Judaism	Semitic	Abraham	Torah; synagogue	Jerusalem, Israel	Ethnic; monotheistic	Conservative, Reform, Orthodox
Sikhism	Indo-Gangetic	Guru Nanak	Guru Granth Sahib; temple	Golden Temple in Amritsar, India; Punjab, India	Universalizing, monotheistic	No major divisions

Terms Review

Acculturation—Occurs when a less-dominant culture comes into contact with and adopts traits from a more dominant culture.

Animism—Belief that objects such as trees, mountains, and rivers have divine spirits in them.

Apartheid—South Africa's English-Dutch imposed government segregating white and black inhabitants.

Assimilation—Final completion of the cultural acculturation process, when a culture group loses all its original traits and becomes fully a part of a different, dominating culture.

Barrio—Spanish-speaking ethnic neighborhood.

Branch of a religion—Large division within a religion.

Carl Sauer—Prominent geographer in the 20th century who championed the study of cultural landscapes and built environments in human geography.

Caste system—System of social levels based on ancestry and job, traditionally in India.

Confucianism—East Asian belief system originally taught by Confucius, stressing morals for all aspects of life.

Creole—Pidgin language that has become the language of the people being dominated by invaders.

Cultural convergence—Occurs when one culture adopts a cultural attribute of another.

Cultural diffusion—Process by which a cultural element spreads from its hearth across space and time. There are two forms: expansion and relocation.

Cultural ecology—Study of a human group's interaction with its natural environment.

Cultural geography—Field of human geography that analyzes how and why culture is expressed in different ways in different places.

Cultural homogeneity—Occurs when cultures become the same, or uniform, and local diversity is decreased.

Cultural imperialism—Invasion of a culture into another with the intent of dominating the invaded culture politically, economically, and/or socially.

Cultural landscape (or built environment)—Tangible result of a human group's interaction with its environment.

Cultural nationalism—Movement to protect one's culture from invasion or influence from another culture's perceived invasion or influence and threat to one's own culture. Highly related to the emotional attachment an individual has for his/her culture.

Culture complex—Unique combination of culture traits for a particular culture group.

Culture hearth—Area where innovations in culture began and from which such cultural elements spread.

Culture (or geographic) realm—Cluster of culture regions in which common culture systems are found. Examples include Latin America and sub-Saharan Africa.

Culture regions—Area in which a culture system is found or is prevalent.

Culture system—Collection of culture complexes that shape a group's common identity.

Culture trait—Single piece of a culture's traditions and practices.

Denomination of a religion—Group of common congregations within a branch of a religion.

Diaspora—Scattering of any ethnic group; originally referred to the Jews.

Dowry death—Murder of a bride by her husband's family because her father failed to pay the dowry.

Enfranchisement—Right to vote.

Environmental determinism—School of thought that believes human activities are controlled by their environment.

Ethnic cleansing—Process in which a racial or ethnic group attempts to expel or exterminate from a territory another racial or ethnic group.

Ethnic enclave—Another name for an ethnic neighborhood surrounded by an unwelcoming, discriminatory, or hostile ethnic group or groups.

Ethnicity—Complex identity created by a people to define their group through actual or perceived shared culture traits, such as language, religion, and so forth.

Ethnic religion—Religion that comprises one group of people or exists in one place and does not seek converts.

Ethnocentrism—Using one's own cultural identity as the superior standard by which to judge others; often causes discriminatory behavior.

Expansion diffusion—Subtype of diffusion in which a phenomenon spreads outward from its hearth while remaining strong in the original location through hierarchical, contagious, or stimulus patterns.

Female infanticide—Murder of female infants.

Folk culture—Isolated group that has had long-lasting culture traits that have not changed substantially over time.

Gender—Category of classifying humans reflecting not just biological but also social differences between men and women.

Gender gap—Difference in social, economic, and political power and opportunity between men and women.

Gender imbalance—Unequal number of men and women in a place.

Genocide—Killing of one racial or ethnic group by another.

Ghetto—Ethnic neighborhood created by government, social, or economic pressures, causing people of one ethnicity to live together.

Independent innovation (or invention)—Invention of the same phenomenon by two culture hearths without each knowing about the other's invention or, sometimes, existence.

Indo-Gangetic Hearth—Hearth near the Indus and Ganges rivers where Hinduism, Buddhism, and Sikhism originated.

Interfaith boundary—Boundary that divides space between two or more religions.

Intrafaith boundary—Boundary that divides space among different groups within a particular religion, such as among branches, denominations, or sects.

Language divergence—Occurs when new languages or dialects grow from one original source because of the migration of original speakers to new lands or contact with new languages.

Language extinction—Occurs when a people's language is no longer used in the world.

Language replacement—Occurs when invaders replace with their own language the language of the people whom they conquer.

Lingua franca—Language used to facilitate trade among groups speaking different languages.

Longevity gap—Difference between life expectancies of men and women.

Maladaptive diffusion—Adoption of a diffusing trait that is impractical for a region or culture.

Material components of culture—Pieces of a cultural landscape that are tangible, such as clothing and architecture.

Maternal mortality rate—Death rate among women giving birth.

Migrant diffusion—Type of relocation diffusion in which the spreading phenomenon's epicenter (or place of most infection or adoption) moves with the relocating group of users or carriers, like the influenza's usual diffusion pattern.

Monolingual state—Country in which only one language is spoken.

Monotheistic religion—Religion based on belief in one god or deity.

Multilingual state—Country where more than one language is spoken.

Nonmaterial components of culture—Pieces of a culture that are intangible, such as beliefs and attitudes.

Official language—Language selected by a country to represent its identity in courts and government proceedings.

Perceptual regions—Area with boundaries defined by people's beliefs, emotions, and attitudes. Often called a vernacular region.

Pidgin language—Simplified version of a lingua franca adopted by a group of people to trade and communicate.

Political ecology—Study of cultural geography through the lens of the relationships government and economic systems create between human cultures and their environments.

Polytheistic religion—Religion based on belief in many gods or deities.

Popular culture—Mass culture that diffuses rapidly.

Possibilism—School of thought suggesting that humans' natural environments present a set of choices from which humans choose their actions.

Proto-Indo-European—First form of language that gave rise to the Indo-European family. Believed to have spread through either the Kurgan conquests or through farming technology.

Race—Classification system of humans based on skin color and other physical characteristics.

Regional identity—Common identification a group of people has with a particular place.

Religion—Set of beliefs and activities created to help humans celebrate and understand their place in the world.

Relocation diffusion—Subtype of diffusion in which the phenomenon spreads through the movement of its users from one place to another.

Reverse reconstruction—Process of tracing a language's diffusion. The process begins with the most recent places of the language's existence and moves backward through time, comparing words with geographic places and groups of people using the same or similar words.

S-curve diffusion pattern—Diffusion often follows this pattern of a slower pace in the innovation stage, followed by a rapid diffusion pattern in the majority-adopter stage, and finishing in a slower-paced "laggard" stage.

Sect—Small group that breaks away from a denomination within a religion's branch.

Secularism—Movement away from control of life by a religion.

Semitic Hearth—Hearth near modern-day Israel where Judaism, Christianity, and Islam originated.

Sequent occupance—Theory that a place is occupied by different groups of people, each group leaving an imprint on the place from which the next group learns.

Shamanism—Any ethnic religion in which a community follows its shaman, or religious leader, healer, and truth knower.

Shintoism—Syncretic faith blending Buddhism with local practices predominant in Japan.

Social distance—Measurement of how "distant" or different two ethnicities or social groups are from each other.

Spatial diffusion—Spread of any phenomenon (such as a disease) across space and time. Cultural diffusion is a form of spatial diffusion in which cultural phenomena diffuse.

Standard language—Acceptable form of a given language as declared by political or societal leaders.

Stimulus expansion diffusion—Occurs when an innovative idea diffuses from its hearth outward, but the original idea is changed by the new adopters.

Sunni and Shiite Muslims—Two major branches of Islam; Sunnis, the largest branch, are known as the orthodox branch supporting only descendants of Muhammad, whereas Shiites support descendants of Ali as religious leaders.

Syncretic religion—Religion blending elements from various religions.

Taoism (Daoism)—East Asian belief system stressing balancing the forces of humanity and nature, taught originally by Laozi.

Theocracy—Government run by a religion.

Toponym—Name given to a place.

Transculturation—Equal exchange of cultural traits between two cultures; a form of cultural convergence.

Universalizing religion—Type of religion that believes that its truth is the one and only truth and is applicable to all humans, a belief often leading to proselytizing and missionary work.

PART 4 — Some Suggested Web Resources for Further Exploration

United Nations Educational, Scientific, and Cultural Organization: http://www. unesco.org/

This is the primary portal for cultural information collected by the United Nations. It contains valuable maps, statistics, and descriptions of cultural issues around the globe.

American Folk: http://www.americanfolk.com/

This site contains interesting information on American folk and popular culture.

Ethnologue: http://www.ethnologue.com/

This site contains a fascinating, online encyclopedia of the thousands of languages spoken in the world.

U.S. Board on Geographic Names: http://geonames.usgs.gov/

This is the official website of the U.S. government's main organ of toponyms. It has searchable databases on place names.

Voice of America (VOA) News Portal: http://www.voanews.com/english/portal.cfm

This site is a radio station run by the U.S. government and disseminated throughout the world. The interesting part of this website is that you can listen to the news (as reported by the VOA) in different languages.

Adherents.com: http://www.adherents.com/

This website contains helpful statistics and graphics related to the religions of the world, though such statistics are often debated. Information on branches, sects, and other divisions are included. It also has links to other websites that focus on religions.

PART 5 Pre-Exam Practice

Terms Review Quiz

Use the Terms Review list or your own memory to determine the extent of your knowledge of key terms and concepts. Remember, the AP exam does not include this kind of exercise, but it is included here as a review tool.

1. _____ Acceptable form of a given language as declared by political or societal leaders.

2. _____ System of social levels separating people on the basis of ancestry and job, traditionally in India.

3. _____ Field of human geography that analyzes how and why culture is expressed in different ways in different places.

4. _____ The tangible result of a human group's interaction with its environment.

5. _____ Unique combination of culture traits for a particular culture group

6. _____ Groups of common congregations within a branch of a religion.

7. _____ Type of religion that exists in one group of people and/or place that does not seek converts.

8. _____ Using one's own cultural identity as the superior standard by which to judge others; often causes discriminatory behavior.

9. _____ Pieces of a culture that are intangible, such as beliefs and attitudes.

10. _____ School of thought suggesting that humans' natural environments present a set of choices from which humans choose their actions.

11. _____ Region with boundaries defined by a people's beliefs, emotions, and attitudes.

12. _____ Occurs when a less-dominant culture comes into contact with and adopts traits from a more dominant culture.

13. _____ Type of diffusion in which the phenomenon spreads through the movement of its adopters from one place to another.

14. _____ Final step of the cultural acculturation process, when a culture group loses all its original traits and becomes fully a part of a different, dominating culture.

15. _____ Area where innovation in culture began and from which such cultural elements spread.

16. _____ Invention of the same phenomenon by two culture hearths without each knowing about the other's invention or, sometimes, existence.

17. _____ Religion based on belief in many gods or deities.

18. _____ Scattering of any ethnic group, originally referring to the Jews.

19. _____ Religion with the largest number of adherents in the world.

20. _____ Occurs when an innovative idea diffuses from its hearth outward, but the original idea is changed by the new adopters.

21. _____ Principal religious text for Muslims.

22. _____ First person to spread teachings of Buddhism; known as the Buddha.

23. _____ Three monotheistic religions originating in the Semitic Hearth.

24. _____ Government run by a religion.

25. _____ Killing of one racial or ethnic group by another.

Multiple-Choice Review Questions

1. Which of the following represents a possibilist interpretation of human activity?

    (A) Shanghai developed into a world city because of its navigable rivers.

    (B) Lesoto's economy has not developed to be globally competitive because of its lack of water access.

    (C) Minnesota's people are usually quieter than Florida's because of the harsher weather people endure in Minnesota.

    (D) Germany's success in gaining land early in World War II was linked to its use of coal deposits in the Ruhr region, which facilitated a more powerful military.

    (E) Civilization was born in arable areas because fertile land created human innovation beyond nomadic lifestyles.

2. A formal caste system of socioeconomic segregation based on family and occupation was prominent in which country's tradition?

    (A) Vietnam   (D) Saudi Arabia

    (B) Russia   (E) China

    (C) India

3. If an Spanish speaker and a French speaker come together to conduct trade and revert to the authentic form of English they both learned in their schools, English is known to them as a(n)

    (A) creolized language   (D) pidgin language

    (B) language branch   (E) lingua franca

    (C) isogloss

4. In the 1800s, Czar Peter the Great of Russia returned to Russia from his travels in Europe and taught his people Western-style dance. This diffusion of Western-style dance is most closely an example of

    (A) cultural convergence   (D) cultural isolation

    (B) sequent occupance   (E) theocracy

    (C) folk culture

5. Which of the following lists religions that all started in Southwest Asia?

    (A) Buddhism, Hinduism, Islam

    (B) Islam, Judaism, Christianity

    (C) Shintoism, Sikhism, Judaism

    (D) Taoism, Christianity, Hinduism

    (E) Judaism, Animism, Buddhism

6. Which of the following is the dominant language family in India?

    (A) Sino-Tibetan   (D) Indo-European

    (B) Dravidian   (E) Altaic

    (C) Afro-Asiatic

7. The above image comes from Beijing, China, and is of a Kentucky Fried Chicken restaurant that bought out and replaced a local family's restaurant. Some might argue this is an example of

    (A) language replacement   (D) ethnic enclave

    (B) creolized language   (E) ghettoization

    (C) cultural imperialism

8. A geographer studying the northern Canadian Inuit culture's intricate river navigation routes is best described as analyzing

   (A) demography

   (B) cultural ecology

   (C) linguistics

   (D) territorial morphology

   (E) boundary classification

9. In which of the following countries has conflict related to its multilingualism escalated to widespread threats of secession?

   (A) United States

   (B) Germany

   (C) Japan

   (D) Canada

   (E) India

10. Which of the following is most closely an example of nonmaterial culture?

    (A) Blue jeans

    (B) Indian naan bread

    (C) Dome of the Rock

    (D) Teachings of Confucianism

    (E) New England saltbox house style

11. Which of the following has the highest concentration of Muslims?

    (A) Vatican City

    (B) Northern Ireland

    (C) Pakistan

    (D) Sri Lanka

    (E) Vietnam

12. The excitement created by attending a Bon Jovi concert diffused in a pattern with an epicenter, or (node), that followed Bon Jovi's band as it toured through Europe between large and small towns in no particular order. About two weeks after Bon Jovi's visit, the excited crowds in each city died down and returned to normal lifestyles, while sometimes listening to his CDs in their homes. The pattern of excitement surrounding the traveling Bon Jovi concert is best classified as

    (A) hierarchical diffusion

    (B) migrant diffusion

    (C) stimulus diffusion

    (D) reverse hierarchical diffusion

    (E) contagious diffusion

13.   Which of the following is a universalizing religion?

(A)   Shintoism   (D)   Confucianism

(B)   Judaism   (E)   Taoism

(C)   Islam

14.   In which region does shamanism currently have the highest presence?

(A)   Western Europe   (D)   South America

(B)   North America   (E)   Southwest Asia

(C)   Sub-Saharan Africa

(Photo by: Aubrey Stoll)

15.   An adherent of which of the following religions would most likely make a pilgrimage to the holy place shown in the above picture from Amritsar, India?

(A)   Islam

(B)   Hinduism

(C)   Eastern Orthodox Christianity

(D)   Sikhism

(E)   Buddhism

16. Which prominent geographer in the 20th century championed the study of cultural landscapes and built environments in human geography?

    (A) Ellen Churchill Semple (D) Joel Garreau

    (B) Walter Christaller (E) Alfred Weber

    (C) Carl Sauer

17. What are the two major branches of Islam?

    (A) Sunni and Shintoism (D) Shiite and Shamanism

    (B) Shiite and Sunni (E) Shiite and Shintoism

    (C) Sunni and Shamanism

18. The simplest component of a culture is a

    (A) culture trait (D) cultural diffusion

    (B) culture complex (E) cultural identity

    (C) culture system

19. Religions that attempt to attract all people to their beliefs are known as

    (A) ethnic religions (D) polytheistic religions

    (B) universalizing religions (E) syncretic religions

    (C) monotheistic religions

20. Mecca, Saudi Arabia, is the holiest site for which religion?

    (A) Buddhism (D) Sikhism

    (B) Shintoism (E) Islam

    (C) Hinduism

19/20

Free-Response Review Questions

Vector 5 diffusion pattern

Time 1: From Large City to Large City

Time 2: From Large City to Medium City

Time 3: From Large and Medium Cities to Smaller Cities

Legend

◯ Large City

○ Medium City

∘ Small Town

→ Spatial Diffusion

● City That the Idea, Innovation, or Disease Has Spread To

Vector 6 diffusion pattern

The maps on the previous page depict the diffusion patterns of two new diseases, vector 5 and vector 6.

(A)   Define *spatial diffusion*.

(B)   Look at the diffusion pattern of vector 5. Define and explain the diffusion type indicated in the map of vector 5's diffusion as relocation, hierarchical expansion, stimulus expansion, or contagious expansion diffusion.

(C)   Look at the diffusion pattern of vector 6. Define and explain the diffusion type indicated in the map of vector 6's diffusion as relocation, hierarchical expansion, stimulus expansion, or contagious expansion diffusion.

PART 6 — Pre-Exam Practice Answers

Terms Review Answers

1. Standard language
2. Caste system
3. Cultural geography
4. Cultural landscape (or built environment)
5. Culture complex
6. Denomination
7. Ethnic religion
8. Ethnocentrism
9. Nonmaterial components of culture
10. Possibilism
11. Perceptual regions (vernacular regions)
12. Acculturation
13. Relocation diffusion
14. Assimilation
15. Culture hearth
16. Independent innovation (or invention)
17. Polytheistic religion
18. Diaspora
19. Christianity
20. Stimulus diffusion
21. Koran
22. Siddhartha Gautama
23. Judaism, Christianity, Islam
24. Theocracy
25. Genocide

Multiple-Choice Answers

1. **(D)**

    Possibilism teaches that humans take the natural environment's opportunities and limitations and innovate from them. It is an argument against environmental determinism, which says that human behavior is directed by the environment. (D) represents possibilism because humans took the coal deposits in the Ruhr region and used them to industrialize and create army technology. The other choices represent the principle from environmental determinism that the environment *directed* human activity and outcomes.

2. **(C)**

    India's formal caste system involved a strict segregation of society based on a person's family and occupation. The untouchables were the lowest caste and suffered almost complete social isolation. Recent political reforms have reduced the effects of the caste system in attempting to create more of a meritocracy, in which people's education and effort play more of a role in economic and social promotion.

3. **(E)**

    A lingua franca is a language used by speakers of different languages to facilitate trade-based communication or some sort of transaction. A pidgin language (D) is a simplified form of a language used by a people dominated by the speakers of that new language, usually in the case of a colonized people. It is not the correct answer to this question because the two groups are using a third language, English, to communicate. The question even stipulates that it is "authentic" English, not a simplified, pidginized form of English. (A) is a pidgin that has been adopted by a people and formalized into a language or dialect, taught even to the children. (B) is a major division in a language family, and (C) is a geographical boundary of a certain linguistic feature, such as word usage.

4. **(A)**

    Cultural convergence occurs when a culture adopts traits from another culture with which it comes into contact. Peter the Great brought the culture trait of Western dance back with him to the Russian people, many of whom adopted that European trait. (B) is the theory that a generation of inhabitants of a space leave behind imprints from which succeeding generations learn, as when occupiers of a region leave buildings behind for the next occupiers to use and adapt. (C) is usually an isolated, unique culture that is not infused with popular culture. (D) implies a culture that is not in contact with other cultures, which is not the case in this scenario of Peter the Great's contact with Western culture. (E) is when religious leaders control a government.

5. **(B)**

The Semitic Hearth in Southwest Asia is home to the origins of the three largest monotheistic religions on the earth: Judaism, Christianity, and Islam. Hinduism and Buddhism have their hearths in the land near the Indus and Ganges rivers, and the Chinese religions (or faiths), Shintoism, Taoism, and Confucianism, started in China.

6. **(D)**

The dominant, native language in India is Hindi, which is an Indo-European language. Dravidian languages also have a presence in India, but not dominance. (A) dominates in East Asia, (C) in Africa, and (E) in Central Asia and Turkey.

7. **(C)**

Cultural imperialism is the diffusion of a dominating set of culture traits or systems that are seen to threaten the existence of local cultures. Moreover, it is seen as a use of cultural invasion as a way to gain dominance politically, economically, or socially over the people in that region. The diffusion of KFC into the region represents the diffusion of Western, specifically American, culture and its threat to local culture—in this scenario, the ouster of a local restaurant. Some may see this as a way for American culture's invasion to pave the way for economic dominance of the region. (A) occurs when a language in a region is replaced by another, (B) occurs when by a dominated people adopts a pidgin as a language, (D) is a region wherein a particular ethnicity is concentrated and surrounded by another ethnicity or group of ethnicities, and (E) is the process of ghetto formation in cities.

8. **(B)**

Cultural ecology is the study of human interaction with the environments. The Inuit's interaction with their landscape is evident in their navigation routes, because they are interacting with their environment, their rivers. (A) is the study of human population and its related patterns, such as birth and death rates. (C) is the study of language origins and diffusions. (D) is the shape of a country; (E) is the analysis of different types of boundaries, such as subsequent and antecedent boundaries.

9. **(D)**

Canada's French-speaking minority (known as Francophones) has pushed for greater political and cultural recognition from the English-speaking (Anglophone) majority-run government and culture. Canadians have been considering a voting referendum on whether Quebec's French-speaking region should secede from Greater Canada. Though there have been tensions in (A), (B), and (E) surrounding multilingualism, widespread threats of secession have not arisen. (C) is nearly monolingual.

10. **(D)**

Nonmaterial culture refers to components of culture that are not physically graspable, such as religious beliefs, communication patterns, customs, and philosophies, such as (D). The other choices are examples of material culture, that which is tangible or physical, such as technology, architecture, food, and clothing.

11. **(C)**

The country of Pakistan was formed in 1947 as a Muslim state in an attempt to end infighting within India between Hindus and Muslims. It is nearly 97 percent Muslim, making it one of the most populated countries in the world with a Muslim majority. (A) is heavily Roman Catholic, (B) has tensions between Roman Catholics and Protestants, (D) is nearly 70 percent Buddhist, and (E) is nearly 81 percent nonbelievers (people who do not identify with a religion or faith).

12. **(B)**

Migrant diffusion is a form of relocation diffusion in which the core (or epicenter) of the diffusing phenomenon follows its wave of diffusion, such as the wave in a stadium, when crowds stand and then sit. The phenomenon tends to die out after a short time and after the wave of diffusion has moved on to new sites of adoption (or infection). The diffusion of excitement surrounding Bon Jovi's concerts is similar in that the crowds in cities where he played were energized by the concert, but that excitement died down shortly after the concert finished. New excitement was drummed up (pun intended) in the next city Bon Jovi went to. (A) occurs when a phenomenon diffuses from large or powerful places (or people) to smaller ones. The question states that there was no order of large or small city in Bon Jovi's pattern, which also rules out (D) because it is a pattern of diffusion from smaller to larger places or importance levels. (C) occurs when the diffusing phenomenon is adapted by the new adopters to fit their needs. (E) is a form of expansion diffusion when the phenomenon spreads according to proximity to the core, regardless of size or importance level. However, in (E), the phenomenon tends to maintain its strength in all places infected rather than weakening, as in migrant diffusion.

13. **(C)**

Islam is a universalizing religion, meaning that it believes its teachings are appropriate for all people. Therefore, like Christianity and Sikhism, it seeks converts. The other choices are ethnic religions, which are based in a particular place or cultural group. Ethnic religions do not actively seek converts.

14. **(C)**

Shamanism is a practice in many traditional societies in which there is a spiritual truth knower, a shaman, who is a guide for the local community or tribe. It has its greatest presence in sub-Saharan Africa, a region in which missionary work of universalizing religions is competing for dominance.

15. **(D)**

The image is of the Golden Temple, the holiest site to Sikhs, located in the holy city of Amritsar, in India's northwest.

16. **(C)**

Carl Sauer was one of the first to realize that humans modified the landscape in ways that told something about their culture. (A) championed the idea of environmental determinism; (B) developed the central place theory; (D) wrote the book *Edge Cities*, which discusses the development of areas outside metropolises; and (E) developed least cost theory.

17. **(B)**

The two major branches of Islam are Sunni and Shiite. Shintoism is a blending of Buddhist teachings and local beliefs in Japan. Shamanism is an ethnic religion that follows a shaman, or holy man.

18. **(A)**

Traits are the basic components of a culture group. They include everything from how a people greet each other to what foods are "good" and "bad" to eat. (B) is the combination of a group's cultural traits into a unique set of characteristics. (C) occurs when a trait is present in several culture complexes; for example, soccer is played by many culture groups. (D) is the process by which traits move between groups. (E) is the set of culture traits an individual or group uses to try to answer the question "Who am I?"

19. **(B)**

Universalizing religions, such as Christianity and Islam, believe their faith is valuable to all people and attempt to show nonbelievers the value of the religion. (A) are religions that attempt to appeal to only one group of people, perhaps in one place or of one ethnicity. (C) and (D) refer to the number of deities worshipped or believed in by a religion. (E) are blendings of elements from different religions.

20. **(E)**

Mecca, Saudi Arabia, is the holiest site for all Muslims, followed by Medina and then Jerusalem.

Free-Response Answers

The following is a list of suggested main points for each part of the question.

Part A

- Spatial diffusion is the spread of a phenomenon, such as a disease, across space and time.

Part B

- Vector 5 is spreading through contagious expansion diffusion, when a phenomenon spreads like a wave through space.

- Expansion diffusion is the spread of a phenomenon geographically from one adopter (or place) to another while remaining with the first adopter (or place).

- Contagious expansion diffusion is the spread of a phenomenon outward without regard to the size of the places surrounding it; places near the origin (or hearth) are affected first. The farther away a person or place is from the origin, the later will it be affected by the diffusing phenomenon.

- Vector 5 is spreading outward from its point of origin to the nearest cities, large and small, in each wave of spread. It is not discriminating based on size, only based on proximity to the point of origin.

Part C

- Vector 6 is spreading through hierarchical expansion diffusion.

- Hierarchical expansion diffusion is the spread of a phenomenon geographically from its place of origin in an outward pattern, like in the contagious pattern. However, unlike contagious expansion diffusion, it spreads outward with respect to size of place or level of susceptibility.

- Vector 6 is spreading outward from its place of origin but is discriminating in its spread pattern to larger cities before hitting smaller places, in a hierarchical pattern.

Chapter 5

Political Organization of Space

Introduction

The lines on the map we refer to as boundaries show which lands belong to which peoples, but long before humans imposed their jigsaw puzzle of division onto the earth, the land was unified as one piece. Throughout history, the often-imaginary lines marking territorial divisions have shifted as humans fought for control over precious land and its resources. In fact, people may have such deep attachments to a territory that they are willing to risk their lives to defend it. Perhaps that is why nearly 200 wars are fought each year, usually conflicts related to territorial claims and desires.

Political geography is the study of human political organization of the earth at various geographic levels. Political geographers study the spatial layout of political organization at, above, and below the country level. Above the country level, political geographers study organizations such as the United Nations, which includes many countries. At the country scale, political geographers look at how a country's government is organized. Below the country level, political geographers might study the boundaries of voting districts. Political geographers study the changing role of the country in the world's political dealings.

> ### Key Questions
>
> ➤ *How do political patterns reflect ideas about how the earth should be organized?*
>
> ➤ *How do political patterns affect human activities and understandings?*
>
> ➤ *What is the evolution of the nation-state from its original form to its modern form?*
>
> ➤ *What forces have shaped the world political map into its current form? How are those forces related to the rise of the modern state in Europe and to colonialism?*
>
> ➤ *How do political boundaries relate to economic, cultural, and environmental boundaries?*

> ➤ *What is the role of the modern country in the contemporary political landscape? How do forces such as ethnic separation, economic globalization, regional supranationalism, and regional environmental problems affect the role of the country in the modern world?*
>
> ➤ *What are the forms and roles of political units above and below the country level?*
>
> ➤ *How do specific political policies, such as racial segregation, affect the organization of spatial and cultural life?*

PART 1 Territorial Dimensions of Politics

Human Territoriality

Territoriality is creating ownership over a defined space. Territoriality can apply to your bedroom or an entire country and often evokes an emotional response. Just as your sibling's entering your room uninvited causes you to feel angry (and even to retaliate), a country's threatening the defined space of another country often provokes an aggressive response. Consider, for example, when Iraq invaded Kuwait's territory and triggered the first Gulf War; or when Germany invaded Poland in 1939 and England and France came to Poland's defense, fearing that Germany would be moving toward taking their lands.

Some political geographers claim that human territoriality is equal to animals' aggressive defense of their territories, such as when a dog runs into another dog's yard. However, American geographer Robert Sack argued that humans are far more complex than animals in their territorial behavior. He posited that human territoriality is contextual and depends on time and place. For example, a country may allow people to cross its administrative border if they have the correct paperwork, and countries enter into and get out of treaties to work together to protect their lands. Such allowances are rare in the animal world.

Territoriality also applies to the geography of personal space. **Personal space** is the area we claim as our own territory into which others may not enter without our permission. A student sitting in a classroom desk, for example, may claim that her personal space extends around her desk like a bubble. If someone invades that space—getting close to her face, for instance—she may feel an immediate sense of anxiety, discomfort, or even anger. How much space is considered "personal" often varies with time and place. For example, people living in small towns often have larger bubbles of personal space than do New Yorkers, who deal with crowded subways and streets. How many times have you accidentally brushed someone's leg

Figure 5.1. A map of the world's countries

or arm and said, "I'm sorry"? This indicates your perception that you have invaded that person's personal space. However, if you walk through a crowded street jammed with people and have to touch people in order to move, your definition of personal space reconfigures, and you may be less likely to say "I'm sorry" every time you make contact with another human. Human territoriality is contextual.

Proxemics is the study of personal space. One commonly established method of claiming personal space is through use of spatial markers, such as a jacket that a man attending a concert places on a seat to mark it as his personal space in the auditorium.

States and Nations

Since first grade, you have probably been referring to England as a country. Political geographers use a more exact term: *state*. In political geography, a **state** is a political unit with a permanent population, territorial boundaries that are recognized by other states, an effective government, a working economy, and sovereignty. **Sovereignty** is the internationally recognized control a state has over the people and territory within its boundaries. Germany, Russia, Japan, Indonesia, the United States, and Mexico are just a few of the nearly 200 states (or countries) on the earth. Some states, such as the United States, have smaller divisions within them that they also refer to as "States." In political geography, the term "state" is used interchangeably with "country."

On the other hand, political geographers use the term **nation** to refer to a group of people who share a common culture and identify as a cohesive group. Language, religion, shared history, and territory are cultural elements that can create such cohesion and form a nation. Usually, people are willing to fight on behalf of their national identity. The United States is often considered a nation, a group of people unified around the principle of being American. Perhaps the constitutional sense of liberty is at the base of this idea of an American nation.

Some geographers argue that the United States is not one nation but comprises many nations within its borders, such as, perhaps, the Mexican American nation, the Islamic American nation, the Jewish American nation, and so on. They argue that the United States is, therefore, a **multinational state**, a state that includes more than one nation within its borders. Russia is a multinational state that contains hundreds of nations within its borders. A state with only one nation in its borders is called a **nation-state**. Japan and Iceland are examples of states that are as close to being classified as nation-states as possible in today's world. On the other hand, when a nation does not have a territory to call its own, it is referred to as a **stateless nation**. The Assyrian Christians of Iraq and the Ughirs of western China do not have their own countries. They are considered stateless nations.

Ethnonationalism and Conflict

Ethnonationalism is a powerful emotional attachment to one's nation that is a minority within a state and feels different from the rest of the state's people. When minority nations feel that they do not have enough **self-determination**, or the power to control their own territory and destiny, ethnonationalism can lead to conflict. For example, the Chechen people comprise a minority nation that live in Russia and have a strong sense of ethnonationalism that has even led to violent conflict with the Russian government. Chechnya is a republic within the Russian state, but the Chechens want more autonomy and feel discriminated against by the Russian government. Terrible violence has exploded over threats of secession, or breaking off into a separate state.

Irredentism

Nations do not always refer to groups of people just within a certain set of borders. For example, the Serbs are a nation, or a group of people that share a sense of brotherhood and identify as a group, but they exist in several countries, not just the land that is considered Serbia. The Chinese nation comprises the group of people identifying as part of that cultural group but not necessarily residing just in China.

Conflict can arise when a nation's homeland is spread into the territory of another state or several states. For example, Hitler believed the German homeland had spilled into Czechoslovakian territory. He wanted to take control of that land in Czechoslovakia to reunite all Germans into one state. A movement to reunite a nation's homeland when a part of it is spread into another state's borders is called **irredentism**. Albania's people live primarily in Albania, but a large pocket of Albanians live in a piece of Serbia's territory called Kosovo. In the 1990s, the Serb government engaged in a ruthless effort to "ethnically cleanse" Kosovo of all Albanians.

Some Recent Conflicts Related to Ethnonationalism

Place	Conflicting Parties	Reason
South Asia, Indian subcontinent	Indians versus Pakistanis	These two parties are fighting over control of Kashmir, a region overlapping each country's sovereignty and homelands.
Palestine, Southwest Asia	Jewish Israelis versus Muslim Palestinians and Arab allies	The stateless nation of Muslim Palestinians and their Arab allies are warring against the Jewish-controlled state of Israel for autonomy in a deeply layered historical conflict.
Southeast Asia	Mainland China versus Taiwan	Taiwan was founded in the 1940s after anticommunists fled the communist government established on Mainland China. China does not recognize Taiwan as a sovereign state and sees Taiwan as an island belonging to it, although Taiwan feels it is independent of China and is its own democratic state.
Former Yugoslavia	Serbs versus all the other nationalities that were once part of "Yugoslavia"	The former Yugoslavia comprised many nations, including Serbs, Croats, Kosovar Albanians, and Bosnian Muslims. In the 1990s, various nations in the multinational state of Yugoslavia warred to break away from the Serb-dominated government in Belgrade. Several newly independent states were created as a result of that war, the bloodiest since World War II.
Russia	Russia versus Chechnya	Chechnya is a territory in the Russian republic, governed by Moscow. The Chechen people want independence from Russia, which has caused massive fighting between the two groups.

Buffer States and Shatterbelts

Sometimes a buffer state or zone is used to try to calm two conflicting states or prevent them from further violence. A **buffer state** is an independent country located between two larger countries that are in conflict. Russia and China have warred over boundaries for centuries, but Mongolia has helped reduce direct confrontation between the two states. A **buffer zone** exists when two or more countries sit between two larger countries in conflict. After World War II, Eastern Europe was a buffer zone between the Soviet Union and Western Europe. However, the Soviets worked to dominate that buffer zone and install communist satellite states in Eastern Europe. **Satellite states** are countries controlled by another, more powerful state. For example, Poland became a satellite state of the Soviet Union, controlled by Moscow almost as tightly as a colonized state. The installation of communist satellite states in Eastern Europe erected what was coined by Winston Churchill as an "iron curtain" boundary between Western Europe and Soviet-controlled Eastern Europe.

A **shatterbelt** is a state or group of states that exists within a sphere of competition between larger states, as Poland was between Russia and Germany in World War II. Often states in a shatterbelt are the victims of invasion, boundary changes, and poor economic development.

Boundaries

Whether it is two states warring or two neighbors on a block arguing over a fence, the locations and definitions of boundaries are at the root of many conflicts at varying scales. Boundaries and their meanings shape our lives. Whether you are crossing into your neighbor's yard or into another country, these human-created lines represent ownership and identity, and they affect human behavior. Boundaries also exist within states at many levels: territories, municipalities, towns, villages, and so forth. *International* political boundaries separate states' territories; this type of political boundary actually extends to define what the state owns above and below the ground. There are several types of political boundaries.

Figure 5.2. Vertical plane of a political boundary, reaching above and beneath the ground

Geometric political boundaries are straight-line boundaries that do not relate to the cultural or physical features of the territories involved. The original boundary separating North and South Korea followed a line of latitude. **Physical (or natural) political boundaries** separate territory according to natural features in the landscape, such as mountains, deserts, or rivers. France is divided from Spain by the Pyrenees Mountains. **Cultural political boundaries** mark changes in the cultural landscape, such as boundaries dividing a territory according to religion or language. Sometimes cultural political boundaries are also drawn according to geometric straight lines. The borders that carved modern-day Pakistan were created to give Muslims a territory.

Frontiers are regions where boundaries are very thinly or weakly developed, zones where territoriality is unclear and not well established. Antarctica is a frontier region at the international scale because it does not have clear boundaries of territorial control. Local communities can have frontier regions between neighborhood boundaries. Whereas boundaries are lines, frontiers are regions.

Another way to classify boundaries depends on how they have evolved over time, rather than just how they were created. **Antecedent boundaries** existed before human cultures developed into their current forms. Many physical political boundaries grew as antecedent boundaries. For example, the states of Kentucky and Indiana grew as distinct cultures around an already present divisor, the Ohio River. **Subsequent boundaries** grow to divide space as a result of human interaction and negotiation after significant settlement has occurred. The division between Canada and the United States is an example of a subsequent boundary. **Superimposed boundaries** are forcibly put on a landscape by outsiders, such as invaders or an organization like the United Nations. The boundary creating the modern state of Israel was superimposed by the United Nations. A **relict boundary** no longer functions as a boundary but only as reminders of a line that once divided space. Perhaps one of the most famous relict boundaries is the Berlin Wall, which no longer serves as an administrative border as it once did in dividing East and West Berlin.

Boundary Creation

There are several steps in the growth of boundaries into final form. **Definition** is the phase in which the exact location of a boundary is legally described and negotiated. **Delimitation** is the step when the boundary's definition is drawn onto a map. **Demarcation** is the visible marking of a boundary on the landscape with a fence, line, sign, wall, or other means. Not all boundaries are demarcated, because it can be an expensive process. One of the longest, most impressively demarcated boundaries is the Great Wall of China, though now it is a relict boundary. **Administration** is the enforcement by a government or people of the boundary that has been created.

Ocean Boundaries

How much of a claim can a country make on the waters that touch its borders? The United Nations has led the world's efforts in creating boundaries of shared waters. In its **Convention on the Law of the Seas (UNCLOS)**, the United Nations has generally paved out the following guiding provisions:

- Coastal states can stake their claims to the sea up to 12 nautical miles from their shorelines. However, ships from other countries have the right to pass through these waters.

- A coastal state can claim up to 200 nautical miles of territory beyond its shoreline as an **exclusive economic zone,** over which that state has economic control, to explore and mine natural resources that may be in the waters.

- When there is not enough water for each country on opposite sides of the sea to have 200 nautical miles of exclusive economic zone, the two or more countries involved will divide up the water evenly, a rule called the **median-line principle**.

Types of Boundary Disputes

Conflicts over boundaries sometimes involve a mix of the following categories. A **definitional boundary dispute** is a fight over the language of the border agreement in a treaty or boundary contract. Japan and Russia have still not agreed on the definition of territorial boundaries surrounding islands north of Japan. A **locational boundary dispute** is a conflict over the location of a boundary, not the definition. The conflicting parties agree on the definition but not on where it exists on the earth or the map. An **operational boundary dispute** is a conflict over the way a boundary should operate or function. For example, two states might disagree about allowing migration across their respective borders. An **allocational boundary dispute** is a fight over resources that may not be divided by the border, such as natural gas reserves beneath the soil.

Territorial Morphology

Territorial morphology is the relationship between a state's geographic shape, size, relative location, and political situation. In other words, factors like shape, size, and relative location affect the political issues facing its people internally and internationally. There are five classifications of geographic shapes of states.

A **fragmented state** geographically exists in several pieces. Indonesia, for example, has more than 16,000 islands within its fragmented boundary. Malaysia is broken into two chunks. A fragmented shape can lead to problems for a state in maintaining unity among its constituent parts, as in East Timor, which broke away from Indonesia.

Elongated states are long and thin in shape. Vietnam has an elongated shape. Sometimes problems can arise with this shape when a state's power base, or capital, loses influence over one end of the elongation. It can also pose transportation problems because of the distances involved.

Figure 5.3. Shapes of various states

A **compact state** does not vary greatly in distance from its center point to any point on its boundary. Compact states can be nearly square or circular in shape. Switzerland has a relatively compact shape. A compact shape is often the political ideal because no one part feels too far away from the center of control.

A **prorupt (or protruded) state** has a piece that protrudes from its core area, like an arm of a leg jutting off from the main body. Thailand has a prorupt shape with its protrusion jutting off from its core. Prorupt states often face problems similar to those of elongated states, because that jutting piece may try to break away or may be invaded.

A **perforated state** has a hole punched in it by another state, like South Africa, which is perforated by Lesotho, a tiny country. In other words, a perforated state completely surrounds another state. Relationships between the perforated state and its perforating state can be difficult and can cause tension, particularly if the perforated state is not welcoming of the perforating state's people.

Unitary and Federal States

A state's size and cultural composition are also factors in its political situation and internal organization. States that are smaller in geographic size and population may be more politically unified, but not always. A **microstate** is a very small state, such as Singapore. Often these smaller homogeneous states will organize using a **unitary governmental structure**, in which one main decision-making body governs the entire state. Regions within the country may have their own local governments, but usually they are weak and serve only as administrative organs of the unitary government based in the country's capital. A unitary government can even take the form of a dictatorship.

A larger, more diverse state often adopts a **federal governmental structure**, with a central government and strong regional governments that share power with the central government; the United States and Germany have this form of government. The regional governments have different names; called states in the United States, Germany, and India; provinces in Canada; and *estados* in Mexico. Federal governmental organization is ideal for countries that may be geographically large and/or have regions that want a sense of self-determination, free from domination by the central government. The United States organized into a federal structure so that each state was given a sense of power and agreed to unify into one country. However, the threat of organizing a multinational state into a federal structure is that some regions, when given autonomy, may choose to break away from the unified state and demand complete independence.

Additionally, a state's relative location, or geographic situation, also affects its ability to survive and thrive. For example, countries that are **landlocked**, or without coastal access to a body of water, must depend on their neighbors to get to water sources for trade and navigation.

One other internal governmental structure is the **confederate governmental structure,** in which a weak central government exists with regional governments holding most of power. The Articles of Confederation was the first document binding together the 13 American colonies, primarily for the purpose of defense during the Revolutionary War.

Political Exclaves and Enclaves

As defined in Chapter 4, an ethnic enclave is an area in which an ethnicity is concentrated and surrounded by another ethnic group or groups. A political enclave exists in a similar way. Similarly, a territorial **enclave** is a state, or part of a state, surrounded completely by another state. Lesotho is an enclave territory surrounded by South Africa, and West Berlin was an enclave within the state of East Germany. The state surrounding an enclave is a perforated state.

When an enclave is a territorial, political extension of another state, it is called an **exclave**. For example, the West Berlin enclave in East Germany was technically part of the West German state, making that West Berlin enclave also an *exclave* of West Germany. Lesotho, though is not an exclave of any other state. It is, in and of itself, a country, and not an extension of another state. Alaska is an exclave of the United States because it is cut off from the rest of the country by Canada.

Enclaves and exclaves can cause conflict over boundaries. Azerbaijan has a Muslim majority, while its neighbor Armenia has a Christian majority. Within Azerbaijan, a minority nation of Christian Armenians lives in an enclave called Nagorno-Karabakh. Because this enclave has fought to be controlled by Armenia, it is also an exclave of Armenia, or an Armenian territory existing in Azerbaijan. Therefore, Azerbaijan is a perforated state, perforated by the Christian Armenian enclave, also an exclave of the Armenian state.

Figure 5.4. A map of Azerbaijan. Take note of its political exclave.

PART 2 — Evolution of the Contemporary Political Pattern

The Rise of the Nation-State Concept

Humans have organized political space throughout their existence in different forms. Early humans organized into clans, tribes, and villages. Conquerors collected such smaller groupings into kingdoms and empires. The ancient Greeks and Romans refined a component of their empires into the **city-state**, in which political space revolved around a central city and surrounding farmland.

In Europe before the 17th century, sovereignty of the rulers depended on the loyalties of the people they ruled rather than clearly defined territories. After the fall of the Romans around 500 CE, European territory was typically divided in a feudal structure according to religion. The feudal structure was based on a system of many rulers exercising control over their own groups of dependent peoples and the dominance of the Catholic Church on everyday life. Therefore, the European political organization before the 1500s was loosely organized and not centralized.

In the 1500s, many western European places began integrating these feudal structures into more-centralized kingdoms. Strong monarchies grew in France and England, where kings developed central powers over their subjects. The loosely organized feudal state began to disappear in England and France as a strong monarchy emerged. With the stronger monarchy came more internal cohesion in the political organization, which led to the rise of nation-states, states that contain one nation, a cohesive group of people linked to their territory through a shared government and common goals. The pattern of integration into nation-states diffused throughout Europe and became a common goal even through World War II. Simply, the idea of linking people who share a strong sense of unity (a nation) under one government seemed to be the best way to prevent ethnonational violence from erupting, as it did in both of the world wars. However, creating political boundaries that match national (or cultural) boundaries was not often in the best interest of the boundary makers, as we will see.

Colonialism and Imperialism

European nation-states began building world empires in the 16th century and competed for territories across the globe through World War II. **Colonialism** is the control by a state over another area or people. Often a state that is colonizing has a more industrialized economy than the region it is overtaking. The first period of colonialism occurred after European explorers, such as Columbus, discovered land in the Western Hemisphere in the 15th century. Europeans raced to form colonies in those lands and extract resources to send back home, an economic system called **mercantilism**. Under mercantilism, a state acquires colonies that can provide it with

Figure 5.5. European colonies in Africa, 1450s–1912

the raw materials to ship back home and use in making products for the population in the mother country. Other motives for colonization were to spread Christianity and to bask in the glory of having more land than other states.

The second major wave occurred in the late 1800s, as western European powers were competing to "carve up" Africa, gaining more land to make them appear more powerful and to feed their industrializing economies. England and France occupied nearly 70 percent of the colonial territory in Africa. Portugal, Germany, Spain, Italy, and Belgium also colonized Africa.

Colonization fueled **imperialism**, the process of establishing political, social, and economic dominance over a colonized area. Europeans acculturated indigenous peoples to European Christianity and culture, even destroying indigenous landscapes and imposing European architecture that signified dominance.

Dependency Theory and Neocolonialism

According to the **dependency theory**, many countries are poor today because of their colonization by European powers. Proponents of this theory assert that former colonies in South America, Africa, and Asia have not been able to heal from the imperial domination established by the European colonizers and are still dependent on them. In most cases, the Europeans drew political boundaries according to the resources available to the colonizers, not according to the cultural (national) groupings of the native peoples. Therefore, when the Europeans left and the lands became independent states, the populations in those states were not unified, leading to violent ethnonational conflicts, as seen in Nigeria and Sudan, for example.

The number of states in the world has increased from 70 in 1938 to more than 200 in 2007. Most of the new states have recently achieved independence from a European colonizer.

Additionally, the political and economic structures established by the Europeans benefited the colonizers, not the local people, in most cases. Educational systems, health care networks, roads, communication lines, and other basic elements of infrastructure were not built in most colonized lands. As a result, many countries that were once European colonies are now in deep debt to their former colonial masters, burdened by loans they arranged with their former colonizers as a means of building up their economies that were, arguably, destroyed by their colonizers. The continued economic dependence of new states on their former colonial masters is called **neocolonialism (or postcolonial dependency)**.

World-Systems Analysis

As developed by Immanuel Wallerstein, **world-systems analysis** looks at the world as a capitalistic system of interlocking states. It posits that the situation in one country is directly linked to that country's role in the greater capitalistic system. Therefore, neocolonialism and its related dependency is not necessarily just a result of internal struggles within a poor country but is a consequence of that country's relationship to a larger system. World-systems analysis argues that the world is divided into three categories and that countries shift among these categories over time:

- The global economic core consists of the industrialized, developed countries that drive the global economy.

- The global economic periphery consists of countries that are underdeveloped and were, usually, once the core's colonies.

- The global economic semiperiphery is a third region in the world system in which countries are between the economic core and the periphery.

Geopolitics

Geopolitics is a branch of political geography that analyzes how states behave as political and territorial systems. In other words, geopolitics is the study of how states interact and compete in the political landscape. Nineteenth-century geopolitical thinker Friedrich Ratzel's **organic theory** argued that states are living organisms that hunger for land and, like organisms, want to grow larger and larger by acquiring more nourishment in the form of land. Adolf Hitler and the Nazis used Ratzel's theory as justification for invading other states to feed Germany's organic hunger for land.

In 1939, Adolf Hitler had the Olympic Village in Berlin laid out in the shape of the German map. In May of that year, Hitler used the viewing room at the Olympic Stadium to make his speech on his geopolitical justifications for gaining more land, or lebensraum, for the German state. By September, he had activated his theory by invading Poland.

Another prominent geopolitical thinker was Halford J. Mackinder, author of the heartland theory. According to the **heartland theory**, the era of sea power was ending and control over land would be the key to power. He believed that Eurasia was the "world island" and the key to dominating the world. Ruling this world island necessitated controlling eastern Europe. Mackinder's theory is linked to the Communists' efforts to dominate eastern Europe and to the U.S. "containment policy"

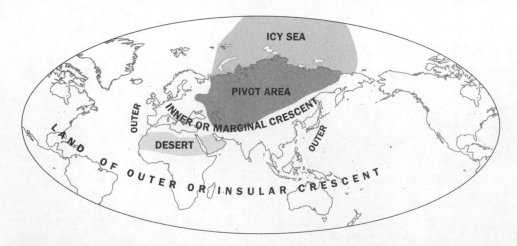

Figure 5.6. Mackinder heartland theory: The "pivot area" shown is the "heartland" in the Mackinder Theory. Mackinder argued that whoever controlled this pivot area would rule the world.

of keeping the Russians from gaining additional territories in the heartland, which the United States believed, based on the **domino theory**, would cause a fall of the world island to the Soviets.

Another geopolitical thinker, Nicolas Spykman, built off of Mackinder's theory and wrote of the "rimland." In his **rimland theory**, Spykman defined the rimland to be all of Eurasia's periphery, not its core of Russia and Central Asia. Therefore, the rimland encompasses western Europe and Southeast, South, and East Asia. He thought it was important to balance power in the rimland to prevent a global power from emerging. His theory is linked to the Vietnam and Korean wars, in which Communists and non-Communists fought for control of peripheral lands in the rimland.

PART 3 — Challenges to Inherited Political-Territorial Arrangements

Core Areas and Multicore States

A region's internal organization of power can affect its level of unity and cohesion. The region in a state wherein political and economic power is concentrated, like the nucleus of a cell, is called a state's **core**. A well-integrated core, one that functions as a healthy part of its state, not in isolation, helps spread development throughout the country. Countries having more than just one core region are called **multicore states**. When these core areas are competing for political and economic power and none is dominant, the result can be internal division within the state. Nigeria, for example, has several core regions competing for control and thus jeopardizing Nigeria's unification. Strong infrastructure development, in the form of roads, communication lines, and so forth, can help distribute the growth generated in a core among the places outside the state's core.

Capital Cities

The capital of most countries is its political nucleus. Some countries have a capital city, called a **primate city**, that is not only the political nucleus but also many times more economically powerful than any other city in the state. Primate cities often exist in less-developed countries, where most of the resources are attracted, like a magnet, to one city that grows and grows and is supplied by the smaller cities in the state that do not get an equal share of the development. Ulaanbaatar, Mongolia, is an example of a primate city that is many times larger and more powerful than the next-largest city in Mongolia. In many such cases, governments are trying to spread the growth and development out among different cities, rather than allowing it to focus on the primate city. Primate cities are also common in old nation-states, like France and Britain. In these places, the primate city has been the cultural center for a long time and still attracts many migrants.

States also move their capital cities for various reasons. A **forward capital** is a capital city built by a state to achieve some national goal. The Russian czar Peter the Great built the forward capital of Saint Petersburg, moving the capital of Russia from Moscow to bring Russia's capital city and its focus closer to Europe; Moscow is farther east and thus farther from Europe than is Saint Petersburg. After the fall of the Berlin Wall in 1990, Germany chose to move its capital city back to Berlin, a forward capital, to show unification.

Gerrymandering

Internal political boundaries often are the subject of debate and manipulation. Electoral boundaries affect voting patterns and outcomes. In the United States alone, considerable debate surrounds the placement of electoral district boundaries. The definition of these boundaries can give one party an advantage over another in competing for a spot in a legislature. For example, boundaries can be drawn to give the number of registered Republicans a majority in a particular district, or registered Democrats in another. Redrawing electoral boundaries to give a political party an advantage is called **gerrymandering**. In total, the spatial organization of electoral geography can have a profound effect on power structures in a state.

Figure 5.7. Political cartoon from 1812 demonstrating voting-district gerrymandering.

In 2000, only 57 of the 435 seats in the U.S. House of Representatives were decided by margins of 10 percent or less.

Centrifugal and Centripetal Forces

Within every state are forces that unify its regions and people and other forces that work to divide its regions and people. **Centrifugal forces** divide a state's people and regions (think "centrifugal," *F*, for "fracture"). **Centripetal forces** unify a state's people and regions (think "centripetal," *T* for "together"). In states that are unified, centripetal forces are more dominant than centrifugal forces. The inverse holds when a state is breaking apart: centrifugal forces are dominant.

Examples of Centripetal and Centrifugal Forces Within States*

Centripetal	Centrifugal
Unifying symbols, such as flags	Separatism in a region
A national pledge of allegiance	Internal boundary conflicts
A strong identity based on language, religion, or other cultural traits	Deep religious divisions

* These examples could be reclassified within a particular situation. A flag, for example, might be a unifying force in the United States of America but a force of division and conflict in a state that has many nations that cannot agree on what the flag should look like. A culture trait like religion can also help strengthen national ties or weaken them.

Centrifugal forces broke apart the former state of Czechoslovakia in 1993 when the Czechs and Slovaks each wanted their own regions, leading to the creation of the Czech Republic and Slovakia. Centripetal forces worked to keep the Canadian French speakers united with the English-speaking Canadian nationality, despite the centrifugal forces calling for secession and an independent French-speaking state. Centrifugal forces tore apart the former Soviet Union, leading to independent states such as Latvia, Lithuania, and Estonia, once a part of the Russian union. **Balkanization** occurs when centrifugal forces break apart a state into smaller pieces. The term is rooted in the violent breakup of the Balkan region of Yugoslavia into smaller autonomous states.

Devolution

States facing centrifugal forces, such as strong regional separatism or internal dispute, often move to transfer more power to regional governments to help

Figure 5.8. Ethnic groups within what was once Yugoslavia

reduce the divisive tensions by giving angry groups more regional power and autonomy. **Devolution** is the process of transferring some power from the central government to regional governments. For example, Scotland was pushing for more autonomy from England. In the 1990s, England devolved more power to Scotland, when Scotland was given its own representative parliament instead of being governed only by England's parliament in London. In France, the Corsicans were a threat to national unity, so France's Paris-based government devolved more power to the Corsicans to keep them from moving toward violently seceding (breaking away). Montenegrins were vying for increased autonomy, and despite Serbia's devolutionary efforts to give them more regional control, the Montenegrins declared independence in 2006.

Supranationalism

Although the current political landscape is characterized by a trend in ethnonationalism leading to newly independent states, a trend toward increased integra-

(Photo by: AP Wide World Photos)

Figure 5.9. A meeting of the UN General Assembly

tion among states, or growing supranationalism, is also evident. **Supranationalism** is the growing trend of three or more countries forming an alliance for cultural, economic, or military reasons. Space–time compression is a factor causing increasing supranationalism. Supranational alliances are created so that states can collectively reach a common goal that they may not be able to reach independently. If a country threatens other states, the affected supranational organizations may impose **international sanctions**, or punishments in the form of economic or diplomatic limits or even isolation. When Iraq was threatening members of the United Nations, the UN imposed economic sanctions on Iraq, including trade embargoes, or complete bans on trade with Iraq.

After the bloody conflict among states during World War I, U.S. President Woodrow Wilson, along with other world leaders, founded the League of Nations. That organization was the precursor to the current **United Nations (UN),** which was formed in the aftermath of World War II. The countries came together as the UN for collective security, trying to ensure that a global war would not happen again. With nearly 200 members, the United Nations is the world's most extensive supranational organization ever established. During the cold war, the **Warsaw Pact** was a supranational organization of communist allies, while the **North Atlantic Treaty Organization (NATO)** was formed to combat the expansion of communist states. The Association of Southeast Asian Nations (ASEAN), another example of political supranationalism, was formed in the 1960s to protect its member states from invasion by China.

(Photo by: Kjetil Ree)

Figure 5.10. The meeting room of the UN Security Council

The United Nations

Formed in 1945, the United Nations is the closest structure to a world government on the earth. Its headquarters and all its main organs, except the International Court of Justice, are located in New York City on a plot of land considered international territory. Bounded by the UN Charter, a constitution of sorts, the United Nations' nearly 200 member-states decide on common issues and policies. The UN Charter states that the organization's purposes are "to maintain international peace and security; to develop friendly relations among nations; to cooperate in solving international economic, social, cultural and humanitarian problems and in promoting respect for human rights and fundamental freedoms; and to be a centre for harmonizing the actions of nations in attaining these ends."

The structure of the UN includes the following main components:

- **General Assembly:** All member-states send a representative to this parliament-like deliberative body. Each member-state has an equal vote in the General Assembly, regardless of the state's size or power.

- **Security Council:** This organ of the UN has 15 member-states that make decisions related to war and peace and sending in UN "peacekeepers," which are the UN's force of troops meant only to be used to defend member-states and their people from threats to their sovereignty on peace-keeping missions. The Security Council also assigns sanctions to punish states for threatening collective security. Currently, 10 states are elected by the General Assembly to rotate onto the council, and five states of the council are permanent members. These five are the Russian Federation, China, the United States, France, and England. Each permanent country has a veto power that can cancel any resolution or action in the council. The Security Council's decisions must be carried out by the general member-ship, as stated in the UN Charter.

- **Economic and Social Council:** This is the arm of the UN that coordinates antipoverty and prohumanitarian efforts throughout the world. It is also charged with promoting cultural awareness and improving global health.

- **International Court of Justice (ICJ):** This is the UN's principal judicial organ located at the Peace Palace in the Hague, the Netherlands. The ICJ settles all legal disputes submitted to it by UN member-states in addition to giving legal advice to the UN. Composed of 15 judges who are elected for nine-year terms by the Security Council and the General Assembly, the ICJ has declared English and French as its official languages.

- **Secretariat:** This is the executive branch of the UN in charge of all administrative issues to keep the UN operating. The head of the secretariat is the UN secretary general, who is appointed by the General Assembly on recommendation of the Security Council.

The UN headquarters in New York has a Meditation Room with a guest book for signatures of people who have visited the room to meditate and pray for world peace.

Critics of the UN have called for restructuring it, including revising the UN Security Council's organization. Some analysts feel that global tensions can be linked to the lack of Arab representation among the Security Council's permanent members. Others call for reducing the UN's bureaucracy and distribution of money.

Palestine and the Vatican are not voting members of the United Nations but are considered "permanent observers."

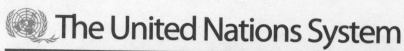

The United Nations System

Principal Organs

Trusteeship Council

Security Council

General Assembly

Subsidiary Bodies

Military Staff Committee

Standing Committee and ad hoc bodies

International Criminal Tribunal for the former Yugoslavia (ICTY)

International Criminal Tribunal for Rwanda (ICTR)

UN Monitoring, Verification and Inspection Commission (Iraq) (UNMOVIC)

United Nations Compensation Commission

Peacekeeping Operations and Missions

Subsidiary Bodies

Main committees

Human Rights Council

Other sessional committees

Standing committees and ad hoc bodies

Other subsidiary organs

Programmes and Funds

UNCTAD   United Nations Conference on Trade and Development

ITC   International Trade Centre (UNCTAD/WTO)

UNDCP [1] United Nations Drug Control Programme

UNEP United Nations Environment Programme

UNICEF United Nations Children's Fund

UNDP United Nations Development Programme

UNIFEM United Nations Development Fund for Women

UNV United Nations Volunteers

UNCDF United Nations Capital Development Fund

UNFPA United Nations Population Fund

UNHCR Office of the United Nations High Commissioner for Refugees

Advisory Subsidiary Body

United Nations Peacebuilding Commission

WFP World Food Programme

UNRWA [2] United Nations Relief and Works Agency for Palestine Refugees in the Near East

UN-HABITAT United Nations Human Settlements Programme

Research and Training Institutes

UNICRI United Nations Interregional Crime and Justice Research Institute

UNITAR United Nations Institute for Training and Research

UNRISD United Nations Research Institute for Social Development

UNIDIR [2] United Nations Institute for Disarmament Research

INSTRAW International Research and Training Institute for the Advancement of Women

Other UN Entities

OHCHR Office of the United Nations High Commissioner for Human Rights

UNOPS United Nations Office for Project Services

UNU United Nations University

UNSSC United Nations System Staff College

UNAIDS Joint United Nations Programme on HIV/AIDS

Other UN Trust Funds[7]

UNFIP United Nations Fund for International Partnerships

UNDEF United Nations Democracy Fund

NOTES: Solid lines from a Principal Organ indicate a direct reporting relationship; dashes indicate a non-subsidiary relationship.

[1] The UN Drug Control Programme is part of the UN Office on Drugs and Crime

[2] UNRWA and UNIDIR report only to the GA

[3] The United Nations Ethics Office and the United Nations Ombudsman's Office report directly to the Secretary-General

[4] IAEA reports to the Security Council and the General Assembly (GA)

[5] The CTBTO Prep.Com and OPCW report to the GA

[6] Specialized agencies are autonomous organizations working with the UN and each other through the coordinating machinery of the ECOSOC at the intergovernmental level, and through the Chief Executives Board for coordination (CEB) at the inter-secretariat level

[7] UNFIP is an autonomous trust fund operating under the leadership of the United Nations Deputy Secretary-General. UNDEF's advisory board recommends funding proposals for approval by the Secretary-General.

Figure 5.11. Organizational chart of the United Nations

The United Nations System

Economic and Social Council

Functional Commissions

Commissions on:
  Narcotic Drugs
  Crime Prevention and Criminal Justice
  Science and Technology for
    Development
  Sustainable Development
  Status of Women
  Population and Development
Commission for Social Development
Statistical Commission

Regional Commissions

Economic Commission for Africa (ECA)

Economic Commission for Europe (ECE)

Economic Commission for Latin
  America and the Caribbean (ECLAC)

Economic and Social Commission for
  Asia and the Pacific (ESCAP)

Economic and Social Commission for
  Western Asia (ESCWA)

Other Bodies

Permanent Forum on Indigenous Issues
  (PFII)

United Nations Forum on Forests

Sessional and standing committees

Expert, ad hoc and related bodies

Related Organizations

WTO World Trade Organization

IAEA [4] International Atomic Energy
  Agency

CTBTO Prep.Com [5] PrepCom for the
  Nuclear-Test-Ban-Treaty Organization

OPCW [5] Organization for the
  Prohibition of Chemical Weapons

International Court of Justice

Specialized Agencies [6]

ILO International Labour
  Organization

FAO Food and Agriculture
  Organization of the United Nations

UNESCO United Nations
  Educational, Scientific and Cultural
  Organization

WHO World Health Organization

World Bank Group
  IBRD International Bank
    for Reconstruction and
    Development

  IDA International Development
    Association

  IFC International Finance
    Corporation

  MIGA Multilateral Investment
    Guarantee Agency

  ICSID International Centre for
    Settlement of Investment
    Disputes

IMF International Monetary Fund

ICAO International Civil Aviation
  Organization

IMO International Maritime
  Organization

ITU International Telecommunication
  Union

UPU Universal Postal Union

WMO World Meteorological
  Organization

WIPO World Intellectual Property
  Organization

IFAD International Fund for
  Agricultural Development

UNIDO United Nations Industrial
  Development Organization

UNWTO World Tourism
  Organization

Secretariat

Departments and Offices

OSG [3] Office of the
  Secretary-General

OIOS Office of Internal Oversight
  Services

OLA Office of Legal Affairs

DPA Department of Political Affairs

DDA Department for Disarmament
  Affairs

DPKO Department of Peacekeeping
  Operations

OCHA Office for the Coordination of
  Humanitarian Affairs

DESA Department of Economic and
  Social Affairs

DGACM Department for General
  Assembly and Conference
  Management

DPI Department of Public Information

DM Department of Management

OHRLLS Office of the High
  Representative for the Least
  Developed Countries, Landlocked
  Developing Countries and Small
  Island Developing States

DSS Department of Safety and
  Security

UNODC United Nations Office on
  Drugs and Crime

ৎ৯ৎ

UNOG UN Office at Geneva

UNOV UN Office at Vienna

UNON UN Office at Nairobi

Published by the United Nations
Department of Public Information
06-39572—August 2006—10,00   0—DPI/2431

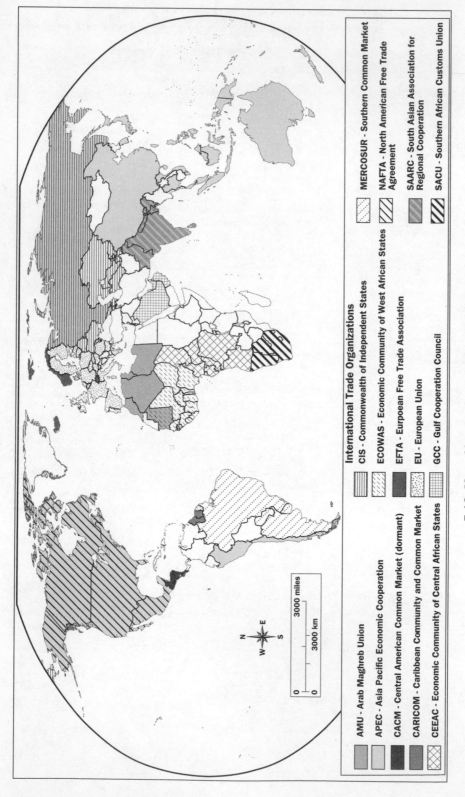

5.12. Map of international trade organizations

International Trade Organizations

CIS - Commonwealth of Independent States
ECOWAS - Economic Community of West African States
EFTA - Eurpoean Free Trade Association
EU - European Union
GCC - Gulf Cooperation Council

MERCOSUR - Southern Common Market
NAFTA - North American Free Trade Agreement
SAARC - South Asian Association for Regional Cooperation
SACU - Southern African Customs Union

AMU - Arab Maghreb Union
APEC - Asia Pacific Economic Cooperation
CACM - Central American Common Market (dormant)
CARICOM - Carlibbean Community and Common Market
CEEAC - Economic Community of Central African States

The Preamble to the UN Charter, Written in 1945

Preamble

We the peoples of the United Nations determined

- to save succeeding generations from the scourge of war, which twice in our lifetime has brought untold sorrow to mankind, and

- to reaffirm faith in fundamental human rights, in the dignity and worth of the human person, in the equal rights of men and women and of nations large and small, and

- to establish conditions under which justice and respect for the obligations arising from treaties and other sources of international law can be maintained, and

- to promote social progress and better standards of life in larger freedom,

and for these ends

- to practice tolerance and live together in peace with one another as good neighbors, and

- to unite our strength to maintain international peace and security, and

- to ensure, by the acceptance of principles and the institution of methods, that armed force shall not be used, save in the common interest, and

- to employ international machinery for the promotion of the economic and social advancement of all peoples,

have resolved to combine our efforts to accomplish these aims

Accordingly, our respective Governments, through representatives assembled in the city of San Francisco, who have exhibited their full powers found to be in good and due form, have agreed to the present Charter of the United Nations and do hereby establish an international organization to be known as the United Nations.

The European Union

Economic supranationalism is the integration of three or more states for achieving collective economic goals. The **European Union (EU)** is an example of economic supranationalism and represents the growth of a European economic community that has been formally developing since the 1950s.

With more than 25 member states, the EU has a population of nearly 500 million.

Figure 5.13. A map of the European Union membership

Historically, the EU started to grow with the formation of the **Benelux**, an economic alliance among Belgium, the Netherlands, and Luxembourg, before the end of World War II. Through Benelux, these three countries benefited from reduced trade barriers, more easily crossable (or permeable) borders, and common goals. Other European countries learned from this idea, and in 1958, the **European Economic Community** (also called the **Common Market**) was formed among some states wanting economic integration and cooperation. Out of the Common Market developed an even larger grouping of states, the European Community, called "Community" with hopes of becoming more than just an economic union. By 1992, the European Union was born with economic, political, cultural, and judicial integration goals.

The EU forms the largest free-trade zone in the world; NAFTA is the second largest.

The EU is perhaps the most powerful supranational alliance in the world, because its member states have bound together their economies, currencies, and environmental policies to create a powerful internal market in Europe. Most member-countries use the Euro, a common currency. Some geographers project that the EU will soon evolve into a military alliance as well among member-states. Nonetheless, its economic integration has created a rival to the economic superpower status of the United States.

The growth of supranational alliances challenges conceptions of state sovereignty. To join such an alliance, states must often give up some powers they have to the organization. Some European countries, particularly England, were reluctant to give up their currencies and use the Euro. The United States' Congress chose not to enter the League of Nations, despite Woodrow Wilson's advocacy for joining it. Congress also did not agree to enter the League of Nations after World War I, in part because the United States did not want to have to abide by the decisions of a supranational organization, which would have meant giving up some sovereignty.

Collapse of the USSR

Following the Russian revolution of 1917, the monarchy was overthrown by the Communists, who created the communist state called Union of Soviet Socialist Republics, or the USSR. The USSR was organized as a federation of states, called union republics, with Russia as its largest union republic; by 1960, the USSR was comprised of 16 republics. Its geographic expanse extended throughout what was the Russian empire into Eastern Europe after World War II.

The effects of the competition between the democratic U.S. allies and the USSR's communist allies, a conflict known as the cold war, led to the eventual devolution and balkanization of what was the USSR. After a period of fierce crushing of political dissent in the 1950s to 1970s, Mikhail Gorbachev was elected as the USSR's leader and ushered in a period of devolutionary reforms, such as allowing more freedom of speech and regional political sovereignty. The destruction of the Soviet-administered Berlin Wall that divided democratic West Berlin from communist-controlled East Berlin foreshadowed the fall of Soviet control of its satellite states and constituent regions calling for independence. By 1991, several union republics had formally voted to secede from the USSR

Other Supranational Organizations	Purpose
Economic Community of West African States (ECOWAS)	Founded in 1975 to create a more cooperative economic union among 15 West African states.
Latin American Integration Association (LAIA)	Formed in 1980 by Argentina, Bolivia, Brazil, Chile, Colombia, Ecuador, Mexico, Paraguay, Peru, Uruguay, and Venezuela to promote free trade.
Organization of Petroleum Exporting Countries (OPEC)	Formed to coordinate petroleum policies among its members in order to secure fair and stable prices for petroleum producers; an efficient, economic and regular supply of petroleum to consuming nations; and a fair return on capital to those investing in the industry. Its five founding members in 1960 were Iran, Iraq, Kuwait, Saudi Arabia, and Venezuela.
Organization of African Unity (African Union)	In a fashion similar to the European Union's integration efforts, the African Union was formed in 1999 with the aim of economically, socially, and politically aligning the African states toward attaining greater efficiency and reducing the strains of their colonial roots.
Arab League	Founded in 1945 in Cairo, Egypt, the Arab League combines voluntary members of primarily Arabic-speaking countries in a supranational union aimed at promoting common interests. In addition to Egypt, founding member-states are Iraq, Lebanon, Saudi Arabia, Syria, and Jordan.
North American Free Trade Association	Made effective in 1994, NAFTA is an economic alliance among the United States, Canada, and Mexico with the aim of fostering free trade throughout North America. The gradual removal of tariffs and trade barriers is the primary aim of NAFTA.

and form their own nation-states. The USSR was declared "dissolved" that same year by its communist government, from which Mikhail Gorbachev resigned. Gorbachev's successor, Boris Yeltsin, became president of Russia, no longer called the Soviet Union.

A New World Order?

During the cold war, in the aftermath of World War II, states were divided into two camps, procommunist and prodemocratic. This "bipolar" world was relatively balanced. A geopolitical transition has occurred since the fall of the Soviet Empire in the 1990s. In this **new world order**, international relations are no longer driven by the bipolar communist/anticommunist groups. Instead, international relations are multilayered and complex. Economically, many poles of superpower exist, including the U.S. economy, the European Union, and the growing Chinese economy. Militarily, the United States maintains superpower status, but it is increasingly challenged by terrorism and other types of warfare. The legitimacy and viability of the United Nations as an agent of collective security has been challenged with the Iraq War, when actions were taken that the UN did not endorse. Therefore, the new world order may be in a disorderly state, with poles of power and alliances reorganizing. It is becoming more "multipolar" in nature.

PART 4   Chapter Review

Terms Review

Administration phase of boundary creation—Phase in which a government enforces the boundary it has created.

Allocational boundary dispute—Conflict over resources that may not be divided by the border, such as natural gas reserves beneath the soil.

Antecedent boundary—Boundary that existed before the human cultures grew into current form.

Balkanization—Division of a region or state into smaller units, usually along ethnic lines.

Benelux—Economic alliance (and precursor to the current European Union) among Belgium, the Netherlands, and Luxembourg established before the end of World War II.

Buffer state—Independent country that exists between two larger countries that are conflicting

Buffer zone—Area consisting of two or more countries located between two larger countries in conflict.

Centrifugal force—Force that divides a state's people and regions.

Centripetal force—Force that unifies a state's people and regions.

City-state—Political space comprising a central city and surrounding farmland.

Colonialism—Control by a developed state over an underdeveloped area.

Compact state—State with little variation in distance from its center point to any point on its boundary.

Confederate governmental structure—Organizational structure comprising a weak central government and regional governments holding the majority of power.

Core of a state—Region in a state wherein political and economic power is concentrated, like the nucleus of a cell.

Cultural political boundary—Political boundary that marks changes in the cultural landscape, such as a boundary dividing territory according to religion or language.

Definitional boundary dispute—Conflict over the language of the border agreement in a treaty or boundary contract.

Definition phase in boundary creation—Phase in which the exact location of a boundary is legally described and negotiated.

Delimitation phase in boundary creation—Phase in which a boundary's definition is drawn onto a map.

Demarcation phase of boundary creation—Phase in which the boundary is visibly marked on the landscape by a fence, line, sign, wall or other means.

Dependency theory—According to this theory, former colonies in South America, Africa, and Asia have not been able to heal from imperial domination and are still dependent on their former European colonizers.

Devolution—Process of transferring some power from the central government to regional governments.

Domino theory—Notion that democratic allies must protect lands from falling to the communists because one such communist acquisition creates others, ultimately resulting in communist domination of the world. This theory led to the containment doctrine, intended to keep the communists from acquiring new lands, such as Vietnam.

Elongated state—State with a long, thin shape.

Enclave—State or part of a state surrounded completely by another state

Ethnonationalism—Powerful emotional attachment people have for their nation when it is a minority within a state, making them feel they are different from the rest of the state's people.

European Economic Community (Common Market)—Supranational economic alliance of European countries wanting to form a European market. Established in 1958, it was a precursor to the current European Union.

European Union (EU)—Supranational organization of nearly 25 member-states in Europe that have integrated for improved economic and political cooperation.

Exclave—Enclave that is a territorial political extension of another state.

Exclusive economic zone—According to the UNCLOS, a 200-nautical-mile area extending along a state's coast to which that state has economic rights.

Federal governmental structure—Organizational structure with a central government that shares power with strong regional governments.

Forward capital—Capital city built by a state to achieve a national goal.

Fragmented state—State geographically existing in more than one piece, or in fragments.

Frontier—Region where boundaries are very thinly or weakly developed; zone where territoriality is not well established and is unclear.

Geometric political boundary—Straight-line political boundary separating territories that do not relate to cultural or physical features.

Geopolitics—Branch of political geography that analyzes how states behave as political and territorial systems.

Gerrymandering—Redrawing electoral boundaries to give one political party an advantage over others.

Imperialism—The process of establishing political, social, and economic dominance over a colonized area

International sanctions—Punishments in the form of economic and/or diplomatic limits or even isolation.

Irredentism—Movement to reunite a nation's homeland when part of it extends into another state's borders.

Landlocked state—State without coastal access to a body of water.

Locational boundary dispute—Conflict over the location or place of a boundary.

Mackinder's heartland theory—Geopolitical theory that Eurasia was the "world island" and the key to dominating the world. Ruling this world island required controlling eastern Europe; linked to the domino theory.

Median-line principle—Statement in UNCLOS declaring that when there is not enough water for each country on opposite sides of the sea to have 200 nautical miles of exclusive economic zone, the two or more countries involved will divide the water evenly.

Mercantilism—Economic system in which colonies are obtained to supply the colonizer with raw materials to ship back home and use in making products for the population in the mother country.

Microstate—Very small state, such as Singapore.

Multicore state—State with more than one core region.

Multinational state—State with more than one nation within its borders.

Nation—Group of people who share a common culture and identify as a cohesive group.

Nation-state—State containing one nation, a cohesive group of people linked to their territory through a shared government and common goals.

Neocolonialism (or postcolonial dependency)—Continued economic dependence of new states on their former colonial masters; the basic principle of dependency theory.

New world order—Multilayered international situation, or landscape, that has existed since the end of the cold war.

North Atlantic Treaty Organization (NATO)—Supranational organization formed during the cold war to combat the expansion of communist states.

Operational boundary dispute—Conflict over the way a boundary should operate or function, such as the conflict over allowing migration across the border.

Organic theory—Friedrich Ratzel's geopolitical theory that states are living organisms that hunger for land and, like organisms, want to grow larger by acquiring more nourishment in the form of land.

Perforated state—State with a hole punched in it by another state, like South Africa perforated by Lesotho.

Personal space—Amount of area a person claims as his or her own territory into which others may not enter without permission.

Physical (or natural) political boundary—Political boundary that separates territories according to natural features in the landscape, such as mountains, deserts, or rivers.

Political geography—Study of human political organization of the earth at various geographic levels.

Primate city—City that is not only the political nucleus but also is many times more economically powerful than any other city in the state.

Prorupt (or protruded) state—State with a piece that protrudes from its core area, as an arm juts off from the main body.

Relict boundary—Boundary that no longer functions as a boundary but only as a reminder of a line that once divided space.

Rimland theory—Nicolas Spykman's theory defining the rimland to be all of Eurasia's periphery, not its core of Russia and Central Asia. This rimland was the key to controlling the world island.

Satellite state—Country controlled by a more powerful state

Self-determination—Power of a nation to control its own territory and destiny.

Shatterbelt—State or group of states that exists within a sphere of competition between larger states

Sovereignty—Internationally recognized control of a state over the people and territory within its boundaries.

State—Political unit with a permanent population, territorial boundaries recognized by other states, an effective government, a working economy, and sovereignty.

Stateless nation—Nation without a territory to call its own.

Subsequent boundary—Boundary that grows after significant settlement has occurred, rather than existing before the growth of human cultures, as with an antecedent boundary.

Superimposed boundary—Boundary forcibly put on a landscape by outsiders.

Supranationalism—Growing trend of three or more countries forming an alliance for cultural, economic, or military reasons.

Territoriality—Control over a space and the assumption of ownership to that space.

Territorial morphology—Relationship between a state's geographic shape, size, relative location, and political situation.

Unitary governmental structure—Organizational structure in which one main governmental decision-making body exists for the entire state. Regions within the country may have their own local governments, but they are weak and usually serve only as administrative organs of the primary government based in the country's capital.

United Nations (UN)—Supranational organization of nearly 200 member-states bound together to create collective security through diplomatic cooperation.

United Nations Convention on Law and the Seas (UNCLOS)—UN document of agreement among coastal states defining how they should divide the earth's bodies of water.

Warsaw Pact—Supranational organization of communist allies formed during the cold war.

World-systems analysis—Viewpoint that the situation in one country is directly linked to that country's role in the greater capitalistic system, divided into core states, peripheral states, and semiperipheral states.

PART 5: Some Suggested Web Resources for Further Exploration

European Union (EU): http://www.europa.eu/

The portal for the EU's official website (to view the English page, select ENG). The site contains organizational charts, maps, biographies, and transcripts of resolutions.

United Nations (UN): http://www.un.org/

This is the official site for the United Nations and all its components. In addition to resources on each of the major institutions governed by the UN, you can watch live Web casts of the UN's components in their sessions, including videos of the UN Security Council. Information on peacekeeping missions and maps are also available on the site.

Central Intelligence Agency (CIA): http://www.cia.gov/

The CIA maintains on its website a database of the world's countries called the World Factbook. This is an invaluable resource detailing each of the world's recognized states and their governmental, economic, and social elements.

Organization of the Petroleum Exporting Countries (OPEC): http://www.opec.org/

This official site of OPEC, a supranational organization of 11 oil-exporting countries.

North Atlantic Treaty Organization (NATO): http://www.nato.int/

This website is dedicated to NATO, a supranational alliance formed to create collective security.

UN Convention on the Law of the Seas: www.un.org/Depts/los/

This site contains information on UNCLOS and its effects on sea boundaries for coastal states.

African Union: http://www.africa-union.org/

The official site of the African Union includes helpful maps, graphs, and information on the union and its missions.

PART 6

Pre-Exam Practice

Terms Review Quiz

Use the Terms Review list or your own memory to determine the extent of your knowledge of key terms and concepts. Remember, the AP exam does not include this kind of exercise, but it is included here as a review tool.

1. _____   Group of people who share a common culture and identify as a cohesive group.

2. _____   Control over a space and the assumption of ownership to that space.

3. _____   Phase in which a boundary's definition is drawn onto a map.

4. _____   State with more than one nation within its borders

5. _____   Region where boundaries are very thinly or weakly developed; zone where territoriality is not well established and is unclear

6. _____   Conflict over the way a boundary should operate or function, such as the conflict over allowing migration across the border.

7. _____   State with a hole punched in it by another state, like South Africa perforated by Lesotho.

8. _____   Economic alliance (and precursor to the current European Union) among Belgium, the Netherlands, and Luxembourg established before the end of World War II.

9. _____   Supranational organization of communist-state allies formed during the cold war.

10. _____   Multilayered international situation, or landscape, that has existed since the end of the cold war.

11. _____ Geopolitical theory that Eurasia was the "world island" and the key to dominating the world. Ruling this world island required controlling eastern Europe.

12. _____ Capital city built by a state to achieve a national goal

13. _____ Force that unifies a state's people and regions.

14. _____ Branch of political geography that analyzes how states behave as political and territorial systems

15. _____ Economic system in which colonies are obtained to supply the colonizer with raw materials to ship back home and use in making products for the population in the mother country.

16. _____ Organizational structure with a central government that shares power with strong regional governments.

17. _____ Statement in UNCLOS declaring that when there is not enough water for each country on opposite sides of the sea to have 200 nautical miles of exclusive economic zone, the two or more countries involved will divide the water evenly.

18. _____ Boundary that grows after significant settlement has occurred, rather than existing before the growth of human cultures, as with an antecedent boundary.

19. _____ State with little variation in distance from its center point to any point on its boundary.

20. _____ Powerful emotional attachment people have for their nation when it is a minority within a state, making them feel they are different from the rest of the state's people.

21. _____ Internationally recognized control of a state over the people and territory within its boundaries.

22. _____   Political unit with a permanent population, territorial boundaries recognized by other states, an effective government, a working economy, and sovereignty.

23. _____   Relationship between a state's geographic shape, size, relative location, and political situation.

24. _____   Process of establishing political, social, and economic dominance over a colonized area.

25. _____   Viewpoint that the situation in one country is directly linked to that country's role in the greater capitalistic system, divided into core states, peripheral states, and semiperipheral states.

Multiple-Choice Review Questions

1. To try to reduce the calls for revolutionary secession from Canada, the Canadian parliament has given Nunavit regions more autonomy, or local control. This situation best represents the geographic concept of

    (A) exclave

    (B) buffer state

    (C) ministate

    (D) gerrymandering

    (E) devolution

Map of Slovakia

2. Which of the following morphological classifications best describes Slovakia, shown in the map above?

    (A) Fragmented

    (B) Compact

    (C) Elongated

    (D) Prorupt, or protruded

    (E) Perforated

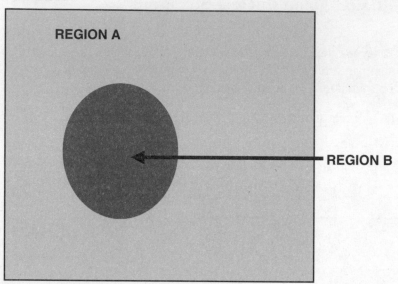

STATE X

REGION A

REGION B

3. Regions A and B both exist in State X shown above. The shaded areas above are both ruled by the government of State X. Region B includes one nation surrounded by other ethnicities living in Region A, that part of State X not including Region B. Based on this information, Region B is best classified as a(n)

(A) exclave

(B) enclave

(C) centripetal force

(D) core

(E) exclusive economic zone

STATE Y

DISTRICT 10

4. District 10 is one electoral region existing in square-shaped State Y, shown on the map above. District 10 was most likely formed through

    (A) gerrymandering   (D) balkanization

    (B) maladaptation   (E) supranationalism

    (C) devolution

5. Which of the following states is NOT a permanent member of the United Nations Security Council?

    (A) China   (D) France

    (B) Russia   (E) Germany

    (C) United States

6. Which of the following is a forward capital?

   (A) Paris, France

   (B) Bombay (Mumbai), India

   (C) Rome, Italy

   (D) Putrajaya, Malaysia

   (E) Sydney, Australia

7. Sikhs in India, Muslim Palestinians in Israel, and Kurds in the former Iraq are all considered

   (A) multinational states   (D) frontiers

   (B) stateless nations   (E) landlocked states

   (C) nation-states

8. According to world-systems analysis, which of the following countries would be best classified as being in the global economic periphery?

   (A) England   (D) China

   (B) Singapore   (E) Colombia

   (C) France

9. The current Canadian governmental organizational structure is best character- ized as

   (A) theocratic

   (B) confederate (or confederal)

   (C) federal

   (D) unitary

   (E) apartheid

10. In its application to the European Union, which state faced criticisms by some of its opponents for not being "European enough" to gain admission to the EU?

    (A) Italy   (D) England

    (B) Russia   (E) Iceland

    (C) Turkey

11. The political boundary dividing much of India from China is classified as

    (A) cultural

    (B) geometric

    (C) physical (or natural)

    (D) relict

    (E) superimposed

12. The United States and its allies entered the Vietnam conflict in part to prevent Communists from gaining control of the Eurasian periphery, because that control would have led to domination of the world, according to some geopolitical thinkers of the time. This justification is most closely associated with which of the following geographic concepts?

    (A) Rimland theory

    (B) New world order

    (C) World-systems analysis

    (D) Neocolonialism

    (E) North–south gap

13. Egypt and Ethiopia have developed a tense relationship related to water from the Nile River. This conflict is best classified as which type of boundary dispute?

    (A) Definitional

    (B) Allocational

    (C) Operational

    (D) Locational

    (E) Demarcation

14. Italy fought against Austria to annex Italian-speaking regions controlled by Austria. This is an example of

    (A) Balkanization

    (B) an exclusive economic zone

    (C) devolution

    (D) irredentism

    (E) colonialism

Irredentism: movement to reunite a nation's homeland when it reaches over another state's borders

15. All the following were included in the UN Convention on the Law of the Seas EXCEPT:

    (A) Coastal states can claim control of waters up to 12 nautical miles from their shorelines.

    (B) Coastal states can claim up to 200 nautical miles from their shorelines in exclusive economic zones.

    (C) Coastal states sharing waters with other states that are less than 200 nautical miles offshore will split the waters according to the median-line principle.

    (D) Ships have rights of passage through all waterways.

    (E) Straits are internationally operated and owned, not belonging to any one country.

16. The state borders drawn by the U.S. government over what used to be Native American lands are examples of

    (A) subsequent borders   (D) natural borders

    (B) superimposed borders   (E) land-grant borders

    (C) antecedent borders

17. Which of the following countries was not a member of the Warsaw Pact established during the cold war?

    (A) Poland   (D) France

    (B) East Germany   (E) Romania

    (C) USSR

18. Which of the following is the usual order of the steps in boundary creation between countries?

    (A) Definition, delimitation, demarcation

    (B) Delimitation, definition, demarcation

    (C) Delimitation, demarcation, definition

    (D) Definition, demarcation, delimitation

    (E) Demarcation, definition, delimitation

19. Which of the following is not a centripetal force?

    (A) Religious variation

    (B) National anthem

    (C) Common heritage

    (D) Common language

    (E) Schools

16/20

20. The Berlin Wall today would represent a(n)

    (A) subsequent boundary

    (B) relic boundary

    (C) antecedent boundary

    (D) natural boundary

    (E) superimposed boundary

Free-Response Review Questions

(A) Explain the *unitary* governmental structure. Give an example of a unitary state, and explain one advantage of having a unitary structure in this example.

(B) Explain the *federal* governmental structure. Give an example of a federal state, and explain one advantage of having a federal structure in this example.

(C) Define *devolution*. Choose a state from either Europe or Asia that has recently experienced devolution, and explain the causes that led the state to devolve.

definition, delimitation, demarcation

Pre-Exam Practice Answers

Terms Review Answers

1. Nation
2. Territoriality
3. Delimitation
4. Multinational state
5. Frontier
6. Operational boundary dispute
7. Perforated state
8. Benelux
9. Warsaw Pact
10. New world order
11. Heartland theory
12. Forward capital
13. Centripetal forces
14. Geopolitics
15. Mercantilism
16. Federal structure
17. Median-line principle
18. Subsequent boundary
19. Compact state
20. Ethnonationalism
21. Sovereignty
22. State
23. Territorial morphology
24. Imperialism
25. World-systems analysis

Multiple-Choice Answers

1. **(E)**

   Devolution is the transfer of some power from the central government to local governments, usually done to reduce ethnonationalism and/or regional separatism. (A) is a piece of a country geographically separated from the mother country and surrounded in another state. (B) is a state that exists geographically between two warring or conflicting states, (C) is a very small state like Singapore, and (D) is when legislators redesign electoral districts in a way to give a political party an advantage in an election.

2. **(C)**

   An elongated state has a long, thin shape, like Slovakia. A fragmented state (A) is splintered or geographically separated into several pieces, like Malaysia. In a compact state (B), no point on the state's boundary is significantly further from the geographic center than any other point. A prorupt, or protruded, state (D) has a piece of land jutting off of a core region, like Thailand. A perforated state (E) has a hole punched in it by another state, like South Africa.

3. **(B)**

   An enclave is a region in which a particular group is concentrated in one area and surrounded by people who are not members of that group. Because Region B is ruled by State X's government, the same as Region A, it is not considered an exclave of any other state (A). (C) is a force that helps bind a country together, such as a charismatic leader, a flag, or national anthem. (D) is a region that dominates a state economically or politically, and nothing in the questions suggests that Region B does so. (E) is the 200-nautical miles off the coast that a state can claim as its exclusive economic zone.

4. **(A)**

   Gerrymandering is the design by legislators of electoral districts to create advantages for a particular party. In linking people registered with a particular party together in one district, gerrymandering often results in very strange-shaped regions. (B) is the adoption of a trait by a population that is impractical for the population. (C) is the transfer of some political power from a central government to regional units; (D) is the breakup of a unified state into various independent subunits; and (E) is an alliance of three or more states for mutual benefit.

5. **(E)**

   The UN Security Council has 15 member states, five of which are permanent, veto-empowered states: China, Russia, United States, France, and

England. Germany was not allowed permanency because of its actions during World War II.

6. **(D)**

A forward capital is a city to which a government moves its capital to achieve a national objective. Malaysia is constructing Putrajaya to replace Kuala Lumpur as its political capital. Putrajaya is being planned from all conceivable aspects to create a city that represents urban innovation.

7. **(B)**

A stateless nation is a unified cultural group without a state to call its own, as in each of the mentioned cases, in which the named group wants its own countries. (A) are states each containing more than one nation; (C) are states each containing only one nation and with political boundaries that match cultural boundaries; (D) are regions that are officially unassigned and unoccupied territories with thinly defined boundaries and undeveloped territoriality; and (E) are countries without coastal access to bodies of water.

8. **(E)**

According to world-systems analysis, the world's states exist in one of three categories: core, periphery, and semiperiphery. A peripheral country is controlled by and serves the countries in the core. Colombia is not in an economic driver's seat, the core; it is not in a state of upward, near-core existence, the semiperiphery; but it is controlled by the core and, as a former colony, serves in a dependent relationship with the core. The other choices are, arguable, in the core or fringes of the semiperiphery near the core.

9. **(C)**

The Canadian government is organized as a constitutional monarchy with a parliamentary democracy that is also a federation of 10 provinces. This means that the central parliament shares power with 10 empowered provincial governments. (A) is a government run by religious leaders; (B) is a structure of a weak central government trumped by more powerful regional governmental units, like provinces; (D) is a structure with a strong central government and weak or nonexistent regional governments; and (E) was the racially segregating governmental structure in South Africa.

10. **(C)**

Turkey, a country that straddles both Europe and Asia, has a large Muslim population and affiliations with the Middle East that have prompted criticism that the country does not share enough of the EU's political-cultural similarities (if they even exist) to be a member-state. For example, Turkey's conflict with Cyprus has been viewed as a human rights issue jeopardizing Turkey's necessary commitment to EU principles.

11. **(C)**

The Himalayan Mountains play a prominent role in creating India's northern border from China. Because this boundary is based on a natural feature, a mountain chain, it is (C). (A) are political boundaries based on cultural aspects, such as language and religion; (B) are geometric straight-line boundaries not based on natural features; (D) are boundaries no longer active in dividing space; and (E) are boundaries applied by outside forces like the United Nations.

12. **(A)**

Spykman's rimland theory is based in the idea that control of the Eurasian periphery would lead to domination of the Eurasian landmass and eventual world domination. Therefore, according to this theory, if lands like Vietnam fell, the rest of the world would have fallen to the Communists in a domino effect. (B) came into existence after the fall of the Soviet Union in the 1990s, after the Vietnam War. (C) argues that states exist in a capitalistic system. (D) argues that the poverty in most newly independent states is linked to the exploitative economic malnourishment engineered by the former colonizing powers. (E) relates to the geographic divide in wealth between countries in the Northern and Southern hemispheres.

13. **(B)**

An allocational dispute centers on fights over resources, such as water, and boundaries. (A) is a dispute over the language in a boundary's creation; (C) is a conflict over how a boundary should function; (D) is a conflict over the location of a boundary; and (E) is a phase in boundary formation involving the marking of a boundary on the territory.

14. **(D)**

Irredentism is an effort by a government to take over (or reclaim) a place or people it believes is naturally part of its state but exists outside its borders. (A) is the breakup or splintering of a unified state into several distinct pieces. (B) is a region of the sea extending 200 nautical miles from a country's coast, unless it overlaps with another's state's zone of control. (C) is the transfer of power from a central authority to local units. (E) is the control by a more powerful country over a place that is less developed.

15. **(E)**

Although straits are open to the passage of ships, they are owned and operated by specific states, which can lead to conflict. The other choices are all a part of stipulations reached in UNCLOS.

16. **(B)**

The borders of western states were drawn by a conquering government to the detriment of the conquered groups. (A) are boundaries drawn after substantial settlement by the people who settled the area, (C) are boundaries created before settlement occurs, (D) are features of the landscape that are used as borders, and (E) is fictitious.

17. **(D)**

The Warsaw Pact was an alliance of communist states founded for mutual protection. (A), (B), (C), and (E) were communist governments during the cold war and originally signed the treaty. (D) is the only country of the five choices that was neither communist nor a member of the Warsaw Pact.

18. **(A)**

First, definition is the phase in which the exact location of a boundary is legally described and negotiated. Second, delimitation is the step when the boundary's definition is drawn onto a map. Third, demarcation is the marking of a boundary on the landscape with something visible, such as a fence, line, sign, or wall. Demarcation is not always reached because some countries choose not to create a physical border between themselves.

19. **(A)**

Religious differences are a major cause of instability within countries. The other choices tend to unite citizens around common values or beliefs and instill a sense of national unity.

20. **(B)**

The Berlin Wall marks the border between East and West Berlin. Although it was superimposed on the people of Berlin after the start of the cold war and was a subsequent boundary (being created after substantial settlement), it is considered a relic boundary because it no long functions as a border.

Unitary: central gov has absolute power
   examples: France; New Zealand; Sweden
   advantages: greater unity

Federal: divided equally
   examples: US; Australia
   advantages: states are empowered and can take charge over their destiny

Devolution: transferring political power to local regions (handwritten)

Free-Response Answers

The following is a list of suggested main points for each part of the question.

Part A

- A unitary state has a strong central government, where most governmental power is concentrated for the entire state.

- Sometimes the regional governments are weak and serve only as administrative units of the central government.

- Usually, the regional governments do not have guaranteed powers.

- The following is a list of some acceptable examples of unitary states: New Zealand, France, Zimbabwe, Namibia, Norway, Denmark, and Sweden. England is often used as an example of a unitary state, but with recent developments in Wales and Scotland, it is devolving into a decentralized unitary state.

- The most obvious advantage of having a unitary state is greater unity resulting from one national body representing the people. Often unitary states are smaller, more homogenous states; however, a multinational state may opt for a unitary organization so that no ethnonational region becomes empowered enough to break away. Although a state facing strong ethnonationalistic tension may play a dangerous game in not empowering its regions with more autonomy, minority nations are not well represented in the unitary government because minority groups may feel even more angered and desirous of secession.

Part B

- A federal state has a government in which powers are divided equally between a central national government and regional governments, usually states or provinces.

- The division of power is guaranteed.

- Examples of federal states include the United States, Nigeria, Switzerland, and Australia.

- One advantage of a federal state is usually seen in a multinational state in which national regions are empowered by a sense of autonomy and power over their destinies, rather than dominated by a central government without adequate representation. A federal state can help bind diverse states by empowering regions with a sense of self-definition and bring government closer to the people. Of course, this can backfire when the devolved power fuels the fires of secession, as seen in the dissolution of the Soviet Union.

Part C

- Devolution is the process of transferring some power from a central government to regional or local governments.

- Devolution often occurs in unitary states with regions that desire greater autonomy and self-definition. England is a classic example of a unitary state that devolved powers to the Scottish people who wanted their own parliament.

- Some strong examples include the USSR, Yugoslavia, and England. Students must include reasons for devolution; in each of these cases, devolution was highly related to ethnonationalism and multinationalism.

Chapter 6

Agricultural and Rural Land Use

Introduction

Like many teenagers in the United States, you may start your day by pouring cereal from a box or popping frozen waffles into the toaster. Imagine waking up and having to roam for most of the day to hunt for your food. Before the domestication of plants, humans were primarily nomadic **hunters and gatherers**, unable to settle in one place for too long before they had to move on to new food resources. Today farms provide humans with the ability to stay in one place and build cities. In fact, fewer than 250,000 people in the world are hunters and gatherers. Instead, most people on the earth practice **agriculture**, the process of growing plants or raising of animals to produce food for sustenance or sale at the marketplace.

Despite the widespread adoption of agriculture, the farming practices used in more-developed countries are substantially different from those used in less-developed countries. Most people in Asia are farmers who can grow only enough food to feed their own families, a type of farming called **subsistence farming**. In more-developed countries like the United States, **commercial farming** predominates, with farms producing food to be sold in groceries and markets, not just to be eaten by the farmers themselves. Worldwide, commercial farming is increasing as subsistence farms are being incorporated into the global farming market.

Key Questions

- *Where did agriculture originate? How and where did it spread?*

- *What are the characteristics of the world's agriculture regions? How do these regions function?*

- *How has agricultural change affected the environment and people's quality of life?*

- *How does diet, energy use, and varying agrarian technology relate to agriculture's origination?*

- *What are different types of extensive and intensive agricultural practices? What are settlement patterns and landscapes related to each agriculture type?*

- *What are land survey systems, environmental conditions, and cultural values linked to each agriculture type?*

- *Why do different agricultural practices exist where they do?*

- *What is the von Thünen model?*

- *What is the status of food supplies throughout the world? Can humans increase the food supply and reduce starvation and malnourishment?*

PART 1 — Development and Diffusion of Agriculture

Origin of Agriculture

How did humans make the leap from being hunters and gatherers to stationary farmers? Geographers generally believe that it was an evolution of knowledge that occurred over thousands of years, in various places, as humans constantly touched and handled plants while gathering their food. Geographers believe that agricultural innovation occurred in and diffused from multiple hearths, or places of origin. According to Carl Sauer, humans first learned how to grow plants through a process of simply cutting off a stem of another plant or by dividing up roots of a plant, a practice known as **vegetative planting**.

Geo Factoid

Women are widely believed to be responsible for discovering vegetative planting because of their typical sociological position as gatherers and medicinal healers.

Later, humans made the leap to **seed agriculture**, which is farming through planting seeds rather than simply planting part of the parent plant. Seed agriculture leads to higher crop yields because there are so many seeds.

Agricultural Hearths

Carl Sauer's theory of a vegetative hearth argues that vegetative farming knowledge first originated in Southeast Asia, where the climate and terrain would have supported the growth of root plants that are easily divided, such as the taro, yam, banana, and palm. From the hearth, it diffused north and east to China and to Japan, and then west toward Southwest Asia, Africa, and the Mediterranean region.

Figure 6.1. Possible cultural and agricultural hearths

Other early vegetative hearths are believed to have emerged through independent innovation in northwestern South America, near the Andes Mountains, and in West Africa.

First Agricultural Revolution

Sometimes referred to as the Neolithic Revolution, the **first agricultural revolution** saw the human development of seed agriculture and the use of animals in the farming process just 12,000 years ago. The growth of seed crops like wheat and rice, and the use of animals such as goats and sheep, replaced the nomadic hunting-and-gathering life that had existed since humanity was born. Human groups were able to stay in one place, grow their populations, and start to build communities. The ability to produce more food without roaming for it increased the carrying capacity of the earth, which charted the path toward the development of civilization. Like the advent of vegetative planting, the first agricultural revolution is believed to have occurred independently in several hearths.

Seed Agricultural Hearths

Hearth	Diffusion Route	Crop Innovation
Western India	To Southwest Asia	Wheat and barley
Southwest Asia (near Tigris and Euphrates rivers)	To Europe (first in Mediterranean regions like Greece and then north through Danube River); North Africa; and to northwestern India and Indus River area	Integrated seed agriculture with domestication of herd animals such as sheep, cattle, and goats, which helped in the farming process
Northern China	To South Asia and Southeast Asia	Millet (a small yellow grain)
Ethiopia	Remained isolated in Ethiopia	Millet (or rather an even smaller millet-like grain known as teff)
Southern Mexico	Throughout Western Hemisphere	Squash and corn
Northern Peru	Throughout Western Hemisphere	Squash, cotton, beans

Second Agricultural Revolution

After the fall of Rome around 500 CE, farming grew into a feudal village structure. During the Middle Ages most farmers worked their lands to feed themselves and their families in an **open-lot system**, one in which there was one large plot of community farmland that all villagers worked to produce a crop to eat. However, as capitalism grew, feudalism diminished and villages enclosed their farmland. This **enclosure movement** gave individual farmers their own plots of farmland, marking a major shift in agriculture. Geographers still debate where and when the second agricultural revolution began, although nearly all agree its most influential phase coincided with the Industrial Revolution in 17th- and 18th-century England and western Europe.

The growing industrial economy and the decline of feudal villages in the 1600s and 1700s caused massive urban migration, as former farmers moved into cities in England and western Europe for work. This caused a great jump in the demand for food from farms to be shipped into cities for the workers.

With this growth in demand came new innovations in farming and transportation technology that dramatically increased crop and livestock yields. New agrarian (farming) technology was invented, such as a better collar for oxen and even the use of the horse instead of the ox on the farm. New fertilizers, field drainage and irrigation systems, and storage systems were invented, all working to help increase farm outputs. Higher farm outputs also worked to encourage the population boom that accompanied the Industrial Revolution.

 PART 2 **Major Agricultural Production Regions**

Subsistence Agriculture

While commercial agriculture has become the dominant agricultural system in core countries, subsistence agriculture remains widely practiced in less-developed, peripheral countries. Subsistence agriculture is divided into three types: shifting cultivation, intensive subsistence agriculture, and pastoralism.

Shifting Cultivation

In **shifting cultivation**, farmers rotate the fields they cultivate to allow the soil to replenish its nutrients, rather than farming the same plot of land over and over. Shifting cultivation is different from crop rotation, in which the farmer changes the crop type, not the plot of land, to keep the soil healthy. Farming the same type of crop repeatedly on the same plot of land leaches the soil of nutrients needed for healthy crops.

Shifting cultivation is often found in the tropical zones, especially rain forest regions in Africa, the Amazon River basin in South America, and throughout Southeast Asia, because the topsoil is thin in these regions, making it necessary to change the plot of land frequently to grow healthy crops. The primary cause of such poor soil quality is the heavy tropical rains that wash away soil nutrients.

The common way that farmers in tropical regions prepare a new plot of land for farming is through **slash-and-burn agriculture**, in which the land is cleared by cutting (or slashing) the existing plants on the land and then burning the rest to create a cleared plot of new farmland, which is called **swidden**. As a subsistence agricultural form, slash-and-burn agriculture (sometimes called swidden agriculture) is not dependent on advanced technology, only on human labor and the presence of extensive acreage, because plots are frequently abandoned once the soil quality becomes poor and new land must be made swidden for a new crop. Often swidden farmers mix various seeds on the same plot of farmland, a practice known as **intertillage**. Intertillage helps grow food for a balanced diet and reduces the risk of crop failure.

The slash-and-burn method has caused environmental problems in some areas. Because of rising population pressures, farmers need to produce more food for more people on less land. Many swidden agriculturists are being forced to reduce the time the farmed land lies fallow, the period the land is not used to produce a crop. When land is repeatedly farmed and not allowed to recuperate, the soils are damaged and never fully regain their nutrients.

Because shifting cultivators use so much land in their farming process (nearly 25 percent of the earth's land) and cannot produce large amounts of food for growing populations, many shifting farmers are switching to more expedient forms of farming that allow them to remain in one place and produce more crops. Shifting cultivation is being replaced by more lucrative farming practices, like cattle ranching, logging, and production of cash crops to sell in the global marketplace. Instead of the rotating, regenerative methods of shifting cultivation, more destructive forms are being used, such as permanent clearing of the rain forests by commercial farming companies.

Intensive Subsistence Agriculture

Shifting cultivation is a form of **extensive subsistence agriculture**, using a large amount of land to cultivate food for the farmer's family to eat. Another category of agriculture is **intensive subsistence agriculture**, in which farmers cultivate small amounts of land very efficiently to produce food for their families. Remember, the intent of subsistence farming is *not* farming surpluses for sale but producing just enough food for the farming family to survive.

Whereas extensive subsistence agriculture is intended for low population densities with extensive amounts of available land, intensive subsistence agriculture is usually found in regions that are highly populated. It is widely practiced in areas where agricultural density is high, particularly China, India, and Southeast Asia. Intensive subsistence farmers make the most use of their small plots of land to feed their families, often showing ingenuity in their techniques, such as the terrace-farming "pyramids" often seen in the Southeast Asian farming landscapes.

Rice is the dominant intensive subsistence agriculture crop in areas such as South China, India, Southeast Asia, and Bangladesh where summer rainfall is abundant. In areas with winters too cold for rice, grains like wheat, corn, and millet are grown

Figure 6.2. Global land use patterns

on intensive subsistence farms. Many intensive subsistence farmers practice **double cropping**, planting and harvesting a crop on a field more than once a year. An example of double cropping is growing corn in one season and wheat in another.

Pastoralism

Another form of subsistence agriculture is **pastoralism**, the breeding and herding of animals to produce food, shelter, and clothing for survival. Pastoralism is usually practiced in climates with very limited, if any, arable land, such as grasslands, deserts, and steppes. Sometimes pastoralism can be sedentary, when the pastoralists live in one place and herd their animals in nearby pastures; or it can be nomadic, when the pastoralists travel with their herds and do not settle in one place for very long. Often involving the herding of cattle, sheep, camels, or goats, pastoralism is most practiced in arid climates in North Africa, central and southern Africa, the Middle East, and Central Asia.

Contrary to popular belief, nomadic pastoralists usually do not wander aimlessly across the landscape. They most often practice **transhumance**, the movement of animal herds to cooler highland areas in the summer to warmer, lowland areas in the winter. Pastoralists usually trade animals with local farmers for food and supplies. Sometimes members of the traveling group plant some crops for use in that location before moving on. However, pastoralists depend on trading their animals for their survival.

Like other forms of subsistence agriculture, pastoralism is declining worldwide as governments work to use dry lands for other purposes, like oil drilling in the Middle East. Pastoral nomads are being confined to less and less land and encouraged to abandon their nomadic lifestyle and incorporate themselves into the global farming economy.

Mediterranean Agriculture

Mediterranean agriculture is primarily associated with the region near the Mediterranean Sea and places with climates that have hot, dry summers and mild, wet winters. California, Chile, southern South Africa, and South Australia are places where Mediterranean agriculture is found. Mediterranean farming involves wheat, barley, vine and tree crops, and grazing for sheep and goats. Olives, grapes, and figs are staple tree crops on Mediterranean farms. It can be either extensive or intensive, depending on the crop. While wheat is extensively farmed, olives are intensively farmed. Mediterranean farming can be either subsistence or commercial, depending on where it is practiced.

Commercial Farming

Commercial farming is different from subsistence farming in that commercial farmers produce crops to sell in the marketplace. Commercial farming types include mixed crop and livestock farming, ranching, dairying, and large-scale grain production. Plantation farming is a form of commercial farming, but it is practiced mostly in less-developed countries.

Mixed Crop and Livestock Farming

Mixed crop and livestock farming involves both growing crops and raising animals. Most of the crops grown on mixed farms are used to feed the farm's animals, which in turn provide manure fertilizer as well as goods for sale, such as eggs. Most of a mixed farm's income comes from sale of its animal products. Further, mixed farms reduce a farmer's complete dependence on seasonal harvests because the animal products are not as dependent on the season as the crops are.

Mixed farming exists widely throughout Europe and eastern North America, usually near large, urban areas where ample land is not available for more extensive practices. Most mixed farms practice crop rotation in which the field is subdivided into various regions, each region growing a different seed and rotating over time. Crop rotation allows the nutrients of the soils to replenish, as different seeds leach different nutrients from the soil.

Ranching

Ranching is commercial grazing, or the raising of animals on a plot of land on which they graze. It is usually extensive, requiring large amounts of land. Because meat and wool are products that are highly demanded, cattle and sheep are the most common animals on ranches. Ranching is practiced in areas where the climate is too dry to support crops, but it is declining in importance. It is most practiced in the western United States, Argentina, southern Brazil, and Uruguay. Ranching is rare in Europe, except for Spain and Portugal. Many U.S. ranches are being converted into "fattening" farms on which fixed-lot cattle are fattened before being slaughtered.

Ranching is quite common also in the tropical deciduous forest regions on the west coast of Latin America and northern Mexico. In some of these areas, such as in western Brazil, it is actually too wet to grow crops. The decline of ranching is partially caused by low grain prices and partially by a system of meat quality standards in the United States that value fat meat over lean. Latin American beef is grass fed, lean, and tough.

Dairying

Dairying is the growth of milk-based products for the marketplace. Dairy farms closest to the marketplace usually produce the most perishable fluid milk products, while those farther away produce goods like cheese and butter. It is the most economically productive type of commercial agriculture practiced near cities in northeastern United States, southeastern Canada, and northwestern Europe. Farms are usually very small and capital intensive. **Capital-intensive farms** use much machinery in the farming process, whereas **labor-intensive farms** use much human labor.

Figure 6.3. Global agricultural regions

The **milkshed** is the zone around the city's center in which milk can be produced and shipped to the marketplace without spoiling. The growth in transportation technology, such as refrigerated trucks, has enabled dairy farmers to locate farther from the city's center, thus increasing the area of the milkshed. In fact, improved technology and feeding systems have led to increases in the amount of milk produced per cow.

Large-Scale Grain Production

Wheat is the dominant grain on **large-scale grain farms**, where the grains are most often grown to be exported to other places for consumption. Large-scale grain production is most common in Canada, the United States, Argentina, Australia, France, England, and Ukraine (which was once considered the "breadbasket" of Russia), although the United States is the world's largest large-scale grain producer. Wheat is the world's leading export crop and is dominated by U.S. and Canadian farms, which collectively grow more than half of the world's wheat. However, many grain farms produce grain to be consumed not by humans but by the animals humans eat. Much of the land in western Europe devoted to grain farming is simply producing grain for animal feed.

Large-scale grain farms grew during the Industrial Revolution, creating large city-based populations needing wheat and other grains for consumption. Large-scale grain farms are usually highly mechanized, thus capital-intensive, operations.

Several technological innovations precipitated the growth of large-scale grain farming. The McCormick reaper, developed in the 1830s, is a machine that cuts standing grain in the field. The combine machine completes all three processes of reaping, threshing, and cleaning in one machine.

Plantation Farming

Plantation agriculture involves large-scale farming operations, known as plantations or agricultural estates, specializing in the farming of one or two high-demand crops for export, usually to more-developed regions. Plantation agriculture was introduced in tropical and subtropical zones by European colonizers who were seeking to produce crops such as coffee, tea, pineapples, palms, coconuts, rubber, tobacco, sugarcane, and cotton. Cotton was particularly important in the southern United States as an export crop produced on plantations by black Africans who were kidnapped and forced into slavery schemes.

Today plantation agriculture is still largely reflective of global power structures. Most plantations exist in low-latitude regions of Africa, Asia, and Latin America but are owned by companies (or individuals) from more-developed countries. Most plantations exist in a location that has easy coastal access for exporting their crops to be sold in foreign markets. Though modern plantations have integrated advanced technology into their farming practices, plantation agriculture is still labor intensive, requiring the estates to hire large numbers of seasonal workers during harvest times. A level of plantation agriculture remains in the subtropical and tropical United States, where migrant workers are used for labor. Hawaii has its own plantations, but there is a strong growers' union and the products are therefore more expensive.

 PART 3 Rural Land Use and Settlement Patterns

Factors Affecting Decisions on Farm Locations

As usual, geographers apply the "why of where" concept to agriculture in analyzing the locations of various farming activities. Why, for example, is a dairy farm closer to the city marketplace than is a grain farm? The factors affecting farming location decisions are physical, political-cultural, and economic.

Physical Factors

Obviously, the appropriate environment for cultivating varies depending on the type of crop. However, farmers can choose to mold the environment as much as possible to fit the crops they want to harvest by adding irrigation systems, greenhouses, and other aids to farming. Usually, farmers evaluate several physical factors in making such decisions:

- **Soil:** A farmer evaluates the depth, texture, nutrient composition, and acidity of the soil in the field, because different crops require different types of soil composition. Most crops require neutral to slightly acidic soils.

- **Relief:** A farmer looks at the shape of the field, or its relief, which includes its slope and altitude. The degree to which the field is exposed to the sun, for example, is a significant factor in choosing a crop. Usually, flatter lands are best for agriculture because more sloped lands can be difficult to irrigate. Altitude also affects temperatures.

- **Climate:** The most influential physical factors affecting a farmer's crop decisions are usually temperature and rainfall, the two components of climate. Different crops require different amounts of water and temperature.

Political-Cultural Factors

The environment, though a factor, does not play a determining role in all agricultural decisions. Political and cultural factors also influence farming location decisions. For example, certain religious beliefs have affected agricultural decisions: Hinduism holds that it is wrong to kill cattle, and it is taboo in Islamic regions to eat pigs. Moreover, immigrants often carry with them their homelands' farming practices and food preferences, thereby injecting their farming styles into

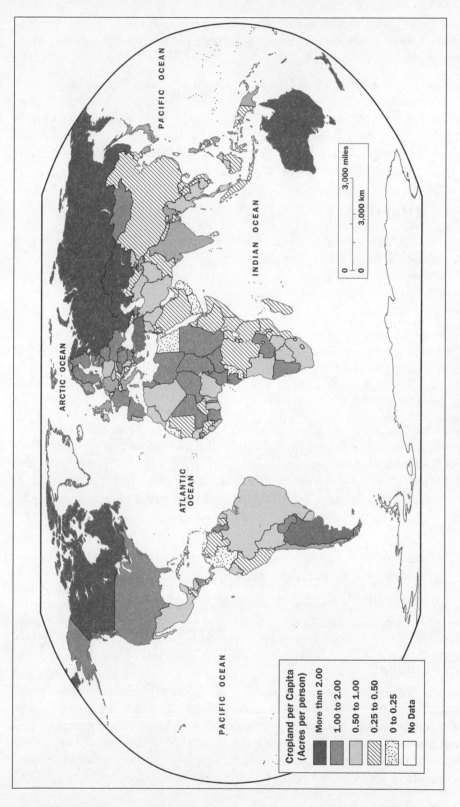

Figure 6.4. Cropland per capita

Cropland per Capita
(Acres per person)

More than 2.00

1.00 to 2.00

0.50 to 1.00

0.25 to 0.50

0 to 0.25

No Data

the agricultural landscapes of their destinations. Food taboos are not always religious. For example, mainstream American culture disapproves of eating horses, even though they are nutritious meat.

Political decisions also impact the agricultural landscape. In less-developed countries, farmers are often financially encouraged by the government to adopt more advanced agricultural technology. During the Green Revolution, discussed later in this chapter, many less-developed countries tried to subsidize the use of the revolution's more-efficient seed types that were more expensive than the common seeds of the time. Another example of political influence exists in the European Union's decision to pay farmers *not* to grow crops in an attempt to eliminate massive surpluses that were driving prices so low that farmers could not survive. In fact, many European countries have agricultural products that are considered national treasures, such as French wine grapes. It is very hard to remove production of one of these crops. In fact, France burns its lower-quality wines instead of allowing farmers to reduce vineyard acreage.

Economic Factors

While subsistence farmers function to feed their families, commercial farmers function in a competitive globalizing economy that has shifting levels of demand for agricultural products. For example, coffee production has dramatically risen in Latin American plantations because of the recent explosion in coffee shop crazes.

Land rent, or the price a farmer must pay for each acre of land, is another economic factor in farming location. Crops sell for different prices, so a farm's location is related to how much money the farmer can make from a crop to pay the rent. Usually, rent is cheaper the farther the land is from the city's center, thus influencing farmers requiring extensive lands (for grain farming, for example) to locate farther out from the city's center to take advantage of the cheaper rent per unit of land.

Von Thünen's Agricultural Location Theory

Johann Heinrich von Thünen was a 19th-century German economist who formulated a model explaining and predicting where and why various agricultural activities would take place around a city's marketplace. In other words, **von Thünen's model** explains and predicts agricultural land use patterns. Von Thünen began by establishing several assumptions on which to build his model. In his model, only one city has one central marketplace where all farmers sell their products in an attempt to make the most money they can. The farmland is all equally farmable and productive, and only one mode of transportation is available. With these assumptions, von Thünen allowed for only one variable to change in his model: the distance a farm location was from the city's market as evident in transportation costs. The model's resulting patterns are as follows:

- The central marketplace is surrounded by agricultural activity zones that are in concentric rings, each ring representing a different type of agricultural land use.

- Moving outward from the city's central marketplace, the farming activities changed from intensive to more extensive.

Von Thünen's land use patterns can be explained through land rent and transportation costs. Land closest to the city's marketplace is more expensive per unit than is land father away from the city's center. Therefore, a grain farmer, who needs lots of land for his or her extensive farming operation, is going to purchase a farm farther from the city's marketplace because land is less expensive farther out. However, a milk producer is likely to buy land closer to the city's center because he or she does not need the extensive land a grain farmer needs to produce the same profit. Additionally, milk spoils quickly, so the dairy farm must be closer to the marketplace so the farmer can be quickly transport milk the to the marketplace for sale before it spoils. Grazing is often the land use farthest outside the city's marketplace in the ring with the lowest land rent because grazing requires so much land and makes the least amount of money per unit of land.

■ The town   ■ Crop rotation with fallow
■ Horticulture and dairying   ■ Three-field system
■ Forestry   ■ Grazing
■ Crop rotation without fallow   ■ Wilderness

Figure 6.5. Von Thünen's model of agricultural land use

Usefulness of the von Thünen Model

Von Thünen's model is useful in comparing real situations to his theoretical farming situation—one that is restricted to only one variable, transportation costs. In the real world, agricultural land use patterns depend on more than one variable. Von Thünen knew his work was based on his theoretical assumptions, so he introduced some variations, such as the existence of a river running through the city and more than one market. Also, he played with the assumption of all soil quality being equal in productivity and introduced the idea of different areas of land having higher-quality soil than others. Overall, the model further illuminates the influence of distance as a factor in human location decisions. Farming decisions, like so many other spatial patterns, relate to distance. Geographers analyze farming land uses in particular areas and compare them to von Thünen's hypothetical situation as a way of explaining what they see and predicting future land use patterns.

Housing Building Materials

Material	Regions Commonly Found
Wood	Eurasia, U.S. Pacific Coast, North America, Australia, Brazil and Chile
Stone	Europe, Egypt, India, western China, Yucatan, Mexico, South-Central Africa, Middle East
Grass and brush	Low-latitude regions: African savanna, East African highlands, upland South Africa, South American highlands, Amazon Basin; northern Australia
Poles and sticks (wattle)	Africa, Southeast Asia, West Africa, Amazon Basin in South America
Sun-dried brick (more traditional; note that brick is often used where wood is not as available)	Middle East, Middle and South America, northern China, African savanna, and North Africa
Oven-baked brick	Modern, contemporary areas in more-developed countries

Settlement Patterns in Villages

The definition of the term *village*, including its size, may vary according to the culture using it. However, historically the shape of a village's spatial layout has related to its function and its environment. In Europe, for example, villages were often clustered on a hillside to leave the flatlands for farming and to offer people protection by being on an incline. Additionally, many early villages were walled to keep invaders out. In lowland areas with rivers and streams, villages were often linear in shape, following the water source, with the farmlands radiating from the linear village. Other villages in Europe, Asia, and Africa were round in shape, with a space in the middle for the cattle. Many villages were built according to a grid plan, with geometric boundaries.

Modern Commercial Agriculture

Third Agricultural Revolution

Beginning in the late 1800s, the **third agricultural revolution** began in North America and saw the globalization of industrialized agriculture and new technologies that increased the food supply. Whereas the first agricultural revolution ushered in the growth of stationary plant and animal domestication and the second agricultural revolution saw new farming and storage capabilities increase food supplies to meet and facilitate a growing and industrializing population, the third agricultural revolution distributed mechanized farming technology and chemical fertilizers on a global level. Importantly, during the third agricultural revolution, farming and food processing were completed at different sites.

Industrialization of the Farming Process

With the advent of the third agricultural revolution, it became more common for commercial farmers to harvest their crops and ship them off to food-processing sites to be packaged for marketing and distribution. Like a factory system in which different parts of the production process are completed by different departments before the finished product hits the market for sale, food production became increasingly "industrialized" with the start of the third agricultural revolution. In the 1700s, the local milk farmer produced, processed, bottled, and shipped the milk to the marketplace for sale. By the 1900s, the milk production process had evolved as part of the third agricultural revolution into an industrialized, agricultural process.

Purity Dairies in Nashville, Tennessee, provides a strong example of this evolution in agriculture. Today this large agricultural corporation subcontracts with local farms to buy unprocessed milk that is shipped to the Purity Dairies factory in Nashville, near the market. At the city-based factory, the milk is processed, packaged, and put on trucks for distribution within the milkshed. The milk farm itself is only one component in this multilayered, agricultural process.

Agribusiness System

The commercialization and industrialization of the food production process has led to the development of a modern farming concept called **agribusiness**, the system of food production involving everything from the development of seeds to the marketing and sale of food products at the market. Agribusiness is the combination of the various pieces of the food production industry, including the farms, processing plants, packagers, fertilizer laboratories, distributors, and advertising agencies. Although the percentage of farmers in the U.S. workforce has markedly declined, the number of workers involved in some way in agribusiness shows that

Figure 6.6. U.S. agricultural regions

food production is still an integral part of the U.S. and global economy. Even the graphic designer drawing the images for a child's lunchbox is part of the increasingly complex agribusiness system.

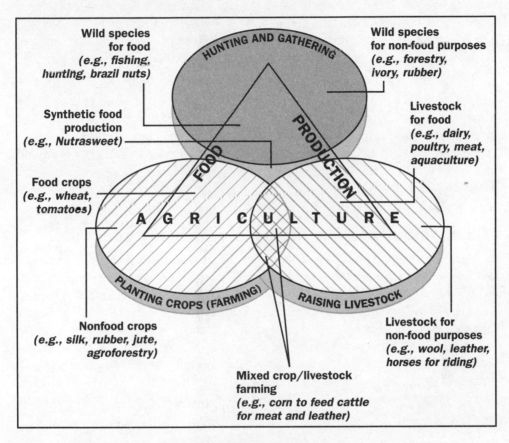

Figure 6.7. The relationship between food production and agriculture

Globalization of the Farming Process

The colonial and imperial campaigns of the 18th and 19th centuries built a system between the core and peripheral regions in the world. European colonizers took over lands in peripheral regions like Africa, South America, and Asia. The Europeans used these colonies to supply their people with raw goods. By the late 1800s and 1900s, the economies of the colonized countries were entrenched in a master-dependent relationship with the colonizers. Even after gaining political independence, former colonies essentially continued to survive by providing crops for export to the core more-developed countries that were once their imperial masters. This neocolonial, or postcolonial, dependent relationship has fueled the globalization of the farming process.

Food sold in grocery stores throughout more-developed countries is often grown in peripheral less-developed regions of the world that ship food to factories for processing and to markets in the more-developed world. Even flowers in your local grocery are often flown in from commercial gardens, called **truck farms**, in tropical zones. Just as a computer production process often involves an international division of labor—with production in Asia, assembly in Europe, and marketing in the United States—the farming process has become a "food production process" divided on an international level into an "agribusiness system."

Truck farming can also refer to intensive commercial agriculture, especially in the context of a core country. Share-based organic farming is a major type of truck farming in the United States and Europe. Organic farms often grow both vegetables and chickens, with the chickens used to produce eggs and to clear and fertilize plots. Pigs are sometimes raised to eat plants that are for some reason unfit for human consumption.

Human Impacts of the Industrialization of Agriculture

The industrialization of agriculture has affected local farmers in both more- and less-developed countries. Local farmers in more-developed countries, such as the United States, have been forced to integrate into the agribusiness system to survive. Often agriculture corporations subcontract with local farmers to purchase their harvests and then process, package, and sell the produce at the marketplace; or the corporation will purchase the local farm to integrate it into the corporation's food production process. Most local flower farms in the United States have closed down because of the globalization of industrial agriculture; the local flower farmers cannot compete with the corporate-owned flower farms in foreign lands that grow and ship flowers to U.S. groceries.

In 1920, about one in three U.S. citizens lived on farms. By 1978, only one in 28 U.S. citizens lived on a farm (Knox and Marsten, 2004, 315).

Many farmers in less-developed countries have been forced to sell their lands to foreign corporations to survive. Foreign corporations often come into these poorer countries and purchase land to grow cash crops for export, such as coffee and rubber. A problem arises from this when the farms become totally export oriented and do not produce food for consumption in their local regions. While corporations from richer countries often own the large farms in poorer countries, they do provide local people with income sources. Yet much of the profits harvested on these corporate farms are channeled directly back to their corporations' already-wealthier countries. These profits are not reinvested in infrastructural growth in these poorer countries in which the export-driven farms are located. Additionally, the communities associated with subsistence farming are changed, because the farming process becomes profit driven and commercialized.

Agricultural Exports

Figure 6.8. U.S. agricultural exports

Green Revolution

An outgrowth of the third agricultural revolution, an effort known as the **Green Revolution**, began in the 1940s and developed new strains of hybrid seeds and fertilizers that dramatically increased the crop output possible on every farm. The Green Revolution began with agricultural experiments that were funded by U.S. charities to find ways of improving Mexico's wheat grain production capabilities to reduce hunger in that region. Scientists soon found new hybrid strains of wheat, maize, and rice that were higher yielding, meaning they were seeds capable of producing more food at a faster pace. Scientists also developed new fertilizers and pesticides to support the higher-yielding Green Revolution seeds because the new seeds required nitrogen-enriching fertilizers and increased protection from diseases and pest infestations. Green Revolution scientist Norman Borlaug won a Nobel Peace Prize in the 1970s for his work to increase world peace through spreading hunger-reducing technology to poorer regions of the world.

The "miracle" of the Green Revolution was in its global diffusion of higher-yielding varieties of wheat, rice, and maize crops. Globally, grain production increased by 45 percent between 1945 and 1990. Asia was able to increase its rice production by 66 percent by 1985, and India was able to supply its own wheat and rice by the 1980s. Hunger and famine were reduced, but not eliminated, through the diffusion of Green Revolution technology. Farmers were simply able to grow more food per unit area of farmland at a faster pace.

The diffusion of Green Revolution technologies has its downsides, too. The technologies have reduced the amount of human labor needed on the farm in some areas. But the higher-yielding crop strains are often more prone to viruses and pest infestations, leading to higher levels of crop failure in some areas. Many of the higher-yielding Green Revolution crops, such as rice and wheat, are not farmable in dryer African regions, where millet and sorghum are grown. Additionally, research in more African-appropriate crops has not kept pace. Less than 5 percent of African farmers use Green Revolution seeds.

Some analysts argue that the Green Revolution has increased economic inequality in peripheral countries. Local farmers in peripheral countries often have a difficult time purchasing the more-expensive Green Revolution seeds and technologies, often driving them out of the market and causing them economic ruin. Mechanized farming also requires expensive fuels to power farm machines, which not only is expensive but also increases pollution and fossil fuel consumption. In some of these countries, governments have subsidized, or helped pay for, the use of Green Revolution technology.

Environmentally, Green Revolution pesticides have arguably caused pollution and soil contamination problems because they drain through the ecosystems in which they are used. Workers frequently exposed to these chemicals have suffered health problems from poisoning. Furthermore, because Green Revolution crops often require more watering, water resources have been strained. Interestingly, Green Revolution seeds are being adopted so widely that the genetic diversity in seeds is rapidly reducing, with local strains being phased out. This genetic uniformity places the food supply at an increased vulnerability to diseases and pest infestations similar to the problem faced with the overuse of antibiotics to which bacteria are adapting and becoming resistant.

Biotechnology

Agricultural **biotechnology** is using living organisms to produce or change plant or animal products. **Genetic modification** is a form of biotechnology that uses scientific, genetic manipulation of crop and animal products to improve agricultural productivity and products. Reorganizing plant and animal DNA as well as tissue culturing are two examples of genetic modification processes in agricultural biotechnology. Recent innovations in biotechnology have led to plant and animal cloning as well as "superplants" that grow at much faster rates, even in nutrient-poor soils, and already have pesticides and fertilizers integrated into their DNA. Scientists have created some crops that are drought resistant and others that are not susceptible to plant diseases. Genetically modified animals are manipulated and cloned to produce larger, better agricultural outputs, such as the "superchicken,"

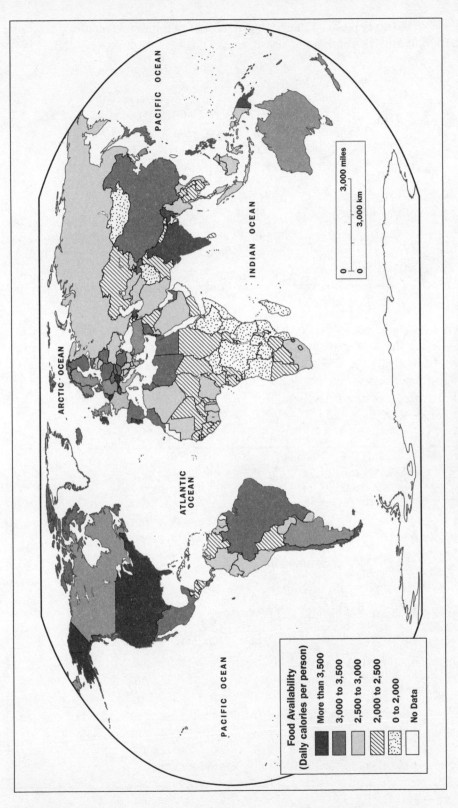

Figure 6.9. Global patterns in food availability

Food Availability
(Daily calories per person)

More than 3,500
3,000 to 3,500
2,500 to 3,000
2,000 to 2,500
0 to 2,000
No Data

which is beefed up to produce more meat at a faster rate. This extension of scientific innovation to all crops and animal products is known as the biorevolution.

The United States produces nearly 63 percent of the world's genetically modified crops. Nearly 33 percent of U.S. corn and 55 percent of U.S. cotton come from genetically modified crops. Among other innovations, biotechnological research is designing bananas containing vaccines against the hepatitis disease.

Supporters of biotechnology argue that in addition to increasing food output, it also reduces costs of farming and can help the environment. Genetically modified crops require less of the expensive fertilizers, thereby reducing the environmental pollution caused by the chemicals. Innovations in agricultural biotechnology are seen by many to be the human innovation to growing population pressures.

There is also criticism of agricultural biotechnology. Cloned plants are often more susceptible to crop diseases and reduce genetic diversity, as discussed earlier. Cloned plants, therefore, require more chemical pesticides and herbicides. Similar to criticism of the Green Revolution discussed earlier, many local farmers suffer because they cannot afford to use newly-invented agricultural biotechnology.

Genetically Modified Foods: Benefits and Controversies

Benefits

- **Crops**

  — Enhanced taste and quality

  — Reduced maturation time

  — Increased nutrients, yields, and stress tolerance

  — Improved resistance to disease, pests, and herbicides

  — New products and growing techniques

- **Animals**

  — Increased resistance, productivity, hardiness, and feed efficiency

  — Better yields of meat, eggs, and milk

  — Improved animal health and diagnostic methods

- **Environment**
  - "Friendly" bioherbicides and bioinsecticides
  - Conservation of soil, water, and energy
  - Bioprocessing for forestry products
  - Better natural waste management
  - More efficient processing
- **Society**
  - Increased food security for growing populations

Controversies

- **Safety**
  - Potential human health impact: allergens, transfer of antibiotic resistance markers, unknown effects
  - Potential environmental impact: unintended transfer of transgenes through cross pollination, unknown effects on other organisms (e.g., soil microbes), and loss of flora and fauna biodiversity
- **Access and Intellectual Property**
  - Domination of world food production by a few companies
  - Increasing dependence on industrialized nations by developing countries
  - Biopiracy—foreign exploitation of natural resources
- **Ethics**
  - Violation of intrinsic values of natural organisms
  - Tampering with nature by mixing genes among species
  - Objections to consuming animal genes in plants and vice versa
  - Stress for animal
- **Labeling**
  - Not mandatory in some countries (e.g., United States)
  - Mixing genetically modified crops with non–genetically modified crops confounds labeling attempts
- **Society**
  - New advances may be skewed to interests of rich countries

(Source: U.S. Department of Energy)

Hunger and the Food Supply

The causes of world hunger exist largely in the distribution of food supplies and people's ability to access food supplies, not in humans' ability to grow food. Although biotechnological research in agriculture promises innovations in humans' ability to further master environmental constraints, it is the social and economic structure inherent in inequality that causes food security issues, undernutrition, and famine.

Undernutrition is the lack of sufficient calories or nutrients, whereas **famine** is mass starvation resulting from prolonged undernutrition in a region during a certain period. In some cultures, women have higher rates of undernourishment than do men because of practices such as men eating first, leaving only scraps for the women to eat. Often a civil war, severe drought, or some other "trigger" starts a period of famine. While food is stockpiling and rotting in some more-developed countries, food shortages and periods of famine are occurring in others areas. Most, but not all, people in more-developed countries have food security, or the ability to access food so that they do not become undernourished.

Nearly 25,000 people in the world die each day because of undernutrition.

The innovative agricultural methods being produced in the biorevolution must be integrated into the agricultural economies of less-developed countries in such a way that people in those countries can afford them and use them to grow more food. Thus, the solution to ending world hunger is believed to exist not just in growing enough food but also in distributing it and empowering people with the *ability* to obtain their needed food and produce **sustainable yields**, or rates of crop production that can be maintained over time.

According to the prominent geographer Ester Boserup, food production methods are derived from human needs. Boserup believed that subsistence farmers want the most leisure time they can have, so they farm in ways that will allow them to feed their families and maximize free time as well. They will change their approach to farming if the population increases and more food is needed. Boserup considered the food supply dependent on human approaches, rather than people dependent on the food supply. This contrasts with Thomas Malthus's theory of human overpopulation outpacing growth of the food supply. Most evidence shows Boserup's theory is true in a subsistence economy but not in a technologically advanced industrialized society.

Desertification and Soil Erosion

Chemical pollution and loss of biological diversity are not the only harmful consequences of contemporary farming. Because of population pressures, farmers in many regions are trying to grow food at faster rates, often not allowing their soils enough time to recuperate from the last harvest before starting another. Such a practice leads to the negative consequence of **soil erosion**, the loss of the nutrient-rich top layer in soil. Some geographers estimate that nearly 7 percent of the world's rich topsoil is being destroyed each decade.

It takes the earth 100 to 500 years to naturally regenerate half an inch of nutrient topsoil. Soil erosion destroys 55 billion tons of topsoil each year.

Another negative consequence related to human overuse of the earth's land is **desertification,** the loss of habitable land to the expansion of deserts. Though desertification can result from both human and natural causes, humans have contributed to the expansion of the Sahara Desert (and others) because of their overly intense use of the land. The loss of forested areas, or deforestation, is caused by humans chopping down wooded areas at rates so fast that the areas cannot regenerate. Some estimates predict that the rain forest centered on the equator will be completely destroyed in less than a century. To try to save precious land resources, governments and organizations have organized **debt-for-nature swaps**, which forgive international debts owed by developing countries in exchange for these countries protecting valuable, natural land resources from human destruction.

Figure 6.10. Percentage of soil degradation by world region

PART 5	Chapter Review

Models Review

Von Thünen Model

Developed by German geographer Johann Heinrich von Thünen, this model explains and predicts agricultural land use patterns in a theoretical state by varying transportation cost. Given the model's assumptions, the pattern that emerges shows more-intensive rural land uses closer to the marketplace, and more-extensive rural land uses farther from the city's marketplace. These rural land use zones are divided in the model into concentric rings.

Terms Review

Agribusiness—System of food production involving everything from the development of seeds to the marketing and sale of food products at the market.

Agriculture—Growing plants or raising animals to produce food for sustenance or sale at the marketplace.

Biotechnology—Using living organisms to produce or change plant or animal products.

Capital-intensive farm—Farm that makes heavy use of machinery in the farming process.

Commercial farming—Growing food to be sold in groceries and markets, not just to be eaten by the farmers themselves.

Dairying—Growth of milk-based products for the marketplace.

Debt-for-nature swaps—Efforts to preserve natural farmland by forgiving international debts owed by developing countries in exchange for those countries protecting valuable, natural land resources from human destruction.

Desertification—Loss of habitable land to the expansion of deserts.

Double cropping—Planting and harvesting a crop on a field more than once a year.

Enclosure movement—As feudalism faded away and capitalism grew, this movement divided the common farm—one the villagers all farmed together—into individual farming plots. Many farmers who did not get private plots moved to the growing cities.

Ester Boserup—Geographer who developed the theory that subsistence farmers want the most leisure time they can have, so they farm in ways that will allow them both to feed their families and to maximize free time. Boserup's theory also posited that farmers will change their approach to farming if the population increases and more food is needed, thus making the food supply dependent on human innovation, rather than humans dependent on the food supply.

Extensive subsistence agriculture—Using a large amount of land to farm food for the farmer's family to eat.

Famine—Mass starvation resulting from prolonged undernutrition in a region during a certain period.

First agricultural revolution—Period marked by the development of seed agriculture and the use of animals in the farming process just 12,000 years ago; also called the Neolithic Revolution.

Genetic modification—Form of biotechnology that uses scientific, genetic manipulation of crop and animal products to improve agricultural productivity and products.

Green Revolution—As an outgrowth of the third agricultural revolution, this effort began in the 1940s and developed new strains of hybrid seeds and fertilizers that dramatically increased the crop output possible from each farm.

Hunters and gatherers—Nomadic people who do not remain stationary but follow herds of wild animals and forage plants for survival.

Intensive subsistence agriculture—Cultivating a small amount land very efficiently to produce food for the farmer's family.

Intertillage—Practice of mixing many types of seeds on the same plot of land.

Labor-intensive farm—Farm that uses much human labor.

Land rent—Price a farmer must pay for each acre of land.

Large-scale grain farm—Extensive commercial grain farm where the grain typically is grown to be exported to other places for consumption.

Mediterranean agriculture—Type of farming involving wheat, barley, vine, and tree crops and grazing for sheep and goats; primarily associated with the region near the Mediterranean Sea and places with climates that have hot, dry summers and mild, wet winters.

Milkshed—Zone around the city's center in which milk can be produced and shipped to the marketplace without spoiling.

Mixed crop and livestock farming—Category of agriculture in which farmers both grow crops and raise animals.

Open-lot system—System of agricultural land distribution in which all villagers worked on one large plot of community farmland to produce a crop to eat.

Pastoralism—Breeding and herding of animals to produce food, shelter, and clothing for survival.

Plantation agriculture—Farming that involves large-scale operations, known as plantations or agricultural estates, specializing in the farming of one or two high-demand crops for export, usually to more-developed regions.

Ranching—Raising animals on a plot of land on which they feed or graze.

Seed agriculture—Developed later than vegetative planting, this type of farming involves planting seeds rather than simply planting part of the parent plant.

Shifting cultivation—Form of extensive subsistence agriculture in which farmers rotate the fields they cultivate to allow the soil to replenish its nutrients, rather than farming the same plot of land over and over.

Slash-and-burn agriculture—Common way that subsistence farmers prepare a new plot of land for farming; system in which the land is cleared by cutting (or slashing) the existing plants on the land and then burning the rest to create a cleared plot of new farmland.

Soil erosion—Loss of the nutrient-rich top layer in soil.

Subsistence farming—Growing only enough food to feed the farmer's own families.

Sustainable yield—Rate of crop production that can be maintained over time.

Swidden—Plot of land prepared by subsistence farmers using the slash-and-burn method.

Third agricultural revolution—Period in which agriculture became globalized and industrialized, and new technologies increased the food supply.

Transhumance—Movement of animal herds to cooler highland areas in the summer to warmer lowland areas in the winter.

Truck farm—Commercial flower farm or garden.

Undernutrition—Case of not getting enough calories or nutrients.

Vegetative planting—Process of cultivating by simply cutting off a stem of another plant or by dividing roots of a plant; developed before seed agriculture.

PART 6 — Some Suggested Web Resources for Further Exploration

United States Department of Agriculture: http://www.usda.gov/

This site provides federal government statistics and processes related to U.S. farming, including an interesting nutritional evaluation called "My Pyramid."

European Union's Agriculture Commission: http://ec.europa.eu/agriculture/info.htm

This is the official site of the EU's branch in charge of agricultural affairs.

United Nations Food and Agriculture Organization (FAO): http://www.fao.org/

This organization is dedicated to ending world hunger. Its mission statement declares, "Serving both developed and developing countries, FAO acts as a neutral forum where all nations meet as equals to negotiate agreements and debate policy. FAO is also a source of knowledge and information."

World Resources Institute (WRI): http://www.wri.org/

Motivated by its mission "to move human society to live in ways that protect Earth's environment and its capacity to provide for the needs and aspirations of current and future generations," the WRI provides useful statistics and projections related to climate change, resource consumption and abuse, farming practices, and more.

Food First: http://www.foodfirst.org/

A nonprofit organization, Food First works to eliminate the injustices that cause hunger. Its website provides information on the Green Revolution, biotechnology, and genetically modified foods, among other topics. It looks at undernutrition and hunger related to the current distribution of resources and food supplies.

PART 7   Pre-Exam Practice

Terms Review Quiz

Use the Terms Review list or your own memory to determine the extent of your knowledge of key terms and concepts. Remember, the AP exam does not include this kind of exercise, but it is included here as a review tool.

1. _____ Planting and harvesting a crop on a field more than once a year.

2. _____ Common way that subsistence farmers prepare a new plot of land for farming; system in which the land is cleared by cutting the existing plants on the land and then burning the rest to create a cleared plot of new farmland.

3. _____ Cultivating a small amount land very efficiently to produce food for the farmer's family.

4. _____ Type of farming involving wheat, barley, vine, and tree crops and grazing for sheep and goats; primarily associated with climates that have hot, dry summers and mild, wet winters.

5. _____ Growth of milk-based products for the marketplace

6. _____ Farming that involves large-scale agricultural estates, specializing in farming one or two high-demand crops for export, usually to more-developed regions.

7. _____ System of food production involving everything from the development of seeds to the marketing and sale of food products at the market.

8. _____ As an outgrowth of the third agricultural revolution, this effort began in the 1940s and developed new strains of hybrid seeds and fertilizers that dramatically increased the crop output possible from each farm.

9. _____ Case of not getting enough calories or nutrients.

10. _____ Category of agriculture in which farmers both grow crops and raise animals.

11. _____ As feudalism faded away and capitalism grew, this movement divided the common farm—one that the villagers all farmed together—into individual farming plots. Many farmers who did not get private plots moved to the growing cities.

12. _____ Developed later than vegetative planting, this type of farming involves planting seeds rather than simply planting part of the parent plant.

13. _____ Growing plants or raising animals to produce food for sustenance or sale at the marketplace.

14. _____ Period marked by the development of seed agriculture and the use of animals in the farming process just 12,000 years ago; also called the Neolithic Revolution.

15. _____ Process of cultivating by simply cutting off a stem of another plant or by dividing roots of a plant; developed before seed agriculture.

16. _____ Form of extensive subsistence agriculture in which farmers rotate the fields they cultivate to allow the soil to replenish its nutrients, rather than farming the same plot of land over and over.

17. _____ Nomadic people who do not remain stationary but follow herds of wild animals and forage plants for survival.

18. _____ Using a large amount of land to farm food for the farmer's family to eat.

19. _____ Growing food to be sold in groceries and markets, not just to be eaten by the farmers themselves.

20. _____ Zone around the city's center in which milk can be produced and shipped to the marketplace without spoiling.

21. _____ Farm that makes heavy use of machinery in the farming process.

22. _____ Raising animals on a plot of land on which they feed or graze.

23. _____ Movement of animal herds to cooler highland areas in the summer to warmer lowland areas in the winter.

24. _____ Period in which agriculture became globalized and industrialized, and new technologies increased the food supply.

25. _____ Efforts to preserve natural farmland by forgiving international debts owed by developing countries in exchange for those countries protecting valuable, natural land resources from human destruction.

Multiple-Choice Review Questions

1. Which of the following agricultural practices is most likely to be found in the Tibetan plateau?

    (A) Slash and burn   (D) Pastoralism

    (B) Mediterranean   (E) Plantation

    (C) Truck

2. According to the von Thünen model of rural land use, which of the following agricultural products would most likely be produced farthest from its London marketplace?

    (A) Fruits and vegetables   (D) Wool and hides

    (B) Feed grains   (E) Wheat and flour

    (C) Butter, cheese, and eggs

3. All of the following are associated with the second agricultural revolution EXCEPT

    (A) the Industrial Revolution

    (B) improved food storage capacity

    (C) the invention of barbed wire

    (D) the enclosure movement

    (E) recombinant DNA splicing

4. All of the following are modern states existing in land postulated to be agriculture hearths EXCEPT

    (A) Ethiopia   (D) China

    (B) Iraq   (E) India

    (C) England

5. Which of the following regions produces the least amount of wheat?

    (A) Ukraine   (D) France

    (B) United States   (E) Greece

    (C) Canada

6. The house shown in this picture is most likely located in which of the following regions?

    (A) Southern Africa   (D) Central Africa

    (B) Northeastern Europe   (E) South Asia

    (C) Southeast Asia

7. Beef consumption is at the lowest level in which of the following regions?

    (A) Italy   (D) China

    (B) United States   (E) India

    (C) Romania

8. Which of the following statements would least support a critical argument outlining the negative side of the impact of the Green Revolution?

    (A) Many of its initial hybrid crops could not grow in African regions.

    (B) It is making developing countries more dependent on Western technology than before.

(C) The original intent of the Green Revolution was to increase the profits of agricultural corporations seeking to expand their markets.

(D) Green Revolution seeds are often more expensive for local farmers in less-developed regions.

(E) The global diffusion of its crops has threatened the genetic diversity in local agricultural landscapes.

9. Which of the following is an accurate statement regarding agriculture and the United States economy?

(A) Agriculture is no longer an important piece of the U.S. economy.

(B) The number of farms in the United States has decreased in the last 50 years.

(C) United States food exports have declined steadily since World War II.

(D) Farming is now an outsourced process in the United States, where nearly all foodstuffs are imported from foreign farms.

(E) Wheat production in the United States has remained stagnant since the start of the 20th century.

10. The seasonal movement from highlands to lowland pastures is known as

(A) slash-and-burn agriculture

(B) Mediterranean agriculture

(C) transhumance

(D) mixed crop and livestock farming

(E) crop rotation

11. Which of the following export-oriented cash crops is often grown in formerly European colonial regions?

(A) Wheat   (D) Corn

(B) Rubber   (E) Millet

(C) Sorghum

12. All the following are assumptions in the classical von Thünen rural land use model EXCEPT:

    (A) Rural land is equally productive, regardless of its proximity to the central city.

    (B) More-extensive land uses will develop farther from the city than intensive farming practices.

    (C) There is only one marketplace.

    (D) Transportation costs are unrelated to distance.

    (E) The land was flat throughout the rural plane.

13. Geographer Ester Boserup would most likely agree with which of the following statements?

    (A) Population growth will outpace the growth of the food supply.

    (B) Population growth is unrelated to the food supply.

    (C) The food supply is adapted by farmers to meet the changing population.

    (D) Farmers cannot affect the level of the food supply.

    (E) Subsistence farmers exist in isolation rather than in community.

14. Which of the following statements accurately applies to agribusiness?

    I. Agribusiness is associated with the vertical and horizontal integration of the processes involved in the agricultural process.

    II. Agribusiness involves the increasingly global division of the agricultural production process.

    III. Individual farmers do not play a role in agribusiness, only corporate conglomerates.

    IV. Agribusiness is contributing to agricultural industrialization.

    (A) I and II   (D) I, II, and IV

    (B) I, III, and IV   (E) I, II, III, and IV

    (C) II, III, and IV

15. A farmer in China is statistically most likely to be a(n)

    (A) extensive subsistence farmer

    (B) nomadic herder

    (C) intensive subsistence farmer

    (D) shifting cultivator

    (E) hunter and gatherer

16. The earliest form of agriculture was

    (A) seed planting   (D) pastoralism

    (B) vegetative planting   (E) the Green Revolution

    (C) agribusiness

17. The use of large amounts of land to grow food to feed only the farmer's family is

    (A) intensive subsistence agriculture

    (B) intensive commercial agriculture

    (C) extensive subsistence agriculture

    (D) extensive commercial agriculture

    (E) ranching

18. The term *swidden* refers to a plot of land formed by what type of agriculture?

    (A) Transhumance   (D) Double cropping

    (B) Truck farming   (E) Slash and burn

    (C) Open-lot system

19. The loss of the nutrient-rich top layer in soil is called

    (A) soil erosion   (D) undernutrition

    (B) swidden   (E) shifting cultivation

    (C) transhumance

20. Biotechnology, or the process of using living organisms to produce or change plant or animal products, is part of which agricultural revolution?

   (A) First agricultural revolution

   (B) Second agricultural revolution

   (C) Third agricultural revolution

   (D) Open-lot system

   (E) Plantation agriculture

Free-Response Review Questions

1. Agriculture has been evolving since its inception some 12,000 years ago.

   (A) Explain the major trends in innovation that characterize the third agricultural revolution.

   (B) Define *agribusiness* and relate it to the third agricultural revolution.

   (C) Explain one positive effect of agribusiness on the individual farmer in the periphery.

   (D) Explain one negative effect of agribusiness on the individual farmer in the periphery.

PART 8 Pre-Exam Practice Answers

Terms Review Answers

1. Double cropping
2. Slash-and-burn agriculture
3. Intensive subsistence agriculture
4. Mediterranean agriculture
5. Dairying
6. Plantation agriculture
7. Agribusiness
8. Green Revolution
9. Undernutrition
10. Mixed crop and livestock farming
11. Enclosure movement
12. Seed agriculture
13. Agriculture
14. First agricultural revolution
15. Vegetative planting
16. Shifting cultivation
17. Hunters and gatherers
18. Extensive subsistence agriculture
19. Commercial farming
20. Milkshed
21. Capital-intensive farm
22. Ranching
23. Transhumance
24. Third agricultural revolution
25. Debt-for-nature swaps

Multiple-Choice Answers

1. **(D)**

   Because of the dryer landscape of the plateau, farming is limited to pastoral activities such as nomadic movements of herders with their animals. (A) is found more in tropical and subtropical zones; (B) obviously, in climates commensurate with the Mediterranean zone; (C) in well-watered tropical zones; and (E) in less-developed regions with climates conducive to cash crop harvests targeted for export.

2. **(D)**

   In von Thünen's model, all land is equally productive. Thus, farming activities requiring the most extensive land use without expensive transportation costs locates farthest from the city's center. Dairying, for example, uses the land intensively and requires expensive trucking to prevent the milk from spoiling, so dairy farms locate close to the city's center. Ranching to produce wool and hides, however, requires extensive amounts of land because the livestock must graze and move about, but it has fewer transportation costs associated with it than a practice such as dairying.

3. **(E)**

   Recombinant DNA splicing is part of the biorevolution during the third agricultural revolution. The other choices were all a part of the wave known as the second agricultural revolution, even (D), which was the closing in of public crops into private properties. This movement caused many people without land to move into the cities to find opportunity in the industrial sector; the enclosure of formerly public crops also led to increased efficiency, related to private property and direct responsibility.

4. **(C)**

   While the other choices are countries located on lands believed to be sites of ancient agriculture hearths, (C) is not believed to be a place where farming first evolved. Rather, farming practices likely originated in southern Europe and diffused northward toward modern-day England.

5. **(E)**

   Greece's Mediterranean climate allows for wheat production but also for farming olives, figs, and other Mediterranean crops that can be highly profitable for the region's farmers, who often do not have extensive lands. Wheat production is dominated particularly by the United States, Canada, and France.

6. **(B)**

The picture is of a house in Lithuania, a northeastern European state. Notice the wood and stone materials, both of which are common in European homes. Wood, in the form of paneling, is not common in African regions, particularly because of the heat and need for ventilation, not insulation. Thus, the combination of wood and stone indicate a place needing insulation from a cold winter, like Lithuania.

7. **(E)**

India's cultural taboo against eating beef is related to a Hindu belief that a divine power is vested in the cow. Hence, beef consumption is lowest in India than in the other states listed.

8. **(C)**

The original intent of the Green Revolution was humanitarian because it was funded by a charitable organization in the United States. Original researchers were sent to Mexico to try to help find a solution to boost Mexican harvests for the benefit of the Mexican people. What developed from their work was a set of technologies that diffused to other less-developed countries as means to boost global food supplies, intentionally in poorer regions. The other arguments are common criticisms of the Green Revolution.

9. **(B)**

As farming has become increasingly industrialized and corporate, the family farmer in the United States has become incorporated into larger farming aggregates. Thus, the number of family farmers has drastically declined as farms have been merged into corporate-owned operations within the industrialized agribusiness system that now constitutes the U.S. farming landscape. (A) is false because agriculture is still an integral part of the U.S. economy, employing in some facet more than 30 percent of U.S. workers. (C) is false because exports have increased since World War II. (D) is false as many consumed foods are of U.S. origin, especially wheat, meat, and dairy-based products. (E) is false because wheat production dramatically increased with the advent of Green Revolution hybrid seeds and improved farming technologies continually being implemented with the modern biorevolution.

10. **(C)**

Transhumance is the movement of seasonal nomads and their respective herds from highland to lowland pastures. (A) is subsistence farming that clears land by first slashing the vegetation and then burning it to prepare the soil for planting. (B) is farming wheat, figs, olives, and other crops in Mediterranean zones. (D) is farming that has both animals and crops on the same, stationary farm. (E) is a farming technique that divides the farm into zones and plants varying seeds in each zone to prevent leeching the soil of its nutrients.

11. **(B)**

Rubber was a cash crop focused on by colonizers to aid the colonizers' industrializing populations. It is still grown in former colonies like India, but it has also expanded to other countries such as China. The other choices were not cash-crop exports in former European colonies.

12. **(D)**

At the heart of von Thünen's conclusions is the variation of transportation costs associated with changing distances from the central marketplace. All other factors are held constant in the model, which results in concentric rings according to transportation costs. The remaining choices accurately state assumptions in the model.

13. **(C)**

Boserup looked at subsistence farmers as having direct power over the food supply and responding to population changes by increasing or decreasing their farming efforts to meet food demands. In contrast, Malthus did not empower farmers with the ability to meet food demands made by what he saw was geometrically increasing population rates.

14. **(D)**

The only statement that does not apply is III, because individual farms do play a role in the process. Many individual farms supply foodstuffs to agribusiness corporations, such as an individual beef farm supplying a meat-packing and distributing company with its raw meat. Perhaps (I) was difficult to understand: integration is the combination of pieces into one unit, so agricultural integration involves the coming together of different pieces of the farming process into one corporate-driven system.

15. **(C)**

While it is industrializing, China is still largely a subsistence agricultural economy. Most of its farmers exist on small plots of farmland that they farm intensively, often employing ingenious tactics like pyramids and terraces.

16. **(B)**

Vegetative planting, the process of simply cutting off a stem of another plant or dividing up roots of a plant, developed before seed agriculture (A). (C) is the modern economic system surrounding agriculture, (D) is the raising of animals by moving from place to place, and (E) is the use of scientifically created fertilizers and pesticides to increase crop yields.

17. **(C)**

Subsistence agriculture is the growing of food to feed just your own family. Extensive agriculture uses large amounts of land, as opposed to intensive agriculture, which tries to maximize yields from small amounts of land. (A) is using smaller plots of land; (B) and (D) are commercial, meaning they raise crops for sale, not just private use; and (E) is the raising of animals for sale.

18. **(E)**

Swidden is another name of a field prepared by cutting down existing vegetation and then burning it to enrich the soil; the process is also known as slash-and-burn agriculture. (A) is the movement of animal herds to cooler highland areas in the summer to warmer, lowland areas in the winter. (B) are commercial flower farms and gardens; (C) is a system of agriculture where the land is distributed in one, large plot of community farmland that all villagers work; and (D) is growing two crops on the same plot of land in a year.

19. **(A)**

Soil erosion is the process of losing the nutrient-rich topsoil needed to raise crops. (B) is a field produced by slash-and-burn agriculture; (C) is the movement of animal herds to cooler highland areas in the summer and to warmer, lowland areas in the winter; (D) is the condition of having too few calories and nutrients in your diet; and (E) is the practice of rotating fields to allow the soil to replenish its nutrients.

20. **(C)**

Biotechnology is an aspect of the third agricultural revolution that relies on scientific means to improve crop yields. (A) started humans on the path to growing their own food instead of collecting it; (B) used industrial advances to improve agricultural output; (D) is a system of agriculture in which the land is distributed in one large plot of community farmland that all villagers work; and (E) are large-scale farming operations specializing in the farming of one or two high-demand crops for export.

Free-Response Answers

The following is a list of some suggested main points for each part of the question.

Part A

- Beginning in the late 1800s, the third agricultural revolution began in North America and saw the globalization of industrialized agriculture and new technologies that increased the food supply.

- Whereas the first agricultural revolution ushered in the growth of stationary plant and animal domestication, the second agricultural revolution saw new farming and storage capabilities increase food supplies to meet and facilitate a growing, industrializing population. The third agricultural revolution distributed mechanized farming technology and chemical fertilizers on a global level.

- During the third agricultural revolution, farming and food processing were completed at different sites in an increasingly "industrialized," mechanical, more corporate-like structure.

Part B

- Agribusiness is the system of food production involving everything from the development of seeds to the marketing and sale of food products at the market.

- Agribusiness is the combination of all the elements of the food production industry, including farms, processing plants, packagers, fertilizer laboratories, distributors, and advertising agencies.

- Agribusiness, an outgrowth of the third agricultural revolution, is the child of agricultural industrialization and commercialization, processes fueled by the globalization of farming technology and mechanization. In other words, the third agricultural revolution saw the growth and development of new farming technologies and transportation systems that have precipitated the commercialization and industrialization of agribusiness.

Part C

- Possible positive effects of agribusiness on individual farmers in the periphery are diffusion of new farming technology to the area (which is also a double-edged sword that can cause farmers harm if the new technology is too expensive for them and makes them unable to compete), growth and development of the local economy, and possible ties to a global marketplace for their farming products.

Part D

- Possible negative effects of agribusiness on individual farmers in the periphery are being pushed out of the marketplace by large corporate farms that can produce more food with more expensive technology and land; loss of subsistence agricultural community; loss of land to multinational corporations in agribusiness and political dealings; water shortages because of intense irrigation needs of the new, large, corporate farms built in the peripheral countries.

Chapter 7

Industrialization and Economic Development

Introduction

Economic geographers study the locations and reasons for economic patterns in the world's human landscape. They analyze the patterns in economic wealth, poverty, growth, and decline. Inherent in this analysis is the genesis of industrialization, which revolutionized economic interaction and moved human resource consumption to a new level. The human and environmental consequences to industrialization and industrialization's impact on varying development levels are carefully analyzed by geographers, partly through the lens of models and theories attempting to explain and predict economic activities. In their quest to understand the "where of why," geographers search for both explanations and solutions to current economic inequalities.

Geo Factoid

Almost half of the people in the world live on the equivalent of less than $2 a day, and about 20 percent live on less than $1 a day. Meanwhile, people in the 20 richest countries on average earn 37 times more than people in the 20 poorest countries.

Key Questions

- *What is industrialization? What is development?*

- *How do natural resources, culture, politics, and history influence the spatial character of economic activity?*

- *What are the key sectors in the economy?*

- *How do places acquire comparative advantages? Where do they exist?*

- *How do key economic models help explain the world's division between core and peripheral economic regions?*

- *What is economic globalization?*

- *How do space–time compression and the international division of labor affect market orientation and the production process?*

- *What are key patterns in economic growth and decline in North America?*

- *What are the modern patterns of economic inequality, and how do they relate to global economic interdependence?*

- *What are the environmental consequences of industrialization and globalization?*

- *What are the socioeconomic and political ramifications of deindustrialization? How is deindustrialization related to the disaggregation of the production process?*

 PART 1 **Key Concepts and the Growth and Diffusion of Industrialization**

Economic Classifications

The system of production, consumption, and distribution is called the **economy**. The economy can be divided into different parts to understand its whole. At its most basic core is its **primary sector**, the part of the economy in which activities revolve around getting raw materials from the earth. Farming, fishing, and raw mining are examples of primary economic activities.

Secondary economic activities deal with processing the raw materials acquired through primary activities into finished products of greater value, such as taking raw corn and processing it into baby food. Factories and manufacturing fall into the secondary economic activity category, taking raw materials and transforming them into finished products.

Tertiary economic activities focus on moving, selling, and trading the products made in primary and secondary activities. Tertiary economic activities also involve professional and financial services, such as banks, carpet cleaning businesses, and fast-food restaurants.

A fourth category of economic activity, termed **quaternary economic activity,** involves information creation and transfer. Quaternary economic activities assemble, distribute, and process information; they also manage other business

Figure 7.1. Percentage of workers in the service sector throughout the world

operations. University research and investment analysis are examples of quaternary economic activities.

Within the quaternary sector exists a subclassification known as **quinary economic activities**, which involve the highest level of decision making, like that of a legislature or a presidential cabinet. High-level government-targeted research is also included in the quinary subclassification.

Industrialization

Industrialization is the growth of manufacturing activity in the economy or a region and usually occurs alongside a decrease in the number of primary economic activities within a country. Even before the Industrial Revolution, manufacturing, a secondary economic activity, transpired. From bread making to clothes making, industrial activity was located nearest the urban cores and close to the raw materials needed in the production process. However, these manufacturing-like activities were small and localized, like preindustrial communities in less-developed regions today.

The amount of world trade since 1950 has increased 20-fold, from $320 billion to $6.8 trillion. This increase in the trade of manufactured goods is three times larger than the increase in the rate of the production of those goods.

The Industrial Revolution

The **Industrial Revolution** began in England in the 1760s, when the industrial geography of England changed significantly and later diffused to other parts of western Europe. In that period of rapid socioeconomic change, machines replaced human labor and new sources of inanimate energy were tapped. Coal began as the leading energy source, fueling England's textile-focused industrial explosion.

What most defined England's Industrial Revolution was the rise of assembly-line manufacturing. Although assembly lines existed first on a small scale in homes where people made goods before the revolution, the 1760s saw the growth of large mechanized factories. Because early factories were powered by coal sources, they tended to clump around the coalfields. North-central England's coalfields fostered major industrial cities such as Manchester and Liverpool. The emergence of many factories led to the development of a clear industrial landscape and working-class housing areas.

Along with this industrial growth, England's transportation infrastructure improved to allow for shipping supplies into urban factories. Further, farming

Figure 7.2. Oil and natural gas deposits

became more mechanized with the infusion of greater technology into the agricultural process. One result of industrialization was the **commodification** of labor, with factory owners looking at their human labor as commodities (objects for trade) with price tags per hour, rather than seeing them as people.

While original factory-like labor was conducted in households, the growth of factories first occurred around water sources, such as rivers and lakes. As coal-powered manufacturing increased, factories could move away from water sources that formerly supplied energy through steam and water-mill methods. Factories could locate in coalfields and occupy larger areas of space, eventually building out, rather than up.

By the 1960s, oil replaced coal as the dominant source of industrial energy in the world. Although the United States, Russia, and Venezuela had been the chief sources of oil, the surge in oil demand allowed for the Middle East to take over the market for oil in the 1960s.

Diffusion of Industrialization

By 1825, the technology of the industrialization in England had spread to North America and countries in western Europe like Belgium, Germany, and France. Again, industrialization thrived in places with rich coal deposits, like Ohio and Pennsylvania in the United States, Ukraine in Russia, and the Ruhr region in Germany.

By the 1920s, the production process in the U.S. automobile factories had broken down into differentiated components, with different groups of people performing different tasks to complete the product, a process known as the **Ford production (or Fordist) method**. Fordist factories built out rather than up, meaning that they were built on only one story so that the product could be transported throughout the assembly line without problems.

Weber's Least Cost Theory of Industrial Location

Where will factories locate? What factors affect industrial location? Predicting where factories will grow was the focus of German economist Alfred Weber's work in the early 20th century. Just as von Thünen studied the locations of agricultural activities, **Alfred Weber** studied the locations of industrial activities by setting up a hypothetical state with several assumptions. Weber's model predicted where industries would locate based on the places that would be the lowest cost to them. Appropriately, his model was called **least cost theory.**

Assumptions in Weber's Model

Weber's model is based on the assumptions that the cost of transportation is determined by the weight of the goods being shipped and the distance to the market; the heavier the good and/or the farther the distance, the more expensive it is to ship. He assumed that industries are competitive and aim to minimize their costs and maximize their profits. He also assumed that markets are in fixed locations. Labor, he assumed, exists only in certain places and is not mobile. Like von Thünen, he also assumed that the physical geography (land quality) and political-cultural landscape are uniform across the model's space. In other words, he assumed a uniform landscape with equal transportation paths and routes throughout the space (no mountains, lakes, or rivers would get in the way). With these assumptions, the location of industry is driven by four factors: transportation, labor, agglomeration, and deglomeration.

Transportation and Distance

Industries wanting to locate where transportation costs are minimized must consider two issues: the distance to the market and the weight of the goods. Distance is a premiere factor in the location of industries on several levels besides shipping. For instance, the distances from the factory to its sources of energy and raw materials are also important. Factories established in the early part of the Industrial Revolution had to locate close to their energy sources, but the invention of electricity and other innovations in energy production and transportation enabled modern factories to locate far from energy sources without incurring high costs.

Early factories also had to consider their proximity to the raw materials they needed. A factory had **spatially variable costs**—costs that varied (or changed) depending on the space in which it was located. For example, a factory using heavy or perishable raw materials in its production process might be built as close as possible to its source of raw materials to minimize the cost of transporting the materials into the factory. **Weight-losing processes** are manufacturing processes that create a product lighter than the raw materials that went into making it. Paper production is an example of a weight-losing production process: many paper mills are located near forests, the source of the heavy wood the factory converts into lighter paper products to be shipped long distances. When weight-losing industries locate near the raw resource supply, they are said to have a **material orientation.**

Weight-gaining processes take raw materials and create a heavier final product. Beverage bottling is a weight-gaining industry. Early factories involved in weight-gaining processes were built near the marketplace because the product was heavier to transport in its final form. When weight-gaining industries locate near the place where the heavier product will be sold, that industry is said to have a **market orientation.**

Some industries maintain the same cost of transportation and production regardless of where they choose to locate. These industries have **spatially fixed costs**—costs that remain the same no matter where they choose to locate. These industries often produce lightweight products of extremely high value, like computer chips. Geographers often refer to these types of industries as **footloose**

industries, because they are not bound by locational constraints and can choose to locate wherever they want. Footloose computer chip industries often locate near advanced university research areas.

Labor Costs

Labor cost is another key factor in least cost theory. Can the factory owner hire the workforce needed for the factory? Included in labor considerations is the availability of industrial capital, which consists of machinery and the money to purchase the tools and workers the factory needs. Sometimes an industry will move to a place to access lower labor costs, even though transportation costs might increase as a result. In the long run, these factories will save more because of the cheaper labor. Such a decision is called the **substitution principle**.

Agglomeration

Weber also focused on the advantages and savings made when industries clump together for mutual advantage, a process called **agglomeration**. Factories that are in the same area can share costs associated with resources such as electrical lines, roads, pollution control, and so forth. In other words, agglomeration has positive effects (usually manifested in lower costs and prices) for both the clustered industries and the consumers of their products, a phenomenon known as an **agglomeration economy**.

An example of agglomeration is the **high-tech corridor**—a place where technology and computer industries agglomerate—established in California's Silicon Valley. Many technology-related companies located in this **technopole**, or region of high-tech agglomeration, to benefit from shared resources, like a highly trained workforce that would migrate there for jobs, similar ancillary activities, or support businesses, like computer repair shops and electrical wiring services. As a consequence of this agglomeration, other areas suffered an out-migration of talented computer engineers and other skilled workers who migrated to Silicon Valley. This negative consequence of agglomeration, when other regions suffer a drain of resources and talent, is called the **backwash effect**.

Related to agglomeration is the theory of **locational interdependence**, which states that industries choose locations based on where their competitors are located. Industries want to maximize their dominance of the market, so they are influenced by their competition. A common sight near a highway exit is an agglomeration of gas stations. The theory of locational interdependence would assert that these gas stations know that one gas station cannot serve all the cars needing gas, so clustering around the exit allows them a slice of the market share.

Deglomeration

When an agglomerated region becomes too clustered, too crowded, agglomeration can begin to negatively affect the industries in the form of excessive pollution, traffic congestion, lack of resources and labor, and so forth. These industries might then choose to move for more space in a process called **deglomeration,** or the "unclumping" of factories because of the negative effects and higher costs associated with industrial overcrowding.

Criticisms of Weber's Model

Weber's theory does not identify the fact that markets and labor are often mobile, and that the labor force varies in age, skill sets, gender, language, and other traits. Some transportation costs, too, are not directly proportional to distance as his model assumes.

 PART 2 **Contemporary Patterns and Impacts of Industrialization and Development**

Development

Why are some countries continually so rich and others so poor? The diffusion of economic growth and the increasingly interconnected world has led geographers to see differences in levels of development in the countries of the world. **Development** is the process of improving the material condition of people through the growth and diffusion of technology and knowledge. Human development is continuous and unending in its drive to improve the human condition. Every place, regardless of size, exists at some level of development. Geographers have grouped countries into identifiable categories, more developed and less developed, based on where they are clumped on the spectrum of development.

More-Developed Versus Less-Developed Countries

More-developed countries are on the wealthier side of the development spectrum, while **less-developed countries** are those on the economically poorer side of the spectrum. Both sides have related challenges, with more-developed countries facing issues such as maintaining economic growth and less-developed countries trying to improve their economic condition. Yet it is difficult to qualify and rank countries according to their level of development. Development is not simply a metric of the amount of money a country has. Rather, economic, social, and demographic factors enter into the measurement.

UN Human Development Index

The United Nations uses a formula to generate the **Human Development Index (HDI),** a measure of development that can be used to compare the various

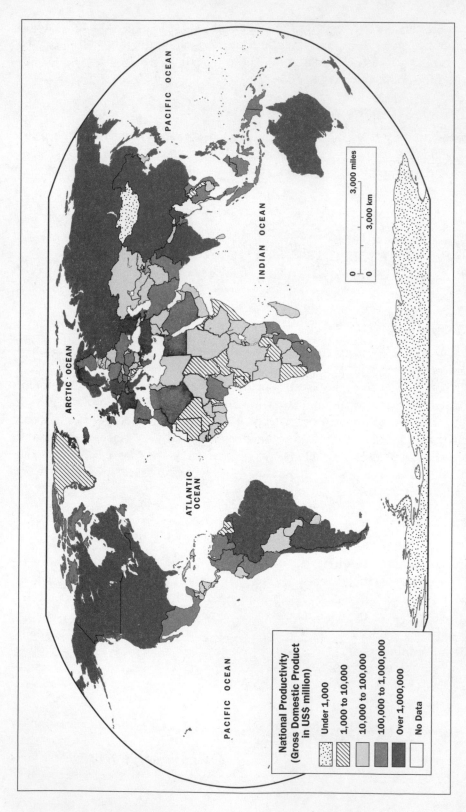

Figure 7.3. National productivity as measured by gross domestic product in U.S. dollars

development levels of regions and countries. According to the UN, the Human Development Index is based on the idea that development is a process of expanding choice. It is an equation that factors into its measurements three areas: life expectancy, average educational levels, and standard of living.

The economic component of HDI is the country's **gross domestic product (GDP)**, the value of total outputs of goods and services produced in a country, usually over one year. GDP per capita is simply the GDP divided by population. In more-developed countries, the GDP per capital is greater than $20,000, and in less-developed countries it is less than $1,000. In the United States, the GDP per capita is nearly $35,000, or $10 to $15 per hour, while in less-developed countries it is 50 cents per hour. (Gross national product includes all goods and services owned and produced by a country overseas.)

Importantly, GDP data are used in calculating **purchasing power parity (PPP)**, a measurement tool for calculating the exchange rates required for each currency to buy an equal amount of goods. In other words, PPP might demonstrate how many colas $1 can buy in Lithuania compared with in the United States. PPP is used to make "apple-to-apple" data comparisons. For example, although the GDP per capita in sub-Saharan African countries is at or below $750, an evaluation of PPP for that income level shows that the buying power in those countries is closer to $4,000 in the United States. PPP puts number comparisons into perspective.

One drawback to using GDP as a factor in evaluating human development is that it is an average that does not reflect the inequality that may exist among people in a country. For example, a country may have a high GDP that is concentrated in one small, elite class of people, while large numbers may be very poor. In fact, in the United States, the richest 10 percent of its citizens holds 15 times more money than the poorest 10 percent of Americans, thus illustrating a large gap between the rich and poor. In less-developed countries, however, the gap is often even more severe. In Guatemala, for example, the richest 10 percent of the population has 75 times more money than the poorest 10 percent.

In addition to GDP per capita, the other three factors used in the UN's HDI equation are life expectancy at birth, educational level attained, and degree of literacy in the region or country. The highest score a country could get on the HDI is 1.000, whereas the lowest is 0.000. In 2006, the lowest country on the list was Niger, with a score of 0.311. The highest country on the list was Norway, with a score of 0.965. The United States ranked eighth among the 177 listed countries.

Informal Sector

Another drawback in using GDP is that many countries do not know and/or do not report data from their **informal sector**, a network of business transactions that are not reported and, therefore, not included in the country's GDP and official economic projections. For example, when parents pay a high school student to baby-sit their children, that transaction is typically "under the table," or not reported to the government. Other examples of workers performing informal-sector economic activities include street vendors selling goods to pedestrians, undocumented aliens working as domestics, prostitutes, and drug traffickers. In many less-developed countries, the informal sector is a prominent portion of overall economic activity, making GDP of limited use in measuring development levels.

The informal sector exists for several reasons. First, the goods produced in the informal sector may be meeting a need that the formal sector has ignored. Second, the goods produced in the informal sector may be in high demand because they are inexpensive. However, because their products are inexpensive, the owners of informal-sector operations, whether they are lunch carts or backroom purse shops, do not make enough money to buy permanent stores and transition into the formal sector. Another part of the informal sector involves illegal immigrants who risk being deported if they and their employers report their earnings to the government.

Other Indicators of Development

Given the problems with solely relying on GDP per capita, geographers sometimes use other measures to analyze economic development, such as access to raw materials, amount of consumer goods, and even the number of TVs and radios per person. Importantly, geographers are beginning to include analyses of women's rights and level of equality as other factors in measuring development levels.

Another interesting indicator of development is the **Big Mac Index**, which compares prices of a Big Mac throughout the world. For example, a Big Mac costs roughly $1.78 in Thailand, where the gross national income per person was $8,440 in 2005. In contrast, the cost of a Big Mac is $3.22 in the United States, where the average income per person is about $42,000. Thus, while Americans earn nearly five times as much as Thais, the U.S. Big Mac costs only two times as much as the Thai version, making it a comparatively expensive meal in Thailand. The Big Mac Index is also used to evaluate exchange rates.

The Development Gap

Geographers are also concerned with the **development gap**, the widening difference between development levels in more- and less-developed countries. Simply put, more-developed countries are improving in their development levels faster than are less-developed countries, and the difference in development levels between the two is widening. In the last decade, the GDP tripled in more-developed countries but only doubled in less-developed countries. The rate of natural population increase fell by nearly 85 percent in more-developed countries but by only 5 percent in less-developed countries.

The world's countries even fall into a regional division based on development, with more-developed countries located primarily in the Northern Hemisphere and less-developed countries primarily located in the Southern Hemisphere. This division is known as the **north–south gap**. Charitable foundations like the Willy Brandt Foundation have called for countries in the north to increase their donations and commitment to less-developed countries in the south to help reduce the widening development gap.

Structuralist Reasons for the Development Gap

How and why do some countries become less developed while others are more developed? Why are many less-developed countries entrenched in their low economic status? Geographers are divided into two camps on this issue. One group of geographers subscribe to **structuralist theories**, which argue that less-developed countries are locked into a vicious cycle of entrenched underdevelopment by the global economic system that supports an unequal structure.

Dependency theory exemplifies this structuralist perspective, arguing that the political and economic relations among countries limit the ability of less-developed countries to modernize and develop. Structuralists see the world's countries as existing in a system, wherein one country's actions directly impact the development paths of other countries in the system. Countries are, therefore, interdependent, not independent.

Immanuel Wallerstein's world-systems analysis (discussed in detail in Chapter 5) is an example of a dependency perspective. Remember, world-systems analysis divides the world into three groups: core, periphery, and semiperiphery. Wallerstein did not assert that all countries can become part of the core, or reach a developed state. Rather, his theory is based on the notion that the core depends on the existence of a periphery. If there is a core, there is a periphery, because the core gains its power through the exploitation of the peripheral and semiperipheral countries. However, the list of countries in the core can change over time, as core countries become peripheral and vice versa.

Dependency theorists point to Europe's colonial occupation of Africa as a reason for continued African poverty. They argue that European colonialism locked African nations into a dependent relationship to their European occupiers. Dependency theory sees little hope for less-developed countries because the dominance of more-developed countries is highly linked to the continued economic and political inferiority of less-developed countries. Dependency theory is criticized for not allowing for cultural and contextual geographic differences.

Liberal Theories of Development: The Rostow Modernization Model

Liberal development theories contrast with structuralist theories and claim that development is a process through which all countries can move. Walt Rostow's **modernization model**, often called the ladder of development, is one such model that assumes all countries follow a similar path of development toward becoming modernized.

Developed in the 1950s, Rostow's modernization model is similar to the demographic transition model in predicting that countries move through stages of structural change to attain development. Rostow's model comprises five stages of development. More-developed countries exist in stages 4 and 5, whereas less-developed countries are in stages 1 through 3. According to the Rostow model, once a country starts investing money in capital—building factories, for instance—its development path is ignited. The following is a description of each stage in Rostow's modernization model.

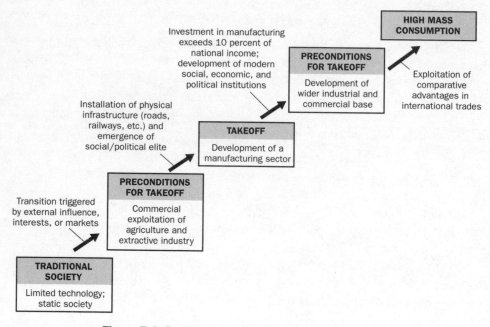

Figure 7.4. Rostow's stages of economic development

- **Stage 1: traditional society.** Economic activity at this stage focuses on subsistence, and the outcome of the activity is consumed primarily by those producing the products. For example, families practicing subsistence farming ate the crops they grew, rather than trading them at markets. Rostow believed that in this first stage, a large amount of national wealth is allocated to tasks that are not economically productive, such as building a military or constructing religious temples.

- **Stage 2: preconditions to takeoff.** As a region begins to develop, a small group of people initiates innovative economic activities that pave the way to economic development. Those few influential people begin to invest in new technologies and infrastructure, such as better water systems and modes of transportation, which sets the stage for economic takeoff. Meanwhile, the region develops surpluses for trading, and productivity increases.

- **Stage 3: takeoff.** The small number of new industries in which the elite invested during stage 2 begin to show rapid economic growth. Industrialization increases as workers shift from agricultural activities into manufacturing jobs created by the takeoff industries. However, the other sectors of the country's economy remain dominated by traditional predevelopment activities like agriculture.

- **Stage 4: drive to maturity.** At this stage the region shows the diffusion of advanced technology beyond just the few initial industries. Other industries experience rapid growth, workers become more skilled and specialized, and the economy begins to diversify and grow in many directions.

- **Stage 5: high mass consumption.** The economy shifts from the dominance of secondary manufacturing jobs to the dominance of service-sector tertiary jobs. High incomes characterize much of the workforce, and masses of people become consumers of produced goods.

Criticisms of Rostow's Model

Some geographers question the applicability of the Rostow modernization model to all countries. After all, the model is based on western European and Anglo-American development patterns and does not account for roadblocks to development, such as the postcolonial dependency on former colonizer that many countries experience while struggling to develop their economies. Another criticism of the model is that it considers each country an independent agent, rather than one piece of an interlocking system of countries.

Reducing the Development Gap: The Self-Sufficiency Approach

To reduce the development gap between rich and poor countries, less-developed countries must build their economies more rapidly. However, geographers debate how to achieve this growth. A method popular in the 1900s is developing **self-sufficiency**, the ability to provide for its own people, independent from foreign economies.

An African woman faces a 1 in 16 chance of dying in childbirth in her lifetime. For a woman in the industrialized world, the chance is 1 in 2,800.

According to the self-sufficiency approach, a country should spread its investments and development equally across all sectors of its economy and regions. Rural areas must develop along with urban areas, and poverty must be reduced across the entire country. The self-sufficiency approach favors a closed economic state, in which imports are limited and heavily taxed so that local businesses can flourish without having to compete with foreign companies.

In the 20th century, China, India, eastern Europe, and Africa were using this self-sufficiency approach to improve development in their regions. However, drawbacks became evident when corruption and inefficiency limited development. In India, for example, the government paid failing businesses to stay open and continue their work. Some economists argue that if the Indian government had allowed those failing businesses to face foreign competition, they would have been forced to improve their products and compete.

Reducing the Development Gap: International Trade

Another approach to improving the economic underdevelopment of less-developed countries is through encouraging **international trade**. This approach pushes a country to identify its unique set of strengths in the world and to channel investment toward building on those strengths. To compete internationally, this approach argues, a country must find out what it can offer the world and capitalize on that good or service.

Eventually, the country will develop a comparative advantage over the rest of the world in producing that good or providing that service. A country has a **comparative advantage** when it is better at producing a particular good or offering some service that is another country. The place with a comparative advantage can fill the market's need for a good or service at a lower production cost than other places can. For example, Japan invested much money and power into developing a comparative advantage in high-technology products. Japan could produce computer chips and such much more efficiently than other places could, thereby giving Japan a comparative advantage in high-technology goods. Japan could then specialize in exporting high-tech products to other countries, which could then trade with Japan for the products Japan needed to survive.

Globalization

Spatial interaction has existed throughout human history, at large and small scales: tribe to tribe, village to village, empire to empire. Along with improved communication and transportation technologies, spatial interaction has increased in speed and distance, leading to a continued trend toward space–time compression.

Globalization is the term used to describe this increasing sense of interconnectedness and spatial interaction among governments, cultures, and economies. Originally, *globalization* was used in reference to the spread of economic activities from a home country to other parts of the world, but its reach has profoundly influenced cultural and political realms.

For example, the globalization of brand-name coffee shops is essentially the spread of an economic activity (the coffee shop), but it is also the diffusion of a piece of American culture. The spread of MTV to other parts of the world is also inherently economic, in the diffusion of music sales and videos, but it is also very much a cultural force. Globalization of Western culture is resented in some places that wish to maintain the "purity" of their cultures without the perceived invasion, or cultural imperialism, of Western forces. Hence, the global diffusion of products and their related values by companies such as Disney, MTV, and McDonalds has given way to phrases such as the "Disneyification," "MTVization," and "McDonaldization" of the world.

Multinational Corporations

Multinational corporations (MNCs), sometimes called transnational corporations, are the primary agents of globalization. MNCs are businesses with headquarters in one country and production facilities in one or more other countries. They are usually **conglomerate corporations**, meaning that one massive corporation owns and operates a collection of smaller companies that provide it with specific services in its production process. For example, a conglomerate corporation might own a bottling company and a food-coloring company. An MNC can also include companies that own completely unrelated businesses, such as one owning not only film studios but also television networks and many other smaller companies.

Usually, MNCs locate their headquarters in core countries and build production facilities in peripheral countries. **Outsourcing** is the practice of an MNC to relocate a piece (or all) of its manufacturing operations to factories in other countries. For example, a company headquartered in the United States, outsources its shoe production process to workers in Malaysia and other less-developed countries. MNCs outsource to take advantage of lower labor costs, lower tax rates, and cheaper land prices in countries outside the United States. Remember the substitution principle: that companies might choose to take on higher transportation costs of moving their industrial location farther from their market because they will end up saving money in the long run by hiring less expensive labor.

New Industrial Countries and the Asian Tigers

MNC headquarters tend to exist in the United States, Canada, Germany, the United Kingdom, France, and Japan. However, several states have climbed the economic ladder and have established an industrialized economy based on manufacturing and global trade, countries geographers refer to as **new industrial countries (NICs)**.

Four East Asian countries experienced rapid economic growth by riding the technology boom in the late 20th century and becoming NICs. Taiwan, South Korea, Hong Kong, and Singapore, collectively known as the **Asian Tigers**, are NICs that followed the growth pattern of post–World War II Japan by developing a global reach for high-tech products. Together with China and Japan, the four Asian Tigers make up the core of the Asian economic engine, known as the **Pacific Rim economic region**.

Figure 7.5. Chinese special economic zones

Foreign Direct Investment

As a tactic to improve their economic development, many less-developed countries actively solicit foreign corporations' investment in their countries, referred to as **foreign direct investment**. Often countries wanting to attract MNCs establish **special economic zones**—regions offering special tax breaks, eased environmental restrictions, and other incentives to attract foreign business and investment. China's communist government has designated special economic zones within its territory to allow foreign companies to have free-trade rights and to outsource. Another related term, **export-processing zones,** refers to regions that offer tax breaks and loosened labor restrictions in less-developed countries to attract export-driven production processes, such as factories producing goods for foreign markets. Often,

Figure 7.6. Asian export-processing zones

export-processing zones are referred to as **free-trade zones**, because duties and tariffs are waived by governments wanting to encourage MNCs to invest in their countries.

In 1982, the global total of foreign direct investment flows was nearly $57 billion. By the year 2000, that number had grown to nearly $1.3 trillion – almost 20 times larger than in 1982!

Maquiladoras

Mexico established **maquiladora zones**, which are special economic zones on its northern border with the United States. MNCs can outsource labor to these maquiladoras, taking advantage of labor costs in Mexico that are far below those required for U.S. workers to manufacture the same products. Additionally, the Mexican government gave tax breaks to U.S. MNCs that located in maquiladora zones, and the products made in maquiladoras could be shipped to U.S. markets tariff free.

The Mexican government created the maquiladora program to create jobs for Mexican farmers no longer able to make a living off the land. Now nearly 500,000 Mexicans work in the maquiladoras, and the areas where the factories re located are besieged by overpopulation and pollution problems. As part of the North American Free Trade Agreement, the maquiladora program is supposed to be phased out.

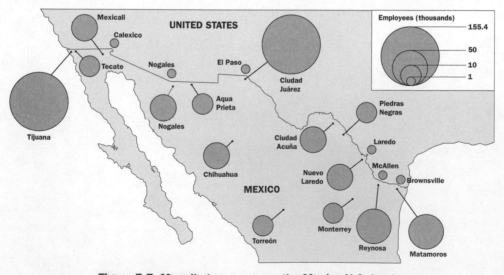

Figure 7.7. Maquiladora zones on the Mexico-U.S. border

Figure 7.8. An example of an international division of labor: Toyota's global assembly process

Toyota's Global Corridors

- ◎ Region
- ● Country
- → Flow of parts and vehicles

New International Division of Labor

With the rise of globalization, the original Fordist assembly-line concept developed during the Industrial Revolution has been split up not only among many factory workers under one factory roof but also among many countries under the **new international division of labor**. The new international division of labor breaks up the manufacturing process by having various pieces of a product made in various countries and then assembling the pieces in another country. Often the total sales of MNCs are larger than the gross national products of the countries in which they operate. Many less-developed countries depend so heavily on investment by MNCs that these foreign corporations wield a large amount of power over governmental decisions.

Free Trade Versus Fair Trade

The effect of globalization on the periphery is a hotly debated topic. While some geographers and economists argue that foreign direct investment is helping to generate increased economic development in less-developed countries, others contend that workers and resources in those countries are being exploited by profit-driven MNCs. According to human rights advocates, many MNCs are not paying workers in the periphery a living wage, enough to survive on in their home countries. Allowing capitalism to direct such spatial interaction, critics assert, is deepening inequality and the development gap.

An offshoot of the debate on globalization is the controversy surrounding the principles of free trade and fair trade. **Free trade** is the concept of allowing MNCs to outsource without any regulation except for the basic forces of market capitalism. Critics argue that free trade only protects the interests of MNCs and does nothing to safeguard workers' rights. As an alternative to free trade, some people advocate **fair trade** policies that favor oversight of foreign direct investment and outsourcing to ensure that workers throughout the world are guaranteed a living wage for their work. In fact, globalization's effect on women in the periphery is a topic of considerable concern, because women often work in the sweatshop-like conditions of outsourced factories.

Structural Adjustments and Privatization

The fight to generate increased socioeconomic development involves organizations such as the World Bank and the International Monetary Fund (IMF), two supranational organizations that regulate international trade and supply money to developing regions in the form of loans. Many of these loans have strings attached to them known as **structural adjustments**, or stipulations that require the country receiving the loan to make economic changes in order to use the loan.

For example, the IMF may issue a less-developed country a loan with the stipulation that some industries in the country that are public goods must be privatized, or sold off to private companies for profit. In many African countries, this involves selling off publicly operated goods, such as water systems, to private companies that begin charging people for the products that were free when owned and operated by the government.

Privatization, the selling of publicly operated industries to market-driven corporations, is one proposed solution to increasing economic efficiency in less-developed countries. However, privatization can cause social hardship for many families that once depended on the government-owned and operated resources being sold off to profit-driven corporations. Further, the movement of foreign companies into local economies threatens the survival of local businesses driven out of the market by the larger MNCs. Advocates of structural adjustments champion the idea that the long-term economic benefits to countries will outweigh the immediate and often difficult side effects of making the economic changes.

Nongovernmental Organizations

To assist in boosting economic development and human rights throughout the world's peripheral regions, nonprofit organizations like *Doctors Without Borders* and *Save the Children* enter the scene. Thousands of **nongovernmental organizations (NGOs)** represent a myriad of causes, including women's rights, health care, the eradication of poverty, and animal rights. NGOs often supply resources and money to local businesses and causes advancing economic and human development. NGOs have also been instrumental in helping combat HIV/AIDS and hunger.

Globalization and the Environment

With the diffusion of industrialization and increased economic interaction, geographers wonder if the increased rate of production and development can be maintained. Fossil fuels and natural resources, including land, are being depleted. With the increase of affordable, efficient transportation methods, humans can travel to places once considered too distant. Consequently, landscapes in exotic and "vacationable" areas are being transformed to meet tourists' desires, often at the expense of local communities and environments. One response to the negative environmental and cultural effects of increasing tourism is to create environmentally friendly tourist operations. **Ecotourism** comprises tourist operations that aim to do as little harm to the environment as possible. For example, instead of tearing down a forest to build a theme park, an ecotourist business might build a tourist attraction around hiking through the forest and celebrating its ecological diversity.

Costa Rica has turned a huge percentage of its land into protected areas that can be used for ecotourism. Many of the activities center on doing something inside the protected area, such as a "jungle swing," where tourists hike into the rain forest and then climb a small tower. At the top of the tower is a guidewire that runs slightly downhill to a tree. Tourists are hooked to the guidewire by a harness and then slide

Figure 7.9. Reported AIDS cases per 1 million people

from tree to tree over the top of the lower canopy. At one point tourists are about a 100 feet above the ground sliding among the trees. The only "damage" to the ecosystem is caused by the wires attached to the trees and the landing platforms they install. As such, Costa Rica is a strong example of the ecotourism movement on a national scale.

The question still remains: Will our rate of resource consumption eventually rob the earth of the natural resources required to keep pace with human development? To protect future generations, many geographers argue that humans must embrace **sustainable development**, a rate of growth and resource-consumption that can be maintained from one generation to another. At its meeting in 1992, the UN Commission on Sustainable Development called for conservation and careful use of resources. The commission focused on caring for the soil, avoiding overfishing the oceans and rivers, preserving the forests, protecting species from extinction, and reducing air pollution. Recycling and alternative sources of fuel were championed at the meeting.

Geographers are also concerned with the rising average global temperature, caused in part by the **greenhouse effect**. When industrial outputs such as carbon dioxide, methane, chlorofluorocarbons, and water vapor combine in the atmosphere, they create a spongelike vapor that transforms radiation into heat, causing the earth's temperature to rise. The greenhouse effect is much like what happens when you park your car with the windows closed on a hot day and return to find it so hot inside that you can barely sit in the seat. Related to the greenhouse effect and depletion of the ozone layer, **global warming theory** argues that the earth's rise in temperature is causing negative consequences, such as premature melting of the polar ice caps, which could cause sea levels to rise and an interruption of oceanic patterns. The merits and impacts of global warming are hotly debated by geographers and other scientists.

Average temperatures in the Arctic have risen at almost twice the rate as temperatures in the rest of the world over the past few decades. Moreover, the warmest global average temperatures on record have occurred within the past 15 years, with the warmest two years being 1998 and 2005.

Industrialization and its diffusion throughout the world are directly linked to these global changes, for industrialization has caused human resource consumption and pollution emissions to dramatically increase. Industrializing humans are abandoning subsistence livelihoods and moving toward consumption-oriented lifestyles in a race toward more "development." Some scholars see irony in the fact that staying up to speed in the global race toward more *development* requires countries to increase their levels of environmental *destruction*.

| PART 3 | Chapter Review |

Models Review

Least Cost Theory

This is Alfred Weber's theory of industrial location, explaining and predicting where industries will locate based on cost analysis of transportation, labor, and agglomeration factors. Weber assumes an industry will choose its location based on the desire to minimize production costs and thus maximize profits. Drawbacks to the model include its assumption of an immobile and equal labor force.

Locational Interdependence

Hotellings theory of locational interdependence asserts that an industry's locational choices are heavily influenced by the location of their chief competitors and related industries. In other words, industries do not make isolated decisions on locations without considering where other, related industries exist.

Rostow's Modernization Model

Developed in the 1950s, this model exemplifies the liberal development ideology, as opposed to structuralist theory. Under the model, all countries develop in a five-stage process. The development cycle is initiated by investment in a takeoff industry that allows the country to grow a comparative advantage, which sparks greater economic gain that eventually diffuses throughout the country's economy. Drawbacks to this model include its not identifying cultural and historic differences in development trajectories because it is based on North American and western European development histories.

Terms Review

Agglomeration—Clumping together of industries for mutual advantage.

Agglomeration economy—Positive effects of agglomeration for clustered industries and for the consumers of their products, often in the form of lower costs to the industries and consumers.

Alfred Weber—Twentieth-century German geographer who created the least cost theory to predict the locational decisions made by industrial operations.

Asian Tigers—Group of new industrial countries comprising Taiwan, South Korea, Hong Kong, and Singapore.

Backwash effect—Occurs when other regions suffer a drain of resources and talent due to agglomeration in another region.

Big Mac Index—Tool for calculating purchasing power parity that compares prices of a Big Mac throughout the world.

Commodification—Giving a price tag or value to something that was not previously perceived as having a money-related value.

Comparative advantage—Ability of a country (or place) to produce a good or offer a service better than another country can.

Conglomerate corporation—Massive corporation operating a collection of smaller companies that provide it with specific services in its production process.

Deglomeration—Unclumping of industries because of the negative effects and higher costs associated with overcrowding.

Dependency theory—Theory that exemplifies the structuralist perspective, arguing that the political and economic relations among countries limit the ability of less-developed countries to modernize and develop.

Development—Process of improving the material condition of people through the growth and diffusion of technology and knowledge.

Development gap—Widening difference between development levels in more-developed and less-developed countries.

Economy—System of production, consumption, and distribution.

Ecotourism—Type of tourist attraction built around an environmentally friendly activity that aims to preserve the earth and its resources.

Export-processing zone—Region of a less-developed country that offer tax breaks and loosened labor restrictions to attract export-driven production processes, such as factories producing goods for foreign markets; sometimes called free-trade zone.

Fair trade—Policies that favor oversight of foreign direct investment and outsourcing to ensure that workers throughout the world are guaranteed a living wage for their work, enough to survive in their home countries.

Footloose industry—Industry not bound by locational constraints and able to choose to locate wherever it wants.

Ford production (Fordist) method—Manufacturing process broken down into differentiated components, with different groups of people performing different tasks to complete the product.

Foreign direct investment—Investment by a multinational corporation in a foreign country's economy.

Free trade—Concept of allowing multinational corporations to outsource without any regulation except for the basic forces of market capitalism.

Globalization—Originally, this buzz term referred to the spread of economic activities from a home country to other parts of the world, but its reach has profoundly influenced cultural and political realms.

Global warming theory—Argues that the earth's surface temperature is gradually rising because of the greenhouse effect, which is responsible for changing global climate patterns.

Greenhouse effect—Rise in the average temperature on the earth as a result of the buildup of chlorofluorocarbons, methane, and other polluting outputs of industrialization.

Gross domestic product (GDP)—Value of total outputs of goods and services produced in a country, usually over one year.

High-tech corridor (technopole)—Place where technology and computer industries agglomerate.

Human Development Index (HDI)—Measurement developed by the United Nations to rank development levels of countries.

Industrialization—Growth of manufacturing activity in an economy or a region; usually occurs alongside a decrease in the number of primary economic activities within a country.

Industrial Revolution—Social and economic change that began in England in the 1760s when the industrial geography of England changed significantly and later diffused to other parts of western Europe. In this period of rapid socioeconomic change, machines replaced human labor and new sources of inanimate energy were tapped. Coal was the leading energy source, fueling the industrial revolution in England's textile-focused industrial explosion.

Informal sector—Network of business transactions that are not reported and therefore not included in the country's GDP and official economic projections.

International trade approach—Method of improving a country's development that pushes the country to identify its unique set of strengths in the world and to channel investment toward building on these strengths. To compete internationally, this approach argues, a country must find out what it can offer the world and capitalize on that good or service.

Less-developed country—Country on the economically poorer side of the development spectrum.

Liberal development theories—Theories that claim development is a process through which all countries can move.

Locational interdependence—Theory that industries choose locations based on where their competitors are located.

Maquiladora zone—Special economic zone on Mexico's northern border with the United States.

Market orientation—Result of locating weight-gaining industries near the marketplace for the heavier product.

Material orientation—Result of locating weight-losing industries near the supply of raw resources.

More-developed country—Country on the wealthier side of the development spectrum.

Multinational corporation (MNC)—As one of the primary agents of globalization, this business has headquarters in one country and production facilities in one or more other countries; sometimes called a transnational corporation.

New industrial country (NIC)—Country that has recently established an industrialized economy based on manufacturing and global trade.

New international division of labor—Division of the manufacturing process across several countries, wherein different pieces of the product are made in different countries, and then the pieces are assembled in yet another country.

Nongovernmental organization (NGO)—Organization not run by a government but by a charity or private organization that supplies resources and money to local businesses and causes advancing economic and human development.

North–south gap—Pattern of development levels in which most most-developed countries exist in the Northern Hemisphere whereas most less-developed countries exist in the Southern Hemisphere.

Outsourcing—An MNC relocating a piece (or all) of its manufacturing operations to factories in other countries.

Pacific Rim economic region—Together with China and Japan, the four Asian Tigers make up the core of the Asian economic engine.

Primary economic activities—Economic activities that revolve around getting raw materials from the earth.

Privatization—Selling of publicly operated industries to market-driven corporations.

Purchasing power parity (PPP)—Measurement tool of calculating exchange rates so that each currency buys an equal amount of goods as every other currency.

Quaternary economic activities—Include assembling, distributing, and processing information, and managing other business operations.

Quinary economic activities—Subset of quaternary activities that involves the highest-level of decision making, such as that of a legislature or a presidential cabinet.

Secondary economic activities—Economic activities related to processing raw materials (acquired through primary activities) into a finished product of greater value.

Self-sufficiency approach—Approach to improving economic development by building a country's independence from foreign economies and fostering its ability to provide for its own people.

Spatially fixed costs—Costs that remain the same no matter where a business chooses to locate.

Spatially variable costs—Costs that vary (or change) depending on the location of an industrial activity.

Special economic zone—Region offering special tax breaks, eased environmental restrictions, and other incentives to attract foreign business and investment.

Structural adjustments—Stipulations that require the country receiving an international loan to make economic changes in order to use the loan.

Structuralist theories—Argue that less-developed countries are locked into a vicious cycle of entrenched underdevelopment by the global economic system that supports an unequal structure.

Substitution principle—Asserts that an industry will choose to move to access lower labor costsdespite higher transportation costs.

Sustainable development—Balance between the pace of human development and the environment that supports that development. A level of development that does not destroy the earth's ability to regenerate its resource supply for future generations of inhabitants of the earth.

Tertiary economic activities—Economic activities that move, sell, and trade the products made in primary and secondary activities.

Weight-gaining process—Process that takes raw materials and creates a heavier final product.

Weight-losing processes—Manufacturing process that takes raw materials and converts them into a product that is lighter than the raw materials that went into making the finished product.

PART 4 Some Suggested Web Resources for Further Exploration

World Bank: http://www.theworldbank.org/

The official site of the World Bank includes valuable data resources, graphs, charts, and discussions related to development levels and economic trends throughout the world.

International Monetary Fund: http://www.imf.org/

This site, like the World Bank's, contains many valuable data resources on economic trends and efforts throughout the world. Particularly interesting is the section on debts owed by various countries.

U.S. Agency for International Development: http://www.usaid.gov/

This is the primary arm of the U.S. government responsible for extending financial assistance to foreign countries. Check out this site to learn more about the countries receiving money from the U.S. government.

European Union Commission on Humanitarian Aid: http://ec.europa. eu/echo/index_en.htm

This is the EU's primary arm for extending financial aid to foreign countries needing humanitarian assistance.

Doctors Without Borders: http://www.doctorswithoutborders.org/

One of the world's largest nongovernmental organizations, Doctors Without Borders has a mission of providing medical care to some of the world's most desperately poor people. The organization provides health care to people who are victims of armed conflict, epidemic diseases, and disasters and those excluded from health care.

Globalization 101: http://www.globalization101.org/

This site contains a look at the key issues related to globalization, sponsored by the Carnegie Foundation for International Peace. The site is very valuable for students and includes lessons for teachers.

PART 5 — Pre-Exam Practice

Terms Review Quiz

Use the Terms Review list or your own memory to determine the extent of your knowledge of key terms and concepts. Remember, the AP exam does not include this kind of exercise, but it is included here as a review tool.

1. _____ Economic activities related to processing raw materials (acquired through primary activities) into a finished product of greater value.

2. _____ Giving a price tag or value to something that was not previously perceived as having a money-related value.

3. _____ Manufacturing process that takes raw materials and converts them into a product that is lighter than the raw materials that went into making the finished product.

4. _____ Occurs when other regions suffer a drain of resources and talent due to agglomeration in another region.

5. _____ Asserts that an industry will choose to move to access lower labor costs despite higher transportation costs.

6. _____ Costs that vary (or change) depending on the location of an industrial activity.

7. _____ Clumping together of industries for mutual advantage.

8. _____ Process of improving the material condition of people through the growth and diffusion of technology and knowledge.

9. _____ Value of total outputs of goods and services produced in a country, usually over one year.

10. _____ Network of business transactions that are not reported and therefore not included in the country's GDP and official economic projections.

11. _____ Industry not bound by locational constraints and able to choose to locate wherever it wants.

12. _____ Pattern of development levels in which most most-developed countries exist in the Northern Hemisphere whereas most less-developed countries exist in the Southern Hemisphere.

13. _____ As one of the primary agents of globalization, this type of business has headquarters in one country and production facilities in one or more other countries; sometimes called a transnational corporation.

14. _____ Include assembling, distributing, and processing information, and managing other business operations.

15. _____ Process that takes raw materials and creates a heavier final product.

16. _____ Twentieth-century German geographer who created the least cost theory to predict the locational decisions made by industrial operations.

17. _____ Growth of manufacturing activity in an economy or a region; usually occurs alongside a decrease in the number of primary economic activities within a country.

18. _____ Place where technology and computer industries agglomerate.

19. _____ Widening difference between development levels in more-developed and less-developed countries.

20. _____ Theory that exemplifies the structuralist perspective, arguing that the political and economic relations among countries limit the ability of less-developed countries to modernize and develop.

21. _____ Ability of a country (or place) to produce a good or offer a service better than another country can.

22. _____ Massive corporation operating a collection of smaller companies that provide it with specific services in its production process.

23. _____ Region offering special tax breaks, eased environmental restrictions, and other incentives to attract foreign business and investment.

24. _____ Organization not run by a government but by a charity or private organization that supplies resources and money to local businesses and causes advancing economic and human development.

25. _____ Division of the manufacturing process across several countries, wherein different pieces of the product are made in different countries, and then the pieces are assembled in yet another country.

Multiple-Choice Review Questions

1. Which of the following best captures a structuralist interpretation of the development gap?

    (A) Less-developed countries fall behind more-developed countries in levels of wealth and development because people in less-developed countries do not work efficiently.

    (B) Less-developed countries are in stages 2 and 3 of Rostow's model.

    (C) More-developed countries have reached higher development levels because of coal deposits beneath their soils.

    (D) Less-developed countries remain poor because they are continually exploited by more-developed countries seeking resources and labor.

    (E) Less-developed countries will develop in the same pattern as more-developed countries have, but it will take time and self-improvement.

2. A factory process transforming raw corn into processed baby food falls into which economic category?

    (A) Primary   (D) Quaternary

    (B) Secondary   (E) Quinary

    (C) Tertiary

3. Fashion Incorporated, a company headquartered in New York, has contracted with a clothing factory in Thailand to make its sweaters. Fashion Incorporated has determined the value of the workers in the factory to be $1.50 per hour of work. This scenario exemplifies which of the following geographic concepts?

    (A) Privatization   (D) Structural adjustments

    (B) Commodification   (E) Deglomeration

    (C) Fair trade

4. All the following are areas of early industrialization EXCEPT

   (A) England
   (B) Ukraine
   (C) the Ruhr region
   (D) Ohio region
   (E) Madrid

5. Which of the following is most likely a footloose industry?

   (A) Automobile production
   (B) Computer chip production
   (C) Steel production
   (D) Bottled-water production
   (E) Paper production

6. All the following are used in the human development index equation EXCEPT

   (A) average income per person
   (B) average life expectancy
   (C) women's level of equality
   (D) literacy rate
   (E) infant mortality rate

7. All the following were Asian Tigers EXCEPT

   (A) South Korea
   (B) Taiwan
   (C) Japan
   (D) Singapore
   (E) Hong Kong

8. Murthy Industries owns a factory located in northern Mexico, on the border with the United States. Given this information, which of the following terms most likely applies to the factory that Murthy Industries owns?

   I. Maquiladora
   II. New industrial country
   III. Special economic zone
   IV. Export-processing zone

   (A) I
   (B) I, II, and IV
   (C) II and III
   (D) I, III, and IV
   (E) I, II, III, and IV

9. Shanghai, China, is industrializing and growing at exponential rates. The urban migration stream into Shanghai is one of the largest in Chinese (and urban) history. As a consequence of this pattern, many smaller surrounding villages and cities are losing talented workers and resources that are being channeled into Shanghai's rapid growth. This situation best illustrates

   (A) backwash effects   (D) footloose industries

   (B) Fordism   (E) ubiquitous industries

   (C) foreign direct investment

10. Which country has been a high-volume destination for global firms from the United States outsourcing their tertiary-sector jobs?

    (A) Mexico   (D) Indonesia

    (B) China   (E) Malaysia

    (C) India

11. Which of the following geographic theories would be used to explain the concept of neocolonialism and postcolonial dependency?

    (A) world-systems analysis

    (B) Rostow's modernization model

    (C) concentric zone model

    (D) locational interdependence

    (E) demographic transition theory

12. Maquiladora areas in Mexico and free-trade regions in China are examples of

    (A) growth poles   (D) special economic zones

    (B) trade blocs   (E) high-tech corridors

    (C) exclusive economic zones

13. Which of the following people performs activities most likely to be classified as part of the informal sector of the economy?

    (A) Broadway-musical dancer

    (B) Janitor at a public high school

    (C) Street hot-dog vendor

(D)   Doctor.

(E)   Newspaper journalist

14.   The IMF agreed to give Kenya a $2 million loan on the condition that the government would sell an electrical company in its northern region to a private corporation. This situation demonstrates which of the following concepts?

(A)   Commodification

(B)   Cumulative causation

(C)   Fair trade

(D)   Arbitrage

(E)   Structural adjustments

15.   Which of the following sectors currently claims the highest percentage of workers in the United States?

(A)   Primary

(B)   Secondary

(C)   Tertiary

(D)   Quaternary

(E)   Quinary

16.   In Weber's least cost theory, what are the two major factors he assumed controlled cost of transportation?

(A)   Value of the good being transported and distance to market

(B)   Size of the market and price of the good

(C)   Durability of the good and size of the market

(D)   Distance to market and terrain

(E)   Weight of the good and distance to market

17.   A company that produces a weight-gaining product decides to locate a factory near its market. This is an example of

(A)   material orientation

(B)   market orientation

(C)   footloose orientation

(D)   locational interdependence

(E)   deglomeration

18. The value of a country's total output of goods and services in that country during a year is called its

    (A) foreign direct investment   (D) inflation rate

    (B) purchasing power parity   (E) gross domestic product

    (C) human development index

19. Allowing MNCs to outsource without any regulation except for the basic forces of market capitalism is known as

    (A) free trade   (D) market orientation

    (B) foreign direct investment   (E) a primary economic activity

    (C) the informal sector

20. As a country industrializes, a decrease in jobs usually occurs in which sector?

    (A) primary   (D) quaternary

    (B) secondary   (E) quinary

    (C) tertiary

Free-Response Review Questions

Globalization has been praised and criticized by geographers and economists.

(A) Define the concept of *multinational corporation (MNC)* and relate it to the new international division of labor. Give an example to illustrate this relationship.

(B) Define *outsourcing*, and explain its effect on economic conditions both in the core and the periphery with reference to two of the following regions:

   •   North America

   •   Latin America

   •   East Asia

   •   Western Europe

PART 6

Pre-Exam Practice Answers

Terms Review Answers

1. Secondary economic activities
2. Commodification
3. Weight-losing process
4. Backwash effect
5. Substitution principle
6. Spatially variable costs
7. Agglomeration
8. Development
9. Gross domestic product (GDP)
10. Informal sector
11. Footloose industries
12. North–south gap
13. Multinational corporation (MNC)
14. Quaternary economic activities
15. Weight-gaining process
16. Alfred Weber
17. Industrialization
18. High-tech corridor (technopole)
19. Development gap
20. Dependency theory
21. Comparative advantage
22. Conglomerate corporation
23. Special economic zone
24. Nongovernmental organization
25. New international division of labor

Multiple-Choice Answers

1. **(D)**

   The structuralist perspective argues that the structure of the world's economy inherently keeps less-developed countries poor at the benefit of more-developed countries. (A) places the blame on the citizens of a less-developed country, which does not hit at the structure of the global economic system. (B) represents Rostow's modernization model, which is the antithesis of the structuralist perspective in that it assumes that all countries can move through the same development pattern and does not account for the economic system of interlocking, interrelated economies. (C) might be related to the structuralist perspective in a weak way in that it hints at resource inequalities, but its relationship to the structuralist perspective is more removed than the clearer relationship of (D). (E) is representative of liberal theories similar to Rostow's modernization model and does not account for cultural and contextual differences within the global economic system.

2. **(B)**

   Secondary economic activities take raw materials gathered in the primary sector and transform them into marketable products.

3. **(B)**

   Commodification is placing a price tag or priced value on something never thought to have a price or value, like a person. (A) is selling a publicly owned business to a private corporation for profit, (C) is moderating free-market capitalism to protect workers' interests, (D) are required changes that a country must agree to make in its economy to receive a loan for which it has applied, and (E) is when companies move out of an agglomerated region because the costs of agglomeration outweigh its benefits.

4. **(E)**

   All the other answer choices were early dominant centers of industrialization.

5. **(B)**

   Computer chip production is not usually tied to any one location and can move around the globe, free of locational restraints, because the resources that go into the final product are not related to one particular place. The other answer choices depend on resources tied to a location, preventing these production processes from moving freely about the world.

6. **(C)**

Though some geographers argue that analyses of women's rights and levels of equality should be included in the HDI equation, those issues are not officially included in the equation.

7. **(C)**

Japan industrialized before the rise of the Asian Tigers, which followed Japan's pattern of industrial and economic development by developing a comparative advantage in a high-tech industrial activity.

8. **(D)**

Located in northern Mexico, this plant is likely in a maquiladora zone, or Mexican factory zone constructed to attract U.S. factories. This zone is also a special economic zone and an export-processing zone because it gives U.S. factories incentives to move there and produce their goods targeted for export. However, Mexico is not an NIC because its economy has not transitioned toward industrialization and dominance.

9. **(A)**

Backwash effects are the negative consequences of agglomeration and growth that pull talented workers and resources from the surrounding regions. (B) is the model of industrial production that breaks down the production process into an assembly line of differentiated operations. (C) is when a company invests or spends money in a foreign country to build a factory or employ its workers. (D) are industries that are not tied down to one particular place but can move freely throughout the world to find the ideal location, and (E) are industries that cannot be separated from their market because their sole purpose is to provide immediate goods to their market (like a dairy farm).

10. **(C)**

India's service-related sector is soaring so high that many U.S. industries are relocating (outsourcing) their service-related jobs to India. Mexico, Indonesia, China, and Malaysia are other places where U.S. global firms are outsourcing secondary-sector jobs, such as factory labor.

11. **(A)**

Neocolonialism and postcolonial dependency describe the continued economic and sociopolitical dependence experienced by countries that were once colonies but are now intricately dependent on their former colonial masters. World-systems analysis divides the world into a core, semiperiphery, and periphery, and it describes core growth as related to an exploitation of the periphery, which supports this exploitative concept of postcolonial relations. (B) assumes that all countries can develop in an equal way and makes no mention of structural impediments to develop as seen in neocolonial explanations of inequality. (C) is a model of urban land use; (D) explains industrial location as related to competition; and (E) explains population change, which could be related to neocolonialism but is not as explanatory of it as is world-systems analysis.

12. **(D)**

Special economic zones offer trade incentives and free trade to companies that locate their industries within the boundaries of the zones. Maquiladora zones in northern Mexico offer U.S. industries special incentives and trade options for locating their factories there, as do free-trade zones in communist-controlled China. (A) are regions experiencing extraordinarily fast industrial growth centered on one particular start-up industry, (C) are areas in the ocean or territorial waters that are exclusively controlled by one country, and (E) are growth poles centered on a high-tech industry.

13. **(C)**

The informal sector of the economy comprises jobs and activities undetected and unreported to the government, the "under the table" operations, such as a hot-dog vendor who takes cash and does not report it to the government. The other jobs are more likely to be reported because they are linked to a greater organizational structure that will pay taxes and health care for their employees.

14. **(E)**

Structural adjustments are changes a country must make in its economy to gain access to the loans it needs; (A) is putting a price on something that has not had a price or been viewed as needing a price before. (B) is the exponential, "snowball" growth that a region experiences once it becomes successful, such as when one city draws all the investment, while the others suffer. (C) is trade that is regulated to ensure that workers' rights are protected, and (D) is when a company produces a product at a very low price and then sells it for many more times its production cost.

15. **(C)**

With the Industrial Revolution in the 20th century, the U.S. economy shifted toward the secondary sector, but the United States is currently transitioning away from the secondary sector in a massive deindustrialization trend that has boosted the service-oriented tertiary sector into dominance.

16. **(E)**
    Weber assumed the weight of the good and the distance were the two most important factors in the cost of transportation. All the other answer choices were not considered in Weber's model.

17. **(B)**
    A company that locates a factory near its market is trying to reduce the cost of shipping the heavier end product as opposed to the lightweight raw materials. (A) occurs when a company locates near its source of raw materials to reduce the cost of shipping heavy raw materials used to produce a lighter final product. (C) describes a company that is not tied to any location by the cost of shipping. (D) is when industries choose their location based on where their competitors are located. (E) is the "unclumping" of industries because of the negative effects and higher costs associated with overcrowding.

18. **(E)**
    A country's gross domestic product (GDP) shows the total of all of the goods and services counted within a country's domestic borders over the course of a year. Usually, the (GDP) is a helpful measure of the country's overall economic strength. (A) is money invested by firms in countries outside of their home country's borders; (B) is a metric often used to compare standards of living among countries; (C) is an equation developed by the United Nations to compare development among countries; (D) is a measure of the devaluation of money and currency.

19. **(A)**
    Free trade is the idea that governments should not inhibit companies but should allow market forces to determine how businesses operate. (B) is the investment by an MNC in a foreign country's economy, (C) is a network of business transactions that are not reported and therefore not included in the country's GDP and official economic projections, (D) occurs when weight-gaining industries locate near the place where the "heavier" product will be sold, and (E) are economic activities that revolve around getting raw materials from the earth.

20. **(A)**
    As industrialization spreads through a country, it usually leads to a decrease in primary-sector jobs because machines make it possible for fewer people to harvest raw materials from the earth while at the same time creating jobs that process the increased amount of materials gathered. (B) Industrialization is a secondary-sector activity, producing goods from raw materials. (C), (D), and (E) are economic sectors that can follow the growth of industrialization.

Free-Response Answers

The following is a list of suggested main points for each part of the question.

Part A

- A multinational corporation is a company, often a conglomerate corporation, which has headquarters in one country and owns production sites in other countries.

- MNCs are the commanding heights behind the new international division of labor, in which production processes are broken down not only under the roof of one factory but also among countries and across borders. A computer's parts may be made in several different countries before it is finally assembled into its marketable product.

- An example of a multinational corporation is Nike, which has its headquarters in the United States but has production sites and factories in other countries.

Part B

- Outsourcing occurs when a multinational corporation sends part of its production process to a site in another country, such as when a modem company outsources its customer service call center to a city in Indian.

- Outsourcing has affected both the core and the periphery in different ways.

- Often the headquarters of MNCs exist in the core countries in North America and western Europe, while their labor-intensive production sites exist in peripheral less-developed countries in East Asia and Latin America.

- The profits reaped are often shipped back to the countries in the core rather than being reinvested in the peripheral production regions.

- The peripheral countries are left with higher pollution levels.

- The core countries' workforces must adapt to the outsourcing of secondary economic activities. They must train for service-sector and high-tech jobs.

- Workers in peripheral regions are often paid much lower wages than what the MNCs would have to pay workers in their headquarter countries (hence, a potential reason the MNCs outsource).

- Workers in the periphery rarely get to buy the goods they are manufacturing, because the goods are produced for export to the countries in which the

MNCs are headquartered. Further, these products are often too expensive for purchase in the less-developed countries.

- Maquiladoras are U.S.-owned factories in northern Mexico. U.S. companies are given incentives, such as lower taxes and lower labor costs, to move their factories into northern Mexico.

- Northern Mexico benefits from the job opportunities provided, though it suffers from the industrial agglomeration—pollution and overcrowding.

- One possible response would discuss the Asian Tigers and the economic growth of China through industrialization and special economic zones.

- Women often suffer the most in less-developed countries because they must work in the often poorly regulated factories that exploit their labor.

Chapter 8

Cities and Urban Land Use

Introduction

While riding atop the tallest Ferris wheel in the world, a resident of London looked down at the sprawling mass of the city whose history spans millennia. The rider wondered how and why London grew and developed in the brilliant way that it did. As the wheel rotated down and the rider's bird's-eye view of the dazzling cityscape, or city landscape, refocused earthward, the Londoner once again became an urban dweller, walking through the "mighty heart" of the urban settlement, almost like an ant in its hill.

Permanent settlements like London developed after human groups learned to practice agriculture. Such permanent places evolved from clans and villages, eventually, into larger urbane city structures that reflect layers and generations of **urbanization**, the growth and diffusion of city landscapes and urban lifestyles. Heavy

(Photo by: M. Paananen)

Figure 8.1. The London Eye, the tallest Ferris wheel in the world

urbanization in more-developed countries is typical, but even in less-developed countries, the number of urban dwellers has grown massively in recent years. Many city governments in less-developed regions are struggling to manage the explosive urbanization. In fact, about 10 million people die each year because of hazardous conditions caused by overcrowding and inadequate infrastructural support in areas experiencing explosive urbanization.

Geographers analyze where urbanization developed and why these places became hearths of urban civilization, or **urban hearth areas**. Geographers analyze the path of urbanization's diffusion from these hearths and the related gaps in urban development among different countries, some of which are nearly 100 percent urban, while others are still largely rural. In addition to analyzing the patterns of urbanization, geographers look into internal spatial relationships in cities. For example, geographers ask why there are socioeconomic ghettos and how a city's transportation system affects its spatial development. Further, geographers compare cities. How does Mumbai, India, compare in organization and development to Moscow, Russia?

Key Questions

- *What is the definition of city, and how do cities across the world vary?*

- *Where are cities located and why do they exist where they do?*

- *What are the paths through which urbanization diffused?*

- *What are the political, economic, and cultural functions of cities?*

(Photo by: Morguefile)

Figure 8.2. A view of the British Parliament from the London Eye

- *What are the differences in the ways cities have grown and developed?*

- *Why are there differences in levels of urbanization throughout the world?*

- *How do urban places interact spatially through communication and transportation?*

- *How do theories like Christaller's central place theory and the rank-size rule help explain and predict settlement geography?*

- *What is urban hierarchy? How and why have cities' rankings changed over time?*

- *What do patterns in urban land use look like, and how do they compare to rural land use patterns?*

- *Where and why do patterns in ethnic and racial segregation exist in urban places?*

- *What types of inner-city transportation systems exist? How do those systems affect city development and spatial organization?*

- *What types of agricultural traditions exist in various urban cultures?*

- *How do comparative models of internal city structure—like the concentric zone, sector, and multiple-nuclei models—explain and predict city growth and development?*

- *How do urban places differ across the world? For example, how do Middle Eastern cities differ from western European cities in layout and design?*

- *What are modern trends in urban development, such as edge cities and gentrification?*

- *What will cities look like in the future?*

PART 1 Defining Urbanism

Urban Population Size

At least 3 billion people, nearly half of the world's population, live in areas considered urban. But what makes a place urban rather than rural? What is the definition of *urbanism*? The answer is that the definition depends on time and culture. The size of a stationary population is part of the equation but varies according to historical context and location. Ancient cities had populations ranging from 2,000 to 20,000. However, Mesopotamia's Ur, one of humanity's most ancient, massive urban civilizations, was home to 200,000 city dwellers, and that pales in comparison to its modern-day neighbor, Baghdad, with a population of nearly 7 million. The size of a city also varies geographically. In Portugal, any population of more than 10,000 people makes up a city; in Ethiopia, a city is at least 2,000 people; and in Norway, a population of only 200 is considered a city. Thus, a city usually is qualified by a population considered large for its time and place.

As of 2005, China, India, and the United States had the largest numbers of urban dwellers in the world.

However, "cityness" is not simply measured by the number of people in a given place. For example, the congregation of people at the Super Bowl may be as large as the populations of some cities, but no one would consider that gathering of football fans a city. The presence of a government and some form of boundaries, though often difficult to determine, are part of the definition of cityness. A city's boundaries often become unclear as the city sprawls and merges with other growing urban places. For example, Cool Springs is a growing urban area near Nashville, Tennessee. Many urban dwellers in Cool Springs consider themselves Nashville citizens, while others call themselves residents of Franklin, another nearby city. Yet Cool Springs is intricately linked to the Greater Nashville economy and culture.

Metropolitan Statistical Areas

Because it is often difficult to determine city boundaries, the U.S. Census Bureau uses the term **metropolitan statistical area (MSA)** to describe a geographic unit of area that includes a central city and all its immediately interacting counties, with commuters and people directly connected to the central city. An MSA is an urbanized region with a minimum of 50,000 people in it. Often the boundaries of MSAs overlap. For example, the cities in what is called the Triangle in North Carolina—Raleigh, Durham, and Chapel Hill—started out as individual cities or towns and have grown into one another, becoming so interrelated that they are now seen as one MSA. Such a massive urban "blob" of overlapping, integrated metropolitan areas, whose distinctive boundaries are increasingly becoming difficult to find, was named a **megalopolis** by the geographer Jean Gottmann, who originally applied the term to the metropolitan areas of Washington, D.C., and Boston.

The U.S. Census Bureau also uses a unit called a **micropolitan statistical area**, an area of the surrounding counties integrated into a central city with a population of 10,000 to 50,000. Many formerly rural areas have been reclassified as micropolitan statistical areas.

With 35 million residents in 2005, the metropolitan area of Tokyo was by far the most populous urban agglomeration in the world.

Economic Diversity

The economy of a place is another layer in classifying it as rural or urban. Economically, cities often have more diversity in economic activities, from dog walking and hair styling to surgery and broadcast journalism. For example, Japan defines a city as a place with at least 50,000 inhabitants, 60 percent or more of whom are engaged in trade, manufacturing, or other nonagricultural activities.

Once ancient humans domesticated animals and began to grow crops, they could produce surpluses of food, leading to permanent settlement and eventually economic diversification, with people performing various jobs rather than just farming. Money developed, records were written, laws were codified, and services were provided. Surrounding farmlands grew to support cities. Traditionally, larger cities have shown a high degree of economic diversity.

Cultural Diversity

A cultural layer also plays a role in defining a place's degree of urbanity, or cityness. A tourist in Paris can visit the Paris Opera House, tour the Louvre Museum and see the Mona Lisa, and eat delicious Indian food. Cultural diversity, complexity, and vibrancy also contribute to a geographer's classification of a place as a city.

A Definition?

Thus, our search for a clear definition of what makes a city has led us to more of a process of comparison than a sentence or two. Geographers use factors such as the size of the population in a given historical and geographic context, economic diversity, governmental organization, delineated boundaries, and cultural complexity to analyze the degree to which a place is considered urban.

PART 2 Origin and Evolution of Cities

Hearths of Urbanization

Where did cities and urbanism, or urban life, begin? The earliest cities were born around 3500 BCE and were spawned from agricultural villages. Earliest hearths of urbanism existed in Mesopotamia, between the Tigris and Euphrates rivers in former Iraq; the Indus River region in modern Pakistan; the Nile Valley in modern Egypt; the Huang He River valley in modern China; and in Mexico and Peru. Several qualities are common among places that were urban hearths: a dependable water supply, a long growing season, domesticated plants and animals, plenty of building materials, and a system of writing and records.

In addition to cities that evolved from agricultural villages, some cities grew as established marketplaces, where traders came together to buy and sell goods from across the region. Many such points of exchange grew near waterways and long-distance overland trade routes. Urbanism spread westward throughout the Mediterranean region because of Phoenician, Greek, and Roman traders, and it spread eastward through overland and caravan trade routes through Persia and Pakistan to India, China, and then Japan. Even at this early stage, specialization began to occur, as certain cities began to focus economic development on the goods over which they had a comparative advantage. Specialization would evolve into a global economic network of specialized cities, each defined largely by its dominant economic specialty, such as Hollywood's specialization in movie making.

Greeks and Romans erected cities as centers of political and administrative control over their conquered regions. Such cities often were built in a planned gridlike pattern. Other cities grew as centers of religious ceremony, such as urban places in China that were determined to be holy sites and designed in geometric shapes to reflect related religious beliefs.

Preindustrial Cities

City landscapes varied significantly across the world before industrialization. However, **preindustrial cities** did share some traits across time and space. Many rural settlements surrounding urban spaces provided agricultural products and foodstuffs to the urban dwellers, who in turn provided various economic functions. Cities have always provided economic functions from their surrounding rural lands. Preindustrial cities served as trade centers and gateways to foreign lands and markets. After the fall of the Roman Empire by 600 BCE, European preindustrial cities experienced a decline in development. Exploration and trade associated with the growth of mercantilism led to a surge in urban growth. Mercantilism is the system in which European governments controlled economic activity and aimed to gain as many new colonies as possible to increase their nations' wealth and supplies. The European drive to grab foreign land and resources fueled the construction and creation of cities in the conquered colonies. Many **colonial cities** contained European imprints, such as wide boulevards and prominent structures evoking classical architecture. Importantly, colonial cities were constructed with the aim of exporting raw resources from the colonial city back to the "mother country." (The colonial city is discussed in more detail in the section on the Latin American city model.)

By the beginning of the 1500s, most cities were located in an arch of trade centers that extended from London to Tokyo, a line of cities known as the **urban banana** because of its crescent or banana-like shape. Thus, the focus of urbanization existed in powerful cities, like London, Paris, Constantinople, Venice, Cairo, Nanking, Hanchow, and Osaka. The urban banana of dominant cities resulted from both site and situation factors. Site factors are the physical and cultural characteristics of a place that help us learn something about the city, factors like arable land, street layout, and building materials. Situation factors relate to how a city fits into the larger urban network, such as proximity to major trade routes and other urban places.

Internally, preindustrial cities often had a diverse mix of economic functions in any given space, rather than the specific zoning that came with industrialization. This meant that shops, markets, homes, and government offices were typically found jumbled together in urban space. However, economic segregation often existed, with the wealthier elite living closer to the city center. Also, in feudal European cities, guilds led to the clumping of certain functions in particular areas of the towns, which suggests the existence of a crude form of zoning, or functional differentiation. Again, though, cultural differences affected internal, urban spatial organization.

Industrialization and City Structure

In 1800, only 5 percent of the world's population lived in cities; by 1950, 16 percent lived in cities; by 2000, nearly 50 percent of the world's population lived in cities. What caused this explosion in urbanization? Largely, the diffusion of industrialization is responsible for urbanizing the world's people, albeit at unequal levels. More than 75 percent of the world's population living in more-developed countries is considered urban. However, only about 40 percent of the world's population living in less-developed countries is considered urban. Specifically, Africa and Asia are the least urbanized continents on the earth, while North America is the most urbanized continent, with nearly 80 percent of its people living in urban places. In 2001, only 35 percent of the African population was considered urban.

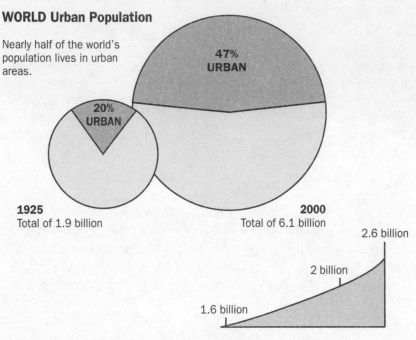

WORLD Urban Population

Nearly half of the world's population lives in urban areas.

20% URBAN

47% URBAN

1925
Total of 1.9 billion

2000
Total of 6.1 billion

2.6 billion

2 billion

1.6 billion

Figure 8.3. Urban growth on a global scale

The European Industrial Revolution and its related imperialism triggered this diffusion of city growth. Urbanization grew in a snowball process, as the growth of factories and urban jobs provided attractive opportunities to rural people struggling to make a living farming. Thus, the Industrial Revolution, which started in England and then diffused to other parts of the world, created a steady rural-urban migration pattern. Supporting this pattern was the demographic transition linked to the second agricultural revolution, which led to an increasing population size to supply more people to work in the cities and fuel industrialization.

Geo Factoid

England's population was 24 percent urban in 1800 and 99 percent by 1999.

Population growth and rural-urban migration led to massively growing urban spaces that were, in many ways, overwhelmed with the influx of urban in-migrants. Manchester, England, grew from having less than 80,000 residents in 1750 to nearly 500,000 urban dwellers just a century later. As industrialization and urbanization spread to North America after it developed in western Europe, the U.S. city of

Figure 8.4. World map displaying global patterns in urbanization

Chicago grew from 30,000 inhabitants in 1750, to 500,000 by 1830, and to more than 1.5 million by 1900. Accompanying those surprising rates of urbanization were challenging social, economic, and cultural changes, such as the growth of slums, hazardous pollution levels, deadly fires, the growth of urban prostitution, and the exploitation of children. Manchester and Chicago were early examples of **shock cities**, urban places experiencing infrastructural challenges related to massive urbanization.

By the mid-1700s, the dominance of land-based trade cities was declining as sea-trade centers like Saint Petersburg and Bombay began to grow rapidly. By the early 1900s, most of the world's greatest cities were American or European industrial cities, like Manchester, Chicago, and Barcelona. The **industrial city** had a different function from its preindustrial precursor. Rather than serving mainly as an administrative, religious, trade, or gateway city, the industrial city's primary function was to make and distribute manufactured products.

Urban Systems

All urban places are part of an interlocking **urban system** of cities that operate within a network of spatial interaction. In other words, urban places are *interdependent*, not independent, and exist in a spider web of interacting parts. Geographers analyze the spatial distribution of cities, trying to determine why the spider web looks the way it does. They wonder how and why cities grow in the geographic locations they do. Why are there fewer large cities than small cities? Do larger cities drain the smaller cities of needed resources, keeping those smaller cities lower on the food chain of the urban system? Do larger cities provide needed services to the smaller urban places in the system?

Christaller's Central Place Model

German geographers were very interested in explaining land use patterns. Recall from Chapter 6 that Johann Heinrich von Thünen studied the geographical patterns of *rural* land use in the 1800s. In the 1930s, the German geographer Walter Christaller proposed the **central place theory** as a means of studying the geographical patterns of *urban* land use, specifically looking to explain and predict the pattern of urban places across the map. Just like von Thünen, Christaller created his model in an isolated state, or ideal world, with assumptions of a flat land surface, a uniformly distributed rural population, equal transportation methods spread throughout the space, and an evolutionary movement toward the growth of cities.

To explain the pattern of urban places across the world, Christaller used four main ideas in his model:

1. **Central places** are urban centers that provide services to their surrounding rural people, collectively referred to as the central place's **hinterland**.

2. The **threshold** is the *minimum* number of people needed to fuel a particular function's existence in a central place. The more unique and special an economic function, the higher its threshold. For example, the threshold of a doughnut shop is lower than the threshold of a neurosurgical center for several reasons. First, doughnuts are eaten, by a large number of people, providing a larger customer base. A neurosurgical center providing brain surgery services has a smaller customer base because fewer people need their services at any one time. Second, the doughnut shop has a lower maintenance cost than a state-of-the-art neurological center. Third, the workforce needed in the neurological center of a hospital requires a higher degree of specialized training compared with the workers in a doughnut shop.

3. The **range of a good or service** is the maximum distance a person is willing to travel to obtain that good or service. The range of a doughnut shop is much smaller than the range of a neurological brain surgery center because a person is willing to travel much farther for lifesaving brain surgery than for a chocolate doughnut.

4. **Spatial competition** implies that central places compete with each other for customers.

With these ideas, Christaller's model illustrated how and why economic functions drive the locational pattern of cities across geographic space. Central places contain economic functions with high thresholds and high ranges that require large populations to serve groups of smaller central places existing around them. Even

- • Village
- • Low-Order Central Place
- • High-Order Central Place

—— Low-Order Market Area Boundary

—— High-Order Market Area Boundary

Figure 8.5. Hexagonal market areas predicted by Christaller's central place theory

the smallest central places, with low-threshold, low-range functions (like the dough-nut shop or a gas station) serve a surrounding population, usually a rural settle-ment. Whereas von Thünen's model resulted in concentric rings of rural land use, Christaller's model predicted a hexagonal pattern of urban central places. In this pattern, smaller central places will be located closer together, because consumers will not be willing to travel as far for lower central place functions, like doughnut shops and gas stations. However, larger central places will be located farther away from each other because consumers are more willing to travel a longer distance to obtain higher central place functions, like brain surgery.

Urban Hierarchy

Essentially, the central place theory predicts that if a population is evenly distributed, there will be a hierarchy of evenly spread central places to serve that population. Such an **urban hierarchy** is a system of cities consisting of various levels, with only a few cities at the highest level and increasingly more settlements on each lower level. The position of a city within the hierarchy is determined by the types of central place functions it provides. The higher the position on the hierarchy, the higher the population being served by the central place, and the more variety of central place functions performed in the city. It is the volume of choices in an urban center that makes it more dominant in the urban hierarchy than a smaller town.

In other words, central places at the top of an urban hierarchy provide functions with the highest ranges and highest thresholds, whereas cities at the lower levels of the urban hierarchy provide lower-range, lower-threshold functions. Providing the highest-range, highest-threshold functions that could not be supported in smaller urban places, Chicago sits at the very top of the urban hierarchy. Actually, some geographers argue that Chicago is a second-level city now, behind Los Angeles and New York.

In the hierarchy, few urban central places are at the top of the hierarchy, while many urban central places are at the bottom. This is logical if you think about it. Few large cities provide functions like those of Broadway and Wall Street in New York City, and many smaller cities provide gas stations and fast-food restaurants. Cities like Chicago sit atop the urban hierarchy in the United States, whereas urban places like Miami and Saint Louis occupy the next level of the urban hierarchy.

Applying the Central Place Theory

The central place theory provides one piece in the jigsaw of understanding and predicting geographic patterns of urban places. Theoretical models like the central place theory can add analytical power to understanding patterns, such as urban growth. Since the 1970s, U.S. urban places in the South and the West have been growing much faster than cities in the old manufacturing areas of the Northeast and Midwest. Many people attribute this pattern to the larger numbers of people, like retirees, moving to those areas for warmer weather and more fun and relaxation. However, the central place theory offers another piece of the explanation.

Over the last 30 years, populations in the U.S. South and West have increased and become wealthier overall. Several factors have contributed to this trend, including increased immigration into the regions from Latin America; construction of military bases and space stations by the U.S. government, and the official ending of legal segregation. With more people and wealth, more services were needed. Several cities stepped up to fill this need. Cities like Phoenix, Atlanta, and Dallas moved up on the urban hierarchy as they grew to offer more central place functions to the newly growing populations. While cities like Atlanta have been important for the past 100 years, their levels of importance on the national level have increased.

As with any hierarchy, as these cities moved up the ladder, other cities moved to fill their places. Cities like Tampa, San Antonio, and Charlotte moved up to fill the new spots. Consequently, some older, manufacturing cities in the Northeast and Midwest began to suffer. Remember, the central place theory assumes that people needing a particular service (from buying a doughnut to getting brain surgery) will travel to the *closest* available option to obtain that service. For example, if a southerner needed to access central place functions, such as neurosurgery, he or she no longer needed to travel to Chicago. Instead, he could go to a major surgery center in Atlanta.

Rank-Size Rule and Centrality

With the existence of an urban hierarchy, there is a pattern in city size distribution across geographic space. In other words, there is a relationship to a city's population size and its place on the urban hierarchy within its urban system. Statistically, this is predicted by the **rank-size rule**, which states that the nth largest city's population size in a region is $1/n$ the size of the region's largest city's population. For example, the fourth largest city in a region is predicted to be one-fourth the size of the region's largest city's population size.

While the urban hierarchy in the United States urban system roughly conforms to the rank-size rule prediction, some urban systems have disproportionately large cities, known as *primate cities*, as mentioned in Chapter 5. Cities with such **primacy**, like Buenos Aires, London, Paris, and Rio de Janeiro, are often much larger than the second-largest city in the country's urban hierarchy. Buenos Aires, Argentina, is nearly 10 times the size of its second-largest city, Rosario, and thus would have a high degree of *primacy*. Additionally, when a city dominates economic, political, and cultural functions more than expected based on its population size, the city demonstrates a high degree of centrality, or the possession of central place functions. For example, Managua, Nicaragua, demonstrates urban centrality because its population accounts for only about 30 percent of Nicaragua's total population, but the city controls nearly 40 percent of the country's economy.

World Cities

Within the network of interacting cities comprising the world's urban system are **world cities**, powerful cities that control a disproportionately high level of the world's economic, political, and cultural activities. World cities, sometimes called global cities, have a high degree of centrality in the global urban system. The group of world cities has shifted with the changing nature of the global urban system. In the 1600s, London, Lisbon, and Amsterdam were world cities in the mercantile economy of that century, and by the 1700s, Rome and Paris had become world cities. In the rising industrialization of the nineteenth century, Berlin, Chicago, New York, and Saint Petersburg became world cities.

Today's world cities are less concerned with serving as administrative centers of power over imperialism and trade. Instead, modern world cities are centers of global financial decisions, flows of information, and multinational (or transnational) corporations driving the global economic and political landscape. Another term related to being a world city is *panregional influence*. New York City is a world city with **panregional influence**, meaning its range extends beyond North America into the other two centers of economic control, Europe/Africa/Middle East and Asia/Oceania. Home to powerful media outlets, financial institutions, global corporate headquarters, and political organizations like the United Nations, New York City is a world city because it influences a larger percentage of world affairs than its share of the world's population would suggest. In other words, New York City is a world city because its global influence is larger than its share of the earth's population. Also, a city can be considered a world city when it dominates a distinct area of global affairs. For instance, Amsterdam is a global financial center, and Milan exerts powerful influence over fashion and design.

Megacities

Though not considered world cities, **megacities** have a high degree of centrality and primacy, thereby exerting high levels of influence and power in their countries' economies. All megacities are large, having more than 10 million inhabitants. Beijing, Cairo, Mexico City, and Jakarta are examples of megacities that serve to connect the earth's world cities with the smaller central places in their countries' urban hierarchies. Thus, Jakarta's businesses and political units connect with New York City's services and bring them to Indonesia's people through spatial interactions in the form of trade, transportation, communication, and even migration.

Modern Trends in Urbanization

In 1950, only 30 percent of the world was urbanized and 83 urban places had a population of 1 million or more people. By 2000, the number of urban places with 1 million or more people had risen to nearly 400. Estimates project that by 2010 nearly 500 such cities will be spread across the earth.

There is an important distinction between level and rate of urbanization. **Rate of urbanization** is the speed at which the population is becoming urban, while **level of urbanization** is the percentage of people already considered urban. For example,

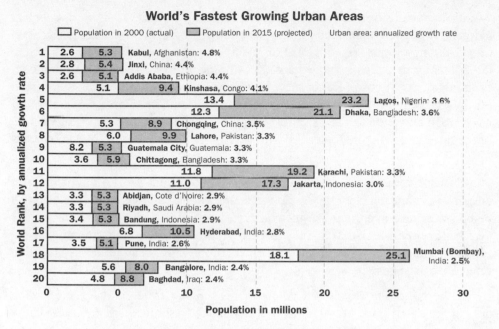

Figure 8.6. The fastest-growing urban areas in the world

the level of urbanization in the United States is nearly 75 percent, meaning that nearly 75 percent of the U.S. population lives in urban places. However, the rate of urbanization in the United States is much lower than the rate of urbanization in China, for example, which is experiencing a rapid rate of urbanization despite its lower level of urbanization, which is nearly 30 percent.

After the communist takeover of China in 1949, Chairman Mao Zedong committed China to agricultural development, not urbanization, and restricted his people's movements into cities. After Mao's death in 1976, his successor, Deng Xiaoping, charted a course of urbanization for China, a course that has led to the doubling of its urban population from 1981 to 2001. Among the less-developed, peripheral countries experiencing high rates of urbanization are Nigeria, Pakistan, Indonesia, and Egypt, where the megacity of Cairo is the focus of urban growth.

An important trend in modern urbanization is its diffusion to less-developed parts of the world and its uneven spread. Overall, the highest rates of urbanization are occurring in places with the lowest levels of urbanization, in less-developed, peripheral countries. In 1950, nearly 60 percent of urbanized places were in *more*-developed countries. By 1980, 19 of the largest 30 metropolitan areas in the world were in the *less*-developed world, indicating a clear surge in the growth of urban cities in less-developed countries. Although rates of urbanization in core countries are relatively low, their levels of urbanization are already high. The populations of most core countries are already above 75 percent urban. In semiperipheral countries, rates of urbanization are also high.

Cities in more-developed countries are fading from the list of the world's largest cities. According to the United Nations, between 1980 and 2000, Lagos, Dhaka, and Cairo, among others, joined the list of 30 largest cities in the world. By 2010, the Nigerian city of Lagos is projected to become the third-largest city on the globe, after Tokyo and Mumbai. European cities like Milan and London will have dropped off the list of the 30 largest cities. By 2010, New York City, Osaka, and Paris will have fallen down the ladder as well. Some projections speculate that nearly all 30 of the largest metropolitan places in the world will be in less-developed countries by 2010.

As we have seen, urbanization in less-developed countries is often focused on one or two major cities with a high degree of primacy and centrality, rather than being spread evenly throughout the country's landscape. Such intensely high rates of urbanization in less-developed countries are straining the infrastructures of the growing cities. Their growth has happened so quickly that these cities are often referred to as shock cities.

Large migration streams of young adults moving from rural areas to urban areas in pursuit of job opportunities challenge already-strained urban places. These young rural-urban migrants are often depressed to find filthy living conditions and demeaning working conditions. Unable to find housing, many new migrants build **squatter settlements (or *barriadas*)**—makeshift, unsafe housing constructed from any scraps they can find on land they neither rent nor own. The 1996 United Nations Conference on Human Settlements estimated that 600 million people were living in unsafe and life-threatening conditions in cities. Further, as much as 33 percent of the world's urban households live in absolute poverty.

Nearly 60 percent of households in Lagos, Nigeria, and Nairobi, Kenya, are not connected to running water.

Models of Urban Systems

As you walk through London, the sense of place you see and feel is quite different from the sense of place you perceive as you walk through Moscow, Russia, or even Nashville, Tennessee. Cities vary greatly in aspects such as their architecture, layout, density, social organization, depending on the political factors, cultural context, and how they have evolved over time.

Although two cities may have similar sizes, economic functions, and standards of living, like Chicago and New York, they can vary in their spatial layout and

Key Finding from the 2001 United Nations Conference on Human Settlements

"A country's global success rests on local shoulders. For the good of all citizens, city and state must become political partners rather than competitors. If accommodation requires new political arrangements, institutional structures or constitutional amendments, it is never too early or too late to begin making changes. . . . Gathering of evidence by putting in place proper information systems and diagnostic tools is a practical first step. Good information will provide the common platform for dialogue among stakeholders—an essential part of the process—as they approach a vision for the future and set priorities for conservation and change. *The main goal is to make the structures of governance more responsive to individuals, households and communities so that both national and local authorities can better serve civil society, each through separate but complementary instruments.*"

unique sense of place. Even as cities become more interconnected with globalization and even as people travel and communicate more frequently among the world's urban places, cities still show the imprints of the generations of people and economic functions that have influenced their growth. Just as the rings within old trees reflect layers of growth, city landscapes reflect the periods of their greatest development. Even the relatively young cities of the United States (compared with ancient cities like Rome) vary significantly depending on their historical eras of growth, their "growth spurt" phases, if you will.

Borchert Model of Urban Evolution

In the 1960s, **Samuel Borchert** studied U.S. cities and linked historical changes to urban evolution. **Borchert's model of urban evolution** defined four categories of cities based on the transportation technology that dominated during the era when the city hit its initial growth spurt and found a comparative advantage in the economy.

In stage 1 of this model are cities that first grew during the "sail wagon" era of 1790–1830 mostly near ports and waterways for transportation. In stage 2, "iron horse" cities were born and grew around the rivers and canals, during the early industrial years of 1830–1870, when the railroad and steamboats were rapidly spreading. By stage 3, the "steel rail" epoch of 1870–1920, the Industrial Revolution was at full steam in the United States. Powered by the steel industry, industrial cities blossomed, particularly around the Great Lakes. Stage 4 cities were born around 1920 and were intricately linked to car and air travel, leading to a maze of road networks and the rapid spread of suburbs. Stage 4 saw the growth of new, more-influential cities in the South.

For example, Pittsburgh began as Fort Duquesne and was on the landscape by 1760. Pittsburgh hit its peak in stages 2 and 3, and then its level of influence began decreasing. The reason a city becomes more or less prominent is related to its comparative advantage. In 1720, Pittsburgh had less of a comparative advantage because no one could reach it by ocean. By 1900, Pittsburgh had developed into a powerhouse because of its central location (situation) and the fact that it had railroads and canals feeding it all the raw materials needed to fuel its industrial revolution.

Such a comparative advantage, though, can weaken as other cities hit their growth spurts and begin to develop dominant comparative advantages. For example, Flint, Michigan, hit its growth spurt and developed a comparative advantage grounded in the Industrial Revolution but lost its dominance as the U.S. economy shifted away from an industrial, factory-based economy toward a more service-based economy.

Cultural and Regional Urban Diversity

Differences among cities often result from their cultural and national contexts. Monuments, temples, and pyramids dominate ancient Chinese and Mexican cityscapes to show the dominance of their governments and religious philosophies, as well as to provide settings for important functions. In contrast, medieval Islamic cities were organized with tiny, winding, dead-end streets into which mosques and government buildings were woven and not prominently displayed. Medieval Muslims believed their buildings should blend into the urban landscape, usually to ensure privacy and protection from outsiders. Visiting Europeans often described such Islamic cities as "mysterious," showing how different the Europeans' outlook on urban structure was from the Muslim view.

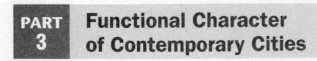

PART 3 **Functional Character of Contemporary Cities**

Basic Versus Nonbasic Jobs

What do cities do, and what types of products do they make to bring in the goods their people need to survive? First, we need to distinguish between basic and nonbasic employment sectors of a city's economy. The **basic employment sector** brings money into an urban place and gives the city its primary function (think *basic brings in* money). For example, Flint, Michigan, was dominated by its

Figure 8.7. Two different urban architectural styles in Shanghai, China, reflecting different influences on the city's urban culture and landscape

Figure 8.8. Islamic architecture often puts windows and openings above human reach and covers windows to increase the privacy of the inhabitants

basic employment sector of automobile manufacturing. The cars made in Flint's basic employment sector were exported to other places, which in turn sent money into Flint's economy for the cars. Chapel Hill, North Carolina, is a small city with a basic employment sector dominated by the existence of the University of North Carolina, a basic employment function that exports information and knowledge in exchange for bringing money into Chapel Hill.

The **nonbasic employment sector** in a city comprises jobs that shift money within the city, not outside the city as basic jobs do (think *nonbasic* does *not* *export jobs*). Teachers, janitors, fire departments, dry cleaners, street cleaners, and air-conditioner repair companies are all examples of nonbasic employment. In other words, the nonbasic sector is largely responsible for maintaining a city's infrastructure.

Usually, the larger the city, the higher the percentage of nonbasic jobs, because these larger cities often have more infrastructural needs, from window washers, dry cleaners, and parking attendants, to expert subway technicians and financial consultants. In a smaller city, gas stations and restaurants may be part of its basic employment sector because residents from nearby rural regions may come into the small town to purchase those services, thereby bringing money into the town from outside.

Since most cities have the same types of nonbasic jobs, it is the basic employment sector that defines a city and gives it more of its unique sense of place and presence in the economy. Steel-mill towns, warehouse port facilities, oil refineries, country music towns, movie industry hotspots—all are examples of elements of the basic employment sector that heavily influence a city's sense of identity. Nashville is defined by its country music industry, an integral part of its basic employment sector.

Multiplier Effect

Cities often try to build their economies around the basic employment sector, which brings in money from the outside. For example, a car factory will bring money in because the cars are produced and sold to people outside the city. In fact, the addition of one basic job tends to give rise to more jobs, including non-basic jobs. This pattern is called the **multiplier effect**. For example, the addition of production line jobs in an automobile factory, which are basic jobs producing a good for export and interaction with other places, creates the need for new janitors, air-conditioning repair people, electricians, and building inspectors, among others—nonbasic jobs. Likewise, adding a movie production company requires nonbasic jobs like carpenters, hair stylists, and costume makers to keep it operating. Thus, the addition of a basic job multiplies the number of jobs within a community. Adding a nonbasic job does not have the same multiplying effect.

Agglomeration

Sometimes a successful industry that generates a multiplier effect becomes a leader in its field throughout the world. When a business achieves such a recognized status as an industry leader, it is called a growth pole, and it often acts as a magnet, attracting other industries and businesses near it to take advantage of its "shine" and innovation. When these businesses locate near the growth pole, it leads to agglomeration. As discussed in Chapter 7, agglomeration is the clumping of industries to take advantage of each other's resources.

For example, the University of North Carolina at Chapel Hill has had success in health research that has led to its becoming a growth pole, attracting other research industries to the area. The resulting agglomeration of research industries has led to a powerful economic multiplier effect, with the number of new jobs skyrocketing and generating new wealth. However, traffic buildup and overcrowding have occurred in the region as a result of the growing Research Triangle Park. Another negative result of agglomeration is the backwash effect; recall from Chapter 7 that this is caused when the growth poles and related agglomeration draw talent and economic growth out of the surrounding regions and do not allow for equal development and the even spread of development throughout the landscape.

Changing Employment Mix of Contemporary Cities

North America's basic employment sectors were once dominated by manufacturing and industrial activities. However, the nature of America's basic employment sector is moving away from industrial jobs and toward professional and financial services. Instead of being dominated by factory-based production processes, modern **postindustrial city** economies are focused more on display and consumption. Old factories are being converted into shopping malls; former waterfront industrial ports are being turned into parks for recreation; old warehouses are turning into art galleries. Postindustrial architecture is often characterized by **postmodernism**, a style that emphasizes diversity and free form rather than the uniformity and symmetry that characterize the classical Greco-Roman roots of Renaissance- and Enlightenment-era architecture.

While the Industrial Revolution changed cities into smog-laden centers of manufacturing and distribution, the modern economy is moving cities back to the Greco-Roman concept of a city, one in which the resources needed by vibrant economic diversity and lifestyles come from centers of production outside the city. Most of the factory-produced goods that Americans buy are now made in foreign countries and shipped into the United States. In exchange, U.S. cities provide services to the foreign production regions, like financial and entertainment services.

Thus, the old industrial cores of the United States, like Chicago and Manhattan, are becoming **deindustrialized**, with their factory-based economies transitioning to economies dominated by the service sector. Such cities have experienced "boom and bust" cycles, in which their service sectors boomed while their manufacturing sectors busted. Some Sunbelt cities, like Austin, Texas, never had any manufacturing base, so their service sectors have boomed without any commensurate bust. Critics of the changing functional nature of U.S. cities worry that if cities become heavily dependent on foreign producers, Americans could be left out economically because they cannot make their own products. Also, factory jobs often offered more security to workers than the increasingly dominant retail and fast-food-type service-sector jobs dominating urban economies. Moreover, factory work required few computer skills and little education. In modern-city economies, people without training and education are left out of the mix, leading to higher rates of crime and unemployment. There are simply fewer factory jobs that provide adequate incomes. Educators are having to analyze and adjust to this prominent economic shift to train students to fill the more highly skilled jobs now in demand.

 PART 4 **Built Environment and Social Space**

Comparative Models of Urban Systems

To understand why cities are spatially organized in various ways, geographers have developed models that explain and predict the internal structures of cities. Most focus on patterns of internal growth within U.S. cities, but some of the following models can be extended to explain and predict foreign cities. Each model described here possesses a **central business district (CBD)**, or original core of its economy, like the nucleus of a cell. However, the degree of influence and geographic location of the CBD varies throughout the models.

Figure 8.9. Three urban land use models

Concentric Zone Model

Developed in the 1920s, the **concentric zone model** was the first model to explain and predict urban growth. Based on urban growth in Chicago, the concentric zone model is the original foundation on which the other models of urban growth were built. The model suggests that a city's land use can be viewed from above as a series of concentric rings, like the rings of a tree trunk that has been cut. As the city grows and expands, new rings are added and older rings change their function and character. For example, a ring of land use that was once where houses were built might become more of a business sector. Old houses may be transformed into offices. The model assumes a process called **invasion and succession (or succession migration)**, in which new arrivals to cities tend to move first into the inner rings, near the CBD. Eventually, people and economic activities in the center are pushed out into farther rings. Invasion and succession is essentially a series of migration waves, with one group moving in and establishing itself.

For example, let's consider the arrival of European immigrants to a hypothetical U.S. city. As German immigrants start to move in (or invade), the English immigrants already living in the city become aggravated and choose to leave, thus making more room for more Germans. This creates a German-dominated center and an English-dominated outer ring. When Italian immigrants decide to move in, they cannot afford to live in the English areas, so they head for the German center. The arrival of new immigrants causes aggravation in the German-dominated core, prompting the Germans to "push out" toward the next ring where the English had settled, thus pushing the English settlers further out. In this example, each new group is looked down on by all the others as the "new guys" who are "ruining" things.

Because of this constant invasion and succession pattern, often a ring known as the **zone in transition** forms just outside the CBD. This ring never becomes developed because investors know it will constantly be caught in the shifting urban pattern. Sometimes this zone of transition is called skid row.

One of the most important components of the concentric zone model is the CBD, known as "downtown" in the United States. In the concentric zone model, the CBD is the land use ring nearest the point of maximum accessibility and visibility in the city, a point known as the **peak land value intersection**. The highest real estate prices and competition for land are found in this model's CBD. Land values decrease moving in all directions away from the CBD, so that the farther out a ring of urban land use, the less expensive the land. This pattern is known as a **bid-rent curve**, which predicts that land prices and population density decline as distances from the central business district increase. A ritzy real estate firm would want to buy a sleek headquarters in the heart of the CBD to show importance in the community and to have access to the downtown's powerful people and businesses. However, a factory would probably not choose to locate in the CBD. Rather, a factory would most likely move away from the CBD, where it can purchase more land for less money to build its horizontal factory.

The concentric zone model shows a pattern in which the architecture and function of buildings match in each concentric ring of urban land use. In other words, the architecture of the houses in a concentric ring occupied by suburban families matches its function to provide families with houses. A suburban-style house is not a likely sight in the heart of Chicago's CBD.

Sector Model

The concentric zone model assumes that a city offers equal access to the CBD in all directions radiating from it. However, in the 1930s, geographers discovered a twist on the concentric zone pattern, known as the **sector model**. The sector model grew out of geographers' observations that there were urban land use zones of growth based on transportation routes and linear features like roads, canals, railroads, and major boulevards, not just concentric zones around the CBD. However, both the concentric zone and sector models feature a strong CBD. The sector model explains that similar land uses and socioeconomic groups clumped in geometric sectors radiating outward from the CBD along particular transportation routes. Therefore, in urban patterns conforming to the sector model, many factories and industrial activities follow rail lines, lower socioeconomic housing follows lines of public transportation, and sectors that service visitors are located along major highways. By the late 1940s, the assumptions of both the concentric zone and sector models no longer applied to urban growth patterns. Therefore, a new model was born: the multiple-nuclei model.

Multiple-Nuclei Model

Unlike previous models that focused on a strong CBD, the **multiple-nuclei model** suggests that growth occurred independently around several major focal points, like airports, universities, highway interchanges, and ports. These focal points may be distant from the "original" CBD and only loosely connected to it, suggesting a reduced dominance of the CBD in urban growth. The multiple-nuclei model recognizes that land use zones often pop up at once, in chunks. Industrial parks, shopping centers, and housing zones are built in one giant sweep of construction and are only very loosely connected to the original heart of the city. In the 1950s, suburban neighborhoods were created overnight.

The model does not suggest that the CBD is necessarily unimportant, but it does show that new areas of intense urban growth (the nuclei) can grow simultaneously around key nodes of access or industry. In the 1950s, geographers saw the growth of **exurbs** (extra-urban areas) or rings of wealthier rural communities that grew just outside of the suburbs and were hotbeds of continued urban growth and development. Early inhabitants of exurbs commuted over parkway systems and commuter rails.

Urban Realms Model

As the automobile became increasingly prevalent in the 1970s, the **urban realms model** was developed to explain suburban regions that were functionally tied to mixed-use suburban downtowns with relative independence from the CBD. This model grew from the increasing independence developed by the nuclei within the multiple-nuclei growth pattern. Beyond simply being focal points of urban growth, these nuclei had evolved into independently functioning "urban realms." The urban realms model recognized that many people's daily lives and activities occurred within a fixed activity space within a portion, or urban realm, of a larger metro region. In these urban realms, one could find suburban downtowns, filled with all the amenities needed for living, including businesses, eateries, medical care, and so forth.

Importantly, many North American city and suburb dwellers want to escape from the bustling pace of modern urban life. Beginning in the 1970s, larger numbers of middle- and later-aged (older) citizens were leaving cities and suburbs and moving to more rural areas and small towns outside the city's busy way of life in a pattern called **counterurbanization**. Plus, with the advent of the Internet and telecommunications technology, people no longer had to commute physically; they could work from home and send everything electronically, a trend called **telecommuting**.

A Comment on All the Models

Importantly, the classic models can be combined to understand a particular city's urban growth pattern. A CBD may be encircled by rings and sectors with a variety of nuclei and realms existing farther from the CBD along a beltway, for example.

Latin American Cities and the Three Models

The classic models can be applied to illustrate urban growth patterns in various cultural settings, such as those in Latin America, especially in formerly Spanish colonial regions. During the medieval period, cities in Europe were laid out in unplanned jumbles of open spaces and intertwined streets, but the 1400s saw a rebirth in Greco-Roman architecture and urban design. Europeans then diffused those classical structures throughout their colonies. In fact, Spain passed a law in 1573 ordering that all its colonial cities would be built according to Greco-Roman designs, with prominent, rectangular plazas dominated by a cathedral and major governmental buildings. These plazas resembled the sectors featured in the sector model.

As with the CBD, a ring of commercial and residential areas formed close to the plaza. The CBD was more important in the focus of Latin American cities because suburbanization was not nearly as strong in Latin America. Instead of rings of wealthy residential areas outside the CBD, as in the suburban rings of North American cities, the zones of the Latin American city model typically decrease in wealth moving away from the CBD. Squatter settlements and abject poverty often mark the rings outside of the centers of Latin American cities. Moreover, Latin Americans traditionally live downtown, giving the inner cities more of a residential nature than is typical of North American cities. Because of the intensity of use, a Latin American city usually has no zone of transition. Further, because Latin Americans people tend to stay in the inner cities (and cannot get loans to move), they tend to upgrade their existing homes, rather than moving out to different neighborhoods as residents of North American cities usually do.

Like other less-developed regions, many Latin American cities have struggled to meet the demands of rapid urbanization. For example, Latin American urban governments are finding it difficult to provide infrastructural support to the growing urban populations. The massive numbers of rural-urban migrants often find shelter by building makeshift homes in the **periferico**, or zone of peripheral squatter settlements. However, industrial parks and government housing projects are starting to pop up in Latin American cities, like nuclei in North American cities, although these urban focal points are less common in Latin American cities because of the limited amount of capital available for development and investment in such projects by developers.

Transportation and Urban Infrastructure

How does transportation infrastructure affect the development of land use and building types? Consider a colonial city built for walking and horse-riding citizens, before motorized transport. The general store, market shops, government offices, bank, and doctor's office were usually located on one block, because people would come to town for their general needs and not be able to transport themselves long distances to obtain each service.

As modes of transportation became more efficient and speedier, the organization and use of urban space changed. Land use and building types could be more specialized and more widespread. As people increasingly used public transportation lines, various districts of urban land use developed along those lines of urban growth, which radiated out from the downtown in a **star-shaped pattern**. Department stores, urban housing zones, and office parks grew around the lines of transportation, which provided the threshold population needed for business to continue. Paris, London, New York City, and Chicago were among the first cities to develop subways and elevated trains to transport massive amounts of people and products into and out of the urban core.

By the 1920s and 1930s, the use of the car had exploded on the scene. City streets were widened and a few parkways were constructed, but the pattern of a strong CBD and zones of straight-line urban growth radiating from it continued until after the 1950s, when the U.S. government enacted the National Defense Highways Act, which ordered the construction of highways to facilitate the movement of military equipment, such as nuclear missiles, during the cold war. Although urban growth continued in the star-shaped pattern established with earlier transportation modes, by the 1970s and 1980s, a new urban form was born with the construction of beltways, or highways that encircled urban areas. With the growth of these outer-belt freeways, people could quickly access areas around the CBD, which led to the growth of regional offices, industrial parks, and shopping centers in new nuclei within the metropolitan complex. Often these new nuclei of urban growth were located in places of urban accessibility, such as on highway exits.

Urban Sprawl

Joel Garreau referred to the self-sufficient urban villages that developed within a greater metropolitan complex, often at highway exits, as **edge cities**. The result of this explosive growth empowered by the growth of highways and beltways is referred to as **urban sprawl**, the diffusion of urban land use and lifestyle into formerly nonurban, often agricultural lands. The pattern of urban sprawl has raised continued problems related to uneven development and changing land use patterns.

Political Organization and Urban Sprawl

The political organization of urban areas largely contributes to the sprawling nature of U.S. cities. Suburbs often fight for independence from the metropolitan government so that their inhabitants can have their own mini-governments and tax bases. A central city surrounded, even strangled, by independently governed suburbs is left with a limited tax base.

Figure 8.10. Edge cities linked to Chicago

If the inner city is predominantly occupied by a lower socioeconomic (poorer) tax base, then the amount of taxes the inner city can collect for its schools and infrastructure is limited. Saint Louis, Missouri, had nearly 1 million residents in 1950, but by 2000 the city proper had only 300,000 residents, because most people had fled to the independently governed suburbs surrounding the city. Many suburbs have legislated their exclusivity, passing **restrictive covenants**, or laws prohibiting low-income housing. The wealthy town of Franklin, Tennessee, has recently passed a law requiring all homeowners to pay a hefty fee to have all their power lines put underground because "it looks better." Obviously, this would be financially impossible for anyone with a low income.

Ghettoization and Uneven Development

Because of political influences, transportation infrastructures, and location preferences, urban sprawl has led to uneven development and **ghettoization**, the growth of areas of concentrated poverty. **Uneven development** refers to urban development that is not spread equally among a city's areas, leaving some areas richly developed and others continually poor and decrepit. Uneven development is often caused by **cumulative causation**, when money flows to areas of greatest profit, places where development has already been focused, rather than to places of greatest need. Agglomeration is another process related to cumulative causation. Opulent skyscrapers and multimillion-dollar malls often exist only minutes from some of the poorest, most underdeveloped regions. Racially and ethnically uniform neighborhoods continued to exist even after the 1960s Civil Rights Act prohibited legal racial segregation.

Urban ghettos originally comprised mostly immigrants, such as newly arrived Irish, Italian, and German people, but even larger African American, Hispanic, and Asian ghettos have emerged since the 1950s. Why and how do modern-day ghettos continue to exist? Several surreptitious practices by real estate developers contributed to the existence of modern-day clusters of economically and racially segregated urban land use zones.

Blockbusting, Redlining, and Racial Steering

Some real estate developers profited from this pattern of ghettoization, preying on racism to sell as many houses as they could. They used **blockbusting** tactics, like placing advertising in African American newspapers and church bulletins, offering an extremely low price for a house in a white neighborhood. When African American families came to look at the advertised house, the malicious real estate agents incited racially charged turmoil in the primarily white neighborhood, urging the white families to sell their homes at low prices and move to the suburban fringes, where they would be "safe" from "invading" minority groups.

Using another form of the malicious blockbusting practice, unscrupulous real estate agents vandalized houses in a neighborhood to induce panic and urge people to move out. Then the same real estate agents would profit from the turnover and clear the land to build large, urban housing structures, which often degenerated into tenements. Blockbusting is now illegal.

Some less-obvious tactics influenced the continued existence of urban ghettos and segregated urban land use patterns. Real estate agents, either intentionally or unintentionally, steered people to certain neighborhoods and not others based on their race, a practice known as **racial steering**, which is now illegal. Further, banks would **redline** minority districts, refusing to give loans to people moving to minority-dominated areas on the grounds that the statistical improbability of successful development in these zones meant the loans would not be repaid. Though redlining is now illegal, the practice contributed to a vicious cycle wherein developers and minority families wanting to develop and improve ghettoized regions could never get money to do so, which only contributed to the continually impoverished character of those zones.

Several real estate trends today contribute to the continued uneven pattern of development in many urban places. The development of gated communities is often based on an underlying fear of crime and, sometimes, racial integration. These types of developments are often constructed with strict regulations and covenants, binding their residents to specific house colors, sizes, and rules, even as to the size of the dogs they can have.

Gentrification

Gentrification is a process wherein older, urban zones are "rediscovered and renovated" by people who move back to the inner city from their suburban fringes.

Gentrification is a trend that is bringing money into urban areas thought to be underdeveloped and poor. Have you driven through your city's inner area and seen a trendy new loft-apartment complex built in an old, abandoned factory warehouse? If so, that is gentrification. Many people see gentrification as a great solution to recharging a city's inner core that was suffering because of **suburbanization**, the growth of suburb neighborhoods and commuter families, and the continued flight of wealthier classes out of the inner city.

However, critics of gentrification see it as only increasing uneven development. They think gentrification is pushing lower-income families from their homes to make way for glitzy, trendy buildings that only the rich can afford. New businesses do come to the region to cater to the rich "gentrifiers," but the people who were living in the neighborhood in the first place cannot afford to patronize the new businesses or buy into the gentrified housing complexes. In this sense, critics claim, gentrification does not help reduce poverty and uneven development but actually pushes the urban poor from their neighborhoods and divides the urban landscape into ghettos and highly priced gentrified districts.

(Photo by: J. Dabu)

Figure 8.11. A block that has been renewed, or gentrified, by investors

Strategies to Curb the Negative Effects of Urban Sprawl

Urban sprawl is one of the greatest challenges facing North American cities. In larger metropolitan cities, you often find suburbs, shopping malls, and industrial parks only miles from the original CBD. However, it is rare to find effective mass transit systems in North American cities. Often this is a result of the high cost of installing subways and other mass transit systems that were not built into the urban infrastructure as the city grew. Some strategists suggest building railways for commuters, more bike paths, government-organized carpools, and special bus lanes. In fact, in Nashville, a new train system is being developed for commuters coming from edge cities into the downtown area.

European cities like London have worked to limit urban development to a particular area. London installed a **green belt** to contain its urban core, forcing all urban development to occur within that boundary and not sprawl. North American cities have a difficult time setting such boundaries because they can attract investors who want to develop these lands and grow the city at the expense of rural lands. Also, city governments profit from new taxes in suburbs. Portland, Oregon, has effectively instituted a boundary to contain urban sprawl. There developers must focus on the land within the established boundary, forcing revitalization of the inner city, not outward growth. Portland also built an effective mass transit system.

Another approach to lessening the negative effects of urban sprawl exists in **street morphology**, or the organization of street patterns. Many newer suburbs are built around cul-de-sacs and loop streets, rather than the traditional grid design of inner cities. Developers tend to favor cul-de-sacs and looping streets to provide privacy for their neighborhoods, reducing traffic and noise throughout the neighborhood by allowing only one or two entrances and exits into and out of the neighborhood.

However, such a street morphology channels all traffic in the same direction toward the major highways. Drivers have no way to escape the traffic, often leading

(Photo by: Derek Jensen)

Figure 8.12. Urban sprawl and its effect on landscape distinctiveness

to backups at the few entrances and exits to the development. Pedestrians cannot walk and cars cannot escape traffic jams by going around the block.

Related to urban morphology are zoning laws. In many shock cities, governments have not effectively created boundaries to channel growth and development into organized sectors, or zones. For example, in some cities experiencing high rates of urbanization, makeshift low-income housing may exist next to large polluting factories. Such lack of zoning contributes to infrastructural decay and problems in functional land use.

Recent Trends in Neo-Urbanism

Recent innovations in neo-urbanism, or the new urban landscape, include **planned communities**, which are neighborhoods with master-planned housing designs, recreational facilities, security systems, and other features that stress uniformity and common identity in the landscape. One planned community in Memphis includes a small grocery store and ice-cream shop, pedestrian-friendly walkways, a Starbucks, and a golf cart for each family in the neighborhood.

Health experts are encouraging North American developers to build pedestrian walkways to help reduce cardiovascular disease, which is increasing in the United States, partly because of Americans' total reliance on automobile travel rather than walking. The Memphis planned community also includes a picnic area and community gathering spot for everyone in the neighborhood to use. In fact, many recent urban designs include **festival settings**, or large recreational areas for communities, such as waterfront parks along the rivers in Nashville, Tennessee, and Louisville, Kentucky. Another feature of the new urban landscape is **office parks,** zones of urban land exclusively set aside for corporate offices and often include incentives to businesses for locating offices in them.

The popular name for neo-urbanism is the livable city movement. Portland, Oregon was an innovator in the movement and is one of the best examples of it. Other well-known examples are Chattanooga, Tennessee; Asheville, North Carolina; and Fort Collins, Colorado. Fort Collins calls itself a "wellness city" and requires a certain percentage of the businesses to focus on wellness. Chiropractors, massage therapists, bike shops, gyms, and other businesses that help people finding "wellness" without using drugs are highly encouraged by the city's planners.

<table>
<tr><td>**PART**
5</td><td>**Chapter Review**</td></tr>
</table>

Models Review

Central Place Theory

This model was devised in the 1920s to predict and explain the growth patterns of North American urban spaces. Its main principle is that cities can be viewed from above as a series of concentric rings; as the city grows and expands, new rings are added and old ones change character. Key elements of the model are the central business district and the peak land value intersection.

Borchert's Model of Urban Evolution

Borchert created this model in the 1960s to predict and explain the growth of cities in four phases of transportation history: stage 1, the "sail wagon" era of 1790–1830; stage 2, the "iron horse" era of 1830–1870; stage 3, the "steel rail" epoch of 1870–1920; and stage 4, the current era of car and air travel that began after 1920.

Sector Model

This model predicts and explains North American urban growth patterns in the 1930s in a pattern in which similar land uses and socioeconomic groups clustered in linear sectors radiating outward from a central business district, usually along transportation corridors.

Multiple-Nuclei Model

Developed in the 1950s, this model explains the changing growth pattern of urban spaces based on the assumption that growth occurred independently around several major foci (or nodes), many of which are far away from the central business district and only marginally connected to it.

Urban Realms Model

This model was developed in the 1970s to explain and predict changing urban growth patterns as the automobile became increasingly prevalent and large suburban "realms" emerged. The suburban regions were functionally tied to a mixed-use suburban downtown, or mini-CBD, with relative independence from the original CBD.

Terms Review

Basic employment sector—Group of economic functions that bring money into an urban place and represent the city's primary functions.

Bid-rent curve—Graph showing the predicted decline in cost of land and population density as you move away from the central business district in the concentric zone model.

Blockbusting—Tactic (now illegal) that contributed to ghettoization; used by real estate agents to get people to move out of their homes because of fear of racial integration.

Central business district (CBD)—Original core of a city's economy, like the nucleus of a cell.

Central place—Urban center that provides services to people living in the surrounding rural areas.

Colonial city—City whose primary identity is as a colony of an invading or conquering imperial power, often showing forced cultural imprints of the colonizer.

Counterurbanization—Increase in rural populations resulting from the out-migration of city residents from their city and suburban homes in search of the peace and tranquility of nonurban lifestyles.

Cumulative causation—Contributing factor to uneven development; occurs when money flows to areas of greatest profit, places where development has already been focused, rather than to places of greatest need.

Deindustrialized—Refers to an industrial city whose factory-based economy has transitioned to an economy dominated by the service sector.

Edge city—Self-sufficient urban area within a greater metropolitan complex; often develops on highway exits.

Exurb—Area of growth outside the central city and surrounding suburbs; its growth is fueled by people exiting the city and suburbs in search of the peace and tranquility of more-rural lifestyles.

Festival setting—Area within an urban place built for community gatherings, such as a park or waterfront.

Gentrification—Process in which older urban zones are rediscovered and renovated by people who move back into the inner city from their suburban fringes; resulting influx of new money raises prices and pushes out lower-income residents.

Ghettoization—Growth of areas of concentrated poverty in urban places.

Green belt—Boundary encircling an urban place and limiting the sprawl of the city, forcing inward development and reinvestment in a city's core.

Hinterland—Area serviced by a central place.

Industrial city—City that grew during the Industrial Revolution. Rather than serving mainly as an administrative, religious, trade, or gateway city, the industrial city's primary function was to make and distribute manufactured products.

Invasion and succession (or succession immigration)—Pattern of inflow of new migrants to the central business district in the concentric zone model and then the related pushing of existing inhabitants outward to rings outside the center, thereby causing changing land use patterns.

Level of urbanization—Percentage of people considered urban.

Megacity—City that has a high degree of centrality and primacy; although not a world city, it exerts high levels of influence and power in the country's economy. All of megacities have populations over 10 million inhabitants.

Megalopolis—Massive, urban "blob" of overlapping, integrating metropolitan areas whose distinctive boundaries are increasingly becoming difficult to find.

Metropolitan statistical area (MSA)—U.S. Census Bureau geographic unit of area including a central city and all its immediately interacting counties populated by commuters and people directly connected to the central city. An MSA is an urbanized region with a minimum of 50,000 residents.

Micropolitan statistical area—U.S. Census Bureau geographic unit comprising a central city and the surrounding counties integrated into it, and having a population of 10,000 to 50,000.

Multiplier effect—Increased economic success and energy created by the addition of new basic-sector jobs.

Nonbasic employment sector—Group of economic functions in a city that shift money within the city, not outside the city as in the basic employment sector.

Office park—Zone of urban land exclusively set aside for corporate offices. Often office park developers offer incentives to businesses to locate there.

Panregional influence—Influence that extends beyond the city's own region into the other centers of economic control.

Peak land value intersection—Point of land with maximum accessibility and visibility in the city, usually the center of the CBD in the concentric zone model.

Periferico—Most peripheral zone of a Latin American city marked by squatter settlements and abject poverty.

Planned community—Master-planned neighborhood with preformulated architectural designs, built-in community gathering spots, and restrictive covenants.

Postindustrial city—City whose economy and urban organization are conforming to the dominance of service-sector, nonindustrial economic functions.

Postmodernism—Postindustrial school of architecture and urban design that frowns on symmetry and balance and looks more toward diversity and individuality in expression.

Preindustrial city—City existing before the Industrial Revolution that served as a trade center and gateway to foreign lands and markets. Often the rural settlements surrounding the urban space provided agricultural products and foodstuffs to the urban dwellers, who in turn provided different economic functions.

Primacy—Degree to which a primate city dominates economic, political, and cultural functions in a country. The degree of primacy is calculated using the formula P_1/P_2, where P_1 is the population size of the primate city and P_2 is the second-largest city in the country.

Racial steering—Tactic (now illegal) contributing to ghettoization; real estate agents would show people neighborhoods and houses according to their race.

Range of a good or service—Maximum distance a person is willing to travel to obtain a good or service.

Rank-size rule—In a region, the nth-largest city's population is $1/n$ the population of the region's largest city.

Rate of urbanization—Speed that the population is becoming urban.

Redlining—Practice (now-illegal) of banks and lending agencies refusing to give loans to people moving to minority-dominated districts because the banks/agencies feared the loans would not be repaid based on the statistical improbability of successful development in the districts.

Restrictive covenants—Special laws passed by communities usually to exert control over the way their neighborhood will look and grow, such as laws restricting how people can use their space.

Shock city—Urban place experiencing infrastructural challenges related to massive and rapid urbanization.

Spatial competition—Assumption in the central place theory that implies that central places compete with each other for customers.

Squatter settlement (or *barriada*)—Makeshift, unsafe housing constructed from any scraps people can find on land they neither rent nor own.

Star-shaped city pattern—Early shape of city growth before automobile dominance in which lines of public transportation radiated from the central business district (or downtown) in a star pattern. The star-shaped pattern of growth maintained the dominance of the CBD.

Street morphology—Layout or pattern of streets.

Suburbanization—Growth of lower-density housing, industry, and commercial zones outside the central business district.

Telecommuting—Modern form of commuting that involves only the commuting of information, not the worker, through use of the telephone and Internet technology, allowing people to send information and communication over long distances. (For example, this book was written Tennessee, sent to California for editing, and then transmitted to New Jersey for publication, all via e-mail.)

Threshold—*Minimum* number of people needed to fuel a particular function's existence in a central place.

Uneven development—Urban development that is not spread equally among a city's areas, leaving some areas richly developed and others continually poor and decrepit.

Urban banana—Arch of the dominant overland, trade-based cities stretching from London to Tokyo in the 1500s before the rise of sea-based trade and exploration.

Urban hearth area—Area where an urban lifestyle and civilization started and from which they diffused.

Urban hierarchy—System of cities consisting of various levels, with few cities at the top level and increasingly more settlements on each lower level. The position of a city within the hierarchy is determined by the diversity and level of central place functions it provides.

Urbanization—Growth and diffusion of city landscapes and urban lifestyle.

Urban sprawl—Diffusion of urban land use and lifestyle into formerly nonurban, often agricultural lands; has raised continued problems related to uneven development and changing land use patterns.

Urban system—Network of urban places; part of an interlocking web of interacting cities.

World city—Powerful city that controls a disproportionately high level of the world's economic, political, and cultural activities. Sometimes called a global city, it has a high degree of centrality in the global urban system.

Zone in transition—Ring of land usually just around the central business district that is constantly in flux and run down because of successive waves of immigration that never allow it to develop a permanent population base and attract development.

Some Suggested Web Resources for Further Exploration

PART 6

Urban Institute: http://www.urban.org/

The Urban Institute researches public policy issues on issues related to urban lifestyle and sprawl, producing reports on issues such as schools in impoverished neighborhoods, environmental problems in urban areas, zoning issues, and more.

Best Practices: http://www.bestpractices.org/

Coordinated by the UN Habitat, this searchable database contains thousands of proven solutions from nearly 150 countries to the common social, economic, and environmental problems of an urbanizing world.

UN Human Settlements Programme: http://www.unhabitat.org/

UN Habitat is the United Nations agency for human settlements. It is mandated by the UN General Assembly to promote socially and environmentally sustainable towns and cities with the goal of providing adequate shelter for all. The website has articles, researched data, and stories related to the UN's work in promoting shelter for the world's people.

Earth Observatory: http://earthobservatory.nasa.gov/

The Earth Observatory page is run by the National Aeronautics and Space Administration (NASA) and provides interesting images related to NASA's research on urbanization and its relationship to global warming and other environmental issues.

UN Department of Economic and Social Affairs (DESA): http://www. un.org/esa/desa/

According to its website, the mission of the DESA is as follows: "Under the overall authority of the General Assembly, DESA coordinates the economic and social work of the United Nations and the UN family of organizations. As the central forum for discussing international economic and social issues and for formulating policy recommendations, the Council plays a key role in fostering international cooperation for development. It also consults with nongovernmental organizations (NGOs), thereby maintaining a vital link between the United Nations and civil society."

Earth Institute: http://www.earthinstitute.columbia.edu/

Issues addressed on this website, run by Columbia University, include challenges facing the planet and its inhabitants, with particular focus on sustainable development and the needs of the world's poor. As its mission states, "The Earth Institute is motivated by the belief that science and technological tools already exist, and could be expanded, to greatly improve conditions for the world's poor while preserving the natural systems that support life on Earth."

PART 7 Pre-Exam Practice

Terms Review Quiz

Use the Terms Review list or your own memory to determine the extent of your knowledge of key terms and concepts. Remember, the AP exam does not include this kind of exercise, but it is included here as a review tool.

1. _____ Makeshift, unsafe housing constructed from any scraps people can find on land they neither rent nor own.

2. _____ System of cities consisting of various levels, with few cities at the top level and increasingly more settlements on each lower level.

3. _____ Growth of lower-density housing, industry, and commercial zones outside the central business district.

4. _____ Graph showing the predicted decline in cost of land and population density as you move away from the central business district in the concentric zone model.

5. _____ Growth of areas of concentrated poverty in urban places.

6. _____ Ring of land usually just around the central business district that is constantly in flux and rundown because of successive waves of immigration that never allow it to develop a permanent population base and attract development.

7. _____   Degree to which a primate city dominates economic, political, and cultural functions in a country.

8. _____   Tactic (now illegal) contributing to ghettoization; real estate agents would show people neighborhoods and houses according to their race.

9. _____   Self-sufficient urban area within a greater metropolitan complex; often develops on highway exits.

10. _____   Contributing factor to uneven development; occurs when money flows to areas of greatest profit, places where development has already been focused, rather than to places of greatest need.

11. _____   Powerful city that controls a disproportionately high level of the world's economic, political, and cultural activities. Sometimes called a global city, it has a high degree of centrality in the global urban system.

12. _____   Urban development that is not spread equally among a city's areas, leaving some areas richly developed and others continually poor and decrepit.

13. _____   *Minimum* number of people needed to fuel a particular function's existence in a central place.

14. _____   Growth and diffusion of city landscapes and urban lifestyle.

15. _____   Urban place experiencing infrastructural challenges related to massive and rapid urbanization.

16. _____   Original core of a city's economy, like the nucleus of a cell.

17. _____   Layout or pattern of streets.

18. _____ Assumption in the central place theory that implies that central places compete with each other for customers.

19. _____ City that has a high degree of centrality and primacy; although not a world city, it exerts high levels of influence and power in the country's economy.

20. _____ Maximum distance a person is willing to travel to obtain that good or service.

21. _____ Massive, urban "blob" of overlapping, integrating metropolitan areas whose distinctive boundaries are increasingly becoming difficult to find.

22. _____ Most peripheral zone of a Latin American city marked by squatter settlements and abject poverty.

23. _____ U.S. Census Bureau geographic unit comprising a central city and the surrounding counties integrated into it, and having a population of 10,000 to 50,000.

24. _____ Arch of the dominant overland, trade-based cities stretching from London to Tokyo in the 1500s before the rise of sea-based trade and exploration.

25. _____ Area serviced by a central place.

Multiple-Choice Review Questions

1. Chicago's relative location near other major city networks gave the urban place a comparative advantage for successful economic growth. This statement best describes Chicago's

    (A) threshold

    (B) site

    (C) situation

    (D) density

    (E) functional zonation

2. Tony and Jacob are brothers who decided to move into an old warehouse in downtown New York City and fix it up into a slick loft apartment complex. Tony and Jacob's actions are most closely classified as

    (A) suburbanization

    (B) urban morphology

    (C) social stratification

    (D) gentrification

    (E) redlining

3. All the following are processes that have contributed to ghettoization in North American cities EXCEPT

    (A) blockbusting

    (B) redlining

    (C) racial steering

    (D) green belts

    (E) suburbanization

4. Tokyo is many times larger than the second-ranked city in Japan, thus making Tokyo a(n)

    (A) periferico

    (B) central business district

    (C) hinterland

    (D) squatter settlement

    (E) primate city

5. All of the following are common preconditions found in areas that became urban hearths EXCEPT

    (A) access to water sources

    (B) access to building materials

    (C) arable land

    (D) a long growing season

    (E) social stratification

6. Which of the following processes most influences the existence of a zone of transition in concentric urban growth patterns?

    (A) Exurbanization   (D) Decentralization

    (B) Successive immigration (E) Zoning

    (C) Agglomeration

7. The Latin American city typically differs from the North American city in which of the following ways?

    (A) The Latin American city often has higher densities in peripheral zones and less population density in the central business district.

    (B) The central business district is more dominant in its influence over its related urban land in the North American city than in the Latin American city.

    (C) The Latin American city typically does not show as strong a trend toward suburbanization as does the North American city.

    (D) The North American city shows more influence of the sector model growth patterns than does the Latin American city.

    (E) The urban realms model is more strongly explanatory and predictive of Latin American urban growth than it is of North American urban growth.

8. Which of the following is the smallest scale of geographic inquiry by the U.S. Census Bureau?

   (A) Metropolitan statistical area

   (B) Micropolitan statistical area

   (C) Metropolitan area

   (D) Census tract

   (E) County

9. Which of the following central place functions is most likely to have the highest range of goods and highest threshold population?

   (A) Used car lot   (D) Steakhouse

   (B) High school   (E) Furniture store

   (C) Hand-surgery center

10. Which of the following is a strong example of postmodern urban landscape?

    (A) Cairo, Egypt   (D) Washington, D.C.

    (B) Brasilia, Brazil   (E) Rome, Italy

    (C) London, England

11. According to the rank-size rule, if the largest city in Country X has 100,000 inhabitants, how many people will live in Country X's fourth-largest city?

    (A) 80,000   (D) 25,000

    (B) 75,000   (E) 10,000

    (C) 50,000

12. The concept of exurbanization is illustrated in which of the following scenarios?

    I. Thirty-three-year-old Marqueze and his wife move from Chicago to San Fransico to take advantage of a new job opportunity.

    II. Twenty-five-year-old Tina decides to move to the heart of New York City to enjoy the cultural vibrancy and diversity during her youth.

III. Fifty-year-olds Margaret and Tom pack up and move to a rural, country-style home outside Louisville, Kentucky, to escape the fast pace of city life.

IV. Nineteen-year-old Marcus decided to move from the city he grew up in to a peripheral farm, both to experience rural labor and to write poetry

(A) I

(B) II and III

(C) I and II

(D) III and IV

(E) I, II, III, and IV

13. Which of the following is an example of a person working in the nonbasic employment sector?

(A) Assembly-line worker in an iPod factory

(B) Video game software engineer

(C) International public relations agent

(D) University medical researcher

(E) High school English teacher

14. Which of the following statements correctly describes the economic employment mix that began to emerge in many U.S. cities after World War II?

(A) U.S. cities have become increasingly dominated by industrial activities.

(B) Workers' unions are reaching their highest level of influence in American history.

(C) Urban jobs are becoming increasingly service oriented and required learned skills.

(D) Most U.S. jobs are being outsourced to foreign labor supplies.

(E) The majority of U.S. jobs are moving from being consumption related to more of a production orientation.

15. Which of the following best illustrates the concept of a shock city?

(A) Chicago

(B) Paris

(C) Madrid

(D) Osaka

(E) Lagos

16. Planned communities would most likely be found in what type of urban setting?

    (A) Transition zones   (D) American suburbs

    (B) CBDs   (E) Ghettos

    (C) Perifericos

17. This model is based on the assumption that growth occurred independently around several major foci, many of which were far away from the CBD and only marginally connected to it.

    (A) Sector model   (D) Urban realms model

    (B) Central place theory   (E) Model of urban evolution

    (C) Multiple-nuclei model

18. Which of the following rivers was NOT a cultural hearth of urbanism?

    (A) Tigris   (D) Rhine

    (B) Euphrates   (E) Nile

    (C) Huang He

19. The star-shaped city pattern resulted from the dominance of which transportation system?

    (A) Beltways surrounding cities

    (B) Lines of public transportation extending from the CBD

    (C) Pedestrian walkways within the CBD

    (D) Interstate highways linking cities

    (E) Roads leading to airports that link cities

20. The area serviced by a central place is called a

    (A) hinterland   (D) threshold

    (B) sphere of influence   (E) redline

    (C) range

Free-Response Review Questions

Urban sprawl has contributed to inner-city decay in many North American urban places.

(A) Define *urban sprawl*.

(B) Explain how urban sprawl has contributed to inner-city decay in some North American urban places.

(C) Choose two of the following categories of solutions to uneven development, and for each, explain one related approach to reducing uneven development:

  • Political

  • Urban morphology

  • Cultural

  • Legal

PART 8 Pre-Exam Practice Answers

Terms Review Answers

1. Squatter settlement (or *barriada*)
2. Urban hierarchy
3. Suburbanization
4. Bid-rent curve
5. Ghettoization
6. Zone in transition
7. Primacy
8. Racial steering
9. Edge city
10. Cumulative causation
11. World city
12. Uneven development
13. Threshold
14. Urbanization
15. Shock city
16. Central business district (CBD)
17. Street morphology
18. Spatial competition
19. Megacity
20. Range of goods
21. Megalopolis
22. Periferico
23. Micropolitan statistical area
24. Urban banana
25. Hinterland

Multiple-Choice Answers

1. **(C)**

   Situation is equivalent to *relative location*, whereas *site* (B) refers to a city's internal features, such as resources and natural landscape. (A) is the number of people needed to support the existence of a central place function; (D) is the number of a certain phenomenon in a given space; and (E) refers to the division of urban space into many areas of use, or zones.

2. **(D)**

   Gentrification is the buildup or renovation of decaying or neglected urban space, usually in an inner city or a formerly industrial region. (A) is the growth of less-dense housing rings for middle and upper-class families within commuting distance to a city's CBD. (B) is the study of urban landscapes and how they evolved into their current forms. (C) is the division of an egalitarian society into various economic and social classes. (E) is the malicious practice of banks not granting loans to people living in certain areas of a city.

3. **(D)**

   Green belts are boundaries that contain a city's development and refocus development and investment energy back into a city's core, rather than allowing the city to sprawl and lose its focus. They help prevent uneven development and ghettoization trends. (A), (B), and (C) are all malicious real estate practices that lead to increased segregation and create ghettos. (E) also contributes to the creation of urban ghettos; suburbs drain the inner city of needed capital and development energy, leaving the core to decay because its predominantly low-income residents are stuck without a tax base for schools and infrastructure.

4. **(E)**

   A primate city is much larger than the next-largest city in the country and is usually overwhelmingly representative of national culture and identity. (A) is a region typically found on the outskirts of a Latin American city and marked by squalor and poverty. (B) is a region in a city that contains the peak land value intersection, the point of highest accessibility and visibility as well as the traditional origin of the city's growth. (C) is the region served by a central place. (D) is a region of a city containing makeshift homes.

5. **(E)**

   All the choices represent preconditions (or traits of urban hearths) except social stratification, which often followed city development. Urban growth led to the division of society along social and economic levels, or social stratification.

6. **(B)**

The constant influx of new arrivals to the city in the concentric zone model brings a new group into the city's center rings, pushing those already living in the inner rings to move outward to rings farther out, forcing a change in function in many rings. Residential rings become commercial rings, and so on. Because of this constant shifting process, there usually exists a ring near the CBD that never develops but is a zone of transition and constant uprooting; often, this is referred to as skid row, and developers avoid investing in it. (A) is the movement of city dwellers out to rural areas beyond the suburbs; (C) is the clumping of industries to take advantage of being together; and (D) is the spread of economic and urban features away from their center around the CBD into becoming more diversely spread throughout an urban space. Though (E) may have been tempting, zoning is the restrictions on land use that can be placed on urban space to segregate office parks from housing areas, for example.

7. **(C)**

Latin American cities tend to grow up, not out, because city inhabitants typically do not have capital and discretionary income to buy new houses; rather, they renovate their current homes. Also, most Latin American cities do not have the development energy and capital that North American cities have. Also, transportation, electricity, and water infrastructural grids tend to focus on the inner city in Latin America, rather than being available for urban sprawl. (A) is reversed, because Latin American cities are denser in the center than in peripheral zones. (B) is reversed, because the CBD is more dominant in Latin American cities and becoming less dominant in North American cities with suburbanization and urban sprawl. (D) is not necessarily true, because many Latin American cities show urban growth that is a mix of the classic models, as in North America. (E) is totally false, because urban realms are more applicable to North American cities than Latin American urban areas.

There is also an interesting cultural trend at work in many Latin American cities: the rich *want* to live in city centers. In contrast, the middle and upper socioeconomic classes in the United States, want to live in the suburbs (though this is changing in many cities). That means that the middle class in Mexico are trying to get *into* the city so they can show they are moving up the economic/social ladder, the middle class in many U.S. cities is trying to get *out* of the inner city for the same reason. Because all the money is in the center of most Latin America cities, that's where the best infrastructure is often found; the opposite is true in the United States.

8. **(D)**

(A)   includes a region of at least 50,000 within a greater metropolitan area (C), while a micropolitan area includes from 10,000 to 50,000 inhabitants of a region within a greater metropolitan area. A census tract is like a neighborhood, whereas a county often includes many census tracts.

9. **(C)**

A central place function with a high range and high threshold must be one that is going to require a very specialized set of customers and workers and is therefore going to attract people to travel far for its specialized services; a hand-surgery center's specialty will attract doctors who specialize and patients who need this specialty and are willing to travel far and wide for it.

10. **(B)**

A postmodern landscape is one that emphasizes diversity of thought and landscape without the obsession with symmetry and form that is found in classical architecture. Brasilia was designed with an emphasis on diversity in form rather than on the balance and emphasis on reason found in Renaissance and Enlightenment forms.

11. **(D)**

The rank-size rule asserts that the fourth-largest city will be one-fourth the size of the largest city.

12. **(D)**

Exurbanization occurs when city dwellers leave their urban homes and urban pace of life in search of more-rural lifestyles outside the central city and beyond the suburbs. Each of these scenarios (III and IV) describes a person in search of a less-urban, more-rural lifestyle.

13. **(E)**

Nonbasic jobs cause a shift of money within the urban place's economy, whereas basic jobs create an exchange of money between the urban place and another place (exports and imports). All choices except (E) are involved in creating a product that will bring money into the city's economy from outside of it. (E) provides a service to the residents and does not bring money in from the outside.

14. **(C)**

The current shift in the employment mix of North American cities is a movement away from unskilled, factory work toward service-oriented employment that often requires some knowledge of technology.

15. **(E)**

A shock city is an urban place usually in a less-developed region that is experiencing rapid rates of urbanization and in-migration. Such growth is straining to a shock city's ill-prepared infrastructure, which cannot provide housing and services, as well as jobs, to the rapidly growing population.

16. **(D)**

Planned communities are master-planned neighborhoods with preformulated architectural designs and often with community gathering spots and restrictive covenants. (A) are the areas outside the CBD that are constantly in flux and run down because of the invasion and succession pattern that never allows it to develop a permanent population base and attract development. (B) are the original cores of cities' economies; (C) are the peripheral zones of squatter settlements and abject poverty on the outskirts of many Latin American cities; and (E) are areas of concentrated poverty in urban places.

17. **(C)**

(A) predicts urban growth in a pattern in which similar land uses and socioeconomic groups are clustered in linear sectors radiating outward from a central business district, usually along transportation corridors. (B) theorizes that cities can be viewed from above as a series of concentric rings. (D) attempted to explain and predict changing urban growth patterns as the automobile became increasingly prevalent. (E) is Borchert's model explaining the growth of cities in four phases of transportation history.

18. **(D)**

Urbanism did not originally spawn from the Rhine river valley in Germany, whereas hearths existed in the other choices.

19. **(B)**

Star-shaped city growth resulted from public transportation systems (mainly streetcars) that extended out from the CBD. Growth took place along these corridors that offered easy access into the city and back out before automobiles became common.

20. **(A)**

The hinterland is the area serviced by a central city. (C) is the distance a person is willing to travel for a certain good or service. (D) is the number of people needed to make a good or service profitable and sustainable. (E) is a practice of not loaning money to individuals or businesses in certain areas. (B) is not a geographic term.

Free-Response Answers

The following is a list of suggested main points for each part of the question.

Part A

- Urban sprawl is the spread of the urban landscape into areas that were formerly nonurban or rural.

- The term *urban sprawl* often includes a negative connotation, implying the unplanned and reckless invasion of rural lands by urban developers and fast-paced, crowded lifestyles.

Part B

- Urban sprawl has contributed to the decay of inner-city zones for several reasons:

- Suburbanization has caused an out-migration of the middle and upper socioeconomic classes from residing in the inner-city zones. This has caused the tax base to be dramatically reduced, causing schools and infrastructure to have less money.

- Sprawl and suburbanization have "strangled" the inner city from being able to grow outward, because many of the newer communities, or nuclei, have seceded and become politically independent from the metropolitan government.

- Poor zoning laws in some areas have allowed housing complexes and industrial zones to be juxtaposed, causing polluted living environments.

- Because of sprawl, the focus of development and renovation is often directed away from the inner-city areas, particularly the fringes between the newer suburban zones and the original CBD—the zone of transition, or skid row.

Part C

- Political—discussion of incorporation and fusing of metropolitan governments with country governments to create one, unified system of support services and tax base; increasing support for mass transit options within the city.

- Urban morphology—discussion of increasing grid-patterned streets and reducing cul-de-sac and one-entrance properties that channel traffic into only a few outlets.

- Cultural—possible discussion of gentrification, though gentrification is not seen by some geographers as a cultural method of controlling sprawl. Other cultural methods might entail our changing beliefs that led to the end of racial segregation in real estate practices or the movement to building smaller homes with smaller environmental footprints and better energy usage.

- Legal—discussion of green belts and zoning laws to restrict out-migration and urban sprawl.

BIBLIOGRAPHY

AP Human Geography

Bibliography

De Blij, Harm J., and Alexander B. Murphy. *Human Geography: Culture, Society, and Space*. 7th ed. New York: Wiley, 2003.

De Blij, Harm J., and Peter O. Muller. *Concepts and Regions in Geography*. New York: Wiley, 2003.

Diamond, Jared. *Guns, Germs, and Steel: The Fates of Human Societies*. New York: Norton, 1999.

Fuller, Charles. *Conquering Human Geography: A Manual for Successful Completion of AP Human Geography*. New York: Wiley, 2007.

Gabrys-Alexson, Randy. *Advanced Placement Student Companion*. New York: Wiley, 2003.

Jordan-Bychkov, Terry G., and Mona Domosh. *The Human Mosaic: A Thematic Introduction to Cultural Geography*. 9th ed. New York: W. H. Freeman, 2003.

Knox, Paul L., and Sallie A. Marston. *Places and Regions in Global Context: Human Geography*. 3rd ed. Upper Saddle River, NJ: Prentice Hall, 2004.

Kuby, Michael, John Harner, and Patricia Gober. *Human Geography in Action*. 3rd ed. Hoboken, NJ: Wiley, 2004.

Norton, William. *Human Geography*. 4th ed. New York: Oxford University Press, 2002.

Nunley, Robert E., George W. Ulbrick, and Bernard O. Williams. *Study Guide to the Cultural Landscape*. 7th ed. Upper Saddle River, NJ: Prentice Hall, 2003.

The Nystrom Desk Atlas. Chicago: Nystrom Herff Jones Education Division, 2004.

Pitzl, Gerald R. *Encyclopedia of Human Geography*. Westport, CN: Greenwood, 2004.

Rubenstein, James M. *The Cultural Landscape: An Introduction to Human Geography*. 8th ed. Upper Saddle River, NJ: Pearson/Prentice Hall, 2005.

Sowell, Thomas. *Conquests and Cultures: An International History*. New York: Basic Books, 1998.

Tuan, Yi-Fu. *Space and Place: The Perspective of Experience*. Minneapolis: University of Minnesota Press, 1977.

PRACTICE EXAMS

AP Human Geography

PRACTICE EXAM 1

This exam is also on CD-ROM in our
special interactive AP Human Geography TEST*ware*®

AP Human Geography

Section I

TIME: 60 minutes
75 multiple-choice questions

(Answer sheets appear in the back of this book.)

Directions: Each of the following questions is followed by five suggested answers or completions. Select the best answer choice.

1. All the following are considered new industrial countries EXCEPT

   (A) Hong Kong   (D) China

   (B) South Korea   (E) Indonesia

   (C) Brazil

2. Which of the following is an example of a quinary-sector economic activity?

   (A) Working at a cash register at McDonald's

   (B) Serving as a researcher for human genetic cloning

   (C) Serving on the U.S. president's cabinet

   (D) Converting crude oil into gasoline

   (E) Plowing land in preparation for planting a crop

3. Chicago has become a world city in part because of its proximity to ports and other places that foster development. This reason for Chicago's historic growth relates to the city's

   (A) site

   (B) sovereignty

   (C) redlining

   (D) situation

   (E) distance decay

4. Which of the following is a valid difference between the urban patterns of the United States and those of Latin America?

   (A) Unlike U.S. cities, Latin American cities have ghettos.

   (B) U.S cities follow a sector pattern, whereas Latin American cities follow concentric zones.

   (C) Gentrification is more present in Latin American cities.

   (D) Latin American cities have more-defined industrial sectors.

   (E) Unlike U.S. cities, Latin American cities show patterns of wealthy residents emanating from the city's central business district.

5. The number of people under the age of 15 plus the number of people above the age of 64 divided by the number of the people aged 15 through 64 is defined as

   (A) carrying capacity

   (B) primary economic sector

   (C) dependency ratio

   (D) age-sex pyramid

   (E) infrastructure

6. Governments such as those controlled by the Taliban in Afghanistan and the Ayatollah Khomeini in Iran are classified as

   (A) landlocked

   (B) parliamentary

   (C) federal

   (D) theocratic

   (E) microstates

7. All the following were original members of the European Community, the predecessor to the European Union, EXCEPT

    (A) France

    (B) Belgium

    (C) United Kingdom

    (D) Italy

    (E) The Netherlands

8. In 1492 Christopher Columbus's voyage took nearly 40 days to cross the Atlantic Ocean, a trip that would take a modern ship less than one week. This difference best reflects the geographic concept of

    (A) distance decay

    (B) uneven development

    (C) stimulus diffusion

    (D) space-time compression

    (E) distribution

9. The arrow on the map above points to a city in India containing the largest number of shrines from which of the following religions?

    (A) Sikhism

    (B) Shintoism

    (C) Buddhism

    (D) Christianity

    (E) Hinduism

X = Headquarters
of United Trucking

10. The region outlined above contains delivery destinations served by United Trucking. Which of the following classifications best fits this region?

(A) Functional

(B) Formal

(C) Vernacular

(D) Mental

(E) Perceptual

11. Compared with the world pattern of crude birth rates, the world pattern of crude death rates shows

(A) more variation because of the vast inequalities in minimal health care throughout the world

(B) less variation because of the general availability of minimal health care facilities throughout the world

(C) equal variation because of the offsetting effect of birth and death rates throughout the world

(D) no variation

(E) high variation because of the high infant mortality in some world regions

12. Which of the following would be most attracted to export-processing zones in less-developed countries?

(A) Transnational corporations assembling products that are bulk reducing or not weight gaining

(B) Multinational firms wanting to build world headquarters

(C) Quaternary-sector workers wanting to find jobs

(D) Technopoles

(E) International lending agencies

13. The second agricultural revolution developed at the same time as

    (A) growing urban markets were demanding increased food production

    (B) improved genetic modification of food allowed for increased harvests in developing countries

    (C) humans were forming communes and practicing open-field farming

    (D) vast shortages in laborers existed because of communicable diseases

    (E) large streams of migrants moved from core to peripheral countries

14. Which of the following most likely explains the diffusion pattern of the iPod depicted in the graph above?

    (A) In the innovation stage, at point A, only a small number of iPod purchases were made, but by point B the number of adopters had grown exponentially as the early buyers spread the word of the iPod.

    (B) The highest exponential growth rate was achieved by point C, where the fastest adoption of the iPod occurred.

    (C) The highest adoption rate occurred at point A because, as a new invention, the iPod aroused excitement.

    (D) Point C represents the late-adopter stage, when adoption of the iPod reached all people in the population.

    (E) The pattern represents relocation diffusion.

15. All the following are true of truck farming EXCEPT:

    (A) Among the most common truck crops are tomatoes, strawberries, and lettuce.

    (B) Most often it is characterized by the use of mechanized farming tools.

    (C) Labor costs are often relatively high on these large-scale farming operations.

    (D) It is the predominant agricultural practice found in the southeastern United States.

    (E) Truck farmers' harvests are usually intended for distant markets.

16. Which of the following places is least influenced by conflicts related to multilingualism?

    (A) Nigeria   (D) Cyprus

    (B) Venezuela   (E) Belgium

    (C) Quebec

17. Which of the following was the first prerequisite for the start of urbanization?

    (A) Formal political organization

    (B) Agricultural surplus

    (C) Monarchial control

    (D) Privatization of land ownership

    (E) Development of currency

18. Which of the following regions is most threatened by desertification?

    (A) South America   (D) Africa

    (B) Australia   (E) Asia

    (C) Europe

19. Which of the following significantly weakened the strength of Mackinder's geopolitical heartland theory?

(A) Ascendance of the United States' international influence after World War II

(B) Existence of a pivot area

(C) Growth of Soviet power in eastern Europe

(D) Influence of Eurasia in world affairs

(E) Rise of Nazi Germany

20. Which of the following factors had the greatest effect in proving the demographic theorist Thomas Malthus incorrect?

(A) Decreased land supply after the Industrial Revolution

(B) Improved fertilizers and crop strains

(C) Increased contraceptive technology in the Western Hemisphere

(D) The decline of the Roman Catholic Church's influence on politics in Britain

(E) Improved trade routes enabling improved food transport and cross-national trade

21. Country X can produce televisions at 50 percent of the cost that Country Y can produce televisions. Country Y can produce pencils at 70 percent of the cost that Country X can produce pencils. Therefore, Country X chooses to produce televisions and trade them with Country Y for pencils. This scenario best reflects which concept?

(A) Substitution principle

(B) Topocide

(C) Foreign direct investment

(D) Footloose industry

(E) Comparative advantage

22. A banking company wanted to open a new branch in the New York City area. In order to study the region, the bank used a map to analyze potential locations. The map the bank's leadership used in its decisionmaking process showed a layer of regional data displaying per capita income; another layer displaying the frequency of bank deposits made; and another layer showing the average value of the deposited amount. With this map, the banking company was able to choose the optimum location for its new branch. All of the following are tools that the bank (or its geographic team) most likely used to create and display this layered map of geographic data EXCEPT

(A) GPS

(B) GIS

(C) remote sensing

(D) desalination

(E) satellite imagery

(Photo by: M. Savage)

23. A pilgrim to the religious site depicted in the photograph above would most likely be a(n)

(A) Taoist

(B) Buddhist

(C) Eastern Orthodox Christian

(D) Muslim

(E) Hindu

24. In the 1980s the demographic trend in China was best characterized by a(n)

    (A) rapidly rising crude birth rate

    (B) falling life expectancy

    (C) decreasing general fertility rate

    (D) increased total fertility rate

    (E) surge in refugees emigrating from China

25. The United Nations Human Development Index is based on the assumption that a country's development

    (A) is directly related to its position in the core or periphery

    (B) is a function of social, demographic, and economic factors

    (C) can improve if countries liberalize trade policies

    (D) is indicated most accurately by its gross domestic product

    (E) is a reflection of its population count

26. The photograph above shows a farm most likely located in which of the following regions?

    (A) Sub-Saharan Africa   (D) North Africa

    (B) Southwest Asia   (E) Southeast Asia

    (C) Eastern Europe

27. All the following resulted from the British enclosure movement in the 1850s EXCEPT

    (A) agricultural efficiency increased

    (B) urban migration increased

    (C) feudal village life was disrupted

    (D) the number of farm owners rose dramatically

    (E) communal fields were consolidated

28. In 1998 an estimated 350,000 asylum seekers were from Croatia. What were their primary destinations in that year?

    (A) Kosovo and Albania

    (B) Germany and France

    (C) Yugoslavia and Bosnia-Herzegovina

    (D) Austria and Hungary

    (E) Macedonia and Romania

29. On which of the following map projections is direction true everywhere on the map?

    (A) Mollweide   (D) Robinson

    (B) Mercator   (E) Miller cylindrical

    (C) Peter

30. Which among the following has the highest-threshold, highest-range central place function?

    (A) Doughnut shop   (D) Neurosurgery complex

    (B) Post office   (E) Department store

    (C) Movie theatre

31. "Women are inherently better preservationists of Earth because women have traditionally been nurturers and men have been destroyers." This argument exemplifies

   (A) economic determinism

   (B) the Gender Empowerment Measure

   (C) ecofeminism

   (D) the convergence hypothesis

   (E) ethnogenesis

32. You would most expect to find a linguistic refuge area in a(n)

   (A) relatively flat country   (D) river bank

   (B) mountainous area   (E) marketplace

   (C) international airport

33. By 2015 life expectancy in several African countries, such as Namibia, is expected to decline by more than 10 years. What is the principal factor causing this demographic projection?

   (A) Cyclical poverty   (D) Infrastructural decay

   (B) Crop shortage   (E) HIV/AIDS

   (C) Ecoterrorism

34. Both Ulaanbaatar in Mongolia and Lagos in Nigeria are examples of

   (A) primate cities   (D) edge cities

   (B) world cities   (E) postindustrial cities

   (C) exclaves

35. A coffee shop and an ice-cream shop are often found on the same block, in close proximity. This is an example of

   (A) deglomeration   (D) purchasing-power parity

   (B) agglomeration   (E) an urban heat island

   (C) an export-processing zone

	Family 1	Family 2	Family 3			Family 4	Family 5		
A			B	C	D		E		

Note: Each square represents one block. Delivery trucks must travel on the road, represented by the shaded region.

36. Based on the linear settlement depicted above, which location would be optimal for a restaurant that offers delivery services, assuming that each family purchases the same amount from the restaurant and that the truck has to return to the restaurant after delivering each order?

(A) Location A   (D) Location D

(B) Location B   (E) Location E

(C) Location C

37. Which of the following is the most accurate title for the map above?

(A) Map of World Democratic Voters

(B) Map of Nuclear Power Reactors

(C) Map of Dravidian Languages Spoken

(D) Map of Avian Flu Outbreaks

(E) Map of HIV-1 Infections

38. The informal sector in a developing country exists for all the following reasons EXCEPT:

    (A) Tertiary economies in the formal sector are not developed well enough to absorb all the economies of the informal sector.

    (B) The demand for informal-sector goods and services keeps prices low.

    (C) Informal-sector workers and businesses cannot afford permanent business sites.

    (D) The government benefits from taxing informal-sector workers and their small businesses.

    (E) The quality of products and the quality of work in the informal sector are low.

39. Two unrelated people are trying to decide whether to travel to Houston, Texas, from their homes in Germany for a special vacation package offered on television. One German decides Houston is too far away, while the other decides to purchase the vacation package. This scenario best demonstrates the effects of

    (A) brain drain   (D) doubling time

    (B) concentration   (E) expansion diffusion

    (C) cognitive distance

Population of A = 1.5 million chickens
Population of B = 6 million chickens
Population of C = 15 million chickens

40. The trend above best demonstrates which pattern of diffusion of the H5N1 or H5N2 strain of the avian influenza virus?

    (A) Hierarchical diffusion   (D) Uneven development

    (B) Stimulus diffusion   (E) Reverse hierarchical diffusion

    (C) Maladaptive diffusion

41. Which of the following is best classified as a centrifugal force?

   (A) National flag

   (B) State-owned news station

   (C) National research laboratories

   (D) Ethnic discrimination

   (E) Common language

42. By 2006 the states of northern Nigeria came under the governance of

   (A) the Sharia law   (D) secularists

   (B) the African Union   (E) Ibo speakers

   (C) Christian theocrats

43. All the following are in the Indo-European language family EXCEPT

   (A) Portuguese   (D) Hindi

   (B) Bengali   (E) Turkish

   (C) German

Population Increases and Growth Rates in Five-Year Periods

	1980–1985	1985–1990	1990–1995	1995–2000	2000–2005	2005–2010	2010–2015	2015–2020
Net population added per year (in millions)	80	87	83	79	76	76	75	72
Annual population growth rate (%)	1.8	1.8	1.6	1.4	1.2	1.2	1.1	1.0

44. The table on the previous page best illustrates which demographic trend?

   (A) Hidden momentum   (D) Doubling time

   (B) North–south gap   (E) Zero population growth

   (C) Counterurbanization

China Population Density

45. Based on the population density map of China above, in which region is extensive subsistence agriculture most heavily practiced?

   (A) Region A   (D) Region D

   (B) Region B   (E) Region E

   (C) Region C

46. In 1990 Iraq invaded Kuwait, in part over an oil resource that Iraq and Kuwait both claimed fell within their national boundaries. This type of boundary dispute is classified as

    (A) locational

    (B) definitional

    (C) allocational

    (D) operational

    (E) subsequent

47. A computer production process involves creating the computer chip in Indonesia and assembling the motherboard in Malaysia. This is, most closely, evidence of

    (A) maquiladora districts

    (B) the post-Fordist production process

    (C) an infrastructure

    (D) the new international division of labor

    (E) a cottage industry

48. Which of the following asserts that ethnic minorities often live in the geographically peripheral regions excluded from the core of a country's power?

    (A) Demographic transition model

    (B) Cleavage model

    (C) Von Thünen's model

    (D) Central place theory

    (E) Locational interdependence model

49. In von Thünen's theory, the key variable in an agricultural location decision is

    (A) labor cost

    (B) value of agglomeration benefits

    (C) climate type

    (D) cost of irrigation

    (E) transportation cost

50. As of 2000 the world's third-largest religion, in terms of number of adherents, is

(A) Sikhism   (D) Christianity

(B) Hinduism   (E) Judaism

(C) Islam

Female Literacy Rates, 2000–2004

	Region A	Region B	Region C
Females Literate in Region (%)	53	73	88

51. Which of the following accurately lists in order the regions in the above table corresponding to A, B, C, respectively?

(A) Asia, Latin America and the Caribbean, sub-Saharan Africa

(B) Latin America and the Caribbean, Asia, sub-Saharan Africa

(C) Asia, sub-Saharan Africa, Latin America and the Caribbean

(D) sub-Saharan Africa, Asia, Latin America and the Caribbean

(E) sub-Saharan Africa, Latin America and the Caribbean, Asia

52. Which of the following cities best represents a forward capital?

(A) Paris, France   (D) Canberra, Australia

(B) Algiers, Algeria   (E) Warsaw, Poland

(C) Putrajaya, Malaysia

53. Which of the following best describes shifting cultivation?

(A) Primarily a subsistence practice, it involves a farmer using a plot and then abandoning it for possible return at a later time.

(B) Usually a commercial agriculture endeavor, it involves rotating one crop type on a plot for another in a sequential pattern.

(C) It is the movement of pastoral nomads from one food source to another.

(D) Only used in wetlands, it is the use of pyramid-style farms for rice farming.

(E) It involves the intensive, commercial integration of crops and livestock into a farming system.

54. Which of the four stages in the demographic transition model are considered "homeostatic" stages, when the forces of demographic change are in equilibrium?

   (A) Stages 1 and 3

   (B) Stages 2 and 3

   (C) Stages 1 and 4

   (D) Stage 4

   (E) Stages 1, 2, 3, and 4

55. An essential difference between the standard language of a people and an official language is that the standard language is

   (A) the chosen, generally accepted variant of a language, while the official language is the legally declared language of a country to be used in all government interactions

   (B) usually spoken by outsiders, while the official language is what is on all official documents

   (C) the form spoken by commoners, while the official language is the "king's form" of the language, taught in the grammar books

   (D) used widely throughout society, while the official language is only used for government documents

   (E) unchanging, while the official language changes with changes in governments

56. Which of the following most accurately matches the country to its territorial shape?

   (A) Russia: fragmented

   (B) Poland: compact

   (C) Singapore: perforated

   (D) Philippines: elongated

   (E) Chile: protruded

57. Where would you most likely find the greatest concentration of feedlots in America?

   (A) Chicago

   (B) California

   (C) Florida

   (D) South Dakota

   (E) Kentucky

58. The seasonal migration of animal livestock from lowland pastures to mountainous regions is termed

    (A) intensive subsistence agriculture

    (B) mixed crop and livestock farming

    (C) double cropping

    (D) transhumance

    (E) swidden agriculture

59. Which of the following strategies was identified by the 1994 United Nations International Conference on Population and Development as the most powerful approach for reducing the global population growth rate?

    (A) Increasing the amount of exports to less-developed countries

    (B) Retracting anticontraception laws throughout conservative countries

    (C) Reducing hunger throughout the world

    (D) Empowering the socioeconomic status of women in less-developed countries

    (E) Enforcing demographic growth rate targets in specific countries through coalition building

60. Which of the following is a true statement about popular culture?

    (A) Technology is reducing the scale of territory covered by popular culture.

    (B) The scale of territory covered by folk culture is often much larger than that of popular culture.

    (C) The heart of popular culture customs is often found in less-developed regions.

    (D) Folk culture is often the result of cultural isolation, while popular culture often results from cultural diffusion.

    (E) Popular culture customs are usually the same from place to place.

61. In Rostow's economic development model, the stage in which workers become more skilled and modern technology spreads to industries beyond the innovating "takeoff" industry is called the

    (A) traditional society

    (B) preconditions for takeoff

    (C) takeoff

    (D) drive to maturity

    (E) age of high mass consumption

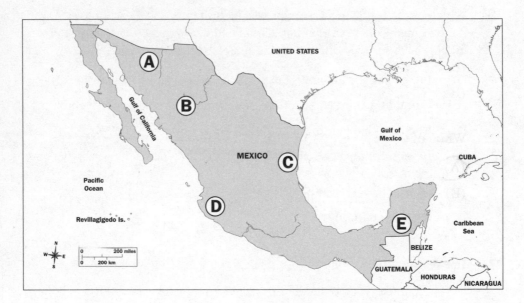

62. On the map of Mexico above, a maquiladora is most likely found at which point?

    (A) Point A   (D) Point D

    (B) Point B   (E) Point E

    (C) Point C

63. The migration of a Hildegarde von Pabst to Dayton, Ohio, from Berlin, Germany, because of a cousin living in Dayton is most closely an example of

    (A) forced migration   (D) periodic movement

    (B) chain migration   (E) a refugee

    (C) internal migration

64. The actual number of live births per 1,000 women in the fecund range refers to

    (A) total fertility rate   (D) infant mortality rate

    (B) fecundity   (E) general fertility rate

    (C) crude birth rate

65. Which of the following correctly sequences Sino-Tibetan languages from largest to smallest in terms of the number of native speakers?

    (A) Mandarin, Cantonese, Wu, Hakka (Kejia), Min

    (B) Cantonese, Wu, Mandarin, Min, Hakka (Kejia)

    (C) Hakka (Kejia), Mandarin, Wu, Cantonese, Min

    (D) Mandarin, Wu, Cantonese, Min, Hakka (Kejia)

    (E) Mandarin, Min, Cantonese, Hakka (Kejia), Wu

66. Which of the following is NOT a usual characteristic of an edge city?

    (A) Accessibility   (D) Suburban sense of place

    (B) Tenement housing   (E) Office park

    (C) Varied urban functions

67. The relationship among power structures, the environment, and economic inequalities is termed

    (A) ecoterrorism   (D) gerrymandering

    (B) political ecology   (E) devolution

    (C) cultural diffusion

68. The focus of the Green Revolution was

    (A) improving crop yields in commercial agribusiness corporations

    (B) reducing starvation in less-developed countries

    (C) inventing new forms of food to add variety to the human diet

    (D) saving undeveloped land from urban sprawl

    (E) encouraging the use of fertilizers less damaging to the environment

69. All the following are factors motivating the conflict surrounding Quebec, Canada, EXCEPT

    (A) language   (D) economic inequality

    (B) sovereignty   (E) colonial roots

    (C) religion

70. Which of the following countries produces the most woven cotton fabric?

    (A) Italy   (D) Egypt

    (B) India   (E) United States

    (C) China

71. The picture above shows an abandoned factory warehouse that was remodeled into a loft apartment complex near the central business district of a major U.S. city. This is an example of

    (A) an edge city   (D) blockbusting

    (B) commodification   (E) gentrification

    (C) counterurbanization

72. A primary differentiation between a state and a nation is that a state is a

    (A) political abstract, whereas a nation is a human group

    (B) mutable concept, whereas a nation is permanent

    (C) fixed geographic item, whereas a nation is not linked to a territory

    (D) product of history, whereas a nation is a product of people

    (E) controversial issue, whereas a nation is more peaceful

73. Structural adjustment programs often encourage all the following EXCEPT

    (A) selling off public resources to private corporations

    (B) higher taxation rates

    (C) closing of export-processing zones

    (D) reducing government expenditures

    (E) charging citizens more for government services

74. Which of the following would have the steepest bid-rent curve?

    (A) Textile factory

    (B) Family desiring a plot of land for a suburban home

    (C) Urban real estate brokerage firm

    (D) Pig farmer

    (E) Trash dump

75. When a barge stops in Louisville, unloads its cargo, and transfers it onto a train to be transported to Ohio, Louisville is referred to as a(n)

    (A) trading bloc   (D) break of bulk

    (B) export-processing zone (E) special economic zone

    (C) shatter belt

Section II

TIME: 75 minutes

3 free-response questions

Instructions: You have 75 minutes to answer all three free-response questions in this section. Take a few minutes to outline your answers. Illustrate your essay with substantive examples when appropriate. It is not enough to answer a question by merely listing facts. You should present a cogent argument based on your critical analysis of the question posed and your understanding of geography.

1. Through the years, geographers have developed various perspectives on cultural ecology.

   (A) Define *cultural ecology*.

   (B) Contrast environmental determinism and possibilism.

   (C) Compare and contrast the spatial distribution of the cities of Chongqing and San Francisco, as shown in the maps below.

   (D) How would the theory of possibilism explain the human constructions shown in the map of San Francisco?

2.   (A)   Define *demographic dependency ratio*.

(B)   Look at the population pyramids below. Describe and explain the demographic trends in fertility and longevity depicted in China from 1950 through 2050 and relate those trends to China's dependency ratio.

(C)   With reference to the demographic trends you identified in part B, forecast any social and/or economic problems facing China related to its dependency ratio.

China's Age Distribution

Population Structures by Age and Sex
Millions

(Source: Population Reference Bureau)

3.   Urbanization is affecting nearly all parts of the world.

(A)   Define *urbanization*.

(B)   Describe and explain the current trends in levels and rates of urbanization in two of the following regions:

• North America

• Southeast Asia

• Latin America

(C)   Explain counterurbanization. Explain the demographic trends linked to current patterns in counterurbanization in the United States.

PRACTICE EXAM 1

AP Human Geography

Answer Key

Section I

1.	(E)	20.	(B)	39.	(C)	58.	(D)
2.	(C)	21.	(E)	40.	(E)	59.	(D)
3.	(D)	22.	(D)	41.	(D)	60.	(D)
4.	(E)	23.	(E)	42.	(A)	61.	(D)
5.	(C)	24.	(C)	43.	(E)	62.	(A)
6.	(D)	25.	(B)	44.	(A)	63.	(B)
7.	(C)	26.	(C)	45.	(E)	64.	(E)
8.	(D)	27.	(D)	46.	(C)	65.	(D)
9.	(A)	28.	(C)	47.	(D)	66.	(B)
10.	(A)	29.	(B)	48.	(B)	67.	(B)
11.	(B)	30.	(D)	49.	(E)	68.	(B)
12.	(A)	31.	(C)	50.	(B)	69.	(C)
13.	(A)	32.	(B)	51.	(D)	70.	(C)
14.	(A)	33.	(E)	52.	(C)	71.	(E)
15.	(C)	34.	(A)	53.	(A)	72.	(A)
16.	(B)	35.	(B)	54.	(C)	73.	(C)
17.	(B)	36.	(C)	55.	(A)	74.	(C)
18.	(B)	37.	(B)	56.	(B)	75.	(D)
19.	(A)	38.	(D)	57.	(D)		

Section I Diagnostic Instrument

> **Instructions:** Use these charts to see where your "weaknesses" exist in the curriculum.

Geography: Its Nature and Perspectives

Item #	3	8	10	22	29	39
Correct/Incorrect						

Population

Item #	5	11	14	20	24	33	40	44	51	54	59	63	64
Correct/Incorrect													

Cultural Patterns and Processes

Item #	9	16	23	32	43	50	55	60	65	69
Correct/Incorrect										

Political Organization of Space

Item #	6	19	28	37	41	42	46	48	52	56	67	72
Correct/Incorrect												

Agricultural and Rural Land Use

Item #	2	13	15	18	26	45	49	53	57	58	68
Correct/Incorrect											

Industrialization and Economic Development

Item #	1	7	12	21	25	35	47	61	62	70	73	75
Correct/Incorrect												

Cities and Urban Land Use

Item #	4	17	27	30	31	34	36	38	66	71	74
Correct/Incorrect											

PRACTICE EXAM 1

AP Human Geography

Detailed Explanations of Answers

Section I

1. **(E)**
   A new industrial country has a strong manufacturing base that enables it to maintain a competitive presence in the global economy rather than remaining a neocolonial country dependent on its former colonial masters. Indonesia is primarily attracting foreign direct investment from transnational corporations, which is a form of neocolonialism. (A) and (B) are part of the Asian Tigers, a group of Asian countries that developed a strong technology manufacturing base that propelled them into a competitive and relatively independent global economic position rather than remaining economically dependent on their former colonial masters.

2. **(C)**
   Serving on the president's cabinet is a quinary-sector economic activity because it involves decisions at the highest level of the government and economy. (A) is a tertiary-sector economic activity because it is service related. (B) is a quaternary-sector economic activity because it involves higher education; jobs in the quaternary sector can also be in financing, technological services, governmental operations, and the media. (D) is an example of a secondary-sector economic activity, which involve converting or processing raw materials (in this case, crude oil) that have been extracted from the earth (which is a primary economic activity) into product (in this case, gas) to be sold at the marketplace. (E) is an example of a primary-sector economic activity because it involves extracting natural resources.

3. **(D)**
   Situation describes a place's location relative to other places, whereas (A) is the physical character of a place. (B) describes a place's ability to control its own territory and internal affairs, (C) is a discriminatory practice used by banks and

lending agencies, and (E) is the decreasing impact a phenomenon has on something as the distance from its origin increases.

4. **(E)**

In Latin American (and western European) cities, the wealthy cluster nearer the central business districts and push outward from the focal point of the city, whereas in the United States the wealthy often live in suburbs outside the central cities. (A) is incorrect because many U.S. cities have ghettos. (B) is incorrect because many Latin American cities also show sector and concentric patterns. (C) is incorrect because U.S. cities show an equal (if not greater) influence of gentrifiers compared with Latin American cities. (D) is incorrect because U.S. cities have industrial sectors that are as defined as those found in Latin American cities.

5. **(C)**

The dependency ratio is a measure of the economically dependent members of the population—people considered either too old or too young to work. (A) is the maximum population that could be supported by a region's resources. (B) is the sector of the economy engaged in direct extraction of natural resources from the earth, such as farmers. (D) is a tool demographers use to illustrate trends in population by gender and age group. (E) is the "backbone of a society," including schools, health care institutions, and transportation systems.

6. **(D)**

Governments ruled by religious authorities are termed theocracies. The Afghani Taliban and the Ayatollah in Iran were religious authorities, both Muslim, who governed their countries. (A) describes countries without coasts on open seas. (B) describes countries with a representative body comprising officials elected at the national level. (C) describes governments wherein the country is divided into districts, each with a sense of protected sovereignty (like the states in the United States) and a national government that represents those subunits. (E) are states that are so small in their state and territory that they are usually only a dot on the map, such as Singapore.

7. **(C)**

The six original countries in the 1958 European Community, which was renamed the European Union (EU), were Belgium, France, West Germany, Italy, Luxembourg, and the Netherlands. By 1973 Ireland, Denmark, and the United Kingdom joined. The EU has effectively improved the economy of western Europe and has made it highly competitive in the world market.

8. **(D)**

Space-time compression is defined as the decreasing effect of distance on the speed of human travel across space, in movement of people and communications. (A) is the decreasing impact a phenomenon has on something as the distance from its origin increases. (B) refers to the negative impact of globalization in causing a growing divide between countries in the periphery and those in the core. (C) is diffusion of an innovation that takes a newer form in the new place to match cultural customs. (E) is a measurement of the way a feature is arranged in space.

9. **(A)**

Amritsar, India, is the city wherein the Sikh's holiest religious site, the Golden Temple, is found. (B) is practiced mainly in Japan and involves the worship of natural elements like rivers, rocks, and mountains. The rest of India is primarily Hindu (E), although minority pockets of Buddhists (C), Christians (D), and Muslims as well as other religious minorities are present.

10. **(A)**

A functional region consists of a node and the places linked to that central point through some sort of movement. In this case the region is created by the movement of United Trucking's services to customers in the places within the boundaries shown in the diagram. (B) describes a place with a uniform trait, such as language, present throughout the area. (C), (D), and (E) describe regions like the Bible Belt or the South in the United States—regions with boundaries marked by people's ideas rather than overtly measurable characteristics.

11. **(B)**

While the crude birth rate reflects varying human decisions related to cultural expectations and requirements, the crude death rate reflects the spread of basic health care throughout the world. Because minimal health care has diffused even to places with very high birth rates, death rates do not display the particularly vast discrepancies among countries that birth rates do, thus invalidating (A), (C), (D), and (E). Further, (C) is illogical in that birth rates do not always offset death rates.

12. **(A)**

Transnational corporations (TNCs, also called multinational corporations) are firms that have different parts of their production processes in different countries. Export-processing zones (EPZs) are special zones, often in less-developed countries, where industrial parks and export-oriented production occurs. Often countries establishing EPZs will grant those regions special tax exemptions to lure foreign direct investment. Typically a TNC contracts with factories to use their low-cost, low-skilled labor to make lightweight products for export to distant markets. (B) is incorrect because a TNC usually establishes its world headquarters in a world city, not in an EPZ. (C) is incorrect because quaternary-sector workers are involved in high-level information processing and decision making, not in industrial assembly; their work is usually found in world cities. (D) is incorrect because technopoles are regions in which technological research and innovation is abundant, for example, Silicon Valley in California. (E) would most be attracted to places with high amounts of capital, such as world cities and global investment capitals.

13. **(A)**

The second agricultural revolution, which occurred at the end of the 19th century, saw improved farming and storage practices that allowed for increased farming efficiency and output to feed the growing urban populations forming to fuel the Industrial Revolution's hunger for city-based workers. (B) refers to the advents of the third agricultural revolution in the 20th century, whereas (C) refers to preindustrial farming practices that colored much of medieval (feudal) times. (D) describes the opposite of what was happening at the time, because improved sanitation and inoculations helped prolong human life and improve health. (E) is also untrue because migrants moved into core countries for industrial work.

14. **(A)**

The graph depicts a typical spatial diffusion S curve. In the innovation stage (point A) the phenomenon (the IPOD) is invented and first used by the innovating class of users, usually a small group. Once the innovation hits the greater community and becomes popular, it enters the majority-adopter stage (point B) with the fastest rate of adoption, as indicated by the slope of the graph. Once the innovation saturates the marketplace, or adopter class, the adoption rate (slope of the curve) lowers and the diffusion pattern reaches the late-adopter stage, when the innovation is adopted by the laggards or latecomers. (B) is incorrect because the highest growth rate occurs in the majority-adopter stage, not the late-adopter stage. (C) is not correct because in the innovator stage, the adoption rate is low, not high. (D) wrongly claims that the IPOD had reached the whole population, but the y-axis of the graph indicates a saturation below 100 percent. (E) is incorrect because it is not possible to determine whether the diffusion represented in the graph was relocation or contagious diffusion.

15. **(C)**

Truck farming refers to commercial farming of fruits and vegetables intended for sale in places where such harvests are not possible (E). The market is now dominated by large agribusiness farms that grow tomatoes, strawberries, and lettuce (A), among other fruits and vegetable crops. These often corporate-owned and operated farms employ the use of machinery to irrigate and process the crops (B). Southeastern U.S. states like Florida dominate truck farming (D), along with California and Texas. (C) is false because migrant workers often supply less-expensive labor on large-scale truck farms.

16. **(B)**

Nigeria (A) has hundreds of local languages, which is one of the centrifugal forces challenging its unity. A major factor influencing the conflict over control of Quebec (C) is the division between French- and English-speaking Canadians, because Quebec is where most French-speaking Canadians are clustered. The political conflict in Cyprus (D) is highly related to the division between Greek speakers and Turkish speakers on the small island. Belgium (E) is highly divided along linguistic lines because the Flemings, the French-speaking Belgians, and the Walloons, the Dutch-speaking Belgians, are in conflict over control of Belgium. By contrast, Venezuela (B) is considered by many to be as near to monolingual as a country can get in today's society. Spanish is spoken by a high percentage of Venezuela's population.

17. **(B)**

The development of food surpluses, or more food than farmers need, allowed a population of nonfarmers to exist. Those nonfarmers could specialize in the fields and conduct the services needed for the development of cities, which were fed by the farmers. After the development of agricultural surpluses, people could perform nonfarming jobs, including those related to politics, and formal political organizations could develop (A). (C) and (D) existed before urbanization. (E) was primarily an outgrowth of the social stratification that occurred as trade grew between farmers and nonfarmers.

18. **(B)**

Desertification is the spread of desert-like conditions into more arable regions as a result of human overuse and, perhaps, environmental shifts. According to de Blij and Murphy's research, South America (A) is at a 20 percent risk; Europe, 9 percent; Africa, 57 percent; and Asia, 37 percent; by contrast, Australia is at an 83 percent risk.

19. **(A)**

The growth of the United States' influence after World War II beyond that of the Soviet Union most significantly challenged Mackinder's theory that dominance of Eurasia would yield world domination for a superpower, because the United States existed outside the Eurasian "world island" that Mackinder defined. (B) was the area of focus of Mackinder's theory, the area of eastern Europe and much of Russia that was considered prime real estate for world domination and that the Soviets dominated after World War II. (D) was the heart of Mackinder's heartland theory. (E) is related to Mackinder's theory because Hitler supposedly subscribed to it.

20. **(B)**

Thomas Malthus lived in England during the late 18th century, when cities were growing explosively as a result of the Industrial Revolution. As urban migration hit a new high mark, Malthus was convinced that the food supply would only grow arithmetically and would not match the exponential growth of the human population "explosion." What Malthus could not see was the Green Revolution on the horizon, when the development of new farming technologies, such as improved fertilizer and crop hybrids, allowed the food supply to grow faster and provide more nourishment for the exponentially growing population. Although (E) may seem reasonable, it was improved farming technologies, not trade routes, that directly proved Malthus's ideas false. If anything, reduced land supply (A) would have supported Malthus's alarmist theory. (C) and (D) are not directly related to Malthus's theory of food production being outpaced by population growth.

21. **(E)**

Comparative advantage is the idea that a region (or country) will produce goods it can make at a lower cost than other regions can and will trade them for goods that other regions can make more efficiently than it can. In this case Country X is better at making televisions, whereas Country Y specializes in pencil production. The two countries will find greatest economic efficiency if each one produces what it has a comparative advantage in producing, and then they trade with each other. (A) relates to industrial location theory—for example, when a company chooses to outsource its factory work and substitute higher transportation costs in exchange for the lower labor costs it will have. (B) is the planned destruction of a place to make way for an industrial center. (C) is the investment of foreign companies in countries outside their headquarters, such as when an American company builds a factory in Indonesia. (D) is a type of industry that does not have high transportation costs and is therefore free to locate wherever it wants; an example is a computer chip manufacturing plant whose final product is extremely lightweight.

22. **(D)**

Desalination (D) refers to the technology used to convert salt-water into potable, drinking water. GPS (A) refers to the global positioning system that activates satellites to pinpoint locations and gather geographic data. GIS (B) refers to geographic information systems that collect, store, and analyze geographic data in the form of layered map displays. Remote Sensing (C) is the process of collecting geographic information from remote locations, most often through satellite collection systems. Satellite imagery (E) is often used to create layers in maps.

23. **(E)**

The temple in the image, with its many statues of gods and goddesses, is most likely a Hindu temple. Another defining feature of a Hindu temple is its peaceful integration into the landscape. Hindu temples are built to house shrines of deities rather than for worship. (A) Taoist temples are usually filled with bright colors, especially red, with broad, curving rooftops and sculptures of traditional deities like the dragon and the carp. (B) Buddhists often decorate their temple complexes with pagoda towers, which are usually tall, with many tiers and slanted roofs. (C) Typically, Eastern Orthodox Christian churches are ornate, with domes and pointed arches. (D) Muslims construct mosques that usually include a central worship building with four towers used to call worshippers to prayer.

24. **(C)**

Whereas the Communist leader Mao Zedong implemented an aggressively pronatalist campaign to raise the birth rate in China, his successor, Deng Xiaoping, realized that high birth rates could destroy China's infrastructure. Thus he imposed a strict one-child policy, which rapidly reduced the Chinese birth rate. As a result, the number of children born per 1,000 women (the general fertility rate) decreased rather than increased (A). Life expectancy (B) was not directly affected. The total fertility rate was forcibly reduced to one child per family in many areas, making (D) invalid. (E) is not a documented claim.

25. **(B)**

The United Nations (UN) measures countries' development with its Human Development Index (HDI), ranking countries up to 1.0, or 100 percent. The equation for the index includes social, demographic, and economic factors, such as literacy rate and amount of education, life expectancy, and gross domestic product. (A) relates to core periphery models. (C) is one side of the economic globalization debate. (D) captures too narrowly the meaning of HDI, because the intent of the UN equation was to broaden analysis of development beyond gross domestic product. (E) is not a factor in the HDI equation because the size of a population is not the sole determinant of the level of human development.

26. **(C)**

The photograph shows large-scale, extensive grain farming, most likely mechanized. This is highly common in places like North America and eastern Europe, especially Ukraine (called the breadbasket of Russia). (A) is dominated by primitive subsistence agricultural and livestock production. (B) and (D) are known for their desert-like terrains and nomadic herding agriculture. (E) is dominated by intensive, primitive subsistence agriculture.

27. **(D)**

The enclosure movement closed in the public field system and consolidated individual strips of land that jutted off feudal villages, forming one large farmstead owned by one or a few farm owners (E). This effectively reduced the number of individual farm owners, making (D) false. Efficiency rose because one owner could push best practice and reduce the chaos that characterized land organization before the enclosure movement (A). People who were pushed off their lands moved into the cities, where they could find work in the growing industrial complexes (B). Thus the number of feudal village communities fell because people lost their lands to the enclosure movement (C).

28. **(C)**

By 1998 the Croats living in Croatia had successfully found independence from their Serb occupiers governing from Belgrade, Serbia. Remember, Croats are a unique nationality, Serbs are a unique nationality, and the Muslims throughout the region are considered a nationality as well. However, following the Croatian victory, many of the ethnic Serbs living in Croatia did not want to be governed by the Croats, who had formed a new government. Therefore, nearly 400,000 ethnic Serbs fled Croatia for their "homeland" of Yugoslavia and Bosnia. Soon thereafter Yugoslavia devolved even further into Serbia-Montenegro, and the dictator Slobodan Milosevic was removed from power by his own people.

29. **(B)**

The Mercator projection, while drastically distorting the dimensions of higher-latitude land masses, accurately displays direction everywhere on the map, making it particularly useful to navigators on sea vessels. (A) is considered an equal-area projection, which accurately depicts the relative sizes of land masses while distorting the other properties of maps: shape, direction, and distance. (C) is also an equal-area map. (D) is considered an average projection in that it distorts all four properties so as not to drastically distort one. While (E) avoids the relative-size distortions of the Mercator projection, direction is only accurate along the equator.

30. **(D)**

In Christaller's central place theory, a high-threshold function requires a large population to make the economic endeavor work; a high-range function draws people from far away to purchase the good or use the service. (D) requires a large population, because a small percentage of people need brain surgery, so it has a high threshold; it has a high range because people would probably travel far for life-saving brain surgery. (A) and (B) are low range and low threshold, whereas (C) and (E) are a bit higher but not as high as (D).

31. **(C)**

Ecofeminism expresses the idea in the quote and is a new facet of study in cultural ecology. (A) is the notion that human behavior and development is dictated by economic factors and causes. (B) is a measurement tool available to geographers to compare the abilities of men and women to excel in economic and political leadership and work. (D) argues that cultures are becoming more similar as regional disparity is being reduced through improved transportation and communication. (E) is the process of all cultures originating somewhere, somehow.

32. **(B)**

A linguistic refuge area is a place that is relatively free from forces of language diffusion and convergence. Mountainous regions such as the Alps, the Himalayas, and the Caucasus Mountains often divide groups geographically and allow for isolation and refuge from invading forces trying to assimilate a people to a particular culture or language. Mountains often provide this geographical separation, preventing language convergence that requires constant contact with other languages or forced change. A marketplace (E), like an international airport

(C), is a place where contact with other languages is likely to occur in trade and thus would not allow for linguistic refuge or shelter from convergence. (A) provides little geographic protection for the forces of diffusion and convergence. (D) is also unlikely to include a linguistic refuge area because riverbanks are often invasion points and centers of cultural contact.

33. **(E)**

Life expectancy in African countries such as Namibia and South Africa is being critically reduced by HIV/AIDS, in some cases by as much as 10 years. While (A) has a cumulative effect that keeps life expectancy low, it is not immediately reducing life expectancy as HIV/AIDS is, although some people argue that cyclical poverty is related to HIV/AIDS in Africa. (Remember, the AP test requires you to select the *best* answer, and cyclical poverty is not as exact as HIV/AIDS.) (C) is the term for the violent terrorist actions taken by environmental activists against organizations linked to ecologically destructive practices.

34. **(A)**

A primate city is a large urban center that is disproportionately representative of its national economic, political, and social power. Often a primate city is found in a developing country where former colonizers set up their colonial headquarters. Both Ulaanbaatar and Lagos are much larger than the next largest cities in their countries and are disproportionately powerful. (B) are economically powerful global "headquarters" cities that generally have populations greater than 10 million people. (C) are portions of a country's territory separated from its main body by the territory of another country. (D) are clusters of new urban settings with varied functions that often exist off highway exits and beltways surrounding central business districts of older downtown regions. (E) are cities in which the dominant economic activities are no longer secondary but have transitioned toward tertiary, quaternary, and quinary sectors. Ulaanbaatar and Lagos are both still in their industrializing phases.

35. **(B)**

Agglomeration is best exemplified in the modern shopping mall, wherein stores are clumped to take advantage of like-minded shoppers who may walk out of one store and be attracted to another. Coffee shops and ice cream shops tend to clump on blocks with the marketing strategy that customers may leave the coffee shop and want ice cream, or may decide against ice cream for coffee or mochas, or vice versa. (A) is the "unclumping" or spreading out of formerly clustered industries that occurs when staying together becomes too expensive or cramped. (C) is a region set up to lure factories, such as maquiladoras. (D) is an equation used to compare the value of a good in two countries; for example, the Big Mac index compares the price of a Big Mac in two places. (E) is the phenomenon of the temperature being somewhat higher in an urban area as a result of industrialization and increased human population density.

36. **(C)**

Location C would be the best location in the pictured linear settlement because it is the median location. The delivery truck would have to travel the least (or a minimized distance) to get to each family if located at point C. The truck would have to travel 11 blocks from point C to get to each of the houses, 12 blocks from point D, 16 from point E, and 19 from point A.

37. **(B)**

This map was created by the International Nuclear Safety Center in 2005 to show the clustered spread of nuclear power throughout the world. Notice that nuclear power is positively correlated with GDP. (A) is incorrect because there are dots in China and not enough throughout India. (C) is incorrect because Dravidian is more widely spoken in India than is indicated on the map, and Dravidian is uncommon in western Europe and the United States. (D) is incorrect because western Europe and the United States had proportionately fewer outbreaks than in China. (E) is incorrect because HIV should be more represented on the map in Africa and less in the United States and western Europe, proportionately, than indicated.

38. **(D)**

The informal sector consists of workers who do not report their incomes or jobs to the government. The government cannot tax informal-sector workers because it does not know officially of their work activities, and the informal sector is not included in GDP calculations.

39. **(C)**

Cognitive distance shapes the effects of friction of distance because a person's perception of distance impacts their travel decision. (A) is massive emigration of educated elites, (B) is a measurement of a phenomenon's spread over space, (D) is the time needed for a population to double in size, and (E) is the spread of a phenomenon from one place to another with the continued addition of adopters along the way.

40. **(E)**

Hierarchical diffusion is the spread of something from large or powerful places to areas that are smaller or less powerful. Reverse hierarchical diffusion is the inverse of that; it is the spread of something from smaller (or less-powerful) places to larger (or more powerful) places. The map shows its spread from A to B to C, each with a larger population of chickens than the other, thus moving from smaller to larger populations. (B) is the diffusion of the basic idea or principle but the failure for the entire concept to spread (e.g., the spread of the idea of a hamburger to India, where it was adopted as a vegetarian burger). (C) is the spread and adoption of a culture trait that does not seem to be appropriate for the adopting population, such as ranch-house architecture in snowy climate regions. (D) is unrelated but describes the gap in development in places, often between more-developed countries and less-developed countries.

41. **(D)**

Centrifugal forces are those that either pull people away from the city's center or pull a state (e.g., a country) toward falling apart and dividing into separate states. (D) can cause people who are being oppressed to become so frustrated that they will try to secede or at least revolt against discrimination by others. (A), (B), (C), and (E) are all centripetal forces, which help bind a state together or pull people toward a city's center. A national flag usually inspires loyalty and unification around a national identity, as does a state-owned news station, which can spin news in favor of the state's power. A national research laboratory could be seen as a centripetal force because of its findings of new health initiatives, but it would not be a centrifugal force in usual scenarios. A common language also binds people together into more of a cohesive whole.

42. **(A)**

Linguistically and religiously divided, Nigeria is nearly split along a north-south axis, with its northern states conforming to Islamic Sharia law and its southern states aligning along Christian lines, thus making (C) and (D) incorrect. Hausa is the dominant language in the north, while Yoruba and Ibo dominate the southern region, making (E) incorrect. (B) is a political, supranational organization similar to the European Union in its aim of uniting African countries in working toward progress.

43. **(E)**

Languages in the Indo-European family are spoken by more of the world's people than any other family, though Chinese, in the Sino-Tibetan family, has the largest number of speakers of any single language. (A), (B), (C), and (D) are all Indo-European languages. Turkish is in the Altaic family, which dominates the Anatolian Plateau region.

44. **(A)**

According to the table, the growth rate declines steadily beginning in 2000. However, between 2015 and 2020, 72 million people will be added to the global population annually. This is a trend called hidden momentum, which is the continuous growth in population despite a growth rate decrease. This occurs because the size of the generation of women having babies is very large as a result of the high fertility rates in the preceding generations. Their mothers and grandmothers had lots of babies. (B) is the divide in development levels that roughly corresponds to the equator, where most of the world's global south population lives in poverty. (C) is the pattern of human migration away from cities into villages and towns. (D) is the amount of time it would take for a population to double in size. (E) is the point at which the natural growth rate equals zero, which is not when no babies are born but is the point when, generally, the birth rate equals the death rate.

45. **(E)**

Extensive agriculture involves farming practices requiring large plots of land, such as wheat farming or animal herding. Intensive agriculture is farming a small plot of land more heavily, as in rice farming. As you move eastward into China's capital interior, intensive subsistence farming increases, and more people live near water-rich, arable lands close to Beijing and Shanghai (regions A, B, and C). Nomadic herding, the movement of animals to find food sources, is an example of extensive subsistence agriculture, most likely to occur in Region E.

46. **(C)**

Allocational boundary disputes involve the distribution of a precious commodity or resource, such as oil. (A) are disputes over the location of a boundary, whereas (B) are arguments over the language in the boundary's definition—for example, the exact height of a boundary's expanse. (D) are fights over the nature of a boundary—for example, how a boundary will be enforced. (E) is a type of border, not a type of border dispute.

47. **(D)**

The new international division of labor is a production process involving outsourcing of some parts of an assembly line to other countries. When one part of a computer is made in one country and another in a different country and final assembly takes place in yet another country, the labor has been divided among three countries. This process is facilitated by improved transportation links and time-space compression, or the reduction of the friction of distance. (A) are production or factory districts in Mexico on the U.S. border where American factories are built to take advantage of Mexico's low-cost labor, usually provided by women. (B) is the new factory production process that contrasts with the original assembly-line process developed by Henry Ford, in which a worker performed one piece of the assembly line process all day. In the post-Fordist assembly line, workers are trained to complete several tasks as a group to increase efficiency. (C) is the "backbone" of a country or region composed of various operations that enable a place to function; examples include the water system, roads, and the electrical grid. (E) refers to manufacturing of goods in homes rather than in factories; this was found in England and the United States before the Industrial Revolution and is often found in less-developed countries that have not yet industrialized.

48. **(B)**

The cleavage model was developed as an explanatory factor in electoral patterns. These patterns often show the power core being dominated by a particular nation (or cultural group) and in tension with minority groups, which are often marginalized politically and geographically. (A) explains and predicts the changes in population patterns in countries, (C) explains and predicts patterns of agricultural land use, and (D) explains and predicts the patterns of city development and their relationship to urban hierarchy. (E) was developed by Harold Hotelling to study the placement of industries in relationship to each other and their markets.

49. **(E)**

The key variable in von Thünen's theory is distance to the marketplace from the harvest site as measured by the transportation cost. He concluded that zones of similar agricultural land use will develop around a central marketplace in relation to the intensity of the farming being done and the cost of transporting the harvest to the market.

50. **(B)**

With nearly 1.5 billion adherents, Christianity is the world's largest, followed by Islam, with 1.2 billion, and then Hinduism, with 757 million. Sikhism, with nearly 22 million believers, is larger than Judaism, with 17 million.

51. **(D)**

Nearly all men and women can read in more-developed countries. Literacy rates for females vary significantly in less-developed regions. In general, more men than women are literate, a pattern true throughout history. However, this gap is lessening in many places throughout the world, though literacy rates continue to be especially divergent between males and females in Arab states, where only 50 percent of females are literate but nearly 75 percent of men are literate. This question requires general knowledge of demographic trends, very accessible through the Population Reference Bureau (www.prb.org). Of the three regions, sub-Saharan Africa has historically had lower literacy rates in general, particularly among women, largely because of that region's earlier stage in the demographic transition. This would eliminate (A), (B), and (C), leaving the correct answer choice dependent on the rates of Latin America and the Caribbean and Asia.

52. **(C)**

A country creates a forward capital when it moves its capital city to a new site to achieve some national aim, such as moving the power base to a more central location. The Malaysian government is currently moving its headquarters from the colonial capital city of Kuala Lumpur to the forward capital of Putrajaya, a move intended to demonstrate the country's economic modernity.

53. **(A)**

Shifting cultivation is primarily associated with subsistence farming, although it is also used by commercial farming systems. It is essentially farming a plot of land and then shifting to another plot to allow the fertility of the soil in the farmed plot to regenerate. (B) is incorrect because shifting cultivation is primarily a subsistence practice. Further, the rotation of crop types in a pattern on the same piece of land is known as crop rotation, not shifting cultivation. (C) describes pastoral nomadism; (D) is intensive subsistence terrace farming often found in China; and (E) describes mixed farming, a technique often found in Europe and North America.

54. **(C)**

Stage 1 is characterized by high crude birth and death rates, leading to equilibrium and nearly a natural rate of increase of nearly zero, which is equilibrium. Stage 2 is when the crude death rate begins to fall as a result of technological improvements in health care, causing the rate of natural increase to rise from its zero position in stage 1. Once a country reaches stage 3 in its demographic transition, the crude birth rate falls toward the death rate, and they finally meet again in stage 4, when the "forces of change," birth rate and death rate, are again equal, or at equilibrium.

55. **(A)**

An official language is the designated language of a government for all government purposes, such as legislation and all records. The standard language is the generally accepted dialect in a language that has various forms. For example, the standard language in the United States is American English, whereas in England, it is British Received Pronunciation. (B) is untrue because the standard language is what is generally spoken by the "insiders" of a population and can be used as a culturally divisive moment when newcomers try to integrate into a region and speak a different dialect. (C) is incorrect because it simply describes what is generally known as the standard language. (D) is untrue because the official language of a country can be (and often is) the standard form of the language. Standard languages can change, with invasion or governmental change, making (E) false.

56. **(B)**

In a compact-shaped country the distance from the center of the country to any of its extremities (or points on its boundaries) is about equal. Russia (A) is more of an elongated shape, Singapore (C) is a compact shape, the Philippines (D) is fragmented, and Chile (E) is elongated.

57. **(D)**

The greatest concentration of cattle feedlots, where cattle are fattened in a mechanized, factory-like process, exists in a corridor from South Dakota to Texas. Feedlots are also found in large numbers in Washington, Utah, Idaho, and Arizona. Some feedlots can hold more than 1 million head of cattle.

58. **(D)**

Transhumance is the practice of pastoral nomads when they circulate with their herds from lowland pastures to mountainous regions in a learned pattern that is often passed down through generations of family members. (A) involves farming one small plot of land to yield high output per acre. (B) is the integration of livestock and crops on one plot of land. (C) is an intensive farming practice using one plot of land to produce two harvests each year. (E) involves clearing unfarmed land by first cutting and then burning the present vegetation, allowing the cleared land to rest for a period, and then planting crops.

59. **(D)**

   The 1994 UN conference related increasing women's rights to lowering birth rates, because women can enter the workforce and find opportunities outside the home. Additionally, increased women's rights lead to better health care for women because women can push for reforms in health care and research that focus on their needs. One of the effects of better maternal health care is a lower infant mortality rate. When babies live longer, parents do not have to have more babies to fill their family needs. (E) may seem like a reasonable answer, but enforcing target goals in specific countries was an approach taken by earlier conferences that did not emphasize enough the significance of the structural change necessary to change birth rates, which are an expression of cultural decisions.

60. **(D)**

   Folk and popular culture are the two primary divisions of material culture, which comprises the aspects of culture that can be seen or are tangible. Nonmaterial culture, on the other hand, comprises the intangible aspects of a culture, such as beliefs. Folk culture represents homogeneity, or sameness, and is usually practiced by those who live in isolated regions, free from the influence of popular culture's diffusion. Popular culture diffuses over wide areas of diverse peoples, while folk culture defines a much smaller group of more-homogenous people, thereby making (B) incorrect. The Internet and television have increased the speed and expanse of popular culture's diffusion, because new ideas can reach farther places faster, thus making (A) incorrect. Popular culture is often spread from the most-developed regions of the world—regions with the capital resources to induce the diffusion— thus (C) is incorrect. Because of the rapid diffusion of popular culture, the actual customs rapidly change from place to place, as new ideas quickly come and adapt to the new people's needs, thus making (E) incorrect.

61. **(D)**

   In the drive-to-maturity stage of Rostow's model of economic growth, the innovation and growth that benefited the society's takeoff industry spread to other areas of the economy, enabling workers to specialize and grow more skilled. During (A) a large number of people in the society are farmers. (B) involves the identification of and initial investment in the infrastructure needed for an industry to take off. (C) is the stage in which the selected industry grows and prospers. By (E) the economy has developed to the extent that consumer goods, such as cars and radios, are produced for consumption by a wealthier workforce.

62. **(A)**

   Maquiladoras are U.S.-owned factories built at any point along the U.S.– Mexico border, such as point A. These factories are built because the maquiladora regions offer companies low-cost labor and other tax breaks. The North American Free Trade Agreement (NAFTA) is highly related to the growth of maquiladoras. The maquiladora regions are also considered export-processing zones.

63. **(B)**

Chain migration is when migrants move to a location because of information from friends or relatives who have made the same migration previously. (A) is when people are pushed from their home regions against their will (e.g., to escape ethnic cleansing) and become refugees (E). (C) is the migration of people within their country or region, and (D) is the movement of people in similar patterns over time, such as traveling from a boarding school to home for the summer holiday.

64. **(E)**

This is the definition of the general fertility rate. (A) is the number of children each woman is expected to bear. (B) is the ability of a woman to conceive. (C) is the number of children born per 1,000 people (not just women) in a given year. (D) is the number of deaths among infants under one year of age per 1,000 live births in a given year.

65. **(D)**

Mandarin, with nearly 875 million speakers, is the largest language from the Sinitic branch of the Sino-Tibetan family, followed by Wu (77 million), Cantonese (71 million), Min (55 million), and then Hakka, also known as Kejia (33 million).

66. **(B)**

An edge city is an urban complex that typically grows off a highway or beltway surrounding an inner city (A). Edge cities often have their own malls, health care facilities, entertainment complexes, and other necessities and conveniences (C). Often manufacturing jobs and facilities exist in edge cities, built in suburban settings (D). A cluster of office buildings on the side of a highway or beltway often forms the heart (or nucleus) of an edge city, and suburban housing and family restaurants grow around the office zone. Tenements, or slums, are not found in most edge cities but are more typical of the original inner-city regions.

67. **(B)**

Political ecology is the arm of geography that analyzes political structures and their relationship to natural resources and habitats. (A) refers to terrorist actions taken by groups frustrated with their perception of corporate abuses of natural habitats, (C) is the spread of a cultural trait across space, (D) is redefining electoral districts to give certain parties an advantage, and (E) is the fracturing of a cohesive state into splinters.

68. **(B)**

The 20th century's Green Revolution was aimed at reducing hunger in less-developed countries by giving farmers in those regions greater access to the fertilizers and seeds they needed to increase their crop yields and improve their farming practices. It did not focus on commercial agriculture or improving profits for agribusiness corporations, as (A) suggests; and it did not focus on improving the human diet (C) or land preservation (D). Although (E) may imply the use of fertilizers that aid in increasing crop yields, (B) is more related to the focus of the Green Revolution.

69. **(C)**

Religion is not a motivating factor in the conflict within Quebec. French-speaking inhabitants of Canada are known as Francophones and English-speaking inhabitants are Anglophones. Quebec was first settled by the French in the 1600s and then taken by the British in the 1700s, making (E) a factor in the conflict. The Francophones desire more control over Quebec's economic and political affairs, which have been traditionally dominated by the Anglophone minority, making (B) another factor. Quebec has traditionally been Canada's poorest province, and this inequality has created tensions that straddle cultural and economic lines, making (D) a factor. Language (A) is a preeminent factor in the dispute, with Francophones seeing their French language as a defining factor in their national identity. They have even created a commission to transfer toponyms from English names into French names.

70. **(C)**

China is the leading producer of woven cotton fabric, a labor-intensive part of the clothing and textile production process. India is second in line, followed by the United States.

71. **(E)**

Gentrification is the upgrading and remodeling of rundown buildings in low-income neighborhoods in inner-city regions. (A) is a suburban complex that has developed on the edge of an inner city, usually off a highway exit. (B) is the process of transforming something not priced into something traded as a product—for example, putting a price on a human working in a factory. (C) is the process of moving away from inner cities toward a more rural, suburban life. (D) is the illegal practice by real estate brokers of stirring up racially grounded fear in residents that leads to segregation and prompts some residents to sell their homes.

72. **(A)**

A state is essentially a country, which is a political term for a sovereign, bounded territory that has a government. A nation, on the other hand, is a group of people with a shared culture and history. A state can change its borders, and a nation can realign its identity, thus making (B) incorrect. (C) is incorrect in its assertion that a nation is not linked to a territory, because nationhood often is tied powerfully to a piece of land; and (D) is incorrect because a state and a nation are both products of history and people. (E) is flawed in its oversimplified suggestion that a nation cannot be controversial; the explosive conflict between the Serbs and Croats in the former Yugoslavia is just one example of a nation steeped in controversy.

73. **(C)**

Structural adjustment programs encourage countries to develop economies that can participate in the globalizing economic landscape through international trade. To achieve such growth, the structural adjustments often end popular, but economically inefficient, practices. This involves all the steps listed except for (C), because a structural adjustment program often leads to the creation of zones to lure foreign direct investment, which can generate growth in a country. However, the program can be quite painful in the short run because people may lose jobs and services that were cut in favor of the "more efficient" economic solutions advocated by proponents of the structural adjustment program.

74. **(C)**

The highest land value in a city is usually found at the point called the peak land value intersection (PLVI), which is near the city's central business district, or city center. The bid-rent curve shows how much a firm or person is willing to pay for land. The stronger the desire to be near the PLVI, the steeper the curve. (C) is a business that needs visibility and accessibility to downtown areas. (A), (B), (D), and (E) require larger plots of land with lower returns on their investments, so it would be illogical, not to mention costly, for them to buy the more expensive land closest to the PLVI. By contrast the real estate firm could afford the property and can expand by building up rather than out.

75. **(D)**

A break-of-bulk is a place where cargo (or people) change from one type of transportation to another, such as from barge to train. (A) is a group of countries that create an open trading relationship through reduced tariffs and improved transportation among their borders. (B) is a region in a less-developed country where foreign direct investment is courted through tax breaks and other incentives to companies. (C) is an unstable zone between two regions of conflicting political or cultural values. (E) is a region in a communist country (such as China) where special capitalistic trade is allowed.

Section II

Sample Response and Scoring Rubric for FRQ 1

Sample Response

    A.   Cultural ecology is the study of the relationship between a human cultural group and its natural environment. It is closely related to human–environment interactions.

    B.   Environmental determinism is a doctrine holding that human activities are controlled by the environment. Possibilism is a school of thought created in response to environmental determinism. One fundamental belief of possibilism is that humans, not the physical environment, are the primary active force. Another belief is that any environment offers a culture numerous possible ways to develop.

    C.   Both cities developed along elongated, hilly sites flanked on one side by water. Both are connected by bridges leading to adjacent land across the water. Both use tunnels for arterial roads. There are differences in street patterns. In Chongqing the streets are laid out to accommodate the rugged terrain. San Francisco, however, shows relatively little deviation from a gridiron pattern. Also, San Francisco covers a much larger land area.

    D.   San Francisco seems to have adapted the environment to fit its gridiron pattern. Possibilists would point to the innovative technologies in the bridges and tunnels that both cities built to adapt to environmental constraints. Also, possibilists would point to San Francisco's parks and the construction of streets through them as human adaptation, molding the environment to fit its needs. Further, the city parks in San Francisco are on the coast, rather than inland.

Scoring Rubric for FRQ 1

PART A: 1 point

1 point for any of the following:

- Cultural ecology is related to the study of human environment interactions.

- It is the study of a human group's interaction with its environment.

- It is the study of the cultural landscape.

PART B: 2 points

1 point for any of the following:

- Environmental determinism sees the environment as directing human action, predetermining the course humans will take.

- Possibilism sees the environment as providing a set of broad constraints that limit the possibilities of human choice.

PART C: 2 points

1 point for accurate similarity; 1 point for accurate difference:

- Both cities developed along elongated, hilly sites nearly surrounded by water, both are connected by bridges leading to adjacent land across the water, and both use tunnels for arterial roads.

- The cities have different street patterns. In Chongqing the streets are laid out to accommodate rugged terrain, whereas San Francisco shows relatively little movement away from the gridiron pattern; also, San Francisco covers a much larger land area compared with Chongqing.

PART D: 2 points

1 point for each of the following:

- Possibilists would point to the innovative technology in bridges and tunnels used by the cultures to adapt to environmental constraints.

- Possibilists would point to San Francisco's parks and the construction of streets through them as indications of human adaptation, molding the environment to fit human needs.

OVERALL SCORE FOR FRQ 1 _____/ 7 points

Sample Response and Scoring Rubric for FRQ 2

Sample Response

A.   The group of people in a country composed of active workers, usually aged 15 through 64, is considered nondependent. The people who are older or younger than the working group form the group considered dependent. The dependency ratio shows the relationship between the dependents and the workers (who take care of the dependents).

B.   These population pyramids illustrate China's shrinking working-age, nondependent population and its growing elderly population. A sharp decline in China's fertility rate was seen starting in the 1980s with the imposition of the antinatalist one-child policy. That policy successfully reduced the number of babies each woman was having, which is the country's total fertility rate. The improvements in medical and industrial technology are increasing the life expectancy of Chinese citizens, or their longevity. This is causing China to have a higher dependency ratio, because a large number of elderly nonworkers are dependent on a shrinking number of people in the working cohort (the nondependents).

C.   Because of its high dependency ratio, China is facing the problem of having too few working-age people to support its growing elderly population. As the number of older people rises, health care costs will rise rapidly and the number of working-age people able to support these rising costs will decrease. Therefore, many older people may not receive the care that they need because they cannot pay for it; they are also more likely to become homeless. Moreover, many jobs may be unfilled because the domestic workforce is not large enough to replace the positions once occupied by the retiring population. This could lead to an economic downturn.

Scoring Rubric for FRQ 2

PART A: 1 point

1 point for the following:

- The dependency ratio is the number of people considered dependent (under age 15 and above age 64) divided by the number of people in the workforce (nondependents).

PART B: 5 points

1 point for each correct description of demographic trend, 1 point for each correct explanation of demographic trend, and 1 point for correct relation of demographic trends to dependency ratio:

- Decreasing working-age, nondependent population

- Rising elderly dependent population

- Decreasing fertility linked to one-child policy

- Increasing longevity linked to improved medical technology and industrialization

- Increasing dependency ratio in China as number of dependents is rising and number of people in the workforce (aged 15 through 64) is decreasing

PART C /4 points

1 point for each correct identification of social and/or economic problem related to China's dependency ratio:

- Higher number of dependents means higher health care costs

- Lower number of workers means fewer people to support rising health care costs

- Potential homelessness and insufficient care provided for elderly people

- Economic downturn because jobs not filled after older workers retire

OVERALL SCORE FOR FRQ 2 _____ / 10 points

Sample Response and Scoring Rubric for FRQ 3

Sample Response

A.   Urbanization is generally equivalent to city building. It is the spread and growth of cities, or the transformation of rural space into urban space. Urbanization includes political, social, and cultural shifts. It is the evolution of a location into a city structure with an urban population that has migrated, usually, from rural areas to supply labor and inhabitants.

B.   "Rate of urbanization" refers to how fast urbanization is growing, while "level of urbanization" refers to the amount of the population that is already considered urban. Although urbanization is increasing globally, certain areas are experiencing faster rates of urbanization because more of their space is becoming urban. Southeast Asia is experiencing rapid rates of urbanization, with many countries industrializing and converting formerly rural places into urban spaces. Southeast Asia's level of urbanization, or the percentage of its people considered urban, is lower than North America's level of urbanization. Simply explained, North America experienced an earlier industrial revolution, therefore it has already developed a higher level of urbanization than Southeast Asia. Since most North Americans are urban already, its rate of urbanization is lower—urbanization has nearly reached 100 percent.

C.   Counterurbanization is the return of city-dwellers (or urban people) to more-rural places because of the pull factors present in more-rural landscapes, including a slower pace of life, less traffic, less pollution, and less noise, among others. It is most likely to be found in more-developed countries among retired individuals, usually older than 55 and in the middle- to upper-income ranges.

Scoring Rubric for FRQ 3

PART A: 2 points

1 point for each of the following observations (2 points maximum):

- Urbanization is the spread and growth of cities.
- It is the growth of city-based populations.
- It includes social, political, and cultural impacts as populations transform into city-based ways of living.

PART B: 4 points

1 point for each of the following correct descriptions and explanations (4 points maximum):

- North America: low rate of urbanization and high level of urbanization; already reached industrial revolution, so population is already largely urban
- Southeast Asia: high rate of urbanization and low level of urbanization (ongoing city building); currently experiencing industrialization and growth of cities, massive urban migration patterns in many countries (although not all; Singapore, for instance, is 100 percent urban)
- Latin America: low level of urbanization and high rate of urbanization; similar to Southeast Asia, with high rates of rural-to-urban migration, causing higher rates of urbanization and increasing levels of urbanization

PART C: 3 points

1 point for each of the following (3 points maximum):

- Counterurbanization is the process of a population becoming less centralized and generally moving from urban spaces into more-rural spaces.
- The factors that influence counterurbanization are higher costs of living in cities, less traffic and congestion in outlying areas, and the availability of improved transportation and communication technology (allowing commuting and working from home in more-remote areas).
- Demographically, most people in U.S. counterurbanization trends are retired (older than 55) and in the middle- to upper-income ranges, allowing them the freedom to be spatially mobile and the ability to move into the "countryside" for a more peaceful retirement than the traffic and congestion in the cities would allow.
- Younger people, in their 20s and 30s, often enjoy the bustle and diversity of the cities. Unmarried people also are statistically more likely to live in urban spaces.

OVERALL SCORE FOR FRQ 3 _____/ 9 points

PRACTICE EXAM 2

This exam is also on CD-ROM in our special interactive AP Human Geography TEST*ware*®

AP Human Geography

Section I

TIME: 60 minutes
75 multiple-choice questions

(Answer sheets appear in the back of this book.)

Directions: Each of the following questions is followed by five suggested answers or completions. Select the best answer choice.

1. The diagram below most clearly illustrates the geographic process of

    (A) deglomeration

    (B) accessibility

    (C) scale

    (D) placelessness

    (E) agglomeration

2. According to the rank-size rule, a country's fourth-largest city is what fraction of the country's largest settlement?

    (A) 1/2   (D) 1/12

    (B) 1/4   (E) 1/16

    (C) 1/8

3. Which of the following countries has a government organized in a federal structure?

    (A) United Kingdom   (D) France

    (B) China   (E) Czech Republic

    (C) India

4. Which of the following religions did not originate with a founder or innovating prophet?

    (A) Buddhism   (D) Taoism

    (B) Hinduism   (E) Confucianism

    (C) Islam

5. Which of the following assumptions underlies push-pull reasoning in human migration selectivity?

    (A) The only category of push-pull factors is economic.

    (B) Some factors in human migration decisions are beyond the total control of migrants making those decisions.

    (C) Push-pull factors are universal truths that apply to all human migration decisions.

    (D) Each place is equal in its original favorability to humans.

    (E) Humans migrate when forced to live in unfavorable places.

Word Usage for Term Meaning "Soda"

Line indicates boundary between two terms' dominance

6.   The diagram above most closely demonstrates the geographic concept of

(A)   language groups

(B)   ideograms

(C)   pidgin language

(D)   the isogloss

(E)   language pollution

7.   All the following are often preconditions for the construction of a federal government EXCEPT

(A)   compact shape

(B)   multiculturalism

(C)   wide expanse of territory

(D)   multicore region (or lack of core)

(E)   regionalism

8. In sub-Saharan Africa,

    (A) caloric intake has reached nearly adequate levels because genetically modified food crops are being shipped from foreign markets

    (B) malnutrition has most affected children in urban areas

    (C) the impact of the Green Revolution has been the highest, though still insufficient to mitigate malnutrition

    (D) agribusiness investments have improved local agricultural economies

    (E) food production has declined since 1980 and continues to drop

9. Which of the following accurately lists regions in order of decreasing levels on the Human Development Index ?

    (A) Anglo-America, western Europe, eastern Europe, Southeast Asia, Middle East

    (B) Anglo-America, western Europe, eastern Europe, Middle East, Southeast Asia

    (C) Anglo-America, western Europe, Middle East, eastern Europe, Southeast Asia

    (D) Western Europe, Anglo-America, eastern Europe, Southeast Asia, Middle East

    (E) Western Europe, Anglo-America, eastern Europe, Middle East, Southeast Asia

10. Bank USA refused to approve loans to people living in a particular neighborhood of Nashville, Tennessee. This is an example of

    (A) blockbusting   (D) ghettoization

    (B) redlining   (E) racial steering

    (C) gerrymandering

11. Approximately how many independent states exist on the earth's surface?

    (A) 2,500   (D) 500

    (B) 1,800   (E) 200

    (C) 1,000

12. A pilgrim wishing to visit the hearth of Islam would most likely visit which modern-day country?

    (A) Iran   (D) Saudi Arabia

    (B) Syria   (E) Lebanon

    (C) Israel

13. After the 1991 Gulf War, the Kurdish people residing in and near Iraq are best classified as a

    (A) nation-state   (D) perforated state

    (B) multination state (E) supranational organization

    (C) stateless nation

14. Which of the following is not one of the key assumptions in von Thünen's agricultural location model of an isolated state?

    (A) The isolated state involves flat, uninterrupted land without barriers to farming or transportation.

    (B) Farmers transport their harvests by accessing the most direct routes.

    (C) Farmers wish to maximize their profits by minimizing their transportation costs.

    (D) It costs more to transport produce longer distances.

    (E) Different soil types and qualities exist throughout the isolated state.

Ethnic Groupings in Former Yugoslavian Regions

	% Serb	% Croat	% Muslim	% Slovene	% Albanian
Serbia	85				
Croatia		75	12		
Slovenia				91	
Bosnia-Herzegovina	32	18	40		
Montenegro			13		6
Macedonia					20
Kosovo	13				77

15. Based on the table above, in the Yugoslavian civil wars, which region was most intensely the focus of Serb irredentism?

   (A) Serbia

   (B) Bosnia-Herzegovina

   (C) Croatia

   (D) Macedonia

   (E) Slovenia

16. Which of the following countries is predominantly Shiite Muslim?

   (A) Saudi Arabia

   (B) Indonesia

   (C) Pakistan

   (D) Iran

   (E) Philippines

17. Which of the following states has only one core region?

   (A) United States

   (B) Japan

   (C) Nigeria

   (D) Malaysia

   (E) India

18. When Dutch traders and Japanese traders meet, they often use English to conduct their business transactions. This use of English is an example of a(n)

    (A) pidgin language   (D) lingua franca

    (B) creole language   (E) monolingualism

    (C) official language

19. On the map of Azerbaijan above, point Z most closely represents which concept?

    (A) Assimilation   (D) Multiculturalism

    (B) Exclave   (E) Multiplier effect

    (C) Ghetto

20. Human geography is best defined as the study of

    (A) where and why human activities are located as they are

    (B) where and why natural forces occur as they do

    (C) populations and birth rates

    (D) human civilizations and their changes

    (E) governments and their impacts on the earth's surface

Demographic Data: Ireland

Year	Total Fertility Rate	Dependency Ratio (dependents:workers)
1970	3.9	10:14
1995	1.9	10:18
2006	1.6	10:22

21. Based on the trend demonstrated by data in the table above, which of the following statements can be inferred about Ireland?

    I.   When children born in the 1960s entered the workforce in Ireland, fewer children were in the generation behind them.

    II. Fewer Irish women were able to enter the workforce in the mid-1990s.

    III. Laws restricting contraception were lessened in Ireland in the 1970s.

    IV. By 2006 Ireland was experiencing an economic downturn

    (A) I

    (B) I and III

    (C) I, II, and IV

    (D) III

    (E) I, II, III, and IV

22. Niamey, the capital of Niger, is located at 13 degrees 31 minutes north latitude and 2 degrees 7 minutes east longitude. This is Niamey's

    (A) relative location   (D) node

    (B) region   (E) site

    (C) absolute location

(Photo by: Davax)

23. Which of the following boundary classifications fits that shown in the picture above?

    (A) Natural-political   (D) Relic

    (B) Subsequent   (E) Antecedent

    (C) Superimposed

24. Based on the map of Bulgaria's economic activity above, which of the following regions contains the most agglomeration of secondary economic activities?

(A) Reka Devnya

(B) Dimitrovgrad

(C) Vratsa

(D) Sofiya

(E) Stara Zagora

25. The image above shows an example of a(n)

    (A) pinyin   (D) shatter belt

    (B) isoline   (E) isolated language

    (C) ideogram

26. Which of the following states is most similar to the concept of a geopolitical nation-state?

    (A) Canada   (D) Belgium

    (B) Russia   (E) Japan

    (C) United Kingdom

27. The Middle East has been called the "crossroads of the world." Which fact would best support this statement?

    (A) Most of the world's oil reserves are there.

    (B) The Strait of Hormuz is an important waterway.

    (C) Parts of three continents intersect there.

    (D) Water bodies surround most of the region.

    (E) It is characterized by regional, tribal conflict over land.

28. The Gravity Model predicts

    (A) population density

    (B) agricultural land use patterns

    (C) urban land use patterns

    (D) birth rates and death rates

    (E) spatial interaction between places

29. Which of the following statements accurately applies to theories of development?

   (A) While liberal models assume that every country can develop along the same projection for growth, structuralist models assume that countries are withheld from growth by constraints built into the global economy.

   (B) Liberal models include the core-periphery models, while structuralist models include Rostow's economic development model.

   (C) Structuralist models reject the theory of neocolonialism.

   (D) Structuralist models assume that economic inequalities between countries are a result of inefficient structure in local or countrywide government policies.

   (E) Liberal models argue that less-developed countries cannot grow economically because the core countries unfairly suppress the less-developed countries' opportunities for economic growth.

30. Which of the following regions has the lowest percentage of urban dwellers?

   (A) Eastern Europe   (D) Southeast Asia

   (B) Middle East   (E) Western Europe

   (C) Latin America

31. Which of the following is true of U.S. agriculture?

   (A) Most U.S. farms are owned by agribusiness corporations.

   (B) Nearly 20 percent of the U.S. workforce is involved in agribusiness.

   (C) The amount of U.S. land devoted to agriculture has decreased.

   (D) The number of U.S. farms has increased since 1900.

   (E) The largest farms, nearly 4 percent of total U.S. farms, account for only 10 percent of U.S. agricultural output.

32. According to world-systems analysis, the world's states

   (A) strengthen when involved in supranational organization

   (B) are divided into a heartland and rim land

   (C) compete for Eurasian dominance

   (D) exist in a mobile structure of economic advancement

   (E) must be seen in the context of a global capitalist economy

(Photo by W. McLean)

33. The photograph above was taken in which of the following cities?

    (A) Mecca, Saudi Arabia   (D) São Paulo, Brazil

    (B) Jerusalem, Israel   (E) Tehran, Iran

    (C) Kuala Lumpur, Malaysia

34. Which of the following correctly sequences the evolution process of boundaries, starting with the first stage and ending with the last?

    (A) Definition, delimitation, demarcation

    (B) Definition, demarcation, delimitation

    (C) Demarcation, definition, delimitation

    (D) Delimitation, demarcation, definition

    (E) Demarcation, delimitation, definition

35. Which of the following statements best describes the growth pole concept?

    (A) Growth poles first cause deindustrialization.

    (B) The growth pole concept only operates at the national or supranational geographic scale.

    (C) The development of growth poles leads to deglomeration.

    (D) Growth pole development is often led by one particularly commanding industry or firm.

    (E) Once a region becomes a megalopolis, growth poles disappear in influence.

36. Which of the following is most likely NOT a significant factor causing the growth of favelas, barrios, and *barriadas* in Latin America?

    (A) Natural disasters   (D) Population increases

    (B) Strained infrastructure   (E) Housing shortages

    (C) Urban migration

37. All the following are regions where ranching is practiced widely EXCEPT

    (A) Central Europe   (D) Southeast South America

    (B) Southern Africa   (E) Central Asia

    (C) Australia

38. Which of the following best defines the cultural landscape approach in geography?

    (A) Each region has a uniquely built environment that is constructed by social processes and their impacts on the surrounding natural features.

    (B) Geography is a result of human processes that shape the earth's features.

    (C) Humans are driven by their environments and consequently shape their surroundings.

    (D) Environmental perception drives industrial development.

    (E) Physical geography is less significant than human constructions in shaping the landscape.

COUNTRY
1. Japan
2. Italy
3. Germany
4. Greece
5. Sweden

39. The table above lists the countries with the

    A. highest natural growth rates

    B. shortest doubling times

    C. lowest percentages of dependents

    D. grayest populations

    E. largest populations of guest workers

40. Which of the following statements most closely aligns with the theory of environmental determinism?

    (A) The physical environment interacts with human groups in shaping the cultural landscape.

    (B) Humans create a series of reactions to the physical environment in which they live and choose from a set of possibilities the best course of action to suit their circumstance.

    (C) The physical environment directly causes human actions to take the forms they do.

    (D) The physical environment may affect human choices, but human groups ultimately can shape the physical environment to fit their needs.

    (E) Resources drive the creation of a set of tensions between the regions of world rich in food and those most needing it.

41. The spread of baseball to China is most closely an example of which process?

    (A) Agglomeration   (D) Balkanization

    (B) Cultural convergence   (E) Conurbation

    (C) Centripetal forces

42. In which place labeled on the map above do the largest number of people live as irredenta of Albania?

(A) Montenegro

(D) Podgorica

(B) Kosovo

(E) Belgrade

(C) Vojvodina

43. Which of the following examples best illustrates the impact of toponyms in contributing to human conflict?

(A) Washington, D.C.

(D) Tokyo, Japan

(B) São Paulo, Brazil

(E) Berlin, Germany

(C) Mumbai, India

44. Which of the following most closely qualifies as a buffer state?

(A) China

(D) Venezuela

(B) Mongolia

(E) Macedonia

(C) France

45. In which of the following regions would the sawah pictured above most likely
    NOT exist?

    (A) Indonesia   (D) Malaysia

    (B) Northern India   (E) Vietnam

    (C) Southeastern China

46. Which of the following processes is most likely to be bulk reducing?

    (A) Automobile manufacturing

    (B) Copper refining

    (C) Computer production

    (D) Clothing manufacturing

    (E) Soda bottling

47. Ukraine, the Czech Republic, Slovenia, and the Republic of Korea shared
    which worldwide demographic trend from 2000 through 2005?

    (A) Highest crude birth rate

    (B) Lowest doubling time

    (C) Highest natural rate of increase

    (D) Lowest total fertility rate

    (E) Lowest dependency ratio

Figure 1

Figure 2

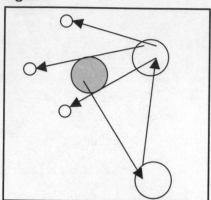

Legend
- Shading indicates node of infection
- The larger the circle, the larger the community infected
- Arrows indicate spatial diffusion path

48. Which of the following accurately describes the infection patterns depicted in each figure above?

(A) Figure 1 demonstrates the pattern of hierarchical diffusion, and Figure 2 shows contagious diffusion.

(B) Figure 1 primarily demonstrates a contagious diffusion pattern, and Figure 2 shows hierarchical diffusion.

(C) Figures 1 and 2 primarily demonstrate contagious diffusion patterns.

(D) Figures 1 and 2 primarily demonstrate hierarchical diffusion patterns.

(E) Neither Figure 1 nor Figure 2 demonstrates contagious diffusion patterns.

49. Which of the following demographic tools is used more as a predictive measurement of fertility in a society?

(A) Total fertility rate   (D) Infant mortality rate

(B) Crude birth rate   (E) Literacy rate

(C) General fertility rate

50. Which of the following is NOT an independent state on the current world map?

    (A) Burma (Myanmar)   (D) Albania

    (B) Yugoslavia   (E) Hungary

    (C) East Timor

51. Subsistence agriculture

    (A) does not include the herding of animals

    (B) is aimed at producing surplus crops for sale in the market

    (C) is becoming increasingly dominant in the world

    (D) is characterized by production of food for consumption by the farmers and their families

    (E) is most practiced in South America

52. Which of the following first focused world attention on global climate change, facilitating discussions by leading world countries to reduce greenhouse gas emissions?

    (A) UNCLOS   (D) Benelux

    (B) Kyoto Protocol   (E) Comintern

    (C) NAFTA

(Source: U.S. Census Bureau, International Data Base)

53. Which of the following accurately contrasts the demographic trends of Suriname and Argentina, based on the 2004 age-sex pyramids shown on the previous page?

(A) Argentina is most likely in stage 1 of demographic transition, while Suriname is likely in stage 3.

(B) Argentina has a higher percentage of women in the fecund range than does Suriname.

(C) Life expectancy in Suriname is higher than Argentina.

(D) Since the 1990s birth rates have changed more in Suriname than in Argentina.

(E) Women have a lower life expectancy in Argentina than in Suriname.

54. In addition to India, which country is home to the largest number of Hindus?

(A) Pakistan   (D) China

(B) Senegal   (E) Nepal

(C) Sri Lanka

55. The picture above was taken on the Paseo de la Reforma, a prominent boulevard in Mexico City, Mexico. This picture most closely reflects which concept?

(A) Agglomeration of industries

(B) Lasting colonial imprints

(C) Communist ideology

(D) Impact of greenhouse gas emissions

(E) Creation of a forward capital

56. The Kentucky Governor's Scholars Program, which offers scholarships covering full room and board to talented high school seniors if they choose to go to in-state universities, was established primarily to prevent

(A) brain drain   (D) immigration

(B) guest workers   (E) intervening opportunity

(C) intraregional migration

57. Diffusion on a microscale often occurs most intensely around the initial adopter, or innovator. This is referred to as

(A) susceptibility   (D) independent invention

(B) maladaptive diffusion   (E) neighborhood effect

(C) stimulus diffusion

58. The push in Northern Ireland to separate from its United Kingdom-based government and reintegrate with Catholic Ireland best exemplifies

(A) devolution   (D) structuration theory

(B) neocolonialism   (E) gerrymandering

(C) centripetal forces

59. Which of the following is true of commercial farming in more-developed countries?

(A) Consumption of a particular food product is usually highly related to its market price.

(B) Commercial farmers face surpluses of their harvests because of stagnant market demand.

(C) The food supply in more-developed countries has remained relatively constant since the 1960s.

(D) Low population growth has not affected agricultural markets.

(E) Farmers in the United States are encouraged by the government to grow surpluses.

60. Newspapers, bakeries, and dairy plants are examples of

    (A) footloose industries   (D) cultural convergence

    (B) ubiquitous industries   (E) bulk-reducing industries

    (C) entrepots

61. All the following are accurate generalizations of human migration in England in the 1880s EXCEPT:

    (A) Streams of migration often produce counterstreams, which are usually small.

    (B) Migrants moving long distances usually travel to one of the great centers of commerce and industry.

    (C) Most migrants travel only small distances.

    (D) Migration is a step-by-step journey.

    (E) Large towns grow more by natural increase than by migration.

62. A major change over the last 30 years in the list of the world's 20 largest (most-populated) cities is that

    (A) no South American city appears on the list

    (B) New York City has fallen off the list

    (C) the dominant presence on the list of Western industrial cities has reduced

    (D) the average annual change is nearly 30 percent

    (E) the average size of cities on the list is nearly 30 million inhabitants

63. Vegetative planting

    (A) is growing plants by dividing roots and cutting stems

    (B) involves planting seeds to cultivate a crop

    (C) is defined as the commercial farming of vegetable crops such as radishes and lettuces

    (D) most likely followed the human discovery of planting and cultivating seeds

    (E) originated in South America

Population and Agricultural Density Measurements

Country	Population Density (people per square kilometer of farmland)		Agricultural Density (farmers per square kilometer of farmland)
	Arithmetic	Physiological	
Egypt	70	3,503	1,401
The Netherlands	398	1,601	64
Canada	3	35	1

Source: Rubenstein, 2005

64. Which of the following statements is directly supported by the data in the table above?

I. Canada has a smaller population than Egypt or the Netherlands.

II. The Dutch use more mechanized farming tools than the Egyptians.

III. Dutch cities are more densely populated than Egyptian or Canadian cities.

IV. Egypt has less arable land per person than the Netherlands or Canada does.

(A) I

(B) I and III

(C) I, II and IV

(D) II, III, and IV

(E) II and IV

65. Which of the following agricultural types is predominantly found in peripheral countries?

(A) Truck farming

(B) Mixed crop and livestock

(C) Mediterranean

(D) Plantation

(E) Organic

66. Feeding Kuala Lumpur's industrial growth has drained other Malaysian cities and regions of valuable workers and resources. This example best demonstrates

(A) cumulative causation

(B) territoriality

(C) the median-line principle

(D) the dependency theory

(E) counterurbanization

67. All the following are considered 21st-century world cities EXCEPT

(A) Seoul, South Korea   (D) Kolkata, India

(B) Istanbul, Turkey   (E) Vienna, Austria

(C) São Paulo, Brazil

68. When Worth Industries was successful in Tokyo, Japan, it drew more jobs to the region, which in turn added more businesses and development. This case study is an example of

(A) multiple-nuclei development

(B) gravity model patterns

(C) the multiplier effect

(D) doubling time

(E) epidemiological transition

69. The process of profits from outsourced factories flowing from the periphery back to the core is known as

(A) machine space   (D) backwash effects

(B) multiplier leakage   (E) terraforming

(C) foreign direct investment

70. The surge in internal migration after 1960 of Mexican women to the border between the United States and Mexico is most influenced by which factor?

(A) The chance of crossing the border

(B) The construction of maquiladoras

(C) Antinatalist policies in central Mexico

(D) Educational opportunities

(E) Forced migration

71. Which type of agriculture is practiced by the most people in the world?

(A) Shifting cultivation   (E) Intensive subsistence

(B) Pastoral nomadism   (D) Plantation

(C) Mediterranean

72. Which of the following is the strongest example of an ecotourism industry?

    (A) Theme park with a roller coaster

    (B) Guided trail hike to view a rain forest

    (C) Beachfront resort

    (D) Oceangoing cruise ship

    (E) Go-cart track

73. A country that enacts pronatalist policies will most directly cause which of the following demographic effects?

    (A) Higher crude death rate   (D) Slower rate of natural increase

    (B) Longer life expectancy   (E) Slower doubling time

    (C) Higher total fertility rates

74. Which of the following best exemplifies exurbanization?

    (A) People in their 20s moving from farms to cities for excitement

    (B) A newly married couple moving from the rural areas to the suburbs to raise their children

    (C) A retired couple moving from their city apartment to a quiet community in a remote, rural village promising greater peace and tranquility from the city's hustle and bustle

    (D) The renovation of a warehouse into a luxurious high-rise loft apartment complex

    (E) The concentration of similar businesses around a shared resource

75. Which of the following central place functions is most likely to have the smallest range of goods and smallest threshold population?

    (A) Research university   (D) Allergy-testing clinic

    (B) Helicopter repair shop   (E) Computer store

    (C) Gas station

Section II

TIME: 75 minutes

3 free-response questions

> **Instructions:** You have 75 minutes to answer all three free-response questions in this section. Take a few minutes to outline your answers. Illustrate your essay with substantive examples when appropriate. It is not enough to answer a question by merely listing facts. You should present a cogent argument based on your critical analysis of the question posed and your understanding of geography.

1. The figure below depicts U.S. intraregional migration during the 1990s.

    (A) Describe the migration pattern shown in the figure.

    (B) State at least two of Ravenstein's laws of migration and analyze the relevance of each to explaining the migration pattern depicted in the figure.

    (C) Explain the combination of factors that work to create the migration pattern demonstrated in the figure. In your response apply the demographic transition model to your explanation of the pattern demonstrated.

2. (A) Define *monolingualism*, and give an example of a monolingual country.

   (B) Multilingualism often reflects strong cultural pluralism and regional division.

      i. Define *multilingualism*.

      ii. Give an example of a multilingual state in either North America or Europe, and explain how linguistic diversity has contributed to regionalism in that state.

(Images Courtesy of Tennessee State Library and Archives, Nashville)

Werthan Mills Plant, circa 1950, was in an inner-city neighborhood in East Nashville, Tennessee.

The luxurious loft apartments at the former Werthan Mills Plant circa 2007.

3. (A) Define *gentrification*.

   (B) Relate gentrification to the photographs above. The modern loft apartments sell for roughly $200,000 each.

   (C) Explain one positive and one negative effect of gentrification as a proposed method of urban renewal.

PRACTICE EXAM 2

AP Human Geography

Answer Key

Section I

1.	(E)	20.	(A)	39.	(D)	58.	(A)
2.	(B)	21.	(B)	40.	(C)	59.	(B)
3.	(C)	22.	(C)	41.	(B)	60.	(B)
4.	(B)	23.	(D)	42.	(B)	61.	(E)
5.	(B)	24.	(D)	43.	(C)	62.	(C)
6.	(D)	25.	(C)	44.	(B)	63.	(A)
7.	(A)	26.	(E)	45.	(B)	64.	(E)
8.	(E)	27.	(C)	46.	(B)	65.	(D)
9.	(A)	28.	(E)	47.	(D)	66.	(A)
10.	(B)	29.	(A)	48.	(B)	67.	(E)
11.	(E)	30.	(D)	49.	(A)	68.	(C)
12.	(D)	31.	(B)	50.	(B)	69.	(B)
13.	(C)	32.	(E)	51.	(D)	70.	(B)
14.	(E)	33.	(B)	52.	(B)	71.	(E)
15.	(B)	34.	(A)	53.	(D)	72.	(B)
16.	(D)	35.	(D)	54.	(E)	73.	(C)
17.	(B)	36.	(A)	55.	(B)	74.	(C)
18.	(D)	37.	(A)	56.	(A)	75.	(C)
19.	(B)	38.	(A)	57.	(E)		

Section I Diagnostic Instrument

> **Instructions:** Use these charts to see where your "weaknesses" exist in the curriculum.

Geography: Its Nature and Perspectives

Item #	20	22	38	40
Correct/Incorrect				

Population

Item #	5	17	21	28	39	47	49	53	56	64	70	73
Correct/Incorrect												

Cultural Patterns and Processes

Item #	4	6	12	16	18	19	25	27	33	41	42	48	54	57
Correct/Incorrect														

Political Organization of Space

Item #	3	7	11	13	15	23	26	34	44	50	58
Correct/Incorrect											

Agricultural and Rural Land Use

Item #	8	14	24	31	37	45	51	59	63	65	71
Correct/Incorrect											

Industrialization and Economic Development

Item #	9	29	32	35	46	52	60	62	66	68	69	72
Correct/Incorrect												

Cities and Urban Land Use

Item #	1	2	10	30	36	43	55	61	67	74	75
Correct/Incorrect											

PRACTICE EXAM 2

AP Human Geography

Detailed Explanations of Answers

Section I

1. **(E)**
    Agglomeration is the process of locating similarly functioning entities, such as the car dealerships, in close proximity. (A) is the inverse process in which geographic phenomena are separated. (B) refers to the general ease with which a given place can interact with other locations. (C) refers to the resolution levels in mapping and geographic research. (D) occurs when a place is indistinguishable from any other place and does not have a sense of being unique.

2. **(B)**
    According to the rank-size rule, there is a regular pattern or hierarchy in the ordering of cities according to size. A country's nth-largest city is always $1/n$ the size of the country's largest settlement. Therefore, the country's fourth-largest city is one-fourth the size of its largest city.

3. **(C)**
    A federal government structure is one in which the constituent regions in the country have protected authorities yielded to them by the central government, which shares power with them. (A), (B), (D), and (E) are unitary government structures, which are characterized by a power concentration in a central government with little or no authority yielded to provincial regions.

4. **(B)**
    Hinduism did not originate with one person or prophet who spread its teachings, whereas (A) was spread by Siddhartha Gautama; (C) is linked to Islam's prophet, Muhammad; (D) is associated with its organizer, Laozi; and (E) was founded by the philosopher Confucius.

5. **(B)**

    Migration selectivity asserts that humans react to new conditions presented in their lives. As a consequence of these conditions, humans often make decisions (or are forced) to move. Push factors "push" people out of a region, or make them want to leave; examples are climate change or high taxes. Pull factors "pull" people to a particular region, or make them want to move there; examples are good schools or better job opportunities. It is important to note, however, that a person's decision to move is not entirely in that person's control. Important influences in the push-pull balance are beyond the individual's control, such as rising taxes or environmental change. (A) is incorrect because push-pull factors fall into several categories, including economic and social categories. (C) is incorrect because a push factor to one person may be a pull factor to another. For example, "being closer to Mother" may be a pull factor to one person and a push factor to another, depending on the person's relationship with Mother. (D) is incorrect because each location has a unique set of features that are valued differently by different people. (E) is incorrect because humans do not always move when forced to live in unfavorable circumstances. Sometimes people do not have the ability to move, as when living under a totalitarian regime.

6. **(D)**

    Isoglosses are boundaries within which a particular word is used. North of the isogloss in the diagram, *Pop* is dominantly used, while south of it *Coke* dominates usage. (B) are symbols in a language that connote the idea being communicated rather than the sound. (C) is a simplified form of a lingua franca (or language used for trade); often pidgins are characterized by simplified vocabulary and grammatical structures. (E) is a derogatory term describing the influx of new words and phrases from other languages or regions into another; typically the word is used by people wanting to keep their language free from outside influences.

7. **(A)**

    Usually states with compact shapes, ideally circular, can fit into a unitary governmental organization because regionalism is not as present as in a fragmented state, for example. The other answer choices set the stage for a federal state, or one that allows for a sense of regional semisovereignty tied to a national government of representation. For example, Australia and the United States have multicore structures (i.e., have more than one power base or region in the country), wide territories, ethnic diversity, and regionalism (i.e., competing regions).

8. **(E)**

    Sub-Saharan Africa's food production has declined and is still dropping as a result of environmental damage related to overfarming and desertification, governmental corruption, disease, and the inability of local farmers to compete in the global agricultural economy. Therefore sub-Saharan Africans have the lowest caloric intake of any people on the earth, making (A) incorrect. (B) is incorrect because malnutrition most affects children in rural areas, which typically lack access to governmental aide and other food sources. (C) is incorrect because the Green Revolution has actually had a limited impact in sub-Saharan Africa compared with other world regions, such as South America. (D) is incorrect, because agribusiness investments and the globalization of agriculture have forced many local farmers out of the competition in the farming marketplace.

9. **(A)**

Following are the Human Development Index levels for the regions in the correct response: Anglo-America, 0.94; western Europe, 0.92; eastern Europe, 0.78; Southeast Asia, 0.71; Middle East, 0.66. This makes (A) the correct order.

10. **(B)**

Redlining is the illegal practice by banks and financial institutions of refusing to lend to people and firms based on their geographic places; it had racist overtones when banks would not give African Americans loans to buy houses in certain areas, keeping those areas all white. Redlining can lead to ghettoization (D), the creation or maintenance of low-income, underprivileged neighborhoods characterized by cyclical poverty. (A) is when real estate agents create racially based fear that leads people to move out of their neighborhoods and that ultimately benefits the agents who sell the homes. (C) is the purposeful redistricting of electoral regions to benefit particular political parties. (E) is the hard-to-trace practice of real estate agents who take people of certain races to see homes in certain areas, leading to segregation patterns and racially grouped living patterns.

11. **(E)**

An independent state is a country. There are approximately 200 independent countries on the earth.

12. **(D)**

The hearth of Islam is believed to be the city of Mecca, which is on the western side of Saudi Arabia near the Red Sea. This is the point, along with the Saudi Arabian city of Medina, from which Islam diffused. Every able-bodied Muslim is called to make a pilgrimage to visit the Holy Mosque in Mecca once in a lifetime. The other choices, though they exist in the Middle East, are not the birthplace of the religion. However, (C) is a tempting choice because it is home to what Muslims believe to be the third-holiest site in Islam, the Dome of the Rock.

13. **(C)**

A stateless nation is a nation or strongly linked cultural group without a state to call its own. The Kurds form a large minority nation in Iran, Turkey, and Iraq. Although they wish to have their own state, the regime of Saddam Hussein in Iraq worked violently against it, and the Kurds face opposition to this concept from their neighboring Arab states. (A) is a country in which the borders of the dominant nation (or group) match the borders of the country, such as Iceland. (B) is a country housing several nations within its borders. (D) is a country whose land totally encompasses the land of another country. (E) is an organization involving three or more countries that are working to promote shared objectives, such as the United Nations or the European Union.

14. **(E)**

The von Thünen model makes all the listed assumptions except for (E), because von Thünen assumed that soil quality and type were similar across the isolated state. By equalizing the soil type and quality, von Thünen focused his model on analyzing farmer's choices based on cost of transportation and land nearest to the market.

15. **(B)**

Irredentism is when one group of people seeks the return of their people (or land) from a region not controlled by them. In the Yugoslavian civil wars of the 1990s, the dominating Serbs longed to keep their fellow Serbs together under one government. Since Bosnia-Herzegovina has the highest percentage (32 percent) of Serbs within it, the Belgrade government of the disintegrating Yugoslavian state wanted bitterly to keep Bosnia-Herzegovina from seceding and forming an independent state. Although the Serbs in Serbia (A) were experiencing irredentism, the bloodiest focus (or cause) of this desire was Bosnia-Herzegovina, where so many Serbs resided outside Serbia. Croatia (C) had a much smaller percentage of ethnic Serbs within its boundaries, as did Macedonia (D) and Slovenia (E). Consequently, their attempted secession from the crumbling Serb-controlled Yugoslavian government was much less bloody than Bosnia's attempt.

16. **(D)**

The two largest branches of Islam are Sunni and Shiite. Iran is nearly 89 percent Shiite, whereas most Islamic countries are predominantly Sunni, as in the remainder of the answer choices. Worldwide there are only about 165 million Shia compared with nearly 1 billion Sunnis.

17. **(B)**

The region of Japan that centers on Tokyo is a clear national core. This area, known as the Kanto Plain, is a highly urbanized region that is the economic and sociopolitical nucleus of the country. (A), (C), and (E) are multicore states, each with several regions that compete for dominance rather than one, clear seat of economic and sociopolitical power. (D) is a fragmented state without one clear core around which activities ambulate.

18. **(D)**

A lingua franca is a language used between two people who speak different languages. When Japanese and German traders meet and turn to English to communicate, English is being used as the lingua franca between the traders. (A) is a simplified form of a dominant language adopted by a people wanting to use that language to participate in the region dominated by that language. When that simplified form of a dominant language, a pidgin, replaces the mother tongue of those people using the pidgin, that simplified variant of the language becomes known as a creole language (B). (C) is the language selected by a government for official purposes and documents. (E) is when only one language exists in a region, which in modern countries is a rarity.

19. **(B)**

An exclave is a region of land separated from but politically controlled by its motherland. On the map, the portion of land marked Z is named Naxcivan (or Nakhichevan) and is an exclave of primarily Muslim Azerbaijan. Notice its position within Armenia, which is primarily Christian. This position has caused much conflict between the two regions, and migrants pass between the two regions. (A) is an extension of acculturation, a process in which a culture group loses some of its original traits when it comes into contact with another more dominant culture group. Assimilation is when authentic, defining traits are lost to complete integration within a new culture. A ghetto (C) is a cultural enclave, wherein people of a similar, often minority and economically or politically oppressed, culture reside or are forced to reside. (D) is the presence of many languages, races, and other culture groups within the same region. When the basic sector of the economy—that which brings money to a region from the outside (e.g., a factory)—is cultivated, the growth of the nonbasic sector doubles; that is the multiplier effect (E).

20. **(A)**

Human geography essentially attempts to answer the questions of where and why human activities occur in the patterns that they do. (B) describes physical geography, which often complements human studies. (C), (D), and (E) are components of human geography but too limited to serve as a definition.

21. **(B)**

The data displayed in the table relates to the decreasing dependency ratio in Ireland after Ireland relaxed its laws preventing contraception, which could be inferred from the table by tracing the pattern of the total fertility rate (TFR). Over the years highlighted, the TFR (the number of children born per woman) steadily declined, allowing more women to enter the workforce because they were not solely having children. By 2006 the combination of more women working and fewer children being born per woman increased the workforce and reduced the number of dependents per worker. This led to an economic surge in Ireland by the turn of the millennium, thus ruling out (C) and (E). Statement I is accurate because the number of children per woman decreased starting in the 1970s, leading to smaller generations of children in the following years.

22. **(C)**

Absolute location is defined as the exact position of a place on the global grid, using latitude and longitude. A location's address, such as 123 Main Street, Brookings, South Dakota 57007, can also be seen as a form of absolute location because only one place on the map can have that exact address. (A) is a location's place relative to other places; (B) is a general term used for a group of places sharing some sense of commonality; (D) is the hearth of a functional region, the focal point of some spreading phenomenon; and (E) comprises a place's physical characteristics.

23. **(D)**

A relic boundary is a boundary that once functioned to divide territory or people but now is only a reminder of that boundary. The remnants of the Berlin Wall are a reminder of a boundary that once divided Berlin. The Berlin Wall was a superimposed boundary when it was functioning but is a relic because it no longer functions. (A) is a boundary that follow lakes, rivers, or natural features. (B) is a boundary created and adjusted along with the cultures affected by it. (C) is a boundary forcibly placed "on top of" a culture and is not sensitive to that culture. (E) is a boundary that existed before the development of the human cultures it serves to divide.

24. **(D)**

Secondary economic activity involves the refining or processing of the earth's resources extracted in primary economic activities, such as farming. Agglomeration is the clumping or clustering of economic activities for economic advantage; the clumped businesses or industries share resources. In Sofiya the machinery and equipment industry, agriculture-processing industry, textiles and clothing industry, chemicals and rubber industry, and power plant can all exchange goods and services to support each other's functions. Additionally, Sofiya is Bulgaria's capital city (evident by its name being in capital letters on the map), having the largest population and available workforce. The other choices, although they have secondary industries, do not have as much agglomeration of secondary economic activities as does Sofiya.

25. **(C)**

Ideograms are written expressions in a language that communicate not a sound but an idea, so they are symbolic representations of ideas in a language. Chinese uses ideograms, such as the one displayed. (A) is the system of using roman letters to write out the phonetics of the Chinese language, instead of using ideograms. (B) is a line on a map that connects points of equal value; isolines often appear on topographic maps and weather maps. (D) is an area where many languages are spoken. (E) is a language that does not show any interaction with other languages and does not belong to a language family.

26. **(E)**

A nation-state is a country in which the boundaries of the state match the ethnographic boundaries of the people within those political borders, a place in which there is ethnic and political cohesion. Japan is most aptly termed a nation-state because it has a relatively cohesive population compared with the other nations listed. (A) exemplifies multinationalism because Canada has French-speaking and English-speaking residents. (B) has thousands of minority nations within the knit of its federation. The population of (C) includes people from prominent minority nations, such as Africans. (D) is geographically and culturally split between the Fleming and Walloon nations.

27. **(C)**

The Middle East is situated at the intersection of Europe, Asia, and Africa, which has resulted in its being both a victim of invasion and a prominent part of trade routes throughout history. Although (A), (B), (D), and (E) are true, they are too limited in scope to explain the comment linking this region to its position as a crossroads of peoples.

28. **(E)**

The Gravity Model is used by geographers to predict the spatial interaction of places, as a function of population sizes of the places in question and the distance between the places. There is no known model to predict population density (A), per se, but the demographic transition model does predict birth and death rates (D), and the von Thünen Model predicts agricultural land use patterns (B). Models such as the concentric zone model and the urban realms model (among others) predict and explain urban land use patterns (C).

29. **(A)**

Liberal models, such as Rostow's economic development model, assume that all countries can develop if they improve practices within their own economies. In contrast, structuralist models of development, such as the dependency theory and core-periphery models, argue that the structure of the international economy controls and limits the growth potential of peripheral countries. (B) has reversed the two ideas, because Rostow's is a liberal model, while core-pcriphery models are structuralist. (C) is not correct because structuralist models embrace the concept of neocolonialism, arguing that countries that were once colonized by core countries are now economically dependent on their former colonial masters. (D) describes liberal models, while (E) describes structuralist models.

30. **(D)**

While Southeast Asia may have large numbers of urban dwellers, it has the lowest percentage (around 40 percent) of urban dwellers, because most Southeast Asians still live in rural, subsistence farming villages. (B) is nearly 60, and (A), (C), and (E) are nearly 80 percent.

31. **(B)**

Agribusiness refers to the system of farming, processing, packaging, distribution, marketing, and sale of farm products. Agribusiness is the food production industry, which accounts for nearly 20 percent of all U.S. workers. (A) is incorrect because most U.S. farms, nearly 98 percent, are still family owned. (C) is incorrect because the amount of U.S. land devoted to farming has increased. The number of U.S. farms has decreased since 1900, making (D) incorrect. The largest farms, comprising 4 percent of the total U.S. farms, accounts for nearly 50 percent of U.S. agricultural output.

32. **(E)**

World-systems analysis asserts that the world's countries are divided into three subgroups: the core, the semiperiphery, and the periphery. The world, according to the theory, is essentially an economic system driven by capitalism and competition for resources. (A) is unrelated and a distracter, although supranational organizations can influence international structures. (B) and (C) are elements of Mackinder's heartland theory. (D) is not necessarily true because it is questionable whether states can move in a fluid manner from the peripheral zones of global power to core positions. Some geographers assert that such mobility is not something that can be achieved by individual states but is more related to global economic structures.

33. **(B)**

The photograph, taken in Jerusalem, Israel, shows the Dome of the Rock, the third-holiest site to Muslims, following Mecca and Medina in Saudi Arabia. It also shows remains of the Western Wall, which is a holy site to Jews because it is believed to be the remains of the western wall of the Temple of Solomon. The juxtaposition of these two holy sites is at the root of the Israeli-Arab conflict. The other answer choices are distracters.

34. **(A)**

Definition, the first stage of the boundary evolution process, is when a treaty or document is written out with a description, and agreement of the boundary is spelled out. At the second stage, delimitation, the boundary is marked on a map. Finally, demarcation (which often does not occur) is when the boundary is formally marked on the land, with a line, a fence, or some other physical marker.

35. **(D)**

Growth poles are regions of extraordinarily high economic and industrial growth that are often initiated and driven around a single firm or industry leading the growth explosion, such as a new factory or research initiative. (A) is false because growth poles first cause heightened industrialization around the process causing growth. (B) is false because growth poles can be local or regional if they apply to a region, like the Ruhr region in Germany's industrial core, or a factory in a town that attracts positive growth. (C) is false because growth poles lead to agglomeration and clustering of like-minded processes around the area of magnetic growth to take advantage of the momentum and to feed the growth. (E) is not true because a megalopolis is caused by or evidence of growth poles.

36. **(A)**

Favelas, barrios, and *barriadas* are squatter settlements on the outskirts of many rapidly growing Latin American cities that are the focus of intense urban migration (C). Unfortunately, these cities cannot adequately house all the migrants (E), and the cities' support services and infrastructures, such as plumbing are strained (B). People are moving to the cities to take part in the industrialization process, coupled with population increases in part owing to improved medical care and farming practices diffusing to less-developed countries in Latin America (D).

37. **(A)**

Ranching is the raising of animals on large tracts of arid and semiarid land (extensive) on which the animals graze. It is usually practiced in more-developed countries on land where the vegetation and soil do not support crops. Mixed crop and livestock farms prevail in central Europe, whereas ranching is prevalent in the other areas listed.

38. **(A)**

The cultural landscape of a region is the imprint of human activity on the earth's surface; it is the fingerprint of human activity on the natural environment. Therefore, the cultural landscape approaches geography through the lens of both physical (natural) and social (cultural) processes. (B) is too limited in that it does not include the nature of human–environment interactions that are at the base of the cultural landscape approach. (C) describes the theory of environmental determinism, which states that people's actions are determined by the climate and natural environment in which they live. Both (D) and (E) are unrelated and not valid theories.

39. **(D)**

Except for Japan, the world's oldest countries are in Europe. These highlighted countries are experiencing "aging populations" in which the rate of natural increase is lowering and the dependency ratio is increasing. (A), (B), and (C) are the inverse of the situation in these countries, because each has a low natural growth rate and the resulting long doubling time and high dependency ratio. Although countries like Italy and Germany have high numbers of guest workers, Japan has strictly regulated the immigration of workers, thus making (E) incorrect.

40. **(C)**

Environmental determinism asserts that the physical environment directly causes human behavior, that humans are driven by their environments to take certain actions. This 19th century theory would have agreed with the idea that warmer areas create more-productive people. (A) is too vague and does not capture the theory of environmental determinism in the more exact way that (C) does. Both choices (B) and (D) more accurately reflect the theory of possibilism, a response to environmental determinism that argues that the physical environment may limit human actions by presenting a set of feasible choices that humans can work with to fit their needs. (E) is unrelated to the topic.

41. **(B)**

Cultural convergence is a result of cultural diffusion, when a trait, such as baseball, from one culture spreads into another culture and is adopted. (A) is the clumping of people and activities in one region for shared benefit, such as the grouping of factories in an industrial park to share resources. (C) are forces that unite a geographic unit, such as a national flag around which people can rally. (D) is the breakup of a country or other geographic unit into smaller (usually ethnic) units, such as what happened in the former Yugoslavia. (E) is the grouping of major metropolitan regions to form a megacomplex (sometimes called a megalopolis) of one urbanized area.

42. **(B)**

Kosovar Albanians longed desperately to be reunited with Albania, although Kosovo was an administrative unit of Serbia. This issue became a flash point in the 1990s as Yugoslavia devolved toward breaking into nation-states. (A) Montenegro is home to most ethnic Montenegrins, who also resented Belgrade's controlling presence. (C) is a region north of Belgrade with few ethnic Albanians; (D) is the largest city and the unofficial capital of Montenegro; and (E) is the capital of the Serb province and was home to the former Serb dictator Slobodan Milosevic's power base.

43. **(C)**

Toponyms are place names. Often human groups will wage war over the name of a place, because names symbolize power structures and history. Mumbai, India, is a toponym that is the result of an ongoing conflict in India over that city's name, which was recently changed from its colonially imposed name of Bombay, given by India's British occupiers. The other answer choices are places not associated with conflicts over place names.

44. **(B)**

A buffer state exists geographically between two potentially hostile or warring states. It is usually smaller and weaker. Belgium, for example, was historically a buffer state between France and Germany, and Mongolia exists as a buffer between potentially hostile Russia and China. (A) and (C) are too large and powerful to be buffers. (D) and (E) do not serve significantly to separate potentially warring neighbors.

45. **(B)**

A sawah is a flooded field in rice farming often found in all the listed regions except (B), which has too dry of a climate for wet rice farming.

46. **(B)**

A bulk- or weight-reducing process is one in which the assembly or production process creates a product that is lower in weight or volume than the original parts. All the answer choices except copper refining are weight-gaining processes, meaning that the final product weighs more than the original parts.

47. **(D)**

Ukraine, the Czech Republic, Slovenia, and the Republic of Korea are so economically depressed and their birth rates—that is, the rates of natural increase—are so low that they are classified as "graying populations." Consequently, they have very low fertility rates, extremely high doubling times, and high dependency ratios, because the younger generations are not reproducing at the levels to match the older generations, thus resulting in more dependents per worker.

48. **(B)**

Contagious diffusion is the spread of an innovation in a wave pattern. The spread pattern moves across space from the hearth or node to the next-closest place, regardless of the size or power of the receiving place. In Figure 1 the phenomenon, perhaps a disease, spreads from smaller cities to larger cities and then to a smaller city. Figure 2 diffuses from the larger cities to the smaller cities, even though the smaller cities are closer to the node than are the larger cities. The remainder of the choices incorrectly label the diffusion types.

49. **(A)**

While all the other answer choices are used to represent past behavior, the total fertility rate represents a predictive measure used to forecast how many children each woman is expected to bear. For example, the crude birth rate (B) reports how many children were born per 1,000 individuals in a society. If the total fertility rate is 3.2, demographers would predict that a woman in the fecund range would produce nearly three children during her fecund years.

50. **(B)**

Beginning in the 1990s the individual pieces of what was known as Yugoslavia began to devolve into independent countries, sometimes through what were violent, genocidal wars. By 2003 the only remaining piece renamed itself "Serbia and Montenegro," which by 2006 had even split into two distinct countries. (A), (C), (D), and (E) remain independent states as of the publication of this book.

51. **(D)**

Subsistence farmers consume what they produce. They do not produce more than what they need, or a surplus, as (B) implies. Subsistence farming often includes raising or herding animals, as in pastoral nomadism, making (A) incorrect. Subsistence agriculture has been steadily declining with the advent of new farming technologies, though it still has a large presence in less-developed countries (C). It is most practiced in Asia, particularly Southeast Asia.

52. **(B)**

The Kyoto Protocol was signed in 1997 by countries that agreed to legally binding commitments to reducing harmful greenhouse gas emissions. This was an outgrowth of the World Climate Program, initiated by the United Nations in 1979. The Kyoto Protocol was simply an overture toward a solution, because the U.S. Senate did not ratify it and President George W. Bush eliminated it from the U.S. radar. (A) established laws for delimiting shared bodies of water; (C) established free-trade relations among North American countries in 1993; (D) was an economic agreement in the 1940s by Belgium, Luxembourg, and the Netherlands that set the stage for the European Union's development; and (E) was created by the Bolsheviks in the Russian realm to spread communism throughout the world.

53. **(D)**

The base of Suriname's population pyramid is much wider than its top, indicating that Suriname is experiencing high growth rates, with more births than deaths. This puts Suriname around stage 2 of transition. Argentina's birth and death rates are more stabilized, placing it around stage 3 (with still some inequality); thus (A) is incorrect. The percentage of women in the reproducing (fecund) range is much higher in Suriname than in Argentina; as the pyramid shows, many more women in Suriname are between the ages of 15 and 40 than are older, making (B) incorrect. Life expectancy is higher in Argentina because it has more people at the top of its pyramid in the older ages than in Suriname, making (C) and (E) incorrect. Because the 1990s were as much as 14 years from the 2004 creation of the population pyramids, you need to look at the numbers for children 0–14 years old. Notice that the bars on the pyramid representing Suriname's children, male and female, 0–14 years of age are longer than the bars representing children aged 0–14 years in Argentina; thus (D) is the correct choice.

54. **(E)**

India is home to nearly 97 percent of the world's Hindu population, but the remaining percentage of Hindus live in neighboring Nepal. Pakistan and Senegal are highly Muslim; Sri Lanka is predominantly Buddhist (97 percent), and China is officially atheist.

55. **(B)**

This picture depicts the boulevard that was constructed in the late 19th century to model the Champs-Élysées in Paris. This Mexican boulevard was built by the Spanish emperor Maximilian, who came to power largely because of the support he had in France. In fact, the wide boulevard, architecture, and roundabout would make one think that this picture was taken in Paris. This shows the noticeable imprint by western European colonizers on the Latin American cultural landscape. (A) is the clumping of similar or related industries to benefit from their proximate locations. Mexico City was not a forward capital city (E) because it has been the seat of Mexican power.

56. **(A)**

Brain drain is the emigration (leaving) of well-educated members of a society for places with more opportunities suiting their needs. The Kentucky scholarship program was established to try to keep Kentucky's high-achieving high school students from migrating to universities outside the state. (B) are workers from other countries who have migrated to work temporarily in a new country. (C) is the movement within a particular region, whereas immigration (D) occurs when migrants enter a region. (E) involves an interruption in the original migration path undertaken by a migrant; essentially it is when something better comes along to prevent the migrant from completing the journey to the point he or she had planned.

57. **(E)**

The neighborhood effect occurs when diffusion is most rapid around the original innovator, or the first person affected by the diffusing element. Most simply, diffusion on a microscale most rapidly occurs through direct exposure to the diffusion phenomenon. (A) is the degree to which a person or place is likely to adopt the diffusing phenomenon. (B) occurs when a trait or phenomenon is adopted in a situation or context in which it should not fit, such as the diffusion of igloo-style homes to Florida. (C) occurs when the main idea or concept spreads but is changed to meet the adopters' needs. (D) is when two places or peoples independently invent the same (or very similar) invention or innovation.

58. **(A)**

Devolution is defined as the movement of power away from the central government in a country to its regional and local (subnational) government bodies. The movement for regional control in Northern Ireland away from U.K. control exemplifies devolution grounded in nationalism. (B) refers to the economic control that former colonial powers exert over their former political colonies. (C) are forces that unify and maintain state structures, rather than tearing down or weakening government models. (D) is the theory that individuals are a product of human structures, such as capitalism, and that humans also shape their structures. (E) is the designing of voting-district boundaries to benefit one political party over another.

59. **(B)**

Commercial farmers in more-developed countries are facing a strange irony: They are growing surpluses because farming efficiency has increased through improved farming technology, but demand for food at their markets is stagnant (and in some cases declining) because of low population growth (making C and D incorrect). In the United States, farmers receive government subsidies to encourage them not to grow surpluses, making (E) incorrect. (A) is incorrect because research shows that people will not switch from wheat products to corn products if the cost of wheat rises (within reason, of course).

60. **(B)**

Ubiquitous industries are found near their markets because of the immediacy of their products, such as a newspaper. They are not examples of (A), because footloose industries have freedom in their choice of industrial locations because they are not related to specific marketplaces and can be transported over long distances for low costs. (C) are intermediate points of trade that facilitate trade between two points or places. (D) is when a trait from one culture is adopted by another culture. (E) is an industry in which the final product weighs less than the raw materials used to create it.

61. **(E)**

Each answer choice except (E) is a generalization made by Ravenstein regarding human migration (human geographers consider Ravenstein's generalizations the only accepted rules on human migration). In the 1880s England was experiencing rapid urban migration, fueled by the Industrial Revolution (B). People were moving from the farms to the cities to find new opportunities. However, in all migration patterns, a reverse stream of people move in a return route—back to the farmlands, for example. It might not be as large as the stream into the city, but it is nevertheless present (A). Most migrants move small distances (C), not having the means or knowledge to leap great distances, and they usually move in steps (D), perhaps from town to town until they make it to their final destinations. However, large towns during the 1880s in England were growing more because of this massive urban migration into the cities than by rates of natural increase, thereby making (E) the correct choice in its inaccuracy.

62. **(C)**

The growth of populations in non-Western, peripheral countries has been the most striking change on the list, as countries such as India, South Korea, Japan, Mexico, Brazil, and China take a more prominent status on the list. In fact, cities in peripheral zones account for nearly 50 percent of cities on the list. (A) is false because Mexico City, São Paulo, Buenos Aires, and Rio de Janeiro are on the list. (B) is false because it is the second-largest city in the world as of 2007. (D) is false because annual growth averages around 15 percent. (E) is false because the average is nearly 15 million, with the largest city, Tokyo at 30 million, being far larger than the next largest, New York at nearly 17.8 million.

63. **(A)**

Vegetative planting is when agriculturalists cut the stems of plants and divide their roots to grow crops. It predated seed agriculture and likely originated in Southeast Asia, making (D) and (E) incorrect. (B) refers to seed agriculture, and (C) refers to truck farming.

64. **(E)**

The table is testing your knowledge of the definitions of arithmetic, physiological, and agricultural densities. While the arithmetic density is simply the number of people per unit of land, the physiological density measures the number of people per unit of farmland, and the agricultural density measures the number of farmers per unit of farmland. Thus, though the Dutch have the highest number of people per land, their ratio of people to farmland is less than that of Egypt's. The arithmetic density of Egypt is only 70 people per square kilometer, while its physiological density is the highest at more than 3,500, indicating that most of Egypt's peoples are clustered on farmable land; this highest physiological density indicates that Egypt has the most people per unit of farmland than the others, proving that it has less farmland per person than the others (statement IV). However, the Netherlands' agricultural density is much lower than Egypt's, indicating that fewer farmers are needed on the farmlands in the Netherlands than in Egypt. This suggests that the Dutch are more mechanized in their farming than are the Egyptians, because the Dutch use machines to reduce the number of farmers to do the same job (statement II). Because the data show ratios, the actual number of people in each country is not known, so statement I cannot be accepted, thereby eliminating (A), (B), and (C). Although statement III is tempting, the table does not specifically indicate any information on urban (city) settlement, so this statement is not supported directly.

65. **(D)**

Plantation agriculture has historically been entrenched in less-developed countries' economies, with its reliance on inexpensive labor to harvest a cash crop for sale in foreign markets. (A), (B), (C), and (E) are found in both more- and less-developed countries. Mediterranean agriculture is found primarily in the region surrounding the Mediterranean Sea, which includes North Africa. Organic agriculture (E) is sometimes found in less-developed countries, when the food is produced for foreign markets where it is sold for a price higher than people living in the countries of production could afford.

66. **(A)**

Cumulative causation happens when modernization and development occur in the area of initial advantage and drain the surrounding regions of investment, labor, and resources. Growth is fed at the expense of more-equalized growth patterns. (B) is the human tendency to claim a part of space and exact control over it, much like an animal marking its territory. (C) is involved when two countries share water space that does not include the 200 miles provided for in exclusive economic zones. According to the principle, the countries must divide the water space in half at the median point. (D) claims that former colonies are still dependent on their former colonial masters, in an economic, not political, sense. (E) refers to the reverse in the trend away from urban migration. Instead, in counterurbanization trends, more people move to suburbs and rural areas to escape cities.

67. **(E)**

World cities are extraordinarily large cities with populations exceeding 10 million. Of the cities listed, only Vienna, Austria, has a population less than 10 million (in fact, its population is less than 2 million people).

68. **(C)**

The multiplier effect is highly related to cumulative causation: one successful industry or a cluster of them acts as a magnet for further development and industry, with more jobs leading to more jobs, and so on. (A) is the urban development pattern that involves many core areas. (B) is a migration theory that states that large cities attract the largest numbers of immigrants and that closer places attract each other more than more-distant places. (D) is the demographic measurement of the time it will take for a population to double in size. (E) is the transition of the causes of death within each stage of the demographic transition model.

69. **(B)**

Multiplier leakage occurs when multinational corporations invest in and build secondary industries, such as factories, in peripheral regions and send most of the profits back to their core headquarters. This contributes to uneven development. (A) is the exponential growth of space needed to feed the growing transportation space associated with cars, trucks, and planes. (C) is the investment of multinational corporations typically in peripheral regions to build factories and export operations to feed the core's needs. (D) are the negative effects of growth poles and agglomeration caused by all the energy in development and industrial growth being focused on one area, thereby draining the surrounding and supplying regions of valuable workers and resources. (E) is the negative restructuring of the earth's physical structure by industrial processes.

70. **(B)**

The Mexican government established its maquiladora program in the 1960s to allow U.S. businesses to build factories on low-cost land on the Mexican side of the U.S.-Mexico border. The program was meant to employ displaced farmers in Mexico and allow U.S. industries to outsource parts of their production processes to lower-cost areas. The labor force in the maquiladoras includes many Mexican women. Although (A) may seem reasonable, that same desire has been present since before the 1960s. (C) and (D) do not exist along the border, and there is no reason for forced migration (E), though poverty and lack of jobs are push factors.

71. **(E)**

Nearly 41 percent of the world's population comprises farmers, and most farmers grow just enough to feed their families with no surplus. In most of Asia and Africa, more than 50 percent of the people are farmers. Intensive subsistence farming involves farming a small plot of land very intensively, or to yield high output per unit area. It is labor intensive per unit area, compared with extensive agriculture, which involves using much land.

72. **(B)**

Ecotourism is ecologically responsible travel that attempts not to harm the ecosystems or well-being of the indigenous people. A trail hike in a rain forest would most likely have the least impact on the local people and environment, whereas the other choices are more invasive to the local environment. Even a cruise ship (D), because it pollutes and disrupts the oceanic ecosystem, is less ecofriendly than a rain forest hike.

73. **(C)**

Pronatalist policies encourage people to have more children, which would lead to a higher total fertility rate, or the number of children each woman is predicted to bear in her fecund years. Higher fertility rates would not likely directly affect death rates (A) or life expectancy (B), though in the long run there could be some interaction between more babies and higher death rates. More babies would lead to higher rates of natural increase and a faster doubling time, making (D) and (E) incorrect.

74. **(C)**

Exurbanization is the movement out of the city to a more quiet, peaceful, rural setting. (A) and (B) represent urban migration, (D) is gentrification, and (E) is agglomeration.

75. **(C)**

A gas station would have a small radius from which it would draw people to use its services, hence a small range. It would also require a small population to exist, hence a small threshold population. The other answer choices would require larger populations to exist, because a small percentage of people use the services rendered by the central place functions in (A), (B), (D), and (E).

Section II

Sample Response and Scoring Rubric for FRQ 1

Sample Response

A. The figure depicts U.S. intraregional migration, which is the permanent movement within a region of a country. The largest flow by far is from the central city to the suburbs, thus indicating a net out-migration from the city. Slightly more people migrate from urban to rural areas (counterurbanization) than from rural to urban areas.

B. British demographer Ernst Ravenstein devised several laws pertaining to internal migration within a country. (Descriptions and applications of any two of the following should be in FRQ.)

   i. **Net migration amounts to a fraction of the gross migration between two places.** As seen in the figure, each of the streams has a countermigration stream, thus affecting the net migration number.

   ii. **The majority of migrants move short distances.** Because of the increase of space-time compression resulting from improvements in transportation technology, modern migrants are more likely to move long distances than were migrants in Ravenstein's time. However, the migration pattern in the figure relates to Ravenstein's prediction because most migrants depicted move short distances. For example, 8 million move between the city and the suburb, a shorter distance than the approximately 1.5 million migrants moving the longer route between the city and rural areas.

   iii. **Migrants who move longer distances tend to choose big-city destinations.** Among the migrants in the figure who move longer distances, more move in a counterurbanization trend from urban to rural areas. This law does not pertain to the figure.

   iv. **Urban residents are less migratory than inhabitants of rural areas.** The figure shows many more migrants moving from urban areas to suburban areas than it does rural residents moving into suburban and city areas. Thus, this law does not apply to the figure.

v. **Families are less likely to make international moves than young adults.** Suburbs are likely to be inhabited largely by families, while cities often attract young adults. Thus the migration pattern in the figure would seem to support Ravenstein's prediction because fewer migrants come from the suburbs than from large urban areas.

C.   People feel compelled (pushed) to emigrate from a location for political, economic, and environmental reasons. Similarly, people are induced (pulled) to immigrate to a new location because of its political, economic, or environmental attractiveness. In the figure the net out-migration from the cities is most likely related to overcrowding in the central city. In this pattern migrants from these cities are moving to the suburbs because they perceive better living conditions outside the urban areas. This pattern fits into the stage-4 prediction of the demographic transition model because major U.S. cities were in stage 4 by the 1990s. After the continued expansion and urbanization of stages 2 and 3 of the model, overcrowding in the central cities led people to seek "more room" in the American suburbs of stage 4, a typical pattern in more-developed countries.

Scoring Rubric for FRQ 1

Part A: 3 points

1 point for each of the following observations:

Note: Students should note that the movement depicted is migratory, which is permanent. Other types of movements, such as cyclic and periodic may be mentioned, but the arrows indicate migration, not cyclic or periodic movement. This is defined in the question prompt.

- Net out-migration from central city

- Largest flow from central city to suburbs

- Slightly larger migration from urban to rural areas than from rural to urban

Part B: 2 points

1 point for each law stated and analyzed.

- Accurate statement of two of Ravenstein's laws and accurate application of it to model (see each law in the sample response above)

Part C: 3 points

1 point for each of the following:

Note: Student must explain the demographic transition model mentioned to get full 3 points.

- Identification of push-pull factors:

   — Push: crowded, expensive cities

   — Pull: lifestyle and space of suburb areas

- Mention of improved transportation technology, thus allowing commuting

- Explanation of stage 4 of model

After surge of industrialization and growth of stages 2 and 3, overcrowding and expense of cities in this developed country push people to suburbs

OVERALL SCORE FOR FRQ 1   _____ / 8 points

Sample Response and Scoring Rubric for FRQ 2

Sample Response

A.   *Monolingualism* is defined as a state in which only one language is spoken. Arguably, no country in the world is truly monolingual because each has a small number of speakers of different languages. One of the closest examples of a monolingual state is Japan, which has strict immigration and naturalization policies.

B.   Multilingualism occurs in a state in which more than one language is in use. One example of a multilingual state experiencing conflict related to its linguistic diversity is Canada. French speakers in the province of Quebec desire a sense of autonomy and self-determination, separate from the English-speaking majority in Canada. Their identity as French speakers is a defining part of their nationalism, even leading to French-only laws within the province and a referendum movement to declare independence from greater Anglo-Canada.

Scoring Rubric for FRQ 2

PART A: 2 points

1 point for any of the following:

- Accurate definition of monolingualism—state wherein one language is spoken

- Possible examples include Japan in Asia; Uruguay and Venezuela in South America; Iceland, Poland, Portugal in Europe; Lesotho in Africa

PART B: 2 points

1 point for any of the following examples

1 point for correct explanation of relation between multilingualism and regionalism

- Example: Student must choose a state and specifically and accurately explain the linguistic diversity in the region and how that diversity contributes to regionalism or cultural division. Possible examples include the following

  —North America: Canada (French vs. English), United States (Spanish vs. English)

  —Europe: Greece (Greek vs. Turkish), Belgium (French vs. Dutch), Bosnia (Croatian, Serbian, Albanian), German (Turkish vs. German), France (French vs. Turkish and English), Switzerland (which has at least three major languages and one minor language)

OVERALL SCORE FOR FRQ 2   _____/ 4 points

Sample Response and Scoring Rubric for FRQ 3

Sample Response

A.   Gentrification is a process of inner-city, neighborhood urban renewal. There is also a resulting social change that occurs with this injection of money into inner-city neighborhoods and the arrival (or return) of higher social or economic groups.

B.   The old Werthan Mills Plant building has been purchased and remodeled into luxurious loft apartments in an inner-city neighborhood of east Nashville. This exemplifies the gentrification process, especially since the renovation has produced housing that is probably too expensive for the existing neighborhood dwellers.

C.   One positive effect of gentrification is that it brings renewed money and attention to decrepit, decaying infrastructures in inner cities. New middle- and upper-income citizens come to the inner-city neighborhoods being gentrified with zeal and a desire to "beautify" and commercialize the regions, generating economic development. One negative aspect of gentrification as a solution to urban renewal is its tendency to push out the people already living in the gentrified neighborhoods. Often these people have a lower socioeconomic status and cannot afford the new high-priced housing units and shops that move in. Thus gentrification can produce greater segregation, rather than unification and integration.

Scoring Rubric for FRQ 3

PART A: 1 point

1 point for the following:

- Gentrification began in the 1970s when decaying inner-city buildings in low-income neighborhoods were targeted for renovation and remodeling by developers and families in the middle and upper socioeconomic classes.

PART B: 2 points

1 point for any of the following:

- The photos show the original factory building around 1950, just as the suburbanization movement was occurring, and its remodeled, modern version.

- Gentrification occurred when a developer moved into this inner-city neighborhood and remodeled and transformed the old factory building into expensive urban-elite dwellings.

PART C: 2 points

1 point for any of the following positive factors and 1 for any of the following negative factors:

- Positives: increased economic energy in neighborhood, more aesthetically pleasing urban landscape, new businesses developed in region, efficient use of space, alternative to urban sprawl, increase in inner-city tax base

- Negatives: alienation and "pushing out" of people already living and working in region because new housing is too expensive and new businesses cater to the rich property owners moving in, political and ideological clashes between original inhabitants and influx of new "gentrifiers," increased segregation of racial and socioeconomic groups, avoiding fixing the inherent problems of cyclical poverty and suburban sprawl

OVERALL SCORE FOR FRQ 3 _____/ 5 points

Index

N

INSTALLING REA's TEST*ware*®

SYSTEM REQUIREMENTS

Pentium 75 MHz (300 MHz recommended), or a higher or compatible processor; Microsoft Windows 98 or later; 64 MB Available RAM; Internet Explorer 5.5 or higher.

INSTALLATION

1. Insert the AP Human Geography TEST*ware*® CD-ROM into the CD-ROM drive.
2. If the installation doesn't begin automatically, from the Start Menu, choose the RUN command. When the RUN dialog box appears, type d:\setup (where D is the letter of your CD-ROM drive) at the prompt and click OK.
3. The installation process will begin. A dialog box proposing the directory "Program Files\REA\AP_HumanGeography" will appear. If the name and location are suitable, click OK. If you wish to specify a different name or location, type it in and click OK.
4. Start the AP Human Geography TEST*ware*® application by double-clicking on the icon.

REA's AP Human Geography TEST*ware*® is **EASY** to **LEARN AND USE**. To achieve maximum benefits, we recommend that you take a few minutes to go through the on-screen tutorial on your computer. The "screen buttons" are also explained there to familiarize you with the program.

SSD ACCOMMODATIONS FOR STUDENTS WITH DISABILITIES

Many students qualify for extra time to take the AP Human Geography exam, and our TEST*ware*® can be adapted to accommodate your time extension. This allows you to practice under the same extended time accommodations that you will receive on the actual test day. To customize your TEST*ware*® to suit the most common extensions, visit our Website at *www.rea.com/ssd*.

TECHNICAL SUPPORT

REA's TEST*ware*® is backed by customer and technical support. For questions about **installation or operation of your software**, contact us at:

Research & Education Association
Phone: (732) 819-8880 (9 a.m. to 5 p.m. ET, Monday–Friday)
Fax: (732) 819-8808
Website: www.rea.com
E-mail: info@rea.com

Note to Windows XP Users: In order for the TEST*ware*® to function properly, please install and run the application under the same computer-administrator level user account. Installing the TEST*ware*® as one user and running it as another could cause file access path conflicts.

Jane Goodall: The Woman Who Redefined Man

"A perceptive and intimate portrait." — *USA Today*

"A thorough, intelligent, and highly readable look at an unusual life."
— *Christian Science Monitor*

"Goodall's story is truly amazing . . . Dale Peterson has done a brilliant job of writing about an equally brilliant person."
— Roger S. Fouts, author of *Next of Kin*

"Peterson's biography sheds new light on the remarkable life of this extraordinary woman." — Peter Singer, author of *Animal Liberation*

"The author's special access is a page-turning primate's reward. Goodall's life story has been so unconventional, it qualifies as wild."
— *Entertainment Weekly*

"Peterson vividly captures his subject's idealism and derring-do." — *Outside*

"[Peterson's] biography takes you deeply and completely into Goodall's many worlds." — *Los Angeles Times*

"The long-awaited, definitive biography . . . Peterson's volume is the one for which Goodall's devotees have been waiting." — *Nature*

"Compelling and detailed." — *Baltimore Sun*

"This thorough and elegant biography traces the unlikely rise of Goodall . . . and places her revolutionary discoveries in context." — *Seed*

"A beautiful book . . . Peterson has achieved the tour de force of conveying Goodall's charisma while explaining the significance of her science — and indeed, why neither would exist without the other." — *American Scientist*

"Captures the spirit of a remarkable woman in science."
— *Library Journal*, starred review

"A loving depiction of a remarkable woman who charmed the world as much as it captivated her." — *Kirkus Reviews*, starred review

"Peterson vividly and significantly enriches our understanding of Good[all] as a scientist, spiritual thinker, and humanist." — *Booklist*, starred rev[iew]

BOOKS BY DALE PETERSON

A Mad People's History of Madness

Big Things from Little Computers

Genesis II

CoCo Logo

Intelligent Schoolhouse

The Deluge and the Ark

Visions of Caliban (with Jane Goodall)

Chimpanzee Travels

Demonic Males (with Richard Wrangham)

Storyville, USA

Africa in My Blood (editor)

Beyond Innocence (editor)

Eating Apes

Jane Goodall

Jane Goodall

*The Woman
Who Redefined Man*

Dale Peterson

A MARINER BOOK
HOUGHTON MIFFLIN COMPANY
Boston · New York

For Wyn Kelley,
for the chimpanzees,
and in memory of Robbie and Kris

First Mariner Books edition 2008
Copyright © 2006 by Dale Peterson

www.houghtonmifflinbooks.com

For more information about Jane Goodall and her continuing
initiatives in wildlife research, education, and conservation,
contact the Jane Goodall Institute at www.janegoodall.com.

Library of Congress Cataloging-in-Publication Data
Peterson, Dale.
  Jane Goodall : the woman who redefined man / Dale Peterson.
    p.   cm.
  Includes bibliographical references and index.
  1. Goodall, Jane, date. 2. Primatologists — England —
Biography. 3. Chimpanzees — Tanzania — Gombe Stream
National Park. I. Title.
  QL31.G58P47 2006
  590.92 — dc22   2006006050

ISBN-13: 978-0-547-05356-1 (pbk.)

Book design by Melissa Lotfy

PRINTED IN THE UNITED STATES OF AMERICA

VB 10 9 8 7 6 5 4 3 2 1

Contents

Prologue

SHE STEPS INTO a halo of light, places a toy stuffed monkey next to a small sheet of notes and a glass of water at the podium. Her face becomes a series of curves — arched eyebrows, finely defined cheeks — and a wave in the hair (thick, an edge of pure white turning into gray and then brown, with lurking strands of honey blond) rolls to the ponytail in back. She wears a simple blue dress with white buttons. Black turtleneck beneath. No makeup other than a little lipstick. And she opens with a greeting from the chimpanzees: noisy inhalations and hooting exhalations building in volume and climaxing into screams.

She speaks, and her hands, fingers spread, move like flags, like signals or semaphores. She has a soft, almost musical voice modulated by an educated accent and polished enunciation. She creates a sense of deep relaxation, a natural, almost hypnotic connection with her audience.

She describes her early love for animals, speaks of taking earthworms to bed and sneaking into the henhouse. She recollects her mother's encouragement. She tells of her childhood reading: the journey Doctor Dolittle took to Africa, for instance, to release circus animals. She loved that bridge the monkeys made with their hands. But then she met Tarzan! And in that childhood and those childish mental images she learned what her future would be. "I vowed that I would go to Africa," she says, "live among the animals, and write books about them." She remembers meeting the great Louis Leakey, then going to find the chimpanzees in their forest. She recalls their names and personal stories. She refers to the hostility she first experienced at Cambridge University, where she was informed that chimpanzees do not have personalities, minds, or emotions. They should be given numbers, not names. . . .

She is a gifted storyteller, and she organizes her lectures around anecdotes, images, and symbols that unfold, one after the other, perfectly. She rarely refers to her notes, animating her talk with gestures and spontaneous sound effects. "Let me tell you a story," she says, "because sometimes stories are the best way to understand things." And she sees the story while telling it: drawing characters with her hands, imitating actions, illustrating thoughts. She speaks of herself at a critical moment, looking up — and looks up. She describes charging angry male chimpanzees with arms bulked out, hair standing on end — and shakes her body in excited ferocity. She speaks of a chimp grinning in fear — and makes the grin. "Imagine we're in a forest, and there are vines hanging down," she says — and she raises a hand and begins tracing vines in the air.

She is a small woman of obvious energy and courage. Against a dark and shadowy background, her face is bathed in light, her hair silvered by the light, and her voice echoes throughout the hall to an audience of several hundred or a few thousand.

The talk ends with an appeal. Perhaps it is the story about a zoo visitor who courageously jumped into a moat to save a drowning chimp named Jojo and then later recalled, "I looked into his eyes, and it was like looking into the eyes of a man, and the expression seemed to say, 'Won't someone help me?'" And she asks her audience rhetorically, "Why am I traveling the world on this crazy schedule, traveling more than three hundred days in the last year? It is because I too have looked into the eyes of chimpanzees at the edge of existence, and felt those eyes say, *Won't someone help?*"

She is a celebrity, a hero, an icon, and her lectures can be evangelistic experiences characterized by rapt attention, spontaneous tears, standing ovations — the works — with, at the end, an enthusiastic mobbing. After the lecture, members of the fundraising institute funnel the excited audience toward the membership and memento sales and the vast stacks of books — copies of almost everything she has ever written. People buy, and then they expect an autograph and, if possible, an exchange of words. As the long line of supplicants creeps forward, her personal assistant organizes: answers questions and, holding open a book to the right page, leans down to communicate special requests. The assistant, standing, gives the impression of being always cheerful. The woman, seated, seems ever patient. She signs and smiles and chats and signs again for as long as it takes — an hour, two, or three.

People approach, lean in closely, act as if they already know her. And she, always perfectly at ease, serene, listens quietly, responds appropriately. "I was on a flight to Arusha," someone says, "and you were there in business class. I talked to you. It was March 2." "Oh, yes," she says, not mentioning the fact that she has flown three or four dozen times since then.

A round-faced young woman with an upturned nose and an open smile says, "I've been working with endangered species." The woman nods affirmatively, with interest.

An older man approaches: "Sometime, if you have a moment after all this, I would like to tell you two stories about my own experiences with chimpanzees. I think you will be interested."

A pair of teenage girls: "We're doing a collection of women's first period stories, and we'd be honored if you would contribute."

Someone else (in tears): "You're my hero. You inspired me to join the Peace Corps."

And: "May the universe bless your work."

"Thank you," someone else says, pulling up a freshly autographed book. "This is one of the most memorable moments of my life."

The line feels endless. The woman listens patiently to everyone.

A young girl with braces on her teeth: "When I was in sixth grade, I had to do a research project. I did it on chimpanzees. And you!"

Another (in tears): "Thank you for everything. I'm just one of your greatest fans."

And: "I just wanted to say, I dressed up as you for Halloween."

The wise woman of silvered hair and serene mien smiles, responds, and handles the books. She writes: *Follow your dreams* and *Remember what my mum said— "Never give up!"* And then, in a neat, plain script, she signs her name: *Jane Goodall.*

PART I

The Naturalist

I

Daddy's Machine, Nanny's Garden

1930–1939

MORTIMER HERBERT MORRIS-GOODALL was a member of the prosperous middle class, a status his family had acquired during the previous
century as a result of initiative, industry, luck, and playing cards.

According to family tradition, some ancient Goodall experienced a more
than passing association with the gallows, as either a hangman or hanged
man; but the family's more reliable record starts with the birth of Charles
Goodall, on December 4, 1785, in the town of Northampton. By the early
1820s, Charles had finished his printer's apprenticeship in London and struck
out on his own as a small-scale manufacturer of playing cards and message
cards. Business was good, and he moved into progressively larger premises
until he built a factory at 24 Great College Street. By this time the concern
was known as Charles Goodall & Son.

After Charles's death, in 1851, his sons, Jonathan and Josiah, began
expanding operations, building more factory space, purchasing new high-
speed color presses, and diversifying their line to include almanacs, ball programs, calendars, Christmas greeting cards, menu cards, memorial cards,
New Year's and Valentine and visiting cards—and playing cards. The company trademark consisted of the name Goodall split in half, stacked four
letters over three, and placed inside a heart:

By 1913, Charles Goodall & Son was printing, packaging, and selling
over 2 million packs of playing cards a year, roughly three times the production of all other manufacturers combined, and by 1915 sales had reached
2.2 million. The two Goodall brothers now running the company, Charles's

grandsons, together took three quarters of the net profits, while a third brother, Reginald — the youngest — having been given no responsibility for running the company whatsoever, was forced to remain content with the final quarter of net profits.

Reginald may have been a prodigal son, and after he married Elizabeth Morris, against the family's wishes, he proceeded to give all their children a hyphenated last name — Morris-Goodall — as if to make a point. He made the point five times before falling off a horse at the Folkestone Race Course in Kent and landing on his head, producing a cerebral blood clot that, on May 3, 1916, proved fatal.

Mortimer Herbert was nine years old at the time of his father's death, and in the years following that unhappy moment the family moved a number of times, eventually settling down when his mother married again. Her new husband, the imposing Major Norman Nutt, DSO (who was said to have led a charge during the Great War by standing on top of a rolling tank and waving his sword), or Nutty, as Mortimer called him, managed the Folkestone Race Course. As an astonishing perquisite of the job, Major Nutt and his family were allowed to move into an ancient manor house built inside the ruins of an even more ancient castle owned by the Folkestone track. By then, however, Mortimer was off to Repton, a public school in Lancashire, where he proved an indifferent scholar. After Repton, he studied engineering and eventually took a job with Callender's Cable and Construction. Callender's had contracts for laying telephone cables all over England, and Mortimer would go around with a test phone to see that the cables were joined up correctly. "That was very interesting," he once recalled, "and it involved traveling and driving the test van, which was right up my street: I love driving."

Driving was his life's dominating passion. His mother taught him to drive when he was fourteen years old, and by his late teens he had bought his first car, a sporty four-cylinder H.E. (made by Herbert Engineering), which in 1930 he traded for a most magical machine.

Aston Martin was started around the time of the Great War as a manufacturer of racecars, producing during the 1920s fewer than a dozen of their superb automobiles per year, on average; the company then began producing sports and touring cars and in the early 1930s picked up production, turning out some 210 cars between 1930 and 1932. But an Aston Martin was still a rare — and very beautiful — object when Mortimer first set eyes on a gleaming white three-seater International on display at the Brooklands Motors showroom at 110 Great Portland Street in London. "It looked so beautiful I was determined to have it," he later recalled, and so when the

crankshaft on his H.E. broke, he sold the vehicle, borrowed against his inheritance, and bought the Aston. As he drove the gleaming machine out of
the showroom, he thought to pause and ask the fellow who had just sold it
to him where the factory was, and thus he learned that Aston Martin assembled cars in a London suburb not far from the showroom.

He found the factory, known as "the Works": four huge brick buildings,
each one inadequately heated by four small coal stoves, with the racecars
under development at the end of one building, their frames strategically situated to avoid damage from rain coming through broken skylights. He
walked onto the shop floor and began asking people for the boss. Someone
said, "There he is," and so Mortimer Herbert Morris-Goodall met the chain-
smoking, Italian-born engineer and racer Augustus Cesare Bertelli.

Mortimer said that he had just bought an Aston Martin International and
wanted to race it. Bertelli said that if Mortimer really wanted to drive com-
petitively, his car would require some very significant modifications. Meanwhile, Bertelli advised, it was important to start out by driving in reliability
trials rather than serious timed races, so that Mortimer could learn how to
handle the car under pressure.

During 1930 and into 1931, Mortimer drove his International in reliability trials as well as a few timed races, eventually achieving credible results
in the long-distance runs from London to Land's End and from London to
Edinburgh. The International, tuned for regular driving, could reach top
speeds of around 80 miles per hour, not particularly fast for competition
cars of that era, but its excellent handling and good brakes meant it could
run at a high average speed under challenging conditions. So Mortimer did
well, and by the middle of 1931 he believed he was ready to drive a real
racecar.

Aston Martin was now trying to make money selling first-rate sports
and touring cars, but the company continued to promote its name with an
official race team, which by the early 1930s was concentrating on the
most challenging and glamorous race of all, the twenty-four-hour Le Mans
Grand Prix d'Endurance. Compared to the other cars running in the Le
Mans Endurance—the Mercedes, Alfa-Romeos, Bugattis, Talbots, and so
on—the Aston Martin racer was a lightweight understatement, but it was
also nimble and reliable.

In 1931, Bertelli transferred Aston Martin's seventh Le Mans racer (identified as LM7) to Mortimer. European motor racing during this classic period
expressed a certain nationalistic spirit, with racecars for each nation painted
one color to simplify the problem of national identification. French cars
were blue, Italian red, German white, and British green. Mortimer's LM7,
therefore, was colored a sweet olive green. It had cut-out doors and wire

wheels, an external exhaust pipe emerging with an elegant swoop on the passenger's side, a long louvered hood kept in place with bolts and a wrap-around leather strap, front motorcycle-style fenders anchored to the brake plates and turning in concert with the front wheels, a tiny glass windscreen, big rock-screened headlamps mounted on short poles, and an aerodynami-cally tapered rear end. Soon after he took possession, Mortimer thought-fully lined the passenger's side of the cockpit with green baize.

Mortimer kept his job at Callender's, and he lived in London, sharing rooms in a Queensgate boarding house with Byron Godfrey Plantagenet Cary, a schoolmate from his Repton days. Their rooms happened to be on one of the lower floors, near the stairs. And, as the two young men noticed, late every afternoon the same stunningly attractive young woman would walk past their open door on the way to her bed-sitter, two floors up. Their door was left open on purpose, of course, and the pair would stand half out in the hall and talk to each other casually around the same time every evening in order to observe the young woman returning home from work.

Margaret Myfanwe Joseph, or Vanne, possessed a striking combination of fine arches and curves in the face, a warm and confident smile, high bright cheeks, and a firm jaw. A certain young man once told her, "Your hair is liked burnished chestnut." Another young man commented on her eyes: "What do you think you are, a green-eyed goddess?" Vanne had come to London in the late 1920s from her family home in Bournemouth, first to acquire secretarial skills at the Pittman Secretarial College, near Russell Square, and then to practice them for the impresario Charles B. Cochran.

Cocky, as he was called, had a small office at the top of 49 Old Bond Street and during the early 1930s was at the height of his career as a show business entrepreneur, creating and producing plays, musicals, and dance revues. Vanne's duties included answering the telephone ("Regent 1241"), typing up letters and documents, and taking dictation. By her own account, she was "absolutely useless" at shorthand and typing, but Cocky, who was famously fond of dachshunds and beautiful young women, may not have examined her secretarial skills very closely. At any rate, she remembered him as an agreeable, generous, and dynamic boss, and "famous actors and actresses, Noël Coward and people like that, used to sit on the arm of my chair and help me with my shorthand." Another benefit of working at 49 Old Bond Street was free admission to most of the major theatrical events in London.

In those days people dressed up for evening events. Vanne wore silk stockings (nylon was yet to be invented), but she could afford only half an evening dress. The other half belonged to her sister, Olwen, who still lived at home in Bournemouth. Thus, before any major show, Vanne had to make sure that Olwen mailed the dress in time. The day after the show, the dress would be posted right back to Bournemouth.

Among his many creative innovations, Cocky introduced a rotating stage to London audiences, for the 1930 Rodgers and Hart musical *Evergreen*. Vanne attended a performance, and because she worked for Cocky, she was able to slip backstage and visit with some of the dancers. As she was chatting enthusiastically, though, the stage began revolving. Someone shouted, "Hey, Vanne, look out!" And before she fully realized what was going on, she was front stage and facing a large, wildly applauding audience. She waved eagerly, as if she actually belonged onstage.

Vanne's true ambitions were quieter and more solitary: "I always wanted to write. I was always practicing writing." Since she was also interested in music (and had played the violin), she would sit in her room, smoke Craven A cigarettes, and try her hand at writing biographies of musicians: the prodigy violinist Yehudi Menuhin, the pianist and composer Frédéric Chopin. "I just loved playing with words, sorting out the sentences, getting the right word for the incident. That's really what it was."

Meanwhile, she began to notice that every time she climbed the stairs in the evening, two young men would be standing at their door and talking to each other. Once, one of them—tall, handsome, with bright blond hair, blue eyes, dimpled cheeks when he smiled—fell down the stairs in front of her. She said, "Now you've done it." He said, "Yes, I've done it too much." It was the only way he could think of catching her attention, but he had sprained his ankle in the process.

Vanne checked on his condition the next day, and so they began talking. After a while he asked if he could drive her to work, and she began accepting rides in his Aston Martin racer. So the friendship brightened. He was kind, laughed a lot, and had wonderful friends, and he introduced Vanne to what she later identified as a "whirly kind of life."

Mortimer's wonderful friends included particularly his roommate and old school chum, Byron Cary, who was the second son of the fourteenth viscount of Falkland. Byron's daughter Sally recalls her father as being "very witty and amusing and all the ladies would rock with laughter at his stories. In fact, one friend had only to see him, and she would start laughing in anticipation before he even spoke." His charm and sociability, however, were lubricated with a good deal of alcohol and hid a deep unhappiness. After the war he ran out of money and never settled into any fully satisfying occupation. Byron's later life, according to his nephew, Lord Cary, was "unsatisfactory" in many ways, "although he was always a devoted father. He was something of an eccentric personality and served a prosperous shipping family for some years as a rather grand Jeeves-type butler."

But that, of course, takes us ahead of the story, into a dark time of destruction and disintegration, through a war and a world gone mad. For now, at the hopeful start of a decade, Byron and his friend and soon fiancée, Daphne, and then Mortimer and his friend and soon fiancée, Vanne, were enjoying the happy, whirly kind of life in London. Vanne loved dancing. Her favorite was the waltz, but she also loved the tango, fox trot, and one-step. After the free shows, courtesy of Cocky, the four of them might find a nightclub in the West End. As for drinking, pubs were considered off-limits to women in those years, so Byron and Mortimer might go into a pub and bring drinks out to Daphne and Vanne, who would be sitting in the car.

Byron may have had a small family income. Mortimer tended to spend whatever he could get, often faster than he could get it. But if they were short of money, Vanne once told me, "there were always things to do. Going for a walk in the park, or going to the museum. Stand in the gallery and get a place for nothing."

Mortimer and Vanne were married on September 26, 1932, at Trinity Church in Sloane Square. After the wedding they crossed the Channel and drove in the green racecar to Monte Carlo, where they stayed at a fancy hotel, watched dreary people losing money in casino games, and ran the car fast on roads snaking into the mountains. They returned to England "just in time," according to Vanne's recollection, for Mortimer to grab his racing gear and run the Aston Martin at the famed Brooklands racetrack outside London. Then they took up a regular married life at 2 Clabon Mews in Chelsea, not far from Sloane Square. It was a small, charming townhouse in a row of similar buildings, consisting of two bedrooms, a bath, a living area, and a small dining room, all on the first floor. The ground floor, formerly a stable, served as Mortimer's garage. And Vanne quit her job to become a full-time housewife and supporter of her husband's rapidly developing career as a racecar driver.

In 1933, Mortimer was asked to add his LM7 to two team Aston Martins, the LM9 and LM10, for the Le Mans Grand Prix d'Endurance on June 17 and 18. The company team plus supporters and friends and family, including the young Mrs. Morris-Goodall, lined up for a photograph outside the Works, and then they climbed into their respective vehicles and pulled onto the highway in a green convoy. They crossed the Channel via Newhaven-Dieppe and then ran east like a small invading force: the three racecars in front (with rubber-bulbed ooga horns and spare wheels bolted onto their sides), followed by some Aston Martin touring cars and an Aston baggage wagon. Before reaching Le Mans, they stopped the convoy and raised a Union Jack onto the radiator of the lead car, and then they roared into town, honking madly. They set up headquarters in the Garage Lenoir and tested out the track: narrow spots and tight S curves, a tree at one corner with a hub-height groove, brick cobbling that got very slippery when wet on the corner known as Indianapolis, and so on.

The Le Mans Endurance was a twenty-four-hour marathon, and the object was to drive as fast and far (as many laps) as you could, starting at four o'clock one afternoon and continuing until four o'clock the next afternoon. Each car had two drivers, and they were required to carry all their tools and spare parts with them, with everything officially identified and approved beforehand—including, at least for the three Aston Martins, a clothesline. Drivers sat in open cockpits wearing leather helmets and goggles, and they drove without safety harnesses or seat belts.

The drizzly morning of June 17 turned dry by noon and intermittently sunny by afternoon, and at four o'clock the starting flag was waved over twenty-six madly whining, rumbling, roaring, spinning, spitting, smoking, accelerating cars. A pack of five Alfa-Romeos took the lead, and after a brief mix-up when the LM10, driven by A. C. Bertelli, spun around and threatened to crash head-on into Mortimer's LM7, the three Aston Martins pulled together into the middle of the pack.

At two o'clock in the morning, Bertelli pulled into the pits and handed the LM10 over to his codriver, Sammy Davis, who at the first turn found the steering mechanism seizing up and nearly crashed; he pulled back into the pits after a lap and located a frozen kingpin close to the wheel hub.

Meanwhile, Mortimer's LM7 had been running reliably around and around at its predetermined pace all evening and into the night, until 3:30 in the morning. Mortimer had by then passed the car over to his codriver, one of the very few women in the race: Leslie Wisdom, known to everyone as Bill. During her run down one of the straightaways, a rod blew through the side of the engine block. So that was the end, and Bill had to leave the car and walk along the edge of the track back to the pits. Various spectators and a few gendarmes had trouble understanding that Bill was a driver, and so they persisted in trying to pull her away from the track, and she persisted in beating them away with her crash helmet and shouting, in her best French, "Voiture bang! Voiture bang!"

As the sun rose on the second day, the front mudguard of the LM10 broke loose. The clothesline had been included in the tool kit for just that sort of eventuality, and so Bertelli, driving at the time, stopped at the pits to secure the flapping part skillfully with a complex web of rope, and then he handed the car over to Sammy Davis. Both the LM10 and the LM9 stayed in the race, at one point skidding around a tree that had been knocked onto the track by a crashed Alfa-Romeo. They finally blasted underneath the finishing flag at 4 P.M. on June 18, with eleven other cars. The LM9 had covered 1,584 miles in twenty-four hours, to take fifth place. The LM10 had gone 1,463 miles, to rank seventh.

Altogether, that was a fine showing for Aston Martin, and it marked the commencement of Mortimer Herbert Morris-Goodall's career as a top British racecar driver. Within a year he was a regular on the Aston Martin team, behind the controls of a new and updated machine. By the end of his career, he had distinguished himself as the only British motor racer ever to have competed eleven times in the grueling Le Mans Grand Prix d'Endurance. He drove in every major competition event in Britain and on the continent, and in 1954 he was part of a team that established several world land-speed records while driving a Healey on the salt flats of Utah. True, Mortimer was never as famous as, say, Sterling Moss, but he was good enough to team up with Sterling Moss, which he did in a Jaguar for the 1953 Mille Miglia.

So the end of June 1933 was the beginning of something very exciting for Mortimer Herbert Morris-Goodall—and his first daughter, Valerie Jane Morris-Goodall, was born approximately nine months later, at 11:30 in the evening of Tuesday, April 3, 1934, in a nursing home in Hampstead Heath, North London.

Though successful as a racecar driver, Mortimer proved less successful as a husband and father over the next few years. For one thing, he was irresponsible about money, which, as Vanne once told me, "just went out and out all the time." Once during those early years the gas company cut off their gas. There was no money, not a penny, and Vanne ran to a Sloane Square bank, took off her emerald ring, and handed it to the bank manager. "The bank manager just laughed. Took my hand in his. Pressed the ring back on my finger. Oh, dear!"

Of course, Mortimer himself had grown up without a father—his stepfather, Major Nutt, always seemed more like an older brother—which may help explain his confusion and disengagement. He responded badly to Vanne's pregnancy, never comforting her during anxious times or offering emotional support, and after his daughter's birth he remained aloof, seemingly indifferent. "For the first year or so she was a baby," he told me, "and so I think until she was a year old there was nothing we could do with her. Then we moved, but I had a job in London, so that when I got home at night she was in bed, and again I didn't see her for about a year." Mortimer, for all his charm, verve, and social grace, was a cool, self-contained, and remote father, a man who, according to his daughter's recollection, "touched me only once" when she was a young child.

What Mortimer contributed to the life of his remarkable offspring, therefore, was more of nature than of nurture, visible not only in certain facial similarities but also, more significantly, in some surprising similarities of physiology. His baby girl grew up to be a woman with a race driver's constitution: good eyesight, high energy, a natural and happy competitiveness, a capacity for intense and extended concentration, a surprising attraction to risk, and an unusual tolerance for physical stress and oscillatory motion — the latter feature protecting her from seasickness in rough weather and the need to tighten her grip on armrests during flight turbulence.

When Valerie Jane was about three weeks old, a nanny arrived at 2 Clabon Mews. She had curly brown hair, blue eyes, and a well-defined and rather pointed face emphasized by a sharp jaw; according to Vanne's memory, she "stood a straight, sturdy five feet without her shoes."

Nancy Sowden was an orphan who left school when she was sixteen, took a job in a photography shop, and attended art school in the evenings. She wanted to paint. But she had come of age in hard times for England's working class. The New York stock market collapse of 1929 led to a global recession, with 2 million British workers unemployed, and Nancy's older sister wisely counseled her to get a steady job with a home attached. Trying to make a career in art was too risky, the sister said, so she arranged for Nancy to become a proper nanny, which required twelve months' formal training (in child psychology, hygiene, nursery management, children's art and games) at the Hampstead Day Nursery and then three months' practical experience at the Swiss Cottage Hospital. After her education was complete, Nancy bought her uniform: brown skirt and tunic with white apron, white collar, white cap (which she hated, because her curly hair meant the cap was never straight), and for colder weather a brown wool coat and a wide-brimmed brown hat. A Hampstead Day Nursery badge identified where she had trained.

Mrs. Morris-Goodall offered the standard compensation: room and board plus a pound a week spending money in return for six and a half days a week of child care. Nancy Sowden accepted the offer, and thus "when Valerie Jane was three weeks old, I started there. That's what I wanted: a small baby."

The townhouse at 2 Clabon Mews, fronted with cream-colored brick and red-brick trim, occupied a quiet little spot on the inside corner of a long U-shaped, cobblestoned alley off Cadogan Square. Nanny and Valerie Jane shared the smaller of the two bedrooms, and every morning after breakfast, in all kinds of weather, Nanny bundled up her tiny charge and gently placed the bundle into a soft nest (frilly pillow and white coverlet) inside the black pram. The infant settled comfortably into place, facing forward, and was rolled out the front door into the light and the moving air and over the bumpy cobblestones. The pram proceeded from bumpy to smooth, sailed past the private Cadogan Gardens, and soon reached Sloane Street, where Nanny and Valerie Jane joined the morning's parade of nannies and prams, all headed for Hyde Park and Kensington Gardens.

The route turned north up Sloane Street, past the women's fashion shops, and through Edinburgh Gate into Hyde Park. Through a maze of walkways, they entered a green, flickering expanse of scampering squirrels, chattering birds, and horses cantering down Rotten Row. As the pram rolled on, the horses went away and the city's noise retreated to a distant din, mild competition with the whispering air that filtered through leaves. Perhaps they turned into the daisy walk, where all the aristocratic nannies sat and knitted next to crested prams; or perhaps they proceeded uphill to the pond, to gaze at boaters stroking the surface and squint against the light on the water. On overcast days the water became slick and gray, with wavering dark bruises pressed into the water where boaters worked their oars or ducks and other waterfowl floated.

At a time when most English parents still believed in physical punishment as an important part of raising children, Vanne was a kind of philosopher of liberal parenting, emphasizing the importance of love and reasoned discipline: "My own early childhood had been a happy one. We had lots of love, lots of discipline, laughter and books." But according to Nanny's memory, her young charge hardly required discipline in any case: "She was a lovely child, very patient and happy, never needed scolding because she never did anything wrong! She was really happy."

Vanne's mother (by then known to everyone as "Danny," a child-friendly pronunciation of "Granny") echoed that positive opinion in a report to Vanne on the infant's progress during a 1934 Christmas visit: "V.J. is asleep in the garden, she is a model baby, no trouble, behaves just as a good healthy baby should. She is wonderfully strong in fact she plays tennis already with her arms, & swims with her legs."

At the same time, there may have been something unusually focused or attentive about the infant's demeanor. Nanny returned from a stroll one day very upset. She had stopped at the front entrance to Peter Jones, the department store, where a big uniformed man grandly welcomed customers and opened doors. "That porter," Nanny reported to Vanne, "was really nasty about Valerie Jane today." The big man had said, "She looks straight through me, just as though she knows all my secrets." Vanne pointed out that such words might be a compliment, but Nanny was not so easily mollified: "Do you think he is afraid there's something peculiar about her?"

There *was* something peculiar, or at least very interesting, about the gift Mortimer gave his daughter on her first birthday. Nanny was "horrified" by the thing. It was a child-sized stuffed toy chimpanzee, with dark shining button eyes, light-colored felt face and felt eyelids, a molded snout marked with a pair of comma-shaped nostrils, funneled ears, white downy chin, silken dark brown hair over the rest of the body, and felt hands and feet with separated thumbs and big toes. When a child squeezed its stomach, the chimpanzee played a music-box tune.

The toy had been produced on special order to honor a real chimpanzee born in the London Zoo on February 15, 1935. The real baby was named Jubilee, in anticipation of the upcoming May 6 celebration marking the twenty-fifth anniversary of King George V's ascension to the throne. Jubilee was, in fact, the London Zoo's first captive-born chimp: important enough to warrant a photographic feature in the *Times* and to inspire Hamley's toy shop on Regent Street to organize the special manufacture of a stuffed toy chimpanzee. Mortimer, on the lookout for a birthday present, happened to pass through Hamley's, saw the toy, and bought it. "I was looking round for a sort of cuddly toy, and I just saw this. There was no other reason. It was just a cuddly toy," he explained. "Took it home. Didn't expect it to have the effect it did have."

"She took to it," Nanny recalls, "and she was always carrying it around." In later years the child used to put her many toy animals and favorite dolls in a row and pretend to teach them things, but Jubilee was always the one who got to sit in her own chair and wear real castoff dresses.

In the spring of 1935, the family—Mortimer, Vanne, Nanny, Valerie Jane, and Jubilee—moved out of London and into the suburban town of Weybridge, home of the world's first and England's most important motor racing track, Brooklands, a three-and-a-half-mile-long loop of concrete poured in 1906 and 1907. Their house, called The Winnats, was located at 27 Woodland Grove, a quiet side street in a suburban neighborhood. The Winnats was a red-brick, three-story Edwardian affair, and Valerie Jane was given her own bedroom, a gabled room on the top floor, while Nanny took one of the five available bedrooms on the floor below.

In Vanne's view, the house was much too big: "The entire contents of the mews flat looked lost in a corner of our new entrance hall, a space we never managed to furnish adequately." Nanny likewise remembers the down-stairs nursery as being "huge," but during bad weather she and Valerie Jane passed many happy hours there. The child loved to color with crayons, dress and undress her dolls, play with Jubilee, and sometimes throw dice with Nanny in the board game known as Snakes and Ladders. Compared to London, Weybridge was quiet—lonely for Nanny, who spent most of her evenings by herself. After she told Mortimer that she wanted a radio for company, though, he bought one, and thus in the daytime, dance band music on the radio became another source of entertainment for Nanny and her charge.

The Winnats had three large oak trees, two at the front, one at the back. There was also a small garden and a small pond at the front, and at the rear a much larger back yard, which included a small flower garden and a surrounding edge of fir trees. From the nursery young Valerie Jane could now, according to an unpublished memoir by her mother, "listen drowsily to the songs of the black birds and the thrushes, the twitterings of all the little birds or the hooting of the owls in the woods behind the Church." In the spring she could smell the wallflowers and lilacs and lilies of the valley, and "it was a new delight to be able to run out into a garden of her own. The place had stood empty for a long time . . . and Nature had taken over the once trim lawns and scattered the long grass with wild sorrel and sturdy little blue bugles, buttercups and daisies and the golden stars of myriads of dandelions." They would sometimes have a picnic in the garden, where Valerie Jane soon became acquainted with "a new world, inhabited by gem-like beetles, spiders and ants, flies, wasps, bees and not least among all these fascinating creatures, the busy earthworms who slid so quickly from her sight beneath the ground."

One evening the child brought some of those earthworms inside, and Nanny came rushing downstairs to inform Vanne: "I think it's quite disgusting. Valerie Jane has taken a bunch of earthworms to bed with her, under her pillow, and she's touching them. I don't know what to do."

Vanne went into her daughter's bedroom to find her lying blissfully in her bed, the evening sun pouring onto her face. Valerie Jane said, "Look!" and moved her pillow to show off the worms.

Vanne said, "Well, Valerie Jane, if you keep these worms there all night, they'll be dead in the morning. They really ought to go into the garden where they belong." The child sighed and looked at the worms. And then together they took them down to the garden, dug a shallow hole, and put them back in the earth.

That rear garden was big enough to run and play in, to line up the dolls and Jubilee for various make-believe enterprises in, to organize snail races in. To have a pet tortoise named Johnny Walker in. (Johnny Walker kept disappearing, and Nanny had to paint the top of his shell bright red so they could spot him more easily.) And to have a dog in.

The dog was a bull terrier named Peggy. According to Nanny, Valerie Jane "could do anything with Peggy—sit on her back, take away her bowl, do anything." Peggy, however, was a fierce dog who would bite strangers coming in through the gate. She bit the postman, for instance, and Nanny had to sew a patch on his trousers. But at night, when Nanny was alone, Peggy always went up and sat with her, and that was comforting.

Occasionally Peggy would disappear, and twice someone rang up from the local pub and said, "Your dog is here. Can you come and fetch it?" Mortimer went to the pub frequently in the evening, so probably Peggy had gone out looking for him.

Mornings in Weybridge, Nanny would leash up Peggy, Valerie Jane might get on her tricycle, and the three of them would follow a sandy road lined on either side with rhododendrons that led to the village shops. Nanny might stop at the newsagent's and pick up her weekly copy of *Nursery World*—and one time Valerie Jane walked away with a small, cheaply illustrated booklet on circus life, with red and black pictures of a clown, ringmaster, animals. When they got home that day, Vanne commented on the booklet, whereupon the child blushed, closed the book, and sat on it. She had stolen it. Vanne took her hand and explained that since she had not paid for the object, she would have to return it. After much sobbing and hiccoughing on the way to the store, Valerie Jane recovered at the last minute, soberly stood on tiptoe, and reached over the counter to hand back her ill-gotten prize.

The women and girls took occasional trips to Brooklands to watch Mortimer drive around the track or to sit in comfort inside the clubhouse and consume tea and pastries, and once Mortimer drove Nanny around the loop in his racing car. But most exciting were visits to the grandmothers: to Vanne's mother, Danny, and Mortimer's mother, Danny Nutt. When Valerie Jane was very small, she would be transported on the train for a couple of hours to Danny's house in Bournemouth. The Bournemouth holidays were short and sporadic in the winter, but in the summer they sometimes lasted all season. Vanne was not necessarily there, however, and thus Nanny and Danny often took charge. In the hot weather they went down to the beach, where Danny owned a bathing hut, and all three of them would splash in the water, eat sandwiches, and dig holes in the sand.

Danny Nutt had the advantage of living in the most appealing of all possible places—the Manor House—and Valerie Jane began going there for short visits as early as April 11, 1935 (when Danny wrote to Vanne, "Bless the little Angel, you will miss her, I know, but you must think how much good it will do her, she will get such a lot of fresh air & come back with rosier cheeks than ever. Tell Nanny not to be afraid to ask Mrs. N. for whatever she wants for V.J."). The Manor House was an eighteenth-century red-brick mansion of two stories, with four reception rooms, eight bedrooms, and four baths. With various corridors leading hither and thither, the old place rambled out to the back before attaching itself to the last standing tower of the ancient Westernhanger Castle. The house, in fact, was surrounded by the remnants of the castle moat and nestled inside a crumbling stone rectangle, the heaps and piles of an edifice that had served Henry II in the twelfth century as well as Henry VIII in the sixteenth. In 1701, unfortunately, an enterprising real estate developer tore down and sold off most of the castle as building material for local barns and farmhouses, which helps explain why it was such a wreck.

It was a fascinating wreck, though, pleasantly melancholic and suitably romantic. As Jane recalled years later, the castle ruins "seemed scary, all gray, crumbling stone and spider webs. There were bats in one room that still had part of its roof." As for the house inside the ruins: "If you walked from one end to the other, you had to go down one or two steps here, up a little slope there, and so on, because different parts had been built at different times." It had no electricity until perhaps the end of the 1930s, so kerosene lamps were lit every evening, and the house was permeated with their sweet and oily smell.

In the country and adjacent to a large farm, the old Manor House was surrounded by gently rolling velvety green pastures dotted with white clots of grazing sheep, some cows, the occasional farm horse, and even sometimes a mare and colt from the nearby racetrack. Danny Nutt was fond of geese, so there always seemed to be half a dozen geese puttering about; and Major Nutt was master of the foxhounds, which meant that a seething pack of floppy-eared, sloppy-tongued dogs was in residence. There were sweet blackberries and bright daisies that turned into little moons at night. The Nutts also kept an enclosure for hens, along with five henhouses, and young Valerie Jane would help feed them and then gather their eggs. Finding the eggs was an adventure in itself, since many of the hens liked to lay their eggs in the bushes rather than in the henhouses.

Mortimer's younger brother, Reginald, usually known as Rex, also lived at the Manor House during those years, and he managed a local stable of racehorses. Valerie Jane had her first experience riding a horse at an early age (about two years), when Uncle Rex lifted her onto a big brown steed named Painstaker. He showed her how to make Painstaker change directions by pulling gently on the reins, and so "I managed to steer him, all by myself," making figure eights around the trees along the road. "I was very proud."

Johnny Walker the tortoise died. He hibernated on the compost heap in the garden, and then there was nothing left but his shell. Next Peggy began disappearing for long stretches of time, educating herself, it eventually became clear, in the art of killing sheep. One day she was brought home in a police van, along with a warning from the sheep farmer, and so she was given to a friend of Mortimer's who had a commission in the Queen's Regiment. The bull terrier became a regimental mascot, "loved, spoiled and cherished," according to Vanne.

Valerie Jane likewise had been loved, spoiled, and cherished, but on her fourth birthday, April 3, 1938, a noisy object unpropitiously turned up in the back seat of a taxi: a baby sister, plump and hungry Judith Daphne. The old pram was dusted off, and Nanny became distracted with a series of new and, from a four-year-old's perspective, unpleasant things: smelly diapers, dirty bottles, demanding shrieks. Valerie Jane was very unhappy. Nanny remembers that once, when she was taking the pair for a walk, the baby in the pram, the older sister shouted out the vilest word she could think of: "Diarrhea! Diarrhea! Diarrhea!" As Valerie Jane has remembered, "Oh, I was jealous. Not so much of Mum, but Nanny. Nanny loved the little baby. And Nanny sort of almost abandoned me when Judy was born. So I went berserk for a while. I became very unmanageable and wild. I did awful things."

Meanwhile, Byron and Daphne Cary, Mortimer and Vanne's best friends and married around the same time, had produced two girls, Rosemary Sally (born on June 18, 1935, little more than a year after Valerie Jane) and Susan Valerie Jane (January 30, 1938, slightly more than two months before Judy). Sally and Sue Cary eventually joined Valerie Jane and Judy to make up a very happy foursome. At the moment, though, only Sally was old enough to appreciate Valerie Jane's troubling ambivalence toward her baby sister — and also to notice the other playmate now turning up.

Dimmy was an imaginary friend, but for Valerie Jane, he possessed enough substance to talk to, look at, and laugh with. Perhaps Dimmy moved at high speed, because according to Vanne's recollection, whenever Valerie Jane talked to him, she spoke very rapidly, in a voice that was "punctuated by little bursts of laughter when they shared a joke together." One day Sally pulled Vanne to the edge of a room to observe this phenomenon. In Vanne's words, "At the door she jerked us to a halt. Her large blue eyes were dark with concern. Valerie Jane was flitting from corner to corner of the room, talking to Dimmy who was evidently flying about near the high ceiling."

Valerie Jane Morris-Goodall, even the four- or five-year-old version, was blessed with an unusually direct connection between her imaginative and analytical selves. From an early age, she seems to have possessed a capacity for focused attention and a mental clarity that was readily transported from inner to outer, from dreaming to waking, from vision to action. Yes, hints, possibilities, and promises were appearing in the life of this young girl—perhaps not so different from the hints, possibilities, and promises many eager parents observe with concern or excitement in their growing children. She had gifts and talents. But how would she use them?

The social and financial advantages that may have seemed to surround this lucky child, heiress to the remnants of a playing card fortune, were flimsier than one might think, and her early environment during the London and Weybridge years was never as promising as her talents. Her father was handsome and charming but irresponsible and usually missing. Vanne, far more stable, sensible, and mature than Mortimer, always possessed a cheerful adaptability and sense of adventure, but during the early part of her daughter's life, she cheerfully adapted to Mortimer and threw herself fully and eagerly into the adventure of their marriage and his racing life. She was, as she once summarized for me, "a flibbertigibbet" during those years. Nanny was like a second mother, but with Vanne gone many evenings, weekends, and holidays, Nanny was gradually becoming the first. So, how, in such a context, would little Valerie Jane escape the prison of self? How would she move from her perfect position at the top of Painstaker and the center of things to a less comfortable place at the edge of the world, striving to push it in a better direction? How would she grow to discover a life beyond the infantile egotism that often distracts so many talented and otherwise admirable adults? Where would she locate and absorb the discipline and moral idealism that a few years later were to become such important parts of her adult personality? What quiet revolution or violent crisis would break through the nursery door and, like a thief or a monster, seize this child and transport her away from the potential damages of the coddled life, and from the sparkling promises of the whirly, flibbertigibbety life?

2

War and a Disappearing Father

1939–1951

MORTIMER QUIT his cable-testing job at Callender's in 1939 to devote himself full-time to racing, and since so many of the important races were continental, he decided to leave Weybridge and settle with the family in France. Thus, in May 1939, little more than a month after England and France signed a treaty that guaranteed the defense of Poland against external aggression, the Morris-Goodall family crossed the Channel and drove on to Les Charmes, a large, four-dormered villa situated at the edge of pine forests near the seaside resort of Le Touquet. A fig tree cast cool shadows over the front patio, and in the back there was an overgrown garden and a big pond filled with frogs. The Morris-Goodalls enjoyed an active stream of visitors to the villa, but Nanny felt, she recalls, "very lonely." Mr. and Mrs. Morris-Goodall were often racing or socializing, and Nanny was afraid of the gardener, who was big and strange and French-speaking. Still, she made friends with the cook, who knew a few words of English.

The children took delight in the sunshine and country smells while remaining blissfully unaware of the dark storm gathering around them. As late spring moved into summer, war seemed a remote fantasy to Vanne as well, although she retained a few images and memories from her childhood during the Great War. She could remember holding her father's hand while walking one chilly dark night under the flickering gaslight of a railway platform, past a large group of wounded soldiers. "Their dingy blankets on the grey stones, the bandaged limbs, the strange smiles on their pallid faces filled me with terror. 'They're home now,' my father comforted me. 'This must be heaven compared with what they have been through out there.'" And she often remembered the story of her brother Eric's lucky escape from death. Eric, eighteen years old, was flying a tiny open plane with an observer seated behind, both of them defended only with a rifle on the observer's knees while they took photographs behind the front lines. They were hit by enemy fire and had to make an emergency landing in France. Eric suffered a smashed ankle. Three decades later he was Dr. Joseph the surgeon, with a permanent limp. Having gone through one Great War that killed three quarters of a million young Englishmen, Vanne thought it impossible that they should endure another.

Making occasional forays into Le Touquet, though, Vanne began to notice how deserted the beaches were and how the shops had begun closing early. She took note of all the English and French soldiers in uniform. And, as she later wrote, "in the little one-room bars in the town, where smoke hung thickly about the customers and weary pianists pounded out their haunting, melancholy melodies, the atmosphere was sometimes dangerously tense, curiously unreal, as though the scene had been set for a Graham Greene spy novel—only as we learned later, the spies who slipped through Le Touquet that summer were real spies. Rumours of their activities whispered over a glass of cognac spread like a contagion through the town."

One morning near the end of summer, a telephone rang at the villa. On the line was Michael Spens, who was engaged to Mortimer's sister Joan. Because his father was lord chief justice of India, Michael had better information than most, and he urged Vanne to leave France immediately.

She booked a passage for Nanny and the children on the last boat out of Bourgogne that same night. As Nanny sat on deck in the bracing night air and held on to the two girls, she was mildly fearful, but she also felt relieved to be leaving France: "I liked the idea of going back to England." Because it was dark, though, and because everyone was quite frantic by then, somehow in the crush and the crowds leaving the boat at Dover they lost the pram.

Vanne, still at Les Charmes the next morning, paid off and said goodbye to the cook, who had come in late and tearful, explaining in a rush of half-comprehended French that the police had commandeered her bicycle. Mortimer, who had been on racing business in Italy, had a hard time getting back to Le Touquet, but within a day or two he and Vanne and the car were crossing the Channel in calm seas and sunny weather. From Dover they drove west along the coast to the village of Hythe and turned north on a country road, finally crunching onto the gravel drive in front of the Manor House in time for afternoon tea: family dogs sprawled on the parlor floor, Danny Nutt seated behind a steaming pot and her best china on a silver tray, and Valerie Jane running downstairs, very excited to see Mummy and Daddy.

Mortimer had three sisters—Marjorie ("a tall handsome blonde," according to Vanne), Barbara (married to Oliver Locker-Lampson, member of Parliament from Birmingham), and Joan—and a younger brother, Rex.

All but Barbara were at the Manor House then, so along with Mortimer's grandfather, Gramps, they joined in for tea, greetings, gossip, and news.

On the final day of August, members of Hitler's elite SS compelled twelve German criminals, freshly retrieved from prison, to dress up in Polish military uniforms and transported them to a forest near the border with Poland. There the prisoners were injected with a lethal drug, shot, and arranged in a pattern to suggest they had been killed after crossing into Germany.

Having established with such rough theater that the Polish were the aggressors, Hitler launched the full force of the German military machine against Poland before dawn the next morning, September 1. Soon flocks of high-altitude German bombers were floating across the border, drifting far behind the front lines, and dropping bombs on the grounded Polish air force, trains and train stations, bridges and communication lines, factories and civilian parts of the cities. The high-flying bombers were supplemented by squadrons of low-flying Stuka dive-bombers with sirens bolted onto their undercarriages to produce an unnerving wail as they attacked Polish forces at the front: diving into a screaming vertical fall, dropping a payload, recovering and evading. On the ground, an army of 1.5 million men crossed the 1,750-mile-long German-Polish border at a dozen places, flooding in from the west, north, and south, on foot and motorcycle, in armored cars and tanks and troop carriers, and soon breathing in the dust raised by a few fast-moving panzer divisions already well on their way to Warsaw.

Two days later, at 11:15 in the morning, Mortimer's family gathered around the recently installed wireless to listen to Prime Minister Neville Chamberlain declare war on Germany. For a few moments after the announcement, Vanne has written, "we stood in shocked silence while the ticking of the grandfather clock edged us relentlessly into the harsh realities of the Second World War."

Chamberlain's September 3 declaration was followed within fifteen minutes by air-raid sirens across London. A false alarm. But the British were already industriously stitching up their blackout curtains. Sandbags were already piled against buildings as protection from bombs. The London Zoo was already closed, partly because of concern about the dangers posed by escaped wild animals. By September 3, more than a million children were already climbing onto special trains that transported them away from London and into the countryside. At the same time Britain had begun reinforcing French defenses, and by the end of September it had sent 160,000 soldiers, along with 140,000 tons of supplies and 24,000 military vehicles, across the Channel.

During the first days of the war, the Folkestone Race Course was closed and its stables, offices, and outbuildings were requisitioned by the army. Men in khaki walked over to the old Manor House and castle and soon gained permission to cover a rectangular stone tower (where Henry II's fair but unlucky Rosamunde was supposedly once immured) with a tarpaulin. They thoroughly washed the old tower down to remove a few centuries' worth of bird mess and thereby transformed it into an officers' mess. Around the same time, Danny Nutt made one of the racecourse bars into a canteen to serve hot tea and buns, cigarettes and chocolate to the soldiers, and Vanne began walking over to help run the canteen every afternoon from two to four—generally a quiet time back at the Manor House, with Judy usually taking her nap, Nanny in attendance, Gramps nodding off, Grace the cook dozing next to the cats in the servants' sitting room, and Valerie Jane visiting the stables to pat the horses and chat with Bob, the groom.

On one of those soporific afternoons, Valerie Jane disappeared. Vanne was late getting home from the canteen. Back in the house at last, she settled into a chair, slipped off her shoes, closed her eyes. Any second now, Nanny would arrive with Valerie Jane and Judy for tea. But soon a half-hour had passed, and still there was no one in the house. Vanne called up the stairs. She looked into the kitchen and found a kettle boiling on the stove, but no Grace to be seen. Tea was always served in the drawing room at four o'clock, and now it was late.

Vanne decided to go down to the stables, but on the way there she met Gramps, who said that everyone was out looking for Valerie Jane. "Nanny thought she was with Bob, and Bob thought she was back at the house with Nanny."

By then it was almost five o'clock, and the child had been missing for nearly three hours. A soldier standing at the stable fence got some of his mates to search, and then, as the afternoon began to turn into evening, Rex, Joan, and Marjorie came home, and the three of them soon drove away in three cars, joining the search. Someone called the police. By seven o'clock, with darkness approaching, the searchers were looking grim. Finally Vanne saw, as she later wrote, "a small, dishevelled figure coming a little wearily over the tussocky field by the hen houses. There were bits of straw in her hair and on her clothes, but her eyes, though darkly ringed by fatigue, were shining." A voice called out, "She's found!" and within a short while the searchers had all gathered back at the stable yard, while Vanne bent down and very patiently asked the child, "Wherever have you been?"

"With a hen."

"But you've been away for nearly five hours. What can you possibly have been doing with a hen all that time?"

"Well, you see, I had to find out how hens lay eggs, so I went into a hen coop to find out, but as soon as I went in the hens went out, so I went into an empty coop and sat in the corner and waited until a hen came in who didn't mind me there."

"So then what happened?"

"A hen came at last. It was a long time, but she came at last, and then she laid an egg. I saw her. So now I know how a hen lays an egg."

The soldiers grinned in relief and amusement and turned away. Rex drifted off to his favorite pub, while Joan went over to take up evening duty at the canteen. Marjorie remained, declaring in a mildly scolding tone, "Well, Valerie Jane, you've given us all a terrible fright. I suppose I'd better ring the police and say they're not wanted. I don't suppose anyone else has thought of it." And then Vanne and Valerie Jane, holding hands, walked back through the gathering darkness to the house.

In her 1988 autobiography for children, *My Life with the Chimpanzees*, a much older Valerie Jane recalled what she had actually seen inside the henhouse. "It was very stuffy and hot where I crouched, and the straw tickled my legs. There was hardly any light, either. But I could see the bird on her nest of straw. She was about five feet away, on the far side of the chicken house, and she had no idea I was there. If I moved, I would spoil everything. So I stayed quite still. So did the chicken." After a very long time, the hen slowly raised herself up from a nest in the straw. "She was facing away from me and bending forward. I saw a round white object gradually protruding from the feathers between her legs. It got bigger. Suddenly she gave a little wiggle and—plop!—it landed on the straw. With loud, pleased clucks, the chicken shook her feathers, moved the egg with her beak, then proudly strutted her way out of the henhouse."

That was Jane Goodall's first research project, done at the age of five.

Mortimer disappeared around the same time, returning later the same day dressed in a crisp soldier's uniform. The Royal Engineers' Stevedore Battalion was bivouacked at the Folkestone Race Course, and the commanding officer had once offered Mortimer an officer's commission. He was gone by the time Mortimer finally enlisted, though, so Mortimer became a private, part of the battalion bedded down in the stables next to his family home. He was soon promoted to quartermaster sergeant, possibly because "I was about the only one that could add up and was reasonable with mathematics."

Vanne, Nanny, and the girls moved out of the Manor House and rented a small house at 10 Earlsfield Road in Hythe. "You would love this little house & everything," Vanne wrote that November to her mother and sisters in Bournemouth. "We sleep to the sound of the sea & a waterfall & it's most cosy." And the fact that it was semidetached, with neighbors only a wall away (unlike Les Charmes), meant that "even Nanny doesn't <u>mind</u> when I go out for the evenings & says so! So we must be safe musn't we?!!"

Nanny, meanwhile, had met the man who would become her husband, Leslie Rillstone, and as Vanne declared in the letter, Nanny "must like Leslie at last," since she was planning to take a break at Christmas to visit him.

Mortimer shipped out to France in December, helping to organize the unloading of ships in support of the British Expeditionary Force, and by March 1940 he was promoted to second lieutenant. Back in England, around the first of the year, a friend of Nanny's living in Devon offered her a place to stay with one of the children, so Nanny and Judy went to Devon. Then Vanne decided to leave the house in Hythe and move in with her mother. She set off with Valerie Jane on the train and arrived at her mother's door early one cold winter's evening just before blackout time. Danny greeted them in the gravel driveway, with, in Vanne's recollection, "a warm stream of light flowing out from the open door beyond." Valerie Jane, running up to hug her grandmother, called out, "Here we are, Danny!"

Soon Nanny and Judy joined Valerie Jane and Vanne and the rest of the family, and The Birches, at 10 Durley Chine Road South, Bournemouth, became home—a real home—for the girls.

Bournemouth was spread across former sand dunes and heath, defined by golden sandstone cliffs above a crashing sea, a curved bay, and a long sandy beach: an appropriate landing place and, with a series of deep ravines (the chines) cutting through cliffs, a natural route for invading forces. Down at the town's beaches, therefore, men were laying minefields and barbed wire and steel barriers, and they armed the cliffs with big guns inside concrete boxes. Inland, other men were removing road signs, hammering antiparachute posts into the middle of fields, stringing out hundreds of miles of barbed wire, and placing long concrete rows of antitank barriers. Bournemouth was closed to visitors, and around forty of the biggest hotels had been requisitioned by the military, while the great pier leading out from the town's central beach was gapped in the middle, rendering it useless as a deep-water landing.

At The Birches, everyone, including Valerie Jane and Judy, had her own personal gas mask laid out on the big oak chest—"the coffin"—in the front hallway, while next to the coffin a row of small suitcases packed with basic necessities stood at the ready.

On April 9, 1940, the Nazis invaded Norway and Denmark. They took Copenhagen within half a day. Within a few weeks Holland and Belgium had been captured, and German panzer divisions were racing across the middle of France, slicing the Allied forces in half. They reached the coast by May 20, then turned north to capture the critical seaports of Boulogne and Calais and rush on toward Dunkirk. For the Allied forces, then, Dunkirk became the final escape hatch. And by the end of May, hundreds of thousands of British troops, along with remnants of the French, Dutch, and Belgian armies, were forming long meandering queues that reached across the beaches right down into the water, waiting patiently to be picked up by a hastily arranged rescue operation: a motley flotilla of nine hundred British Navy and merchant ships, barges and fireboats, paddle wheelers and trawlers, yachts and small motorboats, and anything else that might float.

The wireless in Bournemouth brought news of German advances and Allied defeats and retreat. Mortimer was "somewhere in France," his family knew, and in early June the first of the Dunkirk evacuees showed up. Vanne heard the news one morning from the postman and again from the milkman, so she and Valerie Jane walked down the sloping streets of town toward the sea—at last, in Vanne's words, "halted by the uncanny stillness of the exhausted men, lying there in peace on the warm English pavements far from the sound of guns." Her husband was not among them.

Mortimer, in Le Havre when an air raid scattered his battalion, had been instructed to take the remnants of the battalion transport, one big truck, and drive it into the ocean. The route he originally planned to follow was closed off by the Germans, however, and so he crossed into Chartres—but as he did so, he thought to himself, *This isn't far from Le Mans.* He made a quick detour to the now abandoned racetrack, drove around the 8.3-mile circuit once, and then raced west to St. Lazaire and ran the truck off the end of the quay. In St. Lazaire he joined a group of about twenty other British soldiers of various ranks who had become interested in a British transport ship anchored offshore. A reluctant Frenchman smoking a cigarette was persuaded at gunpoint to take them out to the ship in his small boat.

From the boat, Mortimer called up to a Scotsman on watch, "Can we come aboard?"

The Scotsman shouted down, "There's no room!"

Mortimer responded, "There's only me!" Then he and his twenty companions swarmed onto the already densely crowded ship, which, although strafed and bombed regularly, waited to take on still more evacuees before crossing in a convoy back to England.

Nanny, meanwhile, had become seriously ill ("cysts, several cysts that had to be taken away") and by late May was recovering from emergency surgery in a bed in Furxton Hospital—while Vanne, now alarmingly short of money, had concluded that she could no longer afford Nanny. Nanny was devastated by the news. Worse, while she was still recuperating, the Allied soldiers began pouring in from Dunkirk and the government took over the hospital, forcing her to leave before she was ready. Her older sister fetched her in a taxi, and together they retreated to Bognor Regis.

Naturally, the children were very upset by this sudden change in circumstances. Their grandmother later told Nanny that Valerie Jane used to "cry and cry at night, for weeks, that she wanted Nanny." And Nanny in turn would wake up night after night thinking about her darling Valerie Jane: "I missed her so much! Nearly broke my heart when I left her."

Months later, when she was feeling better, Nanny paid a visit to Bournemouth and heard Valerie Jane and Judy playing in one of the rooms of the house. Then she heard the older girl say to the younger, "She's my nanny, not yours! She was my nanny longer than yours! I'm older than you, so she's my nanny!" Nanny married Leslie Rillstone soon after and went to live with him in Taunton, and together they had two beautiful girls, named Katherine Valerie Jane and Judith Ann, after Nanny's other beautiful girls.

Mortimer phoned home the day he returned to English soil, and he visited Vanne and the girls. But soon he was undergoing an officers' training course, followed by a posting to the 79th Armored Division in Suffolk. Then he was pulled out to work as staff captain in the War Office, and at the end of a year he was promoted to major, which meant he had to stay on for another year.

His brother, Rex, was killed in 1942. Rex had become a flight instructor for the RAF, and during an instruction session a student pilot froze at the controls and the plane went down.

And now Mortimer saw less and less of his family and seldom even wrote—though Vanne remembers that his occasional letters were still "quite good." He turned up in Bournemouth on leave from time to time, but he rarely let anyone know beforehand, and his infrequent visits were typically short. Nine-year-old Valerie Jane described one disappointingly brief visit in a 1943 diary entry:

> Saterday July 10th. . . . We all expected daddy in the after-noon. I had a little preasant for Daddy. We had lunch and Daddy dident come beaucause it was raining hard. We had tea and still Daddy dident come. Then I went up stairs had a bath and dressed up as a fairy (in my nighty). Then fluterd down and waved my wand. Then Daddy rang us and said he wasent coming till to-morrow. Then Olly put a white fur coate on me, then Judy, Mummy and me played pelmanism and then came to bed. Then I wrote this little-book and Mumy blacked us out. Good-night.

July 11th Sunday. In the morning Judy and me went round the blok and home when we came home Daddy arrived stayed to lunch and then went. Then we went for a walk and I climed up a steep clif, then came home had tea played pelmenism and then went to bed and I did my home work. Then Mummy read a bit and I blacked out. Good-night.

In 1944, Mortimer shipped out to India, joining Queen Victoria's Madras Miners and Sappers, and in 1945 he went on to Burma for Exercise Zipper, which was the code name for the invasion of Malaya. But the bomb was dropped, the Japanese surrendered, and he spent a few peaceful years in Kuala Lumpur, returning to England for six months' leave in 1949, taking time off to race at Le Mans. At the end of that leave, on August 11, Valerie Jane, accompanied by Aunt Olwen (Olly), saw him off as he sailed away on the *Eastern Prince* out of Southampton, headed back to Kuala Lumpur. She described the event in a poignant letter to Vanne:

We arrived at Southampton and went to the wrong docks, & met a policeman with dermithitis or some such diasease on his face. We at last arrived at the quay side & there was the "Eastern Prince." Daddy was up on the 2nd deck looking very smart in his hat. He said he would come & see us but had to go to his cabin & we were too late. Olly marched up the gangplank with his parcels & was stopped by a member of the millitary police. Olly asked if the parcels could be given to Major Morris-Goodall, on which piece of information he looked uterly flabbergasted until that person, very vexed, & having lost his hat, appeared, leaping over his fellow soldiers, grabbing said parcels, and calling, "comming in 10 mins." He did not reappear until the band began to play and then Dad appeared on lower deck. The noise was deafening—from the men, and below Dad's rank & dignity so he disappeared, & reappeared on the Poop—or some such place. The noise was deafening as all the men cheered. Then the Millitary Police got ashore, and were promptly booed & booed by the men. Then the gangway was hauled up by the crane & the "Eastern Prince" slowly sailed out of port. Daddy waved until we could no longer see him & the band played.

Mortimer was promoted to lieutenant colonel, and by 1950 he had gone to Hong Kong, as Chiang Kai-shek was being pushed out of China. In Hong Kong, however, the squadron's morale was very low. "We had nothing to do," he later explained. "We were just on standby. We couldn't even lay out a flat bed of ground for them to play football on, or anything like that. And I had a hell of a job to try and keep them ready, and my morale was so low. I was very despondent, very depressed. That was half the reason I wrote that letter. I didn't know what we were in for. We hadn't been briefed for what the operation was, but I had a horrible idea that it wasn't going to be very pleasant, and I didn't know whether I'd get back. All this jammed up, and I wrote that letter."

The letter was to Vanne, asking for a divorce.

3

A Child's Peace

1940–1945

AN EVIL DREAM killed 25 million people and shattered a civilization. It destroyed families, races, cultures, and nations. It built concentration camps and fed millions to the gas chambers, rained fire onto London, Dresden, Hiroshima. It killed Uncle Rex and took away Daddy. But even in the middle of that flaming apocalypse and in the time of a nation's cataclysmic struggle for survival, it was still possible for a child to grow up whole and happy, within the separate peace of a garden, a house, and a secure family.

The garden was a spacious and private place, secured from the curious gaze by a high privet hedge. It was filled with trees (arbutus, ash, beech, birch, chestnut, laurel, pine) as well as flowers and other plants (bamboo, crocuses, daffodils, daisies, dandelions, forget-me-nots, holly, hydrangeas, lavender, lilacs, lilies, mint, pansies, primroses, rhododendrons, roses domestic and wild, and snapdragons). Valerie Jane could find trees to climb, places to hide, and—shadowed by the big arbutus, guarded by a small bamboo thicket, and protected all around by the rising green moat of the privet hedge—a private little hut to enjoy. The hut had curtained windows on either side of the door. When it was hot and sunny, she could open the door and discover cool shadows inside, a dank earth smell, spiders quietly retreating into their dingy boudoirs. When it rained, she could sit inside and listen to the pattering on the roof.

The house, called The Birches, was a rambling red-brick Victorian built in 1872 with a slate roof, gingerbread trim, a small tower over the front entrance, and, leading from the rear of the house into the garden, a high-peaked glass conservatory.

The secure family was one of women only, a matriarchy if you will, likely enough since all the men had gone off to fight their war—and living in a matriarchy had certain advantages. "I was never, ever told I couldn't do something because I was a girl," Jane Goodall commented many years later. The first matriarch was Danny, a strict but loving woman of competence and certitude: a powerful presence with curly white hair. She was, in the memory of her daughter Vanne, "indomitable. Fun-loving. Clever. Charming. And brave as a lion." Danny had struggled and endured, and as the widow of a minister of the Congregational persuasion, she knew her place in the universe.

Danny was born Elizabeth Hornby Legarde, though as a girl she was known as Bess. Her wealthy family moved from Yorkshire to the burgeoning resort town of Bournemouth in 1888, hoping that the southern sunshine and pine-scented breezes would prove therapeutic for her mother, who had already lost a leg and become wheelchair-bound because of tuberculosis. Bess's mother was sometimes seized by terrible back cramps, and the girl, as she got older, would whip her mother's back with a knotted towel to ease them. Bess's brother was also crippled, from poliomyelitis. And her father faltered as well under a devastating chronic disease, a malady described to young Bess as "dizzy spells" — which, as the girl eventually concluded, were identical to the dizzy spells she experimentally induced in her uncle's hens by giving them port wine to drink. Her father's drinking cost him and his family dearly. Once, after rolling his wife in her wheelchair down to the shops of Bournemouth, he left for a few minutes as she was looking over bolts of cloth for her summer dresses and stopped to meet a friend for a quick pint at the local hotel; he returned one year later with a trunk full of Maori artifacts, having shipped out to Australia and New Zealand while drunk.

Bess was a healthy, athletic, vigorous tomboy, who once beat up the local bully after he teased her lame brother. As a young woman she enrolled in Madame Osterberg's College of Physical Education near London, but she soon fell in love with and married the tall, blue-eyed William Joseph, a fiercely eloquent, intellectual minister twenty years her senior. The oldest of four boys from a small Welsh town, all of them ordained in the ministry, William received his divinity degree on scholarship from Cardiff University. He later studied history at Yale University, supporting himself and paying his tuition as an itinerant preacher during weekends and holidays. Back in England, he was posted to a Congregational church in Westbourne, just outside Bournemouth, where he first became acquainted with the Legardes. He became a friend of the family, then a regular visitor, then a suitor, and finally a member by marriage. After he and Bess married, they moved to Oxford, where William pursued another degree, this time in classics, before returning to the ministry in Bournemouth.

Bess affectionately called her husband Boxer, and together they created a warm and lively family, one boy followed by three girls: Eric, Olwen, Margaret Myfanwe (Vanne), and Audrey. But in 1921 Boxer died of cancer. Vanne was only fifteen years old when Bess and the children were turned out of the rectory and given a widow's pension of fourteen pounds a year. Bess's alcoholic father had drunk away most of the family fortune, but she inherited a dozen row houses; after the death of her husband, she began slowly selling the property off, supplementing that sporadic income by managing a girls' sanatorium in Bournemouth.

During happier times, Bess and Boxer had noticed a house that they thought particularly lovely: that red-brick Victorian with its own large garden serenely secluded behind a hedge. They decided that when he retired from the church they would buy the house and live in it. He died first, but in 1938, seventeen years after his death, Bess acquired the property for £2,000 and moved into The Birches with her two unmarried daughters, Olwen and Audrey—becoming, soon after the birth of her first grandchild on April 3, 1934, Danny, since "Granny" was too hard to say. When Vanne and her two daughters moved into The Birches in the spring of 1940, they shared the house with Danny, Olly, and Audrey—as well the PGs, or Paying Guests, a series of elderly female lodgers, some of them evacuees from London.

A physical therapist by training, Olly had a head of curly red hair, an infectious laugh, and a sometimes bawdy sense of humor. Olly was engaged to be married several times, but men were a regular disappointment. At one time she developed the practice of sticking pins into photographs of her ex-boyfriends. Then she stuck a pin into the picture of an ex-beau who soon after had a heart attack, so she stopped. With the children, though, Olly was fun and funny. "Olly always incited everything," Judy recalls. She would come into the kitchen and start making jokes while the children were sitting at the table, eating. She once pushed Valerie Jane's face, already lowered for olfactory purposes, into her bowl of custard. And Danny would scold, "Olly, you're worse than the children." But she had a beautiful, soaring singing voice, and she would play the piano in the children's room and practice her parts for the church choir. The children, playing out in the garden, listened with great pleasure.

Audrey (whose preference for her Welsh name, Gwyneth, was seldom indulged) was quieter than Olly. She had been injured during birth and was mildly spastic. She walked and spoke awkwardly, with effort, and was never able to express herself well or coordinate her hands properly. But if she thought something was wrong, she never hesitated to say so. She was also good-natured and positive, the sort who never said anything demeaning about anyone. She was intuitively sensitive to the feelings and suffering of others, loved to hug, and was always interested in what the children were doing.

The PGs sometimes provided additional drama. One of them, Miss Robinson, would sit in the drawing room and do the *Times* crossword puzzle every morning, but eventually she became increasingly confused, to the point that one morning Danny woke up to find her looming over the bed, kitchen knife in hand. Danny said, "I shouldn't do that, Miss Robinson," and the old woman put down the knife. Danny rang the doctor, who told her to take the children into her bedroom, lock the door, and stay there with them. Medical technicians arrived and removed poor Miss Robinson to a closed nursing facility, and soon her room was taken by another PG.

As Jane wrote many years later, Danny was the "strong, self-disciplined, iron-willed Victorian who ruled over us with supreme authority but had a heart big enough to embrace all the starving children of the world." She always gave herself a cold wash in the morning and was a real practitioner of the stiff upper lip. If you were coughing but not really feverish, you did not require sympathy. And if you seemed to expect it, she would say, "Don't peff." At the same time, she always refused to go to bed before resolving any hurt feelings or strife. "Let not the sun set on thy wrath," she would pronounce.

Danny established "an atmosphere that had become gently permeated by the ethics of Christianity." She quoted from the Bible regularly and went to church every Sunday, as did Audrey and Olly—though not Vanne. The children never said grace before meals, but they always knelt by the bed at night and said their evening prayers.

While Danny was undisputedly the head of the house, Vanne had primary authority over her children, and she always maintained high standards and clear expectations. One did not leave the house without saying where one was going. One got permission to do things. One was considerate of others. One would sit nicely at the table, learn manners, be polite. One went to bed at a certain time and turned out the light at a certain time—but one might also sneak a flashlight under the covers in order to continue reading. "We had lots of fun disobeying the rules," Jane once told me, but the rules were there, and Vanne would always explain why. "They were never unfair or stupid rules."

The children had a playroom next to the drawing room, and they were never at a loss for amusement. As Vanne once recalled, "We had such fun. I don't think I ever thought, 'Oh, dear. We haven't got money for this or money for that.' We had books. We had laughter. We had family jokes. We had masses of affection, love, understanding, sympathy. And things to think about. My mother used to play old songs on the piano, and we used to sing by it. We didn't have many clothes. We didn't have anything much. I can remember putting brown paper in my shoes instead of getting them cobbled. But that would be a laugh. That would be something we'd giggle at."

Vanne's brother, Eric, visited every third weekend. Dr. William Eric Joseph, chief consulting surgeon at Whipps Cross Hospital outside London, was the family's most conventional member, a quiet, serious, stately man with soft brown eyes and big eyebrows. He wore a trilby, walked with that crashed-plane limp from the Great War, and enjoyed taking the luxurious six o'clock Pullman, the Bournemouth Belle, down from London on Friday evenings. He had a penetrating gaze; a stranger in an airport once summarized him as "two eyes and a hat." But Eric, unhappily married to Aunt Peggy, never had children of his own, and when he arrived at The Birches he entered the unfamiliar territory of not only four or five women but two small girls — sometimes four, when Sally and Sue Cary were visiting. Danny treated him with extra care when he came. His breakfast was carried up to him, and the children were told to be quiet and to suppress the usual tendency toward chaos with "Don't do that — Eric's here."

Danny had her small, occasional sources of income. Vanne and the children were surviving on what Mortimer was able to provide — about twenty pounds a month, plus a free railway pass because she was an officer's wife. And of course the war brought its own limitations. Rationing began in January 1940, when the Ministry of Food passed out booklets to limit the consumption of butter, sugar, and ham. Meat was rationed by March, margarine by July. People reused envelopes, saved string, made sure to recycle tin cans and bones and bottles. "If somebody wanted something colored," Vanne told me, "they painted it. They wanted a special drawing, they drew it. Everybody made their own Christmas cards, their own birthday cards. Made their own presents to give to people. We didn't have the luxury of going out and buying things. Couldn't."

Perhaps a reasonable picture of the family's budgetary limitations can be found in the list of presents Danny received for her sixty-fourth birthday, on July 13, 1943, as recorded in Valerie Jane's diary: a coat hanger from Audrey, ten Craven A cigarettes from Olly, a few more Craven A's and ten shillings from Vanne, "drawing pins and onvelops and a home made postcard" from Judy, "a bottel of ink and a home made post-card and a pencil" from Valerie Jane, and, finally, the biggest gift: a check for two pounds from Uncle Eric.

But Danny was an excellent cook who could, as in the miracle of the loaves and fishes, make a tiny bit of food feed many people. Sometimes a single egg would have to satisfy six appetites, and she would spin the egg out to six portions through some kind of culinary miracle involving corn flour. And a treat for the girls was treacle—Tate & Lyle Golden Syrup in a green tin decorated with a golden lion and bees, spread on bread artistically to make portraits of Hitler, Himmler, Göring, and Goebbels. The girls could thus bite off the heads of important Nazi leaders, which was not only tasty but therapeutic.

The German air assault and the Battle of Britain began on August 15, 1940, and night after night flocks of droning dark angels advanced overhead and dropped high-explosive and incendiary bombs onto British docks and air-fields and factories. In bombers the Luftwaffe may have seemed overwhelmingly superior to the RAF, but in fighter aircraft they were on a par. Moreover, the Luftwaffe bombers and fighters were flying at the outer limits of their range, whereas the RAF planes were rising to defend home territory. As well, the British had developed radar, allowing them to track enemy flights at night and in poor weather. Finally, instead of demoralizing the civilian population, the bombing of London had the opposite effect.

Bournemouth was not a strategic target during the Battle of Britain and the subsequent Blitz, although there were airfields nearby and naval stations at Poole, Portland, and Weymouth. Bournemouth was first attacked on July 3, 1940, when a single high-explosive bomb set fire to one house and damaged eighteen. But during the Luftwaffe's extended campaign, German planes often passed over the seaside resort on their way to and from inland targets. If they had any bombs to spare on their return pass, they might drop them randomly over the town before heading out to sea.

Like virtually every other house in Britain, The Birches had its own bomb shelter, a government-issue Morrison (a six-by-five-by-four-foot steel box with solid top and mesh sides), which was situated in a small room just off the kitchen. The shelter included a mattress, some blankets, and a few tins of food (including, as Judy remembers, a tin of pineapple chunks that she always thought must be very tasty); and it provided a safe refuge mainly for the children, though Vanne and the others would often squeeze in, sardine-style, as well. During the first of the air raids, according to Vanne's written recollection, Valerie Jane scrunched deep into her blankets and refused to go down into the shelter. "I'm not going down. I don't mind bombs," she said. And so Vanne had to scoop her out of bed and carry her down. Then one time "a bomb fell with a sickening crunch on the nearby cliff; then another and another, so that the whole house shook and the windows rattled. In the eerie silence that followed there were sounds of running feet and muffled shouts in the road outside. Jane said nothing . . . but the lesson had been learned."

Judy remembers once playing in the garden, looking up, and saying to Vanne, "Oh, look, that plane's dropping papers." And then being picked up and shoved into the shelter, since what she thought were papers were in fact bombs. And once, on a sun-dazzled afternoon, Vanne and Jane watched a damaged German bomber descend rapidly until it was passing directly over their garden "at tree-top level." The mother, gasping "with pure astonishment," was able to see "the pale face of the pilot and the black swastika painted on the side of his plane" — minutes before he crashed out at sea.

"For the most part, we children were not much affected by the war," Jane Goodall later wrote, and indeed, once the most active phase of the Blitz was over in the spring of 1941, ordinary life for many in England was a good deal steadier and safer. And yet the war continued to break the children's peace in unexpected and occasionally distressing ways.

After the Japanese bombed Pearl Harbor, on December 7, 1941, the United States entered the war, and by early 1942 the Yanks had begun showing up in large numbers in Bournemouth. Then, in late May and early June 1944, the family noticed a unusually large influx of American soldiers, accompanied one day by a double column of tanks that came to a rumbling, clattering halt on the road in front of The Birches. The children were not supposed to ask for anything, such as chewing gum, but Judy found she could walk up and down the road chanting, "Gum chum, gum chum," and soldiers would give her gum.

In November of that year, a young American officer named Jack Marshall rang the bell at The Birches and introduced himself to the family. The grandson of a Yale University classmate of Danny's late husband, the Reverend William Joseph, Jack spent several days and evenings visiting with the family. "If we were all busy," Vanne has written, "he would sit, relaxed and happy, with Valerie Jane beside him and tell her tales of snakes and alligators and swamps and the hot steamy world of Florida where he lived." But Jack was soon shipped out to join the fighting in Europe. The young girl promised to write.

Her first letter was taken from his wallet one December day on a snowy field in Belgium and sent back home to his grieving mother in America. It became, as Vanne would write, "the precious link that joined our two families in friendship, for the rest of her life."

In Vanne's written recollection, when Judy was four years old, in 1942, she began waking up in terror, sobbing and crying out that Hitler was going to burn down the house. Her eight-year-old sister came to the rescue by drawing the picture of a tormented Adolf screaming in agony from his own bedroom window, burning up in his own house. Judy tucked the drawing underneath her pillow and slept soundly — for a few nights. But the nightmares started again, this time with Judy waking up from a sound sleep and crying out, "Bury me at the bottom of the garden, but leave my head out!" Valerie Jane soon provided an elaborate colored drawing of tilted, moonlit tombstones in the garden next to Judy's open-eyed, broadly grinning head. The younger sister put that picture beneath her pillow too, and slept well for a few more nights.

When the nocturnal cries and sobs started up a third time, Valerie Jane resorted to more positive imagery. She colored a picture of Judy sleeping peacefully in her bed, half-moon at the window and Mr. Dusky Gloom, brush in hand, painting white clouds onto the bedroom walls. The picture was pasted onto a sheet of cardboard beneath a poem:

> *The Sun, the Sun the mighty Sun*
> *He's shining in the sky*
> *To give us lots of merry fun*
> *Until the day of beauty's done.*
> *Then when shadows haunt the room*
> *Do not think they're witches,*
> *For it's just the Dusky Gloom*
> *Making funny pictures.*

The cardboard with picture and poem was hung on the wall over Judy's bed, and her nightmares ended.

Valerie Jane herself, though never traumatized by the war, was still deeply affected. She lost a beloved uncle. Her father disappeared into the army. And, always remembering the shortages and rationing, she developed a lifelong habit of frugality. Once during her later years at school, her school tunic was worn threadbare. Vanne one day finally commented, "You'll have to go to the secondhand shop and get a new tunic, because yours is really wearing through."

The daughter replied, "Oh, it'll last through the term."

Then, after a month or two, Vanne said, "I'm sorry, but your tunic has worn right through at the back."

"Well, good heavens, Mummy, people don't need to look at my back view, do they?"

Even now, some sixty years after rationing, Jane Goodall continues to eat little and dress simply. She reuses envelopes, steams off uncanceled stamps, plucks an extra packet of sugar from the room service tray left outside a hotel door, saves those small liquor bottles sometimes given out on airplane flights.

Yet possibly the biggest long-term effect of the war on young Valerie Jane was a vision of the extraordinary human capacity for violence, destruction, and true evil. She was five years old when the war began, eleven when it ended. During those years she became increasingly aware of the larger world, catching scraps of information from the radio, from newspapers and magazines, from the occasional news filmstrip, from what the grownups talked about. But it was not until the final months of the war, as the Allies advanced across the face of Europe, that the death camp photographs began appearing in the newspapers. "I was eleven years old at the time," she has written, "very impressionable and imaginative. Although the family would like to have spared me from the horrifying Holocaust photographs, I had never been prevented from reading the newspapers and they did not stop me then." She has never since been able to expunge from her memory or her conscience those images: crowds of starving people reduced to near skeletons and the bodies piled crudely into great heaps. "That such things could happen made no sense."

4 ·

Child in the Trees

1940–1951

IF VALERIE JANE — or V.J., as almost everyone by now called her — felt bad, Vanne would give her a book: "Go and read the book." And she would take herself and the book into her most private refuge, a tree in the garden.

She had two favorite trees, a bushy chestnut named Nooky and a beech named Beech. Beech was the most favored. She would spend hours in Beech, by herself. She loved that tree so much that eventually Danny deeded Beech to her for her fourteenth birthday, presenting a carefully penned declaration (written by Jane, signed by Danny) sealed inside a small envelope that was marked <u>BY PRIVILEGED ORDER</u>:

> DECLARATION. This States Briefly that Elizabeth Joseph Hereby Presents 'BEECH' to V.J.M.-Goodall, on April 3, 1948.

Beech was a useful lookout and a gentle refuge, a child's kingdom of airy solitude.

From her earliest years, this child in the trees loved solitude. She also loved her friends and family, but to an exceptional degree she treasured being by herself. Her rich interior world sufficed, with a thousand active thoughts and visions — a vision, for example, of animals as friends. They were friends with feathers or fur, nonverbal friends to be sure, friends often with four legs and quiet ways but also with a surface quickness and a depth of sense.

She had a small menagerie consisting of various crawlers and creepers. As she noted in a November 1945 letter to her friend Sally Cary, "I have got quite a lot of caterpillars," including a "Lime Hawk Moth," a "green looper (or stick caterpillar) who feeds on mountain ash and he has made a cocoon," an "ordinary cabbige white, who has made a cocoon," a "black hairy tortishell who feeds on nettle," a "little yellowy, orang looper who feeds on lime," and a "green caterpillar who feeds on cabbage, and has turned brown."

She had a "lovely big slow-worm" (legless lizard) christened Ivor Novello, given to V.J. by Audrey on April 3, 1951, as a seventeenth birthday present, and a second known as Solomon. She also had a stable of racing snails, individually identified with watercolor numbers on their shells and kept in the garden, luxuriating in an open-bottomed box: Alice, Andy, Gally, and Jonny. That gallant quartet was made a quintet by Prizewinner, found on Easter Sunday 1949, who was that very day taken with Andy inside a paper bag to church and raced across the gallery railing during, according to a diary notation, a "jolly good sermon" by the Reverend John Short on the theme of "Are you going to give your whole self to God, or only a bit, or none?"

The snails were sometimes fed slugs and accompanied for exercise in the garden by the tortoises, Jacob and Christobel, and a terrapin named Terrapin.

The guinea pigs, Gandhi (or Gandy) and Jimmy, were frequently allowed to wander outdoors but usually harnessed onto string leashes to prevent disappearances into the hedge. Jimmy and Gandhi were joined in 1951, briefly, by Spindle, whose tenure was challenged successfully by Pickles the cat. They were also joined for a much longer period by Hamlette the hamster, who sometimes nested in the armchair's upholstery and one time gnawed through the telephone wire. There was also Peter the canary, secured in his cage at night but often during the day flying freely around the house or even out in the garden.

V.J. regularly fed, cleaned, and exercised her menagerie, often before school in the morning. In a February 1949 diary entry she wrote, "I let Peter out, and then caught him on my fingure, Oh! no, I am so sorry whoever is reading this book, he got on my fingure lots of times, but in the end it grew late, and I had to take the cage up to him." Peter was seriously traumatized in April of that year, when Audrey accidentally dropped his cage: "I dashed down & found Audy had dropped Peters cage & he was crouching on the ground. I caught him & gave him water while Ma rang up the petshop. They said put him in a boot box & take him round if he didn't get better. . . . Peter's mouth was still open, so we took him, under a large umbrella to the pet shop. . . . They said feed him with a matchstick & so we went back & I fed him bread & milk." Sadly, Peter did not survive. His beak was broken, and he had to be put to sleep.

Chase was the only of her dogs whom V.J. actually paid for. She had been given an antique Victorian dollhouse—once Olly's childhood toy, perhaps—which she sold to a collector for enough to buy the black-and-white spaniel in early July 1945. V.J. described Chase in a November 1945 letter to Sally as "sweet" but also "very mischives and bites anything that comes his way. He comes when he is called and also I play a cirtain game with him. I run my fastest away from him and soon he gets tired and sits down. Then I lie down flat, and the minute he see's me lying down he runs straight for me at full speed, with which I hurridly rise to my feet, for if I did not, all the hair of my head would be stuffed down Chase's throaght. He is very greedy, and gobbles down food at a great rate." Most unhappily, Chase was run over by a truck the following summer, as indicated in a July 1946 letter to Sally: "We are very sad, because Chase has been killed. He was in the middle of the road, and a lorry was backing out of a gate (and so could not see him) and he was run over. A man saw him and took him to the vet, but he was dead. It's an awful shame, poor Chase."

Chase was replaced later that year by "a sweet little kitten called Jaffer," who was "just like a dog. He loves me and follows me around." Jaffer was also killed in traffic, as noted a few months later. "This is a very sad piece of news, which made (to tell the truth) me crie! Jaffer was chased into the road by a dog and his leg was run over. The vet came at top speed and put him to sleep." Jaffer was followed by Pickles, who remained a whole and healthy denizen of The Birches for several years.

The child in the trees also became acquainted with horses. As noted, she was mounted on Uncle Rex's Painstaker at the age of two. Later, when she was five, she was allowed to ride a pony named Cherry around in circles near the Manor House stables. By the time she was keeping her first diary, in the summer of 1942, she was enough of an equestrienne to draw pictures of riders mounted on horses and comment about their posture: "This is a good rider exept that his legs are to far back and his reins are to slack for cantering."

V.J. began riding lessons around 1945, taking the local bus every Saturday morning during the school term, two or three times weekly during the summers, from Bournemouth to the small village of Longham and Longham House, a rambling Queen Anne structure surrounded by great elm trees and meadows and with a fifty- to sixty-acre farm, stables, and riding school owned and run by Miss Selena Bush. Miss Bush, or Bushel, as the children called her, was a vital, vigorous woman with a ruddy face, bushy hair, fragments of hay in her hair, and always (so it seemed to Judy) a cat draped around her neck. She was strong enough to toss hundred-pound bags of potatoes and resourceful enough to manage an entire yard full of small children gracefully.

Fifty years later, Miss Bush could still remember the late-autumn afternoon when V.J. first started coming to Longham: "I went in about five, had

a cup of tea, thinking, '*All the young are gone. Peace!*'" But she went outside an hour later to find one small, slight girl still in the yard, standing by
herself, quiet and wide-eyed, as the sky got dark and the stars began to appear. "Isn't it peaceful!" the girl said quietly. Miss Bush called her Spindle,
because of her spindly physique, and she found Spindle always "quite different from everybody else. Completely. She was quiet, for one thing. And
she thought. And noticed. She was always down the meadows with the
horses. When she didn't come back in half an hour, we'd begin to get worried. But after a time it was quite natural, because she would come back with
a frog with a broken toe. Oh, yes, I can remember she was quite different
from everybody else."

Some of the children rode to Longham in automobiles. Some had their
own horses. Since her family did not own a car, Spindle usually went by
bus, about an hour's ride, and she always wore secondhand riding clothes.
"Scruffy old me!" she once described herself. Pony rides cost two shillings
and sixpence each, and the family could afford about one each month, but
Miss Bush made an arrangement for Spindle, and sometimes also for her sister and her friends Sally and Sue Cary. Spindle would groom the ponies and
horses, feed them, and clean the stables and tack, washing the saddles and
bridles with saddle soap and rubbing them down. She shoveled manure,
pulled up weeds, and helped Miss Bush in the potato field, sorting, bagging,
and throwing the wormy potatoes into the sack for Smith's Potato Crisps.
They would pick out a potato caked in mud, and Miss Bush would say, "Oh,
yes, the public will buy a lump of mud if they think there's a potato in the
middle of it."

Spindle worked hard, and soon she was allowed to take clients out for
pony rides. Then she was encouraged to participate in Pony Club events
and gymkhanas, and during her school holidays she sometimes spent the
night at Longham with Sheila MacNaughton, one of two stable hands living
in quarters next to the stables. Sheila was Scottish, and since she tended to
say "Poosh!" when she meant "Push!" the children called her Poosh. Staying overnight with Poosh meant getting up before dawn, sipping tea and
nibbling biscuits, then going out to the fields in the first glorious light of day
to collect the grazing ponies.

Miss Bush had learned to ride on a donkey, she told the girls, and that
gave her all her riding skills, since donkeys are so contrary. Her first pony,
Daniel (black, retired from work in a coal mine), could be the most obstinate creature, and if she had not started with a donkey, she would never
have been able to ride Daniel. Still, and paradoxically, old and graying
Daniel was wonderful with beginners. True, he hated having his withers
touched, and he had the disconcerting habit of stopping in a meadow and

gazing into space for about ten minutes. Those were times, Spindle and Sally told each other, when Daniel was making up poetry. But because he was so good and safe, all the beginners were put on Daniel.

Daniel had been taken as a foal from a feral herd of New Forest ponies, as were several other Longham ponies that Spindle rode, including gentle Imp and canny Chrysler. But the girl eventually graduated from ponies to horses and found she enjoyed competition. Blitz, a former milk horse, blind in one eye, was a lovely jumper. Once she rode Blitz in a local gymkhana and in the middle of a jumping demonstration the horse stumbled and went down on her knees, and the girl slipped out of the saddle and slid under Blitz's neck—but she managed to scramble back up as the horse regained her stride and continued over a ditch and a hedge to the finish line. Then there was Quince. Quince was Poosh's horse, a gorgeous yellow thorough-bred with white socks and a white blaze, and sometimes Spindle would work Quince at jumping. "He would jump what looked like these enormous jumps to us," Judy remembers.

By the age of seventeen, Spindle had grown into a strong enough rider to take a horse named Divot on a fox hunt. As she later recalled, "How exciting! It meant that I would be able to ride with the huntsmen in their 'pink' coats, which in fact are red as red can be. There would be huge hedges and fences to jump; there would be the sound of the hunting horn." Fox hunting was a great challenge, and a chance to practice and show off her skills. As for the fox, well, she gave that slippery, high-tailed goal of fox hunting little thought until, after riding hard for three hours, she at last caught a glimpse of him, "bedraggled and exhausted, just before the hounds seized and tore him up." She was appalled. "How could I even for one moment have wanted to be part of this murderous and horrible event with a whole lot of grown-up people riding on horses, following in cars and on bicycles, while a great pack of baying dogs chased after one poor little fox?"

Perhaps horses taught V.J. to be calm around large animals and to be quietly patient and firmly direct with creatures who cannot talk, but dogs may have taught her other, possibly more important lessons. A year or two after the unhappy demise of Chase the spaniel, she became friendly with two local dogs of less refined parentage, Budleigh and Rusty. Budleigh, or Buds, was a beautiful collie or collie mix owned by Mrs. Churcher, who ran a nearby tobacco and sweets shop. The young girl began taking Budleigh for daily walks, scrambling around the cliffs and ravines and rambling along the beach. She also taught Buds a few basic tricks. Starting probably in 1948, V.J. and Buds were joined by Rusty, an eager, silken-haired, spaniel sort of black dog with a white blaze on his chest and a very sensitive face. Rusty was owned by the managers of the San Remo Hotel, next door to The

Birches, but he must have been bored or unhappy with life at the hotel, where he was regularly tied to the leg of a table.

Rusty, V.J. discovered, was a very intelligent dog who loved attention and was very attentive himself. At first she did not bother trying to teach him any tricks. Rusty was just an eager companion on their daily walks. But then one day, as she worked on getting Buds to shake hands, Rusty, who had been sitting alongside and watching, raised his paw. She took the hint and began teaching Rusty tricks too. After three lessons he mastered the treat-on-your-nose problem, which Buds had only just learned. Unlike Buds, though, after the "Okay," Rusty added the flourish of tossing the biscuit into the air before catching it in his mouth.

Soon Rusty was coming over to The Birches the second he was let out of the hotel in the morning, at 6:30, barking at the front door to be let in. Vanne has written about hearing his "short, sharp bark," and running down the stairs "to find him seated upon the door step, raggety ears acock, intelligent eyes alight, ready, with wildly wagging tail, to bound up to Jane's bed-room." And the young girl began calling him, with great affection, her "Dear Blackness," her "Pig," the "black devil," the "black angel," and so on. "Woken up by the barking of my black angel," she wrote in her diary on June 24, 1951, "and I went down to let him in. As he was so nice & early morningy, I took him for a little walk — after dressing of course. Then — oh, we went on the cliff and round about — and then he went home for his breakfast. I went home for mine."

Rusty would often stay at The Birches, sometimes all day long, return-ing to the San Remo Hotel perhaps for a quick dinner in the evenings and then coming back to the big house and garden and staying until bedtime. He learned tricks quickly, responding to affection as his main reward — both the usual tricks, such as "die for the king," and the unusual ones, such as jump-ing through a hoop and climbing a ladder. He played games, was pushed around in a wheelbarrow, found an object hidden while he was blindfolded, ran through an obstacle course in the garden. And he loved wearing clothes; V.J. would sometimes put him in pajamas and push him around town in an old pram. And yet the dog hated being laughed at. If someone found him too amusing, he would quit the game immediately and walk away, dragging the clothes along behind.

So Rusty learned a lot from the girl who lived across the way from the hotel, but she also learned from him, as she later wrote, "so much about ani-mal behavior, lessons I have remembered all my life." She learned that a dog can think about absent objects. With Rusty at her side, V.J. would throw a ball from an upstairs window into the garden. He would watch where it landed, then turn around, bark until she opened the door to the room, scramble downstairs, bark until someone opened the door to the outside, and go into the garden and find the ball instantly. Rusty was also "the only dog I have ever known who seemed to have a sense of justice." If he did something clearly bad that made the girl appropriately angry or irritated, he would humbly seek forgiveness, rolling onto his back with a submissive grin. But if she became angry or irritated unreasonably, in ways not fully consistent with her usual behavior, he would become visibly upset. For instance, V.J. taught him how to shut a door on command, but one time, when his paws were very muddy, Rusty shut the door without being told to, thereby making a muddy mess. The dog may have felt that V.J.'s quick response—"Bad dog!"—was unfairly inconsistent. He stared at her for a few moments and then walked over to face the wall, nose almost touching it, and refused to move. Only gradually did he respond to her abject apologies.

This child of the trees was a dreamy child, an expansive fantasizer, and she soon harnessed her mind to the wings of language, spoken and written. She started her formal education when she was six years old, in 1940, attending a small school in Bournemouth known as St. Christopher's. Her first teacher was Phyllis Hillbrook, a family friend who came to The Birches for a weekly game of bridge and was called Aunt Phylly.

V.J. was too active and inspired to enjoy the indoor disciplines of any school perfectly, but she adored her teacher. Within a few months, though, Vanne became concerned about Aunt Phylly's reports that the girl was not advancing normally, did not seem to be learning her letters and words as the other students were, was still not moving past the cat-sat-on-the-mat level of competence. But Vanne's growing worries about those reports turned to astonishment when she observed her daughter's behavior at home. One evening after V.J. had gone to bed, Vanne stood "with absolute amazement" outside the open door of her bedroom. "She was reading away as fast as she could read." So Vanne went in and said, "You can read after all!"

"Yes, I could read a long time ago."

"Why on earth have you pretended?"

"You see, if I could read, I would have to leave Auntie Phylly's class. And I'm never going to leave her class, ever."

Vanne laughed. "When you're twelve, you'll still be reading 'D-O-G spells cat'?"

But the girl was, as she admitted many years later, "not at all keen on going to school. I dreamed about nature, animals, and the magic of far-off places. Our house was filled with book-shelves and the books spilled out onto the floor. When it was wet and cold, I would curl up in the chair by the fire and lose myself in other worlds." Before she could read, she listened to her mother reading such children's classics as *At the Back of the North Wind*, the Peter Rabbit series, *The Secret Garden*, *The Wind in the Willows*—and also Stella Mead's *The Land of Never-Grow-Up* (a Christmas present in 1937), Agnes Giberne's *Among the Stars: Or, Wonderful Things in the Sky* (from Olly in 1940), and passages from Harold Wheeler's *The Miracle of Life* (which Danny acquired with cereal coupons and presented as a gift in 1939). The latter volume, a rather encyclopedic collection of experts' essays on biology for young readers, proved to be one of her greatest treasures, and V.J. returned to it again and again as she grew older—always intrigued by the frontispiece illustration of a white-jacketed scientist squinting into a microscope.

But perhaps her very favorite reading from those early years was the Doctor Dolittle books, written by Hugh Lofting. The original of the series, *The Story of Doctor Dolittle*, she borrowed from the local library in November 1942. "I read it all the way through," she later wrote. "Then I read it through again. I had never before loved a book so much. I read it a third time before it had to go back—I finished it under the bedclothes with a flashlight after Mum had turned off the light." Danny gave the book to her that Christmas.

From the first, the fantasy of Doctor Dolittle powerfully expressed this child's ecstatic identification with animals and nature. The good physician kept an entire houseful of pets. "Besides the goldfish in the pond at the bottom of his garden, he had rabbits in the pantry, white mice in his piano, a squirrel in the linen closet, and a hedgehog in the cellar. He had a cow with a calf too and an old lame horse—twenty-five years of age—and chickens and pigeons and two lambs and many other animals. But his favourite pets were Dab-Dab, the duck; Jip, the dog; Gub-Gub the baby pig; Polynesia, the parrot; and the owl, Too-Too." Doctor Dolittle loved animals so intensely that finally Polynesia taught him to speak and understand animal language, a skill that in turn enabled him to succeed as a veterinarian. As soon as the animals realized that he was conversant in their language, they would simply explain what the trouble was, and he would treat them. Doctor Dolittle's reputation as a great empathic veterinarian eventually led him to Africa, where the monkeys had all started dying from a horrible illness. He was too poor to buy tickets to Africa, but a sailor finally lent him a boat, on which he sailed with his friends (crocodile, monkey, parrot, duck, pig, owl, and a white mouse stowaway) for six long weeks over the waves until at last they crashed into Africa.

Eventually V.J. read the entire series. She also loved to read about the adventures of Mowgli in Kipling's *The Jungle Book*. And soon she graduated to the longer, denser adventure series written by Edgar Rice Burroughs and starring Tarzan of the Apes, the lost son of English aristocrats raised in the African "jungle" by an ape mother. V.J. loved to read by the fire in cold, wet weather. And in warmer, drier weather, she would often take a rug, a blanket, snacks, and a favorite book up to the top branches of Beech. "I think I went through all the Tarzan books thirty feet or so above the ground," she later recalled. "I was madly in love with the Lord of the Jungle, terribly jealous of his Jane."

That all her fictional idols were male was not a matter of her own sexual identity but a reflection of the paucity of good adventure fantasies featuring girls and women. ("I dreamed I was a man, you see," she once told me. "All my dreams, I was a man. In my dreams I did male things. That doesn't stop you being feminine.") Like Doctor Dolittle, Tarzan lived in a special intimacy with nature and animals, and daydreaming about Tarzan's life with the apes of the forests led directly to the young girl's determination to go to Africa. It was a romantic, fantastic vision—but soon enough everyone in the family, as well as Sally and Sue Cary, had come to consider it as an established fact that V.J. would someday leave them to go to the forests of Africa. Sue remembers, "She always said that was what she wanted to do, so we always fully believed her."

The Doctor Dolittle and Tarzan series were books of her childhood. By the time she was sixteen and seventeen, she had moved on to Agatha Christie's whodunits, Jeffrey Farnol's romantic bestsellers, Bram Stoker's *Dracula*, Mark Twain's *The Prince and the Pauper*, W. H. Hudson's *Green Mansions*, Shakespeare's plays, and so on. But even at that age she periodically returned to the visions of her earlier years. Among the 129 books she read in 1951, according to a master list at the back of her diary for that year, were seven Tarzans and all ten of the Doctor Dolittle books she still kept in her bookcase.

She also began reading poetry—Rubert Brooke, Walter de la Mare, Alfred Noyes, Wilfred Owen, and Francis Thompson, as well as Browning, Keats, Milton, Shakespeare, and Shelley. Many of those luminaries were her "squidgy poets," as she used to say, whose bumpy or squidgy-feeling leather-bound volumes she discovered in the basement of Arturo's used-book shop in the Westbourne Arcade, halfway between school and home.

She was scribbling letters and words and organizing them into sentences by 1941. She may have written her first story, "The Silly Giraffe" (concerning the tribulations of a gullible giraffe with a gargantuan gullet, a neck so long it reached to the moon), as early as 1941. And by February 16, 1942, she was literate enough to scrawl in pencil her first letter home, composed during a visit to Danny Nutt at the Manor Mouse:

Darling Mummy

the day befor yestoday Mr and Misis Spens broght a big dog called Jacky who is going to live here untill Uncle Micel come back. I dont know how to spell that word. Yestoday Danny Nutt gave me two china dogs and I call them Trouble and Terry. Jublee has got a new dress. I have got a birds nest and a catepiler in a box of calaig leaves. Now I will drow a pictuer of him.

Today I found a ded rook he died of cold. I hop you can read this letter. I had a bold egg for my tea, new bread and real butter. When I went to tea Gremlin came and he stad all night till Gras came with the tea. Mouse sends you her love and a lik. Kincin is giving you his best bone. Jacky and Trouble send you a lik and the Hen's send you a cluck. Eevry body sends you there love.

with lots and lots of love from
V.J.

After she left her first school, St. Christopher's, in the fall of 1943, the child entered a Parents' National Educational Union (or PNEU) school in West Bournemouth, where, according to her first teacher's report on December 21, 1943, "V.J. has applied herself to the new work. Her progress has been very satisfactory."

Her progress continued to be very satisfactory, although an evaluation in the summer of 1944 faulted her otherwise "very good" English essays for being, alas, much "too long" for a little girl of ten years. But she wrote long, and she wrote often, pouring out her thoughts and feelings and the minutiae of her life in letters, diaries, special journals, stories, and poems. In her letters, as she got older, she occasionally experimented with an ironic, high-romantic style; and once, after accidentally jabbing her finger with the nib of her pen, she experimented with the drama of writing in her own blood. She wrote poems, some of them light (such as "Blue Bottom," an ode to a mandrill), some adolescent (as in the one beginning with "A mangled heap of rotting flesh"), and others more interesting and serious. One of her childhood fantasies, she later admitted, was to become England's poet laureate.

Soon after the war began, Sally and Sue regularly went to stay at The Birches during holidays and summers. They became "just part of the family," as Judy recalls. V.J. would invite them to visit, and everyone else would agree. As the invitation was expressed in a November 1945 letter to Sally,

"You must, must, must, must, must, must, must, must, must, must, <u>MUST</u>, come and stay with us this hols. My Ma has written to your Ma to ask if you can, so do write and tell me that you can."

Sometimes Sally and Sue appeared with both their parents, more often with just their mother, but later on the two girls typically came on their own. Their father, Byron, would put them on a train and give a half-crown to the train guard, and then the two girls would ride in great excitement to Bournemouth, leaning out the open windows and letting the train's smoke and grit blow into their faces and eyes. When they arrived, Jane and Judy would be running along the platform to greet them. "It always seemed so sort of free and happy at The Birches," Sally once told me. "We would laugh and have jokes and do funny things. Everything we did seemed to turn out well. It completely changed my childhood, I should think, to be able to go there and be so free."

For at least two summers, in 1942 and 1944, the four girls spent a few weeks together at the beach. The long beach at Bournemouth was off-limits and barricaded against a Nazi invasion, but Vanne discovered a smaller, more obscure beach farther up the coast, at Studland (near Swanage), which was not blocked off. She was able to rent a small cottage for herself, V.J., and Judy, while Daphne and her two daughters took a room in a small hotel nearby. The four friends thus could play together all day: bathing in the ocean, collecting seashells, flowers, and blackberries, spying on farm animals, and so on. V.J.'s 1942 diary describes some of those idyllic days at Studland, including the time the girls visited some pigs and sheep:

July 28. We whent on the bech in the morning and I had my first swim on Sally's rubber-ring then we whent home to lunch then we whent on the beach. But on the way we brout a ruber ring and had my first liy on my back with my leg's kicking it was luvly we came home earlier than Sally and Soue and after tea we whent to the animal field to see them. First of all we hunted for the horse for we had got a carot each for him but we could not find him so we gave them to the pigs. I gave mine to a black one and Judy gave hers to a pink one after that the pigs began to sniff at us then we whent to see the herds. We were walking along when we saw a hen in the road and anuther flew oper the fence and mummy had to pick them up and put them back. Just then the pig's came out of the barbed wire and went along the road till they came to an empty I don't now what . . . [and] when they discuved it was empty they went back through the barbed wire all but one and he ran off down the road ~~becose~~ because he could not find the hole in the barbed wire but just then a lady came and chased him to the gate and pushed him in then I put my hand over the sheep fence and touched one then just as we wher going home we saw a lady peding the sheep and I stroked one and it felt lovly.

Since V.J. was the oldest of this quartet — Sally was more than fourteen months younger, Sue and Judy some four years younger — she became the leader and instigator, the one with the most passionate conviction about what to do and how to do it. "Mostly," recalls Judy, "I was quite happy to trot along and do what I was told. She was bossy, yes, but she did have good ideas and she did organize fun things. Occasionally I'd say, 'No,' and then she was very puzzled."

V.J., in fact, was full of positive energy. "She'd be up before breakfast, long before anybody else," Vanne once told me. "Down into the garden checking a spider's web or checking a beetle, checking anything." And she was typically very focused. "Everything she did," Sally remembers, "she went at it wholeheartedly. And everything was fun. Polishing the brass: normally that's a job that everybody hated doing. The heart would sink. But when we were doing it with her, it was all good fun, and we all enjoyed it. And the brass would be polished. And she'd say, 'Isn't that super?' Everything looked so lovely and sparkling."

No one could afford a bicycle, and so the girls had footraces around the block, rode the bus a lot (and surreptitiously turned the handle of the destination scroll), and went for long walks every day. In very hot weather they might take their shirts off, and V.J. would spray everyone with cold water from the hose. When they got tired of that, they could change into dry clothes, hide in the branches of a tree next to the hedge, and hose down unsuspecting people walking along the street. Rain and gloomy skies sent them into the hut or inside the house to the playroom, where they might all write or scribble in their diaries. They played marbles and assembled jigsaw puzzles. They chatted and planned. In the middle of the room was a table covered with a cloth big enough to hang down almost to the floor, and in the evening they sometimes turned off the lights and played bears underneath the table. Sometimes they made the whole house dark and then rushed around and tried to scare people. Other times they hauled a big mattress down to the bottom of the main stairs and jumped on it endlessly. They telephoned a man named Smelly, who afterward managed to trace the call. And they practiced and performed plays, usually ones that V.J. made up, such as *Handsome Prince Peter and Princess Charming* and *The Farmer and the Pink Pig* (with Sue dressed up in pink underwear to play the part of the pig).

Probably in the spring of 1946, twelve-year-old V.J. organized a nature club called the Alligator Club. Each member was required to take an animal name. V.J., as founder and leader, named herself after a beautiful butterfly, the Red Admiral. Sally, next in age, decided she would be Puffin. Sue chose Ladybird, and Judy, the youngest, became Trout. (In later years, the Alligator Club membership occasionally expanded to include Sally and Sue's little brother, Robert, who, possibly as a penalty for being much younger and a boy, was christened Cobra.) When club business necessitated a walk somewhere, the four members would assemble in order of rank and seniority, with Red Admiral at the head and Puffin, Ladybird, and Trout bringing up the tail, thereby forming an eight-legged ambulating alligator.

A clearing under pine trees near the bottom of the garden became the Alligator Camp, where the girls constructed a fire circle, dragged in some logs to sit on, collected firewood from the cliffs, and stored all their camping essentials (ceramic mugs, tins of cocoa and tea, and a spoon) inside an old trunk. And when Sue and Sally came to The Birches, the club would organize a secret midnight feast. During the day the Alligators hid bits of food from the kitchen, and then at night they gathered their food together and crept out into the garden, dancing around in great whispering excitement and then quieting down to listen to a mysterious rustling of leaves, quarter-hour chimes from the old church clock, and the soft low hooting of the brown owl deep in the murk of the next-door willow. They then cooked up their feast in a camper's pot ("billy can") over a small fire and tried to build an actual campfire.

A big problem with these midnight feasts was getting the "Little Ones," Sue and Judy, or Jif, out of bed without disturbing everyone else in the house. While V.J. and Sally were naturally quiet, Sue and Jif, once awakened, seemed to be very noisy, bumping into things and breathing much too loudly. Red Admiral described one of those midnight feasts in her 1949 diary:

At about 12.15 Sally & I stealthily dressed and then waited for Audy to have her bath. In the end we decided not to wait so we opened our door. Straight away the bathroom door opened & we hurriedly dashed to the shelter of our room. We tried again soon & with better luck. We crept to the Little Ones' room and woke them up. Two disgruntled faces dressed, socks first, making a terrible noise. Jif breathed so heavily we thought the whole house would wake up. After some time I decided to see if the way was clear, but I was just opening the door when I heard Aud go downstairs. We waited till she came up with cup of tea & then crept down one by one me, Sue, Jif & Sal. We then collected various odments & went to the 'serve. We carried the wood down & lit the Billy can. We put on a saucepan of water, but had to take it off so as to have light to kindle the camp fire. It would not work however, & then Jif upset the

water over the can & put it out. It was relit & soon the water was boiling. We had no milk but the tea tasted quite nice. I then made omlette but
fat would not melt & it turned into scrambled egg. It was not bad. We
boiled another saucepan of water for cocoa & toasted bread which tasted
horrid & none of us ate it. We lit two sparklers for light as the torch was
growing dimmer & dimmer. The cocoa was all wishy & then we had
some lovely choc while the can grew dimmer. Then put away some of
the things . . . & crept back like mice. Sally got into my bed & we talked.
Then sleep. Cheerio Pals.

The Alligator Club pursued more serious missions as well, such as raising money for the welfare of old horses. In September 1951 the four girls
cleaned out the glass conservatory, hauled in some cabinets and shelves, and
transformed it into a museum, displaying collections of feathers, seashells,
toadstools, some stuffed birds (found in the house), and, as the centerpiece,
a human skeleton Uncle Eric had fortuitously preserved from the detritus of
his medical school days. "We also arranged the human bones out & they
looked jolly good," Red Admiral noted in her diary. The girls strung up
notices on the outside of the hedge, and Sue and Judy were sent out "to lie
in wait" and persuade people strolling along the street to visit the museum.
Then, once they had seen the exhibition, the visitors were encouraged to
place extra coins through the slot in a round collection box, contributions to
the Society for the Protection of Old Horses at Cherry Tree Farm. By the
time the girls closed their museum, they had raised a total of three pounds,
thirteen shillings, and six and a half pence for equine charity, which, as the
diary notes, was "pretty good."

When holidays and summers were over and half the club had to leave
The Birches, they received in the mail regular editions of the *Alligator Letter,* edited, assembled, published, and mostly though not entirely written
and illustrated by Red Admiral herself. The magazine was filled with quizzes, puzzles, drawings, nature notes, and articles on such subjects as insects'
compound eyes, types of birds' eggs, and animal tracks. The articles, Judy
recollects, were "brilliant, really informative, excellent," but the readers were
expected to respond to the quizzes and puzzles in various ways. When they
did not, which was often enough, they could expect to hear from a Red Admiral who was not amused. As she noted with regal exasperation in an attachment to the *Alligator Letter* for Christmas 1948,

Dear Alligators,
    Please will you send back this number in time. I am getting a little sick
of the magazines trailing back with Puffin and Ladybird on their visites

here. . . . It isn't very encouraging, I can assure you, to spend hours and hours making something, and then just to have it ignored. I never seem to receive your competitions, you always loose them, one of you, and in future, if I don't have all answers—no more Alligator magazine. If you do not want to do this Magazine, please write and tell me, and I certainly will not bother to make any more numbers. Well, I am sorry to have to give you this lecture, but it is for the best, and if I do not have this back, complete with all answers, by the end of November, I shall make it the last. After all, it would be a much nicer club if you all put just a little more effort into it.

Red Admiral

Red Admiral also assigned topics for the other Alligators to write short articles about, and, in a letter written around July 28, 1946, to Sally, she encouraged them to ascend as quickly as possible to the rank of first class by mastering a few basic lessons on type and category:

Don't forget to learn First Class, because you must all pass when you come to stay. If Sue is not sure of no. 2, I will tell her of some things. You have to be able to recognize 10 birds, 10 dogs, 10 trees and 5 butter-flys OR moths:

(10 birds) (1) robbin, (2) blackbird (3) thrush (4) blue tit (5) wren (6) house sparrow (7) gull (8) hawk (9) starling (10) wood-pigeon.

(10 dogs) (1) cocker spaniel, (2) terrier (smooth and wire) (3) collie (4) alsatian (5) bull-dog (6) bull-terrier, (7) pekenese (8) old english sheep-dog, (9) dalmatian, (10) airdale.

(10 trees) (1) oak (2) birch (3) fir (4) pine (5) sycamore (6) mountain-ash (7) plain (8) lime (9) Ash, (10) Horse-chestnut.

(5 butterflies or moths) (1) Red Admiral (2) Six Spot Burnet Moth (3) Purple Emperor (4) Painted Lady (5) Privit Hawk Moth. These are some of the many things. I did not bother to put in ten wild flowers, because there are such a lot that almost everybody knows 7 X 10.

Once a member reached first class, she was allowed to wear the Alligator Club badge, which, however, she had to make herself, according to directions written by Red Admiral in another letter to Sally from the same period. And when the rest of the club was back in town, Red Admiral organized group scrambles on the cliffs and nature walks, getting everyone to look for birds, insects, feathers, shells, and the like. The nature walks became an increasingly serious business, and during those extended periods when the club was dispersed, Red Admiral took many solitary nature walks as well, wandering out to the wild areas along the cliffs overlooking the ocean.

5

Childhood's End

1951–1952

CHILDHOOD'S END appeared in 1951 as a time of melancholy and despair. The young V.J. had discovered a splendid intimacy with nature and dreamed the utterly impossible, childish dream of becoming a Doctor Dolittle or a Tarzan of the Apes, but as she began to mature physically, emotionally, and mentally, she would reasonably have to put aside her childish ways, renounce her foolish dreams, and apply for membership in the adult world. By 1951, school had come to represent that renunciation of dreams and the harrowing march into that alien adult world.

In the fall of 1945, she had matriculated at the all-girls' Uplands School in Parkstone, near Bournemouth. Uplands was a boarding school that took in day students, including V.J. and, later, Judy. All the girls wore uniforms: a simple navy blue skirt and blouse with a white collar, a lighter belted tunic over the blouse, and navy blue knickers under the skirt. Miss M. L. Orr (or Orr Bugs, as she was called by V.J. and her classmates, one of whom remembers a "tall, very strict-looking woman with very thick glasses and boils everywhere") was headmistress.

V.J. described her new school to Sally Cary in a letter written around September 1945: "We have a lovely gym there, bars, horses, ropes and every thing else. Some of the girls are quite nice, others very nice, and others simply stinking (excuse my word please). . . . Yesterday we had a HORRIBLE thing to do for English prep:—explain how to do up and adress a letter."

School days started between 6:00 and 6:30, when Henry VIII (the name V.J. gave her alarm clock) went off, followed by the appearance of Olly, usually, carrying a cup of tea. Between 7:30 and 8:00, V.J. walked or raced up the road to catch the bus and then settled down for the ride plus a short but friendly chat with one of the grownups on the bus. She might find herself chatting to "my old lady," "communist man," "high-voice man," "scarf-man," or "my bowler-hat man" before arriving, finally, at Countess Hoffan'on (the name she privately assigned to Uplands School).

Countess Hoffan'on always started with prayers in the chapel, but if she was lucky, she would arrive too late for that. If not too late, she could skip prayers anyway. Then began the academic classes. In English with Miss Brock, V.J. once rushed into class and "skidded all along the floor but Brock raised an eye & went on babbling while I lay on the floor helpless with laughter while everyone else also roared" (diary for January 1949). Another time, Brock "was lecturing us & I was thumping with my fist & she sent me out. I did not realize why for ages. Then I knew. She thought I was mimicking her. She only gave me a disorder mark" (February 1949). Once the same teacher read out to the entire class "a whole list of my spelling mistakes. Pig! I hate her!" (March 1949). Altogether, between 1949 and 1951, English was a discipline with "vile" exams, "silly" lessons, and "daft" exercises in arbitrary rules of punctuation and meaningless vocabulary.

History was "pretty dull as far as I remember" and "stupid" in 1949, while history assignments during the same year included "an essay on some silly person — Chamberlain I think." Geometry that year was "stupid, silly, idiotic," and "old"; and arithmetic was taught by "dear old Hee Hum-Hum," a personage who was actually "anything but dear . . . in fact a perfect beast."

V.J. was a good student, invariably coming in second or third in her class at end-of-term exams, but her happy and triumphant moments at Uplands were mostly social, not academic, the lighthearted times spent with friends during free periods, lunch, and sports; and although she was never successfully tempted by friends smoking behind the bushes, she enjoyed the usual sorts of school secrets, pranks, and games. Nevertheless, school, as she regularly summarized in her 1949 diary, was "dreary," an experience of "routine and dullness." "Woke gloomily up to the dreary prospect of school, school, school," she wrote on November 29, 1949, "stretching into the future like some monster ready to swallow me up, bit by bit."

By 1951, her penultimate year at Uplands School, V.J. had proceeded to the more advanced academic disciplines, including physics, chemistry, biology, and biology practical. Physics included a good deal of "mucky stuff about calculations" and was on occasion simply "crazy": "I don't believe half of what they say — all about the sun & mirages etc." Chemistry could be "pointless," and even when it had a point, things kept breaking, such as "a whole burette of pottasium permanganate" and "my pipette." Sometimes "all I broke was one beaker," but other times the results were more spectacular: "Suddenly, just as I was writing something, there was a bang, a shower of

Nitric Acid etc fell from the ceiling, & the beaker which had been heating on a wire gauze on a tripod sailed into the sink, all its contents having rained upon Hanly & I's heads." Biology (otherwise known as Bilge) was sometimes interesting, but too often it shared with chemistry the "same boring old Monday lessons . . . in which nothing of interest happened what so ever."

But the diary entries for 1951 take on a new urgency and seriousness, and they begin to communicate real despair at the seemingly interminable prospect of school, school, and school. "Woke up once again to be faced with yet another day," V.J. scribbled on February 2, 1951. "I rose, ate my breakfast, and set off. I suppose that everyone goes through a period of utter despair in their lives? Well, I'm sure going through it. Each successive morning renders me gloomyer than ever, and I only survive on my thoughts of nobler things and continual reading."

"Woke up to be faced by yet another dreary day of torture at that gloomy place of discipline and learning," she commented on February 14, "where one is stuffed with 'education' from day's dawn to day's eve."

"Woke up full of gloom e'en though it was the last day of the week," she wrote on May 4. "It was STILL only the SECOND day of school. Oh the long weary days that stretch out in a never ending procession before me, marring the glorious beauty and freedom of the long summer days ahead."

But the never-ending procession of school ultimately led to what was beyond school—adulthood—and V.J. had begun to mourn the lost glory and freedom of her childhood. Given the depth of her gloom, it is not surprising that by the start of 1951 she was often physically ill. "I woke up about 2.30–3.00 and couldn't go to sleep again," she wrote on Monday, January 15, at the start of a weeklong case of something—the flu, perhaps. "My body was hot, but every time I turned over, I could feel my blood run cold through my arteries and veins. After what seemed ages, Olly came with tea, and I induced her to fetch me some water. Gosh, it was sure good, that fluid with the formula H_2O. She also got me an asprin which I took with the tea (which was foul)." She ate a late breakfast but still felt "mighty queer." She tried to read a little from her old favorite *The Return of Tarzan*, but "I couldn't cope for long, as my head would go all fuzzy."

The next day she was feeling better, even though her body "tingled all over." She ate a little breakfast, brought up by Judy, and then settled down to read *Tarzan Triumphant*, which "proved to be smashing, and is all about a forgotten tribe of creatures started by a servant of Paul, the appostle and a slave girl he ran away with. They are subject to fits of epilepsy, at least the men are, but the women are beautiful." The day after that she read *Strange Conflict*, by Dennis Wheatley, and on Thursday she picked up a "queer book" about past lives brought in by Vanne, called *I Live Again,* finished by lunchtime. After lunch she turned to *Tarzan, Lord of the Jungle,* which had been her first introduction to Tarzan, and "I liked it even better on its second reading." On Friday, V.J. selected yet another Tarzan book, *Tarzan the Invincible.* "I then retired to my bed with this book and read it until my lunch was brought up by which time it was finished. . . . After tea I sat in the big chair and read my big animal book, and went to bed quite early. I found 'Dark Champion' in Judy's bookcase and this I read until it was finished. After that I put the light out."

The next day was Saturday, January 20, and all afternoon she "drove Mummy mad, also Olly I believe, as I felt too floppy to do anything special. I spent (in the end) a long time reading my 'Mammals of the World' which is jolly interesting. I chatted to Danny about monkeys, and then went up to bed. Had supper in bed, and went on perusing my nice animal book. Then I started 'The Wind in the Willows' and presently put out the light. Good night all mankind."

So bad days for school were good days for curling up at home with a book. But the illnesses and sick days were becoming more frequent and more serious. One time Uncle Eric announced that she would have to have her tonsils out, whereupon she scrambled to the top of the tall tree outside the landing window and refused to come down for hours, until it was dark. That dramatic gesture won her a reprieve, and then the emergence of a polio epidemic ended any further talk of tonsillectomy, since raw wounds in the throat might increase susceptibility to infection. (Although no one realized it at the time, she probably did become infected with polio, marked by a fever followed by paralysis—which was, most fortunately, only in the little toe of one foot.) Then she discovered that if she shook her head hard enough, her brains rattled, or seemed to. She was frightened by the rattling and started getting migraine headaches, such as the one on February 5, 1951: "Arrived at school and felt a little dizzy. I then thought I was going to get a migraine. I whispered this glum thought to Scilla before prayers, & then in prayers I couldn't see at all. I got the giggles 'cos Bobhin offered to share with me, & as I couldn't see I pushed it away. She looked so surprised. . . . It was most queer walking to the bus stop, but then it went & headache started."

She had spent the days of her January illness reviewing her favorite fantasy books from childhood, but that year marked the last time she read Tarzan seriously. She still loved being outdoors, going for walks along the cliffs with Rusty, spending Saturdays with Bushel and Poosh and the horses, intently observing quiet nature, eagerly immersing herself in the drama of violent nature. "I woke up and lay happily in bed listening to the wind which was howling outside," she wrote one stormy Sunday. "It was also a rain storm, and I could hear the angry lashings of the wild sea. I got up after this meditation on the merits of a storm, and had breakfast." Setting off with Rusty, then, she "did not meet the wind until I reached the top of the chine, and then it took me about a quarter of an hour to get down. I had to hang onto lamp-posts & shelter behind walls."

Yes, she was still attached to animals and nature, to all the emotions and experiences of her earlier life, but by now the melancholic sense of childhood's end had become a powerful preoccupation. She wrote poems on the theme. On Saturday, January 27, 1951, she woke up "with a feeling of relief that it was not school." The day was "a smashing day," and that morning she wandered by herself around the cliffs, but "all I could think of was a poem"; and she wrote the first stanzas of a poem eventually called "Yesterday," about a bright time, now sadly past, when

> *I was filled with the wonder of living*
> *And the glory of breathing fresh air,*
> *Oh, those were the happiest days of my life*
> *With never a worry or care.*

> *Each day I roamed over the country*
> *And studied the ways of the wild,*
> *And now all I wish is to live them again—*
> *Oh, to be once more a child!*

> *Each day I strayed further and further,*
> *And discovered new wonders untold,*
> *Then hungry and footsore, but happy at heart*
> *At night I returned to the fold.*

> *I returned to the love of a mother*
> *With which my young childhood was blessed*
> *And while my mind pondered deep mysteries of life*
> *My healthy young body found rest.*

> *I was filled with the vigour of living*
> *And glory at my being there;*
> *Oh, those were the happiest days of my life*
> *With never a worry or care.*

That afternoon she and Rusty went out to the cliffs again, and again she was engulfed in a melancholic, creative, poetical mood: "I was so poemy that I could only wander about and had to keep stopping to scribble verses. On the way home I stoped at the patch and wrote the end of the weepy poem. Then I went to the hut and finished the Spirit one."

Aside from its dull routine and sensory deprivation, the problem with school was its irrelevance: it was completely dissociated from this child's burning emotional and fantasy life. And if the ultimate point of school is to prepare one for life, well, then, what sort of life would that be? How could school conceivably allow V.J. to follow her childhood dream: to live among the wild animals of Africa, to study them, to write about them?

School was the force of sanity, of sense and sensibility. School regularized one's behavior enough to mesh with the systems of a factory or an office. At best, school prepared one for a career. For girls, of course, the career choices were still generally confined to secretary, nurse, or teacher. But even if she could find a career that pushed beyond that nurturing triumvirate, what would it be? Academic biology did not lead to field biology, since field biology hardly existed. And to the extent that men—not women— became naturalists or ethologists or zoologists, they did so by studying the birds, insects, or mammals of Europe or America. If an enterprising zoologist wished to study exotic animals—African baboons, for example—he (never she) might expect to study them in a zoo or a laboratory cage somewhere.

The careers advisory lady, on her annual pilgrimage to Uplands School, was completely perplexed by the bizarre idea that a sensible girl might wish to watch wild animals in Africa. But after learning that V.J. also loved dogs, the adviser arrived at a logical compromise solution: the girl could go to photography school and learn to shoot appealing photos of people's pet dogs. One might hope to make a living that way. The advice was not taken, and V.J. remained very worried about what her working career might actually be. She discussed the matter with her mother from time to time. "Then I took a glad departure [from school] and caught a bus Home and had coffee and discussed my career," V.J. wrote on May 2, 1951. The contents of that and a few other discussions on the subject are never revealed in the diary, though, and so we are left with Jane Goodall's later summary: "My mother always used to say, 'Jane, if you really want something, and you really work hard, and you take advantage of opportunities, and above all if you never give up, you will find a way.'"

V.J.'s talents as a writer finally brought some recognition at school, when Miss Orr announced the winner of the 1951 McNeile Essay Prize on May 17. "Went to prayers," V.J. wrote in her diary. "After, Orr Bugs said that she would give out the results of the McNeile. One of them, she said, was outstandingly good, and the owner of said screed, was none other than ME!!! I got the giggles, and felt sick & foul. Nearly fell to the ground. Unfortunately, I was 'going out of prayers' and so had to hear every single member of the Lower IV & III say 'Jolly Good' or 'Congrats' etc."

The prize was two guineas used to buy a book of the winner's choice. The book would be formally presented on Speech Day, which was July 2, a Monday. On that day Vanne and Danny listened from reserved front-row seats to the various speeches. V.J. noted in her diary that she was dressed for the occasion in her "best togs," including nylon stockings on loan from Vanne ("Foul things—stockings"), and she sat next to her friend Hillary. Finally Miss Orr introduced the winner of the McNeile Essay Prize, V.J. stood up and was applauded, and then Miss Orr handed her the prize book, saying, "Well done!" and "That's a very nice book." And V.J., returning to her seat, "got giggles & had to borrow Hilly's hanky."

That Speech Day was possibly the first time V.J. wore nylon stockings, and a summer holiday spent in Germany with Uncle Michael and Aunt Joan provided the occasion for, on August 5, "my first champagne cocktail which was nice." She bought her first girdle, a red one, on November 7, 1951; and on January 17, 1952, Aunt Joan gave her a late Christmas present of nylon stockings ("I felt awful. I don't know why. Embarrassed somehow").

Another mark of approaching maturity was V.J.'s startling change in attitude toward school, beginning with the autumn term in 1951. She had a new English teacher, Miss Ludwig, who on first impression seemed "terribly brainy, being conversant in English, German, French, Latin and Greek, and teaches jolly well." Miss Ludwig had been told that "we'd done no Chaucer, no Keats & no anything else. We are going to do a whole new lot & will be jolly nice. We started reading introduction of Anthony and Cleopatra." The new English curriculum included material on the types of poetry—epic, lyric, and dramatic—which was "jolly nice except that I forgot who wrote all the poems." And that was followed by the study of Spenser's *Faerie Queene:* "We got as far as all the monster's children bursting open after gorging themselves on her blood, & it was smashing."

Biology that term explored heredity and evolution. Classes started with some "rather interesting" lessons on heredity, "all about someone who experimented with peas. Also about people breeding blue from white & white flecked with black, parents." A month later came the session on evolution, "which was great fun as I like learning about it." Practical biology, meanwhile, included dissecting a rabbit. First, in September, the students examined the heart and circulatory system: "My rabbit had wiz vessels all round its heart, & for the first time in my life, I found everything I wanted to find."

A few days later they looked at brains ("wizzard"), and about three weeks later they dissected the rabbit's "urino-genitals" ("rather fun").

At times classes were still uninspired or tedious, such as the double period of biology on November 12, spent discussing the earthworm, which seemed too much time for too small a subject: "80 mins for one tiny little pink creature." But altogether, academic life that term had suddenly and surprisingly taken on a completely new cast and feeling. "Woke up and got up and had brek," V.J. wrote in her diary on Wednesday, November 14. "I caught some bus or other as I always do, and arrived at l'école in my customary mood which is quite gay nowadays. In fact I have come to the startling conclusion that school is quite a nice place after all."

Even the perplexing matter of careers and futures seemed less urgent, although not resolved. As V.J. noted in her diary for January 13, 1952, "This morning I was gloomy about my future but now I am not. The wind brushed my mind clear."

Along with problems of school and her future career, V.J. was starting to confront the problem of the opposite sex: boys and men ranging from the strange to the sinister and from the possibly nice to the perfectly glorious.

Bill was the first in a series of these problems. According to a letter that may have been written in 1948, when V.J. was fourteen, "Bill one day decided that he wanted to see me, and so came on his bicicle from Northbourne." A neighbor saw him standing outside the gate, but at last he came through and rang the bell. "He spoke to Mummy, who answered the door, 'Is it impertanant of me to ask if I am speaking to Mrs. Morris Goodall?'" V.J., he was told, was walking on the beach or along the cliffs. Bill failed to find her but returned to the house later, when V.J. had come back to eat her lunch, a large baked potato plus a bit of meat and tomato. V.J. had "a crumb of potato on my nose," and when she flicked it off, Bill said, "Why did you do that? It looked so sweet sitting there." He also told V.J. she was "inhuman" and that sometimes he could see her floating in the air. "At last I got rid of him, and jolly thankfull I was to. Apparently he came to see me one day when he came out of school but luckily I was not there. I hate him!"

Sinister males included a man who chased her home one afternoon in the autumn of 1950. She had stayed late at school, and by the time she boarded the bus home it was "quite, quite dark," she wrote to Sally. She got off the bus at her usual place and began walking along the road, whistling to herself. When she came to a bend in the road, "leaning against the fence was a shabby old bicycle, and standing beside it, also leaning against the fence, was a young man." V.J. sensed that he intended something improper. "All my nerves sent frantic messages to my brain, imploring it to let me run, and my voice shrieked to my brain to allow it to work, but with an iron will I commanded my brain to take no notice of my screaming feminine emotitutions & walked on, still whistling." She had just crossed the road when

I sensed he had moved. At this my muscles etc., screamed even louder, but I only permitted my brain to allow them to walk a little faster. Even so, he drew nearer & nearer . . . and soon he drew level with me. By this time my cheery whistle had died away, and all my energy was concentrated in walking—almost as fast as I could. Well, when he got level with me, I shuddered from my toes to my head, from my heart to my brain, but when he did the next thing, I thought my last hour had come. First he sort of edged up to me, a sort of leer on his face—an insane leer. Then he started talking gibberish, and by that I <u>mean</u> gibberish, not a string of words, but a string of noises. He also started to fumble—you know where—but luckily he was <u>not</u> indecently exposed, & did not have the chance to carry out this feat. My iron nerve broke down & I frantically told my brain to send an urgent message of speed to my leg muscles. This it did, and the muscles carried out the order with great efficiency. I looked over my shoulder in my mad rush, & saw him walking onward, an insane expression on his face.

Perhaps even more sinister was the man in "orange trousers" who, according to a diary entry, followed "wherever I went" as she climbed around the cliffs on January 22, 1951. Or the same man, dressed in "loud checks" the next day, "who appeared to be following me, but I walked back & up the hill & lost him."

The first of the possibly nice young men was Clive. On Saturday, September 22, 1951, he showed up at Longham and went riding with V.J. Clive also challenged V.J. to a "rock cake" contest, and thus the next Saturday she took in some small currant cakes that had been very hastily assembled and baked the night before. Poosh said V.J.'s cakes had "a nice flavour," while Bushel thought they were "sweet." So even though Clive's looked better, the contest ended as a tie. Both V.J. and Clive were awarded first prize: a piece of candy. Clive joined the army but showed up at the stables several months later, on a Saturday in June 1952, when they went out riding once again. "As a matter of fact we had a jolly nice ride," V.J. admitted in a letter to Sally. "I am absolutely sick of riding with either myself or a lot of stupid kids." Clive telephoned the next day and asked her to go out for a ride in his car. Even though her hair was "frightful," according to the diary, she said, "YES." They drove out to the New Forest, "walked in a howling gale to the

Rufus Stone so my hair was quite straight," and had tea at a small teashop with ponies nearby.

Unfortunately, one of the girls from school happened to see them while they were huddled over their tea, so at prayers on Monday the girl said out loud, "Who was that young man you were out with on Sunday?" V.J. blushed deeply while everyone around her "was in fits." Wendy, another girl in the school, turned to her and said, "Is that the one I know about?"

The one Wendy knew about was George, who showed up at Longham at the start of 1952. Pretty soon George had "winked at me & stroked my hand," and a week later, on Sunday, he spontaneously arrived at The Birches. "Judy came in & said George had come. I was in a filthy mess. My hair was untidy & I had slippers on. It was him. No comb." George hoped to take her for a drive, but she had too much schoolwork, and so they chatted in the drawing room. "I'm sure I was awfully rude to him. I must appologize profusely on Sat."

Finally there was Peter, "a sailor, frightfully brainy, and naturally, being a sailor, can dance frightfully well," who asked V.J. to the Pony Club Dance on January 9, 1952. That morning she was "not at all certain as to whether I wanted to go this evening or not. What will Peter be like! That is the question." In the end, and even though Peter was "hopeless at getting food," the couple had a very good time. They were driven back from the dance by someone's mother and in the car indulged in "great tickling matches." She said he was a baby and "needed his nappies changed," while he "insulted my nose." Then it was home to finish off the day's account in her diary: "Talked. Like Peter. Sleep. Goodnight."

Those three, however, were soon completely outshone by yet another object of interest and affection: Trevor. In contrast to the awkward, uncertain young men, Trevor was balanced, self-confident, and entirely mature. He was, in fact, much older than V.J., and yet at the same time vigorous and charismatic. The Reverend Trevor Davies, B.A., M.A., Ph.D., was a man of obviously high intelligence and serious thoughts who had become minister at the family church in Bournemouth, the Richmond Hill Congregational, during the final months of 1951.

In 1951, as V.J. gradually began reconciling herself to the formal, institutionalized learning of school, her attitude about church shifted in a similar direction. She wrote in her diary on April 15 that Danny and Vanne had gotten into an argument after "Danny said I was always ill on Sunday and I heatedly replied that she wouldn't feel like going if she'd been on a horse working hard every day for about 2 weeks." But only three months later, on July 15, she attended a sermon given by John Short, the minister who was then ending his tenure at Richmond Hill, and found it a "very good sermon about letting Jesus come in, & giving God a chance." She concluded: "I feel very wicked & am resolved to be gooder in future. I do wish he wasn't going just as I want to go to church."

By the time Reverend Davies arrived in the autumn, V.J. was for the first time in her life determined to attend church regularly and to listen. Olly sang in the choir. The rest of the family, including Danny, Audrey, and, when they went, Vanne and the girls, liked to sit in the gallery at the very middle of the very front. When they were fortunate enough to claim those seats, they looked out over the heads of most of the congregation and viewed the minister in his stone pulpit directly, from slightly above. The minister in turn might be looking their way and seeing them lit or silhouetted from behind by a glowing, coruscating wall of stained glass.

Reverend Davies first appears in V.J.'s diary on Sunday, November 11: "Had tea & went to church with Dan & O. Heard Davies who is jolly good, and then went to Lyons & had ice."

The next Sunday, November 18, the new minister spoke again, "and in the prayer he forgot himself and went on, and on. The sermon was jolly good. What is a Christian? You <u>must</u> go to church."

And then two Sundays later, on December 2: "The Sermon was terribly funny, and jolly good, and we all laughed. It was about people thinking they know better than God, and Jesus saying 'Get thee behind me, Satan' to Peter."

During this period, as V.J. turned seventeen and then eighteen, she gradually stopped thinking of herself as V.J. or Spindle or Red Admiral and began thinking of herself as Jane. The change is marked in her correspondence signatures. And yet in many ways her essential character remained consistent. She was always, as Vanne once wrote, "irradiated by her enthusiasms" — and so "it seemed quite in character when she developed an enthusiasm for attending not one but two services every Sunday." By the start of 1952, though, it had become clear to the family that her new enthusiasm for church included a growing one for the minister. Vanne recalled his appearance as she looked across from the front row of the gallery: "Soon it was time for the sermon and as the last notes of the organ died way, Trevor swept up into the pulpit." She saw "a man of medium height with chiseled features and thick prematurely white hair cut neatly to a well-shaped head." He began to speak, and "then I was conscious of the musical tones of his voice with its faint Welsh lilt, and of his charisma which kept the congregation so still. He spoke in the language with which Jane had long been familiar — the language of the poets and the musicians who seek to translate the experiences of the spirit into words and music."

Trevor was the first man Jane had known who could match her own passionate idealism, and she found in his poetic delivery and elevated message a drama to consider. She began taking notes of his sermons, and afterward she would go home to write them down word for word in a special sermon journal. She also started writing her own sermons. Trevor reminded her of her grandfather, the Reverend William Joseph, who was also Welsh and a Congregational minister (and, the thought may have occurred, a generation older than Danny when she fell in love with and married him). Jane began looking through her grandfather's library of philosophy books. She also began practicing the messages of Trevor's sermons. One, on the text of making that extra Christian effort, going "the second mile," provoked her to return home and steep two pots of tea, collect two buckets of coal, bathe herself twice in two tubs of water, and say good night to everyone twice.

By the time spring arrived, Jane's admiration for the new minister had become a wild adolescent infatuation. On Easter Sunday, April 13, she went to all three services, where Trevor was "in smashing form," according to a letter to Sally the next day. "In one of his sermons he said, 'Now tonight I'm going to preach about death. If you don't like it you can go! GO' says he, stretching his hand towards the door. Everyone laughed and we were looking at Audry half expecting she would." Later, after communion, "I SHOOK HANDS WITH HIM!!! I have only just washed my hand. I had to because it was all covered with fudge."

Jane would now wake up "thrilled that it was Sunday," as she wrote in her diary on May 18, 1952. She continued to record Trevor's sermons and take them very seriously—sermons, for example, about faith ("God holds the world in the palm of his hand and everything is bound to work. What an inspiring message of hope"), about "the little things of life and how important they were," and another "jolly good sermon about ropes" where "he got very eloquent towards the end—passionate in fact." That Trevor was so much older (approaching fifty) and happily married, therefore ultimately inaccessible in a physical sense, made this romantic dream all the more delicious, even closer to perfection. She did dream about him, of course. One time she "woke up with Trevor's kiss of dreamland still lingering on my face, and was, therefore, supremely happy."

One Friday evening that spring, Jane discovered that from a certain vantage point she could look across Bournemouth's central gardens and into the lighted window of Trevor's study in the old rectory. She rushed back with great excitement to tell everyone else that she could see her beloved's head as he worked on the coming Sunday's sermon. So now every Friday evening she gathered up any ready-to-be-posted mail and then walked with

Judy or Olly to the post office, conveniently pausing and hoping to spy a white-haired head framed by the yellow square of the rectory window.

Danny, Vanne, and the rest of the family joined in, as they always had, in supporting this latest enthusiasm. Danny promised to invite Trevor and his wife to tea, and Vanne managed to locate a photograph of him, sitting in an armchair and reading a book. Olly bought a frame for the picture, and Jane framed it: "I scrubbed & rubbed all morning till the glass was as clean as I could get it, and even then it wasn't spotless," she wrote in her diary on June 2. "I cut my finger & bloodied everything in the meantime, & had some coffee. Then at last it was finished and really looked smashing."

Trevor and his wife, Alice, finally came to tea on the afternoon of Tuesday, August 12, bringing along their little dog, Kitty. Danny had baked a cake. Flowers had been gathered and placed in vases. And Jane had polished and repolished all the brass and silver, arranged the chairs, told each member of the family what she must say and do, and placed some tiny, downy feathers and cotton threads on "his" chair, so that she would be able to keep forever what his precious bottom had caressed.

Kitty was "sweet," Jane wrote in an August 15 letter to Sally, but Rusty, who was also in attendance, "sulked and lay down by the door all the time." Jane sat in the chair "beside HIM," while Danny and Alice Davies sat on the couch and Vanne sat "behind the tea table on her little setee affair. I wore my white dress—AND he!! said how nice it looked." They "talked about everything under the sun." Jane had "never seen such a lively little man. He couldn't keep still for a second, and he couldn't bear for a conversation to be carried on without him. He <u>hated</u> for his wife to tell a story, and always managed to get his word—or rather wordS in." Trevor, she realized, had "a beautiful long nose and he adores dogs." When Reverend and Mrs. Davies got up to leave and opened the front door, Kitty disappeared—and "do you know! if I hadn't noticed they would have gone off without her! They must have enjoyed themselves. They'd even started the car. Then Trevor & I looked for her, & Audy found her by the [guinea] pigs. 'Oh hurry Trevor' says Mrs. Davies & he came pounding after me, doing exagerated running—you know—knees up & hands up & head back. It was a hoot. The naughty dog made a hole in the wire netting. We did nothing but laugh all afternoon, and do you know! They stayed from 3.45 till 6.30."

When the minister got up to leave, some of the tiny feathers and threads that had been placed on his chair were clinging to the back of his coat. The family tried hard not to laugh at the sight. Then, after he was gone, Jane retrieved a few downy and cottony fragments that remained. In her letter to Sally, she wrote that "I still have them, also his cigarette [and] his match-

stick and his tea leaves. I went to bed on the couch that night with his cush-
ion for my pillow." And since the Reverend Trevor Davies declined to take
sugar in his tea that afternoon, Jane vowed that she would never take sugar
in hers again. She never has.

Such was the final sparkling summer of childhood. Jane had finished school
in style three weeks earlier, having won the McNeile Essay Prize again that
year and having done well in advanced examinations for English, biology,
and history. If her family had been able to afford it, she might have considered university next, but they could not, and she did not.

The next three weeks were spent preparing for three months in Germany
(where she would supposedly be teaching English to a family), which required shopping for shoes and buying a new skirt. She paid a final visit to
school, took a few walks on the cliffs with Rusty, and luxuriated in an "all
night" dream about Trevor. "I kept seeing him," she wrote in her diary,
"wanting to meet him, & then knowing I had curlers in my hair & putting
my hand up and feeling them."

September 7, 1952, was her last Sunday to see Trevor for a long time.
"Got my seat and heard with joy his dear voice in the pulpit again,"
she noted. "Caught his eye. Nice service. Shook hands & asked if I could
say Goodbye in evening." Then, after the evening service—a "lovely
sermon"—she spoke to him again. ("Went in & he told me not to be tearful.
I told him, unbeknown to Ma, about Daddy"—possibly about his letter requesting a divorce. "I felt I should.") Finally, after waiting "for hours," she
met him once again in the front hall of the rectory. "Got into Manse hall &
HE came over." They said their "touching farewells," and he asked her
"was I going to teach them bahth or bath, cahstle or castle?"

The next day, Monday, Jane went to Mr. Barnes's photography studio
and posed for her end-of-childhood portrait. Her brown hair was pulled
back and permed, she was wearing a white blouse and necktie and her best
riding outfit, and black-haired Rusty, a bright splash of white on his chest,
head cocked quizzically, sat faithfully beside her. Two days later she changed
English pounds for German marks at the bank, bought an English-German
dictionary at the bookstore, said some final goodbyes, and stepped on the
2:30 train out of Bournemouth, bound for London, Dover, Germany, and
her adult life.

6

Dream Deferred

1952–1956

JANE'S FIRST TENTATIVE experiment in mature independence consisted of living abroad for three months. Aunt Joan and Uncle Michael Spens at that time lived in Cologne, where Michael had an important post in the administration of the British sector of occupied Germany. Jane had visited Joan and Michael briefly during the summer of 1951, when they first arrived in Cologne. She later recalled gazing over the ruins of that city and seeing the cathedral intact, "rising undamaged from the rubble of the surrounding buildings," which seemed to her "a message symbolizing the ultimate power of good over evil." In any case, after that brief visit, Aunt Joan arranged for her to live with a German family for three months, from mid-September to mid-December 1952, on the theory that she could study German while making herself useful by speaking English with the four children.

She had looked forward to the adventure enthusiastically. "I may be lucky in going to Germany," she wrote to Sally on July 6. However, she continued, "I am only going for one reason—I shall be able to write to Trevor, and I am quite sure he will write back. Then my happiness will pass all belief."

On September 13, Uncle Michael and Aunt Joan met her at the train station in Cologne, and on Monday, September 15, they drove her to Duisburg and the home of the Magis family. The Magises were prosperous merchants, and their house was very big, Jane noted in her diary that night, with a "huge" drawing room containing "2 canaries, plants in window, & massive great furniture." Michael and Joan introduced her to Herr and Frau Magis and their children, two girls, Wiltrud and Helga, and two younger sons, Hans and four-year-old Bubi. Then Jane's "last link with England drove away, and I felt very watery but remained smiling."

She was soon homesick. She thought about Rusty. She worried about the guinea pigs. She dreamed about Trevor. She read a lot, mostly enjoyed the food, played games with the children, listened to British radio on the wireless (especially her favorite program, *Mrs. Dale's Diary*), and once visited the zoo at Duisburg. The grounds were "beautiful," but it was "not nearly as nice as the London Zoo because all the animals looked cold and miserable." She took riding lessons alongside Helga on some good horses but with a riding master who was "very military & bellowed if we got out of place." And she sometimes played with the Magises' dog, Lumpey, a dachshund who had, she wrote to Audrey on September 23, "long hair and is very bouncy. When he wants you to play he comes up and pulls at the hem of your dress. I took him for a long walk over the fields to-day, and he found a dear little baby rabbit—he didn't catch it though."

Jane studied German in the privacy of her room most mornings, and on Sundays she read from the Bible and a book of Trevor's sermons. She struggled with a new family and home, a new language and culture, and the disconcerting novelty of everyday things, including bad shampoo ("comes out of a tube & won't lather or anything"), a strange toothbrush ("very long— the brush part—& the bristles are very, very soft & fine like a babies hair brush. Worse still, you get a whole mouthful every time you brush your teeth"), and an insomnia-inducing bed ("pillow end goes up to steeply").

She may have overcome her initial homesickness, but in spite of the kindness of the Magis family, Jane's return to England on December 17 was a relief. She was met by Vanne in Dover, by Uncle Eric in London, by Judy at the station in Bournemouth, and by Danny at the front door of The Birches, and she picked up Danny gleefully and carried her all the way into the drawing room. Rusty was there as well, but "everyone made such a din," according to her diary, that the dog was "too bewildered to know me at first." The whole family had tea in the drawing room, they talked, and then a tired but contented Jane went upstairs to bathe while Judy hauled up the luggage.

On December 21, her first Sunday home, Jane "woke up very happy." She had "a gay and glorious breakfast and then sallied forth with Judy. We danced down & arrived in good time so got my nice seat" at church. Trevor preached a good sermon about loving-kindness: "Love can be idealism, but kindness must have an object." And then she "pranced home gaily."

Trevor and Alice Davies and their son, Michael, showed up at The Birches on the evening of December 22 for a family meal that included roast chicken, carrots, and mince pie. Trevor, it became apparent, did not like carrots, but the guests stayed until midnight. Best of all, Trevor kissed Jane under the mistletoe. The diary entry is emphatic: "He <u>KISSED ME</u> under M." It was a very public kiss and must have been proper and innocent, though, and Olly demanded that he kiss everyone else as well.

On Christmas day Jane firmly resolved "to keep Christmas spirit all year." But the next year would certainly challenge that vow. She continued in her usual patterns—walks with Rusty, caring for the guinea pigs, events with the family, church on Sunday, and so on—but now she had to face the compelling problem of what to do with her life. A couple of days after her birthday was Easter Sunday, and by Monday, April 6, Jane was confiding to her diary that "in spite of the joy of Easter Sunday after the pensive Good Friday, I felt sadder and more depressed yesterday than I have for a long time. I think it was—or rather is, as I still feel rather melancholy—because I have been looking forward to Easter for so long, and now it is over. Our birthday is over too, and there doesn't seem to be anything left to look forward to . . .—and the thought that . . . I shall have to start earning a living seems almost frightening."

One of her more practical ideas for earning a living was journalism, but Vanne suggested secretarial school, arguing that a secretary could find work anywhere in the world, and by March, Mortimer had agreed to cover the tuition. Thus, in late April or very early May, Jane moved to London and began renting a room in the flat of Agatha Hillier, at 8 Beaufort House, Beaufort Street, in Chelsea. Mrs. Hillier, known to Jane as A.A. (short for Aunt Agatha), already shared her apartment with an apartment-sized dog named Nellie, and soon Jane had hung her favorite picture of Trevor on the wall in her room. From Beaufort Street it was a fair walk or an easy ride on the tube to Queen's Secretarial College in South Kensington, where she started classes on May 4, 1953, learning shorthand, typing, and bookkeeping, with an extra class in "The Art of Writing."

Queen's Secretarial College was founded in 1925 to train young women to operate typewriters. By the time Jane arrived, it occupied a contiguous pair of five-story townhouses at 20 and 22 Queensberry Place (around the corner from the Natural History Museum) and had 125 to 150 students, all women, learning and practicing their secretarial skills in 45-minute periods from 9:30 to 4:00, with 45 minutes off for lunch and one double period a day set aside for typing. The twin townhouses included a posh entryway with a stone floor leading to carpets and the office of the principal, Miss Hill, while the hallways and classrooms were more utilitarian—and often noisy, one can imagine, since typing was learned on large office manuals that signaled the end of a typed line with a dinging bell. To keep the dinging steady and the lessons lively, instructors might choose to play a gramophone record. "Colonel Bogey," with the whistling chorus, was one favorite song.

"I'm very nearly dead," Jane declared three weeks after she had begun at Queen's, in a letter to Sally. "This shorthand is terribly hard work, and also rather monotonous as it only requires learning, learning, learning. The typing is not too bad, but that again, is a little bit automatic." In fact, Jane once told me, she was not at all bored at Queen's, first because "there is something pleasant about learning a mechanical skill, somehow," and second because she enjoyed some of the other students. During lunch hour, she and others would sometimes eat at a cheap restaurant near the South Kensington tube station, and they might walk over to the Museum of Natural History for a quick look at the exhibits.

On Fridays, Jane often took the train or rode in Uncle Eric's car back home to Bournemouth for a relaxed weekend, perhaps including a spirited walk with Rusty across the cliffs and along the beach and, on Sunday, sitting in her favorite spot at Richmond Hill and listening to a sermon by Trevor. Other weekends might find her riding horses at the Chantry, an apple farm in Kent owned by the husband of Deb Seabrook, a good friend of Vanne's. Agatha Hillier was Deb Seabrook's mother, and Seabrook's daughter, Jo, was a friend of Judy's. Jo had two ponies, Joker and Gypsy, which they rode "nearly all the time," as Jane wrote to Sally on May 27. "You can't imagine how super it is to be able to do just what you want on a horse, instead of always having to behave yourself." As an example of what might happen when she was not quite behaving herself, Jane went on to describe "one quite mad ride when we both nearly fell off from laughing." She and Jo had just come back from a dog show and spontaneously decided to take the horses out.

> We got onto the horses as we were, & as I had to take my stockings off, I took my shoes off too. Jo followed suite of course, & so we were sockless, shoeless, johdless, hatless, & saddleless. We went through the orchards (which incidentally were glorious with apple blossom) and Joker kept bucking. That made me laugh, & so I nearly fell off, and then I saw Jo quite helpless with laughter. On enquiring the reason, I discovered that when my skirt blew up (as it frequently did) she could see my suspenders wildly flopping up and down under my knickers. That set me off, and honestly, I've never laughed as much in my life. And as you know it's most queer laughing when cantering. In the end we both had to collapse on the ground, quite helpless & weak. It took about two days to recover from.

In terms of men, it was quiet year. Letters arrived from one or two admirers, including a German fellow named Horst Pelletier, with whom Jane had shared riding lessons the year before. John Barrow, who lived in the same apartment building, sometimes aired his mother's Pekingese and cat around the same time Jane was airing Mrs. Hillier's Nellie, so they occasionally crossed paths. John eventually asked his mother to knock on the door of number 8 and announce that her son had been given two seats for *Pygmalion*— would Jane care to go with him? She went on the evening of February 16, 1954, and found the play "excellent," as she wrote to Sally, while John was "frightfully nice." About a week later they went to a movie, *Runaway Bus*, and "it was very good and very funny." After, they chattered "for hours" outside the door to the flat, while the elderly A.A. fussed about inside the apartment, walking to the door and clattering ostentatiously with the milk bottles, finally calling out "in a horrible voice that it was time I came in." Jane stayed outside another ten minutes and finally returned to "such a blowing up that it was all I could do not to completely loose my temper with the stupid old Victorian creature!"

But John was called up for national service, while Jane had to prepare for final exams and proceed on to the final project, Model Office, which involved real secretarial tasks such as helping Miss Hill, the principal, with school correspondence. When former students wrote, Jane explained to Sally, "we, the poor creatures in the Model Office have to draft nice chatty replies for her—which is an awful job." Meanwhile, in her spare moments at Queen's, Jane had begun amusing herself by drawing cartoon fish with humanoid faces and personalities. She showed some to Mrs. Christie, the Model Office overseer, including a very clever one of a fishy Miss Hill dictating letters to one of the fishy students. Mrs. Christie then showed the drawing to Miss Hill, who "liked it so much that I had an official contract to do her one personally, as she wanted to send it to her invalid mother to cheer her up!"

By the time Jane completed her course at Queen's Secretarial College, on March 6, 1954, she could squeeze out of a typewriter 51 words per minute and scribble shorthand at 110 words per minute. She received top grades in bookkeeping and apparently impressed Miss Hill positively with her fish cartoons. Or did Miss Hill quietly wonder if the creativity involved in drawing fish cartoons and the sobriety involved in being a successful secretary were mutually exclusive? The school's confidential report concluded that Jane was altogether "a clever girl, but rather smug" and "sometimes inclined to behave as if she has nothing to learn." Thus, Model Office "was good for her," since it "showed her how much she did not know!" And in spite of her perfectly acceptable typing, shorthand, and bookkeeping skills, Miss Morris-Goodall was still "quite immature and not really ready for responsibility." She was "very anxious to write" but in time could be expected to jettison that childish fantasy and settle down to a proper career and life: "Will eventually make a good secretary."

• • •

With her Queen's diploma in hand, Jane returned home in time for her twentieth birthday on April 3 and, on April 18, a packed and glorious Easter Sunday service at Richmond Hill. Then, at the start of May, she set off to Oxford to apply for a secretarial position. "I havn't given up the journalism idea by the way," she insisted to Sally in an April 26 letter, "but I have decided that to write anything worth reading I must have lived a few more years and acquired a little experience of life, as they say."

She was not offered the job she had hoped for, and so she settled back in Bournemouth to help with clerical work in Olly's physical therapy clinic for crippled children. The pay was minimal, two shillings and sixpence an hour, and the work was boring. However, as she noted in a June 26 letter to Sally,

> the dullness of the actual work finds recompense in my interest at being up at the clinic & seeing all the cases. Actually one gets a peculiar complex from being amongst crippled children all the time. It makes one realize how damnably lucky one is to have one's body the same as any other ordinary person's. Some of the cases are so pathetic that my heart aches for them, & yet one and all are happy and bright, & they never complain. . . . One little girl is paralysed from the waist down & will never be able to walk. She had polio at 8 yrs old, & as she was such an athletic little thing it got her very badly. But I have never yet seen her with a disagreeable face or a cross voice. It certainly teaches one a lesson!

But finally Jane received a letter from the Oxford University registrar offering basic secretarial work, to start in August. The registrar's office was in the Clarendon, an impressive neoclassical edifice built in 1712 and 1713 by the first earl of Clarendon: three-story and symmetrical, with stone stairs leading from Broad Street up to a great portico of four Doric columns, a classical frieze, and, above that, a roof garnished with monumental sculpted figures in the style of Roman temple statuary.

As soon as she arrived in Oxford, Jane set out to explore the building in the company of two young coworkers. She found it "simply georgeous" on the top floor, as she wrote home to the family, where "one feels on top of the world." They located the entrance to the attic, crept inside, and discovered it to be excitingly "dark & cob-webby, and there were great long spaces with crumbling board beneath. Sheila & I were very venturesome, & got all mixed up in a place where some queer soft stuff lay on the ground between two planks. We couldn't think what it was, & took a handful out to the light with us—but were no wiser. It was white & looked rather like flour that has become clogged with weevils—or whatever those bugs are that used to be in Danny's store of war-time flour & appeared baked in her bread on numerous occasions!"

Jane rented a room in a house at 225 Woodstock Road, and six mornings a week she would take a bus up Woodstock Road to the center of Oxford, then proceed onto Broad Street to the stone steps of the Clarendon. She passed through the iron gates and arch, turned either right or left to choose from the matching oak staircases rising to the first and second floors, and began work, typing and filing mostly, at half past nine in the morning.

She sat in a wooden chair at a wooden desk with a leather top, typed on one of the standard office machines, and wrote by hand with a fountain pen. The ceilings were high, the windows large and arched. All the men came in jacket and tie. The women wore dresses or skirts that draped well below the knee, with stockings and heels — except on the hottest days of summer, when they might wear sandals. There was a coffee break around half past ten, then an hour and a half for lunch, tea in midafternoon, and closing time at six. Saturdays were also workdays, beginning at half past nine and ending at one.

Miss Shearer, Jane's immediate supervisor, was tolerant enough to allow this new employee to bring in her pet hamster, Hamlette, as a squeaky little office companion, but nevertheless it was, Jane remembers, "just very boring filing and a bit of typing. Absolutely at the bottom." Still, exceptional moments occasionally broke the tedium. Once she was asked to find a scholar's hat to fit the emperor of Ethiopia when he came for his honorary degree. Someone sent in the measurements. She shopped around for the hat. But Haile Selassie had a very small head, and in the end she bought the smallest size and padded it with newspaper. Another time — perhaps it was mid-August — some of the registrar's staff were called upon to help time a procession, as Jane noted in one of her letters home: "We have just been out 'processing,' i.e., marching in a long crocodile from the Divinity School to the Sheldonian to give them the means to time such a procession for when the British Association receive their degrees. All the chief members of the corporation were out in full force to-day, including the Mayor, the Mayoress, and the Chief Constable. You've never seen such a ridiculous sight as all of us trailing along pretending we were burdened with gowns, evening dress and the like. All the tourists and sightseers had a wonderful time." But such deviations from the routine were rare.

The compensation for working at a dull job was living in an exciting place. Being in Oxford as a secretary was almost like being a student, with much of the fun and none of the academic pressures. Jane signed up for an evening course in German and enjoyed cutting the class whenever she felt like it, as when, one November evening, there was an influx of "the thickest fog I've ever been in" (as she declared in a letter to the family). After she had missed the German class, she settled down at the library for a while, doing some personal research on unicorns, and then felt her way out through the fog and took a bus home. Riding the bus, however, "set me jumping with fog-fever, as it crept along at about 2 m.p.h. and kept mounting the curb with alarming lurches. The cars in front were making equally heavy weather of it." She got back to the digs, chewed on some bread and a biscuit, and chatted with her landlady, Miss Kersey, who said she "adored wandering about in the fog too." Thus inspired, Jane "sallied forth" and "did some smashing wandering on my own. It was really chronic for the poor wretched motorists, and a wall and a pillar box were knocked flat—only I didn't see them unfortunately. At last I meandered home."

Miss Kersey was "really very sweet," Jane wrote to Sally. She had a kitten, Coco, who spent a lot of time in Jane's room, "which is nice as she keeps me warm." That room was on the ground floor, facing the heavily trafficked Woodstock Road. The first night or two Jane was disturbed by the din, but soon she adjusted and could "scarcely hear the noise save for the annoyance of an occasional extra loud bus or motor bike—this being especially agrivating when one happens to be listening to something on the wireless." Miss Kersey also had some apple trees in her garden, and Jane and the other boarders could pick up the windfall. And unlike Jane's previous landlady, Miss Kersey was tolerant and unobtrusive: "She never interferes with us at all, and we can arrive back at anytime of the day or night without provoking curiosity or wrath—a little different from A.A."

All the residents at 225 Woodstock Road shared the kitchen, and so Jane came to know others in the house. Stuart Ramsden and John Butler were both physics graduate students. Stuart liked music and played his gramophone "half the night," but since he played "super music," no one seemed to mind. Jane had originally assumed, as she wrote to Sally, that the "gorgeous Beethoven proceeding out of his room" came from a wireless, and so she dashed down to her room to find the same station, in vain.

Stuart, John, Jane, and a fourth resident, Eileen, soon became a regular quartet, making frequent weekend excursions around town and into the country, but Stuart, alas, was starting to express a romantic interest in Eileen, thus leaving John and Jane as an uncomfortable pair—uncomfortable, at least, for Jane. "I had a smashing weekend," she wrote to Vanne that December, "but the romance at 225 is progressing too fast for my liking—rather one-sidedly I fear!"

By the start of 1955 the romantic tensions had become more complex, since Stuart had fallen for Eileen while Eileen was in love with a man temporarily living in Canada. "We spend our time either being very happy all together, slightly uneasy in pairs, & rather unhappy when we have heart-to-hearts," Jane wrote home in February. As for John, "At one time John was excellent company to be in—amusing and yet interesting. But now he tries to hide his feelings behind a completely flippant exterior, and it gets mighty tiring, really it does."

But by then Jane had other concerns. For one thing, she was going to be presented as a debutante to the Queen. At the urging of a distinguished sponsor (Uncle Michael), Her Majesty had commanded Jane to appear at Buckingham Palace at 3:30 in the afternoon of March 2 in "day dress" plus hat. Of course Jane would need to know how to curtsy properly, and so that February she took lessons from a petite Hungarian lady in Oxford, who said, "Most people will tell you that when you curtsy, you merely drop your eyes. Instead, you must hold the royal gaze!" And she taught Jane to practice walking gracefully and curtsying with things on her head.

Jane already had a nice evening dress, a lacy, turquoise-and-white one with swan feathers and sequins that Vanne had bought for two pounds—a fashion-show second—but it was not suitable for meeting a queen. "I am just about having kittens over this presentation business," she wrote to Sally on February 17. "It really is driving me off my rocker. As yet, I have nothing to wear, and am, in fact, dashing home this weekend to try on all the dresses in Bournemouth practically. Mummy has apparently got mounds of them out on approval. The whole business really is ridiculous." A week later, though, she was able to inform Sally that "Daddy has turned up trumps over this business, he really has, and I am most grateful to him. Never did I think the day would come when I could walk into the most exclusive and expensive dress shop in Bournemouth, and buy the nicest thing there—AND enjoy it!"

The dress was a lacy swirl of crimson, and she set it off with a lacy black hat and gloves and black shoes. She had her hair done at a fancy shop in Oxford and then showed up at Buckingham Palace on March 2 to discover that someone had mangled her name. Almost everyone else seemed to have a title. Valerie Jane Morris-Goodall might have blended in, but Jane was listed as "Miss Valerie Goodall": the hated first name and only half her last name. So she found the resplendent gentleman who was supposed to read the names and said, "This is wrong. This is not me. You can't do this." He said, "Well, what is it you want to be?" She said, "It's not what I want to be. It's what I *am*."

Jane and the other debutantes were arranged into a long and glamorous queue that ambled across a red carpet toward the throne, where one by one they were presented. The correct name was called out—Miss Valerie Jane Morris-Goodall—and she curtsied to the Queen, holding her royal gaze, curtsied to Prince Philip, holding his royal gaze, and then proceeded along into the palace garden for the debutantes' garden party and thence back to Oxford.

The return to typing and filing at the registry may have felt anticlimactic, but by then Jane had her twenty-first birthday party to think about. A faulty window sash banged shut on both her hands one evening, and although the accident was serious enough to warrant an emergency trip to the doctor, X-rays, bandages, and three days off from work, no bones were broken. She recovered in time to play the elegant hostess on March 26 for her own birthday party at 225 Woodstock Road, wearing the crimson debutante outfit. She was toasted, gave a brief speech, and extinguished twenty-one candles with a single blow.

In spite of such fun, however, Jane was now determined to leave Oxford. She had become, as she wrote home that February, "miserable these last few weeks because of the boredom of this foul job," and she asked Vanne for help locating something less boring and foul. "Do you not think it is time I got something else?" Working as a medical secretary seemed potentially rewarding. Perhaps Uncle Eric knew someone who needed help. Or conceivably a job at the Foreign Office could be "quite fun—10.30 to 5.00, and lots of parties." Uncle Michael might have some ideas. In the end, a family friend, Alvar Lidell (well known in England as one of the reassuring BBC radio voices during the war), set up an interview for Jane at a commercial film studio in London.

Jane took a train to London that April and was met by Judy, Vanne, and Mortimer, who escorted her to the place. The four then celebrated her successful interview at Mortimer's club, the Steering Wheel, and after Vanne and Judy had caught their train back home, Mortimer took Jane out for drinks and a salmon and asparagus dinner at the Sports Car Club. "I have definitely got the job," Jane reported to Sally soon after. "It fills me with dread—at least it ought to and it most certainly will do as the time draws near, as it really is most terribly responsible and complicated. Please pray for me."

Jane left Oxford early in June, spent some time back home in Bournemouth, and by July had settled in London at 88 Redcliffe Gardens, in the borough of Kensington and Chelsea. For thirty-five shillings a week, she was able to afford a dingy basement room with a bed, a chair, a gas ring to cook on, and a window looking onto a bare wall. But she had her favorite books and her picture of Trevor hanging on the wall. She enjoyed the independence of living alone, and she loved her new job, which was certainly more interesting than the last one. "Oh, Sally, I am having such a wonderful time," she wrote to her friend that August. "No more shorthand, no more typing, no more writing other people's stupid letters."

Stanley Schofield Productions occupied the top two floors, above a nightclub and a photographer's studio, of a three-story building at 6–8 Old Bond Street, just a few steps away from where Vanne had worked for Charles Cochran some twenty-five years earlier. You climbed the stairs to a reception office, which was, when Jane started, run by an eighteen-year-old receptionist named Margaret Arthur, who recalled four and a half decades later her first impression of the twenty-one-year-old new employee: "freshly attractive" with "rosy cheeks and blond hair."

Schofield produced cinematic shorts for advertisements, promotions, and educational purposes: films about women's stockings, men's electric shavers, motor racing, motorcycles, medical films about childbirth and the surgical separation of congenitally joined twins, and so on. For the stocking film, a large number of attractive young women were asked to show their legs to Mr. Schofield during private interviews in his office.

Including Jane and Mr. Schofield himself, the company at that time employed some seventeen people, most of whom performed specialized tasks—secretary, receptionist, cleaning person, sound engineer, camera operator, film editor—but Jane was soon working at a little of everything as the studio's main factotum. She entertained customers, projected films, edited and spliced film, selected background music, and even sometimes briefly modeled (providing the hand and arm that poured a jug of milk). Margaret, meanwhile, had concluded that people had more fun upstairs, in the production area, and thus another receptionist was hired and Margaret became a second factotum—and soon Jane's best friend at work. Mr. Schofield sent them both out for a makeup training course at the Max Factor headquarters, so that when the studio produced a piece on Bruce Woodcock (a well-known boxer of the time) shaving with an electric shaver, Jane and Margaret were able to make him up for the shot. At lunchtime the two friends might buy a good piece of cheese and some bread and fruit and then return to the office and eat their lunch on the building's roof. From there they could look down to the busy streets below, and on a sunny day amuse themselves by catching the sun with a small pocket mirror and guiding a beam down to the street. They would select victims at random and provoke them with the beam as they walked along the road.

They dressed smartly. Margaret always wore a suit, with a hat, high heels, and stockings; as Jane recalls, they thought that for a woman to wear trousers to work was "really shocking, totally distasteful." They often traveled on the crowded tube together, thinking it grand to talk about life in "the studio" loudly enough for people to hear them. "We used to show off a bit," Margaret remembers, "and mentioned 'the studio' with practically every other word, and then we'd start off giggling. We were young."

Margaret lived with her family at home, and Jane was regularly invited over to dinner, sometimes to stay overnight. The dinners must have amounted to an important infusion of calories, since with her meager salary (under seven pounds a week), Jane would sometimes skip meals to save money. Still, Mortimer or Uncle Michael would also sometimes treat her to a lunch or dinner, as did a few eager young men, including David from work, Peter from work, and Brian.

Brian Hovington had known and admired Jane in Oxford, and now he pursued her with a quiet persistence in London, taking her to the theater or for coffee in a candlelit place to discuss philosophy and religion until midnight, driving her down to Oxford on the weekend, giving her small potted cacti, building a bookcase for her, painting a picture for her, and wandering with her around Piccadilly Circus on New Year's Eve. Jane had tied balloons to her ears as earrings that evening, and Brian, as she wrote home afterward, "went completely berserk and began spouting Shakespeare and then producing ludicrous extempore verse in the same vein—only absolute rubbish. He pretended to be drunk. It was a hoot." High-spirited Jane enjoyed herself most of the time in most circumstances, and she loved going to concerts and plays with Brian. She also appreciated the meals. But like many of Jane's relationships with men during this period, it was ultimately a one-sided affair, with Brian increasingly convinced that his investments ought to start yielding a return. When Vanne came up to London in March 1956 and Brian insisted on taking both mother and daughter to the theater and a dinner afterward, Jane started to become worried. "I am getting more and more tangled up with poor old Brian," she wrote to Sally that April. "Honestly I don't know what the end of it all will be. Perhaps he will kill himself or me or something!"

It was time to disentangle herself. In May, before Brian drove her down to Bournemouth for the weekend, she felt it important to ask, in a letter to Vanne, "Is it really OK for B. to bring me down?" explaining that "I have decided, even more firmly than when I spoke to you on the phone, that he is no husband for me. He knows how I feel too, so he is just coming down as a kind of repayment of hospitality which I feel is due." She continued bluntly, "If you want to know any reasons for my never marrying him I can let you have a string—e.g.'s television, too settled, too fond of creature comforts, doesn't like books etc., doesn't stand up straight, too fat, not handsom—I could go on for ever, but it boils down to the fact that I just don't love him one bit, so that's that—AND he knows it."

Jane's friendship with Margaret was far less complicated, and the pair regularly succeeded in getting cheap seats to concerts and plays. In mid-September 1955, for instance, they heard the Brahms Second Violin Concerto at Albert Hall, which was, Jane wrote home, "really terrific—and I really and truly think that apart from my darling Mendhelsohn (that looks a bit odd!) violin concerto, I enjoyed it more than any other symphonie."

Jane also attended occasional evening-school classes offered free by the London School of Economics, including a Thursday evening class in theosophy. "There is no studying the great philosophies of Plato, Spinoza, Hegel, etc.," she wrote to Sue Cary in a long, newsy letter dated March 27, 1956. "If we study any recognized philosophy at all, it is the ancient wisdom of the east—she is always quoting passages from the Upanishads and Buddha." Jane found the readings all very interesting, although ultimately perhaps she was more fascinated by the teacher, who was lively and very inspiring. After the lectures, about ten of the students would linger over coffee or tea and "get down to a good old discussion about all sorts of different things."

In spite of the many pleasures of living in London, Jane was once again feeling dissatisfied and restless. Although she loved her job at Schofield, some essential element was yet missing. There was the unsatisfactory matter of Brian; and there was her tiny basement room, which during the gloomy days of winter had become unbearable. When the spring weather came, she gave up on that "vile dark little place," as she described it to Sue Cary in the March 27 letter. "I simply could not endure waking up and wondering whether it was the middle of the night any more."

She soon found a new room at 6 Courtfield Gardens, in South Kensington. It was about as small as the old one and seven shillings a week more expensive, but it had a view: three floors up, it overlooked the middle of a square, with trees, sparrows, pigeons, and an occasional singing blackbird.

But at around the same time Jane moved into her new digs, she received the news from home that Rusty had been run over and killed. "I was so upset when I got Mummy's letter," she finally admitted to Sue, "that I didn't think I would ever be able to go home again—well, you know how I loved him." In fact, she went home that weekend, and faced a grieving family. "There would be long pauses when we all knew what we were all thinking, but nobody said a word about him. When a dog barked, or anything occurred which might remind me of Rusty everyone tried to think of something, anything to say. Really it made it much worse. Danny burst into floods of tears when I set off back to London, but luckily not before."

Rusty had been central to Jane's emotional life, even during her maturing years in Oxford and London, and she was unwilling to consider leaving

England while he was alive. "I was afraid he would think I had abandoned him," she once told me. Now his death brought with it a serious reexamination of her life. She had so far done only the predictable and conventional, had fallen into a staid routine in London with no obvious long-term purpose or goal. Perhaps her disparaging comments to Vanne about Brian—"too settled, too fond of creature comforts, doesn't like books etc."—echoed deeper concerns about what could happen to her. More seriously, she was worried that Brian, still so very assertive, might somehow cajole her into marriage. In any case, after Rusty's death, Jane suddenly felt free to leave England and, at the same time, somehow compelled to. "I have decided that I must go abroad before it is too late," she wrote to Sally on April 26, and "so at the moment I am trying for some sort of job in Sweden."

Olly knew someone who knew a lot of Swedes and might help Jane get a job there. Jane had also written to the well-known author on animals Gerald Durrell, hoping he might have some helpful suggestions. Of course, there was also her childhood dream of going to Africa and living among wild animals. One of her good friends, a classmate at Uplands School named Marie-Claude (Clo) Mange, had written the previous summer and invited Jane to the farm her father had acquired in the hills outside Nairobi, in Kenya Colony, where Clo was intending soon to join him. Jane wrote to Sally about this invitation in the summer of 1955, just after she started work at Schofield: "Clo incidentally is going to join her parents in Kenya and is most insistent that I should go out there and stay about 6 months. If I get tired of this job it would be great fun." So during the crisis following Rusty's death, Jane also wrote to Clo Mange: Was it really all right to visit her in Kenya?

7

Dream Returned

1956–1957

AS JANE RECALLS, one day that spring Vanne came to London and took her out to lunch at a restaurant near Bond Street. During the meal, her mother handed over a letter that had come to The Birches. Jane opened it. It was from Clo, who was now living at her father's farm and confirmed the invitation to Africa. Jane, very excited, wanted to quit her job immediately. Vanne urged her to wait, consider, not be rash—and, apparently, to write to Clo for a reconfirmation. In a letter to Vanne probably written in mid- to late May, Jane remarked that "I have . . . had a letter from Clo & it really is O.K. to go out there next year—though not <u>quite</u> so early as I had hoped." Vanne had been advising her to hold on to her job in London, but as Jane remarked, "I have <u>had</u> to give in my notice under force of circumstances." What those circumstances were the letter never reveals, but we do learn that "things are nicely arranged in my mind & I <u>had</u> to leave here. Stanley [Schofield] has behaved very badly over the whole thing—by which I don't mean he is on bad terms with me at all—but I will explain all over the week-end." Jane had never been able to save money from her meager salary anyway, and so she decided to leave expensive London and move back to less expensive Bournemouth, find hotel work, live rent-free in the garden hut at The Birches, eat cheaply, and thereby save enough to go to Africa.

Margaret Arthur, perhaps inspired by Jane's example of precipitous action, had also quit her job at Schofield, and so the two of them now eagerly prepared to camp out together in Bournemouth for the summer. "Will it be O.K.," Jane asked her mother in the same letter, "if Margaret & I come on the 15th—or 16th June or something? We are as excited as kids over the idea of sleeping in the hut—but don't DARE to tidy it up till we come—that is half the fun. I'm so looking forward to living at home again, especially in the summer."

In the middle of June they rode down to Bournemouth in Uncle Eric's 1937 open-topped Bentley. They soon settled into the garden hut and began looking for work. The hut proved to be rough and spidery, but it was summer, after all, and they kept the place lit at night with candles. Margaret quickly found a job as a housekeeper, in charge of linen and chambermaids, in one of the local hotels—but she soon gave it up, returned to London, and found another job there. Jane found a waitressing job in the restaurant of a hotel called The Hawthorns, located a brief walk up the road from The Birches. The hotel manager was a smartly dressed, dapper little man with a little gray mustache. Jane walked in asking for work, originally thinking she would like to be a chambermaid, and the manager escorted her upstairs to the head housekeeper, who said she did not need another chambermaid. The manager then said (as Jane recalls), "If you can't decorate my corridors, you shall decorate my dining room." They went down to the headwaiter, who was ordered to take her on.

She worked all day and into the evening, serving all meals as well as two afternoon teas, with only one day off every two weeks. She learned to dish out food one-handedly, deftly manipulating the portions with a serving spoon and fork while holding the serving plate in the other hand. She became an expert in transporting several plates simultaneously—up to thirteen—without a tray. To the astonishment of the kitchen staff working one floor below the dining area, she demonstrated that a spindly waitress could fold herself up inside the dumbwaiter and be lowered to the kitchen to fetch salad greens. She made friends with the doorman, who got the idea she liked to drink beer foam and regularly sought her out, bearing a frothing tankard.

Jane worked herself "absolutely to the bone," she declared to Sally in a letter later that summer. "It really is dreadful during the peak of the season," she wrote, and yet, "apart from the ghastly rush of some meals—more especially lunch when we are all up the wall—it is quite entertaining."

Every weekend she came home with a pocketful of wages and tips, which would ceremoniously be added to a growing heap hidden beneath a corner of the drawing room carpet. A roundtrip ticket to Kenya cost around £240, and by October Jane had saved that magic sum. "One evening, when I had been working for four months," she later wrote, "the family gathered around, we drew the curtains (so no one could look in), and counted my earnings. How exciting—I now had enough money, along with the small amount I had saved while in London, for a round-trip fare to Africa!"

Jane had originally booked her passage for December 12, but as she explained in an October letter to Sally, "I am now not sailing until after Christmas because the family were so woebegone at the idea of my going just before." Nevertheless, she quit The Hawthorns in October, relieved to take a break. On her last evening at the job, she demonstrated to an entire staff of waiters, waitresses, and cooks come up from the nether regions and watching through the door her royal curtsy—done with a full tray of coffeepot, milk, sugar, and two cups and saucers on her head. Then she delivered the tray to the entertained hotel guests.

She had lived in the hut all summer while her room in the house was let to a guest. Now that the cold weather had arrived and her room was available once more, she moved all her books and other possessions out of the hut, swept and dusted and straightened up, and finally got ready to splash a fresh coat of creosote on the outside. "This morning I dashed out with great zeal to creosote the hut," she wrote to Sally.

> Pot of creasote in one hand & brush in the other I leapt, sylph-like, onto the table. But oh, most unsylphlike was my descent when the table overbalanced. And I was covered in the most horrid black stuff. Dripping and slightly hysterical I went & dripped in the yard. Mummy & Danny with exclamations of horror dashed out, stripped me, & frantically rubbed me down with bits of cloth. Just then Audrey arrived and was at first horrified to find a completely naked neice, & then furious because I fled to a bath and didn't have it on to show Olly when she came back for lunch! I laughed for some time—but my clothes, I fear, have had it.

Jane had always been the center of attention in her family. She was physically active, sparking with energy, loved a good joke and a laugh, was attuned to the drama of everyday life, and remained socially outgoing yet very self-possessed. But now, as she moved into her early adult years, she had begun to acquire some new qualities as well. First, through no calculation or effort on her part, maturity brought a surprising poise, grace, and symmetry: physical beauty. Second, her growing interest in men began expressing itself spontaneously through an innocent, open flirtatiousness. She was becoming, in a word, charismatic. And the men, caught in various stages of interest, attraction, fascination, and compulsion, lined up.

Brian's persistence slowly and awkwardly faded; he occasionally took Jane out for tea, came to a dinner party once, wrote a check for £40 to contribute to her passage to Kenya. (Of course the check was instantly returned.)

With Hans, a man she met while living in London that spring, Jane had become involved in a mostly telepathic and platonic love relationship, conducted, since he was married, largely through correspondence and impassioned mental experiments. This almost-affair began as a warm friendship that turned briefly hot after the last London School of Economics theosophy class of the season, when they spent a stolen night together in uncon-summated propinquity. "Gosh the absolute heaven of that evening I could never, never have imagined," Jane confided to Sally in the strictest confidence a few days later. "The complete bliss of loving & being loved I have never even dreamed could be so exhilarating, so marvellous, so absolutely divine. To feel the blood rushing through your veins, to feel the intense joy of being with someone who matters a hundred times more than anyone else, even than yourself. Oh Sally my dear just wait until you fall in love. We discussed deep things of the spirit—& we <u>know</u> we have met before in previous incarnations." In spite of such heat and light, the relationship was doomed, in the postal if not the astral plane, becoming by Jane's October letter to Sally "tremendously complicated" and "getting more and more intricate with every letter."

Meanwhile, other suitors had emerged from the woods and begun shaking the branches. Jane's friend from Germany, Horst Pelletier, showed up that summer. Her family seemed to think he was "quite devastating—even Danny thinks so when she isn't frantically asserting that he's a German. But he simply doesn't appeal to me in the slightest." There was Douglas, a young man she met at a beach party, who turned out to be "great fun—the first man of my age I have ever liked and not got bored with." She was seeing Douglas regularly for two or three months. During her final week at the hotel, some guests gave her two tickets for a fancy reception and dance at the Bournemouth Pavilion; she thought it would be fun and "roped old Douglas & got him into a dinner jacket so that I could wear evening dress which was optional. And it really was fun."

By December 3, Jane's love life was complex enough to require coded references in a letter to Sally. Brian was the Shrimp, who remained, among the "tangled threads" of her life, one that had already been "cut through—not clearly and neatly as should have been, but raggedly & uncertainly so that half a strand may yet be left for all I know."

Hans had become the Alpha to her Omega, and together they were a pair who "must never meet again on this plane." He had written that he was exhausted with some extra responsibilities at his job, marketing pharmaceuticals in Europe, and that it had taken nearly six months "to quell physical passion to be able to say 'no' indefinitely." Nevertheless, he hoped "to be strong now so that we can know one another again at a very much higher level later on."

Then came the Mysterious Night (not Knight), who was "the most romantic man I have ever met." Jane often found older men more fascinating than their younger counterparts. They had more to say and gave one more to think about. They had balance and background, gravitas and mystery.

And the Mysterious Night was more than twenty years older, as well as available and sufficiently emotional and idealistic. Jane spent a blissful introductory afternoon with him in London that autumn. They had tea, and Jane concluded that he was "an absolute darling." He said what a shame it was he could not see her on Saturday, but could he have her phone number? She was just on her way to a dance and had to dash off. Then, as she was getting ready for the dance, the phone rang. It was the Mysterious Night. What color was she wearing? he wanted to know. Was it white? He wanted to imagine Jane all that evening, whirling around at the dance. And he said he would call again on Saturday at one o'clock. He did, to ask if she would meet him that afternoon. She would. They went to a movie and had tea together. "And then we walked along the Embankment in the darkness and it was misty and strange and oh! so romantic. He really is such a charming, kind sweet man."

There was also the White Night (possibly Trevor), but alas, the Red Queen (perhaps Alice, his wife) had "put the fear of god into him because he literally does not speak to me. Even Judy commented on this yesterday. He practically ran away. It is quite ridiculous, of course, and also quite stupid."

There was the Upper Shell of the Clam, who remained "elusive" and so would require "patience, patience. The day will come."

Finally, there was the Key, a new arrival named Keith. The Key seemed to be working out nicely that December, and Jane extended the code into an analogy that seems more Freudian than actual circumstances warranted: "At the moment I find it fits the lock rather well and I shall try and keep it in the keyhole for the next few months if I can." Keith had character and balance: a "very strong and independent will of [his] own, and is equally obstinate as I am." He was a captain in the army, "anything but handsom" and no taller than Jane, but when he took her to the Heckey Club Dance that autumn, he looked "smashing" in his uniform: "Somehow I wasn't expecting it. Beautiful skin tight trousers with a red strip down either side, spurs, and all the rest of the outfit plus linked chain epaulettes on either shoulder." He also turned out to be a terrific dancer: "My goodness the man can dance. I found myself doing steps I never dreampt of—& with the greatest of ease. It was quite heavenly."

Jane worked at the post office during the holiday season that year, adding to her savings. She started on December 18, delivering letters along a familiar stretch of Westbourne, substituting for Taffy, the regular postman, who showed her the route the first day. Taffy, Jane declared in a letter to Sally, was "one of the old school—very jolly and an answer for everything," and he teased her mercilessly, stealing a piece of mistletoe in one of the shops and secreting it in her hair.

She came down with a case of red spots, diagnosed as measles, on the weekend, but by Tuesday, which was Christmas, she was back, getting up at 7:00 to begin the mail delivery early. There was very little mail that day, and by then Jane had figured out all the shortcuts, so she was able to start at 7:45, dash through the entire route, and get back to the sorting room by 8:30, qualifying for four hours' pay after less than an hour's work. Back at the sorting room, the supervisor was still having his breakfast, and none of the other delivery people were back. A postman named Zack, "the very handsom second in command," was running the office and in charge of signing Jane out for the day. Zack pushed her about in one of their wheeled sorting baskets and then said that since it was Christmas she ought to be delivered home "in style." Jane climbed into a mail sack. Zack lifted her into the front seat of a big mail delivery van, placed her bicycle in the back, and then drove over to 10 Durley Chine Road South. Parked in the driveway, he tied up the mail sack, hefted it over to the doorway, and rang the bell. When Judy opened the door, he carried the bundle into the drawing room and dumped Jane out of the bag and onto the couch. Vanne appeared with beer and mince pie, and so Zack sat around for some time, drinking beer, eating pie, and chatting.

Later that morning the family opened their stockings, had breakfast, and then went off visiting. Jane rode her bicycle over to Keith's house for a drink; then she visited some other family friends. When she finally got back home, there was the "greatest surprise of all": a little red Austin Healey sports car in the driveway and, in the drawing room, Daddy. Vanne always invited him for Christmas, and this year he actually came.

"Of course he only stayed a few hours. The stupid man had driven all the way down with the hood down, & so arrived quite frozen. It was a pity we wern't having the turkey at lunch time really, but it couldn't be helped," Jane wrote in the same letter. Mortimer had brought two bottles of burgundy and a box of crackers, as well as nylons for Vanne, Judy, and Jane and a regular array of wrapped Christmas presents. They all listened to the Queen's Christmas address on the radio, and then he left.

On New Year's Eve, Jane and Keith went out to a dinner and dance. Keith wanted to dress formally, with tails, so Jane decided to wear her turquoise-and-white dress with the swan feathers. Several of the feathers had fallen off and needed to be stitched back on, and then the entire dress had to be ironed, which was "absolute complete & utter murder," and Jane was "only just ready in time." Still, the effort and panicked rush were worth it, since Keith seemed to be "entranced" when he saw her, and during the evening he overheard a couple of enthusiastic comments about the dress, which "of course he wallowed in!" The dinner was "excellent" and the evening "heavenly." They started with two gins and had a bottle of wine with dinner, which was followed by postprandial liqueurs and finally, to call in the New Year, a bottle of champagne. The music was perfect, and the band played "all the right types of dances—no rock and roll or jiving," while Keith once again showed himself to be an excellent dancer. The dance was over by 2:30, and they finally returned home to The Birches, where they took orange juice and coffee into the drawing room and Keith proposed marriage.

But the vision of Africa, wild and glorious Africa, was too forcibly on Jane's mind by then, and in two and a half months—on Wednesday, March 13—she took the boat train from Waterloo station to the Southampton docks, along with Vanne and Uncle Eric. A porter delivered her luggage to the quay, goodbyes were tearfully expressed, and then twenty-two-year-old Jane Morris-Goodall walked up the gangplank of a 576-foot, 17,000-ton, lavender-hulled, red-and-black-funneled passenger steamship, the *Kenya Castle*, bound for Mombasa by way of the western and then southern shores of Africa.

A receptionist checked her ticket and handed over her passport, and Jane was escorted to her cabin. The vessel's engines and propellers began to rumble and churn, a horn blasted, and then, at four o'clock in the afternoon, the *Kenya Castle* disengaged from her moorings and slipped down Southampton Water in the direction of the Channel and the ocean.

The next day Jane began her first letter home: "It is now 4 P.M. on Thursday and I still find it difficult to believe that I am on my way to Africa. That is the thing—AFRICA. It is so easy to imagine I am going for a long sea voyage, but not that names like Mombassa, Nairobi, South Kinangop, Nakuru, etc. are going to become reality."

As she wrote those words, the *Kenya Castle* was jostling through the Bay of Biscay, and the sea had turned rough enough to challenge the stomachs of most passengers. Diners had been rushing out of the dining hall in various states of gastric dysphoria ever since breakfast time, and all Jane's cabin-mates were by late afternoon "languishing in misery" on their bunks. Jane, meanwhile, spent the afternoon out on deck, relishing the weather, delighting in the rough seas, locating a

> favourite spot as far forward as one can get. There one gets more movement than anywhere else. Sitting there watching the waves is simply heavenly. One is right in the teeth of the wind and no one else goes there

at all because it is so cold. Just under the ship the sea is dark inky blue, then it rises up a clear transparent blue green, and then it breaks in white and sky blue foam. But best of all, some of this foam is forced back under the wave from which it broke, and this spreads out under the surface like the palest of blue milk, all soft and hazy at the edge.

Jane's four cabin-mates included an unsympathetic "old girl" who came on board with a fur coat (she was soon to be known as "Old Fur Coat") as well as three "very nice" younger women. First was Helen Patterson, who had attended Uplands a year or two after Jane. Second was Pam, "a very pretty girl — & rather mad like me." And the third, Sue, seemed "the nicest of the lot." Sue slept in the bunk directly below Jane and quickly developed the friendly teasing habit of tugging on a loose piece of dressing gown or sheet corner. Jane retaliated by dangling a stray end of dressing gown belt and tickling her bunkmate's face at unexpected moments, or by pointing the cabin air blower so that it blew a stream of air into her face.

Within a week, as the *Kenya Castle* approached the equator, the weather turned "absolutely sweltering," as Jane described it in her second letter home. Everyone's regular clothes "now consist of shorts & blouse or bathing dress — and bare feet until the decks get too hot to bear." Several passengers had gotten blisters on their feet, and some were in sickbay with sunburn. Jane herself had gotten a slight burn the first day out, when there was "such a breeze I didn't realize how strong the sun was." But now, a week later, she was contentedly turning brown. She experienced some occasional wistful thoughts regarding the family back home, and now and then she felt mildly concerned about the state of Pickles the cat and the progress of Clara the caterpillar. But she was also having the time of her life. "It really is absolutely heavenly, this trip, well worth all the money saved. I really didn't think it was going to be such fun," she reported. She was delighted to have seen her first shark and flying fish, and she was pleased to discover a quadruped on board, a "poor little dog" who was "nearly dead of heat yesterday," chained up in a section of the deck cordoned off for ship officers only. She began taking the dog for strolls around the ship, and she spoke to the purser, who directed someone to rig a shady awning over the dog's resting spot.

That was satisfying, but Jane's predominant pleasures onboard the *Kenya Castle* were social. The rejected Keith from Bournemouth wrote unhappy letters, which periodically appeared at various mail depots as the ship sailed south and around the Cape. Jane certainly felt sorry for him and perhaps mildly guilty, but within her first couple of days at sea she had met a new Keith, a twenty-six-year-old British engineer on his way to Uganda. He was "not a bad chap" and "not a very good dancer" but was nevertheless very energetic. "This morning," she noted in her second letter home, as the ship approached the equator in highest heat, she and Keith had played three games of deck tennis "while most people lay gasping in the shack."

Her young cabin-mates had likewise quickly paired off with suitable young men: Helen with Peter, who was a "very nice lad" returning to his position with the Kenya Police; Pam with Pat, a "quite good fun" man Jane often referred to as Ginger Top; and Sue with Dennis, a surveyor who was "tall & thin with yellow hair, a beak nose, and lazy manner and rather interesting." Jane and Keith plus those three couples and a few others—Mossy Face, for example, a "most amusing character," who planned to work in a leper colony for three years, and a married couple from Scotland—made "a crowd as mad as one could wish" who had "great fun all the time." There were dances most evenings, some of which were "really funny because the old ship was tossing & pitching so that one slid madly from one side of the floor to the other." Deck tennis during the day. Swimming in the open-air pool. Parlor tricks. Brief shore leave at Las Palmas, in the Canary Islands. And so on. For a costume ball one evening, Jane appeared as a Hawaiian princess, wearing a "grass skirt" made from strips of green crepe paper, a top consisting of Pam's bathing suit top covered with cloth maple leaves originally used as table decoration, a garland of white crepe-paper flowers around her neck, white beads around her ankle and green beads around her wrist, and, of course, a flower tucked behind her ear. "I was a great success."

Jane was still discovering the extraordinary effect she could have on people, especially men. And she was soon reporting to the family back home, with amazement and amusement, surprise and pride, that "I am being chased by practically every officer on board! With the exception of the Captain. The first & second officers, the Purser & the Doctor are the main ones."

Before the ship had reached Cape Town, in fact, Jane had begun having long and earnest discussions about life with the ship's doctor, a man named Reg. "He really is a darling—& incredibly handsom in his way," Jane informed the family—and a couple of months later she confided to her friend Sally that he was also "a real old rogue," who had begun by asking "if I was prepared to go to bed with him, & after I said no, he was very sweet & never once pestered me." But when his "semi-fiancée" came onboard at Cape Town and turned out to be "the most attractive woman I've seen for a long time," Jane felt, if only temporarily, "desolated," since she thought her "happy flirtation was finished with."

The *Kenya Castle* pulled away from Cape Town at 8:18 P.M. on March 22, scheduled to arrive at Durban in two days. They were sailing close to shore now, and the next morning Jane sat out on the deck, working on another of her letters home and regularly raising her eyes to observe

the coast of <u>AFRICA!</u> drift by. It is a fascinating coast line. This morning it was bleak grass covered downs reaching down to the sea, where great breakers dashed clouds of foam into the air as they broke on the jagged rocks at the water's edge. Occasionally there would be a tiny group of native huts or a lonely Coast Guard station, tiny & white against the rolling green hills. Now the land is more civilized—little villages, roads, factories sometimes appear. The slopes are more wooded & a lovely pale yellow beach runs out to meet the waves.

By the evening of April 1 the boat was pulling away from Dar es Salaam and drawing north through the Zanzibar Channel, while Jane was gathering with her cabin-mates, friends, and acquaintances in the grand dining hall for a fancy farewell dinner. At five o'clock the next morning, having completed its three-week, 9,000-mile journey from Southampton, the *Kenya Castle* nestled into berth in Mombasa harbor, and by 11:50 the customs shed finally opened and passengers were allowed to proceed down the gangplank. Jane spent the afternoon wandering with friends under an oppressive sun in 98-degree heat, poking through the Arab markets and pausing for a refreshing orange squash in one of the hotels, and then returned to the boat for a final shower, final farewells, and a final disembarkation before boarding the train for Nairobi.

On the train she shared a compartment with Helen, Pam, and Sue, her former cabin-mates. Next door was a compartment containing six men, including some friends from the boat and Ken, the fiancé Sue had come to join in Kenya. After moving into the compartment with the men in it, they "rollicked along" and "were all more than gay," as Jane later wrote home, partaking of an excellent dinner and desserts as well as a bottle of wine from Biera, a bottle of gin from Cape Town, and some Kenyan beer known as Tusker.

While the young women were washing and dressing the next morning, the train stopped at a station, where they observed four Maasai warriors, with spears, orange robes, and enormous rings in their ears, peering through the window with apparent fascination. But the half-dressed Englishwomen inside observed a group of Maasai women beyond the peering warriors, half-dressed themselves and washing under a tap, so "we decided to carry on!" The train started up again. They had a "smashing breakfast" and sat down to watch the vast, rough, semibarren landscape (occasionally animated with wildebeests, Thomson's gazelles, and ostriches) roll past.

The train reached Nairobi at 10:45 that morning, which was Saturday, April 3, 1957—by coincidence, Jane's twenty-third birthday.

Jane was saying goodbye to her friends from the boat when her old school chum Clo emerged from the crowd. Accompanied by her boyfriend, Tony, and her father, Roland Mange, Clo helped gather Jane's luggage together, and then the four of them left the station, tossed the luggage into Roland's enormous International Harvester truck, and found a hotel where they could sit down and order a meal.

Clo had left Uplands a year before Jane and gone home to Switzerland, so they had not seen each other for almost six years. They had corresponded occasionally, sent cards and small presents to mark birthdays and significant holidays, but were they still good friends? Jane's mild concern was happily alleviated during lunch at the hotel, when, after the two of them happened to look across at a man sitting at a nearby table who was eating from his knife, they broke into wild, hysterical giggles. Clo "hasn't changed at all," Jane reported in her first letter home from Kenya, while Clo, in an appended note to Vanne, confirmed that they had "exactly the same feeling of uncontrolled giggles as we had in our extreme youth."

After lunch Clo's father drove them on a long climbing dirt road that rose from Nairobi's 5,000 feet to the South Kinangop Highlands at 8,400 feet—with time out to pause at the Rift Escarpment and appreciate a cool, quiet, long, and hazy view across Kenya's Rift Valley. Finally they arrived at the Mange farm, Greystones, where they were greeted by Mrs. Mange, six dogs, two cats, and a birthday present and long letter for Jane from Keith back in Bournemouth. After supper Clo walked in with a big round cake, frosted pink and white with three elaborate pansies on top, shimmering with the flames of twenty-three candles. The house lights—oil lamps—were extinguished, and Jane made her quiet wish before blowing out the candles with a single breath.

8

Africa!

1957

ARRIVING IN AFRICA seemed in some ways like coming home. "I really do simply adore Kenya," Jane wrote to the family back in England after she had been there about a week. "It is so wild, uncultivated, primitive, mad, exciting, unpredictable. It is also slightly degrading in its effect on some rather weak characters, but on the whole I am living in the Africa I have always longed for, always felt stirring in my blood." Or, as she described the feeling to her friend Sally in a letter written at the end of May, "Right from the moment I got here I felt at home. Out here I am no longer mad—because everyone is mad."

Jane was surprised by how cool it was in the highlands—cold at night, requiring fires in the fireplaces—when Nairobi had been so hot. Still, the farm, Greystones, was "absolute <u>heaven</u>."

Clo's father, Roland, was French and had at one time been a rubber planter in Singapore. When the war came, he volunteered to serve in the British navy, in the submarine service, but he was captured by the Japanese, held prisoner for a few years, and emerged a physical and mental wreck. The family remained in India for about two years because he was simply too ill to travel, and then he had another two years of medical treatment in Europe. Finally a friend said (as Clo has paraphrased it), "Look, why don't you come out to Kenya, where I've got a lot of farms and business? I'll find you a pyrethrum farm. Little white plants. It's an insecticide. A very healthy life, you know—because you can't stay in Europe." Roland was persuaded that sunny Kenya would be better for his health than gloomy Europe, and so he acquired the 160-acre farm known as Greystones.

The main house was a large bungalow of stone and cedar with a corrugated iron roof, stone floors, fireplaces in every room, two bathrooms, no electricity, and (in Jane's assessment) "thousands of dogs"—six, actually: a dachshund named Regus; two Dobermans, Schnokey and Trigger; an Alsatian, Flicka; and a pair of mutts, Sally and Patch. With all those dogs mixing occasionally with two Siamese cats and, outdoors, a herd of cows, seven horses, numerous rabbits, chickens, turkeys, and oxen, and one "darling baby chameleon," Greystones seemed gloriously "mad" — an adjective on the short list of Jane's highest expressions of praise.

Patch soon began visiting Jane in her bed at night. He was, she remarked teasingly in her second letter home, "a most romantic lover. Every night he wakes me up, very gently, at about 2.30. He then creeps into my bed and makes love to me until I want to go to sleep again."

Still, on her first morning there, April 4, Jane and Clo excitedly set off for Nairobi again to have lunch and take a bath at the Muthaiga Club before changing into cocktail dresses, having tea, pursuing a "smell tour" of the club garden ("some smells are heavenly out here"), and attending a cocktail party, where a twenty-four-year-old Frenchman named Marc de Beaumont "was most taken with me," while a "white hunter" offered her a ten-day safari as soon as she earned the money to pay for it. On their return trip from Nairobi, they sighted springboks and a hyena, and the next day they toured a neighboring farm, stopping to watch "a most beautiful Laurie bird — dark blue shining plumage above and when it flew the undersides of its wings were brilliant crimson." While watching the bird, they sighted an entire family group of colobus monkeys ("very glorious creatures — black & white with lovely bushy tails"), not to mention "masses of hawks, storks, cranes, honey birds & many others." Soon after that, Jane saw her first giraffe. "They are even taller and more impressive than I had imagined." One of them wandered right into the road, then "walked away in a most condescending & stately fashion."

On Friday of that first week, Ivor Yorke-Davis, who owned a farm adjacent to Greystones, took the two young women and his son, Hugo, to Nairobi to see an afternoon film, *The King and I.* But while they were driving down the road, "all very gay and jolly," as Jane wrote in her second letter home, the engine of Yorke-Davis's Mercedes conked out. Father and son disappeared under the hood of the vehicle and tinkered for a long while, and then Hugh began walking toward Nairobi, intending to fetch a tow truck. Soon, though, a "very, very handsom" man driving a Land Rover stopped, got out, and offered to help. For the rest of the morning he "practically took the car to pieces," while Jane and Clo entertained themselves by "admiring his bottom & feeling sorry for him because he was getting filthy & oily & we knew he was on his way to Nairobi to meet his girl friend." Hours later, the car seemed more hopeless than ever and obviously required a tow into town. They borrowed a rope from a passing truck. Jane climbed in with the driver of the Land Rover, and Clo and Ivor rode together in the defunct Mercedes. They picked up Hugo only a few miles down the road, walking toward Nairobi. It had started raining by then, and soon it was pouring, with a thick bank of fog swirling in and great clouds of flying termites swarming into the mix. By the time they arrived in town, it was dark and they had missed the film, so, after dropping the Mercedes off at a garage, they proceeded directly to the Muthaiga Club to wash and change. Then it was off to dinner at the Nuit St. George, followed by a full night of champagne and dancing at the Mogambo Club. They left the Mogambo at 4:30 on Saturday morning, and Jane and Clo were back at Greystones by dawn, taking tea and then falling into bed.

At the end of that first week, during another excursion into town, Jane and Clo visited a pet shop that happened to be selling bush babies (*Galago senegalensis,* a widely distributed nocturnal primate), and they were "such darlings" that Jane was instantly compelled to buy one for four pounds—a lot of money for such a tiny creature, but, as Jane explained to her family, "he was so sweet." She named him Levi, and he soon appeared to adjust to life with his new mother in the cool climate of a new home. He was soon taking "flying leaps onto me from any strange place, & clings with his tiny hands. They have teeny-weeny nails. He really plays with me, hiding behind cushions & leaping out at one's hand. He loves sleeping under my jersey."

Clo was an attractive young woman: blond, buxom, full of life. One contemporary remembers her as "rather wild" and "quite sexy." Jane had poise and self-confidence, energy and passion, a lean, trim figure and a lovely sculpted face. "Everyone found her tremendously sexy and attractive," Clo told me. Jane "could get any man she wanted"—mainly because she was an "interesting companion" and a "really brave girl" who had "extraordinary self-control" and a very effective gaze. It is the gaze that Clo found most impressive. "Occasionally if she wants something she looks at you in a particular way, and she gets calmer and calmer and deeper and deeper, and you sort of give in. I think she has hypnotic qualities. She'd have made a very good hypnotist. Oh yes, she uses her gaze—I call it her 'look'—a lot, with great success."

Around this time Clo's neighbor Ivor Yorke-Davis decided he was in love with Clo—passionately so, he confided to Jane—and he offered to divorce his wife if only Clo would agree to marry him. At the same time, Tony, Clo's boyfriend, concluded he was more interested in Jane and was soon driving her down to Nairobi and out into the countryside.

Jane, however, decided that Marc de Beaumont, the young man she had met on her first night in Nairobi, was her "boy friend." Marc was the "'right' kind of person," she informed the family with some small irony: twenty-four years old, well traveled, with a wealthy father, but unspoiled and working to earn his own living as a taster on a coffee plantation. Marc came up to Greystones to visit Jane on Easter Sunday, and within a couple of weeks he had taken her out to tea in Nairobi, then to the cinema and dinner at a restaurant known as The Equator, where they shared a cozy candlelit table in the corner and ate lobster and chicken and he worked on teaching her some French words. "He was very French and rather sweet," Jane wrote, "and we flirted like mad with our eyes all through the meal." It was enjoyable going out with a Frenchman, she thought, if only because he knew one wine from another. After dinner, they proceeded on to the Mogambo Club and "danced and danced, and went on flirting." He drove her home on a very peculiar route and at one point claimed the car had gotten stuck. Jane told him he was "very naughty," and he laughed and took her home.

That successful date was followed by a much less successful one at the annual ball of the Polish Association of Kenya. The dance hall was festively decorated but the lights were kept burning brightly, which destroyed the atmosphere, Jane thought, and the whole thing was so boring that they left early. On the way home, Marc revealed himself as "a typical Frenchman" who had "his own very definite ideas about what should happen when he took a girl home after a dance." Jane was annoyed, and that was the last she saw of him for some time.

In the meantime, she and Clo spent a week at the end of April and the beginning of May in Thompson's Falls (now Nanyuki), staying at the farm of Yolande and Francis MacDonnell, friends of the Manges'. In Thompson's Falls, Jane met a man named Bob. She had lunch at his farm and made friends with his three dogs. After lunch they wandered into the woods looking for colobus monkeys, who soon appeared, according to a May 6 letter, "especially for my benefit." Bob was "terribly shy with girls," Jane wrote, and as a result of a riding injury had hurt his ankle and walked with a limp, mostly noticeable when he wore riding boots.

Clo remembers Bob as "very good looking" and "awfully nice." From Jane's perspective, though, Bob's most engaging feature was his horse, a large and powerful animal given him because no one else could handle her. At more than seventeen hands, or six feet high at the withers, Fire Fly was larger than any horse Jane had ever ridden—and she was "rather mad" to boot, with "a shocking reputation at T. Falls." But Jane, of course, was eager to ride that very animal, and the next day Bob showed up at the Mac-Donnells' riding another horse and leading Fire Fly. It took half an hour to put on the saddle, but once Jane had mounted her, to everyone's surprise Fire Fly rode "like a lamb." Jane was delighted, proud, enamored. "I havn't ridden such a horse for a long time—she is a big horse, and there is an in-credible sense of tremendous strength and power about her whatsoever she does."

Marion and Hobo Swift, neighbors of the MacDonnells', had organized a hunt along the lines of an English fox hunt, only in pursuit of "buck" or jackal rather than fox—and Bob assured Jane that they seldom caught any-thing at all. Against the warning of Yolande MacDonnell, Bob agreed that Jane could ride Fire Fly in the hunt. Riding clothes would be important, of course, and since neither Clo nor Jane had any, they hastily cobbled together suitable outfits. Clo borrowed gloves from Yolande, put on long socks and breeches that had belonged to Yolande's first husband, and wore the leather jacket of her current husband. Jane had her own gloves, and she borrowed jodhpurs and boots from Marion Swift. Neither had a proper hunting hat, alas, and when they showed up at the hunt, several of the "snobby people—of which there are quite a few round here—made remarks in loud voices." Jane and Clo apologized to the hunt master for their hatlessness. Bob soon appeared with a horse for himself, Cinderella, and Fire Fly for Jane. They saddled her up, but Jane had not realized that she should not mount Fire Fly by stepping directly into the stirrup. When she put her foot in, the great beast dashed back, reared up, and fell over backward. Jane was able to leap clear, fortunately, and the saddle was unbroken, but the accident confirmed everyone's opinion that Fire Fly was dangerous. "Put that bloody horse away," Marion Swift yelled, "and have one of mine!" Someone else shouted, "Leave that brute behind, for God's sake!"

Jane, stung by these comments, "remarked calmly" (as she reported home) that she had no intention of riding any other horse. Bob gave her a leg up, and she mounted Fire Fly once again. People had begun drinking by then, and they were making additional "rude remarks about my horse and how it wasn't safe." So Jane and Bob rode their mounts "away from the vul-gar crowd" and quietly reassured each other that their supposedly "mad" horses were "the best of the bunch." As it turned out, Fire Fly ran beauti-fully in the hunt. "She never put a foot wrong, she never got away, she never kicked a hound (supposedly one of her vices), she never refused a fence." The principal sources of danger were ant bear dens, hidden under high grass and a serious hazard for galloping horses. Fire Fly dropped a hind leg down one hole but instantly recovered.

Two people from the hunt eventually apologized for their earlier re-marks, and several others declared that they could not believe Jane had ridden the notorious Fire Fly. Later, the master of the hunt offered to in-troduce her to a millionaire owner of racehorses, and she and Bob began planning her horsy future in Thompson's Falls. They would take a weeklong ride out into the wild country. She would learn to play polo. She could manage and train horses, including Fire Fly and a powerful horse named Opera who was too much for the man who regularly rode her. The only minor complication was a lack of appropriate riding clothes; and to that end, by the middle of May, Jane had bought a jockey cap and had herself measured for jodhs and breeches. "Of course, I can't afford any of this," she explained to the family, "but it is an investment really, and will last me for years."

Although Jane was indeed longing and plotting to work with horses in Thompson's Falls, and although she had already concluded that she loathed Nairobi, she still needed to earn a living and thus began working in town as a typist for a British-owned construction firm, W. & C. French. Her first day on the job was Monday, May 6, little more than a month after she arrived in Africa. Commuting between Greystones and Nairobi every day was out of the question, and so she took a room at Kirk Road House, next door to Nairobi Cathedral. Kirk Road House cost sixteen pounds ten shillings a month, meals included, and it was a "hostel": a collection of long, low wooden huts, each divided into half a dozen or more two-occupant rooms connected by way of covered verandas, with communal lavatories and bathrooms, a club room, and a "rather nice" dining hall.

The only problem was Levi, the bush baby. The hostel was run by a married couple, and when Jane arrived, the woman told her that pets were not allowed. Jane persevered, asking (as she reported home in a May 6 letter) if the reluctant woman "hadn't better see Levi before she said I couldn't keep him," and when the woman did look over the tiny primate, she was "so delighted" she declared she would try to persuade her husband that this particular pet was acceptable. Jane had already made a good impression on the husband ("already winked at him when I first arrived"), and so Levi was allowed. Jane and her bush baby moved in.

Her roommate, a young woman named Linda, said she loved animals, which was a good thing, since on Jane's first evening there she let the bush baby out for his nightly scamper and he instantly leaped onto the sleeping roommate's mosquito netting, startling her awake. The next morning he attacked her leg as she was getting dressed.

Jane started taking him to work, an arrangement that seemed acceptable—although one of her bosses was, according to a letter home, shocked ("eyes nearly popped out of his head") to see Jane's cardigan moving all by itself during dictation one morning. Still, Levi slept most of the day—only to become active for much of the night. He was turning out to be (Jane wrote to Sally on May 28) "oh such a darling, such a jumper, such an acrobat—&

so very naughty. He <u>adores</u> pulling my hair." But Linda appreciated the naughty nocturnal creature less and less. Finally she announced that it was either her or the bush baby, and since Kirk Road House did not officially allow pets, Levi had to go.

When Bob came down from Thompson's Falls for the weekend, Jane asked him to take care of "my darling." Bob already had his own baby tree hyrax, so perhaps Levi would have a friend. But when Bob took Levi back to Thompson's Falls, Jane was bereft—and implacably hostile toward her roommate. "Honestly," she confided in the letter to Sally, "we havn't spoken a single word since then. . . . Ugh! Ugh. Ugh. I feel like commiting a murder."

Jane was still excited to be in the Africa of her dreams, but at the same time she was uncertain where those dreams would take her next. If she had followed Levi to Thompson's Falls and followed through on the plan to start working with horses, she might have become a trainer, a jockey perhaps, a polo and racing devotee, and then? Marriage to one of the rich and horsy members of the colonial establishment? Jane had all the necessary skills, social and otherwise, to enter such a world and succeed superbly in it, but she was too unconventional and independent to have tolerated it gracefully for long. No, her dreams were of an Africa that was wilder, rougher, more elemental, closer to nature and animals, and the key to entering that continent would not be found among the social set of Thompson's Falls or anywhere else in the complacent circles of the pale elite. Rather, it would be found, simply, in the person of one brilliant and eccentric fifty-three-year-old white man who had grown up with Africans, who thought of himself as a white African, and who served as curator of Nairobi's natural history museum, the Coryndon (known today as the National Museums of Kenya): Louis Leakey.

Louis Seymour Bazett Leakey was born two months prematurely to Harry and May Leakey, pioneering British missionaries, at Kabete Station, Kenya, on August 7, 1903. He was their third child, after two daughters, Julia and Gladys. His reserved and fragile mother soon bore a second son, Douglas, and placed all four children in the care of a Kikuyu nanny, Mariamu, who delighted the children with wonderful fables about the animals all around, especially the quick hare who always outsmarted the arrogant lion and the avaricious hyena. His father baptized, preached, translated the Bible into Kikuyu—and inculcated in his children a love of nature and natural history.

The children had egg and feather collections, an aviary, and a house full of orphaned baby animals: bush babies, duikers, gazelles, genet cats, hares, hyraxes, mice, monkeys, and serval cats. Louis also played with the neighborhood boys, all members of the Kikuyu tribe, and he learned to speak their language and play their games. He acquired stalking and hunting skills from a Kikuyu friend, Joshua Muhia, learned to throw a spear and wield a war club, and at adolescence was taken with his age group to endure the secret and painful circumcision ritual required of every Kikuyu boy before entering manhood. "In language and in mental outlook," Louis recalled in his early autobiography, *White African* (1937), "I was more Kikuyu than English, and it never occurred to me to act other than as a Kikuyu." Having become a Kikuyu man at age thirteen, he moved out of his parents' house and into his own bachelor pad, a mud-and-wattle house layered with white clay, which he built on mission property and decorated with his collection of birds' skins, eggs, and nests and animal pelts. This son of missionaries thus grew up speaking, thinking, and dreaming in Kikuyu, though at the same time he taught his friends to play football, was tutored in Latin and mathematics, and spoke French with his parents and siblings at dinnertime.

Museum work, anthropology, and archaeology enabled Louis to combine those two disparate worlds. He learned specimen collection and bird classification from Arthur Loveridge, the first curator of Nairobi's natural history museum, who periodically stayed at the Kabete mission while on collecting expeditions; and he was inspired to become an archaeologist after receiving as a gift H. N. Hall's *Days Before History,* a children's adventure book set in prehistoric Britain and based on the experiences of a youthful hero named Tig. The book's illustrations included drawings of flint weapons and tools that reminded the young Louis of the pieces of glassy stone he regularly stumbled across in recently dug or washed-out areas. He began collecting fragments of obsidian, and when he finally, with trepidation, showed his collection to Loveridge, the curator confirmed that some of the specimens were indeed Stone Age implements. "Once I had received this assurance that my 'bits of black stone,' as my father called them, were really things that had been made by Stone Age man, I started collecting with doubled keenness," he wrote. And by the time he turned thirteen, Louis had set upon his life's course: "I firmly made up my mind that I would go on until we knew all about the Stone Age" in East Africa.

In 1919 the family returned for a couple of years to England. Louis, now sixteen years old, entered a public school, Weymouth, in Dorset. He found it hard to make friends, however. The restrictions seemed absurd, and nearly all the other students appeared, as he once wrote, "appallingly childish." And yet, although he had never written an essay, never attended a theater, and proved embarrassingly bad at cricket, he was determined to attend his father's university, Cambridge. The Weymouth headmaster said he ought to settle for a job in a bank, but Louis proposed entering on a course of studies that would include modern languages and anthropology/archaeology. Modern languages required two foreign languages. Louis knew "only French" and so was at first discouraged, until he observed that nothing in university regulations implied that the two foreign languages should be European. He submitted Kikuyu as his second modern language. When Cambridge administrators protested that Kikuyu lacked writing or literature, Louis countered that the Bible had been translated into Kikuyu—by his father. When it became apparent that no one at Cambridge was capable of teaching him the formal niceties of Kikuyu, Louis settled on a tutor who agreed to be taught the language—by Louis. When university officials finally tried to locate experts to examine him in his chosen language, they were given a list of two top Kikuyu experts in Britain—one of whom was the examinee.

At Cambridge, Louis was the first undergraduate to show up on the tennis courts wearing shorts—and also the first to be thrown off the courts for "indecency." He was an eccentric and an iconoclast, in short, ultimately saved from the scorn ordinarily directed at social outsiders by his physical vigor, handsome features, and exceptional intellect. He distinguished himself at university, but not before taking a year off to manage, as second in charge, a difficult fossil-hunting expedition into southeastern Tanganyika. He gave his first public lecture to an audience of one thousand at Cambridge University's Guildhall while still an undergraduate, twenty-one years old; went on to finish his studies with the highest possible honors (a double first); and in the summer of 1926, when he was twenty-three, returned to East Africa as the head of an archaeological expedition. During the next four decades, Leakey's diggings and pluckings of ancient artifacts and fossilized skulls and bones—his life's work—ultimately revolutionized paleoanthropology and helped shape the scientific world's vision of human evolution as a tree with roots in the garden of Africa.

When Jane met Louis Leakey, in May 1957, he was an eminent scientist (Ph.D. from Cambridge, honorary D.Sc. from Oxford, full-time curator of the Coryndon Museum, recently elected president of the third Pan-African Congress on Prehistory, author of eight books, and so on), though not yet the celebrity he would become. His brown hair had turned white, his trimmed mustache was gray, and he had lately begun to put on weight. He had also developed his longtime habit of dressing in one-piece khaki coveralls with missing buttons, overloaded pockets, and flapping knees. His teeth were bad, and he tended to stink, perhaps as a consequence of infrequent bathing and frequent cheroot smoking. As always, he spoke enthusiastically and endlessly with a "soft voice" and "sing-song inflections" (in the words of his biographer Sonia Cole), while his laugh was "quiet and staccato, like a bronchitic gasping for breath."

Leakey was by then very well known among white Kenyans, and given Jane's interests, perhaps it was inevitable that the two would eventually meet. According to Jane's later account, one day that May someone told her that "if you are interested in animals, you must meet Louis Leakey." In a letter to the family, Jane declared that "Clo told me about him." Since Clo had met Dr. Leakey once or twice, she promised to introduce Jane to him, but Jane, impatient perhaps, telephoned the museum on her own. To a voice on the other end of the line, she said, "I'd like to make an appointment to meet Dr. Leakey." The voice responded, "I'm Dr. Leakey. What do you want?"

Louis Leakey invited her to visit the museum at ten o'clock on Friday morning, May 24, which happened to be a bank holiday in Nairobi, so Jane had the day free. And for the "whole morning," as she soon wrote home with boiling excitement, the great man guided her around the museum, "pointing out why one species of antelope had its head set on a particular angle, or one type of pig had horny developments in one place and another sort in another." He showed Jane the museum's large collection of snakes, about which she was "naturally very interested." He told her about his experiments on lungfish that demonstrated their astonishing tolerance for drought. ("These remarkable creatures have been proved [by Leakey] able to remain in their dried mud holes without a drop of water or a bit to eat for—you just couldn't guess—3 whole years!!!!! They were still alive, but very weak, and Dr. Leakey decided it wasn't fair to make them survive longer.") Louis Leakey seems to have talked almost nonstop that morning, and he told Jane "so many fascinating things, that it would take me pages and pages," she declared, to write them down.

After that two-hour tour, they sat down for coffee. Louis asked Jane to work as his secretary starting in September, since his previous one had left to watch gorillas. He also asked, "Can you ride?"

Jane said she loved to ride horses.

He looked at her closely and asked, "Are you good with dogs?"

Jane responded very positively.

"Would you be interested in living at my house while my wife and I are away, exercising the horses and seeing that all the animals are all right?" The animals included, he said, horses, dogs, bush babies, a tree hyrax, a python, and a garden full of other snakes; and the offer, as Jane wrote home, "absolutely took my breath away." Naturally, Louis added, he would first have to discuss the idea with his wife, Mary.

Meanwhile, Jane agreed to gather spiders for the museum, since the resident entomologist, Robert Carcasson, was "not frightfully keen on them" himself; and so after work the following Monday, she returned to meet with Carcasson, talk about spider collecting, and be given the necessary equipment. Louis happened to be staying late at the museum that day, and he took the opportunity to show Jane another two hours' worth of specimens, reaffirming that he wanted her to become his secretary in September. ("He says he doesn't care about my shorthand and typing—only spelling!!!! Which, as I told him, is a positive HOOT! Whereat he informed me that he couldn't spell either.") Jane learned, as she wrote home, a "terrific amount" that time, and she left with spider-collecting jars and preserving fluid as well as copies of two books Louis had written.

The spider collecting did not get very far. Jane dutifully trapped a few, but after the first two she found she could not bear to kill them.

Louis met Jane at the museum again the following Friday, and this time he took her out in his Land Rover to Nairobi National Park and, according to a June 6 letter home, "put me through my paces," asking her to identify, in the drizzle-dimmed late-afternoon light, the animals they were seeing: Thomson's gazelle, Grant's gazelle, wildebeest, impala, dik-dik, and so on. They also stopped at the chief game warden's house to see his eight-month-old lion, an orphan named Prince, who turned out to be a "really lovely creature" and "absolutely gigantic, particularly the size of his paws," stretched out in front of the fire, lazy and serene like a well-fed housecat.

The house-sitting offer never quite materialized, but the promise of a secretarial job was repeated and confirmed. One day in June, while Jane was again visiting the museum, Louis declared that he ought to give her an official shorthand test, and so he invented a sample letter about a fossil tooth from some antique species, spelling out the species' Latinate name. Afterward he said, "Well, you got that down all right, didn't you?" She said yes, and that was the end of the shorthand test. Then he asked if he ought also to give her a spelling test. Jane smiled and said that if her future work for him depended on a spelling test, then perhaps he should not. He smiled back and did not give the test.

Finally, having covered the matter of employment for September, Louis "thought deeply" and then very boldly "proposed a glorious scheme" for August. He and Mary were planning an archaeological expedition to Olduvai Gorge in Tanganyika, and if it were possible to add enough water and food for another person, would Jane like to come along? As she wrote home a few days later (on June 20), "If—& a big IF—they can take enough water & food for one extra, they will take me!! IF, IF, IF. But that fact remains that he is trying hard to work it for me, & if I go it will be miles from anywhere in lion & rhino country, working very hard at digging up bones, very rough conditions—& absolute heaven." Louis also loaned her some chapters of the unpublished manuscript for his study on the Kikuyu to read, which was, she recognized, "an honour."

On Friday afternoon, June 28, Louis telephoned Jane at work to announce that he intended to come over and pick her up after she was done for the day to pass on some more chapters of his book. At 4:30 that afternoon he appeared in his enormous safari truck, gave her three more manuscript chapters, and asked if she still wanted to go on the expedition to Olduvai. Jane was eager to go, and so Louis said he would talk to his wife that evening. If she vetoed the idea, that would be the end of it. But if she thought it might be possible, then Jane would have to meet Mary on Sunday morning at a Langata Pony Club "drag hunt" (horses following hounds following a dragged scent trail rather than a live animal).

Langata was the Nairobi suburb where the Leakeys lived, and during the ten- or twelve-mile drive out there that Sunday morning, Louis cautioned Jane about Mary. He would have to be careful not to call Jane by her first name in front of his wife, he explained, since Mary would consider such a thing "dreadfully familiar." Indeed, they had had a terrific battle over his previous secretary, because Mary thought she had been flirting with Louis. "She takes violent dislikes or likes to people for no reason at all," Louis concluded, and so Jane (as she wrote home) "began to be petrified of meeting Mary."

The problem with Mary was more complicated than Louis was letting on. Although he and his wife worked superbly together as a professional team, partners in the great Leakey family enterprise of fossil-hunting and paleoanthropology, they were much less successful in their personal partnership. Louis's extroversion, charm, and great vigor happened to combine with a quiet emotional neediness and even, one can imagine, an abiding loneliness. "Woman came to him like moths to a flame," one observer has noted. "And he enjoyed it; he was a real human that way." Louis Leakey's several affairs had included a serious and recent one with his previous secretary, who, in the assessment of his son Richard, nearly became "the third Mrs. Leakey."

In 1954, while Louis was in London at the British Museum studying a collection of pig fossils, he began the affair with the young and attractive Rosalie Osborn, who moved to Kenya in the summer of 1955 to become his secretary at the museum. Mary had tolerated Louis's previous affairs, but this one was much more serious. Mary soon began consoling herself with alcohol, which Louis found intolerable, and by the end of that year their house at Langata was the scene of bitter and noisy quarrels. The Leakeys' three sons, Jonathan, Richard, and Philip, each responded differently to the familial chaos. Richard, the middle son, almost eleven years old at the time, appeared to be the most affected. When his parents fought, Richard would confront them, screaming, "For heaven's sake, stop this! Please don't shout at each other!" And when Louis began threatening to leave, his young son pleaded, "Daddy, please don't leave me. Don't go, Daddy."

Then Richard fell off a horse and suffered a severe concussion, from which he recovered slowly. Louis was filled with remorse and became concerned about how the family stress was affecting the boy and how Richard would cope with a divorce. In the end Louis ended the affair with Rosalie, who continued to work at the museum until February 1956, whereupon, as Louis had arranged, she went on a fossil-hunting and fish-collecting trip to Rusinga Island in Lake Victoria. A few months later she began a preliminary attempt to study mountain gorillas in Uganda. But with only minimal results after four months on the gorilla front, Rosalie returned to England at the beginning of 1957, worked at the British Museum for a time, and finally enrolled as an undergraduate at Newnham College, Cambridge University, to study zoology.

Jane was only a month younger than her secretarial predecessor, and Louis may have been hoping, perhaps in spite of his better impulses, that she would turn out to be another Rosalie. Jane, who was impressed by and already tremendously fond of Louis, would have been shocked and upset to understand the complex dynamics of the situation she was moving into, and it was probably best she did not.

They stopped at a village shop to buy soft drinks for the Pony Club and then proceeded to the Leakey house, where they met five big dalmations and a pair of wild hyraxes, then picked up Richard (then twelve) and Philip (just eight years old, sometimes known as Peanut). Accompanied by the two boys, Louis and Jane drove on to the Pony Club event, where Jane met Mary: "a small, lean woman, with blackened teeth, a perpetual cigarette, & short wavy hair," who seemed "a little distant" on that first introduction. Jane was next introduced to a nineteen-year-old friend of the Leakey family's, Gillian Trace, who would be going on the expedition to Olduvai.

There was no extra horse for Jane, so she rode along with Louis as he followed the progress of the drag hunt in his Land Rover, which was "wonderful fun," since he was so skilled at handling that seemingly indestructible vehicle. "The sun shone—& I was so happy," she wrote home.

When they got back to the Pony Club meet, Mary encouraged Jane to ride a "wicked little pony" named Shandy, who was notoriously skittish and tended to walk backward when mounted. No one told Jane about Shandy's reverse inclinations, and when she did mount the horse, Shandy felt, as Jane now recalls, "very odd to me as she went back." Everyone was laughing at the sight, but Jane got off and said she thought the horse was in pain. She removed the saddle and discovered "a big pink saddle sore." Perhaps it was that event, more than anything, that gave Mary a positive first impression. They found a sheepskin or something comparable to put on the horse, and while Louis and Mary drove back to the house with Philip, Jane rode cross-country with the two older Leakey sons, Jonny and Richard, and "a very nice girl" around fourteen years old. Jonny was then sixteen and, as Jane put it, "dead nuts on snakes." On the ride back, in between the moments when Jonny would leap off his horse to gather up frogs to feed his snakes, he and Jane "talked snake." Richard distracted himself by chasing butterflies.

Back at the house, they found that Louis and Mary had already started eating lunch. Louis asked Jane if she was hungry, and she replied, "Fairly." Mary declared, "That means 'starving,' only she's well brought up." Jane, very alert to any signals of favor or disfavor emanating from Mary, thought that comment was a "good sign."

After lunch, the visitor was shown the family fish, swimming around inside nineteen different tanks in the house. Then Jonny hauled out his python: twelve feet long and ill-tempered enough to bite the boy's arm. Undeterred, he proceeded to show off his four-foot-long Jackson's tree snake, interesting though not poisonous, followed by an equally interesting and perfectly deadly boomslang. Next they went outdoors to look at the snake garden. Jonny, barefoot, stepped around his slithering collection of poisonous night adders and puff adders. He was "not a polite child," Jane concluded, and "indeed, none of them are." The boys were all "treated rather as grown ups and a little spoilt."

While they were being entertained by barefoot Jonny and his poisonous snakes, a phone call interrupted with the urgent message that a leopard had just killed a neighbor's Irish wolfhound. Louis was asked to come over and set a trap; a leopard might prove useful at Tsavo National Park just then, because overenthusiastic hunters had recently wiped out most of the predators controlling baboon and wild pig populations. So it was back into the Land Rover once again, with Louis and the two younger boys, both wielding butterfly nets, off to borrow a leopard trap—a wood-and-wire-mesh contraption around eight feet long and nearly five feet high—and transport it to the aggrieved neighbor with the dead Irish wolfhound. That neighbor was "an old boy with heart trouble," Jane noted, who had a "beefy" son-in-law. The old boy, the beefy son-in-law, Louis, Jane, and six African employees on the farm unloaded the trap and began hauling it over rocks and streams, through thorn thickets and dense woodland, following the trail of the leopard and the dead dog he had recently dragged away.

It was very hot, and the undergrowth soon turned resistant, so they put down the trap and waited. Then Louis went off to see where the trail led and consider how best to proceed. Next the six Africans left, following the same trail. Finally Jane and the old boy and the beefy son-in-law began following cautiously behind. Suddenly they heard a great ruckus. Catching up at last, they learned that the Africans had just sighted the leopard trying to haul his kill into a tree. The leopard had fled, dropping the Irish wolfhound—who now lay there on the ground, enormous and "really ghastly" to contemplate, with "all its guts hanging out & two holes in his throat where the leopard must have killed him."

The idea was to bait the trap with the wolfhound in the vicinity of the hungry leopard, and so, while the old boy and his son-in-law kept watch over the carcass, the rest of the group returned to the trap and began laboriously hauling it over large boulders and through forest and uncooperative thickets back to the dog. The six Africans included three who were too old or weak to be useful, so the labor party actually included three African workers, Louis, and Jane. "Honestly," she wrote home afterward, "I havn't worked so hard for ages, & the going was ghastly." It was slow, hard, hot labor of the pushing and pulling and grunting and resting-every-five-minutes sort, but in the end, after they had reached the spot and set the trap with the wolfhound inside and were certain it worked, Louis said, "Thank you." He and she then walked back to the Land Rover together, apart from the others, which for Jane was "reward enough."

Back at the Leakey house once again, Louis said to Mary, "Well, she can work, anyway." And then they all sat down to tea, although Louis periodically jumped up to find something new to show Jane, including a young tenrec, who was, so Jane wrote her family, "oh the funniest darlingest wee animal you ever saw in all your life."

Mary Leakey drove their guest back to Kirk Road House in Nairobi that afternoon and on the way there declared, "I hear you might like to come with us to Olduvai."

Jane replied that she wanted "nothing else in the world more."

Mary said, "Well, I think it would be an excellent plan—providing Gillian doesn't mind."

9

Olduvai

1957

ON MONDAY, JULY 1, Louis, Jane, and Gillian Trace met for lunch on the roof of the museum. Louis cautioned the two young women about conditions at Olduvai, including the scarcity of water. Water would be trucked in only once a week, he explained, and they would each be allowed a small bowl of it for daily ablutions plus a frugal weekly bath in a canvas tub. Louis went through the list of things they would need for the expedition. And did they prefer milk or hot chocolate? Would they like brandy to drink after dinner? (They said, "Orange squash, thank you.") He wondered if there was any food they could not eat and whether either had ever had her appendix removed. There was not. Neither had.

Jane returned to her typing at W. & C. French so excited she could barely sit still.

On Tuesday she and Gillian had lunch in town and spent some time, while drinking coffee and eating hog dogs, discussing Louis's instructions and considering what they would do about their hair while at Olduvai. With almost no water for ordinary washing or bathing, they anticipated having "dirty greasy hair," as Jane put it, and so debated whether it would be better to cut it short, and therefore have it clumped and stringy, or to pull it back. They jointly decided "to turn ourselves prim by tying it back"—and thus began Jane Goodall's trademark ponytail.

Bob came down from Thompson's Falls that weekend for a Friday dinner and dance and a Saturday driving tour of Nairobi Park, bringing extra blankets, pillows, and sheets for Jane and agreeing to take care of Levi the bush baby for the rest of the summer. Jane's boss from W. & C. French lent her his folding camp bed. The Leakeys agreed to provide a mattress and mosquito netting. So everything seemed just about ready, except for "sensible bush pajamas," which she hired a Nairobi tailor to produce.

Finally, on Monday morning, July 15, the expedition set off. Their safari van was a Land Rover, Jane wrote home a few days later, but with a back compartment that seemed two or three times as large as the rear of an ordinary Land Rover. The vehicle was packed so thoroughly that Jane and Gillian could only fit themselves in horizontally on top of a heap of supplies, bedding, and dog baskets with a pair of dogs. Gillian failed to appreciate being "a dog pillow or eiderdown," and so she may not have enjoyed the ride so much, but Jane was perfectly content and soon settled down with the warm and affectionate canines. Together the three of them could look through the little window into the front cabin, where Louis and Mary sat.

They rendezvoused with the African staff (six men under the direction of Heselon Mukiri, Louis's lifelong friend and colleague) and their truck, then proceeded in a caravan until it was nearly dark. They set up tents, ate steak-and-kidney pudding under the stars, and were awakened at 6:30 the next morning by the cook, Muli, with hot tea followed by breakfast. It was chilly that morning, and as the road took them on the long ascent to the high rim of Ngorongoro Crater, it became downright cold; and with the Land Rover ahead, the truck laboring behind, they entered a soft and mysterious white world of swirling fog.

At the top of the rim they stopped at Ngorongoro Camp to pick up a two-hundred-gallon water tank on a trailer. The truck to tow it arrived soon after—but with a broken spring, which was with much effort extracted. Louis and Mary took the Land Rover back to Arusha to find a replacement spring, leaving the African staff with the truck and Jane and Gillian with a Serengeti park warden, Gordon Harvey, and his wife, Edith, who provided lunch.

The Harveys were "utterly charming," Jane thought, and their small government house "most delightful," with a magnificent view that included, in the evenings, buffalo and rhinos grazing and cavorting. After lunch Mr. Harvey drove Jane and Gillian down a half-built road to the game-filled plains at Ngorongoro Crater's center. Halfway down, where the finished portion of the road ended, the warden pulled out his good binoculars and pointed to some remote dots that he insisted were hippos, rhinos, lions, and so on. Jane and Gillian took turns looking through the glasses but were "no wiser really!" Then they drove onto a narrow side trail into a "whispering" bamboo forest to check on the camp water supply. They finally returned to the house for late-afternoon tea with the Leakeys, who had just returned from Arusha with a new spring for the truck.

Louis and Mary were eager to move to a lower and warmer elevation for the night, so the Leakey expedition—overloaded Land Rover and newly repaired truck towing the trailered water tank—pulled away from Ngorongoro Camp at around 5:15 and proceeded down to the lower plains of the Serengeti, which, Jane wrote home, "rise & fall and are covered in golden sun-baked grass and clumps of shrub & thorn trees." The wind "shrieked" noisily that night, but they could hear, in the cold darkness, the distant roar of a lion and the shivering whoops of hyenas.

As they emerged from their tents the next day, the rising sun's glare illuminated calmly grazing herds of eland and gazelles all around. After breakfast they turned off the dirt track and drove overland, raising a billowing wake of red dust as they proceeded slowly and bumpily along, finally (after a stop to repair a flat tire and a slowdown to observe "the most beautiful cheetah who walked along beside the car, quite unafraid, before turning rather disgustedly from our noisy machine & bounding leisurely into the nearby thorn thicket") arriving at the edge of Olduvai late in the morning. They spent the rest of the day setting up camp at the bottom.

Olduvai Gorge is a pair of irregular gashes — a 25-mile-long, 300-foot-deep main ravine intersected by a 15-mile-long side ravine — on the East African plains, an environment of howling winds, swirling dust, high heat, low rainfall, prickly vegetation, stinging scorpions, and a sample of mammals that includes hyenas and jackals, lions and rhinos. Maasai herdsmen named those plains *ol duvai*, meaning simply the "place of wild sisal." But in 1911, when a German entomologist named Kattwinkel wandered into the region chasing butterflies, he was surprised by — and, it has been said, nearly fell into — a precipitous ravine that suddenly appeared in the middle of flat dry land marked by scrub, acacia, and wild sisal. Kattwinkel looked down into the gorge and noted some exposed fossils. He put down his butterfly net, gathered a few crates' worth of the odd stones, and eventually sent them back to Germany for analysis. The fossils included remnants of a previously unknown species of three-toed horse, which was a startling enough find to warrant another look.

Two years later the German colonial administration sent out a geologist, Hans Reck, with instructions to conduct a complete geological survey of German East Africa, giving particular attention to volcanic sites in the Rift Valley and to the gorge at Olduvai.

Reck set out with only a general idea of where the gorge might be, and so with an expedition that included some one hundred African porters, the tall, blue-eyed German "of a sunny disposition and upright character" walked into the plains of East Africa, up the steep rim of the ancient caldera Ngorongoro, and then down again, until he finally located it. Geologically, Reck soon concluded, Olduvai Gorge was significant, if only because it ripped through a series of ancient sediment beds all the way down to a bottom layer of black volcanic siltstone (which he identified as Bed I), which was covered by a striated series of four mostly red and reddish brown sandstone layers (Beds II to V), each representing a distinctive era of sedimentation at the bottom of an ancient alkaline lake. Reck could only roughly estimate the ages of those five sedimentation layers; with new dating technologies, later geologists clarified that the bottommost layer, Bed I, was more than 2 million years old, while the top layer, Bed V, was around 20,000 years old. Later geologists also agreed on a hypothetical sequence of events, beginning with those five eras of lake-bottom siltation and followed by a catastrophic earthquake that drained the lake. A seasonally flooding river cut the gorge and thereby opened Olduvai's quiet theater of time.

The gorge also happened to slice down along a former shoreline of the prehistoric lake, revealing an astonishing treasury of fossils from lakeshore fauna. Reck spent three months in 1913 gathering fossils, and he returned to Berlin with, among many other remarkable finds, fossils from a previously unknown elephant species (*Elephas recki*, in honor of the discoverer) and an entire human skeleton that had been buried in a crouching position.

In Berlin the Olduvai skeleton created great excitement—but how old was it? Was it merely the remains of a contemporary human from a comparatively recent burial, or was it, as Reck believed, an immensely ancient skeleton from an ancient burial? Reck insisted that he had found the skeleton in the ancient Bed II, but the Olduvai man looked anatomically modern. The kaiser himself was curious enough to help finance another expedition in 1914 in order to sort out the matter, but a war intervened, and by the end of the war Germany no longer possessed German East Africa, which had become League of Nations territory under British control. The collapse of the postwar economy, moreover, ended all hope for a German expedition back to Olduvai.

When Louis Leakey was an undergraduate at Cambridge, he conducted a study of African bows and arrows that required him to examine European museum collections, and while he was visiting the Berlin Natural History Museum in 1925, he made a point of looking up the well-known Dr. Hans Reck. Although the Olduvai skeleton had been sent off to scholars in Munich, Reck showed Louis many of his other fossils from East Africa; and Louis, after announcing his intention "to spend the rest of my life studying the prehistoric problems of East Africa," blurted out that he would one day look for artifacts and fossils at Olduvai—and Reck would simply have to come along.

Louis's third major expedition into East Africa, underwritten in 1931 by, among other organizations, the British Museum (which sent along its own man to be responsible for all mammalian fossils), aimed to find the legendary Olduvai Gorge and included enough in the budget to take along Hans Reck. It is possible that no European had actually seen Olduvai since Reck left in 1913, and so aside from contributing his valuable expertise as a geologist, the German might prove useful in explaining how to get there. In fact, Reck's old route was comparatively simple, but it seemed to require walking with a hundred African porters. Louis thought it would be possible to drive, and he sent Captain J. H. Hewlett, a skilled cross-country driver who was reputedly among the best shots in Africa, to find a route. Hewlett returned claiming success, and around midday on September 22, 1931, four Europeans and a staff of eighteen Africans set out from Nairobi, driving three large Chevrolet trucks and one ordinary Chevrolet car, all packed to the bursting point with tools, equipment, spare parts, fuel, food, and water. They drove south on a rough and dusty track until it ended, whereupon the caravan proceeded across rolling, open plains, the radiators boiling over, the vehicles churning in low gear at an average of five miles an hour, until, after a few days, they plowed through patches of wild sisal right up to the northern edge of the gorge.

During his three-month dig at Olduvai in 1913, Professor Reck had found only fossils, not a single human artifact. However, he had assumed that African Pleistocene handaxes and other implements would be made from the same material as European Pleistocene artifacts: flint. He could readily identify flint, which was rare in Africa, but he failed to imagine that early Africans might have used hard minerals common there, such as obsidian and quartz, and so was left with the impression that Olduvai contained no artifacts. Louis, who had been picking up Stone Age obsidian tools in East Africa since he was a boy, thought differently. Before their 1931 expedition, he had wagered Reck ten pounds that they would find an artifact within their first twenty-four hours at the site. Louis won the bet, discovering at dawn on their first full morning a perfect obsidian handax in situ. "I was nearly mad with delight," he recalled five years later, "and I rushed back with it into camp, and rudely awakened the sleepers so that they should share in my joy."

Every ten days they hauled back to Nairobi a truckload of fossils, carting away the mineralized remains of an astonishing horde of extinct species: peculiar-looking remnants of ancestral antelopes, crocodiles, elephants, fish, flamingos, hippos, horses, turtles, and so on. Olduvai was magnificent, a "veritable paradise for the prehistorian as well as the palaeontologist," as Louis was later to write. For the next twenty years Louis and his second wife, Mary (they were married in 1936), returned for brief exploratory ex-

peditions, gradually surveying the entire gorge for surface exposures of artifacts and fossils and eventually determining the best sites for future, more
intensive study.

By the start of the 1950s, the Leakeys were funded well enough to begin
conducting their research in depth—literally—digging first at two sites
known as BK and SHK, in Bed II. Site BK eventually yielded more than
11,000 artifacts and enormous quantities of fossils, many of them beautifully preserved, with whole skulls and sometimes nearly complete skeletons.
An abundance of pig species was to be found in that portion of Bed II, some
of them gigantic, with tusks as long as a man's arm; and there were giant
herbivores, including, for instance, *Pelorovis oldowayensis,* a buffalo-like animal with curved horns spanning almost 8 feet. In fact, the Leakeys located
the fossilized remains of an entire herd of *Pelorovis oldowayensis,* apparently
trapped in a swamp and slaughtered by ancient human or prehuman (hominid) hunters—with the evidence for this slaughter, a large number of stone
tools, scattered around the dismembered fossil bones.

Tools mean toolmakers, and the existence of all those relics among the
fossils of extinct animal species indicated that the toolmakers were contem-
poraries of the extinct animals. As Louis must have realized on the first day
of his first Olduvai expedition in 1931, it should be possible to find not
merely artifacts but actual fossils of ancient humans or even hominids ancestral to *Homo sapiens.* Reck's Olduvai skeleton was later confirmed to be
the comparatively recent skeleton of a modern human, but the Leakeys
found a few hominid skull fragments in 1935, and in 1955 at site BK they discovered some hominid teeth—a lower canine tooth and a child's molar, appropriately shaped for a three-year-old child but twice the size. But until
1959, when the Leakeys first began digging into Bed I, their hominid finds
from Olduvai were rare, and in the summer of 1957, when Jane and Gillian
Trace joined the team at Olduvai, they were still digging, sifting, dusting,
and cleaning the trenches in Bed II at BK and SHK.

They began work on July 18, spending their first two days roughing out an
area at site BK, removing the covering layer of soil with pick and shovel,
and then, once they were down to the fossil bed, chipping away at that con-
glomeration of soil and stone with hunting knives. Whenever a fossil bone
was found, Louis would bring out dental picks for the close work, and if a
fossil proved fragile, they would coat it with wet strips of toilet paper and
plaster of Paris before removal. One day Jane found a tooth that looked as
if it might be from a human—or was it from a female baboon? And she
spent another day gathering tiny mouse bones and teeth. There were times
when, holding a fossilized bone in her hand, she would be (as she wrote

forty years later) "filled with awe by the sight or the feel of it. This—this very bone—had once been part of a living, breathing animal that had walked and slept and propagated its species millions of years ago. It had belonged to a creature with a personality, with eyes and hair and its own distinctive scent, its own voice. What had it really looked like? How had it lived?" But the "great aim," she reported to the family that July, "is to find the man who made all the tools—primitive pebble tools & the beginnings of the more evolved hand axe."

Every morning they woke at dawn and then, after breakfast, walked the mile or so out to the dig. They took coffee for a midmorning break and returned to camp around noon to spend the hottest three hours of the day in the shade of a tarpaulin, cleaning and sorting and labeling specimens and resting. Around the middle of the afternoon they would walk back to the site to continue excavations.

At the end of the workday, Gillian and Jane loved to climb up the sides of the gorge and wander over the plains. "Admittedly we <u>don't</u> meet lion & rhino around every bush," Jane wrote. "But we do see Gazelle and dear little dik-dik—klipspringers walking on the extreme tips of their one modified toe of each foot, jackals, mongooses, & an <u>occasional</u> snake. I am disappointed there are not more of those." They also found endless ticks, clouds of small, pesky, hair- and ear-invading flies, and the occasional scorpion. Nocturnally their camp was sometimes disturbed by thieving jackals and lurking hyenas, and diurnally by a pair of semi-tame ravens named Hansel and Gretel. A tawny eagle maintained a nest within sight of the latrine, which had a two-sided sign in front. One side said ALL CLEAR, and the other said BIRD WATCHING.

Heselon Mukiri and the rest of the African staff camped by themselves with their own fire and tent cluster. Louis and Mary bunked down with the two dalmatians in the back of the truck. And Jane and Gillian shared a tent. They soon established a small museum, primarily of skulls and dung samples, in their tent, and at night they pulled their camp beds outside so they could listen to the eternal chorus of insects and the sporadic cries of animals while surrendering to sleep under the stars within "the whole immense vastness of Africa and the Serengeti with the mysterious universe all around and very real," as Jane phrased it. Ordinarily there was a cool breeze at night, and when, on occasion, the breeze turned into a howling wind, they would simply pull the blankets up around their ears.

The food was good, Jane thought, and they all ate "most tremendously." The expedition supplies included live chickens; one night they reveled in a grand feast of roast chicken and potatoes, "superbly cooked with stuffing & all, over a camp fire in the middle of wildest Africa!" Jane was also pleased because the others seemed to share her feelings about insects. "If we see a spider or beetle while we are digging it has to be rescued & taken to safety." And Louis, dear Louis, continued to be his "utterly adorable" self. "With his grey hair tousled & falling over his forehead & his grey eyes twinkling, he looks for all the world like a naughty little boy." Louis was agreeable ("so sweet"), considerate ("Nothing is too much trouble"), and enormously accomplished ("There is nothing he can't do"). In general Jane found the atmosphere of the camp absolutely congenial, very "friendly & joking & oh so pleasant—until dinner time."

Louis could "hold anybody in rapture," his son Jonathan once told me, but he was especially charming and charismatic when his audience consisted of adoring and attractive young women—Jane and Gillian, for example. Mary could not possibly compete. Instead she lavished her affection on the dalmatians, Victoria and Flicker (otherwise known as Toots and Bottom-Biter), and when the day's labor was done, in the cool of the early evening, Mary would sit down, uncork the brandy, and pour herself a glass—followed by several more. By dinnertime she would be drunk. According to Jane's letters home, Mary would stagger up to the table, quite "blotto," and because she was traditionally in charge of spooning out the vegetables, servings tended to be very erratic: "One is liable to get ½ a bean & 6 potatoes—whilst all the cauliflower goes on the table."

Dinners were often tense, and Mary made them more than usually so for an entire week by complaining about the soup, saying it was too thin. In response, Louis thickened the soup one night with powdered milk, but when they tipped the soup jug, the contents only dribbled out slowly. Too thick. Mary was "staggering about even more than usual" the next evening, while Jane and Gillian were feeling rather lightheaded and giggly. When the soup was poured, it was thicker than ever and plopped out in "a thick, solid sick-ey looking mess"; Jane and Gillian, breaking up lumps of powdered milk with their spoons, looked at each other and burst helplessly into a stifled explosion of laughter. Jane feigned an attack of coughing, while Gillian made the excuse that she had just burned her mouth with the soup.

In spite of the tension at dinnertime, being at Olduvai was a wonderful experience for Jane, one of the supremely memorable times of her life. As her letters home make entirely clear, the work, small dangers, and minor constraints simply made Olduvai that much more exciting and pleasurable. Her childhood dream had been transformed into waking reality.

Perhaps one of that reality's best and most dreamlike moments happened late one afternoon in August. Jane and Gillian had taken the two dalmatians out for an evening stroll along the bottom of the gorge. Toots and Bottom-Biter started chasing a mouse, and soon all four of them were milling about under an acacia tree, looking for the elusive rodent, when Jane experienced a strange sensation of being watched—and she heard, as she wrote home a few days later, a small voice inside her head say, "Jane, there's a lion up there under the tree." She turned around to see a powerful young cat only a hundred yards away, surveying them and then softly growling, "warning us not to come closer." The dogs had not sensed the lion's presence, fortunately, and Jane quietly instructed Gillian to grab one of them and walk very slowly away. Then she collared the other and began following Gillian. After they had walked only a few steps, Jane felt "so thrilled I wanted to dance for joy"—although the lion was slowly following them. Then Toots began limping: she had a thorn in her foot. They stopped to remove the thorn. They continued, but Toots soon got another thorn, and then another. Jane kept looking over her shoulder to observe the young male lion, who followed them for the first hundred yards and was still observing them quietly. Gillian whispered anxiously that they should hide in the thickets at the bottom of the gorge, but Jane insisted that they stay visible and calmly climb the side of the gorge to the open plains above. So they climbed. Toots bolted away at one point and ran back into the gorge, and the two young women called for her again and again; when she finally came back, they looped their belts onto both dogs and dragged them back across the open plains in the direction of camp. It was getting dark by then, and they finally met up with Louis and Mary in the Land Rover, both of them appropriately worried, the former "with his gun," the latter "boozed."

"Gosh, it was fun," Jane concluded.

Near the end of the summer, Jane and Gillian took a couple of days off to visit Gordon and Edith Harvey and their son Hamish (temporarily home from Oxford) at Ngorongoro Crater. It was a wonderful break, in part because of the opportunity to take hot baths. Or, as Jane put it, "<u>BATHS</u>!! I can't tell you how wonderful it was to lie & wallow in half a bath of hot water."

After the visit, Hamish drove Jane and Gillian back to Olduvai and stayed on as a guest for a few days—joined by the three Leakey boys, who showed up accompanied by two young friends, Ian McRae and Nick Pickford, and a family friend, Jean Hyde. It was a "full camp" and "such fun," Jane wrote.

One Sunday morning, Louis, carrying his gun for protection, amused the young guests by leading them through the thickets in the bottom of the gorge to a tiny water hole, looking for rhinoceros, finding some signs of a mother and infant. A day or so later, in the evening, Jane and some of the other young people took off from work early to continue that hunt, minus Louis and his gun. They walked up the gorge farther than before, finally arriving at an area that looked and then smelled "more and more rhino-y." They spied recent tracks and fresh dung. After walking a little farther, Jane decided to climb up the side of the gorge. Everyone else followed, whereupon someone said, "There he is," and a dark and massive armored beast appeared, trotting right along the trail they had just left: snorting, sniffing, and squinting. He was "petrified, poor chap, looking around with his short sighted little eyes, & vainly sniffing" as they observed him. "We are so very thrilled that at long last we have seen _our_ rhino."

At night all the young people slept outside, making the Olduvai camp "rather like a dormitory." Jane and Gillian had for some time wanted to set their mattresses halfway up the side of the gorge, high above the camp — too far away, Louis considered, to be without a gun. Hamish had brought a gun, though, and so the young women pulled a tarpaulin and their mattresses up the side of the gorge, built a campfire, and for a few nights slept tightly together for warmth. One night — among the last at Olduvai — Louis, leaving his wife and dogs asleep in the van, "poddled" up and quietly shared a thermos of tea with the campers. He crept up the slope a second time around 3:30 in the morning to show Jane the Pleiades and Orion, while Gillian and Hamish slept. Finally, as Jane wrote home, "the dear midnight ghost poddled back down the slope to his horrible stuffy little box where the stars were shut out & Toots had to be covered every time she woke."

It was near the end of her stay at Olduvai — perhaps on that same starry night — that Louis first began describing his grandiose plans to sponsor studies of the African great apes: chimpanzees, bonobos, and gorillas. Fossil discoveries would eventually yield many important lines of inquiry about the human past. Tooth size and shape would provide clues about ancestral diets. Skeletons would suggest critical facts about gait, locomotion, and so on. But what could one learn about our deepest ancestors' everyday behaviors and social lives? What was life actually like for human ancestors — before metal, before fire and cooking, before language and speech? Louis Leakey's patient excavations were drawing him into an abyss, down past the upright, large-brained, recognizably _Homo sapiens_ hunter and gatherer, down to a place where the human ancestors shifted form, morphed into mute prehuman creatures who would ultimately lead right back to the ancestors of modern apes. Modern apes are humanity's closest living relatives, in other words. And if, Louis reasoned, it was possible to identify any fundamental behaviors that modern apes and modern humans held in common, then one could logically conclude that those behaviors would have been shared by their common ancestor.

Of course, field studies of the great apes would be difficult and dangerous. There were no good precedents. No one had done it successfully. Few had imagined it might be possible. The apes were wild animals, powerful and dangerous, and they lived normal lives only in the most remote forests. It would require courage, endurance, and a complete disregard for convention for any scientist to succeed in such a study. . . .

"I remember wondering," Jane later wrote about that conversation with Louis, "what kind of scientist he would find for such a herculean task."

A few days after they returned to Nairobi that September, Louis spoke again about the need for a scientific study of apes living freely in a remote forest, and Jane, in exasperation, blurted out, "Louis, I wish you wouldn't keep talking about it, because that's just what I want to do."

"Jane," he responded, "I've been waiting for you to tell me that. Why on earth did you think I talked about those chimpanzees to you?"

Louis had decided that his ape study should focus on chimpanzees, and he knew where it should take place. Early in the century German colonial authorities had demarcated a rich piece of forest at the edge of Lake Tanganyika where chimpanzees lived. When the British took over the administration of Tanganyika Territory at the end of World War I, they continued protecting that forest, which was known as the Gombe Stream Chimpanzee Reserve. Louis had learned about the place in 1945, after talking with a Cambridge University anthropologist named Jack Trevor, who had made a brief excursion down to the Gombe area. And since the chimpanzees in that reserve were undisturbed by human intrusion—hunting, for example—they might be comparatively easy to observe.

Soon after they returned to Nairobi, Jane described Louis's proposal to her family back in England (though she was confused about the location, having placed the site in northern Kenya rather than along a lake in Tanganyika). "I adore working for Louis!" she wrote with typical enthusiasm, apparently enclosing a carbon copy of one of Louis's letters, then commenting,

> He wrote this letter for me to pop in this morning. You see what he says about me working to be a Research Assistant? Well, he is getting hold of a very wealthy man & is going to try to get enough money to create such a position for me to fill. Isn't it super! And there is the rarest possible chance that little me <u>may</u> have the chance to go right out into the wilds of the Northern Frontier for two or 3 months to study a strange tribe of chimpanzees who may be a new species, or sub-species. That is too heavenly to even think about. He says (Louis) that it might be hard as I'm a woman & one has to get the help of the D. C. [district commissioner] there. So I said he was to leave that part <u>entirely</u> to me!!

As the rest of her life would demonstrate, Jane was the perfect candidate for such a project, but in fact she was not the first person Louis had considered. As early as 1946 he had tried to send a man to study the chimpanzees on the shores of Lake Tanganyika, but the unfortunate fellow "failed utterly," according to Louis. And, as mentioned, Louis had also sent his previous secretary, Rosalie Osborn, out to look at gorillas living on the forested slopes of the Virunga volcanoes in eastern Uganda.

He had learned about the Ugandan mountain gorillas from a German-born businessman, Walter Baumgartel, who had purchased, sight unseen, a half interest in Travellers Rest, a tottering, tin-roofed hotel near the three-way border crossing between Uganda, Rwanda, and the Belgian Congo. Baumgartel arrived in March 1955 and was soon distracted from the unpleasant state of the hotel by reports of wild gorillas living in the volcanic forests nearby. Joining forces with a handsome middle-aged tracker of local renown, Roveni Rwanzagire, the hotelier set out to find the gorillas. Baumgartel first sighted a small family group—adult male, female, and offspring, emerging from a bamboo thicket and crossing a stream—and from that day forward he was convinced of the apes' "touchingly human" qualities. Gorilla-watching became his passion.

But the hotel was disintegrating physically and failing financially. Baumgartel remodeled the interior, painted the exterior, planted trees and put in a garden, blasted a new and deeper outdoor latrine into the volcanic rock. And he decided to exploit the gorillas as the hotel's primary attraction for tourists. Tourists would appear in great flocks to see gorillas—of that Walter Baumgartel was certain—but why should the gorillas wish to see tourists? He began trying to feed the apes, leaving various foods on paths and other open places where he had seen them. He tried sugarcane and, when that failed, sweet potatoes and bananas, then corncobs, then salt; but nothing, it seemed, would entice the apes into the open. In desperation, Baumgartel decided to hire an assistant to conduct the feeding experiments more extensively and perhaps even begin a modest scientific study of the animals. Early in 1956 he wrote to the well-known curator of the Coryndon Museum in Nairobi, Dr. Louis S. B. Leakey, seeking his help and offering to provide any suitable person with room and board in exchange for gorilla-attracting services.

Leakey wrote back: "I have found a suitable person for you, provided you do not insist on having a man." He had ended his affair with Rosalie Osborn by that time, and he may have hoped to find her an engaging occupation away from Nairobi. By late spring or early summer, after her fossil- and fish-collecting expedition to Rusinga Island, she was on her way to Travellers Rest. Osborn was, according to Baumgartel's written recollection, a "Scottish lass of twenty-two." She had no scientific training, but she turned out to be "an alert, competent, resolute young person" with "a natural gift of observation." Soon she was camping out in the high volcanic forests with Roveni Rwanzagire and his trackers, looking for gorillas.

Her first sighting occurred as she was sitting on the forest floor quietly eating her lunch. Looking up, she saw a gorilla seated in a tree, quietly looking down at her. "A penny for your thoughts," she said, but the gorilla turned and disappeared. Not long after that, Osborn started finding the apes more regularly, but the story of her first contact was somehow transmitted back to Scotland, where it appeared in an Edinburgh newspaper under the headline: "Scottish Lass Lunches with Young Gorilla Man." Osborn's mother, who had believed her daughter was still typing letters for Dr. Leakey within the safe confines of the Coryndon Museum in Nairobi, read the article and immediately contacted Rosalie, demanding that she leave the gorillas and return to Kenya.

Walter Baumgartel sought a replacement by placing an advertisement in a Nairobi newspaper ("three months free holiday to lover of wildlife willing to assist in experiment with gorillas") and soon hired Jill Donisthorpe, who surprised Baumgartel (unfamiliar with English names) by also being a woman. But she was older and more mature than Rosalie, and she proved herself tough and competent. She had good luck finding the gorillas and helped develop the Travellers Rest program of gorilla tourism, taking out two or three guests at a time—but she left after eight months.

Meanwhile, Baumgartel had begun thinking of his hotel as a global nexus for international scientific gorilla studies, and thus he applied to the London Zoological Society for financing. On behalf of the society, the eminent Sir Solly Zuckerman soon sent back a curt dismissal. As Baumgartel paraphrased it, "Our amateurish effort did not justify financial support."

After Rosalie Osborn's gorilla work in Uganda came to a close in late 1956, Louis began corresponding with Geoffrey Browning, the British district commissioner for that part of Tanganyika, who would authorize any visits to the Gombe Stream Chimpanzee Reserve. Apparently Louis may have hoped to send Osborn to study the Gombe Stream chimpanzees, and when he proposed such a project to Jane in September 1957, he was already aware of the district commissioner's one big restriction: that no European woman would be allowed into the Gombe forests alone.

After Jane enthusiastically accepted his proposal, Louis began casting around for funding. That autumn he wrote to Sherwood Washburn, an anthropologist at the University of Chicago, asking for his support in a grant application to various foundations. The Chimpanzee Project, Louis explained, would examine "the social life and behaviour of chimpanzees in their natural surroundings in an area where they are living in open parkland country, with a few forest galleries along rivers, to which they proceed at times. They also go down to the lake shore." The study would take four months, although it might be renewed and extended for some additional period, and it would be important mainly for anthropological reasons. In his letter to Washburn, Louis also noted that Miss Jane Morris-Goodall—"from the point of view of her personality and interests, and, by the time I send her, from the point of view of her training also"—was most certainly a "highly suitable candidate." Washburn seems never to have replied.

Louis also, like Walter Baumgartel, wrote to Sir Solly Zuckerman and applied for ape research funds from the London Zoological Society—unsuccessfully. In sum, even the distinguished Dr. Louis S. B. Leakey found it difficult to persuade established scientists or reputable institutions to support such an exotic proposal, particularly given the dual problem that the primary investigator was, first, uncredentialed, and second, female.

Louis was not particularly moved by contemporary prejudices against women. His intuition suggested that women might prove superior to men at studying animal behavior. They were probably more patient than men, he thought, and perhaps they would appear less threatening to wild animals and less likely to provoke male aggression, especially among the humanlike primates. And, as is so often the case, Louis's intellectual biases were happily congruent with his emotional ones. He happened to like women, and they—many of them—happened to find him spellbinding.

He also maintained a healthy skepticism about the value of credentials and formal education. In fact, the number of successful field studies of wild animals was extremely small in 1957, meaning that formal education would by necessity require the acquisition of theory largely untarnished by fact. Louis was less interested in the former, more in the latter. As Jane later phrased it, he was looking for someone "with a mind uncluttered and unbiased by theory." Still, a university degree of some sort might at least serve as a significant union card, and Louis must have anticipated how reflexively the scientific establishment would dismiss anything attempted or accomplished by an uneducated young amateur of the female sort.

Louis continued his search for financial support over the next couple of years, while Jane began wondering how she could overcome the Kigoma district commissioner's restriction. Fortunately, Browning had failed to specify who—or of which sex—the protective escort of the European woman researcher should be. In early January 1958, therefore, Jane sent a letter to her best friend from childhood, Sally Cary, inviting her to become a second on the expedition. Sally had sent Jane a clothesline for Christmas, so the letter began with thanks for the gift and "the information that you really are still alive." Her note would by necessity be "a very hasty scrawl," Jane continued, and "something in the nature of a proposition"—but only a "'Do you think you <u>might</u> <u>if</u> it came off' sort of thing."

> <u>And</u>, most <u>important</u>, it is to be kept a <u>strict</u> secret. Please don't let me down. Of course, <u>if</u> it comes off, it needn't be a secret. Now, listen. At the North end of Lake Tanganyika, 400 miles from civilization, Dr. Leakey, in 1933, found a troup of Chimpanzees living under odd conditions—open bushland with forest galleries instead of dense forest or jungle. These <u>may</u> be a new genus. They have never been studied yet, but the area was made into a chimp reserve against the day when time & money should be available for a field study. Leakey wants me to do it. Either alone or with another girl. For three months. And if we get the cash I'm doing it. And the only girl I'd take with me is you. It would mean your fare out here—as there's no extra money. After that you would be kept—& <u>possibly</u> have a small salary. When that was over you could <u>easily</u> earn your fare home—that I promise you.

The expedition would begin in May or June of that year, Jane believed, and Sally would need to raise only about £100 to fly out—or £80 to sail on the Union Castle line through the Suez Canal, plus another £3 for train fare. It would be "the most tremendous opportunity of your life," Jane declared, and she ended the letter with "Think about it & let me know."

10

Love and Other Complications

1957–1958

AFTER THEY RETURNED from the Olduvai expedition that September, Louis found Jane a room in Mary's Hall, the women's dormitory for the Nairobi Technical Institute (now Nairobi University) on Protectorate Road, a mile and a half from the museum. Jane considered it, as she wrote home, "so <u>heavenly</u> to have my very <u>own room</u> again that I nearly burst in excitement." It was not only "the nicest digs I've <u>ever</u> had" but also, at six pounds a month, wonderfully cheap—a tenth her secretarial salary. She could buy breakfast at the institute, eat lunch at the museum, and fix a light supper right in her room. Since the building was new, only three other young women were living in that wing; and although the place was locked up at night, the woman in charge gave her a key to the back door. "So WHAT could be better, & who could be more lucky than me?"

At first, working as the Coryndon curator's personal secretary was everything she might have hoped for. The hours were flexible. Jane could work late one evening and leave early the next day or, alternatively, enjoy a long weekend. The letters she typed for Louis were about interesting subjects, and the social atmosphere of the place was, she announced to her family, "super," with all the staff "charming & great fun, everyone mad."

The Africans working there, including Heselon Mukiri, were soon "roaring with laughter" over Jane's tortured attempts to speak Swahili. The museum entomologist, Robert Carcasson, promised to teach her all about spiders. The resident ornithologist, John Williams, said he would help her figure out bird classification (although Jane was alarmed and distressed by her first look at the collection: so many drawers full of dead birds). The office manager and accountant, Gerry Hellings, seemed agreeable as well. As for the museum technician and handyman, Norman Mitton, Jane immediately liked him. Though not particularly well educated, he was among the most intellectual of the museum staff, she thought, someone who loved music, knew the meaning of the word *solipsistic,* and could quote Shakespeare. He was "an absolute sweetie" who was, Jane soon concluded, "madly in love with me." Norman was eager to show her how to make casts of bones and skulls, and he and Louis began building a large outdoor cage for Levi the bush baby, who was now back with Jane.

There were periodic visits from Very Important Personages, and so Jane had the pleasure of watching ostrich courtship rituals in Nairobi Park with Louis and a visiting American neuroanatomist, of entertaining a "charming Portuguese professor," of escorting yet another visiting VIP on a "lovely day" to visit Gamble's Cave, the site of one of Louis's earliest excavations, and so on.

Life at the museum was exciting indeed. Almost daily there was something new to think about or do. Someone would ring up asking how to feed a baby hawk that had fallen out of a tree. Louis, who happened to be an expert on handwriting, would be called as a government witness at court in Nakuru—and, of course, take along his personal secretary for the day. There would be another phone call: while digging the foundations for a teacher's college outside Nairobi, construction engineers had discovered human bones. Louis and his personal secretary would hop into a car and speed out to the site, only to conclude that the bones were merely about three hundred years old but historically interesting nonetheless, since, in contrast to modern funeral practices among the people of that region, they had all been buried in a shallow grave along with their beads. It was late in the day by the time Louis reached these preliminary conclusions, but Jane enjoyed herself thoroughly. She found the project engineers charming, and she even won a pint of beer by walking a considerable distance while balancing a bowl full of dental picks on her head.

Louis told Jane he thought she could go out the next day and take charge of the removal of the bones. However, when he told Mary about the plan that evening, she was at first positive but then, after drinking a bottle of brandy, negative. The bad mood turned into bad words and then shouting, with Mary finally locking herself for a very long time in the bathroom and, after an alarmed Louis tried to force the door, bolting out of the house and driving off into the night.

Mary's volatile moods and erratic behavior became less mysterious as time passed and Louis began in various ways to declare his love to Jane. One Sunday morning in October, she was awakened by a loud banging on the door. She put on her dressing gown and opened the door . . . to find a hand reaching around the corner, dramatically offering the romantic token of a single red rose. "He really does behave like a child over this," Jane wrote home, "and I begin to see why Mary has taken to the brandy."

At first Jane excused Louis's behavior, telling the family back home that since he was "such a complete darling and so childish," she found it hard to get really angry. But he was soon becoming less of a darling. "Old Louis really is infantile in his infatuation and is suggesting the most impossible things," she wrote. One time he was scheduled to travel by train to Mombasa to serve as an expert witness in court, and he invited Jane to meet him on his way back for a daylong visit to Tsavo National Park. Just before leaving on Thursday, however, he gave her a train ticket and said they would meet at midnight on Friday, so that they could camp out at the park entrance to be ready for an early start the next day. "In actual FACT," Jane believed, "it would have been O.K. I know I can trust him. He's much too fond of me for any monkey business." Still, what would people at the museum think if they learned about such a rendezvous? What would Mary think? And since he had given her the ticket and described the plan at the last minute, in a room full of museum trustees, Jane had been unable to refuse reasonably.

Louis telephoned her at the museum on Saturday, wondering why she had failed to appear at the Tsavo station, but with someone else in the room, she could only excuse herself weakly and gracelessly. She arrived at work the following Monday full of dread, expecting Louis to be furious. And when she heard his Land Rover, with its rusted-out muffler, pull into the parking lot around noon, she panicked. "I quite lost my nerve & my head & obeyed blind instinct." She ran through the ornithologist's office, through the entomologist's office, and down to Norman Mitton's room in the basement. Legs trembling, heart hammering, she gathered her courage for a few minutes before walking back upstairs "to face the music."

"Why did you lie to me?" Louis demanded.

She explained that it was not always possible to talk privately over the telephone.

He said coldly, "You have let me down—let me down by not speaking the truth," and then he left the room.

Jane, feeling humiliated, returned downstairs to her friend and ally Norman for support. But finally, as she was leaving the museum for lunch, Louis found her. "I've come to apologize," he said. "I was rude and beastly, and I'm sorry."

Jane said she was the one who should apologize, and they both went to the museum kitchen and had lunch.

She spent that evening with friends, returning much later to her room at the institute to find a note from Louis on her pillow: "I had to come back to tell you how I love you." It made her feel "quite ill," she wrote home, to think that he had actually come into her room late at night—although a few days later she was able to see some humor in the event, particularly after Norman confessed that he had driven slowly past her room the same night, intending, perhaps, to protect her from Louis.

At the age of twenty-three, Jane was still discovering how attractive she was to men, and it sometimes amused her, certainly gave her a quiet pleasure, to note the strange power she had. "Does my work fascinate me or is it the hearts thrown at my feet?" she asked rhetorically at the end of a seventeen-page letter home written in November. She answered: "Oh, the work—the atmosphere & nice & interesting people at the Museum, staff & otherwise, the fact that I can have animals, talk animals, study animals. And also that I can get time off when I want or need it."

Hamish Harvey, the Serengeti warden's son whom Jane and Gillian Trace had met at Ngorongoro during the summer, showed up at the museum one day that October. He had been drawn to Nairobi by a romantic attraction to Gillian but soon was forced to conclude that the interest was not mutual. Jane spent an entire day serving as "chief comforter" to Hamish, whose "faith in human nature was shattered."

She skipped breakfast one morning to see him off at the airport. When he learned that she had not eaten, he said, "Oh, I'll fix you up with my aunt"—his maternal aunt, Eve Mitchell, who was also at the airport. So Jane had breakfast at the Mitchell house, right next door to the women's dormitory of the Nairobi Technical Institute. In the months to follow, Eve became a sympathetic friend, and in fact Jane considered the entire Mitchell family "delightful" and began breakfasting at the house regularly, sometimes babysitting the three children as a return favor.

At Ngorongoro Crater that summer, Jane and Gillian had briefly met the son of the Ngorongoro Camp manager, a young man named Brian Herne. Jane's initial impressions of Brian were not positive. As she recalled a few weeks later, at first they "hadn't clicked at all."

For one thing, Brian was a white hunter, that is, a professional big-game hunter and safari guide: a member of an elite group of skilled colonial outdoorsmen who made a business of escorting wealthy European and American clients into the backcountry in search of living animals—a bull tusker, a black rhino, a large lion, a record buffalo, a great-horned antelope—for the thrill of transforming them into dead trophies. The fact that he loved to hunt big game and was in fact the youngest licensed professional hunter in Kenyan history remained a source of genuine concern for Jane—although

Brian remembers none of that: "Neither hunting nor my safari lifestyle was ever an issue between us." In any event, he soon became, as she put it years later, "my first real love."

Brian was a good-looking (dark brown hair, bright blue eyes), tall (six foot one), trim (165 pounds), and vital nineteen-year-old. And if, when Jane first met him, his height and vitality were temporarily obscured by a full-body cast, inside of which various broken bones were repairing themselves, his position of extreme vulnerability probably made him even more interesting. Jane has always responded very positively to physical vulnerability, particularly when coupled with a gritty sort of courage.

Brian had been traveling in a truck down the Kilima cha Tembo (Elephant Escarpment), one of a series of steppes above Lake Manyara composing the western wall of the Great Rift Valley, when the driver attempted to downshift but failed. The brakes went, and the truck accelerated around a half-dozen hairpin turns before sailing off a cliff. The driver was killed, and Brian wound up in an Arusha hospital before returning to recuperate in the company of his parents at Ngorongoro Camp. The body cast was sawn off at summer's end, and Brian, although able to hobble only a few steps at a time, felt fit enough to drive his brother's noisy red MG to Nairobi to meet up with his friend, the lovestruck Hamish Harvey. When Brian got to Nairobi, though, he first stopped at the Coryndon.

Louis and Jane heard and then saw the old MG pull up outside the museum. "Anything to do with you?" Louis asked, but she thought not. Then Heselon appeared at the door to say that a lame young man was looking for her. She and Brian sat on the stairs of the museum's back entrance as he explained that he was trying to find Hamish but had lost the address.

Jane "spoke beautifully," Brian recently recalled, though with a "rather plummy" accent. She was a "pommy"—an English-born recent arrival to the colonies—and seemed to be "the ultimate greenhorn in the wilds of Africa." Still, she was attractive, energetic, and interesting, and Brian showed up at the museum a second time.

Jane wrote home that at first she had thought him "very young" and with "an external layer of the typical hard bitten and tough white hunter about him," but after they spent some time together, she found it "incredibly easy to get through that layer" and locate "the character underneath," which was "one of the very nicest I've come across out here. Loyal, honest, faithful, etc., etc." And while he still took pleasure in killing big wild animals, he was perfectly gentle with small tame animals. In any case, Jane was pleased when the young man hobbled up to her room one day, and she soon realized that she liked him, and his family and friends, a lot.

Family included Brian's younger brother, David, who was the assistant manager of a large coffee estate near Arusha. Like his older brother, David was bold and sometimes inclined to trouble—which inclination took the form of a serious car accident while Brian was in the plaster cast that summer, followed in November by an unfortunate conflict with ten armed Maasai warriors, resulting in a broken arm and a severe knife wound to the head. Other family included Brian's uncle and aunt, Bill and Molly Legg, who lived in Nairobi. Bill Legg worked as an accountant for the railroad, but he was also a talented musician with his own dance band, the Melodians. Bill and Molly really liked Jane, Brian recalls, and she regularly visited their house, where Brian stayed when he was in town.

Brian's friends were a youthful and rowdy bunch of Kenyans: a few of them, like him, professional big-game hunters (including the handsome David Ommanney and the redheaded, droopy-eyed Derrick Dunn); all of them, Jane soon decided, "quite utterly and completely mad" but also interesting, thoughtful, and kind. "They are incredibly decent to each other, this crazy bunch. It is so nice to see. They will do <u>anything</u> for each other & never let anyone down, although they are so mad." And so she was quickly swept up in a season of all-night parties and dancing, of fast driving and immature adventures: pilfering beer glasses and a flag from the Kenya Regiment, shooting out Nairobi streetlights, stealing traffic lights, rearranging road signs in the dead of night.

One of Brian's friends told Jane that, as she proudly reported home, "Brian was very lucky to have a girl friend he could take out with the crowd because most <u>nice</u> girls were scared of driving fast & didn't like doing mad things. But I was what they needed!" Jane, as Brian remembers, was "daring and game to try anything." Once they visited some friends who seemed to spend all their spare time fixing and tuning up cars and motorcycles and talking reverently about "doing the ton," that is, reaching 100 miles per hour. Jane said she would love to do the ton and soon found herself hanging on behind Brian on an AJS motorcycle. They accelerated on a cracked and bumpy ribbon of asphalt road outside Nairobi until the red needle pointed to 105. Jane was ecstatic.

She also valued Brian's thoughtful side. He was capable of sitting quietly next to her under the stars: "the first person I've met out here I have <u>liked</u> sitting alone with," she wrote home. He liked to dance; they learned to tango. Although both were regularly penniless, they still occasionally went out to dinner and to the cinema. Brian recalls seeing *Carve Her Name with Pride,* a film based on the life of Odette Hallowes, a British Special Operations courier who was tortured by the Gestapo, and "Jane was so overcome by the film she burst into tears, saying her life seemed so worthless by comparison."

Once, after a strange wedding (the English bridegroom had trouble pronouncing the Italian bride's name) and boring reception, they went with some friends to dance at the Blue Posts Hotel at Thika, an elegant colonial inn with a great expanse of lawn and garden running down to the scenic Chania Falls. Between dances, Jane walked around with a glass of beer balanced on her head, picked up a full glass in her teeth and chugged the contents, did match tricks, and so on. The hotel had a large outdoor swimming pool, and eventually she declared it was time for a swim. It was a chilly night and no one had thought to take swimming suits, but soon some of the group were stumbling through the darkness, getting lost, climbing a fence or two, and tripping through a vegetable garden. When they finally reached the pool, Jane stripped down to her underwear and dove in, followed by Brian and one other person, while the rest of the group stood around, clothed and shivering, at the edge. "It was quite heavenly," she later reported to the family.

Still, that general period was not a particularly heavenly time for Brian. His injuries had left him not only in pain but also underemployed and nearly broke. His employer, Lawrence-Brown Safaris of Tanganyika, paid him a nominal monthly sum, but as long as he was unable to run a hunting safari, it was not much. Jane wangled a small income for him through Louis—a few pounds for collecting rhinoceros tickbirds and buffalo horns for an American museum—and in January 1958 they started fantasizing about a partnership. It would be Herne & Goodall, Ltd., Jane thought, providing animal-oriented articles and photographs to American magazines.

That April, Brian took a Dutch photographer named André Gunn on a photographic safari that included a few days with Jane at Carr Hartley's 22,000-acre game ranch at Rumuruti, in north-central Kenya. Hartley was a physically powerful man who captured big-game animals by racing alongside in a vehicle and lassoing them, and he managed a successful business supplying African wildlife to zoos and film companies. Jane, however, found his operation, as she wrote home, "almost worse than I had thought possible." ("Tiny cages. Filthy. Stinking. Every animal marked, scarred or wounded in some way. A poor impala that could hardly walk. No shade—oh, ghastly.") But she had the opportunity to watch a professional photographer work, while Brian began to demonstrate some photographic talent himself. They helped Gunn film two northern white rhinos who were trotting around and wallowing in a grassy swamp on the ranch. One of the beasts, Jimmy, was completely used to people (and "quite the most charming rhino that ever lived"), so Jane climbed onto his back while Brian took a picture.

Jane and Brian began working on an article about the ivory trade, and then they bought an enlarger and began struggling with, or squabbling over, other articles they hoped to write. Jane described the creative process in a letter to the family: "He thinks he can write articles, and I know very well I can write them better." Brian would tell her to make some notes on a subject so that he could write it out. And she would immediately sit up all night and write the entire piece. He would look it over, endeavoring to find mistakes, and then write it out again with a few small alterations. She would retype it the next day, "having re-altered all his alterations." Of course, these were intended to be popular pieces for a nonscientific public, and Jane encouraged her mother to think of an English periodical that might be interested in illustrated articles about, for example, working at the Coryndon. Or about bush babies or bat-eared foxes.

The source of Jane's expertise on bush babies was Levi. But bat-eared foxes? One Sunday evening in December, Brian had come to her room with a large box under his arm. Inside were four baby bat-eared foxes, orphans from the Serengeti. He handed her the tamest of the four. "He is so small & so very sweet," she wrote home at the time. "I felt he would miss his family so I slept in my sleeping bag on the floor & he curled up in a box on its side — & slept so long as my hand was laid in there beside him — which gave me a cramp! He kept waking up & playing. We had a few hours of sleep between us!"

Louis soon got her a legal permit to keep him. Jane bought a small green collar and leash, and she put a dirt-filled box in her room, which the smart little animal soon learned to use as a litter box, more or less. But the fox liked to dig. He would try to get to the bottom of his little box, and when asleep, instead of making the usual little running twitches with his legs that dogs make, he made little digging twitches. He was an obsessive digger, and thus was named Chimba ("to dig" in Swahili). Predictably, Chimba became Jane's constant companion: lying peacefully next to her on the bed as she read *The Oxford Book of Mystic Verse*, wildly dancing around her room and snapping at moths, energetically excavating the dirt box, blissfully sleeping at her feet while she typed away in her office at the museum. He was an endearing little creature of kisses and wags and expressively flattened ears, and he turned out to be very friendly with dogs. He "fell in love with" David's dog, a Border collie named Gringo, and he quickly became good friends with Brian's springer spaniel, Hobo.

Jane and Brian were soon in love, and by January, Jane was writing to her mother about some of the affair's complexities. "Brian, in a lot of ways, I could marry," she began. "But one of the reasons why I'm writing you is to reassure you that I am not on the verge of getting engaged or anything dopey like that. For one thing Brian has no intention of marrying for at least another 3 years. And he would have to change a <u>lot</u> in those 3 years before I could marry him. The point is that I <u>do</u> love Brian. He is in a state of worry at the moment — and honestly that poor boy has been through hell personified in his life." Still, Jane concluded, "I have yet to find a more honest & essentially good hearted & big hearted man than my Brian. If he didn't love hunting, & if he <u>did</u> love music & literature, he would be <u>ideal</u>."

Louis, meanwhile, was starting to become quite impossible — telephoning Jane's friend and neighbor Eve Mitchell to remind her to wash Jane's sheets, cut the stems of the roses he had put in her room, and so on. "But we've had a little talk & he's promised to stop doing this," Jane reassured her mother. "When he acts normally, without trying to hold my hand & saying that he thinks one day I might love him back, I begin to like him again, & be sorry for him again. The endless cycle."

Jane possibly was looking for the love of a father she never had. Louis, apparently, was hoping for the love of a lover. "Oh, yes. He <u>is</u> in love with me," Jane wrote in another note to her mother. "He has been sweet & kind & helpful — & for that I am grateful. But what does he expect & hope — & with no right? Simply that one day — to quote — 'you will love me as much as I love you'. What right has a man of his age, already on his second wife, to expect & even <u>hope</u> for such a thing?" She continued, "Oh it's all my fault of course. When I first knew him I admired him — as you know. At Olduvai I was really & truly sorry for him. I still respected him & trusted him. In a way he has never abused my trust — but I can never describe my utter & complete physical <u>revulsion</u> when I discovered that he expected me to be in love with him — <u>never</u>."

Jane's ongoing emotional battle with Louis eventually reached a climax. Jane nearly left the museum, and she and Louis finally "thrashed it out," resulting, as she wrote home, in his promise to be "merely a father to me" and her promise that she would "trust him with everything as he valued my friendship more than anything else in the world." She took Louis at his word, and was able to report home that "it is so pleasant now."

Though not as immediately as Jane had expected, Louis did finally transform his passion into a more tempered and paternal kind of love. Jane soon was referring to him as "Papa" — and later, as he began to guide and advance her life and career, "Fairy Foster Father."

Mary Leakey, meanwhile, may have begun to realize that Jane was not intentionally competing for her husband's affections and thus that her brandy-stoked hostilities were misplaced. In December, perhaps as a peace offering, she gave Jane a fish tank with four guppies, two swordtails, and "a mouthbreeder & his wife (so called because when danger threatens the babies mama pops them all in her mouth until the coast is clear)." Jane was also invited for weekend visits to the Leakey house at Langata, with the expectation that she would school Mary's notoriously temperamental and backward-walking horse, Shandy. Jane was entirely delighted with the challenge. "I got blisters again," she wrote home at the time, "but I love battling with a horse. When life is full of problems and difficulties and you havn't a clue where you are being taken, it is wonderful just to be able to battle with a horse, make him go where you want, no matter how hard it is."

Soon Shandy was jumping nicely, and by February Mary had persuaded Jane to take him to a Pony Club meet one Sunday. The chief instructors of the club were Major and Mrs. Piper, and Jane found the event "gay & carefree & everyone happy." The young riders had "much bigger horses" than their Pony Club equivalents in England, "& they ride better, on the whole. More confidence." There was a treasure hunt in the morning, followed by a picnic for the children and a full luncheon spread for the grownups. After lunch came the jumping. "Eventually I got on my devil & he knew at once that it was jumping," Jane wrote afterward. Unfortunately, Shandy, perhaps overexcited, reverted to his old retrogressive ways. "People were laughing & leaping out of the way—& suddenly he wizzed, through a row of chattering old ladies, towards two tables laden with mugs of beer, tea, cakes, etc. The panic was comic. Everyone grabbed something from the table & by the time we hit them not much damage was done. Richard threw a bucket of water at our tail but Shandy didn't much seem to mind. So Major Piper came to the rescue with a hunting crop. That did the trick." Shandy eventually did jump, and even "fairly well"—that is, "relative to Shandy, not normal equestrian standards!"

In any case, the Pipers were so impressed with Jane's handling of Shandy that they decided to give her a horse of her own: a large mare, three-quarters Arabian, one-quarter thoroughbred, named Ghazle. The Leakeys agreed to expand their stables to accommodate an additional horse, and so Jane soon had another reason to make the trip out to Langata. She could take Ghazle into the countryside and watch the sun set across the plains with the Ngong Hills at the horizon, something "so breathtakingly beautiful" that when she "suddenly came face to face with it through a break in the trees even Ghazle stood motionless, her ears pricked."

In late February or early March 1958, the women's dormitory of Nairobi Technical Institute advised Jane that she was required to vacate her room. As Jane put it, "On Saturday I received a notice kicking me out of my room." Levi the bush baby was living at the museum, so perhaps someone had objected to the bat-eared fox. In any case, Jane and her fish and fox were invited to move into the Leakey house, and she was soon finding life at Langata "rather fun." Situated on five acres with a sloping grass lawn that provided a sunset view west to the Ngong Hills, the house had been built during the Mau Mau uprising in the early 1950s, in the style of a fortress—concrete block and stucco with a tin roof and a sturdy protective mesh over the windows—around an interior courtyard.

Jane found there was a lot of work to do there, what with schooling Shandy, cleaning Ghazle, and building her stable, but "it's a good life & I love the Leakey kids. Mary is still very tricky & needs exceptionally careful handling—I may lose any minute. I just keep my fingers crossed." But given Mary's brittle tectonics of mood and character and Louis's complex and sometimes overbearing personality, Jane was surprised at how stable and agreeable the three Leakey boys were. Jonny, the oldest, was shy and mildly awkward, rather hard to penetrate perhaps, but "full of charm, has a delicious sense of humor, and a real love of all animals." The middle child, Richard, was a "real charmer, very intelligent, very quick off the mark." One evening, Jane recalled for her family, she and Richard sat together on a carpet of grass "under a beautiful full moon and talked philosophy—and he's only 12. His ideas happen to be <u>identical</u> to mine—reincarnation, etc."

Of course, living a dozen miles outside Nairobi presented a transportation problem, which Jane sought to solve by buying an eight-horsepower 1948 Morris for eighty-five pounds and learning how to drive. It happened that an old racing-world friend of Mortimer's, Ernest Stapleton, was serving as Kenya's chief of traffic police. By February, Ernie Stapleton was giving Jane driving lessons. In April she passed her test, and thus the famous Mort Morris-Goodall's pretty, long-haired daughter was photographed for a 1958 issue of *AM Magazine*, holding her pet fox and being handed her driving papers by Ernie Stapleton as they stood together at the open door of a gleaming Aston Martin.

By then, however, Jane had decided that Stapleton was "vile," a conclusion based on his furtive invitation to dinner while his wife was away, other inappropriate advances, and his dramatic confession during a driving lesson that he was terribly ill with an incurable disease called Jane.

Then there was Pip—Major Piper, from the Langata Pony Club—who was a "real flirt, in a highly amusing way," Jane thought, although he was also "in love with me—horribly much." Soon (perhaps it was after that bit of "crazy" roughhousing in the Leakey stables, involving flung wet tea towels and many handfuls of sopping pondweed) his attentions became more and more emotionally charged.

Even Gordon Harvey, the Serengeti park warden Jane and Gillian had met during the summer of 1957, the man who drove them down into Ngorongoro Crater that day in the middle of July, had fallen into the web.

When the Leakey expedition left Ngorongoro on the way to Olduvai, Gordon had placed a small radish into the twisted sleeve of Jane's cardigan, a mysteriously evocative token; and when the withered radish fell out two days later, she understood the message and felt, as she wrote later, surprisingly "melancholy." Jane liked Gordon a lot, and when he visited her in Nairobi, in April 1958, she once again noticed how "handsom and so very sweet" he was. He had prepared a picnic lunch with radishes, and they jointly confessed that whenever they saw a radish they thought of each other. "The birds sang and the sun shone," she informed the family back home,

> and we leant against a shady tree, and talked about animals and things for a long time—until 3. He asked me what had happened to him—he was not young any longer, and he had had a happy married life. This sort of thing he had not dreamed possible. I would never realize what it had meant to him, my just walking into his life, from nowhere. I would never realize how often, when he was out on safari, miles from anywhere, how he longed for me to be with him, to share the animals and the little things of life that are so important. He was so utterly sincere, so honest, so touching. I loved that lunch time.

Jane's attractiveness to men, including middle-aged and married ones, is easy to understand. She was young and good-looking. She was extroverted, constitutionally unrestrained in her feelings and sympathies. She enjoyed the attention, and she liked the men, many of them. But in the end their serious responses to her and her less-than-serious flirtations could be troubling. "What the devil am I to do with all these middle aged married men?" she asked her mother in bemused exasperation. "They hang in multitudinous garlands from every limb and neck I've got, and most of them are so charming. Hey ho. What did you do some 24 years ago Mummy? I bet you never guessed when I lay so small and waxey in your arms!"

11

The Menagerie

1958

"DO PLEASE FORGIVE ME for the long silence," Jane wrote home on April 2, 1958. "I really do have an excuse this time — at least, a sort of one. The most <u>vile</u> and <u>horrible</u> things have been happening. Really horrible this time. Chimba is dead. He was <u>stoned</u> to death by a European and 4 Africans."

Chimba had vanished from Jane's car one morning when she had pulled up in front of the Leggs' house to fetch something before going on to the Coryndon. She and Brian hunted for her beloved pet everywhere they could think of, but finally she left for work while he continued the search. As she was eating lunch at the museum, Brian appeared, "trembling all over," to deliver the news: "Your fox is dead." Nearly in tears, he explained that some schoolchildren had seen a white man and four Africans stoning Chimba to death, and he had found the little fox inside a concrete culvert on Ngara Road. At first Jane "couldn't think." Brian went off to bury the animal, but as soon as he left, "the horror swept over me." All the museum staff were aware of the situation by then, and "there were <u>many</u> wet hankies."

Jane and Brian spent that first evening printing and enlarging photographs in the museum darkroom in an attempt to avoid thinking deeply about what had happened, and the next day Jane reported the killing of a collared and licensed pet to the police and the local RSPCA. Then she and Brian rode horses out from the Leakey house in Langata. Jane must have been "in a very strange & edgy mood." She began making disparaging remarks to Brian about hunting, and finally they rode off in opposite directions, meeting sullenly some time later back at the stables. Jane had agreed to drive Brian back to Nairobi, but her car stalled, so she left it on the road, walked back to the Leakey house, and asked to borrow the Land Rover. Brian, still furious from their earlier argument, decided to walk or hitchhike the several miles into Nairobi. She caught up with him and told him to get into the Land Rover. He refused. She drove on—then stopped, blinded by tears, beside the road. He caught up and started to drive. After a while "I collapsed beside him" and began screaming irrationally, "Stop them! Stop them! They can't do it!" He drove her back to the Leggs' house and carried her to bed, but she wouldn't keep still. She said Brian had killed Chimba, then that it was all her fault, and so on. She was so hysterical that the Leggs at last bundled her into their car and drove her to the hospital.

She was given a shot and three turquoise-colored pills to swallow. "Have you spat it out?" the nurse asked. She pulled one of the pills from her mouth and said, "No, there it is."

Jane stayed in the hospital overnight in a sedated daze and left in the company of Brian and his uncle, Bill Legg, at around noon the next day, whereupon she took to bed at the Legg house for another day. Life at the Leakey place in Langata, in the meantime, had gone from good to bad. Mary had one evening descended into a sodden, shouting rage that ended in the middle of the night with her trying to jump out a window. Then, on the day following Chimba's death, after Jane borrowed the Land Rover and wound up under sedation in the hospital, Mary ungraciously reported the vehicle stolen.

Fortunately, an apartment was becoming available at the start of April in the two-story building right behind the Coryndon Museum, maintained to house museum staff and known as the Museum Flats, and so Jane was able to move directly from her temporary sanctuary into one of the Museum Flats. Her new place—ground floor on the right side of the building—was pleasant and spacious, with parquet floors and cream-painted walls: sitting and dining room, kitchen, two good-sized bedrooms, a tiled bathroom, and, opening onto a garden and flowering shrubs at the back, a large veranda. It was unfurnished, but someone from the museum lent her a table, two chairs, and a bed and mattress, and she soon began decorating. She placed two stuffed birds on a window ledge, a serval cat skin on the floor, and, on the walls, framed photographs of one rhino and two big cats (taken by Brian) as well as two African masks, two drums, two horned antelope heads, and one polished woodcarving of a stretch-lipped Ubangi woman, all temporarily liberated from museum storage.

Robert Carcasson (the museum entomologist) and his wife and son lived in the flat directly above, and Jane imagined that her upstairs neighbors might be disturbed or amused by the new sounds emanating from below. She wrote to Danny in mid-April, "First I've been singing snatches of opera, interspersed with 'Stop it!' in a very loud voice when Levi bites my foot.

And then I got the giggles over a book I was reading! Soon I shall start on T. S. Eliot or Shakespeare, in a loud voice, no doubt!" The Carcassons soon returned the favor, however, by playing Beethoven's Fourth Symphony on their record player—though not quite loud enough for Jane's taste. She found it pleasant to be living by herself again and to have enough space for large-eared, round-eyed, bushy-tailed little Levi to bounce around to his heart's content, knocking over cups in the kitchen and jars in the bathroom and, at mealtime, leaping after a loosened pack of popping grasshoppers. Levi was soon joined by the fish in the fish tank, brought down from Langata and placed in the sitting room, followed by a big and "really beautiful spider—a great hairey thing with very thick legs" that someone had donated to the museum and Jane agreed to keep. The spider, named Circe, inhabited a large jar in the kitchen.

As noted, in January 1958 Jane had written to Sally Cary about a three-month expedition to the shores of Lake Tanganyika to study chimpanzees. Louis, meanwhile, was having trouble convincing anyone to spend money on an expedition managed by his unqualified secretary, and thus, the project was postponed. For her part, Sally was never enticed by Jane's peculiar offer of an expedition to find exotic apes—but she did go to Africa. She boarded the *Kenya Castle* on April 2, sailed through the Suez Canal, and arrived in Nairobi within three weeks. She took a job as a teacher at a small school in Nairobi and bunked with Jane at the Museum Flats.

By the time Sally showed up, around the fourth week of April, Circe had been joined by another big spider in another big jar, as well as a green tree snake, sometimes loose and sometimes curled up in a third big jar. By the middle of May, though, Jane had given the two big spiders their freedom and the green tree snake had spontaneously disappeared, leaving the menagerie reduced to Levi and the fish once again—a good thing, because she had decided to meet Brian at the coast for a weeklong holiday, so Sally would have to care for them.

Seasonal rains had descended on Nairobi by then, so the weather was sometimes chilly and often damp, and when Bill Legg took Jane and Brian to the train station, they drove through a downpour and streaming streets. The station was flooded, with water flowing knee-high through the parking lot and rippling ankle-high across the floor of the station restaurant and bar, but Jane, wading about with her shoes off and her skirt hitched up, made friends among her fellow waiting passengers and took the whole situation in good cheer, even as the lights went out, the station closed down, and the train finally pulled away nine hours behind schedule.

The weather was dry and deliciously hot in Mombasa, and Jane and

Brian were soon driving around town and down to the sea. "Oh how lovely it was to hear the waves again," she rhapsodized in a letter home, "to feel the sea breeze on one's face, damp with spray, and to breath sea air once more. It was very hot that first night—one couldn't even sleep with a sheet over one—it's unheard of to use a blanket at night."

They camped on the beach near the resort town of Malindi, taking occasional showers at a posh hotel nearby (the Sinbad, owned by a friend of Brian's family), diving into waves, and sitting on the sandy shore while eating sweets and biscuits and drinking City beer. One day they rented a dugout canoe and paddled across a mile of open water to a reef, a comparatively level expanse of rough rock containing many small ponds and pools and channels. "It would take days," Jane wrote, "to describe all the fascinating things we saw there—the giant shells, the brilliantly coloured fish, the strange anemones, starfish, and sea urchins." Brian caught a three-foot-long moray eel, which they first intended to eat but then decided not to, and so they tossed the creature back in. They gathered shells and watched the many crabs emerging from their tiny burrows in the sand.

But perhaps the most significant event of that rejuvenating coastal holiday happened back in Mombasa, near the end of the week. On Thursday evening, following some obscure, twisting streets, Jane and Brian located an Arab trader named Kombo, eating curry by candlelight, who was known to offer animals for sale. Kombo showed them a mongoose, "the sweetest little thing," Jane thought, whom the trader placed on his table and proceeded to play with. The trader also had two bush babies for sale, but of a larger species than little Levi, and possibly not appropriate companions for him. After much negotiation, Jane and Brian bought the mongoose for twenty shillings, and the next morning they took delivery of "a large gourd with many holes in it through which a small pinkish nose kept being thrust." That same morning they located, in another part of town, a group of African women baking bread and offering a small vervet monkey for sale. The monkey was "so sweet and friendly to us, complete strangers after all, that Brian said I must get him." They bought the monkey for another twenty shillings and named him Kombo, in honor of the trader who had sold them the mongoose.

Poor little Kombo caught a cold that same day, with a temperature, cough, and runny nose, and they gave him aspirin, a tiny drop of brandy, and a taste of cough medicine. On Saturday, Jane and Brian left the two animals for a short while in the hotel room of Brian's parents, each tied to a different piece of furniture. When they returned from lunch, they found that the mongoose had slipped out of his collar and crawled into the monkey's arms. "Since then they have been inseparable," Jane wrote to her family, although at night Kombo was sleeping in her bed. "You see, how else can I keep him warm?"

When, very late on Sunday night, Jane arrived back at the Museum Flats with a monkey and a mongoose, Sally emerged sleepily, wrapped in her dressing gown, and seemed not in the least surprised by the two new pets, who were put with Levi in the second bedroom.

Jane christened the mongoose Kip, and at some point around the start of June, Kip, Kombo, Levi, and the fish were joined by a six-week-old cocker spaniel, scion of distinguished lines from both Kenya and England and given to Jane by the East African Kennel Club. Predictably, the puppy was "adorable—white and orange, round and fat and fluffy," and she was very good her first night in the apartment. The puppy was named Tana, in reference to a crocodile-infested river in Kenya that Brian had always wanted Jane to see.

The Carcassons kept a large black-and-white dog, Happy, who spent two weeks with Jane and her pets while his own family took a vacation in May and afterward began coming down to visit the expanding menagerie with some regularity.

The Fleetwood family, who lived in the second-floor flat adjacent to the Carcassons', had a pet named Boozy—a greater bush baby (*Galago crassicaudatus*), in contrast to Levi, who was a lesser bush baby (*Galago senegalensis*). But Boozy soon discovered that life was very interesting down in Jane's place, and although little Levi was intimidated by the bigger Boozy, Boozy became good friends with Kombo, the monkey. The pair would frequently sit hugging each other, with Boozy licking Kombo's face "while he shuts his eyes in bliss." Boozy was "incorporated into our family," although her membership was at first limited to evening hours between 6:30 and 10:00.

Jane, Brian, and Derek Fleetwood soon built a large outdoor cage on the veranda to house some of the animals, but in the meantime most of them (with the exception of Kombo and the fish) stayed in the second bedroom at night, while Jane and Sally and Kombo (the latter curled up under Jane's blankets) shared the first, and the fish swam and shimmered in their own watery space in the sitting room. On weekday mornings Tana might accompany Jane to the museum, where she mostly slept in her box or looked up, a brown-eyed study in adoration, waiting to be comforted on a warm lap.

Three afternoons a week, Sally was free from work and watched over the animals. On weekends Kombo might be tied up in the garden on a long string, with Kip and Tana loose and playing around him, so the animal room could be left open for ventilation and cleaning. In the evenings Jane at first tried leaving all the animals loose in the kitchen and sitting room, but that proved too chaotic. It was hard to eat supper. "There would be Kombo and Kip helping themselves from my plate, a bush baby stretching out and seizing handfuls from my fork as they sat on my shoulder, and two pleading eyes from such a charming little puppy face on the floor, that a few tit-bits had to be spared in that direction as well." Soon most of the animals were fed in their own room, while Sally and Jane enjoyed their supper in peace—except that little Levi, who preferred not to eat in the presence of Kombo, took his meal in the sitting room, and Tana consumed hers in the kitchen. Once all were fed, the animals could visit the main parts of the flat—although after Kombo smashed two vases and one framed photograph and became hard to control, he was tied to the kitchen table.

One day Tana disappeared. Kip, the mongoose, squeaking and tearing about, helped Jane in her frantic search through the garden until the puppy was finally found in the kitchen cupboard, curled up and fast asleep among the saucepans. Kip got into trouble when he broke and ate three of the four last eggs; then he refused to sleep with Tana, as he ordinarily did, and insisted on crawling into Jane's bed instead, which made her usual bedmate, Kombo, very jealous, but Jane was simply too tired to keep a determined mongoose out. In the morning Kip refused to get up. "In the end I just stripped the bed and exposed him to the hard light of the morning. Once up he had a lick and a stretch and felt fine and on top of the world." In sum, the menagerie was a lot of work. "But," Jane wrote home around the second week of June, "can you imagine how paradisical (if that is the correct word?) it is for me having all these animals around?"

Around the third week of June, Dinkie, a prickly hedgehog, joined the family. Kip, who would crack eggs open by flicking them through his back legs against a wall, had lately begun practicing the same technique on bottle tops, pens, shells, and other small objects. Now he tried it out on a balled-up hedgehog. The hedgehog was bigger than the mongoose, though, so Kip had to suffer "getting his tender parts pricked and doing really high handstands," while Dinkie "doesn't seem to care two hoots."

A friend of Bob Carcasson's happened to have a surplus of Siamese kittens, and so near the end of June, Nanki Poo arrived. Jane's family continued to expand that summer, with the addition of a black-and-white laboratory rat from Sally's school (kept in a glass tank); a greater bush baby wife for Boozy, named Slosh (arriving in August); a mongoose wife for Kip, named Mrs. Kip (in early September); and a vervet monkey wife for Kombo, named Thimble. Then, of course, there were routine visits from Hobo (Brian's springer spaniel) and Gringo (David Herne's Border collie).

• • •

While her animal family grew so rapidly, Jane's relationship with Brian became increasingly problematic. Brian's moods that summer shifted rapidly and were hard to forecast: gusts of jealousy and storms of rage interspersed with flashes of sunny calm. "I seem to be spending most of my time at present having tremendous rows with Brian," Jane wrote home on July 25. "He is for some reason in a worse state than he has been all the time. He gets het up & enraged over absolutely nothing. You can tell when he walks in the room whether or not he is going to erupt. 3 days ago he removed all his belongings, for the 4th time! from the flat, & stalked home in the hot sun carrying all his bedding." Jane finally decided that the end had come—but then "the next evening when he crept round with his tail between his legs—what could I do but forgive him once again. Yesterday evening he had supper with us & we printed some photos, & he was in a delightful mood. But this evening he was vile again—he has gone off to work on his car in a vast rage."

The menagerie was to some degree self-contained and self-sustaining, with Sally as well as one or two sympathetic neighbors in the Museum Flats helping out with the feeding and caring, so Jane was still able to see a good deal of Brian that summer: a weekend in Mombasa, another weekend spent visiting Clo and her fiancé in the Kinangop, an afternoon wedding, an evening spent dancing, and so on. They began frequenting a drive-in cinema in town, a place that intrigued Jane in part because of its various promotions. At one point the drive-in offered free admission to any woman who appeared at the gate driving a car. Jane practiced driving with Sally on her lap, hoping that they could both get in free—though in the end Sally was too tired on the night they had planned to try it out. Another time they got Sally admitted for a child's price by tying a bright red ribbon in her hair and placing a big doll in her arms, while Jane made herself invisible by curling into a ball on the floor of the front seat between Brian and his friend David Cairns.

Jane's car was falling apart, however, with dangerously unreliable steering, nonfunctioning headlights and wipers, bad points, hard-to-find spare parts . . . and, as a mechanic explained one day with great seriousness, "I'm sorry, madam. You have old-fashioned nipples." Old-fashioned nipples or not, she continued making regular excursions to the Leakey house in Langata to feed, exercise, train, and jump Ghazle. She also regularly drove the menagerie, except for Dinkie and the rat, out to Langata for a picnic and exercise—"Teddy Bear Picnics" that Sally remembers with fond nostalgia: "We used to drive out for a picnic out on the plains of Langata, taking all the animals in the car with us. We would open the doors when we got there, and they would all disappear: monkeys into the trees, Kip into the bushes, and dogs and the cat and everything else wandering out. They would all disappear. Then we had our picnic, and when it was time to go home, Jane would hoot on the horn, and they all came zooming back and got into the car."

In mid-August, Jane and Sally alternated tending the menagerie and taking one-week portions of a two-week Coryndon Museum specimen-collecting expedition to Kenya's Kakamega Forest. Accompanied by Jonny Leakey and Derek Fleetwood, Jane had her first taste of living in a real tropical forest and an interesting foretaste of what life would be like only two years later at the Gombe Stream Chimpanzee Reserve in Tanganyika. They all slept in a cabin, which was dry and roomy but invaded by ants. Jane at first was, as she wrote home, "not very keen" on them. But the table and food safe were ant-proofed (their legs placed in cans of water), and thus confined to the floor, the ants turned out to be "better than any broom at clearing up the floor after meals."

Jane found Derek Fleetwood less agreeable, slow and uninspired and "so ghastly—clumping around in boots and smoking a pipe," but Jonny Leakey was his usual thoughtful, resourceful, agreeable self. He and Jane usually went off on their own during the days, engaged in such things as turning over stones and rotten tree trunks looking for snakes and insects. Once she left Jonny by a small stream where he was intending to catch frogs and wandered into the forest beyond, when "suddenly I found myself in the midst of the strangest and weirdest chorus imaginable. I had heard of the chorus of the Colobus monkeys before, and heard it in the distance, but never before been actually surrounded by them." Then "all the birds also began shouting," and Jane felt a sudden and perhaps irrational fear: "a sudden horrible feeling that there might be a leopard somewhere, but I don't suppose there was." But the fear passed and was replaced by curiosity and wonder at the "many rustlings and strange noises—mainly drips from the eternal dampness. And at night there are even more noises: the high pitched trill of the forest cricket, the croaking of toads, and 'glup-glup-glup' of the musical tree frog, the squeaking of bats, the odd noise of the Poto—and so on."

Meanwhile, Jane had saved up enough money from her salary to buy a plane ticket from London to Nairobi as a gift to her mother, so Vanne lifted off from the first city on September 2 and settled down into the second on September 3, "fresh as a daisy after having had several good sleeps," as she quickly reassured Danny, Olwen, and Audrey back in Bournemouth.

Vanne had been longing to see Jane again, but she was also worried, in a maternal fashion, about Jane's well-being and (as she had put it in a letter written back in April) "the Brian problem." Brian was away when she arrived, and Vanne informed the family in a letter of September 10 that she was "shocked by her [Jane's] appearance when I arrived as she is terribly thin & on edge. But I really think that even after a week of fairly early nights, a little food & no Brian she looks better. I think it is mostly caused by the worry of her difficult situation out here & that there is nothing which can be put right." In spite of such problems, however, Jane still had "masses of energy," Vanne thought, and was leading her usual "mad whirl" of a life. A shopping trip into Nairobi, for example, would "have to be seen to be believed. Sal perches in the back with <u>Hobo</u> a larger springer spaniel on one side, LUCKY, a huge black and white dog on the other side, TANA, the small spaniel (a dream of cream & brown silk) on the floor. I sit in front clutching perhaps one or two mongooses called Kip & his wife, & yesterday KOMBO the monkey in addition. The mongooses like to travel inside one's dress!"

Vanne soon met two of Brian's best friends in Nairobi, Dave Cairns and Micky O'Brien Kelly, and found them both "absolutely sweet." Both young men came to supper at the flat one evening and impressed her with their excellent manners and the fact that upon arriving they "immediately took off their coats, donned aprons & cooked the bacon & sausages & eggs!" In contrast to their English counterparts, Vanne concluded, Kenya-born men were "more mature."

As for Brian, who was not expected in town for another week, she could only report that everyone she had met so far described him as "a boy of great charm, and he has only to suggest something and everyone (including Jane) follows him. The extraordinary part of it is that he is only 20!" Still, and most significantly, Vanne added with double-underlined emphasis, "<u>no engagement likely.</u>"

When she finally did meet Brian, around the middle of September, her initial conceptions and concerns were generally confirmed. Brian "would make a wonderful film star," she wrote, even though "he is not my cup of tea." Jane remained "<u>very</u> attached to him," but Vanne considered much of that attraction to be based on the unhealthy emotional appeal of melodrama: "always a SITUATION!!" She elaborated: "Either Brian is dying, or cross, or about to commit suicide, or going to sell his car, or abandon Jane, or wring Leakey's neck or go off into the blue, or just martyr himself in a quiet corner. OR he is on top of the world and all is well. The latter situation seldom occurs."

But if Jane's boyfriend provided a contrary mix of pleasure and turmoil that autumn, so did the menagerie. Vanne stayed in the flat's second bedroom, which meant that the previous occupants had to be rearranged (though several of them were already well settled into their open-air quarters: the wire-mesh cage on the veranda). Soon after Vanne's arrival, Levi and Mrs. Kip wandered off and disappeared. Jane and Sally spent many hours searching and calling for them, and finally Louis came down to the flat "with a very worried face" and urged Jane to write an SOS to be broadcast on the local radio station's nine o'clock news. The mongoose, Mrs. Kip, never returned; Levi, the bush baby, finally "staggered" back into the flat the next morning, "half dead," according to Vanne, who set to nursing the pathetic creature back to health.

A few weeks later Kip made the mistake of scrambling up the stairs, entering one of the second-floor apartments, and jumping into a baby's pram. The baby's mother, being "a Yorkshire fish wife type," as Vanne put it, yelled down at Jane from her veranda. After Kip invaded the pram a second time, the woman lodged a complaint with the Nairobi public health authorities, who soon referred the matter to the Coryndon Museum trustees, who spoke to Leakey, who assured everyone he would look into it. At the same time, a city inspector was directed to visit the apartment. Jane, as Vanne reported back to the family, "exercised some of her fatal charm on the man, and we have heard no more" . . . until, that is, Kip ran up the stairs a third time and leaped into the pram once again. "Down came the fish wife, arms akimbo, skinny body alive with hatred of us and ours, and told Jane that if her damned mongoose came in to her flat again she'd wring its bloody neck!"

The mongoose was confined indoors, and since he was used to having the freedom to dig all day long in the garden, confinement was hard—for him and, during the hours she managed the flat, for Vanne. Around the same time, the dogs also required special attention, Hobo from a bite on the eye, Tana from a minor episode of distemper following her vaccination, and Gringo with "tick fever." Happily, however, responsibility for the care and maintenance of Jane's menagerie was distributed evenly enough that Vanne still found plenty of time to go shopping, work on a novel, socialize with Jane and Sally and their friends, and, with Louis Leakey's help, see some small and interesting portions of a vast continent.

During a trip to England that spring, Louis had arranged to meet Jane's mother. Vanne had taken a morning train from Bournemouth to London on Tuesday, April 1, and they met in the early afternoon at the main entrance to Harrods department store. He had booked a table at a nearby restaurant, and they ate, as Vanne reported back to Jane, "a very good lunch," during which "he told me lots and lots of things about Kenya and you and his work and you again." Vanne felt she "could have sat there all day hearing tit bits about you" and was therefore entirely "loath to tear myself away." She considered Louis to have "a wonderful flow of conversation and a very strong personality which I liked."

When Vanne went out to Nairobi that September, Louis, who enjoyed playing the gracious host, arranged a number of small trips for her into the countryside. There was a visit to the Leakey house at Langata while their animals were being photographed (with an awkward introduction to Mary, who managed to emit an approximation of "How do you do" from inside a stable, being altogether "so rude that Leakey had to apologise to us for her"); a quick drive to Limuru through the Kikuyu reserve and into the White Highlands ("where a good many English people have settled & made the place as English as possible — dull!"); and a daylong expedition through "miles and miles of real African country," descending to the floor of the Rift Valley with Mary's aunt Toudy and two overdressed, "absolutely typical American ladies" to visit the spectacular Olorgesailie Prehistoric Site (where Louis and Mary had in 1942 stumbled upon an astonishing, enormous cache of large stone hand axes, cleavers, and round bola stones in a remote area of sandy desert plains).

Then, in October, Louis provided Jane and her mother with a weekend float in his research vessel, the *Miocene Lady,* on Lake Victoria. Leaving on a Friday morning, the pair were driven by Brian and Dave Cairns to the port of Kisumu, where they met the boat's skipper, Hassan Salimu, and his second mate, Hamisi. During that glorious weekend excursion on the second largest freshwater lake in the world, Jane and Vanne spent a day exploring the uninhabited, monkey-filled island of Lolui. It was, for Vanne at least (as she then wrote home), a "dream which will live in memory forever," where mother and daughter "sailed on and on and on, under a tropical sky, and landed on an uninhabited Island, and slept to the sound of a million croaking frogs, the faint plop of hippos wallowing, and were awakened at dawn by the most lovely skies I have ever seen. We returned on Tuesday and Nairobi seemed as dull as the old Bull and Bush after a glimpse of paradise."

Louis also took Vanne on a brief excursion to Olduvai, which she described to Danny in a November 5 letter. Jack Evernden, a geophysicist from the University of California at Berkeley, had gone to Kenya with the intention of gathering rock samples from the various layers of Olduvai for subjection to new dating techniques; the young American needed help in finding the gorge. As Louis explained to Vanne, he had wanted to take Jane along as well but could find "no excuse except that he wants to take her!" Since Vanne was not a museum employee, excuses were unnecessary; and so, at 9:30 on Tuesday morning, October 28, Louis, Jack Evernden, and Vanne "tore off the horizons" in the Land Rover. They reached Ngorongoro Crater by sunset, ate a supper cooked by Louis ("a most delicious one as all his meals are"), and camped under the stars, with their camp cots set up next to the vehicle, Louis on one side, Evernden on the other, Vanne in the middle. "I hardly slept that night, the crickets produced their own symphony, the moon came up and turned our camp into a brilliantly lit stage, and before very long the birds began to sing again and we had to sit up and watch the dawn breaking the night sky."

Evernden turned out to be "the nicest type of American," Vanne thought, and they all "got on very well." And after a breakfast of fried eggs, bacon, and tea, they packed up and set off into the Serengeti, which "far exceeded in strangeness and beauty what I had expected." The Land Rover rolled across "the dried up shimmering Serengeti plains," where they saw "cheetah slumbering under a thorn tree, and passed of course Ostrich, wildebeest, giraffe and all the charming antelopes."

Olduvai Gorge itself, from which Leakey and Evernden began digging up stones to be transported back to America for dating, produced in Vanne "a profound melancholy. It was so silent, so utterly remote, so dry, and there on the face of the cliff, for those who could read it, was the story of the centuries. One felt small, lost, finite."

When all the rock samples were finally gathered, the three of them returned to their second night's camp, at the bottom of the gorge, where Louis fixed for Vanne a "private bathroom (a bowl on a soap box) with mirror, and hot and cold water. We all had a good wash but even a good wash cannot remove the red dust of Africa from hair and nails and feet." They gathered wood, built a fire, and settled down for a "wonderful dinner" and an evening of sipping coffee in front of the fire before turning in for the night. At dawn the next day, they climbed the side of a cliff to watch the sunrise, and then, on the return trip, spent an additional day exploring the vast floor of Ngorongoro Crater and a final, glorious wandering, lingering, and viewing day traveling back to Nairobi.

In such a fashion, then, Vanne was caught in some of the drama and pleasure of Louis Leakey's life and personality, and an important friendship began. It was a straightforward and ordinary one at the time—but then (as Vanne may have begun to realize on the day she ran into Mary Leakey at the museum without quite recognizing who she was, until a significantly scowling Louis appeared on the stairs), no friendship with Louis could be entirely simple. "I have never," Vanne wrote to her mother and sisters after that minor epiphany, "been embroiled in so many intrigues, so many cross currents of fevered emotions, so many secrets to be kept from almost everyone, and so many comings and goings which may or may not be divulged. One's head literally reels with it all, and sometimes the only possible refuge is bed!!!!" Still, because Louis had followed through on his promise to think of

Jane paternally, he and Vanne now found that they shared at least one compelling mutual interest: the future of her young daughter and his young protégée.

They discussed the Brian problem, and they also considered Louis's long-standing plan to send Jane on a brief expedition to study chimpanzees at the edge of Lake Tanganyika. Louis was still applying for the necessary funding and still fretting about the obstacle erected by Geoffrey Browning, the district commissioner in Kigoma, who refused to allow any European woman into the Gombe Stream Chimpanzee Reserve "alone"—that is, without a suitable European companion. "Louis told me all this one day," Vanne once wrote. "I shall never know why I suddenly and without the slightest premeditation heard myself say how much I should like to go to Gombe." Vanne would thus serve as Jane's required companion.

But since Louis's attempts to find a grant had so far achieved nothing, it was, as Vanne explained in a letter to Danny, "impossible to forecast Jane's future." The sensible move was for Jane to return to England for a few months to rest and repair and prepare herself. She could take a job in London, and once again Leakey would help. "Louis is now busy getting Jane a job in London," Vanne wrote to the family in mid-November, "for the period after Christmas and before she comes out here again. He's just like a magician. Want a job? British Museum? Zoo? Natural History Museum?"

Vanne had gone to Kenya intending to stay only three months, and Jane had already planned to return with her to England. They booked their passage on British India's *Kenya*, to sail from Mombasa on November 30 and, after a passage through the Suez Canal and stops at Aden, Port Said, Malta, and Barcelona, finally descend the gangplank in Southampton on December 20, just in time for Christmas at The Birches.

Sally was to stay in the flat for another few weeks, until January 17, meeting her grandmother in the meanwhile and returning with her via Europe. Sally and some of Jane's friends at the museum had agreed to help resettle much of the menagerie in various new homes, except for the rat, who was soon back in place as a school science pet; Levi, who fell ill and died that December; Dinkie the hedgehog, who was released; and Boozy and Kip, who would be flown to England at the end of December to join the family in Bournemouth.

Vanne prepared her mother, Danny, in advance about Kip. "Now although at first sight Danny you may not entirely take to him because he dashes about in what may look to you a mouselike fashion, he is no more like a mouse than Rusty was, and in fact tiny though he is, his character is such that he makes himself felt in no uncertain fashion." Vanne illustrated her point with an example:

Imagine—two huge dogs are having a bit of a rough and tumble, beautiful little blonde Tana joins in, and perhaps the large fat Siamese so that there is a fearsome jumble of legs and frolicking bodies. Kip busily engaged about his pursuits at the far end of the room spies the fray, and immediately without thought he dashes into it, just ankle high to everyone, but so fierce that soon the dogs hide their heads from him and the cat leaps away. If he cannot get his own way he's likely to draw himself up to his full ridiculous height and scream defiance.

Jane bade farewell to the museum staff on Saturday morning, November 22, spent the evening washing and packing, and then left with Brian in his Land Rover at half past noon the next day. They were planning a last safari together. Vanne believed that her daughter would "say goodbye to Brian forever before we sail," and both Jane and Brian shared that depressing expectation.

Brian understood that Jane intended to return to Africa, perhaps within a few months, but if she had her way, she would be returning to a different place and in a new capacity, to follow through on the plan of studying wild chimpanzees on the shores of Lake Tanganyika. It was a crazy scheme, certainly, one that even Brian, who must have appreciated Jane's energy and endurance and her capacity for focused determination, considered improbable. Jane had told him of the plan only a couple of months earlier, and Brian knew enough of the area and situation to harbor some perfectly sensible misgivings. "At the time I very much doubted that she could live by herself in such a place with only a few Africans to assist her," he has recalled. Jane, after all, still knew very little about "life in the bush," and she still had not learned any Swahili. "Moreover, I happened to be familiar with some of the terrain farther south east of Kigoma on the shores of Lake Tanganyika, for I had spent several months there and knew that it was a difficult and little known country."

For the moment, in any case, they drove east in the direction of Mombasa, with the intention of having a final safari together at Tsavo National Park. They pulled up around six that evening at the park entrance. Tsavo was closed during the winter wet season, owing to the danger of washed-out roads, but after the park director examined a personal note from Louis Leakey, he "immediately spread his arms wide," as Jane wrote to Sally on December 1, "& said the Park was ours! Of course!" Thus, aside from a few game rangers, Jane and Brian were now possibly the only two people within 8,000 square miles of wilderness, and they drove out to a spot known as Mzima Springs.

"There one is, in dry almost desert country, sweltering hot, and surrounded by burnt looking scrub," Jane wrote. "Suddenly, before one's astonished eyes, there is a splash of luxuriant greenness—palm trees, flowers, bright green grass. You reach the place and getting out of the car, hear the music of rippling water. There, from the seemingly barren rocks, sweet ice cold water trickles out, across the water-worn pebbles, and so forms a most enchanting hippo pool." Soon, around a dozen enormous hippos "regarded us with their piggy little red eyes, waggling their stupid little red ears. One had the most horrible expression, and she turned her head as we came to the water's edge and gazed long and malevolently at us. The reason for her rage became apparent when a little toto popped up his head beside her. He too gazed at us, but so curiously. He was a little poppet. Then we saw an evil looking form slide into the water—Brian says there are very few croc and I was lucky to see one just there."

They had lunch, dangled their feet in the water and, in spite of a big notice that said BATHING PROHIBITED, had a quick bathe in a pool right above the hippo pool—first tossing in stones to assure themselves there were no crocodiles. Mzima means "alive" in Swahili, and the place was definitely alive, as Brian recalls, with a constant stream of animals passing through their camping spot to the water, "including numerous rhino, elephant, zebra, impala, hartebeest, and other game, while a chorus of lions roared around the clock." They camped overnight, and three times they were awakened by rhinoceros, one only ten yards away. Jane fled for the safety of the Land Rover, followed by Brian, but as she later wrote, "I can't describe properly the thrill of waking up & those tremendously loud sounding footsteps. The ground seems to shake. And seeing the huge beasts so close, ghostly in the moonlight. It was quite wonderful." In the morning, after a breakfast of tinned pears, they watched a great troop of baboons descend to the water. "One old dog sat, hands on his knees, regarding us, waiting to see what we were going to do. He looked so like an old budda on his throne."

From Tsavo they proceeded to the coast, paused for a day or two to splash in the surf at Malindi, and finally drove on to Mombasa. "I have NEVER enjoyed a week's holiday more in my whole long life," Jane summarized in her December 1 letter to Sally. As for Brian, he was "so absolutely charming this last week that I fell in love with him all over again—as I knew I would of course."

Vanne and her luggage arrived in Mombasa by train on Saturday, and on Sunday, Brian, joined by his mother and friends, accompanied Jane and Vanne onto the *Kenya* for the final round of hugs, kisses, and salutations. A band played, an anchor clanked, ropes were untied and tossed and drawn aboard, and a blaze of multicolored streamers was cast, fluttering, into the breeze. Washed in tears and the warm airs of the ocean, Jane and her mother waved vigorously as they left Africa, for a year or perhaps forever.

12

London Interlude

1959–1960

JANE WAS HAPPY to be home, in England and London, and she immediately went to St. James's Park to gaze at the ducks and then strolled along the Embankment to take a gander at the Chelsea artists and their work. It was so exciting to be walking in (as she wrote to a friend in Nairobi) "the greatest city in the world with the feeling that you are 'home' again." Back in Bournemouth, The Birches was "so exactly the same that I could hardly believe I had been away at all."

It was a cheerful, celebratory Christmas that year, with "no boozing!" which made for a wonderful contrast from Kenyan Christmases. But the technically sober household was still in a merry state, with the family and two visiting friends producing music: Judy alternating piano with clarinet, one of the friends playing a flute, the other a violin, and Olly singing beautifully. Jane, to keep her end up, walked about reciting her favorite lines from Shakespeare "very passionately to anyone who would listen—but mostly to no one in particular." And Uncle Eric, who had just gotten a tape recorder, secretly recorded and then played back an afternoon's auditory proceedings.

On New Year's Eve, Jane went back up to London, wandered around Piccadilly with a friend, and had a Chinese meal, and the next morning at 7:15 she collected Kip and Boozy from airport quarantine and returned with them to Bournemouth. The family cat, Figaro, was disconcerted by the arrival of two strange new animals, but the mongoose and the bush baby boldly made themselves at home anyway. Kip explored the terrain of house and garden in a few fast, furious minutes, while Boozy established home territory in the kitchen hallway, where she was "terribly friendly, leaping onto all and sundry with passionate embraces and loving kisses." Jane had caught a bad cold, and so she stationed herself on the floor in front of a hot coal fire in the family room, hands frozen, legs toasting, where she could listen to Judy practicing Beethoven on the piano in the other room and glance fondly over at Olly, sprawled asleep in her chair with a book about elephants spread open over her face.

On Monday, January 5, 1959, Jane once again took a train to London, where she settled into a new flat and saw about her job. Number 19, The Lodge, Kensington Park Gardens, was actually her father's flat, but he came and went according to his own inscrutable schedule, and the place was spacious enough to include at least two daughters. In fact, Judy, by then a student at the London Guildhall School of Music, was already living there, and Jane was soon settled in. She could fall asleep to the chiming clock of a big gray church across the road, and she could gaze out the window, over the tree-tops to a lovely view stretching away to Holland Park or into the iron-fenced, gated gardens directly below.

From the flat to work—at the London Zoo—was a forty-five-minute walk, and on her first day Jane arrived early and casually wandered around the zoo, looking at moose, elk, peacocks, and eagles. She saw, as she wrote home to her mother, a fish eagle, "looking so bedraggled compared to his lucky cousin" that she had seen, "proud and free," very recently, and a bate-leur eagle, "seen so very often soaring over the African landscape." She spent the whole afternoon listening to a strange yet familiar new world, to "the familiar roar, last heard across Serengeti Plains, of the hungry lion. The barking grunts of the deer, curious screeches and cries from the birds. Soon the hyaena will probably start laughing, and then I shall be really homesick!"

She worked next to the birdhouse, inside a large old building that had been the veterinarian's sanatorium until he was moved into modern quarters, whereupon the place was turned into the library and production studio for the Granada Television and Film Unit of the Zoological Society of London. The unit had been created in the mid-1950s with the intention of producing serious animal behavior films for scientific purposes and, for more general consumption, a weekly television program featuring inhabitants of the zoo. The TV show, a half-hour segment broadcast live every Sunday and known as *Zootime*, was produced and presented by Desmond Morris, a promising and telegenic young zoologist who had been doing research at Oxford University on bird courtship and display but in 1956 was persuaded to leave that post to become head of the unit. His wife, Ramona, became a researcher for the show.

Desmond had been lured to London with the promise that he could make those serious animal behavior films, but instead he found himself becoming a television personality with a successful and demanding weekly show to think about. Frustrated by this unforeseen development, he threatened to resign, thus persuading the zoo administration to make him curator of mammals, with his own research department and Ph.D. students, and to enlarge the Granada Television and Film Unit. With a new viewing theater, editors, and cameraman, the unit began attending in earnest to the more serious, scientific aspect of its mission while continuing to broadcast *Zootime*. Desmond still ran and presented that show, but by January 1, 1959, just as Jane was about to start work at Granada, he moved into his new office in a new building as curator of mammals, although Ramona stayed on at the unit to continue doing background research for the television show and manage a library of black-and-white films on animal behavior.

Ramona was officially the unit's film librarian, and she had hired Jane as her assistant, mainly to carry out the tedious job of shot listing: viewing all the library's cans of films and cataloguing all the animal shots according to species and behavior. Ramona remembers Jane's introductory interview in early January—she was wearing her mother's fur coat. And Desmond, who seldom had occasion to wander into the Granada building once he became curator of mammals, still vividly remembers dancing with Jane at the 1959 staff Christmas party, held on December 18 in the television studio. "What Ramona and I are always sort of ashamed to admit," he recently told me, "is that neither of us, in fact nobody in the unit, saw Jane's potential. We, none of us, realized that she was going to become the enormous success that she did later. She was very attractive, a beautiful young blonde, and she was working away doing boring shot-listing jobs in the library. But she didn't make anything special about her passion for apes. We knew that she'd been to Africa or something, but she didn't sort of say, 'I'm dreaming of. . . .' There was no 'I want to be a great pioneer of chimpanzee research.' None of that. She did her job."

Perhaps Jane was memorable mainly for showing up for work with a pet mongoose and a bush baby. Boozy was given a nice big cage at the unit that spring and was soon briefly featured in a film. By October, Kip was trying his hand at show business as well, appearing in a significant role in a film about animal play.

Jane maintained a sporadic correspondence with her friend Bernard Verdcourt, a botanist who had arrived in Nairobi to direct the herbarium associated with the Coryndon Museum during the summer of 1958. At some point in 1959, Bernard traveled to London to conduct research at Kew Gardens; he occasionally visited Jane and gave her a few small plants with which to decorate her office space. Then in November, back in Kenya once more, he sent by air freight a male bush baby who was meant to be a companion for Boozy. Jane named the male Bishop and (as she soon wrote to Bernard) took him in his traveling "house" to the unit for a first introduction to Boozy, who "in a very forward and immodest fashion, leapt into his house, growling, and terrified him. I'm sure he thinks her a brazen hussy!"

The pair had an on-again, off-again relationship. On that first day, brazen Boozy decided to lick bashful Bishop all over. ("He was terrified, but loved being kissed.") But within a few days they had begun to fight viciously. Jane, afraid they would kill each other, tried leaving them together in a strange place with their cages touching, but in December she finally placed Boozy under the care of an acquaintance in Oxford, where the pet was "thoroughly spoilt" (according to a January 21 letter to Bernard) and fed baby mice for three months. In mid-February, Boozy came back to Granada and was briefly featured on a television show having to do with primate hands; late in the day, Jane took her in to meet Bishop once more. She let them both out of their cages, expecting a fight. Instead they started licking each other—before being placed back into their respective cages for the night. Jane patiently expanded on that approach, following a late-afternoon, two-hour visiting session with a night in separate cages, for four days. On the fifth day, keeping her fingers crossed, she left them in the same cage overnight and found in the morning that all was well. Two evenings later they were mating.

Aside from the mongoose and bush babies, Jane took a pet budgerigar named Tango to work. This smart little Australian parakeet—greenish yellow, with blue cheeks and tail feathers—stayed outside his cage all day long, and when Jane was typing would hop on her head or peck at her moving fingers.

At lunchtime, Jane loved wandering around the zoo—although, as she wrote to Bernard Verdcourt, "there are some animals which I can't bear to see caged, especially the African ones." She made friends with the gardener, who brought her roses in the summer, and with some of the animal caretakers. One of the keepers let her spend time inside the cage with "my best boy friend": Alex the orangutan. "I really do adore them—if Orangs weren't so difficult to watch in the wild I should really love to study their habits. They are charming creatures—when young, anyway." She would also go to the birdhouse to collect food for Bishop, and on occasion the head keeper allowed her to feed grapes and mealworms to Horatio, the zoo's giant hornbill. Horatio was actually a very tame bird who would sometimes try to return the favor if he liked the person feeding him. Grapes, Jane discovered, were more fun in that regard than mealworms.

Back in Kenya, meanwhile, Louis Leakey had still been unable to locate an institutional sponsor for his proposed Chimpanzee Project, and so he finally turned away from the typical sources of funding to ask for a grant from his atypical American friend Leighton Wilkie, an imaginative and practical man who in 1933 had invented the metal-cutting band saw and then made a fortune through his DoAll Company, which manufactured and distributed cutting machines. At one point in his career, Wilkie created a mobile museum of tools, "Civilization Through Tools," and in 1951 he and two brothers established a philanthropic organization, the Wilkie Brothers Foundation. Then, while touring southern Africa in a large and well-appointed mobile home in 1955, he attended as a nonprofessional observer the third Pan-African Congress on Prehistory, held that July at Livingstone, Northern Rhodesia (now Zambia). The meeting included some seventy African-based scientists, most of them committed to understanding human prehistory through prehistorical artifacts, and like many other conference attendees, Wilkie was particularly impressed by two presentations.

The first was a paper by Raymond A. Dart of the University of the Witwatersrand, South Africa. Three decades earlier Dart had discovered in a block of quarried limestone the fossilized brain cast, skull, and facial fragments of a fascinating creature: about six years old, according to the teeth, and combining in a striking fashion the features of human and ape. This was the first in a veritable flood of fossil discoveries that would map the ancient existence of a widely distributed group of creatures with human posture, humanoid faces and teeth, and ape-sized brains. Dart named his newly discovered hominid *Australopithecus,* or Southern Ape, since the first fossil was found in southern Africa. In his 1955 paper at Livingstone, he described the evidence for an australopithecine osteodontokeratic (bone, tooth, and horn) culture. He described the analysis of hundreds of thousands of fossilized mammalian bone fragments found in the limestone among australopithecine fossils, and he suggested that those human precursors were using mammalian skeletal material as weapons — as tools of war. The skeletons of other mammals, Dart insisted, would have provided the australopithecines with "an adequate predaceous armamentarium," which thereby constructed the "foundations of that particulate anatomical and physiological experience which, in my opinion, was an essential apprenticeship for the ultimate acquisition by man of speech." By wielding bones as killing tools, in short, our apelike ancestors began their gradual march into the human present.

Louis Leakey, who served as president of the 1955 Pan-African Congress, gave the other memorable presentation. At the urging of some delegates, he agreed to demonstrate how to skin and butcher a freshly killed animal with stone tools. To provide a specimen, a delegate who lived in the area went hunting one evening, shot a small antelope, and put it in his kitchen before retiring for the night. Next morning he discovered that his cook had already skinned it and was starting to cook the meat, so he shot a second antelope, which was left under guard at the office of the Rhodes Livingstone Museum that night and in the morning taken outside, into the museum courtyard. In the shade of a tree, Louis knelt beside the carcass and set to work, starting with some blocks of flint that had been softened by an overnight soaking in the courtyard fountain. Using two of those pieces, he chipped out a rough hand ax, a chopper of the sort he was finding at Olduvai, and began to skin the carcass. As the work became more demanding, he paused to produce a second tool, a cleaver, sharp and refined enough to finish the job. Finally, Louis deftly chipped out a sharp, single-edged blade and with that instrument cut the skinned antelope into pieces small enough to cook. Just as he was finishing, someone in the audience standing around him shouted out, "Now what about eating a bit?" Without hesitation, Louis picked up a leg and bit off a piece. His audience was "amazed," according to his biographer Sonia Cole, by this demonstration of "how quickly it was possible to make the necessary equipment and butcher an animal."

Raymond Dart was one of the patriarchs of African paleontology, and Leighton Wilkie was so impressed by his presentation that after the conference he began underwriting, via the Wilkie Foundation, the scientist's studies in South Africa. He also began funding some of Leakey's work, starting with a check for $1,000 in 1955 and another for the same amount in 1957 to help with the digging at Olduvai. The support continued—another $1,000 in 1958 and again in 1959.

On February 12, 1959, after Louis received notice of that year's grant from the Wilkie Foundation, he wrote to Leighton to thank him and to ask for another. The second grant would underwrite his Chimpanzee Project in Tanganyika, which was supposed to begin in September of that year. Louis included a proposal that mentioned Jane—as one of two "research workers"—but naturally avoided mentioning her secretarial background and lack of a scientific one. Miss Jane Morris-Goodall "has worked in Kenya with Dr. Leakey," it informed Wilkie, and "is at present doing further training in London. She has already shown considerable ability in getting into close contact with wild animals, and in living under very rough conditions in the wilds." Louis mentioned that Jane would in addition be conducting a shorter study of vervet monkeys on an island in Lake Victoria. The vervet monkey study would cost around £250, he estimated, while the four-month-long Chimpanzee Project would require only £800, which would cover living expenses, no salaries, for the two persons concerned.

In a quick, enthusiastic response written on February 18, Leighton Wilkie noted that the foundation was prepared to send $3,000 to underwrite the "very interesting" Chimpanzee Project. He was in fact so enthusiastic about

Leakey's idea that he also offered to lend, for chimp-study purposes, a large Jeep and a custom-built land yacht. The Jeep was of a "new wide tread style" with a cab over the engine and "two spacious beds which can be opened up and covered with a canvas canopy," as well as a built-in 2,500-watt generator, sufficient to supply power for cooking in an electric oven and on an electric frying pan and for boiling water in the built-in water tank, not to mention running the power winches at both ends. Wilkie understood that the Gombe Stream Chimpanzee Reserve was situated in very rugged country, but he wished to assure Louis that the Jeep "will have the latest facilities for getting over rough ground."

The second vehicle, the land yacht, might require some assistance from the first in order to negotiate the most formidable terrain, but once it was located within the chimpanzee reserve, it would provide a unique facility for researchers. In order to avoid alarming any wild animals, it was going to be perfectly disguised as an elephant: wrapped inside a gray, rubberized skin and fronted with a full-size artificial elephant head, currently being produced by a Hollywood firm that had supplied similar creations to the film and television industries. Altogether, Wilkie continued, he was convinced that the yacht could be camouflaged well enough that it would "even fool elephants," and it certainly ought to allow a photographer to approach wild baboons and chimpanzees closely. "Since elephants," he summarized, "may be found in nearly every environment of East Africa, and since they have no enemies except man, we have a feeling that our scheme will work."

Louis declined the wide-tread Jeep and elephantized land yacht but accepted the money.

That good news was soon overshadowed by some of the greatest news of Louis's entire professional career. On July 17, 1959, Louis and Mary were starting their yearly excavations at Olduvai, and they had for the first time decided to start digging in the lowest strata of the gorge, Bed I. Louis was ill with the flu, and he stayed in bed that day while Mary went off with their two dalmatians to sniff around some nearby Bed I exposures. At a place near the junction of the main and side gorges, she casually looked over some recently rain-exposed materials on the surface until her gaze rested on a fragment of fossilized bone projecting up to the surface.

"It seemed to be part of a skull," Mary wrote in her autobiography, *Disclosing the Past,* "including a mastoid process (the bony projection below the ear). It had a hominoid look, but the bones seemed enormously thick—too thick, surely. I carefully brushed away a little of the deposit, and then I could see parts of the two large teeth in place in the upper jaw. They *were* hominid. It was a hominid skull, apparently *in situ,* and there was a lot of it there. I rushed back to camp to tell Louis, who leaped out of bed and then we were soon back at the site, looking at my find together."

In Langata the Leakeys happened to live next door to a successful husband-and-wife team of wildlife and natural history cinematographers, Armand and Michaela Denis, and that summer they had agreed to allow the Denises' cameraman, Des Bartlett, to film some of their excavations. Bartlett, accompanied by his wife and young daughter, was due to arrive in another couple of days, so Louis and Mary had to content themselves with a superficial examination of the half-buried skull fragment before covering it over gently with a protective pile of stones. After Bartlett arrived and set up his cameras, the digging began in earnest, and for the rest of their time at Olduvai that summer, until August 6, the excavations concentrated on slowly and methodically removing, sifting, and washing a substantial volume of soil around the first discovered piece. Ultimately they recovered four hundred fragments, which Mary painstakingly glued together into three major interlocking pieces that together presented a haunting visage, at once apelike and humanoid, with an upper palate notable for its large grinding molars.

Louis was at first "rather disappointed" with the thing, according to Mary's account, because he believed it might be yet another sample from one of the already thoroughly dug-up group of australopithecines. By that time Raymond Dart, his associate Phillip Tobias, and several of their colleagues had retrieved fossil specimens from more than three hundred individual members of what was being called the Australopithecinae subfamily, divided into two genera, the *Australopithecus* and *Paranthropus* lines. If Louis and Mary were holding a fossilized sample from a known australopithecine, it would be interesting, of course, but not the sort of spectacular discovery he was hoping for. It was still a superb find, though. A substantial portion of the skull was recovered in good condition, and the excavations also turned up a leg bone (tibia) from the same skeleton, as well as many stone tools and numerous bones from archaic antelopes, birds, amphibians, pigs, reptiles, and rodents. All the larger animal bones were scattered about, whereas the pieces from the hominid skull were embedded within a single piece of earth one foot wide, one foot long, and six inches deep. Expansion and contraction of the surrounding clay would account for the skull's localized fragmentation over time, while the scattering of tools and all the other bones powerfully suggested that the owner of the skull was the maker and manipulator of the tools, used to prepare and consume the animals.

Finally, after an extended comparison of his skull with samples from the two known australopithecine genera, Louis concluded that he and Mary had found the remains of an individual from a third genus and, as he was soon to announce, "the oldest yet discovered maker of stone tools." To name the new genus, Louis combined the ancient Arabic name for East Africa and the Greek for "human." For species identification, he Latinized the last name of Charles Boise, who was among his steadiest financial backers at the time. The great discovery of July 1959 thus became *Zinjanthropus boisei.*

Louis immediately moved to introduce "Zinj" to the world at large. He wrote a brief piece for the August 15 issue of *Nature*, although a printers' strike in London held up that announcement until September. Later in August, he and Mary placed their three major pieces of fossilized skull into a wooden box and flew with the box on Mary's lap to Leopoldville (now Kinshasa) in the Belgian Congo (now the Democratic Republic of Congo) for an opening presentation on August 22 at the fourth Pan-African Congress on Prehistory. At the congress, the Zinj skull created a great buzzing commotion, although many delegates expressed serious reservations at Dr. Leakey's insistence that it belonged to a new genus. Still, the distinguished Raymond A. Dart declared himself very pleased about the discovery, particularly that it had been made by Louis and Mary. Dart's younger colleague, Phillip Tobias, was also fascinated by Zinj, and in a smart gesture of collegial generosity, Louis offered Tobias the job of writing a technical report and analysis. The offer was accepted, according to Mary, "with amazement and delight." (Tobias ultimately presented an extremely thorough analysis concluding, alas, that the fossil was a specimen from one of the two already well-known genera, albeit a new species, and thus he changed the skull's name to *Australopithecus boisei,* an alteration that Louis finally accepted.)

Louis and Mary had privately taken to calling their skull Dear Boy, while Tobias accidentally created a popular name for it during the Pan-African Congress by noting that the enormous molars made it look like a child's wooden toy, the Nutcracker Man. So while the rather obscure and academic debates about naming and grouping the skull kept all the specialists entertained, for the public at large this same fossil became simply Nutcracker Man.

The discovery of Zinj or Dear Boy or Nutcracker Man was widely publicized (thanks in part to Des Bartlett's film showing the fossil's methodical excavation and reassembly, presented on BBC television as part of the Armand and Michaela Denis series *On Safari*), and it soon helped elevate Louis and Mary to the realm of scientific celebrities. Louis had already been invited as a featured speaker, one of a group of fifty distinguished international scientists, to celebrate the centennial of the publication of Darwin's *Origin of Species*, scheduled to take place from November 24 to November 28 at the University of Chicago. That institution sent Louis a plane ticket to make the journey, his first to the United States, and he took advantage of the free passage to spend a short time in England, taking along Dear Boy in his box. In London, Louis theatrically presented the wonderful thing to a packed, tremendously enthusiastic assembly at the Academy of Sciences — walking into the room carrying the leather-strapped wooden box under his arm, setting down and unstrapping the box, pulling out the three pieces of skull, each in its own plastic bag, unbagging and then assembling them, encasing the finished skull inside glass plates from an old aquarium, and finally proceeding to tell his audience all about (in the language of an attending newspaper reporter) "Mr. Nutcracker." Jane, Judy, and Vanne attended the lecture and afterward had dinner with the distinguished man. It was, Jane wrote to Bernard Verdcourt on November 7, "the gayest meal I've had for a long time. He was in a wonderful mood."

Louis expanded on that happy moment by informing Jane that the grant from Leighton Wilkie had finally come through. As she relayed the news to Bernard, "the Chimp project is fixed for next June."

Louis wisely left the box and three precious pieces of fossil locked away in London and then, taking only a plaster cast of the original palate, flew to the United States, where he found an overwhelmingly positive reception once again. At the University of Chicago, he spoke on "The Origin of the Genus *Homo*," using that opportunity to introduce his discovery and to remind everyone that Darwin himself had speculated that the African great apes were probably humankind's closest modern relatives and that Africa was the "most likely continent in which to search for evidence of human evolution." After Chicago he traveled on to Salt Lake City, lecturing twice at the University of Utah. Local notices informed Mormons that they were allowed to attend "but must not believe." A number believed anyway, apparently, since the distinguished paleontologist was invited back to the University of Utah several times during the next decade, finally in 1971 to receive an honorary degree.

Louis gave a total of sixty-six lectures at seventeen different universities and scientific institutions during this trip, but his major coup happened at National Geographic Society headquarters in Washington, D.C., where he met with the society's president, Melville Bell Grosvenor. After he and Mary had finished their excavation of Zinj in the summer of 1959, Louis had written to the society, proposing an article on the subject for its glossy popular magazine. The society turned down his proposal at that time, but Armand Denis had been able to arrange the meeting with Grosvenor.

Louis appears to have been eloquent and convincing, and Grosvenor penciled him into the schedule of a November 9 meeting of the National Geographic's Research and Exploration Committee. "It was voted," the minutes tell us, "that the Committee recommend a grant to Dr. Leakey of $20,200." In return the society would acquire exclusive American publication rights to the Zinj story, as well as permission to send out its own writer and photographer.

Financing for the Leakeys' research had until then come in the form of regular but comparatively small grants from a number of sources, altogether neither steady nor substantial enough to keep Louis and Mary from running regular overdrafts on their personal bank accounts or, more significantly, to enable them to expand their Olduvai work into the major scientific operation it could be. The National Geographic grant marked the beginning of a long-term relationship between Louis and Mary Leakey and the society, and it lifted the family operation out of its genteel poverty. Relying now on a substantial team of assistants and laborers, Louis and Mary were able to put in some 92,000 person-hours at Olduvai during the next year, in a single season doubling the total amount of time and labor invested in the operation over the previous thirty years. And Louis's first *National Geographic* article, "Finding the World's Earliest Man," which appeared in the magazine's September 1960 issue, demonstrated clearly the Leakey drawing power and marked the rise of Louis's personal star.

Louis left the United States in the middle of December 1959, flying back to Kenya. Once again he stopped briefly in London. Jane reported in a December 19 letter to Bernard that "I saw Leakey during the past 2 or 3 days—he took Ma & I out to dinner, & to the theatre." He also confirmed at that time that the chimpanzee expedition to Tanganyika was a certainty: "My 'chimping' is all fixed—honestly Bernard, if I stop & think about it, I get simply terrified—not of the actual job, but of the responsibility—at the Primate Research meeting in America Leakey told everyone he had a person who was ideal for the task & better than anyone they could find. He tells me his reputation is at stake."

As we have seen, Louis had received the grant for the Chimpanzee Project several months earlier, in March. But now, and in spite of his reassurances to Jane, he may have been contemplating a serious betrayal. While he was in the States, he had attended a dinner in Cincinnati given by George Barbour, a geology professor and the dean of students at the University of Cincinnati. Barbour was a kind, sympathetic man who had invited a young woman named Cathryn Hosea to the event. He telephoned her, as Hosea remembers, to say, "A friend of mine, Louis Leakey, is joining us for dinner" and to express the opinion that Dr. Leakey might be able to connect her with a job opportunity.

Hosea immediately liked Louis. He seemed "so kind, such a gentleman." Following the meal, he lectured at the University of Cincinnati, and she was overwhelmed, struck not only by his greatness but by his patience and apparent humility, his "incredible willingness to stay and be asked questions. If a child wanted to ask a question, he would get down on the floor to give an answer."

Louis knew by then that Cathryn Hosea wanted to get to Africa and was looking for some kind of anthropology job, and at the end of the Cincinnati lecture he told her he was going to the University of Chicago next and arranged to meet her there. She attended the Chicago lecture, and then they met in his hotel room. They sat on the bed, talking about Africa. Louis had long before developed his skills in simple performance tricks, minor acts of prestidigitation and string figure manipulations, which had served him well when meeting new people in Africa and elsewhere. Now, talking to the young woman, he pulled out some string and began demonstrating a few string figure stories. At the same time he told her about a group of chimpanzees living in a very remote place beside a lake, and then about his desire to send someone there to study the apes in their natural environment. Years ago he had sent a man out there, Louis declared, but the poor fellow simply did not have the staying power and patience. Now Louis had decided to send a woman, because women had more patience. It would be an exciting, demanding job in a very remote, very inaccessible place, and therefore she would have to have her appendix out. Was she prepared to do that?

While continuing to demonstrate the shape-shifting string figures, Louis also mentioned his young secretary at the Coryndon Museum. As Hosea recalls the words, he said, "There is a young girl in my office who wants the job in the worst way. But she doesn't have the credentials."

Louis went on. Miss Hosea would need someone, another non-African, to accompany her. That was, unfortunately, one of the requirements of the stuffy colonial administrator, though ultimately not so significant. More importantly, she would always have an African support staff, and therefore in spite of the remoteness of the place she would be safe and well cared for as she studied the wild chimpanzees. It was going to be a unique, extremely challenging job.

At some point in this discussion, Louis stopped talking and fiddling with the string figures, handed her the string, and said, "I want you to do what I just did." It was a typical L.S.B. Leakey test of observational abilities, and she repeated the sequence of figures he had just produced. He said, "You'll do just fine. How would you like to come to Africa to do an ape study?"

Louis thus offered her the very job he had long been promising to Jane. He seemed to be entirely serious about the offer, and during the months that followed he maintained a steady correspondence on the subject with Cathryn Hosea while keeping it secret from Jane in London. His explanation to Hosea was straightforward and reasonable: she had credentials—an undergraduate degree in anthropology. Louis, of course, had an iconoclast's intuitive disdain for the abstract navigations represented by an academic degree, and he understood only too well that the qualities fundamental to success in a long-term field study were passion and character. The job would require above all an unteachable endurance and a high tolerance for isolation, tedium, and danger. Jane had already shown that she was a suitable candidate on that level. She could do the job. But, after all, what would that job mean if no one was interested in the results? Whoever went out to conduct this project would be representing him, and she would need not merely to find the apes, to watch them, to learn something about them. She would also have to succeed in convincing others, scientists above all, of the value of what she had done. How could that young, pretty, enthusiastic, animal-loving former secretary of his, now living in London, possibly translate any observations from the forests of Tanganyika into a result that would be respected by the scientific community at large?

Jane, meanwhile, was keeping her own secret, and although it was not a betrayal, she recognized that Louis, if he learned of it, might be disturbed.

The secret's name was Robert Young, and she met him at the Troubadour, a coffeehouse at 265 Old Brampton Road, Earl's Court. The Troubadour was a rambling place with exposed beams on the ceiling, antiques on the walls, and a downstairs room with pillows on the floor and a small stage where poets could be poetic and musicians musical. Jane and Robert—she would soon call him "Bob"—both happened to attend a downstairs concert of flamenco guitar sometime in the autumn of 1959. He was twenty-six, a classically handsome actor, who, as he recently recalled, "saw her across a crowded room." He went over, spoke to her, and discovered "an instant liking." Jane, he soon decided, was "an extremely interesting, fascinating woman." She was ambitious. She had plans, goals, the courage to do whatever she wanted to do, an entire attitude that was, in his opinion, "way ahead of her time."

The attraction was mutual. One Monday evening, probably in late January or early February, Robert went to Jane's flat, and while Jane, Judy, and a friend named Chris worked on dinner in the kitchen, he spoke to Mortimer in the sitting room, asking in an old-fashioned way, "May I marry your daughter?" Mortimer looked at him blankly and then said, "Which one?"

Robert was appropriately amused. According to Jane's account of the exchange, written soon after in a letter home, Mortimer then "frantically" reviewed all the things a father was expected to say at such a moment. He wanted to know Robert's profession and how he might expect to support a family. Robert said he was an actor. Mortimer said he thought that was a "rather precarious" way to make a living. Robert replied that motor racing was a precarious sort of activity too, and when Jane's father insisted that for him motor racing was merely a hobby, Robert replied that a hobby in which you could kill yourself was even worse. Jane, Judy, and Chris eventually went in to find the two men engaged in "deep and happy conversation."

Jane recalls telephoning her mother soon after that event to say, "Guess what? Your daughter has gotten herself engaged." Robert then traveled down to Bournemouth to meet the rest of the family, and Danny wrote in her diary afterward that "we all found Robert charming. He and Jane seem to get on very well together, but I wonder how it will work out. Never mind. So long as they are happy nothing else matters." The uncertain tone of that comment suggests an underlying mood that may have been general among the family. Robert remembers meeting Vanne and finding a subtle barrier of polished reserve—in his words, "When I walked through the door, her face didn't light up with pleasure."

Possibly the family had doubts about the stability and practicality of Robert Young's chosen profession. Of course, there was the more obvious concern about how his future as an actor might integrate with Jane's plans to study chimpanzees in Africa. He was fascinated by her zoological interests and ambitions, but "I wasn't exactly the sort of guy to be sitting in a tent watching his beloved with chimpanzees for days on end." At the time, though, no one imagined that Jane would spend the rest of her life studying chimpanzees in Africa, and the plan they discussed among themselves was that she would go to Africa, do her research, then return to find work in England or Europe, perhaps take a position at a zoo somewhere.

In a March 3, 1960, letter to Bernard Verdcourt, Jane confessed that although she and Robert got along "really wonderfully in every way, and our interests are almost identical," nevertheless "our occupations just couldn't be further apart—of all the unlikely things, he acts." She continued, "He, of course, wants to marry me before I go out, but this I will not do. First I have got to find out whether I can live without Africa. He says he is willing for me to go on going back to Africa to do field studies for as long as I like, but somehow this doesn't seem right. He knows that this particular study, even if it takes 3 years, must be completed."

So a new love interest and the engagement were complicating developments that spring. At the same time, though, Jane was also preparing in earnest for her chimpanzee study. Back in October 1959 she had happened to run into John Napier, a comparative anatomist interested in primates and employed by the Royal Free Hospital of Medicine. Napier came to the unit to view one of the films in progress, and she knew him by reputation, having once or twice heard Louis mention the name. So she talked to the man and soon found him to be interested in her plan to study chimpanzees. Napier agreed to give her a two- to three-month private tutorial, a course in primatology (as Jane explained in a letter to Verdcourt) "specially designed for me — he has already given me a lot of books. It is the one thing which makes all the difference to my contemplation of the job before me."

By the end of March 1960, Jane had quit work at Granada Television and Film and returned home for a couple of weeks before beginning that personalized tutorial in primate studies. In the meantime, she had been poring over the books and papers Napier had given her, focusing on earlier primate research to see what she might learn.

In the early twentieth century, a few people, most obviously Carl Akeley of the American Museum of Natural History and Harold Coolidge of Harvard University, had traveled to Africa as members of specimen-collecting expeditions that collected several dead gorillas, and at the same time a few others had initiated original studies of the behavior and psychology of apes in captivity. In 1912 the Prussian Academy of Sciences established a primate research station at Tenerife, in the Canary Islands, where Wolfgang Köhler experimentally documented creative problem-solving among chimpanzees: moments of apparent insight and the spontaneous fashioning of useful tools and makeshift ladders to retrieve remotely dangled bananas. During the same period, Robert Yerkes of Yale University acquired what he believed were two baby chimpanzees (one may actually have been a pygmy chimpanzee, or bonobo) and began raising them. In a 1916 article in *Science*, Yerkes described his vision of an international string of primate breeding and research stations in the warm parts of the world, where apes and monkeys, as "infrahuman organisms," could be encouraged to "contribute importantly to human welfare" and thereby become "servants of science." He then founded, in 1930, the Yale Laboratories for Primate Biology at Orange Park, Florida, conducting behavioral experiments with apes as a means of thinking about the biologically based aspects of human psychology.

Robert Yerkes believed that apes were guided by a constellation of human-style emotions and that they were probably capable of rational and symbolic thought. Indeed, there was "no obvious reason," he once wrote, "why the chimpanzee and the other great apes should not talk." To test that proposition, a chimpanzee baby named Gua was taken from the Orange Park station and placed in the home of the psychologist Winthrop Kellogg and his wife, Luella, who proceeded for several months to raise him alongside their own infant son, Donald. Donald eventually began speaking while

Gua remained mute, although the Kelloggs believed that he understood the meaning of around one hundred words; the experiment was prematurely terminated, rumor has it, when the human baby began making chimp noises.

Determined also to examine the natural behavior of wild apes, Yerkes sent a young Yale psychologist named Harold C. Bingham to the Parc National Albert in the eastern Belgian Congo to study mountain gorillas in the summer of 1929. Bingham, accompanied by his wife, Lucille, and a group of African assistants that at one point included some forty porters, spent about two months in the field, following gorilla trails and examining nests. The Binghams did watch gorillas directly on a few occasions, but their observations were very limited and also biased by the observers' fear of the observed, particularly on the day when an agitated male gorilla provoked an anxious Harold Bingham to shoot him dead.

Following the Bingham expedition, Yerkes sent another Yale psychologist, Henry W. Nissen, into the bush of French Guinea (now Guinea) for nine weeks in 1930 in pursuit of chimpanzees. Nissen hired three African assistants and a half-dozen porters and guides and then set out on his self-described "one-man expedition" to find the wild apes. Since there were no good precedents for observing apes in their natural state, he had little idea how to go about it, and so he tried whatever he could think of, a trial-and-error approach that he later described fancifully as a "gradually" acquired set of "methods and techniques" based on "time-honored modes of naturalistic work."

Among those time-honored modes, Nissen tried hiding in blinds, only to discover that the "sharp-sighted" chimpanzees were sensitive to "artificial anomalies in the bush." He considered using "lures" (that is, the "presentation of chimpanzee delicacies at the same spot over long periods of time") but decided against that approach because of time limitations. He was certain that it would be easy to surround a group of chimpanzees with a circle of hired African helpers and inhibit the apes' movement for a day or so, long enough to acquire basic information about group size and composition, age, sex, and so on—but the few times he tried to encircle chimps with forty hired Africans his plans were thwarted, he thought, by the "inexperience and stupidity" of his crew (and also, perhaps, by the pandemonium created when he fired his gun, lit grass fires, and with a club-wielding gang of helpers pulled a baby chimp out of the trees). Nissen found ordinary tracking of the apes discouragingly unproductive, since the ground was usually too hard for footprints and any trails pressed into the grass or brush seemed to go every which way. Ultimately the American psychologist resorted to listening for the hoots and cries of chimps and the excited drumming noises they made by kicking and punching tree roots, then following those sounds. When he got close enough, he would leave his African assistants behind and approach by himself, steadily and stealthily, and sometimes he was able to watch a few chimpanzees through binoculars.

Nine weeks was too short a time to learn much of anything reliable or significant about wild apes, and some of Nissen's conclusions were simplistic or simply wrong (such as "the chimpanzee is nomadic, having no permanent home" and "the chimpanzee group is composed of from four to fourteen animals"). But because his was the first methodical study of wild chimps, many of the observations were at least useful by virtue of their novelty (chimpanzees sleep at night in arboreal nests, rise early and are awake during the day, spend a good deal of their waking time searching for fruits and nuts and other foods, are afraid of water, and so on). And even when his commentary amounted to a bland recitation of the obvious, the Yale investigator had, following Yerkes' example, perfected a ratiocinative writing style that regularly managed to obscure that problem ("Urine was not found as often as were feces which fact is easily explainable by the difference in the nature of the two substances").

Finally, Robert Yerkes launched a third Yale psychologist into the tropics in pursuit of primates. This time the psychologist was a young man named Clarence Ray Carpenter, and the primate species was a monkey known as the mantled howler monkey, which Carpenter began studying on Panama's Barro Colorado Island in 1931. Carpenter observed the howler monkeys and later spider monkeys on Barro Colorado until 1935; in 1937 he joined an expedition to Thailand and commenced a four-month study of white-handed gibbons; and later in the decade he created his own primate research site by releasing a few hundred imported rhesus macaques on a Puerto Rican island. Although his chosen primates were monkeys and gibbons, not great apes, Carpenter was the first and until the 1950s the only person to conduct a successful long-term scientific field study of wild primates.

Which of her predecessors' limited studies did Jane become familiar with during the spring of 1960? She certainly read Wolfgang Köhler's 1925 summary of his work on captive chimpanzees, *The Mentality of Apes*. That book, she once informed me, "was my bible. He thought of chimps in the right way, and I still count his writings as giving some of the best ever descriptions of chimp personality." As for Robert Yerkes' pair of protégées who tried to study great apes in Africa, she did not bother with Harold C. Bingham's 1932 report, *Gorillas in a Native Habitat*, which mainly describes not finding gorillas; she did review Henry W. Nissen's earnest and antique 1931 monograph, *A Field Study of the Chimpanzee*. She was, however, "shocked" at Nissen, "traveling with all those porters and seeing nothing!" And at one point she lent his report to Robert Young, who told her, as she reported back to Vanne, that "the more he reads the more worried about me he gets."

While Jane was studiously preparing herself that spring, Louis stopped communicating. In fact, ever since his trip through London on the way back to Nairobi in December, as Jane wrote to Bernard on March 3, 1960, "I have not heard a word from Leakey, and nor has Mummy, and we are getting a little worried. What is he doing at present? Is he digging or politics-ing, or what? The old devil. I dare say all the arrangements are satisfactorily clear in his own mind, down to the last detail, but maybe he doesn't realize that we should like to know just a few of them. Please don't mention it to him though—that would offend him, I'm sure."

While Louis had gone silent in his correspondence with Jane, in fact, he was still exchanging letters with Cathryn Hosea, who was agonizing over that amazing job offer of studying wild chimpanzees in Tanganyika. The young American longed to go to Africa, but she had never been before, and the lack of a concrete vision of what the project might entail, combined with Louis's unreasonable insistence that she commit herself for five years, finally led her to decline what she nevertheless recognized was "the opportunity of a lifetime."

Jane's engagement to Robert Young was made public in the "Court and Social" section of the *Daily Telegram and Morning Post* on May 13, 1960: "The engagement is announced between Robert William, eldest son of Mr. and Mrs. R. W. Young, of The Orchard House, Charlton Kings, Cheltenham, and Valerie Jane, elder daughter of Major and Mrs. M. H. Morris-Goodall of 10, Durley Chine Road, Bournemouth." Around the same time, Louis finally contacted Jane to inform her that preparations for the chimpanzee expedition were complete. And so, on May 31, 1960, she said goodbye to Robert. It was a temporary separation, they assured each other. As she and Vanne left for the airport in a car, there were "desperate tears," as Robert remembers, but he consoled himself with thoughts of her return and their eventual marriage.

13

Lolui Island and the Road to Gombe

1960

MOTHER AND DAUGHTER took a four-prop Vickers Viscount 833 out of London, ate a chicken lunch over the Alps, and, after refueling in Rome, arrived in Nairobi the next day. Eve Mitchell put them up in her house on Protectorate Road for two nights, and on the third they moved into a small hotel, the Ainsworth, near the museum, waiting for permission from the Tanganyikan authorities to begin their journey to Gombe.

In a letter postmarked June 7, Vanne told the family in England her impression of what happened next: "It came through on the telephone just now & was most disappointing. Leakey had had the area investigated by D.C.'s, police etc & they found that two lots of fishermen were having a private dispute over the fishing rights right on the shores of our corner of the lake." He reluctantly informed Vanne and Jane that for their own safety, the expedition would have to be delayed. That story became the regularly repeated official reason that the pair were told to go back three spaces from the chimpanzees of Gombe and advance instead to the vervet monkeys of Lolui Island. As Jane wrote in her popular book *In the Shadow of Man*, the news that "there was trouble among the African fishermen on the beaches of the chimpanzee reserve" amounted to a "first setback." But then Louis resourcefully "put forth the suggestion that I should make a short trial study of the vervet monkeys on an island in Lake Victoria."

Around the end of July 1960, Louis communicated to the project funder, Leighton Wilkie, a slightly different version. Just when his "research worker arrived here in Nairobi from training," he learned that "political agit[at]ors had stirred up anti-white trouble on the shores of the lake at the Chimpanzee Reserve," resulting in the delay and change of plans. Whatever the case, Louis had been intending for things to happen precisely that way for at least a year and a half, as he had unambiguously informed Wilkie early in 1959.

He had described in a February 12 letter of that year his "vervet monkey project (see second attached enclosure), which would be conducted by the same research worker, partly before and partly after the chimpanzee project."

Lolui was the uninhabited island Jane and Vanne had visited during their glorious weekend excursion on Lake Victoria back in the fall of 1958, and now, as then, they traveled to the port of Kisumu, where they were met by Hassan Salimu and his young assistant, Hamisi. Hassan, the captain of Louis's vessel, the *Miocene Lady,* was someone everyone appears to have liked and admired. Mary Leakey described him in her autobiography as "almost a member of the family" who had once saved Richard from drowning. Vanne referred to him in letters to Bournemouth as "our stately little captain," "a respected and popular figure wherever he went," and "the marvelous Hassan."

Louis and Mary had been exploring Miocene-era fossil deposits on some of the islands of Lake Victoria since the 1940s, and a benefactor's gift of £1,600 in 1948 had enabled Louis to buy a secondhand forty-two-foot twin-engine cabin cruiser in Mombasa and have it shipped by rail to Kisumu. Rechristened the *Miocene Lady,* it contained belowdecks the wheel and engine controls, two bunks, a hanging lantern or two, and portholes just large enough for the slender Jane to squeeze through experimentally. It was a "most charming little boat," Vanne thought, and in October 1958 she had written in some detail of their earlier journey out to the island after an evening start from Kisumu and a hot and buggy night's anchorage.

They woke up around 4:30 that morning, wrapped themselves in blankets on deck, and watched the night dissolve into dawn. Around 5:15, Hamisi raised anchor, Hassan started the engine, and they set off, accompanied by a half-dozen pelicans, "all yellow beak, fawn wing tips and the first sun lighting up their feathers with rose." Around 7:00, Jane and Vanne, feeling chilled, went down to the cabin, where Jane fried up bacon and eggs while Vanne mended a tear in her jeans. After a midmorning coffee, with Jane taking the wheel for a while, they sailed past Rusinga Island; and after a lunch of chicken roll and banana, around 2:00 in the afternoon, they sighted Lolui, a faint bluish gray anomaly at the horizon. The water became "calm and oily, and although the tropical sun was beating down on us, we were still cooled by a soft breeze. Jane and I trailed our toes in the warm water, and then lay on the cabin roof, dazed by the magnitude and beauty of this vast lake on which one sails on and on and on, so that the ever changing hills, brooding in the heat, the glittering light and the dreamlike quality of the haze which sometimes almost obscured the land, had a hypnotic effect on us."

By 3:15 they were close enough to discern the green of trees and scrub and the amber of a sandy shore, an island "long and low, wooded near the shore and covered with grasses on its rounded summit. It looked hot." Covering only about nine square miles altogether, Lolui had a sporadically rocky, high-grassed interior marked with pockets of bush and trees and patches of wild cucumber, and a protective outer belt of dense scrubby thicket and forest that was penetrable through a few natural gaps and hippo tunnels. The hippos wallowed in shallows offshore, and an occasional crocodile was sprawled on the narrow beach. Lake flies and mosquitoes swarmed around the edges; small lizards flicked and darted about on the rocks.

On this second trip to the island, they arrived on the afternoon of Saturday, June 11, 1960. Jane's field journal from Lolui opens on Sunday, June 12, with the confession of a late start.

> Did not wake up quite as early as I intended, but was on the island by 7 am. Ma stayed behind to make some bread & tidy up. . . . I walked along inside the forest belt. After about 20 minutes I noticed a movement in the branches. Lifted the field glasses—slowly—it was a mature female with very pink, large conspicuous nipples. Sat down on a tussock so as to steady the glasses. 3 monkeys were feeding from the tops of two trees bearing dark coloured fruit. After I had watched them for 5 minutes the male began to make his threatening bark. 5 or 6 barks and then the more angry sound—the bark repeated 3 times with the breath drawn in between—rather the effect of a pig grunting. The mouth was opened fairly wide.

A more typical day began earlier, around 5:45, still dark, when Jane would wake and get dressed, whereupon Hassan would creakily row her ashore in the dinghy. Passing from the beach through the island's ring of scrub in the pale morning mist, Jane entered the high-grassed interior and took up her station, binoculars in hand, notebook on lap, waiting for the first light to rouse the monkeys.

Jane would return to the boat for breakfast around nine o'clock, watching to see if the monkeys were coming down to the lake for a drink. (One time she spied them not merely drinking but hopping out into the water, up to their necks and possibly swimming.) After breakfast mother and daughter would go back to the island, Jane to her watching post (wearing her long-sleeved pajama blouse when the mosquitoes and flies were particularly bothersome, fighting off the sun with a hat she had woven from leaves) and Vanne to specimen-gathering (wearing a green tennis hat to shade her eyes and a knife on a string around her waist, and armed with a large butterfly net, a killing jar, and a dozen bags for storing dead insects).

Vanne usually went back to the boat around two o'clock for a lazy, warm, midday period of pinning up insects, pressing flowers, and writing notes before returning to the island around six, an hour before sunset, for a final bout of collecting. "and all that time," she wrote in a June 26 letter to the family,

> Jane is seated almost motionless, on an anthill or a hummock of grass, staring, staring, remembering, noting, waiting & watching her monkeys!! The sun beats down, ants wander over her, her nose peels, her forehead peels, but she is there, never stopping her work for a single second. Happier than I've ever seen her. She's brown now, & in an odd mixture of scarlet, brown freckles and a sort of orange haze overall. Wish I looked like Jane, her skin, her pony tail, her khaki slacks & blouse are all ideal for her job. She melts into the landscape & would stay here for a year if she could. She loves the monkey families, & the other night dreamed, & woke, expecting to find her outflung arm covered in soft brown monkey fur!!

After sunset, once the monkeys had sleepily nestled into the trees, Jane and Vanne would return to the boat for supper, their single hot meal of the day. And then, under the swaying light of the lantern, Jane would spend an hour or so writing up her field notes, getting mosquito-bitten and sleepy, and finally listening to the nine o'clock news on the radio—faithfully done because Louis planned to send a safari message on the news program to tell them when to return to Nairobi—before turning in for the night.

Jane began that monkey study as she would the chimpanzee study: without serious precedent, established preconception, or standard method. No one had studied wild vervet monkeys before. Few had studied wild primates before. There was little to build on, almost everything to learn, including the most fundamental issue of how to approach the research subjects for observation in the first place.

In his nine-week 1930 chimpanzee study, Henry Nissen had considered solving the approach problem with three "time-honored modes of naturalistic work"—blinds, baiting, visual tracking—and settled on a variation of the third, using auditory rather than visual clues. His approach amounted to a hunter's technique, closing in with stealth, quietly and carefully creeping closer until he was within observational range. Stealth worked for him, to some degree, but it always holds one significant disadvantage: once the observed subject recognizes the presence of the observer, stealth becomes threatening, since it typically indicates a predator preparing to attack. Intuitively, Jane chose to approach the vervet monkeys using a fourth technique, the sort of thing she had done as a young girl observing birds and small wild animals along the Bournemouth cliffs: proceeding openly rather than secretively. Of course, she still had to learn the wild monkeys' tolerance for such an approach: how close to go, the sorts of movements to make or avoid making, the kind of clothes to wear. Some of that learning process was recorded in her field notes, such as this entry from June 15: "At 2.15 an adolescent entered the two tall bushes nearest to my tree, and I was too close for him. He started to give a warning call, and soon an adult female, a male & another J[uvenile] had joined it. I curled up & pretended to go to sleep. Soon they all stopped."

But if her first problem was *how* to study—how to get close enough to make good observations—the second was *what* to study. She began by describing every obvious aspect of the vervet monkeys' behavior in detail: resting positions, locomotion, grooming, mating, eating, calls. She spent hours considering the distance between the troop of monkeys she watched and a neighboring troop. On the morning of June 21, she was fortunate enough to watch her monkeys emerge from the ring thicket onto the beach and have a bath, "the enchanting spectacle of the whole troop playing at the edge of the water—& going right in!"

Yet Jane's primary, though unexamined and unplanned, method was not to assemble a broad and general portrait of Lolui Island's vervet monkey inhabitants as a species, but rather to understand the species through an understanding of individual members. Thus, her overarching task was to develop a mental dramatis personae of the monkeys: to recognize individuals and to describe their individual behaviors and interactions. Recognizing individuals required noting and remembering distinguishing features, and her earliest notes include "adult male—very handsom creature in its prime," "mature female with very pink, large conspicuous nipples," and so on. Then, once she recognized individual monkeys, Jane gave them names. By the fourth day of her study the small infant who kept appearing in the arms of "the huge female" became Sammy. By the thirteenth day of the study, Sammy's apparent mother was Bessie, while one of the smaller adult males became Pierre and a large adult male became Brutus. And on that same productive day, the "very obviously pregnant" young female with nipples "very small in comparison with the other adult females" was named Lotus. By the sixteenth day, Lotus had appeared holding a baby, who was then named Glock:

Then I made out the animal who was near me. A smallish creature sitting just above & to the right of Sl.T.II [Sleeping Tree the Second] all alone! Watched it for about 10 minutes. Kept very still. Then it moved upwards—and it was Lotus—& she had had her baby!! I was thrilled.

She sat for a further 10 minutes in full view of me. Ate about 3 berries. The little object was blackish & still wet. She didn't appear to give it a lot of attention, but put her arm round it every so often. Then she stood up again, paused while the infant (Glock) got firmly into position, and sat where the baby was completely obscured by a branch.

Louis's safari message was broadcast over the evening radio news on June 25, giving them just a few more days at Lolui, and on her final morning there, Wednesday, June 29, Jane recorded waking up and feeling "very miserable as we had to go." She and Vanne made a final trip onto the island and a farewell visit to the monkeys before returning to the *Miocene Lady*. Hamisi raised anchor at around ten, and they arrived at Kisumu by the middle of the next day, June 30, setting off by car at the end of the afternoon and arriving in Nairobi around midnight.

Back in Nairobi, Jane wrote up a report of the vervet monkey study for Louis, and on Sunday they met at the museum. Jane presented him with the report, and he read it in her presence, with, she then reported back to the family in England, "great sighs . . . coming across the room, very foreboding!" In the end, he concluded that it was "fine," although she would obviously need to return someday to finish the study. Still, Jane was pleased with the results of her very first fieldwork: "All in all I think our little expedition was very satisfactory."

Mother and daughter then began shopping for supplies and equipment for their expedition to Gombe (as Vanne wrote: "Kit bags, haversacks, tents, chairs, water bottles, jugs, plates etc., mosquito netting, creams, oh & a mass of other things"), and by Monday evening they had sorted and stacked it all at the museum. Early the next morning, Tuesday, July 5, they watched as Bernard Verdcourt oversaw the final cramming of things into the Land Rover. Louis handed Jane a working revolver that had once belonged to Sir Evelyn Baring, the former governor of Kenya (and was soon to begin rusting, untouched, at the bottom of a tin trunk at Gombe). With the staff providing what Vanne considered a "royal send off" and with Bernard at the wheel, assigned to deliver them to the Tanganyikan port of Kigoma, they pulled out of the museum driveway, navigated through the outskirts of Nairobi, and turned south.

The four-day trip to Kigoma went about as smoothly as one could expect, given the fact that their ancient vehicle, with failing brakes and worn-out springs, was so severely overloaded it would teeter precariously whenever Bernard tried to pick up the pace. But after three days, one emergency brake repair, and a patched puncture or two, they reached the edge of Lake Tanganyika, the legendary inland sea that the British explorers Richard Francis

Burton and John Hanning Speke had been taken to see by their African guides hardly more than a century earlier. Burton, in *The Lake Regions of Central Africa* (1860), described "an expanse of the lightest and softest blue, in breadth varying from thirty to thirty-five miles, and sprinkled by the crisp east wind with tiny crescents of snowy foam." Beyond the breathtaking stretch of scintillating blue, the explorer saw in the distance mountains of a land that within twenty-five years was claimed and exploited as the personal property of the king of Belgium. Burton raised his eyes to observe "a high and broken wall of steel-colored mountain, here flecked and capped with pearly mist, there standing sharply penciled against the azure air; its yawning chasms, marked by a deeper plum-color, fall toward dwarf hills of mound-like proportions, which apparently dip their feet in the wave."

When Jane and Vanne first set eyes upon that same grand vista, on July 7, 1960, the sun was going down, and so they searched for a place to camp. But whenever they stopped the Land Rover, as Vanne wrote home, "we found ourselves smothered in tsetse flies & flew for our lives!" Finally, after passing a vast papyrus swamp and crossing a stretch of water on a small, hand-drawn ferry, they escaped the swarming, biting insects and found a burned-over area where the soot soon covered their shoes and clothes, beds and blankets, food and water. At dawn they set out on their final run, passing through bush and forest and mile after mile of small cultivated plots before descending a long hill into Kigoma.

Kigoma amounted to one main street with a large open market at the top and running downhill through a brief business district of small shops to the administrative heart of things—dusty square, railway station, and an old German fort now containing government, postal, and police offices—and down once more to the docks and harbor at the bottom. The town had two hotels, and the overloaded Land Rover was soon parked in front of the more promising one, which was the cool and rather spread-out Regina Hotel, with a pleasant little dining hall and a long stone veranda overlooking the harbor. It was run by an overweight Greek and worked by a staff of two Africans, both dressed in long white robes and red fezzes. On Saturday, as Jane and Vanne soon discovered, the government offices were closed, but they nevertheless located the district commissioner, who gave them the latest bad news. Recent events on the other side of the lake were causing serious concern on this side, and as a result their planned excursion to the Gombe Stream Chimpanzee Reserve would have to be delayed once more.

On the other side of the lake, the Belgians had run a highly profitable colony (producing in 1959 almost a tenth of the world's copper, nearly half its cobalt, and about seven tenths of its industrial diamonds) that was tragically unprepared for independence. With an openly racist, segregated administration, the Belgian Congo had by 1959 produced only 136 black secondary school graduates; it was run by a civil service of nearly 5,000 Belgians and 3 Congolese, and a 25,000-man Force Publique consisting of white officers and black soldiers.

On June 30, only a week earlier, political power had formally been turned over to a new Congolese administration, with Joseph Kasavubu as president and Patrice Lumumba as prime minister, whereupon members of the Force Publique garrisoned in Leopoldville (now Kinshasa) protested vehemently against the continuation of the Belgian officer corps. Prime Minister Lumumba met with the angry soldiers and on July 6 dismissed all senior Belgian officers, elevating his own private secretary (a former army clerk named Joseph Mobutu) to chief of staff and former sergeant Victor Lundulawas to commander of the Force Publique. This arbitrary change in command provoked mutinies throughout the country, and the army disintegrated into an armed rabble that turned on their former colonial masters with a bloody ferocity, precipitating a mass exodus of refugees. Thousands fled across the new nation's borders to the north, south, and west, and several hundred more began crossing Lake Tanganyika to the east.

In Kigoma, the district commissioner was worried, as he told Jane and Vanne, that the violence in Congo would spread across the lake—and just as they returned to their hotel to contemplate this latest setback, the two women were induced to consider the arrival, from across the lake, of hundreds of traumatized Belgian refugees. The Regina Hotel was overwhelmed, and to make more room, Bernard moved into Jane and Vanne's room, an inconvenient twist they all accepted with good humor.

The hotel had only two baths and two lavatories for around sixty people, and the lavatories were broken. And now, with themselves and all their expedition equipment, plus Bernard and all his equipment, their single small room would, as Vanne wrote home, "have to be seen to be believed." The room was small and square, with two white-painted cast-iron bedsteads "festooned by greyish mosquito nets, two very thin straw mats on the floor, an ancient washstand with cracked ewer, some thin sheets, ½" dust under the beds, mosquitoes on the prowl, and all our stuff all over the rest of the floor. Bernard's boxes of food, coats, thermos flasks, a dilapidated type writer, 6 towels, which might have been white in 1900, camp beds etc. & down the middle the camp bed on which Bernard sleeps!! It's a HOOT!! Luckily it doesn't bother any of us but it would be nice to feel slightly less grimey!"

During the next couple of days, Vanne and Jane worked down at the dock, greeting refugees, making sandwiches and ladling soup, feeding children and doling out fruit, cigarettes, chocolate, and beer. The Belgians, mostly women and children, looked "so pathetic & white & utterly lost & dejected," Vanne thought. Jane later recalled cutting up two thousand sandwiches' worth of canned Spam in one evening, noting that "I have never been able to face tinned Spam since." But within a short while the displaced Belgians were packed onto trains and sent east to Dar es Salaam, and Kigoma returned to its normal state: hot, dusty, and sleepy.

The chimpanzee expedition still awaited official blessing, however, and given their limited funds — little more than £100 deposited in a Kigoma bank account — Jane, Vanne, and Bernard decided to check out of the hotel and set up tents on the grounds of the Kigoma prison, on a bluff overlooking the lake. It offered a beautiful view, accompanied by a pungent citrus aroma rising from the prison's small orchard and the whine and nick of endless mosquitoes. For the rest of the week they slept on the bluff by night and by day wandered around the markets, wrote letters home, and began making friends with some of Kigoma's important people. These were mainly government employees and their spouses, "very friendly and hospitable," as Jane later wrote. Someone introduced them to Bimje, the owner of a small shop, and from Bimje's shop they stocked up on a few essentials. Around the same time they hired a cook, Dominic Charles Bandora, who was, Vanne assured the family back home, "a very good type with stacks of references & known to our Bank Manager."

Finally permission was given for the expedition to proceed, and thus, in the early morning of Thursday, July 14, they packed up their tents. Louis Leakey had shipped a small aluminum boat by rail from Dar es Salaam, and Bernard drove Jane down to the railway station to locate its motor, which they found at last in the parcels office inside an enormous cardboard carton marked with red chalk LEAKEY. Bernard returned to the prison to fetch Vanne and the rest of their supplies, and then they met at the docks with the game warden for western Tanganyika, a yellow-haired man in his mid-thirties named David Anstey. They transferred their collection of boxes and bags onto the Tanganyika Game Department launch and tethered the little aluminum boat onto the stern.

The *Kibisi* was a steel-hulled, diesel-powered vessel with cabin and sleeping accommodations, big enough to accommodate all their supplies plus Jane, Vanne, Dominic Bandora, and David Anstey. With a growl and a puff of dirty smoke, it pulled away and headed north, with Jane and Vanne waving to a diminishing Bernard Verdcourt standing on the dock next to the worn and now underloaded Land Rover. "It was very sad watching our last link with the fantastic life of Kigoma disappearing behind us," Vanne soon wrote back to Bernard, and years later she admitted to being "suddenly overwhelmed by depression."

But the lake was (and still is) simply beautiful. The second deepest lake in the world, Tanganyika probably also ranks among the cleanest. The waters are surprisingly clear, like warm, rolling liquid glass—"so unbelievably clear," Jane wrote in the opening entry of her Gombe field journal, "that I could scarcely believe it." Even better, she noted, there was no bilharziasis (schistosomiasis), the snail-borne parasitic scourge of so much otherwise promising fresh water in Africa, which meant that people could bathe and swim in the lake.

It was a bright, blue-domed day, yet still hazy enough that the mountains of Congo twenty-five miles to the west were invisible, and a sharp breeze chopped the water as they followed the irregular coastline north, moving from one rocky headland to the next, looking east to the sometimes sandy, often rocky shore backed by a wall rising steeply above the lake before terminating at a high plateau. Small streams plummeted down to the lake through deep rugged ravines and forested valleys, and for the first seven miles of their journey, much of the steep land had been cleared and, in places, cultivated. Occasional houses and small fishing villages were lodged in the valleys or wedged into precarious niches.

Within an hour the *Kibisi* had reached a rocky outcrop that David identified as the southern boundary of the Gombe Stream Chimpanzee Reserve, and the shore was marked now by a wall of emerald vegetation. Jane was experiencing, according to her field journal, the irritation of a "foul sore throat, turning into a cold," but psychologically she felt, according to her first popular account of that journey, "neither excitement nor trepidation but only a curious sense of detachment. What had I, the girl standing on a government launch in her jeans, to do with the girl who in a few days would be searching those very mountains for wild chimpanzees?"

David Anstey, who was about ten years older than Jane, once told me that with her hair tied up in a ponytail, she looked "incredibly young" and her voice seemed rather "girlish." But he had no doubts about her capacity to do whatever it was she had set out to do. "I didn't really think about it. All I was thinking was whether the situation over in the Congo would send baddies, vagabonds, hooligans, murderers, or what-have-you across the lake and knock her in the head." True, the chimpanzee research expedition may have seemed a little unusual to some people, but David Anstey was used to eccentric women arriving in the territory and doing "all sorts of odd things": studying grasses, researching ticks, flying airplanes. "So I don't honestly believe I thought whether she was a bit strange." Actually, David was much more impressed by Vanne. Vanne, he thought, provided a prime example of what he sometimes called "the imperial grit," which to him meant that "she instilled respect. She was not a silly fluffy woman. She was down to earth, in charge." Yes, Jane's mother was "an impressive lady."

Passing the forested shoreline, they observed fishermen all along the beaches, with their main commercial catch—small, silvery, sardinelike fish known as *dagaa*—spread out in patches on the sand, making it look "white-washed," as Jane put it in her journal. And every so often, along that forested stretch, "a stream cascaded down the valleys between the ridges, with its thick fringe of forests—the home of the chimps."

At last they reached a headland, a stream, a small bay, and on the shore a small crowd of people: part of a Tanganyika Game Department encampment and fishing camp called Kasekela village. The *Kibisi* dropped anchor, and the crew and passengers rowed ashore and were greeted first by two Game Department scouts and second by a stately, white-haired old man rather splendidly attired in a red European overcoat, worn like a robe. The old man was Iddi Matata, the unofficial head of Kasekela. Matata greeted the new arrivals ceremoniously, giving a long speech in Swahili, while the two women responded, as David Anstey had advised them to, by presenting him with a small gift. With such formalities complete, David, the two scouts, and the two women attended to the sweatier business of transferring everything from the launch to the beach and then, with some help from Matata's six children, setting up camp.

Dominic's tent was erected on a spot just above the beach, while Jane and Vanne's larger tent was hauled several yards up a path and raised in a flat clearing, an excellent spot shaded by a few oil palm trees and separated from the beach by a fringe of scrub. Their tent—big enough to include a separate washroom at the rear and a raised-flap veranda at the front—enclosed two camp cots side by side and facing north, with the lake on the left. From the steeply rising land to their right, "a little bubbling stream" (so Vanne wrote in a letter home) "tumbles down right behind our tent, and it is so clean and runs so fast that we wash our feet in it, or sit them in it to cool off." Vanne also found a small pool of water deep enough, she thought, to wash her hair, which by then was "so stiff with dust that it stands up like a halo."

They spent the afternoon unpacking and arranging, setting up and digging in. Louis had supplied them with extra mosquito netting, some of which now could be placed over the entire front of the tent, and they also had mosquito booties to wear while sitting around the fire at night, although Vanne was relieved to report (prematurely, as it turned out) that there were "no mosquitoes." They were soon provided with a decent latrine, "a sweet little lav," which was a deep hole in the ground surrounded, for modesty purposes, by a palisade of woven palm leaves.

It was around five o'clock that first afternoon, according to Jane's journal, that one of the game scouts, Adolf Siwezi, came to report that some of the fishermen had seen a chimp. So Jane and Adolf rushed down to the beach, where they walked until they found a group of fishermen gazing at the ape. The dark creature was a considerable distance away and obscured by vegetation but still unquestionably a chimpanzee. As Jane and Adolf tried to draw nearer, however, it moved away into deeper forest, and although they climbed a nearby slope and spent some time quietly searching, they failed to see the ape again. It was getting dark, and so they returned to the beach and walked back to the camp.

Dominic cooked an excellent dinner that first night: soup, a stew with potatoes and onions, canned oranges, and coffee. The two women ate in the company of David Anstey, and then, after what Jane described in her journal as "long chats, & helpless endeavouring to hear the news" on a portable radio, mother and daughter "thankfully retired to bed."

14

Summer in Paradise

1960

"I WISH you could be here—even just for a day," Jane wrote to the family in England about a week after she arrived at Gombe. "It is so beautiful, with the crystal clear blue lake, the tiny white pebbles on the beach, the sparkling ice cold mountain stream, the palm nut trees, the comical baboons." She continued:

> I have seen a timid little bushbuck leading his two ladies across a grassy patch, each one following exactly in his footsteps. I have seen seven buffalo feeding peacefully at the top of one of the mountain ridges. I have found a beautiful monkey with black fur and a bright red crown on the top of its head & watched the troop for an hour, the mother with her tiny baby clinging round her middle, the old man resting in the shade, and some of the young bloods prancing round from branch to branch. And a tiny kingfisher, no bigger than a sparrow, and brilliant as a jewel. Can you wonder that I should be happy here? It is the Africa of my childhood's dreams, and I have the chance of finding out things which no one has ever known before.

Some thirty years later I visited Jane Goodall at Gombe, sitting down with her one evening before a small fire on the beach at almost the very spot where she had set foot for the first time on July 14, 1960. We were sipping postprandial Scotch and waters, savoring a cool breeze flowing off the lake, listening to the rush and clink of water sifting a slope of pebble and sand, and drifting under a cold black universe warmed by the glowing Milky Way. Louis Leakey originally sent her there, Jane said, because he had spent so much of his life digging up the remains of hominids who lived along ancient shorelines, and he thought modern chimpanzees living at the edge of a lake would indicate something about the lives of his own study subjects. As it happened, living on a shoreline was irrelevant to the chimps. "But wasn't I lucky? Of all the possible places I might have been in Africa studying chimps, to come here to this paradise!"

The paradisiacal quality of Gombe is a gift from Lake Tanganyika. The lake not only defines and nourishes the forest ecosystem, it provides people with food to eat, water to drink, and after a hot, exhausting day in the mountains, the perfect place to splash in. When Jane and Vanne arrived, David Anstey told them not to bathe in the lake because the fishermen would be shocked, and so that first summer they sometimes washed in the stream behind their tent or took a warm evening bath in a canvas tub at the rear section of their tent, with the back flap drawn open far enough for them to gaze at, beyond the shifting screen of trees, the lake's sheen under a setting sun. But after the early years people at Gombe have regularly indulged in the pleasure of an evening bathe or swim in the lake.

Gombe is also paradisiacal because it happens to have a relatively low human population density. In one or two unlikely spots deep in the forest, you can find signs—a few large stone circles—of long-ago human dwellings located in apparently deliberate obscurity. One theory suggests that those circles mark temporary settlements of Arab slave traders from an earlier time. An alternative story is that Africans escaping from German conscription during the first world war moved back into the forests and are responsible for the circles, even though large stones are not a traditional building material in the area. But Gombe was obscure and underpopulated long before the Arab traders and German colonialists arrived, since the African people originally living in the region, the Waha, regarded its special topography, its forests and the wildlife therein, as sacred ground: an abode for earth spirits, the *bisigo* and *mashinga*, who required serious deference. Around the turn of the twentieth century, German colonialists mapped out the boundaries of Gombe, thus preserving the integrity of those sacred forests by defining them as legally protected chimpanzee habitat, and after World War I the English civil administration continued to enforce that protected status.

During the 1930s and 1940s, *dagaa* fishing on that part of the lake became an increasingly significant commercial enterprise. *Dagaa* swim in great schools and find light strangely attractive. When the moon is full, they spread out broadly in the water, distracted by the flickering, rippling emanations from above. On darker nights, with the moon waxing or waning, the fishermen took advantage of that weakness by burning fires on the parapets of their boats, producing a focused light that drew the little fish into the fishing nets. The fires, of course, required wood, which was often taken from the trees of Gombe, and so one of the early jobs of the British-run Tanganyika Game Department was to enforce limits on tree-cutting at Gombe — a task that became increasingly irrelevant by the late 1940s and early 1950s, as the new storm-proof kerosene lanterns, Tilley pressure lamps, replaced wood fires on the fishing boats.

When Jane arrived in 1960, Gombe still contained an exceptionally abundant sample of East African forest fauna: not only a healthy population of some 160 chimpanzees (the eastern subspecies, *Pan troglodytes schweinfurthii*) but representatives of a half-dozen other primate species, including olive baboons; red colobus monkeys; blue, red-tailed, and vervet monkeys, and needle-clawed bush babies. The reserve's other mammals included two small herds of buffalo, numerous bushbucks and bush pigs, some hippos, the occasional hyena, a few reclusive leopards, a number of smaller animals such as civets, genets, and elephant shrews, and various kinds of mongooses, rodents, and squirrels. Lions were no longer in evidence by the time Jane arrived, and since that time the hippos and buffalo and lurking crocodiles have vanished as well. But birds in great variety and profusion remain, and it is still possible to find the terrestrial and very large (up to six feet long) Nile monitor lizard, as well as chameleons, frogs, geckos, lizards, skinks, terrapins, toads, and tortoises, and the rare Ujiji round-snouted worm lizard. Gombe also contains venomous giant millipedes and scorpions as well as assassin bugs, beetles, grasshoppers, safari ants, spiders, termites, tsetse flies, and wasps — and an endless supply of malarial mosquitoes.

Every paradise has its serpent, and at Gombe the python is king, growing up to sixteen feet long, with teeth as big as a large dog's but curved backward to assist in swallowing prey, which can include bush pigs and bushbucks. Gombe's two dozen snake species include several poisonous ones, ranging from the mildly venomous (burrowing adders, night adders, sand snakes, and vine snakes) to the seriously so (black-and-white forest cobras, black mambas, boomslangs, bush vipers, Lake Tanganyika water cobras, puff adders, and spitting cobras).

Bush vipers are arboreal, but they seem to prefer the lower, bushy regions of Gombe vegetation; since they are small and produce comparatively small amounts of venom, their bite is unlikely to kill a full-size human. The boomslang, another arboreal snake, happens to be rear-fanged, with fangs that are grooved rather than hollow, meaning that the snake has to chew on prey in order to inject venom; moreover, the venom is slow-acting, so a victim has several days to locate a snakebite kit.

Those two are the good ones. Others are not so good. The aggressive and very poisonous Lake Tanganyika water cobras, which prefer rocky shoreline, are, luckily, rare at Gombe, where much of the shoreline is open sand or pebble shingle; and the black-and-white forest cobras, glossy black above and custard-yellow below, with a black lip and black chin band, are nocturnal and secretive, therefore seldom seen. Puff adders, not that rare or secretive, are fast-striking reptiles that prefer to ambush small prey along an animal path. They are sometimes slow to move out of the way of a person striding along the same path—a good reason to stomp your feet. Spitting cobras appear in a whole spectrum of color schemes, such as a lovely lemon-yellow body with a dark neckband, and their spitting—a finely sprayed venom aimed at any glittering target, including an anxious person's eye—is a defense mechanism; but they can also inflict a lethal bite. Black mambas as long as six feet have been seen many times at Gombe, and their distinctively flat head, which is shaped like a coffin if viewed from above, ought to be a clear reminder that a direct bite can kill you within half an hour.

Jane always kept a lookout for snakes, as well as for buffalo, who could be unpredictable and dangerous, and the rare leopards, about whom she held, as she once wrote, "an ingrained illogical fear." But her vision of living so close to nature was always intensely, fundamentally positive, and so for her perhaps the most challenging aspect of the place was its rugged topography.

Gombe is a long, thin rectangle, with the long sides defined by the lake-shore on the western edge and the edge of the Rift Escarpment to the east. Water drains off the escarpment's high plateau, forming more than a dozen active streams that break, splash, and tumble down through the forest to-ward the lake, maintaining in the process more than a dozen deep ravines. Gombe's rugged terrain gives its acrobatic chimpanzees a special advantage over the weaker, plodding, upright human apes. Chimps can climb a tree as readily as people can run on level ground, and if a branch breaks, they are strong enough to catch themselves on the way down and tough enough to survive falls from a considerable height. Any cliff or ravine that presents an impossible barrier to the human follower requires a momentary pause for the chimp being followed, who will soon find just the right vine or tree to serve as a convenient ladder and bridge from A to B.

Nevertheless, Gombe's extreme verticality provides some unexpected advantages to humans. For one thing, it is hard to get very lost, since down-hill is a reliable compass pointing west. For another, although the terrain makes it difficult to follow chimps over long distances, the high peaks and deep valleys provide exceptional long-distance viewing opportunities. Once you find the right observation point, with a good pair of binoculars you can peer into and beyond treetops, onto and over ridges, and down into the pockets of forest below.

. . .

The reserve's social challenges were perhaps more serious. A couple of days after they arrived, David Anstey met with an aggressive and noisy crowd of around twenty people, fishermen and villagers from Mwamgongo, to the north, with another sixty people hanging around to observe. Some of these people used to live on the shores of Gombe, and in the days before kerosene pressure lamps they cut firewood for the fishing boats. Now the spokesmen from that crowd were saying that they wanted the land for themselves, and they argued that the two European women were probably government spies sent to exaggerate the number of chimps in order to justify continuing to keep Gombe off-limits to the local people.

Anstey handled the volatile situation well, and the meeting concluded with an agreement that Jane would do her chimpanzee-watching accompanied by a few hired assistants. First would be a subchief of Mwamgongo village, a man named Htwale, whose task was to check on Jane's activities: to look over her shoulder to verify that she did her job correctly and honestly. Her second minder, another resident of Mwamgongo, the "tall and lean and silent" (as Jane wrote home) Rashidi Kikwale, would serve as a guide and porter. And finally there would be the "good-humored" Adolf Siwezi, one of the Tanganyika game scouts stationed at the reserve, whose job (as she noted in her field journal) was "to go where I told him, and . . . to tell me of any bad rumors among the fishermen." Siwezi was already paid a salary by the Game Department, and Jane agreed to pay Htwale and Rashidi Kikwale two shillings a day each for their services. She would also occasionally hire yet another resident of Mwamgongo, a chief's son named Mikidadi, for tasks in and around camp.

That was the compromise David Anstey patiently negotiated—after which he left, taking the *Kibisi* back to Kigoma. Jane had visualized walking through the forests among wild animals by herself, immersed in nature and gloriously alone, and so she went to bed that night (according to her later writing) "depressed and miserable." But when she woke up the next morning, her depression had vanished, and she decided to make the best of things. "I do hope it's all going to work," she wrote home.

In fact her first couple of weeks at Gombe provided a surprisingly fruitful introduction to the apes, since chimpanzees living in the northern end of the reserve were excitedly grouping around their own fruitful discovery, an enormous *msulula* tree coming into season. The tree was located in the northernmost valley of the reserve, Mitumba Valley, and David Anstey had been told by the game scouts that they had heard chimp cries and seen nests in the area. Thus, early in the morning of July 17, Jane's third full day at the reserve and first day officially watching chimps, she, Rashidi, and Adolf took the little aluminum boat north along the shore and beached it at the mouth of Mitumba stream, where they were met by the Mwamgongo sub-chief, Htwale, who asked Jane exactly where she intended to go for her chimpanzee study. When she pointed to the forest and the hills rising above it, he said that as a consequence of being ill he would not be able to accompany her that day. "Later," Jane was eventually to recall, "I found out that he had expected that I would merely ride up and down the lake-shore in a boat, counting any chimpanzees I saw. The idea of clambering about in the mountains did not appeal to him at all, and I never saw him again."

So now her minders were reduced to two, a more agreeable number, and according to the field journal entry for that day, they quickly "set off up the forested valley following the shallow, fast running stream" of Mitumba.

It was very beautiful and very cool, with thick vegetation, many wild oil palms, and yet easy to walk through. We saw two bush pig. They were on the track ahead of us, and only moved a little when we approached. We stopped to look up through the trees at them and they trotted unhurriedly away. I have only seen the tracks of bush pig previously. We saw many buffalo prints but no buffalo. At 8:30 we heard the cries of a party of chimps from the forested slopes to the North of the river. . . . Soon after this we saw several chimps feeding in a tree.

They located an ideal hillside observation point, far enough away that the chimps continued feeding undisturbed, high enough that Jane could peer into the tree through her binoculars and make out a few shadowy shapes, a boiling in the leaves, an arm or two.

There must have been about 10 animals, but as the tree in which they were feeding had thick foliage, and as the animals kept climbing down to the ground & then up again, it was hard to make an exact count. I could see no animal which could be classified as a young chimpanzee, though one or two were definitely much smaller than the large adults. Feeding was fairly intensive—on the whole the berries were picked off the branch by hand and then eaten. Occasionally the food was taken from the branch directly into the mouth.

After she had watched them for about twenty minutes, the entire group except for one climbed down out of the tree, and then another group—or was it the same one?—appeared and climbed into the tree and began feeding. The chimpanzees in the tree broke out into a chorus of hoots and screams regularly, six times during the first hour, and near the end of that time Jane was able to see three apes clearly. Then, at 9:45, the whole group descended from the tree and seemed to disappear into the underbrush. About ten minutes later, Jane and her two companions moved closer to the tree in order to get a sample of the berries.

> This was a mistake as they were still in the lower trees nearby and we startled them. They did not go away for about 20 mins, however. We heard them moving about, cracking twigs, and I heard the low grunts which approximated to the sounds made by captive chimps when eating a looked-forward to meal, or some special delicacy. Only one animal did we see during this time—it climbed a low tree. But it was only possible to distinguish a dark object.

During that first week Jane pursued the chimpanzees from dawn to dark, spending two nights out in the forest in a sleeping bag (with Rashidi and Adolf warming themselves by a fire) in order to watch chimps as they woke up in the morning.

Large numbers of the chimps were climbing up an adjacent palm tree to get into the enormous crown of the *msulula* for its red-and-yellow berries, but Jane's observations were inevitably limited by distance and obscured by leafy obstacles, and she confessed in an early journal entry to "a mood, a depression" that settled in. "How can I ever see any behavior? All I see is chimpanzees stuffing themselves with various types of food." But then she consoled herself with the fact that already she had made "one or two pertinent observations as to their behaviour whilst feeding in the trees." Although they were "remarkably agile in the branches," in general the chimps seemed to move around very little while eating. It was very easy, Jane thought, "to look at the food tree, which I <u>know</u> bears 15 chimps, & yet see no movement for at least a minute."

Also, she noted, they often hung on to a higher branch with a hand and arm while eating. One female that morning hung by a single arm for fifteen minutes, changed to the other arm, and hung by that for another ten minutes. Most of that time the female appeared to be watching her watchers and occasionally eating a bit of fruit. And other times the chimps would recline, leaning against a branch, for instance, and "propping themselves up on one elbow whilst lazily picking fruit & eating it with the other hand."

Perhaps the most interesting observation Jane made during those first days at the *msulula* tree was that the chimps seemed to gather in a very confusing, almost random fashion. A certain number would clamber up the palm tree ladder into the *msulula*. Some of them would climb down again. One mixture of adults and juveniles, males and females, would start something. A second mixture would finish it. Some quite large groups would appear in the tree, but then very small groups might also appear—and sometimes only a single individual. Even more interesting—and confusing, perhaps—when the chimps were not in the tree but rather moving around somewhere in the green maze of the surrounding forest, they would sometimes call in hooting, screaming choruses, as if separate groups were keeping in touch with each other; Jane would sometimes hear multiple groups of chimps calling from all around. How unlike monkeys! The vervet monkeys of Lolui Island, for instance, traveled around in stable troops that remained consistent in number and structure. Jane also used the word *troop* to describe the strangely mixed and matched chimpanzee social units she was puzzling over that July, but those groups appeared to be structurally completely different from monkey troops. Her journal entry for the morning of July 20 gives some idea of how confusing the chimpanzee grouping system was:

> There was no sign of movement until about 7:30 when 5 chimps climbed into the food tree and began feeding. They made no sound at all. They remained there for about an hour, and then left, one after the other, and mostly swung down the left side of the tree, only one using the palm ladder. After they had disappeared there was a chorus of hoots and calls, and these were repeated from 4 separate and distinct localities. During the next half hour there was a good deal of this calling between one troop and another. Usually only three troops were involved. These calls did not include screaming.
>
> At about 9 am 3 chimps climbed into the tree. Two (one a male) left almost immediately and then 6 climbed up. Again many of them used branches to the left of the tree rather than the palm ladder. For ¾ hour these 7 fed quietly, with only one outburst of calls, including screams. Then at 9.45 they all climbed down and disappeared.

The *msulula* tree was soon stripped of its attractive berries, and by the end of July, Jane and her two assistants were scouring the reserve, looking for and generally failing to find an equivalent viewing opportunity, exploring in the process several of the streams to the south, to the north, in the middle. A journal entry for August 10 provides one example from that discouraging time:

> At 2 pm I happened to see two chimps—miles and miles away. They were moving in a tree, but almost as I saw them they vanished. They were right at the top of the furthest away mountain. The wind had died down a little by now. At 2.30 pm heard chimps—over the top of this

same mountain. Then again, even further away, and once more, so far that it was scarcely audible. As it would have taken well over an hour to get even to the top of the mountain, I abandoned the idea of going after them. It was 3.30 by then & we returned!

Adding to the frustration of trying to observe distant and obscure chimps was the more immediate problem of the field staff, Adolf and Rashidi. In a letter written in late July or early August, Vanne summarized the state of affairs for the family in England. "The chimps by the way are not being at all cooperative," she began, "and Jane is rapidly becoming in a state. The country is so mountainous that they are almost impossible to find. It is dry too, so they cannot be tracked—add to that the fact that she has two people with her wherever she goes and you can imagine how frustrated she is—especially as they cannot seem to be able to get up early in the morning and she can outwalk them and outclimb them so well that she tires them to the point of open mutiny daily!"

Jane continued to walk and watch tirelessly from dawn until dark, and she wrote up the field journal every evening, finishing around 10:30. Even on Sunday, a day off for the men, she would write letters, collect specimens, and wander onto the beach or into the forest around her camp looking for chimps. Both Adolf and Rashidi, it should be said, were very able and skilled men—but Jane's energy, stamina, and determination were simply very hard to match.

The journal tells this story more slowly. She was awake by five on July 18, for example, ready to leave by six, but no one had showed up at camp to meet her, so "I got very annoyed." When Adolf finally appeared at ten minutes to seven, "I ticked him off."

On the night of July 19, the three of them slept out near the *msulula* tree in Mitumba Valley. Jane ate a can of beans for dinner, and in the morning she may have eaten nothing—or perhaps she had one of her usual spare breakfasts: a piece of bread and a cup of coffee. She was content to continue watching chimps indefinitely, but by midmorning Rashidi began complaining that he was famished. "It transpired that Rashidi was dying from hunger," she wrote, "and so, against my will, I thought I had better return to camp. I don't want to be a slave driver! This is the trouble with having to be accompanied on my observations—people do need food and things & I must try to remember."

Along with that considerate thought, Jane may have realized that for some people, getting up before dawn requires mechanical assistance. She gave her alarm clock to Adolf on the evening of July 20, and it worked well enough that on the morning of the twenty-first they set off at 6:45 according to plan. But that afternoon, while Jane was watching chimps, Adolf and Rashidi spent most of the afternoon sleeping after a long lunch. And when Adolf failed to appear by 8:45 on July 22, Jane decided she was "fed up" and left without him, climbing by herself up the Kakombe stream, which ran behind her tent.

On August 5, Rashidi demonstrated his "extraordinarily good eyes" by being able "to make out the progress of the animals up the opposite mountain." But when they reached camp that evening, Rashidi "was too tired even to accompany me back to the tent. Oh, for someone who would walk." And by August 6 both Adolf and Rashidi were too worn-out to function at all.

> We continued for another mile but saw nothing. Adolf and Rashidi then had to rest. I got fed up & went on up the stream until it became very narrow. To give them their due the boys followed me.
>
> We then returned. Rashidi kept saying he was tired & blundering along like an elephant. Saw nothing—not even a monkey. However, just as we got to the beach heard chimps calling—from Nyasanga Stream where we had been earlier. Rashidi collapsed. I told him he could return but he preferred not to. So I set off with Adolf. They were fairly high up in the mountains where it is very rocky. Adolf did not wish to go up the river again, so he & Rashidi lay down under a large mango [tree] & I set off alone. I went as far as I could, & I climbed up the mountain, but could not hear them. So, after listening for about ½ hour I decided to return. Would have liked to go further but the country was so precipitous I thought it was asking for trouble on my own. I MUST get a good boy who is willing to work—to get up early, walk all day if necessary, & stay out late.
>
> Returned to the two slumbering beauties. Heard no chimps. Set off back along the beach. It was frantically exhausting. I've never known such a long 2 miles.

While Jane was preoccupied with disappearing chimpanzees and an exhausted field staff, Vanne was working on another problem, which was the attitude of the local fishermen and the Mwamgongo villagers living just outside the reserve. Louis Leakey had understood that Jane and Vanne would be living among people who might properly be suspicious of their motives and resentful of their presence, and he had advised Vanne, as she put it in a letter home, that "the surest way of making friends is to give them medicine." Thus, he had made sure that their expedition's cartons and cartons of supplies included substantial amounts of bandages, aspirin, cough medicine, Elastoplast, and Epsom salts.

Vanne made it known that she would provide simple medical attention for anyone who needed it, and some people brought in an old man with two deep ulcers in his leg, "the most ghastly livid swelling on his ankle that I have ever seen. The whole leg swollen to the knee, and the bad part, swollen to the size of a tangerine, and all red and yellow." Vanne was afraid he might lose the foot and declared that he should go to the hospital at Kigoma, but the old man, already emaciated and very ill, was unwilling to make the trip. So Vanne washed and soaked the leg daily with hot water and antiseptic. The ulcers began to drain, and within three weeks the swelling had disappeared and the sores were clean and beginning to heal.

That was the clinic—quickly institutionalized with four poles and a circular thatched roof overhead. Soon after Vanne had treated the old man with the tropical ulcers on that first day, two more people arrived with wounds to be dressed. While she was doing that, she became aware of about twenty more patients lined up for treatment. On the clinic's second day, thirty people arrived, wanting medicine for "coughs, colds, constipation, headaches, backaches and other ailments which I don't understand and for which I dish out indiscrim[in]ate aspirins which seem to them like magic."

A week later sixty clients lined up, including two men who appeared in clean white clothes, having walked several miles to request cough medicine for their babies. Vanne took on a volunteer assistant, one of Rashidi's sons, named Jumanne, an eager and helpful eight-year-old who would mix the Epsom salts, pour the water for aspirin, cut up pieces of Elastoplast, and keep an eye out for anyone trying to move through the queue twice. Those ongoing morning clinics, as Jane has written, "not only cured many maladies but, most importantly, helped us to establish good relations with our new neighbors."

As the summer progressed, the weather became increasingly hot and humid: "suffocating by 9 A.M.," Vanne wrote home. She found her head and hair to be "permanently wet & hot," and every day, in the hottest part of the afternoon when everyone else was taking a siesta, she would put on some loose cotton clothing, walk down to the stream, and sit in the water. "It's very shallow & rustles over smooth stones, but it's gloriously cool."

But Vanne sometimes felt overwhelmed, by both the heat and her responsibilities. "There is always something happening," she wrote. When she was not responding to a crisis at the clinic or, on occasion, entertaining surprise visitors, she was dutifully trying to gather specimens—insects and plants—or, less dutifully, poking at her typewriter. People coming up and down the lake for one reason or another would regularly stop by, and since communications with the outside world were very limited, these visits were often by necessity surprise events. David Anstey might show up in the *Kibisi* on wildlife business. Friends from Kigoma might drop in for a day. Or perhaps Father Guertz, "the White Father," might be cruising up or down the lake in his speedboat on mission business and decide to pop in for a moment, as he did one afternoon in early September, accompanied by two nuns. The lake was too choppy to beach the boat, so they anchored offshore and waited to be fetched in a dugout canoe. The two nuns (one of them around eighty years old) "lifted their skirts & stepped nimbly from one rocking boat to the other, and were paddled ashore." After hopping from the canoe onto the beach, they trod up the path to the tent for a brief treat of orange squash and biscuits before proceeding on their return journey to Kigoma. "I'll never forget Father Guertz in a big bushhat, long khaki gown, & the two sisters with their coifs floating out in the breeze as they literally hurtled over the waters to disappear immediately round the distant headland," Vanne wrote.

Sometimes surprise visitors were a pleasant diversion, but other times they were not. Vanne, in any case, was often distracted by the onerous chore of specimen-collecting. She had agreed to do it and felt obligated to keep at it routinely, but as the summer progressed and the hot weather expanded, her inspiration wilted. She expressed her frank opinion about the matter one day in a letter home:

> I can't find <u>insects</u> & I go up & down in the boiling heat trying to get just ONE for the box. As for plants—well they drive me <u>MAD</u>! I loathe collecting them now. Of all the dreary occupations a botanist's must be one of the worst . . . You fold them neatly, & they jump out of the folders. You put the leaves <u>flat</u> . . . & by the time you've shut the folder, the leaves are all back to front again. You do them in the sun & die of heat. You wait till it's cooler & just as you get them safely in the press, the wind blows & away go half the flimsy insides, out come the flowers!! You get berries & they bulge, you get a prize specimen & when you go to change the paper next day the press is alive with ANTS!

And then she summarized: "From this you'll gather that plant collecting is not my forte!" Insects, she thought, were a lot more fun than plants, but still, "I'm always glad when butterflies elude my net, so have decided that entomology has not lost an embryo genius either."

Writing was the one thing Vanne really looked forward to. When they had first arrived at Gombe, someone had built a wooden table for her, which was placed at the open and be-flapped front, the veranda, of the tent. To reduce the dust, she hired someone to carry buckets of pebbles from the beach and spread them around the tent's entrance. With pebbles at her feet, a canvas flap over her head, and the forest at her back, Jane's mother sat at her rickety wooden table that summer, facing north but with a view of the lake glistening away to her left, and typed. She typed long letters to her mother and siblings in England. She also worked on her novel. However, the sweat dripping off her hair and face and from her hands was threatening to rust the typewriter, and the ribbon was starting to fade—and would be gone by the end of August.

And while the ribbon was going faint, so was she. By August 13 she had (according to Jane's field journal) a "very bad" throat that rapidly got worse. It was serious enough to warrant a trip to Kigoma and an "injection" of some kind at the hospital on the fifteenth. The mysterious ailment quickly moved on to Jane, who by the morning of August 16 was "beginning to feel strange" herself, although she still felt fit enough to go out into the mountains with Rashidi, looking for chimpanzees as usual. But it was an extremely hot day, and they climbed for what seemed like many miles, up and down, approaching a "completely sheer ravine," following the sounds and signs of chimps until they reached a high point and sat, waiting. "I was feeling very strange by now," Jane noted in her journal. "Things were unreal. I lay down for a moment, & only a sort of instinct saved me from missing two chimps."

In terms of chimpanzee-watching, that afternoon was actually very productive, but their journey back to camp near the end of the day was "a real nightmare," and when Jane found her temperature registering 101, she retired to bed. Both mother and daughter were "lousy all day" on August 17, and by the next day Vanne had a temperature of 105. Jane's was 104, and she was feeling "not much better. Dismal." By August 20, she noticed, a "strange rash of pink blisters developed all over me & got worse as the day went on." Their temperatures seemed to go down a little on the following day, and by August 22, a Monday, Jane thought she was "very much better but horribly weak. Head throbbing, etc." During this time, Dominic pleaded with the two women to see a doctor in Kigoma, but neither felt well enough to make the journey, and so he administered to them by, in Jane's words, "constantly fussing over us." One night he found Vanne collapsed and unconscious outside the tent and took her back to bed.

Vanne's retrospective description of their two-week ordeal, written for the benefit of the family in England, was lighthearted and amusing, perhaps partly in an attempt to reassure her relatives that she and Jane had never been in any serious danger. Within a few days, she wrote, "neither of us could stand without holding on to something. It was a hoot!!" So they lay down side by side in their hot tent, which slowly became "dustier & dustier—the leaves piled up in the corners & the rush mat became sticky with sugar & orange juice." Each morning Jane would ask her mother for the thermometer, and after a half-hour or so Vanne would "pluck up the courage" to indicate where it was. "Another hour of silence & stillness would probably pass & then Jane would stretch an arm out very slowly to reach the thermometer." Taking their temperatures, Vanne concluded, "was the only intellectual enjoyment we had! It occupied a very long time & we took them about 3 times a day when we felt strong!!"

Dominic brought them constant cups of tea and "other dainties," most of which went unconsumed, but after the first two days Jane decided that she had to maintain her strength, so she insisted on a hearty evening din-ner—sausages, peas, potatoes, and soup—and forced herself to sit up and try to eat some of it. So now, Vanne went on, they had both learned exactly what it was like "to lie in a tent, under a tropical sky & stagger about like they do on the films in the grip of a FEVER!!!!" Vanne described what they had been experiencing as a peculiar "lake fever" of some sort, "or rather a fever caught from the natives of this area who often get these fevers and put it down to—guess what—THE WEATHER." She continued in this be-mused vein: "It is so funny to see them look round at the blazing sky and say that their fever must be due to the heat or the climate, or the lack of rain or something. The weather is as good a scape goat here as in England."

Actually, the weather was about as logical a cause of their condition as "bad air," which was the traditional prescientific theory among Europeans— as the Italians used to say, *mala aria*. Malaria, however, was the one diagno-sis Vanne resisted stubbornly: "It was not malaria & no one seems to know what it was, but the fishermen here get a lot of it, & I'm always dishing out fever pills now." In mid-July, just before they went to Gombe, the doctor they visited in Kigoma had insisted there was absolutely nothing to worry about in the realm of "tropical fevers" of any sort; but now, on the advice of several friends and acquaintances in Kigoma, Jane and Vanne began tak-ing the standard antimalarial prophylactic of the time, Paludrine—which Vanne always referred to as her "fever pills."

In spite of the continuing effects of what was most probably, in fact, ma-laria, Jane forced herself to go looking for chimpanzees on August 23 and 24. "Woke up at dawn," she wrote in her field journal on Wednesday the twenty-fourth, "but did not feel able to get up. Head hurt too much." She stayed in bed until around 7:30 and then sipped a cup of tea and discussed "how miserable everything was" with Vanne. "I then set off up the mountain. Several times thought I couldn't make it. Earth kept vanishing & head throbbed like an engine. However, I got up to the ridge at last."

She was feeling mildly better the next day, and after a brief relapse considered herself by August 30 to be "almost recovered."

15

David's Gift

1960

IN THE MIDDLE of the summer that year, after a month of climbing one by one through the dozen jagged valleys that cut through Gombe's tangled rectangle from east to west, Jane began concentrating on the area just beyond her own camp, a region inscribed north to south by the Linda, Kasekela, Kakombe, and Mkenke valleys.

On August 16, the same day she started feeling the preliminary effects of malaria, Jane and Rashidi were exploring some forest above the Linda valley. At around 1:30 in the afternoon, as they were sitting quietly at a high point and gazing over an open area where two chimps had recently passed by, Jane watched quietly as a third chimp, an older, "very handsom" male distinguished by his white beard, happened to approach within 10 yards. It was a remarkable encounter, with the ape seeming to register a complex sequence of emotions, from surprise to shock to calm curiosity as, for a moment, observed became observer. Jane described it all in her field journal:

> Then I heard a measured tread, & down the hill, straight towards me, came a very handsom male chimp. White beard, palish face, long black shining hair. He got to within about 10 yards, & suddenly saw me. His expression was one of amazement. He stopped abruptly. Stared. Put his head on one side & then on the other, and then turned & cantered off into the thicker undergrowth. We could hear his progression. Once out of sight, he walked again, made a complete semi-circle, until he was below us & in a line with the point where we had interrupted his journey. He then climbed up a small tree until his head was visible, and peered at us again. Having satisfied his curiosity he then climbed down & proceeded down the ravine.

After her malarial fever subsided, in the final week of August, Jane continued exploring the mountains and valleys just beyond her camp, perhaps at first because she was too weak to go any farther. But soon she was enjoying many hours of excellent chimp observations from there, which was a welcome and striking change from the depressing dearth of observations earlier in the month. It was, in fact, a real breakthrough.

"Did Mum tell you how many chimps I have been finding, up behind our own mountain?" Jane asked proudly in a letter to the family written late in the month. "I've discovered more—since my fever, in about 5 days, than in all the dreary weeks before. I've seen them walking along paths, I've seen them resting under trees, I've seen them playing. I've seen them 12 yards away, walking along, unconcerned." And while thus so productively occupied, she was surprised, early in the afternoon of August 26, by a second close encounter with a white-bearded older male.

> At this point I became aware of footsteps very close to me. I looked up and saw an old male, with a white beard, approaching along the track. He came to within 10 yards and then turned to the edge of the pocket. Miraculously he never saw me. He carefully lowered himself over the edge—very precipitous just here. As soon as he had gone I moved cautiously foreward & was able to see him lowering himself down the precipice by means of a tall tree growing there. When he reached the bottom of the tree he covered the next steep slope with a sort of sideways movement. Then the slope lessened and he walked solemnly along the baboon track with a normal 4-legged lumbering gait. Once every so often he would swing his legs through his arms, using his arms as crutches.

Was he the same white-bearded male she had seen ten days previously?

During the final week of August, Jane began "risking official displeasure" by going out alone. She was partly motivated by an unwillingness to let her African companions see her "in my weakened state," while she was still recovering from the malaria. But at the same time she was delighted to be walking around by herself and tired of coddling and compromising with two men who were unable to keep up with her. And in any case she had always believed that a single person would be less threatening to the wild apes.

She soon found an excellent observation spot. By following the Kakombe stream behind her tent and then moving up an unpleasantly steep hill (an ogre of a climb, soon named Ogre) onto a high ridge, she reached a rocky overlook from which she could spy down into the forested pocket of the Kakombe valley or look over to the ridge beyond. From this high overlook, moreover, it was an easy walk across high ground to a second excellent view down into parts of the Kasekela valley and beyond. In the journal, Jane first identified that favored viewing place as "my vantage spot," but soon she was referring to it as "the peak" and then "the Peak." In the mornings now she typically climbed directly to the Peak, sat down, and scanned a large part of the Kakombe valley through her binoculars. By the middle of September she had organized a secondary camp at the Peak: a tin trunk containing a kettle and coffee, a blanket and sweater, and a few cans of beans.

Her solo forays into the mountains lasted only a short while, though—altogether about a week between the end of her malaria and the arrival on September 1 of two new African assistants, Soko and Wilbert, who were essentially replacements for the fading and fatigued Adolf and Rashidi.

The two new men came to Gombe through the agency of a Kenyan named Derrick Dunn, who had dropped by earlier in August. Derrick was a friend of Brian Herne's whom Jane became acquainted with in Nairobi during the fall of 1957; she once described him in a letter home as "square faced, droopey eyes, huge, and not very intelligent," but those negative first impressions, she continued, were absolutely wrong. He was actually "one of the nicest men I've met out here" and "very clever."

During her first winter in Kenya, Jane had become good friends with Derrick and his wife, Joy, and their two young children, Michael and Valerie Ann. Derrick farmed in Kenya, but like Brian he was also a white hunter working for Lawrence-Brown Safaris in Tanganyika. Now, during the summer of 1960, David Anstey happened to mention to Derrick that Jane had set up a camp and was chasing chimpanzees at Gombe, and thus on August 13 he showed up at the reserve's pebble-and-sand shore with his safari client in tow.

Jane was pleased to see her old friend. Vanne found the client, a wealthy older American overly eager for his whiskey and cigars and dressed in an Ernest Hemingway sort of safari outfit, mildly comical and slightly awkward, but she was nonetheless delighted with the generous amounts of food they brought—including chocolates and ginger ale—and especially glad Derrick had come "so that," she wrote to the family in England, "I could revise my opinion of him." Derrick, in fact, "couldn't have been nicer or more helpful to Jane," she thought. In the end, having recognized Jane's deep frustrations with the progress of her chimp research, he paid for two of his top trackers from the safari business to go to Gombe. On August 28, therefore, a telegram was delivered to Gombe that said, "Soko and another arriving 1st September for you."

Jane was, as she wrote in her journal at the time, "completely mystified" by the news. But when the two men arrived, she decided that she "felt <u>very</u> pleased & happy. At long last I shall be able to get down to some <u>real</u> work."

On the morning of September 3, their first working day together, Jane was "so looking forward to it" that she woke up at 4:45. "It is impossible to describe the elation with which I heard the boys waking up at 6," she wrote in the journal. She lit the fire for tea, and then, after a quick and simple breakfast, they "fairly shot up the mountain—I was thoroughly exhausted at the top! Climbed the peak, & no sooner there than heard chimps calling to the left—fairly close & from the first patch of forest inland from the pocket."

Jane continued exploring the central area of the reserve beyond her camp, and she continued using the Peak as a starting place. The men's physical fitness may have been more important than their tracking skills, but in any case Jane now made good use of her new field staff, having them scout and plan, sending one to look for chimpanzees in one place while she accompanied the other to another place, and in that way effectively expanding her ability to locate the elusive creatures. Once they found a good viewing place, her assistant would quietly back off so that Jane could worm in closer.

Wilbert, who was very tall and, according to Jane's later writing, "always looked immaculate even after scrambling on his belly along a pig trail," had trouble adjusting to the food in camp, and he and Soko were not getting along very well, so he began sleeping in Dominic the cook's tent. But Soko left after only two weeks and was quickly replaced by a third tracker hired by Derrick Dunn, a short and vigorous man who went by the nickname Short. After Wilbert left, around the middle of October, Jane and Short typically went out separately, agreeing to meet at various times in various places to trade information. Short continued at Gombe until Jane left for her first holiday from chimp-watching, on December 1.

As she had done with the vervet monkeys on Lolui Island, Jane approached the chimps openly but subtly, moving in as close as their signals of comfort and discomfort dictated. She also dressed quietly, avoiding unnatural patterns or colors. And when the apes were clearly distracted or distressed by being looked at, she would do her best to pretend she was not really interested in looking to begin with. She might try to behave as if she were just another innocently foraging primate, ostentatiously scratching herself or pawing away for food—as on October 15: "The first chimp went close to the trunk and hid in the leaves, watching me. I began to look for insects, digging in the ground with my hand & pretending to eat." It was a technique she called "my baboon act."

But time and again the watched would turn to stare at the watchers — with mild curiosity, perhaps, or anxiety. "Suddenly, the two females saw us, got up, moved a little way back towards the trees they had left, stared at us again, and went out of sight," Jane wrote on September 7. "They walked about 100 yards & then stopped," she noted on September 9, "each in a little patch of shade. The first old boy sat with his knees up, his arms folded across them, and his chin on his arms. Only the other large one did not look quite at ease. The other two both sat very comfortably, and they all stared at us." September 11: "I thought we could get closer to the 5 in the pocket & possibly see them nest building, but this was a failure. As we got round they climbed down & disappeared."

On a few rare occasions, however, the apes seemed not to mind the new primates in their forest. On September 14: "After a while they saw us and paused to stare. Did not appear to mind, and did not hurry, but continued their leisurely ascent." And especially on September 16, when an "old & grizzled male with white beard," sitting down only about 15 yards away, watched her very calmly: "Absolutely no fear. Scratched one shoulder & then the other. Rubbed his chin."

Jane studied everything she could think of, including what the apes looked like. She labored over basic physical descriptions, as with this field journal entry for September 9: "This was the very first opportunity I had of seeing the male genital organs closely. The testicles of the old man were enormous, hanging down like a great bag. The penis, which was not erected, was a dull pink."

She tried to identify the sounds chimps made and assess what those vocalizations might actually mean. For example, this entry from September 12:

At 12.45 there were calls, hoots & screams, from near the top of the mountain, and low hoots from lower down, in the karonga [ravine]. From 1 pm onwards, until the 5 chimps from the top of the mountain came down, there was an almost continual screaming, about every 10 to 15 mins. Each occasion was a series of high pitched, fairly short, loud screams. Pain or fear? Pretty sure it was the same animal. The voice had a hoarse vibration. Often this scream was accompanied by calls from the rest of the group, & frequently there was a response from the animals lower down. These appeared to split into two groups, one lot moving further up the karonga. It sounded as though there was only one chimp near the bottom — the calls were always those of a single animal, & always sounded the same — low pitched rather mournful hooting call. Mournful, because the "ooh" was long drawn out.

Or this entry from September 13: "The call was two two-syllable sounds: 'Ooh-huh ooh-huh'—i.e., low hooting call. At 7.30 the above sound was repeated, then louder 3 times, & low again for another 2. At 8.15, a rather high pitched series of scream-like calls 'ooah-ooah whah-whah'—repeated several times."

She described and analyzed how the chimpanzees moved. September 8: "It was very steep, & they all went rather fast, using a movement that was almost like the 'crutch walk' but consisted of moving both arms forward together & then bringing the legs forward together. As they touched the ground, the arms moved off again, giving a 'bounding' effect."

She gathered as much data as possible on what they ate, starting with collecting—and tasting—samples of things she had seen them eat. September 20: "Inside the case, which is thick & hard, is an acorn-like nut encased in bright pink oily fibres. These taste rather like the palm nuts. The nut, which is also oily, has the most unpleasant, bitter pungent taste—I could not get rid of it for a long time." October 15: "The place where they stayed so long was where a new type of berry was growing—fruit I should say. Round & purple with a small stone. Also the tree with the yellow flowers—there were no flowers so they were eating shoots." And Jane continued collecting and examining whatever she could find from the other end. September 18: "The feces were dry, dark brown, and fibrous. Contained many stones from a small purplish fruit. We opened one of these small stones & found it oily. Also several brown nuts, looking rather like peeled acorns, & of the type which we had noticed along the Linda River the day before. They are the inside of a hard case."

She described where the chimpanzees slept, in arboreal nests, and watched how they constructed those nests. September 9:

After this we were lucky enough to see a chimp making its nest. It was not close, unfortunately, & we could not tell which sex. But it squatted in a leafy tree, near the top. It then rapidly pulled small leafy branches towards it, from each direction, treading on them to hold them in place. It then sat down for a moment: stood up & pulled off a branch from higher up which it incorporated into the nest. This it did 4 times, with about ½ minute between each picking. It then lay down, hardly visible. Another couple of minutes & it reached out & picked a very small bunch of leaves which it appeared to place under its head. Then it stretched right out so that its feet projected beyond the structure of the nest.

And eventually (on November 18) she tried stretching right out in one of those nests for herself: "Very comfortable & springy indeed."

She was intrigued by the imaginative and apparently happy play of young chimps. As recorded on October 26: "They had their mouths open—the chimp laugh—tickling each other? Only twice during 45 mins of play did I hear a sound. Once a small scream—(Ahah ahah ahah). When 2 were wrestling. Often they dropped, still gripping each other. And on one occasion I heard a soft panting 'hoo-e-hoo-e-hoo.'" And October 27: "The child amused itself quietly: climbed up the tall thick branch above its mother, crawled along underneath where it bent over at the top, hung down by its arms, or one arm, kicking its legs. Turned upside down. For some time it climbed around with a sprig of leaves clasped in its left leg where the knee bends. Often it reached down, hanging by one arm and leg, and patted its mother's head or the leaves."

She was curious about the obviously close, affectionate relationships between mothers and young offspring, as evidenced, for example, during the following moment on September 22: "After eating two fruits—all of which, incidentally, were picked by hand from the tree—right or left apparantly impartially—the mother reached out—right arm, and picked up her child. She held it to her breast—in exactly human fashion—right hand behind its shoulders, left cradling it, & for about 5 minutes it suckled—from left breast only."

She was fascinated by the occasional tense and complex encounters between species—between chimps and baboons, for instance, as on September 14:

> At 2.30 we suddenly saw 4 adult chimps—certainly 2 large males, and almost certainly 2 females, surrounded by a troop of baboons. All at once several of the baboons ran forward, and the chimps also ran forward. It looked as though they were being chased. The two smaller ones climbed right up two small trees. The large male in the front stopped near a tree for a moment, and the one behind climbed a few feet up a tree, paused, climbed down, and suddenly rushed after the baboons near him. The other large male followed his example, turning on his tormentors, & running for several yards on his hind legs. There was quite a lot of noise—hard to sort out. The low grunting, growling noise of the chimp, mixed with the barks of baboons and one screaming.

One hundred sixty chimpanzees inhabited the full reserve, but in the valleys and hills just beyond Jane's camp there lived only four or five dozen apes altogether—few enough that, as they were becoming familiar with her, Jane could reasonably anticipate learning to recognize individuals on sight. But it was hard to make out distinctive individual features. For one thing, she was still watching most of the time from a considerable distance. Moreover, because of limited funds, her binoculars were second-rate, and thus she was often left squinting unproductively into a chromatic blur. On September 5, though, Jane made a routine trip into Kigoma and found that the British district officer, a man named Michael Beardmore, had a much better pair of field glasses, which he generously lent her. They were of German manufacture, "very small & light, 7 X 25, special for bird watching. Vast improvement. First class."

In any event, the difficult process of making identifications took months, as Jane continued to watch and carefully describe her subjects, noting whenever possible any distinguishing marks. The following methodical description of a mother and her infant, entered in the journal on October 24, gives a taste of the problem and process:

> She was dark faced & a little grizzled. Small bald V. Dark mark on left side of her face, behind & below eye. She was keeping mostly in the same place, reaching out—either hand—& pulling the sprays towards her, picking off fruit with lips. Her breasts were not noticeably large, nor were the nipples. I find a note that her face & hands gave a "grey" impression, rather than black. The infant very small & very pale faced. Large white rump patch. White mark on top of head, left side. (Thank god for a distinguishing mark at last!)

But with the new, hardworking, skilled, and motivated field staff, with the increasingly comfortable familiarity between observer and observed, and with the improved field glasses, Jane was slowly beginning to make out distinctive features and marks and to conclude that she could recognize a few individuals. And by September 12 she was confident enough to begin tentatively trying out some names. As she wrote less tentatively a few days later, in a letter to the family, "But my chimps are so lovely now. I know where to find them, I know some of them by sight. I know the hideous Sophie with her son, Sophocles. I know the bearded grizzled old Claud, and an almost bald old lady who, I think, must be Annie. They are getting used to us."

By the second half of September, Jane had surpassed the number of days—sixty-four—spent in active fieldwork pursuing chimpanzees by her significant predecessor, Henry W. Nissen of Yale University, in 1930.

Nissen, with his gun and grass fires and club-wielding African helpers, with his aggressive and ultimately blundering approach to the problem of studying wild chimpanzees, never thought of the species as a collection of individuals with individual personalities. He preferred instead to conceptualize the species as a biological monolith, a simplistically coherent unit about which simple and definite laws of behavior might readily be deduced, such as "the chimpanzee likes company," "the chimpanzee is nomadic," "the wild chimpanzee is an early riser." And yet nothing Jane had done or seen so far actively contradicted or overtly surpassed Nissen's general conclusions about the apes: that chimpanzee group size varies substantially; that they wander a lot, seek out a variety of fruits and berries and other vegetable matter to eat, rest during the midday heat, build tree nests in the evening to sleep in, and so on. In most ways, she was that summer and autumn still busily confirming the general conclusions of her scientific predecessor.

Then George Schaller showed up.

George Schaller—tall and lean, clean-cut and good-looking, poised, very smart—had been a graduate student in zoology at the University of Wisconsin when, in January 1957, Professor John Emlen asked him if he would consider something bigger and hairier than birds, his chief interest, since the National Academy of Sciences was looking to fund field research on wild gorillas. Schaller impetuously agreed to give up birds in favor of gorillas and immediately set about reading everything he could on the latter, thus quickly discovering how very little anyone knew.

Schaller reviewed nineteenth-century exploration and hunting narratives, Carl Akeley's accounts of killing gorillas for science and regretting it, and Harold C. Bingham's brief monograph describing his unsatisfactory 1929 expedition, in which the anxious researcher shot a gorilla. He eagerly awaited the latest reports from Uganda by Rosalie Osborn and Jill Donisthorpe, those two courageous if untrained enthusiasts supported by Walter Baumgartel of the Travellers Rest hotel. Rosalie Osborn had observed mountain gorillas in the Ugandan Virungas between October 1956 and January 1957; Jill Donisthorpe had continued that work until September 1957. But when their typed reports finally arrived in Wisconsin, the young George Schaller found himself, as he has written, "truly depressed." He clarified: "Here someone had made a serious attempt to study gorillas for a whole year, but the amount of concrete information about the behavior of the apes which these investigators obtained was minute."

Schaller and his wife, Kay, accompanied by John Emlen and his wife, Jinny, arrived in East Africa in February 1959, and over the next six months the two men proceeded to conduct a general survey of mountain gorilla distribution—a very ambitious task at the time, partly because their definition of "mountain gorilla" included the thousands of apes we would today identify as eastern lowland gorillas. Once the survey was finished, in August, John and Jinny Emlen went home, while George and Kay Schaller hiked into the Belgian Congo portion of the Virunga volcanoes and set up housekeeping in a teetering, tin-roofed, three-windowed cabin at Kabara meadow in Albert National Park. As it happened, Kabara was the very place where the reformed specimen collector and taxidermist Carl Akeley had camped out in 1926, seriously ill but gamely intending to study gorillas. From that failed attempt, a simple flat marker—Akeley's tombstone—remained, weathering at the edge of the meadow.

Kay Schaller took on the essential tasks of support, maintenance, and logistics in their mountain cabin, while George spent his days wandering, sometimes alone and sometimes in the company of a park guard, through the damp and chilly volcanic forests, looking for gorillas. And finding them.

Like Jane, George Schaller developed a technique of approaching the apes by appearing openly if unobtrusively and projecting himself as a quiet, nonthreatening presence, hoping that their curiosity would overcome their fear. He walked slowly, tried to seem boring, never carried a gun, and avoided as much as possible staring directly at his subjects. Like Jane, he found the apes "more annoyed and excited on seeing two persons than one," so when he went out with one of the park guards, he would ask the guard to withdraw when they found gorillas. Like Jane, he understood that the puzzle of the species as a collective could best be solved through understanding, and therefore recognizing, individuals. Like Jane, he intuitively thought of his subjects as sentient creatures with humanlike emotions, and again like Jane, he gave them names that sometimes mnemonically identified their appearance but also marked them as distinctive personalities: Big Daddy ("easily recognizable by the two bright silver spots on his gray back"), D.J. ("the striving executive type who had not yet reached the top"), the Outsider ("roamed slowly around the periphery of the group"), Splitnose, Junior, Mrs. September, Mrs. Bad-eye, Mrs. Greyhead, Max, Moritz, and so on.

George Schaller's gorilla work in the Virungas was a spectacular breakthrough, arguably the first intimate scientific study of wild apes, and he was therefore almost uniquely qualified to understand and advise Jane as she labored in isolation at Gombe. His original plan had been to study gorillas for eighteen months following the population survey, which would have kept him and Kay in the cabin at Kabara until February 1961. But the same political storm in the Belgian Congo that had delayed the start of Jane's research in mid-July 1960 prematurely precipitated the end of his, and the Schallers wisely left their cabin and crossed the border into Uganda, where Kay moved into a women's dorm at Makerere College in Kampala while George did a couple more months' worth of gorilla work in southwestern Uganda.

Louis Leakey contacted George by telegram that September, just as he was finishing up, and asked him to stop at the Coryndon Museum when he was next in Nairobi. As Kay Schaller recently recalled, they finally located Louis in his office, sitting behind his desk and "looking very biggely-browed and grumpy." The white-haired curator "looked up at us as if we were the most unwelcome people in this world," but then, "as soon as George said who he was, he was just extremely kind."

George Schaller remembers "a rather bulky man full of enthusiasm and dressed in a sort of jumpsuit and delightedly showing me some fossils that he had found. In my ignorance, I could not have appreciated them enough, but I greatly liked his enthusiasm for things." In any event, Louis soon persuaded them that they must go see that Jane Goodall person and the chimpanzees she was watching in Tanganyika, and thus the Schallers drove their Volkswagen bus from Nairobi to Kigoma and established themselves by Saturday, October 8, 1960, at the Regina Hotel.

On Thursday, Jane had received a telegram from Louis, informing her that the Schallers would arrive in Kigoma in two days. So she took the boat into town on Friday, had a skin infection on her leg attended to at the Kigoma hospital, and, the day after, met George and Kay Schaller at their hotel for tea. As Jane noted laconically in her field journal, "Very favourably impressed by them."

Jane and the Schallers returned to Gombe on a hired boat that Sunday, arriving at noon, and after lunch at the camp, Kay and Vanne visited while Jane and George set off up the mountain to find chimps. Unfortunately, they were nowhere to be seen. Some hooting cries and calls from somewhere down in one of the forest pockets—that was it. They returned to camp early and "had a very pleasant and interesting evening," according to the journal. The next day was "still unlucky" in a chimp-finding sense, even though Jane took her guest "all round the usual haunts." Still no chimps. "But I learnt a great deal from him, & we had some very interesting conversations," not to mention "another extremely pleasant evening." The Schallers took a boat back to Kigoma the next morning, October 11.

George and Kay Schaller recall only a few faint details from that long-ago visit to Gombe. Kay recollects liking Vanne: "She and I started talking a lot during the day while Jane and George were up on the trail, and I've admired her ever since." George remembers Jane as a "quiet, attractive girl" who, as he learned very quickly, "was good at climbing hills and very determined to get on with her work." He was also surprised by the brevity of the project—only four months—and by the pathetic inadequacy of her equipment, including the borrowed and still not very good binoculars, nonexistent telescope, and bad camera. With a decent grant, he thought then, she would be able to get more information; and he left her the small gift of a polythene sheet to use as a quick shelter from the rain while looking for chimps.

Precisely what their "very interesting conversations" consisted of, Jane never wrote down, but in any event she was most certainly upset because her chimpanzee study was drawing to a close. She was afraid of failure and of disappointing Louis. And what *had* she done so far to justify further funding, a longer study, more support, more time in the field? In a letter to the family back home, she mentioned the Schallers' visit and noted that it was "really nice to talk to someone who really understood what I was doing, & why, & who didn't think I was completely crazy." And she summarized what may have been George Schaller's most important comment: "George said he thought that if I could see chimps eating meat, or using a tool, a whole year's work would be justified."

Schaller's year of close gorilla observations had confirmed that those apes ate a highly fibrous vegetarian diet: typically, the ground-level plants they wandered through. Chimpanzees, most everyone seemed to agree, favored a rarer and richer vegetarian diet that focused on fruits and berries and nuts. Indeed, the chimp diet seemed not very different from a human diet, with the very important exception that the hairy apes were not supposed to be hunters or meat-eaters. Nissen had described dozens of vegetable items that appeared on the menu of the chimpanzees he studied, but no meat. Chimpanzees, like gorillas, were vegetarians.

At least that was the consensus, although Schaller smartly recognized that no one actually knew for certain. And Jane, now alerted to the possibility of a hidden, carnivorous aspect to her apes, was perhaps more than usually attentive when, around 7:40 in the morning of October 30, a Sunday, she sat next to Short on the Peak and witnessed, through her binoculars, a wild drama in the trees below. It was hard to make out what was going on, since the foliage was very dense in that particular spot, but she steadied her glasses onto a violent boiling in the branches, listened to some "angry little screams," as she wrote in the field journal, and finally made out three chimps, one of whom was holding "something which looked pink."

At first she thought the pink object was a newborn infant. She continued to study the excited little drama below. She made out a fourth chimp nearby. She saw three baboons "very close"—heard some screams and a violent crashing through leaves as the chimp holding the pinkish object seemed to chase after a big gray baboon who had approached very closely. And then down on the ground she could make out two large and grayish bush pigs milling around the base of the tree. A younger chimp happened to move from a low spot in the tree onto the ground, and then, screaming, he precipitously rushed up into another tree. "It was being chased, I'm sure, by one of the pigs," Jane wrote in the journal, although she also noted that she might conceivably have been mistaken. What sounded like the "grunting" of pigs could have been the "growling snort" of a baboon.

At around eight o'clock that morning, she noted two chimps sitting next to each other in the tree. One of them, a big male, seemed to be eating away at the pink object. "Suspected meat," she wrote. Meanwhile, five baboons were crowding in aggressively; the second chimpanzee, Jane now saw, was a female with a small infant. Noisy skirmishes with the baboons, screams and snarls, chases and counterchases, continued on and off for the next hour and a quarter, but the two chimps sat together, and once every few minutes the female would tentatively reach toward the male with the mysterious object in his hands. Jane "began to wonder if object was honey in some form — was she dipping her hand in & licking fingers? Did not appear to be putting hand to mouth."

The male climbed down to some lower branches, followed by the female with the clinging infant. Five minutes later the male moved to another branch, followed again by the female and her infant. Ten minutes later the male moved a third time, and again the female moved up next to him. At around 9:20, after some aggressive harassment from a large baboon, the male chimpanzee with the strange pink prize "nonchalantly moved out onto a completely bare branch at the top of a tree," where Jane could see more clearly.

> The object was meat. He carried it in his left hand as before, close to his chest. In his right hand were 2 or 3 twigs with leaves on them. He sat on the branch, his left hand, with the meat, on his "lap". He lifted it to his mouth & seemed to "suck" rather than bite, at the limp end. There was no hair or fur on this meat. Unless he had plucked or skinned the thing, it was a baby of some sort. No head. Two bits hanging down that looked like legs. But impossible to know what it was. About the size of a small rabbit. After biting or sucking at the meat he put his hand down, & took a bite of the leaves from the bunch in his other hand. He had a pale, slightly mottled face, with conspicuous white beard & very pink "flabby" testicles.

Now the female with her small infant climbed up to a branch opposite the white-bearded male, and Jane watched her beg for a piece of the prize. She turned around and "presented her bottom to him," a sexual and submissive gesture, then sat down on the branch to face him. He drew the meat

away, securing it under his arm. She reached over and touched it. He ignored her. She stretched her right arm out and placed her fingers on his lips.
She touched his right hand and then his mouth once again. He took another
bite of the meat and again held it away, tucked under his arm. Once more
she reached out to touch it. From time to time the female would pluck a leaf
and put it in her mouth, but mostly now she simply stared at the white-
bearded male—or at the meat—as he continued slowly chewing away at it,
alternating bites of green leaves with bites of pink flesh. That intense little
episode lasted about ten minutes, until the male moved away once again,
with the persistent and supplicating female and her baby following.

"It was very exciting to see," Jane reflected on her discovery that evening, as she wrote it all out with a careful longhand in the journal, "but it is
rather like a detective book with not only the end chapter missing, but the
beginning as well. We have an unidentified victim, we do not know how he
met his death, & we are not sure of the murderer. Most frustrating."

But she would eventually conclude that the victim was an infant bush
pig—hence the rushing, agitated two adult pigs at the base of the tree. And
he met his death, as dozens, even hundreds of subsequent observations
would ultimately reinforce, at the predatory hands and teeth of a chimpanzee. That day's observation was a seminal moment, the first clearly recorded
eyewitness account of carnivory among wild chimps—and within a very
short time, less than a week, it would be followed by a discovery that was
even more startling.

It had been clear since the pioneering work of Wolfgang Köhler, during the
second decade of the twentieth century, that chimpanzees in laboratory
cages are smart enough to solve novel problems, such as obtaining out-of-
reach bananas, by using ordinary objects in creative ways as tools. George
Schaller may have been disappointed that he never found wild gorillas using
tools, but he was aware of a couple of casual reports indicating that at least
some groups of wild chimps did so in the course of their daily lives.

In 1948 an American adventurer named Harry Beatty successfully followed a group of chimpanzees through the thickets of a Liberian forest and
watched in amazement as some of them paused to use stones as hammers,
pounding hard walnuts onto stone anvils in order to crack them open; his
brief note on the behavior was published in a scientific journal two years
later. And in a 1956 popularized memoir, the English gorilla hunter Fred
Merfield described watching through binoculars as a group of eight chimpanzees sat around the entrance to a bees' nest and used sticks or twigs to
dip for honey: "Each ape held a long twig, which it poked down the hole
and withdrew coated with honey." Beatty was following chimps near the far

western edge of their range in West Africa; Merfield's single, brief observation took place in Central Africa. But Jane could hope to observe some similar behavior among her eastern chimps.

The great moment took place on Friday, November 4. Since Short had gone into Kigoma on an errand, Jane was wandering in the mountains on her own. She started up the Kakombe valley behind her camp, but, following the auditory trail of cries and hoots, she moved north, walking on a high ridge trail above the Linda valley. She was passing within 100 yards of a termite mound when, at 8:15, she happened to notice a "black object" in front of the mound. Jane "didn't remember seeing a tree stump there," as the journal indicates, and so she looked more closely and realized it was a chimp. "I quickly dropped down, & crawled through the sparse dry grass until I reached a tree with greenery sprouting at the base." Looking through the screen of those leaves, she observed the ape, about 50 yards away, "picking up things" from the termite mound and putting them in his mouth. Eating. His back was turned toward her. Jane carefully moved around to get a better view, while the chimp turned around, facing her—but still not aware, apparently, that he was being watched.

> Then, very deliberately he pulled a thick grass stalk towards him & broke off a piece about 18" long. Then, unfortunately, he turned his back on me again. (He picked off the grass with his right hand.) After some minutes he climbed onto the top of the mound, but still with his back to me. Then he got down—after peering hard in my direction, & vanished down the hill. After 5 mins or so, when I thought he had seen me & gone, he appeared, wandering away nonchalantly, away from me. Then he stopped, put up his left hand up onto a low branch, stood up, & looked around. Apparantly changed his mind, for he turned round & came straight towards me. As he walked along, he gave the impression of "swinging along," his head slightly swinging from side to side. Fairly bald. Face not too dark. White beard.

When the white-bearded chimp had come within about 10 yards of where Jane was sitting, he "suddenly saw me & stopped dead for a second. I can't say exactly how, but his whole face registered a sudden shock." Then he bounded away, racing quickly down the slope in the direction of the forest pocket.

Ants, bees, beetle grubs, crickets, moth caterpillars, and wasps all provide significant dietary protein for the chimpanzees of Gombe, as Jane eventually concluded, but the mound-building termites, *Macrotermes bellicosus,* are the most important insect food of all. From October to December, members of this species' colony develop wings and emerge from their mounds through narrow tunnels to swarm away and found new colonies. The winged termites are large and plump, and they provide bundles of nutritionally attractive protein to anyone (including baboons and other monkeys, chimps, small mammals, birds, and humans) who can catch them. But only chimpanzees have developed the technique of fishing deeply into the termite mounds in order to catch the nonwinged members of the colony, mainly the soldiers. The chimps select a long stem of grass or a suitable strip of bark or palm or a twig; modify it to create a long, smooth, and flexible probe; and then insert the tool deeply into one of the narrow, twisty exit tunnels of the mound. The colony's soldier termites, antagonized by the intrusion of a foreign object, reflexively clamp on with their mandibles and, thus attached, are pulled slowly back out. And the chimps, having assiduously drawn out the termite-laden probe, then swipe it through their lips and gobble down the helplessly clinging insects.

Jane's first sighting of a termite-fishing chimpanzee, that white-bearded male hunched with his back toward her at the mound, was followed two days later, on Sunday, November 6, by a more detailed observation at the same termite mound. This time, however, there were two chimps, both male. Just as she saw them, one of the males moved away from the left side of the mound and out of sight, while the other continued sitting, to the right of the mound and still visible. There was little cover for Jane's approach, just tall grass, and the sitting chimp appeared to see her. But then, after a moment of concerned observation, he calmly returned to the more important activity of fishing for termites.

> After a few minutes (it was 8.45 when I got there) he looked in my direction, peered, got up, climbed to the top of the [termite] hill, and gazed directly at me. Then he got down, resumed his original position, & continued eating termites. I could see a little better the use of the piece of straw. It was held in the left hand, poked into the ground, and then removed coated with termites. The straw was then raised to the mouth & the insects picked off with the lips, along the length of the straw, starting in the middle. Occasionally his head was bent right down to the ground. He chewed each mouthful. Occasionally sat with his lips open as he poked up a new load.

Jane realized that she was watching the same male she had seen two days before, the white-bearded one — only now, closer up and in the bright sunlight, his beard appeared more gray than white, and she described him thus: "Grey beard, fingers looked greyish, dark face, only a little bald. Very handsom." She watched him for around three quarters of an hour, whereupon the second chimp, after laboring on the far side of the mound, appeared once again and then left. The first chimp, the gray-bearded one (and a few lines after the above description she coined a name for him: Greybeard), followed his companion a short while later. Jane waited until they had been gone for fifteen minutes, and then she moved down to "examine the scene of the repast." But the minute she arrived there were some low hoots and then loud screams, begun by one of the chimps, continued by them both. "So—they had been watching me had they! I pretended to eat termites—which must have infuriated them!—& then quietly moved away & sat down."

Greybeard was, as Jane later confirmed, the same male she had surprised two days earlier when she witnessed termite-fishing for the first time. He was also the same chimpanzee she had seen a week earlier with a pink piece of meat in one hand and leaves in the other.

It was the season for termites, and during the days that followed, she observed on several occasions different individuals fishing intently at the mound, though not Greybeard. On November 9, however, she happened to spot him walking through an area just below where she walked, and they both stopped. She sat down, and he eventually sat down as well: knees up, directly facing and casually observing her from a spot where, as Jane wrote in the journal that evening, "I was able to observe him excellently." After looking at her, he groomed his right wrist and his knees, looked up at her again, reached with his left arm under his right to scratch his back. "He then spent about 5 mins stroking his beard with his left hand, (like a man thinking), & rubbing his thumb along upper lip. During this he occasionally glanced casually at me. He is a very nice chimp."

Indeed, when she stumbled across the gray-bearded male once more (this time he was sitting in a tree, facing away from her), on November 26, Jane acted as if she had run into an old friend—and invented, in an apparently spontaneous moment of inspiration, his full name: "Hastily I backed away & moved round to where a group of 3 trees offered some cover. Cautiously I looked for the chimp. He had not moved. And it was David Greybeard!" She quietly watched the ape for several minutes, he continuing to face away from her, right leg hanging down, left leg up and bent at the knee, looking very relaxed. He continued in that position and posture, occasionally looking back in her general direction but not appearing to notice her.

He then moved into another tree in which there sat a second chimp, and Jane very carefully and slowly tried to creep through some trees and bush for a better look. She became slightly disoriented in the process and emerged to find the two chimps directly ahead instead of over to the right where she had expected, and only 30 yards away. Much closer than usual. "David Greybeard was half way up the tree. He had his back to me, but as I sat down he turned to face me. He was <u>perfectly</u> aware of my presence—as he had been all along. He must have got a good laugh out of my creeping round."

The other chimpanzee in the tree, another male, seemed less relaxed, a little anxious perhaps, and he picked his nose from time and time, occasionally peering at her and shifting his position. Jane recognized this second male as one of David's regular companions, and she gave him the name Jonathan, in reference to the Biblical friends: "Jonathan, below, was more cautious."

David climbed down out of that tree, while Jonathan moved higher, reaching a point where he was obscured by leaves. David walked a short distance to the left, climbed an adjacent tree, sat casually and openly in view of Jane, again with his left leg hanging, his right leg up, and his right arm resting on the knee as he quietly gazed in Jonathan's direction. "While David was sitting in his third and last tree and Jonathan was up in his tree, a large male baboon walked past below them, between them and me. He glanced at me casually & went on. I felt that it was the proudest moment of my whole life—all 3 accepted me."

David Greybeard was almost from the very beginning less afraid of Jane than the others, calmer, more sedate. More intrigued, perhaps. David was, as Jane summarized two and a half decades later, "the first chimpanzee I saw eating meat, the first to demonstrate the use of tools, and the first to permit my close approach in the forest." And his quiet, almost musing and thoughtful tolerance of her presence "did much to speed up habituation in the early months." He was the first chimpanzee at Gombe whose curiosity overcame his fear, in short, and his gift to Jane—that relaxed, chin-stroking acceptance of her alien, ghostly, ponytailed appearance in the woods—helped to calm the others around him and ultimately to tame the responses and attitudes of the entire community.

16

Primates and Paradigms

1960–1962

JANE REGULARLY SENT Louis reports from Gombe, including a weekly carbon copy of field journal entries, and after she had seen tool-using at the termite mound a second time, closely enough to be certain of what was going on, she passed on her account. Louis had spent most of his life searching for the tools of ancestral humans, and he believed—as did many of his professional peers—that tool-using and toolmaking essentially defined "human." Tools made the man, as Leighton Wilkie liked to put it, echoing a phrase coined by the Scottish historian and philosopher Thomas Carlyle. The discovery that chimpanzees were not only using but fashioning their own tools therefore came as a profound surprise to Louis, and he cabled back to Jane the memorable response "Now we must redefine 'tool,' redefine 'man,' or accept chimpanzees as humans."

Jane's study was scheduled to end by December 1, 1960. The field journal was due to be finished at that date. In the ordinary course of events, her work at Gombe would have become an amateur's snapshot in the grand album of scientific progress. But the meat-eating and tool-using observations of October and November constituted a complete validation of Jane's work and style, her untrained and possibly eccentric approach to the study of animal behavior, and they demonstrated to Louis the importance of his continued involvement.

He was very excited by this turn of events, filled with enthusiasm and expansive visions for his young protégée, and during Jane's December holiday in Nairobi that year he unveiled his next wild scheme, which was to enroll her in a doctoral program in ethology at Cambridge University. She would need that diploma as a ticket, a union card, he insisted, to give her chimpanzee research the credibility it deserved. To be sure, getting her into graduate studies at Cambridge would be an impressive trick, since she had no undergraduate education—the ordinary prerequisite—but that obstacle was a minor one to Louis's way of thinking. Jane in turn promised Louis that if she were given the chance, she would work very hard to earn the degree. As she candidly and bemusedly expressed the whole idea in a December letter to Vanne, "His plans, I must say, are all rather exciting, if they come off. If they do, then you really <u>could</u> squish all the other Ma's with a Dr Goodall in the family!!!"

The second phase of Louis's Project Pygmalion was to send Jane to America, where she would study captive chimpanzees living in seminaturalistic conditions at Robert Yerkes' primate center in Orange Park, Florida. By the spring of 1961 that deal was all properly arranged, including a stipend to cover her expenses. "It sounds as if I'm really off to Florida. Isn't it fun. I hear from Leakey they will pay me a 'stipend,'" she wrote home in March, adding, "What exactly is a 'stipend'?"

Finally, there was the matter of getting more money for further Gombe work, and for that Jane's powerful mentor turned to the National Geographic Society in Washington, D.C. Louis's first *National Geographic* article, "Finding the World's Earliest Man," had just appeared in September (of 1960), and a second was in the works for October 1961. Meanwhile, in late February, Louis had visited the United States for the second time, giving high-profile lectures at the Smithsonian Institution, the National Academy of Sciences, and the National Geographic Society. At the Geographic Society's Constitution Hall, Dr. Leakey gave two presentations on "Finding the Earliest Man." Coordinated with the showing of a film on East Africa and the Olduvai excavations made by Des Bartlett, Louis's talks—and his dignified presence and offhand manner, his appealing "eccentricity and unabashed corniness"—entranced the audiences and left the powers at the National Geographic convinced, as the society's president and magazine editor, Melville Bell Grosvenor, phrased it in a letter to the filmmaker Armand Denis, that the man was "an <u>extraordinary</u> find."

On Friday, February 24, Louis met with the National Geographic's Research and Exploration Committee to lobby for continued funding for his own work and now, additionally, for a small sum to keep the Gombe chimpanzee study going. In a February 27 follow-up letter to that meeting, he reviewed his arguments on behalf of the chimp project. His underlying reason for the work currently being done by "one of my research assistants, Miss Jane Goodall," he wrote, was anthropological: "vital to me in my study of early primate evolution because it will help me to build up an idea of Proconsul behavior under similar ecological conditions." This, of course, was the same justification Louis had offered in his much earlier proposal, the one that had failed to excite anyone other than Leighton Wilkie. But now he could declare that his research assistant had "already achieved observations that are fantastically important to science" and even to articulate some of them—without specifically mentioning the discovery of chimpanzee tool use, an observation he was reluctant to announce prematurely.

The National Geographic's Research and Exploration Committee voted to award Louis a grant of $28,000 to continue the digging at Olduvai, a highly unusual assignment of $7,800 to replace his salary at the Coryndon to pay for a year's leave, and a third grant of $1,400 to support several more months of Miss Goodall's work at Gombe. And so, with that generous underwriting, Jane was able to concentrate completely on her chimpanzee-watching. She set aside her Yerkes-in-Florida plan, and she postponed her date of arrival at Cambridge University until after the chimpanzee termite-fishing season would be over, in December. It was a propitious opening to a brilliant career . . . even if that career was a year late in getting started.

In his original proposal to Leighton Wilkie two years earlier, Louis had described a four-month Chimpanzee Project that would send Jane to Gombe in September 1959. Wilkie had, by the middle of March 1959, mailed Louis a check for $3,000 to underwrite that project. The check was cashed, but—possibly because Louis was thinking of replacing Jane—the project remained unorganized for a full year. In the meantime, Leighton Wilkie provided funds to support another chimpanzee research expedition, this one led by a real scientist rather than Louis's secretarial amateur, the creative and determined Dutch ethologist Adriaan Kortlandt, who had soon produced some impressive results.

Kortlandt first publicly revealed his findings in an article for the September 1962 issue of *Scientific American* entitled "Chimpanzees in the Wild," describing an expedition that swept across "the breadth of the continent" during a period of "some months" in early 1960 before settling on the "perfect spot" to study chimpanzees, a banana and papaya plantation at Beni, on the eastern edge of the Belgian Congo. The article remains vague about dates and durations, so one must consult the author's later writings to learn that "some months" means around two and that by the time Kortlandt had established himself at the Beni plantation and organized the construction of viewing stations, he had only about seven weeks left for watching chimps. In any case, he finished his preliminary research at Beni by the end of June 1960, around two weeks before Jane began hers at Gombe.

An observer of wild animals starts with two problems. First is finding the animals. Second is getting close enough to make good observations without causing them to run away. Jane chose to solve the second problem by observing semi-openly from far away while patiently and subtly reducing the distance and in that manner building a fragile sense of comfort and trust between observer and observed. She was slowly taming them, in essence, or *habituating* them. By contrast, Kortlandt felt that after he had arrived at the Beni plantation, there was not enough time for habituation. He therefore decided on the alternative approach of complete hiding: watching the chimps from secure observation stations without, he hoped, their recognizing what was going on.

The Beni plantation was an excellent place to watch chimpanzees in part because it was edged by a steep forested hillside. The apes, living in their usual sort of forest environment, often emerged into the open area of the plantation in order to steal cultivated bananas and papayas. The plantation owner, exceptionally tolerant of such simian thievery, had never shot at them or otherwise tried to drive them off, and thus they were used to moving from natural thicket to artificial clearing for extended and somewhat leisurely feasts. It was an unusual opportunity for the chimp watcher.

Kortlandt took note of the apes' established pathways from forest to fruit and built five blinds at strategic places. One of them was a high nest, constructed in a tall tree at around 80 feet. A second was a 25-foot tower. The other three were closer to the ground, each designed carefully "as a kind of basket so that the apes could look through and see that nothing was hiding in this newly-grown 'bush.' Day by day more and more leaves were added. Eventually the chimps accepted that nothing was hiding there—but then I was there." The 80-foot-high tree perch gave the ethologist panoramic views of the area and any chimps wandering about, although it had the disadvantage of swaying so hard in the wind that some days he was unable to use his binoculars. It was also a terrifying place to be during a thunderstorm: "I could only pray that I would not be electrocuted." Nevertheless, as soon as the chimpanzees appeared in the field, Kortlandt wrote, "I did not dare come down before nightfall lest I betray my presence and so permanently drive them away." On days the researcher spent in the ground-level blinds, a male chimp would on occasion approach as close as 10 feet to inspect the structure, peering intently and, Kortlandt imagined, "able to see my eyes through the peep hole." When that happened, the chimp proceeded to scratch himself—"because of uncertainty," Kortlandt assumed—and then "walked away without either fleeing or attacking, perhaps wondering what those grey-blue eyes in a heap of rubbish could mean. Such moments provided me with the most profound experiences of my professional life."

During seven weeks inside the blinds at Beni, Adriaan Kortlandt achieved a total of fifty-four successful observation sessions, sighting as many as forty-eight or forty-nine chimpanzees during a single period, observing aspects of chimpanzee social life, noting for the first time an array of complex chimpanzee gestural and postural communications, and producing the first photographs and film of these apes in the wild. He returned to the Beni site in 1963 and 1964 for another six months' research altogether—and over a lifetime claims to have been responsible, either directly or indirectly through his students, for more than three years of field research on wild chimpanzees at several locations across Africa.

So the significant ape studies of Adriaan Kortlandt—and George Schaller—predated Jane's research at Gombe. Both men were, like Jane, the spiritual or intellectual inheritors of a naturalist tradition, driven to study animals of any kind, not necessarily primates, perhaps by the same sort of emotional complex that motivated Victorian naturalists to put on their walking shoes and wander intelligently, with ripe and patient curiosity, into God's wondrous creation.

Schaller went to Africa in 1959 to study gorillas in order to expand zoological knowledge—not because gorillas were an interesting species belonging to the primate order but because they were an interesting species within the animal kingdom. In other words, he would have been more or less equally prepared to study birds or sea otters or lions or giant pandas, which he eventually did.

In Europe, the traditions of Victorian naturalism and the emerging discipline of zoology were modified during the twentieth century by a small group of men who ultimately pressed the study of animal behavior into a more analytical, experimental, and quantitative mold and in the process invented a discipline they called ethology. Like American zoologists, European ethologists were interested in penetrating the mysteries of all animal behavior and so were neither especially attracted nor averse to primate studies. Adriaan Kortlandt was educated as a geographer and psychologist before turning to the ethological study of cormorants, and he switched to chimpanzees, it appears, simply because they presented another set of interesting problems in animal behavior.

Jane's own naturalism was an intuitive and untutored one, and she was sponsored by Louis Leakey, who originally promoted the Gombe study as an anthropological exercise. But within a short while she would join the European school of ethology, beginning her formal graduate education in that discipline at Cambridge University.

A few other ethologists turned to the study of captive and wild primates (monkeys mostly) during this general period. But the real energy behind primate field studies, an impetus pushing the remarkable first wave of eager young students off to the tropics to study monkeys and apes, occurred in the late 1950s and early 1960s largely as a result of changing paradigms within the disciplines of psychology and anthropology, perhaps especially in the United States, where primates came to be seen as particular animals who could serve as mirrors to enhance the study of humans.

Yale University's Robert M. Yerkes originally foresaw, in the 1920s, a new psychology—or a psychobiology, as he preferred it—that would study captive and wild primates, apes mainly, as a way to enter the cage of the human psyche. But Yerkes' voice was forgotten during the 1930s and 1940s, overwhelmed in his own discipline by academic herding and the fashion of behaviorism, first articulated in 1908 by John B. Watson, an experimental psychologist at Johns Hopkins University. Watson labored to establish experimental psychology as a hard science, like physics and chemistry, that would start with simple questions and build its edifice out of simple answers; that relied on small, easily bred, and easy-to-handle animals like rats and pigeons to provide models for human learning and behavior; and that possessed an irrational faith in its vision of the human mind appearing at birth as a blank slate, unmarked by instinct or inherited inclination, written upon solely by the chalk of learning through experience. Behaviorism provided good employment for an entire generation of experimental psychologists as well as several generations of rats and pigeons, although how effectively it advanced our knowledge of the human mind remains unclear.

The important change began in the early 1930s, when young Harry Harlow, having just completed graduate work on rat learning at Stanford, arrived as a newly hired psychology professor at the University of Wisconsin and found that Wisconsin had no decent rat laboratory. The junior faculty member was forced to improvise, and so he began conducting a few experiments on some primates—a couple of orangutans, one overfed baboon—at a small local zoo. But the orangutans, Maggie and Jiggs, had real personalities, as did the baboon, Tommy, who soon became obviously infatuated with one of Harlow's students, Betty. Betty was very attentive to Tommy, but as Harlow was to describe the case succinctly, "No rat would have fallen in love with Betty."

With the help of a few students, Harlow converted an old box factory into his first monkey laboratory, and he was able to acquire a few South American spider monkeys and capuchins along with some rhesus macaques from India. With primates, the young researcher soon began to see some surprising hints of mental complexity: problem-solving that seemed creative, for example, advancing not along elaborately constructed chains of stimulus and response but rather through lightning-fast moments of insight. Meanwhile, Harlow needed more primates, and his creative solution was to try breeding them. He found that the monkeys reproduced well enough, and as soon as possible he would remove the babies from their mothers and place them in diapers for sanitary reasons. But why were those baby monkeys dragging around and obsessively clinging to their cloth diapers?

Classic behaviorism, hypothesizing that all behavior derived from constructions of simple responses to environmental stimuli, presumed that the stimuli had a value, positive or negative, based on the organism's few basic physiologically derived needs—for relief from hunger, from cold, from pain, and so on. According to this concept of motivation, no mammal was born with anything as complicated and amorphous as a need for affection or a mother's love. Instead, infants learned to behave *as if* they loved their mothers, when in fact they had merely learned to respond actively to the provider of milk, their central source of relief from the physiological experience of hunger. So the question naturally arose: what sort of physiologically based relief were cloth diapers offering those monkeys in Harry Harlow's cages?

During the 1950s, Harlow stunned his profession and the American public with a series of experiments famously culminating in the clear demonstration that given a choice between a doll-like "surrogate mother" that was soft and fluffy and padded with cloth and a second that was hard and cold and made of wire, baby monkeys always chose the cloth mother, even when a bottle of milk was offered at the wire mother. Cuddling, in other words, was very important. As the psychologist described the issue in a speech before the September 1958 meeting of the American Psychological Association (just after that organization had elected him president), "Psychologists, at least the psychologists who write textbooks, not only show no interest in the origin and development of love and affection, but they seem to be unaware of its presence."

Harlow's rise in academic psychology marks the decline of the behaviorist paradigm and a renewed appreciation for the complexity of the human psyche and the usefulness of primates as models of human behavior—at least in the laboratory.

Among North American anthropologists, a parallel shift in orientation took place during the same period. As noted, Louis Leakey had promoted the idea that one could speculate intelligently about the behavior of ancestral humans through triangulation: the concept that the basic patterns of behavior modern humans share with their closest living relatives, the modern great apes, probably existed among their common ancestors. But Louis's thinking was not unique.

Alfred Kroeber of the University of California at Berkeley argued as early as 1928, in an article entitled "Sub-human Culture Beginnings," that cultural anthropologists should look at primates in order to further their thinking about human cultures. And Harvard University's E. A. Hooton proposed, in two books of the late 1930s and early 1940s (*Apes, Men and Morons* and *Man's Poor Relations*), that physical anthropology could be advanced through the study of primates in the wild. Still, for reasons both pragmatic and paradigmatic, primate field studies did not become a significant anthropological tool for another couple of decades.

Pragmatically, the 1950s saw technological developments—such as jet travel and new antimalarial medicines—that made research in the remote tropics easier and safer, while the postwar prosperity in the United States made such an endeavor more feasible.

Paradigmatically, two things happened. First was the final demise of the idea that human evolution began with an abrupt expansion in brain size. According to this old view of human evolution, the development of a large brain was the single significant change that led to a suite of other distinct human characteristics: upright walking, tool-using, fire-building, language, culture, and so on. This paradigm also meant that the upright-walking, small-brained, apish-looking creatures whose remains were being dug up by such people as Raymond Dart in South Africa, fossilized remains of the so-called australopithecines, were best considered as mere ancestral apes and not immediate members of the hominid line. It also meant that considering the behavior of living apes or even living monkeys might not prove very relevant. Why waste time studying small-brained animals, even primates? The large-brain paradigm held sway among some scientists even into the 1940s, mainly because of a handful of apparent fossils found in 1912 at the Piltdown quarries of Sussex, England. Those apparent fossils included the spectacular find of a modern-sized human skull in intimate proximity with an ape-sized jaw, suggesting that Piltdown man (as the putative original owner of those bones was called) must have been the missing link, the direct evolutionary line leading from ape to human.

During the 1920s and 1930s, as an increasing number of hominid-looking yet small-brained fossils were dug up, however, the Piltdown remains became increasingly anomalous. Then, in 1949, a new technique for dating fossils revealed that the Piltdown skull and jaw were only a few hundred years old. That information, combined with a panel of experts' conclusive demonstration in 1953 that Piltdown man was actually a clever fraud, ended most serious belief in an abrupt evolutionary break between ancestral humans and ancestral apes. In other words, the earliest humans were far more apelike than scientists had previously imagined.

At the same time anthropologists in the United States were becoming increasingly aware of developments in quantitative biology, and in 1951 the anthropologist Sherwood Washburn proposed a "new physical anthropology" that would incorporate recent advances in genetics and biology into the anthropological study of human evolution. Washburn had met Raymond Dart in Africa in 1948 and was allowed to examine some of Dart's *Australopithecus* specimens. Financed by a Ford Foundation grant, he returned to Africa for the July 1955 Pan-African Congress on Prehistory in Livingstone—the same meeting attended by the enthusiastic American industrialist Leighton Wilkie and presided over by the distinguished Louis Leakey, who showed everyone how to skin an antelope carcass with stone tools.

After the conference was over, Sherwood Washburn found a comfortable spot at the Victoria Falls Hotel, where he could pursue his passion for dissection and comparative anatomy. Washburn was dissecting baboons killed by government wardens in the interests of what was once called "vermin control." But according to one of his students, Irven DeVore, the dissections did not take long, so Washburn had a lot of time on his hands. "He sat out there on the veranda sipping Pims Number One and Two and watched baboons come in and raid the gardens in the hotel, and in the process he became much more interested in their behavior than their anatomy. He came back and got a bigger Ford grant, which ultimately took me to Africa, and he and his wife and son joined us for the last half of the stay."

Washburn returned from that 1955 trip to Africa determined to promote the behavioral study of primates as an anthropological exercise, and in March 1959 he and DeVore commenced their joint research on the behavior of olive baboons in Kenya. (They were, incidentally, following by almost a year the British psychologist K.R.L. Hall's pioneering field study of baboons in South Africa and by a few months the first field study of common langurs in India, begun in October 1958 by another of Washburn's anthropology students, Phyllis Jay.) By the time DeVore arrived in Nairobi and visited the Coryndon Museum to get Louis Leakey's advice on where to find the baboons, Louis had already sent Rosalie Osborn out to study gorillas—with only modest results. Louis, DeVore recalls, "knew nothing about behavior. What he did know was largely the kind of stereotype stuff you get from white hunters at a bar in Nairobi. So none of us had much hope when he sent another secretary out: Jane Goodall."

But while Louis Leakey was sending young secretaries out to watch apes, Sherwood Washburn was beginning to send young graduate students out to study almost any kind of primate—monkeys, mainly—in Africa and Asia. Savanna-dwelling baboons were among the first subjects partly because they were so easy to see, with the ones in Nairobi National Park already used to being watched by humans sitting comfortably inside cars. And Washburn still entertained the enormously optimistic notion that a few brief field studies of various primate species would reveal a "primate pattern," an underlying structure of behavior common to almost all primates, including humans.

In concentrating on apes rather than monkeys, Louis was far ahead of the anthropological pack—as were, by then, the Japanese.

Japanese primate studies had developed in isolation from and to some degree in advance of Western primatology, and they began with mayflies. Around the start of World War II, Kinji Imanishi observed that the mayflies skittering around the Kamo River, which passes through the middle of Kyoto, were segregated into habitats according to species. One species favored the warm and shallow edge waters, another preferred a colder habitat under rocks at the churning middle of the river, and so on. Such habitat segregation, Imanishi hypothesized, might serve as a way to reduce the competition between similar species. He finished writing out his first thoughts on the subject in *The World of Living Things* (1941) before being sent off to the front lines. Imanishi expected to die in the war, and he considered the book to be an intellectual last testament to a new way of thinking about the natural world that he hoped others would be inspired to continue after he was gone.

Fortunately, he survived and thus was able to develop what he called "animal sociology" in person, traveling around Japan to study several species while encouraging others to do the same. By the late 1940s, one of his students was following Japanese deer, and another did research on captive rabbits. But in December 1948 two others, while following feral horses, happened to come across a troop of Japanese macaques (*Macaca fuscata*). As a result of this chance encounter, a number of Imanishi's students, starting with Junichiro Itani and Kisaburo Tokuda, began puzzling methodically over the social lives of the macaques. And although much of the early animal sociology research concentrated on nonprimate species, some clear successes with Japanese macaque studies during the early 1950s led Imanishi and his students to focus on those monkeys—especially once it was recognized that understanding primate societies would provide the best route for speculating about the origin and structures of human society. In 1956 the Meitetsu Railroad Company of Nagoya built the Japan Monkey Center, and with that as an institutional home, Imanishi's animal sociology was finally transformed into a distinctively Japanese primatology.

If Japanese primatology was to become a route for exploring human social systems, then its best subjects ought to be those species generally understood to be humankind's closest relatives, the great apes. Imanishi had originally intended to study the orangutans of Southeast Asia, but, among other things, Japanese primatology had developed a method of attracting animals through provisioning: baiting the observation area with food. Orangutans, habitually solitary and extremely arboreal, did not seem to be good candidates for provisioning. Also, the three African apes—gorillas, chimpanzees, and pygmy chimpanzees (bonobos)—were considered to be even more closely related to humans than orangutans were.

Kinji Imanishi wrote to Walter Baumgartel at the Travellers Rest hotel in Uganda, rather poetically, in the late 1950s: "We have already heard in Tokyo of you and your gorillas. We have been dreaming for many years of watching the natural life of gorillas in Africa, and we have been told that you hold the secret of the Mountain Gorillas in your hand." Then, in 1958, Imanishi and Junichiro Itani traveled to Africa to survey eastern and mountain gorilla habitat, and in 1959, about a year before George Schaller began walking among mountain gorillas from the Belgian Congo side of the Virungas, Masao Kawai and Hiroki Mizuhara went to observe the same apes from the Ugandan side, using Travellers Rest as their base.

In 1960, Junichiro Itani returned to Africa to continue the preliminary work begun by his colleagues Kawai and Mizuhara, unwrapping his expedition's supplies at roughly the same time George Schaller was wrapping up his work—prematurely, as a response to the turmoil enveloping the Congo. But because of that turmoil, Itani decided against continuing the Japanese mountain gorilla study. He turned to an alternate ape.

There were plenty of wild chimpanzees living in forests along the eastern edge of Lake Tanganyika, in the politically stable Tanganyika Territory, and the ambitious young primatologist started looking there for a good place to begin a major chimpanzee study. When he contacted Louis Leakey in the summer of 1960, Itani learned of the ideal place to set up such a project: the Gombe Stream Chimpanzee Reserve. Chimps were plentiful at Gombe, the white-haired anthropologist confirmed, and since they had for many years been protected from hunting and other sorts of human intrusion, they were relatively easy to approach. It was true that Louis had already sent his own research assistant down to the reserve (a young Englishwoman named Jane Morris-Goodall), but her project was a short-term exercise, not well funded, perhaps not all that serious, and in any event due to end in a very short time . . . at which point the Japanese could set up their own project. According to Toshisada Nishida, one of Itani's students from that period, Louis "promised" that the Japanese would be able to study chimpanzees at Gombe.

Junichiro Itani was a great scholar and prolific writer, the author of many books both scholarly and literary. His father was a famous painter, his mother a well-known poet of haiku and other traditional verse. Another of his former students, Takayoshi Kano, has said, "My first impression of Professor Itani was that he was a very gaunt, rather meager-looking man. But the eyes peering from behind his glasses were gentle, and his lips always tilted into a slight smile." Itani was patient, never upset with his brash young students. And while working with him on a monkey study, Kano continues, "I came to know his power and capabilities. He could run very swiftly up and down steep hills, following monkeys all day long without being tired at the end of the day. I was amazed at the amount of information Junichiro Itani was able to put in his notebooks. It seemed as if he could write at twice the speed and gather ten times the information that I could. As a matter of fact, I was tormented with a sense of inferiority every time I worked with him in the field."

After speaking to Leakey, Itani was persuaded that the Gombe Stream Chimpanzee Reserve would be an excellent place to begin the Japanese chimpanzee project, and then, ignoring Leakey's instructions to the contrary, he went to see the place for himself. Taking one of the local water taxis out of Kigoma, he arrived on the beach at Gombe late in the afternoon of Thursday, September 29, while Jane was out in the mountains, and walked up to the camp. Vanne had just sat down to begin working at her novel when the unexpected visitor appeared, and she was not entirely pleased at the surprise interruption. She said *jambo* (hello) a little "coldly" (as she recounted in a letter home), removed her reading glasses, and somewhat tersely asked what he wanted. He said he was "Japanese, a Dr. . . . ?" Vanne never did get the name. Then, in Vanne's words, "the penny dropped." Itani explained that he was a scientist studying primates in Africa. Eventually he went on to confess that "Dr. Leakey told me *not* to come here, but I came!"

Vanne offered him a chair. Dominic brought tea. The late-afternoon light began to fade. Finally, after the last of the tea was gone, the guest politely announced that he should go. Vanne asked him how he proposed to do that. He said, "By boat." Vanne ventured that "perhaps there might not be a boat."

Then Jane returned from her chimp-watching, and so the three of them sat down for dinner. Afterward, at around nine o'clock, mother and daughter suggested to their visitor that he should spend the night, and they offered to lend him a blanket. He said (as Vanne reported), "No blanket. I have my bed with me. It is my habit in mountain to sleep in it!" Vanne looked curiously at his "tiny haversack," but he began pulling from beneath his jacket a loose shirt that, it became clear, would serve, spread over a patch of rough grass, as his bed. Just then, however, they heard the sound of a boat moving across the lake, and so in great haste they all ran down to the shore, signaled the boat, and "we said goodbye & watched him disappearing on the inky lake."

It is evident from Vanne's letter as well as from Jane's very limited comments in her field journal that their meeting with Junichiro Itani was slightly awkward. Louis never explained to Jane that he had recommended Gombe as a future site for the Japanese. Itani soon after returned home, and the next year, 1961, Imanishi himself went to Africa at the head of the large and well-funded Kyoto University Africa Primatological Expedition, which was oriented toward studying chimpanzees and prepared to set up operations at Gombe starting in June.

By then, of course, support from the National Geographic Society had ensured Jane's presence at the reserve, forcing the Japanese to establish their base elsewhere. They chose a place called Kabogo Point, in western Tanzania, and for the next couple of years were cursed by a paucity of chimpanzees. In 1963 they moved their operations to Kasakati Basin, managing to sight wild chimps there frequently enough to identify some individual males and make a number of decent observations—but not enough to habituate their subjects. The chimps remained elusive, secretive, skittishly afraid of the human observers.

Imanishi retired in 1964, and Junichiro Itani, now head of the Kyoto University expedition, patiently and methodically began its reorganization. He started by establishing two more base camps, at Filabanga and the Mahale Mountains, and then he began encouraging different methods of approaching wild chimps at the different sites.

Workers at Kasakati had tried the traditional Japanese method of provisioning, planting banana and sugarcane as a temptation for the chimps, but after elephants got there first and ate up the bananas and sugarcane, the researchers turned to an experiment in what has been called "impressing" chimps. Itani went to Kenya and bought from an animal dealer an infant chimp named Brucy. The director of the project carried Brucy back into Tanzania and began displaying him openly at Kasakati, hoping that when wild chimpanzees saw a person and a small chimp together, they would conclude that the person was not dangerous. Unfortunately, Brucy was absolutely terrified of wild chimps, and whenever those big hairy shadows appeared at the edge of the dark forest, he would scream frantically and try to hide. The experiment was not successful.

At Filabanga, the Japanese attempted a more ordinary habituation: walking openly through chimpanzee habitat and hoping that eventually the wild apes would simply get used to their presence. That experiment was unsuccessful as well.

Finally, at the Mahale Mountains base, they tried provisioning once

more. The director of the Mahale project, Toshisada Nishida, recently recalled that when he began his work, the chimpanzees ran away whenever
they saw him. Even at a distance of 200 yards they ran away. The local villagers had never hunted them—chimpanzees were too much like humans to
eat, they said—but the apes were still extremely wary of people. However,
some of the local people also told Nishida that when in the past they had
planted sugarcane, the chimpanzees had appeared and eaten up all their
crops, and so he began to think that a cane plantation might attract chimps.
The head of the village showed him exactly where they had previously cultivated sugarcane—a big stretch of land now covered with thick elephant
grass. Nishida was working with a very small budget, only about a thousand
shillings (less than $150) a month, but he hired about forty people from the
village to clear the grass and plant sugarcane. He found that the cane grew
slowly and was regularly destroyed by rampaging bush pigs, rats, and termites. But after about six months, starting in March 1966, a tempting enough
crop had emerged that the chimpanzees began feeding on it—and a few humans with binoculars and notebooks gathered around to watch. Eventually
the other base stations were closed and the researchers began concentrating
their efforts at Mahale.

In the years following Nishida's 1966 triumph, the Mahale Mountains
camp became among the most successful and important long-term ape
research sites in the world. The Japanese are credited with the important
discovery of an encompassing chimpanzee social system based on the territorial *unit group*, what Western researchers usually call "community"; and
starting in the early 1970s, Nishida and his good friend and colleague Takayoshi Kano surveyed Zaire by car, boat, bicycle, and on foot to map the habitat of that rare, pacific, and famously sexy ape species known as the pygmy
chimpanzee, or bonobo. Kano proceeded to establish his own important
study of bonobos from the village of Wamba, in north-central Zaire.

But back in July 1960—when Kortlandt had just pulled up stakes at Beni,
when Jane was just putting down stakes at Gombe, and when Junichiro Itani
was deciding to turn from gorillas to chimps—George Schaller, having
ended his mountain gorilla work at Kabara, took some time off to crawl
through the underbrush in Uganda's Budongo Forest with a Cambridge anthropology student. On at least one occasion they sighted large numbers of
chimps and then found themselves surrounded by an invisible but aggressively screaming group of those apes, an adventure Schaller later described
dramatically in *The Year of the Gorilla:* "Without warning the hooting began, this time all around us in the obscurity of the undergrowth, drawing
closer and closer until the sounds seemed to come out of the earth itself.

Not a single animal revealed itself, and this, coupled with the high-pitched screeches that appeared to erupt from the throats of a thousand furious demons, brought fear to our hearts."

Schaller may have entertained the ambition of conducting his own chimpanzee research project, perhaps at Budongo. At Gombe, as Jane reported with some lighthearted amusement in a letter home, he "admitted as much" — that "he had only come to look at [chimpanzee] habitat, the possibilities of the Reserve and, mainly, to spy on me!" But if George Schaller had ever hoped to establish a chimpanzee study site at Budongo, that opportunity was taken within the next year or so.

In early 1962, Vernon Reynolds, a young, London-based anthropologist, and his wife, Frances (or Frankie), set up housekeeping in a Ugandan forest service bungalow and — with the advice and encouragement of Adriaan Kortlandt as well as funding from the Wilkie Foundation — began eight months' research at Budongo with the single objective of observing chimpanzee behavior. On one of their first forays into the forest, the Reynoldses experienced the sort of very exciting, unnerving encounter that Schaller had reported. They came within 10 yards of a surprised and then alarmed chimpanzee and were soon surrounded by an apparently hostile, wildly screaming group of chimps in the trees. But after that initial spectacular introduction, the arboreal apes turned from aggressive to shy and soon learned to disperse and disappear quietly whenever the terrestrial, upright-walking apes approached. As Vernon Reynolds has written, "More and more often, as the days went by, the response of the chimps on spotting us was that they all quickly descended the trees, usually in silence, and made off deep into the forest along their own network of tracks which criss-crossed the undergrowth of the forest floor."

The Reynoldses had concluded that a person could get seriously lost in the 138-square-mile Budongo Forest, and so they hired a tracker already familiar with the place, a man named Manueri, and the three of them always went looking for chimps together, typically following their calls and noisy drumming on tree roots. However, the chimps never became comfortable with that trio of chimp-watchers — too many people, possibly — and the people eventually settled on a daily effort to approach their shy subjects by stealth. The researchers dressed in camouflage clothes and covered their heads and hands and binoculars with camouflage netting, and in that fashion were sometimes able to watch feeding chimps from a distance of about 60 yards before, inevitably, one of the apes saw them and the group slipped away. Still, the Reynoldses formed impressions and gathered data. They described locomotion styles, estimated nest heights, studied group size and composition, and summarized food sources (concluding that 90 percent of the apes' diet consisted of fruit, with the remainder leaves, bark, stems, and insects), and so on. But during the eight months this 1962 project lasted, the researchers never saw chimpanzees hunting or eating meat, never found even a hint of tool-using, and, perhaps most significantly, were never able to recognize individuals. For all they knew, they were seeing different individual chimps each time they went into the forest.

Since those early days, that brief sliver of time at the turn of a decade when modern field primatology began, Adriaan Kortlandt has taken to wondering publicly why his own first study at Beni has not received greater attention and to commenting on what he regards as the "parochialism," "isolationism," and "occasional anti-scientific attitude" of Jane Goodall and her work. Having the wit to select such a good site as Beni (where chimpanzees were already provisioned by the plantation's banana and papaya crop), Kortlandt was able to begin his "close-distance observation and testing within a few days," as he has written, possibly starting in April 1960. By comparison, Jane's chimpanzee research, starting in the middle of July 1960, was (according to Kortlandt's assessment) much slower and therefore far less productive per unit of time, requiring "8 months until the first male became habituated, and several years until the mothers especially had lost their shyness."

Certainly their methodologies were different. Kortlandt, working within the mainstream of European ethology, promoted a more direct and experimental style of studying wild animals, the establishment of a kind of natural laboratory that combined close observation with "ethically sound and harmless experimentation." In his best-known experiment, done sometime after the 1960 Beni study, Kortlandt placed a realistic, mechanically activated, stuffed leopard (sometimes with a chimp doll in its paws) in areas where wild chimpanzees would find it, as a way of testing the apes' "anti-predator defense technique." Elsewhere he gathered data on wild chimpanzee food interests by setting out egg-laden nests, chameleons fixed in nets, and a freshly killed small forest antelope "made to look as though it were alive." Kortlandt discounts the question of whether wild chimpanzees might be confused or frightened by chameleons inside nets. He is unimpressed with the issue of whether the freshly killed antelope "made to look . . . alive" actually looked more alive to humans than to chimps. His experiments were, he insists, quick and effective ways to acquire valid scientific information about the lives of wild chimpanzees—whereas Jane's alternative methodology, her preference for quiet, patient, long-term naturalistic observation on the ground, amounts to a luxurious and inefficient "St. Francis of Assisi approach."

They may also have had ideological differences. What Kortlandt has described as Jane's "occasional anti-scientific attitude" may be more the dislike of a certain kind of science, where the scientist works as a manipulator and voyeur: elevated, protected, distanced, hiding behind the curtain. That stance establishes a universe in which observer prevails as operator while observed endures as object. Jane's alternative style placed observer and observed in the same field, not only literally and physically but also, I believe, psychologically and intellectually.

Adriaan Kortlandt has identified himself as "the first human being to observe chimpanzees at close quarters in the wild," which (if we discount the strong likelihood of numerous unrecorded encounters between, say, indigenous Africans and chimps) may be true. His closest observations, those few occasions in 1960 when male chimpanzees approached one of his blinds and tried to peer inside, were very special times when "a shiver went down my spine," indeed "the greatest experience of my professional life." But only a few months later Jane was approaching wild chimpanzees—still regarded by most people as terribly dangerous beasts—in the open, on foot, unarmed, lightly clothed, often alone, always unprotected.

In short, Adriaan Kortlandt's solution to the problem of watching chimpanzees took great ingenuity, whereas Jane's solution took great courage. And while courage is obviously no measure of scientific accomplishment, it might be said that Kortlandt's early emphasis on observing apes from inside blinds meant he never followed them into their forest home. That limitation alone might account for the fact that even as late as the spring of 1962, when he was drafting the article that appeared in a September issue of *Scientific American,* he could write that wild chimpanzees have a "natural vegetable diet" and wonder why they did not make tools.

17

The Magical and the Mundane

1960–1961

VANNE LEFT GOMBE on November 12, 1960. Louis sent out Hassan Salimu, the captain of the *Miocene Lady,* on assignment to be the captain, more or less, of Gombe, and with Hassan now in charge, Jane's first stretch of chimpanzee-watching came to an end on November 27, a Sunday.

Her friend Derrick Dunn showed up from Kigoma that evening, bringing along a loaf of bread, some beer, and two live cockerels, who were supposed to become the central ingredients in a curry. Derrick and Jane soon ate one of the cockerels, but the other was, as Jane wrote home, "quite exceptional." When he arrived, his legs were bound with string, which he pecked through within an hour, and when Jane retired to the back of her tent for a bath in the canvas tub, the bird stalked right in to watch. He started talking to her, and when she talked back — in chicken language — he became argumentative. Even though Jane considered him to be "the last animal I should ever have imagined being a friend of mine," the feisty young cock was given a reprieve from the curry and a name, Hildebrand.

On the morning of December 1, the tent was taken down, "de-lizardized," and folded, and Jane and Derrick plus all their supplies and luggage and Hildebrand were lined up on the beach and waiting for a boat by nine o'clock. In Kigoma, after depositing most of their things at the government offices in the old German fort, the Boma, they stayed overnight at the home of Jane's good friends, the young and newly wed Colin and José Lamb.

The next morning Hildebrand was left in the care of José while Jane and Derrick pulled away from Kigoma in a minor caravan, sharing a bagful of hot samosas in a Land Rover, with three of Derek's African assistants following in a truck. It took them well over a week to get to Nairobi, owing to unforeseen delays caused by punctured tires, a broken axle, and a shattered windshield, as well some foreseen ones, such as a three-day luxury but gunless elephant-hunting safari in Tanganyika. "Luxury" refers to the fact that Derrick was assisted by his best tracker, Soko, and an excellent cook, Elias, and had taken along first-class tents and a refrigerator so they could have cold drinks in the evening. The elephant-hunting compensated for the luxury with three hard days of walking along a path formed by dinner-plate-sized footprints through a hot, tsetse-infested environment of woodland and savanna. It was altogether an exhausting enterprise, culminating on the third day with a grim fifteen-hour marathon in pursuit of a randomly wandering big bull tusker who alternated feeding with pushing over trees. They finally got close enough for Derrick to call out to the magnificent pachyderm. If Jane had not been along, she was certain, he would have been shot, but because she was there he was instead given a name, George, and left intact.

After finding George, they stopped for a couple of days at Derrick's farm in Kenya and eventually, accompanied now by his daughter, Valerie Ann, made it to Nairobi by Tuesday, December 13. Louis was "delighted to see me," Jane wrote home, and she and Valerie Ann were invited to his house in Langata that evening for a "special supper" (Mary was not around), after which he and Jane talked until one in the morning.

On Sunday, January 14, 1961, Jane returned to Gombe by herself—the requirement that she be accompanied by a second European had by then been quietly forgotten. Along with Hassan Salimu, the camp staff included Rashidi Kikwale and Dominic Bandora, who was soon joined by his wife, Chiko, and young daughter, Ado.

The full complement of supplies, including everything that had been stored in the Kigoma Boma, as well as Hildebrand and his new mate, Hilda, arrived on the *Kibisi* six days later, on the afternoon of January 21, and Jane's tent was quickly erected, with the chaos of unorganized supplies placed inside, just in time for a prodigious rainstorm that night. It was, she wrote to Vanne and the rest of the family, "lovely to lie hearing the rain on my new roof."

The next day Jane came down early from chimp-watching in order to make the camp "ship-shape." Hassan had built a henhouse, which she placed to one side of the tent's entryway—the "veranda"—where it doubled as a sideboard, with six large tins containing sugar, flour, and other supplies on top. Beside the henhouse was a small storage cabinet, named Norman (having been built by Norman Mitton of the Coryndon). Dishes and cups were stored on top of Norman. In the middle of the veranda, Jane put her new camp table, good for eating meals on in bad weather but otherwise useful as a writing desk, just high enough for her to reach comfortably while sitting on the bed, supported by two pillows and a folded blanket.

In the sectioned-off rear of the tent, the washroom, she kept a large box for extra supplies. Derrick had given her three waterproof ammo boxes, one of which was now situated next to the large supply box and filled with various "oddments required daily," including batteries and antimalarial Nivaquine. The second ammo box, containing various foods—biscuits, spaghetti—was set out on the veranda beside Norman and the henhouse. The third was balanced at the top of the bed, where it served as a bookcase. Jane also kept two trunks in the tent, a blue one containing all her papers and a black one filled with things that would be required only rarely. On top of the black trunk sat her alarm clock, a can of baby powder, and an elephant carved out of ivory named George, presented by Derrick as a souvenir of their day chasing the real George.

Aside from straightening up her tent, there were other pressing chores to take care of. The boat needed painting, cream and green, and rechristening as *Soko Muke* ("Chimpanzee Woman"). There were plants to gather and press and preserve and moths to collect—*dudus,* she called them (preferring the Swahili for "insects"), attracted to the light of a pressure lamp and trapped in a net.

But by early March a large rat had begun eating the *dudu* nets, as well as sheets and blankets, and although he or she was caught in a rat trap by the middle of the month, another large rat soon took up the cause. Meanwhile, Jane discovered a "magnificent brood of red centipedes" in the tent's bathroom, and when she picked her sweater off the ground one afternoon, "a large and most elegant scorpion peered beligerantly at me from one sleeve!" A big crocodile showed up at the shore that spring and ate one of Iddi Matata's ducks. And around the same time Jane saw at last the leopard she knew was living somewhere in the area. "I heard a strange sound," she wrote home, "unlike any sound I can describe. And the first I saw of him was his tail above the grass—held up & over his back a little, which surprised me. Then the nice fellow walked into a clearing made by grazing buffalo & I had a lovely view of him. He is very beautiful—large and dark."

Hildebrand was one of the bright spots in camp, "the craziest kind that ever came out of an egg," she described him in a February 17 letter.

He does great displays at tent pegs, ending up by flying on to a guy rope, immediately losing his balance, & pretending the skrewy landing is all part of the plan. He runs full tilt at trees, chairs, me, Hilda—stopping & crowing at the last minute. The old idiot began crowing when I got up this morning—long before dawn. I opened the door to show him that any light filtering through the crack came from my hurricane [lantern]—but this made him strain to greater vocal effort, so I hastily closed him in. At least it was then muffled slightly! Poor old Hilda!

Poor old Hilda, however, was working on her own project, which by March consisted of a baker's dozen eggs and around the start of April the same number of black fluffy chicks. But the little chicks were soon disappearing one by one, as a pair of gigantic Nile monitor lizards began zipping in and nipping away at every opportunity.

Meanwhile, Derrick was sending Jane unrequited love letters and, one time, a big box of artichokes from Arusha, as she had once remarked to him that if she were a millionaire she would eat artichoke hearts weekly. Unfortunately, Derrick's box was unaccountably delayed in the mails, so at Gombe it was finally opened to reveal "a glorious sea of purple flowers!!" Hassan, who had never seen an artichoke before, declared enthusiastically that "he has sent you lovely flowers!!!"

Then there was the lingering heart-in-thistle of Jane's engagement to Robert Young. Jane had written her fiancé two long letters near the end of 1960 declaring, as she later summarized, that "everything was rather hopeless" and she "didn't see how it could work." But for a time it seemed as if those letters never made it to London. Finally, in March, she received his letter acknowledging that (as Jane paraphrased for Vanne) "he respects my views," while describing his own discouraging predicament, including long-term unemployment, a painful back requiring him to lie on the floor of a friend's apartment, and the distressing words of a well-respected physician friend who had just returned from Africa and was "most sorry to hear" that Bob's fiancée "was living with Dr. Leakey who had now left his wife."

Aside from rare visits with her Kigoma friends, Jane's social life in the spring of 1961 was entirely African—the company of Hassan, Rashidi, and Dominic supplemented by occasional visits with Chiko and little Ado, as well as Iddi Matata and others from Kasekela village. Iddi Matata might show up to chat or ask for medicine, and he and Jane soon became "great buddies," as she phrased it in her March 4 letter to the family. Since her Swahili improved with daily practice, she was by then convinced she could understand most of what he was saying.

Jane now went into the mountains alone in pursuit of chimpanzees, while the Tanganyika game scout officially keeping track of her at this point, Saulo David, sometimes went up for short periods later in the day. Jane communicated with him via notes inside plastic bags that described where she had gone, and so, according to a late-January letter to the family, "he has a sort of paper chase each day—rather fun for him!" And since she was now on her own and walking through some very wet vegetation, she often pulled off her trousers and knotted them around her waist, keeping them relatively dry beneath a polythene sheet. When it was raining, she sometimes removed her shirt and knotted that around her waist beneath the polythene too, thus presenting both her top and bottom halves to the elements.

Her letters home during the early months of 1961, often headed with the cheerfully light and simple return address "Chimpland," usually reveal high energy and an excited pleasure in the small events of her daily life, seldom a hint of lowered spirits. But it was still a time of great solitude. As Jane reflected forty years later in her autobiographical *Reason for Hope*, "I missed Vanne for her companionship, for the long talks we had enjoyed by the campfire, the discussions of new observations." Jane also treasured and embraced her solitude, since "always I have enjoyed aloneness." Nevertheless, she was not always her usual self. As she commented wryly at the start of one letter home in late February, "Just mad, she is. Quite skatty & round the corner." The letter proceeded to encapsulate her day: "I got up at 5 today. It was dark. The stars were big. And a chimp killed a hare, and ate it. They have returned, returned over the mountain. I am here, and they have come back over the mountain. A rainbow is arched over the Congo Hills. The top of the bow is lost in the clouds of heaven. Is God wanting to break his promise? The water in the stream is singing. It is singing, and I cannot catch the words. I know the words, but I cannot hear them. I cannot say them." Then, having listened for the words of the stream, her rising thoughts were returned to terra firma by a mundane query from Dominic: "I am having eggs for supper. Dominic has just asked me. So, I'm normal—the eggs did it you know!"

In *Reason for Hope*, Jane writes of becoming "totally absorbed" during this particular period of "Solitude" (a chapter title) in the experience of being in nature, a "forest existence" that came to envelop her. It was a time when "aloneness was a way of life," when "I was getting closer to animals and nature, and as a result, closer to myself and more and more in tune with the spiritual power that I felt all around." And then, in special moments, a peculiar, vivid, and certain awareness of life in nature would sweep over her. "The longer I spent on my own, the more I became one with the magic forest world that was now my home. Inanimate objects developed their own identities and, like my favorite saint, Francis of Assisi, I named them and greeted them as friends. 'Good morning, Peak,' I would say as I arrived there each morning; 'Hello, Stream' when I collected my water; 'Oh, Wind, for Heaven's sake, calm down' as it howled overhead, ruining my chance of locating the chimps." There were "enchanted nights when I stayed up on the Peak in the moonlight" and days when "I loved to sit in the forest when it was raining, and to hear the pattering of the drops on the leaves and feel utterly enclosed in a dim twilight world of greens and browns and soft air." But most of all, during this period, she "became intensely aware of the being-ness of trees. The feel of rough sun-warmed bark of an ancient forest giant, or the cool, smooth skin of a young and eager sapling, gave me a strange, intuitive sense of the sap as it was sucked up by unseen roots and drawn up to the very tips of the branches."

The forest was also, of course, alive with chimpanzees, and on January 31, only a couple of weeks after her return from Nairobi, Jane witnessed a drama that was far more exciting, she soon wrote home, than any behavior she had ever before seen—"more than the meat, more than the termites." She had begun the morning in the Linda valley watching a large number of chimps, some feeding, several youngsters playing wildly in the trees. It was hard to see more than an arm or leg, a face or foot at any one moment, but they appeared to be chasing one another or perhaps playing tag. Then they disappeared. Jane moved closer to watch a smaller and more sedate group—five adult males and a single adult female, feeding by themselves in the trees. Those apes climbed down, then climbed again into a single tree and "rested peacefully"—until all at once, quite suddenly, as Jane described it, "the rest of the party appeared—seemingly out of thin air! All the children and at least one more male & a young lady of skittish temperament. The romping began all over again—the poor grown ups just had to lump it. The games went on for an hour. I could see better this time—wrestling, chasing—all silently, as it had been all morning."

Then it began to rain. The large, chimp-filled tree was about 100 yards down a grassy, tree-studded slope, and Jane expected the apes to seek shelter beneath it or some of the other trees on the slope. Instead, they all remained inside the glistening foliage . . . until finally one older male with a pale face (whom she christened Paleface) climbed down and sat in a hunched posture in the grass under a tree, facing Jane. It was raining harder now, and Paleface was soon joined by a "tubby" younger male who sat beside him.

The rest of the apes in the tree now climbed down to the ground as well, and soon they had assembled into two groups, about 50 yards apart from each other and 100 yards down from the crest of the grassy slope. "It was most organized," Jane commented in her letter. The first group, centered on Paleface, consisted of at least a half-dozen individuals, including one or two other mature males and a mature female with an infant clinging to her back. The second group, over to Jane's left, seemed to gather around a second mature male, one she identified as Bare Bum, and it included at least five chimps—though the grass was very high there, which meant she was able to

see only hints and glimpses of their dark figures. Both groups began ambling slowly up the hill in the pelting rain, some 50 yards apart but moving
in parallel, single-file processions, the mature female and her clinging infant
at the head of Paleface's group, Bare Bum heading his over to the left.

The field journal entry for January 31 (mistakenly dated January 30)
continues this tale:

> As the two processions neared the top, one from the left hand group sud-
> denly charged over to the other group, running through the long grass,
> swinging his arms in a scything motion as he neared them. Small "whaah-
> he-whaah's". One of the right hand males, Paleface, as he reached the
> top, ran towards a bush, stood up, & swiped at it with his right hand in
> passing. He then turned & charged back down the hill, diagonally, leapt
> at a branch, broke it as he ran, waved it, & ran, holding it, on down.
> Reached a tree, some 50 yds down, swung round it & climbed up. By
> now many of the chimps had climbed trees. The rain was falling hard,
> & the following exhibition now has a dreamlike quality. One by one the
> large males began charging down the slope, leaping at branches & taking
> them along. Sometimes they called out. Usually it was silent. Once one
> charged after another. They both climbed up a tree & leapt down. One
> took his branch & charged off with it. The other leapt from a height of
> about 18', & the branch merely split, & remained attached. He ran off
> to another tree & up. Often they leapt into trees only to hurl themselves
> down again, with or without a branch. The calls were usually as they ap-
> proached a tree. Often one would go after another, but they never tried
> to touch each other at all. Many times they stalked off on their hind legs,
> but the momentum soon brought them onto all fours. Probably only the
> 5 mature males were "dancing" but it was impossible to tell. Certainly
> only the mature animals, & I did not _see_ a female dancing. I should say
> it is most unlikely. And all this in a pouring rain with the thunder rolling
> above, & vivid lightning flashes. It really was like a dream.

That remarkable performance, which Jane had already begun thinking
of as the Rain Dance, continued for about a half-hour, with the rest of the
group sitting quietly, like an audience, in the trees near the top of the slope.
At around two o'clock in the afternoon it ended, and the big males left the
grassy slope and climbed into the trees, sitting there and seeming to glance
now in the direction of the single human member of their audience. "I felt
all the time that it was for my benefit. I wonder?" Jane wrote in the journal.

After about fifteen minutes, Paleface quietly descended from his tree and
starting walking up the slope. "Then they all climbed down & made their
way slowly up the hill. Silhouetted on the skyline several climbed trees &

sat. Others disappeared over the crest. Paleface was the last to go. He stood up, holding a sapling in his left hand, looking back at me. His giant silhouette against the grey sky was impressive. Awe inspiring. The actor taking his curtain call."

The Rain Dance was one of Jane's great observations from her early period at Gombe: a magical moment, a bright epiphany. It would be too easy, however, to pull a soft focus over the larger period, to promote the romantic but false idea that her entry into the magical world of Gombe was itself a bit of magic—the easy result of great intuitive powers and calm attentiveness, perhaps, or the revolutionary consequence of a feminine approach to sterile old masculine science. In truth, very little of what she did was easy or quick. Yes, Jane often made spontaneous, intuitive choices. Yes, she projected an unusually calm and accepting persona. Yes, it might be possible to say that her innovations in the study of animal behavior, previously a man's serious business, included in some ways a characteristically feminine style. But the real force behind her early success at Gombe, the style or approach or technique that ultimately led to fundamental breakthroughs in understanding the creatures she moved among, was neither especially masculine nor feminine but rather neutral and sexless: a determined struggle against seriously adverse conditions and a seemingly boundless capacity for slogging, dogged, hard work. Struggle. Hard work. Those were the mundane keys that unlocked the door to Gombe's magical world.

Adverse conditions included the weather. While Jane experienced some breathtaking moments of appreciation for the great natural beauty of the place, there were many other moments in which all that lush tropical beauty became inverted, like an overturned bowl, and created, as she described it in a February letter home, the "high powered tropical greenhouse" experience, making clothing and bedding continuously damp, promoting the growth of mildew on books and papers, complicating even such an ordinarily simple task as personal correspondence via stuck-together envelopes, sticky hands, and slippery fingers. There were daily rains and poundingly violent storms; and then, naturally, things tended to rot—clothes, for example, as well as canvas bathtubs and human legs and feet. The latter problem added to the medicinal requirements of camp. Aside from the twice-weekly Nivaquine to shield against malaria, there was now a daily dose of vitamin C, twice-daily multivitamins, gentian violet to spread over the skin ulcers on her legs, and Whitfield's ointment pressed between the toes, an area that had gotten very bad by the first of May, when she asked for advice on treating "this horrid thing on my toes" from Olly. "I presume it's athlete's foot—sort of white & fungus-y between the toes. It's from being in wet shoes all day long for 4 months. But suddenly it's gone <u>under</u> the nails—all the cuticles. I discovered it today—will my toe nails drop off? <u>What</u> can I do?"

Jane had occasional severe headaches and sporadic fevers to contend with and an extended period of extreme insomnia ("WHY—I just cannot imagine. It's most odd"). Yet she continued, as ever, to rise before dawn and work until late into the night. Often now she was seeing chimps daily, on good days for hours at a stretch, and in that way continuously expanding her already extensive knowledge of the minutiae of their daily lives. Her journal from this period amounts to a masterpiece of laboriously recorded precise detail. (April 14: "As he was grooming her chest she idly ran her fingers through the hair on his arm with her right hand, but not for long. Then both put their left arms up & groomed each other. She seemed to be merely flicking through his hair with short downward movements. He ran his fingers in a circular movement through the long hair round the arm pit. All at once he must have found something, for he brought both hands to the job. She stretched up the other arm in ecstasy. He 4 times put something in his mouth. Then his other arm went up & she groomed him again.") But aside from several lucky moments, her sightings that spring often resulted in the frustration of watching evasive creatures seriously obscured by vegetation and blurred by distance.

Distance was the real problem. There were exceptional moments when either she accidentally stumbled right into a group or, conversely, a group inadvertently wandered uncomfortably close to her—with both situations typically resulting in angry calls and retreating apes. But 100 yards, Jane wrote home, was still "not far away" for her. And when she was fortunate enough to get as close as 25 yards, she would still have to rely on the binoculars and, in the end, might not see very much more than the general outlines of a mother and infant, as in this April 10 entry: "Saw head of adult. . . . And saw the child. It was walking off along a branch away from me. Branches moving nearby. Ma just stared at me for awhile, then either lay back, or moved slightly. Hardly saw her. She scratched occasionally. Only about 25 yards away. <u>Sickening</u> I could not see properly. Child returned. It too out of sight."

At such distances it remained hard to identify individuals, and Jane went for weeks without seeing many chimps she was certain she had seen before. With a few exceptions, they all looked like strangers, while the ones she had so hopefully and confidently named the previous autumn had vanished. Jane's old friend David Greybeard, to be sure, was very distinctive in appearance, and she had seen him plenty of times at close quarters last November—but where was he now? Jane was not to look on his face again until April 9, when she accidentally came within 3 yards of him, feeding in a tree. Three yards may have been too close even for placid David, and when he seemed to withdraw, she decided it would be simply "rude" to stay and gawk, and so she moved away.

> He was eating leaves. He <u>must</u> have known I was coming. Anyway, he looked at me, & I looked at him. He went on chewing, but very slowly as though preoccupied. After a minute he climbed deliberately to a lower branch & pulled a higher one down so that he was quite obscured. Well, I didn't know what to do. I couldn't stay—it was—well, RUDE. Silly I know, but I couldn't. I <u>knew</u> he would not like it. So, without looking, I moved on. Some 30 yards off I stopped. He was still there. Remained for 10–15 mins, but I could not see much—he didn't want me to! Then he went. Grass too long to observe crossing.

While Jane was going out on her exhausting dawn-to-dark searches, back in camp a few chimpanzees began, tentatively and occasionally at first, dropping by. On February 24 at 6:30 in the evening she saw an adult male "climb down palm close to camp! Beside road! Paused to look at me. Vanished." And on February 26, after she came back in the evening, Jane learned that a male chimp had during the day "visited" Chiko.

Two palm trees in the clearing near Jane's tent had started producing nuts, while a tree at the higher side of the clearing had sprouted some yellow blossoms with edible seeds. March 8 was a discouraging day up in the mountains, but when Jane came down to camp that evening she was greeted by an enthusiastically grinning Saulo, who informed her that five big chimps and a young juvenile had been "all over camp" at nine o'clock that morning, mostly feeding on the palm nuts. Chimps were sighted in camp on March 12, then again on March 15, when Saulo saw a large male and two juveniles intent on feasting in the "yellow-flower tree."

At last, after reports of chimpanzees feeding in the camp palms for two days in a row at the end of the month, Jane decided on the afternoon of the third day, March 30, to look for herself. It had been an uninteresting morning at the Peak, and she took the trail back down in the rain and turned a corner into the camp clearing at around one o'clock, to find two chimps in a tall palm on the lake side of the tent. Both stared at her in apparent alarm before climbing down and hastily scampering behind the tent and out of sight. Keeping the tent between herself and the two apes, Jane slowly entered it, quietly stepped into the washroom at the rear, and discreetly peered from underneath a flap to see one of the apes only about ten yards away, a big bearded male standing in what was now a heavy downpour and looking up, wistfully perhaps, at the tree he had prematurely abandoned.

He sat down for a few minutes, scratching his chin and regularly turning his head to look back at the palm tree, and then he stood up and walked "deliberately" back to the palm, climbing up on the side away from the tent (so that Jane could only see his hands moving up the tree) and feeding high up and on the far side (so she could see nothing at all). After the chimp had been up there for over an hour and the rain had eased a little, she tried poking her head out from under the front flap of the tent, craning her neck to look up into the top of the tree—only to see a dark-haired ape craning his neck to look down. Ten minutes passed. Jane once again peered out from under the front flap. Once again the big ape peered down at her. She retreated to the washroom, from where, in another five minutes, she watched him appear at the bottom of the tree and then evaporate into the forest.

On April 3, her twenty-seventh birthday, Jane started the day well before dawn with a mountain climb in the moonlight to see, as she described it in a letter home, "8 dear little chimps in their nests." Among them was "one poor young lady" who, "while it was scarcely light, was woken from a deep sleep by an amorous suitor. With a scream horrifying to hear she leapt out of bed—no time to make up or anything. Dear me! From the sound of things she was not permitted a peaceful breakfast either!" All the apes left after that rude awakening, and Jane climbed into their nests to examine them. But soon she heard the calls of more chimps and, following them, was led right back to camp. It started raining, and Jane found Dominic dodging the rain and "cursing the fire" because it was ruining her birthday cake. He told her she could ice the cake and put in the candles as soon as it had cooled, but the rain kept hammering down, and since it was her birthday, Jane retired to her tent, sat on her bed, and began writing a letter home . . . only to be interrupted by an unusual noise. She looked up to see a big male chimp dangling from the lower end of a palm frond just outside the tent. He was climbing up the palm, and as Jane quickly lay down on the tent floor for a better view, a second appeared on the other side of the tree—only about 5 yards away. Just then the male in the palm saw Jane and let out a few low hoots, whereupon the one below dashed across the grass and into the yellow-flower tree. Both of the chimps made "angry loud calls—at me?" But the "old man" in the tree, after making a "funny little cross hoot to himself," simply continued as he was before, "stuffing nuts into his mouth." And the other one just moved a little higher in the yellow-flower tree. After perhaps twenty minutes, the palm-tree chimp climbed down, and then they both disappeared. "This is the way to watch chimps!" Jane declared to the family.

At first she did not take the occasional chimpanzee visits to camp seriously. They consisted of only one or two apes briefly appearing, feeding, and disappearing. Primarily, it was good entertainment for the staff. "It gives D[ominic] & H[assan] great fun," she wrote home in a letter of April 9, but it also meant, she added as a hopeful afterthought, "if I ever had to stay down for a day there's the chance it might not be a chimpless day!" Dominic, in fact, had once tried to make the palm tree more attractive by hanging up a few bananas, and Jane tried suspending a block of salt and, for a brief while, a dead rat.

By the middle of that month she was once more getting good enough observations in the mountains to begin trying to identify and name individuals again. She discovered Mike ("Large black faced male, not a very conspicuous beard, but pale chin, not very bald—small upright bald line to the left side of brow, small dark ears") on April 18. And William ("Very large, round chin & large mouth. A most comical chimp. Fond of hanging lower lip down—very pink. Black face. Not very bald. Distinctly white beard. Dark ears, little larger than Mike's") on the same day. Wilhemina followed on April 31. Lord Dracula on May 4. Lucy, Henrietta, and Fifi on May 5.

May turned out to be a bad month for finding chimps in the mountains, though—but a good month for watching David Greybeard in camp. Jane felt certain it was David who entered camp on May 5 and May 6, while she was searching in the mountains. On May 7 he appeared early in the morning, while she was still inside her tent. She heard a rustle and then watched a hairy form race up the tree and begin plucking and consuming the ripe palm nuts. Jane immediately dashed off an excited note to her family. "Have to write a few words," she began,

> because it can't be true. It can't. David Greybeard is up the palm. I am sitting outside the tent. D[ominic] is washing up after my breakfast—which I ate sitting outside the tent. I have walked all round the tree taking pictures—sadness—only one film & that, I think, spoiled by damp. Even from directly underneath. We have talked. Can it be true? My filming difficulties, re. termites—are as good as over. I can just walk up the ant hill & film David G. This is unique. I can get my own fabulous pictures. Only the sad thing is it's not salt he's after—it's palm nuts & they are nearly finished. Still, as I proved the other day, he doesn't mind me up in the mountains either. I keep looking up & not believing it's a chimp—not a real one. How I wish you were here, Mum. He'd soon take food from your hands, come here when you called! He's sitting contemplating now, scratching his chin. I have just been under the tree talking in a loud voice to him. He didn't even look! Rayed out below are: 1 tin baked beans, open. 1 plate salt. 1 plate sugar. 1 glass lime juice!!! I am drinking coffee! Isn't it too ridiculous for words?

That night Jane pulled her camp bed and its draped mosquito netting out of the tent and situated them strategically under the palm tree, and when the ape came back the next morning, May 8, she experienced "the strangest awakening I've ever had!" David climbed halfway up the palm before stopping to peer under the mosquito net. Then, with only a brief pause to scratch himself, he continued climbing all the way to the top and the still-productive cluster of ripe palm nuts. Jane readjusted the net and lay back in her cot "inwardly roaring with mirth. Chimp watching in bed!!"

So it went. Jane continued the daily climbs and attempted observations of all the wild chimps hidden in the forests and mountains outside of camp, but she was amused and delighted by the cameo appearances of a chimp who seemed to like coming into camp — by this time attracted not only by the occasional nuts in the palm tree near Jane's tent and the figs in a fig tree near Hassan's tent but also by the possibility of a few ripe bananas, which had become a standard offering by mid-May. Some of the bananas were "demolished" on the spot, "skin & all," or the big chimp might run off a short distance with more clutched in his hands and perhaps a single banana stuck in his mouth for safekeeping, making him look "like an old boy with a cigar drooling from his mouth!"

Jane also periodically ran into David outside of camp, sitting in the forest, obscured in the tall grass, or lolloping along a trail somewhere. On May 14, for instance, just as she was about to begin her climb up the hill known as Ogre, pausing for a moment to think about a new spot for her *dudu* trap, she heard a whispering in the tall grass ahead. She stopped, listened, moved closer. As she declared in the field journal, "I knew what to expect." And then: "Sure enough a black head appeared!" It was "Dear David G," who "stopped & regarded me in an offhand way, scratched his leg, and moved into the track." It looked as though he was about to head down the trail in the direction of camp, so Jane quietly stepped aside and "waved him on." He paused, scratched himself, crossed the path hesitatingly; she, responding to his hesitation, turned around and began ambling back toward camp — soon to discover that he was following her. "It was like taking a dog out — if I stopped I heard him behind me, & he stopped. Did not see him."

She reached camp ahead of him, with time enough to fetch the camera and toss a few bananas beneath the palm tree. She sat down on the floor of the tent's veranda, and ten minutes later David walked up. He hardly glanced in her direction before grabbing four bananas and sitting down with them, about 6 yards away and facing her. The handsome ape gobbled the fruit whole, scratching himself from time to time, before finally moving to within 5 feet of her to grab a fifth and final helping.

David was "a lovely specimen," Jane wrote home. "All his hair, scarcely any baldness of the forehead, long cheek hair, dark handsom face—<u>very</u> handsome chimp."

Although she admitted it only retrospectively, the first five months of 1961 were exhausting, and a thinner than usual Jane left Gombe for a rest in "civilization"—Nairobi—at the end of May. The holiday was refreshing, with Jane sleeping past dawn in a real bed at the Ainsworth Hotel and seizing the opportunity—assisted by some efficacious medicine from Olly and open sandals in dry weather—to cure the rot between her toes.

The Coryndon was very different from what she remembered, with Louis's old office now, she wrote home, "spick & span & shining" and taken over by a bookkeeper, an extension to the library completed, and a modern telephone switchboard installed, "which no one can work, & which is a menace." Mary Leakey was no longer speaking to her, Jane discovered, while Louis (who absurdly offered Jane his office dictaphone to tape-record the chimps) was simply his same old "mad" self—yet "so amenable and pleasant," she considered, "that I havn't even told him he's mad." She renewed several old friendships and spent time catching up with Clo, who was by then having serious problems (as suggested by the marks or bruises at her throat) with her marriage to Francis Erskine. Jane and Clo attended a posh affair at the YWCA one afternoon and found themselves underdressed, which put Clo "in a great flap" because "half the gathering were her relatives." But Jane simply imagined all the sheer-stockinged, high-heeled, long-gloved society dames and denizens "climbing up my mountains, or meeting a buffalo, and was vastly amused at the ensuing mental picture! I also keep noticing chimp gestures amongst my fellow <u>Homo</u> groups! There are many similarities!"

By the afternoon of June 16 Jane was back at Gombe, where she found that Dominic and Chiko had been joined by a second baby daughter and a young nephew. Meanwhile, Hilda was "brooding like mad," Jane informed the family, sitting regally and fluffily over more than a dozen eggs, while Hildebrand and the growing offspring were defensively bunching up together on the other side of the henhouse at night. One of the young hens snored, Jane discovered, and it sounded, she wrote to Vanne, "just like you!!!"

But the big news was a dramatic and welcome change in the physical environment. The long heavy rains were gone. Fires and tramping feet had conquered the high grass. And the terribly oppressive humid heat had been replaced by an agreeable dry heat. As Jane now confessed, writing on July 13 to her friend Bernard Verdcourt, "there were times, during my last session here, when I wondered if I could possibly exist through those 4 months. But

I think it was because of the continual rain & the long grass. Life was so difficult, and then, between the rains, it was _so_ hot & humid. I think it got me down. I came back this time rather full of foreboding. But, although as yet I've not had as _much_ fun with my chimps, already I hate the thought of going!" There had been lots of "beastly" ticks that June, but around the start of July they simply vanished. "One day I was plucking them from me all day—feet, legs, bottom, waist, bossom, arms, neck, hands. The next day—not even _one_."

Now, though, there was a wind problem: very strong and very noisy, often making it nearly impossible to locate chimps from their calls and even, when located, difficult to watch them properly, since the shuddering wind would shake the binoculars. So generally the chimps were harder to find. However, they were being "utterly charming & friendly," as she wrote to Bernard. They seemed less anxious, easier to approach. Although the wild apes had been "reasonably tame before," they now were "suddenly more so," and she was seeing them more closely and getting ever surer of her identifications.

She spotted David Greybeard in the forest for a short while on June 22, according to the field journal, and on July 6, upon her return at the end of the day, she was informed that he had briefly visited camp with three friends, two male and one female. David then disappeared for several weeks, but meanwhile Jane made another friend in the mountains, a big male (possibly the one she had named, many months earlier, Winston) who one afternoon in July moved closely around her for an hour and a half and sat down in the sun with his back to her "for ages" only 10 yards away. On another excellent day early that summer, Jane spent about two hours lingering peacefully just across a small gully from a large group—four adult males, two adult females, two adolescents, and an infant or young juvenile—all resting and interacting on open ground. One of the males "yelled at me once when he first saw me," Jane wrote in a July 5 letter home, but the rest of the group just continued peacefully as they were. The other three males (Hollis, Huxley, and Mike) groomed each other. One of the adolescents (young Hugh) lay down next to one of the adult females and played with the baby. "It was all so utterly heavenly. This is real success. This is like George [Schaller] & his Gorilla. And I never thought to be able to do it. But my gosh, it's taken long enough!"

On July 14, Jane sent a letter to the family marking "the anniversary of the first arrival of the Morris Goodall Chimpanzee expedition!" and summarizing her accomplishments over the previous year. That great day of first arrival, exactly a year before, "does seem a long time ago in many ways," she began, and yet she could still, at times, look at the peaks & valleys & see them with my early eyes, & how different they seem now. Then they were alien, strange, confusing—a challenge. And indeed, so they were in the rains. But now—now life is so wonderful. The challenge has been met. The hills and forests are my home. And what is more, I think my mind works like a chimp's, subconsciously. For when I take a track through the forest, selecting one from a maze of little trails—sure enough if chimps are around, some old chap will be on the same road. It's happened <u>so</u> often. And I can't put it down to my cleverness at all—often it's a very <u>bad</u> track—for me. And often I choose one which I think I took before, & find it's another—& there is a chimp. It's most peculiar.

But while she would continue to be amazed that "my mind works like a chimp's," perhaps her most impressive accomplishment was to recognize that chimpanzees have minds in the first place. For Jane's greatest, most remarkable discovery during her first year of watching and wandering among the chimpanzees of Gombe was not that these apes eat meat, make and use tools, dance wildly in the rain, and all the rest, but rather that they do such things as active and willful beings with personalities, beings who inhabit an intellectual world similar to our own, who possess, as we do, a vibrant emotional and mental reality complete with the standard mysteries of ego, love, pain, and death. That slowly appreciated truth was the real magic behind her first year at Gombe.

18

A Photographic Failure

1961

SUPPORT FROM the National Geographic Society was always generous but never free. The National Geographic expected in return for its money first publication rights to any written results and photographs. From the start the society's magazine staff had been preparing for the likelihood of a richly illustrated article about Miss Goodall and her work on the Louis Leakey Chimpanzee Project. In his original application for funds to support that work, Louis implied, by presenting only the best and most atypical scenario ("as many as 23 chimpanzees . . . feeding calmly around her, within 15 or 20 feet of her"), that Jane was regularly getting roughly ten or twenty times closer to her chimpanzee subjects than she typically was, and that taking good pictures would be a simple matter—once *he* allowed it ("I have forbidden her to carry cameras" in order that she "go unrecognized by the chimpanzees as [long as] is feasibly possible"). But, Louis continued, elaborating on the fantasy, it would be necessary to extend her time in the field, if only because so far no pictures had been taken. He expected that after a year of his research assistant's sitting completely still, the chimpanzees might develop a tolerance for her as a minor novelty. At that point, "I shall have her start different operations, using a telephoto camera, an ordinary camera, and possibly a cine camera . . . for by then they should be so used to her as not to mind so much."

The National Geographic staff were enticed by the image Louis was producing, but they wanted their photographs as soon as possible. They also wanted a skilled professional from their own staff to shoot them.

During his visit to Washington in late February 1961, Louis had discussed that issue with Melville Bell Grosvenor. Grosvenor was a near contemporary of Louis's, only a couple of years older, and they shared an attractive tendency toward optimism and youthful enthusiasm. Grosvenor's "eternal boyishness," according to a staff member of the time, "made him a wonderful guy to work with. He was approachable, salable on new ideas. He was warm, generous; he could be reasoned with. He woke up with stars in his eyes believing the world was a wonderful exciting place." And Louis and Mel, as they were soon calling each other, appear to have actively liked each other. Louis had little trouble selling Mel on the idea that the Chimpanzee Project required a woman photographer. He was willing to accept a *National Geographic* photographer for Gombe, Louis declared, provided they could find someone suitably female.

Within a couple of months Louis had returned to the United States for a brief visit on May 5 to the society's headquarters in order to select, with help from Grosvenor, the lucky person who would get to photograph life and chimps at Gombe. That the person had to be female simplified their chore a good deal, since the two to three dozen members of the magazine's illustrations staff included only two or three women, none of them photographers. Nevertheless, Louis and Mel jointly stalked the halls until they located a young assistant illustrations editor, Mary Griswold, whom Louis found congenial.

Years later, Mary Griswold Smith wrote about the auspicious moment when President Grosvenor and Dr. Leakey appeared in her office, with the latter inquiring solicitously, "How old are you, my dear?"

"Twenty-seven," she said.

"Good, good," he responded, smiling broadly and rubbing his hands together enthusiastically. "She'll like that. She's the same age."

So, in one of Louis's typically impulsive gestures, Mary Griswold was chosen to be the photographer, and Melville Bell Grosvenor announced in a May 9 note to his father, Gilbert H. Grosvenor, the chairman of the board, that she would be leaving later that month. She would be expected not only to take top-quality still photographs but also to produce useful film footage.

Jane was alarmed by the idea of any photographer, male or female, coming in to take pictures. "Not many people are lucky enough to do the sort of work they <u>really</u> want to do more than anything else," she wrote in a March 24 letter home. "I have my two, in one—animals & writing. Arn't I just too lucky for words." However, she continued, Louis had "sold his soul to National Geographic. That's why I'm anxious, if at all possible, to steer clear of it." Jane was seriously concerned both about having a second person in camp or near the chimps and about somehow losing credit for what she had achieved: "I'm not at <u>all</u> keen on the Nat. Geographic woman photographer. (1) I can't imagine such a person fitting in here, (2) I want to do my own photos—or have a jolly good try first. Why should she [take advantage of] all my months of hard work for her results?" And if an outside photographer turned out to be absolutely necessary, she would prefer to have someone she already knew, namely Des Bartlett, who had recently filmed Louis's Olduvai excavations.

Within a month Jane had become even more emphatic. "I have made up my mind NOT to have the Geographic woman," she wrote to the family near the end of April. "I can't go into all my reasons now, but I'm not having her." Instead, she would take the pictures herself.

> They will not be as good as hers would be, IF she was able to get anywhere near the chimps & photograph them. Leakey keeps saying that she would only do "far away" ones, so as not to disturb them—i.e. 100 yards. He just does not realize that 100 yards is not far away & they comparatively seldom allow ME any closer, unless in thick trees where they can remain hidden. As for taking pictures of me with the chimps—what does he think. He hasn't a clue how very tricky my chimps are or he wouldn't suggest any such thing! It is hopeless trying to explain any of these things because he won't listen to things he doesn't want to hear.

And in a letter written around May 6, she reported to the family that she had just received "an even crazier letter from Leakey who is trying to make me believe that for a telephoto lens you have to have a tripod!" She continued: "Well, either way he's batty! 1) You don't. 2) If you do, does he think chimps will allow strange ladies and their tripods to invade them?! I can see a big battle ahead! I'm rather looking forward to it."

On May 10 an editorial staff member named William Graves sent a detailed note to his boss, Melville Grosvenor, on the subject of "Miss Griswold's East African Assignment," circumspectly remarking that "I have a suggestion you might consider worthwhile." He began by reminding Grosvenor about the challenges of life at Gombe, reaffirming emphatically the choice of Griswold for the job and tactfully avoiding any reference to her inexperience as a photographer, a filmmaker, or a traveler in Africa. He then proceeded to suggest there might still be serious problems of a pragmatic nature. For one thing, there was all that bulky photography equipment to tote around. For another, she might be required to function by herself in the field, with perhaps only the support of an African assistant. Did Jane's African assistants speak English? Probably not. Mary Griswold, in short, would most likely discover that she needed extra help—and even, conceivably, "minor protection." Graves reminded Grosvenor of Louis Leakey's story that he had many years earlier sent a "grown man" out to study the chimpanzees of Gombe and "the man simply could not take it and gave up."

The solution? Graves thought that the society should hire Richard Leakey, Louis's seventeen-year-old son, to assist Mary Griswold. Richard had grown up in Africa, was thoroughly experienced with rough conditions there, was resourceful and competent. Richard had also spent a good deal of time in the company of Des Bartlett and was himself an "ardent photographic student." He happened to be saving money for his university education and thus should especially appreciate the opportunity to earn something extra. But possibly the biggest advantage of hiring Richard Leakey to assist Miss Griswold was that his father would have no reason to object: "He is undoubtedly no stranger to Miss Goodall, and would certainly not be looked on by Dr. Leakey as a distraction or hindrance to her work."

Graves's suggestion seemed such an excellent one that by the time Grosvenor relayed it to Louis, in a long and thoughtful letter sent at the end of the month, the Mary Griswold part had been removed altogether. Grosvenor began by noting somewhat apologetically that they had "hastily assigned" her to the job and were now "reluctantly" concluding that it might be "unwise to send someone inexperienced in working with wild animals." The rest of the letter concentrated on the matter of someone who was not similarly inexperienced, namely Richard. "We certainly understand your reluctance to permitting most photographers from accompanying Miss Goodall into the field," the distinguished president and editor sensitively conceded, "but perhaps Richard would be acceptable since he is no stranger to her. He knows the animals and would not be unduly alarmed being alone with them in the jungle." The National Geographic would offer a guaranteed and very generous minimum pay of $800 for about two months' work, and if Richard were to succeed exceptionally, he might make a lot more. "Richard could do very well if he were to put his mind to it!"

Grosvenor described the subjects they were hoping to get pictures of—and the package that had already been sent by air express: a wide-angle Rolleiflex camera and a substantial bundle of high-speed Ektachrome 120 film and special shipping cartons. James H. Godbold, the magazine's director of photography, would be writing soon, Grosvenor promised, to elaborate on the equipment, and it would be good for Jane and Richard to experiment with a few rolls of the film while she was in Nairobi and rush them back in the shipping cartons to Washington. Finally, once Jane and Richard had disappeared back "into the jungle," they could send out their exposed films weekly, which would enable the Geographic to monitor the quality of their pictures and the functionality of their equipment continuously.

Louis returned from a visit to London near the end of the first week in

June to find the letter from Mel Grosvenor in his museum mailbox, and he immediately fired back a brief and seemingly irritated response. Although he could appreciate the logic of their decision not to send Mary Griswold, he began, his son Richard was otherwise engaged and could not suddenly change course at such impossibly short notice. Slipping into a schoolmarm's scolding tone, he then proceeded to chide the National Geographic Society president for his ignorance: "I do not think you perhaps fully appreciated (although I did try to explain it to you) that Jane Goodall is only here in Nairobi for one week and this is only the second time out of the bush in more than a year." Thus there was no time to find anyone else to accompany her, and thus Louis himself had decided to equip Jane with extra cameras so she could take the pictures on her own.

Jane actually was taking a two-week break in Nairobi, but by the time Louis had responded to Grosvenor she had only one left, which was just long enough to try out the wide-angle Rolleiflex, sent, as the Geographic director of photography explained in his own letter, so that "Miss Goodall could get better coverage of the chimpanzees when they were ten feet or closer."

That camera made everyone unhappy. As Jane candidly commented in a June 10 note to the family in England, "Geographical, at vast expense, have sent me a completely useless camera—a wide-angle Rolleiflex which makes things very close further away!!!! Are they not mad?" As Louis put the matter bluntly in a second letter to Grosvenor, written on June 12, "We tried out the camera which you had sent but it is far too heavy and clumsy, and Jane will not take it with her into the field. What would you like me to do with it and the films that go with it?"

While Jane was in Nairobi, Louis bought her a simpler and more straightforward Retina Reflex, costing some eighty pounds, for use at Gombe. This piece of equipment Louis described in his second letter to Grosvenor as a "camera round her neck," and he hoped that the National Geographic would reimburse him for its cost and see fit to supplement it with an additional camera plus tripod and large telephoto lens for long-distance shots.

In Washington, someone in the editorial department was soon writing a note to Louis apologizing for the mix-up and sorting out the matter of returns and reimbursements, and someone in the shipping department was soon wrapping up a Nikon 35mm camera with three lenses: 50mm for normal distances, 105mm for medium distances, and a 300mm telephoto attachment for treetop and other long shots. The full package included an electric motor drive energized by eight C-type batteries in a battery case, a General Electric exposure meter, an aluminum tripod, caption cards, film shipping cartons, 15 rolls of Kodachrome film, and a Globe-Trotter carrying bag. It was shipped to Nairobi by air express on June 22, a week after Jane had returned to Gombe with the more portable Retina around her neck.

The failure of the National Geographic to find a suitable photographer was good news from Jane's perspective, since she seemed to have won, by default, the who-will-shoot-the-photos battle. "For the present," she wrote home in June, "I hold the photographic baby in my own lap." She herself would be the female photographer.

The Nikon camera plus telephoto lenses plus motor drive plus tripod remained in Nairobi that summer, but the instructions on how to operate it, written by the magazine's assistant director of photography, Joseph B. Roberts, went to Gombe. "Now," the note announced, "for the shortest correspondence course in photography ever written. I presume that you have had considerable camera experience on previous scientific studies."

Roberts had apparently composed his "shortest correspondence course" with no ironic intent, but the intimidatingly detailed instructions gave Jane a "raging headache." She described her reaction to the letter in a July 5 note to the family in England. "The only real news I have is quite horrifying," she began.

> A long letter from National Geographic with details of the equipment they are sending me—camera with 3 lenses & 1 tripod & automatic controls. It makes me feel so utterly helpless & dependent. It's a good thing you weren't here when it arrived, Ma. I was still awake at 3.30, & taking painocils for a raging headache! Have recovered a bit now. The man presumed I was already an experienced photographer after photographing my other scientific studies! It's bad enough having to battle with mountains, heat, tired body <u>and</u> chimps—let alone tripods & lenses & lengths of wire, etc. If they only realized the conditions—& this includes dear L.S.B. For instance, yesterday I was inching my way up a mountain side, clinging onto rocks & roots. And I bumped into some chimps. Well, there they sat, yelled at me a bit, ate a bit, scratched a bit, & went on their way. Wonderful view. Super photos—if I could have taken them. But as I really hadn't enough hands & feet to secure me to the mountain's surface, <u>how</u> could I take out my one simple little camera? Let alone if I'd had millions of lenses & tripods stuck all over me!

Five weeks later, on August 14, Jane replied to Joseph Roberts, apologizing for the delayed response and explaining that the Nikon and all its associated equipment were still in Nairobi and that she was not intending to use it until later, since at the moment she was afraid of upsetting the chimps with "a determined effort at close-up photography." She informed Roberts that a test roll of film was being sent separately in one of the special cartons he had provided. And she excused herself in advance for the "very disappointing" quality of the pictures on that roll, noting that in the time since she had received his letter and the film, she had experienced "the worst month of my entire research period!"

Jane went on to describe the two primary problems in photographing chimpanzees at Gombe. First was the unmitigated up-and-downness of the place. Second was "the attitude of the chimps." Although they were not frightened by her, she noted, they did not like being watched. And she was still finding it difficult and "often not possible" to approach closer than 50 to 100 feet. There would be times, especially as ripe fruits appeared, when closer photography ought to be possible, and she had already built hides near several fruit trees. When the second camera, the Nikon, finally arrived, it could be used in the hides. "I am not in the position of having had previous camera experience I'm afraid," Jane confessed at the end of the note, but she was still confident that when the chimpanzees at last began to show themselves again, she would be able to "get the sort of pictures you are wanting — as well as the sort I must get for my report — habitat, nests, positions, etc."

It was a forthright letter, but the contents must have been discouraging for an illustrations staff to contemplate. Jane still had not touched the Nikon, which remained inside a box in Nairobi. She confessed to knowing nothing about photography. She admitted that the apes — temporarily, one hoped — had disappeared. And she had exposed only a single test roll in two months. The technical assessment, once the test roll was developed in the magazine's photo laboratory, was even gloomier. Of the thirty-seven exposed frames on the roll, the assistant illustrations editor, Robert Gilka, summarized in an internal memo, sixteen were so underexposed they were "unreadable," ten had been ruined by camera motion, and six more turned out to be otherwise useless. That left a single exposure that the magazine "might possibly use": Jane sitting on a hillside and looking through her binoculars in the hope of seeing chimps.

Both Jane and Louis had already concluded by then that a second person was necessary, although they remained unconvinced about the need for a professionally trained one; and by the middle of July, Jane had nominated her sister, Judy, for the job. Judy had no more photographic training or experience than Jane did, but unlike Jane she would be able to focus solely on taking pictures. Also, since Judy looked a little like her sister, perhaps if she dressed in the same clothes, the chimps would be fooled into thinking she was the same person they were already used to.

Louis first presented the Judy idea in a brief and amiable July 17 note to Grosvenor, arguing that Jane's sister already had "some experience of color photography" without specifying exactly how much or what sort. (In fact her experience was, like Jane's, limited to the occasional snapshot produced by pressing a button on a small box.) Judy would, Louis continued, undoubtedly need "extra training" to use the fancy Nikon plus telescopic lenses and tripod that the society had recently sent, and hence he proposed to arrange for tutoring from Des Bartlett before sending her on to Gombe in October. Judy was currently an employee of the British Museum of Natural History, but Louis felt he could arrange for a minor leave of absence — if the National Geographic would cover her plane tickets and the cost of her food and perhaps provide some compensation for lost salary during her leave. . . .

Unfortunately, the usually receptive Melville Bell Grosvenor was on vacation in Canada when Louis's new proposal reached society headquarters, and it was therefore dropped onto the desk of a less receptive vice president and associate editor named Frederick G. Vosburgh. Vosburgh was by then starting to acquire a reputation among the magazine's editorial staff for "inflexibility and conservatism, rather than imagination" and as a "stickler for accuracy." Famously, he once stopped the presses in order to restore a missing comma (for the July 1964 issue), at a cost of $30,000. And, as the person considered "responsible for keeping [Grosvenor's] excesses in check," Vosburgh predictably responded in the cool negative to Louis Leakey's latest wild scheme, declaring soberly in a return note that "the production of satisfactory photographs for the National Geographic requires considerable experience as well as aptitude, and this assignment would tax the skill of even a professional photographer." He ended his formally cordial reply by reminding Louis that "it would certainly simplify matters" if one of the professional photographers on the staff went to Gombe for a few weeks or even a few days. Perhaps Jane could invite a friend to stay during that period "for the sake of convention."

That was a logically expressed no, but Louis took it as a challenging maybe, and he quickly responded. Reverting to the schoolmarm's scold ("I don't think any of you fully realise . . ."), he began by inventing a geographical fantasy. Jane's camp could be reached only by boat, he noted, and the space available in the camp clearing was so very tiny, with strict rules against expanding it by cutting trees, that there could be "absolutely no possibility" of a professional male photographer coming out accompanied by—

for convention's sake—a woman to be Jane's companion and chaperone. Not enough room for the extra body.

Moving from the fantasy problem, he proceeded to detail the real one. The chimps were shadowy creatures living inside shadowed forests: a photographer's nightmare. Louis and Jane were anticipating a few occasions during the next several months when the apes might expose themselves while feeding in a few large fruit trees, whereupon their images could be captured from a distance via telephoto lenses. Jane was carrying the small round-the-neck Retina Reflex he had recently purchased for her in Nairobi, but the bigger Nikon with tripod and lenses would be "quite impossible" for her to use by herself. He then reviewed his tempting vision of what such photographs and the resulting article might mean to *National Geographic,* in terms of both scientific import and popular drama. And he concluded with a threat. If the magazine staff was not willing to risk a tiny sum of money for a few photographs on this spectacular story, he would look elsewhere for support, since "it has got to be done."

In a subsequent letter to the society vice president that August, Louis noted that they were caught in an unhappy "deadlock"—which he had just preemptively broken by selling first rights for the story and pictures to a British weekly newspaper, *Reveille,* for £300.

Jane began preparing for her sister's arrival. She organized the construction of a few grass-and-palm-frond hides big enough for one camera and two crouched siblings, conveniently located near important fruit trees and termite mounds. And she wrote and advised Judy about such essentials as anti-malaria medicine (Nivaquine, begun two weeks before arrival), good binoculars ("most important"), a pair of sunglasses, and the proper clothes (a pair of canvas gym shoes, lightweight jeans or shorts, and at least one good "bush shirt" with breast pockets).

And then she worked on taking a few pictures on her own. She spent a wonderful night that August sleeping out with the chimps under a full moon, cooking herself a dinner of porridge and beans and coffee over a campfire as the chimps went to sleep in their nests. "I have seldom been happier than I was then," she wrote home late in the month. "My chimps below me, I curled up in my blanket and slept till 5, then went down as close as I could get & saw them getting up." But then, before she could get any good shots, the chimps disappeared.

She was able to photograph a big crowd of banded mongooses, perhaps fifteen or twenty of them. They were "so like Kip," she noted: "the same sort of small squeals, only deeper—not chirp-y like his. The same busy little digging & scuttling. Believe it or not, they came up to within 3 <u>feet</u> of me & never knew I was there!!" She stood "still as a statue—to my great cost as I was being bitten all over by tsetse's!" Then she took a picture. "But I think it was too close! And the 'click' sent them all scampering away."

In early September the chimps finally came back in significant numbers. There were exciting days in which, as she wrote to the family, "all the gents are in fighting fettle," so that "everywhere they go they charge around, swiping at trees & yelling & screaming and flinging their arms about." There was a special moment of watching young juveniles dance: "2 little children, 2 years old, <u>dancing</u> yesterday. I can't really call it anything else. They were pacing up & down, a distance of 6 yards or so, passing each other, turning, & repassing, walking bipedally, & stamping down each foot—sort of Conga step, bringing the arm down in time, & nodding their heads." But that lasted only a brief while, and Jane was unable to get any pictures.

Even "my <u>darling</u> David Greybeard," gone for much of August, had reappeared by September 3. Then, on September 12, during a special moment that was quickly turning into a spectacular scene for a photographer, Jane's camera seized up. "But oh, what a tragedy," she wrote home a couple of days later. "William 12 ft away, standing up with one hand on a tree, saying, very gently, 'hoo' & then sitting there gazing up at the trees looking for figs—Mike, the same distance, chewing a lovely pink wadge of palm nut fibres & fig pips. Mrs. Maggs followed by her baby. It was no use for anything else—they were on a safari & did not stop. But superb for photos. And it is the first time in 2 months I've had the opportunity. Makes you weep." Frantic, Jane packed up and shipped her Retina to Nairobi for what she hoped would be a quick repair.

Waiting for Judy with slowly mounting anxiety about the swiftly passing time ("Help! how time flies" she began her journal entry for September 19), Jane spent her nights in an often turbulent and wakeful fret. "I despair of 2 things," she wrote to the family in midmonth:

1)—seeing mating (2) Jif [Judy] or I getting any photos—it's not a question of the <u>capabilities</u> of taking them—it's getting in the right place at the right time. Really one needs about 6 people, all with telephotos, all sitting in all possible places, in hiding, every day for a couple of months! As it is, Jif will have to hopefully dash from hide to hide, & they'll never go the right way at the right time. What a life.

Seeing mating, it turned out, was the easy part. As Jane noted in a letter of September 22, "<u>MATING</u>!"

Judy, meanwhile, arrived in Nairobi on September 15, was met by Louis at the airport, and spent a few days developing her picture-taking skills with the Geographic's tripod-mounted Nikon. Then, carrying the Nikon, she flew to Dar es Salaam, took the two-day train west to Kigoma, and rendezvoused there on Saturday, September 23, with Hassan, who took her up the lake to Gombe. Jane had planned to greet her sister upon arrival at the reserve, of course, but that afternoon one of her favorite chimps, Mike, was busy mating and she simply could not tear herself away from the opportunity to watch, so she arrived in camp late.

Judy was startled, she later told her mother, to see how very thin her older sister had gotten. "Skeletal" was the operative word. But the younger sister nevertheless had a wonderful introduction to the apes the very next day, which began, before dawn, with a walk in the moonlight up to the Peak.

Jane soon summarized Judy's remarkable first day of chimpanzee observations in a letter home. "More than 25, all spread out over the Pocket [below the Peak]. Mating! Walking on hind legs! Dragging branches! And today, making a nest!" The particularly dramatic mating, involving five very eager males lined up to take turns with a single sexually receptive female, was recorded in mostly detached and sober detail for the field journal but recollected with a good deal less detachment and sobriety for the family back home. ("Then a female jumped up into a big tree, followed by her 5 year old child. With yells & shrieks, full of the joys of life, 5 large males bounded up after her. All masculine strength and virility they swung from branch to branch, calling wildly, huge and black in the cool clear morning. One of them bounded up to the lady. She screamed—but played the game all right. Well, she coped with No. 1. He sat beside her for a moment, then swung away, out of the tree.")

Unfortunately, though, the newly arrived female photographer was distracted by a severe sunburn. She spent her first couple of weeks at Gombe in a tender state, with puffy, then pink and peeling skin, and was additionally preoccupied, as Jane wrote home positively, with "getting to know the lie of the land, & finding her feet."

In truth, Judy was mostly without a camera those first couple of weeks, because a still Retina-less Jane took over the Nikon, thinking she would be able to get closer to the chimps. Indeed, along with getting some clear if somewhat distant observations of mating, she managed to creep within 20 feet of three adult chimps, Mike, Pooch, and Humphrey, and watch them quietly for at least an hour one afternoon. It could have been an excellent chance to get some really clear shots. "Unfortunately," as she explained in a letter to Louis, "the pictures will be no good as there was scarcely any light owing to approaching storm, & the intervening tangle of vines, while not impeding one's view, was bad for photography. And I dared not use a lower shutter speed as I had to hold the camera at such an odd angle my arm was shaking."

It was a pleasant change to have Judy around, though. They enjoyed their evenings together, eating meals by the campfire. Judy, who always had a good appetite, experimented with (as Jane wrote home) "enormous plate-fuls" of *dagaa* and discovered the pleasures of crisply cooked termites. Al-though Jane's supply of butter had gone rancid, the pair began baking po-tatoes in the embers of their fire. They spent happy times discussing the standard sisterly things, such as what to do with Jane's overgrown "yards of sun-blond hair," which could be woven into plaits, spun into earphones, or cast into a ringleted crown. And while Jane labored over the field journal late into the evening (absently nibbling on cake, papaya, or a bit of choco-late and sipping coffee) and then stayed awake half the night with insomnia, Judy was, as Jane informed the family, "the sleeping beauty. What a child for sleep. Certainly all night & at least half the day. She just leans back on the hill side & snores softly!!"

Jane's Retina was eventually repaired and returned to camp, but then the Nikon succumbed to Gombe's intense heat and humidity. On October 4, David Greybeard appeared, as Jane noted in the journal, "walking straight towards me. He climbed a small fig some 30 feet ahead, & thence into a low palm. Made happy little grunts. Moved round behind. I got ready to take pictures, though light v. bad. After 5 mins (more grunts & low 'hoo's') he reappeared & climbed down. Shutter stuck!"

Judy then commenced her photographic efforts, sitting patiently for very long periods inside one of the grass hides, sweltering and sweating. And since she could see only through the single front hole, she was unable to recognize the great creature who one time pounced onto her hut from be-hind. "I can remember thinking my end was nigh," she told me. "I heard this heavy sort of body lumbering around the hut towards me. I thought, 'My goodness, it's a buffalo!' I heard this thing coming closer and closer, and I couldn't see because I only had one little lookout in front. And it came closer and closer and went all round the edge very slowly and ponderously. Finally, it came into my line of vision, and it was a Nile monitor lizard. One of the really big ones. I heaved a sigh of relief. The old adrenaline rush."

Some fishermen brought to camp an orphaned baby vervet monkey one day that October, and Jane and Judy bought him for a very small sum, so the tedium of Judy's days in the hide was now relieved by the companionship of a tiny monkey on her shoulder. At the same time the monkey, named Moshi, made being quiet in the hide a lot harder.

Then the rains came, and that year they seemed heavier than usual. October 20 was, according to the journal, "a horrid day." October 21 was the "worst day for weeks." As a result of a wrenched knee and fever, Jane stayed in camp on the twenty-second, her first complete day in camp for months. "It rained hard" on the twenty-third. On the twenty-fourth, she found the chimps and stayed with them the entire day "but learnt nothing new—& got very wet!" So it went, and by October 29, Jane, feeling "lousey" and having a fever, went to look at some termite nests but when the fever got worse returned to camp. October 30 was a day of "Rain, rain, rain."

On November 1, Jane's camera once again broke, so Judy had to take it into Kigoma for repairs.

"Dear me, how it does rain here to be sure," Jane wrote to the family on November 3, describing the state of things during the previous few weeks. "I really have ceased worrying over photography & begin to laugh instead. Hordes of frogs, not even gracing Chimpland in the long rains, have arrived to celebrate the 'water water everywhere.' Only there are plenty of drinkable drops." As for the chimps, she continued, "What pray, is a chimp? I fear I've forgotten. Quite honestly, the last few weeks have been a waste of time, except that we have termite pictures." The termite pictures were taken on November 2, a day auspiciously marked in the journal with "At last some pictures."

Judy may have left for Kigoma with the broken Retina by then, and since the termite season was upon them, Jane stationed herself at the hide near the mounds, fortified with a supply of bananas. But before disappearing into the hide that morning, she left some bananas on top of one of the mounds. David Greybeard showed up around 9:30, climbed to the top of the mound, and began eating the bananas. Jane shot a few pictures, but the clicking of the camera alerted the white-bearded old male, and so, after consuming some of the fruit, he deliberately marched up to the hide to see what was going on. In a letter to the family, Jane detailed that encounter:

He sat on top of the hill, gave the hide a passing glance, & set to on the bananas. "Click" went the camera. He glanced across. Ate another banana. "Click". Another look. "Click". Banana. No attention. Etc. But, having finished the bananas he very slowly & deliberately climbed down & proceeded up the 30 feet of path to the hide. The "door" is a low hole across which grass is pulled. Slight pause outside—then a hand grasped the "door", pulled the grass to one side, & a face looked in. (The hide is just big enough for 2 people & you can't stand upright.) Well, he said "hoo", retreated a couple of steps, paused. Then marched solemnly back & got on with the main business—termite eating.

After an hour of termite-harvesting and eating, much of which Jane was able to observe clearly and occasionally to photograph, David climbed down from the mound to pick up a banana skin he had earlier dropped by accident. At that point Jane crawled out of the hide and held up a banana.

He didn't like me doing that. Anyhow, I threw it—it misfired & fell about 4 feet away. Well, I didn't think he'd paid much attention. But after 5 mins he began shaking a branch. This got more & more violent. Then he climbed a tree & shook that. Then, wildly hitting everything, he arrived at a small tree over the hide & shook that till I expected him through the roof at any moment. Then he sat. Then he leapt down, drummed a few times, & returned to the hill. I could not decide what it was all in aid of. Then, after 5 mins, he began to march up the path again. And got the banana. All this because he was annoyed that the banana was too close to me for his liking!! Well, he vanished. The walls are very thick. I heard much rustling just outside, where there is a lot of long grass. But could not see. Silence. Then fingers appeared—literally 5" away from my foot. Again, I wondered what on <u>earth</u> was going on. It was a banana skin Jiff had poked out through the grass, & he wanted it!! It was terribly funny. Then he went back to termite eating again!

November 2, however, was the single really good day of photography that entire season. The following day, as the journal indicates, was more typical and "quite useless." In a brief and desperate November 9 note to Louis that included an expression of alarm because she was out of money and overdrawn on her bank account in Kigoma, Jane wrote, "Life is depressing—wet, chimpless, and, it seems, impecunious. We are doing our best, but I cannot—repeat <u>cannot</u>—contend with FATE. What else is it that makes it <u>pour</u> when I get close to chimps, or else my camera fails—the new one."

Ten days later Jane wrote to Louis again, with "Land of Rain" as her return address. "I can't remember when I last wrote," she began. "Had I been ill with a weird fever that left spots all over my face? Well, I got vaguely better from that—now I have developed SHINGLES. I fear that this time, being unable to get the right stuff in Kigoma, I shall be left with <u>holes</u> in my cheek (as it's akin to chicken pox)." The failure of photography felt like a failure in life, and Jane's usual optimism had, along with her health, started to collapse. She reviewed the circumstances conspiring against photography: continuing rains, flooding rivers, blanketing clouds, nonfruiting fruit trees, rotting plant samples, sticking cameras, stinking dead fish on the beach, sisters slipping in the mud and sliding down mountainsides on their bottoms, and so on. "I hate to write such depressing news," she concluded, "but you had better be warned—it has made me feel that my entire work has been a failure. This, I suppose, is not true, but I just can't help feeling miserable about everything."

The year sputtered to an end. The journal entries became markedly shorter—soon, by November 12, winnowed down to a single sentence: "Stayed in camp with shingles." November 13 was two sentences. Nothing was written for the next three days, while an entry for Friday, November 17, continued the unhappy tale with seven laconic sentences: "Saw David in palm tree on other side of the stream. Took sixteen pictures—mostly back view! Stayed for about 20 mins then climbed down. Sat under tree for a minute & peered at me. Walked off. I re-crossed stream & saw him walk across open space towards the Ridge. Long grass made pictures impossible."

After a grand farewell party with the camp staff and local friends, Jane and Judy packed up and on December 5 left Gombe. Some acquaintances in Kigoma had agreed to adopt Moshi, the baby vervet monkey, and the sisters then headed by train to Nairobi, where they were met by Louis Leakey, who in turn telegrammed Vanne: "Girls arrived safely stop one thin one fat."

By December 14 the contrasting sisters were seated on a plane that circled monotonously above London. They looked out the window into a gray foggy world until, finally, after a fog emergency detour to Hurn, only a few miles outside Bournemouth, they were delivered by taxi to the familiar home at 10 Durley Chine Road South, where in lieu of the proverbial red carpet a tatty red towel was spread across the front doorstep. They were thus swept back into the bosom of home and family, in time for Christmas and Jane's new life as a doctoral student at Cambridge University.

Meanwhile, all their exposed film—one roll of black-and-white and twenty-three of color—was flown on to Washington, D.C., for development. Robert Gilka, in a December 13 internal memo, noted that aside from one good picture of "a large chimpanzee dining at an ant hill," the photographs were "not exciting"—although they might conceivably prove "adequate" for a short article about Miss Goodall's work. The next day Melville Bell Grosvenor reviewed the pictures and responded more emphatically and even less positively. The pictures were simply, he scrawled across the memo, "not suitable for publication in NGM."

On January 2, 1962, Gilka sent a letter to Jane and Judy (the "Misses Goodall"), officially breaking the bad news that "a lack of good pictures of the animals in the native habitat" was "so serious as to preclude attempting to illustrate a story." However, he continued (searching for a silver lining, however attenuated it might be), certainly the young ladies "tried hard," and he was sure that in the process they "learned a great deal about photography." Some of the pictures might prove useful to Jane in any future lectures she might give, while the experience must have been good preparation for future photography work. He wondered, incidentally, what had happened to the valuable Nikon camera that had been lent them, and he certainly hoped that one day either or both of them would be able to visit the society's headquarters in Washington, where, he was sure, they would discover how interesting the building and physical plant were and would also appreciate witnessing at first hand the National Geographic Society's impressive editorial operation.

In short, the editorial staff of *National Geographic* had firmly decided not to publish the story of Miss Jane Goodall and her chimpanzee research.

19

A Different Language

1961–1962

IN BOURNEMOUTH, Jane bought a new typewriter with a sticky space bar at Classic Typewriters, and on Thursday, December 14, 1961, in a less-than-reliable secondhand car known as Gertrude, she set off for Cambridge to begin her university career.

First, of course, she needed a place to live. She found a prospective landlady, Mrs. Tweedie, who along with Mr. Tweedie owned and managed a rooming house for young women at 1 Magrath Avenue. They were "awfully nice people," Jane remarked in a letter home, and she was pleased with the proposed digs, an agreeable bedroom with shared bathroom and a spacious kitchen and cupboards. Hot water was included in the rental price, which was two pounds fifteen shillings a week. She soon moved in.

Cambridge University at that time consisted of twenty-six semi-independent colleges, three of which—Newnham, Girton, and New Hall—were for women. Jane registered at Newnham, and she was soon trying to find her tutor, Patience Burne, who never seemed to be in her office but was, according to the acting librarian, Mrs. de Plage, "young, pretty, efficient, pleasant, and also, the official librarian, but does 101 other things which is why she, Mrs. de Plage, is acting librarian."

Jane's important task during the next three years, spending roughly half her time at Cambridge and half at Gombe, would be to transform herself from an enthusiastic amateur into a distinguished professional, complete with significant initials after the name. She had no undergraduate education, but her work at Gombe had already been such an impressive accomplishment that the academic administrators at Cambridge were persuaded, on the recommendation of Louis Leakey, to ignore that lack and also to assume that her basic research for the doctoral degree was done. Thus, she was merely required to write up, in appropriate format, her results. It was a reasonable if extremely unusual shortcut.

On those matters, Jane, and Louis before her, had corresponded with Professor William H. Thorpe, who directed the Zoology Department's Sub-department of Animal Behavior at Madingley. Madingley is a small village around three miles outside Cambridge, and the Sub-department of Animal Behavior began in 1950 as the Ornithological Field Station, serving Thorpe's interest in birds. Birds could be observed and experimented upon better in the open spaces and expansive buildings of Madingley (a field and trees, a long low brick building, an old blacksmith's shop, and several dozen aviaries) than in the limited confines of Cambridge proper. But the birds of Madingley were soon joined by other animals—hamsters and monkeys, for starters—which accounts for the change in name.

Jane now sought out William Thorpe in his Madingley office—finding him, as she once recalled for me, "like a professor," being "rather austere," "very dignified," and also "very rigid." Their first meeting was not auspicious. While Jane tried to explain herself and her ideas, the professor's myna bird, flying freely about the office, landed on her and began pecking. The bird drew blood, but Jane, believing such avian harassment may have been a test of some sort, deliberately did not react. She failed to warm up to the professor, though, and thus was relieved to learn that he had decided to turn her over to his immediate subordinate, Robert A. Hinde, the curator of Madingley and the person working with monkeys.

So she met Professor Hinde at 2:15 one afternoon that mid-December in his private apartment at St. John's College, "where I was regaled with black Nescafe and frozen stiff as he doesn't appear to like warmth!!" she wrote home. "Dr. Hinde is 100 times nicer than Thorpe—he is NOT vile!!! Nor is Thorpe vile—simply not so nice." Regarding Hinde, she quickly concluded, "I shall get on O.K. with him."

During that first meeting, Hinde candidly admitted that he did not "know a thing about chimps," but he nevertheless promised to "help me as much as he can." They planned out some lectures Jane might attend, about one a day, which were not actually required but could be helpful and, as Jane thought, "ought to make just the right amount of break from sitting writing about chimps all the time!" Meanwhile, Jane decided to type up a quick report on the red colobus monkeys at Gombe. Hinde had said, "pathetically" (Jane thought), that "he doesn't at all know the lines I've been working on," and so she decided a report on the monkeys would provide a fair sample of those lines, and she would be able to say that "I worked along the same lines with the chimps, but 100%—no, 75%—more thoroughly." But what lines, exactly, were they? As she confessed to the family, "I feel helpless when confronted by animal behaviourists—they speak a different language from myself—except for dear old George [Schaller]."

The different language Robert Hinde spoke was ethology, a term Jane first heard in the summer of 1961, while she was still at Gombe but starting to worry about her academic career at Cambridge. In a letter of July 21, she wrote to Vanne, "Is there such a word as ETHOLOGY? If so, what does it mean?"

Vanne responded by wondering if the word in question was actually "ethnology," but in an August 11 letter, Jane set her right: "The word was ethology—not ethnology, which (oddly enough) I know! I feel it may be a misprint for ecology."

Oskar Heinroth, the director of the aquarium at the Berlin Zoological Gardens during the early decades of the twentieth century, coined the word *ethology* and was the first to articulate its general mission: a scientific study of animal behavior that would operate through comparative methods, like the already well-established discipline of comparative anatomy. The peculiar behaviors that characterized any species, Heinroth asserted, were as fixed and distinctive as anatomical features; and just as distinctive anatomical features could be compared and contrasted between species (enabling, for example, an informed expert to speculate about evolutionary relationships), so too could distinctive behavioral features be compared and contrasted for similar purposes.

Heinroth outlined his vision of ethology in a 1911 publication, and he set about creating a great encyclopedia on European bird behavior. In that ambitious task, he was assisted by his wife, Magdalena. The couple chose not to have children, forwent their normal holidays, and in general devoted themselves obsessively to cataloguing the vast variety of bird behaviors, finally publishing, between 1926 and 1933, four illustrated volumes on *Die Vögel Mitteleuropas* (*The Birds of Central Europe*). Heinroth's work ultimately fused a new, scientific way of knowing onto the old European naturalists' fascination with the ways of nature, and three other gifted persons—Karl von Frisch, Konrad Lorenz, and Nikolaas Tinbergen—launched ethology as a viable discipline during succeeding decades.

Karl von Frisch was born in Vienna in 1886, into a wealthy Austrian family who kept a summer home near the hamlet of Brunnwinkl. The boy's impressionable personality and imagination were deeply affected by the pastoral world around Brunnwinkl, by the fields and woods and lakes, the insects and birds and small animals, and when his father purchased and began renovating an old mill, the young naturalist built his own museum in the mill's upper rooms in order to house his natural history collection: beetles, butterflies, moths, fossils, stuffed birds, pressed flowers, and so on.

In 1905 von Frisch matriculated at Vienna University, intending to follow his father into the medical profession. But attracted by the zoological lectures of his uncle, Professor Sigmund Exner, and distracted by the insistence of a Professor Otto Korner that fish were incapable of perceiving sound, von Frisch turned from medicine to zoology. Korner's supposed proof that fish were deaf was simple. He kept fish in a tank, subjected them to various sounds, such as his own whistling and operatic arias sung by a well-known soprano, and noted that they never reacted to the sounds. Young von Frisch, believing that the fish had no special reason to respond to professorial whistles or opera singers, set up an alternative experiment with blinded catfish, whereby he offered them food treats just after whistling. Within six days the catfish had learned to lunge assertively for food—whether or not food treats were offered—as soon as the whistling began, thereby demonstrating that catfish could hear and would respond to a sound when it was in their interest to do so.

As a young lecturer at Munich University before World War I, von Frisch became involved in another zoological controversy on the issue of animal perception. Since insects were small and simple forms of life, people reasoned, they should have small and simple perceptual experiences. What could such insignificant organisms actually see? At best, probably mere shades of gray. Spending the summer of 1912 in Brunnwinkl, von Frisch observed honeybees emerging from their hives and zeroing in on the brilliantly colored flowers of the garden. How could anyone imagine that such gloriously hued flowers provided merely a bland spectrum of gray for bees? Bees must have good color vision, von Frisch thought, and he set about proving it.

He began by teaching the honeybees to feed at a dish of sugar solution he always placed on a square piece of blue cardboard. Once his bees were reliably feeding on that artificial source on the blue cardboard, he removed the sugar solution and set out a matrix of cardboard squares, all of them various shades of gray except for the single blue square—and soon he found that the bees inevitably flew to the blue square, where they would begin searching for the missing food. The honeybees, then, were able to distinguish blue from shades of gray. Using the same sort of reasoning and experimental testing, von Frisch went on to demonstrate that bees could see several other colors, although they were insensitive to red and so frequently confused red squares with dark gray or black squares. He also eventually discovered that bees could see ultraviolet, invisible to people, and in fact were very sensitive to that color.

At the courtyard garden of the Munich Zoo, Karl von Frisch established a colony of bees, marking the forager bees of the colony with dabs of colored paint to distinguish them from other members of the hive. He also fashioned a glass-sided observation hive, enabling him to see what the bees were doing inside. One day in the spring of 1919, the young zoologist happened to observe a scout honeybee fly away from the hive, find a newly filled container of sugar solution, and then sail directly back home. Peering through the glass side of the hive, he witnessed an astonishing event. "I could scarcely believe my eyes," the zoologist would recall years later. "She performed a round dance on the honeycomb which greatly excited the marked foragers around her and caused them to fly back to the feeding place. This, I believe, was the most far-reaching observation of my life."

Suspecting that he had witnessed a communication between the successful scout and the other foragers, the modest, reserved young man "calmly smiled to myself" and proceeded, during the rest of his life, to design and carry out an extensive series of extraordinary experiments that ultimately deciphered the language the bees communicated with. By moving the source of food in various directions and distances away from the hive and then by observing a successful scout find that food, return to the hive, and dance on the honeycomb, von Frisch showed that the specific choreography of a honeybee dance communicated a message regarding the quality of a food source and its direction and distance from the hive.

Bees, hardly a half-inch long themselves, will forage farther than six miles from home, and their capacity to orient themselves well enough to fly back and forth between the hive and a single remote food source, such as a flower, and to communicate precisely to each other about that remote food source and its direction and distance from the hive, is remarkable. Karl von Frisch's decoding of the dance of the bees was no less remarkable, a lifetime accomplishment based on patient and ingenious experimentation that in 1974 finally earned him a Nobel Prize, an honor he shared jointly with ethology's two other founding luminaries, Konrad Lorenz and Niko Tinbergen.

Born in Vienna in 1903, Konrad Lorenz was, like Karl von Frisch, a prosperous physician's son who spent his youthful summers in a state of pastoral bliss. The Lorenz family home was a big mansion in the small village of Altenberg, a few miles outside Vienna and close to the Danube marshes. Young Konrad loved animals, and his parents tolerated the many household pets he acquired—birds, a dog, fish, a lemur, imprinted wild geese. . . . *Imprinting* was a term Oskar Heinroth had coined to describe the process by which the hatchlings of certain bird species, during a critical developmental period, become powerfully inclined to follow any moving entity—hen or duck or person—as if that entity were their dearest biological parent. Imprinting, for Heinroth, was not only interesting but useful. It meant that if the hatchlings were exposed to him at the right moment in their lives, they would follow him everywhere, which of course enabled him to observe them very closely. The only problem was all those imprinted birds stubbornly taking up residence beneath his office chair.

When Konrad Lorenz was only six years old, he and a playmate, Margarethe (Gretl) Gebhardt, played with a pair of just-hatched ducklings in the Danube marshes—and the fluffy little things became imprinted on Konrad and Gretl, while Konrad, as he joked many years later, became imprinted on the ducks. Boy and girl grew up, married each other, and had children, and Lorenz dedicated his life to studying the behavior of animals, mainly birds. Imprinting became an essential element in his scientific modus operandi.

To satisfy his father, Lorenz studied medicine, first at Columbia University in New York, then at the University of Vienna. While in Vienna, though, he happened to stroll past a pet shop with a large dark bird in a cage. The bird was a jackdaw, and the medical student, moved by pity (he "suddenly felt a longing to cram that great, yellow framed throat with good food"), bought him, named him Jock, and took him home to Altenberg. Jock was allowed the freedom of an upstairs bedroom and would frequently fly through a hole in the bedroom wall into the attic and from there onto the roof. Lorenz would follow Jock onto the roof and sit there for hours, patiently filling his diary with notes on the life of a jackdaw. Meanwhile, his closest friend during his student years, Bernhard Hellmann, read the first volume of Heinroth's *Die Vögel Mitteleuropas* and decided that Lorenz's diary entries were comparable. With the connivance of Gretl, Hellmann temporarily stole his friend's diary, typed a copy of the notes about the jackdaw, and submitted them for thoughtful consideration to the great man.

Oskar Heinroth recognized Konrad Lorenz's promise, and Lorenz was very pleased to find in Heinroth an important mentor. As a medical student at the University of Vienna, Lorenz had concentrated on comparative anatomy, and it had early on occurred to him that a person could apply the same thinking and methodology to fashion a science of comparative behavior. So it was serendipitous that Heinroth had already defined such a science. The young man's diary notes were finally published as "Observations on Jackdaws" in an early 1927 issue of the *Journal of Ornithology,* and Lorenz's career as an ethologist began. He married Gretl that year and completed his medical studies the next, but by the summer of 1928 an entire colony of jackdaws was nesting in the attic and on the roof of the Lorenz house at Altenberg, and Konrad Lorenz was regularly stepping out onto the roof, roosting alongside the jackdaws, and studying their social interactions.

Lorenz turned his attention next to herons and then, during the late 1930s, to graylag geese. Wild geese are evasive creatures, normally very difficult to observe, but Lorenz incubated eggs taken from nests and imprinted some of the hatchlings on himself, soon establishing a flock of about twenty geese, some fully wild and some imprinted birds still retaining most of their wild behaviors. The imprinted geese Lorenz gave names to; the others he simply numbered. But since his named geese were treating him as a parent, he took his parental duties seriously. He would wake up at dawn, call his children, and go swimming with them or follow along in a canoe. As much as any person can, Konrad Lorenz became a goose, and he was able to observe every aspect of their normal lives—courtship, mating, nesting, and the rearing of young—from a close and intimate perspective, discovering a rich social system and a complex vocabulary of behaviors and displays, the most interesting of which were those that seemed most predictable and most characteristic of the species. Those were the instinctual behaviors—automatic, stereotypical, innate—and so Lorenz was fascinated not only by the myriad details of his animals' intimate lives but also by a larger pattern: the possible structure and meaning of instinct.

Nikolaas Tinbergen was born in 1907, in The Hague, Netherlands. His father was a secondary school teacher, and the family loved to spend their free time outdoors, vacationing regularly in a region of heath and pine forest growing over glacial sands near Hulshorst. There Niko demonstrated a passion for watching animals in their unguarded moments and sketching and photographing their behavior. But he was an indifferent student, preferring outdoor sports and nature exploration to the sedentary gloom of institutionalized education. School, he felt, was merely an unpleasant inhibition, and he was careful to keep his grades just high enough to avoid additional restrictions on his time spent outdoors. He finished secondary school in 1925 and decided he would follow his athletic interests and become a physical education teacher. Wise friends, however, knowing his special talents for nature study, persuaded his parents to send him to work on a scientific bird migration study for three months at Volgewarte Rossiten, in eastern Germany. Upon returning, he enrolled as a student of biology at the University of Leiden.

In the summer of 1930 Tinbergen began his first ethological research, on the digger wasp (*Philanthus triangulum*), plentiful in the sands of Hulshorst, trying to answer a seemingly simple question: how did a digger wasp, emerging to forage from one of thousands of seemingly identical holes in the sand, find its way home again? For that work he received a Ph.D. in

1932, and after marriage and a year-and-a-half honeymoon on a Dutch expedition to Greenland (where he studied the reproductive behavior of two bird species), he settled into a minor academic position at the University of Leiden. The ethological method in Holland, particularly as understood by Tinbergen and his colleagues during the early 1930s, was inspired by Karl von Frisch, the great man who, in the words of one commentator, "founded the art of making an animal answer questions." And the Leiden group, following von Frisch's example, worked on questions of animal perception, how animals recognize objects and situations significant to them.

But perception could be understood only through observing behavior, and the focus of ethology, the study of behavior, had by then become—following Lorenz's example—those behaviors that seemed automatic, predictable, and characteristic of a particular species in its normal environment: instinct. In November 1936, Lorenz himself was finally invited to give a lecture on instinct at Leiden. But the enormous impact of that lecture on Tinbergen resulted not so much from any ideas expressed as from the professional friendship that followed. As Lorenz would later say, he and Niko Tinbergen "clicked immediately."

In the fall of 1937, Tinbergen and his wife and child were invited to spend several months at the Lorenz home and research center in Altenberg, where Tinbergen worked on a number of interesting experiments to examine the fears of geese. The Dutch ethologist strung a wire 30 feet above the ground and then passed flat paper cutouts across the wire—flying profiles—while examining the response of a flock of goslings below. He passed circles, squares, and stylized profiles of a number of birds as they might appear in flight. Mostly the shapes passing overhead produced no effect on goslings clucking away on the ground—except when Tinbergen passed along the flat profile of a common predator, a hawk or a falcon. Graylag goslings can see well, and clearly they were not mistaking the appearance of those rough shapes for real predators. What, then, did they find threatening about them? Tinbergen refined his experiment by creating a simple shape that when pulled in one direction resembled the profile of a long-necked, short-tailed goose in flight but when drawn along the wire in the opposite direction mimicked the profile of a short-necked, long-tailed hawk. And indeed, the goslings were unmoved by the sight of the model going in one direction, but the same model passed in the other direction caused a tremendous commotion of alarm-piping. Tinbergen's conclusion: the goslings had an instinctive response to the general profile of their natural predator. It was a brilliant experiment (though, as it turned out, with a wrong conclusion; since hawks are much rarer than waterfowl, the goslings were responding in alarm to the novelty of the shape overhead), marking the start of a lifelong friendship and collaboration.

Konrad Lorenz and Niko Tinbergen presented contrasting and complementary personalities and intellectual styles. Both were passionate about learning through the closest possible contact with their animals—Lorenz by living openly among them as "an adopted alien member and protector," Tinbergen by watching carefully as a "non-participating hidden observer." Lorenz was an expansive, imaginative sort, a talker who could be impressively and deeply informed on a subject but impatient with the details; Tinbergen was more the careful analyst, a thoughtful listener who liked to clarify and verify. Lorenz was a brilliant observer of animals but disinclined to experimentation; Tinbergen had a talent for posing interesting problems and testing them with elegant experiments. In the end, according to Gerard Baerends, one of Tinbergen's colleagues in Holland, "their contributions to ethology were complementary. They mutually appreciated this and recognized that they needed one another. It made them become and remain close friends."

In 1949 Niko Tinbergen accepted a faculty post at Oxford University, and in 1950 William D. Thorpe (inspired by Tinbergen's experimental method) established Cambridge University's Ornithological Field Station at Madingley in order to test certain Lorenzean ideas on the nature of instinct.

Thorpe was studying a common British bird known as the chaffinch, which proclaims its territorial presence by repeating a sweet but brief song consisting of "two or three phrases and a terminal flourish." But the chaffinch song is done with regional dialects. Chaffinches from the London area produce a song generally characteristic of the species, and yet in particular ways it sounds different from chaffinch songs coming from Wales or other parts of the British Isles. Thorpe considered it likely that the regional accent was a learned thing, and thus the species seemed to present an interesting puzzle on the relationship between innate and learned behavior. What portion of the chaffinch song was innate and how much was learned? Could they be differentiated?

During nesting season in the spring and early summer, Thorpe and his associates would prowl the countryside around Madingley searching for chaffinch nestlings. They would snatch the birds from their nests five days after hatching, carry them into the laboratory, and rear them according to various experimental protocols. Some were raised in total isolation from their own kind inside strictly soundproof boxes, unexposed to any sort of bird song. When they reached the age of singing, the isolates' attempts at song were recorded and subjected to a sound spectrogram analysis. These birds did sing, as it turned out, but their productions were rudimentary, missing the pure tones and distinctive phrasing of a normal chaffinch song. In other experiments, hand-reared and isolated chaffinches were played tape-recorded songs from other species, to which they proved unresponsive; but when isolates were exposed to tape recordings of their own species' song, they responded very actively, demonstrating the bird's innate responsiveness to its own song. Thorpe also found that chaffinches had a critical period of learning sensitivity, in the fall, when they could quickly memorize all the important aspects of their song.

At Oxford, meanwhile, Niko Tinbergen continued with his own various research projects while conducting seminars and nurturing graduate students. He was becoming a distinguished and internationally prominent figure, but according to John Krebs, one of his students from a couple of decades later, he was refreshingly unpretentious: "I never felt, in talking to him, anything other than a colleague and an equal, one whose views were to be judged and appreciated in the same way as those of more senior colleagues." The former student additionally recalls Tinbergen's impressive athleticism, particularly in evidence the day he was lecturing in a steeply tiered lecture hall. Having noticed an undergraduate at the very back of the hall rudely absenting himself within the pages of a newspaper, the Dutch ethologist, all the while coolly continuing his lecture, "leapt onto the front-row bench, strode two benches at a time up to the top row, grabbed the newspaper, scrunched it up into a ball, and then strode back down to the front as though nothing had happened."

The task of ethology, as Tinbergen soon came to define it, would be to study behavior using "objective scientific methods"—in pointed contrast to Konrad Lorenz's often naive and typically unabashed subjectivity. Lorenz happily named his favorite subjects, those who had been imprinted on him, and he deliberately chose to describe certain behaviors among his subjects with evocatively human terms—"love," "betrothal," "marriage"—thus carelessly promoting a vision of geese as more like humans than they are. Lorenz's ethology remained in many ways a lone philosopher's brilliant but idiosyncratic creation, whereas Tinbergen promoted an enterprise less idiosyncratic, more collective: a scientific way to knowledge, structurally designed to reduce the influence of any single observer's subjectivity. The faithful practitioner of Tinbergen's ethology would start (as Lorenz certainly would) with very thorough, repeated, and direct observations of the animal's behavior in as natural an environment as possible, with the observer remaining as open-minded as possible. Having observed thoroughly, the good Tinbergenian ethologist would proceed (as Lorenz generally would not) to describe quantitatively, to test experimentally, and finally to assess methodically—ultimately asking *why?* at four different but interrelated levels of explanation.

Tinbergen's "Four Whys" can be summarized as causation, development, function, and evolution. Although these four questions, or levels of explanation, are ordinarily applied to a piece of behavior, one could just as easily apply them to a piece of anatomy, such as (to consider an example favored by Robert Hinde) any person's thumb. Why does your thumb work differently from your fingers? The answer might be explored in terms of immediate causation: because of a dynamic architecture of bone, muscle, and sinew. It might be considered an issue of development: because your thumb grows to distinguish itself from the fingers at certain embryonic stages. One might analyze the question functionally: your thumb enables you to hold on to some things firmly and to pick up other things readily. Or one might examine it in terms of its evolutionary significance: you possess a thumb because that odd digit evolved among your ancient ancestors, primates still living in the trees, providing a powerful grip and thereby improving their chances for survival against the demands of gravity. A good Tinbergenian ethologist would be prepared to consider all four ways of asking *why?* and to recognize them as independently useful yet interestingly interrelated.

Jane's adviser at Cambridge, Robert Hinde, was trained in ethology at Oxford by one of Tinbergen's colleagues, the ornithologist David Lack. The war had interrupted Hinde's education. In 1940, at age seventeen, he signed up for the RAF and was trained as a pilot, and he flew convoy escort and reconnaissance missions until 1945. He finally returned to civilian life as an overaged undergraduate at Cambridge—and hated it. He took a room somewhere away from the center of town, found he could not understand the lectures very well, and was, as he once told me, "overawed by people who seemed infinitely younger than me—I was then at the great age of twenty-three—by how clever they all were." Twice he approached his tutor's door and quietly rapped, resolved that he would declare his intent to leave Cambridge and become a commercial airline pilot. But each time his tutor said, "Come in!" the anxious young man ran away down the stairs. "I reckon that's the only decision I ever made in my life. And a very good one it was, too."

So instead of flying he watched birds, leaving Cambridge in 1948 to start his doctoral work at Oxford with David Lack. Interested in, among other things, what Lorenz described as "releasers"—signals or events that provoked instinctual behavior—Lack had demonstrated that male robins were provoked to fight each other by a splash of red; indeed, that they would attack a cluster of red feathers while ignoring the realistic effigy of a brown-breasted intruder. Hinde's own study at Oxford was obviously influenced by Lack's ethological orientation, but at the same time the young man developed an important friendship with the newly hired lecturer from the Netherlands.

Many years later, Niko Tinbergen recalled having been "fortunate" in getting to know the young Robert Hinde and of following him about "while he observed birds in the wood, dressed in his long grey RAF coat." Hinde in turn recalled meeting Tinbergen at a time when the pioneering ethologist was still free enough to "talk with me and teach me. This had a profound influence on me, and has coloured my research ever since."

After Hinde completed his graduate work at Oxford, he was hired by William Thorpe to serve as curator at the Ornithological Field Station at Madingley, and thus Hinde—now Dr. Hinde—moved back to Cambridge in 1950 and continued working as an ethologist studying the behavior of birds. But why birds, always birds? Why this peculiar concentration on a single group of animals? The ethology of Konrad Lorenz and Niko Tinbergen had been applied mainly (though not exclusively) to birds partly because of the accidental fact that birds (along with insects and fish) were among the few wild organisms in biologically impoverished central Europe that a person could readily locate and, with a little effort, watch closely. And birds were particularly convenient because the imprinting instinct of several species allowed researchers a quick and remarkably close access to the researched.

The basic principles of ethology, however, ought to apply to any animal, including humans, although the problems with turning the spotlight onto *Homo sapiens* were considerable. Among them was the political one. In the bloody context of mid-twentieth-century history, any scientific enterprise hoping to increase human self-understanding would be perceived as politically dangerous and thus under pressure from the prevailing winds of political justification or the countervailing winds of political correctness. The conceptual problems of ethologizing humans also included the obvious likelihood that human behavior would prove more difficult to parse than that of, say, graylag geese. Tinbergen himself was concerned, as he once wrote, about the "uncritical application of our results" to human behavior—and he may have been particularly distressed by the success of one of his students, Desmond Morris, in popularizing ethology by broadly speculating about what its discoveries might suggest about human nature.

In any case, Robert Hinde switched from birds to monkeys during the late 1950s as a result of some interesting communications about humans with a London psychiatrist named John Bowlby. Bowlby believed that early family disruptions might account for subsequent juvenile delinquency. He was familiar enough with ethology and Lorenz's work to wonder if human children underwent a critical developmental period, roughly comparable to the imprinting period among some birds, during which they made a fundamental sort of identity attachment with important adults—or failed to do so in the absence of important adults. Bowlby's concerns were not merely theoretical. At the time London hospitals maintained a standard policy of very strictly limiting visiting hours for the parents of pediatric patients. Based on his own observations and retrospective study, Bowlby had become convinced that the policy was clinically destructive, and he hoped to support his conviction with experimental data. He located funding and enlisted the support of Hinde, who agreed to study the matter experimentally. But since one could not ethically study human children in any obvious way that would provide good scientific data, Hinde turned to other primates. And since the nonhuman primates most easily acquired at the time were rhesus monkeys, he settled on that species, setting up a colony at Madingley that consisted of six social and breeding groups, each containing one adult male, three or four females, and their offspring.

Hinde's rhesus macaque study at Madingley may have been the only primate behavioral study in England at that time, and so by default he became the person to tutor the young observer of wild primates named Jane MorrisGoodall as she worked to gain a doctor of philosophy degree.

By the time Jane arrived at Cambridge at the end of 1961, Robert Hinde was a formidable presence. He was "incredibly handsome," as one of his former students recalls, with "piercing blue eyes," a "craggy" face, and "silverygray" hair. He was also proud, certain, serious, smart, rigorous, and demanding. Undoubtedly he was one of the few male teachers of his era who readily took on, taught, and nurtured many women students, but he also, in the words of another former student, "frequently had young women break down into tears. He was not aggressive, but he was very smart—and he could make you feel completely stupid. He would ask a particularly penetrating question and look at you with those penetrating eyes." Some of his male students, according to the memory of one, would jokingly declare that they counted their own chest hairs before and after a seminar with Hinde: a quick and ethological sort of technique to measure loss of virility during face-to-face encounters with the volatile, exacting, silver-haired alpha male.

Jane was, as ever, poised, self-assured, and, in this context at least, very stubborn. By virtue of her fieldwork at Gombe, she was already the world's foremost expert on chimpanzees. It was clear from the start, as Hinde recently told me, that she was "a very dedicated young woman." Indeed, her matriculation at Cambridge was actually an exciting opportunity for the university and for Robert Hinde. "The fieldwork that had been done before Jane was, I think, of a fairly limited sort, and Jane had much greater insight into the animals" than any of her predecessors, Hinde now declares. He continues: "Personally, [Jane's association with Cambridge] was a tremendous opportunity, because it gave me the chance to get out there to Gombe, and there was a whole string of students who subsequently came through Madingley to work with Jane in East Africa."

"He is a dear, really," Jane wrote home that February. And, particularly in contrast to the stiff and formal William Thorpe, he was surprisingly "youthful," she once told me. In their private tutorials in his apartment at St. John's College, for example, Hinde would sprawl on the floor in front of the fire, avidly reviewing and discussing her work. "I found it rather strange, him lying on the floor on his tummy." Although their association was always properly professional, entirely focused on her work, apparently it was of a sufficient heat and light that some of the other students concluded they were having an affair, a theory Jane learned about only years later, to her great surprise. "It absolutely dazed me" to hear that. "I'd no idea."

Yet she was also, she has written, "terribly in awe" of him in her early days at university. During their regular conferences, she would say little as he patiently "pointed out the flawed reasoning behind some attempt to describe and quantify a portion of the data, or explained just why it was that certain words were not acceptable in the scientific circles of the time." On occasion he would tell her that "I'd better go and do a lot of reading before I continued to make a fool of myself (not that he put it quite in those terms, but his meaning was clear)." She often left those sessions "filled with frustration and sometimes despair. Back in my digs I would hurl everything into the corner of the room: page after page, written so carefully, now marked all over with Robert's comments and criticisms. How desperately I longed to give it all up and go back to the chimpanzees and the forests." The next day, however, she would wake up feeling very different about the whole thing. "Even if I didn't agree with everything he said, I would realise why he had said it and where I had failed in my confused attempts to describe the behaviour of the chimps. Then I would gather up the scattered pages and, with renewed enthusiasm, tackle the problem afresh."

One basic problem was reconstituting her raw data, that day-by-day, minute-by-minute narration recorded in her handwritten field journal over a year and a half in the forests of Gombe, into scientifically acceptable form. But with Hinde's guidance, Jane sorted out her field journal, first by creating an index, then, piece by piece, by summarizing her information as quantitatively and objectively as possible. For her, it was not so easy or reasonable. As she wrote home in January, "It gets rather depressing—the only things people here appreciate are graphs & statistics!" Nevertheless, she threw herself into the work with characteristic energy and focus, and within a couple of months she was able to report to her friend Bernard Verdcourt in Nairobi that "I have, at last, begun to settle down in Cambridge. I wasn't at all happy here at first—I felt it was a mistake coming here."

Robert Hinde's goal was to teach Jane the language of ethology, which meant, over the short term, to encourage a writing style that would be recognized for its veracity and validity and to help shape her first reports on the chimpanzees of Gombe into a standardized and quantitative format. A longer-term task was to standardize the data collecting at Gombe.

Hinde once described Jane's original method as "narrative": the detailed stories and observations of her field notes, gathered and transcribed each evening into the field journal. "The advantage of a narrative account," he conceded, "is that it's flexible and you can record things that happen only once in a long time. The disadvantage is that you don't know you've recorded everything all the time. There are particular items—chimpanzee copulation, let's say—that it's important to know how often it happens and when. And so it's better to have, for many purposes, a check sheet in which for every consecutive time interval you enter what the chimpanzee has been doing. It was that sort of check sheet that I introduced her to." Based on certain preestablished categories, the check sheet would force Jane, or any other observer, to record timed snapshots of chimpanzee behaviors.

Over the next several years, Hinde introduced his standardized check-sheet data collection to Gombe, traveling to the research camp three times (in 1968, 1970, and 1972) and, far more importantly, sending out a large number of students to work there. While Jane continued with the narrative accounts as well, Hinde's data-recording system meant that researchers became in some ways interchangeable, while the gathering of knowledge about chimpanzee behavior became to a degree genuinely collective. By the late 1970s and early 1980s, when Jane was writing her great book on the Gombe research (*The Chimpanzees of Gombe*), well over a hundred people—students and staff and colleagues—had participated in the research, and she could draw not only on her results but on theirs as well, which amounted to a great wealth of relevant information.

Ultimately, though, Hinde's most ambitious project was to turn Jane Goodall into a person who not only wrote like a scientist and acquired data like a scientist but who thought like a scientist. What constitutes thinking like a scientist? On that question, their deepest conflict of opinion and their most serious and extended battle of wills emerged.

Ethology had by tradition focused on behaviors that seemed to be representative of a species—predictable communications of honeybees, stereotypical courting of graylag geese, distinctive territorial aggression of male robins, and so on. Ethologists had preoccupied themselves with those animal behaviors that were typical, while atypical behaviors were much less interesting or even altogether irrelevant. It may be true that insects and fish and birds behave much more predictably than large mammals to begin with, so that the discipline of ethology, having started with some convenient small organisms of central Europe, simply presumed that others would likewise prove to be primarily puzzles in typicality.

Jane was content in her first scientific writing done at Cambridge to report on the typical behaviors of chimpanzees, such as their standard feeding behaviors ("In its wild state the chimpanzee spends between six and seven hours of the day in active feeding, and a considerable amount of the rest of the time in moving between one food source and another") or their usual nesting style ("The time taken for the construction of a normal nest varies between one and five minutes. A nest consists basically of a main branch or branches forming the 'foundation,' over which smaller branches or 'crosspieces' are bent"). Knowing the typical was an essential part of understanding chimpanzees. At the same time, however, she was strongly drawn to consider the great mystery of the atypical: for instance, the peculiarly friendly behaviors of that gray-bearded old chimpanzee she had named David Greybeard. In other words, while ethology had traditionally focused on the species instead of the individual as its fundamental unit of study, Jane was intuitively more focused on the individual.

Jane's naming of her subjects was a problem, because it implied a humanlike individuality, and she often, and quite proudly, recalls her own stubborn naiveté in the matter. "When I first got to Cambridge in 1961," she recently wrote,

> I had no undergraduate degree. I had not been to college, and there were many things about animal behavior that I did not know. I had not been taught, for example, that it was wrong to give names to my study subjects—it would have been more scientific to give them numbers. I was dumbfounded by this practice. For one thing, I did not think of the chimps as "study subjects" but as individuals, each with his or her own personality. I was learning *from* them, not only *about* them. On a more practical level, I would never have been able to remember who was who if they only had numbers!

From an ethological point of view, moreover, focusing on individuals suggested the disturbing possibility that at least some kinds of animals might have, like humans, actual individuality—possibly with humanlike personalities, emotions, and even perhaps minds. "I was also reprimanded at Cambridge," Jane has written, "for ascribing personalities to the different chimpanzees—as though I had made up the vivid and unique characteristics of the various members of the Kasekela community! Only humans have personalities, I was told. Nor should I have been talking about the chimpanzee mind—only humans, said the scientists, were capable of rational thought. Talking of chimpanzee emotions was the very worst of my anthropomorphic sins."

To assume that some animals behaved in certain ways as the result of personalities, or because of emotions or minds, was in the early 1960s considered unscientific—or at least unethological. It might very well lead to the kind of sloppy thinking of certain nineteenth-century enthusiasts who announced that beavers' amazing engineering works proved the existence of a sophisticated beaver mind, whereas simple experimentation will show that beavers build their elaborate constructions because of an innate response to the sound of running water. (A mechanical recording of running water will cause beavers in a dry room to build dams around the loudspeakers.) Ethology's method was to seek truth in formal parsimony: a careful scouring of small facts, a deliberate building of knowledge piece by piece, establishing patiently, brick by brick, an edifice of the demonstrably true while avoiding or leaving for a later stage generalizations about the possibly true. The discipline achieved some remarkable results that way, and yet perhaps it had simultaneously come to rely too fully on its preconceptions, such as that instinct and simple learning could by themselves explain most animal behavior.

"Fortunately," Jane continues in her written recollection of that longago intellectual battle, "I had had a marvelous teacher in animal behavior throughout my childhood—my dog, Rusty." Thus she simply "ignored the admonitions of Science"—until the day her own peculiar ideas became accepted as part of that same Science.

PART II

The Scientist

20

First Scientific Conferences

1962

IN AUGUST 1961, while Jane was still at Gombe—before she had begun her studies at Cambridge—she received her first invitation to a scientific conference: a symposium organized by the American anthropologist Sherwood Washburn, sponsored by the Wenner-Gren Foundation, and scheduled to take place the following July at the foundation's castle in Austria. Louis had previously told Jane about the castle, which added an aura of exclusivity to the invitation. In fact the conference would be, as Jane could read in the soliciting letter, a "select" meeting of important "specialists" in relevant fields—anatomical, anthropological, biological, genetic, primatological, psychological—on the topic of "Classification and Human Evolution."

Jane was amazed by the invitation. As she wrote home on August 3, "My future is so ridiculous. I just squat here, chimp-like, on my rocks, pulling out prickles & thorns, and laugh to think of this unknown 'Miss Goodall' who is said to be doing scientific research somewhere. Much better to be ME, I think to myself—just go out and live like the chimps—none of this scientific talk for me!!"

But Louis Leakey would take part, as would Jane's tutor from her London days, the primate anatomist John Napier. Sherwood Washburn planned to present a paper, as did his recent collaborator, Irven DeVore. Washburn, DeVore, and a third conference participant, the British psychologist K.R.L. Hall, had all conducted preliminary field studies of baboons in the late 1950s, but aside from those three, Jane would have been the only field researcher at the conference. She would already have had more hours of field experience than the other three combined. She would also have been one of the very few women there, certainly the only participant without an undergraduate degree, much less an advanced degree. It was a distinct yet intimidating honor to be invited, in short, and Jane may have felt relieved to note that the conference dates (July 8 to July 21, 1962) made it impossible for her to attend, since she was already committed to watching chimps at Gombe during the summer of 1962.

Sherwood Washburn, a Harvard-trained physical anthropologist with an expertise in anatomy and natural history, was, as one of his former students has written, of "slightly below average height" and "lean and wiry rather than skinny." As a teacher and speaker, he could be "crystal clear, dynamic, and sweeping in vision"—and that clarity and sweeping vision, combined with his "contagious enthusiasm," led to the big revolution in physical anthropology.

Inspired by the recent excavations of *Australopithecus* fossils in South Africa, Washburn declared in 1950 that it was "an auspicious moment to reconsider the problems of human origins." As he then argued in his 1951 essay, "The New Physical Anthropology," understanding human evolution required a multidisciplinary approach, because evolution itself was multidisciplinary. Natural selection, the operating force of evolution, provokes change not in single, isolated characteristics (a shift in the structure, say, of bone or brain, biochemistry or behavior) but rather in functional complexes (an alternation in the structure of bone *and* brain *and* biochemistry *and* behavior). Any meaningful study of human evolution therefore would require an understanding of such functional complexes, and it would necessarily do so through interdisciplinary efforts. "The new physical anthropology has much to offer to anyone interested in the structure or evolution of man," he concluded, "but this is only a beginning. To build it, we must collaborate with social scientists, geneticists, anatomists, and paleontologists. We need new ideas, new methods, new workers. There is nothing we do today which will not be done better tomorrow."

As a comparative anatomist who had experimentally examined the developmental associations of muscle and bone and sinew, Washburn originally tended to describe functional complexes anatomically, and his writings in 1951 hardly even hinted at the potential for adding primate field studies to the new physical anthropologist's toolbox. When Washburn attended the 1955 Pan-African Congress in Livingstone, Northern Rhodesia, he planned to further his studies of primate anatomy by dissecting baboons. His intentions, he declared at the time, were "80 percent anatomy and 20 percent behavior." But from his vantage point at the Victoria Falls Hotel, he suddenly found himself watching, with increasing fascination, the behavior of living baboons. As he wrote to a colleague at the University of Chicago, "I see now that a totally new level of primate behavior description is possible, one which recognizes both the generalities about the species and individual peculiarity. This would take fully a year in the field to do for baboons, as getting to know one of the big, wild troops would be a major task. However, I've learned so much on obvious things such as locomotion that I can't believe the literature contains the statements it does."

In his writings and teaching, through his many graduate students, and through his energy and fundraising abilities and tireless organizing of crossfertilizing conferences, Sherwood Washburn was the individual most directly responsible for ending the old physical anthropology (devoted to human measurement and racial typology) and establishing a new physical anthropology that would focus on humankind as a single species and ask the big questions, including the evolutionary one: where did we come from? The answer would somehow, Washburn knew, require a general vision of the human primate emerging from an ancestral primate.

He turned to baboons as a focal species for behavioral studies largely through serendipity and convenience. They were the primates visible from the porch of the Victoria Falls Hotel. And, as his student Irven DeVore would soon discover, they were the primates a person could readily watch from inside a Land Rover and within commuting distance from Nairobi. Washburn may have hoped that a year of studying baboons would solve the primate problem, revealing the underlying structures of nonhuman primate behavior and thereby illuminating human behavior and behavioral evolution. But the primate problem would turn out to be far more complex than anyone imagined. Baboons were not particularly representative of the primate family, which consists of two or three hundred different species of monkeys, apes, and prosimians. A year of study would not provide anywhere near enough data to unravel the dynamics even of baboon society. Nevertheless, the much broader study of monkeys, apes, and prosimians living freely in nature soon became an intellectual and inspirational core to Washburn's new physical anthropology.

Before the war, only three people had initiated serious and methodical field studies of wild primates, all three of them students of Robert Yerkes: Bingham, Nissen, and Carpenter. After the war, Japanese animal sociologists under the leadership of Kinji Imanishi were the first to take up primate field studies, beginning in 1948 with their early interest in the social lives of Japanese macaques. By the start of the 1960s, more than fifty researchers from nine different countries were involved in primate field studies — and yet it was still actually possible, as of 1962, to read all the important field reports during a single college semester, and still theoretically possible to gather together all the important field primatologists in the world under a single roof.

Sherwood Washburn tried to do the latter, more or less, by co-organizing a second conference that focused on primate field studies. Taking place at the Center for Advanced Study in the Behavioral Sciences of Stanford University, it was to be a weeklong affair (September 5–12, 1962) that marked the start of a longer (nine-month) Primate Project. The project would involve seminars and discussions and papers presented by the co-organizers, Washburn and a Stanford psychiatry professor named David Hamburg, and by two of Washburn's former students, Irven DeVore (baboons in Kenya) and Phyllis Jay (langurs in India), as well as K.R.L. Hall (baboons in South Africa), Hiroki Mizuhara (macaques in Japan), Frances and Vernon Reynolds (chimpanzees in Uganda), and George Schaller (gorillas in Belgian Congo). In addition to this important core group, about two dozen others —notably Clarence Ray Carpenter, Harry Harlow, Adriaan Kortlandt, and Jane Morris-Goodall—were invited to the conference in September.

Just as she was settling in at Cambridge, in mid-December 1961, Jane received her invitation from Sherwood Washburn to attend that conference. Once again, however, because she planned to be working at Gombe at that time, she was forced to decline.

Around the same time she turned down Washburn's second invitation, though, Jane received two more invitations to scientific conferences, both planned for the spring of 1962, when she would still be in England. The first, a three-day symposium entitled "The Primates," was at least convenient. Organized by John Napier and sponsored by the Zoological Society of London, it was scheduled to take place from April 12 to April 14 at the society's headquarters in Regent's Park, London—an inexpensive train trip from Cambridge. The second conference, on the less simply expressed theme "The Relatives of Man: Modern Studies of the Relation of the Evolution of Nonhuman Primates to Human Evolution," was also less convenient. Organized by a Yale geneticist named John Buettner-Janusch and sponsored by the New York Academy of Sciences, this one was supposed to take place on April 27 and 28 in New York City. Jane was concerned about whether she could afford to get there, but Louis Leakey wrote to her about it, insisting that (as she reported to the family) "I simply MUST go."

The New York Academy of Sciences sent Jane £160 to help defray expenses, while the National Geographic Society, suddenly regretting the earlier rejection of her photographic efforts and now eager to rekindle her interest, added another £200, providing she would agree to slip down to Geographic headquarters in Washington before going to New York. In the end she made a small profit from the trip.

At Cambridge, meanwhile, Jane proved to be an industrious student and a quick study. By March 1962 she was finishing her first scientific papers, on "Feeding Behaviour of Wild Chimpanzees" and "Nest Building Behavior in the Free Ranging Chimpanzee." While developing her ideas on these two subjects, she consulted with her old boss at the Granada Television and Film Unit of the London Zoo, Desmond Morris. Morris, as mentioned, had been trained as an ethologist under Niko Tinbergen at Oxford, and he was by then well informed on the behavior of zoo animals. Thus Jane wrote to him for ideas on chimp nest construction. "I was thinking about the various reasons for the construction of a new nest every night," she began, "—you know, greater protection from predators, or the fact that fresh leaves are softer and warmer than old ones. For various reasons these do not explain the behaviour—even though they may have been the original cause of it. So I began to wonder whether, perhaps, it was simply habit, like a dog turning round and round before he lies down." And on at least one occasion that spring, she dined with Desmond and his wife, Ramona, and enjoyed an invigorating conversation after the meal, returning, as she expressed it in a March 6 thank-you note, back to "my 'prison' inspired & set too to do some really hard work."

On April 11, Jane took the train from Cambridge to London, and in the evening she met John Napier at his laboratory at the British Museum of Natural History for a pre-symposium party. Napier's laboratory was a big square room with two white-topped anatomical dissection tables in the middle, which now supported wine, nibbles, and napkins. Around the walls were cabinets with dissecting tools and shelves with skulls and other anatomical objects, a few pictures of anatomical joints, and Napier's favorite photograph, showing the difference between human and chimp precision grips: human passes grape to chimpanzee, the latter reaching out of her cage and grasping the tender orb with a short thumb. A young woman named Alison Bishop attended the party and was struck by the photograph, partly because she had the day before taken her Ph.D. oral examination in zoology at Yale University on a subject closely related to Napier's interests. Her dissertation, "Use of the Hand in Lower Primates," would consider whether the evolutionary development of the primates' grasping hand and binocular vision, both of critical importance for a tree-dwelling mammal, were essential features that led to tool use, object manipulation, and the evolution of intelligence. Napier was the big expert on the anatomy of precision and power grips among primates, and so his work was a critical precursor for Bishop's study.

Alison Bishop was still reeling from jet lag when she arrived at Napier's laboratory that evening, and feeling, as she recently told me, "green and young and not knowing what the great Professor Napier would be like." She looked around and thought Napier must be that enormous man in the corner with the gray hair and beetling gray eyebrows, but then she asked someone, "Where is Professor Napier?" The person responded, "You see that rather handsome young man with the very black hair over there? The one who's doing card tricks on the table? That's Napier."

Everyone, Alison recalls, was "very jovial," in part because "there was a sense of occasion. There really had not been a primate conference before. It was the feeling that a field might be opening." Against one wall, she now noticed, someone had propped a poster board with some blurry black-and-white photographs pasted to it: pictures, she could see upon closer examination, of chimpanzees using sticks or twigs and poking them inside termite nests. People were "kind of buzzing around" the photographs, she remembers, but it was not until she chatted with John Napier that she began to understand.

He: "Did you see those photographs?"

She: "Yes, really interesting. Never would have imagined chimps fishing for termites."

He: "But you don't understand—this woman has redefined humanity. I asked her to the conference because Leakey said so. But it's quite extraordinary. This woman that nobody's ever heard of has appeared here on Leakey's recommendation, and look what she's been looking at."

She: "Oh, you mean that chimps using tools to fish for termites isn't just interesting, it's redefining humanity!"

Alison Bishop soon met Jane Goodall. They talked a little, but the pony-tailed young woman seemed no more interesting or memorable than anyone else there. "I was more struck by the people who were old and famous and I'd heard of. She just seemed like a nice woman. Only in those days we called [unmarried female] people 'girls.'" Jane seemed like a "nice girl."

On April 12, the first day of the "Primates" symposium, Jane shared the stage with eleven other speakers, three of whom had done significant field-work. K.R.L. Hall would talk about baboons. Adriaan Kortlandt would speak on the "Protohominid Behaviour in Primates." And Louis Leakey's former secretary and lover until early 1956, Rosalie Osborn, now an undergraduate student in zoology at Newnham College, Cambridge, would present her "Observations on the Behaviour of the Mountain Gorilla."

Jane was aware of Rosalie Osborn and her past relationship with Louis, but although they were both Newnham students, the two women scarcely knew each other. In any case, Osborn's talk was notable for its lack of fresh information. While it was true that her project amounted to the first concerted attempt to study gorillas since Harold Bingham's 1929 expedition, like Bingham she had not seen that much of the hairy creatures, and thus she now had not much to report. She concluded her talk with the modest admission that "the observations made during the pilot study form insufficient material from which to make generalizations and draw conclusions. Comparison with Schaller's study will be interesting and his work may throw fresh light on the interpretation and significance of these observations."

Jane's talk followed directly, and it was, by contrast, fresh and richly detailed. For the first time she publicly revealed her discovery that chimpanzees make and use tools, but her first scientific presentation focused on a related subject that was more general, less provocative—chimpanzee feeding behavior, about which she could draw on a substantial collection of original observations. Over a period of fifteen months, she had directly watched wild chimpanzees for approximately eight hundred hours, some three hundred of which involved feeding activity. She was able to summarize how much time the Gombe chimpanzees spent eating, describe their methods of finding and retrieving foods (including, as an incidental aside, the tool use involved in fishing for termites), detail some individual differences in "feeding mannerisms," and identify the types of foods commonly eaten—including sixty-one different vegetable foods, four different insect species, and the meat of mammals.

Her description of meat-eating was fully elaborated:

During the fifteen months spent in the field, observations on the eating of meat were made on three occasions and on one occasion part of the foot of some species of monkey was found in fresh chimpanzee faeces. The hunting or killing of the prey was not observed but on each occasion attention was attracted to the scene by loud chimpanzee calls, twice mingled with those of baboons. Once the prey animal was a very young bushpig, once a bushbuck about one month old, and once a small unidentified mammal. In each case these animals when observed had been decapitated and disembowelled.

In each instance the prey was taken up into a tree and was in the possession of a mature male chimpanzee. The male with the unidentified animal was half-up the tree when he saw the observer and moved away. The chimpanzee (identified as "Sam"), with the bushpig, remained in a tree for three hours before moving off with the remains in his mouth, whilst "Huxley," with the bushbuck, fed in his tree for six hours before moving away, again carrying the remains of a carcass in his mouth.

Initially, flesh was pulled from the neck region, the chimpanzee using his incisor teeth. From time to time the sound of bone being gnawed was audible. Between each bite a mouthful of leaves was invariably eaten. A female chimpanzee, which was allowed to feed from the bushbuck, also ate leaves between each bite.

The acquisition of meat creates the unusual situation in which one member of the group only is in possession of the food. The behaviour of the other chimpanzees towards the one with the meat suggests that the liking of flesh is not merely an abnormality of one individual, but is common to all members of the group. Not only do the others sit close to the chimpanzee with the meat, watching his every movement, but many of them actually beg from him, stretching out their hands to touch his lips with their fingers.

Jane was the first to observe that chimpanzees eat meat, and the descriptions of this activity were an important part of her contribution. But primate carnivory was a more broadly significant theme that day. Raymond A. Dart, famous as the discoverer of *Australopithecus*, followed Jane's talk with a presentation on the "Carnivorous Propensity of Baboons." And later in the symposium some of Irven DeVore's films of baboons were shown, including a very dramatic sequence of males eating meat, with a vivid close-up of ripped flesh, dangling intestines, grinding teeth, bloody snouts.

This professional conference was more formal than a similar event might be today. For starters, people were dressed up. Alison Bishop recalls the time as sartorially "just another era, way, way back." The men wore suits and ties, and she had arrived in high heels and stockings, a black suit with a long skirt, white gloves, and a pillbox hat with a little veil. She really loved that hat, which was, she thought, "terribly cute." The formality extended to behavior as well, and in this case the behavior of symposium attendees was strictly regulated by an official chairman: Solly Zuckerman, the powerful secretary of the Zoological Society. His 1932 book, *The Social Life of Monkeys and Apes,* was still considered the single significant theoretical synthesis of pre–World War II primatology.

Zuckerman, born and raised in Cape Town, South Africa, had studied anatomy at Cape Town University, where (despite a minor if memorable humiliation at the hands of his final examiner, Raymond A. Dart, from the University of the Witwatersrand) he passed with honors and received the senior medal in zoology. In 1926 the young man secured a position as research anatomist at the London Zoo, where he did postmortem assessments of dead zoo animals. The zoo was producing a lot of dead baboons at the time, mainly because of a gross error in the creation of its baboon colony. Established in 1925 on an artificial cliff face known as Monkey Hill, the collection had consisted of around one hundred hamadryas baboons, all but six of whom were adult males (a management choice probably based on the idea that the males—big and dramatically fanged and caped, with pink buttocks—would appeal to a zoo-going public more than the smaller and less gaudy females). Hamadryas baboons normally live in harem societies, family units consisting of one adult male and a plurality of adult females plus offspring. The males acquire and maintain their harems by herding the smaller females. And so, of course, with ninety-some adult males fighting over those half-dozen adult females, the competition was intense. Illness and injuries reduced the colony to only fifty-six individuals by 1927, whereupon thirty additional females and five young males were added to the mix—with explosive results. The old resident males fought viciously over access to the newly arrived females, and within a month half the females had been killed in the process.

As the zoo's research anatomist, Solly Zuckerman was eager to explore his interest in the relationship of the baboon menstrual cycle to hormone production, but he also became curious about baboon social behavior and so began watching the daily drama at Monkey Hill. In 1930 he returned to South Africa for three months to gather specimens and study chacma baboons in the wild, at one time spending a total of nine days observing a single group. Nothing he saw during that quick visit to South Africa countered his already established conclusions about the baboons of the London Zoo, and when he examined the existing zoo and field literature on other primate species, he found little to challenge his idea that the world's monkeys and apes were almost identical, sociologically speaking, to baboons. Thus, by pressing into the theoretical grinder his field notes on South African baboons and observations of northern hamadryas baboons crammed into a pathologically abnormal zoo colony, adding hormonal and anatomical studies, and pushing into that mix every other zoo and field note he could find on primates in general, Solly Zuckerman produced in 1932 his grand theory of primate behavior: that the social glue of primates is female sexual attractiveness, with attracted males fighting each other for dominance and forming alliances and hierarchies for the prize of access.

Even before publication of his book, Zuckerman had been invited by Robert Yerkes to become director of his ape research colony in Orange Park, Florida. Arriving in the United States early in 1933 to assume his new position, however, the South African anatomist quickly concluded that the North American psychologist was an austere and humorless bore, and an unhappy stay at the nonsmoking, nondrinking Yerkes household in New Haven (with nearly raw eggs for breakfast on the first morning, accompanied by unfortunate comments about the noise Zuckerman made stropping his razor in the bathroom) was followed by a disastrous visit to Florida. The Orange Park research station had "enough apes to satisfy the most avid researcher," Zuckerman remarked years later, "but absolutely no real scientific purpose that I could discern in the endeavour." On his first evening in Florida, staying once again with the Yerkeses, he endured, after a "severely simple dinner" and an inauspicious introduction to pumpkin pie, a migration to the fireside, where the psychologist asked the anatomist if he enjoyed being read to. His honest reply—that he could think of nothing he liked less—produced a long silence, followed by awkward attempts at further conversation until everyone went to bed. The next day Zuckerman learned that Mrs. Yerkes habitually read aloud to her husband in the evenings as an important family ritual.

Back in England, Solly Zuckerman soon found an academic post at Oxford University, where his talents were, during the next several years, more appreciated. He had a first-rate mind, which, combined with even more impressive social abilities, yielded over time a remarkable network of connections among the rich, the famous, and the powerful. By April 12, 1962, the day he chaired the symposium on primates sponsored by the Zoological Society of London, Solly Zuckerman had risen to become chair of the Department of Anatomy at Birmingham University and chief scientific adviser to the Ministry of Defence. For his services during the war, among other things, he had been knighted, so he was now also—an éminence grise with an impeccably tailored suit and a perfectly parted field of wavy hair—Sir Solly.

To Alison Bishop, sitting in the audience and peering out from beneath her pillbox hat and little veil, he appeared "a square, wide, impressive man" with "red face and white hair, and a position—you know, always being centered in the chair in front of the room, doing the summing up."

According to Desmond Morris, also a member of the audience that day, Zuckerman was "very hostile" toward Jane, privately dismissing her as one of the "amateurs"—a perspective Desmond and others found outrageous. "Those of us who knew Jane," he now recollects, "were just in awe of the risk she was taking and the effort she was making to do these studies. She was bringing back information about chimpanzees which was, to us as students of animal behavior, tremendously exciting. We were learning things from her about chimpanzees which we couldn't have learned any other way. This was the point. Her study was unique." Other people had done primate field studies by then, of course, and they would return to the comforts of civilization and write up their results, but Jane was different in what Desmond identifies as her "thoroughgoingness": her total dedication. "We realized that she had got in close in a way that for the first time she was seeing chimps as they really are. It was that fearless determination to get out there at any risk that was the really admirable thing about her."

Protocol at the symposium meant that any questions asked of a speaker were addressed not to him or her but to the chair, who then turned and restated the question for the speaker to answer. During his study of hamadryas baboons at the London Zoo thirty years earlier, Zuckerman had noted that the adult baboon males were herding females to form harems, and so, based on this flimsy bit of evidence, he had concluded that a harem system was characteristic of all primate societies. After Jane's talk, Desmond Morris raised his hand to ask whether she had noticed harems among the chimpanzees. His question was simply ignored by the chair. Desmond asked a second time, and when the question was ignored once again, he turned to Jane and repeated his question for the third time, breaking with protocol to ask her directly. She answered. While it was true that chimpanzee males will compete vigorously for the opportunity to mate with a fertile female, she noted, ultimately many males will typically have mated with that female. In other words, chimpanzees display a promiscuous sexuality, and the males do not acquire stable harems.

At the end of that day's presentations, Sir Solly began his official summation with the barbed comment that "there are those who are here and who prefer anecdote—and what I must confess I regard as sometimes unbounded speculation." He supposed it was "not entirely a matter of personal taste whether one regards this sort of study of primate behaviour, or of primate evolution, as constituting a real contribution to science or not." But, the great man continued, if one were to disregard the anecdotes and the speculations, one would find that all the important generalizations revealed during the day's proceedings confirmed to an astonishing extent his own basic conclusions.

First was the concept of "dominance relations," which turned out to be an issue of as "over-riding importance . . . as it was when I emphasized it thirty years back." Second was the matter of primate sex ratios, which, just as he had long ago discovered, inevitably become skewed as a result of the "drastic elimination of males" during their violent competition for females. (And although Miss Goodall "appeared to question this generalization" in her presentation, her study animals did not provide a fair sample of wild chimp behavior, because they happened to be a "special group of chimpanzees living under very favorable conditions, plagued by few predators and enjoying abundant food.") The third generalization that Sir Solly had made three decades earlier was that primates were "territorial animals"—a concept, so he found to his own clear satisfaction, fully substantiated by "some of the precise observations which have been brought to our attention at today's symposium." And finally, as Sir Solly once again had noted thirty years earlier, all the monkeys and apes in the world are vegetarians and fruit-eaters, not carnivores or omnivores. While it may be true that baboons had been seen eating meat on some rare occasion, he continued, such observations were fundamentally misleading, since the baboon is certainly "a non-carnivorous animal in most places where it exists." As for Miss Goodall's most peculiar account of chimpanzees eating meat, it would be "a useful point to remember," he lectured in a coolly patronizing style, "that in scientific work it is far safer to base one's major conclusions and generalizations on a concordant and large body of data than on a few contradictory and isolated observations, the explanation of which sometimes leaves a little to be desired."

In spite of what anyone may have seen or heard or imagined that day, in other words, Sir Solly Zuckerman could assure the audience that neither baboons nor chimpanzees eat meat to any significant degree. Primates do not eat meat.

After the conference, Desmond Morris received a conciliatory note from Zuckerman, justifying his avoidance of the question about chimpanzees and harems. "I realize that you were only trying to provoke discussion," Sir Solly declared, "in the same way that you appreciate, I'm sure . . . my anxiety lest a subject which has been usually marked by unscientific treatment should continue in the unscientific shadows because of glamour."

On Monday, April 23, eleven days after her London talk, an anti-scientifically glamorous Miss Jane Morris-Goodall flew to Washington, D.C., to see for the first time the National Geographic headquarters and also take in the National Zoo. At the zoo, a photographer snapped a publicity shot—Jane's first—of her holding the zoo's eleven-month-old chimpanzee, Lulu, the pair of them flanked by the Geographic's Leonard Carmichael and Melville Bell Grosvenor (with Lulu reaching back to tweak Carmichael's mustache).

From Washington, Jane traveled to Yale University in New Haven for a brief visit with her new acquaintance and colleague Alison Bishop, starting with an afternoon picnic shared by about a half-dozen graduate students. Jane was still wearing her National Geographic clothes—suit and skirt, nylons and heels—as Alison remembers, while everyone else was in jeans and other casual attire. But it had gotten warm, and after a while their elegant English guest disappeared behind a bush to peel off those burdensome stockings and shoes, an act that at the time seemed daring. They spent the night in Alison's student apartment, Jane sacked out on the floor, and early the next morning set off for New York, finding their way to 2 East 63rd Street, the neo–Italian Renaissance building that sheltered the New York Academy of Sciences, for the Friday and Saturday meetings on "The Relatives of Man: Modern Studies of the Relation of the Evolution of Nonhuman Primates to Human Evolution."

Like Sherwood Washburn's primatologically oriented conferences on human evolution, this was characterized by a tremendous diversity of approaches: anatomical, behavioral, biochemical, ecological, immunological, paleontological, physiological, and so on. Alison Bishop presented her first scientific paper, "Control of the Hand in Lower Primates," while Jane gave her second, "Nest Building Behavior in the Free Ranging Chimpanzee."

Her talk seemed to go well, except that the reading light at the podium had burned out, so when her slides were projected onto a screen and the house lights dimmed, she could no longer read what she had written and was forced to extemporize. "Luckily," she commented in a letter written a few days afterward, "I knew my subject well enough to get away with it, but it was annoying, all the same." Still, the meeting in New York was altogether "very interesting and profitable," she thought. "Profitable in that I met a great many people whom I have long wanted to meet, and with whom I was able to have stimulating discussions."

After the conference Jane flew back to England, returning to finish up the term at Cambridge. From there it would be back to Gombe for several months. Alison Bishop meanwhile got married and thereby turned into Alison Jolly—who then turned to field studies of lemurs in Madagascar and a long and distinguished career as a primatologist.

The conferences of 1962 marked Jane's professional debut as a scientist. In some ways, they also marked the debut of primatology as a modern science.

Sir Solly Zuckerman remained forever convinced that the primate problem had already been solved—by himself—and that it was mainly a masculine melodrama on the themes of sex and violence. Yet even by the early 1960s modern primate studies were beginning to reveal and revel in almost the opposite sort of story. Instead of great simplicity, an inclusive pattern of behavior characterizing all members of the family, the new research and reports from the field were starting to show (beyond the unifying principle of evolution through natural selection) great diversity, an astonishing variety of ways in which the world's many primate species had adapted to their great diversity of environments. The recognized styles of primate social life would come to include not only stable harems but also solitary individuals, monogamous pairs, promiscuous pairings, and perpetually shifting (fission-fusion) groups within stable communities; and the theoretical springs and gears driving primate behavior would expand beyond the hormone-motivated sex and dominance of Zuckerman's world to encompass an indefinite number of further possibilities, such as adaptability, affiliation, choice, kinship, learning, maternity, paternity, planning, and politics. Jane's own vision of primates (at least chimpanzees) as emotional and deliberative animals with real personalities and active minds would come to seem increasingly relevant and finally—following the manifestos of Donald Griffin, *The Question of Animal Awareness* (1976) and *Animal Thinking* (1984)—commonplace.

Solly Zuckerman's big contribution had been to think about primates from combined vantage points, hormonal and behavioral. Perhaps the most significant of his several errors was to assume that a brief field study would suffice. It was Zuckerman's contemporary and Robert Yerkes' student Clarence Ray Carpenter who, watching howler monkeys in Panama, originally set the standard for methodical and extended field studies. But it was none other than Jane Goodall who so decisively demonstrated that any significant understanding of primate behavior would require an act of radical immersion over extended time.

Zuckerman's clever dismissal of Jane's first scientific presentation as, in essence, glamour parading as science foreshadowed the stubborn prejudice that pursued her on occasion through much of her professional life: the idea that her legs were too nice, her hair too blond, her face too fine, her manner too feminine for anything she said or wrote to be taken all that seriously. But one interesting thing about the new primatology was how many women were already climbing Monkey Hill to take up positions as field researchers and academic leaders. The new primatology, especially primate field studies, was a science in which women would become increasingly important, and today the practitioners are about equally divided in gender. Women started becoming primatologists for a number of reasons, one suspects, not least of which was the fair encouragement offered by such important senior male figures as Louis Leakey, Robert Hinde, and Sherwood Washburn. But also, of course, there would soon appear some very visible female models and mentors, including the increasingly celebrated Jane Goodall as well as several other important pioneers, such as Alison Jolly and (also participating in the 1962 New York conference) Cynthia Booth and Phyllis Jay.

Ultimately, of course, Jane *was* glamorous, and it would be under the lens of *National Geographic* that her natural glamour was artificially multiplied many times over. In the process, primatology would itself metamorphose into one of the most seen and often mis-seen of the sciences, while Jane would become among the most visible scientists of the twentieth century and possibly the best-known woman scientist in history. Meanwhile, the primates would turn out to possess their own compelling glamour, and through the media's magic machinery they would come to provide an ever-expanding popular audience with the most thrilling sort of education and entertainment: that of gazing very deeply into nature's mirror.

21

~~~

A Photographic Success

1962

AS WE HAVE SEEN, the National Geographic Society first became interested in Jane Goodall's story through the encouragement of Louis Leakey. The society had supported Louis's Chimpanzee Project, while *National Geographic* magazine prepared to feature it in an article illustrated with the usual excellent color photography. When the pictures taken by Judy Goodall were discovered to be inadequate, however, the magazine staff turned down their option via Robert E. Gilka's mildly patronizing note in January 1962.

That rejection was a mistake, as the magazine's executives quickly realized—encouraged in their realization by Louis Leakey. In early December 1961 he had solicited a grant of £400 to support Jane during her first year's work at Cambridge University ("to write up her results," he put it, playing down her student status). The Geographic's Research and Exploration Committee had tentatively declined that request, asking for more details about Jane and how the money would be spent.

In a response dated January 5, 1962, Jane's mentor pulled out the stops and produced what may have been the strongest recommendation of his life, and hers, for the first time placing Jane emphatically center stage—no longer "one of my research assistants." He summarized several things he had written earlier, but now he strongly emphasized the significance of her own work, and for the first time he revealed Jane's discovery of chimpanzee toolmaking and toolusing:

As regards the importance of Miss Goodall's research, I do not want to give away too much of what is, after all, her own special series of discoveries, but since you ask for a brief resumé of her research, I suppose I can confidentially give you the following information, but please treat this as highly confidential as it is her work which is of the very highest scientific importance, and all the credit is hers.

1. She has observed wild chimpanzees for eighteen months in their natural habitat at closer quarters and in more detail than has ever been done for any wild primates hitherto.

2. The number of hours of direct observation far exceeds that of George Schaller on the gorillas a year or two ago, which was then the most important work done.

3. Miss Goodall was able to establish such good relations with the chimpanzees that she has had them living their normal lives, mating, grooming, nursing their babies, playing, and all their other activities . . . at very close quarters indeed.

4. Miss Goodall has magnificent notes as well as a photographic record of something previously, I think, unheard of, namely, chimpanzees at certain seasons of the year regularly making a primitive tool for the purpose of catching termites. This discovery is of the very highest scientific importance.

5. She also has examples of the "tools" so made for this purpose and I have in my possession some black and white prints of the photographs of this unbelievable discovery taken by Jane.

6. Miss Goodall has a number of records of chimpanzees eating the flesh of mammals including juvenile wild pig and bush buck, and on one occasion the dividing up of such flesh amongst the troop by an old male.

7. Miss Goodall has an exceedingly complete record of the mating behaviour of chimpanzees in the wild, which is certainly unique.

8. Miss Goodall has records, I think new to science, of chimpanzees excavating with their teeth into a cliff face for saline earth at certain times of the year.

9. She has records of some fantastic "rain dances" performed by male chimpanzees with green branches torn from trees at the onset of tropical storms.

All this and much else makes the work she has done completely outstanding and somehow I must raise the money to enable her to write it up quietly without having to try and earn enough to live on at the same time as writing it up.

Louis's recommendation had the desired effect: an immediate posting of £400 to Jane, combined with a renewed, suddenly intense interest in her work. On January 16 the society's vice president, Melvin Payne, passed on Leakey's statement to Leonard Carmichael, the chairman of the Committee for Research and Exploration, commenting that "the resumé of her work is quite exciting, and I know you will find it of particular interest." Carmichael was so impressed that he began lobbying for his own trip to Gombe.

Within a week, President Grosvenor had also caught the enthusiasm. "The significance of these studies is extraordinary," he wrote, "not to mention the excitement of Miss Goodall sitting there with these chimpanzees making friends with them and their unconcern when she is there. It would make a fabulous story for our magazine and we must make every effort to get it."

By January 23 a plan was shaped and a proposal set in motion. Grosvenor first sent a copy of Louis's statement to the photographer David Boyer, in order to "show you why this idea is so exciting and important to the magazine. These behavior studies are new—the fact that a chimpanzee uses a small wooden tool that it has made itself to dig for termites. Think of that!" On the same day Grosvenor cabled Louis to ask if Leonard Carmichael could visit Gombe for a few days in mid-February. That telegram was followed by letters to both Louis and Jane. To Louis, he announced that "we are as enthusiastic about the results of Miss Jane Goodall's work as you are and we feel we must find a means to publish the article."

A fuller proposal was included in Grosvenor's longer letter to Jane. "Dr. Leakey has written fascinating letters telling something of your extraordinary studies and discoveries of chimpanzee behavior," the society president began. "So important is this work that we feel we must publish an article in National Geographic about it."

Jane must certainly be very busy right then, he acknowledged, "embarked" as she was "on the preparation of your technical reports" that the Geographic had been so "pleased to support" (referring to the £400 recently sent). However, he wondered if she would also be willing to write an article for the magazine telling the story of her experiences with the chimps and her latest discoveries concerning their behavior. And, since it was "essential that new color photographs be made by a professional photographer," would it be possible for her to take a short break from her report-writing in Cambridge to return to Gombe in mid-February, to help the photographer and accompany Dr. Leonard Carmichael? Naturally, Grosvenor concluded, the society would be prepared to cover all her expenses as well as provide another $1,000 "in appreciation for your undertaking this task," not to mention a further $2,500 for writing the article and assisting in the photography.

Louis responded immediately, commenting in a return letter that the proposed visit of Leonard Carmichael to Gombe was "completely out of the question unless he has a lot more time available than the schedule sent to me." Louis proceeded to enumerate the difficulties. It would take three to five days to get to Kigoma from Nairobi. Another three to five days in returning. There was no road from Kigoma to the research site. The country was impossible to walk through. There would be no boat, since the one Jane had been using was out of service until her return in the summer. And finally, of course, since Jane was in England in order "to write up her results," she could not be in Africa, and without her a visit to Gombe would be useless, since "no-one else knows the exact places to go to find the chimpanzee troops."

Louis's letter reached Washington by January 30, and Grosvenor immediately provided a copy to Carmichael while offering his colleague some consoling remarks ("Don't be discouraged yet. I think by helicopter or float plane and the use of a boat you could get into that site") and summarizing, as it had now started to come into focus, the real obstacle: Louis. "It's a funny think [*sic*] the way Louis likes to keep this chimpanzee site so exclusive," Grosvenor noted to Carmichael. "He won't let us send in photographers with Jane Goodall simply for prudish reasons. It is rather ridiculous, I feel." But perhaps Louis Leakey was not all that important anyway. It was really Jane Goodall they were after, and perhaps she could be pried away. "I am hoping that my letter directed to Jane Goodall herself may produce some results."

Jane's response echoed, though more gracefully, Louis's. She informed Grosvenor that she was actually working for a Ph.D. degree at Cambridge, and, she added, February, the middle of the rainy season, would be the worst time for photography. "The grass is at its very highest—over 12 feet in many places—and the observer is generally soaked to the skin all day long. In addition, all the normal buffalo tracks are overgrown, and it is almost impossible to travel around to any great extent."

Any serious and worthy suitor will tolerate a gentle rejection or two; and so it was with Melville Bell Grosvenor, who wrote to Jane on February 13, inviting her to come to Washington to meet with the staff and the Research and Exploration Committee. The society would pay for the trip, and Grosvenor was sure they would be able to "firm up details" about their new plans to have a photographer at Gombe by June.

That invitation was followed less than a week later by a more detailed one written by Robert Gilka, the assistant illustrations editor, noting that since Jane was already planning to come to New York for the Academy of Sciences primate conference in April, he hoped she would also drop by in Washington for a brief visit. Gilka, of course, had written the unfortunate January 2 rejection letter to Jane and Judy—but now he was humbly asking for "a second look at the pictures you and your sister took last year and which I returned to you earlier."

In mid-March, two National Geographic Society alpha males, Dr. Leonard Carmichael and Dr. Thomas W. McKnew, and their wives, having just completed a brief trip to various spots of interest in East Africa and on their way back to the States, arranged to meet Jane in London. She took a morning train from Cambridge and had lunch with the four of them, and Carmichael returned to Geographic headquarters in Washington to report that he and McKnew had "interviewed" her and "were most favorably impressed by her scientific knowledge and her personality." Meanwhile, the society sent Jane a check for £200 to make sure she visited Washington in late April before attending the New York Academy of Sciences conference.

How else could they dramatize their interest in Jane and perhaps stimulate hers in them? On March 22 the board of trustees voted to honor her with the Franklin L. Burr Prize for the Increase and Diffusion of Geographic Knowledge, a prestigious award that included $1,500 in cash. Louis was in Washington just then to deliver one of the society's public lectures (on Friday, March 23); that same day, he met with President Grosvenor, who agreed to underwrite research at Gombe for another year at "up to $5,000."

Louis then proposed a solution to the problem of getting a photographer for Gombe. A year earlier he had objected to sending a male photographer to Gombe for reasons of propriety, but he had lately become acquainted with a talented young Dutchman, Hugo van Lawick, who in fact had produced the very film used to illustrate the very lecture Louis had just given. This van Lawick fellow would be the best person to photograph the Gombe chimpanzees "because," Louis said (according to a paraphrase made after that meeting), "he is familiar with wild animal behavior. In addition, this man lives in Nairobi and can get to the chimpanzee site within a few days." Louis also pointed out that "the timing is most important as it may be several weeks before the chimps will become accustomed to Miss Goodall and begin eating fruit and hunting for termites."

Naturally, since Hugo van Lawick was male, there remained the old matter of propriety—the resolution to which was simple, Louis now declared. Along with underwriting the Gombe research and paying Jane's expenses, the National Geographic could pay her mother's expenses as well, so that Vanne could go out to Gombe once more, this time to serve as "chaperone."

Baron Hugo van Lawick was born on April 10, 1937, in the Dutch East Indies (now Indonesia). His father, a pilot with the Dutch fleet, was killed in an airplane crash when the boy was four years old, at which point his mother moved the family to Australia, then England. Hugo and his mother and brother spent the war years in London and Hull, where they endured frequent air raids, and then in Devon. In London, Hugo was given his own gas mask and a wooden rattle to carry around, the latter to be set in motion, he was told, as a warning to others in case of gas attack. In Hull, their household garden included an air raid shelter made from piled sandbags, but Hugo later remembered only sitting in the garden with his mother and neighbors, all drinking tea and chatting while the planes and the V-1s and V-2s passed overhead. After the war ended, his mother took the younger brother to Holland, while Hugo stayed in Devon, because he enjoyed boarding school there. The family's aristocratic titles were not accompanied by wealth, however, and when his mother found she could no longer afford the school in Devon, in 1947, Hugo joined the rest of the family in Amersfoort, Netherlands.

Hugo had always been interested in wildlife, and by the time he was fourteen or fifteen he had joined a nature club of perhaps a dozen boys of the same age, who once a year went on a three-day trip. Their first trip was to a national park in Holland. Two of his friends took along small, rudimentary cameras, and they were sighting small animals (birds, deer, frogs, snakes) and trying to take pictures of them, an activity that, because of the simplicity of their equipment, required a lot of creeping. Hugo knew nothing about taking pictures, but he was good at creeping, and his friends told him what to do: "When you get up to that tree, press the knob."

He eventually decided that through photography he could pursue his dream of a life close to nature. His family was by tradition militarily inclined, but his mother supported him in this ambition, so Hugo, after finishing national service in the Dutch army, joined a film company as assistant cameraman and started making commercials. He worked in a film laboratory for three months, and then he worked for a while as a still photographer before leaving for East Africa in November 1959.

Hugo loved Africa from the start, and he soon found work as a cameraman for the Nairobi-based filmmaking couple Armand and Michaela Denis, who were by then famous in Europe for producing the first nature films for television. When that job ran out after a couple of years, Hugo, needing the money, joined the Kenyan Game Department and helped catch rhinos in heavily poached areas and release them into national parks. Then, having saved up enough to survive for about a month without working, he tried freelancing as a photographer.

While he worked for the Denises, Hugo became friends with one of their neighbors, Richard Leakey, and now Richard's father, Dr. Louis Leakey, invited him to stay at their house in Langata. After two days at the Leakey house, Hugo happened to be standing behind Louis when the telephone rang: long distance from America, someone at the National Geographic, talk about Louis's next American lecture and how to find someone to make a background film for it. Hugo made that film in a couple of months, in the process positively impressing Louis and the National Geographic.

But he had been away from Holland for two years by then, and now he had enough money from the Geographic film to return home to visit his mother. It was at his mother's house that he received the April 4, 1962, letter from a Geographic staff member complimenting him on his camera work for the lecture film and proposing to give him $100 a month as a retainer, enough to ensure his availability, and offering additional payments at the magazine's usual rates for any still and motion-picture work they used. Meanwhile, the letter went on, Hugo should come to Washington immediately, at the Geographic's expense, "to familiarize you with the photographic requirements and needs" and "to discuss equipment, film, and photographic techniques which you would find of value."

Hugo cabled his acceptance and booked a flight out of Amsterdam for Monday, April 16. When he arrived at National Geographic headquarters in Washington, however, the young Dutchman was disconcerted to be asked so seriously about his still-photography skills, since he had done mostly motion pictures. Then someone handed him a camera and said, "Well, go into Washington and take some photographs."

He said, "I photograph animals, not people."

The person said, "Oh, it's the same. Photography's photography."

Hugo was very shy in those days, and the thought of wandering into a city and randomly photographing strangers terrified him. But he went off, tried some shots, came back, and sent his film into the lab for development. Disappointing results. Next he wandered over to the National Zoo, to photograph not animals but rather people watching animals. First he saw an attractive young woman looking at some sort of animal, and he took a couple of pictures, but then a jealous boyfriend showed up, inquiring aggressively, "What's going on?" Hugo next found what seemed to be a less fraught situation, a grandfather popping sweets into his granddaughter's mouth. He snapped a picture, and the man looked over and smiled. But when Hugo took a few more, the man abruptly got up and walked away.

It was an animal photograph that finally landed Hugo the job. He photographed a pelican being fed at the zoo, and Melville Grosvenor decided that he really liked the pelican picture.

The National Geographic hired the young Hugo van Lawick and agreed to support a Gombe sojourn for Jane *and* her mother—also to pay Jane another $2,000 for a 7,500-word article on her work at Gombe, plus $200 per picture for any of her photographs used. And the magazine's associate editor, Frederick G. Vosburgh, personally emphasized while she was in Washington that April (a week after Hugo) "the importance of being concrete rather than general, of using the first-person pronoun, and the personal-narrative approach, with plenty of anecdote and a bit of humor."

As Jane noted in a letter to Desmond Morris that March, a short while after Louis had told her about the new plan, she was

> feeling happier than I have felt for a very long time because at long last there is the prospect that I shall get a really suitable photographer. This man is, at the moment, climbing about mountain forests in Africa to see how much equipment he can reasonably carry, and is also experimenting with flashlight on various sorts of monkeys and other animals to see just how much effect it has on them, and how long they take to get used to it. The thought of someone like this, who is really desperate to [photograph] the chimps and who is, in addition to being a first class photographer, wonderful with animals — well it's just too good to be true.

The reigning powers at *National Geographic* must have been satisfied as well, although they still proposed to send their own backup photographer to Gombe, someone who was already scheduled to be in Nairobi that summer, directing photography for an article on the Leakey family. As Robert Gilka explained to Jane in a May 10 letter, Miss Mary Griswold was "a self-sufficient young woman" and "an experienced photographer," whose sole purpose would be to "shoot some of the necessary photographs of your camp life. She would not attempt chimpanzee pictures because this would be an intrusion on your study."

Mary Griswold was the same assistant illustrations editor who had been so casually selected by Louis and Melville Grosvenor to photograph Jane and the chimps a year earlier, only to be as casually deselected a few weeks later. This second proposal to send her out to Gombe was as ill-considered as the first, as Jane implied in a May 15 response to Gilka: "Do you really think she would get very much better pictures than Hugo and myself between us? The other thing is that I don't, quite honestly, see what she could take — my camp is empty and deserted all day."

Once again Miss Griswold was cut from the program. Since there was still the Leakey family story to direct, however, she went to Kenya anyway and thus ran into Jane in Nairobi, probably on June 28, outside a downtown restaurant. They shook hands and briefly registered a mutual lack of fascination with one another. Mary judged Jane to be "sort of frail" and thought she "probably wouldn't last."

. . .

By July 4, Jane and her friend Derrick Dunn were driving south out of Nairobi, through the Serengeti and past the mist-shrouded Ngorongoro Crater, getting lost on rough and disappearing roads, arriving late and exhausted that night at Singida, where they took a room at a hotel notable for its broken toilets. The next day Jane boarded a train at Itigi and spent a night in Tabora—where her old friend and camp cook, Dominic Bandora, showed up, short of money and disappointed, he said, that Vanne was not there. And the next morning Jane and Dominic caught a train west to Kigoma, which, to their delight, was also carrying Hassan Salimu.

The British-run United Nations trusteeship of Tanganyika had become the independent nation of Tanganyika some eight months earlier, on December 7, 1961. Although modern Tanzania would not be formed until the unification of Tanganyika and Zanzibar on April 26, 1964, independence for this former German colony and British mandate was a glorious event. Jane noticed that she was the only European onboard the train (other than "an insipid White Father trying to buy bread at 7 A.M., but he seems to have got out at one of the little places in the middle of nowhere"), and when Jane, Dominic, and Hassan arrived at Kigoma later in the day, she observed that the former Regina Hotel had been thoughtfully renamed the Lake View, while nearly all the civil service posts with offices in the Boma had been taken over by Africans.

Jane reached Gombe by Monday, July 8, and immediately wrote to Louis: "My word, but it's good to be back here. Even when the chimps are scarce, it's still good."

As a result of some recent, unusually heavy rains, the lake was high, which made it difficult to walk along the beach and explore the areas north and south of her camp at Kasekela. The small aluminum boat was handicapped by a dead motor; Jane borrowed a small dugout canoe and practiced her paddling. The grass, normally dry and burned out by midsummer, was still wet and green and tall, in places as high as 10 feet. In addition to the unseasonably tall grass, there was the seasonal challenge of high winds, which made it hard to find chimps by sighting their leafy perturbations or hearing their cries and hoots. And the tent, supposedly overhauled by Ahamed Brothers in Nairobi, was now rolled out to reveal a rip in the washroom roof, a missing mallet, the same old rotten guy ropes, and hardly enough pegs to fasten it down. ("So you can tick off dear Jimmy Ahamed when you see him," she instructed Louis.)

Still, she loved being back in the forest and living once again in a tent. "People often seem horrified when they hear that I lived in a tent for 18 months," Jane wrote to Thomas McKnew at the National Geographic that summer. "But I love a tent—and I think, particularly, that to be under canvas in a heavy rain storm is one of the most wonderful feelings there is."

Near the end of July, Jane and Hassan set up a temporary camp on the beach near the northern end of the reserve, at Mitumba Valley, thinking that the great *msulula* tree there should be in fruit and attracting large numbers of chimps. They hauled up a few blankets and a couple of boxes containing the bare essentials, and someone from Mwamgongo village was hired to keep Hassan company during the days while Jane was out looking for chimps and trying to get some good shots for the magazine article. Her attempts at chimp photography in Mitumba were disappointing, but that disappointment was compensated for by nights that were "so perfect," as she informed Thomas McKnew.

> We were on the beach so that I sat by my small fire looking out across the dark mystery of the lake at night. All around were the sounds one comes to love in Africa—the secret rustlings in the long grass, the never ending chirping of the crickets, the low voices of the Africans over by their fire, and, over all, the whispering and sighing of the lapping at the shingle. Up above the stars were so brilliant that some kind of radiance illuminated the whole dark sky—the darkness was somehow <u>alive</u>. After a long hot day, crawling up mountain slopes with the grass above my head—it was like another world.

Most positively, Jane found that the chimps who had been comfortable with her before remembered her now, as she remembered them, and so she was able to pick up her study where she had left off more than six months before.

When she arrived, the game scouts living at Kasekela informed her that David Greybeard had regularly been visiting a large fig tree near their village, and Jane soon found him there, up in the tree. He was still tame, tolerating her walking around the tree, looking up, pointing a camera at him. He was, as Jane wrote to Louis on July 17, "the same old David as ever, and just as amenable, bless him. I couldn't help laughing when I saw him, sitting up there in the great fig tree, chewing peacefully on his fig wadge. . . . Dear old David G!"

David's high rank in the chimpanzee hierarchy combined with his weakness for the amenities of camp (such as bananas) and his calm tolerance of Jane's presence meant that three other males—Ugly, Charlie, and Goliath—were soon drawn into the camp as well. Goliath was the largest, "a real giant," as Jane described him in her first official report to the Geographic Society, and also apparently the community's dominant male. Without the mediating presence of David Greybeard, both Ugly and Charlie were still overtly anxious and suspicious about the actions and intentions of the strange pale ape with the ponytail. But suddenly Goliath had become as calm and seemingly indifferent to Jane as David Greybeard was.

One day I was passing through camp on my way from one observation point to another. By great good fortune I stopped for a few minutes as I had some plants to press. Whilst I was in the tent I heard a crash in the oil nut palm overhead, peered cautiously out, and there was Charlie up in the tree. As he was on his own I took care that he could not see me.

He had been up there for 5 minutes or so when I heard a low sound [chimpanzee vocalization], as used when a companion is sighted. I therefore went to the back of the tent and peeped out behind—just in time to see Goliath proceeding round through the front. I remained in the bathroom part and looked out through the mosquito netting window. Goliath appeared in the veranda of the tent, and looked in. He immediately observed some bananas on the table just inside, came in, picked them up, looked all round, walked out, and sat eating them just outside. At this point I emerged from the bathroom for my camera, and distributed some more bananas in the tent. Charlie had just come down from his tree, saw me, and moved a little way up the slope opposite. I then went back to the bathroom. Another couple of minutes and Goliath again walked into the tent (unfortunately, as there was no sun, it was almost pitch dark inside, much too dark for a photograph). He filled the tent with his huge form. For at least a minute he gazed intently at the camera lens, and quite definitely knew I was there. Took his bananas, stood up, looking on the table again, and then went out. He sat up in the "kitchen" eating his haul, quite unconcerned that I sat in my veranda, some 10 yards away, watching him.

So now, as Jane added in an August 9 note to Leonard Carmichael, she had two completely "tame" chimps, David and Goliath. They were her "pals," regularly visiting camp and her tent, looking for whatever tasty things they might find—not only edible bananas but also suckable cloth. One time she found the two males inside her tent, and

I don't think I've ever seen anything so funny in my life. They were both standing, with looks of dreamy contentment in their eyes—Goliath with a rather ancient tea towel hanging from his huge mouth, and David with the cook's apron (his pride and joy) dangling from his bearded lips!! They sat down, reclining, sucking away in ecstasy. Suck, suck, suck. And finally plodded off up the mountain, one after the other, still trailing their prizes along, and stopping, every now and then, to suck again!!

Every bit as remarkable as the apes' absence of fear in Jane's presence, of course, was her lack of fear in theirs. Her casual attitude about them makes it too easy to forget that David and Goliath were extremely strong and quick and, like most chimpanzees, emotionally volatile. Goliath especially had always seemed explosively temperamental. "I wouldn't like him to get angry with me as I've seen him with one of his females," Jane acknowledged in the same August 9 letter. "He's the only male I've observed being really rough with a female. He gets these terrible fits of temper over nothing at all. He is more excited and nervy than any other male when another group of chimpanzees arrives—thumping trees and shaking branches and leaping about and screaming with twice as much intensity as everyone else. He yells at me in exactly the same way!"

The National Geographic had given Jane new photography equipment (camera, lenses, tripod, and film) for her own use, and after her week back in the forest, she dispatched four exposed rolls of film to Washington. By early August the staff had developed and reviewed these preliminary exposures. Robert Gilka, who a year earlier had "always seemed so horrid" (as Jane phrased it for the family in England) "when beastly letters used to come from him saying everything was wrong," now was far less horrid. He wrote, "Your first shipment . . . is the best you've done so far. Good going! In the 4 rolls are the first really readable pictures of the animals in the trees. I feel sure that at least one of David G. will wind up as an illustration in your article, and there is a sequence of one chimp out near the end of a limb, reaching for food, which may also make the grade."

There had been one especially bad moment that summer. Jane had clicked off a number of frames with an excellent view of David and Goliath grooming each other, but the film had been improperly loaded and did not wind. Nonetheless, with that first positive response from Gilka, she could reasonably conclude that "the jinx must be over."

At the same time, David Greybeard was becoming ever more comfortable with Jane and familiar with her camp. On August 17 she was awakened at dawn by the big ape sitting next to her bed and calmly finishing off the banana he had just pilfered from her wooden storage crate. "He IS a devil!" Jane wrote home that same day. "I shooed him off & closed my eyes." Five minutes later, however, she was roused by "a stealthy foot fall." David again. When she shouted at him this time, he hastily left the tent, "spitefully" banging on the table as he went. The day's big event, however, happened around noon, when once again the handsome, white-bearded male wandered into the camp clearing. The moment was, Jane stated enthusiastically, the happiest: the proudest, of my whole life to date. David G—yes—he has TAKEN BANANAS FROM MY HAND. So gently. No snatching. The first time I held one out he stood up & hooted, swayed from one foot to the other, banged the tree, & sat down. So I threw it to him. The next one he came & took. Even when I stand upright he takes them. I even got Dominic to come & get a picture—unfortunately he was just a second too late & D. had taken it from my hand.

In the meantime Hugo van Lawick was making his way down from Nairobi—and mildly anxious about his new situation. He had caught a glimpse of Jane one day in June 1961 when she went to the Denis house in Langata for photographic advice, but she may not have noticed him. And now he may have been wondering, would the two of them, forced into the intimacy of a small camp in a thick forest, get along? Jane's mother, the designated chaperone, was not due to arrive for a couple of weeks.

Hugo had intended to reach Gombe by August 15, but he arrived a few days later. As Jane remembers it, he first saw her coming down from a day partly spent in burned grass, her face blackened as a result. He later told her he thought she had done that deliberately to impress him.

Hugo had also come influenced by rumors, emanating from Sir Solly Zuckerman, that Jane had invented the stories of chimpanzee meat-eating, but within the first week after his arrival he saw an episode of predation and carnivory. Perhaps that was the "most exciting observation" Jane described in her official report to the National Geographic for the end of August, the hunting and killing of an adult colobus monkey:

> Two adolescent chimpanzees caught the prey, one sitting close to the monkey aparantly to attract its attention whilst the second ran swiftly along the branch upon which the monkey sat, leapt at it, and killed it immediately. I was unable to observe exactly how the killing was done, but it was instantianous as there was no sound from the prey. 4 other chimpanzees then climbed into the tree and all but one female got a piece of the carcass. The young male who did the killing was left with the larger share—there was no fighting and almost no sound. The killing was done at 7 A.M.—at 1 P.M. a mature male passed me still with a small piece of meat in his mouth.

Jane soon found the newly arrived photographer to be agreeable, and like her, he was completely dedicated to his work. Naturally, their joint confinement at Gombe required some mutual habituation. He was a heavy smoker, and she disliked his smoking. Hugo did not mind the spartan conditions of the camp, but he was interested in food, whereas she lived on, as he later recalled for me, "pretty well nothing." Yet on the whole, Hugo van Lawick's integration into camp and life at Gombe proceeded smoothly. Jane soon summarized the matter to her friend Bernard Verdcourt: "We are a very happy family. Hugo is charming and we get on very well."

By early September the happy family included Vanne, who arrived with her suitcase "full" (as she wrote home to her brother, Eric) "of gorgeous medicines thanks to you." Vanne concentrated on running the dispensary and other occupations back in camp, while the two young people kept themselves busy with the task of harvesting light.

Jane was taking as many still photographs as she could with her own camera—"very keen," as she expressed it to Verdcourt, "to get as good a photographic record as possible—& we have been incredibly lucky so far." Hugo was not only taking still photographs for the article but also exposing movie film for any future Geographic-sponsored lectures. "But oh dear—" Jane wrote of his task, "what a ghastly paraphernalia to carry around. Tons & tons it seems like. The method is that I find a place where, with luck, the chimps may return, & then the next day I help Hugo get the stuff there. At crack of dawn, we build a rough hide, and I leave him with my blessing and carry on my own observations undisturbed."

Hugo's tripod was made mostly of wood, and he had to lug around that heavy, bulky object along with cameras, several lenses (including a three-foot-long 600mm lens), and metal storage magazines. But the main problem was lack of light. He used film rated at 16 ASA, very slow, and yet often in the forest shadows he was unable to film at all unless he was working up close with a very short lens. A lot of things he simply could not capture on film.

Still, Jane's previous work presented him with a photographer's dream, since the chimps' increasing tameness around her to some degree generalized into a tolerance for Hugo as well. As she wrote to Leonard Carmichael, "The chimpanzees have become so much tamer since last year, and they have accepted the presence of Hugo van Lawick with his tripods and lenses in the most wonderful way. The method I have always followed—never hiding from the chimpanzees, never following them when they have moved away from me, and never appearing particularly interested in them—has, at long last, paid dividends."

Did Hugo appreciate how remarkably she had managed to draw back the veil on the lives of those wild apes? "I hope he realizes how lucky he is," Jane confided to Bernard Verdcourt "—coming now at a time when he can reap the results of my months of patience. If I didn't like him I should hate to think of it!! I am jealous of my chimps!"

· · ·

Robert Gilka wrote separate letters to Hugo and Jane on September 14, declaring that he was especially pleased with one image of Jane handing a banana to David Greybeard in front of their tent. They were "off to a fine start," and he was eager to suggest other sorts of pictures he would like to see.

He hoped Hugo would concentrate on the camp, but it would be especially good if he could get a photograph of Jane standing in the nearby stream and shampooing her hair. It might be a slightly intimate picture (and Gilka expressed a confidential concern in his letter to Jane that Hugo might be "too embarrassed to ask you to do this for him"), but President Grosvenor himself had requested the photograph "because of its 'roughing it' information." Gilka also wanted more of Jane out "in the field," where she should be presented in the posture of "either studying chimps or simulating the study of chimps," in order to give their readers "an idea of the lay of the land and the kind of vegetation there." He asked for more photographs of the African fishermen on the shores of the lake. He hoped they would be sure to capture images of animals other than chimps, such as the Cape buffalo, since pictures of that sort "give us variety and show our readers additional information about the area in which you are studying and the possible dangers in that area." A chimpanzee rain dance would be nearly impossible to photograph, obviously, but Gilka wanted Jane to get some detailed representations of the trees and branches for their staff artist to use in his creation of a rain dance painting. "So, don't conserve film; it's really the cheapest tool with which you are working."

By September 26 Jane had mailed off another package of exposed film along with a response to Gilka's letter. He would soon be looking at the stills of her shampooing her hair, Jane noted, and Hugo was planning to try more sudsy shots in a more forested area. "You needn't worry about him being embarrassed," she added. "I havn't noticed it yet!"

She also remarked that the chimpanzee originally identified as Ugly had been renamed Hugo, since the ape was not ugly and also, when scratching his back on a tree trunk, he would get an expression on his face exactly like Hugo's during moments of intense concentration. The main news, however, was negative. They were going through a "very, very bad spell," photographically speaking, since the fig season had failed, and it was during the appearance of concentrated fruit that the chimpanzees ordinarily congregated, offering the best opportunities for "all the 'intimate' pictures of chimp life." Instead, the unhelpful chimps had disappeared, and as a result she had been able to get "practically nothing."

Four days later things had gotten worse, and Jane wrote to Gilka that there were no more stills to send, because of developments that were "the most frustrating I can think of." She was particularly upset by her recent experience of getting "really in amongst my black hairy friends—20 feet and closer. They stay there, that close, for an hour or more." And yet she had been unable to get any decent pictures. "There are so many twigs and things between them and me that it just isn't worth it, and, into the bargain, it is very dark. I've taken a few black and whites, but not even a complete roll."

Hugo had managed to take several photos of the African fishermen working over their *dagaa*, although the fishermen had angrily demanded five shillings for each picture taken. Jane had gone down to the beach and palavered with them, reminding them that they were all getting free medicine from Vanne when they were ill and offering prints of any close-ups once they were developed, whereupon (Jane reported to Gilka) "their faces lit up." So now, she was asking, would he return a few color prints from the batch of film Hugo had just sent off? "It means so very much to them, most of whom have never seen a photograph of anyone, let alone themselves. In particular the bloke with the net, the ones turning the fish, the one playing the pipe—and any others who have close ups."

Gilka honored the request, and he remained optimistic about the photography. "The picture business is well in hand, so relax on that score," he advised Jane in a return letter.

In fact the magazine staff was by then preoccupied with other matters, one of which was the nagging possibility that Jane's story would soon be old news. When the society had declined Louis's request for £300 to underwrite Judy's photographic efforts in the summer of 1961, he had arranged for an English weekly newspaper, *Reveille,* to finance that fall's sisterly expedition. The English paper thereby acquired first rights to an illustrated article for a popular audience, and Jane and Judy had been interviewed by a *Reveille* reporter when they returned to England in December.

The paper had been slow in releasing the story, though, and in the meantime Jane had read her first scientific paper at the London Zoo symposium, in April 1962, which was attended by several newspaper reporters. Jane and Judy were both, according to Louis's subsequent assessment (in a letter in July), "pestered by pressmen" at the event, and both declined to give interviews. But the symposium chairman, Sir Solly Zuckerman, was not so inhibited, and for a full hour he talked to the press about his own views concerning Miss Goodall and the wild chimpanzees. As result, some "very misleading reports appeared," which "caused Jane great annoyance." Several newspapers in England had printed "fictitious and highly coloured articles," whereupon *Reveille* was moved at last to publish its own three-part series. Meanwhile, the editor of *Reveille* believed he had acquired full syndication rights, and so by June 18, 1962, *Woman's Day* and *Woman* in Australia were releasing their own sensational "Jane and the Apes": the tale of "a real-life Jane, with no Tarzan to help her," who "faced dangerous wild animals and unfriendly natives while living in the African jungle, far from civilisation and her London home."

By the fall of 1962 *Life* magazine had taken up the chase. After a photographer for *Life* failed to get permission from the National Geographic to visit Jane in the field, he wrote to her directly, announcing in October that a note from the Geographic giving him full permission to photograph at Gombe had probably already arrived and he was soon to follow. Jane's father sent her a letter at the same time, declaring that the *Life* person had contacted him as well, and Mortimer believed that Jane would quite like the chap. The enterprising American then appeared in Nairobi at the Coryndon Museum, asking Louis Leakey for directions to Gombe. It was Leakey who at last discouraged the determined photographer from his dogged pursuit.

Vanne left Gombe around the end of October, Hugo on November 4. Approximately a month later, Robert Gilka, satisfied finally with a portfolio showing clear photographic success, turned the Goodall file over to the magazine's editorial department. By December 19, William Graves, from the editorial staff, was writing to Jane, assuring her that "from the photographic standpoint there is more than sufficient material to make a fine layout" and encouraging her to put down camera and take up typewriter. "I'm sure you realize that the process of preparing a story for publication in the Geographic is done with extreme care and that the time involved is considerable," he began diplomatically, before getting to the point: "In short, we need the manuscript from you as soon as you can possibly send it."

Graves reminded Jane of her discussion with Frederick Vosburgh about *Geographic*'s preference for a "first-person, anecdotal type of article which includes not only the remarkable and hitherto-unknown scientific data you have gathered on chimpanzees but also a little of your dramatic personal experiences while making the discoveries. In fact, not a little of the personal drama but a lot." And even though she and Vosburgh had agreed on a 7,500-word manuscript as their "rough goal," Jane ought to realize that more was better than less. An extra one or two thousand words would be ideal.

But on the same day that Graves was composing his letter urging Jane to *hurry up, please*, with the article, she was seated somewhere in the Gombe camp, probably at the table in the open veranda of her tent, typing out her own note to Vosburgh to announce the draft's near completion.

Chimpland.
19 December 1962.

Dear Mr. Vosburgh,

Excuse the frivolous address, but as I shall have left here before I could receive an answer to this letter, my correct postal address seemed unnecessary.

I have nearly finished a first draft of an article for your Magazine. It will, of course, be too long! What I am writing to ask is this: would you prefer me to sit down when I get back to England and reduce it to the approximate length required? Or would you rather first see it as it is so that you can see the sort of material. I feel this might be better—it would be discouraging if all the parts which I decided needed shortening were the very incidents you subsequently might think in need of filling out! (Excuse grammar—It's too late I think). . . .

I expect you will have heard from time to time how well things are going here. The season has been far more profitable than I hoped it could be. Have you also heard that I am returning next year? The family have given up—they imagine that I shall still be coming back to watch chimps when I'm old and tottering. But it's taken so long to get the chimps really used to me that really it's only just starting to be worth while. Well, perhaps that's putting it too strongly. It has occurred to me that this may alter your plans about when the article should be published. If it is decided to hold it over until the end of next year's research—well, the sooner I know the better!

It's too late to wish you a happy Christmas, but I can wish you a very happy New Year.

With best regards,
Jane

22

Intimate Encounters

1963

JANE'S OPTIMISM about completing that article was premature. When she returned to England in the middle of January 1963, rushing from London to Cambridge to locate a place to live for the term, the piece was still unfinished and very much on her mind.

Patience Burne, her adviser at Newnham College, found her a room in a renovated fourteenth-century farmhouse with thatched roof and exposed ceiling beams, in the village of Comberton, a half-dozen miles outside Cambridge. Cross Farm had central heating plus a coal fire and a sitting room, which Jane would share with a married couple. The agreeable landlady, Lyn Newman, kept goats, geese, and sheep in a paddock behind the house, and in a converted dovecote she worked on her own books (her first and at that time only being a popular appreciation of domestic geese, *Field with Geese*). "I am so happy here. I can really work. It is absolutely heaven," Jane was soon writing to Louis Leakey.

During the final week of January she "glued" herself "to my room and typewriter solidly for about a week, and got shingles—but also got the thing into the post yesterday," which was Monday, January 28.

William Graves gave the typescript a quick first read and pronounced it "delightful"—as he wrote immediately to Jane—with "my only suggestion being that you are far too modest in your approach to the subject. As you probably know, Dr. Leakey long ago betrayed you to us by praising your work and its great scientific significance."

Graves soon began expanding on those opinions for the benefit of his colleagues in Washington, declaring that the work was "outstanding . . . not only for its great scientific value but for its sense of drama and poignancy. It combines startling scientific discovery with rare adventure and humor." There was still the small matter of Jane's "modesty"—her unwillingness or inability to point out her own "remarkable courage" as well as the "fantastic significance" of her discoveries and their "potential effect on the whole concept of early man." In the latter category, Graves was thinking particularly about the chimpanzees making and using tools, which Jane had described in some detail yet without making much of what Louis Leakey had previously announced to be its ultimate significance. Thus, Graves concluded, they should ask someone, possibly Leakey himself, to write a prefatory note that would summarize "what an enormous contribution Jane Goodall has made to science and what she risked to do it. These are things she will never say about herself but the things our readers should know right off. It would put a fine article and a courageous act in clearer perspective."

Other readers in the editorial department agreed that the article was beautifully written and exciting and that Jane's unassuming style required an expert of appropriate stature to write some introductory comment. But who would the expert be? "Not Leakey, please," Frederick Vosburgh scribbled emphatically at the bottom of one document circulated during this discussion.

Louis Leakey inadvertently contributed to the debate when, on March 21, he sent a memo to the Geographic's Committee for Research and Exploration stating that Jane's observation that chimpanzees were making and using the termite-fishing tools left scientists with only "two alternatives, either they accept chimpanzees as man, by definition, or else they must redefine 'man.'" He went on to describe the previous summer's conference at the Wenner-Gren castle in Austria, where two dozen internationally known scientists found themselves compelled "to work out a new definition of man, in view of Jane Goodall's discovery. This they did and while the new definition includes the making of tools, it has other criteria as well, thereby eliminating chimpanzees from inclusion in the term 'man.'"

It was an exciting thought, and Graves immediately wrote to Professor Sherwood Washburn for further details and an exact wording on the current definition of *human*. But when Washburn was finally reached by telephone, he replied (according to a written paraphrase of the conversation) that "contrary to Dr. Leakey's memorandum," the Wenner-Gren conference did not even try to agree on the definition of *human*. Miss Goodall had been invited but unfortunately was unable to attend, and although her observations of chimpanzees using tools were received "with great interest," they were nevertheless insufficient "to cause a great scientific revolution in the concept of man." Since anthropologists had been thinking in terms of stone axes or other heavy objects requiring substantial alteration, perhaps it was necessary to reconsider the definition of the word *tool*. Yet altogether, Washburn thought, it was a "mistake" to emphasize those observations of tool use while Jane's study included "such a wealth of material on many varied aspects of chimpanzees' behavior."

The editorial staff at *National Geographic* soon concluded that the chimpanzee tool-using issue had "become too complex"—and also that some expert other than Dr. Leakey should write an introduction to the article. Leonard Carmichael was a logical alternative, and thus he was soon drafting his own three hundred words introducing Jane as a "modern scientific zoologist" and "charming young Englishwoman" who had intrepidly "journeyed into the African forest" to live "alone" for several months among the "powerful and potentially dangerous" chimps, learning in the process many new things about humanity's closest relatives. At great personal risk, she had produced a "unique scientific record."

Back at Cross Farm, meanwhile, Jane was responding to a flurry of editorial suggestions for the article and working on her doctoral dissertation while writing a chapter for a book edited by Irven DeVore. DeVore's book collected the papers presented during the nine-month Primate Project at Stanford; Jane had agreed to contribute by mail her report, "Chimpanzees of the Gombe Stream Reserve." As she wrote to Thomas McKnew at the Geographic on February 4, "I have really got my nose to the grindstone, annalysing my field notes so that I can contribute the chimpanzee chapter to the primate behaviour book which is being written at Stanford. The idea of having to write the whole thing in 2 months is terrible—but nothing can detract from the fascination of annalysing my data. The more I learn and think about chimpanzees the more wonderful they seem!"

But the chapter was long and the term short, and even as the latter ended in mid-March and Jane packed up and left Comberton for a final week's holiday in Bournemouth, she continued feverishly laboring over the former, typing away until two every morning and seeing the family only during an occasional hasty meal. Then one day her most recent romantic attachment, a young man from Cambridge named John King, rang the bell at 10 Durley Chine Road South, briefly met Vanne, and then whisked Jane away to meet his family at their home in Cheshire. John's parents were "extremely pleasant" and "sort of countrified," with a "glorious" pair of Labradors, Jane soon reported back to Vanne, although the family must have been "slightly dazed at the way I vanished upstairs to my typewriter between each meal."

John escorted her to Gatwick airport for her March 25 flight to Nairobi, and on the theory that it would make the young couple less miserable, his parents went along. They gave Jane "large kisses" as she left for the plane, and John vowed to see her again as soon possible. He was already making plans for a trip to Africa.

At the back of the plane, Jane found an empty pair of seats she could luxuriate in by herself, but she was far too excited to sleep. "Thoughts, thoughts, thoughts," she scribbled, ballpoint pen on a thin sheet of paper in front of her. "Lectures, dominance, John, Hugo, dominance, undone map, etc., etc." The Stanford book chapter was still incomplete, and her developing intimacy with John was now a problem as well. The flight landed at Entebbe and took off again, tracing a bumpy trajectory in the direction of Nairobi, and while a large woman dressed in pale mauve seated nearby vomited into her airsickness bag, Jane finally resolved to level with poor Hugo, to tell him about John immediately. But in Nairobi, once she saw Hugo—with that bright, hopeful smile on his face—she realized it could not be done that way. Also, Hugo had just done a thoughtful and generous thing: he had taken her old gray dress from its storage wardrobe and replaced it with "two simply exquisite dresses" from Holland.

Regarding the problem of Hugo's romantic expectations, Jane informed the family back home that "the situation worsens hourly—but my mind is made up. Well, it very definitely is at the moment."

After a couple of days in Nairobi, much of it spent reworking the Stanford chapter before dropping it into the mail, Jane traveled to Dar es Salaam and gave a short lecture to the Tanganyika Society. Then, on the two-day train from Dar to Kigoma, she caught up on her correspondence, worked on photographic captions for the *Geographic* article, and continued to worry about her romantic entanglements. John was ascendant, Hugo descendent, and the latter's persistence, she now thought, was bound to have an increasingly negative influence within the intimate confines of camp. Of course, "the situation can't be tense all the time," and she and Hugo would strike "some sort of working compromize." But the end of their time together, she could imagine, might become "quite ghastly."

Dominic had maintained a research presence at Gombe while Jane was in England, and now she returned—stepping out of the little aluminum boat onto Kasekela's pebble shore—to find he had done just "splendidly" (as she reported home), having recorded chimpanzee events in a daily log while collecting chimp dung in jars. Hugo arrived soon after, along with the camp manager, Hassan Salimu, and a new cook, Anyango, whose culinary contribution would allow Dominic a few weeks' holiday. Rashidi Kikwale also returned from his home in Mwamgongo village. With everyone reunited, the tents reerected, and the machinery of camp life restarted, Jane and Hugo prepared to resume chimp-watching, photographing, and filming.

It was near the end of the rainy season, which meant that the lake was still high and the grass thick. There were wet and blustery days, even a few downright chilly ones. But Jane found, while out following chimps one "grey cold day," that she could change the weather. "By using a vivid imagination," she explained to the family, "I was able to hunch my back, close my eyes, and slowly the sun came out, warming my back with its happy glow. But when I chanced to open my eyes—cold grey clouds enveloped me again, and the shy sun hid his face with miraculous speed." And she was soon able to report that "the most fantabulous things are happening here"—frequently back in camp. While she was in England, several of the chimps had continued coming into the camp clearing, enticed by that wonderfully reliable food resource: bananas. So now Hugo set up his tripod and motion-picture camera right there, and the neighborhood was photogentrified by the removal of small trees and bushes and the dispersal of the kitchen and *choo* (latrine).

As Jane could read in Dominic's report, the chimps who came into camp for bananas had also found other good things. Goliath, for instance, had one time grabbed two squawking chickens, run up a tree, and eaten them. Another time, William had pushed a hen off her nest and snatched her eggs, popping them into his mouth. Jane read the egg-stealing account on the very day she noticed some black weaverbirds building their baggy nests in the camp palm tree. Within two days, after they had nearly finished the job while Hugo had filmed the process, an "evil minded" Jane (as she described herself in a letter home) made the connection: "Wouldn't it be wonderful," she mentioned to Hugo, "if William, when the palm tree is ripe, happened to notice those nests?"

Soon after, Hugo was filming some of the camp's usual events—David and Goliath greeting each other, Mr. McGregor yelling and catching thrown bananas, baboons aggressively challenging William—when he observed Goliath gazing up in the direction of the weaver nests in the palm tree, an excited state of mind signaled by lofting body hair.

With lightning speed the cameraman rushed to get the fronds in silhouette—Got the murderer climbing the trunk, pulling down a frond, hand over hand, and then, very carefully, with two fingers, feeling inside the nest on the end. He then repeated the process, let the fronds swing back, the nests undisturbed, and climbed down. Wasn't it super! The birds have not deserted, and we now see a contemplative expression come over Goliath's face when he looks at the nests—the same sort of expression you see on the face of a housewife when she gazes towards the kitchen where her cake is in the oven, and looks at her watch. "When will it be done". In fact yesterday when Goliath returned he sat resting in a tree, one foot dangling down, gazing with delighted anticipation at the little nests whose owners are working so industriously to provide the rapacious creature with a tasty h'oerdoevre (the effect of that sentence, I fear, is sadly lost by my inability to spell this common culinary dish!).

The close friendship of David and Goliath continued to amaze Jane, and she soon observed them inside a thickly overgrown area holding hands, then tickling and chasing each other in circles, wrestling, and laughing in apparent delight. This sequence of events happened one day after she had followed the pair across a stream and into a dense thicket.

David lay on his back under a low tangle of vines. Goliath flung himself beside him. After a moment I saw they were holding hands. They began to play with each other's fingers — at first gently, then more actively. And after about 4 minutes they began to wrestle. There they were, two old gents (and I believe now that David is much older than I suspected) playing about like two year olds, roaring with laughter and tickling each other in the ribs. After a couple of minutes David couldn't stand it any longer and with a final guffaw he jumped up and ran round in a half circle. Goliath followed a little way and then sat to eat a reed. Then David sat down by a sapling with open space round it. Quite light. Goliath once more flung himself at D's feet and sprawled, face down. Suddenly he put one hand on D's foot and held it. D at once put a hand on G's hand. And the fun began all over again. I got one picture — oh how I hope it comes out — of David sitting up, leaning slightly back, head thrown back, and simply shrieking with laughter whilst Goliath, almost hidden behind, tickled under his arms. Twice again D broke away and ran in a circle — and twice again the playing started with holding hands and playing with each other's fingers. It was so completely fantastic that I simply couldn't believe it was actually happening.

The emotional intimacy of these two friends inevitably melded into an important political alliance. They supported each other, protected each other, fought alongside each other — in aggressive encounters with the baboons, for example. And as Jane soon realized, Goliath would come to David's aid even when it was, by her reckoning, unnecessary. David by then would accept Jane's touch: an occasional, careful, chimpish grooming. But once she stretched out her hand to groom David's back when Goliath was present, resting on the ground about 20 yards distant. Hugo, who was quietly stationed farther away and filming the apes, suddenly shouted, "Look out!" And Jane looked up to see Goliath advancing, body bulked up and hair standing out, eyes wide-open. "It was like an apparition in a nightmare!" she wrote home. "I have never seen him look so huge." She took her hand away, and Goliath returned to his resting spot. But then she thought to experiment and began grooming David once again, whereupon "at once G rose & advanced threateningly, & went back again when I stopped."

As Jane and Hugo enticed more and more chimps into camp with bananas that spring, they were suddenly blessed with a thousand opportunities for close observations and images and at the same time cursed with a hundred potential catastrophes. Soon as many as twenty chimpanzees were daily emerging from the trembling trees and dark thickets and slouching along the path, while the local baboons were starting to show up as well. Chimpanzees are immensely strong and quick, and their flexible shoulders and long reach give them the capacity to grab and punch and pummel as well as bite and tear; but baboons, especially the big males (twice the size of adult females), with their doggish snouts and long, sharp, dagger-shaped canines, can also be very formidable foes.

One day Hugo managed to get some excellent footage of a fight between three big chimps—David, Goliath, and William—and some big baboons. Then, while the three apes withdrew into a tree, Jane and Hugo tried to drive away the aggressive monkeys by hurling stones. Hugo yelled threateningly and ran toward the worst of the lot, chasing him into a position right below the tree where the three apes were perched. Unfortunately, the chimps must have interpreted Jane and Hugo's behavior as a threat against them, and they became enraged. "At once, with screams of excitement," Jane wrote to her friend Bernard,

> the 3 swung down. David was really mad. He came for me, mouth open, upright. I ran round the tent—he after. Luckily, he tripped over a guy rope! I dived into the bathroom—he followed. I went into the tent & held the flaps closed. Obviously he was not really serious 'cos he could have pulled them open! Hugo, meanwhile, had been charged by G (who doesn't much like him anyway). He rushed into his tent which luckily has mosquito netting which closes with a zip. He closed it—the chimps were very puzzled by this. G stopped—then ran back to my tent where David was about to go in again, having gone round to the front. Hugo peeked out & thinking I'd had it if Goliath joined David, he emerged & threw a stone. Unfortunately this <u>hit</u> G who turned & came after him full speed. Hugo just got back into his tent in time. This time William joined in. (Before he had been having a private fight with a baboon!) Goliath hit one of the tent poles & climbed halfway up the next—there are two in the veranda. Then the two glared at Hugo, hair out, through the net. Hugo had the bright idea of offering Wm his greatest treat—he got an egg & put it out, in his hand, under the netting. William's whole expression

changed, his hair fell, & he took the egg gently. This calmed G. David, meanwhile, got tired of keeping me at bay in the bathroom & wandered out. Cautiously, Hugo & I emerged. David approached—I greeted him. He peered into an empty box. Rather apprehensively I picked up the box & walked past G who was on the path, glaring. No reaction. Of course, they all followed, & arrived just as the big banana box had been opened! We did not dare stop them—they had a hell of a feast!

The camp was also attracting rats, who collected food in Jane's tent and carried it over to Hugo's tent, where they were trying to build nests. Jane and Hugo used a snake bag to catch one of the rodents, intending to kill him, when suddenly "bingo—it was out! Like an arrow it rushed back to my tent!"

But baboons were the real nuisance, and Jane was starting to see the brash, brawling monkeys rather as the chimps did. True, she had named some of the baboons—and in doing so, she often honored her National Geographic friends and correspondents. There was baboon McKnew (after Thomas McKnew, vice chairman of the board), baboon Poggenpohl (art editor Andrew Poggenpohl), and baboon Silcott (Phillip B. Silcott, with whom she had been corresponding about photographic captions). But at the same time she was increasingly upset with them. Not only were they fighting with the chimps, but soon they were going after weaverbirds as well. Jane heard a crashing outside her tent one day and emerged to find that the baboons had destroyed three of the nests, along with the eggs. "To hell with them," she wrote home angrily.

By the end of May and the start of June, some of the baboons had become so pushy that they were displacing the chimps. Jane was particularly incensed with baboon McKnew, who, intimidated by the alliance of Hugo and Goliath, had been going after the sweet adolescent chimp Evered. "Honestly, if you'd seen McKnew yesterday threatening Evered," she wrote home, "going right up & keeping on opening his mouth in a threat yawn in the little fellows face & hitting bushes at him. Just taking it out on him because he couldn't cope with Hugo & Goliath together."

Within a decade the Gombe baboons, with their distinctive personalities and remarkable social lives, would seem as personally and scientifically interesting as the chimps, but for now Jane's sympathies were decidedly with the chimps. Meanwhile, after reading her description of how the contretemps with baboons provoked some chimps into a violent attack against humans, the Geographic's executive vice president, Melvin Payne, expressed his serious concern. "I know you have complete confidence in your friends, but I have a continuing apprehension that they may suffer a momentary lapse and forget their friendship with you," he wrote to Jane on May 28. "There is, of course, always some risk involved in a field study of this nature, but I urge you and Hugo not to take chances by way of experimentation which might inflame the chimps and cause them to harm either of you."

Jane hastened to reassure Payne. "I know you think that I am rather foolhardy in my attitude to the chimpanzees. In actual fact, although I do have implicit trust in David Greybeard, I do not have this trust for the other chimpanzees at all." She noted that she actually mistrusted Goliath a lot. "I have never pretended a friendship with him. He is slightly mad and not very intelligent." She wished, therefore, to stress that she and Hugo would continue to "take great care not to alarm or provoke him in any way."

Of course, Goliath had already been alarmed and provoked by that stone thrown by Hugo, and the enormous ape now held a grudge against the smallish man, chasing him a number of times in subsequent weeks. Finally Hassan traveled to Kigoma and oversaw the construction of a metal cage as a protective retreat. The cage, Jane wrote in a July 20 letter to Payne, was "foolproof." It had two doors and a forward projection with some netting to drop in front of Hugo's cameras. In an emergency, he could "nip into the cage and close the door."

In early July, Gombe hosted its first visitor from the National Geographic Society, Joanne Hess, who, as secretary for the society's lecture committee, was partly responsible for overseeing production of a film made to accompany Jane's public appearances and lectures (planned to take place after the publication of her article). Louis's son Richard chartered a plane in Nairobi and flew with her down to Kigoma. Gombe was "beautiful," as Richard once recalled, and he was "tremendously pleased to have the experience of going there." Joanne Hess spent a full and exciting day there; more than twenty chimps appeared in camp, and Jane noted in a subsequent letter to one contact at the Geographic that she believed "Joanne enjoyed her visit here." Apparently Richard did as well, but he returned to Nairobi with some critical opinions, which were communicated to his father.

In a letter to Jane written on August 21 — typed, "to be sure you can read it" — Louis registered his profound concern. Not only were the people in danger from the chaos wrought by banana feeding in camp, he thought, but ultimately the chimpanzees were as well, since if a person was seriously injured, surely "some interfering officer" from the police or Game Department would be ready to shoot a chimp. Louis emphasized that he "felt desperately and I still feel that you must not take any risks because of your desire to get the best possible information and pictures." Also, he argued compellingly, Jane's own safety was ultimately vital to the welfare of the chimps.

Jane was stung by Louis's expressed concern and implied criticism. He had never visited Gombe, and it seemed unfair that he should criticize her based on limited information from others. "If only you came you would see for yourself that things are not as Joanne and Richard painted them," she wrote. "If you could only SEE my chimps for yourself. O.K.—we didn't quite know how to cope when 20 chimps arrived, the first couple of times," but now "there is not the slightest danger of anything happening at all. I mean that."

The cage, she assured Louis, was not so much "a means of escape" but more a method of "removing temptation from the chimps—if they get excited we do not have to try and get out of their way." As for the safety of the chimps, "Louis, can you really think that I honestly havn't thought and thought about the safety of my chimps?" She had already had discussions with the Game Department over a plan to keep the fishermen's temporary huts away from Kasekela beach, as a way of reducing potential conflict between apes and humans; and for the long term, she had decided, the way to protect the chimps and their forest would be to make Gombe "pay just a little" through tourism. Tourists coming to see the chimps.

"So," she summarized optimistically, "all is planned. The attraction is provided—the chimps themselves. Their safety is planned." Moreover, she intended to put all the money she made from the lecture film back into the reserve. It would be enough to build a small hut for visitors, perhaps four at a time, down by the lake. A covered walkway would lead from the hut to an observation cage, and she would hire a scout to inform any visitors when the chimps had come. "Louis," she pleaded finally, "you had faith in me when the whole project was seemingly hopeless and futile (to me). Do not suddenly lose it just when things are better than I ever dared to hope. The results I am getting now are the sort of things I never dreamed of getting."

The provisioning of chimpanzees with bananas at Gombe would long be a target of criticism, some of it reasonable, much of it ill-informed. But since no one else had succeeded in studying wild chimpanzees to the degree that Jane had already done, there were no alternative examples to consider.

George Schaller had managed to get close to wild gorillas in Uganda and the eastern Belgian Congo without feeding them, but gorillas are temperamentally far more sedate than chimps. Adriaan Kortlandt had watched chimpanzees at Beni in the eastern Congo from inside a series of stationary blinds, but those animals had moved into the clearing only to feed on cultivated papayas and bananas. The chimps, in other words, were lured by provisioning even before Kortlandt arrived. And the Japanese, in the summer of 1963, were still trying to habituate wild chimpanzees in a number of ways. They eventually succeeded in the Mahale Mountains through provisioning with sugarcane.

Jane's inclination had always been to "tame" the wild chimpanzees as one might tame a wild bird. Reduce distance. Gain trust. Offer food. Intuitively, she moved to achieve an intimate connection with her chimps: to participate in their lives and perhaps thereby to follow her childhood dream of living close to nature and wild animals in the style of Doctor Dolittle. Following such dreams and intuitions fortunately happened to converge with reasonable science. Nothing about Jane's provisioning approach was egregiously unorthodox or blatantly unscientific. Provisioning, in fact, fit perfectly well into the manipulative traditions of European ethology and was, for example, arguably far less drastic than Konrad Lorenz's practice of imprinting wild geese as a prelude to studying them.

A few later critics would suggest that banana-feeding made the Gombe chimpanzees more aggressive than they would otherwise have been. While that may well have been true locally and temporarily—the result of a new and rich resource suddenly appearing in a circumscribed area, an ape's Klondike—in the long term it was not. The banana-feeding regimen was never substantially different, ecologically, from a prolific, unusually reliable fruit tree in the forest; and later studies now offer us the comparative perspective, demonstrating that chimpanzees across Africa, whether provisioned or not, develop similar social systems and display similar styles and levels of violence.

In any event, the bananas were a great draw during the spring and summer of 1963, and they had the important effect of accelerating habituation and bringing in some of the more fugitive members of the chimpanzee community, particularly females, adolescents, and youngsters. Just as Karl von Frisch had opened his beehive for observation by putting in a glass side, so Jane's banana-feeding ultimately created a window on the forest, allowing her to peer effectively into the otherwise occult social lives of her chimpanzees. Banana-feeding moved her observations beyond the occasionally rich if serendipitous encounter with one or a few individuals. It soon brought up close a much larger cast, an expanded dramatis personae of Gombe, and it provided the opportunity for a whole series of wonderfully detailed portraits, close observations, and intimate encounters.

"My chimps. Honestly Lyn, I just cannot believe it is all true, these days," Jane declared in an August 4 letter to Lyn Newman, her Cross Farm landlady.

I can't write out, on paper, all the fantastic things I am learning about their social behavior. We now have 21 regular visitors to camp! This means that for the first time I can get continuity in my observations. Up in the mountains it is lucky if you can see the same two together more than once or twice in a fortnight, and even a month. Now things are simply too perfect. We even have walkie talkies (a very recent acquisition with which we are childishly thrilled) so that I can rush down from the mountains when an interesting group appears in camp, or near camp.

But it was not the results, the scientific data, that she found thrilling, Jane insisted. "It is the chimps. More and more they amaze me. I used to think that I knew at any rate <u>something</u> about them. I now know that I knew next to nothing. They cannot be thought of as animals—they just cannot."

She had even found, Jane continued, that the males had

a sort of "gang warfare" system! Goliath was sitting with us one day—suddenly all his hair came out, his eyes nearly started out of his head, and he got up and rushed away down the path and out of sight. . . . We looked in the direction he had been staring—and there, like a group of vile Teddy Boys, were Hugo (a chimp!), Hugh and Mr. Worzle. They stood, glaring down at us, rushed up, straight past us, and after Goliath. At the corner they stood, lost . . . and, after searching in the bushes, came for bananas. About 10 mins later we suddenly saw Goliath. He had been in a big circle and was up a tree half way up the opposite slope, hiding and peeping down at the gang. He was there for a whole hour, just watching—once Hugo moved out for some reason—Goliath at once climbed down so as not to be seen.

And yet the really exciting observations that spring and summer, Jane thought, focused on mothers and their young. Since several males ordinarily mated with a single female during her fertile times, paternity was never obvious for the human observers at Gombe. Probably not for the chimpanzees either. The adult males would sometimes move with the females and adolescents, sometimes even play with the young, but they tended to prefer each other's company, making the females and their dependent offspring the important family unit. And now Jane was getting some wonderful extended observations of such families. There was, for example, the mother Olly—"a dear old soul. Quite hideous, but in a gentle kind of way—the poor thing has a huge goitre (probably) on her neck"—with her "darling little daughter of about 1 year," named Gilka (in honor of Robert Gilka from the Geographic). Also her older offspring, Evered, who may have been seven or eight years old. Evered was "quite independent. But loves to go around with

Mum and small sister from time to time. He really loves his sister, and spends hours playing gently with her. So does Olly."

Then there was Flo, "the most hideous old bag in Chimpland," as Jane put it. Flo was "small, all out of proportion, and skinny. She has spindly legs, a large piece torn out of one ear and a beak of a nose that makes her look like some prehistoric stone age woman." She was at once among the ugliest, by human standards, and sexiest, based on the behavior of the males, of Gombe's females. And now Flo was toodling in regularly with her offspring in tow or hanging on: "3 year old Fifi and naughty clever little 6 year old Figan." Jane considered this a "fairly close family, always together." Fifi displayed "an unusual amount of affection for her mother," and even though she had grown to be nearly as big as Flo, she continued suckling until the end of July. Flo was "a rather spoiling sort of parent for she still allows the great lump [Fifi] to ride about on her back."

Some two weeks before, however, such tranquil scenes of domesticity had been shaken by a major tremor. Flo began cycling into estrus, evidenced by her first sexual swelling since, apparently, the conception of Fifi, some three to four years earlier. Flo's condition became a big red flag attracting a large number of absurdly excited males. Jane elaborated on the dramatic events in her letter to Lyn Newman:

At this point I should interrupt myself to say that Flo, despite being so almost incredibly ugly, has what is vulgarly known as "it". The boys just love her. The prize greeting (which is filmed) was between Flo and David. Flo arrived. Hugo, Goliath and David immediately dashed up. Hugo embraced her. Goliath embraced her. Then, lastly, her very best boy friend David. He also flung his arms around her—then, very deliberately, "kissed" one nipple, reached round, and tweaked the other!!! Anyway—that is Flo. And so, when she became really "interesting" she acquired an enormous following. It was she who introduced to our "banana club" so many new members. . . . The second day of her swelling she staggered wearily into camp after lunch, just longing for a banana. Rushing after came the bald headed Mr. McGregor, Mr. Worzle, Huxley (who has just got a blind eye), Hugh, Humphrey, Charlie, Mike and Ben—not to mention Hugo, Goliath and, of course, David Greybeard. Poor thing—they wouldn't leave her alone. The most superb courtship displays, dancing upright, swaying from side to side, hair out, arms swinging. She obliged—anything for a bit of peace—but little Fifi couldn't stand it. She followed her mother about like a little vengeful shadow—just let one of those men dare make advances to her Mum. And up she rushed, jumped onto Flo's back, and pushed and pushed with all her might. Sometimes she succeeded in interrupting things—at which

the male moved off as though he couldn't care less, leaving Flo scratching in a rather frustrated way—after all, she had waited 3½ years!

While Flo was enjoying or enduring those intimate encounters, Jane herself
was becoming the object of increasingly intense interest. For one thing, the
National Geographic staff had begun to recognize just what an exceptional
article they were about to publish, and President Grosvenor decided that
the magazine should give everyone associated with that "magnificent" article more money than had originally been agreed upon. Jane's remuneration
"should not be less than" $7,000, he insisted in an internal memo, while
Hugo would receive $3,500 for his photographs and Louis Leakey $2,500
for the "encouragement of Jane Goodall and the coaching he gave her in
the production of this article." Even with that significantly increased sum,
Grosvenor continued, they were still paying Miss Goodall less than Sir Vivian
Fuchs received for his account of a two-thousand-mile journey across Antarctica. "Yet this young woman's feat in studying these chimpanzees under
these conditions is no less dangerous or unique."

Geographic's August edition had gone to press by the middle of June, and
by July 5 Mary Griswold was composing a congratulatory note to Jane and
Hugo: "The big day has finally arrived!" The issue was printed and bound,
she informed them enthusiastically, and an advance copy was on its way.
Griswold also cautioned them that even though it seemed "unlikely your
chimp companions will tip our hand to other magazines," the two humans
should nevertheless "keep [their advance copy of the] Magazine and its contents confidential until after the issue has been mailed out generally."

The desire both to maintain confidentiality in the summer of 1963 and to
make the biggest possible splash was natural—and unpleasantly frustrated
by the surprise appearance in July of a *Harper's Magazine* article, written by
the journalist John Pfeiffer and revealing (as an unhappy July 26 missive
from *Geographic* staff member Franc Schor phrased it to Jane) "the most
important parts of your article."

Pfeiffer had originally represented himself to the society and to Louis as
wishing to visit the Leakey family excavations for research on "a book about
prehistoric man," and he "did not stop to think" (as he later phrased it in an
abject apology to Louis and Mary) that the agreement might not "also apply
to Goodall's work." Jane had given him an interview in Cambridge after
glancing at "one or two documents—unfortunately, I can't remember what
they were—which convinced me he was genuine." She spoke mostly about
things she had already revealed in her two scientific lectures: chimpanzee
feeding and nest-building.

But Pfeiffer had also interviewed others, including Sir Solly Zuckerman, and now Jane, feeling betrayed, was working herself up into an uncharacteristic rage: "Is there nothing that one can do about it?" she wrote to Schor. "Anything I can do? I would love to fight him to the death. I am really mad about it—in fact, one could almost say . . . 'She has been with her chimps too long'—because I feel like tearing out his hair, and things like that."

Yet in spite of such occasional, peculiar intrusions from the outside world, life at Gombe that July continued at a pace steady and serene. It was chimps during the day, and then after dark (once the apes had retreated to the trees, woven their nests, crawled inside), it was eating meals, listening to news on a whistling radio, and then quietly sitting by the fire, warmed by flames and embers and bathed in the indecipherable conversations of insects. At such times, Jane wrote home, the bigger world outside seemed "so far and remote, and our conversation is mostly—chimp—chimp—and more chimp. Hugo loves them as much as I do, and we have got some simply wonderful film as a result."

Their advance copy of *National Geographic* finally arrived, and Jane was able to pull back those golden covers and contemplate her early years of labor at Gombe, so agonizing and passionately pursued then, so miraculously represented now by a parade of small print and big pictures, thirty-seven glossy pages long.

Unfortunately, some of the color reproductions were a disappointment. As she wrote to Lyn Newman, at first they were "simply horrified by the pictures. We have got a bit more used to them now—but the quality, when compared with that of black and white, does give one a shock." Still, discounting a few technical problems in reproduction, the photographs gave an unprecedented glimpse into the forest world of wild chimpanzees, and they succeeded as the visual yin to a textual yang.

Jane's text demonstrated unmistakably that for all her understated stylistic tone, the work at Gombe amounted to a major scientific breakthrough, while the photographs revealed a softer but more startling aspect. First, they conveyed how close she had gotten to the wild creatures. They were sauntering into her camp. Snatching bananas out of her hand. Accepting her touch. The photos also suggested, with fair accuracy, Jane's personal courage and casual vulnerability. She was young, slight, pretty, female, and she exposed herself to the tropical elements with bare arms and bare legs and, on her feet, mere black-and-white sneakers, or no shoes at all. Finally, the photos effectively communicated a mood. They expressed how Jane felt, which can be described as embracing or experiencing a romantic closeness to nature. Indeed, the article opened with the most serenely romantic image of all, a two-page spread bled to the edges: Jane wrapped in a blanket and writing notes in a barely visible booklet or journal, warmed by the flickering tongues of a small campfire before her, softly illuminated and silhouetted by a lake and sky, silvery blue and yellow-streaked gray, beyond. Altogether, the article was a great success, creating a story both personal and scientific while establishing Jane Goodall as one of the magazine's great icons. Only in context, perhaps, did the negative side of the bargain with *National Geographic* become apparent.

Context. The feature article for that August issue was not Jane's but rather "The Magic Worlds of Walt Disney," a long and forgettable piece on an entertainer's secrets for generating popular fantasy. More generally, *National Geographic*'s own urge to entertain, its deliberate pursuit of popularity — through bright colors, posed tableaux, smiling exoticisms, and a long-standing editorial policy of avoiding controversy or advocacy — kept it frequently, during the postwar years, in danger of becoming little more than golden-edged furniture for middle-class American households. Still, from an accountant's point of view, *Geographic*'s editorial strategy was terrifically successful, having by the summer of 1963 attracted some 3 million subscribing members and perhaps at least that many readers, or lookers; and one might justify the magazine's approach as an egalitarian attempt at accomplishing the society's original mission, which was "the increase and diffusion of geographical knowledge," with *geographical* understood very broadly.

In any case, the pictorial style and editorial character of *National Geographic* may have been ideally suited to presenting Jane's story, since it combined breakthrough science with an uncommonly entertaining life, and she could only be grateful for the society's steady financial support, as well as that final bonus of celebrity.

At the very end of the month, the National Geographic Society mailed out to its regular subscribers 3 million gleaming, gold-framed copies of the August issue, enough magazines to pile a stack 15 miles high, and Jane's celebrity began. Soon she was receiving messages from readers and lookers all over the world, people who were piqued or inspired by the article and who now hoped to provoke a small but possibly intimate encounter with Jane of the Apes.

An older man from California noted that the image of chimpanzees making and using tools "hit" him, although "being a Catholic priest, 40 yrs, and besides, having been Chaplain of big Chicago State Hospital for 'INSANE' for 13 yrs maybe I notice things out of line faster." He was moved to question the state of Jane's soul: "I thought to myself, gee here is a beautiful young lady, brains, ability, plenty God given talents, HOW MUCH DOES SHE GIVE 'GOD' IN RETURN??? ... You are working hard for your

Doctor of Philosophy, how hard are you working for YOUR CROWN IN HEAVEN??"

A woman from Connecticut wrote to say that she had "been conducting cancer research on my own body and have subjected myself to a great number of tests and experiments." At this point, she had "endangered my health to such an extent, that I am now fighting for survival to complete my work." Her "only hope in this battle" was to find out the exact names of the eighty-one different kinds of chimpanzee foods referred to in the article.

"Whenever I think of Africa and Apes," a young man from Pennsylvania declared, "a funny feeling charges up and down my spine." In the forest behind his home, he liked to "dive through the trees free as an Ape." He had also built some high platforms in the trees, where he sometimes slept at night; and now he had decided that after graduation from high school he would go to Africa and live among the apes, just as Jane was doing. In such a way, the apes would learn to accept him as their own. He was sure not to "have much trouble following them because I am built like one. After I get in contact with them I could get cameras and other equipment and record their habits and daily life."

A young woman from Lima, Peru, wrote that her heroes since childhood had been the great ethologists Konrad Lorenz and Niko Tinbergen. She had earned a B.A. in psychology from Reed College in the United States, and since the *National Geographic* article had "kindled the fire within me to new dimensions," she was wondering whether Jane would like an assistant. "Miss Goodall," she implored, "if there is but the remotest possibility [of a job] I'll be delighted to hear from you and give you any amount of information about myself—I can understand you'd want to know as much as possible before being stuck with me somewhere out in the sticks. I am sure that you would not be sorry but you have no way of knowing this. I am a keen observer and love to 'rough it' and am convinced that I could be a great help to you."

Desmond Morris sent his congratulations on the article. So did Stanley Schofield, Jane's old film-producing boss in London, who also wanted to know, "Is there any chance of accompanying you on your next trip?" Sir Julian Huxley, the distinguished zoologist and grandson of the famous Victorian biologist T. H. Huxley, made the same request. Malcolm MacDonald, the son of Britain's first Labour Party prime minister, himself a former MP and cabinet minister and now Kenya's governor-general, wrote to say he had been so astonished by the article that he was going to have it bound in leather and placed in a position of honor on his bookshelf; and he invited Jane and Hugo—Flo, too, if she could make it—to stay with him next time they passed through Nairobi. The influential German zoologist Bernhard

Grzimek also wrote, proposing to collaborate with the filmmaker Alan Root in making a movie of Jane's work at Gombe. He believed they could "succeed in our country to raise quite a lot of money for scientific research and conservation in East Africa, preferably in Tanganyika."

Grzimek's letter was alarming, actually, since his plan was already in process with support from the Tanganyikan government, while Hugo was racing to finish his own Gombe film for the National Geographic Society. As Hugo described the situation to a contact at the society on September 1,

> I hope this illustrates how great the interest in a chimp film is, for Dr. Grzimek is not the only one trying to enter the Reserve. I trust the Society realises this. I will have spent nearly a year of my life here and I was willing to do this on the conviction that I could prove to the Society it would be well worth while to put this film into world wide distribution. We <u>may</u> be able to keep out photographers for a short while, but certainly not for long. This country is screaming for money and tourist publicity. It boils down to the fact that if we do not get this film onto the market soon in the very near future we will fish behind the net.

"Since the publication of the August issue," Jane declared on the same day to her own Geographic correspondent, "a number of journalists, photographers, and even a writer, have done their best to come to the Reserve." Meanwhile, editors from a number of major publishing houses in the United States and England had dashed off letters and telegrams, saying things like "Your fascinating account of life among the chimpanzees leads me to believe that the subject might serve as a basis for a popular book."

So it went. So the ceaseless clamor and desire of the world, the human world, began arriving at Gombe that summer. Jane did her best to put it off and away. With the help of Louis in Nairobi and Melvin Payne in Washington, who corresponded strategically with various Tanganyikan officials, the determined Dr. Bernhard Grzimek was discouraged. The enterprising journalists and photographers were, one by one, turned away. And the importuning book editors were, in a couple of cases, put on hold. As Jane wrote on November 27 to Paul Brooks, an editor at Houghton Mifflin Company, her eventual American publisher,

> As regards a book—I really and honestly can't tell you anything about that just at the moment. I feel quite helpless about it. I had a letter from Geographic Society (because a number of publishers wrote them to ask about the possibility of a book) suggesting that I should make no commitments at present because there was the possibility that the Society

might want to publish a book. This I should not be happy about for various reasons, but if they really insist there is little I can do about it, being,
as I am, indebted to them so greatly. However, when I have sorted things
out a bit more I will contact you again.

Jane's newfound celebrity would never seem to end, nor would the
clamor and desire of the human world; and that fading year, 1963, turned
out to be Jane's last really private and peaceful moment in the forest, the last
time she could expect to savor such sweet solitude and the surprising and
sometimes intimate encounters with her beloved chimpanzees.

23

Love and Romance,
Passion and Marriage

1963–1964

VANNE WAS NO LONGER described as a chaperone by anyone, and so her official status (though still underwritten by the National Geographic Society) had become ambiguous by the time she saw Nairobi airport through the clouds on Wednesday, July 10, 1963. By three o'clock in the afternoon she had deplaned and been met by Louis Leakey. She had dinner with him, "slept like a top" in her downtown hotel, and the next day shopped "nonstop," checking items off a list Jane had prepared.

Several days later Vanne found the little camp at Kasekela to be "just exactly the same as ever," she reported to the family after a dinner of sausage and banana fritters, typing away in the flickering light of a pressure lamp surrounded by fluttering insects. "The sun rises over the hills, the chimps come and then don't come, and with their coming and going spirits lift and fall." Dominic, as usual, had his share of *pombe*, the local brew, and became "mildly merry," and Hassan, in his new tent, was the same dignified and reliable man "as he will be for ever and ever." Anyango, the new cook, was "anxious to please," and of course the dispensary patients "roll up for their medicines."

Perhaps the family in England was most curious about Jane's love life, and Vanne was at first cautious in her assessment: "I don't think Jane has made up her mind—I haven't asked her," she wrote. And she found herself assessing their camera-toting camp-mate coolly, in the analytical manner of a potential mother-in-law: "Hugo is if anything the more philosophical of the two this year & is full of beans," but "I want to see more of Hugo to find out which is the real Hugo—the worried moody creature of last year or the buoyant, successful one of this!"

After a few days, though, Vanne was reporting that Jane and Hugo were "very happy with each other, and Jane is calm and happy. They discuss work and work and more work, and really and truly look very happy together. Jane is calm with Hugo and Hugo is good tempered all the time." As for John King, Jane's handsome prince from Cambridge, he was "OUT — absolutely and completely." John had "written some VILE letters," as Vanne put it, and Jane was now saying that she knew "as soon as she left England that he was no good."

Vanne summarized the situation this way: "Hugo therefore has lasted longer than all the others in that his charm has survived a flit to England, a long separation and then a further stretch in Chimpland."

Vanne was still working on her novel, a romantic adventure entitled *Beyond the Rain Forest*, and by late August she had written almost 80,000 words, which was about full length for "a normal sized novel" she thought. She had "tidied up" all the old chapters, written two new ones, and partially filled out another couple. There were three more to go, and she hoped to finish it soon. Like most novice novelists, perhaps, she was struggling with self-doubt. "The more I look at it the less likely it seems to me that anyone else will want to do so," she declared. But the most obvious obstacles to completion were the chimps and her responsibilities regarding them.

"We have a huge hide just near the tents these days," she explained to the family, "and an elaborate system of warnings of the approach of chimps. Whistles blow from various look outs, Hugo then races to his cameras in the hide, Jane comes pelting down from wherever she is, I look wildly round the tents to see that nothing of interest to David such as jumpers pillows etc, are lying about anywhere, and dash for the hide." Inside the steel-caged hide, Jane would then sit next to Hugo "with her little tape recorder ready to give it a running commentary of everything that transpires during the visitation." Hugo, meanwhile, "adjusts his mighty tripods, cameras are loaded, vast lenses, three on each camera, are trained." Vanne would crouch right behind Hugo, running his tape recorder for him, "ready to record every sound the visitors make — whimpers, screams, tantrums if they can't get bananas, grunts of pleasure" — and poised with pencil over paper "to note down numbers of steps (bipedal), all wees, defecations, matings, and who carries what with which hand, and there we are."

Thus prepared, all three people inside the hide would await the arrival of their guests. "The first black shape appears down the path, or racing down the slope, or bumbling up from the stream, and presently we have a whole group, mothers, babies, males, adolescents, right in front of us." Alternatively, it might be that "only a single chimp comes rather nervously up to the holes in which the bananas are hidden, eats till his tummy is as round and full as a drum of sweets, and then departs." The chimps would some-times hang around for up to an hour after eating, resting and digesting; some of the big males would "lie down for a snooze quite near us or out in the open," whereas "the ladies usually retire to the bushes."

September came, and Vanne found even more obstacles to her writing. Hugo had been ill since early June. In late August he was coping with severe fevers, probably malarial, but still refused to rest. He was working every day, and even though his temperature ranged as high as 103 and he was barely able "to hold the camera steady," he was "still on the ball!" Jane had a stiff neck for a couple of days in August, and Hugo, very ill himself, was "most attentive in rushing after her with pillows and things, glad I imagine to be able to do a little looking after instead of being looked after by Jane and me." But by September, Hugo had become so feverish that he was spending much of the day prostrate in the big tent shared by Jane and Vanne, rather than in his own smaller, hotter one. Of course that made it hard for Vanne to write there.

Things got worse. Both Vanne and Jane came down with malaria, and Hugo's case turned so serious that he was shipped off to Kigoma to see a doctor, who concluded that he had been taking the preventative rather than the curative kind of malaria medicine. Hassan, meanwhile, was suddenly in-capacitated with severe back pain, so he also went to the doctor in Kigoma, and Dominic was laid low with some mysterious ailment eventually diag-nosed as sleeping sickness. Fortunately, it could be treated. Hassan's back pain was labeled sciatica and also treated, with some success. Vanne's and Jane's malaria waned. And by the end of the month, as Jane wrote in a Sep-tember 30 letter to Melvin Payne at the Geographic, Hugo was "now just about recovered—though so thin that there is hardly anything left!"

Between the interruptions and fevers, Vanne continued pecking away bravely at her novel, and she was now far enough along to be able to imag-ine the end. *Beyond the Rain Forest*, published in 1967, opens with young, sensitive, and idealistic Sarah Lovell, "a slender figure in blue jeans with her dark hair drawn back into a pony tail," arriving in Africa to locate her long-absent father, Dr. Matthew Lovell, who had left his family and a medical ca-reer in England to live in the African bush, operating a rural clinic while pursuing the secret of a rain-forest-encircled volcano, Mount Vala. Happily reunited with her father at last, the sharp-minded Sarah becomes infatuated with the dashing if insensitive Mark Howarth, a Kenya-born white hunter, but his flawed character is soon revealed. In the end she courageously sets out, accompanied by her father's resourceful assistant, Hassan Olalle, on a difficult journey through the rain forest and up to the summit of Mount

Vala, where the mysterious secret is revealed. Is it, as some have thought, diamonds? Or, as others are certain, gold? No, it is a blue flower, an ordinary-seeming plant with extraordinary medicinal properties: a great scientific discovery with the potential to improve human welfare.

The novel is about fathers, not lovers, and more an adventure than a romance. Of course, Vanne was experienced and smart enough to be suspicious of romantic love in any case. She had been bitterly educated by her own failed marriage to a man who seemed, in retrospect, a typical representative of his sex. Her sister Olly, so bright and funny and cheerful, had also been painfully disappointed by romance and men. In fact, that very summer Olly had been betrayed by (in Vanne's phrase) "the vile D.," her long-standing fiancé. That July, in one of her early letters home, Vanne had tried to console her wounded sister with some hard conclusions about the other sex:

Men are not <u>sentimental</u> (as opposed to having sentiment) & never like jogging backwards in their memories unless it suits them to do so. By nature they are not monogamous. That all sounds like a treatise but is meant as some sort of comfort. Think of the millions of women who have to share their husbands. A man so often has a wife plus a girl friend. Perhaps the faithful sec. of an office or some old old friend of his wife's—his wife's sister—the colleague in a lab. So many situations there are—women are too possessive perhaps—they want everything. They're greedy—I often think it might help society if a man or a woman were allowed two wives or husbands providing all were looked after & cared for. End of that.

Jane's own thoughts and feelings about men, and about Hugo, during this time were never written down, or at least not preserved. While Vanne was at Gombe, Jane never wrote home, leaving that agreeable but time-consuming task to her mother. And she was so completely engaged in her work with the chimpanzees that she may not have had the extra energy to analyze her feelings about the cigarette-smoking Dutchman who shared her camp and probably, after Vanne left in mid-October, her tent. Yes, he was good-looking and charming. He told funny stories. They shared an abiding love of animals and some compelling mutual goals. They had a lot to talk about—mainly their ideas about and plans for Gombe and the chimps.

And yet perhaps the most exciting, even romantic moment of that year happened on October 11, a day when David Greybeard wandered into the camp alone and then wandered off again, moving up along the Kasekela valley. Jane followed, and since there were no other chimps around, she did not bother to slip on her shoes or take along the binoculars. "He was in a lazy and tolerant mood," she wrote the next day to Melvin Payne at the National Geographic, and

> after he had vanished through a thick tangle of vegetation I found him sitting (seeming to wait) when I finally crawled through after him. We sat and ate leaves side by side. And then I found a palm nut, nice and ripe and red, and felt sure David would appreciate it. So I held it out on my outstretched palm. Now David is a past master at affecting to ignore completely what he considers foolish actions on the part of his would-be human friends. He gave my offering a scornful glance and turned away. I held my hand a little nearer. For a few more moments he continued to ignore me. And then, suddenly, he turned towards me, reached out his hand to the nut, and, to my astonishment and delight, held my hand with his, keeping a firm warm pressure for about 10 seconds. He then withdrew his hand, glanced at the nut, and dropped it to the ground.

Jane went on to analyze the act's significance from David's perspective: "I have explained in my reports how chimps sometimes hold each others hands—normally the subordinate animal holds out its hand when wanting reassurance and the dominant animal, if feeling friendly, reaches out to clasp the hand of the other. David did not want the nut. But there was this strange creature, holding out its hand, making an offering. So he took it, reassured me, and then demonstrated his complete lack of interest in my offering by dropping it to the ground."

That intimate moment became for Jane an emblematic event, marking the culmination of years of careful work, the slow and painfully cautious approaching, the less slow and less cautious tempting and provisioning, the whole brave labor of taming a community of wild apes. "If it had not happened to me I think I would never have believed it possible," she concluded. David Greybeard had, very gently, held her hand—in a manner that was at once an unexceptional chimpanzee gesture of reassurance, a clear communication between species, and an event that Jane would proudly remember forty years later as "the most significant of my life," the moment when she recognized intellectually and emotionally the evolutionary closeness between chimps and humans.

At Geographic headquarters in Washington, the typed aerogram describing this great event was soon being circulated along with an attached memo: "I suppose it was inevitable—Jane is now holding hands with David Greybeard." Thomas McKnew read the aerogram and memo, then penciled in his own sly comment at the bottom of the latter: "I trust this is as far as it will go in the interest of science."

Jane had a surprising passion for animals generally and, more particularly, for the individual chimpanzees she had come to know at Gombe, and she had mastered the trick of describing that passion in ways other people could understand and sympathize with. She would portray herself as ambitious at science, intellectually engaged in serious research, rationally determined to advance her own career and our understanding of humanity's closest relatives, and so on. But it was passion, not ambition, that had taken her as far as she had gone; and passion, more than anything else, was keeping her there now.

For her, the chimpanzees of Gombe were no longer "animals" at all; instead, they were sentient, thoughtful creatures who now seemed about as interesting and emotionally complex as people—but who at the same time were vulnerable, helpless before the arrogance and ambitions of their technologically enhanced *Homo sapiens* siblings. Jane's passionate attachment to the apes was therefore doubled by an assumption of responsibility. She not only wanted to be with the chimpanzees but, knowing the dangers of the world beyond, felt compelled to protect them. "You would fall head over heels in love with all my darlings," she insisted to Louis late that summer, proceeding to describe her own responsibility for their future welfare at Gombe: "Never, never think that I will let anything happen to them through what I am doing. I KNOW it is right. I KNOW that I can work the reserve the way it must. I KNOW that I shall come back here time and time again until the problems that remain are hardly worth mentioning."

The problems created by the banana-feeding regimen that summer were relatively minor, but the potential problems from other sources were manifold and expanding. Tanganyika was an impoverished country, desperate for money, and there had been talk lately about the timber value of Gombe's big trees. The fishermen wanted more room on the shore for their encampments. There was always, with a rapidly growing human population, the likelihood of future agricultural encroachment. Moreover, Jane and Louis were becoming increasingly aware of many other kinds of destruction that might be brought by insensitive tourists, intrusive journalists, overeager scientists, and so on—the very people who had been attracted by Jane's accomplishments yet might best be discouraged by her continuing presence.

She was now seriously worried about what would happen when she returned to Cambridge. The university's Board of Research Studies had in the past allowed her some exceptional leaves, but starting in 1964 she was expected to spend significant time there. She was thus dreading the coming year, and in the fall of 1963 Louis began lobbying for her to be granted additional time away from Cambridge. But even if the Board of Research Studies forced her to reside in Cambridge for only one term during 1964, she would still need to be away from the chimps for three months. Hugo had his own career and relationship with the Geographic to think about, so who would be in charge at Gombe when she was not?

Louis first proposed a young man in Kenya named Alec MacKay, who might serve as a caretaker and at the same time study baboons. Jane was originally pleased by the suggestion. "One of the greatest reliefs," she wrote to Louis on October 20, anticipating MacKay's appropriateness, "will be that I can simply leave my tent, etc., if someone is coming to take over when I leave. . . . If Alec is suitable . . . then it is a God send and answer to prayer." But a day later she was feeling far less positive—not so much about the man, whom she had never met, as about his plan to study baboons. She sent Louis a "hasty P.S." on October 21: "Alec, or anyone else, must <u>NOT</u> have as his <u>job</u> a study of the baboons. . . . I thought I had made it <u>quite</u> <u>clear</u> that my work had reached the stage where it would be <u>WICKED</u> not to continue observations on the chimps. <u>Detailed</u> observations." In short, she concluded, "I want an ASSISTANT CHIMP OBSERVOR. . . . This is all very important. Please don't get money for someone to come & study those revolting baboons. If you only knew what a menace to us & our work they are!!!"

Alec MacKay, in any event, soon took a job at the Coryndon Museum, and thus, "Alec unable to come," as Louis cabled on November 2. Jane wrote back immediately, describing herself as "rather shattered" at the news. "The thing is that I <u>CANNOT</u> leave here until someone comes to carry on my observations and therefore I shall lose my PhD." Perhaps, she went on, Louis ought to talk to a friend of Hugo's, a "young zoologist in Holland whose aim has always been to do something like this."

The "zoologist in Holland" was actually Hugo's friend's friend, someone named C.H.B. Sars, who was twenty-five years old and studying wildlife management at an agricultural college in Ontario, Canada. Louis wrote to young Sars immediately, offering him the job of Gombe camp manager and promising a decent salary with all transportation and other expenses paid; but even before Sars had a chance to consider the offer, Louis was having doubts. Ontario was far away, Sars an unknown quantity. What if he were flown all the way to Africa and then proved unsuitable? "I have asked Sars to cable," Louis wrote to Jane, "and I am assuming, I hope rightly, that Hugo knows enough about him to be certain he can do the job. . . . You will agree the wrong man would be worse than no man at all."

Jane, meanwhile, was feeling so desperate that by November 8, after some "very, very serious consideration" and intense discussions with Hugo (they had "talked and talked and talked about it, and thrashed it out from all angles"), she had decided to give up her Ph.D. work at Cambridge. Of course it "would be wonderful," she wrote to Louis, to continue getting advice and supervision from Robert Hinde.

> But Louis, this work is SO important. With every succeeding day I am more and more impressed by these creatures I am studying. I cannot risk losing such valuable ground just for the sake of a worldly tag. . . . Just think—two days ago we were in the middle of a rain dance. Couldn't film it because it was too dark and wet. But to be able to see exactly how it started, all the movements, every thing in complete detail, and the sequence—well, that is something I never imagined. It was started by your namesake—did Mummy tell you? Leakey is a splendid fellow and I hope to send you his photograph in the near future! One super thing today—Flo trod in a pool of mud (one that I was getting ready to take plaster casts of foot prints in!!) and removed her foot, peered at it, picked up a handful of leaves and wiped it clean. And last week Fifi pulled down some leaves to wipe a sticky mouth. And twice, in one week, mature males and females playing, laughing—the male tickling the lady's bottom at the end!!!! And one female very pregnant—think of a tiny new born baby! And our favourite Figan, now that Flo is no longer attractive to the men, has abandoned his grown up role and is back with Mum and small sister. Even the suckling facts have startled Robert—that Flo's milk dried up just after—or just during—her first sexual swelling since the birth—or conception—of Fifi (about 3 years now). And that there was no weaning behaviour—she still let Fifi suck, though there was quite obviously no milk. I could go on for several pages, but will desist!

She would not leave Gombe without a replacement, and now she could hardly bear the idea of leaving the chimpanzees at all, of dropping, even for a short while, the many threads of connection and knowledge she had so patiently taken up. And anyway, was having those three little letters after one's name really so very important? "Of course, it would be a nice thing to have," she conceded. "But the only thing that matters to me, for the rest of my life, is the setting up and financing of this Research Station, and a comparative study in West Africa. I don't think a PhD will vitally affect either of these issues—be honest in thinking about it. It really won't, will it?"

Louis was in London, attending to his own work at the Natural History Museum—and now, alarmed at Jane's passionately stated intent to drop her academic work, he rushed to Cambridge and met with Robert Hinde and

William Thorpe. They assured him that they expected the Board of Research Studies would soon grant Jane permission to be absent from Cambridge after her first term in 1964, from the middle of March to the end of the year, although that was, as Louis now wrote to Jane, "provided that you do TWO things.—Keep TWO more terms during 1965.—and Hand in your THESIS before the end of the last TERM of 1965. Which is the DEAD LINE FOR IT."

As for the issue of an immediate replacement at Gombe, Louis continued, he had decided against Sars and had instead followed through on reports of a young man working at Kew Gardens, an English botanist with a Polish family name, Kristopher Pirozynsky, "who might be willing to go out for a time and keep an eye on your camp and your interests while doing research on botany and plant fungii himself."

Pirozynsky was soon vetted by Jane's mother and sister, then given his yellow fever and smallpox shots. Louis arranged with Tanganyika's chief game warden, Bruce Kinloch, to provide Jane's replacement with the legal status of honorary game warden. The National Geographic Society agreed to pay some $3,000 to cover his plane tickets and expenses and a small salary. And, Louis concluded, after he had explained everything to Jane in a long and thoughtful letter, "I do hope that all this now sorts out your problem and that you will be able to leave the young man . . . with the reasonable certainty that he will protect the chimps and record any really startling events."

Jane telegraphed back on November 20: "Delighted for botanist to come stop please cable probable date of arrival stop Jane."

Kristopher Pirozynsky arrived in Nairobi sometime during the first week of December, and Richard Leakey flew him out to Kigoma around the eighth or ninth. At Gombe, Jane spent a few days checking him out (he seemed "a most reliable and satisfactory caretaker for Chimpland," she reported back to Melvin Payne) and filling him in before leaving with Hugo for Nairobi on December 15.

By that time, Jane later wrote, she and Hugo were "very much in love." They had even talked of marriage but then wisely wondered whether their newfound passion was "simply the outcome of being thrown together in the wilds, far from other European society." So they decided "to test our love" for the three months Jane would be away in Cambridge.

On the day before Christmas, Jane was back with the family in Bournemouth, and on the day after Christmas she received a telegram: "Will you marry me stop Hugo."

Jane answered yes and thus added a wedding to her already demanding schedule. Joanne Hess of the National Geographic was arriving at Bourne-mouth on December 28 with a half-edited lecture film. For the next couple of weeks she and Jane would review Gombe footage recently shot by Hugo, working toward a final film that would support Jane's first big public lecture, to take place at the 3,500-seat Constitution Hall on February 28. Jane now had to prepare that lecture—as well as a more "scientific" one for Monday, March 2, to members and guests of the National Academy of Sciences.

"Joanne and I have been working on the film from 8 in the morning until midnight every day," Jane wrote to Melvin Payne on January 7. "By now we are both just about dead beat—but the film is down to the right length. I am so hoping that the lectures—both the Society one and the small scientific one—will be successful to justify the faith which you and the Society placed in me and my chimps!"

She was back in Cambridge around January 10, working on her doctoral thesis while laboring over the wedding plans. She and Hugo had chosen a date: March 28, Easter Saturday. "It was all decided in a hurry," she confided in a February 3 letter to her best friend from childhood, Sally Cary,

and you can't imagine the cables and express letters that went whizzing—and still whiz—between here and Africa, Africa and Holland, Holland and here. My goodness. 7 letters all at once from Hugo. 1 express—did I like emeralds!! So back went a cable—"love emeralds love you"!!! Back came a cable—what size was my finger? Back went an answer—No. J. Another cable—can't find J on the card I was given. Then an urgent one—please cable names and addresses of your parents for the announcement of engagement (there are two cables, both saying this, one from Africa, one from England. They crossed!!). Then a cable from Holland—please what are Hugo's full names. Then a cable from Africa to Holland—have I got christening cards. A cable back to Africa—please cable Jane to ring me. Cable to me—please ring my mother tonight. Horrors! Was I panic stricken. I got through at last, and his mother sounded quite sweet—but the poor thing was in such a muddle, all Hugo's letters having contradicted each other. Was I going to see them before the wedding. Was it a white wedding. Did Hugo really need christening cards—they were burnt by the Japs in Indonesia?!! Oh, I can't tell you what a muddle. And in the middle of all this frantic cables from Africa to Washington, Washington to Africa and to England and from England to Washington about films and tapes and more films. My whole life since I last saw you has been snowed under by showers of express or registered letters and cables! Not to mention film and paper!! I am exhausted in the extreme.

She found a white wedding dress that was "really quite superb" at a shop called Bride's Corner, close to home. The wedding would take place in the Chelsea Old Church, in London, where she had been christened. Vanne and Jane had talked to the vicar. Aunt Marjory (Mortimer's sister), who was a Cordon Bleu cook, would cater the reception. Uncle Eric would get drinks at cost—bubbly wine, not champagne, which Jane considered "just a snob value waste of money!" Finally, they printed up and sent out the announcement:

> Mr. M. H. Morris-Goodall and Mrs. M. M. Morris-Goodall take pleasure in announcing the forthcoming marriage of their daughter Valerie Jane with H.A.R. Baron van Lawick. The wedding ceremony will take place on Saturday the 28th of March 1964 in London by the Reverend C. E. Leighton Thomson, M.A. C.F. (T.A.) in the Chelsea Old Church at 1.30 P.M.

Jane was by then feeling unusually fatigued, and on March 13 she was examined for possible schistosomiasis at the Tropical Diseases Hospital in London (where, by coincidence, she met Richard Leakey, who had been temporarily paralyzed by a flea). She was well enough, however, to participate in the wedding, which unfolded beautifully among arum lilies and daffodils, reflecting a bride in white and bridesmaids in yellow. Big color photographs of chimpanzees—including David, Goliath, Flo, and Fifi—enlivened the walls of the reception hall, and the cake was topped by a clay model of David Greybeard. Louis, unable to attend, was represented by the daughter of his first marriage, Priscilla, and a granddaughter, eight-year-old Alison Davis, who was one of the two bridesmaids, and he gave a rousing congratulatory speech by tape recording. A day earlier the Research and Exploration Committee of the National Geographic Society had awarded Jane a second Franklin L. Burr Prize, this time for $2,000, and Jane was informed of the honor and money in a telegram read aloud at the reception.

As Jane wrote a few years later, she and Hugo "agreed afterward that we had never been to a wedding we enjoyed more."

24

Babies and Bananas

1964

BARON HUGO and Baroness Jane van Lawick, originally intending to honeymoon in Holland for six days, instead cut the nuptial holiday down to three as a result of two exciting letters they received in early March about one special birth.

"*Flo amekwisha kuzaa,*" Dominic had written: "Flo has had her baby." A note from Kris Pirozynsky, dated March 1, elaborated: "Flo has a baby! We have not seen her since early February, but to-day she came again with Fifi. Attached to her was a tiny infant. Probably not more than 3 or 4 days old —the umbilical cord still dangling from its belly."

After a short while in Holland, therefore, the happy couple boarded a plane for Nairobi. It was a "fantastic" flight, Jane wrote home. "I have never had such excellent service since the time Jif & I went 1st Class. Food superb. Smiles & help from all Hostesses. . . . Iced eau de cologne towels in the morning to freshen up. Nuts, crisps & cocktail biscuits at 7. It was all quite amazing." And, as if royal treatment were now standard, they were met at Nairobi airport by a shiny pair of government limousines, one for their luggage, the second for them, whisking them off to State House as guests of Malcolm MacDonald, Kenya's governor-general.

Independence had come to Kenya Colony on December 11, 1963, a moment marked in Nairobi by a parade some quarter of a million people long and broad, hours of splendid tribal dancing, a dramatic lowering of one flag and raising of another, a proud assembly of paternal dignitaries, and so on. Kenya then entered transitional status, a twelve-month gestation period before it would emerge a year later as the Republic of Kenya, led by President Jomo Kenyatta. Malcolm MacDonald had been selected as the white-haired, pale-faced midwife to assist in that gestation and birth. Elected a member of Parliament at the age of twenty-seven, appointed a cabinet minister by the age of thirty-three, he had been sent by Winston Churchill to serve as high commissioner to Canada in 1941, a prelude to two and a half decades in high-level colonial diplomacy and administration. And now, as Kenya proceeded from independence to full statehood, MacDonald had been brought in as, in the words of one historian, an essential figure of "outstanding political deftness."

He greeted Jane and Hugo upon their arrival at State House, ordering coffee and biscuits and peevishly accepting tea and no biscuits. The guests were shown to their "sumptuous suite," as Jane put it, and had dinner that evening with Mrs. MacDonald and her daughter, since "H.E. was tied up with Prime Ministers."

The following evening was taken up by a twenty-guest dinner to honor a retiring air force commodore. Jane wore a new black dress and let her hair fall loose around her shoulders, making, she thought, a strong impression. She sat to the left of the governor-general, with the commodore's wife on her other side, and the three of them "talked chimp nearly all through dinner — the wife joining in & being nice & interested." After dinner the women removed themselves for a civilized coffee and liqueur before the fire while the men followed MacDonald out to the garden, where, Kenya-style, they all stood in a row and urinated.

It was raining hard in Nairobi, and the rains extended south into Tanganyika and all the way to Gombe. The countryside was wet, rivers were flooded, and after Jane and Hugo had driven three quarters of the way to Kigoma, they were forced to turn back. They put the car, their supplies, and themselves onto a train and finally arrived at camp on April 14. They were soon joined by Jane's newly hired secretary, Edna Koning, who had boarded the last passenger train liable to operate for some time, given that the tracks near Kigoma were covered by 20 inches of still-rising water.

The tiny object of all that rushed and rained-on effort, Flo's baby (christened Flint), was, Jane wrote to Melvin Payne at the Geographic, "simply the most adorable little object you ever saw." Jane, of course, had been "heartbroken" that she had not been there to witness the birth or the baby's first days, but Kris reported that she had not missed much. For the first five weeks Flint hardly moved at all, remaining a small blob of squinting face and tiny hands that grasped Flo tightly. Then, according to Kris (as Jane relayed to Payne), two days before she and Hugo arrived, the infant began looking around "with intelligent focused eyes" and also began moving his arms. So, Jane concluded, "I think we were lucky and timed our arrival fairly well. He should take his first crawl in a couple of weeks!"

Jane was intending, she reassured Payne, "to start work on another article in the not too distant future." In the meantime, though, aside from the new baby, there were several other urgent matters, including the training of the new secretary. Edna Koning was the person who had sent Jane an impassioned message from Lima after the appearance of her chimpanzee article in *National Geographic*. It was an interesting letter, at once emotional and reasonable, but Jane may have been more intrigued by the almost perfect typing—and now the young woman was settling into camp as a secretary. In Nairobi, Hugo and Jane had acquired a "super tiney weeny tape recorder" and "the only typewriter like ours in Nairobi," and Edna's primary task would be to reduce Jane's labor by transforming tape-recorded day notes into a typewritten evening journal. She would also handle the professional correspondence, starting with thirty letters to publishers hoping for a book about Gombe and the chimps.

Jane's habit had been to spend many lamplit hours each evening transcribing the day's scribbled notes into the more permanent record of a field journal, and it was a great relief to have Edna take over that chore. But far more pressing than the transcription problem was the provisioning one.

The old Banana Club method of feeding the chimps—scattering basketfuls of fruit across the ground in a fairly haphazard fashion—had reached its logical conclusion the previous year. In order to reduce the squabbling and hoarding among chimps as well as their regular conflicts with baboons, Jane and Hugo planned to refine their control over the dispersal of bananas. In February, while Hugo was still in Nairobi, he had designed and ordered for £150 ten steel banana boxes that could be opened remotely with wires and levers—but when he and Jane showed up at Gombe in April, the steel banana boxes were not there. At the same time, Kris said that more chimps had been wandering into camp and had been boldly sauntering into the tent to find whatever was attractive inside, such as clothing and bedding. Kris had stuffed everything he could inside boxes. But then Goliath initiated a new fashion of chewing on canvas, and within a short while several of the chimps were gathering together in canvas-chewing groups, gnawing away at the tent, camp chairs, and camp bed. From canvas they graduated to wood, and by the time Jane and Hugo arrived that April, the apes had finished off a chair leg and the back of a cupboard. Far more disturbing, they had also started raiding the fishermen's temporary huts on the beach and pulling out some of their clothing, creating the immediate possibility of a serious incident.

Clearly, Jane and Hugo realized, they had to locate the banana dispersions farther away from the beach and the fishermen's huts, and they soon found an excellent site about a half-mile up from their old lakeshore camp, on a slight ridge. It was, she wrote home, the "most delightful shady place, palm trees overhead, and a lovely open space opposite where, we thought, when the long grass was trampled or cut down, Hugo would be able to film the chimps admirably."

Using sheets of corrugated iron, Hassan built a chimp-proof banana store and a shaded sleeping hut big enough for a couple of African assistants. Once that construction was done but before they moved their tent and supplies up there, Jane and Hugo thought to show the new Ridge Camp to the chimps. "So we filled the store with bananas," she wrote home, "and I came here at crack of dawn ready to seduce early chimps which might pass with delicious bananas. No chimps passed." Hugo, still down at the old Lake Camp, contacted Jane by walkie-talkie around nine o'clock that morning and said that several of the apes were down there. He wondered whether to try tempting them onto the trail and up to the new place. She said he should. "So he picked up an empty box—one they sometimes have bananas in, walked past them—they ignored him—and then held the box up and sort of waved it at David. Good old David, immediately hoodwinked, gave screams of delight and anticipation." Jane was soon hearing Hugo's frantic and breathless voice on the walkie-talkie: "They're coming!" She quickly began flinging bananas "all over the place as the excited screams and calls approached—and they came—a long string of black creatures all rushing after a panting and disheveled Hugo who was still brandishing the empty box. With yells of pleasure they fell on the new banana supply."

Now that the apes had been introduced, it was time to ready the site for human habitation, first by leveling a meadow of tall grass. A small army of fishermen, hired and organized by Hassan, showed up with *pangas* and sticks and proceeded to cut, beat, and trample down the grass. They were soon joined by Jane and Hugo, who, having decided that trampling was best, held hands and danced in a trampling waltz. The next day they leveled a square of earth and erected their tent, soon piling all their equipment inside. They draped polythene over their books in bookshelves and locked up almost everything else in wooden boxes and crates. They also started folding up their beds and locking away their bedclothes every morning. ("I dread the day," Jane wrote home, "when they suddenly realize that the clothes we are actually wearing are as good to chew as the ones they steal from broken into boxes and stores!!")

Meanwhile, the rain continued to fall, at one point coming down that spring "as I never imagined it could rain." Lazy little Kakombe stream was "transformed into a raging hurtling river, with enormous boulders being dashed along," and Kigoma was cut off from the outside world, which meant that the town shops soon ran out of several essentials.

Along with the mail and equipment from the National Geographic, a new tent intended for Edna's use was stuck in the floods somewhere between Kigoma and Nairobi. Without her new tent, Edna had to use the old one, still down at the Lake Camp. Kris had returned to England and his job at Kew Gardens by then, so Hugo and Jane could luxuriate by themselves in their tent at the new Ridge Camp. Naturally, they loved their "new little home" in all its romantic seclusion and blissful privacy. "It is really most super—we have our cosy supper and coffee round the fire—did I tell you we have bought a really elegant coffee percolator—one of those glass ones that push the coffee up and then let it down again? It is really most handy for out here because all you have to do is light a small flame, and remember to time it. And it makes good coffee. Then we come back to our cosy tent here."

By the end of May, though, the rains had let up and the first mail train had been able to plow through the water into Kigoma. Edna's tent finally arrived and was quickly erected up at the Ridge Camp. The new arrangement was, Jane wrote home on June 1, "rather sad—better really, from work points of view, but not so nice and cosy for us in the evenings when we had our own special little tent." Still, it was "the most heavenly tent imaginable." Poles in the middle and at the sides elevated the canvas roof high enough for a person to stand upright everywhere inside. Yellow mosquito-net windows on all sides provided "such a nice warm light all the time" and kept things breezy and cool during the day, and the rear of the tent opened into a smaller extra room with its own mosquito-net windows. The extra room was supposedly a washroom, but it was big enough to hold a trunk, a wooden stand, and a bed, and so it became Edna's bedroom, while the main room served as a daytime storage area for books and papers, plant specimens, and extra clothes and a general workspace.

The Lake Camp, with its rather tattered, A-shaped canvas structure down near the beach, remained for some time the location of the clinic and dispensary. At the end of a hard day, Jane and Hugo would settle down before the fire at the old camp, tomato juice in hand, "only to be brought off our feet by a string of patients." And every third night, approximately, an "extra large mob" (as Jane phrased it in her June 1 letter home) would appear, all of them "madly inventing ailments" while eagerly begging Edna to play her guitar. The two main instigators of this group were also guitarists, and after Edna had played a few songs, she would hand the instrument over to them. Then, "surrounded by an admiring circle," they would play their favorite African songs until supper was announced, whereupon Dominic "shoos them all away." But, Jane thought, "how they love it." And as a result of Edna's guitar and their hosting of the guitar nights, Jane and Hugo were frequently given hens' eggs as gifts.

Not enough eggs, though, since old, bald-headed Mr. McGregor had developed "an absolute passion for eggs. If we even half open a container with eggs in it, when he is anywhere around, he simply rushes up, taking the shortest possible route even when this is straight through the tent and over someone's legs, scattering wadges and cardboard in his wake, and grabs the eggs." McGregor first revealed this strong passion when they were sleeping down at the old camp and one morning handed a couple of eggs to Dominic to boil for breakfast. The chimp happened to be "miles away calmly eating a pile of bananas," but he "suddenly leapt to his feet, rushed, upright, to Dominic (who he is normally scared of) and snatched away the eggs—albeit with rather a trembling hand at his own audacity!"

So McGregor was the big bad egg thief; but there was also Pooch (who "will dare much for an egg") and Fifi ("manages to get one very frequently") and little Gilka, who liked to steal them as well, although since her mouth was too small to contain an entire orb, she would crack them, watch the contents pour out, and chew over the wet shells before spitting them out.

The birth of the Ridge Camp marked the beginning of a new system for banana provisioning (with a few eggs occasionally tossed in). Since the steel banana boxes Hugo had ordered in Nairobi had not yet shown up, he and Jane began experimenting with various alternative ways to distribute bananas, hoping, as ever, to reduce the jostling chaos.

First they tried hiding the fruit in trees and various containers—but most were soon found by a small band of determined specialists. Moreover, the chimps were still getting into everything else, and now that they were encouraged to come in and actually hunt for bananas, they were becoming even more intrusive and destructive. A chimp named Marina had gotten into the habit of pushing Jane aside whenever she opened the banana storage box, in order to dive in headfirst. Marina also ate Jane's moccasins and Hugo's gym shoes, and even tried Edna's wooden-soled leather sandals. Then Peter Pan (soon known as Pepe) smashed open two big coffee thermoses as well as a large flashlight, just to see, it seemed, whether there were any bananas inside.

When, by late June or early July, Hugo's steel banana boxes still had not arrived, Hassan began constructing a few concrete boxes with steel lids, which he planted in the ground at the new camp. Positioned so that the lids would drop open, the boxes were baited with bananas and the lids drawn shut by wires tightened remotely with levers. The remote levers were pinned into position, so that by pulling the pins, anyone could slacken the wires, allowing the lids to drop open and expose the bananas. The new devices may have seemed a little Rube Goldbergish, but theoretically, at least, they enabled a person to release a controlled amount of fruit from a comfortable distance. Jane announced hopefully to Melvin Payne in a July 9 letter that as a result of the new system "already the situation is vastly improved, and we are able to cope relatively easily with the largest of groups."

It was clear that the Ridge Camp and provisioning area were satisfying to the chimps. They seemed more relaxed away from the beach and farther into the forest, and Jane was soon watching several new individuals appear. The chimps were "more at home" there, she reported to Payne, and thus she was seeing more play among the mature individuals. In fact, so many new behaviors were cropping up that it was hard to keep track of them all. By July 9, Jane and Hugo had already twice watched the chimpanzees closely as they reacted to snakes. They were now observing the chimpanzees drumming: percussively punching and kicking the thin, high roots of a particular species of tree. They had seen Flo display just the way the males did: charging, dragging vegetation, slapping the earth or a tree. And they were discovering new chimp foods, including weaver ants, caterpillars, and a swarming kind of termite. The weaver ants were being consumed in "large quantities," and Jane and Hugo soon discovered that they "have a most exotic flavour, and we are planning ways of marketing them as tropical delicacies!!" When the termites swarmed, the chimps would stand in the treetops and try to snatch them out of the air with one or both hands. "The chimps look rather strange when they feed in this way—rather as though they are signalling!"

But certainly the most important focus of attention that year was little Flint, who offered Jane and Hugo an unprecedented opportunity to record the development of an infant chimpanzee in the wild. By early July, Flint had, as Jane wrote home, "lots of teeth, upper and lower—about 6 in each jaw" and was taking "his first tottering steps—so far, not more than two before collapsing. However, he progresses, because, at first, he cried as soon as he collapsed so that Flo gathered him to her breast immediately. Now he keeps quiet, gets up, and tries again."

Flo was occasionally carrying Flint around on her back, while Flint was increasingly interacting with other members of his family, especially sister Fifi. "Fifi now takes him more and more often, and is allowed to keep him for longer and longer periods. As she sometimes runs off with him and carries him up tall trees, with poor Flo puffing in pursuit, we can't help feeling that this might be one of the reasons for the suspected high rate of infant mortality!"

Flo and her offspring had been important before, as members of the study community, but now they seemed central. The family also appeared to be one member larger than Jane had previously believed. As she expressed her thinking to Payne, "We have also come to the conclusion that one of the adolescent males, some two or three years older than Figan, is also a son of Flo." Obviously, it was not possible to be certain, but Jane and Hugo had seen enough evidence to justify renaming the chimpanzee Faben, so that he fit in alliteratively with the rest of Flo's family.

One important point is that Faben is the only adolescent male, with the exception of Figan, who is allowed to touch, and even play, with Flint. He is continually moving about with Flo, plays frequently with both Fifi and Figan and, believe it or not, with old Flo! The other day he was tickling her in the ribs until the old girl shrieked with laughter! And only yesterday we saw a never to be forgotten sight: Flo, Faben, Figan and Fifi (not to mention dear old Flint clinging on for dear life under his Ma) all chased each other round and round and round a palm tree, grabbing at each others ankles as they went. We all agree that we have never seen anything funnier.

Soon Flint could, as Jane wrote home, "walk about 4 steps without falling over." Then, as she noted in a subsequent letter, "Flint can now walk! Tottering to be sure, but at least 6 steps, or bounds rather, before total collapse. He has found that the faster he leaps the more likely he is to reach his objective without losing his balance."

While Jane still regretted missing the first six weeks of baby Flint's existence, she and Hugo had begun eagerly eyeing the recently expanded Melissa with the idea that her forthcoming baby would help fill in the observational gap. On September 8, Melissa appeared at last with a tiny bundle who could not have been, Jane was sure, more than two days old. "The mother seemed completely dazed," Jane remarked in a September 24 letter to Melvin Payne, "as though she couldn't understand at all what had happened. She walked only a few yards at a time, supporting the infant carefully with one hand and also with her thighs — she walked all the time with very bent legs. The entire placenta was dangling from the umbilical cord — on one occasion this became entangled in the vegetation and Melissa had to stop and unwind it."

The following morning Jane and Hugo observed some of the other chimps' first reactions to a new baby in their midst. Four-year-old Fifi seemed "particularly interested, and kept approaching closely, peering, and sniffing at the placenta." David Greybeard, also very curious, "went very close, and peered and peered." So did Flo. And a childless adult female,

Circe, reached out to touch the new infant, whereupon an apparently alarmed Melissa "immediately grabbed her hand, and rushed to Goliath for reassurance." Flo's oldest son, Faben, was also "tremendously curious" about the new arrival, but soon his "continual peering worried Melissa who kept reaching out her hand to him, presenting [herself in a sexually receptive posture] and generally trying to appease him yet keep her distance."

Melissa was less wary of the two humans hanging around, and they were able to watch and photograph the new baby closely—though not closely enough to figure out what sex it was. Hoping it was female, though, Jane and Hugo had decided tentatively to name her Jane. Still, the baby was

the ugliest little creature you can imagine and, [compared with] Dominic's and Kristopher's [earlier] descriptions, completely different from Flint when he was a baby. Flint, apparently, had a very pale and pretty face, and was very sparcely covered in hair on his head and back, and more or less naked below. This infant has a strangely marked face, dark around her eyes except for pale eyebrow streaks, and pale around her mouth. In addition she has thick hair on her head, back, and outsides of legs and arms. We have not been able to see the underside yet.

Assuming that baby Jane did turn out to be female, this new opportunity to compare the development of a male and female from early infancy would add to the data on sex differences. And compared with Flint, baby Jane would provide an interesting parallel to a somewhat older opposite-sex pair, two-and-a-half-year-old Gilka and Merlin, who was about a year younger.

Merlin, Jane thought, was "really 'little boy' through and through," and she found his style of play to be much more "rough and tumble" than Gilka's. "He litteraly 'flings' himself into games, onto other chimps, and, in fact, into everything he does, including begging food from his mother. In this latter he is invariably successful which is a measure of his persistance since Marina is extremely fond and possessive of her food!" Merlin was also, at such a young age, extremely fascinated by Circe's sexually swollen bottom and "was continually running up to embrace it, and even tried to mount her by half climbing up her legs!"

Meanwhile, the birth of Flint had placed young Gilka in a difficult social situation. Her brother, Evered, was growing up and therefore spending less and less time with his mother and younger sister, so Gilka was now often deprived of his company. At the same time she was discovering that her one-time favorite playmate, Fifi, was suddenly interested only in playing with her little brother, Flint. As a final blow to her infantile sphere of happiness, Gilka's mother, Olly, was starting to wean her. Jane described the process in her September 24 letter to Melvin Payne:

> This weaning has a very marked effect on Gilka. When the breast is denied to her she whimpers, and she usually approaches Olly, when she wants to suckle, stands in front of her, and whimpers. If Olly does not want her to suckle she stands up and either gently bites her wrist, or "play bites" and nuzzles at the child until she stops whimpering to laugh. If the whimpering continues . . . Olly takes Gilka ventrally, carries her a few steps, sets her down, and again tickles her until she laughs. Several times that worked, but twice Gilka continued to cry. This seemed to affect Olly considerably—she returned to the child, gathered her up in an embrace and sat holding her on her lap. Then, when Gilka tried to suckle and the breast was again denied, Gilka moved away crying. But she had only gone a few steps when Olly reached out, drew Gilka back by one arm, embraced her, and allowed her to suckle very briefly.

Poor Gilka. No wonder, then, that she was becoming friends with a young baboon. While it was true that juvenile baboons and chimps frequently played together at Gombe, usually the play was fleeting and lopsided, since the young baboons were ordinarily afraid of their chimp counterparts. But Gilka played very gently with her new friend, Goblin. One time the baboon presented a little bottom to Gilka, who went up and thoroughly inspected it. Having done that, she turned to present her own little bottom for the edification of Goblin, who mounted her and made a few playful thrusts. Then they "nuzzled each other in the neck, play biting," after which Goblin "embraced her from behind and ticked her in the ribs, she throwing back her head and laughing. She tickled him in a similar way."

Goblin soon turned out to be female and thus was renamed Goblina. That was convenient, since (as Jane realized after getting a good look around the start of October) Melissa's baby, Jane, was male and so was rechristened Goblin, in honor of his gargoylish face. In her typically positive way, Jane wrote in an October 26 letter to Melvin Payne that even when they had believed Melissa's baby was female, it was interesting to compare the two infants; but now that they recognized the baby was male, comparisons between the two ought to be "even more interesting."

By late November a third baby was born: Mandy's Jane. She was, Jane wrote to Louis Leakey at the time, "the most gorgeous little girl." Her appearance was a "splendid" event, which, following the birth of those two little males, should provide "really first class comparative material now." Among the many interesting possibilities for comparison was the clear difference in mothering styles between Melissa and Mandy. Melissa, in fact, "never goes out of her way to make things easy for the baby." Mandy was almost the opposite, "so concerned for the well being of her infant that, when eating and therefore having two hands in use (or, rather, if she is eating and happens to need both hands for the job!) she holds Jane pressed closely to her by means of her foot—which she may hold in the most uncomfortable looking position for ages."

Such a wealth of observations now, made possible largely by the banana-feeding system, which brought out of the forests and into the open a dynamic community of apes. And by August 10 those steel banana boxes Hugo had so long ago ordered in Nairobi finally arrived in Kigoma. Jane wrote to the family that she expected soon to have "13 chimp proof boxes," whereupon "we can stop this silly game of hiding in all sorts of places where bananas shouldn't be hidden—such as under the [tent] ground sheet!"

By September 24, Jane was informing Melvin Payne that the steel boxes had been set up in the provisioning area, along with some additional cement boxes, and they all were working "superbly, and we have no problems at all with our feeding." The steel boxes operated as the cement boxes did, with lids that dropped open when the wires were slack, wires pulled taut with remote levers, pins to hold the levers in place. "Everything goes smoothly," Jane added, "and we havn't had one crisis since all were ready."

That assessment was overly optimistic, of course, since the new banana-dispersal system drastically underestimated the determination, intelligence, and strength of the chimps. For starters, one of the males, J.B. (short for John Bull), had already begun digging the boxes out of the ground and was pulling on the wires. The boxes were reset and embedded in cement. But by early December 1964, J.B. was breaking the wires, and the camp staff members were forced to work at night by lantern light, placing the vulnerable metal sinews inside metal pipes—blissfully unaware that their hasty repairs to the banana-dispersal system were merely the barest beginning.

25

A Permanent Research Center

1964–1965

ON THE AFTERNOON of March 3, 1964, the soon-to-be-married Jane Morris-Goodall and Hugo van Lawick sat at a round table in the president's office of National Geographic headquarters in Washington, D.C., face-to-face with President Melville Bell Grosvenor and a half-dozen other senior executives, to discuss future plans, including a second chimpanzee article, a television special, and a book.

Robert C. Doyle, the man in charge of National Geographic's new television division, introduced the matter of the television special, announcing that they already had almost enough footage from Gombe for a full hour.

Jane introduced the matter of a book, a popularized account of her work, mentioning that the American publishing house McGraw-Hill had already offered her an advance of $100,000 and wondering whether writing such a thing would conflict with plans anyone might be harboring. Yes it would, President Grosvenor warmly responded, since the society also intended to publish a popular book about Jane's work. He coolly reminded Jane that they had already "invested substantial funds in research grants and other assistance" on her behalf, and it would not be "cricket" for a commercial press to "cash in on the results of this investment." He pressed his case: over the long term it would surely prove to be to Jane's "advantage" to continue her close working relationship with the National Geographic Society, even though $100,000 might at first glance seem "impressive."

Actually, in 1964 the sum of $100,000 was a hugely impressive advance for any publisher to offer an unpublished author, and the society's executives may have been jolted by the figure. Thus, although Jane was bound by a literary release giving the society very broad rights over her future written output, it would still have been important for them to imply more clearly what sorts of "advantage" a continuing relationship with the society could provide. It was, in short, a very good time for Jane to introduce her other plans and fantasies—especially those embodied in the brief, rough-draft proposal for a "Permanant Research Center" at Gombe.

Such a center was justified, the proposal asserted, because Gombe was among the best places on the continent for studying wild chimpanzees; because a study of at least ten years was essential for understanding them fully; and because the Gombe chimpanzees were otherwise threatened with extermination by human encroachment. The research center would require an annual budget of perhaps £2,000 to £3,000—salaries and food for scientists and staff, gasoline for the boat, bananas for the chimps—and a one-time capital investment of between £5,000 and £10,000 to pay for equipment and the construction of an observation building and living quarters. The observation building would be a small, three-room affair with a flat roof on which scientists might gather for observation purposes. Situated at some distance away from the lake, it would overlook a large area of forest and be surrounded and protected by a 10-foot-wide water moat. The living quarters, located about a half-mile from the observation building, might consist of six inexpensive, prefabricated aluminum "rondavels," three for scientists and three for staff. This cluster of buildings would be surrounded by another protective 10-foot-wide moat—as would, finally, a piece of land set aside for the vegetable garden, hens, and goats.

Jane emphasized her plan's tentative quality as an idea in progress and apparently solicited neither comment nor commitment. None was recorded. Probably none was given.

In fact Jane's ambitions were far grander than that little proposal suggested. She and Hugo were working on a proposal to the World Wildlife Fund in Holland that would establish a permanent station at Gombe as well as a whole string of "chimpanzee reserves," where the apes might be simultaneously protected and studied, across Africa. And if the WWF did not come through, perhaps Jane and Hugo could hope for practical support from the pioneering ethologist Konrad Lorenz, now director of the Max Planck Institute for Behavioral Physiology in Seewiesen, Austria. Jane had written to Lorenz earlier that year and received a warm response, including "a standing invitation" to visit him and the wish that "you will find the necessary finance to set up a permanent field observation center. I regard it as absolutely vital that a long-term observation of group behaviour in your chimpanzees should be made possible. We do this with greylag geese for 10 years now, and we got more from it than we dared to hope."

Jane had also been assured by the president of the New York Zoological Society that it would be, as she put it in a March 11 letter to Louis, "extremely interested in the research center." Then there was the Geneva-based International Union for the Conservation of Nature (IUCN), which, as she noted in a letter home that summer, could "almost certainly" make available a "very large amount of money" for the furtherance of their "chimp reserves across Africa scheme." And if none of those leads fulfilled their promise, there were more.

How, then, did the National Geographic Society fit in?

It was becoming distressing, even galling, to realize that the National Geographic Society had, through a few grants, now being called "investments," combined with a small piece of paper known as Jane's "literary release," managed to gain such a complete lock on her future career. Especially disturbing was the prospect of that popular book Jane was now supposed to produce for the society. Of course she was grateful for the organization's support and fond of some people she had gotten to know there. Still, they were now asking a great deal in return. A May 3 letter to the family in England expressed the problem this way: "We are in a huge flap about what to do about asking the Geographic what they want to do about the Research Center here. Because IF they say they want to finance it, will this put me under even more of an obligation re. this wretched book? It is all so complicated—yet we must do something soon—the end of the year looms horribly close."

Hugo had signed the same all-embracing literary release that Jane had, and he too was beginning to feel the chill. Part of the problem was that he was distinctly unhappy with how the first chimpanzee lecture film had turned out—too much frothy human interest, not enough serious science—and the prospect of the upcoming television special did not seem very bright either. Hugo had big ambitions of his own, but as a subcontracting cameraman, subject to the regime and manipulations of distant writers, editors, and producers, what could he hope for? The National Geographic owned and controlled everything he had filmed at Gombe.

When a letter from staff member Joanne Hess arrived at Gombe in early May, announcing that she would appear on June 13 to begin three weeks of additional filming for the Geographic television show, Jane's and Hugo's vexations and anxieties acquired more focus. They had developed the mistaken impression that Konrad Lorenz and Niko Tinbergen were coming to East Africa that June and might visit the research site, so they were perturbed about Hess's suddenly announced descent because they imagined it might clash with the greatly hoped-for one of Lorenz and Tinbergen. At the same time, Jane anticipated a real conflict over the television film. "I can forsee the most terrible upsets, clashes of will, sulks, bad moods and loss of temper all round," she wrote home. "If Joanne thinks she can firmly say 'Hair washing scenes at the big fig tree in the next valley at 10.0 tomorrow'—well, she is mighty mistaken!"

To reduce any possibility for the worst sorts of human-interest shots the newly married couple could imagine, they planned to hide their canvas baths (of which there were two, so that they could sit side by side every evening and scrub each other's backs) and tell the visitor that their tubs had worn out, so they were forced to bathe less photogenically in the cold mountain stream. Yes, they were now seriously upset, and the fantasy about how to respond developed even further: "We are already collecting large numbers of evil looking spiders and centipedes to lay around casually in her tent, in an endeavour to shorten her visit."

The reality of Joanne's visit was bad enough. Richard Leakey flew her down from Nairobi to Kigoma and then escorted her up to the camp, privately telling Jane and Hugo that she was already upset, expecting that they would not cooperate. So Jane and Hugo were forewarned. But they were also busy, and so experienced the new demands on their time as a series of arbitrary and burdensome interruptions. "There is scarcely time to breathe," Jane wrote home at the time, "and when there is, there are so many things left over from ages ago to be done, that the time is lost! We get quite desperate, Hugo and I, wondering how we can ever get everything done." Joanne, of course, was merely doing her job, which meant in large part producing more human-interest footage—just the sort of thing Jane and Hugo really hated, since everything had to be posed, scripted, reenacted. If Vanne was not there to dole out medicine to a long line of clinic supplicants, Jane could do it. The fishermen? Bring them in for a chat. Jane sleeping overnight at the Peak? Too bad she never took a pressure lamp with her, because a pressure lamp would provide good contrasting light. "The film is absolutely the end. How anyone ever writes a script to it I can't imagine. However. Apart from going to Kigoma I have decided to do it all—it is so ghastly there is no use quibbling over whether or not I have a pressure lamp at the peak, etc., etc."

Anticipating exactly that sort of unpleasantness, Louis Leakey had at the start of June sent Jane and Hugo a pair of letters that were uncharacteristically long and ("to make sure I get all my points across") typewritten.

He explained his own theory that Joanne Hess's trip had been "timed especially for the dry season," when she could get shots of chimpanzees against a lighter background, providing the sharp contrast essential because the television show would be seen on millions of black-and-white sets in the States. Black-and-white television required higher contrast.

He reassured Hugo that the television film was being "professionally edited" and that the Geographic Society was "most emphatically not slap happy about the editing." At the same time, however, Hugo should realistically understand that "what is required for TV film for America is utterly unlike anything that you and I would call good. If it was, it would never get a good sponsor on a serious network. As you know quite well, the film on Olduvai has about 11 minutes of serious stuff in it, and even that not the way I wanted it, and a vast amount of padding. The Geographic, for their American films for TV, have got to provide what the TV sponsors want, and I know I am right when I say this."

As for the book problem, as far as Louis knew, the National Geographic had not suggested that the book Jane wrote for them would have to be the only popular book she could write. Of course they wanted one for their own popular series, but it would be "not at all the sort" anyone would write for an "ordinary book type" publisher—such as McGraw-Hill. The National Geographic would naturally expect to release theirs first, but "in view of all the money they have spent and the money they hope to continue to spend," Louis thought, that expectation was "only fair."

Finally, Louis tackled the matter of Jane's proposal for a permanent scientific research center at Gombe. Even though he and Jane had casually discussed it several months earlier, he was completely surprised ("I had no idea")—and seemingly displeased—that she had taken the initiative of presenting her scheme to the National Geographic Society without consulting him first. In any case, it was premature to plan anything of that kind until she had finished her doctorate and had much more free time. "If it is to be a success, it will involve a lot of travelling, a lot of very slow—and at times frustrating—discussions at Dar es Salaam, and perhaps in America and London." And even though there had been talk that the government of Tanganyika ought to declare Gombe Stream a national park set aside for research purposes, who knew what would happen? "Nobody—and I mean nobody—is going to provide funds until they know in writing that the land on which the centre is to be built has been agreed to by the Government concerned, that the full plans have been approved by the Government concerned and, even more important, that really first class research people to man the centre have been found and have accepted the job."

In short, Louis concluded, Jane should set aside this foolish talk about a permanent research center until her Ph.D. work was done. It was far more important to concentrate on finding someone to help Edna Koning manage the day-to-day operation of the place while Jane was back in Cambridge next year. "That, at least, would be my advice."

Edna Koning was Dutch, born in Jakarta (then Batavia), Indonesia, just before the war but imprisoned with her parents for three years in a Japanese concentration camp. They escaped and resettled in Holland for two years, moved to England for one, and then to Peru, where Edna attended an English school before getting an undergraduate degree in psychology from Reed College in the United States. When she had first written to Jane, back in 1963, she was twenty-four years old and doing office work in Lima, but she had always wanted to study animal behavior. "To join a field trip as an assistant to a professor studying birds, insects, or whatever has always been my ambition," she wrote, before asking whether Jane could use an assistant in the chimpanzee research and declaring candidly that "I can think of nothing that I would rather do (and I'm sure you'd find no better or more capable person!!) than to join you." So Jane had hired her as a secretary, and she demonstrated her potential soon after she arrived in mid-April.

Edna, Jane reported back to the family, "is turning out just fine. She is not 'tough' yet, and I'm not sure she ever will be really tough. But she is keen, interested, observant, intelligent, and great fun. So, all in all, we feel she is a great success. She adores the chimps, and we certainly feel that she will be able to cope at the end of the year. If she agrees to stay on, that is. We asked her, point blank, if she felt she wanted to go on with this sort of work, and she said yes. I hope she does."

For the moment, the main task was to organize, to *systematize*, the chimpanzee research in a way that would make Jane to some degree replaceable. True, in some ways she would be very hard to replace. But the artificial banana-feeding site provided a standard base of operations and observations, and any researcher at Gombe could readily contribute to background data collection at the site on (1) times of arrival and departure for every individual, (2) composition of each group, and (3) direction from which they came and to which they departed. Additionally, the feeding site records would include data on (4) the reproductive status of every female, (5) any illnesses and injuries, (6) and the comings and goings of the baboons. Such were, in fact, the standard daily records, begun as early as 1963, when Flo first appeared at camp in a sexually attractive state, bringing along with her a crowd of eager suitors.

In later years the daily records would expand to include a large number of other data, such as (starting in 1969) a survey, routinely checked every two minutes, of grooming and play. And in the summer of 1964, with Edna looking on, Jane began her daily analyses of the chimpanzees' food intake by studying their outgo—a visual analysis of dung contents, in other words, which seemed to work best if one washed the dung in water to sort out the solid remnants. "Dung swirling" was what Jane called the technique, and when first mentioning it to the family in a letter of late June or early July, she declared it to be "rather fun, but time consuming."

Dung swirling was, as Jane wrote to Lyn Newman that August, a "fabulous method of finding out exactly what the chimps eat all the time," and she proceeded to describe the technique in detail: "All dungs are collected each day, from here and from my wanderings. These are then put in a tin with lots of tiny holes in it, water poured over, and the tin swirled round and round. More and more water is added until only the contents of the dung are left. All clean and nice. This is then spread out on sieves, and we can examine it carefully." Lyn would be "absolutely amazed," Jane went on, "at the amount of whole and totally undigested food [that] comes out. Leaves which look as though they had been picked straight from trees, whole fruits, whole insects." And, among other things, the dung swirling had clarified just what omnivores those chimps were. As Jane phrased it in the same letter, "Poor Solly Zuckerman. You know he hates the idea that any of the primates are great meat or insect eaters. Well, since we began the swirling technique not one day has passed but that either ants or termites have been found in at least one dung. In four weeks, they have eaten meat five times. In addition they ate caterpillars daily for two weeks. And they nearly all love eggs and baby birds. Horrid of them, but interesting."

Of course, every new system and technique added a new level of responsibility and work, and by midsummer Jane, Hugo, and Edna were laboring virtually nonstop at least every other night up at the Ridge Camp. Their hot dinner would be carried up in open thermoses that rapidly cooled (all the stoppers having been lost) and reheated over the Primus stove, and then Edna might whip up pancakes or fudge, or Jane might produce a banana custard. And without the time-consuming luxuries of bath and fire, Jane explained to the family, they could get "so much work done." It was "all very nice & cosy in the work tent, and I love it up here."

But Edna had soon proven so valuable in assisting with the scientific work—note-taking, record-keeping, dung swirling—that Jane needed someone else to take over the secretarial work. She described the problem to Melvin Payne on July 9, noting that "the overall work has increased so tremendously that we are all three going flat out from about 6.30 A.M. until midnight nearly every other day simply in order to keep everything up to date." Jane was willing to cover Edna's expenses out of her own pocket, but she hoped the National Geographic would agree to provide for someone else, a second assistant, who would be taken on strictly for "secretarial purposes."

And while Edna, during Jane's future absence, could be responsible for maintaining the continuity of chimpanzee observations and records, she ought—and also eagerly wanted—to have her own research project to think about. What sort of study might that be? "We have got a baboon person,"

Jane wrote to Louis on September 8. "Edna is now really keen, and she is shaping well. We are giving her a trial period on the baboons and, when this is written up, and with some film on them, we feel absolutely convinced that money will be forthcoming." Edna in fact began her preliminary study of one of the Gombe baboon troops, consisting of around fifty individuals, on September 9. By the time she wrote up her first detailed report in December, she had managed to accumulate some 150 hours of direct and impressively detailed observation.

A new secretary, Sonia Ivey, was soon found in England, but the prospect that young Edna Koning would be joined for the next year by a young female assistant only clarified the importance of making the Gombe architectural environment more substantial than canvas tents. Jane loved living in a tent, but most people did not, and thus she returned to the idea of solid buildings, the sort she had envisioned in her original plan for the permanent research center.

By early August, in fact, Jane had stumbled across, as she soon described it in a letter home, the "IDEAL site for the future research building." It was about a half-mile farther up the Kakombe valley from the Ridge Camp, high enough that the trees thinned out into open meadow, presenting "the most magnificent view stretching right across the valley and over the distant mountain slopes."

A couple of weeks later Jane and Hugo hosted a pair of important scientific visitors from the Max Planck Institute ("Konrad Lorenz's institution," as Jane reminded the family in an August 21 letter): Hans Hass, a biologist and diving pioneer, and Irenäus Eibl-Eibesfeldt, an ethologist. The two scientists watched the chimps at the Ridge Camp banana-feeding station and were, according to Jane, "most enthusiastic" when shown the site for the future research center. Indeed, they were "tremendously impressed with everything here—the work, the chimps, and the future plans." They spent some time "enthusiastically plotting" with Jane and Hugo ways to ensure that Konrad Lorenz and Niko Tinbergen might be induced to visit Gombe themselves that autumn. They congenially agreed "to spread the news abroad—that the chimpanzee research station at the Gombe Stream reserve is a 'must.'" Hass generously promised to provide Hugo with "millions of contacts in all the right television places." And Eibl-Eibesfeldt firmly announced that he would send future doctoral students from the Max Planck Institute to Gombe to carry out "certain specialized studies"—which was, Jane thought, just the thing needed to "give life to the research station, give it standing, and keep it going."

Jane also described the new site and some new plans for a two-building center in a letter to Louis, and she even sent along some drawings of what the proposed buildings would look like. Louis responded on August 19 with another of his long typewritten letters. He had definitely not changed his mind on the principle of the research center. It would require far more time and planning than Jane could afford right now; and of course it would be necessary to get permits from the Tanganyikan government. Still, he could see the logic of a simple, basic structure or two to shelter Edna and whoever else would assist her in the next year. "I entirely agree," he conceded, "that some kind of a building to take the place of tents is <u>necessary</u> in order to keep equipment and everything else safe from the risk of loss and breakage by the Chimps."

Louis Leakey had an enormous reservoir of pragmatic knowledge and a sense about how to do things — cook a meal, organize a safari, outfit an expedition, run an archaeological dig, establish a research camp — in remote places. And like most people with specialized knowledge, he enjoyed exercising it. So once he had acknowledged that buildings, not tents, would be appropriate for the next year at Gombe, he moved into planning exactly, in increasing detail, what sort of buildings they might be.

To be sure, now was not the time to put up something permanent, he went on in the same letter, but one could still imagine a temporary structure or two, resistant to the weather and the chimps. Obviously, one would start with the accommodation building, which could be made from poles and grass: thatched, rectangular, perhaps 15 feet wide, 40 long, with a steeply pitched roof and (for protection against the chimps) strong wire mesh rolled all around the sides and roof and doubled over the sides. Inside, this building could be partitioned into bedrooms, a living and dining room, and a workroom or laboratory. Jane had described to Louis two buildings that she thought would cost between £2,000 and £3,000 to erect, and Louis could not imagine the Geographic agreeing to such an expense right now. But a thatched structure of the sort he imagined ought to cost far less. Grass would be free. Poles could be taken from the reserve, bought in Kigoma, or acquired cheaply elsewhere and shipped by rail to Kigoma — but in any case, they would not be expensive. That left only the doors and frames, wire mesh, and a small expenditure for nails and twine. Naturally, one also wanted a suitable lavatory, which could be linked to the accommodation building by a wire-covered walkway. All told, Louis figured, the thing might be built for about £200 to £300 — one tenth what Jane had been talking about.

A smaller observation building might be constructed later, out of more lasting materials, when Jane and Hugo had a good deal more time. Louis agreed that it might be possible to build it out of concrete blocks, either manufactured on the spot or purchased ready-made in Kigoma. Of course, Jane would need to hire a first-class African *fundi* (skilled worker or expert) and about four assistants and be prepared to pay for their transport and two months' worth of food; but before he could estimate the cost of that building, Louis would need to know what size concrete blocks one could get in Kigoma, whether they were solid or hollow, and what they cost, as well as the availability and price of cement, sand, corrugated iron, timber. . . .

Two days later (August 21), Louis typed out yet another very long letter to Jane. He had been thinking. If one used aluminum sheeting to prefabricate a slightly larger accommodation building in Nairobi, it would still cost only around £670, with the smaller observation building an additional £225. The two units could be shipped from Nairobi to Kigoma by rail and boat; and even though one would need to hire someone to supervise the purchases and loading, one would still have spent only perhaps £1,200 to get everything to Kigoma. Additional costs of floating the prefab units up the lake to Gombe and hauling them up to the site would add £300, making a grand total of £1,500, which was still, Louis summarized with possibly a small note of triumph, "a long way below" what Jane had estimated. . . .

A month later Louis had identified the brand name of the prefabricated unit he was considering: a Uniport, manufactured by the Booth Trading Company, Ltd., of Nairobi. Since the Booth Company's Uniports consisted of bolted-together aluminum sections, for aesthetic and insulation purposes it would be important, Louis thought, to fix grass around the walls and roof, then protect such thatching from the chimps with "rat wire." Perhaps the observation building might still eventually be built out of reinforced concrete. . . .

Several weeks later (on November 2), the Booth Trading Company, Ltd., gave Louis a description of two rectangular, gable-ended Uniports, one of them 30 by 14.5 feet and including double doors, nine windows, and enough partitions to divide the interior into four rooms, the second a 15-by-14.5-foot unit with a single door and three windows. In addition, Booth identified a smaller, roundish (or polygonal) aluminum rondavel structure, called a Miniport. All three prefabricated buildings, plus shipping fees to Kigoma, plus transportation and food for an accompanying *fundi*, would require exactly £1,253. . . .

Louis was just then completing his application to the National Geographic for the next year's support of Jane and her work at Gombe and Cambridge, but time was short and he was rushed. Otherwise he would surely have padded the estimate with additional figures for the transportation of 5,500 pounds of aluminum up the lake from Kigoma to Gombe, for concrete to make foundations, for labor, and so on. Instead he simply forwarded the figures provided by Booth Trading. Thus, when the Committee for Research and Exploration met later in the month, it recommended a grant to Jane in the amount of $13,428.20, divided into $9,920.40 (or £3,543) for her chimpanzee study during 1965 and another $3,508.40 (£1,253) for "prefabricated huts." The recommendation was approved on November 19, 1964.

Hugo, meanwhile, had been nursing his own plans, and in a letter written that September to the Geographic Society's second-in-command, Melvin Payne, he described one of them.

Hugo was convinced that he could make a spectacular alternative to the film that the society's television czar, Robert Doyle, was currently putting together, and so now he proposed to Payne that he be hired to edit a second film for television, perhaps taking advantage of some of the same footage used in the first but still distinctive enough that it would not "in any way" compete with the first. Rather, his would be a "scientific documentary" that focused entirely on the apes and left Jane and her story entirely "out of the picture." Hugo was certain there would be a good market for this more serious film in Europe, even perhaps "in certain quarters" in the United States. And if the society agreed to support the endeavor, he would like to work on it in England during 1965, while Jane was finishing her degree work at Cambridge.

He went on to describe other ideas, such as a television film on insects, based largely on footage he had already taken for the society—but it was, he concluded, rather urgent to settle soon on the second television film so that he and Jane could make plans.

Hugo was respected as a photographer and cameraman, but what did he know about film editing? And why should the National Geographic consider making a film that would undoubtedly compete with one they were already producing? Anyway, Doyle was perfectly capable of producing a second television program on the chimpanzees, if it came to that. Moreover, why should anyone at the Geographic rush any decision as an act of charity, to help Jane and Hugo plan their next year together in England? Payne circulated Hugo's letter to relevant staff members and, in an attached memo, proposed a meeting with the following comment: "As things have worked out, we seem to be a Committee for the Direction and Welfare of Baron and Baroness Hugo van Lawick. I think we ought to get together in a few days and talk this thing over."

Payne finally got back to Hugo a few weeks later, in a letter dated November 18, vaguely apologizing for the delay, agreeing that there was "a definite need" for the sort of scientific documentary Hugo had proposed, but pointedly arguing that it should remain "collateral" to the film Doyle was preparing. Payne reminded Hugo that the cost of acquiring all the footage on the Gombe chimpanzees had been substantial; the additional expense of sending Hugo to England, paying his usual retainer, and then providing a salary for a professional film editor to assist him would not be justified by the "very modest payments" European television networks typically made for such programs. Hugo could certainly stay on at Gombe until Jane left in April, at which time he might work on some other projects, photographing various animals and insects in Africa. In addition, he might be allowed to take over a "basic preliminary editing" of the film to support Jane's planned 1966 lecture in Washington. It might be possible for Hugo to do *that* work in England during the latter part of 1965.

A telegram from Melvin Payne to Louis Leakey reached Nairobi on November 20: "Janes future program including prefabs approved today stop please advise her." Louis did, while placing an order with Booth Trading Company for two Uniports and one Miniport.

Booth Trading required three to four weeks to fill the order. East African Railways would then take an average of twenty days more to transport the prefabs by rail and ferry (across Lake Victoria) from Nairobi to Kigoma. At Kigoma, a standard water taxi could ferry the whole load up to Gombe. Perhaps East African Railways would be willing to expedite the shipment; but in any event, Louis calculated it would reach Kigoma in the second week of January, and he instructed Jane and Hugo to get ready. In order to avoid wasting time, he urged them in a December 7 letter to decide exactly where the structures would be erected, clear and level a sufficient area, hire a *fundi* experienced with concrete, hire additional labor, haul up bags of cement from Kigoma as well as gravel and sand from the lakeshore, and pour the foundation slabs.

Hugo took over the supervision of this job, and by month's end the bulk of the preparations—clearing, leveling, and hauling—was more or less complete. Jane, meanwhile, was occupied by "millions of chimps," as she put it in a letter to Lyn Newman, while working hard on a scientific paper and her second *National Geographic* article.

The three aluminum buildings arrived that January but remained neglected and unassembled inside their wooden crates at the Kigoma railway offices because of an even more important arrival: three alpha males from the United States.

Louis had organized it all. As he had informed Jane and Hugo in December, the important three members of the National Geographic Society's Committee for Research and Exploration—Dr. Leonard Carmichael, Dr. T. Dale Stewart, and Dr. Melvin M. Payne—would be flown in a rented twin-engine plane from Nairobi to Kigoma on the morning of January 21, taken by Hugo in the little aluminum boat out to Gombe, spend three nights there, and return to Kigoma on the morning of the twenty-fourth for their flight back to Nairobi.

Hugo had been discouraged by Melvin Payne's rejection of his television documentary idea in late November, but he was still encouraged by his own certainty on the matter. "Do they [not] realise they have the material to make one of the greatest animal films ever made?" he wrote in frustration to Louis early that January. Now, naturally, Hugo was starting to think of the upcoming visit as an opportunity. Perhaps during a relaxed and intimate moment, as they all sat around a campfire in the evening drinking coffee or sipping Cointreau, he could make his case directly to the powerful Dr. Payne.

Hugo had written to Louis in some detail about how such a campfire strategy might unfold. And in another of his lengthy typed missives, Louis responded thoroughly, describing what might be a fair strategic approach to the Payne problem but finally advising caution. Hugo had been thinking about "surprising" Dr. Payne with his new idea—and Louis was certain that Payne would be "much more likely to refuse to commit himself at all, or even to comment, if the idea is jumped on him." Also, there was the matter of language: "Hugo, please try to avoid any use of the word 'documentary' with reference to films. This word is already anathema in the United States, and is rapidly getting so also in England where it is becoming synonymous with second-rate and dreary."

Louis wrote to Jane around the same time, advising her about preparations for the upcoming visit. The visitors were not expecting "comforts," although they would obviously appreciate "good food and drink, beds and sheets, and mosquito nets." Perhaps Jane misread those words and concluded that the three gentlemen *did* expect comforts. She was, in any case, acutely aware that they could be enormously important to the future of the chimps and the research center, and therefore, as she described the situation in a January 4 letter to Lyn Newman,

you can't imagine the bustle and preparation that is going on. We have even brought a shiney black modern lavatory seat!!!!! This will be laid tenderly over a hole in a box over the normal hole in the ground which serves us here! They have to be coddled like babies—not allowed to eat any fresh green food in Africa, all water must be boiled (even the water here which we have drunk, unboiled, for years!). Not to put even a finger into a lake or stream because of bilherzia. It must be horrid to be them!

Vegetation was cleared, tents tidied, mats laid down. A fence and path were organized between the guest tent area and the *choo*, with its new wooden box and glistening black seat.

Along with creature comforts for the three distinguished arrivals from America, Jane was also thinking about the comfort of creatures. How would the chimps react to three new upright apes in camp? She erected fences and strung up screens consisting of mosquito netting dyed a dark color. On their first day in camp, the visitors were kept under wraps—or behind mosquito nets—so that alongside Hugo, they turned into (she phrased it in a letter home) "four vaguely visible objects" who were "clicking away" with their cameras. That worked for the first day, but by the second

our resolutions were overcome as, one by one, all the chimps accepted our VIP's with a nonchelant stare and a turned back. It was quite unbelievable. It was as though they all knew that, perhaps, their future depended on the impression they made. Olly couldn't have cared less. Figan straight away brushed past Payne, nearly pushing him off his chair. Mac D[onald], timid little Mac D[onald], gave them a noncommital stare and continued to scrounge in the tent for bananas. Circe didn't mind. And even little Jomeo, . . . for whom we still hide in tents, came bouncing along the path whilst we were all standing out in the field! So. Our gentlemen from the States enjoyed two complete days of freedom.

Not only were the chimps well behaved, but so, in general, were the men. "They were very good," Jane wrote home afterward. "Did what they were told." They seemed not to mind the handleless mugs, the breakfasts abandoned and gone cold because of early-arriving chimps, the drinking water unboiled and taken directly from the stream. And Dr. Leonard Carmichael, that "great giant of a man," when asked whether he would like hot water to wash or bathe in, politely said that his thermos cup of shaving water went a long way.

Carmichael, tall and very self-possessed, was the one who had once, on the streets of Washington, deflated the aggressive attentions of a mugger by stating politely, "I'm sorry, but you must have the wrong man." And Carmichael was the one who, harboring a long-standing interest in primates and primatology, had so industriously lobbied to visit Gombe two years earlier. When he first showed up at camp, though, Jane found him hard to take: "so pompous and ready to pounce on every word I said—how did I know—why did I say so—was this justified—etc, etc, etc." In fact he was simply "being silly." When she asked him at what age a laboratory chimp would first walk, instead of answering the question, Carmichael "spent 5 minutes giving a discourse on the origin of walking, and how infants new born walked by movements of their limbs through space, and walking originated by the C and then the S shape of swimming organisms—and it went on and on. In point of fact he didn't obviously know the answer to the question, and he would never admit it!"

Finally, after a long discussion about the significance of one chimpanzee's particular movements, the big man pontificated that when Jane was working on her scientific article or her doctoral thesis, "I should say this or this, and not that or that." Completely exasperated, Jane curtly declared that "I wasn't writing a thesis, but talking to him." That stopped him short, and "from that moment onwards," Carmichael was "a completely changed man. He stopped being terrified that every opinion he gave would appear in reference to his name in some or other of my papers. He became human. He talked about chimps like we do. He commented on a satisfied expression on Gregor's face. He began extasising about Flint (only I'm sure he spelt it differently!) And we had fun. I think he rather likes it that I stood up for our views, and wouldn't be talked down, and even ventured to disagree with him on more than one topic!"

Dr. T. Dale Stewart, the director of the Smithsonian Institution's Museum of Natural History, had, like Carmichael, arrived in an analytical mood. But when Stewart lengthily elaborated on his favorite theory about the evolution of speech—the upright posture of early humans reducing pressure on the vocal organs and so on—Jane simply disagreed. Next morning Stewart mentioned that he had spent much of the night "thinking and thinking about the vocal organs and—this, that and the other." Carmichael chimed in. He also had been "thinking during the night" about something they had conversed about the day before. "So both learned gents had had food for thought. And began to enjoy themselves, and relaxed, and told jokes, and we grew to really like Carmichael. And what a brilliant man he is to be sure."

As for the third alpha male, the National Geographic Society's executive vice president and secretary, Dr. Melvin Payne, what of him? "Payne, dear Payne," Jane wrote home, "has emerged in his true colours."

Payne had been at first "oh, so pleasant and charming. So full of praise for the work here." But then Hugo introduced the issue of future films, and Payne, suddenly put on the spot, turned defensive. Or was it offensive? His face, Jane thought, "twisted with cynical malice. It honestly sent shivers up my spine." And so the conversation began, astutely observed by Jane and soon paraphrased: "Well, if Hugo thought it was a good idea to spend £5,000 of his own money and edit a film, Payne wouldn't dream of stopping him. But he couldn't guarantee that Joanne wouldn't pull the whole thing to pieces for the lecture. What did Hugo and I know of Constitution Hall lectures." This unpleasant and rather one-sided discussion continued.

Every question was either circumnavigated or firmly squashed. Every plea was answered with a sneer. Oh yes, with a disdainful shrug of the shoulders, oh yes, we could certainly edit a film for the BBC at some point, unspecified, in the future, after Doyle had finished messing about with the material. We could certainly do just what we liked with that—cold sneer. After all, was the implication, what did it matter what sort of film we concocted for some paltry, little-paying concern like the BBC with its trash.

Talk veered onto the topic of Jane's popular book. She was already obligated, she understood, to produce a book for the National Geographic Society, but would they then let her write a second popular book, something of her own, later on? Dr. Payne was "even worse" when it came to that subject. "He had no idea that Grosvenor had ever said he disagreed with my writing a second book after writing the Geographic book. How could [Payne] say that, when he was there at that ghastly round table discussion when Grosvenor said it was out of the question that any but the Geographic publication ever be written we just don't know."

And when Jane declared herself unhappy that her first lecture film was being shown to scientific audiences, Dr. Payne "nearly exploded with rage." Still, she was "livid too" over the issue, and later on, sitting around the campfire, when the topic of that first lecture film was brought up once again, she took the opportunity and "regaled Carmichael and Stewart with the examples of unscientific things which had crept into the film. Stewart was on my side in a flash. Carmichael looked into the fire for a long time, and could only say that anyway it served to interest people in chimps and in conservation. He was on our side too." Payne, though, merely sat there, "silent with rage."

Finally there was the matter of Edna's ambition to study baboons. What did Dr. Payne think about the chances that the National Geographic would sponsor baboon research? He was certain they would not, since there was already "quite enough animal research." Jane turned to the other two men, asking their opinion. They in fact were "most enthusiastic," which left Payne once again "silent in his bitterness. He doesn't like baboons."

On the bright side was the issue of a permanent research center. Leonard Carmichael, Jane reported to the family in England, was "so impressed that he feels this place MUST be put into a permanent footing." He added the further thought that the U.S. government was budgeting millions of dollars for primate research on captive animals; some of that money ought to be available for studying wild primates. Carmichael also expressed his certainty that he could find "qualified people" to take over at Gombe while Jane and Hugo were elsewhere, "because he feels as we do that there must be a continuity of observations, and the records must be kept. He was, in fact, wildly enthusiastic."

Melvin Payne may have been less so, but he did, on the way back to Kigoma, make the very useful observation that their 12-foot aluminum boat was too small for the lake and therefore dangerous.

Within a few days of the important trio's departure, Jane finished a draft of her second article for *National Geographic* and mailed it off to Frederick Vosburgh in Washington. It was a relief to be done, but the important thing just then was chimpanzee news. Circe showed up in camp with a new baby—named Cindy, once her sex was figured out. A few days later Madam Bee appeared, having been mysteriously absent for about five months and now arriving out of nowhere with her youngster, Little Bee, in tow, plus a tiny newborn. Jane described the event in an early-February letter to Mary Griswold at the Geographic: "We had been talking about her and saying we felt she must be dead only minutes before she arrived, because I dreamed about her last night!! Little Bee was still well, but Mama was very nervous. The new infant is 'Tiny Bee.' It really is most exciting—the 5th baby this season—the 2nd this year!"

The bliss of those two new babies was soon counterbalanced by a horrible death. Mandy was the last of the three mothers to give birth in 1964, and at the time Jane considered her to be an unusually "good" and solicitous parent, "so concerned for the well being of her infant," as she expressed it in a note to Louis that December. "It will be fascinating," she wrote then, "to see whether Mandy's solicitude has the effect of retarding the baby's development, or the opposite."

Little Jane had cut her finger early in January and for a while was unable to grasp things. But solicitous Mandy coddled her infant even after the finger got better, supporting her so much that she appeared to have lost the habit of clinging tightly to her mother. Perhaps it was that little cut, then the coddling, that resulted in a torn arm—as one day mother moved suddenly and baby fell. "Mandy came down the slope with a big group," Jane reported to Melvin Payne on February 13, "and when she was way up we heard agonized screaming. And then we saw it—little Jane, her 3 month old infant you remember—had one arm dangling loose, all the inside of her lower arm torn off from the elbow and dangling down over the little hand." Whenever Mandy moved, the infant screamed in agony. "She turned to the comfort of the nipple and suckled, but could find no relief. Mandy, of course, didn't understand at all, and when Jane screamed she pressed her close, adding to the infant's pain. It was about the most ghastly thing I've seen in a long while." Two days later they saw Mandy again, carrying the body of her baby and flicking away at a seething cloud of flies. Mandy appeared in camp two days later, this time alone, "her breasts very tight and swollen, but otherwise showing no ill effects. But sometimes she sits and stares and stares at one or other of the other infants."

By mid-February, meanwhile, all three of the aluminum prefabs were bolted into coherence, and the workers began attaching bamboo and grass thatching to the outsides. The bigger rectangular Uniport would serve as living quarters, the smaller Uniport was to be the work and observation building, and the much smaller Miniport, situated down the trail a short distance, would serve as the banana storehouse. With those first buildings up, the permanent research center Jane had imagined a year earlier had taken on a rough physical form. She soon reinforced its conceptual form with an official name: the Gombe Stream Research Centre.

Of course Jane was saddened by the prospect of soon leaving Gombe in order to take up her studies once more in Cambridge. "The saddest part to miss," she declared to the family on February 17, "will be the evenings at the new site over the ridge. It will be so simply glorious to have supper up there in the sunsets—which are simply glorious at the moment, and every night offers some new and beautiful painting." She was also unhappy at the prospect of an extended separation from Hugo, who was preparing to go off on his new assignment: still photography for a book about East African fauna the Geographic was planning.

As February ended and March began, thirty of the remote-operated banana boxes were carted up to the new camp and set in place, just about ready for use. Sonia Ivey, the new secretary and assistant, had arrived at the end of 1964 and was now thoroughly settled in. And Edna was, as Jane reported home, "full of life and fun" and "working really hard"—while Jane and Hugo were "quite frantic here with so little time left." Madam Bee had by then started coming into the banana-provisioning area regularly, bringing little Little Bee and tiny Tiny Bee, who had been rechristened Honey Bee. "How sad that we shall miss the story of Little Bee and Honey Bee," Jane wrote. "But how lucky to have someone to record it all and know that the facts will not be lost for ever."

26

Gombe from Afar

1965

WHILE JANE AND HUGO pulled down their tents and packed up their belongings, Edna and Sonia moved into the prefab accommodation building,
which was soon named Pan Palace in honor of its constituent aluminum
pans and the chimpanzees' scientific name, *Pan troglodytes*.

Jane and Hugo left camp on March 18, drove from Kigoma to Nairobi,
and stored their supplies and equipment at Louis's place in Langata. Between March 25 and April 5 the pair stayed in a tourist lodge at the Masai
Mara Game Reserve for a short holiday while Hugo began photographing
animals for the Geographic's planned book. They then made a brief detour
down to Dar es Salaam, where Jane gave a lecture and film show for President Julius Nyerere, but by April 11 they were back in Nairobi, Hugo returning to his animal photography and Jane preparing for the flight to England.

In Jane's vision, future research at Gombe would eventually spread beyond the study of the chimpanzees to include almost every other living
thing in the reserve, starting with the baboons. By December 1964, in fact,
Edna had completed a three-month preliminary study of one baboon troop,
and in late March 1965 she received word that the Geographic Society's
Committee for Research and Exploration had approved a £1,162 grant to
support her baboon project during 1966. Members of the committee were
also thinking about a magazine article on the subject, while Hugo was
already thinking of himself as the photographer for such an article and perhaps as the cameraman for a film to support Edna's future lectures at Constitution Hall. He had already shot some film footage on the baboons—and
on the insects.

Gombe, partly because it was situated in a mixed zone between eastern
and central African ecosystems, happened to be "the best insect area I know

of in East Africa," Hugo wrote to Melville Bell Grosvenor on February 2, 1965. Hugo had been trying to photograph insects all along, he explained, but in the past he had encountered two kinds of difficulty. First, insect filming was regularly interrupted by the importunate arrival of chimpanzees, which he was supposed to be filming. Second, his own entomological ignorance meant that he had concentrated on the most obvious things, such as eating and moving, with very little on the insects' full life stories as well as their many unusual behaviors. "And some of these unusual cases are fascinating. For instance there exists a caterpillar, which, before pupaeting, bites the spines off its back and sticks these in front and behind him on the twig. Having thus formed a barricade, it pupaets." So, would it not be a good idea to bring an insect expert to Gombe?

Hugo already had one such person in mind. Malcolm MacDonald had written to Jane and Hugo about his talented nephew, a young man who wished to take a year off before starting his undergraduate studies at Oxford University. John MacKinnon had "no official qualifications" on the subject of insect behavior, but he was still "very advanced in his field" and had conducted on his own initiative a study on the effects of irradiating hawk moths. If the Geographic agreed to sponsor a study of Gombe's insects, beginning in August, Hugo believed he would be able to join MacKinnon in later months and "film the results." Also, and not incidentally, John MacKinnon could serve as a "responsible male companion" for those "two girls looking after the chimpanzee affairs."

By the middle of June, Hugo learned that the National Geographic had agreed to his proposal and would contribute $1,500 to cover John Mac-Kinnon's expenses for the year, starting in August. Hugo would supplement the insect studies with photos and film, which might be used for a magazine article or a television or lecture film. And if the insect stills justified an article, then perhaps MacKinnon would be asked to write the text, and therefore "he should be instructed to take copious notes so that this information will be available."

So the Gombe research was moving in two new directions—baboons and insects—and Jane, back in Cambridge and learning about such new developments through the mail, must have been pleased with the accumulating evidence of the National Geographic Society's commitment. During this same period she heard another piece of good news. The society had also approved spending up to $3,000 to buy a new boat and was recommending a 16.5-foot fiberglass Boston Whaler. An attractive brochure picturing the proposed purchase was dropped in the mail, along with a note to Jane from Leonard Carmichael, stating that "when the question of your new boat was considered, Dr. Melville Grosvenor, who is as you know a former naval officer and a great authority on small and large boats, suggested that a so-called Boston Whaler might be very useful for you."

The Boston Whaler, propelled by a new 40-horsepower outboard, would be far faster than their old aluminum tub but also, and more importantly, much safer. Jane was never inclined to worry much about untoward events, the inevitable slippage and breakage of things, and perhaps she failed to appreciate that additional aspect of the new boat. But watching and managing Gombe from afar really required thinking about and planning for potential disasters.

Perhaps Hugo was right to be concerned about the welfare of the two very young women then running the research. Of course, Edna and Sonia had the support of a competent and reliable African staff. But then, would the staff remain as reliable as they always had been? Hugo must have asked himself that question after receiving an April 13 telegram from Edna: "Domenic departed without permission second time shall we fire please advise." Dominic, according to Jane's later account, soon retired and moved back to Kigoma with his family.

Hassan was a stalwart member of the staff, but his back was bad because of "a certain amount of osteo-arthritis," requiring a combination of drugs and physical therapy, as the Nairobi doctor had informed Louis (who paid for the consultation) the previous December. Hassan was now back at Gombe, and the drugs did help a little.

Well, if something went really amiss at Gombe, Hugo could straighten it out. Hugo was planning to stay in East Africa photographing animals until June, at which point he would move to England to start editing Jane's second lecture film for the Geographic. At least until June, then, he might be on call in an emergency. Meanwhile, in a letter of April 21 to Melvin Payne, he suggested some of the photographic successes he had achieved so far: decent shots of jackals, spotted hyenas, wild dogs, hunting lionesses and fighting lions, as well as various mongooses, impalas, and a baby elephant suckling at his mother's breast. But it was not really a good time for photography, given the recent appearance of some intense seasonal rains—and then, by the start of May, Hugo had begun to feel very ill.

He returned to Holland for a few days and then flew on to England to have himself examined and repaired. "He looks rather ghastly," Jane wrote to Mary Griswold on May 10, "and I am anxiously waiting for the results of his visit to the Tropical Diseases Hospital."

Hugo's association with the National Geographic Society often had an uncomfortable edge. They had once offered him a full-time staff position. He refused, choosing to remain a freelance subcontractor who was paid a $100-per-week retainer plus additional money whenever film he had exposed, still or moving, was used. But he kept having new ideas, proposing new plans, and then, unfortunately, needing more money. As one Geographic employee scribbled at the bottom of an internal memo during this period, "I am not unsympathetic to Hugo's problems, either personal or professional, but at the same time I have the distinct feeling that he is—perhaps unconsciously—beginning to take advantage of our well-known generosity." And now the question arose, who would be responsible for him while he was ill? Melvin Payne informed Hugo in a May 12 letter that the Geographic had decided to continue his $100-per-week retainer for up to four weeks' worth of hospitalization "should this be required. I earnestly hope that it will not." At the same time, Payne took the opportunity to remind Hugo rather sternly how much they had already spent on the chimpanzee film: a "very large sum of money . . . not only in the fees paid you as a photographer, but also the cost of the film and its processing, combined with incidental expenses incurred by you on the assignment." It was a figure "far beyond that which we anticipated," and thus, "to avoid piling any more expenses than are absolutely necessary on top of this present cost," Payne wanted him to limit himself strictly to two months' editing work on the lecture film. They would pay him a total of $200 per week during that period.

Hugo was treated for possible amoebic dysentery. After significant dental work in addition, he began recuperating in London at 1 York Mansions on Earl's Court Road, a flat Louis rented and sublet to Judy while she worked at the British Museum. She in turn sublet extra rooms to other young women, who all agreed to vacate whenever Louis was in town, so the place served as a pied-à-terre for him as well as for the Morris-Goodalls and van Lawicks.

Back at Gombe, meanwhile, Sonia Ivey was experiencing severe back pain, and on May 16 she informed Louis by telegram that she was coming to Nairobi for medical treatment and probably would not return to Gombe. In Nairobi, Louis hastily located a temporary replacement for her, a young Swiss woman named Mireille Gaillard, or Milly, who left for Kigoma at the end of the month, with the plan that she would assist Edna until John Mac-Kinnon showed up at the end of August.

Sonia arrived in Nairobi during the first week of June, in great pain and presumably walking with difficulty, as she lugged her personal gear plus one of the two Gombe typewriters, which had also broken down. Geographic funds would get the typewriter fixed, but who would pay for fixing Sonia? The chimpanzee research at Gombe was still officially a Louis Leakey project, which meant he was ultimately responsible. "Sonia is here and quite definitely unwell," he wrote to Jane on June 8. "The doctors who actually examined her have both gone off for a weeks leave (blast them!) and their partner informed me that she has both a slipped and disintegrating disc." She was actually employed by the National Geographic Society, Louis continued, but since the Geographic had everyone sign a release absolving the organization of any responsibility for illness or accidents, Louis was paying for her first week of hospitalization out of his own funds ("ex gratia, but not as a right"). Now, however, he was worried about his and Jane's financial responsibility for Gombe from afar, and he asked Jane to send him "any correspondence, copies, etc. of what you told Sonia when you appointed her, or what terms she agreed to in letters written to you," so that he could "sort out what your commitments are to her over this hospital business."

While Sonia was in the hospital in Nairobi, Edna (now assisted by Milly) continued with the chimpanzee observations, periodically sending out to interested parties—Louis in Nairobi, Jane in Cambridge and Comberton, Melvin Payne in Washington—a series of informal letters and slightly more formal reports. Of particular interest that year was her information on the four surviving infants born in 1964 (Flint and Goblin) and early 1965 (Cindy and Honey Bee).

Circe's infant, Cindy, around five months old by June 9, when Edna assembled her first report, was "developing her teeth nicely." She was becoming increasingly active, Edna concluded, "but Circe still holds her back a lot."

Melissa's Goblin, born the previous September, was now moving away from his mother for increasingly extended periods, up to five minutes at a time.

Flo's Flint also seemed to be developing normally, though he was often distracted by his mother's playing with the big males. Typically, such a play session would start with the male tickling Flint and his older sister, Fifi. Once they began laughing in glee, Flo could not resist joining in: tickling, laughing, rolling around. One time Flo played with old Huxley, a combination that was, Edna thought, "a lovely sight!" But then Flint, becoming "frightfully jealous," leaped on top of the two adults and whimpered for attention. The "big, dominant often grouchy Mike" also played with Flo and Flint. "He played very sweetly with Flint. At one point during that playing, Flint was on [Mike's] back and Mike got up and very carefully walked a little circle with Flint riding piggy back! Mike really seemed to enjoy it."

Mike had done a strange thing that spring with another youngster, the two-and-a-half-year-old Merlin. The chimp Hugo, a mature male who was somehow "in a frightful mood," happened to be sitting at the provisioning site when little Merlin left his mother, Marina, for a moment to approach the grouchy and volatile old guy, turning finally and presenting his white tufted backside in his own tyke-ish version of a friendly greeting.

> Hugo just looked at him so little Merlin backed up a bit more. Then Hugo grabbed his leg and sort of twisted it. Merlin shrieked with surprise and turned to face Hugo. Hugo then grabbed little Merlin and started display-ing with him as if he were but a branch. He hit him up and down on the ground, dragged him and finally threw him forward. Poor Marina in her condition was not up to it to come to Merlin's aid. Instead she escaped up onto the roof. But Mike — at the moment the most dominant male — came down his tree about 20 yards away and rushed up to Merlin with all his hair out. . . . I thought that would be the end of the little one but instead Mike gathered Merlin up in his embrace, turning his back on Hugo who came displaying down again and flapped at Mike. It was quite, quite in-credible. After a bit Merlin went out of his embrace and towards his Ma. On his way he passed Hugo [to whom] he gave one little defiant bark!

Merlin was one of Jane's favorites, but now, in the spring of 1965, his mother was very ill, emaciated and moving very slowly, and on May 9 she disappeared — along with Merlin. After a month had elapsed with no sign of either Marina or Merlin, Edna concluded that both were dead, noting in her report to Dr. Payne that "I wish we could have saved at least little Merlin!"

Marina's older daughter and son, six-year-old Miff and eleven-year-old Pepe, were still alive, however. Miff, young enough to have spent nearly all her time with her mother, somehow survived Marina's death and now regu-larly appeared at the banana site alone. But poor little Merlin had still been very small, nursing, completely dependent. How could he possibly have outlived his mother? And yet Merlin returned to the provisioning site a month later, in mid-July, an event Edna described in a July 21 letter to Louis Leakey:

> I had quite given up hope on him and his mother Marina. She had not been for about 2 months and her daughter Miff, who was always with her, had come here alone. But all of a sudden the little one — only about 2½ years old, appeared in camp with his brother. Everybody [chimps] was delighted to see him and embraced him. Since then he has stuck with his sister Miff who seems to take care of him. His mother must have died. How that little thing could possibly have survived seems a real miracle! But it was certainly a happy moment to see that little face again!

Merlin's sister saved his life by adopting him that summer, remaining over the next year his almost constant companion, spending many hours each day grooming him, patiently waiting for him to catch up as they moved from place to place, and lovingly taking him into their shared nest at night.

During the spring and summer of 1965, Jane (reading about such far-off events in the letters and reports sent her way) remained mainly holed up at Cross Farm in Comberton, dutifully pounding away on the typewriter at her doctoral dissertation. "I am absolutely flat-out on infant development," she had written to one correspondent soon after she arrived, "and have nearly got it worked out. Which is super, as its a big chunk of material." As usual, however, she was vastly overcommitted.

Back at National Geographic headquarters, Jane's draft for her second magazine article (tentatively entitled "New Discoveries Among the Wild Chimpanzees") was batted around by the official readers. One considered it to be "equally spectacular as the first Goodall story" and "full of valuable discovery," and recommended that the magazine "hustle this into the first issue possible, depending (sob) as always on the pictures." A second found it "extremely dull" and concluded that "the author needs help." A third thought it required "a somewhat more delicate discussion of the chimps' sex life. These animals are too close to human, and the details get a little too explicit." Finally, Frederick Vosburgh rolled all the opinions together and on May 11 sent the manuscript back to Jane with the summary comment: "The gist of our opinion is that a great deal of work must be done on this story before it is up to the standard of your first fine contribution." He wanted it fixed up and cut in half.

Jane's first impulse was to turn the whole thing over to her mother. Vanne, after all, had been to Gombe, knew most of the chimps and all of the people in the story, and was certainly an excellent writer. Finally, though, Jane realized it would be quicker and simpler to revise the article herself, which she did by June 21.

In Washington, the editorial readers seemed pleased with the revised version. As one wrote, "This is a very good article and a unique anthropological document. Jane Goodall writes clearly (though she doesn't know how to use commas), she has plenty to tell, and something is happening all the time." Around the same time the society had located suitable sponsors — Britannica and Aetna — for the television film, which was now scheduled for broadcast on the CBS network on December 22. The society decided to publish the article in the same month.

Meanwhile, Jane was just completing another burdensome project, a chapter on "Mother-Offspring Relationships in Free-ranging Chimpanzees" for a book collection, *Primate Ethology,* being assembled and edited by Desmond Morris.

Then someone on the *Geographic* editorial staff began to think that her "New Discoveries" article should be tightened a little more. An editorial assistant named Andrew H. Brown was flown to England to convert Jane to that line of thinking—with, as he reported back to headquarters on July 27, little success. "Jane was fussy in limiting my . . . editorial discretion to dramatize sentences or incidents." She refused to open the story with the chimps noisily charging up the hill to the new camp. She firmly insisted "on the conservative use of words and presentation of situations so that there could be no possibility of misinterpretation by scientific readers." Brown would have preferred to describe chimpanzee Mike as standing "low on the social totem pole," but Jane argued that the word *totem* was burdened with "so many specialized anthropological meanings that it was unacceptable." Nonetheless, Brown informed his colleagues that the current version of the article had been "approved overall and in detail by the authoress." So now it was *really* finished, and Jane could turn her full attention back to the doctoral dissertation.

Except that she had a few lectures to plan. She had agreed to give one big talk at a symposium sponsored by the Wenner-Gren Foundation, to be held at its castle in Austria that coming September. She was scheduled for another on October 27 at the Royal Institute in London. There were the Constitution Hall lectures in Washington to think about, scheduled for February of the following year, along with an expanding series of other American lectures and appearances being arranged.

During this time, as Lyn Newman later reported, Jane was so focused on her work that she hardly ate. "She lived on Nescafé and the occasional apple," according to Newman. "I cooked one meal a day for her to make sure she had enough food." By the end of July, Jane was so overwhelmed with her endless and solitary literary labor, and perhaps with the nightmarish vision of never-ending projects and responsibilities, that her body gave out. Her doctor pronounced her anemic and announced that it was (as Hugo put it in a July 30 note to Louis Leakey) "high time she had a holiday." By August 2, Hugo was explaining to Andrew Brown in Washington that Jane was in hospital and would be there for at least a week, more probably two or three. The physician had hinted that he might well "forbid her to do any more work for two months."

After Jane underwent several days of tests and consultations in London, her physician concluded that she was suffering partly from a minor infection but mainly from exhaustion as a result of overwork, and he prescribed bed rest for six weeks. That was not possible, but Jane did return home to

Bournemouth for a few days in the middle of the month, preparing to leave in early September for the Wenner-Gren symposium. Planning also for a happy and relaxed holiday after the conference, Hugo rented a little country chalet close to Konrad Lorenz's Max Planck Institute in Seewiesen.

Hugo described such problems and plans in a letter to Melvin Payne, noting that "unfortunately due to the large amount of work she must have ready by December it will not be possible for her to have a complete break" during the Austrian holiday. However, they were pursuing other strategies to lighten her burden. Perhaps, for example, the academic administration could be persuaded to give Jane another term at Cambridge, enabling her to turn in the thesis next March rather than in December. Also, they would make the pile of typing ostentatiously thicker with lots of photographs.

Around the same time, Louis wrote to Jane's Cambridge supervisor, Robert Hinde. Jane was not only "physically ill," he declared, but "in a considerable state of mental worry" and "trying to do far more than can possibly be necessary for her Ph.D. thesis." Louis reminded Hinde that after nearly five years of fieldwork, Jane had already produced eight thousand pages of typed journals and commentary. Since everyone could agree that the essential goal was for her to recover her health, Louis thought it reasonable—assuming she ran short of time before the December deadline—that she be allowed to add a brief introduction and conclusion to "<u>the very considerable amount which she already has prepared</u>" and hand that in.

Back in Nairobi, meanwhile, Sonia Ivey's physician had written pessimistically about her "prolapsing lumbar disc," concluding that "she can return to some activity, but must continue to be very careful, wear her corset, do her exercises & refrain from any strain or bending." Sonia was determined to return to Gombe, however, and she finally persuaded Louis to agree; but Louis, increasingly concerned about his own liability in such matters, required her to sign a waiver before she left: "I, Sonia Ivey, having been duly informed. . . ."

John MacKinnon had arrived in Nairobi by then, and he and Sonia traveled to Kigoma together, arriving on August 26 with her personal gear and his very large suitcase. Louis shipped back to the reserve the once malfunctioning typewriter, now fixed, and a chair for Sonia so that she would no longer have to sit on a battered old oil drum while typing.

While fragile Sonia returned from Nairobi to Gombe, fragile Jane left England for Austria, accompanied by Hugo, to attend the Wenner-Gren symposium on "Primate Social Behavior" from September 2 to September 12 and report on "Expressive Movements and Communication in the Gombe Stream Chimpanzees." She arrived at the castle, the Burg Wartenstein, with some dread, fearing that she might never feel at ease among the distinguished scientists there. But she already knew a few of them: Irven DeVore, Sherwood Washburn, and Irenäus Eibl-Eibesfeldt (who had visited Gombe a year earlier). And she soon found she got along well with most of the others, including David Hamburg from Stanford University, Phyllis Jay from the University of California at Berkeley, Peter Marler from Rockefeller University, and Hans Kummer and William Mason from the Delta Regional Primate Center in Louisiana.

Indeed, Jane was having a fine time. The castle was, she wrote to Louis, "a fantastic place for a conference." Wine was decanted liberally at the dinner table while "thousands of concepts evolved," and after dinner the conferees retreated to the chapel garden for classical music. Jane considered it her first really serious professional conference, and it was uplifting to find that she was accepted as a peer, as an important scientist herself. The only problem was Hugo, who was miserable: awkward and glum and apparently feeling isolated. He disappeared the second evening after dinner, and Jane found him lying on the bed, smoking a cigarette and very angry. He began verbally attacking her for the fault of "being happy." Jane considered his reaction to be "jealousy, pure jealousy," as she once told me, and she "cried for hours." For the first time, she began to think their marriage would not last.

On the final evening of the symposium, Irven DeVore and Sherwood Washburn sang an amusing, mildly obscene song about chimpanzees to Jane, and then she and Hugo moved on to their post-symposium holiday at the rented chalet. They had also rented a sporty little MG for the duration, "grossly extravagant" Jane admitted in her letter to Louis, but still a lot of fun, and "the open air is just wonderful." Their chalet was located in "really beautiful countryside," she wrote home, and they did plenty of pleasurable holiday things: rode a cable car into the mountains, walked into the pine forests, ate wild blueberries and raspberries, and made friends with "a chatty pig." Hugo was in a much better mood now, and he spent some time spinning out elaborate plans to establish a big naturalistic aquarium, tourist center, coffee shop, and marine research station on the Indian Ocean near Mombasa.

Together they visited Konrad Lorenz at the Max Planck Institute to show the lecture film Hugo had just edited. The institute was "so beautiful and quiet," Jane thought, "with the lake and the calls of the geese." And the famed Dr. Lorenz, though he was not feeling well ("pains in the abdomen"), proved to be "completely delighted with the film." He was "terribly quick to pick out the different chimps. And we can certainly rely on his whole hearted support. It made us laugh that he is so like Louis. Just as quick to jump to conclusions and maintain that something is so because—well, it <u>must</u> be!" They also spent a pleasant evening at the home of Irenäus Eibl-Eibesfeldt—or Eibl, as Jane called him—and his two houseguests, Hans Kummer and Bill Mason, who were now identified as Jane's "castle" friends from the symposium. Kummer had been studying hamadryas baboons in Ethiopia, and Hugo and Jane, in a burst of postprandial enthusiasm, decided they should look at those baboons too. Kummer was intending to return to Ethiopia in a few months, and Hugo declared he could go out there in a couple of years to film the animals. Jane added that she would conduct her own comparative primatology on the terrestrial monkeys.

In that manner Jane and Hugo informed and entertained themselves during their September holiday, with no recorded spark of anxiety fanned by the thought of her thesis looming and undone in England, and with only a few hints, remarks, and small acts directed toward the continuing problems at Gombe—particularly those described in a long letter dated September 8, which they had just received from Edna.

Edna wrote that John MacKinnon was turning out to be "a nice chap" who was "very eager and very enthusiastic about his work." He had been exploring the reserve and catching butterflies, and always came back "scratched or bitten and hot and saying he hates the country and certainly hates insects! and then he gives a big laugh. He seems to be doing well." MacKinnon had already learned several of the chimps' names, was adept at setting up the banana boxes, worked every evening writing up his reports, and, with four sisters of his own, was able to cope with the inevitable teasing from Edna, Sonia, and Milly. Also, someone had lent them a phonograph and some records, and so now they were listening to "lovely glorious classical music in the evenings. Beethoven, Bach, Pucinni, Vivaldi, Paganini and Mendelssohn have all enraptured us with their glorious music. You feel quite civilized when listening to them quietly!"

But the tape recorder was not working.

Also, there was the boat problem. Since the National Geographic had not delivered that promised Boston Whaler, the Gombe residents were stuck with the aluminum dinghy, and its motor no longer worked. "Our motor was hurt in Kig[oma] with some big waves that came up," was how Edna phrased it.

Also, Hassan had left because of a death in the family.

And what was Milly doing there? Milly had written to Louis early in

August to announce that because her father had just had a third heart attack, she would be departing for Nairobi almost immediately. But she kept postponing her departure, and as time passed it became clear that her father was not so seriously ill. Now, in her September letter, Edna confirmed it: Milly's father was actually "alright."

The Sonia issue was more complicated, if only because Sonia wanted to be there. Still, she had reinjured her back during a bumpy boat ride, and, as Edna now reported, "it all hurt in exactly the same places where it did before," making her once again "an invalid." Sonia was unable to bend over and could not open or close any of the banana boxes. She could sit for only half an hour at a time, even with the new chair. She needed to rest an extra two hours each day. She was not supposed to be walking up or down hills. And she remained in a perilously vulnerable state: "Any jar can bring the disc straight out again, and if it does it might be permanent her surgeon says."

But certainly the most upsetting news had to do with the chimps. All the chimps had been ill that summer, information Milly had passed along casually in an August 25 note to Louis: "Every single one has a cold, they even passed it on to Edna and me, but it seems to trouble the chimps much less than us." And Flint, as Edna was now reporting, had failed to recover. All the other chimps' runny noses had gotten better, but Flint's cold turned into something worse, pneumonia perhaps.

> He was frightfully weak, would not hold onto Flo who was very good supporting him and she herself seemed very worried often looking down on him. He just sat tottering on the ground groaning, felt very hot and his eyes were not very bright. You can imagine in what a state Milly and I were! We tried to get a penecillin tablet into him but Flo was extra wary with him and it was impossible. Yesterday he seemed slightly better. Got a b[anana] and ate some of it, also he suckled again. So I am just praying that he will pull through. He is a strong little fellow full of the love for life so he should. He was funny with other chimps. Absolutely could not tolerate to be touched and wraahed and bit at anybody who came near him. Poor thing he must have been so miserable. I was too sick about it to write to you.

Flint recovered. Yet the whole episode was a reminder that chimps are susceptible to almost every disease that plagues humans (and vice versa)—and a warning.

Louis wrote to Jane and Hugo on October 11, after they had returned to England, about his own concerns. "I have nightmares that one of these days some human disease will be introduced to the chimps now that they are in such close contact with humans, and that they will be wiped out. I am not joking—this could happen, and I am not at all convinced that the girls appreciate the danger." Louis, in fact, was increasingly aware of the many, many things that could go wrong at Gombe managed from afar, and he emphatically pressed Hugo to "tell me what you have done about insurance for Edna, Sonia . . . and Hassan and the other men. This is terribly important, as should any of the staff meet with an accident, the financial implications could be very drastic and lead to endless trouble." He also strongly encouraged Jane to develop stricter policies to protect the chimps from disease. He wondered whether everyone going to Gombe should have a tuberculosis examination beforehand. And he argued that any person working there who contracted any infectious disease, even a cold, should be "banished to the shore camp, and not run any risk of infecting the chimpanzees."

Jane agreed, in a quick response to Louis's letter, that the chimps were at risk from human diseases and that they should "take as many precautions as possible." She also thought it was important to keep casual visitors away from the provisioning site or at least limit them to not more than one at a time. In truth, however, such rules were almost impossible to maintain from a distance. Edna had brought "various young men to the site several times—this we strongly disapprove of but we cannot enforce this rule unless we are there."

Louis would remain responsible for the chimpanzee research at Gombe until the end of the year, and he would submit the Gombe budget and grant request for 1966. Once Jane finished her degree, though, the grant money would start going directly to her, along with most of the accounting, legal, logistical, managerial, and medical headaches. So from Jane's perspective, insurance and a stricter policy regarding human-chimp contact were very good ideas, important for a Gombe run from afar—particularly now that her scheme for a permanent research station was developing.

Along with Edna Koning on baboons and John MacKinnon on insects, a third researcher, a young Englishwoman named Caroline Coleman, was due to arrive in November and begin a six-month study on chimpanzee play behavior as part of her work for a Ph.D. Jane and Hugo were also, as Hugo wrote to Louis that August, hoping to find someone to study facial expressions and analyze chimpanzee vocalizations. Altogether, he and Jane believed that "the research is bound to start growing fast and while the going is good we feel we should encourage specialised studies to be carried out on the chimps." Of course, housing all the new people required several more

Miniports. Hugo sent Louis £60 in that same August letter and instructed him to order one for John MacKinnon. "Could you therefore please have one railed to Kigoma with two windows, a door with lock, and plenty of nuts and bolts," he wrote.

Louis did; and then he put into the final version of the 1966 Gombe budget a request for funds to buy eight more. By the end of October, Jane and Hugo were presented with further evidence of the society's generosity and support: a bonus of $2,500 to Jane as "compensation for unusual demands on her time and for her cooperation" on the forthcoming magazine article, a bonus of $1,900 to Hugo for the same article, a lump sum of $10,000 to Jane for her help on the television show, and another of $3,000 to Hugo for his. The alpha males in Washington were apparently happy with the soon-to-appear article, while they must also have been relieved that the television show was finally wrapped up, and they were now looking forward to many future adventures and productions with the van Lawick-Goodalls. Hugo, they agreed, would return to photographing for the East African animal book. Jane could join him but should also start writing her popular chimpanzee book.

Hugo made a quick trip near the end of October to the society's headquarters to show the results of the chimpanzee lecture film he had edited and also to persuade important people, especially Melville Grosvenor, that it was, in spite of his minimizing the usual "human interest," just right. Then, in mid-November, he flew from London to Nairobi, took a room at the Ainsworth Hotel, and discovered himself feverish and broke. He cabled the Geographic: "Safari delayed am in bed with fever badly need 1500 advance expenses. . . . Regards." But the fever receded while the Geographic proceeded to cable the necessary funds, and so he was off.

Jane, meanwhile, was by November 5 (as she wrote to one correspondent) "working flat out on the final stages of my PhD thesis" and by December 16 had (she wrote to another) "just surfaced!" She was finished, and so she could relax long enough to appreciate the December issue of *National Geographic*, with a lovely picture of herself (Baroness Jane van Lawick-Goodall) on the cover, along with Flo, Fifi, Flint, and a huddled and hairy bunch of others.

The CBS television special, *Miss Goodall and the Wild Chimpanzees*, followed on Wednesday evening, December 22. But before the flickering icon of a young Miss Jane Goodall could excite the phosphorus inside the screens of 20 million North American television sets, the actual Jane was back in Nairobi and catching up with Hugo. She failed to sleep "a wink" on the flight from London, according to her first letter home, but it was still a "good journey" and she thought Hugo looked "very fit" — though he "defi-

<u>nitely</u>" needed a session with the dentist. Still, the dentist would have to wait, since they were just then rushing frantically about, rummaging through the storeroom at Louis's place in Langata, "carrying bundles & tying on mattreses," packing up all the essentials for their overland trip down to Olduvai for Christmas and the New Year and then "TO THE CHIMPS!! To sort out various muddles!"

The protagonist wakes.

Mortimer, Vanne, and Valerie Jane outside the flat at 2 Clabon Mews, Chelsea

The two sisters, Valerie Jane and Judy

Feeding the birds

With Nanny,
Judy, and Jubilee

The family (left to right): Judy, Olly, Danny, Audrey, V.J., Eric, Vanne

The Alligator Club (top to bottom):
Red Admiral, Puffin, Ladybird, Trout

On Daniel at Bushel's

Ready for school,
late 1940s

The Reverend Trevor Davis

Rusty loved getting dressed up.

Mortimer and his nineteen-year-old daughter at dinner, London, 1953

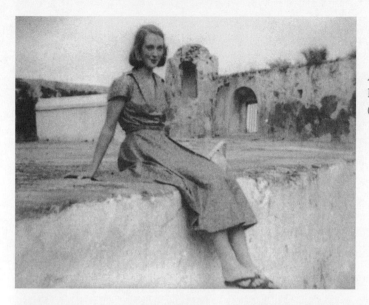

At Fort Jesus,
Mombasa, May 1958
(*Courtesy of Brian Herne*)

Dancing with Brian Herne
at Ngorongoro Crater
(*Courtesy of Brian Herne*)

In the dugout canoe at
Malindi, May 1958
(*Courtesy of Brian Herne*)

left: Louis Leakey at Olduvai Gorge, circa 1957

below: Vanne and Jane try out their life jackets while sailing from Mombasa to London, December 1958.

In the tent at Gombe with Vanne, preserving specimens

Vanne with new arrivals at the clinic

Following chimpanzees
at Gombe

Recording field notes by lamplight

Easter Saturday, 1964, in Chelsea
Old Church, London

Jane and her baby son, Hugo Eric Louis van Lawick, with Jubilee, England, 1967

In the Serengeti
with George Dove,
a good neighbor
and great friend

Hugo gives Grub a
swimming lesson.

Hugo feeding Grub in the Serengeti, 1968

Grub helps with the laundry at Gombe, summer, 1968.

Grub with his childhood hero, Maulidi Yango

Robert Hinde and Melissa
visit camp at the same time.

Left to right: Yasini
Selemani, David
Riss, and Jumanne
Mukukwe
(*Courtesy of Caroline van
Zinnicq Bergmann*)

Derek Bryceson visits Gombe.

Maternal love: Fanni and Fax

Maternal labor: Flo, Flint, and Flame

(Courtesy of Patrick McGinnis)

Flo, pregnant with
Flame, summer 1968

Males J.B. and Humphrey make their presence known.

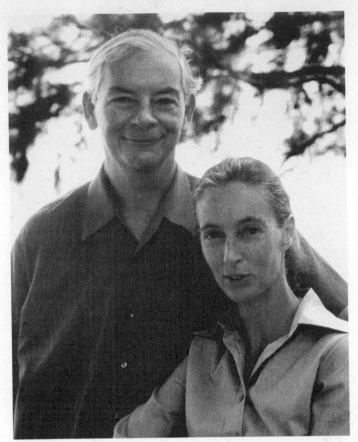

Jane and Derek in 1976

Derek's widow in 1981, receiving condolences from Mwalimu Julius Nyerere, first president of Tanzania

Visiting the chimps at LEMSIP, 1988.

On the road with Mary Lewis
and Mr. H

Secretary-General Kofi Annan names Jane a UN
messenger of peace.

A giant peace dove flies in the Grand Tetons. (*Courtesy of David Gonzalez*)

The family gathers, 1997. Standing: Grub and his daughter, Angel; Maria; Jane; Judy and her daughters, Pip and Emma. Seated: Olly, Vanne, and Merlin. Whiskey is on guard.

27

A Peripatetic Dr. van Lawick
and the Paleolithic Vulture

1966–1967

HUGO'S HALF BROTHER Michael, recently arrived from Holland, was camping near the Leakey digs at Olduvai in December 1965, and Jane and Hugo caught up with him at Louis's usual campsite in time for tea on Christmas Eve. Immediately after tea, they all went out to look for animals and soon found a cheetah and her eight cubs. Then they returned to camp and settled in for a chicken dinner, balloons Jane had brought from England, wine, and a happy tearing-open of cards and presents. It was a very pleasant Christmas Eve, and the next day they moved some distance away from the Leakey camp, set up their own camp, and celebrated all over again.

By early January, Jane, Hugo, and Michael had driven down to Kigoma and proceeded on to Gombe, where Jane hoped to sort out the "various muddles."

The young Swiss woman, Milly, had left sometime in October. Sonia had gone on a healing and rejuvenating holiday in Kenya, intending to come back in February and stay for several weeks, until a replacement could be found. Edna was still there but had made up her mind not to do the baboon study and was now planning to leave for good on January 13.

Since John MacKinnon was occupied with his work on insects, Edna's departure would leave only twenty-three-year-old Caroline Coleman, who had arrived just two months previously, to keep the chimpanzee observations going. And so Michael, who was quiet, artistic, and moody, agreed to stay at Gombe to draw insects and keep John and Caroline company while Jane and Hugo, after three days at the reserve, left for the 5,700-square-mile Serengeti National Park so Hugo could photograph animals.

They spent most of January on the Serengeti and then enjoyed, as Jane wrote to Lyn Newman, "5 glorious days down at the bottom of the crater" before climbing finally, in their heavily loaded Land Rover and trailer, up "the most frightfully steep road you can imagine." At the top of the rim they stopped at Ngorongoro Crater Lodge, where they were greeted by someone at the desk who said, "Oh, I think there is mail for you," and passed over two large envelopes sent by Louis from Nairobi, with, Jane estimated, nearly a hundred letters in them.

Louis's accompanying note informed them that several applicants for the secretarial position would be waiting to be interviewed at the Ainsworth Hotel in Nairobi on February 6 and also that a telegram from Professor Thorpe named the date of Jane's Ph.D. oral examination in Cambridge: Wednesday, February 9.

Jane arrived in Cambridge on the evening of February 8, and on the next day she and her work were tried before a medievally costumed jury of academic superiors. After it was over, she waited out in the hall for the results, feeling, as she later told me, "sick" with apprehension. Robert Hinde finally appeared.

"How did I do?" she asked.

"You passed. You didn't have any doubts, did you?"

"Yes!" she said.

The next day, in a small gesture of gratitude, pleasure, and triumph, she sent a brief telegram to Louis, "We had a pleasant flight," signed by "Dr. van Lawick."

Dr. van Lawick caught a Sunday, February 13, flight to Washington, D.C., and began her American lecture series on the following Thursday evening before 3,500 people in the grand auditorium of Constitution Hall. Jane was "Bambi-like," according to a reporter for the *Evening Star,* who also noted that the recent television special had scored higher ratings on national television than *Tarzan of the Apes.* And, in a "romantic story twist," the man who had gone into the "jungle" to film Jane and the apes, Baron Hugo van Lawick, had stayed on to marry her, thus transforming her into Baroness Jane van Lawick-Goodall. She was a scientist, a scholar, and a courageous beauty among the beasts. "On listening to her impeccably turned Cambridge accent, it is difficult to equate this scholarly woman with a scene dominated by dozens of powerful and unpredictable beasts. Yet she has named most of them, has won their confidence and can discuss the habits of each at length."

After two more Constitution Hall appearances the following evening (at

5:00 and 8:30), she moved on to Ohio for a presentation at the Cincinnati Natural History Museum, and from there to the Maryland Academy of Sciences and then the Philadelphia Academy of Sciences. She proceeded to the South and to the West Coast for talks in the vicinity of Tulane and Stanford Universities before returning to the East Coast, on March 6, to lecture at the Boston Museum of Science and then the New York Zoological Society.

Vanne and Hugo had attended Jane's Constitution Hall lecture as guests of the National Geographic Society, and Hugo had accompanied Jane during some of her travels around the country. He also received his weekly retainer during this time (until March 1), provoking Melvin Payne at the Geographic to huff in an internal memo: "We are certainly not going to pay him a retainer to act as Jane's 'Prince Consort.'" Still, Hugo was present and presumably useful during the February 24 meeting of the Committee for Research and Exploration, when the Chimpanzee Project budget for 1966 was presented and reviewed. Louis had submitted that budget the previous year, but the committee postponed its formal review until Jane became Dr. van Lawick and was officially in charge. Aside from a minor change in Louis's final version—a request for six prefabricated aluminum Miniports instead of eight—the budget was more or less the same . . . except that Jane had tacked on an "Additional Grant Request."

As she now explained to the committee, the additional request was necessary as a result of her and Hugo's increasingly peripatetic existence. At the end of April they would return to Gombe in order to check up on "how smoothly things are running" as well as introduce Caroline Coleman to a revised system of data collection. Naturally, Jane would also be working on her popular chimpanzee book, while Hugo would be filming insects. Around the middle of July, they intended to move their operations into the Serengeti, where Hugo would be taking pictures for the Geographic's East African animal book while Jane hoped to complete the chimpanzee book and then "to analyze for final scientific publication all of the data collected to date—in far greater detail than time permitted for the Ph.D. thesis."

In the past their research assistants at the Gombe Reserve had been able to contact either them or Louis in an emergency, as when Sonia hurt her back. But Louis was withdrawing from his day-to-day association with the Chimpanzee Project, while Jane and Hugo would be more remotely located. Thus, in order to ensure that things continued to run smoothly, Jane was first requesting a set of radiotelephones that would connect their car, wherever it was, with Gombe. The radiotelephones were expensive—about £1,000—but necessary, she thought. Second, she hoped that the Geographic would support someone to serve as their "reliable contact" and factotum in Nairobi. They had already found someone for this position: Mike Richmond, who worked at East African Film Services in Nairobi. For £10 per month, Mike would make himself available to forward messages and mail, run errands, and take care of some of the routine work with which Louis had previously been stuck. And third, because Hugo's work meant that "we shall be constantly moving our camp . . . depending on where the animals are," Jane needed a reliable shelter for writing the book and her other scientific work. In January she had tried working inside a tent, which turned out to be less than ideal, "owing to heat, wind and dust." She was now proposing that the Geographic buy her a Volkswagen bus, which could be turned into a "traveling office," with a table, chairs, cupboard, filing cabinet, and air conditioning.

Those unusual requests added another $7,056 to the budget, bringing the estimated total for 1966 up to $20,900. But since the National Geographic had yet to advance a penny for the popular chimpanzee book Jane would soon write, the additional costs were minor compared to what might have been expected. After a short discussion, the committee approved Jane's full proposal and budget.

Jane and Hugo returned to England and by March 11 were writing thank-you letters to their Geographic associates from the flat in London. But if their original intent had been to rush back to Africa, the itinerary was complicated by an invitation from the San Diego Zoo, planning to celebrate its fiftieth birthday in early April and hoping Jane and Hugo could attend.

They left for San Diego on March 30 and "had a fantastic time" (as Jane described it in a letter to Leonard Carmichael) serving as the central celebrities in an enormous celebration. Best of all was the children's birthday party on April 3, by coincidence Jane's own birthday, which featured a 100-yard-long birthday cake laid out along the zoo's primate section. "I had to cut the first piece! It was quite a performance, and the children loved it — so did all the great apes who were all given pieces as well." Jane and Hugo were then honored guests at the Safari Supper, held at the San Diego Convention Hall for members of the Zoological Society. With almost four thousand people in attendance, it was the largest indoor dinner in the city's history (according to Sheldon Campbell, an organizer of the event, later writing to Melville Grosvenor). After the meal they showed the lecture film Hugo had edited, with Jane providing commentary. "The applause at the end of the film and Jane's presentation," Campbell wrote, "was spontaneous and lengthy." If, back at Geographic headquarters, Hugo's lecture film may have been considered a competitor to Robert Doyle's recently broadcast television film, then Sheldon Campbell inadvertently added to the conflict with his subsequent comment to Grosvenor: "It is a far superior film to the one used on television by CBS, and the San Diego audience was quite manifestly enthralled by it. The 'comedy' scenes were among the funniest, I am sure, that these people have ever seen, and there was no question in the minds of astute observers that the film would be greeted elsewhere with the same response."

Jane and Hugo caught an April 8 flight back to England, where she polished up for publication a final version of the lecture she had given at the Wenner-Gren symposium, while he packed and otherwise prepared for Africa. They flew to Nairobi around April 18, staying at the Ainsworth Hotel and engaging in further packing and preparations. Mainly they had to locate radiotelephones; order six new aluminum Miniports from Booth Trading; buy a telescope, tape recorder, cutlery, and camp chairs; and place an order for a Volkswagen bus modified to become Jane's air-conditioned traveling office. The vehicle they settled on—the only one in stock—was light gray on the outside and very cozy on the inside. No air-conditioning system would work properly without running down the battery, and so they bought an electric fan instead. The bus would be converted to an office by Jane's specifications within a month, they were told—and so Jane and Hugo left on April 24 for a safari to Tanzania's Manyara National Park, doing six days of photography for the East African animal book, after which they drove to Dar es Salaam to show the new lecture film to President Nyerere.

When they at last headed for Gombe, the roads were flooded, so instead of driving, Jane, Hugo, and an engineer supposed to install the radiotelephone system and antenna at Gombe were flown down by Mike Richmond. The single-engine plane was, unfortunately, "much too overloaded," as Jane soon wrote home, which meant a lumbering and uncertain flight. Thick banks of fog made the trip simultaneously "hair raising" and "tremendous fun," from Jane's perspective, but soon they were all safely back at camp with their mattress, boxes, new typewriter, and luggage piled into a heap inside the smaller rectangular Uniport, which had lately been named Lawick Lodge.

Michael van Lawick was still there. Sonia Ivey was now gone for good, replaced as secretary by an older woman named Sally Avery, who shared Pan Palace with Caroline Coleman. Both of them were "living in luxury" there, as Jane phrased it in her letter home. Caroline was "doing excellently. She is a very conscientious and neat person, just as we thought. Very thorough, and everything is kept quite up to date and ship shape. She is rather extravagant in her tastes, but we don't think she is spending more money than she should. And she certainly likes the chimps. She is a bit tired at the moment as they have been having a terrible two months—chimps here the entire day through with scarcely a moment to even have a cup of tea or visit the choo!" As for Sally Avery, she appeared to be "working out fine." She was "sweet actually, and also loves the chimps. Very quick typist, does shorthand so Caroline dictates the notes which saves the tapes."

John MacKinnon was also there, still working on his insects and now living a short distance away from the Ridge Camp. John had assembled and settled into his own little aluminum rondavel the previous November or December, and he was now living at a beautiful little spot slightly above the ridge, with a pleasant view of the lake.

The chimps were also doing well, Jane thought—except that, most frustratingly, the recent rule against touching any of them was being ignored by the camp staff: "So far as we can see, even Caroline has been touching them. It really is hopeless." Also rather hopeless was David Greybeard, who "when he comes he takes one by the hand and leads his victim to a [banana] box." David was "too dim" to understand that the boxes were opened by a remote handle, and so "you sit with him at the box held in his iron grip, and he gets progressively more livid because you don't open the box." So now, after David was allowed his ration of bananas for the day, everyone was forced to go inside the buildings and stay there until he had given up and left.

Most of the rest of the chimps were fine. Little Flint was turning into "an absolute dear mischevous wicked imp. Never still for more than a few moments at a time, and always up to some mischieve." His sister, Fifi, was, in an amusing way, "worse than ever. Really wicked. She has developed a pashion for throwing, with very bad aim (I know I spelt that wrong!). But she doesn't just throw one stone. She collects stones until her hands are full and then goes stamping off towards the poor female she is about to attack, scattering her stones all round her." But Merlin—the wonderful little "boy," three and a half years old now, who had been orphaned the previous summer and adopted by his older sister, Miff—had sadly failed to thrive. Miff was still taking care of him. Jane and Hugo followed the pair one evening and watched Miff build a nest while Merlin ate caterpillars before climbing into the nest and snuggling up with his sister for the night. But he was now "a most sad and pathetic little chap."

> He is actually smaller than Flint, except that his limbs are longer. But, even worse than his skeletal form, is his apathy. We watched Master Flint trying to play with him this afternoon—it was quite horrid. Flint jumping all over him, and Merlin just crouching down, taking it all—rather like a mother being attacked by a male. He does all sorts of peculiar things—for instance, when he grooms himself, which he does all the

time, he pulls his hairs out by the roots, with his teeth. He is like an old neurotic little man.

And then, near the end of May, Jane and Hugo witnessed a spectacular drama of predation and meat-eating from start to finish. She described it for the family:

> MEAT-EATING. Saw Hugo (chimp) hitting a baboon (young, not baby) in camp!! He had it by leg and was bashing its head up & down on the ground. Saw the <u>whole</u> meat-eating sequence. Hugo being selfish. Mike chasing all others away from him—& getting the liver—JB begging from Mike & crying when he couldn't get any. Hugo carrying the carcass over his shoulder. . . . Lying asleep with it. Suddenly getting up & leaving it on the ground. The others, his faithful persistent followers, staring in disbelief & then all with one accord pouncing on it. Mike, Goliath, JB & Huxley & David. They <u>all</u> grabbed it & pulled. Mike attacked them all & finally got it. Rushed off, flailing it. But the others rushed after him and grabbed it again. Guess who got the best bit?—David!! Up a tree with a rump & one leg.

David sat up there chewing away at the prize, his back turned to the rest of the group, occasionally doling out tiny bits to some lucky supplicants: a "tiny splinter" to Goliath, a "bare bone" to Flo, and "3 tiny bits of cartilage" to Mandy. Mike, meanwhile, was lying back on a branch and holding the baboon's head above him with his foot, then, with one free hand, grotesquely grooming the disembodied head. Mike shared some of his portion with JB, but stopped sharing, whereupon JB gave up—or appeared to—and reclined farther away on the branch and just above Mike. But all of a sudden JB "rushed past Mike, shot down the tree, & was gone. I peered, wondering what he had seen. Mike was staring after him with ½ open mouth." Then she saw: "Mike's share was gone!" It was "the prettyest bit of snatch & run robbery I ever saw!"

Jane soon inserted a polished recollection of the whole episode into the chimp book she was working on—only she changed chimp Hugo's name to Rudolph, in order to avoid any confusion with Hugo the person. She was "plodding on with the book," she informed the family on June 4, having already produced "in a semi-sort of way, 5 chapters." Still, she found the National Geographic's expectations irritating: "Awfully difficult doing it the way they want—beginning with now, and sort of darting backwards and forwards like a grasshopper." As a kind of mental vacation, she would occasionally think about the book she really wanted to write: her own version of a popular book about the chimpanzee work, which she privately called "the real book"—and now, at last, she had thought of the name for it. In the same letter home, she asked if it was appropriate to "patent" a book title, "because I have thought of another title for my book—the real book. I only hope that this one has not also been used before, though both Hugo and I feel that it really <u>must</u> have been. 'In the Shadow of Man'—super, don't you think?"

By then people seemed to be in the mood for attaching words to lots of things. For instance, they had decided to call the new Boston Whaler, which had finally arrived, *Pink Lady*. Then there was the new Ridge Camp *banda*—a shaded, open-air dining area consisting of a concrete floor, low walls, and a thatched-over aluminum roof on poles—soon named Troglodytes Taverne. Other improvements at the Ridge Camp during this time, such as painting the inside of Pan Palace sky blue and cream, building long bookshelves onto one wall and a new deck for Sally to do her typing on, and so on, inspired a new name as well, and Pan Palace became, experimentally at least, Chimpanzee Castle. The urge for renaming even extended to the chimps, when Melissa's two-year-old Goblin was turned into Goblin Grub. As Jane wrote home that summer, the extra name was added "because he always, always has a dirty face."

While the humans were engaged in this peculiar flurry of naming, the chimps also kept themselves busy. Three youngsters—Fifi, Figan, and Evered—had figured out how to remove the attachment pins from the remotely located lever handles that kept the banana boxes shut. The pins were replaced with screws, but the same three soon learned to unscrew the screws. Although the older chimps never quite grasped exactly how it was done, they soon realized that the three younger chimps figuratively held the key, and so the older ones, upon seeing the trio of geniuses fiddling at remote handles, would gather around the boxes and wait for them to fall open. In turn the youngsters, finding their ingenuity exploited, did their best to open the boxes unnoticed by the others. "The record," Jane reported to Melvin Payne, "was when Figan strolled to a handle, opened the screw, but then sat, gazing in all directions but the box, and with his foot idly on the handle— thus keeping the lid closed. Only when none of his superiors were near the box did he release the handle and go to collect his well-earned meal!!"

The technology race continued. Mike Richmond in Nairobi was soon ordering forty new boxes that would be made from a combination of steel and fiberglass, to be encased in concrete and locked with an electrical system powered by a car battery. Buried electrical wires would connect the boxes to four control panels inside Lawick Lodge, thus enabling human researchers inside (and looking out the windows) to present bananas methodically outside by pressing numbered buttons. "It all seems weird," Jane wrote home later, after seeing a prototype box in operation, "but should really fox cunning little devils like Fifi!!"

Meanwhile, Jane continued to struggle with the book for the National Geographic. By early July she was sending typed "final chapters" to her mother for feedback: "Hope you can read this lot and send comments quickly, as the sooner I get it off to America the better—plenty of time to correct their corrections! and make sure that there are no sordid mistakes." The book, Jane wrote to Lyn Newman, had turned into a project "almost as bad as the thesis!" Nevertheless, it was then truly almost, almost done, or, to be more precise, "in its last but one stage now, all but the last 2 chapters which are in their last but two stage! Mind you—the Geographic havn't seen it yet—I may well have to do the whole thing over again! Not enough 'human interest' or something!"

Hugo left Gombe on July 2 and spent about ten days in and around Amboseli National Park, photographing elephants and colobus monkeys, followed by a few more days elsewhere pursuing oryx, gerenuks, and steenboks. On July 25 he returned to Gombe, whereupon he, Jane, and Michael flew to Nairobi and began packing for another safari. Jane was celebrating "the fact that for the first time in 6 years I do not have a weighty work hanging over my head." And now, in Nairobi, she had her first opportunity to look over the customized VW bus the National Geographic had paid for. It was "absolutely super," she wrote to the family in England. "Our first little house."

Leaving Nairobi at the end of July and heading south into the great East African plains, their safari caravan consisted of two vehicles, the Volkswagen traveling office (christened Satyre) and Hugo's Land Rover (Troglodyte). Jane had her first experience of driving a vehicle on the rough roads and tracks of the great plains, and "it was fun," she wrote home a few days later. Satyre was "super to drive, but rather like being in a very rough boat—when one meets the waves head on. Or on a bucking horse!"

Originally they had planned to start Hugo's photography work in the Ngorongoro Crater, and they arrived at the rim at dusk but were quickly persuaded by "the rhino man, who works there," that they would have better luck in the Serengeti, so they turned around and set up their first camp on the way down from Ngorongoro to the Serengeti. "And oh! the wind. We could hardly get out—it nearly blew us over."

A day or two later, while traveling into the central Serengeti, they made a discovery that was, as Jane wrote home, "so exciting we can hardly believe it (and it is a dead secret at the moment till published in Nature). A NEW TOOL!!!!!"

A great fire had been spreading across that part of the Serengeti. The day before they had kept away, since it was "all black and horrid," but now (on August 2, the day before she described the events in her letter) they returned with the intention of revisiting "a handsom male ostrich with the reddest of necks," who was guarding a nest with five eggs. The first time they had seen him the fire had just passed, and Jane and Hugo could hardly believe that the bird and the nest and eggs had survived, but they had.

Then Hugo noticed a high circling and swooping congress of fowl in the distance and drove across the rough, burned-over ground to see what the attraction was. Approaching the spot, the two vehicles spooked away a hyena, who thus left an abandoned ostrich nest and some very large white eggs to the noisy delectation of about twenty vultures. Most of the birds were big and of the usual variety: white-backed vultures, Ruppell's griffons, lappet-faced and hooded vultures. But two were the smaller and "rather pretty" Egyptian vultures, with white bodies, and "feathers up the neck, and then just a bare patch round his cheek which, like the beak, is bright yellow. And bright yellow legs." As Jane, Hugo, and the rest of the group cautiously approached this avian assembly in their vehicles, they could see that only six ostrich eggs remained unbroken, while

the big vultures were squabbling round the broken eggs, picking up the remains of the yolk. Suddenly one of the little Egyptian ones did something strange. Our first thought was that he had a bit of a chick. And then we saw he had a big stone in his beak. Well—you can guess the rest. Between them, they broke three eggs. They took the stones in their beaks, reared up as high as [they] could go, and with a sudden downward movement threw their stones directly down towards the egg. Often they missed. One managed in 6 goes. The other, once, took about 12. He was a hoot. He was eating one egg, and seemed more or less to finish it—a lot ran onto the ground of course. There was a whole egg about 5 feet away. Standing by his old egg and looking at the new, he picked up the stone he had cracked the old egg with and threw it to the ground—by his old egg. Picked it up and repeated. Picked it up, took a couple of steps, threw it down. Did this three more times before he got to the new egg!!! Either sort of displacement or perhaps because it was heavy for him, and it was a means of getting it there. The latter not very likely. Because, to our utter astonishment, he was able, once he had cracked the egg, to get hold of the little indentation and actually raise the whole egg—about 3 or more pounds—from the ground and bang it down. And the Egyptian vulture is one of the very smallest of the vultures. Once they had cracked open an egg, the other big vultures pushed in and drove them away. Until we drove a bit closer, and then the big cowards flew away and we could watch the little ones open another each. Then they were full and flew away. Isn't it FANTASTIC!

Jane and Hugo understood at once that they were watching a rare instance of an animal using an object as a tool. They had been recording new cases of chimpanzees using and sometimes preparing objects as tools at Gombe, such as crumpled leaves serving as sponges and a palm leaf as a fly whisk. But other than the chimps, they could think of only four other animals known to use objects as tools: California sea otters swimming on their backs with flat stones pressed to their chests, cracking shellfish by smacking them down on the stones; Galápagos woodpecker finches using twigs or cactus spines to probe for grubs; sand wasps wielding small stones for engineering purposes; and marine crabs clutching stinging sea anemones as shields or weapons to discourage intruders. So this new observation, Egyptian vultures using stones as projectile hammers, belonged to an exclusive list, and Jane immediately determined to write up an account of the discovery and send it to *Nature* in England (which in June 1964 had published her two-page piece on the Gombe chimps' tool use).

Seeing that three of the abandoned giant ostrich eggs were still intact after all the birds had gone, Jane and Hugo picked them up and toted them back to camp. Jane wanted to taste one, and Hugo chipped a hole into the shell and "gurgled" out the contents into their biggest frying pan. "It came out looking thick and dark red and [altogether a] thick glutinous jelly. With some froth at the end. However, determined to try something I have wanted to try for years, I tipped half into a smaller pan (equivalent of 10 or so hens eggs, the half was) and beat and beat it. And scrambled it." At first it looked "like a rich too wet cake mixture," but after further scrambling the consistency altered, until it finally resembled that of an ordinary egg. "Well, believe it or not—it tasted simply super—in fact, it tasted like particularly well scrambled hens eggs! Everyone has always said how rich it is, etc—maybe they got their eggs when they were nearly hatched, or something. Ours wasn't rich, oily or in any way different from a free ranging hens egg."

During the next three weeks they continued looking for Egyptian vultures hanging around ostrich eggs, and in case they should find vultures without eggs, they carried with them the two intact eggs. They saw no more of the vultures in the Serengeti, though, and after a time they moved out of the park and over to Olduvai. They were soon lucky enough to find three Egyptian vultures there, which they then provoked with the two weighty orbs. "And Hugo got the most fantastic stills, and film, and I got a really good (I hope) bit of film on the 8 mm," Jane wrote home. "It was quite fantastic—especially the first of the two eggs we put down. . . . Because two of the birds (a pair) were opening it at once, and each wanted to stop the other. Oh it was funny. One nearly hit the other on the head with its stone."

By then Jane and Hugo had started planning their itinerary for the next several months. Hugo was still working on the East African animal book, but in the meantime George and Kay Schaller had arrived in the Serengeti to study how lion predations affected the other Serengeti animals. *National Geographic* quickly enlisted Schaller to write a "Life with the King of Beasts" article, and Hugo was asked to take the photos. He hoped to start working on them next year—after he had finished with the hyenas.

Hugo had become friendly with a Dutch scientist named Hans Kruuk, who, with his wife, Jane, was studying hyenas and their predatory impact in the Serengeti and Ngorongoro Crater. *National Geographic* had signed Kruuk for a hyena article, and Hugo had also been assigned as photographer for that.

But while Hugo was photographing hyenas and then lions, what would Jane do? Having finished the National Geographic's popular book on chimps, she decided that her next big writing project was to transform her doctoral dissertation into a scholarly monograph for publication, and she believed she could do that in the shelter of the Volkswagen while accompanying Hugo on his photographic safaris in the Serengeti and Ngorongoro. She also planned to conduct her own special research project on Serengeti mongooses. Meanwhile, of course, both Jane and Hugo were thinking they might produce something significant—perhaps an article for *National Geographic*—on their discovery of the Serengeti's paleolithic vultures.

In the final week of August they returned to Nairobi, staying in, as Jane wrote to the family at the time, the "most horrible hotel," the Agip. Jane, Hugo, and Michael spent three days in town, unpacking and repacking, reading the piles of mail that had accumulated, responding as necessary. They went to pick up the forty electrically operated banana boxes ordered several weeks earlier and found them not entirely finished, and so drove away with only twenty. Jane mailed off her chimpanzee book manuscript to the National Geographic. They met with Louis and told him about the tool-using vultures. And they rendezvoused with Phyllis Jay, another of Jane's "castle" friends from the Wenner-Gren conference. Finally, Jane sent off, on August 26, a dramatic telegram to Melville Bell Grosvenor: "Exciting news we discovered vultures using tools to open ostrich eggs stop this only second recorded avian tooluser stop recorded on stills and cine regards."

At the same time Hugo mailed the society ten rolls of stills and two reels of motion-picture film on the same subject. Having gotten no response by late October, he followed up with a note to Joanne Hess, explaining that he thought the National Geographic should pay for some of Jane's expenses during his photographic safaris, because she was doing work that would be "of great value for picture legends and story writing, which I alone could not manage in addition to photography. For instance we have about 200 pages of behaviour notes on the animals photographed, and could very soon if need be write one or two small factual articles. (I especially think here of course of the vultures using tools.)"

Around the same time, Jane sent one of her regular reports to Melvin Payne, summarizing the latest events at Gombe (including the installation of the new banana boxes, which were now "working wonderfully"), describing her plans (including the part-time mongoose study in the Serengeti), and explaining the logic of her accompanying Hugo on his photographic safaris. "One exciting result of my accompanying Hugo was, of course, that I was with him when we saw the Egyptian Vulture tool-using. We still find the whole thing hard to believe. When you consider that, apart from chimpanzees, possibly a gorilla, the sea otter, and the Galapagos Woodpecker Finch, no other vertebrates, so far, have been see using tools in the wild—well, it really does seem a fantastic piece of luck that Hugo and I have been able to observe a fifth!!" She attached to that report a copy of the scientific paper she and Hugo had written of the discovery, which they were about to submit for publication in *Nature*.

But aside from a single courtesy response to Jane's telegrammed announcement of August 26, sent by a lower-ranking staff member, no one from the National Geographic responded to any of their tool-using vulture news. And as if to express that yawning institutional indifference even further, several rolls of Hugo's photographs on the subject were lost.

Perhaps the absence of a response demonstrated not indifference so much as distraction and a growing alarm about Jane and her increasingly peripatetic existence. The question of whether the society was still getting its money's worth out of Jane reached the point, by the end of 1966, that an accountant in the business office was instructed to add up everything spent so far on her and the Chimpanzee Project, including the two Franklin L. Burr Prizes. He arrived at a grand total of $60,531.23. That odd number was handily, and strangely, rounded off to an even $76,000 by Melvin Payne when, during a meeting of the Committee for Research and Exploration on the morning of December 8, he expressed his serious concerns about "becoming a patron of Miss Goodall and not just supporting her scientific research."

Dr. Payne was not alone in his anxiety. Gilbert H. Grosvenor, son of Melville Bell and associate editor of the magazine, noted that "she is branching out more and more. . . . The chimpanzee study is important and we were wise to support it. The question is how far we want to go in supporting her studies of other animals in other places." T. Dale Stewart also weighed in. Although Jane was "going into other areas which will enlarge her perspective," he was nevertheless "not too happy about her going with her husband to study other animals." Thomas W. McKnew observed that as far as the chimpanzee research at Gombe was concerned, "she is becoming more of an administrator and less of a working scientist and is supervising an expanded operation involving other investigations." In the end, the committee approved Jane's request for a grant of $23,909 to sustain another year of research at Gombe, although Leonard Carmichael officially requested that Dr. Payne tell Jane and Hugo about their discussion that day. "She should know about the concern of the Committee as regarding the expansion of her activities and the fact that our research funds are limited and that, while we are interested in her work, we do not want to support a diffuse project."

The committee's worries about their peripatetic Dr. van Lawick were reasonable. Her approved chimpanzee research budget for 1967 would raise the combined investment in her and Hugo to more than $150,000—a considerable sum when the society's entire annual research budget was only $750,000. Moreover, during that same meeting the committee also reviewed a distinctively assertive application for $25,000 submitted by John Owen, the director of the Tanzania National Parks, to assist in the legal transformation of Gombe from reserve to national park.

Several months earlier, both Jane and Louis Leakey had sent to their favored contacts at the Geographic confidential letters regarding the Owen problem. As Jane wrote to Leonard Carmichael on May 5, when John Owen had previously applied to the Geographic for funds and been turned down, he had become "extremely angry" and seriously contemplated "banning all Geographic photographers from the Tanzania National Parks." Louis, writing on the same day to Melville Grosvenor, described the situation in direr terms. As a result of past rejections from the National Geographic, Owen had become "somewhat vindictive, or at least hostile to the Society and its projects." Turning Gombe Stream from a reserve into a national park would certainly increase its importance, long-term stability, and physical protection. But when the realignment took place, Louis warned, Gombe would "automatically come under his [Owen's] complete and direct control. He would then, I think, try to prevent the continuation of Jane's research work." Such an event would be, of course, "tragic."

In response to these warnings, Melvin Payne sent a telegram directly to Owen, advising him of serious "rumors" attributable to "idle gossip" and asking for a "word from you dispelling this most disturbing report." Owen responded quickly, emphasizing in a return letter how much he appreciated Payne's "friendly tone and the concern it shows to remove any misunderstanding that may have arisen between us." But since such matters were very difficult to resolve effectively in writing, he suggested that they meet during his upcoming trip to the States and discuss them in person.

Thus, early that November, John Owen, Melvin Payne, and Melville Grosvenor met for a private and informal lunch at Geographic headquarters, during which Owen pointed out how the society had benefited financially from its access to the Gombe Stream reserve for many years. The three men also discussed the future of society photographic projects in the Serengeti and other Tanzanian parks, and they came to a tentative agreement that Jane would be exempt from park entry fees and Hugo would be classified as a researcher rather than a photographer, giving him camping privileges. He might also be required to pay only £10 per week in picture-taking fees, rather than the usual £50 for professional photographers, unless any of his material was subsequently used for television or commercial films.

When John Owen's grant application was reviewed by the Committee for Research and Exploration a month later, Dr. Payne explained the situation bluntly: "Owen personally is an aggressive man and, if we do not assist in this project, he may not be sympathetic to our research programs." Owen had made it quite clear that "he expected the Society to have a part in transforming the Reserve into a park," Payne went on, and in fact he and Dr. Grosvenor had already "assured" the man that the National Geographic Society "would give some support." Although a number of other participants in that December meeting grumbled that such "pressure" for a grant was "not desirable," in the end they yielded, and a check for $25,000 was soon made out to Tanzania National Parks.

Such complications, doubts, and extra expenses may help explain why no one at the society or the magazine had so far shown the slightest interest in the tool-using vulture story. But on the day before Christmas, *Nature* published "Use of Tools by the Egyptian Vulture, *Neophron percnopterus*," by Jane and Hugo van Lawick.

The news quickly spread into other English publications and then rippled across the Atlantic, into the *Washington Post* by December 27 and *Time* by January 6, 1967. On the same day, Charlene Murphy from *Geographic*'s illustrations department sent the following telegram to Hugo in Nairobi: "Additional pictures needed for magazine rock throwing vultures stop suggest using motor drive camera stop please advise prospects stop editorial will advise text length when photographs in hand letter follows."

Murphy elaborated in her letter that an article in a "local newspaper" had "aroused some interest here," and certain senior staff members wished to know whether Hugo was continuing his observations and photography of the paleolithic vulture or working on something else and planning to attend to the subject at a later date. Hugo's misplaced rolls of film were soon found. And Jane and Hugo began working in earnest on their third *National Geographic* article, "Tool-using Bird: Egyptian Vulture Opens Ostrich Eggs," which finally appeared in the May 1968 issue.

28

Epidemic

1966–1967

ON THE SAME DAY that Jane cabled Melville Bell Grosvenor in Washington to announce the discovery of the tool-using vulture, August 26, she sent him a second telegram revealing a second piece of exciting news, the birth of Olly's baby, named in honor of the Geographic president himself: "Baby grosvenor born to chimp olly stop mother son and sibling gilka thriving."

Accompanied by Phyllis Jay, Jane and Hugo and Hugo's half brother Michael returned to Gombe on September 1, taking twenty of the new electrically operated banana boxes. John MacKinnon had finished his year of insect studies by then, and Caroline Coleman and Sally Avery were in charge of camp management and the chimp observations. But Caroline was worn-out by the climate and work and had also developed a compelling interest in a Kigoma bank manager. Meanwhile, Sally had injured her right leg in an accidental collision with a chimpanzee; according to the doctors she saw, the injury had precipitated arthritis in her leg, and the medicine she took to alleviate the arthritis had precipitated kidney complications. "I fear we are losing Sally," Jane wrote home. "She may have to have a kidney operation. It is a long story, and she <u>may</u> be O.K." Still, the new banana boxes with their spiffy electrical locking system, operated by pushbuttons from inside Lawick Lodge, were "quite <u>fantastic</u>."

The chimps seemed generally fine, although Merlin, carried about and attended to by Miff, was still weak. Interestingly, Merlin had been joined by a second orphan in the community. A mother named Bessie had disappeared—probably died—leaving her two female offspring, Bumble and Beattle, on their own. Just as Miff had adopted Merlin, so Bumble, the older sister, adopted little sister Beattle. As for the new mother and baby, plain old long-faced Olly was a "super Mum," and the newborn baby was "so gorgeous." Yet tiny Grosvenor was "an amazingly vocal infant—he protests vigorously every time Olly moves when he is trying to have a snooze. Likes his comfort!"

Actually, Grosvenor screamed a lot, particularly when his mother moved, as if her motion caused him pain. Jane had suspected something was wrong from the start, and the screaming grew worse. Then one day, when the mother bent to get some bananas from a box, the baby, clinging weakly, almost dropped to the ground.

Early the following morning, Olly arrived at the provisioning area clutching her howling infant, who was now making no obvious effort to hold on to his mother at all. Indeed, except for his head and face, tiny Grosvenor appeared to be "quite paralyzed." Still, Olly held on to the baby "most tenderly, and seemed almost to pluck up her courage to move, because she hated it screaming." When the mother left later that morning, carrying the baby and accompanied by her four-year-old daughter, Gilka, as well as an early-adolescent female named Gigi, Jane followed. Olly climbed a tree and began nursing the infant. Gilka and Gigi also scrambled into the tree, playing together. Then Gilka approached the baby, still in his mother's arms, and began attempting to groom him. From ten to eleven that morning it rained, and after the rain Olly descended from the tree, carrying a baby who was now ominously quiet and motionless.

Next morning Olly and Gilka showed up at the provisioning site together, with Grosvenor's dead body draped around Olly's neck like a fashionable fur piece. After they left camp, Jane followed them for six hours, watching Gilka desperately try to play with and groom the corpse of her little brother and even attempt to hug and carry it, with Olly then rushing to rescue the object from young Gilka's overeager attentions. "It was unutterably horrible. And the stench was enough to make one sick." But eventually the chimps scuttled into pig tunnels through dense thickets, Jane crawling after (with "the stench of death clinging closely to the tangled vines and leaves") until they finally disappeared.

Around lunchtime on the next day, Olly and Gilka arrived back in camp without the dead baby. It had been "a most tragic affair," though; and, adding to the gloom, Merlin looked as if he would not survive the rains. He was now severely emaciated and half hairless, having neurotically plucked most of the hair from his legs and much from the rest of his body. He shivered a lot, and his face turned blue in the rain. He was still cuddling up in the night nest with Miff, but Jane was certain that Miff would soon end that arrangement: "Already, as he climbs up to join her, he is starting to whimper — as a youngster whimpers when it approaches to suckle and fears it will meet with no luck. Poor little scamp."

. . .

Hugo's East African animal book photography took them away from Gombe by September 17, when he, Jane, Michael, and Phyllis drove the Land Rover and VW bus north to Murchison Falls Park in Uganda. It was enervatingly hot there during the middle of the day, but the discomfort was worth it, Jane informed Lyn Newman, given "the lovely scenery" and the presence of many hundreds of elephants. Early in the morning elephants wandered into their camp and gently investigated the tents and guy ropes with their trunks.

By October the safari had moved on to Queen Elizabeth National Park, and then, as of October 19, they were back in Nairobi. They picked up the last twenty electric banana boxes and, on the twenty-fourth, their new research associate, a recent graduate of San Diego State College in California named Alice Sorem.

Jane and Hugo drove the banana boxes and Alice down to Kigoma by November 1. Back at Gombe, they learned that Caroline Coleman would be married and gone by February, while Sally Avery would be leaving in early December. At the same time, Anyango, the cook, had just returned from a mission hospital, where a surgeon had removed an "abdominal mass." He was now recuperating but still looked very weak, so Jane and Hugo decided to send him to Nairobi for further tests.

Two visitors arrived at Gombe around November 10, a text editor and a picture editor from the National Geographic, flown down to review last-minute changes to Jane's book. Jane wrote home that the text editor was "one of the nicest Americans I have ever met," while the picture editor was "rather a brash, pleased with himself, young man—but he's been quite fun to have around." Still, the significant thing was—"what a surprise—the book is going to be a really nice book." Her text had been reorganized but not fundamentally altered. "If it stays as is, the writing is all mine, and the only things they have cut are 'human interest'!!!!!! And they have asked for more on pink ladies [estrous females]!!!!!! And the drawings have been made by a man who draws animals—and, the ones we have seen, will really benefit the book. You will have to wait and see, but most of them are quite enchanting. There are also going to be paintings—but not by Geographic staff artists. They have hired the top illustrator in the whole of U.S.A.!!!!!"

All those exclamation points in the good-news part of Jane's letter may have been erected as conceptual palisades against the bad news, which was appalling. It had started with the appearance in camp of Gilka, Olly's four-year-daughter, who was now showing her own alarming ailment: a paralyzed wrist. Next appeared the "ghastly cases" of Faben (eldest son of Flo) and Madam Bee. "Oh how horrid it is," Jane wrote. Faben's right arm and Madam Bee's left were "completely useless" and "just trailing and dangling." Without that arm as locomotive support, Faben had taken to walking upright, and it was "uncanny, spooky and ghastly to watch him." Madam Bee, still clutching her baby, Honey Bee, got around on two legs and one arm, limply dragging the other limb along.

After seeing Faben, Jane and Hugo guessed that the disease was polio, and when Madam Bee arrived, they felt certain. There were other casualties. The frail orphan Merlin had last been seen in September dragging a useless foot. He was now probably dead. Miff and J.B. had also disappeared. Other chimps seemed to have experienced at least temporary symptoms of paralysis: Olly had trouble walking on a foot, Sniff had a dangling hand, Melissa had a stiff neck, David Greybeard was unable to put weight on one leg.

Then there was Pepe. Jane had been attending to another chimp when "suddenly poor Alice (what a start in Chimpland for her) gave me a whistle. I went up the slope and found her in floods of tears." Alice wanted to know who that chimp hunched on the doorstep of Lawick Lodge was. As Jane reported home, "I felt sick." Pepe was entirely paralyzed in one arm, partly in the other, and his legs were weak. "And he was moving in a squatting position, his bottom just off the ground, waddling forward on one bent leg after the other. It was so horrible."

Pepe shuffled weakly into camp the following day and then noticed Humphrey, who stared at Pepe with his hair raised and his face twisted into an expression of fear. "And Pepe just looked up, his mouth wide open with fright, and then turned and stared behind him. What was this thing terrifying Humphrey? How could he know it was his pathetic self."

Hugo took the boat to Kigoma, where a physician confirmed that a few human cases of polio had recently been seen in town and in two villages between Kigoma and the reserve. The villages were at that time within habitat range of the reserve, and chimps would sometimes appear on their peripheries, so perhaps the virus, which spreads orally, had been transferred through discarded food scraps. But now, of course, an immediate and obvious worry was that the virus might transfer back from the chimps to humans, and so Hugo arranged for a supply of oral vaccine to be brought down on the same plane that would soon fetch the pair of National Geographic editors.

In mid-November the first batches of vaccine arrived and were distributed to everyone at Gombe. On November 22, Anyango, weaker than ever, departed for tests, and a few days later Louis Leakey radiotelephoned with the news that Anyango was dead. He had been working at Gombe for a long time, and he was well liked. News of his death, apparently from cancer, saddened everyone. Until the second week of December, however, everyone was distracted by the continuing threat of paralysis or death from polio. Since the disease has an incubation period of about three weeks, no one could be sure of having escaped infection until at least three weeks after starting the course of oral prophylaxis.

As soon as all the people at Gombe had started taking the oral vaccine, Jane and Hugo began distributing it to the chimps, inserting appropriate doses into bananas and taking care that every chimp who came to the feeding area got enough but not too much. "We have a big vaccination chart," she explained to the family, "and mark off those that have taken it." But it was a "ghastly business," full of "tactics and worry and tension." More than half the chimps who had taken their banana-laced dose had done so "without a second thought." Among them, Flo and her young offspring Fifi and Flint had been "good—though Flint gave us heart attacks because he took it out of his mouth, and kept sniffing. He knew something was wrong. But obviously didn't mind it." Among the rest of the chimps, "our worst horrors came when giving it to females who come seldom and in big groups—what if a male charges a female, making her drop her vaccine, and he eats it—and has already had just one dose. We presume he would get polio." At any rate, by the second week in December they had vaccinated three fourths of the familiar crowd, not counting small infants. By that time, however, Mr. McGregor was dead.

Bald on top of his head and across his neck and shoulders, the egg-loving chimp was perhaps thirty or forty years old when Jane first encountered him, and during their early acquaintance he was belligerent. If she accidentally approached too closely, he would threaten by shaking a branch or suddenly jerking up his head. The combination of age, appearance, and personality reminded her of the grouchy old gardener in Beatrix Potter's *The Tale of Peter Rabbit*, which accounts for the name. But now dear old McGregor was stricken, and in the final week of November he emerged from the forest with both legs paralyzed. "He managed to pull himself up to camp," Jane recalled in a December letter home. "He was moving either by sitting upright and inching backwards using his arms as crutches, or by pulling forward on his tummy—when the vegetation was strong enough—or by rolling, or, somehow by using his arms to pull his body up and turning head over heels. He had lost bladder control, and all his legs etc stank of wee. He was surrounded by clouds and clouds of flies. He <u>loathed</u> the flies. We flitted and flitted and took him food."

Once he made it to camp, the old male seemed to take refuge there, hanging around for the next several days, laboriously dragging himself with his powerful arms up into a low-branched tree to make his nest for the night and then, in the mornings, lingering late before descending with great difficulty. While he was in his nest, Jane and Hugo passed up eggs inside palm-frond baskets, palm nuts balanced on the ends of sticks, and speared bananas. At first he resisted, but within a couple of days he had adjusted to the point that, once down from the nest, he would lie back and allow Jane to drip water into his mouth with a sponge. The seething cloud of fat shiny flies obviously tormented him, and Jane started killing them with a hand-squeezed aerosol. That too frightened the old guy at first, but soon he was behaving as if he appreciated the gesture.

The chimpanzees were less charitable with this disturbingly transformed member of their community. They stared intently, and then, perhaps out of fear or intolerance for such a shocking violation of normalcy, some of the big males made aggressive displays around him. McGregor's terror in those circumstances was "pathetic." Goliath one time moved up to McGregor on the ground, put his nose right down to the ape, and sniffed. "Gregor just lay, and then, fearfully, reached a hand to Goliath," but Goliath stared and sniffed once again and walked around the broken figure. The worst incident happened after McGregor had finally settled into his night nest, and an excited Goliath, hair ferociously bulked out, entered the tree and began thrashing about in violent threat displays. "And Gregor was clinging on, really for his life, and bowing his head as branches broke around him and his nest—made with such labour and difficulty—was destroyed. At last he really was forced to abandon his nest, and swing lower. His screams and fear face were horrible—at first it was just fear—no sound at all. Then Goliath stopped (it was his fifth display) and sat near the ground." McGregor lowered himself as well and tentatively stretched one hand toward Goliath in a submissive gesture. Goliath accepted the gesture and reassuringly "patted and patted his hand. And all was over. But it was so ghastly to watch."

Within a short while, the typical reaction to McGregor had changed from aggression to avoidance, with the other chimps moving away whenever the smelly, fly-infested ape painfully crawled or wriggled or rolled their way. Everyone, that is, except Humphrey. In the past, Humphrey and McGregor had been such regular companions that Jane believed they were probably brothers. And now, with McGregor suddenly struck down, Humphrey seemed simply "lost." During that terrible moment when Goliath had so vigorously threatened McGregor with displays in the tree, Humphrey, nearby, had overcome his own fear of Goliath to leap into the tree and display back, albeit ineffectually. And although he never groomed or touched his old friend, Humphrey slept nearby every night. In the daytime he sat around camp, never very far away from McGregor, as if waiting patiently for his friend, or brother, to snap out of it.

Jane and Hugo had nurtured the small hope that McGregor would recover, but in the end they concluded they would have to shoot him. The appropriateness of that decision was reaffirmed when McGregor wrenched one of his arms, leaving only a single limb with which to yank himself about. Now he was unable even to lift himself into a tree and so was left, helpless, sprawled out weakly on the bare ground.

Early in the evening, with their lamp flickering and McGregor half asleep, almost snoring, in a "deep wheezy breathe," Jane and Hugo tried to inject him with morphine, but he batted the syringe away. They tried again. Again he batted it away. They left him and returned to camp for a nine o'clock dinner. Later that night, Jane, flashlight in hand, crept back down to see her old friend.

> He opened a sleepy eye as I approached. I gave him a banana and he grunted and ate it, with a few wadge leaves. Then he reached to a little bit of twig, and bent it down under his chin. Why hadn't I thought of it before—of course, he couldn't reach anything and he wanted a nest. So I picked him a huge pile of green branches. And even with all this crashing around, and torch shining, he was not afraid. I put the pile by his good hand—he at once bent in branches under his head and neck, using good arm and teeth and chin. And then sank his head onto his curled up good hand and closed his eyes. And so I left him.

Next morning Jane took down an egg and Hugo a gun. McGregor, still lying pathetically on the ground, quietly accepted and ate the egg. "He quite trusted Hugo behind him, just a couple of feet away. And he never even jumped or jerked—as the bullet ended his misery, his head just sank slightly lower, and he lay, as if still asleep. It was much worse for us."

"The whole affair has been like living in a nightmare as one after the other of the chimps comes back, after an absence, crippled," Jane wrote in a December 15 letter to Leonard Carmichael. "We have 7 affected now, three really badly. And, almost certainly, between two and four deaths."

She and Hugo stayed on for several more days, until it seemed as if the epidemic was at last under control. Then, on December 19, leaving Alice Sorem and Caroline Coleman in charge, they set off by Volkswagen and Land Rover for Nairobi, carting along the formaldehyde-preserved body of McGregor, which upon arrival they placed in a deep freeze until an expert could be found to conduct the postmortem. Naturally, they had been too overwhelmed and despondent to do anything about the upcoming holiday, even to scribble a note home. As Jane finally wrote in a brief and late Christmas aerogram to the family, mailed from Nairobi on December 23, "Bells and trees & plum puddings all seemed so out of place." Still, she refused to dwell on past horrors. And the bad news they received in Nairobi—that Hugo's vulture photos had been mislaid and the Geographic had just decided to hand its George Schaller lion photo project over to someone else—was, after all, trivial in comparison to what they had recently endured.

To celebrate Christmas, Jane, Hugo, and Michael planned a brief safari to Lake Baringo, in Kenya. And because he was "all alone and sad," their Nairobi friend and contact, Mike Richmond, was invited to go along.

Louis's new "gorilla girl" (Jane's phrase) from America had also appeared in town on December 22, and she soon met Jane. Dian Fossey was a tall, dark, bony, slightly awkward occupational therapist, who had approached Louis the previous March after a lecture he had given in Louisville, Kentucky. She had actually met both the Leakeys three years before, during an East African safari that included a brief visit to Olduvai, and, amazingly, Louis remembered her name: "Miss Fossey, isn't it?" And: "Please wait until I've finished with all these people."

Louis was looking for someone to study mountain gorillas in the style of the now famous Jane Goodall. Thus, after the lecture hall had cleared, he and the twenty-three-year-old American proceeded to his room at Stouffer's Louisville Inn for an hourlong interview, during which he did most of the talking, that terminated with a job offer. Louis agreed to raise the money and also remarked that, given the remoteness of where Fossey would be camped in the Virungas, she ought to have her appendix taken out. He was not serious, but she thought he was and so arrived in Nairobi that December slightly lighter. Louis took the young woman to meet Mary over lunch at their home in Langata, and Mary looked up to declare dryly, "So you're the girl who is going to out-Schaller Schaller, are you."

The idea was, as Fossey later recalled, "intimidating." Of course George Schaller had studied some of the same gorillas for a year during 1959 and 1960, but he was an experienced and trained zoologist, thoroughly prepared and provisioned in his Kabara meadow cabin, and accompanied by his wife. Fossey, by contrast, was inexperienced, untrained, unprepared, and unaccompanied. That December the appropriately anxious "gorilla girl" was staying at the Ainsworth Hotel and preparing for her expedition with a big shopping spree for supplies and camping equipment. She had also just acquired a battered old canvas-topped Land Rover named Lily, but she still seemed, as Jane explained to the family, "stranded" at the Ainsworth. So Dian Fossey was invited to go along on the Christmas safari as well.

Including a cook named Benjamin, the group of six camped in a tree-shaded spot situated above Lake Baringo and "miles from anywhere," with a view of "unspoilt Africa" and roving dik-diks, mongooses, and vervet monkeys. They all climbed down to the lake across great black pumice boulders replete with "the most fascinating agama lizards." The lizards were "very tame," Jane thought, and were given their own Christmas treats of marmalade custard and a bit of fried egg.

Jane decorated the inside of her traveling office with balloons and crepe-paper streamers, a little tree made of wire and strips of palm leaf with "sparkly things" on it, and various presents laid out on the table. She iced a tinned currant-and-nut cake, wrapped it with a "super-duper paper frill," and stuck on top four little plastic animals: chimp, gorilla, baboon, and vervet monkey.

They had a great Christmas dinner, according to Jane, lubricated with two bottles of "Pouille Fouis — how _do_ you spell it? Poo-y Foo-y!!" Outside in the moonlight, they feasted on roast duck with roast potatoes and peas, and a tin of briefly enflamed Christmas pudding with custard. Then they went back into the bus and opened presents. Hugo gave Jane "the most _exquisite_ just off white scarf with a heron hand painted — doesn't _look_ hand painted, except that it looks too superb to be anything else. The sort of scarf I have always wanted." They tried to time their Christmas toasts with those of the family back in England but had trouble figuring out the time difference between the two places, thus "got completely tiddly drinking toasts every hour — from 7 onwards — so that we should be sure to drink one at the time you were drinking to us." Jane's currant cake was divided six ways, with the four plastic animals on top distributed in four directions. The gorilla, of course, went to Dian Fossey, and she "was really delighted with it. We were so glad we had taken her along with us, as she entered the spirit of everything."

As is so often the case with the spike of first-impression enthusiasm, this one moderated over time. The safari returned to Nairobi by December 29, and then on January 3, Jane and Hugo flew with Dian down to Gombe. Almost twenty years later Fossey wrote, in _Gorillas in the Mist_, that Jane had "kindly invited" her to the research site in order "to show me her methods of camp organization, data collecting, and, as well, to introduce me to her lovable chimpanzees." Still, she may not have been "an appreciative guest," Fossey went on, since she was keenly distracted by anxieties about her upcoming trip to the mountain gorillas. Jane's account of the visit, written in a mid-January note to her mother, is more direct: "We got slightly annoyed with her."

Jane had thought Dian was "really excellent when we first met her — and, as you know, we took her on safari for Christmas. But — and don't mention this to Louis who is so pleased. She seems to have the most romantic notions in her head." Dian kept insisting that the meadow at Kabara, where George and Kay Schaller had stayed in the old Akeley cabin and where she also planned to stay, was an "alpine meadow" and she was going to take a cow up there. She would put a bell around the cow's neck, keep hens and several pets, and tame all the ravens. Then she would make bramble jam from the blackberries. True, when Jane first went to study the chimps, she had harbored "romantic notions too," but they were more realistic: "how I would be able to move about with a chimp group, be accepted by them as another chimp, practise climbing through the branches—you know, a glorified Tarzan type of thing." Also, and more alarming, Dian "had not even read George's book carefully. Nor has she, during the past 3 years since she planned to study gorilla, bothered to learn <u>anything</u> about primates." Dian had said to Jane that she "couldn't think why gorillas didn't eat wild blackberries" and that she was certain "George was wrong" on that score. Jane pointed out that George Schaller had in fact written "detailed descriptions of a big male eating wild blackberries!"

Dian Fossey finally left Nairobi in her overloaded Land Rover on January 6, starting her 600-mile journey east to the Virungas, and Jane remained in town, using Louis's museum office while she searched for a secretary to replace Caroline Coleman. She quickly found one: Suzanne Chaytor, "a very nice girl," as she soon wrote to her mother. Some additional time spent with Chaytor during the new few days confirmed that initial reaction. She was "a very self-effacing person, well educated, top drawer, interesting and intelligent, good sense of humor—and fun."

There were other positive developments. First, Alice Sorem (doing "EXCELLENTLY" at Gombe) would soon be joined by Patrick McGinnis, "quite a buddy of hers—male," who had also studied zoology at San Diego State College. Second, a phone call from Washington had just confirmed that Jane's book was nearing completion, and the title had been changed from *My Friends the Chimps* to *My Friends the Wild Chimpanzees,* which was an improvement. Earlier, editors at the Geographic had entirely redone the final chapter, putting in "a lot of rubbish about conservation in general" and cutting what she had written about chimpanzee conservation, and they had, "believe it or not, added a whole long bit about the polio—which I had especially said I did not want to put in!" Now, however, they were accepting Jane's version of that chapter, including a paragraph she really valued, "defining what I mean by friendship with a chimp." Moreover, they were including some comparative illustrations of human and chimpanzee musculature, drawings of hand positions and locomotion styles, and so on. In sum, "compared to what we thought it would be like, it will be excellent. Only trouble is, they have used a number of ideas we had for our own book!!!!!!"

But the nicest bit of serendipity that January was an offer from an American millionaire named Royal Little to fly them all down to Gombe so that he could see the chimps for himself. Thus, in mid-January, Jane, Hugo, and the new secretary, Sue Chaytor, flew to the camp in Safari Air's fastest charter plane, a twin-engine Skyknight. Royal Little and the rest of his group—his son and daughter-in-law and an "oldish woman—someone's aunt"—showed up the next day.

Sleeping accommodations at camp were, Jane thought, "a bit tight." Royal and the oldish aunt took over the two bedrooms in Pan Palace, and the son and his wife were given Lawick Lodge. Caroline Coleman was sent into Kigoma to be with her fiancé. The rest of them—Jane and Hugo, Sue Chaytor and Alice Sorem—slept on a row of mattresses laid out in the workroom of Pan Palace. But just as they were settling down, the camp's semi-tame genet wandered in, and since Royal Little had earlier mentioned that he hoped to see the little creature, he was called out—providing a moment of great amusement for the rest of the group. Jane thought Sue would be seized by "an apoplectic fit" at the sight of him dressed in his millionaire's pajamas, which were made from a "sort of chill-proof stuff." They had a close-fitting navy-blue top with a tight white collar and tight long sleeves with white cuffs. The pants, into which the shirt was carefully tucked, reversed the color scheme, being all white except for a navy-blue waistband and then, puckered tightly just below the calves, navy blue cuffs. "It really was the biggest hoot!" Jane concluded. Also amusing was Little's habit of dropping four spoonfuls of sugar into every glass of champagne he drank, something "only a millionaire could get away with."

Such eccentricities may have been funnier in the seeing than the telling, but they did provide some always-welcome comic relief. The chimps, meanwhile, provided real relief, and the two days of millionaire-style chimp-watching were "most successful." Not many of them actually showed up, but the "mums came—plus Flo of course! Babies played. Flo and Gigi had a fight, and Worzle stomped on Flo. Mike displayed and threw a rock almost into the party watching him! And they could be out all the time. Sniff and Fifi sat looking in at the windows, and Pooch played a sort of Peek-a-boo with Royal that delighted him. They had a colour polaroid, took a picture of Fifi, showed it to Flint—and he delighted them by kissing it!"

Best of all, Pepe showed up once again, after a long absence, looking better. Last time he had been in camp, his appearance had terrified Humphrey, and the terror in Humphrey's face had in turn terrified Pepe. This time around, Pepe could move by walking upright on his hind legs, rather in the way that Faben had successfully adapted to his paralysis in one arm. Pepe was attacked and threatened when he reappeared, but since Faben had now been accepted back into the community, Jane was certain Pepe soon would be as well.

So the epidemic was over. By January 27, 1967, Jane was confident enough to announce that fact to Leonard Carmichael, providing a final account: four dead chimps, two of them (McGregor and MacDonald) shot; and another five suffering partial paralysis (Faben, Madam Bee, and Pepe in one or both arms, Gilka slightly in a wrist, and Willy Wally to some degree in a foot). Mr. McGregor was still in the deep freeze in Nairobi, Jane noted, and "we have now found virologists willing to examine parts of his brain and spinal cord in an effort to determine, for certain, whether or not he died of polio." The final autopsy would turn out to be technically inconclusive (brain and spinal cord tissue should have been frozen while they were fresh) but pragmatically irrelevant, now that the chimpanzees of Gombe were once again safe and enduring.

29

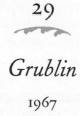

Grublin

1967

JANE WAS seven months pregnant by the start of 1967, but she had managed to keep her condition a secret from almost everyone, including close friends and family. Louis must have noticed when she appeared in Nairobi near the end of December. Vanne learned around that time, perhaps by way of Louis. Judy eventually found out when someone at her job in the British Museum of Natural History asked how she liked the idea of being an aunt.

From their camp in Ngorongoro Crater, Jane explained in a February 11 letter to Lyn Newman that "we were keeping it as a surprise—or that was our plan. But, of course, such things are hard to keep secret!!" At any rate, so far there had been "no complications, little alteration to my normal mode of life, no harm from bouncing or jolting over the roads of east Africa!"

Certainly Jane would continue to live her life at the same passionate, breakneck pace. That was her inclination and nature, and any baby of hers would need to adapt quickly to bouncing and jolting over the East African roads. At the same time, she had decided not only to expand her study of infant development in chimps to include the human species but also to start her own mothering project according to the chimpanzee principle of close and extended physical contact. She and Hugo had even discovered a hospital in Nairobi where mothers were allowed to keep babies from the instant they were born. It was a "darling Catholic one, which is small, but specializes in child birth." And the sister in charge seemed to understand completely that "for someone who studied chimpanzee infants it was most desirable that she be able to study her own!"

In the meantime, Jane and Hugo were having a splendid time inside Ngorongoro Crater, which was "wonderful—a little world of one's own." They were camped beside a narrow, muddy creek known as the Munge

River, on the other side of which the hyena-watching Dutch scientist Hans Kruuk and his wife, Jane, were holed up in a one-room cabin.

By then the van Lawicks were concentrating on tool-using vultures. In Nairobi they had acquired a supply of ranched ostrich eggs and emptied the contents by punching holes in the ends and blowing. The blown contents, heated and scrambled, made several good breakfasts, while the empty shells could be saved and transported without rotting. To return the emptied shells to their original weight, about three pounds, Jane and Hugo poured plaster of Paris inside. So, living in the Ngorongoro Crater and armed with their collection of blown and weighted ostrich eggs, they got to work.

After sighting a solitary Egyptian vulture, they would place one of the eggs on the ground, about 30 yards away. The bird would notice the egg, and after a little preening begin moving toward it, picking up a stone, throwing it down, and picking it up again every few seconds while gradually approaching the big white target. This premature throwing turned out to be a common aspect of the behavior, as if, Jane later wrote, "the sight of an egg [was] so stimulating that the birds could not wait to reach the target before they started throwing." At last the bird would arrive within a stone's throw of the egg and let fly. It typically took several tries, but after a few minutes the vulture would have cracked a hole in the side of the egg and cocked his head to peer into the interior. Finding none of the usual delicious soppy mess, the determined little vulture would pick up more stones and continue pummeling the orb for another thirty minutes or so, until it was a heap of small fragments. During this process the bird often moved back several yards, searching for and selecting new stones, as if operating on the principle that the right stone would finally yield the desired yolk. Over time Jane and Hugo found that the vultures would search for good stones as far away as 50 yards from the egg and that, once within striking distance, they would succeed in hitting the target about half the time. The thrown stones weighed an average of five ounces, with a range from half an ounce to one pound two ounces. Not all of the Egyptian vultures threw stones, though. Some of the immature birds would merely peck away at the ostrich eggs, ineffectually, suggesting that stone-throwing was a learned behavior acquired by imitating successful adults.

It was an ethological game of cat-and-mouse with the vultures, but one evening that February the van Lawicks, along with their cook, Benjamin, and his assistant, Thomas, found themselves on the anxious end of a bigger cat-and-mouse game. The cats were lions, the first of whom was sighted in the fading dusk by Thomas while he was outside cleaning the lanterns. The lion was about 30 yards distant but stalking steadily closer, and Thomas instinctively if inappropriately threw himself to the ground. Benjamin, working inside the kitchen tent, saw Thomas dive down and then saw the lion, and he told Thomas to get up and walk slowly back to the kitchen tent. Thomas did so, and they closed up the tent and peered out through a gap between flaps.

Jane and Hugo were inside their office tent, about 30 yards away from the kitchen tent, with one entire side raised up. Since it was nearly dark and they were partly blinded by the brilliant light of their gas mantle lantern, they failed to notice the lion. Benjamin called out "Look!" while shining a flashlight beam at the stalking beast. Unfortunately, the flashlight was dim, and Hugo left the tent to see what Benjamin was trying to illuminate. Benjamin shouted something Hugo could not understand, and he walked out farther, until at last he noticed, about 20 yards distant, a big tawny cat creeping in. He hastened back to the tent, intending to make a dash with his heavily pregnant wife from canvas shelter to steel Land Rover. The vehicle was parked only 10 yards away, but as they soon discovered, it was blocked by the trajectory of a second lion, also stalking in their direction.

They dropped the raised side of their tent and then lit the gas stove, preparing to produce flaming torches from rolled-up pieces of paper if the lions tried to enter. Since the tent had no window and they lacked a flashlight to shine out through a gap, Jane and Hugo could only wait inside and listen. Next they heard from the kitchen tent a radio turned on full blast, then yelling and banging on pots. Then silence.

Hugo decided that the lion next to the Land Rover had moved away, and so he once again thought to run for it. But then, starting to open that side of the tent, he heard the sneeze of a third lion right beside the car. He and Jane called out to Benjamin and Thomas but heard no reply. Still, Hugo reasoned, if the Africans were being mauled, he and Jane would hear screams.

Then they heard the sounds of canvas ripping. The ripping stopped. Silence. Then the sound of running footsteps. Hugo, convinced that one of the Africans had already been attacked and the other was fleeing with a lion at his heels, started to light some of the paper, intending either to throw it at the lion or, better yet (he thought dramatically), to set the tent on fire at the bottom, pick up the whole thing from the inside, and walk with it over to the car. Now, however, they heard not one but two car doors slam, and Hugo peered out from the tent to see both Benjamin and Thomas with that weak flashlight inside the car, while the lions were investigating the kitchen tent.

Hugo and Jane raced to the vehicle and jumped inside. With the four of them now safely inside the Land Rover, Hugo tried to chase the giant cats out of camp by driving at them. The lions may have concluded that the big machine just wanted to play, though, because they began leaping and pouncing about, playing right back. Finally Hugo managed to drive the trio out of camp and into the darkness, although when he looked back, he saw that the tent had caught fire. They put it out with a fire extinguisher and that same night moved into the little cabin on the other side of the creek, vacated by the considerate Hans and Jane Kruuk.

Nairobi had been "frantically hot" that year, Jane wrote home to the family on February 26, and she and Hugo were just "dripping with sweat" in their rooms at the Devon Hotel. But a day or two earlier they had noticed in the newspaper an advertisement for a house in Limuru, about 18 miles out of town and in the cooler highlands. They had gone out that evening to look it over and put down their deposit the next day.

"Now the great thing about this house, for us," Jane enthused, "is that it is fully furnished!" It was built of stone with a tile roof, a smaller second story, and to one side a recently added guest wing, all situated on more than eight acres of land with a spectacular 80-mile view to the front, as well as some recently planted avocado trees, two vegetable gardens, a four-horse stable, and a "lovely front lawn—just asking for lush flowers around it." Inside and up a carpeted staircase was the master bedroom and an alcove with its own writing desk, which was "a wonderful place to work with the 80 mile view." Aside from bathroom and lavatory, the second floor included an additional, smaller bedroom. The downstairs centered on a long dining and living room, with fireplace and mantel and, to the front, a windowed veranda. The guest wing included its own small bedroom, bathroom, and lavatory, while to the rear of the house there was a big kitchen, a fourth bedroom, and another veranda. Stretching across the entire length of the house, with windows and a tiled floor, this latter room was "really lovely," Jane thought, and might be used for almost anything, such as "sitting in, eating, having a party, for children or pets—or anything else you can think of!"

When she and Hugo were given their tour of the house and reached that beautiful back veranda, the previous owner turned to Hugo and said, "It's a good room for the wife to sit with her sewing." Sewing was not a traditionally feminine activity Jane would be interested in, but she was nevertheless just then working on her maternal perspective. She had received in the mail some "darling little baby clothes" from the family, and she and Hugo had shopped in Nairobi, where they "did manage to get nappies!" Also "a little pair of sheets and a nice soft blanket. And one dear little sort of siren suit thing."

Labor began a week ahead of schedule, at around two o'clock in the morning of March 4. Jane reached the hospital by four o'clock, as she noted in a letter to Lyn Newman, and the baby began to reach for the light of day around 8:20. The mother had no anesthetic, and "the first part went quickly & smoothly." Then "things slowed down." The baby was supposed to have been born by 9:00 but did not finally emerge until 9:45. Everyone was "frightfully surprised I didn't get too tired to finish off the job!! Trouble was I had, apparently, a 'lazy' uterus. Also, which was most annoying, he had a large head and I had to have thousands of stitches."

That inconveniently large head, the mother wrote a day after its emergence, had been "slightly squashed" but was now "almost in its correct shape." The baby also had "quite pronounced jowls at birth but these are 'rising' towards his cheeks. A rosebud mouth. Really! One ear is pushed out in a funny shape, but we think that that, also, is correcting itself."

The father had missed the birth, having been curtly dismissed and sent back to bed by an officious night nurse who was positive there were many hours yet to go. Thus he was discussing income-tax issues with his accountant when the seven-pound package arrived; but he quickly learned, as he wrote to Melville Grosvenor the next day, that both mother and infant were doing "exceedingly well." And in spite of the unfortunate sequence of initials, the parents soon settled on Hugo Eric Louis van Lawick for a name, thus covering both families (first sons were always Hugo in the van Lawick family, and Jane thought her sweet but childless Uncle Eric would appreciate a reference) while honoring Louis Leakey, the man "who brought us together and has done so much for us."

Although neither mother nor father had "really seen new born human infants before," Jane wrote, their baby was clearly "an advanced sort of baby. People say that at 2 days old he could have been 2 weeks! He is very good." As for her plan to be like a chimpanzee mother from the very first day, unfortunately, the hospital administration had "gone back on its word" and would not allow her to keep the baby in her room. "Hugo & I have given up. They all refer [the issue] to more and more inaccessible and unapproachable sisters & mothers. And, as I hope to be out in 2 more days, or 3 perhaps, we have resigned ourselves to all the possible repressions & fixations and complexes etc, etc which may develop in his personality as a consequence."

After Jane had been out of the hospital for a week, still staying in the Devon Hotel and waiting for the house in Limuru to be ready, she was combining her new maternal duties (including washing "nappies [and] other little garments") with arranging interviews for a new secretary to replace the already discouraged Sue Chaytor and hosting their newly arrived research assistant from San Diego, young Patrick McGinnis.

McGinnis had graduated with a B.A. in zoology in 1965, after which he

spent a semester discovering what a terrible mistake dental school was before returning to zoology graduate studies at San Diego State. There he
developed a relationship with Alice Sorem, and Alice, a few months after
starting work at Gombe, had convinced Jane to take him on as an additional
research assistant. The young man's immediate impression of Jane when he
showed up at the Devon Hotel that March, as he recently recalled, was of "a
very down-to-earth, natural person." She was "just so serene about everything. Nothing seemed to put her in a flap. And I just warmed to her immediately."

Hugo was, Jane wrote home, "trying to do the work for both of us,"
which included "accounts, shopping, repairs & equipment, correspondence
& shopping for the Reserve, coping with Pat—and trying to get some of
his own photography done between whiles." By the end of the month they
had found a promising secretary: an Italian, fluent in English and French, by
the name of Nicoletta Marashin. She was a "fast typist" as well as a "very
charming girl" who "would have done the work for nothing."

Little Hugo had his smallpox shots on April 1, and the next day he and
his mother and father—along with two big German shepherd dogs (Jessica
and Rusty), a Siamese cat (Squink), and some toy bears on a string—moved
into the house in Limuru. On April 3, Big Hugo flew down to Gombe with
Pat McGinnis. And a few days after that Jane and Little Hugo caught an
overnight flight to England.

The baby's arrival at The Birches in Bournemouth set off a quick flurry
of nickname coinages, with Vanne becoming Grum, Olly turning into Grolly,
and Danny, his great-grandmother, becoming Grand Granan or Grunkle.
Olly had borrowed from the local library a book on child development, and
that document confirmed, as Jane soon wrote to Lyn Newman, that Little
Hugo was "very precocious" and getting to be "more a person each day."
He was christened in the same London church where Jane and Hugo had
been married, the Chelsea Old Church, at five o'clock in the afternoon of
Friday, May 5. That major event was followed by a party at the flat in Earl's
Court.

Mother and baby returned to Nairobi by the morning of June 1, finding
their home in Limuru (as Jane immediately wrote home) "so welcoming—
full of flowers from Hugo." Also getting full of puppies, with the first of
seven delivered from Jessica just as Jane, holding Little Hugo, stepped out
of the car.

It was good to be home, in spite of some leaky faucets and a surprising
evening chill. The month of June, however, became a time when all Jane's

logical if abstract theories about infant development yielded to the more particular, less logical reality of diapers, demands, moods, and missing maternal sleep. On the flight back to Nairobi, Little Hugo had been "so good," sleeping soundly for almost the entire trip, and then back home in Limuru he "behaved angelically." For a day. But then, suddenly, he would cry and cry "for no reason," although every time Jane picked him up and walked around with him, he would stop. Why? A flower placed at the end of his cot seemed to quiet him, Jane noticed, and sometimes he would become blissfully intent on scratching away with his little fingers at the label on his cot.

By the middle of June, she was writing to the family about a "miracle" that had lately unfolded. "He is now a model baby. He wakes up between 6.45 and 7.30 A.M. He feeds, plays, and goes to sleep till about 11. Again he plays, feeds, plays, and sleeps till after lunch. He then is fed and goes for a walk round the garden, looking at all the flowers (in his pram) and sleeps until about 5.30. Then he kicks by the fire, has his bath, and is fed up in our room at between 6 and 7. He at once drops off and sleeps until about 11 or 11.30. He feeds, plays in bed with us, and then sleeps throughout the night!!!!!!"

That miracle lasted eight nights, but by June 25, Jane was forced to conclude that it may have been merely an "isolated patch of lovely peace. After the 8 nights he became ghastly—crying & crying."

Still, the baby was beautiful. And, sleep-deprived or not, Jane devoted her full attention to observing this interesting new subject. Developmentally, in fact, June was a busy time. At the start of the month the baby had "stared at his rattle, gets hands to it, & when they touch it he holds on & waves it a moment." He said his first _b_ sound. He learned to hit his bears. By June 10 he was reaching out to touch and stare fixedly at flowers, books, pictures, faces, and hands. He enjoyed playing with fingers, his mother's ring, the toy bears on a string in his crib. He loved hitting Big Hugo in the face and roaring with laughter. He loved being bounced on his parents' bed. And when someone held the rattle up close, he would press his hands together and then separate and shake them about, fingers out, with the fingers of one or both hands slowly creeping into a grasp around the fascinating object, until it was held, gazed at, and drawn up to his mouth. By the middle of the month, Little Hugo had decided for the very first time that "he <u>loved</u> things on a spoon. He tries to grab the spoon & push it in if I don't push it into his mouth the minute he opens it. From ½ egg cupful of solids he has risen to a sherry glass per feed!"

Little Hugo, by the end of June, "<u>adores</u> being swung upside down, holding his ankles; & by his hands round and round. He looks startled &

then, when you put him down, he <u>roars</u> with laughter!" His diet by then had expanded to include "all <u>sorts</u> of things. Egg custard, apricot custard, chicken broth, mixed vegetables, fish dinner, egg cereal—my!"

On June 23 Big Hugo left Nairobi in a two-vehicle convoy that arrived in Kigoma four days later, transporting Nicoletta, the Italian secretary, as well as a guest researcher named Peter Marler, his wife and two children, and one of his students.

Jane had met Peter Marler, a zoologist from Rockefeller University, at the Wenner-Gren conference of 1965, so he was another of her "castle" friends. He was now planning to study chimp vocalizations and facial expressions. The Marler entourage had arrived in Nairobi by mid-June and stayed at the Limuru house for about a week, thus giving Jane the opportunity to form first impressions. Peter and Judith Marler were "very nice and easy to have around," she had written then, and their children were "nice." The student was "obviously brilliant," although he startled everyone, especially Nicoletta, with the awkward habit of "sitting at table with face almost <u>in</u> food & frequently bursting into loud melodies—hummed!"

After those seven departed for Gombe, mother remained home with baby for a few more days, hoping that a final new chimpanzee observer, Patricia Moehlman, would materialize. Moehlman was scheduled to arrive on June 20, according to a confusing telegram from her mother, but when she failed to appear by the end of the month, Jane and the baby flew down to Gombe on their own.

After arriving at camp that evening, Little Hugo went to sleep in his safari cot, peacefully unconscious in the new dining hall all through an evening's commotion of nine people (including the pilot) chattering and laughing, and he spent the rest of the night in a steel cage inside Lawick Lodge. He had already received his smallpox and polio shots, and his mother had brought along vitamin D drops and a measuring spoon for his Monday dose of malaria medicine; but that cage may have been the most important prophylaxis. Constructed from welded steel bars and heavy wire mesh, painted baby blue, padded on the bottom with foam rubber, decorated at the top with hanging birds and stars, and wrapped in mosquito netting, the cage was big enough to include mother, baby, and furniture (safari cot, pram, baby bouncer, chair) and strong enough to exclude the chimps if they ever happened to mistake Little Hugo for food. In fact, some of the chimps had peered in the windows of Lawick Lodge, but only Fifi, probably out of curiosity, had tried to reach in through the window and touch the baby.

In general the chimps were fine. David Greybeard had disappeared into the deep woods some time before, in the company of Olly, but Gilka soon showed up in camp, and as Jane wrote to the family, her partially paralyzed hand was "very good now and she has learned to make the most of the muscles she has." Willy Wally appeared, but with one leg still not functioning, he was "pathetic." He moved around with the use of only three limbs, keeping the thigh of his bad leg drawn up to his abdomen, a peculiarity the other chimps disliked and took advantage of. Even Fifi attacked him, throwing a stick when he had his back turned, then leaping at him and biting him in the middle of the back. Flint, meanwhile, developed "a thing" about Peter Marler. "He runs up & hits him at the slightest provocation! Doesn't like his beard!" Flint had also started throwing stones at people and some of the other chimps. "He is undoubtedly copying Fifi—she gathered up 8 the other day—destined for Pooch but most of them landed almost on top of Fifi!"

By the end of July, Little Hugo had "a bit of a cold," while all the chimps had likewise caught colds. "They all sit round from morning to night snuffling and picking and eating stuff from their noses, sneezing, and starting all over again."

Fifi had reached adolescence that year, and now, in late July, she was having her first really clear signs of estrus: a swelling and pinkness that thoroughly excited the males—and Fifi as well. As Jane wrote home in a letter of late July or early August, Fifi "rushes up to all the males as they arrive and insists they mate her, pushing her bottom at them time and time again." However, interestingly enough, she would not allow her little brother, Flint, to play at sex ("do his baby thrusting") with her. Nor was there any obvious sexual interest between Fifi and her two older brothers, Figan and Faben. That was "fascinating," Jane thought, since it suggested a chimpanzee incest taboo.

The new chimpanzee observer, Patti Moehlman, finally arrived in July. She could play the guitar, and so, with her musical help, they all celebrated the full moon on July 21, which was "great fun," Jane concluded.

Pat McGinnis, who had been mainly categorized in Jane's mind as "Alice's boy friend," had by midsummer been shifted into another mental category, "the best person we've had here so far. His notes are excellent & he is so nice." And Nicoletta was also "working out very well indeed." Jane was impressed by how diligently she poked away at the typewriter from dawn to dusk. She was fast, too, though not fast enough. There was too much typing to do, mainly because of all the tape-recorded notes being generated by Hugo and Peter Marler. With movie cameras and audio recorders, they produced by the end of that summer nearly two hundred reels of movie film, most of it accompanied by synchronized sound. That, combined with their extensive tape-recorded notes, was supposed to serve as raw data for Marler's attempt to analyze chimpanzee communication via sound, facial expression, and gesture. But poor Nicoletta could not keep up with the transcriptions, so many of those tape-recorded notes were mailed back, untranscribed, to New York.

By the start of August, meanwhile, Little Hugo had figured out how to raise himself up on his knees and, with nearly straight arms, propel himself forward. With a rabbity kind of locomotion, he could now span the length of an entire mattress in just a few minutes. That was a good thing and undoubtedly consolation for whatever was waking him up every night. Another Little Hugo problem was the verbal labor required to distinguish him from Big Hugo. Jane had tried to simplify the process in her letters by writing the baby's name with a small *h*, so that "Little Hugo" could be "hugo," but obviously that was more successful in writing than in speech. Soon, however, the problem was solved. Before Jane showed up with her baby that summer, Gombe had only one classically messy eater: Melissa's baby, Goblin, who had been renamed Goblin Grub in honor of his comic eagerness to press more food into his mouth than that small opening could tolerate. Little Hugo proved even messier, and so he was nicknamed Grublin.

Jane was still struggling with his sleeplessness, though. "I am exhausted to a T!" she wrote on August 6. And, on August 18, "He is driving us dotty—waking up at 3 again, and for 3 nights running, waking up twice—3 and 5 or 3 and 6. It is ghastly but I don't know what I can do about it. Perhaps it's the moon." Nevertheless, the baby was undergoing so many remarkable changes and advances, it was impossible not to be adoringly entranced.

Meanwhile, David Greybeard, accompanied by Olly, finally arrived at the banana-provisioning site in the middle of August, causing Jane great pleasure and relief. Other visitors to the camp during the month included Irven DeVore, who showed up with his wife, Nancy, for three days, and the Tanzanian minister of agriculture, Derek Bryceson. Hugo took the Boston Whaler into Kigoma to fetch the minister and his entourage, and Bryceson, who had been badly crippled in a plane crash during the war, had to be hoisted up to the Ridge Camp in one of their old camp canvas chairs strapped to poles.

But probably the most unusual and certainly the most upsetting visitor that month was Worzle, a mature male with very human-looking whites to his eyes, who arrived "covered in sores & can hardly walk," as Jane wrote home on August 10. "We fear some ghastly disease," she added, and she soon managed to acquire a skin scraping, which was sent to Nairobi to be tested for leprosy. Just to be certain, Jane took a second skin scraping when she and Hugo returned to Nairobi at the start of September, and soon she received the laboratory report, dated September 5, from Dr. G. C. Dockeray: "I have examined the scales from the chimpanzee and found no leprosy bacilli."

Other news at that time was not as positive. Jane also learned on September 5 that Dian Fossey (along with her two chickens, Lucy and Desi) had been forcibly evacuated from her camp in the Virunga volcanoes. She had been taken down to park headquarters at Rumangabo, imprisoned, and "earmarked," as she later phrased it, for the personal attentions of an important military general. She was put on display in a cage, urinated and spat upon, and probably raped. After two weeks she had talked her drunk and disorganized captors into allowing her, accompanied by Lucy and Desi and a half-dozen armed guards, to drive her old canvas-topped Land Rover across the border into Uganda, where supposedly she would fetch $400 in cash. Once across the border, however, she raced into the driveway of Walter Baumgartel's Travellers Rest hotel, leaped out, and ran through the hotel until she reached the farthest room, where she dove under the bed. Baumgartel had the presence of mind to telephone the Ugandan army.

A few days later Louis Leakey met Fossey at the airport in Nairobi, where he provided her with a week's rest, recuperation, and refitting. "She had a pretty thin time, but she is completely undaunted," he wrote to Melvin Payne at the Geographic, adding that his protégé's immediate goal was to get right back to the gorillas. With new permits and equipment, she had by mid-August set off once again for the Virungas, this time to the Rwandan side, where she established a new camp just across the border from the old one. "I still think he [Louis] is absolutely foolish to have allowed Dian Fossey to go back to the gorillas," Jane wrote home.

Fossey's harrowing experience was a reminder: how fragile the scaffolding of political stability, how delicate one's own physical security. Still, unlike the former Belgian colony now struggling as the new nation of Zaire, the East African stretch formerly under British dominion—Uganda, Kenya, and Tanzania—remained welcoming, peaceful, and stable. And at Limuru, that first week in September, the flower garden was "not so full of flowers, but is still super," while the vegetable garden was producing beautifully: beans, carrots, corn, onions, peas, rhubarb, and a few strawberries. Jane and Grublin were raiding the strawberry patch and finding about four new ripe ones every day. Grublin had just learned to crawl properly and even, with the help of a chair or some other stable object, to practice his upright stance and sidle a bit, as if he were intending soon to toddle on his own. And he was also starting to enjoy the outdoors and at least one of the dogs.

. . .

By the second week of September, Hugo, Jane, Grublin, and Alice Sorem, on vacation from the chimps, had settled down in a camp centered on the one-room cabin on the Munge River in Ngorongoro Crater, preparing to start Hugo's next National Geographic assignment: photographing the spotted hyenas being studied by Hans Kruuk.

Grublin's first tooth—lower left incisor—was showing a white edge through the pink of his gums. He had got the hang of the baby bouncer and had learned to gum his food directly off the spoon. He had plenty of toys to play with, such as the standard teething rings and his bears on a string, but he often preferred film cartons, camera batteries, empty envelopes, baby-food tins, an ashtray. He had a playpen with a foam rubber mattress floor and, for mealtimes, a blue baby chair and new plastic pelican bib with a food-catching pocket. The baby, Jane summarized for the family back in England, was having "the most extraordinary life" and "thriving on it 100%."

She then described a typical day in the life of six-month-old Grublin, starting with an eye-rubbing wake-up at dawn inside the Volkswagen bus, surrounded by herds of zebras and wildebeests moving out to the grasslands after a night in the forested hills. Flamingos are flying above, calling out "with their plaintive haunting cry" and splash-landing on the lake, then "dancing their graceful display, wings up, leaping up and down as they hunt for their insect breakfast." But then, "suddenly the peace is broken." Jane and Hugo sight a herd of zebras racing into the hills with a pack of hyenas in close pursuit. "Every so often the little herd stops and the stallion wheels to attack the pursuing hyenas. They vanish into a hollow of the hills—and next thing some vultures have landed."

Babe in arms, Jane and Hugo leap out of the Volkswagen and into the Land Rover, clip on their safety belts, and lurch off to follow the action. Meanwhile, a second Land Rover, belonging to Hans and Jane Kruuk, is raising a trail of dust and racing to the same place. They count forty-two hyenas, faced off into "two snarling whooping groups, both with tails up aggressively" and battling over a just-killed zebra. One of the groups actively feeds on the carcass, while the other advances fiercely in a tight pack.

As it turns out, the zebra has been killed by members of the pack Hans calls the Munge Clan, who during their chase were drawn into the territory of the Scratching Rocks Clan. Now the Scratching Rockers, advancing in a coordinated group, are chasing the Mungers off their kill. "There are short individual skirmishes all over the place as one hyena after another gets a piece from the kill and rushes off, vainly trying to get away far enough to eat its spoil in peace. The high pitched nervous giggles of these animals sound from all directions." The scattered Munge Clan regroups, however, and returns in force, enlarged now by stragglers returning after having finished off pilfered chunks of flesh. Their first attack "is repulsed with dreadful snarls and erect bristling manes and tails," and the Munge hyenas break and retreat. But again they reassemble and again advance, trying once more to reclaim the zebra kill—this time succeeding for a brief moment before being driven off for a final time by the Scratching Rockers.

Soon only the zebra's head and a heap of splintered and strewn bones remain, and Hans interrupts the feeding by driving his Land Rover onto the carcass remnants, forcing the last of the animals away. Hans collects the jaws of hyena kills for later analysis, and so now he gets out of the car and, wielding a knife and an ax, severs the zebra's jaw. "The hyenas stand round watching—knowing, by now, that the rest will be theirs." Hans casually tosses a few scraps in their direction as he works, and they wait patiently until the human wipes the blood off his hands, climbs back into the vehicle, and drives off. The Munge hyenas close in once more, while the Scratching Rockers linger and watch, until, in scattered twos and threes, they saunter away.

Grublin loves being in the Land Rover. As soon as the motor was turned on that morning, he started singing "loudly and shoutingly," and his happy noisemaking had blended in with the whooping, yelping cacophony of the battling animals. And now, after the hyenas have gone, Hans drives over in his Land Rover, smiling at Jane and Hugo through an open window as he says, "Young Hugo was certainly giving encouragement to the hyenas."

Big Hugo finally drives Jane away from the bones and tatters of zebra, as Grublin sags into a sleeping, songless bundle. They reach the Volkswagen bus at last, and mother hands over baby, "all cosy and rosey in his new yellow suit," to father. The two Hugos drive back to the cabin and breakfast, while Jane follows in the gray VW bus, pausing momentarily to search for dung from a white-tailed mongoose. She rolls and bucks through the grass and over the dusty earth, past the serenely grazing herds of zebras and wildebeests, until at last, at eleven o'clock that morning, she reaches the little cabin in the shade of a great fig tree.

Early that afternoon, Jane, Hugo, Alice, and Grublin climb into the Land Rover and drive off to the vultures' bathing hole, where as usual they find a flapping congregation of about forty birds, this time including four Egyptian vultures named Lame, Number Two, Yellow, and Mottled. Today's experiment is to bait the stone-throwing birds with an especially large egg made out of fiberglass and around six times bigger than the normal ostrich egg. And, yes, for Egyptian vultures, size matters. The birds, "most excited," industriously and patiently pummel the monster egg with stones for a long time, until, as a consolation prize for a job well done, Jane and Hugo remove the fake big egg and replace it with a half-dozen domestic hens' eggs. Finally, with the experiment finished—and the birds gone, the giant egg all scratched and chipped, the area littered with a mess of thrown stones, and the hens' eggs flattened—the experimenters gather all the thrown stones, label them, and return to the Munge cabin.

After supper Hugo checks his cameras and three-bulb flash and tape recorder, and he and Alice drive off in the Land Rover, intending to find lion cubs. For Grublin it's bath time, after which Jane loads up the gray Volkswagen bus with baby cardigan, bag for dirty nappies, basket, bedding, binoculars, clean nappies, clothes, cocoa, coffee, cups, kettle, oranges, thermos, and a spare little nightie. All set. With Grublin in her arms, she starts the engine, and away they go. Grublin is singing and gazing at the sunset and the "black silver-fringed shapes of the wildebeeste and zebra clustered thickly on either side of the track."

She pulls up beside the Land Rover, shuts off the engine, and the peace of dusk descends. Jane and Grublin retire to the rear of the bus for a final evening meal. "He is nearly asleep now," she thinks, "but not too sleepy for his last suckle—well, last for a while anyway. Oh dear—was it the right last time—or the left. Must have been right—or not? Ah, yes. The left window is open. Never got round to closing it. So it must be right." Then Grublin is making his contented suckling noises, his eyelids drooping, his breathing settling, his head nodding. Into the cot he goes, with blanket laid loosely across and mosquito net draped around.

Now Alice quietly moves into the VW while Jane climbs out and into the Land Rover, joining Hugo to follow hyenas. At 7:45 the first edge of the moon peers up from the crater rim, and soon the great round yellow disk rises, but now the hyena pack they have been following divides and then divides once more, and by 10:15 only two animals are visible, lying in the grass. In another ten minutes Jane and Hugo are watching only one. It is a quiet moment for sipping coffee . . . but just as she reaches for the cups and thermos, the resting hyena comes alert, ears suddenly raised, and takes off running.

We are off. About 30 yards off a second hyena is flat out after a wildebeeste, [and] the animal, seeming to know it is the end, is giving stricken bellows. Our hyaena joins the pursuing one, and we see a third, then a fourth, rushing to the scene. The wildebeeste runs frantically to a herd and tries to escape, dodging amongst the others. But the hyaena are not to be fooled. They stick, like true hunters, to the original quarry. With eyes only on the speeding animals we have heed for the ground ahead as the speedometer needle creeps up towards 30 m.p.h. — no mean speed for travelling over rough pot-hole (actually hyaena, jackal and fox burrow!) infested country. Luckily for us there are no holes in the way.

Hugo's three-bulb camera flash is mounted on a board on the door of the Land Rover, and now he switches on the battery. "The wildebeeste makes a sudden turn. The landrover swings round and — click flash — Hugo in a superhuman manner takes a picture at the very moment that the wildebeeste is thrown. It is in mid-air with a hyena biting onto it somewhere." Hyenas are rushing in from all directions, and the downed wildebeest bellows for three minutes while being eaten alive, still crying out as the hyenas are "running off with pieces of gut, giggling as they are chased." But now from out of the dark night a second pack of hyenas rushes in — soon followed by Jane and Hans Kruuk in their Land Rover.

They have just witnessed another Munge Clan kill in Scratching Rocks territory, and now the Scratching Rockers arrive, so the Munge hyenas are alarmed and scrambling. A snarling whooping giggling chaos is followed by momentary resolution, and the human observers conclude that the entire Munge Clan has been driven off the kill. All but one, they soon correct themselves. "Look," Hugo says. "It's a hyena they've got."

With unbelieving horror we watch a scene of tribal warfare carried to extremes. A pack of hyaena deliberately, and in cold blood, murdering one of their own kind. A Munge hyaena that did not get away. We have never seen anything so horrible before. The moans of the tortured wildebeeste are still ringing in our ears, and we are still trembling slightly from that terrible scene. But this is infinitely more gruesome. Surely the hyaena has more brain than the wildebeeste, can feel more. And soon the tragedy that is taking place under our eyes has been dragged out for nearly 10 minutes. And still it goes on. The mauled animal is growling and screaming horribly. One hyaena has it by the scruff of the neck. Another has one ear. A third has it by the rump.

At first the attack on the captured Munge hyena had been partly obscured by a raging circle of Scratching Rockers, perhaps ten or fifteen animals, but now most of them have gone off to feed on the wildebeest, so

we can clearly see the details of this murder. The individual holding the ear growls and shakes it as would a dog a rat. The other two follow suit. The stricken hyena screams. All is still again. Then this is repeated. And again, and again. Now a fourth adult joins in. It takes hold of a leg. The four animals pull, all in different directions. The screams are ghastly. The hyaena holding onto an ear lets go suddenly—the ear has come right off. Soon after this the stricken beast is left alone. He turns to lick his wounds—but he is so mutilated that he seems just to give up. He cannot stand. A few hyaenas go over and sniff him—he growls but cannot move away. We feel sick.

Then Jane sees headlights from the VW bus moving their way, which is a great relief, since "I cannot bear to watch this mutilated animal any longer." Hugo drives over to the bus, and Jane sees little Grublin howling in Alice's arms. Jane moves into the VW and takes the bawling baby in her arms, whereupon he soon quiets down and settles back to sleep.

Hugo drives Alice in the Land Rover back to the cabin, where she will sleep. He returns to the hyenas, takes more photos, and at last returns to Jane and Grublin in the gray Volkswagen. Outside the bus, he pauses for ten minutes, watching shapes and shadows illuminated by his headlights: two young lions prowling around the bus. They sniff. One roars. They slink away. Then Hugo shuts off his car lights and joins Jane and Grublin inside the bus. He starts to undress, muttering to himself as his elbow accidentally hits the door, his head hits the roof, his toe is stubbed on the gas cooker stowed away beneath the head of the bed—finally waking up the baby, who starts screaming.

The baby quiets down, and now Hugo lights his final cigarette of the night, its tip glowing red and wavering in the darkness. Little Grublin gazes in fascination at the moving red star, suckles a little, falls back asleep. His mother carefully lowers him into his cot, but "he is teething. He cannot bear his cot another moment. He must convince us he is in agony. He screws up his face. Opens his mouth, and yells." He screams, he wails, he bellows, and then, after Jane gathers him up once again and softly places him on the bed right beside her, he sleeps. Fifteen minutes later, all three have fallen asleep.

Outside the full moon gradually sinks lower in the sky. There is the distant roar of a lion. A moaning whoop of a hungry hyaena. A sudden yelping chorus, high pitched and ethereal, of the gold jackals. A chorus is repeated way over to the north, and then to the east. Then silence once more. Hugo and Jane and Grublin sleep until morning.

30

Promise and Loss

1968–1969

IT HAD BEEN a bad week for Mrs. Crisp, private secretary to Louis S. B. Leakey, starting with an incident at 7:30 on Tuesday morning, February 6, 1968. As she prepared to enter a side door of the Coryndon Museum, wild bees swarmed down from a hollow in a nearby tree and stung her seven times in the head and four or five times on the body. She beat them away, rushed into the building, slammed the door, and began experiencing, as she wrote in a letter to her absent boss, a "peculiar feeling round my heart."

Almost as upsetting as the bees was the telephone call two days later: an imperious voice on the line belonging to Lady Listowel, speaking in fractured English and being, Mrs. Crisp thought, "exceptionally rude." Lady Listowel's relative, a young man named Geza Teleki, was arriving at the Nairobi airport on Saturday night, and surely Dr. Leakey should have arranged for someone to meet him there. And since Dr. Leakey had just hired young Teleki for one year (which was complete news to Mrs. Crisp), why had no one yet booked him a room in a hotel?

Mrs. Crisp booked Mr. Geza Teleki for one week at the Ainsworth Hotel and then wrote him an explanatory letter and passed it on personally with a cover letter to the airport's duty traffic officer. So she had done her best. She intended to rest over the weekend, but she had arranged for "the Teleki person" to be waiting for her at the museum first thing Monday morning, whereupon "I will deal with him."

On Saturday morning, however, Mrs. Crisp received a call from Mike Richmond's secretary, informing her that Mr. Richmond, acting on behalf of the van Lawicks, planned to meet Mr. Teleki at the airport that night, had booked a room for him at the Devon Hotel, and at the start of the week would be flying him out to Ngorongoro Crater. In her second letter to

Louis, Mrs. Crisp supposed that twelve bee stings with seven in the head was "a bit much for anyone," even though she herself had a "natural resilience" to such constitutional shocks. But there remained the irritation of Lady Listowel's call and the mystery of Mr. Teleki's coming: "How all this muddle occurred and where Lady Listowel got the information that you had engaged him for 1 year, I don't know."

As soon as Louis received Mrs. Crisp's first letter on the matter, on February 13, in Baltimore, Maryland, he dashed off a cable to Nairobi: "Teleki responsibility of mike richmond. . . . he going chimpanzees."

Thus Mrs. Crisp failed to meet Geza Teleki that time around, and in any case she was not in the mood to appreciate his charm and good looks. Had she done and been so, she would have seen a tall, lean young man with an aquiline nose and thick dark hair combed straight back from the forehead. His single physical flaw, an occasionally drifting right eye, only added to the haunted, romantic effect, which was packaged with an air of thoughtful intelligence and substantial self-assurance.

That self-assurance was among the few remaining benefits of his family's past social and political prominence in Hungary. His ancestor Count Samuel Teleki von Szek had during 1887 and 1888 become the first European to make it alive through Kikuyuland, walking 3,000 to 4,000 miles across what is now Kenya and in the process honoring friends by naming Lakes Rudolf (now Turkana) and Stefanie (Chew Bahir). A couple of generations later, Geza's grandfather, Count Paul Teleki, served as prime minister of Hungary during World War II, while his father was minister of education. Both were outspoken anticommunists, and as the Soviet tanks rolled in during the final months of the war, the Telekis traded the last remnants of their fortune for a fast ride out. In that way Geza Teleki, instead of becoming a Hungarian count, became an American citizen, joining the Boy Scouts and working on a B.A. degree in anthropology from George Washington University.

During his undergraduate years he attended a number of lectures Louis Leakey gave in Washington, D.C., and when he started graduate work in anthropology at Pennsylvania State, Geza began writing to the great man, begging to be taken on one of the Leakey digs in East Africa. Louis finally agreed to meet him for an interview, which took place over a bottle of sherry in a room at the Jefferson Hotel in Washington, across the street from Geographic headquarters. Louis seemed mostly interested in Geza's practical talents. What had he done in the Boy Scouts? Could he fix a car? Could he cook? When Geza answered yes to the last question, Louis told him to make them both lunch. There was a hot plate in the room as well as pork chops, potatoes, and beans. Pork chops, potatoes, and beans are not difficult to cook, of course, but by the time Geza had finished preparing their lunch, Louis had finished off enough sherry to ruin his midday appetite.

Geza wanted to dig at Olduvai, but a couple of months later Louis telephoned him from Nairobi, saying (as Geza recalls), "Get on an airplane. Goodall needs a person." And that was how he came to be in Nairobi in early February 1968, missed by Mrs. Crisp, met by Mike Richmond, staying overnight at the Devon Hotel, flying out to the Ngorongoro Crater to meet with Jane and Hugo. It was, he thought, like a fantastic dream: coming out of New York and (after that brief pause in Nairobi) dropping through the shimmering, ambiguous haze down onto the burnished grass plains inside the crater with all those wild animals roaming around.

He planned to spend a brief time at the crater, getting to know Jane and Hugo and becoming informed about the chimpanzees and chimpanzee-watching and what would be expected of him, before slipping off to Gombe, where he was supposed to join forces with Alice Sorem, Pat McGinnis, Tim and Bonnie Ransom (working on baboons), and two recently enlisted short-term volunteers, Carole Gale and Sanno Keeler, from a Quaker school in Nairobi known as Friends World International (FWI).

Hugo had by then ended his weekly retainer arrangement with the National Geographic Society, and now, with that steady source of money gone—and the pictures taken for the East African animals book and the vulture and hyena articles finished and being polished by the editors in Washington—he was financially insecure yet photographically free to turn to a project of his own choosing. This was to be an illustrated book on East African carnivores, supported by an advance from a British publisher. While he worked on the writing and photographs (mostly the photographs) for that book, Jane labored in earnest on her scientific book, a project Robert Hinde had persuaded her to take on. When circumstances and the one-year-old Grublin allowed, she sat in the shade of her work tent writing, rewriting, expanding, contracting, assessing, analyzing: transforming her dissertation into a monograph for scientific readers.

Geza began helping Hugo. February turned into March. And then, earlier than anyone had expected, the rains began and the weather turned bad. One night they had to rescue themselves, their tents, and half their possessions while the Munge River raged dark and cold up to their knees. By March 20, Hugo was writing to Frederick Vosburgh of the Geographic that "the rains are so heavy that we are virtually cut off in the Ngorongoro Crater and are unable to move our camp out." Geza was marooned by the floods, an impassable road, and an impossible airstrip, along with the rest of them. Still, it was not so bad. They were safe. They had food. He had gotten used to helping Hugo. And he was probably looking forward to whatever lay ahead at Gombe—especially because Jane and Hugo had agreed to take on another person to assist with the chimp-watching, a young woman who had recently received her B.A. in geology from George Washington University and who happened to be Geza's important friend: Ruth Davis.

Finally the weather relented, and Geza made it out of the crater and down to Kigoma—by plane and accompanied by Hugo's mother, Moeza, who had been visiting her son and daughter-in-law at the crater and intended to take that same plane as it returned to Nairobi. At Gombe, Pat McGinnis met Geza and Moeza for the first time. Although he found Hugo's mother to be "very Dutch," precise and reserved, that reserve melted significantly on their flight together in a single-engine plane back to Nairobi, when they were shaken and introduced to their own unfathomable fragility by a nightmare storm so violent that even the pilot was sweating. As Pat now recalls, after landing in Nairobi, "we didn't pick up our luggage. We went straight to the bar."

Pat went to Nairobi to meet his parents and take a two-week holiday from Gombe, and near the end of that break he finally met with Jane—the van Lawicks were temporarily back in Limuru from the crater, drying off and attending to business—and confirmed some details of an ongoing piece of bad news, which she in turn summarized in an April 15 letter to Melvin Payne. A flu epidemic around the start of the year had caused the deaths of two mothers, Sophie and Circe. Their orphaned offspring soon succumbed as well. Sophie's little Sorema was adopted by her five-year-old brother, Sniff, and with his support she survived for two weeks. The other orphan, Cindy, lasted for about a month and a half. Another victim of the epidemic, Pooch, was "without question, my favourite young female," and everyone had been eagerly anticipating her first baby. "The other victim is one whom I still cannot believe has gone, and hardly like to write of it even now that he has gone for over three months, David Greybeard."

By the time Geza arrived at Gombe, the flu epidemic was over. Geza had never met Sophie, Circe, Sorema, Cindy, Pooch, or David Greybeard, so their collective absence would have been a fading abstraction for him. In any event, the newly arrived Hungarian American was soon dealing with another problem, which had started to look more like a crisis by the time Pat McGinnis returned from his holiday in the third week of April. The provisioning system was out of control.

The banana-feeding in camp was supposed to mimic a very good food source in the forest, and Jane and Hugo had spent years tinkering with their dispersal system, perpetually trying to outsmart the chimps with ever more sophisticated technology. However, there was always the inherent difficulty of maintaining an ideal level of attraction: keeping the food source interesting for the chimps but not overwhelmingly so. Lately Gombe researchers had reduced the attraction by putting bananas into the boxes only every other day, but several of the chimps had figured out that pattern and would show up in force on the alternate days. At the moment, in the spring of 1968 the researchers were loading the boxes according to a more confusing schedule, which was seven out of fourteen days but not necessarily alternate ones. Still, as many as three dozen excited chimps were showing up and hanging around the site each day, obviously hoping for some of that magical banana manna. Worse, one of the baboon troops had been drawn by the bananas, so now a few dozen baboons had joined the crowd. The situation had become, in Geza's retrospective assessment, "exceedingly chaotic."

Ruth Davis appeared at Gombe around the start of June, and she was able to observe the matter with a fresh perspective. "How remote the rest of the world seems!" she wrote in her first letter home to her parents, on June 4. "Here we are in our world of bananas and chimpanzees and nothing else seems real." She was "slowly getting into the swing of things" and had done some observations and record-keeping when the situation was "relatively calm," but "I don't know if I will ever be at ease on an exciting banana morning when there are 30 chimps and 50 baboons, all fighting and carrying on like crazy!"

In a June 22 letter she elaborated. The chimps would arrive in the early morning, and if it was a banana day, they would eat from the forty boxes for approximately two hours, whereupon a group of banana-satiated apes would sit or lie around for another few hours while one of the observers took notes on their social interactions. "We carry a small tape recorder on the shoulder and record who comes in from what direction, and then what they do when they are here. These include things like displays, attacks, matings, groomings, greetings, etc." Typically an observer would tape-record notes for two to three hours and then be relieved by a second observer, while the first would go inside Pan Palace and transcribe and chart the notes. At the moment two and a half observers worked on this project — Ruth was the half — and the standard procedure was to watch the chimps at a single place: the provisioning site.

"When the chimps first come in and usually all during feeding they are very excited," whereupon one sees "all sorts of wild action going on." It could sometimes be "scary," Ruth wrote, "when one of these big black hulks comes charging at you, with his hair all out and sometimes waving a huge palm frond!" But the real problem was the baboons, and on most days all the apes — chimps *and* humans — were "plagued by the presence of 50 ugly, repulsive, disgusting and frustrated baboons." Ruth had never liked baboons, and now that she had gotten to know the big, sharp-toothed, dog-shaped monkeys better, her initial dislike had coagulated into disgust, so that "now I find their movements and actions so repulsive that sometimes my stomach actually turns over while watching them."

Only one person in camp could intimidate the baboons, and that was Geza, partly because he was big and self-possessed, partly because he had a good aim with stones. The baboons quickly learned which humans to fear and which not to fear, and Ruth, being comparatively slight and a terrible shot with stones, was among the not. In fact she had already been attacked by a baboon, an episode that happened one afternoon after all the hairy apes had left camp and only a few of the doggy monkeys remained. She was standing outside, and a male baboon was walking past, perhaps 2 or 3 yards distant. "Things were so quiet that it didn't even occur to me that anything might happen. So this baboon walked by and passed me, then all of a sudden, for no reason whatsoever, turned around and jumped on top of me! Needless to say, I was taken quite by surprise, started to fall to the ground with this creature still on me, then regained my balance, threw my arms into the air and lunged forward. Then this growling monster moved off (but, even then, only a few feet)." Fortunately, she was only scratched on the elbow.

Jane and Hugo had intended to return to Gombe around the first of May, but with the rains so heavy and the roads flooded, they pushed back the date a month. Jane was overwhelmed with transforming her dissertation into a monograph, and that task also kept them stuck in Nairobi until the middle of June, when the typescript was finally dropped off at the post office.

Jane had met another student from the Nairobi-based Quaker school FWI, Dawn Starin, who volunteered to help out with Grub. She also hired an old friend of Jonny Leakey's, someone she had, coincidentally, spent a few days with at Olduvai eleven years earlier: Nicholas Pickford, who was now married to a South African woman named Margaret. Nick, born and raised in Kenya, was tough, pragmatic, and resourceful, which made him a good candidate for general manager at Gombe. Thus, when Jane and Hugo finally assembled their vastly overloaded two-vehicle caravan and headed south, they shared the Land Rover with Grub and Dawn, while Margaret and Nick followed in the VW bus. They arrived "dead as a doornail" at Kigoma on Sunday, June 30, parked the vehicles, transferred all their luggage and supplies into a water taxi, and took off, chugging north over the flickering waters of Lake Tanganyika.

Grub enjoyed the boat ride, even though the lake swallowed his favorite toy. Jane had other things to think about, and when they finally arrived at

Gombe, as she wrote to her family the next day, they were met by "gloom," "hurried conversations, stopping when Hugo & I appeared," and "delegations & despair."

The latest news was "grim, grim, grim." First, it was by then undeniably clear that David Greybeard was dead. And Pooch. Also, Faben had not been seen for three months. But the worst news had to do with the banana-feeding system and the disastrous crowding of chimps and baboons: "Baboons attacking humans. Baboon had a tooth broken by Geza throwing a stone. Ruth attacked."

Jane was "utterly horrified," as she later told me, to learn how bad the situation had become. Everyone assembled for a quick meeting, and soon they had all agreed to load the banana boxes only during the night, when the chimps were asleep. They would keep the boxes closed whether they were full or empty, so that the chimpanzees would never be able to tell which ones to concentrate their frustrations on. And there would be significantly fewer banana days. They would henceforth be putting out the bananas only one day in every five or six.

Cutting down the banana days by nearly two thirds constituted a significant change in the system, but another change proved to be far more important. Jane and Hugo were informed that several people wanted to follow the chimps out of camp and study them during their wanderings in the forest, an idea Jane quickly embraced. As she wrote home enthusiastically, "You know how I have always wanted people to try & follow the chimps? And none ever have? Well—Geza, Ruth, Carol (& our two temporary FWI students . . .) all want to follow, lone following. Lone climbing about in the mountains. It is so exciting now—2 people follow each day, & one stays in camp." There was other promising news to relate in the same letter, such as the surprise return of Faben: "Today FABEN came BACK! So exciting!" But lone following of chimps into the hills and valleys and forests—that was the thing. And since the observers would keep standardized behavioral notes during those outings, the research at Gombe would henceforth have two sorts of data to draw on. The general records accumulating at the provisioning site would be the A Records, and the data they would start gathering while they followed particular individuals—on general behavior, food choices, group associations, encounters with other species, travel routes, and so on—would become the B Records.

Ruth Davis had blue eyes, full dark eyebrows, well-defined lips and chin. Her long brown hair was straight (but with a tendency to curl, so that when subjected to Gombe's heat and high humidity it went frizzy, which she hated) and on dressy occasions styled in a flip. When, during the first week of June, she heard on the camp's shortwave radio that Robert Kennedy had been assassinated in a hotel in San Francisco, she found it hard to imagine (as she wrote home a few days later) "what the poor U.S. is coming to." Nevertheless, she felt she was already "living so close to nature," and the entire civilized way of life back in the States seemed "rather absurd to me now and I often think of what people there, living in a world of steel and concrete, are missing."

To be sure, the food that close to nature was not always what she had been used to. Some of it was, admittedly, "very, very good," but other culinary offerings were "extremely gross." She was surprised at the variety available, and their daytime food was decent and sufficient: eggs, bacon on occasion, and jam and honey and cheese. Tangerines had recently come into the market, so they had tangerines. And bananas. But certainly their best food was the bread, baked every other day. Dinner was another story. They got fresh food only once a week, on Kigoma Day, which was every Thursday. On such a day, whoever went shopping in Kigoma would bring back "a most delicious fresh fish," as well as passion-fruit juice and some spicy little meat-filled pastries: samosas. So it would be fresh fish for dinner on Thursdays, but, most unhappily, "<u>every other night</u> of the week" they were eating canned steak, presented in one of three possible modalities: as a stew, as a "most inedible curry piled high with repulsive fried bananas," or as "some kind of a meat pie."

Apart from the food, Ruth really appreciated Gombe. She found the latrine "most delightful." It was a seat over a hole in the ground, surrounded on three sides by a little thatched fence. But how wonderful to look out the open fourth side! You could enjoy a great view, which made one's *choo* experience very "aesthetically pleasing," particularly under a milky canopy of stars at night. Also she started taking baths in a small pool at the bottom of Kasekela stream, an excellent little spot. Bathing that way, out in the open in a little natural pool, was the "most delicious experience," and "I don't think I ever want to use a bath tub again!"

Ruth quickly became enamored of the chimps, and she soon tried to follow some of them, on her own, onto the higher slopes. At such times the chimps were "so oblivious to me" that she felt as if she were simply a "part of nature." She thought, "What a great life they have!" And she found herself envying them. "How beautiful it would be to build a nest at night high in a palm tree and lie in it under the African sky, with the lake below and only the sounds of the wild African night!"

When Jane and Hugo finally appeared at the end of June and agreed that people could follow the chimps out of camp, Ruth immediately ordered new sneakers from Kigoma, in order to get around better. "I have been out exploring and experimenting the last couple of days," she wrote home soon after Jane and Hugo arrived, "and, lord, how beautiful it is! Every now and then it is just so great to stop and not move a muscle and just listen to all the sounds." It was difficult getting around in the dense thickets down in the valleys, and up on the slopes the tall grass could be extremely slippery. Still, of the several types of grass at Gombe, some of the tall grass was a "soft, delicate" sort. "Can you ever imagine what it is like to walk along through this soft, swaying grass that completely envelopes you, i.e. is about 10 feet high???" Naturally, in the coarse and thick parts of that 10-foot-high grass a person could get almost stuck, and that might be worrisome. When plowing through the high grass like that, it was impossible to see much of anything, and it would be bad to run into an unhappy buffalo under such circumstances.

Within a few weeks (according to a letter of July 27), Ruth had become "so involved with these animals that I never want to leave them. And this experience, at least for me, is getting deeper and deeper." At the start she had been afraid of some of the male chimps, but now the very ones she had originally feared she found particularly compelling—especially the two brothers Charlie and Hugh, who, it was true, regularly went after people during raised-hair moments of irrational excitement. Ruth had been "scared to death" of them originally, and for a long time had trouble even telling them apart. Those two chimps rarely let anyone follow them, but she now was able to follow them easily, and she had the powerful sense that Hugh actually liked her. One time as she was following the big male into a valley, he came up and sat down right next to her, as if expecting to be groomed.

The art of chasing chimps through the tall sharp grass, dense thickets, and thorny vines required a person to assume "all sorts of contorted positions," and at the end of the day Ruth would wander back into camp "aching from head to foot. Besides being all scratched and bloody, full of thorns and splinters." And sometimes she would get lost, confused, and even a little frightened—as happened on August 23, according to her journal. That day she had tried following Humphrey, and indeed she kept up with him for some time; he met up with Goliath and Faben, and so she was hurrying along behind the three of them when they just evaporated somehow. Ruth continued plowing through thickets, but

after approximately an hour of this nightmare I became somewhat panicky—or, more truthfully, just neurotically uncomfortable. I began feeling disoriented and my movements were not well controlled. At this point I managed to crash my head into a sharp branch and got a small bloody gash on the side of my forehead. Perhaps it was just my state of mind at the time, but for several seconds all I could see was darkness with stars whirling in front of me. I then proceeded to pass out. When I came to (which I think was not long after) a monstrous baboon was standing about two feet away from me.

She asked herself, "How long had he been there? What was he thinking? What was he going to do?" Temporarily unable to move, she felt "somewhat terrified." She stirred. He produced a startling flash of white eyelids and made a yawn threat, showing his teeth. She tried to return the threats: grunting, groaning, making faces. "Fortunately, he dashed away. Warm blood was trickling down my face. At this point I decided the Record B was certainly not worth this. All I wanted to do was return, but god what I had to go through." She saw a buffalo then, and to avoid him took a path down to the beach. She finally jumped into the lake to cool off, and then, exhausted, dozed off on the shore for a while, dreaming of baboons. Then she walked down the beach. When she reached the beach house where the van Lawicks were staying, Grub, seeing her, began to cry.

Whatever the irritants, obstacles, and potential dangers, though, Ruth loved what she did. She loved being in the forest and following the chimps, the big males especially. "Having spent so much time alone with Hugh in the woods," she wrote home one day, "I am getting to know him in a very much deeper way than I know the other chimps. This is also becoming true of Mike, the big boss (!) and they are now my two favorite animals, in fact, two of my most favorite beings in the entire world!"

The van Lawicks also had a good summer. They were living down on the beach in Marler Mansion, a three-room hut on the beach built the summer before for Tim Marler, now fixed up for Grub's sake with steel mesh nailed around the outside, which turned the place into another chimp- and baboon-proof cage. This new cage was "gigantic," Jane wrote home, and the house was surprisingly "cool and beautiful" inside. Baboons passed by all day long, and a stray kitten seemed to come with the place, making Grub roar with laughter by pouncing on and playing with his toys.

But Grub was content just being near the water. He was "wild on the lake" and "never so happy anywhere." He would step into the water fearlessly, held up by his little red water wings, delighted by the sparkling water and lapping waves, and he loved to go sailing in his boat, which was actually a yellow plastic paddling pool. He refused to talk and shook his head stubbornly if asked to, which made his mother worry, since he was now one and a half. Nevertheless, Grub was happy to imitate a donkey or make baboon and chimp noises. He could tell the difference between Mummy's shoes and

Daddy's shoes and was able to pile four tins on top of each other and identify a few dozen named things by pointing at their pictures.

Robert Hinde and yet another of Jane's "castle" friends, a professor of psychiatry from Stanford University named David Hamburg, arrived around the middle of July, and as Jane wrote to the family on July 19, both men believed that "what is going on here is the most exciting thing in animal behaviour that is going on anywhere in the world." Robert was "madly going to help us get funds and people"—Cambridge zoology graduate students supported by grants from the Science Research Council in Britain. And David Hamburg was "pretty sure" that considerable sums would be available for the production of scientifically oriented films on chimpanzee development from the National Institute of Child Health and Human Development in the States.

Alice Sorem, meanwhile, was having trouble with her infant development study. But Pat McGinnis had already been accepted as a Ph.D. candidate at Cambridge University, and although he had started working on the red colobus monkeys, Jane and Robert soon converted him to the chimps. As Jane wrote home, "Pat we have persuaded, thank Goodness, to return to the fold. He has given up his colobus (thankfully I know) and is going to do six months of sexual behaviour, go to Cambridge for 6 months, return here for two years of sexual behaviour, write up for a year in Cambridge, and leave with a PhD—at least, there seems little doubt of that."

Robert had come to Gombe planning to computerize the data collection system, but in order to do that it was necessary to produce punched data cards. As Geza recalls, "You were supposed to walk around with a stupid box with this bunch of keypunches. You were supposed to stick your card into that thing and do your observations by literally punching the keys to make holes in the cards." To Geza's thinking, the worst part of the proposed system was that "carting this incredible gizmo around would totally make it impossible for you to at the same time make any written or tape-recorded notes." But Robert had never been to Gombe before, and so he had come with a theoretical vision of chimpanzee-following uncomplicated by the reality of high grass, sharp thorns, impenetrable thickets, steep mountains, precipitous ravines, and smart animals far more competent at navigating the three-dimensional maze than any person could ever hope to be. Some of the people at camp questioned the sense of his proposed new system, and he finally agreed to try it out first for himself. Geza remembers the result: "I can close my eyes and see him walking into camp. He looked like hell. I mean, he was torn up by thorns. He was bleeding from head to toe. His clothes were torn. He looked like he'd come out of a concentration camp, okay?"

Still, with Robert's collaboration, Gombe finally settled on a new, if noncomputerized, system for data gathering. For A Records, a researcher at the feeding station, speaking into a portable tape recorder, would try to note all individual interactions within a group. For B Records, the researcher—either at the feeding station or out in the forest—would follow an individual as long as possible and make continuous tape-recorded observations of that individual's behavior. In both cases the tape-recorded notes were punctuated by an automatic one-minute (or sometimes half-minute) interval beeper; and then at day's end, everyone would record those beep-segmented audio notes as category entries on complex and cross-referenced check sheets, in that way establishing several kinds of standardized and calibrated data (who did what to whom when, how often, for how long, and so on).

Altogether, Jane concluded, Robert's visit was "a huge enormous success," and the man had "gone down well with everyone." Margaret Pickford considered him a "sweet poppet." Nick liked him. Others were "thrilled with his intellect." In turn, Robert seemed fond of Grub and had "quite fallen for Geza's Ruth—who is willowy, quiet and intelligent." But the professor from Cambridge was simply "most dashing," Jane thought, while bathing in the lake in his black bikini underwear. "He keeps away from others for the bathing, so you see the elegant figure with the tiny black strip around his loins, in the distance. . . . Alice saw him once thus, and I'm sure was quite bowled over."

Aside from the visit of David Hamburg and Robert Hinde, perhaps the most significant event that summer was Flo's pregnancy and subsequent delivery. Jane wrote in her July 19 letter home, "Do you know that FLO IS PREGNANT!!! Can you believe it? Nova lost a baby in November. Palace lost a baby two weeks ago—she disappeared just before it was due, and came back a week later with no baby. But Flo won't!"

Flo was Gombe's most skilled and successful mother, even though at the moment her two youngest, Fifi and Flint, were not reacting well to her pregnancy. Flint, just weaned, had regressed and was now, as Jane wrote home in late July, "going through a real baby stage." He was clinging to and riding on his mother constantly. FWI volunteer Carole Gale spent six hours following the pair one day and reported that whenever Flo slowed down to rest or eat, Flint would begin whimpering and push her until she moved on—at which he would climb onto her back. When she once dared to descend from a tree without holding him to her breast, he "flew down after her in the most terrible temper tantrum." And if Flo groomed anyone but him, Flint would starting whimpering and push himself in between. But the "really ridiculous thing," Jane declared in late July, was when adolescent Fifi chose to spend time with her mother and little brother. When Fifi was around, she wanted her mother's full attention. So if Flo was grooming Flint, Fifi would pull her hands away and whimper "like a small spoilt child!"

Perhaps Flo was such an affectionate and attentive mother that her off-spring found it hard to leave the nest. In any case, given the interesting dynamics of that little family, everyone looked forward to the birth of the new baby. Alice Sorem wanted to observe Flo during childbirth, which meant that she began following Flo daily that August. Alice, as Jane wrote home around the middle of the month, was "really redeeming herself" after a bad start on the infant development study. She had by then followed Flo for nearly a week straight during daylight hours. Flint was still riding on Flo's back, and perhaps Flo kept caroming along the narrow tunnels in the thorny thickets to discourage him. It discouraged Alice even more, particularly on the day Flo raided a beehive. When the bees swarmed after Flo, she ran right back in the direction of Alice and then took off, leaving the bees behind to sting the person. Still, aside from the few occasions where they became temporarily separated, Alice managed to keep up with Flo for ten days—only to lose her on the critical morning of August 22, when baby Flame was born.

The infant was, Jane wrote home two days later, "the sweetest little girl"—and, typical for Flo's family, she was almost completely pink and (aside from down on her body, a little hair on her head, and a few long white hairs on her chin and upper lip) hairless. To everyone's amazement, Flint behaved "beautifully" upon the arrival of this new member of the family, although Fifi, while curious ("peered, and several times just touched a hand or foot"), did not seem to be "as overjoyed as we had hoped."

Dominic Bandora, the original Gombe cook, turned up on the beach one night that summer, happy to talk about his family (his daughter Ado was *mkubwa sana sasa*—all grown up now) and looking for work. As Jane wrote home, "Since we have to get another cook, we have re-employed the old rogue."

Ruth also wrote home about Dominic. "He is a small, funny old man, extremely proud and an excellent cook." Perhaps most important from her perspective, his return meant that the food got better. "What a difference in our meals since he has been back!" He was even producing decent apple pies and chocolate cakes for dessert.

"We're vastly expanding here," Jane wrote proudly to Desmond Morris on September 10, 1968. She and Hugo now had six students working full-time on the chimpanzee observations. Two were concentrating on their own Ph.D. projects after completing a full year of work on the general records. One would be going to Cambridge University "under Robert's wing, which is excellent." In addition, "two Berkeley-ites," Tim and Bonnie Ransom, had recently finished a baboon study ("and a first class one that will be quite shattering"). Another of Robert's Ph.D. students from Cambridge, Tim Clutton-Brock, would soon be arriving to start research on Gombe's red colobus monkeys. In fact, Jane continued, the Gombe Stream Research Centre had gotten so big they had even taken on a full-time administrator and his wife; and starting early next year, they would be hiring a senior scientist to supervise the Ph.D. students' work while working on his or her own research project.

Naturally, that expanding population created its own set of problems. People were occasionally getting on each other's nerves, which was perhaps inevitable in such an isolated place but exacerbated by a shortage of living and working space. Pat and Alice had their own little rondavels, but the rest of the chimp-watchers were left, for example, trying to do their typing—a noisy process of transcribing notes from the tape recorders—in the 14-by-14-foot workroom of Pan Palace. Moreover, at least three of them were sharing the tiny kitchen space at Pan Palace for their breakfast and lunch, cooking on a single gas ring.

But possibly the most serious and persistent concern that summer and fall was Patrick McGinnis's draft status. Although Pat had proven himself to be (as Jane mentioned in a letter to the Geographic's Leonard Carmichael) "the best researcher we have had to date," his draft board in San Diego had decided that it was time for the young man to begin a close and active study of human agonistic behavior in Vietnam. Jane had twice written to them explaining the importance of Pat's chimp work and requesting a deferral, but the board members were unmoved. In the end she enlisted the help of Dr. Carmichael, who happened to serve as chairman of the committee on scientific personnel for the U.S. Selective Service System. In the meantime Geza Teleki received a notice in the mail that his draft status had also changed to 1-A: ready for induction into the United States Army.

But aside from the occasional personnel problems and draft worries of Patrick and Geza, by the time Jane and Hugo packed up near the end of September, they must have felt they were leaving the chimpanzee research in capable hands. During the third week of the month, Hugo flew back to the crater to resume his photography. A few days later, Jane and Grub flew out of Kigoma to join him. Jane would return to Gombe for comparatively brief periods two or three times during the next several months, checking up and sorting out, but for the most part she managed the research from a distance: from their camp in the crater, from their camp in the Serengeti, from their home in Limuru, and from her family home in England.

Another young researcher from San Diego, Cathleen Clark, dropped in at the crater that October, staying for a couple of weeks to help with the hyena photography and get her immigration papers fixed before going on to join the Gombe group. Cathy made a good first impression. "We both like her most frightfully," Jane wrote home on October 21. The American was "prepared to rough it" and did not take vitamin pills or expect caviar twice a week.

And by late October, Jane had also settled on the senior scientist for Gombe, a former doctoral student of Robert Hinde's named Michael Simpson. "I shall be returning to Gombe in two weeks," Jane wrote to Leonard Carmichael on November 22. "All is going splendidly there—and we have found a man for the post of Senior Scientist who will be arriving in January." Dr. Simpson, she continued, was a "very sound scientist" who "will be excellent in his capacity of supervising research students at the Gombe."

Flo's infant, Flame, died in February 1969. As Jane wrote to Carmichael on March 5, "We don't know what happened, but presume she got the flu-cold type of thing which all the chimps have been suffering from." Flo herself had been ill enough to go missing for five days, and when she returned, she was accompanied by Flint and Fifi but not Flame. "We are all terribly upset, because I can't conceive of Flo being able to survive another pregnancy."

Meanwhile, Jane had been persuaded by Frederick Vosburgh to write yet another article on the Gombe chimpanzees for *National Geographic*. It would be her third on the chimps, her fourth for the magazine, and by early April she had produced a rough draft. She wrote of Merlin being orphaned, the birth of Flame, little Flint as Flo's problem child, the males' continuing competition for dominance, Grub's life in the cage, and the hazards of research that took young researchers away from camp and out into the forest—where Geza Teleki was charged by a raging bush pig and Ruth Davis was butted and treed by an aggressive buffalo. The draft may have combined too many disparate stories, but Jane was most concerned, as she declared to Vosburgh, that it "seems to have rather a lot of the tragedy of the chimps." Still, in the interests of *Geographic*'s reading public, she had tried to temper the sad parts with some strategic editing: "I actually had to take out several of the deaths about which I had written and try to substitute them with happier things!"

In any event, the magazine's editorial staff rejected Jane's submission. One reader referred to the lack of focus. Another wanted the article to clarify more "<u>why</u> from a <u>scientific</u> point of view all the work is done." But

Jane's own worry, that much of the story was too sad for ordinary readers, was the theme of a third objection: "Much of the material is depressing, if not downright gruesome, with vivid details of polio and influenza among the chimps and mercy killing of sick ones."

Vosburgh informed her in early June. Jane, replying late in the month, accepted the rejection but at the same time suggested that she might soon have some happier stories for a future article. It was likely that Fifi would soon have a baby, which ought to result in an "excellent story," particularly if Flo was still alive. And the ancient lady herself "might even surprise us by producing again herself, though, for her sake, I hope not." Indeed, Jane continued, in spite of the gloom of her recent failed attempt at an article, things at Gombe were actually "going very well," since "we have the best team there that we have ever had."

Pat McGinnis had finally been deferred by his draft board, and so he was now on his way back to Gombe after his two terms at Cambridge. And Geza Teleki, who had returned to the States for academic reasons, would be returning to Gombe in January 1970, at which point "he will be married to Ruth Davis (the one charged by the buffalo in the article)."

Geza had left in March, taking a sun-and-swim vacation at the coast with Ruth before going home for his draft physical, which he failed because of bad eyesight. Then he stayed in the States to begin writing up a thesis on chimpanzee predation and meat-eating.

Ruth, after about a month's vacation from Gombe—first with Geza, then with Jane and Hugo in the Serengeti—returned and began working on her own special project, which was to study the relationships between six of the adult males. This meant she had to follow individual males over much of their range—a very challenging task.

On Sunday morning, July 13, 1969, she left camp following Mike. When she failed to show up for dinner that evening, everyone became concerned, then worried. They began a search, which was discontinued at one o'clock and resumed at dawn the next day, assisted now by several fishermen. One of the researchers took the boat into Kigoma and informed the police, who sent a team of twelve men out to help in the search. National Parks was notified, and they flew in a search plane. The village of Mwamgongo, to the north of the park, was also alerted, and so reinforcements came from that direction as well.

Jane and Hugo had gone to Holland for the wedding of Hugo's brother Godert, which was to be followed by three scientific conferences for Jane in London—their first time away from Africa in eighteen months. In their absence, Pat McGinnis notified Louis Leakey by telegram on Tuesday: "Phone jane that ruth has been lost for 3 days." Louis contacted Jane and Hugo, who immediately telegrammed Ruth's parents in Lynchburg, Virginia.

Mr. and Mrs. Davis were at the time being visited by their other daughters, Jean and Ann, along with their spouses and children, which meant that during the next few days the extended family shared an excruciating wait. "The phone was ringing all day, and then it would also seem to ring in the night," Ruth's sister Jean has recalled. "We lived on coffee. We hardly ate. We weren't sleeping." Around dawn on Saturday morning, July 19, the phone rang once again. Jean was sleeping on a small cot, and Ann shook her awake. Ruth had been found.

Pat McGinnis was with the group who found her. She was lying at the bottom of a waterfall in Kahama valley, her head severely fractured. She must have died quickly. Pat and the rest of the small search party built a makeshift stretcher out of branches and vines and carried the body down to the beach, where it was picked up by a boat and taken into Kigoma. Ruth's tape recorder was discovered next to her body, and later on people played back her taped notes to figure out what had happened. According to the notes, she had first followed Mike that Sunday morning, and after he disappeared she had met up with Hugh and Charlie and so followed them. At around 3:30 in the afternoon, however, she had lost their trail and decided to turn back, intending to walk out of the mountains and down to the beach. She last described a small clearing in the forest corresponding to a small clearing just above the waterfall where she was found . . . and so there, one imagines, she lost her balance and then, tragically, her life.

Mr. and Mrs. Davis decided that Ruth should be buried at Gombe, the place she loved, and thus they began their hard journey. They flew to Washington on Sunday evening, July 20, arriving late because of thunderstorms, bunking down finally in the Jefferson Hotel, staying awake only long enough to watch on television the American astronauts take their first steps on the moon. By Monday evening they were on a plane to London.

Hugo met them at the Nairobi airport on Wednesday morning, July 23, and within a short while the three of them had boarded a Piper Cub four-seater and set off for Kigoma. "The flight was a most fantastic one," Mrs. Davis wrote in her journal. "We never flew high enough to lose sight of the land and the African landscape was like nothing ever dreamed of." After a brief touchdown at Hugo's photography camp in the Serengeti and a refueling stop at Tabora, they arrived late that afternoon at Kigoma. The chief of police met them at the airport and drove them down to the docks, where they boarded a big trimaran used by National Parks for tourist transportation. Many flowers from people in Kigoma were brought onboard, and then Ruth, inside a simple wooden coffin with a nicely crafted wooden cross, was carried onto the boat as well, and all the flowers were arranged around her. Then the boat left Kigoma harbor and headed north. "It was a long, very difficult and sad trip."

By the time they finally arrived at the shores of Gombe, around 7:30 that evening, Mrs. Davis was so tired she could hardly walk. But people on the beach greeted her and her husband warmly and led them to a room in Marler Mansion, where they could rest. After a short nap they felt better and so joined Cathy Clark, Tim Clutton-Brock, Carole Gale, Pat McGinnis, Nick Pickford, Michael Simpson, Hugo, and the recently arrived Loretta Baldwin for a special dinner prepared by Dominic. Dominic had also picked several bouquets of wildflowers for the occasion, and he served up a first-rate pork roast with potatoes, a vegetable, and a custard and fruit dessert that was delicious. After dinner they went to visit Ruth, who had been placed in one of the thatched aluminum rondavels for the night, with all the flowers heaped around her. "Somehow I feel that this must be all a dream," Mrs. Davis wrote, "and I will awaken soon to find everything normal. I can't believe we're here and somehow can't believe what has happened."

Around noon the next day, a group of some two dozen additional mourners ("black, white and Indian who had come to help us say our farewell to Ruth") arrived from Kigoma on the Parks trimaran, and then Hugo said it was time. Cathleen Clark led the way, and the procession moved along the beach for a while and then turned up, crossing a small bridge and following a steep path until, about halfway up the hill, they came to a level clearing, grass and a few trees, with a view of the lake. Ruth was there already, and after some words and a reading by Father Prew from Kigoma, she was lowered into the earth. Later in the day her parents returned to the spot by themselves, and, as they could see then, "the sunset is beautiful where she is and there is a beautiful view of the lake."

Mrs. Davis hoped that "the chimps come there to visit."

31

Hugo's Book

1967–1970

BACK IN 1967, Hugo's big chance — his opportunity for artistic independence — had arrived in the form of Sir William Collins, the principal owner of a publishing house known as William Collins and Sons. Sir William — or Billy, as Jane and Hugo quickly came to know him — was the publisher of Vanne's romantic adventure novel, *In the Rain Forest,* released in England early that year.

Billy Collins, who had learned about Jane's work in the early years from his friend Julian Huxley, also hoped to publish her popular book about chimpanzees. Of course, after the first *National Geographic* article appeared in the summer of 1963, Jane had been showered with eager queries from publishers, but Billy was her first and most faithful suitor. It would be a few more years before she actually had time to write that book, distracted as she was by turning out articles, chapters, papers, films, lectures, and the popular book she wrote for the National Geographic Society. But she always kept in mind "the real book" she would one day write.

Hugo also hoped to write a book, and perhaps it was the idea of a family package, his book followed by hers, that finally persuaded the van Lawicks to sign with Collins. Hugo once described the situation this way: "A lot of publishers had approached Jane asking for a book on chimps, which we knew was going to be a big seller. But we knew nothing about publishing, and I suggested to Jane, 'Why don't we first do one book and through that we'll find out how it works and then do the chimps?'" Collins was the publisher who agreed to that approach — with Houghton Mifflin of Boston soon following suit for North American rights.

Billy Collins went to Nairobi around June 1967 and met with Jane and Hugo at the New Stanley Hotel. He was tall and handsome, with longish hair and bushy eyebrows. When the weather called for it, he wore a cape. He was a dramatic, dynamic, decisive man, and when Hugo and Jane met him for the first time the conversation was, Hugo has recalled, pleasingly succinct. What did they want to do? he asked. They told him, and he said, "That's fine." How much money did they want? They told him, and he said, "That's fine."

The first book, Hugo's, would feature, in text and black-and-white photographs, a half-dozen East African carnivores: spotted hyenas, golden jackals, wild dogs, lions, leopards, and cheetahs. These were among the most beautiful, intelligent, and socially complex animals of the plains, and of course they were all killers. Jane and Hugo had been "horrified," as she later wrote, to see the hyenas eat their prey while it was still alive. At least as chilling was the sight of wild dogs disemboweling their living prey. Lions, leopards, and cheetahs are sometimes thought to be nobler beasts, since they often kill by crushing a windpipe and suffocating their victims, which might seem to be a cleaner approach; but a death by suffocation can take ten minutes or longer, and "who are we to judge which is the more painful way to die?" Unlike humans, of course, who kill for sport and with the ability to understand the suffering they inflict, East African carnivores "kill in order to eat and to live in the only way for which evolution has fitted them." The carnivores thus might be described as "innocent killers"—which would be the title of Hugo's book.

Hugo was still on assignment for the National Geographic during 1967. Only when he ended his regular connection with the society and began working independently, in January 1968, could he begin the searching, watching, waiting, coffee-drinking, cigarette-smoking, picture-taking, and writing that finally resulted in *Innocent Killers*.

Jane and Grub accompanied Hugo to Ngorongoro Crater that January. Jane always loved the moment of starting the descent into the crater, passing through the swirling clouds of the caldera's high rim and, as their vehicles ground slowly in low gear down the steep, rough, rutted road, seeing the green floor a half-mile below start to take shape out of the attenuating mist. From so high above, the 100 square miles of Ngorongoro's floor at first appeared flat and unpopulated. But she and Hugo would soon be pointing out "the dark masses of the wildebeeste herds and the single black spots of solitary rhinos." As they continued the descent, they would spy clusters of grazing zebras and "the pale sandy-coloured herds of Grant's and Thompson's gazelles." The soda lake on the crater floor would be flashing silver-blue in the sun—pink at the edges from thousands of flamingos. Hidden in the emerald forests just beyond the lake would be elephants, buffalo, herds of eland. Predators, seldom as obvious as their grazing prey, would be down there somewhere as well: lions, hyenas, three species of jackal, several species of mongoose, as well as servals, leopards, wild cats, civets, genets, and a few cheetahs and wild dogs. Descending into that world was a breathtaking experience, and it was a pleasure to set up camp there, to live intimately with wild animals in such a wilderness, to stay for weeks or months in green, sun-warmed canvas tents and the little cabin on the Munge River.

Hugo was always anxious to get photographs, but his vision for *Innocent Killers* was of much more than a mere book of pictures. He intended to do research and make original observations about his six carnivore species, and he would use a conceptual modus operandi similar to the one Jane had used with the chimps. Start with an open mind. Identify individuals. Understand personalities. Follow the interactions of individuals with extended and careful observations; proceed to understanding the complex social behaviors. That conceptual approach had worked nicely with chimpanzees, and it made a suitable stylistic approach as well, since the lives of individuals could inspire a narrative that ordinary readers might appreciate.

More practically, Hugo's approach involved a lot of driving and then a lot of sitting. When a full or bright moon provided enough light, Hugo would be bouncing about in the Land Rover behind a ghostly parade of large, rather doggy-looking nocturnal animals as they loped through the rough grasslands. Once they discovered their prey, the hyenas would begin moving faster, and one might hear the pounding of hooves, then see, emerging from the darkness, a small, frightened herd, a dozen zebras galloping, swerving, kicking—the car bolting and jolting and the zebras bounding, pursued by a whooping nemesis of dark bodies and shimmering eyes. On darker nights, when driving was too difficult, Hugo would sleep (he was a remarkably sound sleeper), wake just before dawn, and, with a couple of thermoses of hot water, climb into the Land Rover and start the engine. Then he was off to keep watch over the grass-covered entrance to the jackals' den while quietly murmuring notes into the tape recorder.

7:50. We arrive at the golden jackal den, find Jason and two puppies in the open, presumably hunting.
7:54. Jason grooms one puppy. It runs off.

Next to him on the car seat would be an open aluminum suitcase with his various cameras, lenses, and filters, each in its own baize-lined compartment. Hugo might draw out a Hasselblad fitted with a 500mm lens, attach it to the special mount on his car door, and focus on the den entrance. He would spoon some instant coffee into a plastic mug, pour in the hot water, add two or three spoonfuls of sugar, sit and sip coffee, chain-smoke ciga-rettes, and wait.

Hugo began his research that year with Ngorongoro's spotted hyenas and, when there was time and daylight, golden jackals. For the spotted hye-nas, he could take advantage of his earlier work in support of Hans Kruuk's article for *National Geographic*. Although he would not be allowed to use any of those photographs (or would have to ask or cajole and probably pay for any the society might choose to release), working on Kruuk's study had given him an essential understanding of the animals and their social system. People commonly considered hyenas to be the big ugly scavengers of East Africa, gruesome and giggling as they picked over the leftovers of more at-tractive beasts. In fact, with data from thousands of separate observations, Kruuk had shown hyenas to be bold predators. In the Serengeti, both lions and hyenas made their own kills; in Ngorongoro Crater, lions seldom both-ered killing for themselves but instead scavenged the remains of hyena pre-dations. Kruuk also verified that spotted hyenas live in matriarchal societies, with the powerful and aggressive females (as big as the males, weighing up to 130 pounds) remaining within their own stable social units, which he called clans, while the males were relatively peripheral, sometimes migrating from one clan to another. Finally, he confirmed that the matriarchal clans—eight within the confines of the crater—were distinctly territorial, with the resi-dent females violently defending their home ranges against aggressive in-cursions from females of neighboring clans.

Hugo ultimately focused on hyena life from the perspective of the com-munity of around eighty individuals called the Scratching Rocks Clan, but in 1968 he had just begun the photography and research when June arrived and he and Jane had to return to Nairobi and Limuru. Jane finished her chimpanzee monograph at last and mailed it off around the middle of the month. "Well that is the end of that. Thank goodness it's done," she wrote home to the family on June 16, and that evening she and Hugo celebrated.

After spending the summer at Gombe, Hugo and Jane returned, with Grub-lin, to the Munge River camp at Ngorongoro Crater around the final week of September and Hugo resumed his work on the spotted hyenas. Jane was busy with her own projects. But they took along Nick and Margaret Pick-ford to help Hugo, and Jane soon found that she could pitch in as well. Hugo was starting to make progress.

"We've all been flat out on hyena!" Jane wrote home on October 12. The hyena work would start around 5:45 in the evening, with Nick and Margaret and Hugo climbing into the Land Rover, strapping themselves in and their crash helmets on, and then roaming roughly over the grasslands, prowling about in search of hyenas who were prowling about in search of prey. They spent moonlit evenings watching the dramatic and violent aspects of hyena life, while Jane and Grub concentrated on the more sedate and domestic side of hyena life, settling down in the VW bus in front of a den and quietly watching from the front windows as the lowering sun turned the brown grass gold and the pups and their mothers emerged and frolicked. By then Jane and Hugo had identified and named several individuals of the Scratching Rocks Clan, giving the pups such names as Walpole, Toffee, Fudge, Coal, H.H., Coke, Sheltie, and Woolsey, and naming "the great fat old Mums" Coffee, Mrs. Brown, Mrs. Wart, Mrs. Straggle, Sloop, and so on. "Oh to see these gross old ladies, their stomachs only inches from the ground, gamboling after each other and frolicking with the pups in the moonlight! It is a sight that must be seen to be believed! One old bag played with 6 young ones. Often she was completely obliterated save for an occasional glimpse of a paw. And then Mrs. Brown, always digging for her youngsters."

Nick and Margaret left in mid-October, and the same little Piper Cub that came to take them out brought in the mail, supplies (beef, pork, lamb, tomatoes, lettuce, bananas, a crate of oranges and apples, two boxes of canned goods), and a young journalist from England. Timothy Green was writing a book called *The Adventurers* that would devote a quarter of its contents to Jane and Hugo as a fair sample of interesting "contemporary travellers." Just as Green climbed across the wing of the Piper and dropped to the ground, Hugo bounced up in the Land Rover, ready to be observed and written about. The journalist saw "a short young man, with rather unbrushed dark brown hair, a face burnt red-brown by the African sun, and tired eyes that seemed constantly slightly screwed up in defense against the strong light. He wore a khaki slipover shirt, shorts and dusty plimsolls." Soon they both noted a rising plume of brown in the distance, marking the advance of a second vehicle. A Volkswagen bus pulled up, and Tim Green met Jane, who appeared from out of the bus, barefoot, in jeans and a light blue shirt, as "a tall, very slim girl with long blonde hair, tied simply behind her head with a band." Jane then drew from out of the bus "a blond haired little boy, with a rather dirty face, dressed in a red and white tee shirt and brown shorts."

The van Lawicks left the crater and returned to Limuru by mid-November so Jane could have some necessary dental work in Nairobi: seventeen replacement fillings. "I shan't tell you the cost," she wrote home on December 7, "because dentistry is exorbitant out here. But Hugo & I felt it must be done." Hugo's turn for exorbitant dental work would come a month later.

In the meantime, they learned that the Geographic Society had agreed to fund Jane's grant request for Gombe in 1969 minus her own salary, which meant she was now an unpaid volunteer. It also meant that she and Hugo would have to rely almost entirely on Hugo's advance payments from Houghton Mifflin and Collins for *Innocent Killers,* although that money was rapidly running low and he had not yet finished his first chapter, on the first of six killers. Their increasingly tenuous finances also meant that although Jane would continue monitoring the work at Gombe and make a number of visits there, she and Hugo could not afford a three-month sojourn with the chimpanzees in 1969 like the one they had so enjoyed during the summer of 1968.

They were, as Jane summarized finally in a post-Christmas letter home, "pretty broke at the moment." They had bought a small, silvery foil tree but were reluctant to buy any Christmas decorations—and so were grateful that the family had sent decorations that made the silvery tree "glistening and glittering and winking at me as I sit writing this." For Christmas dinner they had duck, pudding, and wine, followed by a cake that Jane had decorated in an innocent-killer theme: ice-blue frill and three blue candles with a plastic lion, lioness, leopard, and jackal. One can imagine that Hugo secretly felt there was too much innocent killer that Christmas, given the year's dismal progress on the subject, but by then Jane had decided, as she explained in her letter, "to help Huog [sic] write his hyena chapter," and the effort was already forcing her to type "three times as fast as I am able" and therefore make plenty of mistakes.

There was still much to do on hyenas and jackals, but starting in 1969 they moved on to a third innocent killer—wild dogs (or Cape hunting dogs), which required moving their camp from the Ngorongoro Crater to the Serengeti, where the dogs were. Hugo went first, around the beginning of January, accompanied by two volunteer assistants, Roger Polk and Jean-Jacques Mermod. Vanne flew out to Nairobi that January, intending to do some grandmotherly babysitting, and Jane, Vanne, and Grub reached Hugo's camp in the second week of February.

Vanne immediately wrote home, "Well here we all are on the famous Serengeti Plains—camped on some high ground overlooking a beautiful deserted soda water lake." The camp consisted of eight green tents arranged in a crescent and nestled in a thin grove of flat-topped acacia trees and thorn scrub on a slight hill sloping gently down to the lake. Lions, warthogs, ostriches, and giraffes occasionally ambled or rushed through the trees and scrub, and from their tents the van Lawicks could watch a seemingly endless procession of herbivores on the plains. Yearly, after the spring rains turned the brown grass green, scattered herds of zebras, gazelles, and wildebeests would gather in bush land to the north and west of the park and then, oriented by memory and the smell of rain, migrate in great grazing columns south and east into the fresh grassy plains to eat and to calve until the rains and the green feast were over. "For a few weeks," Jane later wrote, "while the herds remained in the vicinity of our camp, we lived our lives to the constant accompaniment of the mellow lowing and honking of the wildebeests and the wild bursts of zebra calls which sound somewhat like speeded-up and hysterical versions of donkeys braying. The splendour and freedom of those hundreds of miles of unspoilt country, the sunrises and sunsets over plains made black by thousands of animals, the roaring of lions and the weird whooping calls of hyenas at night, are things which I shall remember as long as I live." Also during the migration, thousands of wildebeests would run, dance, buck, and pirouette crazily through the area, churning into the alkaline lake below, swimming wildly and drowning by the hundreds.

That beautiful and sometimes fatal lake was known as Legaja, a name supposedly indicating in the Maasai language a peaceful, sacred place undisturbed by human noise. It was an evocative name, even though no one was sure how to spell its English transliteration. In her letters, Jane experimented with Legadja, Legarga, Lagarja, Lagaja, and Legaja. Legaja became the official version for *Innocent Killers*, but Hugo changed it in a later book to Lagarja. A tented safari camp for tourists on the other side of the lake was called Ndutu, and Hugo finally, by 1986, solved the orthographic puzzle in time for his grand book of photographs, *Among Predators and Prey*, by describing that potent if unpotable body of water as Lake Ndutu.

At the moment, however, it was still Legaja, and the important puzzle was a canine one: where were the wild dogs? They were being elusive. The Serengeti's wild dogs are nomadic hunters who cruise the plains in small packs, crossing vast areas with no clear territories. A pack stays in one area only when there are puppies and a den to support. Once the young are mature enough to travel, the den is abandoned and the growing pups join the rest of the pack in their nomadic wandering. For the kind of close and long-term behavioral study Hugo had in mind, therefore, it was not enough to sight a trotting pack on the horizon. He needed to find a den with dependent puppies inside. In each of the previous three years during the spring, he had sighted wild dogs with puppies and dens near Lake Legaja; but now, so far, he was having no such luck.

Hugo decided to try searching in a small plane, and having arranged to fly with Hans Kruuk, he left before dawn one morning while the rest of the camp still slept in their tents. Jane and Vanne woke around seven, had tea, and had just started their breakfast when a couple of Land Rovers roared into camp. Out climbed six "ghastly pseudo rich safari types," as Vanne would describe them in a letter home. "There's a Land Rover up the road!" various members of the group announced ("shouted with glee," according to Vanne's assessment). "It's a complete write-off!" "Blood all over the place." "Belongs to van Lawick." "Whoever was in it can't have gotten far."

Vanne drew aside one of the women in the group and, nodding in Jane's direction, discreetly declared, "That is his wife." The woman stared blankly at Vanne for a moment and then turned to Jane and said, "My dear, with all the blood! Well, people with concussions wander off." She continued, "I'm just warning you—he's probably wandered into the bush, and it's full of lions and hyenas."

Vanne, Jane, Grub, Roger, and Jack set off in the Volkswagen and finally arrived at the spot near a rain-swollen stream where the Land Rover, minus Hugo, was cocked into a hole in the road. Jane, alarmed, began wandering around, looking for a bloody trail and footprints, while Vanne searched the car, where she found only three little wads of bloodied toilet paper and a single smear of blood on a door. Roger headed for Hans Kruuk's camp in the VW van while the rest of the party spread out and searched along the rushing stream, calling into the tall grass, the weedy wallows, the thorny thickets.

At last they heard the noise of an engine, which was soon followed by the sight of the VW with Roger inside and Hugo at the wheel. After he had crashed the Land Rover, Hugo explained, he had walked the final mile and a half to Kruuk's place in order to have his two-hour flight looking for wild dogs. He had bumped his nose in the accident; there was a little blood. And he had no idea why anyone would be upset, although he was upset, because he still had not found the wild dogs or their den.

Over time Hugo, Roger, and Jack sighted a number of roaming packs, and whenever they located one, they would work in relays—relieving one another at ten in the morning and four in the afternoon—trying to track the tireless trotters by car. They had help as well from an eccentric but generous and resourceful man named George Dove, who ran the Ndutu safari camp on the other side of the lake. Dove organized game-watching trips for tourists, and he instructed all his drivers to report any dog sightings. Whenever a pack was seen, he would drive over to the van Lawick camp right away to let them know. In that fashion, Hugo and his volunteers gained some useful information about the roaming packs—but they still failed to find the puppies and dens.

During the early months of 1969, Jane was working on the article for *National Geographic* that had been solicited by Frederick Vosburgh. Vosburgh's interest, however, was not shared by others in the editorial and executive departments, and although Jane felt compelled to honor Vosburgh's request, she never felt the same enthusiasm for this article that she had for her previous *Geographic* efforts. Lack of enthusiasm might help explain why the manuscript she submitted in early April was so rambling and rough, even without a title. And part of that lack may have been a result of her increasing preoccupation with *Innocent Killers*.

In fact, Jane was by then in the process of rescuing Hugo's book. His plan to carry out original research on the behavior of six different carnivores, with good photographs and an accessible text, had been far too ambitious, and so he and Jane reconsidered and repackaged the concept. It would be two books, not one, they decided, and the first volume would consist of an introduction and three chapters featuring hyenas, jackals, and wild dogs. Also, Jane would be officially responsible for some of the writing.

Jane wrote to her childhood friend Sally about some of those decisions on April 11, 1969: "Now that Hugo is no longer free lancing in a tied-to-the-Geographic manner (if you see what I mean) money is difficult. But his book—or rather two books—are going to be really first rate and super duper." It was true that they still had to return to the crater for more work on the hyenas, but she had taken over the writing of the hyena chapter, and their publisher had already agreed with that arrangement: "Billy Collins thinks it will be fine to have one chapter by me."

By April the van Lawicks were back at the house in Limuru, dusting themselves off from the Serengeti, sending Grub to a local nursery school, taking care of business and correspondence, meeting with various Gombe people in transit, and on April 12 seeing Vanne off at the airport for her return flight to England.

They returned to Lake Legaja near the end of the month, to find their camp overrun by delicate little tree-dwelling rodents with large eyes and fluffy tails—dormice—who were "all very sweet," as Jane remarked in an April 28 letter home, but "just as bad as rats." Upon their arrival in camp, she spent a day and a half in bed recovering from the flu. When she finally felt ambulatory, she opened her suitcase and saw that the rodents had already finished off two of her three sweaters. She found another dormouse inside a jam jar, and one leaped out of Grub's toy box and clung to his leg before running off. The cute little rodent had just torn half the innards out of one leg of a stuffed bear.

Unhappily, the explosion in dormouse numbers at camp was counterbalanced by an implosion in numbers elsewhere. The Serengeti rains had ended early that year, which meant the grass was drying prematurely. Ordinarily the migration would have kept tens of thousands of herbivores in the area until the end of May or early June, but now, with the grass already brown by the end of April, the herbivores were leaving, making life difficult for the carnivores. Hugo, Roger, and Jack now had three vehicles and spent their days spreading out in a coordinated search across enormous areas for wild dogs, still with little success. The three of them had started that January "full of enthusiasm," so Hugo later wrote, but as the weeks and months passed without locating wild dogs with puppies and a den, "our hopes gradually ebbed."

In May an appearance of the bubonic plague caused Tanzanian health authorities to quarantine the town of Arusha, Jane and Hugo's usual source of food and other supplies, and thus by late May they were getting low on food.

In spite of all the infestations, desiccations, frustrations, and complications, though, Grub was having the time of his life. He was always eager to see wild animals, and even after the herbivores had left he could count on the resident herd of eight giraffes, an old bull rhino who wandered about, and the spring hares bounding across the ground after dark. Once a rare striped hyena ambled into camp. Another time they found, while driving about in the dark, a tree full of nocturnal bush babies, their reflective eyes "shining like red Christmas tree lights" as they leaped across the branches of the tree. And as Grub ate his evening supper on the tent veranda, he was continuously entertained by "long strings of graceful flamingoes" flying past, "silhouetted against the red or golden sky, and giving their strange creaking calls as they headed for a night's feeding on the lake." Grub also had his toys, including a small wheelbarrow he loved to charge around behind and a kickball that he was skilled at activating. And then there was George Dove, always a good friend and a reliable source of chocolates and other treats.

In fact, the van Lawicks were starting to see a good deal of Dove, a big, hearty man who was full of stories. A former Kenyan farmer turned safari guide, he had reddish blond hair and beard and a spectacular set of waxed and pointed mustachios. According to one visitor to Ndutu camp during that period, Dove's whiskers were "easily ten inches long" and he "moved them around like range-finding antennae as he talked, sometimes pointing straight ahead, sometimes pointing them out to the sides, sometimes up in the air alongside his ears." Other observers said that he would use the whiskers to signal mood. If he was angry or otherwise in a bad mood, he would turn the ends down. When he was happy, he would turn them up.

"I'm sure there is not a kinder man anywhere than Grub's Dov," Jane wrote home on May 7. "He came in the morning, bringing huge boxes of fresh food, chocolate for Grubby, petrol and water." Yet perhaps even more significantly, Dove was a very practical man who could, as Hugo could not, fix cars. He spent hours one day getting the stalled VW bus to start and repairing a loose wheel bearing, and he also fixed up Hugo's wrecked Land Rover.

Jane and Hugo made a quick trip from the Serengeti back to the crater to gather a little more material on the golden jackals, and by the end of the month Jane had figured out the introductory and jackal chapters and was typing frantically against the usual impediments of time, a faint ribbon, and a strong gusty wind blowing papers around. By June 3 she had mailed a draft version of nearly the entire chapter on jackals to Billy Collins, with the rest to follow in ten days.

Now, with the jackal chapter done and the introductory chapter well under way, she really only had to worry about hyenas and wild dogs. "The wild dog news is still nothing. Hugo has searched and searched," she wrote home on June 13. Still, they had already gotten a good deal of information just from watching the nomadic packs, and she believed they had already produced perhaps three quarters of the writing. Since Billy had extended their deadline by a year, they now had until early 1970 to finish, which gave "plenty of time to hear news of one of our known packs, and so change a bit of the chapter."

Jane and Hugo left for Europe at the start of July 1969, first to Holland to attend the wedding of Hugo's brother Godert. They were alarmed and distressed to hear on July 15 that Ruth Davis had been missing for three days, and were profoundly saddened to learn on July 19 of her death. Hugo was back in Africa by then, and as noted, he met Ruth's parents at the Nairobi airport and accompanied them to Gombe for the funeral. Jane wrote to the parents early that August: "I find it impossible to find words that can adequately convey my distress. This accident shouldn't have happened. I cannot help but feel in some way responsible; but for my work there, Ruth would have never gone to the Gombe."

Ruth's death led to a significant change that summer in Gombe protocol. When, a year earlier, Jane and Hugo had first discussed with Gombe researchers the new idea of B Records and following the chimps away from camp, they had all acknowledged the dangers and considered a buddy system where every researcher following chimps would be accompanied by an assistant from the African staff. Everyone had rejected the idea then, settling instead on the policy of carrying around small safety kits with signal flares, snakebite antidote, and so on. But after Ruth's death, Jane instituted the buddy system, which had the important long-term effect of bringing the African staff at last into the daily labor of chimpanzee research.

For the rest of the summer Jane stayed with Grub in England, working on a paper about the chimps while doing what she could to help Hugo with his book. And Hugo, after his brief time back at Gombe, returned to the Lake Legaja camp in the Serengeti, where, to his amazement and delight, he and the latest volunteer assistant, Jeff Schoffern, finally located a wild dog den.

During the past two and a half years, Hugo had regularly seen one particular pack, led by an old male named Genghis, roaming the plains. This time Hugo and Jeff found and followed the Genghis pack once again, trailing behind them in the Land Rover and watching as the pack chased, captured, and ate a gazelle. After about fifteen minutes the terrified antelope was transformed into a scattering of bones and the pack was moving again, with Hugo and Jeff quietly following. Genghis, leading the pack, "trotted steadily for some three and a half miles across the flat plains and then, ahead of us," Hugo reported, "we saw another wild dog appear as if from the ground and rush towards the returning hunters."

That was Juno, one of the pack's four adult females. Her tail was wagging, and as Hugo quickly noticed, "her teats [were] heavy with milk." As the returning pack crowded around, Juno ran frantically from one to the other, "pushing her nose up at the mouth of each, and uttering high-pitched squeaks." She was begging for food, and her peculiar behavior caused some of the hunters to regurgitate convulsively some of the undigested meat they had just consumed: food for a mother unable to hunt because she was guarding pups at the den. After eating, Juno peered into a dark hole in the ground and whined. Then she descended until Hugo could see only her tail, whereupon she reversed direction and emerged with eight little pups in tow. "The pups moved faster than I would have expected for such young creatures, but had obvious difficulty in remaining upright on their wobbly legs and outsize paws. Their ears were large, like those of adult wild dogs, but still completely crumpled, and their dark faces were lined and wrinkled, and more reminiscent of old age than youth."

Once the pups had come out of the den, the entire pack, squeaking noisily, closed in. "As the pups stumbled and wobbled hither and thither, so the grown dogs followed, every few moments pushing their noses under the pups and then, with a flicking movement of their heads, turning the youngsters on to their backs." With the adult dogs licking away at their tender bellies, the little puppies lay back with all four legs kicking gently into the air before finally scrambling upright and trying to stagger away. "Often three or even four of the adults gathered to nose and lick the same small pup, pushing each other out of the way, their squeaks following each other faster and faster until the sound resembled the twittering of birds."

The discovery of the Genghis den that August day was a breakthrough, and over the next six weeks, as Hugo and Jeff spent day after day watching the den, they developed a fuller understanding of the individuals and their personalities and the pack's social dynamics. They discovered, for example, that wild dogs, in the fashion of wolves, operate with two different and parallel social hierarchies, male and female. The male hierarchy was harder to figure out, and Hugo and Jeff never did so entirely. They did know that the old leader, Genghis, was top dog and the fast-running Swift also ranked high, while the six other males were lower in rank. The female hierarchy, with only four adult females in the pack, was more obvious: Havoc at the top, Black Angel second, Lotus third, and Juno ("by far the most submissive") at the bottom.

Near the end of September, Jane, back in the Legaja camp, wrote to Louis Leakey that Hugo had gotten "simply super stuff on wild dogs" and that "it was so nice that he got a den in the end, after all that hunting and searching in Feb, March and April." Hugo had accumulated enough new information now, she thought, that "he is about to disprove most current theories about wild dog social structure." By then, however, the pups had grown big enough to run with the adults, so the Genghis pack was leaving its den and returning to its nomadic phase of existence. Jane and Hugo thus pulled up stakes at Lake Legaja and returned to the crater for a final month "to get the final data on the hyenas."

But first they went to Gombe to check on the chimps and chimp-watchers. The ranks of the Gombe researchers had been recently expanded by three new arrivals—Anne Shouldice, Neville Washington, and (coming to take up the baboon study) Leanne Taylor. They were expecting a fourth, David Bygott, by the end of October. Anne Shouldice would stay for the better part of a year, working on general records and mother-infant relations, becoming in the meanwhile acquainted with and then married to the senior scientist, Michael Simpson. Neville Washington left after a shorter stay, around four months, which he spent examining the dynamics of spacing between chimpanzees in a group. And Leanne Taylor nearly left right away, after discovering an enormous black mamba inhabiting the rondavel she was supposed to live in; but Pat McGinnis went in with a snake stick and a machete and decisively decapitated the trespassing reptile, so Leanne stayed.

Jane, Hugo, and Grub—accompanied by Hugo's honeymooning brother Godert (Godi), his new wife, Bobbie, and George Dove—arrived at Gombe around the start of October, and as Jane soon reported in a letter home, Neville Washington was at that point "working out well," while Anne

Shouldice seemed to be "very clever, coming to grips with the problems involved—and the others like her." Michael Simpson was also suddenly "much more cheerful." In short, everything seemed fine and normal—except that Nick Pickford had announced he would be gone in three weeks. His wife, Margaret, had left him by then, and he was planning to depart in the company of researcher Cathleen Clark, but his hasty departure would leave Gombe without a camp manager. It was, Jane commented with apparent irritation, "not much notice!" Godi and Bobbie had been intending to return to Holland at the end of the month, but they agreed to take over the camp management and stay at least until January. As Jane declared to her readers in Bournemouth, "What a weight off our minds!"

Back in the Ngorongoro Crater, the grass was just turning green from new rain, and "my dear hyenas [are] perking up," as Jane phrased it hopefully in an October 14 letter home. Now she expected to get her final data on the hyenas, including especially, she hoped, direct observations of mating, whereupon she could at last finish the hyena chapter. But (as she wrote home eleven days later) the hyenas were "not being at all co-operative. Not at all." It had been good to see "all the familiar faces again" and also "to recognize grown children, and to find a lot of so called young males now with cubs!" And Hugo had gotten pictures of some "most spectacular hunts." But they still had not seen mating—or, as she phrased it in a teasing reference to Danny's Victorian-style expression, "I am not going to get an answer to their 'that certain behaviour,' which means a lot of things in the book will have to be described but not explained—except as a guess. Hey ho."

The van Lawicks were now very seriously low on money. Perhaps, Jane suggested in her October 25 letter home, Vanne could approach Billy Collins and ask "in a nice sort of way whether he would be prepared to make us a LOAN!" She and Hugo were "worried"—and, according to her next letter home, in mid-November, Hugo at least was "frantic with worry!"

By then they were back in Limuru, and Jane was back at the typewriter. Billy Collins had also wanted a children's book, and by assembling the best of Hugo's photographs of little Grub with some commentary by Jane, they had just produced one, which was going to be entitled *Grub, the Bush Baby*. Hugo was now busy writing up his wild dog chapter for *Innocent Killers,* and Jane was frenetically typing out her hyena notes from the crater, rewriting the jackal chapter, and hoping to get going soon on the introductory chapter, whereupon finally she would "get down to my dear hyenas!"

"We are in a most hectic rush with Hugo's book," she wrote to Melvin Payne on December 1, "—which should all be with the publisher by 1st of January. Of course it won't!"

• • •

During the second half of December they made another visit to Gombe, finding, as Jane reported to the family, that Bobbie was two and a half months pregnant; that Godi had "done wonders" there with repairs, new furniture, and new latrines; and that the three new chimp people—Anne, Neville, and David Bygott—were all "working frightfully well." Everyone took Christmas day off, exchanged presents, went swimming and water-skiing, and imbibed "heaps of booze." So the Gombe Stream Research Centre seemed once again whole and promising, and Godi and Bobbie insisted that since Bobbie was pregnant, they would avoid bumpy roads for another month, which meant Gombe would have a camp manager at least until the end of January.

On the afternoon of December 30, Jane, Hugo, and Grub left Gombe, had supper at the Red Lion in Kigoma, and then drove north and east all night long, finally arriving at Lake Legaja by the afternoon of December 31 and then, on January 1, celebrating Christmas with George Dove and his wife, Mibs, at Ndutu camp—before returning once again to Limuru and their continuing labors on *Innocent Killers*.

The deadline had been extended to January 13 by then, and in a letter written on the eighth, Jane described their frantic state: "The dog chapter is getting so interrupted, the hyena chapter not started. The bibliography, glossary, index all to be done. The captions mostly to be done." They had sent an air freight parcel to Billy Collins ("photos, layouts, captions, drawings—almost 200 photos, 8 x 10, and some even 10 x 12") that had not yet arrived in London, which was an added worry. And Hugo was suffering from "the most terrible, horrible, awful malaria." Robert Hinde had by then persuaded Jane to write a scientific chapter for a book on animal tool use. It was an end-of-February deadline, but Jane was unsure whether he wanted her to focus on tool-using primates or all tool-using animals. Also, she had recently learned that Dian Fossey had assembled a collection of gorilla photographs taken by Bob Campbell—"super photos," actually, "though rather monotonous, they being gorillas." Jane urged Vanne to see if she could persuade Billy Collins to publish Dian's popular book (*Gorillas in the Mist*), so that he could time its release to avoid competing with the release of her own popular book (*In the Shadow of Man*).

By January 10, Hugo had "risen shakily from his malaria, or whatever it was."

By January 21, Jane was expressing relief that Billy had finally found the photographs. She hoped he was "really pleased" with the introduction and "will be pleased" with the jackal chapter.

A month later Jane and Hugo were back at their camp at Lake Legaja and about to meet Billy Collins. Jane was still working on the tool-using paper and the hyena chapter, the latter still a "welter of hyenas," as she described it on February 20. But Grub was now recovering from malaria, and Jane was feeling "most queer this morning, sort of headachey and sick as though I'll get flue again which is, of course, an utter impossibility. At least I sincerely hope so." In fact, Billy's visit to their camp coincided, as Jane noted a few days later, with her own terrible illness: "Flu, malaria—I just don't know. Sweating buckets daily, limp rag head, eyes—the lot. Couldn't have been worse."

The mysterious illness lasted more than a week, and at the end, once she was clearheaded again, Jane concluded that she had to rewrite the hyena chapter. "I have been shut in the VW, day and evening, redoing the hyena chapter—which, as you know, I wrote when I had flue," she declared in a mid-March letter home. "Anyway, I'm much more pleased with it now." She had also just finished an epilogue. She had completed the picture captions. She had done a new layout for the hyena chapter, since Billy had said they could add more photos. She was finished with the bibliography. And, finally, she was now "trying to think of titles for chapters—ugh—and frantically trying to get a few more photos of us for publicity."

The annual migration had arrived in that part of the Serengeti by then and was "all around the lake, thickly. And believe it or not, those stupid idiotic wildebeeste have been crossing the lake again, drowning and orphaning hundreds of calves again. Isn't it ridiculous of them." But Billy Collins, as Jane reported happily, was "very keen on the book now." He was also "crazy" about the wild dogs and had even decided to finance Hugo to make a film on them. And through "fantastic luck," they had recently found the Genghis pack while the dominant female, Havoc, was in heat and mating. So if all went well, Havoc would have her pups and the pack would be tending a den in about eight weeks, enabling Hugo to do his film and release it not long after the publication of his—or, by then, *their*—book.

32

Regime Changes

1970–1972

AT THE START OF *1970, the Kasekela chimpanzees at Gombe were living un-der Mike's regime. Mike was the undisputed alpha male, having managed in 1964 to remove the big and powerful Goliath from that position without a fight. Mike in fact had deflated and defeated the reigning Goliath and several other high-ranking males of the community through a technologically assisted per-sonal drama. He began stealing empty ten-gallon kerosene tins from Jane's tent and then, during his charging displays, rolling two or three of the bright silvery objects in front of him, making a fearsome and confounding racket.*

Mike was a relatively small chimpanzee who probably would not have achieved the highest rank among males through physical force or ordinary intimi-dation. It seemed clear that he was using the rackety cans deliberately to enhance his stature. One time, for example, while a half-dozen other mature males sat grooming each other about 10 yards away, Mike quietly got up, moved into Jane's tent, grabbed two empty cans by their handles, and then, walking upright, car-ried them back to his previous spot. He sat down. For a few minutes he stared at the other males, all of them higher-ranking, who continued grooming each other and ignoring the socially inferior Mike. "After a moment Mike began to rock al-most imperceptibly from side to side, his hair very slightly erect. The other males continued to ignore him. Gradually, Mike rocked more vigorously, his hair be-came fully erect, and uttering pant-hoots he suddenly charged directly at his su-periors, hitting the cans ahead of him. The other males fled."

Mike repeated that performance several times, and after Jane and Hugo re-moved the kerosene tins from camp, he acquired other artifacts, such as boxes, chairs, tables, and tripods, to amplify his personal drama. When one by one those were secured, Mike turned to natural objects, such as palm fronds. In that manner he continued to make his impressive displays, until eventually even an ordinary, unassisted charge by Mike was enough to unnerve all the other adult males. They all developed a habit of submission to the clever one, and they became subordinate to him, indicating his eminence with gestures of respect and allowing Mike first access to such important resources as food and sex. Thus, small but smart Mike became in 1964 the top-ranking male of Gombe, the king, the wizard, the president and prime minister.

By 1970, however, Mike was six years older and physically less prepossessing. His hair had become dull and thin. His teeth were ground down, his canines broken. The continuation of his regime depended more on social habit, less on his power or unassisted capacity to unnerve an opponent. In fact, one of Flo's sons, Figan, was beginning to ignore Mike's charging displays—a small yet irritating act of disrespect. Mike would compress his lips and draw his face into a terrific scowl, bulk out his hair, stand upright and swagger, stomp and slap on the ground or at a nearby tree, tear up vegetation, throw rocks, and charge with great ferocity right past Figan, but the nervy upstart would remain lackadaisically turned away, refusing to bow or scurry. Mike, clearly upset at such a lack of deference, was starting to display more and more often at Figan and would sometimes, perhaps to emphasize his regal displeasure, yank on a branch Figan was sitting on.

Soon a second young male, Evered, began showing comparable insubordination, also ignoring Mike's charging displays. As he had done with Figan, Mike now began displaying more directly and frequently at Evered, seemingly trying to provoke some sign or act of respect.

By the start of 1970, meanwhile, Jane had found a new general administrator for Gombe, a young American named Gerald Rilling. As a result of childhood polio, Rilling walked with crutches, but he was a "plucky man," she commented in a letter home, who "has the determination to go to places like this." Gombe's senior scientist, Michael Simpson, was due to leave in a few months, but Jane had located a replacement for him too, a former student of Konrad Lorenz's named Helmut Albrecht, on leave from Amsterdam University. And the researchers already associated with Gombe at the end of 1969 would be joined by Geza Teleki, who planned to start a Ph.D. study on chimpanzee ranging. David Bygott, already at Gombe, would be joined in the next few months by fellow British graduate students Anne Pusey and Richard Wrangham. Harold Bauer, from the University of Manitoba, was scheduled to arrive in late July. After him would come several others from a variety of backgrounds: Ellen Drake, Margaretta (Mitzi) Hankey, Nicholas Owens, Stephen Rowlands, and Sean Sheehan. The Gombe team would soon be gathering information on a half-dozen aspects of chimpanzee behavior and simultaneously acquiring data on baboons and other monkeys, snakes, birds, fish, and vegetation.

"We firmly believe," Jane wrote on January 10 to Leonard Carmichael, "that the Gombe Stream Research Centre, despite some 'teething troubles,' will become one of the most important primate research centres in the field—and here I mean, of course, 'the field of field research'!"

But while Jane was expressing such strong optimism about Gombe's future, the National Geographic Society's alpha males were in the opposite sort of mood. They wanted out. Upon reviewing Jane's 1970 grant application that February, Carmichael resorted to a metaphor about the geometrics of scientific discovery that he had come to favor when discussing Jane's work: "The 'curve' is flattening out." Melvin Payne, now the society's president, agreed, adding, "We should start a positive program of reducing our support to compel the Goodalls to seek funds elsewhere." He then suggested that the Research and Exploration Committee cut the annual grant from the request of around $40,000 down to $25,000. Gilbert Grosvenor, a son of the former president, Melville Bell Grosvenor, inserted his own opinion that "the Society has made . . . Goodall world-famous. Now [she] should be able to obtain substantial support from sources other than the Geographic." And when they informed Jane of the reduction in her grant request, he continued, they should also stress their expectation that "the reduction [should not] detract from the field research. If curtailment is necessary, adjustments should come from the funds allocated for salary and expenses for herself and her husband."

Jane was unable to conceal her disappointment when she learned about the reduction. Particularly upsetting was the message that she and Hugo were again expected to forgo their own salaries. She wrote to Carmichael on March 9, expressing both gratitude at the "very welcome news" of the grant and dismay at its diminishment, since "the Gombe Research (and you will recall that this will not be the first year I have had no salary) has cost Hugo and myself considerable financial hardships through loss of time on other work." She was certain to be "intimately involved with chimpanzee behaviour . . . for the rest of my life," she declared in a subsequent letter, but without a salary, she and Hugo "cannot devote more than a certain proportion of our time to Gombe research without sliding into bankruptcy."

It was uncharacteristic of Jane to worry about money so publicly or to give the appearance of being imperfectly grateful. Clearly she and Hugo were weathering a stormy financial stretch just then. But in spite of her anxieties about the withdrawal of support from a once generous and benevolent regime, and in spite of her gloomy worries about "sliding into bankruptcy," she would soon, in fact, be able to imagine sunnier conditions ahead. For one thing, there was the David Hamburg connection.

Dr. David A. Hamburg, slight and sharp-featured, with a pointed chin, a high forehead, and a soothingly rational demeanor, was a research psychiatrist who, because of a long-standing interest in the biology and psychology of human stress, had become curious about human evolution. What were the ancestral precursors, he wondered, to contemporary experiences of stress and anxiety, which often seemed so dysfunctional? When he was invited to spend a year at the brand-new Center for Advanced Study in the Behavioral Sciences at Stanford University in the mid-1950s, the young psychiatrist listed human evolution as one of his interests. On his first or second day at the center, as he recalls, "a little man" knocked on his office door and introduced himself, saying, "I see you're interested in human evolution. That's my field. I'd love to talk to you."

It was Sherwood Washburn, the physical anthropologist, who was then teaching at the University of Chicago. Washburn had recently returned from studying baboons in Africa with his graduate student Irven DeVore, and soon the three of them were running a seminar on biology and behavior.

After that year at the Center for Advanced Study, Hamburg took a position with the National Institutes of Health, where, inspired by Washburn's thinking, he continued to entertain the idea of studying primates. Of all the nonhuman primates, chimps were the most obvious candidates to model human behavior and physiology, he thought, since chimps are genetically closest to humans. Both Washburn and DeVore had told him they believed no one would ever study wild chimpanzees. Too dangerous. But Hamburg thought he could create a seminatural laboratory for chimp studies, something that would avoid the jail-like setting of most animal laboratories, have lots of space, and be sufficiently appropriate in other ways for scientists to expect the chimps within to behave normally. The problem was that no one knew what behaving normally meant for chimpanzees.

Then one day in 1960 a colleague introduced Hamburg to Louis Leakey, who talked about Jane Goodall. As Hamburg recalls, "He said she was intelligent, courageous—and inexperienced. That was what he wanted: someone with a fresh eye, no biases, no preconceptions." Louis talked about the dangers and difficulties of habituation, how terribly hard it was to get the powerful apes to accept a human observer. In fact, Louis continued (happily proceeding into dramatic embellishment), his young researcher had developed the ability to sit perfectly still for long periods of time when she was around the chimps, and she had taught herself to take notes almost motionlessly, using a handwriting so tiny—almost microscopic—that at the end of the day all her notes would still fit into the palm of her hand.

Hamburg was fascinated. He wrote to Jane, and they began corresponding. At the same time, Stanford University's Department of Psychiatry lured him out to California with a job offer, which he took mainly because the university agreed to set aside twenty-seven acres of land for that semi-natural chimpanzee laboratory he dreamed of. Once he was back in California, Hamburg got in touch with his friend Sherwood Washburn, who was by then teaching at the University of California at Berkeley. They decided to organize a conference at Stanford's Center for Advanced Study, to take place over nine months in 1962 and 1963, and they invited a cluster of people who, although they came from very different disciplines—biology, anthropology, psychology—would focus on primate field studies. Jane was invited to join this Primate Project, as noted, but she had made the previous commitment to be at Gombe. She contributed a paper instead.

Hamburg finally met Jane in person at Burg Wartenstein during the conference on "Primate Social Behavior" in September 1965. Hugo was there as well, and Jane's talk was accompanied by a showing of one of Hugo's chimp films. As Hamburg recalls, "We were just totally—even the experienced primatologists, which I wasn't—blown away by the film. Not least by the number of similarities [the chimps showed] to humans in posture, gesture, vocalizations." And upon hearing Jane speak, Hamburg became more than ever convinced that her work was "enormously significant" and that "clearly this was a person gifted not only at observing but at explaining." Jane, he saw, was not merely a "dedicated field worker, which she was, or animal lover, which she was—but also a highly intelligent, highly articulate, thoughtful, curious person." And he had the insight that "she could be a terrific teacher."

Dr. David A. Hamburg was soon transformed into David, then Dave, and Jane began regularly inviting him to visit Gombe. He regularly turned her down. He had two young children. He was busy building up the new psychiatry department at Stanford. He was "not a field person in any way." But finally, during the summer of 1968, he went. Jane told him during the middle of his visit that she believed she would finally "wind up at Gombe," as he was later to recall the words, and that when she did visit Gombe, she always hated to leave. But there were so many problems and obstacles: the shortage of money, the increasingly tenuous nature of the National Geographic's support, the fact that Hugo needed to work elsewhere.

Near the end of his stay, David brought up the subject once again. "Would you like to stay if you could?"

She certainly would.

He said, "There's a chance, at least a chance, that I could help you with it." He might be able to help get funding, and he could begin sending out colleagues. Possibly postdoctoral students. Maybe graduate students.

Over the ensuing months they actively corresponded, enlivened by the "wonderful enthusiasm" that they shared about making Gombe into a long-term field station with Jane in residence—and also affiliating Gombe with the seminatural laboratory Hamburg intended to create at Stanford. "It was a very attractive vision," he recalls, "a fantasy."

In mid-May 1970, Hamburg chaired a UNESCO-sponsored meeting in Paris on the subject of human aggression, and Jane flew out to give a paper. They must have discussed their important plans for a new regime based on the affiliation of Gombe and Stanford. Hugo, writing to Jane from the Serengeti on May 18, the day she left for Paris, wondered about "what news Dave Hamburg will have on the affiliation plans?" But the news must have been still indefinite; Hugo, writing to Jane in England more than a month later, commented about their plans for Gombe in the following manner: "Danger—if Geographic pulls out, the whole thing collapses."

Yet even if David Hamburg failed ultimately to establish alternative support for Gombe, there was still the book, the popular chimpanzee book, *In the Shadow of Man*, which might earn some substantial money, if Jane could ever find time to write it.

Jane and Grub had gone to England in late April, perhaps partly to give her time to work on the book, but also for Grub's benefit. Having spent so much of his life among adults in exotic places, he was still shy around children his own age in more normal circumstances. A couple of months in nursery school at Bournemouth might help. It might also be good, Jane and Hugo thought, for Grub to learn about life in England. He knew how to imitate the sounds of a chimp, a hyena, and a lion, but he still did not fully appreciate that cows went moo and ducks quack. Perhaps he should learn a few other English things as well, such as that there was no need to hit the garden bushes in Bournemouth with a stick to scare away snakes. Also, of course, it was important for him to get to know his extended family in England better.

The sad news in England was that Louis Leakey was ill. He had experienced a mild heart attack on January 31 at Olduvai but, ignoring the nausea and chest pains, continued on his usual frantic schedule and flew to London on February 5. Upon landing, he decided that he was about to collapse and called for an ambulance, which whisked him to the flat in Earl's Court. Vanne called a doctor, who instantly sent him to the Princess Beatrice Hospital, where he had a second and far more serious attack. He remained on the critical list for a week and finally was discharged with the prescription of avoiding all "agitation, anxiety, and anger." When Jane arrived in late April, the great man was still unwell and no doubt feeling agitated, anxious, and angry over the restrictions on his activities as he lay in bed at the London flat.

Jane was not feeling well either. Perhaps it was a continuation of the mystery ailment she had experienced in February, flu or malaria or something else, only now, in addition, some tiny creatures were crawling around under her skin. In June she submitted to specialists at the Tropical Diseases Hospital in London, who instructed her to take, as she phrased it, the "kill or cure" treatment for pernicious parasites. Meanwhile Grub had come down with whooping cough, and Danny was unwell, perhaps with a gallstone. It was not an easy time, and the long separation from Hugo left Jane, as she confessed in an affectionate and emotional letter to him on June 6, feeling "so desperate & depressed sometimes."

The parasites, or possibly the cure for them, made her feel "GHASTLY," she wrote to him a week later, and then, just as she was hoping "to get a good bash at my poor chimp book," the galley proofs of the index for *Innocent Killers* arrived in the mail, requiring immediate attention. The galley proofs combined with her illness were "all most frightfully frustrating for my book," she wrote on June 20.

But then, remarkably, she found that she was able to "think well" while lying in bed. In fact she was bursting with ideas and words, and so she was able to produce the first two chapters in two days. She began "rushing through, just assembling material in its correct chapter," putting together a quick if rough draft, intending to "cut, add, rearrange as necessary" at the end and hoping "to get one chapter per two days into more or less its final form. Several are in that stage already. I have just finished Chapter 10, but that is not as good as it sounds — in my outline that was Chapter 8. So I have at least six, and possibly there will be another 8 to go. I do not think the book will be too long, though, as the extra chapters are not very long. It makes the facts clearer to divide them up a bit. And I now have a complete clear week ahead, so, with luck, I can rush it through to the end before I go to London."

Jane had always thought of Figan as especially intelligent; he was also patently ambitious, eager to make his way into the higher ranks of male society. Figan had developed an impressive charging display, and he possessed, she thought, a characteristic "audacity." Eleven years old when Mike deposed Goliath in 1964, Figan was obviously "fascinated by the imaginative strategy of the new alpha." Mike had intimidated everyone by incorporating those empty kerosene tins into his charging display, and interestingly enough, none of the other adults seemed curious about how he did it. Young Figan was the single individual who peered

*behind the wizard's curtain, the one member of his community who appeared cu-
rious about Mike's magic. Young Figan was twice observed experimenting with
rolling the kerosene tins himself, though only when he was discreetly out of sight
of all the big males.*

*Figan was future alpha-male material. His only obvious weakness was what
Jane considered a "very highly strung nature." He was sensitive. During times
of raging social excitement, for example, he would occasionally rush off in a
panic, screaming, clutching his scrotum, running to nearby chimps for a reassuring hug.*

*Even for someone with intelligence and real ambition, like Figan, getting to
the top is not easy. Whom you know can be as important as who you are. Affiliations are extremely important, not merely because a friend or ally might help out
in a critical moment, but also because a friend or ally will at least not side with a
rival and attack you. Lucky for Figan, then, that he had the advantage of a natural affiliation with his older brother, Faben. During the polio epidemic of 1966,
Faben had lost the use of an arm; with that limitation, the bigger and older sibling had been dominated by the smaller, younger one. At that time the two brothers spent little time in each other's company, but they still occasionally met, because both were sometimes drawn to visit their old mother, Flo.*

*Lately, though, the brothers had been spending more time together, and in
July 1970 their natural affiliation proved significant in a major fight with Evered.
While the two young upstarts, Figan and Evered, had begun quietly failing to
recognize the leadership of Mike that year, they had also started testing and
challenging each other. Who could intimidate whom? The rivalry remained generally hypothetical and inconclusive until a day in July when Figan, traveling
with Faben, happened to meet up with Evered high in the top of a tree. Other
members of Figan's family — Flint and Flo — were there as well.*

*The brothers cornered Evered, and with Flint barking and swinging around
the lower branches and ancient Flo calling out in her hoarse old voice on the
ground, Figan grappled with Evered in the high branches. Finally Evered either
fell or was pushed and plummeted to the ground. With his face torn from the corner of his lip, split into a grotesque sort of artificial grimace, he fled screaming
into the forest, with Figan and Faben chasing right behind.*

*Evered's terrible injury healed quickly, but for the next several months the
presence of Figan made him act very anxious. Old Mike was still the alpha
male, and he remained in that privileged niche for about six months longer. Although neither Evered nor Figan seemed to fear or respect him now, Mike often
traveled with some of the older males — Humphrey, for example — who remained
his occasional friends or passing allies. Humphrey was particularly important in
the political dynamics of Gombe, since he was a big and aggressive bully, which*

meant that both Figan and Evered were appropriately cautious in his presence, while Humphrey remained, as he had been for years, surprisingly submissive to Mike.

Figan was still ambitious, but he could not always count on the support of Faben. Indeed, Faben sometimes spent friendly time in the company of Humphrey. Meanwhile, Evered, over the next few months, began to regain his self-confidence around Figan. And what would happen if or when Humphrey sensed Mike's growing weakness and became tired of the current regime?

Who, in short, was going to organize and win the next coup d'état?

Jane and Grub flew to Nairobi at the start of July 1970 and were soon back in the Serengeti with Hugo, living in tents next to George Dove's Ndutu Lodge. Harold Bauer and Geza Teleki were also at Ndutu then, intending to meet with Jane before heading on to Gombe.

Loretta (Lori) Baldwin, also on her way to Gombe, showed up at the Serengeti camp next, and since she had picked up some of the same parasites that Jane had recently been treated for, she stayed for a couple of weeks while recovering. Geza and Harold went off by plane on July 22, but Nick Owens from Cambridge had by then arrived, ready to study the play behavior of baboons at Gombe, along with his friend Stephen Rowlands, who was going to spend three months with the Gombe birds. Jerry Rilling also arrived around this time, on holiday from his job as camp administrator, and Anne Pusey from Oxford and Dr. Helmut Albrecht, the senior scientist from Amsterdam University, were expected soon. "Half of Gombe always seems to be with us!" Jane commented in a letter home.

Still, by July 25 she was able to report that she had gotten down to the chimp book's final two chapters. By August 9 she had four chapters to go and was distracted by "a <u>huge</u> stack of mail." And a while after that, she had reached chapter 14, "which leaves 7 to go!!" She added, "That will surprise you since it was only 13 in all when I left, wasn't it?"

In other words, the book was growing faster than Jane could write. Meanwhile, she took time off in the middle of the month for a quick trip to Gombe, where she found everything fine and everyone well—except for Gilka, whose nose had started to grow. "What I particularly wanted to talk to you about was Gilka's nose," she wrote on August 30 to Louis. Seeing the young chimp's grotesquely swollen nose had been "such a shock," and Jane thought that medical intervention was essential. It might be yaws or some other horrible tropical disease, and aside from the natural urge to ease a friend's misery, she would have to prevent whatever the chimp might conceivably have from spreading.

While Gilka's nose was a new source of worry and distraction, though, Jane finally finished a fair draft of the chimp book and posted it to Billy Collins in London. She received a message on September 8 that Billy was pleased with the typescript, and so she and Hugo celebrated. Around the same time she was invited to become visiting associate professor in the Department of Psychiatry at Stanford University. And about a week later their first copy of *Innocent Killers* arrived in the mail, fresh off the press.

"Have you seen Innocent Killers?" Jane wrote home proudly on September 16. "Our copy has just arrived, and we think it has been produced really beautifully, and that the price, for the book, is amazingly cheap." She was still in the Serengeti with Hugo, and although she had taken a few days off to go dog-chasing with her husband, she was now "tied to my typewriter all day," with accounts, reports, various abstracts, and final editing on the chimp book. In a week she would be in England working on the promotion of *Innocent Killers*, and then it would be "off to my fate in America, which I can't tell you how much I hate the idea of. Hey ho. Anyway, such is life, and the chimp book off my mind has lifted away some clouds that have hung for 6 years, so I don't really mind much about the rest any more."

On October 16, Hugo flew out to Gombe with two veterinarians and a surgeon to look at Gilka, whose enormous nose, to everyone's relief, was diagnosed as the result of a treatable fungal infection. Then he went back to the Serengeti and started his photography work for the sequel to *Innocent Killers* (tentatively entitled *Stealthy Killers*), on big cats. Grub meanwhile settled back into nursery school in Bournemouth, while Jane boarded a plane for the United States. *Innocent Killers* was published simultaneously in England (by Collins) and in the States (by Houghton Mifflin), and so part of Jane's "fate" in America was to promote the coauthored book there. The promotion included the usual radio and print media interviews as well as network television appearances with David Frost and Dick Cavett and on the *Today* show—all of which apparently went well, except that on the first of two *Today* appearances, she failed to mention the National Geographic Society as her main sponsor. The oversight prompted Melvin Payne to telephone her after the show and give her a "mild 'scolding'" (as he described it in an internal memo at the Geographic).

Another purpose of Jane's trip to America was fundraising. The L.S.B. Leakey Foundation, which had been established in 1968 by some of Louis's wealthy friends and admirers in southern California, was helping Jane raise money for Gombe by organizing lectures in southern California and elsewhere. She also spent the first part of November in northern California, staying with the Hamburgs and giving lectures at Stanford and Berkeley—

and meeting with important grant-money people, guided now by David Hamburg. Since they were looking for money that would support the affiliation between his planned seminatural chimp laboratory in California and her research center in Africa, they were applying jointly.

Jane's American tour ended in Washington, D.C., with a presentation on Tuesday morning, November 24, for the National Geographic's Committee for Research and Exploration. David Hamburg was a guest at that meeting, and although he and Jane had not yet acquired the necessary funding for their big plan, she was still confident enough to describe it to Leonard Carmichael in a letter written a few days later. "I think the affiliation of the Gombe Stream Research Centre with Stanford University is a happy one," she wrote on November 30, "and I look forward to the results of this association. I do feel it a great honour to have been awarded a position on the Stanford faculty. I think too that the new outdoor chimpanzee facility at Stanford will become very meaningful as our research progresses, particularly for those students working on such subjects as reproduction."

So the grand new regime, the affiliation with Stanford and a stable financial future for the Gombe Stream Research Centre, seemed a good probability by then. A serious concern about Gombe's political future did not begin to emerge until the van Lawicks were back in East Africa at the end of December, whereupon John Owen, the director of National Parks, summoned them to his office at the Serengeti Research Institute (SRI) to inform them that some people had been "upset" by *Innocent Killers*.

Ever since Gombe's official transformation in 1968 into a national park that happened to support an ongoing chimpanzee research project, Jane and Hugo's continuing presence there had relied on the joint pleasures of National Parks and the SRI, so Owen's opinion was important. At the same time, though, National Parks and the SRI were both undergoing their own regime changes, as government officials sought to improve the representation of Tanzanians within what had recently been colonial institutions. The SRI during the 1960s and early 1970s had its own tennis court and gliding club—but no Tanzanian scientists. The first scientific director of the institute, Hugh Lamprey, would be replaced in 1972 by a Tanzanian, Tumaina Mcharo, and by late 1970 John Owen was also on the way out. He still retained the old imposing presence, however, and now, when Jane and Hugo asked him to explain why some people were upset by *Innocent Killers*, he said that he really did not know. He leafed through the book and then commented vaguely about a reference to Hans Kruuk as a "young Dutch scientist"—a small clue that their popularized wildlife studies in the Serengeti might be regarded by some—Kruuk, for example—as poaching on the scientific studies. In a letter home, Jane summarized her thinking: "Of course, it boils down to straightforward jealousy—and we had expected Hans to get upset. Because his book isn't published yet." In any case, Owen agreed that the right thing would be to arrange a future meeting where everyone would "try and sort it all out."

With that problem postponed, they rushed down to Gombe, arriving by New Year's Eve and settling in for a three-week stay. Jane wrote home immediately: "Gombe has NEVER, NEVER been better. I am really so excited about it. Albrecht is superb, Geza is subdued, Harold a bit of a problem, but a solvable one. Anne is fitting in excellently & wants to stay 2 years & do analysis, Wrangham is super, Mitzi getting on very well, generally working on analysis. Everyone adores Helmut (Albrecht). SO—isn't that nice." There was even a little happy gossip to relate: "You'll be amused to know, Ma, Geza & Lori are having a passionate affair!"

Jane summarized some of the chimp news and gossip a week later, in a January 7, 1971, letter to Joanne Hess at the Geographic. Flo was "fine" and Goliath "very old." Fifi was still "her old self." Flint had become "a terror." Gilka's nose was "not yet subsiding though she is taking her medicine daily." And the old regime, with Mike as alpha, shakily held: "Mike still boss (but worried again by Figan)."

Mike's regime ended later that month, on a day that began with the alpha male peacefully feeding on bananas in the provisioning area. The morning's peace was broken when Humphrey, backed by his temporary ally Faben, rushed up a slope into the feeding area and began brutally pounding on Mike, who scrambled up a tree. The previously submissive Humphrey dragged the older male out of the tree and down to the ground, where he struck and stomped on him, with Faben joining in. But now the big attacker seemed "almost shocked," as Jane later wrote, by his own heated audacity, and he and Faben vanished into the forest, while poor old Mike remained on the ground, "utterly shattered" and "giving soft calls of fear and distress."

That was the end of a six-year reign, and Mike's status dropped immediately. He went from being the highest-ranking male to one of the lowest, to the point that even some of the adolescents felt bold enough to confront him. Mike was now so lacking in confidence that he only rarely tried to defend himself.

So Humphrey became alpha male. But even though his victory was swift and sure, it was "hardly glorious." Mike, after all, was older and weaker and about twenty pounds lighter than Humphrey, and the new leader's quick ascent to the top had involved "no grim determination to succeed" and "no hard-won series of battles against a powerful adversary." In spite of his formidable size, strength, and temper, Humphrey "never became a truly impressive alpha." Instead he re-

mained a "blustering bully, lacking the drive, intelligence and courage that had been so impressive in both Mike and his predecessor Goliath."

Humphrey also lacked the social skills and political sophistication of those predecessors. He had no really close friends to count on, only the occasional alliance with Faben. In fact, Humphrey was probably able to achieve alpha-male status among the Kasekela chimps only because the larger community was just then starting to divide, with some members now preferring to spend time in the southern part of their range, leaving Humphrey, in the northern part, able to avoid the more troublesome and ambitious members of the male hierarchy. Particularly troublesome were Hugh and Charlie, two full-grown males, probably brothers, who traveled together and maintained a close, mutually supportive relationship. But it was Humphrey's inability to form long-term, reliable affiliations with other powerful chimps that ultimately doomed his regime to a relatively short (eighteen months) and tumultuous duration.

Figan proved to be the biggest problem. Even though Figan maintained an outward show of deference, Humphrey acted as if he understood very well where the real threat to his power lay, and in Figan's presence he would frequently emphasize his own vigor and strength through "bristling and magnificent" displays. On his own, Figan, in spite of his cunning and clear ambition, might never have been able to challenge Humphrey — but eventually Faben experienced a change of heart and cast his lot with his brother, so in future months Figan and Faben began to form their own tight and effective affiliation.

By the start of 1971, David Hamburg was working on an additional affiliation, for both Stanford and Gombe, with the University of Dar es Salaam. He went to Gombe in late January, and then he and Jane traveled to Dar es Salaam to meet with the person who would soon become their friend and important ally in that capital city, Abdul S. Msangi. "I liked him and respected him from the start," David has recalled of Msangi, who was professor of zoology and dean of faculties at Dar es Salaam University. Jane and David gave lectures at Dar es Salaam, and Gombe was officially opened to Tanzanian students.

The harmony in Dar es Salaam became more important as the dissonance with John Owen and others at the Serengeti Research Institute increased that spring. Owen gave up his position as parks director to a Tanzanian, Solomon ole Saibull, but for another year he remained unofficially in the background, and he was still powerful enough to join with others in what Jane characterized evocatively in a March 4 letter home as "the battle." As she mentioned then, Owen appeared to be "trying to push me out of Gombe, etc.," with the "etc." possibly referring to a parallel effort to push Hugo out of the Serengeti. "It's just so idiotic and horrible," Jane wrote to Joan Travis of the Leakey Foundation in California a couple of weeks later, "—and I hate being accused of all the things that I have been accused of (such as stealing scientific information, [intellectual] poaching, deliberate deception) and not be able to do a thing about it because they refuse to put anything on paper, and just say things vaguely." In any case, the whole experience enabled the van Lawicks to find out "who your friends are"—and they were not, unfortunately, among the administratively powerful at the SRI. It would be "thanks to David Hamburg . . . [that] the Gombe problems will sort themselves out," Jane continued in the same letter—although, as for Hugo's projected sequel to *Innocent Killers,* "we'll just have to manage without Hugo doing lions, leopards, and cheetahs!"

David's final plans for the seminatural chimpanzee laboratory in California—officially called the Stanford Outdoor Primate Facility—described a six-acre, circular enclosure divided (like a sliced pie) into four separate pens of one and a half acres each, with a main observation and shelter building in the center. That building would be a moderately elevated tower, so that observers standing on top could see into every part of the four pens, and it would include, down below, a feeding area, an area to trap and isolate individual chimps for various purposes, toilet and washing facilities for people, and so on. It was important that the place also provide, in the slightly mechanical language of the original grant proposal, "conditions under which chimpanzees are likely to function effectively and display the full range of their behavioral repertoire." Based on an understanding of the wild chimpanzees at Gombe, such conditions would include a chance to climb (a few artificial trees), an opportunity for visual isolation and shade (artificial bushes), access to nest-building materials, a variety of foods and feeding locations, and other forms of variety and enrichment (chimp movies, perhaps, projected onto the sides of the central building).

Of course the big enclosure would be expensive. Just to get the physical plant up and running—with roads, fences, buildings, water, electricity, and so on—would cost an estimated $162,000. But finally David found an organization that seemed willing to fund that plan and to underwrite Jane's own dream at Gombe. The Grant Foundation, established during the Depression by the five-and-dime-store magnate William T. Grant, liked to support interdisciplinary studies of child development; David argued that understanding chimp development was one important way to gain insights into the development of human children.

The van Lawicks visited Jane's family in England in April and Hugo's family in Holland in May, and in the last week of May, Jane made a quick trip back to the States, meeting with some of her National Geographic supporters in Washington to talk about a future television film and also, on May 25, to present to the Committee for Research and Exploration her 1971 grant request, this time for only $15,832. It was unanimously approved.

At the end of the month Jane learned that the Grant Foundation had agreed to fund much of the budget at Gombe for the next year, with possible extensions after that, and that the foundation's president, Douglas Bond, was making plans to visit Gombe to see for himself what was going on. On the first of June, from Hugo's family home in Holland, Jane wrote a letter to Bond, welcoming his visit and clarifying her own plans. She intended to be "based permanently at Gombe" and to make twice-yearly forays to Stanford University, in spring and fall, with her fall sojourn lasting around two months, during which time she would teach and contribute to the chimpanzee research at the Stanford Outdoor Primate Facility (which she preferred to think of as "Gombe West"). She concluded with an inspired and enthusiastic image: "Sometimes I have the feeling that The Grant Foundation is like some kind angel that has swooped down out of the sky and scooped Gombe out of the financial mire!"

The good news continued. Jane learned that *Ladies' Home Journal* had paid $5,000 for rights to publish an excerpt from *In the Shadow of Man* sometime that fall. She was informed that she would soon be honored with the Stott Science Award from Cambridge University. David called her in Holland on June 5 to confirm that the Grant Foundation had officially agreed to fund the Stanford Outdoor Primate Facility and to confirm her salaried position as a Stanford professor. And, as she had recently heard from Gombe, Fifi had had a baby.

The van Lawicks were back at Gombe by July 12, whereupon Jane reported to the family in England that "Fifi's baby is quite fantastic—about twice as big as he should be for his age—& he is called Freud! I suddenly thought he had to be!" Madam Bee had also given birth. Bee Hinde was the baby's name, honoring Jane's Cambridge mentor. Winkle was about to produce a baby, to be named Wilkie. And Passion was expecting one soon as well, an infant who, following the alliterative tradition, was going to be Professor Hamburg (then shortened to Prof).

The human version of Professor Hamburg was already at Gombe by July 19, although he was suffering from swollen ankles and badly infected tsetse fly bites. That month marked Jane's eleventh year since first arriving at the shores of Gombe, and on July 22 they all celebrated. Other than Jane, only two people present in the summer of 1971 had been there in the summer of 1960—Dominic and Rashidi—and Jane made a short speech in Swahili and gave them each a small present. Then, as everyone sat drinking coffee after dinner, she reminisced about the early days and all the changes and developments. She spoke of David Hamburg's new role and the importance of "the super student group of today," while David followed with his own "super string of remarks about the significance of the work, its evolution, its future." Later in the evening, Hugo gave some brief comments about the early days. Finally they all drank a toast to Vanne, followed by a special toast in honor of "two of the most wonderful old ladies we have ever heard of—Danny & Flo!"

"The only things wrong," Jane confided to her readers in Bournemouth, "were 1) Helmut who sat gazing at Mitzi in strong silence as he does every evening & never, _ever_ says a word and 2) Hugo who is always in a bad mood on our anniversaries here!"

But Jane was still worried about being "kicked out of Gombe" as a result of shifting regimes in the Tanzanian government and National Parks, and so she and David were only too happy to reinforce their new connection with the University of Dar es Salaam. At the request of Professor Msangi, they both traveled to Dar in the first week of August to give a chimpanzee talk. It was a "triumphant" moment, as Jane recalled in an August 7 letter to the family. Msangi had advertised it "superbly," and when they arrived at the auditorium he gave a "_superb_" introduction. So many people showed up that they had to move into a bigger auditorium, where Jane spoke to perhaps five or six hundred altogether, without a microphone. David, who sat at the rear, said afterward that he could hear every word. Msangi was "glowing," and said "how delighted he was that students from Dar were about to take part in this historic & exciting research!" Even more importantly, perhaps, Msangi then reminded Jane that he was eager to start on the Swahili translation of _In the Shadow of Man._

Shadow was released on both sides of the Atlantic at around the same time. In London, the _Sunday Times_ began a four-week serialized abridgement of the book on September 5. As Vanne reported, "The Shadow of Man has created a stupendous sensation in the Sunday Times. My dearest little love— what a triumph. It isn't any good trying to tell you how proud I am of your success and of the qualities in you that have made it all possible—they've all been bruited all over this world by far more eloquent pens than mine."

By the third week of September, Jane was back in England and publicizing the British edition. She flew to New York on September 23 for a _Today_ show appearance on the next day, which began the publicity for the American edition, and then continued on to California and her life as a professor and lecturer in the human biology program at Stanford. She wrote home on September 28, "Sorry not to have written before, but heavens—have I been busy!" At least she had her own office and telephone and typewriter, as well as secretarial help, which was "super. Today, for example, I got 70 envelopes all typed out for me!!"

There was a quick trip to the Frankfurt Book Fair in Germany and then to London in mid-October. By the start of November, Jane had returned to the States for a solid week of book promotion in New York with, as she wrote home, "a morning of autographing in 3 of the major 5th Avenue bookstores—including one that is supposed to be best in the States. A really fabulous place, Scribner's. Books displayed rather as though in an old fashioned oak library! Very elegant & charming sales people. . . . Anyway, the book seems to be doing well—&, though the TV people here are rather nasty & impersonal compared to most of the British ones, I think it all went fairly well." That was a modest understatement. The book was a galloping success, with major reviews, much serious attention, and terrific sales.

Of course, *In the Shadow of Man* was Jane's second book about her life and the Gombe chimpanzees written for a popular audience, since the National Geographic Society had compelled her to write *My Friends the Wild Chimpanzees* first, in 1967. But the Geographic production had turned out to be something of a magazine-book hybrid, and its tabloid morphology, wide and tall and thin, suggested and even defined a wide and tall but thin reading experience. *My Friends the Wild Chimpanzees* was marketed directly to society members, never sold in bookstores, and so in that sense too *In the Shadow of Man* was really Jane's first significant popular book about her work with the Gombe chimps.

She had for a long time thought of *Shadow* as her "real book," as we have seen. And now, in this book, her personality and her distinctive writing style seemed fully liberated. *In the Shadow of Man* was first of all an adventure story, a modestly told tale of courage and determination. For many readers, the most exciting thing about Jane's story was that she was a woman who had shown herself braver than most men. Smarter too, since she had the intellectual vigor to defy common sense and received wisdom, in the process placing herself at the heart of the new science of primate-watching. So *Shadow* was in part an iconic representation of female courage and, from there, of feminine and feminist achievement. But it was also a compelling piece of popularized science. Jane's earlier accomplishments—living with wild animals, getting to know them individually, discovering the meat-eating and the tool-using—had by then achieved general currency. In this book, those events were the mere beginnings of a story that drew readers deeply into an emotional, social, and political universe inhabited not by humans but by their siblings once removed. *In the Shadow of Man* presented, in short, the tale of Jane van Lawick-Goodall's astonishing discovery of intelligent life beyond our own.

Shadow was soon ascending the bestseller lists in both England and the States. By mid-December 1971 its increasingly celebrated author had met privately with the Queen Mother, after which the van Lawicks flew to Amsterdam, where they showed Hugo's wild dog film to the Dutch queen and prince. *In the Shadow of Man* was soon being translated into foreign-language editions, ultimately forty-seven in all; and the American version, at least, has remained continuously in print since it first appeared. The book significantly contributed to Jane's popular reputation as a scientist. It might also have made a significant contribution to her bank account (beginning with Houghton Mifflin's advance of $100,000), except that she assigned the bulk of its earnings to an irrevocable trust, with Grub as the sole beneficiary.

Jane, Hugo, and Grub were back at Gombe by the last day of the year, and as she had come to expect by then, everything there was "fine," with only a few problems between a couple of the researchers.

David Hamburg had gone to Gombe as well, and as usual his presence was "very soothing for everyone," according to a January 3, 1972, letter Jane wrote while flying with him from Kigoma to Seronera, on the way to "fateful meetings" at the offices of the Serengeti Research Institute. Someone in the Tanzanian vice president's office was refusing to sign immigration clearances for foreign researchers, and as Jane soon discovered, all the foreign researchers at SRI had the same problem the Gombe people were having. It was a "stormy meeting," she told her family in a January 10 letter, with some of the foreign SRI researchers being "tactless and hopeless with the people who matter."

Jane described the meeting in more detail in a January 13 letter to Robert Hinde, declaring that she and David "kept out of everything, and just sat in a corner listening." In the process, they "learned a great deal" and also "had several excellent sessions with key people." Finally they were invited on to Dar es Salaam, where they had "even better sessions." David "got on wonderfully" with President Nyerere's new science adviser, Professor Wasawo, and their old friend and ally at the University of Dar es Salaam, Abdul Msangi, organized a grand luncheon at one of Dar's big hotels on the beach, having invited several department heads from the university. Then David "gave a really brilliant lecture—which was full—I mean the auditorium was full."

And so, assisted by David Hamburg's negotiating and affiliating skills, a new regime at Gombe was at last, by the start of 1972, established, supported, and stabilized. It may have been with some feelings of personal triumph, combined with gratitude and relief, that Jane wrote on January 22 to

Leonard Carmichael, filling him in on the latest research and chimpanzee gossip and announcing the Gombe Stream Research Centre's final independence from the National Geographic Society: "May I . . . take this opportunity of letting you know that, for the present year, we have managed to raise sufficient funds to keep the Gombe research running and shall not have to burden the Society for an immediate request for financial support."

33

Abundance, Estrangement, and Death

1972

STARTING IN 1972, the Gombe Stream Research Centre was expanded and enlivened by the arrival of undergraduates from Stanford. First came a couple of students sent out by biology professor Paul Ehrlich to study butterflies. "Paul Ehrlich's crew are madly collecting butterflies and caterpillars," Jane wrote home from Gombe on January 3, while "Grub is very busy helping to get and raise caterpillars!"

Following the Ehrlich lepidopterists came two human biology undergraduates, Catherine (Cay) Craig and Donna (Dede) Robbins, committed to a six-month stay and allowed into the country officially as visitors. By January 13, as Jane remarked in a letter to Robert Hinde, the pair had "settled in very well indeed," and, she added, "they are two really super girls, and will make a big difference in this time of shortage"—referring to the temporary shortage of personnel as a result of continuing difficulties in acquiring immigration clearances for long-term researchers. Cay and Dede would contribute to the maintenance of general records at Gombe and participate, when the opportunity arose, in more specialized studies. They would be replaced by five additional human bio students that summer. Three more would arrive in December 1972 and early January 1973, followed by a half-dozen more later in the year . . . and so on.

The human biology major at Stanford was another development inspired largely by David Hamburg, who, along with several colleagues, had persuaded the Ford Foundation to underwrite a new undergraduate concentration that was supposed to bridge the chasm between biological and cultural studies. Human biology would focus on "the kind of biology uniquely related to what it means to be human"—which meant that in addition to the more obvious mixture of biological and social science offerings, the human bio major might offer courses in primatology and primate evolution. The

Stanford Outdoor Primate Facility, or Gombe West, the place to observe captive chimpanzees living inside a six-acre pie-shaped pen located in the grassy hills behind Stanford's linear accelerator, was thus an important feature of the human bio major (although the chimps would not be there until the spring of 1974). Meanwhile, a number of human bio students were being given the spectacular opportunity to go to Gombe East, to design their own research projects, and to observe wild chimpanzees or baboons under the direction of one of the world's great pioneering primatologists.

They studied Swahili for a year. Got their passports and visas in order. Submitted to multiple inoculations. Located the smallest possible Philips portable tape recorder, plus spare batteries and microphones. Packed their jeans and other utilitarian summer clothes (and, for the women, modest one-piece bathing suits), cameras and binoculars (and extra silica gel to protect the delicate instruments from fog and fungi), wristwatches (reliable and moisture-proof), typewriters (if possible), extra carbon paper (since all reports were done in quintuplicate and the Chinese carbon paper available in Tanzania was inked on both sides), multiple pens, underwear, socks. And then, powered by Ford Foundation money, they were magically catapulted to the other side of the world, arriving finally in an astonishing and mysterious new place of intense light and heat and color.

Gombe's connection with Stanford was paralleled by its connection with the University of Dar es Salaam. Jane began periodically crossing to the other side of Tanzania to give lectures there, while a small number of undergraduates from Dar crossed in the opposite direction to participate, alongside the Stanford undergraduates, in the chimp and baboon research.

"My students are just great," Jane wrote home to the family on May 22, 1972, referring to the Stanford and Dar undergraduates as well as the graduate researchers Anne Pusey, Mitzi Hankey, and Richard Wrangham. "The Stanford & the Dar—Anne, Mitzi—full of enthusiasm, being so nice, helping in the kitchen again. Super. Richard has done a really splendid paper on the banana feeding system & how it affected group size, etc. I feel really proud of him. It is so exciting to have this group—they are going to make a fantastic contribution in the long run. The baboon study (I have become their 'teacher' already) is going very well. Both Stanford boys want to stay a year to do PhD degrees! The two from Dar want to return next summer. Isn't it super!"

That invigorating infusion from afar was supplemented by an exciting local expansion, as several of the African staff became important members of the research team. As noted, the African staff at Gombe had begun to accompany researchers as a safety measure, a policy begun in the summer of 1969 after Ruth Davis fell to her death while following chimps alone. These were men from nearby villages who showed up looking for work. Some had a few years of formal education. Few spoke English, and none wrote English. None could claim to have the slightest scientific education. But after years of supporting the researchers, the African workers had come to recognize the individual chimps and baboons and to understand the fundamental logic of their behavior as well as anyone, and by the start of 1972 the best of them were enlisted in the research and given higher salaries and new titles. They became field assistants, and five of them (Hilali Matama, Eslom Mpongo, Sadiki Rukamata, Kassin Selemani, and Yasini Selemani) served as chimp specialists, while a sixth (Apollinaire Sindimwo) was the resident baboon expert. "Our Tanzanian staff is really becoming an exciting project," Jane wrote home that January. "We have 5 followers—field assistants now—who have got higher salaries, and go out following chimps . . . often all day. They are super at following. They also take accurate records—check sheets on very simple things, and written notes on fights and anything special. We are learning a lot in this way, and they are so proud."

During the next several months, the number of field assistants doubled and eventually nearly tripled, while the supporting staff (building construction and maintenance, cooking, domestic work, nighttime security) expanded comparably. And as the African staff grew, so did the number of specialized researchers. Jane continued her own long-term work on the social relationships of the adult males and mother-infant relations, and a postdoctoral researcher named Bill McGrew arrived in November 1972 to begin studying the behavioral development of young chimpanzees. Between January 1972 and May 1975, a second postdoctoral researcher, Larry Goldman, came to look at chimpanzee play behavior, while sixteen British and North American graduate students started or finished or otherwise carried on with their own in-depth studies of some sixteen different aspects of chimpanzee and baboon life.

The researchers and undergraduates and field staff adhered to what Jane called "the spirit of Gombe," which was the spirit of scientific collaboration. Information about what was going on among the chimps and baboons was a resource to be shared rather than hoarded. If one person saw something (a fight, a hunt, mating, a friendly gesture, or some other event) or someone (a particular chimp or baboon) important to another person's research project, the information was passed on freely. To be sure, much of the data sharing was done automatically, since the data collection system was producing its own official record, an epic code-poem on the lives of Gombe's wild denizens. But much of the data sharing happened informally, since the researchers and students often compared notes during the day. Also, each evening, after a long day traipsing through thorns and thickets, they assembled around the great dinner table (place mats and napkins rolled

inside napkin rings, Jane seated at the head) to eat, drink, recite happy dog-
gerel on the subject of promiscuous young females, perform short skits on
the problem of oversexed adolescent males, or simply gossip about the day's
primate adventures.

Physically, the research center had already been expanded to accommodate
its new abundance. During the fall of 1971, Jane and Hugo's friend George
Dove had arrived with his favorite experts and workers and completely re-
built the place, transforming what had been a few scattered huts and tents
into a coherent and substantial research station.

"Upstairs," at the provisioning site, Dove left the two main camp buildings intact, with Lawick Lodge remaining as an observation building and
Pan Palace continuing as the banana storehouse and provisioning center.
But now, along a winding path up and away from the camp meadow, he
poured some circular concrete foundations and bolted several prefabricated
aluminum rondavels on top: residential huts.

"Downstairs," at the beach, was the old Marler Mansion, the three-room
beach hut that had already been turned into the Cage, baboon- and chimp-
proofed with wire mesh to make sure little Grublin did not become the object of a successful predation. South of the Cage, perhaps 150 yards along
the beach, Dove oversaw the construction of a long, low stone building divided into four small, interconnected administrative offices. Between the
stone offices and the Cage, he built the Mess: a roof on posts, four low
stone-and-concrete walls, wire mesh from the tops of the walls to the bottoms of the roof, and, embedded as a mosaic in the front doorstep, an hon-
orific portrait of David Greybeard. Finally, north of the Cage a hundred
yards, Dove began work on a beach cabin for the director and her family: a
simple stone-and-wood rectangle with a full front veranda, thatched roof,
open meshed sides, and several rooms that became fewer once Jane experimented with removing interior walls. Dove also redug and redid the latrines
and brought in generators and thus electricity, enough to run a refrigerator
and a few flickering beacons for late-night insects and typists.

He even managed to improve the mood of the baboons—or at least that
of the big old male Crease, who usually hung around, trying to steal food
and generally being a fearful pest. People at Gombe were continually trying
to chase him away, while the old baboon, flashing his nasty teeth, chased
right back. But George Dove, instead of chasing the baboon, fed him, and
now, at the start of 1972, Jane concluded that "the difference is incredible."
Old Crease had become "very benign"—although he still expected to be
fed, and so every morning she slipped him a piece of toast.

• • •

Jane now began spending eight or nine months a year in residence, as Gombe's scientific director, only flying off periodically to fulfill her responsibilities as a professor at Stanford and Dar es Salaam. The beach cabin was behind schedule, unfortunately, and with Hugo temporarily away, Jane and Grub finally moved in around the end of March, when the place was still, as she wrote home on March 30, "nowhere near ready."

Their first night in the cabin, she came back from dinner in the Mess and found young Grub "wide awake." She worked for thirty minutes while he lay open-eyed and quiet but still completely awake. "So we put on his slippers & sweater & he came & sat on the beach while I had a moonlight swim, & then we drank Milo, & finally went to bed about 11.45!! But next morning up as usual and going strong at 7.00 pm! He has amazing vitality."

Vitality was an important thing to have at Gombe, since the hothouse environment inevitably took its toll. In Jane's case, rampant pathogens sometimes combined with physical exhaustion to produce shingles or bad fevers, the latter sometimes symptomatic of (as she wrote home on May 25) "malaria or flue or something evil." Or (on August 14), it would be a "cold, cough, sore throat—fever. I staggered out twice, thinking I was better—one morning to watch baboons, one evening to go to a meeting. The second really finished me off & I had to retire to bed, not just stay in the house. The worst was that at night as soon as I lay, the cough got worse & worse." Grub, at five and six years old, was also very vulnerable, of course, and he periodically succumbed to similar illnesses.

Grub had occasional nightmares, including one of being attacked by Crease. In reality, as Grub recently recalled, Crease was never fully mollified by those daily rations of toast. The big old baboon would sometimes come to the beach cabin and slam his whole body against the door, and on more than occasion he succeeded in breaking through the door and getting inside, where he rampaged about in search of food. Worse, once when Grub was climbing a tree, Crease appeared out of nowhere and lunged right at him. Fortunately, Hugo was nearby, and he came running, grabbed his son, and pulled him out of the tree just in time.

The baboons on the beach occasionally swam or waded or even played in the water when the weather was calm, but people could get away from them by dashing deeper into the lake. The chimps were different. Much worse. Once a chimp ran up a tree and tried to snatch Grub off his father's back. In fact, several of them were very aggressive toward him, and for some reason Flint was always trying to grab him. They were of a similar age, similar size. Among Grub's earliest memories is the time he went up to the chimps with his mother and father. Jane had brought along a bunch of toy plastic bananas, and she told Grub to hand them to Flint. Grub was reluctant, but she said (as Grub remembers), "No, no, go ahead and give them to him." He walked a few steps closer, always holding on to his mother's hand, and offered the toy bananas. Flint tottered up, took them, and walked away, but after sniffing the bananas he started coming back. Jane said, "See what he does. He wants to thank you." Grub reached forward, feeling mildly apprehensive. Flint put out his hand, and so Grub put out his hand—which the little ape suddenly grabbed and bit. After that Grub did not want to have any more to do with the chimps.

Then there were snakes. One time Grub was chasing a butterfly that vanished into a bush. He pulled open the bush and saw, emerging from within, the head and then the body of a great black snake—probably a black mamba—which now reared back, ready to strike. Grub let go of the bush, which closed on the snake, and ran backward. Another time, when he was playing in the heavy surf after a storm, the boy caught hold of something that was slippery, like a fish or an eel. But then a big wave broke and churned back into the lake, and as the foaming water drew away, the long, brown, black-banded water cobra he had just grabbed slid away in front of him.

Because of the dangers, Grub was constantly watched by a responsible adult. It was Jane during the best part of the afternoon; other times, an African babysitter or a volunteer from among the European and American residents took over. Grub developed a great fondness for one babysitter in particular, Maulidi Yango, who had originally been hired to help clear the trails. As Jane later wrote, Maulidi had "a splendid physique" and was "strong as an ox" yet also "easy-going, with a great sense of humour," and he became her son's "childhood hero" and later his good friend. Grub made friends with the African children as well, including one who soon became his best friend, Sofi, a son of the staff member Juma Mkukwe.

Grub soon identified his favorite element and lifelong passion: water and fish. From the first he enjoyed playing in the lake, and by early 1972, as Jane wrote to the family, he had learned to swim "like a little fish"—entirely underwater. Hugo had first learned to swim underwater as well, so it seemed perfectly normal, and Grub was so pleased with himself that it was hard to keep him away from the lake. Soon he had flippers and a mask. He also had his own bowl of fish, about twenty of them, swimming around inside a crystal ball of water and shells from the lake; and for his sixth birthday that March, Hugo brought him a tank complete with pump and filter, which was set up in the Mess.

On occasion Grub was allowed to stay up late for the weekly after-supper film show, which began that May after Hugo brought in a projector from Nairobi and they began renting a share of the feature films imported weekly by the single cinema in Kigoma. Someone from Gombe would take the boat into Kigoma to collect the reel on Monday, and after a Monday evening showing it would be rushed back to Kigoma by a deadline of nine o'clock Tuesday morning.

In mid-July 1972, the Monday night film show included a Walt Disney cartoon, and Grub stayed up for that. Since he was then wide-awake, he was allowed to see the feature as well: *Kidnapped*. He "really did enjoy it very much," Jane reported to the family back home, "especially the fighting and the creeping about on the highlands and hiding in the bracken and behind water falls."

One day in May, a park warden named John Savage brought over his son and a pair of rabbits for Grub to play with. The rabbits stayed and became housetrained, and soon, when Grub and Jane returned from supper at the Mess, the pair would be sitting cozily side by side in the armchair. The rabbits sometimes hunted and ate spiders, but they also liked to nibble on the rush carpets. They were chewing up "all our possessions" by July 4 and had also suddenly become "very sexy—constantly mating." Grub thought that was "great fun," and so "at all hours of the day" he would cry out, "Mummy—come quickly!" or "Jane—come—the rabbits are mating." There were soon baby rabbits in the cabin, four at first, three after the mother ate one, and Jane and Grub were able to watch them grow hair after three days and open their eyes after five.

If life was a great bubble of playful pleasures for the boy that spring and summer, it was still pricked occasionally by the small thorn of scholarly discipline. Jane had enrolled Grub in a correspondence program around the start of February, and school was not always easy. "He just sets his mind against the thing," she explained to the family on March 12, "has that silly smile, drops his pencil on the floor, does a wrong letter with a very hard pressed pencil, and an even horrider smile! Oh, what times we have. And then I really get exasperated and stalk off, and he does the thing perfectly with no trouble at all." According to a letter written later that month, Grub's academic experience had not improved: "He gets through school fast, so it only takes about an hour each day unless he is in a MOOD! Then we sit for 2 hours, him saying he won't do it, me saying Oh then we just have to stay here, what a pity. Then he does it for a few minutes just before I strangle him!"

By early June, Jane thought she could see progress. Grub was "very healthy at the moment, brown as 20 bunnies" and "quite good about school. We have done all the writing, more than all the reading . . . & at the moment we are sticking little squares of paper on a card for his hard work." And by July 28 he had made enough progress in school to earn "thousands of gold & silver stars" and a "super report. He is very excited & pleased about his progress & is, I think, looking forward to starting his new term, now that my immediate hectic-ness is over."

Jane's immediate hecticness was partly the result of finishing a chapter on chimpanzee culture for a scientific book. During the last two weeks of July she managed to produce it by running one of her typical literary marathons: two weeks at the keyboard from nine in the morning until half past midnight.

Inevitably, there were other professional obligations, such as the Adolf Meyer Memorial Lecture for the annual meeting of the American Psychiatric Association in Dallas that spring. That conference of some 3,500 psychiatrists generated (as she admitted afterward in a May 6 letter to her friends Joan and Arnold Travis) an unusual level of stage fright: "I really was *very* scared." But her reputation in the States was on the rise, and by the middle of May she had received the formal notification (printed in an old-fashioned, elaborate script and addressed to "Sir") of her election to the American Academy of Arts and Sciences as an honorary foreign member. She wrote home: "I have yet to find out exactly how significant it is, but I feel fearfully honoured!"

Jane had for years been rushing from crisis to crisis, deadline to deadline, task to task. From her earliest times at Gombe she had felt an enormous pressure to produce scientifically and communicate popularly about the chimps. In previous times the load and pace had often seemed hard to bear, but now, with the increasing size of the Gombe project and her own spreading fame, she was busier than ever. A March 23 letter to Robert Hinde, typed out near midnight in a sprint against flickering light bulbs and the generator's curfew, gives some indication of her normal raft of tasks by then:

> I have been feeling completely frantic. A paper to be finished—deadline 1st March. Still only a draft. 8 seminars to prepare for Stanford. One big lecture. Another grant application. Constantly working on bits and pieces for the Gombe West application. Student problems daily. Staff meetings. Seminars. Visitors, visitors, visitors. . . . And believe it or not, I am getting an average of 50 letters per week. And I have entered Grub for a postal primary school, and so am become a teacher also. And now, with Hugo away, there are constant interruptions—I sympathise with him now more than I did before! And I think he'll be horrified at the lack of work done by the carpenter, etc., while there has been only me supervising, because I simply can't do any more.

. . .

Yet Jane's blossoming success and fame may have rankled her equally ambitious but seemingly less successful husband. Hugo, as she candidly reported home that January, was "very depressed."

For one thing, there were the comparatively tepid reviews and modest
sales of *Innocent Killers* to brood about. It was clear by then that the book
would remain forever in the shadow of *In the Shadow of Man*. For another,
John Owen and the SRI administration had recently scuttled Hugo's plans
to study and photograph the Serengeti big cats for the sequel to *Innocent
Killers*. True, he had another good idea for the second book. During the
summer of 1970, Hugo and his assistant James Malcolm had watched an os-
tracized wild dog puppy, a runt who was pluckily trying to keep up with her
roaming family pack. As she faltered and fell back and a group of excited
hyenas closed in, Hugo and James could bear the cruel drama no longer, so
they interceded. They picked up the little pup, whom they named Solo, and
fed and nurtured her, and once she had gotten stronger they began trying to
return her to the pack. The full tale eventually became *Solo: The Story of an
African Wild Dog*, which Collins released in 1974. So the two-book deal
with Collins was eventually resolved in that way (with Jane privately writing most of the text for *Solo*), but in the meanwhile, what could Hugo do at
Gombe? He was officially the research center's administrative director, but
he was at heart a filmmaker and photographer, and to enjoy Gombe he
needed to be operating a camera.

During the previous year, he and Jane had often discussed their scheme to
edit some scientific and educational films for distribution to universities, based
on all the early chimpanzee footage he had taken at Gombe. David Hamburg
had been confident that the U.S. National Institute of Mental Health would
support such a worthy project. However, Hugo's chimpanzee films (some 30
miles' worth by then) belonged to the National Geographic and were held
in the society's vaults in Washington, and so he and Jane would have to persuade the society to cooperate. Jane had broached the idea to Melvin Payne
while she was in Washington that May, and he (after being reminded by an
associate of the economic value of that vast footage, or mileage, and that
Jane was "probably the 'hottest property' in her field") decided that the society might allow Hugo to edit and produce the series but would retain possession and marketing rights: to hold the films "exclusively under the Society's imprimatur, as a part of our 'stable' of films for educational purposes."

Hugo had also thought about making a movie on Flo's family. In late
May 1971, when Jane had communicated this idea to Payne, it seemed particularly interesting, because Flo's daughter Fifi was about to give birth to her
first baby, Freud, and Hugo might be able to produce a triple-generational
story on the chimps—provided the Geographic would release some of the

archival footage on Flo and Fifi. Payne replied that once again the Geographic would insist on remaining "a principal in the project."

Jane also passed on Hugo's request for permission to take still photographs of chimps at Gombe for personal use. Since he was no longer employed by the society, Hugo hoped they would allow him that freedom. But Payne, after consulting with his colleagues, decided otherwise. Even though Hugo was not an employee of the society or otherwise obligated to it, he could not have permission to take chimp photographs for personal use, since "we zealously guard our right of first refusal on photographs of Society-sponsored field research." (Although Hugo was independent by 1971, the society still provided Jane an annual grant for her Gombe work.)

The National Geographic Society's insistence on drawing such a tight cord around past, present, and even future photos and footage from Gombe must have been deeply frustrating for Hugo. In late February or early March 1972, however, he finally sold the wild dog film to a company known as Metromedia, for a sum Jane later described (in a note to an acquaintance) as "astronomical." Hugo was suddenly wealthy — or wealthy enough, at least, to keep on filming. Metromedia acquired in the same deal first options on his next four films, and now he was planning two of them, based on a pair of subjects abundant at Gombe: baboons and insects. He was already starting to study the baboons, Jane wrote to Joan Travis on March 6, and he was "full of plans" for that "fabulous insect film."

By 1972, of course, the National Geographic Society had stopped sponsoring any of the field research at Gombe, and so it was hard to imagine how anyone there could object this time around. But Jane still decided to inform President Payne (in a May 12 letter) about Hugo's plans to film baboons and the fact that a limited amount of chimp footage would also be taken, since the two species often interact. Perhaps recognizing that the society no longer had any strong legal argument for control over the light reflecting off Gombe and its denizens, Payne resorted to a moral one. "Somehow," he wrote, "it seems improper for Hugo to commercialize the institution which Gombe now represents in pursuit of purely commercial gain without consideration as to the Society other than some form of tacit approval. Necessarily this matter takes on personal aspects." Gombe, he went on, would have been "quite a different thing" without the society's past support, while much of Hugo's "undoubted success as a photographer" should likewise be credited to that same great generosity. In view of such facts and generosity, Dr. Payne concluded, he did not consider it unreasonable to suggest that the National Geographic Society ought to retain, at the very least, an option to bid on commercial television rights for the two films once they were finished.

Hugo responded coolly that the baboon and insect films could be made in several other places, and the only reason he wished to film at Gombe, "apart from Jane, Grub and myself wishing to stay together as a family, is that it makes it possible for me to contribute more fully to the organisation and running of Gombe if I am on the spot." He was unmoved, in any case, by the idea that he owed the National Geographic Society anything.

Hugo's career had just taken a dramatic turn for the better, but at the same time his marriage to Jane was taking a quiet turn in the opposite direction. Jane's family back in England could intuit that things were going badly—mainly because she had virtually stopped mentioning his name in her letters home. As she once recalled for me, Hugo took no clear pleasure in her success and had little interest in her career as a scientist. He also maintained a perhaps typically masculine need to control things, and Jane, and she was not very controllable. There were other stresses. They had come together with a powerful shared interest in animals and animal behavior, but within a few years they had become increasingly aware of significant parts of their lives where there was little mutual pleasure or agreement. Hugo never shared Jane's more intellectual inclinations, her love of classical music and poetry, for example, and he remained indifferent to her spiritual or religious interests. As Jane watched, Grub one day asked Hugo a childish question about God. Hugo, confidently an atheist and a materialist, happened to be sitting with some friends at the time, and he simply laughed at Grub's question, while the friends soon joined in. That seemed a cruel, almost unforgivable offense to Jane.

Jane and Hugo became distant and then estranged during 1972. If they had shared a suburban house somewhere, they might have begun sleeping in separate bedrooms. Instead they began sleeping in separate parts of East Africa, with Hugo going back to the Serengeti once his Gombe films were finished. Grub stayed mostly with his mother, who had always been the nurturing parent and primary caregiver. Perhaps Jane saw in the drama with Hugo and Grub parallels to her own childhood experience with a distant and then disappearing father—and perhaps she also saw the parallels to what she knew of chimpanzee family life. Adult males can be wonderfully sensitive and attentive to young chimps, but the strongest and most intimate bond of chimpanzee family life is always between mother and child.

The Gombe research had identified a normal weaning process for chimps, which begins when the youngster reaches an age of four to five years and lasts for a year or more, until the mother's milk has dried up. Weaning must be a traumatic time for the youngster, who begins pestering his or her mother for extra care and reassurance, soliciting hugs, grooming, and so on.

Flint, for example, constantly pestered Flo for grooming, even while she was pregnant with Flame. When Flo finally gave birth, Flint became less demanding—but only for a brief while. He soon returned to his needy ways, whimpering in distress and drawing her hands away from the new-born sibling. And after little Flame died, Flint became needier and more persistent, and old Flo, seemingly without the energy to do anything else, usually gave in.

Flo's grandson, Freud, was "very well indeed," Jane wrote to Leonard Carmichael on January 22, 1972, while Flint had become "quite avuncular" with his sister Fifi's baby, frequently carrying the tiny nephew about and playing with him. Still, Flint remained "peculiar" in his inability to grow up. Or was it old Flo's inability to make him? The young chimp would be eight years old at the start of March, but he was still creeping into his mother's nest at night and still clambering up and trying to ride around on her back.

Weaning, of course, is not the end to mother-child relations, and chim-panzee mothers remain physically close to their preadolescent progeny and continue to maintain important associations even when their offspring are mature and independent. For instance, when Flo's grown-up son Figan found himself in desperate straits that year, he was suddenly very much in need of his mother's comforting presence.

Even though Humphrey retained his alpha status into 1972, clever and ambitious young Figan was still a rival, so there was a lot of tension be-tween the two males. Figan did his best to avoid Humphrey whenever he could, while Humphrey, upon meeting Figan, would burst into one of his spectacular, hair-bristling displays of bulk and power. But Figan may have recognized that while the big bully stood at the top of the heap, Evered would eventually turn out to be a more serious rival, and thus during 1972 Figan seemed mainly preoccupied with the struggle to intimidate and domi-nate Evered. At some point around the start of the summer, the pair of them had a serious fight high up in a tree. Evered was able to enlist the support of one of the senior males, though, and with two against one, the fight ended with Figan crashing out of the tree and falling 30 feet to the ground. Evered displayed high in the branches in a sort of victory celebration, while Figan sat on the ground screaming and holding a broken or badly sprained hand, which kept him lame for weeks. As Jane wrote years later, Flo was "incredi-bly ancient" by then, shrunken and slow-moving. Nevertheless, upon hear-ing the "frenzied screaming of her son, at least a quarter of a mile away, she leapt to her feet and, with all her remaining hairs standing on end, raced to-wards the sounds—so fast that her human follower was left far behind." Ar-riving on the scene, Flo could do nothing practical to help Figan. "But her very presence calmed him. His frantic screaming gave way to soft whimpers as he limped towards his mother. And when she began to groom him, he quietened altogether, relaxing under the reassuring touch of her fingers just as he had throughout his infancy and childhood." Flo moved away finally, with her grown son Figan following, careful to keep his injured hand from touching the ground.

Flo was still capable of small bursts of the old energy and self-confidence. Since her teeth were gone, she was sometimes given extra bananas at the provisioning site, and when she approached the beach cabin, Jane might step out and hand her a boiled egg. One time Crease, lurking near the cabin, tried to snatch away one of the eggs Jane had just given her. Then Flo, though old and frail, "bristled up at once, stood upright, and ran at the baboon, flailing her arms and actually hitting him," whereupon Crease executed a strategic retreat and "sat watching from a respectful distance as the ancient female slowly savoured the eggs, one at a time, chewing them with leaves."

But by the end of the summer Flo was worn down, apparently ill, and severely emaciated, having become (as Jane wrote home on August 16) "quite literally, a skeleton with some hairy flesh around it." Perhaps she found it comforting to have Fifi and Flint around, Jane supposed, except that Flint was being "the most ghastly pest." He would still try to climb on her back and ride his pathetic mother, and now she simply toppled over from the weight. In fact, she was so weak that she spent most of her time listlessly lying on the ground. Yet still Flint would go up to her with an unhappy pout on his face and push at her, doing his best to prod her into moving on. Or pull at her, trying to solicit more grooming. Flo was dying, and Jane could only wonder, *What will he do when she is gone?*

Both Robert Hinde and Irven DeVore were visiting the research center when Flo's body was discovered in the third week of August. Jane later wrote that it was a "bright, clear morning when I received news of her death." The body was sprawled facedown in the gurgling flow of Kakombe stream, and when Jane turned it over, she saw a face peaceful and composed. "Although I had known that the end was close, this did nothing to mitigate the grief that filled me as I stood looking down at Flo's remains. I had known her for eleven years, and I had loved her."

Flint was sitting in a tree overhead when Flo's body was discovered that morning, and after Jane turned it over, he approached and bent over to gaze into his mother's eyes.

On the first night, Jane watched over the body to protect it from nocturnally scavenging bush pigs, thinking that Flint's "grief might have been worse had he found his mother's body torn and partly eaten." For the next few nights the old matriarch's body was taken into the Cage and stretched out on a pallet alongside the sleeping (or trying to sleep) Irven DeVore. Just before dawn the body would be returned to its position at the edge of Kakombe stream, so that Gombe researchers could keep track of Flint and observe the reactions of Flo's other progeny.

"In many ways it was a great relief," Jane wrote home on September 8. Flo had been "so decrepit and sad that we dreaded her having to face the rains." But it was wrenching to watch Flint's reaction. "He has gone into deep depression. Occasionally he goes about with Fifi or Figan, but then he leaves them, and stays alone, hardly moving, hardly eating, all day long." Flint took to sleeping on the ground near the spot where Flo died—and Jane once watched him climb a tree and stare into an old nest where he and his mother had spent the night several months earlier.

When Jane and Grub left for Nairobi around September 12, Jane was hoping that Flint might respond positively to a dose of antibiotics. "We're trying to arrange a plane to take some medicines down to him," she wrote to Joan Travis from Nairobi on the fifteenth, "but it may be too late. He won't eat or anything. Poor poor little Flint."

It was too late. Flint died around the same time Jane wrote those words. She and Grub flew to England on the twentieth, and after a brief visit to the family home in Bournemouth (where Grub would remain with the rest of the family for a term of school), Jane departed again on September 25, bound for California and Stanford. She had written an obituary of Flo, which was published in the Sunday edition of the *Times* on October 1 and included, along with a photo of the ancient mother and a second of her grieving son, a final tribute to little Flint. Flo, the grand old matriarch of Gombe Stream, with "her torn ears and bulbous nose, her occasional spells of wild sexual activity, her dauntless, forceful personality," had "contributed much to science." Flint's death was "a tragedy in every way," although simultaneously it stood as "testimony to the depth and significance of the affectionate bond, which can unite a chimpanzee child to his mother." As a mother herself, Jane continued, she had "learnt much wisdom during my years of association with Flo. I owe her a personal debt of gratitude and, for me, Gombe can never again be quite the same."

It was the first obituary for a nonhuman ever printed in the *Times,* and Jane might in ordinary circumstances have been pleased to learn of its appearance that Sunday. Perhaps Vanne telephoned from England with the news. At the same time, however, any possible pleasure over that minor triumph would certainly have been obliterated by other, major news: the great Louis S. B. Leakey had died the same morning.

Louis had gone to London a few days earlier, flying out from Nairobi late on September 26 and settling into his usual London residence, the flat on

Earl's Court Road. He intended, with Vanne's assistance, to polish up the second volume of his memoirs before proceeding to America at the start of October for another grueling series of fundraising lectures.

Louis had recently turned sixty-nine, and he was neither well nor taking good care of himself. He had lost thirty pounds since his serious heart attack in February 1970, yet was still overweight. Chronically painful arthritis and failed hip replacement surgery had for the past few years forced him to hobble about with the assistance of a cane. And then, in January 1971, not a year after the first heart attack, he had experienced another troubling episode, which his doctor in Nairobi described as an embolism and for which he prescribed time off at a lower elevation. Louis therefore took a holiday at sea level in the company of his African driver, Clemente, and a bevy of attractive young women. The women donned their bikinis and snorkeled in the Indian Ocean while the old man relaxed on shore, and by January 18 he was feeling better. Before returning to Nairobi, though, Louis introduced his friends to the ruins at Gedi, a sixteenth-century Arabic settlement. As Clemente escorted them about the site, Louis sat down to rest in the flickering shade of a mango tree. It was very hot and still, and perhaps the bees were attracted by his sweat. He had just gotten up to examine some aspect of the ruins when, as he later recalled, "a swarm of bees attacked me en masse. It was perfectly horrible, [a] terrible, terrifying experience. I was alone. The bees simply came in their thousands upon thousands all around me and mobbed me."

The white-haired figure fled, staggering madly, balancing himself with his cane, swatting at the swarm, shouting for help, and then running into a wall, banging his head, and toppling to the ground. He struggled, still trying to escape the bees, and finally was rescued by his young friends. An emergency medical flight took him to a Nairobi hospital, where he lay paralyzed and partially blind. Within a week he had begun to recuperate, although his right hand and arm were still not working, so he could not easily write. Still, he was slowly regaining the use of extremities on his left side and was soon sending a tape-recorded message to Vanne and her family in England that described the catastrophe while confirming his plans to get on with his lecture tour in the States, because "I do need the money so desperately badly."

As always, he had a thousand ideas and a dozen major enterprises under way or in sight. He had books to write, articles to finish, conferences to attend and organize, archaeological digs to support and start. He maintained directorships at the museum and its associated Centre for Prehistory and Palaeontology, and at the Tigoni Primate Research Centre (which he had founded in 1958) outside Nairobi. He was still funding and overseeing the

Calico Hills archaeological dig in California (which he had begun in 1964). In Kenya he had recently hired a young woman to observe DeBrazza's monkeys, another to study black-and-white colobus monkeys, a third to reconsider the taxonomy of wildebeests. Jane and Dian Fossey were already thoroughly established in their respective ape studies, of course, and now Louis had to locate the money to send his third ape woman, Biruté Galdikas, off to the orangutans in Borneo. He planned to get his fourth ape woman started on a study of bonobos in north-central Zaire. It was all endlessly stimulating but also perpetually costly.

Louis was released from the hospital after about a month, though still paralyzed in the right arm and leg. After a couple months' rehabilitation, he flew to California for his spring lecture tour, beginning on April 30 in San Francisco with a press conference and dinner, to be followed the next day with an address to a University of California symposium. But while attempting to climb out of a car on his way to dinner that evening, he pitched forward and landed headfirst on the pavement. He recovered with some dignity, and the next day gave his symposium address. But at the end of the afternoon, as he and other speakers were answering questions while seated on a stage platform, Louis's chair tipped off the edge, and he crashed onto the stage, striking the back of his head. He had some bad bruises and an apparent mild concussion but nevertheless was up the next day and continuing the lecture series.

After three weeks of almost daily presentations in California, Louis gave his final one on May 25, at the University of California at Riverside. He was alert during the event but at the end had to be helped off the stage and escorted back to the car. By the time the car arrived at his Los Angeles base, the home of Joan and Arnold Travis, he was disoriented and unable to walk, so Joan Travis called in a neighbor, Charles Carton, who happened to be a neurosurgeon. Dr. Carton grasped the urgency of the situation, and by May 29 the old patriarch was stretched out on a gurney under the bright lights as Dr. Carton peered through access holes at the surface of his brain. The surgeon excised two blood clots, one of which looked fresh, apparently a result of the fall in San Francisco. The second clot, directly beneath the first, could have been produced during his fall at Gedi, when Louis was swarmed by bees. Removal of the clots reduced pressure on the brain and had the miraculous effect of ending, for the most part, his paralysis.

By the end of June he had improved enough to board a plane and fly to Washington, D.C., where he intended to request from the National Geographic a small grant to get Biruté Galdikas launched. He was forced to stay longer than planned, since a high fever and sudden bladder infection took him back into the hospital. Even though the committee members appeared reluctant to start backing another of those interminable ape studies, they finally agreed. The Wilkie Brothers Foundation promised an additional sum, and more would come from the Jane and Justin Dart Foundation, so now the total appeared sufficient. Louis returned to East Africa and rendezvoused with Galdikas and her husband for final preparations.

Still, money, or the lack thereof, had always been a source of worry for Louis, but it was now more so than ever. The Leakey Foundation, recently created to help promote his particular vision and projects, was getting sidetracked by conflicts among the trustees and the unhappy consequences of an economic recession in the States. And so Louis's lecture series during the fall of 1971 took on a greater than usual urgency, as he returned to give talks in Washington, New York, Chicago, Denver, and Los Angeles, followed by three weeks of more standard peregrinations up and down the state of California.

He was back in Nairobi by December and from there flew on to Addis Ababa, attending the seventh Pan-African Congress on Prehistory. Back to London for Christmas. Philadelphia after Christmas. Return to Nairobi. Brief visit to Olduvai. Return to London in February, and finally once again to America: to Ithaca, New York, where, during three weeks as a visiting professor at Cornell University, he dropped a fireplace log onto his left big toe and broke it. He returned to Nairobi by the end of April, isolated, prone to angry outbursts, entirely estranged from Mary, and now hardly on speaking terms with his son Richard, yet still as imaginative and grandly ambitious as ever. Assuming that his unreliable legs and high blood pressure could tolerate the climb and altitude, he was planning to visit Dian Fossey at her mountain gorilla camp. He was envisioning a major archaeological expedition into Kenya's remote Suguta Valley. He had lined up his fourth ape woman, Toni Jackman, for the bonobo study in Zaire and by June was busy giving her (as he wrote to Jane on the twenty-fourth) "some intensive instruction on what to do and what not to do and how to become aware of the presence of dangerous animals and what to do in an emergency."

He had also gotten an advance from an American publisher to write the second volume of his memoirs, *By the Evidence.* The first, *White African,* had done reasonably well, and therefore, perhaps, if he could produce a substantial piece of the second, Collins in England might also come up with a solid advance. But he needed help with the writing.

Louis and Vanne had coauthored an earlier book, a popularized survey of evolutionary theories and discoveries entitled *Unveiling Man's Origins* (1969), for which he had found the publisher and she had done most of the work. "The Old Men," as she privately referred to it, was Vanne's second book, begun directly after the publication of her novel. Louis had then connected her with a publisher for her third, an illustrated collection of chapters by six experts that would draw together "some of the skeins of modern scientific and metaphysical thought concerning human evolution." And now he was asking her for help in writing his memoirs. Vanne did not relish the task, but she could not turn him down. As she described her thinking in a letter to Jane, "I know about Louis—all the good and the bad, but when you are in continual discomfort with a leg that won't work properly, when you have two metal plates in your head, when your hands no longer function and you can only scribble illegibly for a moment or two, and when you're kicked by your family even if it's largely your fault, it must be terrible. And after all that I've been lumbered with the Memoir manuscript!!!!!!!!!!!!!! How could I refuse."

Louis and Vanne, working with a friend of Louis's, had put together about five chapters of the book in April while he was in London. Then, starting in late July, he and Vanne spent three weeks holed up together at the friend's cottage in Hampshire, by the end of which time they had sent off fifteen chapters and were closing in on the remaining three. When he returned to London near the end of September and met Vanne at the flat on Earl's Court Road, the manuscript needed only a few finishing touches. Still, Louis felt tired. On Saturday he submitted to a routine electrocardiogram, which seemed normal, although his blood pressure was high. Then, on Sunday morning, October 1, while he was getting dressed, Louis was struck down by a massive heart attack. At the hospital, Vanne stayed by his side until about nine o'clock that morning, when she left him in the care of a nurse. A half-hour later he was dead.

Biographer Virginia Morrell has described the relationship between Louis and Vanne as an "intimate" one, and I would agree, although certainly the word has more than one commonly understood meaning. My impression is that they were intimately close friends, drawn together by mutual admiration and interests, a common attachment to and ambition for Jane, and, during the later years, some collaborative work and Vanne's maternal sympathy for an aging friend during his painful last years. Morrell also recalls the rumor that Vanne and Louis had a long and secret shared history, going back far and deeply enough to make Jane Louis's biological daughter. But there appears to be absolutely no supporting evidence for that rumor and substantial contradicting evidence, including the fact that when Louis first met Jane, in 1957, he treated her as he did many other attractive young women who came under his sway: as an intelligent and interesting person who was also romantically and sexually fair game. Not the behavior of a father toward his long-lost daughter.

Louis's body was sent back to Kenya and, during a quiet family ceremony, lowered into the earth beside the graves of his missionary parents in a small village churchyard at Limuru. A more public memorial was held two days later in All Saints' Cathedral of Nairobi, where an enormous, bustling throng of friends and admirers of all races and social classes gathered to hear the eulogy delivered by Charles Njonjo, the attorney general of Kenya. "It was always his great gift," Njonjo said of Louis, "to merge himself, quite unaffectedly, into any segment . . . of mankind. And he would wish to be remembered, not in terms of any race or nationality or tribe, but as a member of the human species."

34

Friends, Allies, and Lovers

1973

"WE SURE NEED a resident practising psychiatrist here at Gombe," Jane wrote, half-joking, to a psychiatrist colleague of David Hamburg's during the summer of 1972. "Can't you spare us a year! The things people get upset about." Fortunately, she would soon be supported on matters practical and personal by a competent friend and ally: Emilie van Zinnicq Bergmann, who arrived on the last day of 1972 to take Hugo's place as general administrator.

Emilie Bergmann was Dutch, pretty, with rich dark hair, a broad and pleasant face, and a passionately forthright manner. She had been working as a veterinary technician with large farm animals and sharing with some students a big house near Utrecht, in a village where Hugo's brother also happened to live. In 1971, Jane was invited to speak to a gathering of about 150 people at the house, and twenty-one-year-old Emilie cooked dinner for all of them. Afterward Hugo took her aside and said (as she recalls the words), "Well, you seem to be pretty handy. Wouldn't you like, sometime, to come to Africa?"

Emilie had always dreamed of going to Africa. And thus, at some point near the end of 1972, she approached Hugo's mother, Moeza, who lived not far away, to ask if she thought Hugo and Jane were serious about the invitation.

By the third week of December, Emilie had flown to London to meet with Jane. Grub was in Bournemouth, recovering from pneumonia, and directly after Christmas, while he stayed there to recuperate, Jane and Emilie caught a nonstop 747 to Nairobi. Emerging sleepy and dazed into a bright African morning, they were flown in a small, bouncy plane to George Dove's Ndutu camp. Emilie remembers how exciting it was to soar so close to Mount Kilimanjaro and then to sight, down in the midst of the rolling plains, the lake and camp and landing strip. The strip was covered by grazing wildebeests and zebras, and before they could land, Dove had to drive out in his Land Rover and chase the animals off. After the plane landed, Jane and Emilie settled into camp, with time for a relaxed lunch. Later that afternoon they drove out on the Serengeti to look for wild dogs.

They had a "festive dinner," Jane reported home, and then "collapsed into bed. It apparently thundered & hyenas whooped—I heard nothing at all! Except a foul mosquito." Jane had been very favorably impressed by Emilie in London, and she remained completely positive now: "I think Emilie will be a tower of strength," she wrote home on December 31, as they flew on to Kigoma.

Grub, having recovered from the pneumonia, took another nonstop 747 to Nairobi on January 23. A Stanford student named David Riss had already arrived in Nairobi by then, about to begin his six-month stint at Gombe, and he met Grub at the van Lawick house in Limuru and then flew with him to spend a short time at the Ndutu camp with Hugo.

Twenty-one-year-old David Riss was lean and athletic, with thick brown hair, light blue eyes, an easy smile, a soft voice, and a gentle, uncomplicated personality. He was a premedical student who planned to go into family practice, but in the meantime he had enrolled in the human bio program and thought going to work with Jane Goodall in Africa sounded like a wonderful thing to do. At the Ndutu camp, as he remembers, Hugo smoked endless cigarettes, drank plenty of Scotch, and seemed always out on an adventure. In fact, Hugo's whole life seemed like one big adventure. During the day they would look for animals to photograph. In the evenings David would sit with other guests inside a tent, sip Scotch, and listen to Hugo spin out entertaining stories about, for example, young newcomers to the Serengeti who were foolish enough to let their feet dangle outside the tent at night or who otherwise got mangled or killed by lions or hyenas when they least expected it. David would then slip beyond the comforting glow of the tent, stumble through a confusing darkness to the latrine, and sit there in a Scotch-infused daze while listening to the rumble and whoop of real lions and real hyenas.

Jane showed up at Ndutu on January 25 to fly with Grub back to Gombe, and David Riss followed a few days later. His first task there was to record what the chimps were doing, identify what they were eating, and mark down where they were going; he was given a map of the trails so he could pinpoint where any animal was at a given time. From the first, he enjoyed being out with the wild chimps, and he thought everyone at Gombe made "a really good team" with "a lot of enthusiasm." At the same time, he was distracted by a surprisingly sudden and strong interest in Emilie.

He finally passed her a short note on the subject, dated Sunday, February 25. "My dearest Emilie," the note began.

From the minute that I set my eyes on you that wonderful day, february 6th, 1973, I knew that somehow I must have you for the rest of my life: I knew from that minute that you were the only girl for me; that I loved you, that I needed you, that I would marry you. The three weeks since that magical day have confirmed and amplified my love for you. You are one of the prettiest, most understanding, most compassionate, most exciting and most loving women that I have ever met. My heart has glowed thinking about you more than it ever has. You are the center of all my thoughts. When I am following chimps, it is hard to concentrate on the damned animal: you are always on my mind.

He hoped they could spend their lives together, he went on, and he knew that she loved him too. She showed it in the way she had offered to mix up some chocolate milk for him. "Emilie, dearest Emilie, my Emilie," he concluded,

come to P[an] P[alace] tomorrow and we will elope together, with the hooting and the branchwaving and the grooming of the wild chimps and the wahoos of the primitive baboons to say farewell to us, Emilie and her lover David. And so, until that moment, I must go up to my room and await your reply. It will be a sleepless and agonizing night, a long and worrisome night, a night that I shall always dimly regard . . . but, hopefully, it will be the night before the most important and happy day of my life . . . the day that you and I commit ourselves to each other, and our love.

Jane, meanwhile, was burdened by what she called "the dog book," meaning Hugo's book for Billy Collins, *Solo: The Story of an African Wild Dog*, which she had agreed to write. "I am beginning to be depressed about the thought of the dog book," she wrote home late that January. "I so hate the idea of doing it. However, I dare say it will be okay once I start it."

She was also receiving bad news on the financial front. For one thing, partly as a consequence of a sudden burst of inflation in Tanzania, Gombe's local accounts in Tanzanian currency had shrunk—or disappeared. As she wrote home on February 3, "Now we find we are 19,500 shs overdrawn! Worry, worry. Money sent to us in August for a guest house ($5,000) has been spent! Money given us by Paul Ehrlich for his house—gone!" A note from the accountant in London announced that Gombe's general operating funds, still in British pounds, were due to run out around June, whereas the anticipated renewal of their main source of funding, from the Grant Foundation, would not occur until November. Jane had also received a telegram and letter from David Hamburg in California, who was now, as she put it in a February 11 letter home, "very depressed." Although the Grant Foundation had provided seed money for the construction of the outdoor primate research site at Stanford—Gombe West—he had been expecting a big grant from the National Institute of Mental Health (NIMH) to support daily operations. But now "Nixon's cuts in the scientific research budget have been even worse than anyone thought," which meant that he was "not even sure we'll get a penny of our NIMH grant—after all that work. Isn't that ghastly! And he's having to implement great cuts."

Jane began cutting costs at Gombe East, although since the place was already run so frugally, the cuts were mostly symbolic. She also began writing to anyone she could think of who might be able to help. Gombe was eventually rescued by a few significant gifts, and by early that summer Jane would be dancing—literally—in relief and pleasure at the receipt of a telegram announcing an early renewal of the Grant Foundation grant. Nevertheless, as she was in the process of discovering, how-to-pay-for-it-all was a lifelong treadmill. And while the money headache was becoming chronic, the matter of permits and clearances for researchers, of regular permission to visit and work in the country, was starting to look the same. Had not those problems already been solved?

At the end of February, Grub went to stay with Hugo in the Serengeti while Jane went to Dar es Salaam and checked into the Kilimanjaro Hotel. It was extremely hot there, and the hotel's air conditioning was not working, but she still enjoyed a stunning view of the harbor from her veranda. Having concluded that the coolest spot in her hot room was dead center, she moved the coffee table there, placed a couple of pillows on the floor next to it, set her typewriter on top of it, removed all her clothes, sat herself down on the pillows, and began pecking out the story of Solo. In between bouts of dog book typing, she spent a couple of days, as she later phrased it, "battling away for Gombe."

She visited the prime minister's office and talked with "a very nice man" named Mr. Chambo, and she had lunch at the home of the new director of Tanzania National Parks, Derek Bryceson (who had earlier, when he was minister of agriculture, made a brief stop at Gombe). A tall, white-haired Englishman who had been badly crippled in a plane crash during the war, Bryceson was a close personal friend of Tanzania's president, Julius Nyerere, and his house was located on the beach right next to Nyerere's house, facing a protected inlet of the Indian Ocean, with palm trees, a sandy beach, a boat, and a big aquarium inside. Jane liked the house, and she found Bryce-son a sympathetic listener. After lunch they went to a "dainty tea" and spoke with Tumaina Mcharo, the new director of the Serengeti Research Institute, and Myles Turner, the former Serengeti park warden who had recently become Tanzania's "chief anti-poaching chap."

Jane liked and trusted Derek Bryceson, who was far more open and sympathetic to her and her Gombe problems than his predecessors in the Parks directorship, John Owen and Solomon ole Saibull. Ole Saibull held the position for only a few months, so the comparison was really with Owen. "Gosh," she wrote home, "Derek is a different kettle of fish."

At around midnight on her second night at the Kilimanjaro Hotel, Jane set aside the dog book manuscript, rolled a sheet of hotel stationery onto the typewriter's cylinder, and finished a letter to the family in England describing the last two days in detail. She looked out the window and noted, just beyond a dark and grassy margin, the harbor. "It is so utterly glorious. You look right into the harbour, and the sea is almost directly below the window. There are a number of big ships riding at anchor, and at night, when they are all lit up, and especially if there is a moon (which there isn't now) it is absolutely exquisite. Air conditioning or not, I really like the hotel." She listened to a great eructating choir of frogs in the grass below her window, gazed out once more to the harbor, where everything seemed "still so beautiful," but now even somehow better: more mysterious and dreamily inviting, looking "like a fairy land out there, with the water shining and rippling, and the almost unreal illuminated cargo boats and one passenger liner. And, occasionally, an Arab dhow slips past silently. Or a little lit tug chugs busily on its errands. Or a tiny speed boat races by, the engine quite lost below the chorus of frogs."

Jane spent the next week in a tent at Ndutu camp, typing away at the dog book from 6:30 in the morning to 6:30 in the evening until it was done. It was "another marathon over," she wrote to the family on March 10 (while in flight to Gombe with Grub). And with that worry behind her, she could now consider others before her, including the mild fear she often felt, whenever she was gone from Gombe, that "some dire mishap will have taken place in my absence. I hope not!"

But at Gombe everything was fine. Indeed, the only problems now were Jane's unending administrative duties, which amounted to "letters daily about clearance, permits, finances, supervision, recommendations—and on and on and on." She seemed always stuck at the desk in her little office at the beach cabin, never seeing the chimps, only occasionally some of the baboons when they happened to wander up to the cabin and gaze quizzically through the window at her "frantically tapping fingers."

In early April she flew to England with Grub, and, while he stayed there with the family for a few weeks, she went on to Stanford to begin her first human bio lectures, on Monday, April 16. The funding news regarding Gombe West was still "very grim," she reported in an open letter to everyone back at Gombe East, but by the end of the month the situation appeared less grim, as she began traveling, giving public lectures, and appealing for funds. A trip to San Francisco raised $25,000, the gift of a single donor, and other potential donors were expressing interest. Moreover, if it was true that President Nixon's lack of interest in general scientific research helped account for the recent cuts in federal funding, then Nixon's latest political problems, centered on a sordid attempted burglary of Democratic Party headquarters at the Watergate Hotel in Washington, may have seemed rather perversely promising.

David Riss's warm friendship with Emilie Bergmann was developing happily, if quietly, and in the meantime David had begun studying three top-ranking males—Figan, Faben, and Evered—and the relationship between them. Besides following, watching, and taking notes on that ambitious trio, he thoroughly reviewed all the old records, going back as far as 1963. He was also lucky enough to witness a significant realignment in the male hierarchy involving those three.

When David had arrived in February, Humphrey was still alpha, having bullied his way to the top a year earlier. But an important competition for status was taking place between two of his underlings, Figan and Evered, both physically smaller but possibly more intelligent and more ambitious than Humphrey. While superficially subservient, they were obviously waiting for their chance to climb to the top of the male social ladder—at the same time, it seemed, recognizing each other as the most significant competitors for the next rung.

Although Evered had thrown Figan down from the treetops in 1972, Figan had recovered from his injuries and was clearly feeling better. Humphrey had formed a temporary alliance with Evered; the pair of them now spent more time together, grooming each other and, when occasion demanded, supporting each other in charging displays and fights. One time Humphrey and Evered combined to attack Figan. The beating was not decisive, however, and whenever Humphrey was alone—without Evered in sight as support—he avoided Figan. But when all three males converged in the forest or at the provisioning area, tension and hostility invariably erupted, usually expressed with vigorous charging displays, the allied pair seemingly doing their best to impress and intimidate Figan and Figan trying to return the favor. With arms, shoulders, and torsos bulked up, hair bristled, faces curled into a grim mask of fury, they violently crashed through the vegetation and rushed back and forth again and again and again, tearing branches, tossing huge rocks, scattering any innocent chimp bystanders in panic.

With such a formidable pair of foes allied against him, Figan might never have made it to the top—except that after Flo's death, late in the summer of 1972, he had grown closer to his brother, Faben. Perhaps the disappearance of their mother aroused new feelings of family solidarity in the siblings. Faben had never joined forces with anyone against his brother, but neither had he predictably supported Figan. But in the months following Flo's death, the brothers became good friends and tight allies, almost always together; and it was during this period that Faben became, as Jane once wrote, "utterly committed to supporting Figan in his quest for power."

In late April 1973, without warning, Figan and Faben together set upon Evered, who scrambled desperately into the refuge of a high tree. For half an hour the brothers chased and displayed, while an obviously terrified Evered screamed and whimpered and crouched defensively in the tree before finally managing to escape.

Four days later a large group of chimps, including males, females, and juveniles, began bedding down for the night, bending branches and weaving together their leafy night nests after a long day. Humphrey, having already made his nest, was relaxing peacefully in it. Figan had been feeding in a tree some distance away from the main group, but now, in the cooling air and lengthening shadows, he paused, as if in thought. Then (with Faben already settled in nearby and watching) he calmly and quietly descended from his feeding tree and began moving toward a big tree that contained many of the others. As he approached, his hair began to rise, until he seemed actually to double in size. And then, in an exploding instant, he was up into the branches of the big tree and raging, charging about, leaping and swinging and rushing from branch to branch. With a chaos of screams and cries and whimpers, others scattered out of his way, some of them jumping out of their nests to safety. Figan chased and slapped an older, low-ranking male before—having at last generated the perfect rage—he sprang down on top of Humphrey, who was unprepared and still sitting in his nest. The pair, grappling now in a swaying embrace, spun and toppled out of the tree, crashing to the ground, where Humphrey finally pulled himself loose and raced off, screaming, into the darkness.

Humphrey was a powerful male, fifteen pounds heavier than Figan, but Figan had surprised him. Even so, Figan probably would not have dared to attack Humphrey without the presence of his brother Faben in reserve, watching and capable of joining him immediately if he needed support.

After that decisive beating, Humphrey became appropriately deferential to Figan, and so now Figan's final target was Evered. Figan and Faben together located the upstart in a tree one hot, wet afternoon in late May. The two brothers displayed and raced around the base of the tree, throwing rocks, dragging branches, and then together they ascended and jumped onto the terrified Evered. All three fell to the ground. Evered broke away and fled up a hillside and into a second tree. The brothers displayed wildly beneath that tree for another hour, with their victim clinging to his precarious refuge until, finally, Figan and Faben moved away.

With Faben as his reliable ally, Figan had at last become alpha male, a position of supreme importance recognized in gesture and deed by every other member of the community.

"Do remember to save Watergate papers for me—send them off—the good ones like from the Sunday Times. That would be super," Jane wrote to the family on May 20, after she had returned to Africa, having just spiraled down, with Grub, into Hugo's camp in the Ngorongoro Crater.

It was hard to know where that peculiar Watergate affair in America might lead, but by the time Jane and Grub made it back to Gombe for the final week of May, Nixon's problems may have seemed irrelevant, given all the tremendously good news that suddenly seemed to drop right out of the sky. First came the information that Hugo had been awarded two Emmys in the United States for his wild dog film, narrated by Jane and titled *Jane Goodall's World of Animal Behavior: The Wild Dogs of Africa*. Then came two telegrams from David Hamburg, announcing that he had been given two grants to support Gombe West. And finally, another telegram informed Jane that the Leakey Foundation would provide an emergency grant to assist Gombe East through its tight spot. "I simply can't believe it! How simply fantastic, and marvellous and wonderful—and SUPER!" Jane enthused in a May 27 letter.

In the same week Derek Bryceson visited Gombe, accompanied by the Canadian high commissioner. Jane was "desperately hoping they would see good chimp things," but Bryceson was so crippled he could move only laboriously, with the assistance of "a stick and will power." How, she wondered, would he get up the trail to the provisioning area? She planned to have people haul him up in a chair or on a stretcher, but Bryceson walked all the way, and once he finally made it up there, more hairy creatures lumbered and dashed out of the forest and into the provisioning clearing than had been seen "in the past FIVE months!" The tall, white-haired man with a sweet smile and a personal grace that overcame any physical lack of it "couldn't have been more impressed and delighted—and delightful for that matter."

Bryceson also gave two short but well-received talks, one in English, for the students, on the subject of Tanzanian politics, and the second in Swahili, for the staff, about the future of Tanzania's national parks. He helped Grub fish for crabs and catfish, and he recommended a good book for Jane, Solzhenitsyn's *Cancer Ward*. He was simply "a marvellous person," who would do, Jane was convinced, "more than any other single person in Tanzania could do, at this point in history, to save our wildlife."

In the third week of June, Jane found it necessary to return to Dar es Salaam for four days, hoping, as she described the case in a letter to Joan Travis, to "sort out a few more clearance problems." The trip was another big success. Jane showed a National Geographic chimpanzee film to the Tanzanian parliament, and then she had, as she later described it in a letter to Robert Hinde, "the most fabulous talk with the President." She had met Julius Nyerere six years earlier, when he seemed "lonely and ill." But this time he "radiates strength together with an amazing quality of gentleness which makes his personality quite unique in my experience." Most importantly, President Nyerere declared emphatically that Gombe would not be turned over to tourism—and at the same time he agreed to write the preface for the Swahili edition of *In the Shadow of Man*. Of course, that productive meeting with the president had been arranged by her new friend, Derek Bryceson, and Jane was now anticipating "several such trips [to Dar es Salaam] a year in order to keep Gombe afloat."

Bryceson spent part of July in England. In London he met Vanne, who gave him a package for Jane: some paperback copies of *Shadow* and a bundle of ponytail clips for her hair.

Emilie Bergmann had always loved animals and felt comfortable around them, and her role at Gombe in some ways amounted to a continuation of her earlier job as a veterinary assistant. When she arrived, Gombe had a semi-tame mongoose. Although everyone called the mongoose Minnie, he was actually a male, and he fit right in. He played with the chimps, for instance, and he was smart, quick, and aggressive enough to intimidate the big baboon Grinner. But Minnie had a soft, affectionate side as well, and he started crawling into bed with Emilie at night, which she thought was just fine—until, after about a month, she realized that Minnie was full of fleas.

Giant monitor lizards also sometimes made ghostly nocturnal visitations, and Emilie would get up to chase them out of the garbage dump. Bolivar, the bush pig, might snuffle and snort around the base of the palm nut trees at night, sniffing out scraps left by the baboons. And there were the snakes. Mambas slipped into people's aluminum huts most often, for some reason, and since it was a national park, generally the practice was not to kill any living creature, including mambas. Thus Emilie might be sitting in her hut at night, working by the light of a kerosene lantern, and she would see a moth fluttering about. A gecko would skitter out from the shadows and eat the moth. Then a mamba would emerge and eat the gecko, and at that point Emilie would say to herself, *Oh, it's time to shut off my light.*

There was the morning when Emilie, just getting up, still not dressed, was washing herself with water from the basin in her room, and Figan the chimp happened to be coming down the trail next to her hut. He stopped, turned, and looked straight into her window: a hairy voyeur. Emilie quickly covered herself and shrieked, "My God, Figan, what are you doing here!" Later on, she thought, *Why the heck would I worry about Figan seeing me? If I tell this to people, they'll think I'm a little weird.*

Of course, it was not that weird. Everyone—researchers, students, and staff—found it natural to identify closely with the chimps, and that identification probably made their research more creative and ultimately more accurate. Some of the students had tried sleeping in chimp nests at night, just to know what it was like. The next day they might joke about being nostalgic for the old nest and feeling "nest-sick." They occasionally threw parties featuring chimp foods, like termites. And Cambridge graduate student Richard Wrangham, who was researching chimpanzee foods and gastronomical ecology, one day decided he would see if he could survive on a chimp diet. To make his experiment more authentic, he thought that he would also walk around naked, like a chimp, and he asked Jane for permission to carry out the full protocol. Jane, typically very tolerant of creative thinking, accepted his proposal, except, she said, he would have to wear a loincloth in deference to human sensibilities. Richard agreed to that limiting condition—and then, sensibly, decided against doing the experiment.

The only administration Emilie had done before was keeping track of cows. Now she was running an entire camp, watching the money, keeping the records, paying taxes and workers' compensation, sending reports to the government, dealing with immigration authorities, and so on. The "so on" might include some odd tasks, such as cleaning up Flo's and Flint's skeletons (which, like all chimp remains at Gombe, were preserved as scientifically valuable material). But Emilie was also regularly taking the boat into Kigoma, going to the bank, paying bills, buying diesel fuel for the generator, ordering cement and corrugated iron for building projects, and bargaining for all their food at the market. Having a generator meant they could have a freezer, so it was possible to buy frozen things. There were times when they had no meat, and that was fine. But when meat was available, she would get it as fresh as possible, which meant, often, still alive. She might buy a live goat and chickens or ducks from one of the local villagers. A new student might come up to her and say, "You can't kill that little goat!" And she would say, "Fine. You've been eating meat for the last three weeks. You never questioned it then. So here, take the goat back to the village."

In short, Emilie held a position of great responsibility as Gombe administrator, and she always needed to stay alert and on top of things. Also, given her veterinary background as well as her control over the keys to the dispensary, people frequently came to her first when there was a medical emergency. She remembers the time when the Stanford student Jim Moore said, "I think I've just been bitten by a very poisonous snake, and there's nothing anyone can do. I just want you to know I've been bitten." "What am I going to do?" she asked. He said, "I don't want you to do anything. I don't want you to tell anybody. Just sit here with me." She sat with him, and fortunately none of the preliminary symptoms (slurred speech, labored breathing, drooping eyelids) appeared—a lucky but not unusual reprieve, since little or no venom is actually injected in three quarters of poisonous snakebites.

She comforted Jim Moore on another occasion, after a scorpion bit him on the testicle while he was getting dressed. She plunged a hypodermic full of penicillin into student Chuck de Sieyes's buttock. And when Craig Packer showed up one day with the end of a rotten thorn deeply embedded in his foot, she spread a bit of black goop she had once used to treat horses' hoof infections onto the injury. When Craig's foot was no better a day later, she called on the real embedded-thorn expert, field staff member Hilali Matama. With the injured Stanford student lying facedown on the ground, with Emilie pinning him down from one side and Anne Pusey from the other, Hilali wiggled and worked the thorn out, using a long, sharp kitchen knife and two sharpened sticks.

In the staff village, someone's wife had a nervous breakdown and left the village and her little baby; the husband, not knowing what else to do, took the baby to Emilie. Emilie kept the infant with her for a week, comforting him as well as she could and feeding him by bottle. Later the mother wrote from Dar es Salaam, thanking Emilie and sending twenty shillings to cover expenses. Another woman in the staff village—the wife of baboon expert Apollinaire Sindimwo—dreamed about snakes while she was pregnant, and the local witch doctor interpreted the dream to mean she should have an abortion. The woman asked Emilie for help, and so Emilie took her to the Catholic mission hospital in Kabanga when she was ready to deliver.

Another time Dominic woke her up in the middle of the night, saying, "Mama Emilie, Mama Emilie, my granddaughter has died! We have to go and get her! I have to take her home!" In the darkness they climbed into the boat, and she drove to a village near Burundi, met the mother and picked up the dead child, who was wrapped in a fresh white sheet, and then, with all of them in tears, took Dominic, the mother, and the girl's body back to Kigoma for the funeral.

By the second half of July, Derek Bryceson had returned from England. When he visited Gombe again, they all—researchers, students, staff, and staff family members—sat on the beach before a fire one evening, ate goat and rice off communal plates, drank numerous toasts, and celebrated Gombe's thirteenth anniversary. Derek gave, as Jane later reported to the family, "a super speech," which was followed by a "nice" one by Dominic, and then she took her turn, endeavoring to say something appropriate in Swahili, "which would have been OK if only my Swahili was better—well, it's almost non-existent!"

Jane had practiced and used Swahili for years, but roughly. She was inspired by Bryceson's mastery of the language, which she would now strive to emulate, and also by his vision of and dedication to the future of Tanzania. And the more she knew him, the more she found to admire. He had been born in China on the last day of 1922, educated in England, and in 1939, when Europe was in flames and England preparing for invasion, he had enlisted as a fighter pilot in the Royal Air Force, at age sixteen. In 1942 his plane was shot down, and in the crash his pelvis and legs were shattered so completely that doctors were convinced he would never walk again. He learned to get around with a cane and went on to study agricultural science at Cambridge University. Together with his young wife, Bobbie, Derek moved out to Kenya and then began farming a 1,200-acre plot at the base of Mount Kilimanjaro, in Tanganyika. After three years of farming he met the charismatic Julius Nyerere, leader of an independence movement and political party, the Tanganyika African National Union, and soon became among the first white settlers to endorse Nyerere's vision of a democratic, multiracial society tempered by an African-style socialism. Bryceson and Nyerere became close friends, and when the African politician sought credit to build a house in Dar es Salaam, the English farmer accompanied him to the bank and backed the loan. Nyerere built his house on the beach directly next to Bryceson's; and after Nyerere was elected president of Tanganika, in 1962, and of the United Republic of Tanzania, in 1964, Derek Bryceson became the only white member of the first cabinet.

Derek was a brave and decent man, in short, and he had also recently revealed himself to Jane as a thoughtful, sensitive person who loved literature and music and shared her thirst for the life of the mind and spirit. He encouraged her to indulge her love of Shakespeare by reading *Hamlet* aloud to Grub; and it was probably Derek's influence as well that caused her to read

Bible stories to her son and talk to him about such things as baptism and the Christian concept of a Holy Trinity. It was only an unfortunate side effect of the new regimen that Grub became confused about the ghost in *Hamlet* and the spirit in the Holy Trinity and so had a bad nighttime scare, having seen a wavering curtain in his room that looked like a ghost. But, the frightened boy needed to know when he crawled into bed with his mother, was it the God ghost or the *Hamlet* ghost?

Jane always welcomed allies wherever she could find them, but especially that summer she may have felt she needed one more than ever. "I still feel that I shall go stark staring mad soon," she confessed to Robert Hinde in a letter of August 8. "What with the 2 papers I've just finished, plus the students, plus the staff, plus politics, plus Grub. The other night, as I tossed and turned at 3.30 worrying about the pile (waist high!) of unanswered mail, I almost got up and burnt it." She was not expecting Derek to help in any particular way, but he was someone to confide in, after all, and he was older — a mature fifty-one years compared to her youthful thirty-nine — and seemed so strong and sure of himself. Derek, Jane wrote home, "not only knows and understands the Tanzanians, but he has great wisdom, and all the students love him. So do the staff." The students, she added, were "so much more prepared to listen to him when it comes to questions of relationships with the local people than to listen to me. So many things which are necessary for the successful running of a place as big as Gombe depend on discipline — which, suggested by me, is interpreted by some as 'Colonialism'!"

Discipline was not a concept Jane would have thought about too seriously on her own initiative. Her style of running Gombe and dealing with Gombeites was more democratic, supportive, creative. She preferred to reason rather than demand, persuade rather than dictate. As Emilie recalls, when Jane was in residence, she would come to dinner at the Mess almost every night and "listen to everybody's stories very openly. She would never say, 'No, that isn't the way to look at it.'" The students, Emilie thought, were "so honest" and making "honest, gut observations." But they were not yet scientists — or, as Emilie put it, not yet "spoiled" by the expectations of a scientific discipline. "They were just making really honest observations. So when they came down and said, 'Well, it was just like my sister,' or 'just like my father,' she wouldn't say, 'Well, you can't look at it that way.' And I think she just gave everybody so much chance to express exactly what they had experienced that day, and she wanted to hear about that. I thought there were always very good, very honest observations."

Perhaps Jane felt too close to the students' age and generation, too sympathetic to their ideas, opinions, moods, and fashions. Derek belonged to a different generation and could bring a contrasting style. Not surprisingly, having climbed to the top of one particular hierarchy, he believed in the hierarchical virtues: authority, discipline, knowing one's proper place. Jane remained open to the students and researchers, socially accessible and on a first-name basis. She was "Jane" to them, while Derek, by contrast, remained respectfully "Mr. Bryceson"—although some eventually ventured to call him "Mr. B." Derek, Jane later wrote, had "a wonderful sense of humor," but at the same time he had a "strong and forceful character" and was "honest to the point of brutality."

Derek's mission was to improve the value of Tanzania's parks and thereby perhaps improve the lot of ordinary Tanzanians. He was planning a new project to import park rangers from elsewhere temporarily into Gombe, where they would receive training in scientific data collection as a way of increasing their general professionalism. Rweyongeza Mwenera, a graduate of Mweka College of African Wildlife Management and Gombe's current park warden, was already starting a research project on the social associations of chimps living to the south of the Kasekela community. More generally, Derek expected that administrators and others associated with the parks, particularly foreign researchers and guests, should gain the respect of ordinary people in Tanzania, in part by respecting ordinary people's traditional sensibilities. Those sensibilities included modesty and also, in the case of the new students and researchers coming so casually into hard Africa from soft parts of the world, haircuts.

Haircuts were not as irrelevant as they might at first seem. President Nyerere was promoting a utopian political and social program of Ujamaa (Familyhood) that stressed government-managed agricultural development along with personal self-reliance and egalitarianism. Ujamaa would nationalize industries, create communal villages, break down class barriers, and promote the dignity of individuals. It also meant that Tanzanian leaders were required to maintain the highest moral standards in their dealings with ordinary citizens. "There must be a deliberate effort to build equality between the leaders and those they lead," Nyerere had declared in 1967. "For a Tanzanian leader it must be forbidden to be arrogant, extravagant, contemptuous, and oppressive." It was a grand moral vision, and perhaps Nyerere himself—known affectionately as Mwalimu, or Teacher—was the person most successful in embodying it. He went to church every Sunday. He seldom traveled about in big shiny cars with a large escort or group of bodyguards. He never wore ties or fancy suits or put carnations in the buttonholes of the simple jackets he did wear. He was not interested in personal pomposity, in other words, and he promoted a concept of modesty in dress and style for Tanzanian society at large. Unhappily, his reasonable thoughts on the subject were sometimes unreasonably interpreted and enforced—as when, in early October 1973, immigration authorities at Kigoma harassed two students just arrived from Stanford, one for his shorts, the second for her bell-bottom trousers, or when, around the same time, Kigoma police gave two Gombe staff members cold-water dousings for similar cases of sartorial malfeasance.

Derek may have been echoing Mwalimu's teachings on personal propri ety by wanting everyone at Gombe to have a decent haircut, and Jane quickly picked up the idea. As she noted in a July 5 letter to the family, Richard Wrangham had just come back from a term at Cambridge "WITH LONG HAIR." She had decided she would instruct him to "cut it or leave," add- ing, "How I loath this part of administration." And, as she wrote a day later to Derek, she was also firmly determined "to REFUSE" to allow elephant researcher Iain Douglas-Hamilton to visit Gombe, given his own tonsori- ally overextended condition.

At first Emilie did not really understand Mr. Bryceson's emerging role at Gombe. She felt protective of Jane, and when she saw Derek getting closer to Jane, she was suspicious. But she also realized what a privilege it was for them all to be there doing what they were doing. "That's why," she remem- bers, "I kept reminding the students all the time, all of us, even myself, that we couldn't change the world we were living in, that we were within the Tanzania National Parks, that it was a fine line to walk." And so, with Mr. Bryceson coming in one day, Emilie lined everybody up. "OK, guys," she said, "we're going to have haircuts."

Emilie worried that Jane was working too hard, and since Jane kept so much to herself and seldom complained, it was hard to know whether she was ill, had malaria, or was merely tired.

Derek likewise worried, and he thought Jane needed a vacation. He came into Kigoma on August 7 to attend some Parks Department meetings, and Jane met him there. The two of them paused in town after the meetings to locate an inner tube for Grub, so he could paddle his fishnets into deeper water. Derek had found a place that specialized in patching up old inner tubes, and that afternoon they sat down at the tire-patching place, patiently waiting and negotiating and waiting some more for the inner tube. But it took a very long time, and when they finally got into the boat and back onto the lake, it was dark. They revived themselves with ginger wine and toma- toes and then, as the round white face of the moon rose and cast its light across the black water, passionate kisses.

Derek returned to Dar es Salaam, and Jane and Grub followed for a full week's holiday. Grub had the time of his life, finding it liberating to roam and play on a beach where there were no baboons and chimpanzees to worry about and spending the best parts of his days searching through tide pools for shells, crabs, and little fish to feed to the bigger fish Derek kept in his aquarium. Jane found it hard to remember (as she wrote to him during her bumpy return flight to Kigoma) "spending a day like Sunday—just doing nothing except fun things—for <u>years</u>!" They had spent that afternoon in Derek's boat, riding out to the reefs through a rough sea and then snorkeling, but as Jane noted in a second letter accompanying the first (which was a rather generic note of gratitude), "You know, I would 100 times prefer to go on the sea in bad weather than not to go on the sea at all. It was much worse for you—you always have the sea & you can pick & choose. But just to see the corals again, & the fishes—just to smell that glorious tidal smell—to see the octopus & the worms & urchins & brittle stars. For me it was fantastic." Their final night together, she went on, was "sad, but it was happy too. I hated it when you had to go off out into the cold—of course, it wasn't cold but you know what I mean. It was so good to wake up & find you there so close and strong."

Writing a love letter was dangerous, of course, since both she and he were still married, if unhappily, to other people. "I shan't actually write more letters like this—there is no point," Jane went on in the same note. "You know it all, and there is always a risk. We don't want to spoil something that is beautiful & so ultimately good. We both would hate it."

In any case, they had very little time left before she had to leave for England and then Stanford. They spent a few glorious days together in September, including more snorkeling adventures at the reef—"a real piece of heaven," as Jane phrased it in a letter to Derek written hours after they had finally parted and while she waited with Grub in the transit lounge of Nairobi airport for their flight to England. Now she was left with "a broken watch, a beautiful pen, a suitcase full of carvings, boxes of shells, a book and the still warm feeling of kisses." Their time together was receding into the past, and she was once again pulling away with "a torn feeling, a sense of unreality—and the memories."

By the end of the month Jane was unpacking her bags in a rented house at 455 Seale Street, Palo Alto, a short drive in her rented car from the Stanford campus. It was a "really super house," she soon concluded (writing to Derek), with a garden that was especially notable for two fig trees that bore green figs and were also "fitted with birds & jet black squirrels—including a baby who can't climb properly yet. He is so funny. And a pair of exquisite humming birds." The yard was surrounded by a tall, dense hedge, creating enough privacy for her to sit outside in the morning sun "scantily attired" and write her first letter to Derek while noting that her sunburn and coral-reef scabs were almost gone and thinking how wonderful it would be if only he were there to enjoy the figs, the squirrels, and the hummingbirds.

The hummingbirds were zeroing in on a feeder that Jane set about moving closer to the house, by small daily increments, anticipating the pleasure that a spin and flicker of emerald at the window would bring to Grub, who was due to show up soon in Vanne's company.

By October 11, Vanne and Grub had arrived, and within a few days Grub started school. He hated the first day, cried on the second, and only reluctantly attended on the third—but returned home in great exhilaration, announcing to his mother, "You see, Jane, when the boys like you they fight you!"

He was reading, doing arithmetic, and painting. Besides fighting with other boys in his spare time, he made friends with two who lived just around the corner, and back at school he soon felt confident enough to resist the schoolyard bully. This was a person who seemed (as Grub told Jane, who recounted the words for Derek) "always naughty," and when he had spat onto a stone and then thrown it at people, Grub, who really hated spit, grabbed the stone and lobbed it onto the school roof. The bully rushed him, fists clenched, shouting, "Why did you do that?" But Grub stood his ground and stared intently at the unpleasant aggressor until he turned away.

Jane had a tape recorder, and that device, combined with first-rate secretarial assistance at Stanford, allowed her to buzz right through the piles of correspondence that had so weighed her down at Gombe. Life was still very hectic, what with the human bio lectures to produce, students to confer with, funds to raise, a chapter for a book and a memorial piece about Louis Leakey to write, visits to make, and talks to give. But she could always find time for the activity now central to her emotional life: communication with Derek, which included occasional long-distance phone calls and regular love letters, sealed and marked "confidential" and placed inside the envelopes of more businesslike letters. There was also even a physical rendezvous. Derek had been offered a weeklong guest lectureship at Rhode Island University around the end of November, which he was able to combine with brief talks about Tanzania in New York and then, on December 14, at the Stanford Faculty Club in California.

But this new love was leaving them both very unsettled. "I am so emotionally upset," Derek wrote on October 8, "that even ½ bottle of Black label would not put me to sleep. I cannot help thinking about you all the time. I don't know any way to love you—once started, you could not have stopped it or lessened it. You are here all the time, yet not here. Perhaps I'll end up by going mad! Maybe already a bit along that road?" "I long for the time," she declared back, "when I can see you, look into your eyes, feel your strong arms around me, kiss you, feel safe and so exquisitely happy in your love. We have so much to share & give each other. So much to talk about. No, it is not a dream, beloved. It is the truth we have both been waiting for." But their anguish over the pain of separation was complicated by concern about their approaching reunion. Certainly they both wanted to be together for the rest of their lives. That was the future they longed for, but how, in truth, could they seize it? They both worried over that, again and again and again, but with drastically different perspectives.

Jane was caught between the guilt of concealment and the fear of revelation—and of the suffering the latter would cause to those she cared about, particularly Hugo and Grub. "What am I worrying about?" she asked rhetorically. "The future, of course. Derek, Hugo—at least at the moment— is more dependent on me than he has ever been. Despite the Emmys, despite his recognition. If I am sharp with him he is abjectly miserable." Hugo was subject to terrible depressions, and she feared what he might be capable of. At the same time, he was changing, becoming more independent, losing interest, drifting away. Similarly, Derek's wife, Bobbie, had been spending more and more time in England, retreating from the African climate, which she found hard to take—and possibly from Derek as well. Therefore, Jane counseled Derek, they should be patient and trust in fate or providence. "We must either wait—wait for the passing of years to wreak (I hope) their change in him. Or for the benevolence of fate. My hopes, my faith, my trust—my life—are in the hands of the shooting stars, the wishbones, the ultimate & certain goodness of the providence which brought us together."

Derek had no desire to wait patiently or to trust in providence and the shooting stars. Instead, he pressed for action. He wanted Jane to leave Hugo as soon as possible, end her professional association with Stanford and America, and place herself under his protection and care. He had seen how exhausted she had been when she returned from the spring trip to California, and it was clear that she had been exploited and beaten down by those self-centered Americans. "Jane, oh Jane, my dearest," he wrote, "cannot you see now why I <u>hate</u> you going over to the USA for all this time in this way. Knowing that you will not look after yourself, knowing that those who should will not be looking after you, knowing that there are so many people who will take advantage of this, and seeing it all happen, just like that. Can't you see now why I get half crazy with concern and worry for you? Knowing that I should look after you properly." Derek distrusted and perhaps even disliked Americans, and while Jane was attached to Stanford and her American fame and financing, her professional associations with that far-off place seemed to him at best an irrelevant distraction. As for the extra money coming from her position at Stanford and her fundraising lectures in the States, well, "Damn money. I don't want you to go around chasing money. Leave this to me and we'll muddle along okay."

Derek was a lot more like Hugo than Jane appreciated at the time. Or was it that both Derek and Hugo were emotionally like most men? Hugo had been unnerved by Jane's success and fame and charisma—jealous, perhaps. She was inevitably exciting to others, invariably the center of attention, and thus forever drawing attention away from him. But Derek, with his own high status and great accomplishments, should not have been threatened by hers. No, Jane thought, Derek was simply misguided and misinformed. He did not understand. And so she reasoned with him. "You are right about parts of American society being evil—but you really need not fear for me!" she wrote, continuing on a positive note: "There are still good people. There are still great areas of wilderness—puma and coyote and grizzly bear. . . . And there are so many people who hate the decadence and who are fighting to preserve the American country from pollution and to try to reclaim the human dignity which is swamped literally swamped—in the decadence." As for her work at Stanford, she pleaded strongly in a later letter,

> Please try to understand that, whilst I may get a bit tired, I'm doing this because I LOVE it, and WANT to do it. The walls of this unique in the world chimp facility are up—it has taken 4 years of hard work—on & off—& they are up. The group of chimps [soon to be transferred there] has just produced its 2nd baby. The students are getting more & more bright, better & better people. I just begin to feel I've mastered the art of teaching. Derek—this is as much a part of me as the work at Gombe. Please understand. This is what is worrying me to distraction about your letters. Dearest, dearest, dearest Derek. I don't WANT to be stopped from doing this work, I'm not yet ready to stop from doing it—just as the efforts are bearing fruit.

But Derek's perspective was not subject to change through rational discussion. "You know my aim," he wrote. "It is to have you as my own, to present to the world and to [be] proud and happy. Nothing you can do can change this dream." Of course, that dream ultimately meant she would need to end her strange and irritating habit of disappearing into the cruel vastness of North America, and he was determined somehow, at some point, to stop that, no matter what she wanted. It was for her own good, and to protect her against the evils of the world was his essential right and duty as a lover and a man. "I will not allow this to happen to you again," he declared emphatically, perhaps even ominously, "—whatever I have to do to stop it.

This is where I am ruthless!! When I see something that has to be done, I do it. And I shall not again just allow you to go off and let yourself be subjected to the battery that you get in your USA trip. It is horrible for me to see. I could suffer lots of things but not this, and I will not let it happen again. Whatever I have to do to stop it, I will do."

35

*Things Fall Down —
and Sometimes Apart*

1974

HAVING RETURNED to East Africa by the first days of 1974, Jane and Grub made a brief safari to Ruaha National Park with Derek Bryceson. As they were flying to the park in a four-seater Cessna, a small plume of smoke began rising out of the instrument panel. They observed that writhing little spirit for the next forty-five minutes, until at last the Ruaha River and the ranger camp, rest house, and landing strip hove into view. Just as they were about to land, however, a herd of zebras wandered onto the strip. The pilot pulled up, but instead of circling and waiting for the zebras to clear off, he lost his nerve and dropped down for a crash landing on the far side of the river.

Derek, seated in the copilot's seat and now feeling the rapid descent, looked up from the instrument panel to see a scattering of rough earth, brush, and trees and said, "You're not going to try to land here!"

The pilot said, "Yes!"

Derek shouted, "Well, *don't!*"

At Gombe the year 1974 began quietly, with a temporarily small group of foreigners — two researchers, five students, and Emilie — in residence. The two researchers were graduate students from the University of Edinburgh, and both were interested in sex. Caroline Tutin was finishing a study of sexual behavior among the chimps, with a special interest in consortships, while David Anthony Collins was starting to look at sexual consortships among the baboons.

As Caroline was confirming, chimpanzee sex is often promiscuous. The classic case is a single female who, having entered the fertile phase of her cycle and advertising that fact with a pink and swollen perineum, attracts a rowdy scrum of males. A second sexual style for chimpanzees—the consortship—is, for a few hours to several days, monogamous and more serene. In a consortship, one lucky or clever male, not necessarily high-ranking, finds himself near an attractively fertile female at a moment when the other males are distracted or elsewhere, and he persuades her to accompany him on a quiet honeymoonlike safari. Persuasion is not automatic, and thus the drama opens on the theme of male certainty overcoming female uncertainty. He gazes at her significantly and shakes a leafy branch, a gesture that at Gombe means something like *Follow me*. The female may be reluctant or perhaps distracted by a young offspring. The eager male shakes the branch again, with greater emphasis. Possibly her reluctance or distraction continues, and he rattles the branch a third time. If she continues to ignore his signal, he may bound over and pummel her with his hands and feet. In that way, oscillating between positive and negative reinforcement, the certain male persuades the uncertain female to follow. He leads her—and her young offspring, if any—on safari into an unfamiliar part of the forest, where he is less likely to run into the other males and she is more likely to cling to him for protection. In this cozier place, he becomes her protector and even her gentle friend, and in return she mates with him exclusively. He grooms her studiously and submits on occasion to her minor inclinations (to sleep later than usual, perhaps, or to go here and not there), and when they do have sex, it is much quieter, less frantic, and far less frequent than what she would expect ordinarily. Perhaps they mate only five times a day.

The Gombe baboons have somewhat comparable consortships, and Tony Collins, who had originally wanted to study chimps, by 1974 had realized that he loved the baboons. He found that his subjects offered every bit as much soap opera as the chimps and even, particularly with their feisty, uncoordinated infants, plenty of comedy. Unlike chimps and their often confusing temporary group formations within the larger stable community, baboons live in more obvious *troops,* where all members remain in continuous visual or auditory contact with one another, making their social world smaller and easier for human observers to comprehend. Also, baboons grow up much faster than chimps. "If you take an old Charlie Chaplin film and run it at normal speed," Tony once told me, "you have chimp life. If you run it at fast-forward, you have baboon life."

Tony and Caroline compared notes and shared anecdotes with Emilie and five Stanford undergraduates: John Crocker, Julie Johnson, Jim Moore, Lisa Nowell, and Sara Simpson. New Year's Day was a holiday, of course, and everyone assembled groggily "upstairs" for a special brunch, during which Tony and Julie Johnson demonstrated ancient mandarin dueling tech-

niques. That was fun. At the same time they were anticipating the appearance of three more Stanford students in about a week and Jane's arrival,
along with Grub and possibly Mr. Bryceson, in five days.

Julie Johnson had been staying in Jane's beach cabin during her absence,
and early in the evening of January 5, in anticipation of Jane's return, she
rushed around the cabin cleaning and straightening up. Then, instead of
tossing all the trash onto the trash heap, she made an efficient shortcut to the
long-drop latrine and pushed everything through the circular passageway.
Having tidied up the cabin and moved her belongings back to her little aluminum rondavel, Julie began preparing for a hut-warming party. She had
some rare Vermont cheddar her parents had just mailed out, and she had recently purchased in Kigoma an expensive quart bottle of Black & White
whisky, a luxurious alternative to the usual Tanzanian Konyagi. She found
some tin cups to drink from. She pulled out the cheese. Where was the
whisky?

Julie and some of her recently arrived guests, flashlights in hand, re-
traced her footsteps to the latrine. "Yeah, it's down there!" someone confirmed, shining a flashlight into the hole. "I can see it!" The party took place
anyway, with spirits on loan from Lisa Nowell, and soon Julie was inspired
to issue a reward for anyone who could retrieve the fallen bottle: "OK, anyone who gets the whisky out of the *choo*, I'll match that bottle."

Next morning, January 6, Tony, Julie, and Lisa took the boat out with
the intention of fetching Jane and Grub from the Kigoma airport. On the
lake, they turned south, revved up the motor, and began the journey—only
to be waved down at the ranger post and park headquarters at Nyasanga, a
half-mile south of the research station. When they beached the boat, they
heard the news just in over the rangers' two-way radio: a plane carrying
Jane, Grub, and Mr. Bryceson had crashed.

The plane was wrecked, but Jane, Derek, Grub, and the pilot survived, although Derek was damaged by way of some cracked ribs. Within a short
while, Jane and Grub were back at Gombe and Derek was in Kigoma, de-
tained for a few days on Parks business. As for Julie Johnson and the fallen
bottle of whisky, she watched the flickering of flashlights on the trail at night,
signs of people on their way to try out various contraptions—mechanical
pinchers and snatchers and so forth—until, on January 17, Jim Moore and
Caroline Tutin finally retrieved it by borrowing Grub's fishing pole, fashioning a loop at the end of a line, skillfully lowering the loop down to the
right spot, and drawing it tightly around the neck of the bottle. The precious object was swaddled in toilet paper, carried down to the dispensary,

and swabbed and sterilized with methylated spirits, and after a thorough inspection, its contents were pronounced fit for human consumption. "The verdict," Emilie wrote in her journal, "was that 12 days seasoning in a choo did not impair the flavor of the whisky."

Jane wrote to her mother about the crash only several days after the event, reassuring her in a letter from Gombe that it was all really "a silly thing" and apologizing for the tardiness of her letter with the notion that "I thought I couldn't tell you because you'd all worry—I thought I'd tell you later. But now I find that the crash has been in the papers and on the radio—and it was STUPID of me to think you wouldn't hear about it from someone else."

Once she realized the plane was going to crash, Jane went on to explain, she had remained "quite calm and collected. I did not even have time to feel frightened. I only remember, as we raced down at 80 mph onto this tiny space where it was obvious we'd hit a tree (which we did) that soon I'd be dead. So I held onto Grub tighter." The plane dropped and bounded onto rough ground, losing a wheel, hitting the tree and a termite mound, and then careening, skidding, spinning, ripping, and finally grinding to a stop onto a buckled wing. Jane was able to push open a door before it had fully stopped, and Derek reached up and turned off the engine. The pilot said, "Jump out quickly—the plane is going to burst into flames," and he leaped out and vanished. Jane unbuckled Grub and instructed him to climb out the door and run away from the plane, which he did. But Derek, already severely limited by his paralyzed legs, was stuck in his seat, which had been wedged into place by fallen luggage, while his door, on the downward side of the plane's resting tilt, was jammed shut. Jane desperately clawed away at the luggage, hurling the pieces aside. "Have you lost your purse or something?" Derek asked mischievously, looking back to smile at his little joke. She climbed out Grub's door while Derek dragged himself up and through the pilot's door, headfirst, and dropped on the ground.

By the time everyone had crawled out of the wreck, the park staff, who had seen the crash from their side of the river, had waded across (in spite of the crocodiles) and rushed to the plane, expecting to haul out mangled bodies. Relieved to see everyone generally intact, they gathered up the luggage and began carrying it back across the river, with Jane and Derek and Grub following.

After reaching the Ruaha rest house, the three of them changed into dry clothes and then relaxed with cups of tea, reflecting on the interesting fact that they were still alive. The crash in fact may have had a salutary effect on Jane. As she expressed the idea in her letter home, "Since so few people ever crash at all, and certainly so few survive the kind of ruined plane that we got out of—we feel confident that we are now safe. The people here have been telling us that God wanted us to finish our work to help them in Tanzania. It is like an omen, and I feel quite strange about it." She continued: "For me, Africa has always been the ruling force of my life, I suppose. Now it is even more than that. Lots of things seem to have fallen into shape after nearly being dead—you know, you suddenly realize that it could happen (death, I mean) at any moment. So [you think about] what is best to do with the life entrusted to you."

Among the things seeming to fall into place was the issue of what to do about Derek and Hugo, a conflict that had previously left Jane hesitant, uncertain, and counseling patience. During a romantic walk out to look at elephants on the evening after the crash, she agreed with Derek that they should divorce their spouses and then marry.

At the same time, however, they were facing a complicating press of events. The crash would soon become a news item on the radio, forcing both of them to act decisively. Derek would have to explain the situation to his wife, Bobbie, and two grown children. Jane would have to meet with Hugo and describe the new reality to Grub. And the vision of endless explanations, recriminations, tears, anger, trauma, pain, and divorce left Jane enervated and in a state of inner turmoil.

She communicated some of her anxieties to Derek in a mid-January letter. The weather had been particularly dramatic and capricious at Gombe, she wrote, and while "snuggling into the bedclothes and wishing so much you were there, snuggling beside me," she had gone to sleep listening to the rain "pounding on the roof and the wild clamour of the waves." She added, "We've had grey skies & seen terrific storms sweeping towards us over the lake, with rumblings of thunder and sizzling lightning—and then, by a strange magic, the sky has turned from glooming black to white fluffy clouds and blue with no rain." Indeed, the great storms and magical clear spells at Gombe now seemed rather like the dramatic interior weather of their lives. "How will you be feeling when you get this letter? Worried, anxious, tense—or something of the sort. A major crisis? A worrying atmosphere? Or will you be feeling happy about things, happy to get a letter, thinking about the next time we can see each other? Why doesn't our telepathy work better—Why don't I <u>know</u>?"

As an alternative to telepathy, a two-way radio was installed in Jane's beach cabin, supposedly to enable emergency communications with the outside world but also to improve her personal communications with Derek while he traveled around the country on Parks business. Naturally the personal communications could never be *too* personal, since anyone else with a radio set would be able to eavesdrop. "I almost hate the radio telephone," she wrote in frustration to Derek on February 26,

> because we can't <u>say</u> anything. Or even find out anything. . . . Oh dar-
> ling. I do wish I knew if something additional is wrong and, if it is, that
> I could be with you more concretely than right now. I'm afraid my set
> won't work. The aerial looks <u>so</u> low. I'll try it on Thursday if I have a
> battery. I keep praying and praying that things will not go too wrong. If
> they do, we shall never be able to forgive, let alone forget. It would put a
> very, very heavy burden on our relationship. What is it I am frightened
> of? I don't know.

Among the things she feared was the possibility that Hugo or his mother, Moeza, would move to take Grub during a divorce. Fortunately, Hugo was so far behaving reasonably. In fact he had been in West Africa that January, filming the story of an attractive young woman, Stella Brewer, who was try-ing to return formerly captive chimps confiscated in Gambia to a forest in nearby Senegal. When he returned around the start of February, he told Jane (as she relayed to Vanne in a February 10 letter) that they had to "make up our minds about the future," wondering "would I leave Gombe for him." It had been an "upsetting" discussion, not surprisingly, but nevertheless they finally "covered everything & decided, quite calmly, how it wasn't any good." As Jane noted in the same letter, she suspected that Hugo had devel-oped a romantic interest in Stella Brewer. He had been "so cheerful, & so enthusiastic about Stella & all her family, that I feel sure something is up. Which could be <u>super</u>. Only he wouldn't say."

Of course Jane also feared the psychological effect a divorce could have on Grub. But he seemed to be "very happy about things" and in a "super & calm mood." Many of Grub's playmates at Gombe had fathers with extra wives, and Grub had said he thought it reasonable for Hugo to take a second wife, who could take vacations from wifehood whenever Jane went to Ndutu and whenever Hugo came to Gombe.

Once those painful discussions with Hugo were over, the air (as Jane concluded optimistically for Vanne on February 10) was "much clearer & I really think that all may be well." Actually, though, her conversation with Hugo had been rushed, and she was not able to tell him everything until a month later, in early March—when he once again behaved sensibly. "I've told Hugo, one more step," Jane reported back to Derek on March 4. "He wrote me such a nice, nice letter (before I told him the one more step). It made me cry all over again and hate—I don't know what I hate."

But while her fears about Hugo's reaction were proving unfounded, there were now so many other things to worry about. A pain in Grub's tooth was waxing and waning by the end of February, and Jane worried about how she could get him to a dentist in Dar es Salaam—until she finally remembered that the mission hospital at Kabanga, 60 miles by taxi from Kigoma, had a dentist on staff, Sister Kate. Jane could not bear to see Grub in pain; her vision of pain in a dental office was exacerbated by memories of her own childhood dentist, who had been (as she once described him) a "torturer." So Emilie made the appointment with Sister Kate, and in the early morning of Friday, March 1, she and Grub set off in the rain for Kigoma, with Grub prone at the front of the boat like a figurehead, draped in a shiny plastic mac and gazing down into the water, obviously pleased about the adventure.

"Don't worry if I'm not back until eight o'clock," Emilie said. But Jane did worry when they had not appeared by seven-thirty and darkness was closing in. She had eaten supper alone, but at eight o'clock she walked over to the Mess, joining the researchers and students for a dessert of caramel custard. They chatted about many things in order to distract her from her anxieties and told her not to look at the clock, but she noticed that their eyes also strayed in that direction. By nine o'clock everyone was considering the many ordinary things that might quite innocently have delayed the boat's return. At last Jane, undone by a raging headache and occupied with a swirl of fragmentary thoughts and images too terrible to complete, returned to her cabin. She changed shoes and pulled out her strongest lamp, some tools, and a rope, intending to walk down the beach to the ranger post, where the Parks boat was tied up, borrow it, and drive slowly to Kigoma, looking for a drifting, broken-down vessel. She was nearly overwhelmed with fear and dread by then, and Tony Collins and Grant Heidrich (recently arrived from Stanford) agreed to accompany her. The three of them set off for the ranger post, walking along the shore—but after about ten minutes they heard a boat. They shouted, and then they heard Emilie's voice cry out that everything was all right.

Back on shore and up at the Mess, Grub was eager to fill everyone in. He had had two teeth removed, upper left and upper right molars, as everyone could see when he opened his mouth, and he had had a super time because he had been so good. Emilie confirmed that he had been "absolutely fantastic, and Sister Kate couldn't believe how good and brave he'd been." He had even led Sister Kate by the hand to help her develop the X-rays. Then, on the taxi drive back to Kigoma, he had seen a clump of giant bamboo alongside the road, and remembering that Jane was looking for bamboo to hang curtains on, he asked the driver to stop so they could cut three enormous poles (far too big, unfortunately, for curtain rods). That delayed them, but mainly they were so late getting back because Sister Kate had been tied up by an emergency and thus was not able to look inside Grub's mouth until late in the afternoon.

It had been a nice little adventure for the boy but a nightmare for his mother. As Grub slept that night, Jane lay wide-awake, "partly worrying about you" (she later wrote to Derek), partly worrying "about Hugo, about things in general, and partly relief from the worry about Grub." She finally wrapped herself in a blanket, fixed herself a "minute tot of Biscuit," and went down to the beach to observe "the most spectacular storm" she could ever remember.

At first everything had been serene, a windless warm night domed by black sky and twinkling stars. But over the lake, Jane could see, the sky was "inky black, and the lightning was almost continuous over the Congo mountains. Flickering, flickering, flickering to the north, to the south, to the west." Suddenly there came a "blinding fork streaking down to the mountains, or far out into the lake, followed by crashes of thunder that were deafening and made me jump in spite of anticipating them. And still the stars twinkled overhead, and no breath of wind to stir the warm night air." The whole scene was "quite glorious and very awe inspiring and I longed for you to be there to share the sheer majesty of it." A half-hour later, though, "the stars were swallowed up, one by one, faster, faster. And then I heard the wind coming. A far off whispering that quickly became a roaring sound. And the flat, gentle lake erupted with little wavelets that soon were crashing breakers as the wind came whistling and raging across the lake."

Jane raced back to the cabin to draw canvas over the open windows, anchor various papers, and place other things under cover, and she had barely completed these precautions when "the first great drops of rain began hurtling out of the wind and the sky and the thunder was right overhead, and I was sure I could hear lightning hissing into the turbulence of the water." After a final kiss to her sleeping son tucked beneath his covers in the other room, she crawled back into her own bed and imagined herself lying there comforted by Derek, the two of them "listening together to the voice of the elements—a Voice which seemed to be reminding us that we were but pawns, that we should act as best we could on the promptings that came, that we should make the most of the moves offered by That which is greater than us."

By the end of March, as Jane left for her spring term at Stanford, the situation with Hugo had "turned out well—amazingly and unbelieveably well," as she expressed it to Derek, writing on the flight out of Dar es Salaam after a long, silent goodbye through windows at the Dar airfield. And in Arusha, as the plane took on more passengers, she could look out the window once more and still imagine him clearly: Derek in his blue shirt, standing there looking at her as she looked back at him. "And the love in your eyes and my eyes, through the dirty old window, still so shining & clear that I expected a man who walked between us to pause & feel before him, as if he's seen a strand of spider web gleaming and glistening with beauty in the morning sunlight. That shows the dream-state I was in when I left you. All unreal except our love."

She spent a few days at home in Bournemouth, where her grandmother, Danny, was recovering from a bronchial pneumonia that had taken her, she told Jane, to the very brink—until Saint Peter pushed her back. Meanwhile, Hugo telephoned from Nairobi, gloomily updating Jane on the latest news concerning Stella Brewer (who had just sent him an ambivalent letter) and more positively agreeing that the divorce could be taken care of quickly in Holland. Then she left for America, flying BOAC through blue skies and turbulent air above a great sea of thick white clouds. "What can I do to shake off this terrible depression?" she asked herself (writing the question to Derek), then closing her eyes to soothe away the irritation brought by billows of cigarette smoke wafting back from the smoking section. She dozed, drank a cup of tea, attended to her business correspondence, reread Derek's latest love letters, and then transported herself into the paradise of her own imagination: all the wonderful sounds and sights that she and he would someday share.

But it was spring in California, a beautiful time in a hopeful place, and Jane was soon happy just to be among friends—David and Peggy Hamburg, for example, who warmly invited her over and took her out for family dinners—and with chimp people and the human biology students and Gombeites past, present, and future. "I saw John [Crocker] who arrived yesterday," she reported to Derek on Monday, April 1, "looking just as he did when I said goodbye to him in Kigoma! Dear John. That did me good. I saw both the Nancys, Merrick & Nicolson, and then the graduate students—Anne [Pusey], Barbara [Smuts] & Harold [Bauer]. And Cathy Pickford, who's doing weaning. And they were all so excited about their analysis, and Gombe news and things. It really was nice."

Jane had a room in the Stanford Faculty Club, on campus, and by her fortieth birthday, on April 3, with her first lecture over, she could look around and savor the experience of a California spring: blossoms bursting, birds warbling, a crisply fresh breeze drifting by. A hostess on the flight to California, recognizing her as the celebrity author of *In the Shadow of Man*, had presented her with a bouquet of carnations, which were still fresh and fragrant in her room. The woman who ran the Faculty Club had provided a bouquet of apple blossoms. And that morning, while walking to her office through bright sunlight, she met two interesting animals, a "beautiful" dog and a pigeon. The pigeon seemed "very tame" and looked "exceptionally brilliant with a glossy sheen of many hues," which reminded her of peacocks and then of Derek, which put her into a daydream, making her mildly disoriented, and so she took the wrong turn and had an "extra long walk which was nice!"

Derek had given her a bejeweled pendant, a fish. She could talk to the fish, which she wore all the time, or merely look down and experience "a warm & happy feeling" to see the little fellow there, "with his tail flirting and his little green eye winking." She also had her own richly imaginative mind as a place for retreat. As she had always been able to do, Jane could close her eyes and drift into a bright, dreamlike state, a self-induced trance, and thus become her own audience in one of what she called her "imagining sessions." She sometimes described them for Derek's benefit:

> You will be up—you will have finished on the radio—maybe you will have talked to Grub. Or, at least, you may have heard news of Grub. Perhaps you are in the little house, looking at your fish, or feeding them. Or perhaps you are already out & in the town. Or perhaps you are somewhere quite different. So let me imagine you here with me instead. At least I know where I am. So you come to me, and I can put my arms around you, and feel your hair under my hand, and kiss your warm alive lips and feel our love, through & through & through.

And then, of course, she waited for his letters to come. She saved every one, and she pored over them again and again, taking consolation from words that were—mostly—thoughtful, loving, and supportive. Though sometimes not.

On Good Friday, April 12, for example, she woke up feeling (as she soon reported back to Derek) "miserable." Then the sun shone warmly through her window, and she had some tea and settled down to take care of urgent professional correspondence. There was a knock on the door. Mail. A letter from Derek. She felt much happier. Then she read it and "felt much, much, much worse." She attempted to return to her work, but now she was unable to concentrate. "There are limits to self control," she wrote, and "right now I am so miserable, and lost, and lonely, and—yes, frightened. I do nothing, nothing, nothing but make people unhappy. What the hell is the point of my staying alive any more. It's been getting worse & worse & worse, and now when even you say I am cruel & make you unhappy for a stupid reason— Derek, how can I feel there is any point to anything any more. Hugo is unhappy, Bobbie is unhappy, Mum is worried, all kinds of other people will be—well, I don't know what they'll be." In addition to everything else, a beautiful rendering of Beethoven's Fifth Piano Concerto was being played on the radio while she wrote, and the slow movement always made her cry.

Jane endured many worries that spring, many anxieties, many fears, but her deepest and conceivably most rational fear was that Derek would turn away from her, or possibly turn her away from him. So far they had spent only a few days together on a few occasions, with a ten-day rendezvous in America the previous December their longest unbroken stretch together, and thus the sweeping intensity of the affair—conducted mainly at a significant remove, through heated correspondence and the occasional long-distance telephone call—was remarkable. It was equally remarkable that they were both risking so much on the strength of such a short and sporadic relationship, attracted and caught as they were by the idealized images they held of each other. They were happy, almost desperately so, whenever they spent time together, days as well as nights, but what if their idealized images of each other proved false or insufficient? "I sometimes dread that you expect too much," Jane had written a month earlier, "and that you will be disappointed and begin to regret the suffering that we are now causing. Yet it's too late to turn back."

Her fear that he would be disappointed had a particular focus, one that may have existed ever since—was it only a few months ago?—he had declared he would, for her own good, do anything in his power to break her ties with America and Stanford. The same conflict had arisen again, because as a result of persistent efforts by Dave Hamburg and other Stanford friends, Jane had been invited to give the keynote address at a meeting of the presidents of fifteen top American philanthropic foundations, who apparently wished to be told how to spend their money. It was an honor and an important opportunity. The problem was that this new commitment, already made on her behalf, would require Jane to stay in America another three days, until May 4, and Derek had already planned to meet her in London on May 1. In a rather agonized letter to her, he announced that he could hardly bear the further separation. He considered that sort of American conference a foolish waste of time anyhow, one more meaningless thing that kept his beloved on the other side of the ocean for far too long. He wanted her to break the commitment, and if that meant offending those who had made such an effort to bring the opportunity her way, so be it.

The deeper problem, as Jane understood—and feared—was his lack of interest in the American side of her professional work. She feared as well that such a lack of sympathy for her ambitions could easily become a destructive disregard for herself and the integrity of her desires. Or was it all simpler than that: a case of mere male possessive jealousy? "Oh darling—" she pleaded,

> don't you see what is going to happen if, when I miss you so much anyway, you make me feel guilty on top of that? Don't you see what will happen to the future if you always do that when I have to be away? Perhaps this was what was lurking in my mind when I wrote you a letter about being worried about being different to how you wanted me to be. I have never lied to you, I have never pretended to be what I'm not—I said, right at the beginning, that I would have to go on doing my work in America—because I felt it was important. . . . If, for as long as we live together, I cause you this kind of agony, how can it work out? If I start feeling like a criminal when I come here to do what I feel I have to do—how can it work out? Darling Derek—don't you see what I mean? I know you think America is wicked, that they are all out to exploit me. But don't you see what they have done for me too?

It was a season of great inner turmoil. But Jane always tried to keep her personal life private, and thus the researchers and students and staff back at Gombe only occasionally became aware of a few odd moods and only gradually cognizant of two important realignments. First they learned about Hugo. Later, about Derek. And while Jane privately struggled to bring some kind of order to her personal chaos, the general research operation at Gombe hummed along like a machine, as productive as ever.

Three new Stanford students had arrived at Gombe on January 11—Curt Busse, Grant Heidrich, and Kit Morris—and on January 26, Larry Goldman showed up as a postdoctoral researcher focusing on chimpanzee play behavior. His wife, Helen, also came, agreeing to serve as a caretaker and a teacher for Grub. As Jane reported in a letter home written around the first week of February, she was soon proving herself. Grub had had a "SUPER school with Helen. She is working VERY hard & he is reading like a dream. It's amazing. Helen is not too happy, but getting happier daily—& Grub is what is making her day."

Around the same time David Riss came back. David had completed his time at Gombe the previous summer, graduated from Stanford, and been accepted into medical school, but he was taking a year off to experience life and write up his research at Gombe for publication. He was available, in other words, and Jane invited him back, much to Emilie's delight. David was there by April 6, and he quickly joined forces with Curt Busse to study male dominance, aggression, feeding, and ranging behaviors. Later David and Curt concentrated their joint study on the life of a single male, Figan, and together the pair of determined humans managed to follow that one tolerant ape for fifty days straight ("from nest to nest": from when Figan stepped out of his nest in the morning to when he climbed back in at night), accumulating during that record-setting longitudinal observation a wealth of quantitative data eventually summarized in an article for the scientific journal *Folia Primatologica*.

Also during this period, Derek Bryceson decided that Gombe—and the overworked Emilie—could benefit from the help of someone who would take over the National Parks' aspect of administration. He had already tried, and failed, with an unsuitable male candidate, who was there briefly near the end of 1973 and made a quick mess. To Derek's credit, he now challenged tradition by choosing a woman for the job. Jane mentioned this move in a letter home postmarked January 16, 1974: "Derek is going to try & get us a girl Tanzanian this time—& help Emilie."

Women seldom took jobs or had careers in Tanzania at that time, and Marietha (Etha) Lohay was one of the very few women working in Parks. She was born on December 12, 1948, in the village of Mamaissa, in the Arusha region, to Lohay Massai, a farmer and trader in livestock who had three wives and fifteen children. Her mother, Boi, had four children; Etha was the youngest. As a young girl she took up embroidery as a hobby, but most of her time was spent looking after her father's cattle. She dreamed of becoming a nurse, but as she traveled from her small village to Dar es Salaam for secondary school, she would pass by Lake Manyara National Park and see all the animals. When she left school and got her first nursing job at a hospital, she quickly found that she did not like the sight of blood, and then, remembering all the interesting animals she had seen at Lake Manyara, she thought she would try working in the Wildlife Department. She went to the Ngorongoro Conservation Area and asked the conservator if any jobs were available. He said (as she remembers the conversation), "You would be the only lady around the men in the bush. It won't be convenient. Let me look for some other ladies who will be joining Ngorongoro Conservation, so you can be together with them."

He located two other ladies and then sent the three of them to Mweka College of African Wildlife Management to earn certificates. After the course was finished, they began working at Ngorongoro as guides, escorting tourists into and out of the crater. Later the three women decided to join Tanzania National Parks. Then, early in 1974, Etha was asked by the director, Derek Bryceson, if she would like to work at Gombe. She said, "Okay, but I haven't been there, so I would like to see the place first." She stayed at Gombe for two weeks around the start of the year, returned to Arusha to pack, and near the end of April the young, inexperienced, very shy and sweet-looking African woman took her place as the National Parks administrator, working alongside Emilie.

Etha stayed in her own little aluminum hut and ate dinner with the students and researchers. She soon felt comfortable there, and she found she liked everyone. The administrative work was "rather heavy," but a lot of people helped out. Dominic, the cook, was very kind. He would say, "Oh, what kind of food would you like to have? Can I prepare a nice egg bread for you?" or "Okay, let us go and have a cassava food at my place," and his wife would prepare that. And Sadiki Rukumata, the assistant cook, always asked Etha what kind of food she liked. Dominic and Sadiki were never gloomy. They kept on smiling. Then there was Anne Pusey, perpetually helpful and full of good advice. She was also very polite, and Etha liked her very much. Another person she liked was Craig Packer, who used to tease her but was also "cheering me all the time, laughing, smiling. He was very happy with me." Helen Goldman kept trying to improve her Swahili and so would ask, "Etha, what is this? What does this mean? How do you say this in Swahili?" Then there was Emilie, Etha's most important colleague, who was invariably supportive and always said things like "Hi, Etha, what are you doing? Is there any problem? What can I do for you?"

Derek Bryceson was Etha's boss, of course. She did not work that closely with him, but she remembers him as "not difficult." Perhaps he was for other people, but with her he was "quite okay." But Emilie remembers, still with some passion, the time Etha fixed up her hair for a party with the students, combing it out and frizzing it up a little. Mr. B. said, "Well, what are you trying to do? Afro-Americanize yourself?" Etha was a proud woman, and the comment made her very sad, Emilie could see, and that in turn made Emilie angry.

Derek could be brusque and authoritarian. He could be brutally frank. He could decide things without informing people or educating them about the logic behind his decisions. Some students thought he was remote, arbitrary, and unappreciative. But then, he had many responsibilities, many things to worry about. He was an important man.

Jane left America at the start of May, arriving in England by the fourth, spending a few days with the family in Bournemouth, and then meeting Hugo in Holland, where they applied for and were granted a divorce. As she wrote to Joan Travis in California, "Hugo & I went through with our plans—it took 5 mins in a courtroom in the Hague. We are great friends. Still."

When Jane returned to Gombe at the end of the month, she found that, as she soon wrote home, things were going "jolly well." There had been lots of births among the baboons, and the morale of the researchers was "very high." As for the new administrator, Etha Lohay, "everyone loves her." She worked "all the time" and seemed "efficient and clever." The students also appeared "very pleased" to hear about Jane's divorce from Hugo: "Not quite congratulating me, but jolly nearly!" One of them, Kit Morris, had had a "super" chimp observation, having watched two female chimps, Athena and Miff, steal a recently killed bushbuck away from a group of about ten baboons and then climb a tree to consume their bloody loot. A few minutes later, Figan (that "crafty fellow") showed up and, obviously not wanting the females to run away with the prize, approached submissively and begged obsequiously for half a minute until he could get close enough to grab the entire thing for himself. It was, Jane thought, "typical Figan."

Grub too seemed in very good spirits, and he was for the moment in less of a "fishing mood" and more of a "tree climbing mood." He was climbing around, jumping, and swinging on vines. Jane had decided to devote every Saturday evening to Grub, and on their first Saturday they sat on the beach and cooked supper over an open fire. Then they went back into the cabin, he got into bed, and she read to him from *The Lord of the Rings*.

The only problem was the rat—a very big rat, an "enormous RAT," who kept walking across Jane's bed as she tried to sleep. The rat multiplied, and by June the cabin was swarming with them. As Jane and Grub prepared to fly out to Ngorongoro Crater to spend time with Hugo, she instructed Emilie to set out a few rat traps in the cabin while they were gone.

At Ngorongoro, it was actually very good to see Hugo again. Now that he and Jane were no longer married, their relationship seemed a good deal more satisfactory. Hugo confided in her about his latest advances and retreats with Stella, and she gave him advice about how to deal with the situation. Jane wrote home on June 21, "It is such a relief to be just friends with him—I can't tell you. He keeps doing the things that used to make me feel so trapped & desperate—& I feel so happy that it doesn't matter any more. We are getting on famously, and it is super for Grub." Grub became ill at Ngorongoro, and it was cold there, but he still had a wonderful and exciting time, and he wrote all about the trip in his first rather grown-up missive to Vanne and Danny: "We kept on going out looking at hyenas. One got pierced by a rhino and then it was smashed onto the ground. It was crippled. Then there were some lions nearby. They started to kill the hyena because lions don't like hyenas. But all the other hyenas ran up to protect him & threatened the lions. He wasn't dead the next morning but we know he's going to die."

When Jane and Grub finally returned to the cabin at Gombe, they spent some time carefully locating the rat traps, none of which had been sprung. "And if someone had <u>wanted</u> to trap Grub's & my toes, they couldn't have arranged the traps more skillfully—Just under the bed, just hidden by curtains & bedspread," Jane wrote home. "It was so funny. However, so far no rats have been caught, at least no fingers & toes either—& I <u>think</u> the rat herself has gone."

As if it were a case of Biblical plagues, though, the rats were soon replaced by snakes. Gombe now seemed to be inundated with them. First there had been the unsettling experience of Emilie's visiting sister, who, while sitting meditatively in the *choo*, was confronted by a big cobra rearing up most alarmingly between her legs. She hopped onto the seat, jumped right over the snake, and burst out the door, running. Then a graduate student named Juliet Oliver, while working in her office, looked up and into the mouth of a enormous green snake of some kind. Finally, one of the researchers spotted the baboon Ebony confronting a coffin-headed black mamba. Gombe, as Jane summarized in a July letter to Derek, had gone "a bit snakey!"

On July 20 she flew off to another Wenner-Gren conference at Burg Wartenstein, this one on "The Behaviour of Great Apes: Perspectives on Human Evolution." She and David Hamburg had organized it, and three recent Gombe alumni—David Bygott, Pat McGinnis, and Bill McGrew—presented papers there. The Japanese team working in Tanzania to the south of Gombe, in the Mahale Mountains, was represented at the conference by Junichiro Itani and Toshisada Nishida, while all three of Louis Leakey's ape women—Jane, Dian Fossey, and Biruté Galdikas-Brindamour—were present. The conference, as Jane later characterized it for the family, "<u>really</u> was fantastic," and they had all most genially toasted Louis, wishing he could have been alive to see "his 3 girls all together at such a gathering."

Jane returned to East Africa by early August and spent eleven glorious days with Derek in Dar es Salaam and Ruaha National Park before dropping back into Gombe near the middle of the month. Curt Busse and David Riss finished up their fifty-day follow of Figan on the nineteenth, and so, as Jane wrote to Derek, "Figan probably feels neglected today!" At the same time Gombe was being visited, photographed, and generally immortalized by a glamorous American actress named Candice Bergen, who was trying her hand at photojournalism, having been commissioned by *Ladies' Home Journal* to do a piece on Jane of the Apes.

So the summer of 1974 slipped by, with Jane and Derek mostly apart and communicating by letter and over the two-way radio. Sometimes his radio voice emerged crisply, and sometimes it came in whistly and wavery, "as though," Jane wrote to him, "I were listening in a swoon with blood rushing past my ears in cycles."

By the start of October, Jane had flown off to California once more, leaving Grub with Vanne and the rest of the family in Bournemouth. Arriving with a high temperature and extreme congestion, she crawled into bed in her rented house at 1551 Walnut Street, Palo Alto. Soon, though, she was feeling better, enjoying the house, and sending Derek letter after letter. As ever, she loved teaching and her interactions with students. As ever, she took pleasure in experiencing and observing the natural world around her, even when it was small and nearly tame—a back-yard hummingbird, for instance, who "has found his feeder and comes so close—he has just been here, a tiny, quivering scrap of feather, his wings vibrating. And now he's flown onto a little branch, and is singing his funny whirring song—which might be pretty, if you could slow it down." And as usual when she and Derek were apart, Jane thought of him often. ("Sometimes when I'm looking at something beautiful, or listening, I imagine you are right beside me, & see your face, or [hear] your voice saying something, and then a big smile comes over my face, & I sit like a Chesire cat!")

The despairing moods that had sometimes gripped her so fiercely during her previous two times in California seemed mostly in the past, perhaps partly because Derek's letters were now much warmer and more positive. That October he was focused on the painful end of his own marriage, since Bobbie, having spent most of the year in England, was returning to Dar to proceed with the divorce. Although Derek's marriage had been on the decline before he met Jane, she continued to be pained by the thought of Bobbie's pain, finding it "hard to concentrate," as she wrote to Derek, and "wondering how it will go, how terrible it will be—for her—for you. How she will cope with having to taste once again the near presence of you. I feel so, so, so sorry for her. After all, I can imagine what I would feel like, losing you. I should curl up, inside, and quietly my spirit would stop living."

By the middle of the month, Vanne and Grub had come to California. Vanne looked worn and was suffering from a severe headache, because during the flight an overhead bin popped open and a two-pound tin of marmalade fell out and knocked her on the head. Grub, though, seemed in good spirits and arrived bearing a toy plane that dropped gunpowder-cap-activated bombs; Jane quickly bought more caps, and so he went around dropping bombs and then making friends with the boy next door. Still, Jane could not help worrying about how her divorce might affect him. Vanne reported that the boy had refused to talk about Derek in Bournemouth; when she had mentioned that Jane and Hugo were no longer married, Grub had adamantly insisted otherwise. Jane's conclusion (written to Derek): "You see, he really is troubled & upset." At the same time, though, "he talks happily about you to me—without any pretense," and she could only wonder and imagine what he really felt.

Vanne and Grub had been in California only briefly when Jane, over-worked as usual, fell ill again. Perhaps, she thought, it was a resurgence of her old malaria. In any case, as she reported to Derek, "I simply felt horri-ble the evening before, simply awful all day yesterday." And yet she kept on working. She gave two lectures, met with students to discuss their various projects and concerns, and finally "came home & collapsed!"

At the end of the month she was still feeling ill, "all hazy" and "can't seem to properly wake up," but nonetheless she climbed onto a plane bound east—for a frenzied series of dinners, interviews, lectures, lunches, meet-ings, and symposiums in Philadelphia, New York, and Chicago, before re-turning to more of the same in California. Jane was dreading the pressured parts of the trip, but at least now, on the plane, she could buckle herself in and seize a peaceful moment alone: close her eyes, withdraw from the rush and whirl of plans and obligations, the thoughts and memories and anticipa-tions of "doctors, lectures, dinners, & not being 100% & having to buy a dress," and focus instead on pleasant, meditative images of a peaceful future with the love of her life. The flight was full, every seat taken. But as the plane raced and lifted and the planet turned, Jane, still exhausted and ill, smiled quietly to herself and pressed a ballpoint pen against a sheet of plain white paper. "At the moment you will be in Gombe," she began. "I wonder how it is going."

She wondered about so many things. She wondered about Etha and Tony, and about Gilka, poor dear Gilka, with her swollen, fungus-infected nose. She wondered whether Ebony would make a good alpha male for Beach Troop. And also how Freud and Fifi were doing. Then, having won-dered, she began wishing. She wished the trip east was over, for example, instead of merely beginning. And she wished so much that Derek could be there sitting next to her, at that moment, smiling his sweet smile and looking at her with those bright eyes. "There are times," she continued, "when I long for the wide African skies and clean air, and the animals so much that tears come to my eyes. Africa. And now Africa is inextricably interwoven with thoughts of you so I cannot think of the country without thinking of you. Though the reverse is not true! I love you."

36

Domesticity and Disaster

1975

LEAVING GRUB in the hands of the family in Bournemouth, Jane met Derek in London soon after Christmas, and together they flew to Dar es Salaam.

She reached Gombe by January 3, 1975, and by the middle of the month she was, in a letter to the family, wishing Vanne a happy January 24 birthday and reassuring Grub that the fish in his aquarium were still alive and much bigger. The fish known as Spotted Jane had gotten "quite big," and both the eels were "fine" and seemed "to like one another very much." It was lonely there without Grub, Jane continued, and indeed life felt very odd without him. She found herself frequently whispering in the cabin at night, imagining him there in his bed, asleep.

But the big news right then had to do with one of Jane's favorite people at Gombe, Emilie, who had recently been admitted to the human biology program at Stanford and was scheduled to leave Gombe at the end of May. Emilie had already begun her own research project. "I always thought she would," Jane declared proudly, and she concluded the letter with a pleasant bit of gossip: "Don't mention to <u>ANYONE</u> who might know the people — but she & Dave Riss are <u>very fond</u> of one another."

After returning to Africa at the end of January (accompanied by his newly hired British tutor, Simon Stuart), Grub spent the first week of February with his mother in Dar es Salaam. Jane's quiet civil marriage to Derek may have taken place during that week, and she began moving some of her things into his house at 99 Old Bagamoyo Road. She also delivered eleven hours of lectures at the University of Dar and attended to a few Gombe business matters — and to a few small domestic matters, such as the fleas on Derek's little dog, a silky Pekingese named Beetle. Then, after someone's big dog killed the peacock belonging to President Nyerere, she began writing her letters with a peacock-quill pen.

By February 9, Jane and Grub were back at Gombe, where a new spirit of domesticity was inspiring renovations on her cabin. The walls of a lengthwise corridor were knocked down and some crosswise walls were extended, which ultimately increased the passage of light and air and the use of space. Her old study had been a small room across the corridor from her old storeroom. It had been (she wrote home) "so tiny & claustrophic—whatever I did, it was horrid." But with the corridor walls mostly gone, the cabin was "cool & lovely now," and she could sit in her new combined study and storeroom and "look out at the ferns & things, cool and green." The bedrooms as well were bigger, and Grub now had the space to build a feather, shell, and bone museum he called the Pit. At the same time, all the little domestic accoutrements the Bournemouth family had at one time or another contributed as gifts—ceramic badgers and hedgehog, dishcloths, mugs, napkins, tea cozy, tea towels—were thoughtfully set in place.

Jane still stayed up most nights until one or two in the morning, picking and sorting and rattling away like a factory worker at an assembly line of paperwork, but she no longer felt overwhelmed by it. And by placing a little food outside each evening, she could work and simultaneously be haunted by some lovely apparitions drifting in and out of the shadows and moonlight: civets, genets, and a beautiful white-tailed mongoose who would come sniffing right up to the kitchen window.

Derek arrived near the end of the month, bearing gifts from Dar, including a typist's chair, making Jane's office "fantastic now," as she wrote home, and "fit for kings & queens." He also brought more objects for the beach cabin domestication project: decorative bits of coral and shells, baskets, curtain material, mounted posters for the walls.

Most importantly, he brought gifts for Grub's birthday, which was celebrated three days early, on March 1, because that was a Saturday, when the students and researchers had the afternoon off and could enjoy the party. It started as a bright and sunny day, and since Grub had already gotten his biggest present, a new fishing rod, he used it to fish all morning, catching one big enough to feed Jane and Derek at lunchtime. Jane spent most of the morning drawing his birthday card, five pages on the subject of fishing; and then, at three in the afternoon, the birthday party began. It included apple bobbing with *strychnos* balls (hard-shelled, tennis ball–sized fruits of a certain *Strychnos* species at Gombe, favored by the chimps), a scavenger hunt, a sack race, a dizzy game of blindfolded stick-the-pin-on-the-fish, and prizes of chocolate squares. Then Jane cut the cake. Derek had brought along some Tanzanian whisky, and Jane thought the cake was particularly good with a bit of that splashed over, though Grub took his piece plain. Then Derek, Jane, and Grub ambled back to the cabin, sat on the veranda steps to try some apple pie, and went for a swim. Finally, just before teatime, Grub opened his other presents: fishing net, fishing line, fisherman's knife, pen-knife, a few toy cars, and Legos from President Nyerere.

Jane described Grub's birthday celebration to the family in England four days later, by which time the weather had shifted from clear and sunny to gloomy and wet. Ever since the party, in fact, it had been raining—or, as Jane wrote, "It has rained & rained & rained. Floods in the mess, waterfall by the house, leaks in the roof, drenched people, drenched chimps, drenched baboons." Figan and Faben, after a particularly wet and cold day, had constructed a bigger night nest than usual and then climbed in together, cuddling up and sleeping "in contact." It was "amazing," Jane thought, a behavior never seen before, and the person who saw it was Emilie, who (Jane reminded her readers) would be leaving to study at Stanford at the end of May. "I'll miss her," Jane remarked. "She is a _really_ good egg. She follows & follows. . . . Having got back, soaked, from one follow, she went out again. After my own heart!"

Jane was immobilized by malaria during the second half of March and lay in bed sweating and shivering and drinking orange juice. A recently arrived student from Stanford, Michelle Trudeau, located some soup, and Jane started drinking that. Derek showed up and gave her more soup. On Monday, March 24, he took her back to Dar es Salaam, where he thought she would recover more quickly, and she did seem to improve rapidly there. She spent a morning wandering quietly through tide pools, another morning swimming at the coral reef. She and Derek caught some interesting fish to accompany the fish already in his aquarium, and then, at the local dog pound, they found a suitable companion for Beetle. Spider, as Jane wrote home early in April, was "_exactly_ the dog we have been looking for." She was about nine months old, small, shorthaired, and pale yellow; she smiled and vocalized a lot, and looked very "_pretty_."

Jane, seemingly recovered, returned to Gombe with Derek by Friday. They found Grub "very perky" and the cabin "spin & span & ship shape," and together they all observed Easter with a nice dinner. But on the Monday after Easter, March 31, Jane felt very ill once again—some kind of "gastric flu," possibly, which made her very weak, unable to eat or move around or do much of anything.

She was "miraculously" better on April 3, her forty-first birthday, and she, Derek, and Grub celebrated the occasion privately, cooking a fish-and-cheese-sauce dinner and enjoying a fruit pie for dessert. Grub had drawn a chimp card for her birthday and written a story about a big battle between Vikings and Saxons, and after the dinner and the pie were finished, Jane felt content and really herself once again. Just fine. The next evening she celebrated her birthday a second time, with the students and researchers, everyone assembling at the Mess for a "sumptuous repast." But while she was "madly celebrating," she was "struck down again"—and now forced to pretend otherwise for Derek's sake, since he "simply HAD to leave. Poor man, he had cancelled all kinds of vital things to be with me so much and try to get me better in Dar!"

With Derek gone, she spent two more days flat and helpless in bed; a third day in bed, eating a little, feeling slightly better; and a fourth quietly sitting up and recuperating, walking around, eating a bit of porridge for breakfast and scrambled egg and toast for lunch.

Jane described her illness to the family in England in a letter postmarked April 9. By then she was well enough to attend to some chores, the most pressing of which was the production of a paper on chimpanzee intercommunity relations, due to be a chapter in a book summarizing the previous summer's Wenner-Gren conference. By the final few days of April the paper was "finished!" as Jane pronounced in a hasty note to the family, written a few sleep-rounded hours after she had cut and taped the thing into final draft form and crawled into bed to review the result at 4:30 A.M. Some thirty-one pages of single-spaced text plus tables and references, it was, she concluded, "very interesting." If only she had not been working in such a "frenzy," she would have "really enjoyed working on it," and in fact she had anyway. "Much too human, the chimps! And we know so much more about inter-community interactions than I thought we knew." Jane had been ill during most of the month, she admitted, and therefore had become rather gaunt, but now, she assured everyone back in England, "You'll be pleased to know I'm fatter again, after getting so thin!"

By May 1 she could declare positively to her California friend Joan Travis, "Whew! I have emerged!" But she was also finishing a major section of Gombe's annual report as well as putting the final touches on an article she and Derek had written for *Africana* magazine on the subject of poaching and trophy-hunting. She was eyeing a pile of correspondence, around two hundred letters requiring her thoughtful response. And she needed to prepare for the regular field assistant seminars, as well as for meetings with chimp people, baboon people, mother-infant and feeding behavior people, and a series of "catching-up, making-up-for lost ground talks with all the students." The students numbered eighteen just then, counting the graduates. Two new graduate students (Richard Barnes and Barbara Smuts) had come onboard that March and were now working alongside another six already established graduate researchers (Tony Collins, Helen Neely, Juliet Oliver, Craig Packer, Ann Pierce, and Anne Pusey) as well as nine Stanford undergraduates (Jim Baugh, Carrie Hunter, Phyllis Lee, Susan Loeb, Emily Polis, Joan Silk, Kenneth Stephen Smith, Michelle Trudeau—with Emilie Bergmann) and a tenth undergraduate from the University of Dar es Salaam (Adeline Mrema).

Then Grub fell ill. In a letter dated "May 3 or 4," Jane reported to the family that he had been "collapsed on his bed" for the past four days. "Poor little scrap," she declared, he had been prostrate with a "horrible cough, fever going up and down," and was "limp and half the time (bad luck for me) irritable." She was doing her best to instruct him in "the art of being a grateful invalid rather than a crusty one," but with little success so far. Perhaps he had picked up whatever evil pathogen she had just jettisoned, or possibly he was wrestling with a different disease altogether, since his cough was so much more severe than hers had been.

A terrible catastrophe unfolded on the afternoon of May 12. A water taxi filled with people and chugging along the lake past the research station, about 200 yards from shore, caught fire, exploded, and capsized. Several people on the shore heard the explosion, and as Emilie remembers, she, Tony Collins, Helen Neely, and Steve Smith climbed into the little research boat and raced out to the site of the disaster. By the time they reached it, the wooden vessel was upside down, drifting, looking to Emilie like a big brown whale. They began diving into the water, trying to pull people out. But people living along the lake generally did not know how to swim, and the water taxi had a roof, which meant that many passengers were trapped in an ugly swarm of baggage and bodies between the inside of the boat and the underside of the roof, or, if they escaped from there, were sinking.

Emilie and Steve dove into the water, pulled people out, and handed them off to Tony and Helen, who attempted mouth-to-mouth resuscitation. Emilie and Steve would catch their breath while balancing on top of the wooden boat, dive back in, pull more bodies out. But no one survived. The water was far too deep to dive down and reach the bottom, but it was also almost perfectly clear, and even without goggles Emilie could look down and see beyond a screen of fine bubbles the scattering of children and adults and pots and baskets, maybe a sewing machine, all strewn on the bottom of the lake. It was the saddest thing she had ever seen.

And was it another knot in the same strand of evil fate or bad luck that brought—a week later, at around 11:30 on the night of Monday, May 19,

1975—a 30- to 40-foot-long open boat carrying a gang of forty armed men onto the pebbled shores beneath the ranger station and park headquarters at Nyasanga?

The forty intruders, dressed in gray military fatigues and carrying rope, hand grenades, and AK-47s, stepped through the moonlight and mist and spread onto the murk of dry land, stabbing the night with head-mounted spotlights and barking in French and an African language, possibly Lingala. Nyasanga, half a mile south of the research station, was home to three rangers and their families as well as two researchers, Americans Ann Pierce and Jim Baugh, who were studying the southern community of chimps. The invaders spent a few minutes there, capturing two of the park rangers and binding them with rope. The third escaped, while the panicked screams of the rangers' families alerted the Americans, who stumbled into the night to investigate just as the men and their two captives got back on the lake, the big boat noisily churning water with a pair of outboard motors and heading north. The Americans found the third ranger, who told them to flee, and so, after hastily snatching a few essentials from their huts, they retreated into the hills—but then, reconsidering, started moving north through the forest, planning to warn people at the research station.

The boat and the forty men were faster, scraping onto the pebbles below the staff village a few minutes before midnight. Upon hearing the sound of a motor above the surf, the night watchman, Venas Garaba, descended to the beach, where he was overwhelmed by the gang, who pointed their AK-47s and demanded in rough Swahili to know where the *wazungu*, the white people, were. Venas, once described as effeminate ("simpered and always spoke in a high falsetto") and fearful ("so afraid of walking around at night that his voice trembled in the dark") proved himself full of courage. *There are no white people*, he said. They demanded that he tell them where the director of the research center lived. *There is no director*, he insisted. But then someone noticed a flicker through trees, and so a smaller party of men, dragging Venas along, moved quietly across Kakombe stream and up the path to the source of the light, which was a lantern in Emilie Bergmann's little aluminum rondavel, illuminating her desk and papers and typewriter as she stayed up late working.

They burst inside, and after a vigorous struggle tied her hands behind her back with rope. Then, pulling and prodding the terrified Emilie, they continued up the path. The next hut they reached belonged to Tony Collins, who happened to have left a day earlier, on vacation with Juliet Oliver at Ruaha National Park. With bright lights the men peered through the window mesh and confirmed that the hut was deserted.

They reached a T-junction in the trail, turned right, and arrived next at the hut of Stephen Smith, a bearded, square-shouldered Stanford under-graduate, who blocked the entrance and fought, keeping them all at bay while screaming for help. Steve's shouts alerted Michelle Trudeau and Carrie Hunter, who shared another hut not far away. Michelle ran to find Etha Lohay, and Carrie—tall, strong, and toughened by what she thought of as Gombe's Marine combat training raced through the shadows to Steve's hut, to find herself suddenly surrounded by armed men she had never seen before. Some of the men hit her with their guns while others only pointed them, shouting an angry, confusing welter of words. Carrie was overwhelmed by fear, hers and theirs—since she could see that they were frightened and jumpy. They wore uniforms, but she could also see how young and undisciplined they were, and looking at the guns pointed at her, she knew things could go very wrong at any second.

The commotion soon brought down someone from another hut: Barbara Smuts, a small, smart, determined graduate student from Stanford, who, thinking Steve had been bitten by a snake, ran toward the shouting and was soon seized, bound with rope, and forced to her knees.

By then Michelle had reached Etha's place, calling out (as Etha remem-bers), "Etha! Etha! There are thieves about the hill, and Steve is yelling! He needs help." Etha, wearing only her white cotton nightdress, said to herself, *Oh, if they are thieves, then what do I do?* She had the keys to the Parks safe and the research safe, and she clutched them in her fist, intending to get help, to find the night watchman. She and Michelle began rushing down the hill, and since the trail looped and branched, it was possible to avoid the area where Steve was shouting. But then Michelle stumbled, fell, and cut herself, while Etha, pressing on ahead, collided with a second party of intruders, who were moving up the trail. They said, "Where are you going?" She saw their headlamps and the grenades and guns, the latter now pointed at her, and she answered, "I'm going down." "What are you going to do there?" She had no answer. Then they asked her, "Where are the *wazungu?*" She said, "I don't know."

Michelle, getting up from her fall and seeing Etha in the darkness ahead, surrounded by several armed men, slipped off the trail into the forest and hid. Etha was hauled back up the trail by two men, first to her own hut, where they shone lights inside, peering in through the mesh screen. "Where are you taking me?" she demanded, and then: "I'm not going!" But they showed her a gun and pushed and pulled her back onto the trail and over to Steve's hut, where she saw her good friend Emilie, crying. Emilie looked at her and said, "Etha, what's this?" Etha replied, "Emilie, I don't know! We're in the same pot!"

Steve was dragged out of his hut with hands tied behind his back. After ransacking the place, ripping out bedding and clothing but leaving his money and passport behind, the gang proceeded back through the dark matrix of forest trails, hauling their prisoners along. Pausing to raid Emilie's hut for more bedding and clothing, they continued down (randomly strewing along the path her typewriter and a portion of her clothes) until they reached the research center storehouse. They raided it for food and supplies, and then they tried to break into the generator room. Pounding on the door failed to break it open, although it did create enough noise to be heard by Jane. With a sore eye and therefore in bed earlier than usual that night, she was inside her cabin some 200 yards north up the shore. Steve's shouts had been so remote (and filtered by the forest and masked by the nearby slap and hiss of surf) that she had so far heard nothing unusual. Derek had left a day earlier, and only she and Grub were in the cabin. And she, listening now for a minute to the distant repetitive percussion, opened her eyes and sat up. Then, concluding that the noise was caused by some relatively ordinary event of the night, such as a family quarrel and a slamming door in the staff village, she lay back and closed her eyes again.

In front of the storehouse, some of the men were speaking to Etha in French, and she was struggling to grasp their words and talking back in English. "I don't know French," she told them. "Who are you?" someone demanded, "Tanzanian or what? Don't you speak French?" She said again, "I don't speak French." And then, "I speak English and Swahili, that's all." They looked at her. "Okay. You go!"

She ran away, turning off immediately into a thicket. Stripping away her white cotton nightdress in order to be less visible, she then rushed back up the trail to warn people. First she reached the hut of Adeline Mrema, and the two of them began alerting anyone else they could find—Richard Barnes, Larry Goldman, Helen Neely—warning about the gang of thieves and telling them to take their valuables and hide.

Meanwhile, the armed thugs had moved their hostages down to the beach in front of the staff village, placing the four bound students in the big boat but leaving the three captive Tanzanians—Venas and the two rangers from Nyasanga—on shore, and were questioning people from the village. Every person questioned courageously repeated the lie: *There are no more white people. There are only those four. No more. No more.* Rashidi Kikwale, as village head, kept the keys to the boathouse, and even under the guns and a barrage of threats he refused to give them up, finally declaring that the raiders would have to kill him first. Someone struck him against his right ear with a gun, knocking him to the ground and permanently damaging his hearing, and then they tore the keys away. They unlocked the boathouse, carried the aluminum research boat down to the lake, and tethered it to the stern of their long boat, filling the smaller vessel with all the clothes, bedding, food, and other supplies they had just stolen. At around 1:15 in the morning, they started the motors and turned back onto the lake, heading west, in the direction of Zaire.

Etha and Adeline, coming back down the trail now, saw some lights and then heard the boat race away. They stopped. Etha said, "Oh, my God!" and started crying. Adeline said, "Okay, Etha, cool down, cool down. Let us go." So she stopped crying. "Fine," she said. "Let's go." And they went down to meet with the others, to verify who had been taken, to account for the safety of everyone remaining, to find the staff people and their families, to talk to Jane. Jane wrote a note asking for police help and sent it via the park rangers, who had a boat at Nyasanga and could run into Kigoma; and then, as everyone concluded, there was nothing else to do but stay alert until after dawn, when the Parks people and the police would be awake and receiving calls on their radios.

Carrie Hunter, Barbara Smuts, and Steve Smith had been dropped into a dark pool of cold water in the bow of the boat, along with various supplies and dead chickens. But Carrie and Barbara were untied now and able to move, while Steve, still bound tightly, was sinking into the water and becoming seriously chilled. Carrie and Barbara began pleading with their captors in French to untie Steve. In response, they were beaten with guns and told not to talk. Emilie was in a drier place, propped farther back, and during the seven-hour ride to the other side of the lake, she traded a few words of French with some of the men around her, enough to confirm that she and the others had been kidnapped for ransom.

Next morning and on the other side of the lake, they were forced to climb up a steep cliff to an encampment anchored precariously on the mountainside. A small army was spread out on a high ridge there, and below that, in a steep and narrow valley, isolated, guarded by soldiers, were three bamboo huts, two for the captives, the third for their guards.

On their third day, the captives were escorted to another bamboo hut and made to sit down in a small anteroom. Looking around, Carrie soon discovered in a random pile of things a book by Niko Tinbergen, *The Herring Gull's World*. It may have been the only English-language publication in the entire camp.

The four students were taken in to meet the generals, six of them. The generals sat up high; the students were placed down low. The generals seemed confident and well-fed, and they wore clean and sharply pressed uniforms theatrically overadorned with clusters of medals and ribbons. One of them explained methodically in French that they were leaders of a Marxist rebel army, the Parti de la Révolution Populaire (PRP), fighting under the supreme authority and inspired leadership of Laurent Kabila. Their goal was to remove President Mobutu and his entire government and army from Zaire and establish a Marxist society, a social paradise where wealth would be distributed equally and where all citizens, from the highest to the lowest, men and women alike, would become comrades in the revolution and have the same access to everything important, such as education, medical care, and shoes. The students themselves would soon be educated in the tenets of revolutionary Marxism, and they would be fed and cared for. But they were captives, after all, and no one would have the slightest hesitation about shooting them dead in an instant. They were there to serve the revolution as valuable hostages, and the PRP was going to make certain demands: for money (half a million American dollars in small bills or the equivalent in British pounds); weapons, including large-caliber guns, and ammunition; and the liberation from jail of certain political prisoners being held in Tanzania. Also, although it was not a demand, the PRP intended by this bold act to reach a better understanding with President Nyerere, a socialist himself, after all, who should give them the right to travel through his country and trade in the Tanzanian markets. Finally, since the students knew proper English, they were going to write out their own ransom note, articulating clearly all of these demands, and if that note should give even the tiniest hint about where they were being held, they would be killed instantly. In any case, the demands had a sixty-day deadline, after which they would be killed anyhow. Were there any comments or questions?

Speaking in French, Carrie and Emilie protested. They were nothing but impoverished and lowly students. They were not famous scientists. They were not important people. No one cared about them. No one would miss them. And therefore the PRP, as enlightened as it might be in most significant things, was not going to get far with its demands for a big ransom and guns and the plan for leveraging President Nyerere. The generals' spokesman asked if there was anything else they wanted to say, and Carrie said, "I want that book," referring to *The Herring Gull's World*.

On the other side of the lake, Jane, operating the two-way radio, reached Parks headquarters in Arusha by seven o'clock in the morning on May 20. Thirty minutes later she was talking to Derek in Dar es Salaam. Thirty minutes after that, Derek was meeting with the Tanzanian minister for home affairs, who immediately informed the defense and security ministers of the kidnapping and ordered the inspector general of police to fly by helicopter to Kigoma. Derek then flew in a Parks plane out to Kigoma, arriving by 4:30 that afternoon, to be met at the landing strip by Jane.

Five students had been on holiday from Gombe at the time of the kidnapping. A sixth had left for home two days earlier. Therefore, only eight white students and researchers now remained. Since the kidnappers had deliberately taken only *wazungu*, those eight students and researchers plus Jane, Grub, Grub's tutor, Simon, and another British citizen who had recently come to replace Simon were evacuated to town for their own safety. The next day the students and researchers were allowed back to Gombe, under heavy police escort, to gather their personal belongings and any important records. Jane and Derek, meanwhile, spoke by telephone to the U.S. embassy in Dar, and then they flew in the small Parks plane across the lake, scouring the green hillsides and cliffs and half-hidden villages at the eastern edge of Zaire, desperately hoping for a glimpse of some kind of military encampment down below and perhaps the sight of four white captives. They found nothing.

Derek and Jane returned to Gombe, which by then was crowded with police, and spent the next two days alongside the other displaced *wazungu*, disconsolately packing and meeting with the remaining Africans—including Etha Lohay, who bravely agreed to stay on as Parks administrator for the time being, and the Tanzanian student, Adeline Mrema, who said she would remain a while longer as well. Many of the supporting staff—carpenters, night watchmen, kitchen workers, messengers, and so on—were no longer needed and were now unemployed. But the field staff, roughly a dozen skilled, tough, very astute chimp and baboon watchers, declared that they were ready to carry on.

By Friday, May 23, Jane, Derek, and the other *wazungu* were back in Kigoma, where they opened a message from Dave Hamburg and the president of Stanford University, instructing all the Stanford students to leave for supposedly safer quarters in Nairobi and declaring that they were no longer authorized to do further research in East Africa. Most of the students and others from that group decided that they would go to Dar es Salaam instead—they could stay in the guest cottage adjoining Jane and Derek's house—expressing solidarity with their kidnapped friends and hoping they might help in some way. They set off by train, while Jane, Derek, and Grub took off in the Parks plane.

Back in Dar, Derek phoned the American and Dutch ambassadors and invited them to meet with him and Jane at their home the next day to consider strategies. It was during that meeting, on May 24, that a message was brought in to the American ambassador, a distinguished and imposingly tall African American named William Beverly Carter. Ambassador Carter relayed the news to everyone else in the room: one of the four kidnapping victims, Barbara Smuts, was in Kigoma. Members of the PRP had transported her across the lake during the night and deposited her on the shore just before dawn, whereupon she had walked into town and located the police. She was physically unharmed and would be flying to Dar es Salaam on a chartered plane the next day.

Sunday evening at the city airport, the twenty-four-year-old American graduate student, utterly exhausted, wearing faded jeans and a plain white cotton blouse, climbed out of a small private plane, was surrounded by a swirl of reporters and bulb-flashing photographers, and was then greeted warmly by a small crowd of people who included Jane and Derek, the American ambassador, and others from the American embassy. Barbara and Jane, according to a reporter for the *Times,* "hugged each other emotionally." And then the fatigued student was "whisked" off to the American embassy, where Ambassador Carter had insisted she should stay. As everyone soon learned, she was carrying letters addressed to President Nyerere and the U.S. and Dutch ambassadors, as well as to Jane and the parents of the remaining hostages, stating that they were all in good health and being cared for appropriately, more or less, but that they would be killed if demands were not met: for money, arms, and the release of certain political prisoners.

At the end of the month David Hamburg arrived in Dar, officially representing Stanford University and bringing with him Carrie Hunter's and Steve Smith's fathers. Jane had been allowed to spend a couple of hours with Barbara Smuts and her mother, and as she reported in a letter home, written probably on May 31, Barbara was "much better, and was able to tell us all sorts of details about the rebels," including the fact that they frequently shook hands with the students, fed them three meals a day, and talked a good deal about "the rights of women," which meant partly that whenever the PRP took over a new area, any soldier who raped a woman was summarily executed. Jane went on to say that Dave Hamburg had retired to the Kilimanjaro Hotel to recuperate from jet lag, exhaustion, sore throat, sinus trouble, and some kind of stomach ailment, but now he was feeling better and describing himself as "mentally . . . much, much better." Indeed, Jane thought, she could sense "quite an atmosphere of hope"— although there were still various odd problems she could only hint at, such as the fact that the American ambassador, who was six feet seven inches tall and "like a character from Graham Greene," had so far "handled the whole thing in a most peculiar—and utterly foolish—way."

It was still unclear what anyone in Dar es Salaam could do, and the leaders of the PRP had apparently not given much thought to the logistical problems of negotiation and communication over long distances. At the same time, various parties in Dar were experiencing their own problems in negotiation and communication.

To begin with, soon after Ambassador Carter had "whisked" Barbara Smuts off to the American embassy, a conflict developed over political sovereignty and responsibility. According to Derek's confidential report, President Nyerere had been allowed to meet for a short while alone with Miss Smuts; as a result of that meeting, the Tanzanian president concluded that the American ambassador had not been forthright about some details of the situation. Nyerere thus became, in Derek's words, "very angry with the U.S. ambassador." At the same time, the American embassy issued a statement declaring publicly that (according to a reporter's paraphrase) "the primary responsibility for coping with the kidnappers and effecting the safe release of the students . . . rested with the Tanzanian government." In quick response, the official position of the Tanzanian government was published in a government-owned newspaper: that although Tanzania maintained a serious humanitarian concern for the welfare of the students, its leaders would "categorically reject any responsibility for their release or whatever happens to them." As a Reuters news report neatly summarized, "Tanzania Washes Its Hands of Students' Kidnapping."

Nyerere had decided, officially at least, not to negotiate with the kidnappers. Meanwhile, the U.S. secretary of state, Henry Kissinger, sent explicit instructions to Ambassador Carter not to negotiate with the PRP either. The United States was at the time encouraging President Mobutu to back a war against a Soviet-oriented Marxist regime recently established in Angola, on the western side of Zaire, and thus could not afford to associate with Marxist rebels on the eastern side. By the time David Hamburg arrived on May 30, there had been such a serious breakdown in communications between the U.S. embassy and the Tanzanian government that Derek, complaining about a "virtual boycott" of information from the American side, asked David to intervene.

Derek and Jane decided to try on their own initiative to contact the kidnappers. Jane had composed a personal letter to the three captives, reassuring them that everyone loved them, that their parents and other family members were arriving, that their fellow students were all very concerned and sent their love, and that they should have hope. "Please try not to worry about your future," she wrote. "Everything is going to be all right. All the world feels certain that your captors are humane people. We are doing all that we can do. Please believe us and have faith." The letter would naturally be read by the kidnappers as well, and Jane obviously intended it as an opening in communication with them, sending indirectly their way a few vaguely positive comments, such as "Surely they must know that this is their chance—that by treating you well and by returning you safely to your families, the world will be most impressed in their favour. On the other hand, if they harm you, the world will be shocked and the whole operation could bring them to a much worse position than they were in before they started it." The letter went on to detail the developing situation at Gombe, and it optimistically suggested a few mental projects having to do with research that Emilie, Carrie, and Steve might wish to consider as they waited for the help that would most certainly come. "We send all, all our love," it concluded. "And we're telling you not to worry. It's all going to be okay."

The letter must have been difficult to compose—and now, how to mail it? The general location of the PRP encampment was known by then, and on June 1 Jane and Derek flew to Kigoma intending to hire a freelance courier. With help from the head of the Kigoma police, they finally found someone who agreed to take it (plus some Dutch cigars for the PRP from the Dutch ambassador), but then the irrationally bold man rationally changed his mind.

On the other side of the lake, meanwhile, the nights were wet and surprisingly cold. At first the captives slept in individual bamboo cots, each covered with a single light blanket and with a small fire smoldering beneath. They would turn over, facedown to the fire, to get warm, but soon they would be smoky and choking and unable to breathe. They would flip over and become unbearably cold. They would flip over again, warm up again, and start to think about the fire below and worry about going up in flames. After Barbara left, the remaining hostages were placed together in a single hut. Steve by then was using a sleeping bag that had been taken in the raid on Gombe, and Emilie's mattress, also taken, was now placed on a cot that Emilie and Carrie shared.

The kidnappers had raided the storeroom at Gombe partly to get food for their captives, so in addition to small rations of *ugali*, a cassava root paste, they ate a good deal of canned tomato paste, occasional potatoes, a little rice, and periodically a small piece of chicken—a wing or a leg, which they would split three ways. The chicken was extremely tough, and Emilie preferred to crack the bones and suck the marrow, leaving the bits of meat and gristle for Carrie and Steve. Once every couple of weeks they were given a single cooked egg, which they split three ways. Twice during their captivity they were brought hot coffee sweetened with milk—a great treat.

Their days were taken up with hours of reeducation, during which one of the generals, Alfred Nondo, lectured and hectored them in Swahili, covering such subjects as Marxist-Leninist thought and the history of Laurent Kabila and his PRP. They were told to contemplate their French-language copies of Mao Zedong's *Little Red Book,* and they were required to read a few small treatises that had been printed in Swahili. Paper was in short supply, and the hostages were each given a sheet of onionskin paper and a pen, then told to sit at bamboo tables and write out, over the wavy ridges of the bamboo, notes on their reading.

During this time of daily reeducation, they also looked around them to learn more about what the Marxism of Kabila and the Parti de la Révolution Populaire really meant—and noted that among other hypocrisies, the frequently stated concerns about the rights of women were seriously contradicted by stories from the three African women who brought them hot water in the mornings and food at mealtimes. Those women were themselves captives, two from Zaire, the other from Tanzania, taken from their villages and forced to serve a few privileged members of the PRP as sexual slaves. But one of them was stealing food meant for the hostages, and since the students needed to maintain their strength for an escape attempt, they decided to risk reporting the thefts. They followed established procedure for complaint-making and were told reassuringly that such pilfering would cease and the offending woman would be given a period of reeducation, which soon was revealed to consist of imprisonment inside a suspended cage for twenty-four hours.

It was important to establish some control over the details of their lives. Thus, when instructed to study their printed pamphlets, they sat out in the sun on the little pad of earth supporting their hut and held the pamphlets upside down. At the same time, *The Herring Gull's World* became an important source of solace. They each read it privately, but they also read it out loud to one another, and they found themselves profoundly absorbed by the world of herring gulls, and consoled too by one another's presence and voice and the music of familiar English words spoken aloud, like poetry.

To keep up their morale and their strength, they sang at night and tried to exercise twice daily, mornings and afternoons. Steve and Carrie would have to drag Emilie out of bed in the mornings to do this; and then all three would go out into their little green niche overlooking the lake, face the hazily distant blue-and-yellow edge of Tanzania, and do jumping jacks, push-ups, and sit-ups. One day they happened to look up to the ridge behind them to see jumping silhouettes, hundreds of them, and concluded that the entire army was out doing jumping jacks. Perhaps their example had inspired someone up there, and for the next couple of days, the whole PRP seemed to be following their lead in daily calisthenics. It was funny. If they had not been hostages, it might have been funnier.

Jane updated her family on the Dar es Salaam situation in a June 13 letter. She and Derek were still trying to have a message delivered from Kigoma to the kidnappers. Their relationship with Ambassador Carter was "now good." Dave Hamburg was "helping everyone" cope with the situation.

Michelle Trudeau was dealing effectively with the worried fathers of Carrie and Steve, while "the poor USA ambassador is going crazy with those poor fathers sort of pressuring him to do things all the time, when he [already] is. No one [is] blaming those poor fathers—just that it does make things so difficult for everyone, them being here, everyone feeling so sorry for them—awful for them, nothing to do. We're having them to lunch in a couple of days." At the same time the American and Dutch ambassadors had both received new messages from the kidnappers, passed through the regular post, repeating their demands and suggesting that a small white-flagged boat putter across the lake for negotiation purposes.

The idea of sending ambassador-level negotiators in a small marked boat was not a compelling one, and it became much less so once President Mobutu decided to simplify everything by killing everyone involved, kidnappers and hostages alike. He sent his Lake Tanganyika gunboats, recent gifts of friendship from the United States, into action with orders to shell any settlements along the shore that looked as though they might be Marxist training camps. Periodically, therefore, Emilie, Carrie, Steve, and the army on the ridge above them were being shot at from the lake. And when the PRP leaders finally concluded that they would have to send their own emissaries across the lake, they had to paddle quietly in a small canoe on a dark night in order to sneak past Mobutu's restless, spotlighting gunboats.

The first two emissaries successfully slipped across one night, but upon reaching dry land and civilization on the other side, they were challenged and soon scuttled by alcohol and loose women. The second set, General Alfred Nondo and a sidekick, paddled across the lake and beached at Kigoma by dawn. From Kigoma they rode a train for three days and two nights across the country to Dar es Salaam. In Dar Friday morning, June 20, they took a bus from the train station to the Commerce Bank building downtown, and finally they walked up several flights of stairs and introduced themselves to the Marine guards at the American embassy. General Nondo was dressed in dark jeans and a dark shirt; according to Tony Collins, who had met him in Kigoma, the man was young, handsome, athletically built, and charming. His subordinate was a small, round sort who said very little.

By that time the negotiators for the students had split clearly into two camps. Of course the American and Dutch ambassadors had taken charge from the start, and in spite of Henry Kissinger's cable unambiguously instructing Ambassador Carter not to deal with the Marxist rebels, he courageously chose to do so. "Once you start thinking of one life as different from a thousand lives," he insisted, "you've lost it all." In the other camp, President Nyerere, while officially rejecting any responsibility for the students' welfare, had enlisted Derek as the spokesman for Tanzania and instructed or allowed him to take a somewhat complicated position, which was to negotiate but without agreeing to the primary demand, a ransom, on the theory that paying money would only encourage more kidnappings.

David Hamburg had arrived with a simpler goal, which was to free the students as soon as possible in any way possible, and he soon found a determined ally in Ambassador Carter. David had previously been warned by Jane and others that Derek Bryceson was (as David later told me) "a very difficult, irascible person" and "anti-American." From the first, he found that early characterization to be almost tragically accurate. David's initial encounter with Derek was "unpleasant," and their working relationship remained that way throughout the crisis. Worse, Derek actively worked to manipulate them all and to control Jane, to keep her isolated and out of the picture. Jane had little or no status in the world of Tanzanian politics to begin with, other than as his wife. Now Derek did not allow her to communicate independently with David or others directly involved in the case. Jane accepted her secondary role, respecting the intense pressure her new husband was under while loving him passionately and trusting him totally, and uncritically, to do what was best. She was shattered and dazed, I believe, profoundly disturbed by the kidnapping and worried about the fate of the students, but she characteristically kept her deepest anxieties private and looked on the positive side of things.

David Hamburg had gone to Dar es Salaam under enormous stress and was really "counting on Jane," but Derek immediately made it very clear that he was, "to put it kindly, going to minimize my opportunity to talk with Jane alone." David tried a couple of times to speak to her privately on the telephone, but even communication at that remove was extremely difficult to accomplish and "minimal." In David's assessment, Jane always had a capacity for "wishful thinking," and in this case, he believed, she simply did not accept how "real and terrible" the threat to the students actually was. He continued to have faith that somehow, if she could "really come to understand and accept the gravity of the situation, she might somehow be more helpful." At the same time, though, how could she help? She might have become involved in an international effort among scientific groups and others to pressure the kidnappers publicly; but David also recognized the sad truth that "there wasn't an awful lot she could do under the circumstances."

David Hamburg kept flying back and forth between Dar and Kigoma, developing plans and contingencies, talking day and night to everyone he could think of, trying to make contact with the kidnappers. He had bad diarrhea the entire time and was rapidly losing weight. His room in the Kilimanjaro Hotel was electronically bugged. And Ambassador Carter, "a wonderful man," several times expressed his own frustration that as a result of

Derek's strange and stubborn resistance, he was unable to reach President Nyerere or anyone else of importance in the government. Derek Bryceson had become, David concluded, "a wall" separating him and the U.S. and Dutch ambassadors from the rest of the Tanzanian government.

At noon on Friday, June 20, Derek received a phone call from the American embassy requesting that he go there immediately. When he arrived, he was greeted by the Dutch and American ambassadors and David Hamburg and informed that two men had walked into the embassy that morning, claiming to represent the PRP and carrying letters from the hostages. Derek agreed that they should all remain inside the embassy and begin negotiations at once. And so the two ambassadors, David, Derek, and a translator sat down with General Nondo and his sidekick. Ambassador Carter opened the talks diplomatically by welcoming the kidnappers and introducing everyone else, and then he turned to Derek and asked him to speak first.

Derek lectured the two men in Swahili for three hours—their turn for reeducation—enunciating at length the Tanzanian position and explaining emphatically, as he later wrote, "how Tanzania does not believe that they can really be PRP if they behave in the way that they had, that they were alienating Tanzania and that they must return the students at once unharmed." If they were to return the students, then they would "gain considerable international good will for their humane actions," while it was certain that their own people held in prison in Tanzania would be released. Derek was offering, in other words, a trade, hostages for hostages; and at the end of the three hours he believed that "a good relationship was building up." He had exhausted himself, though, and asked for a recess, during which he retired with the two ambassadors and David Hamburg to consider what to do next.

In that private huddle, Derek argued forcibly that the discussion was really "going well," but now it was "vital" for them to adjourn for the day so the PRP emissaries could have time to absorb all the things he had just told them. Not surprisingly, since no one else had yet been given an opportunity to say much, no one else agreed. David Hamburg voted for discussing the kidnappers' specific demands next, whereupon Derek begged for adjournment until the next day, convinced that, given enough time, he could win the students' freedom without anyone's paying a ransom. Hamburg also pressed for bringing the students' fathers into the discussions. Derek vehemently protested, insisting that the fathers could only ask that the kidnappers' demands be met immediately, which would automatically sacrifice any "flexibility" in negotiations.

Derek was overruled, and the negotiators returned to the larger meeting with the two fathers, whereupon the conversation quickly slipped past the other demands and landed directly on the subject of the ransom. Hamburg announced that he needed that night and the next morning to contact sources in the United States to find out how much cash could actually be raised. Then the meeting was adjourned.

By Monday the ransom had been negotiated down to $460,000. That amount in British pounds, small-denomination bills, had been collected over the weekend, based on credit from Carrie Hunter's father, and it was already stacked inside a strongbox and being flown to Kigoma, along with Derek, David, Mr. Hunter, the two PRP emissaries, and two Marines from the U.S. embassy. At dawn on Tuesday, a fishing boat containing the box of money, the two PRP men, David, and the embassy Marines set out from Kigoma harbor, but as the vessel approached the far shore, signaled in by flashing mirrors, one of Mobutu's gunboats appeared and started firing shells into its path. The boat immediately turned around and headed back to Kigoma. According to a *Los Angeles Times* account, Mr. Hunter had been able to watch the whole scene unfold from his vantage point on a high bluff near Kigoma and was "furious" at the failure of the exchange. It was necessary to regroup and recalibrate.

Derek returned to Dar, and so now, as Jane wrote home at the time, Carrie's father and David Hamburg waited anxiously together in Kigoma while she and Derek were as anxiously gathered with Steve's father in Dar. "I wish I could be there to greet Em," she wrote, "—but at least she'll have Dave H. which will be super for her. Sometimes I dread what this will have done to her. At other times I'm sure she'll be okay." In any case, she continued, "we'll all go round the bend if we have to wait much longer."

A large box of British pound notes was finally exchanged for human hostages on Friday, June 27—but the kidnappers betrayed everyone by releasing only two, Emilie and Carrie. They held Steve Smith in reserve and announced additional demands: international publication of one of their pamphlets and the release of at least two particular prisoners still held in Tanzanian jails. Mr. Smith, Jane wrote home in a letter postmarked July 5, had been planning to go to Kigoma to meet his son, but then came the devastating news that he was still a prisoner on the other side. "We do feel that Steve will be okay, though," Jane declared. "Just that it is going to take time—hopefully nothing else—to get him back. Isn't it lousy, though, for him to be left on his own. Awful for Em and Carrie—and absolute hell for his parents. Sitting around, waiting, trying to do things but managing to get very little done, has become a way of life. Pray God not for much longer."

As Jane observed in the same note, Emilie and Carrie remained safe in Dar es Salaam, and they looked "remarkably fit (more fit than me!) and, apart from Em's feet (she got blisters from running down the hill in her excitement at knowing she would be released) nothing wrong with them." It was "absolutely super to have Emilie back" and also "so nice" that David Riss had arrived in Dar just in time to greet her. Indeed, Jane and Derek had asked Emilie and Dave Riss to stay with them in their house, but Emilie wanted to be near Carrie, who had joined her father at the Kilimanjaro Hotel.

Jane and Derek had managed to greet the two just-released women as they were being debriefed at the American embassy, but to welcome them personally and joyously, they went to the Kilimanjaro Hotel. They knocked on Emilie's door first. No answer. After a few minutes, they tried Carrie's door. Her father drew it open and stood there looking at them with, Jane thought, an "utterly shocked" expression on his face. She peered past him to see Michelle Trudeau and the American ambassador, and she could hear Emilie speaking to someone on the telephone. But after an awkward pause, Mr. Hunter quietly but firmly shut the door in their faces, leaving Jane and Derek outside, expecting the door to be opened again. It was not, and after two minutes that "seemed like 10," they walked back down the long corridor and left the hotel.

The next day they sent Emilie a "big bunch of flowers," and she and David Riss came over to the house almost immediately. "So we had a good chat, but when I asked Em about the door shutting, she went funny and said they were frightened. Oh well. No one is themselves these days."

One week after the release of Emilie and Carrie was July 4, America's Independence Day, and several of the students had been invited to celebrate at the American ambassador's place. To get there, they borrowed a car from Mrs. Van den Burgh, the wife of the Dutch ambassador.

David Riss was appointed driver, and Emilie, Michelle, and Tony Collins climbed inside as passengers. David had been reluctant to drive, because one consequence of the British colonial past was that all highway traffic in Tanzania traveled, from an American perspective, in the wrong direction. Now, going around a corner and seeing a big Land Rover looming nearly on top of them, he swerved right when he should have swerved left. The crash transformed the new car into an old concertina, gasoline dripping away underneath, headlights pushed back into the middle of the engine compartment.

Ambassador and Mrs. Van den Burgh were soon contacted, and while Tony, miraculously unhurt, stayed with the car and waited for the police to arrive, they took the other three students to the Aga Khan Hospital, where David was treated for a broken ankle and deep cuts on his face. Jane rushed to the hospital and reported in a July 8 letter home that Michelle looked "simply ghastly, with one side of her face enormous, and a terrible black eye, closed shut." But Emilie by then had decided she was bleeding internally and would probably die, and when she finally was able to spend time alone with David, she said to him, "Why don't you just say that you'll marry me, because we can't do anything any more. I've got kidnapped. I got carcrashed. And I think I'm going to die, so you might as well say that you're going to marry me."

Steve Smith was released by the kidnappers about a week later, after the Tanzanian government acceded to their final significant demand and released two PRP detainees. A few days after his release, Ambassador William Beverly Carter received word that an angry Henry Kissinger had canceled his next appointment, as ambassador to Denmark, and was reassigning him to the U.S. Information Agency, with a loss in both salary and status. David Riss and Emilie Bergmann were married on September 2, 1976, fourteen months after the car crash. Laurent Kabila, the leader of the kidnappers, drove President Sese Seko Mobutu out of office and off the continent some twenty-two years after the kidnapping, thereby becoming president of Zaire, which he renamed the Democratic Republic of the Congo. He was shot dead by one of his own bodyguards less than four years after that, on January 16, 2001.

37

A New Normal

1975–1980

AFTER THE LAST HOSTAGE was returned in late July 1975, Jane wrote to Joan Travis that "slowly things will sort themselves out—though they will not return to normal to me for a very long time, as my 'normal' is no more, so I shall have to create a new one!"

At Gombe, the new normal included Etha Lohay, who would stay on as administrator until a replacement could be found. Adeline Mrema, the Tanzanian undergraduate from the University of Dar es Salaam, also continued working there for a while longer. Meanwhile, the Tanzanian field staff moved front and center. Jane had recently appointed a young man named Emmanuel Tsolo do Fisco as senior field assistant, and he became responsible for the combined daily research and reporting activities and also translated between Swahili and English. The field staff who worked on chimpanzees were a core group of six: Rugema Bambanganya, Petro Leo, Hilali Matama, Hamisi Mkono, Eslom Mpongo, and Kassin Selemani. Hilali Matama had been the first field assistant, hired back in 1968, and he now headed the chimpanzee team. A small man with a guileless, youthful smile, wide mouth, and mildly bulbous nose, Hilali was loved and admired by the students for his impressive physical endurance and agility, and also, according to Craig Packer's recollection, "the most remarkable, imperious dignity."

The field staff for baboons consisted of one person, Apollinaire Sindimwo, whose labor was soon supplemented by that of two others, Peter Nyabenda and Moshi Katota. While most of the Gombe field staff were local men from Lake Tanganyika villages, Apollinaire, or Apolly, was a Hutu from Burundi. In Craig Packer's assessment, Apolly was "impeccable" in everything he did. He could be "quite contemplative and philosophical—at times, almost poetic." He also managed to maintain "an objective, no-nonsense attitude about his work." But the man's "most impressive talent" was his capacity to follow baboons through the forest "without ever letting a hair get out of place. Whenever the baboons go romping down a steep ravine through thorny vines, I always end up with muddy trousers, torn shirt, scratched face, and mangled shoes. Apolly comes out immaculate, ready to dine with royalty."

After the kidnapping, Apollinaire's study of baboon swimming was the single specialized research project left. But the major task of maintaining general long-term records for the baboons and chimpanzees—A Records, based on observations at the camp provisioning area, and B Records, from the regular follows of individuals—continued entirely as before. At the provisioning area, a member of the field staff was stationed with two clipboards to hold the charts and check sheets (for attendance, health, feeding, grooming, play), as well as binoculars, a timer, and some blank sheets of paper on which to take notes. Outside the provisioning area, teams of two, a first and second observer, went out daily to follow and report on target individuals. Since the first observer was supposed to write up a final report, he carried paper and pen or pencil. He also wore an accurate wristwatch. The second observer took along charts to mark down association and travel patterns and kept the timer to mark one-, two-, and five-minute intervals. And because their work often ended at dusk or after dark, both men also carried flashlights in their pockets.

Jane kept in touch with the field staff during daily two-way radio conversations. She also regularly visited Gombe to confer with them and to review their daily reports for accuracy. At first her visits required government clearance. While there, she and Derek, who usually accompanied her, would be guarded by members of the military field force stationed at Gombe. And at least during the summer of 1975, getting there was not so easy. The pilot supposed to fly them out in early July suddenly became ill ("said his bones ache," Jane reported in the first week of the month, "something to do with oxygen, and he needs a medical"), while a second attempt was dogged by aggressively bad weather. "Our trips to Gombe seem ill fated," Jane wrote home during the July 23 flight. "The weather this time. We're sitting in the little plane (called a Reim's _Rocket_ for some extraordinary reason) & we've been plodding around the skies since 8.30 A.M.—trying & failing—to find a way through rain & clouds to Gombe."

They finally had to return to the Serengeti for refueling and then find a hole in the weather through which they could crawl back to Dar.

In the coming years, the all-Tanzanian field staff would continue to document ordinary life among the chimpanzees of Gombe: a generally peaceful existence spiced by small daily adventures in foraging and hunting, sex and socializing, and leavened by tickles and laughter, gentle play with the young, and relaxed times spent lolling about in the company of friends. Certainly there were moments of social strife and dramatic excitement and even, on rare occasions, as when brash young upstarts challenged the established male hierarchy, serious fights—which typically ended once the loser admitted defeat by running away or signaling submission.

But the field staff also began to document some less common events, such as the cannibalism practiced by an adult female, Passion, and her two offspring, Pom and Prof. Jane and Derek made it out to Gombe in August and September 1975; by September 24, Jane was referring, in a note to Joan Travis, to "a super 5 days there with Derek." The work of the field staff was "going very very well," she continued, "even if they have to record unpleasant, gruesome, behaviour!" Actually, "all sorts of ghastly things" had recently been happening among the chimpanzees, including the first in what would become a series of disturbing attacks: "I expect you heard about Passion seizing, killing and eating Gilka's adorable little infant? Oh dear."

Although the Passion family's opportunistic cannibalism continued sporadically during the next few years, it was always very odd, apparently abnormal behavior. Even the other chimpanzees seemed to fear and possibly abhor this rogue female and her offspring. By contrast, another kind of violence documented during the second half of the 1970s, male-dominated warfare between adjacent communities, eventually appeared to be a normal aspect of chimpanzee behavior. Jane mentioned one piece of that puzzle in the same September 24 note: "The Kasekela chimps have killed Madam Bee, by repeatedly attacking her."

The killing of Madam Bee was witnessed by Hilali Matama and Eslom Mpongo on September 14, when, alerted by the raging sounds of violent conflict, the two men came upon the horrific drama of four powerful adult males—Figan, Jomeo, Satan, and Sherry—murderously assaulting the older female, who had been crippled by polio. As the human observers appeared on the scene, Jomeo was dragging Madam Bee down a slope before turning to jump on her and strike her with an open palm. Then Figan stomped on her and dragged her. Madam Bee, trembling severely, attempted to stand up, but Satan tossed her back down to the ground, stomped on her, and dragged her. Figan began hitting and stomping on her. Jomeo picked up her limp body and slammed it down before jumping on her and rolling her down the slope. Screaming, she weakly attempted to escape, whereupon Satan knocked her to the ground and pummeled her with his hands and feet. And so it went, with the four males screaming, displaying, kicking and hitting and dragging, stomping on and smashing Madam Bee until she collapsed and lay helplessly inert and then feebly rolled away into some dense under-brush.

After the killers left, Hilali and Eslom crawled into the thickets, hoping to find the beaten female, but they were not successful. Nor was Jane, brought to the scene soon after. Three days later a search party sighted Honey Bee, Madam Bee's second daughter, moving around in the branches of a tree. Madam Bee was subsequently found on the ground below, barely able to move and severely injured in several different parts of her body. As the mother slowly died from her wounds, Jane later wrote, her daughter "tried to comfort her, gently grooming her and keeping the flies away."

The war of Kasekela against Kahama was rooted in events that began, perhaps, in the 1960s, a period when Jane was becoming familiar with a large number of chimpanzees, including some dozen and a half adult males who periodically showed up for bananas and were sometimes sighted in the forest. During the second half of the decade, it became apparent that some of those males tended to prefer the northern portion of their large range, while others maintained a mild preference for forests to the south. By the start of the 1970s, the males were dividing into two social groups increas-ingly attached to the two geographical areas. The pattern was not clear at first, partly because of Gombe's complicated landscape and partly because chimpanzee social life itself is so complicated. Among chimpanzees, group size and composition vary constantly, as social and ecological circumstances dictate, from a single lone male or female, or a female with offspring, to a group of five or ten or twenty or more. That sort of generally relaxed, "fission-fusion" society is unusual but not unique. Humans act the same way. For chimpanzees, though, the system characterizes only interactions among individuals who are members of the same larger community and who, by virtue of that membership, inhabit the same piece of land. Chim-panzees are territorial animals, in other words; and when the original study group of males began to divide socially during the later 1960s and early 1970s, they were also dividing territorially.

There were eight northern males then, including six in their prime—Evered, Faben, Figan, Humphrey, Jerome, and Satan—and two past their prime, Hugo and Mike. The southern subgroup consisted of four males at the height of their physical powers—Charlie, Dé, Godi, and Willy Wally—along with the past-his-prime Hugh, the downright ancient Goliath, and the adolescent Sniff. By the start of 1973, those two groups of males had essen-tially completed their split into two separate territories, with one group ranging over a section of forest to the north, centered on the Kasekela val-ley, and the second taking over its own area to the south, centering on the

Kahama valley. Three adult females—Madam Bee, Mandy, and Wanda—also gravitated into the southern region and became members of the Kahama community.

By 1974 the occasional peaceful interactions between the Kasekela and Kahama communities were replaced by a steady state of xenophobia and mutual hostility and punctuated by a series of opportunistic killer attacks. On both sides of their shared border, adult males (occasionally accompanied by an adolescent male or a female) formed small, coherent gangs that patrolled territorial edges, sometimes pausing to gaze intently into the sizzling puzzle of a foreign land. When a patrolling group from one side happened to encounter a group from the other, the result was a cacophony of hoots and cries along with aggressively threatening gestures. If their numbers were approximately equal, both groups withdrew deeper into the flickering safety of home territory, but when one group discovered a clear numerical superiority over the other, all caution and restraint vanished. After nearly four years of male patrols and raging gang attacks, from early 1974 to late 1977, the chimpanzee war ended with a complete victory for one community and the complete annihilation of the other. By 1978, with Kahama no more, members of the Kasekela community, male and female, were traveling and eating and sleeping in an expanded territory that included all of what had once been Kahama lands.

"The kidnapping and its aftermath of bitterness and misery affected all of us who were part of it," Jane wrote years later. But she had known that humans were capable of harming their fellow humans in so many imaginative ways, and so the kidnapping was one more jarring confirmation of her own species' already well-established capacity for evil. By contrast, the chilling acts of cannibalism and the ferocious warfare among the chimpanzees of Gombe altered forever her vision of what those apes were capable of. During the first decade of her research, Jane had believed that chimpanzees were somehow, in their own peculiar way, hairy versions of the Noble Savage, "for the most part, rather nicer than human beings." Now, emphatically and remarkably, the second decade demonstrated that chimpanzees, like humans, possess "a dark side to their nature."

Jane also, during the summer of 1975, turned to creating a new normal in Dar es Salaam. Grub was young enough to remain perhaps largely unaffected by the kidnapping and was in perfectly good spirits and fishing at every opportunity, but his mother and Derek resumed homeschooling that summer. He was "doing mostly pretty well at school," Jane reported to the family in England on August 19, "though I despair of teaching him to spell." Derek was having some success in teaching him mathematics, while she was working on the reading. But now they were discussing formal schooling in England alternating with holidays in Africa, which the boy agreed was "quite a good idea."

Jane also fixed up a new office in the Dar house, taking over a large and airy upstairs room, putting in a desk, new bookshelves, and an armchair, and turning an old wardrobe into a new "sort of filing cabinet for reprints and storage place for journals." The front windows looked out to the Indian Ocean, although it was necessary to peer through bougainvillea and some palm trees. But all that vegetation filtered the sunlight, and the collective result, Jane summarized, "couldn't be a nicer office."

Meanwhile, Derek spent much of that summer campaigning for his usual seat in the Tanzanian Parliament as a representative of the large Kinondoni constituency in Dar es Salaam. Indeed, he had gone off the day before, Jane mentioned in the same letter, to attend a party meeting during which a list of twenty-three candidates had been shrunk down to two, Derek and a Tanzanian woman. Derek was a clear favorite to win in the general election, which in fact he soon did, thereby retaining his status as the only democratically elected white politician on the entire continent.

With that gentle smile, the tall, lean, and permanently damaged body, the brave and certain manner, and the distinguished head of fine white hair, Derek possessed his own celebrity in Tanzania. Jane, during her years in Dar es Salaam, was generally the lesser-known spouse, recognized and respected not as Dr. Jane Goodall, the great pioneering ethologist, but rather as the Honorable Derek Bryceson's charming if slightly exotic wife: Mama Bryceson or Mrs. Bryceson or Jane Bryceson. That was another part of the new normal. And while Derek was winning the election and representing the Kinondoni constituency in Dar, Jane was losing some of her own constituency in the United States, which until then had been the primary source of her fame, funding, and intellectual sustenance.

The crisis of the kidnapping had produced a secondary crisis. The early conflict between the American embassy and the Tanzanian government about how to respond was worsened, I believe, partly by Derek. Derek was "nastier than he had to be," as David Hamburg once phrased it, while mentioning a "prevalent speculation" that Derek really wanted the Americans out of Gombe and was using the kidnapping as "leverage to get us out." A less elaborate theory held that Derek's unpleasantness was a consequence of his being "genuinely and sincerely anti-American." Whatever his motivations, clearly some aspects of his style and behavior alienated some of the American contingent during that stressful time. And because Derek had expected and received the love and loyalty of his new wife, Jane, and had successfully isolated her, she too, much to her own mystification, became an object of animosity.

"This whole kidnapping business is so side-making," she wrote home in a letter postmarked July 18, after all the hostages but Steve Smith had been released. "The Americans don't really tell us what they're doing—we just found out that Mr. Hunter is going to Kigoma today. Why? The students said things were looking optimistic—but we're not in the picture." The hotel door closed in her face and Derek's that month was an expression of a deep bitterness, one that, instead of diminishing over time and as the crisis reached an end, simmered slowly into a more poisonous brew.

By October 6, Jane had returned to California to complete her teaching obligation at Stanford, where she found that some of her associates at the university, once so supportive, were now less so. To start with, the house rental she had arranged in nearby Palo Alto was canceled by one of her academic colleagues—apparently as a deliberate gesture of dismissal. She thus spent her first night in town sleeping on the carpet in an unfurnished emergency sublet, waking up the next morning riddled with flea bites. Her written recollection of that final semester describes a "devastating" time that "taught me so much about human nature." Many of the people she had previously considered "true friends" revealed themselves to be "fair-weather friends." Some of her former students "came from long distances to spend time with me, boosting my morale to no end." Others did not come, while several of her professional colleagues, apparently discerning shades and shapes of truth within the fog of rumor, shunned her in various ways and to varying degrees.

"Most of the rumors were about Derek. It was true that he had hoped the students' release might be secured without payment—just because of the precedent that would be set. But the idea that their death would have been a preferable alternative was absurd." Other rumors were essentially speculations about what she might have felt (concerned more about chimps than about students) or done differently (openly defied her husband and taken a more public role).

A more particular idea, that she had deftly "slipped into the jungle" when the kidnappers showed up, is contradicted by all first-person accounts as well as a detailed summary of events compiled the next day. Yet Jane's supposedly slippery escape into "the jungle" was twenty-three years later printed as established fact in an article published by Stanford's alumni association. It is not clear what good Jane could have accomplished by confronting the forty thugs with machine guns or offering herself as an alternate hostage. Such hypothetical acts might conceivably have made her a better research station director—and simultaneously a much worse mother, since she also had the safety of eight-year-old Grub to consider. In any case, she was in bed at the time of the kidnapping, a significant distance away from the commotion, and became aware of what had happened only after the boat was racing away in the direction of Zaire.

That October, Jane learned from a friend another reason for the hostility: a rumor that she was personally wealthy but refused to contribute to the May 19 Emergency Fund, established to retire the bank loan that had paid the ransom. In fact Jane had assumed that the ransom was paid through pledges and contributions made when the students were held captive. Now, hearing for the first time about the existence of the fund, she contacted the person in charge of it, David Hamburg. They met on October 10, at which time he told her that (as she wrote a few weeks later) "our financial wizards have put you down for $25,000."

She could not easily get that much money. The major portion of earnings from *In the Shadow of Man* was held in a trust fund for Grub. She received nothing for her ongoing contributions to Hugo's television films. Her Stanford teaching salary mostly took care of living expenses while she and her family were in California.

Still, there was what she had earned from public lectures during the previous three years, kept in an account at Stanford identified as the "Primate Research Account" and intended for unanticipated research expenses. She agreed to donate any of her lecture income held in that account—only to learn that it had all already been spent, without her knowledge or consent, "for kidnapping expenses." She agreed to contribute $6,000 from various fundraising lectures planned for that fall. Offer accepted. She wrote a check for $14,000 but postdated it for the end of the year, explaining to David that her personal account would not cover that amount until that time. And when she received a telephone call from her bank the next morning, October 11, informing her that the big postdated check, already being processed, was about to bounce, she wrote and mailed two more checks, one immediately good, the second postdated. Jane also offered to become more publicly and personally involved in the efforts at fundraising in California to pay the ransom loan, only to have that final offer ignored.

During the worst of this uncertain, unsettled period, in the fall of 1975, two of Jane's old and good friends, Prince Rainier di San Faustino and his wife, Genevieve (or Genie), who lived in San Francisco, came down to visit her at the Faculty Club, bringing a great bouquet of flowers. Over dinner, they suggested that she could solve her financial problems by forming a tax-exempt charitable foundation that would, in the style of Louis Leakey's L.S.B. Leakey Foundation, generate a steady income for Gombe and related projects. Thus the Jane Goodall Institute for Research, Conservation, and Education was conceived. Trustees and board members were discussed and selected in 1976, and the letterhead was designed by July of that year. The organization's tax-exempt status was officially certified by the U.S. Internal Revenue Service by June 1978. But it would be another few years before the Jane Goodall Institute provided, on its own, any significant financial sustenance for the Gombe research.

Jane went home to England for Christmas and was back in Dar es Salaam by January 1976. By then Grub was living with Vanne and the rest of the family at The Birches in Bournemouth and attending a local school, and his absence made the house in Dar quiet and lonely. Jane was regularly reminded of him by so many objects still scattered about the house: toy airplanes, plastic horses and plastic men with guns, fishing lures, books. And also by his special little schoolroom next to her office, which, as she wrote to him that January, "I don't like going into because I always feel so sad you are not here. Though I am glad someone else is teaching you spelling & writing and not me." She urged him most strongly to write all about it: the lessons, games, gym, fellow students, good teachers, and so on. She would be seeing him soon — for two weeks in April, when she would visit Bournemouth — and he could look forward to a whole wonderful summer in East Africa, in Dar with her and in the Serengeti with Hugo.

Derek's dog, Beetle, had died the year before, but that January, Spider, the yellowish, shorthaired mutt rescued from the dog pound the previous April, gave birth to eight healthy puppies. Jane and Derek kept one of them, an eager waggler named Wagga, and Jane regularly took her, Spider, and any other dogs who cared to show up for walks along the beach in front of the house. Since the pup suffered from some kind of skin ailment, Jane gave Wagga her first bath, with warm water prepared for the medicinal washing. She described the rest of that experience in a June letter to Grub: "So — I got the soap all on, and she was quite good, standing there shivering with her tail for once not wagging, but tucked tightly between her legs." And then, suddenly, as Jane was getting ready for the rinse, Wagga decided to take off. "Well, of course, with the soap on and all nice and lathery she was as slippery as an eel — and you know how slippery they are! So off she went." Wagga shot off and scurried under the fence into President Nyerere's garden, where, in spite of the enticements of whistling and banging on food plates, she stayed for hours, until she finally slunk back into the house and had to be washed all over again.

In July, Grub was able to learn about the new waggle-tailed puppy in person — and also to walk along the beach, examine all the tide pools, find exotic shells for Derek's shell collection, gather bait for fishing, and of course fish, sometimes from the shore and sometimes from a boat.

Hugo arrived in Dar around the middle of August and took Grub out for more fishing, and then the two of them left for a couple of weeks of fossil-hunting and other adventures in the Serengeti, leaving Jane to recover, as she wrote home at that time, from "being a Mama and abandoning all Gombe work!" But by September 12, Grub had played with the dogs for the last time and taken his last looks at the fish in the aquarium, and then he was a little speck of boyhood flying back to England again for another term of school, leaving Jane feeling bereft and now trying to recover from not being a mama.

The sadness she felt about Grub's departure was soon expanded by the news that Billy Collins, her old friend and English publisher, had died. A month later she heard the far more intimate and affecting news that Danny, her grandmother, was also gone. Derek had received a telegram in the afternoon of October 27, while Jane was teaching at the University of Dar es Salaam. As she wrote home the next day, they had spent a "very, very tearful evening" together at home, followed by a night where "sleep was impossible." Still, eventually she fell into a doze and had a vision, or perhaps a dream, of Danny: "The little figure of recent years, sitting up in bed and saying, 'Oh I am a silly old thing. No use to anyone. Don't think of me like that, oh dear me no.'" But as Danny continued to chatter in that vein, she was gradually transforming, turning younger and younger, until she was a youthful Danny with dark hair and bright "twinkling" eyes. With a mischievous look, she said brightly to Jane, "I've found him, you know." Jane, uncertain, asked, "Do you mean Daddy or Jesus?" And Danny said, "Wouldn't you like to know!"

Danny was ninety-seven years old when she died, and she had been seriously ill for some time. Although her passing marked, as Jane phrased it in the same letter, "the end of an era," it was not an unexpected end. And so Jane's life in Dar es Salaam, with the dogs and the beach, with Derek and the coming and going of Grub, with the regular visits to Gombe and the constant labor of collecting and preserving the data, continued in its new normal course. And by the end of that year, the problem of how to pay for the new normal, at least for the next few years, was more or less solved.

Jane's estimated budgets for Gombe during the second half of the 1970s ran at around $25,000 per year. She had expected the Grant Foundation money to end soon, though she learned near the end of October 1976 that the foundation would continue funding Gombe at a smaller level, tentatively $10,000 to be divided over the next three years. And Gordon Getty, a new friend she had met through the Leakey Foundation, spontaneously donated $5,000 around the same time. Jane hoped to earn most of the remainder through her continuing public lectures in the United States, which she organized through the Leakey Foundation, and through additional grants from that organization. Meanwhile, with what may have been some desperation, she decided to appeal once again to old friends at the National Geographic Society, and thus on October 15 she typed out a formal application for a society grant to study the "Behavior of Free-living Chimpanzees at Gombe, Kahama Community," requesting a modest $2,011.81 for the following year.

The society's Committee for Research and Exploration met on the morning of December 7, 1976, to consider grant applications. Whereas in earlier times Jane Goodall had been the star and darling of such proceedings, now the committee deliberated her case in a starkly different mood. Jane had given up her position at Stanford, committee members noted, and the "overall project" at Gombe "is now out of Dr. Goodall's direct control." The committee moved, seconded, and declined Jane Goodall's application. Later that morning, however, Dr. Melvin M. Payne, chairman of the committee, urged everyone to reconsider, reminding them of the National Geographic's "long association with Dr. Goodall and the pioneering studies she carried out." And thus the committee moved, seconded, and this time unanimously accepted the application, thereby contributing to the Gombe Stream chimpanzee research project slightly more than $2,000 for the year 1977. That grant was renewed and modestly expanded for the year 1978. And in May 1979, having paid her a reasonable additional sum for the text and photographs, *National Geographic* published its fourth Jane Goodall article (third on the chimpanzees), this time a splendid and thorough summary of the evidence for cannibalism and intercommunity warfare: "Life and Death at Gombe."

With finances stabilized (albeit precariously), Jane could concentrate on the work of running Gombe. By the start of 1977 she was using an electric typewriter, which eased the burden somewhat; but, as she wrote to Joan Travis in a February 18 letter, "The only problem is that the field assistants are getting too good!! I'm getting so much information—to cope with it is more than a full time job." She had already hired a young Tanzanian woman, Gudilla Tarimo, to help sort and translate the raw data, and she was beginning to use the services of a part-time typist, Diana Francis. Nevertheless, Jane continued in that same letter, "all the time, I'm trying to think of more efficient ways of sorting, storing, and so on."

Aside from handling the daily tide of data from Gombe and keeping up with her regular correspondence, Jane was by then also trying to assemble her Gombe annual report for the previous year and hoping to finish a scientific article on chimp infanticide and cannibalism. "Havn't done anything except the Infanticide, and sordid letters, and sorting piles & piles of Gombe data," she reported home in a January 23 letter—but at least the article was "finished." Within another couple of weeks, it was actually finished and in the mail (and eventually published in the journal *Folia Primatologica* as "Infant Killing and Cannibalism in Free-living Chimpanzees"). At the same time, she was, according to a February 10 letter home, hoping to find someone "to analyse my maps (chimps' range)." It would require about thirty hours per month or more but also might be "quite fun, putting a grid over the map, etc."

Then the proofs of a book written by Stella Brewer, Hugo's one-time romantic interest, arrived in the mail. About to be published by Collins in England and Knopf in the United States, Brewer's *The Chimps of Mt. Asserik* told the story of her courageous if quixotic attempt to reintroduce captive chimps into the wilderness of Senegal, West Africa, and it urgently required a nice introduction by Jane. Another task.

That was soon followed by work on a first draft of the new article for *National Geographic*. Still, as of March 9, after much "wallowing in my annual report" and thus not being able to "think straight" (as Jane phrased it for her mother), that onerous task was nearly done. In addition, she had found yet another likely assistant, Carole Ganiaris, who lived only a couple of houses away.

But the big project for that year—and for the next several, as it slowly became clear—probably began in July. Jane first mentioned it then in a letter to Grub: "I am so bogged down by trying to read years and years of journal notes—for this book. My eyes are squilt!" The book, which she began calling her "monograph," was originally meant to be an updating of the original scientific monograph, *The Behaviour of Free-living Chimpanzees in the Gombe Stream Reserve*, published back in 1968. Although Jane now was approaching the end of her second decade of chimp research, she hoped to produce a full summary that would be at once complete and compact. Of course, that would be difficult. As she explained to an associate at the National Geographic in a March 20, 1978, letter, "18 years of research crammed into a volume slim enough to come within reach of student pockets is some task!"

Within a couple of months she had realized that the thing would probably be much longer: "I plod on with my monograph (think maybe it will have to be in 2 vols!!)," she wrote to Joan Travis in May.

She was working on a chapter about chimpanzee aggression by mid-June, according to a letter home: "Have worked out how to do it, which is the main thing, but tallying up all those threats and fights is a bit tedious. Never mind—the end is in sight, and it's beginning to be fun—to see how

Goblin, for instance, has changed in the last couple of years." A year later, on the first of July 1979, she reported that "Chapter I and II—or 1 and 2 really—of the Monograph are, to all intents and purposes, done."

And by September 23, 1979 (just after Grub had returned to England following his usual summer holiday in Africa), she was "knee deep in the monograph again—after a GHASTLY evening. The whole thing was lost. ALL of it. 1 year's work. Not seen since Grub arrived." For a paranoid moment she had imagined that perhaps Hugo, when he had come to pick up or deliver Grub, had destroyed it as an act of sabotage. "However, it was Grub's rat hunting that was to blame. I suddenly remembered I'd said he could remove all the klobber from the bottom of my cupboard. If he put it back. He did put it back—& the monograph!! Phew. All night long I searched the house in my imagination."

Jane was flying out to Gombe regularly during these years, trying to spend a few days there each month to consult with and review the work of the field staff, deal with problems, and watch and follow chimps. The Kasekela-Kahama war was over by the end of 1977, and her trips to Gombe were typically "truly fantastic super," as she reported home, or "really amazing, for me, this time." Gombe was almost never disappointing, almost always a source of renewal and discovery.

But Jane's more interior and intellectual labors in the office on the second floor of the house in Dar es Salaam—sorting, analyzing, thinking, writing about Gombe—were really the center of her new normal life. And gradually the monograph came to represent the center of the center, the repository for all she had learned and was continuing to learn about chimpanzees.

She employed a series of very satisfactory assistants. After Carole Ganiaris worked for about a year, there was, starting in March 1978, Rosemarie (Rosie) Fief, who lived in the guesthouse. Rosie was partially replaced in January 1979 by Neil Margerison (who helped with the records), then more fully in March 1979 by Heta Bomanpatell. Heta soon moved into the guesthouse, and by September she was living there with her new husband, Prashant Pandit. Yet even with the best assistance of the best assistants, the work was inevitably a struggle against the inertia of language, the sticky obstinacy of a tropical climate, and the silent resistance of a thousand unforeseen interruptions and inconveniences.

The climate in Dar inclined to high heat and seasonal wetness, generating a sometimes oppressive atmosphere that could turn on a whole screeching factory of cicadas or suddenly cause typewriters to stick. Derek might go outside and try clapping his hands to shut up the cicadas, but then the humid wind and rustling palms might try to smother the sound of his clapping.

The thousand interruptions and inconveniences ranged from visitors for coffee or tea or lunch to longer-term guests; to occasional interviews or private lectures in Dar; to a plumbing catastrophe after Jane and Derek returned from Christmas in England at the start of 1978, when "the whole upstairs was flooded! About 3" deep. Worse, it has just poured down two walls—down onto rows of books and files, and into Grub's wardrobe where we keep lots of sheets, materials, and so forth. Oh my oh my, what a time we had."

Periodic shortages of various essentials were randomly interspersed with periodic surpluses of mosquitoes and social obligations (dinner parties with members of the diplomatic corps, for example); and in the summer of 1979, Jane and Derek took time out to attend a state reception for the British royal family. They had a "most informal chat" for about ten minutes with the Queen, who may have been tired. "She said she'd seen one of the films on T.V.," Jane informed the family, and then she chatted with Derek about Tanzanian politics. "All pleasant, but the almost uncanny part was the way she turned on & off. It was almost as though a computer inside her was sometimes a bit late dropping the next penny in the slot, & the smile & interest faded, then suddenly—zoom—there it was again, in a flash!" They also chatted with Prince Philip, having been told that he was fascinated by chimps but soon concluding that he was "not interested in animals one tiny bit." Later that year the interruptions and inconveniences included inconsiderate neighbors playing loud music half the night and an inconsiderate typewriter breaking down, first from failures in electricity, then from a failure of rubber: a little piece that might best be replaced by emergency express from Mr. Sparks's typewriter shop in Bournemouth.

And while the two dogs, Spider and Wagga, were always among the great pleasures of Jane's life in Dar, they too must occasionally have seemed more like a pair of worry-inducing canines or even, possibly, inconvenient quadrupeds. Spider had the bad habit of scrabbling under the fence into President Nyerere's property, where she liked to climb into the garbage and eat until she was bloated and disgusting, with scrapes on her snout and grease on her fur, as well as, at least once, bits of chewing gum stuck all over her face. And Wagga suffered from some kind of skin ailment that never healed completely, no matter what new remedy Jane experimented with.

Spider was spayed in October or November 1979, and the event was "very traumatic for me," Jane admitted in a letter to Vanne, although within a few days the dog was much better. Then Wagga, racing along the beach with Spider and rushing into a yard belonging to two dogs named Lucy and Angus, fell into a toothy territorial dispute with one of them and retreated home with a bad cut above her eye. "Oh dear, I am bored of saline drips!"

A few weeks later Jane was hauling Wagga back to the vet's office again, this time for a serious operation. "What a morning," she wrote to the family later that day. First Wagga was tranquilized, then she was knocked out with an anesthetic. "Into the vein it went. In 1 minute Wagga a) went totally limp as I held her & b) stopped breathing. It was AWFUL. I was sure she was dead. For 4 min (seemed like 4 hours) Gail gave her artificial respiration (sucking) etc. And finally she took a breath—Phew! What a 4 min.! Well, then came 1 hour of horrible surgery. Thank goodness I had her done. She had 'cystic' ovaries—and this may have caused her skin."

Wagga recovered soon enough. But even when both dogs were in the best of health, they were still likely to sniff out trouble of some sort. If not barking and snapping at a suspicious stranger on the beach or bounding heedlessly onto Lucy and Angus's property, they might be trotting down the beach to the fenced property of Apollo Milton Obote and inciting his seven dogs to explode in a frenzy.

Apollo Milton Obote had been Uganda's first prime minister when that nation acquired independence on October 9, 1962, but in 1966, after opposition leaders charged him with financial corruption, Obote dismissed parliament, invoked martial law, and appointed himself Uganda's first president. In January 1971 he was replaced in a coup d'état by an erstwhile supporter in the military, Colonel Idi Amin. Amin established himself as the second president of Uganda, while Obote was made a guest of Tanzania through the generosity of President Nyerere, and thus he settled down in Dar es Salaam in a house on the beach, languishing in a sorry state of seven-dog exile.

Amin's reign of terror in Uganda is legendary. The country was already fractured by competing tribal and religious allegiances, and Amin consolidated his control first with mass executions in the army. He next drove out the nation's entire East Asian population, giving his friends and supporters first choice of the many businesses and other properties left behind. He then organized the torture and execution of anyone in the country who still seemed loyal to Obote or potentially disloyal to himself, ultimately murdering about 300,000 real and imaginary opponents before turning his attention to international affairs with a surprise military attack on his southern neighbor, Tanzania, on October 31, 1978. The tactical advantage of surprise was insufficient, though, and the invasion was soon repelled. Tanzania, hastily assembling an army of 50,000 men, retaliated with a counterinvasion, bloodily pressing all the way to the capital city of Kampala and finally, on April 11, 1979, toppling the Idi Amin regime. The infamous president was forced to seek asylum in Libya, accompanied by his four wives, several of his approximately thirty concubines, and around twenty of his children.

Shortages had been common enough in Tanzania for years, but the war made them worse. By Christmas 1978 there was little or no toilet paper, rice, salt, sugar, and flour in the country, and after the war was officially over, in the spring of 1979, shortages of some essentials continued and even became more serious. As Jane remarked in an August 5, 1979, letter home, "Tanzania is running out of petrol. I mean really — not like shortages — the crude oil supplies are finished." Moreover, she continued, "with no petrol there will be little food in the shops — it cannot be carried to town. Derek is very anxious about harvesting. It is all a MISTAKE — someone has made a stinking mess."

A year after the war had ended, when Jane arrived back in Bournemouth from her usual American lecture and fundraising expedition "more alive than dead" (as she put it in a May 11 note to an American acquaintance), she opened a telegram to learn that "our favourite dog was dead of distemper, in spite of inoculations. She, Spider, was a very special dog for us (as dogs tend to be) and somehow it makes it worse because I have a wish that it was our second dog who died and not Spider, and so added to feeling so sad about Spider I feel guilty about Wagga, because, of course, I love her dearly too. Life deals out such blows."

When Jane and Derek flew back to Dar es Salaam near the end of May, they discovered that Wagga too was dead, the victim of an epidemic of canine distemper. Jane wrote home as soon as she could bear to put the words on paper (May 26): "Both the dogs are dead. That dog flu. Both of them. . . . And the dog next door, that super Whiskey, has nerve problems, after living through the disease, and her lower jaw just snaps up and down all the time. The house is so bleak and empty — and it just seems impossible to believe — yet it is, of course, true."

In the same letter she mentioned that "Obote leaves for Uganda tomorrow." Possibly Apollo Milton Obote was also indulging himself with the hopeful thought that he too could return home to a new normal. Indeed, he was soon triumphantly stepping off the plane back in Kampala and quickly being reseated as his nation's interim leader. And when he lost the general election for president, carried out near the end of that year, Obote simply used his loyal troops to recount the votes until he had won, whereupon he embarked on a four-and-a-half-year trajectory of normal dictatorship, maintaining his hold on power by utilizing his predecessor's well-polished tools and techniques of corruption, patronage, torture, and murder.

Jane and Derek's marriage had during the first five years passed through its own rather normal trajectory: from a beginning marked by intense romantic passion to a less intense yet steadier and more pragmatic middle stage. By the end of the decade, however, Jane had quietly concluded that the marriage would not last. Possibly the central problem was that Derek's once attractive male protectiveness had turned into an oppressive male possessiveness. Derek, in short, was socially jealous. He could not bear for Jane to have friends and a social life separate from him. He would not even allow her to balance her own checkbook. It was so much the way Hugo had been, Jane began to reflect with some amazement, and she started privately to wonder how or why she had twice fallen into the same emotional trap. . . .

But by early 1980 Derek was experiencing digestion problems, then abdominal pains that were serious enough for him to make an appointment with a specialist once they were back in Dar es Salaam. Writing home on June 8, Jane mentioned that "D goes off to his revolting barium meal tomorrow. We can't believe there is anything wrong because he still looks so well. If there is anything wrong I will ring you up."

There was something wrong. The X-rays showed an abnormal dark mass, and so Jane and Derek rushed back to England to find a top London surgeon to operate. The surgeon was very encouraging before the operation, according to Jane's account in *Reason for Hope*. After the surgery, however, he drew Jane into a darkened hospital room—at around nine o'clock in the evening—and informed her bluntly that Derek had cancer. Although he had removed the tumor, it had already metastasized. No further treatment would help. Derek had about three months to live. He hoped Jane was staying with a friend or relative. "Take a taxi, won't you?" he concluded, before patting her on the shoulder and walking out.

By the time Jane left the hospital, it was late and raining. She took the tube to some faraway destination, walked for a significant distance through the rain, and eventually arrived, completely soaked and shaken, back at the home of Pam Bryceson, the widow of Derek's recently deceased brother. After a warm and sympathetic hug, a change of clothing, a sit-down before the fire, a bit of food, a glass of whisky, and—for the first time in her life—sleeping pills, Jane went to bed.

The next evening Vanne showed up from Bournemouth. "After a weep & a whiskey," as Jane later phrased it in a letter to her National Geographic friend Joanne Hess, "we started to talk." They made plans. There were witch doctors in Africa who had access to a whole rich pharmacy of therapeutic herbs; Jane called a good friend in Dar es Salaam, who agreed to pursue that possibility. They had also heard of a "wonderful root" in a village in India; an "old Indian nanny" was put to task on that account. And the next day they heard that Hephzibah Menuhin, the classical pianist and sister of the famed virtuoso violinist Yehudi Menuhin, had survived a serious form of cancer for the past five years. Jane went to see her and thus learned about a controversial substance called laetrile and a physician in Germany, Hans Nieper, who dispensed it. Desperate for the tiniest gleam of hope, Jane seized on this one. Hephzibah "gave me books. She proved that what I knew was right—that 'nothing to be done' was WRONG."

They booked seats on a flight, and by the start of July, Derek was lying in a bed in room 513 at Dr. Nieper's Krankenhaus in Hanover, West Germany. After Derek underwent five days of tests, pills, and laetrile dripped intravenously, Jane was full of enthusiasm, convinced that the treatment had miraculously deactivated his cancer cells. "D feels no pain at all," she wrote to Joanne Hess. "We are so excited. Still another few weeks here. Diet terribly important. But the great hurdle is crossed. The path lab report indicated a FAST growing type of cancer. This seldom responds to Laetrile. But the blood tests indicate that, in fact, it was a slow growing kind. Which is SUPER." Naturally, there was still a "long way to go, as Dr. N says," but Jane was sure of the positive future and just wanted to share with all their friends at the National Geographic "the happiness of proving the London chap wrong."

After about a month they had one "scare" (as Jane put it in an August 22 letter to Mary Griswold Smith at the Geographic), after Derek "developed what Nieper called a 'nodule'—one of the metastases, I suppose, on the colon and we were terrified of an obstruction. That night I know there was a miracle of healing. Because I felt it. And next morning Nieper said 'Oh, your nodule has regressed.' Phew!"

Jane was desperately trying to find hope in an apparently hopeless situation, but the surgeon in London had been right. Derek lived for three months after his surgery, during the first two of which, according to Jane's recollection in Reason for Hope, "we truly believed that he would get well. We believed it absolutely." Still, the false hope they embraced brought true benefits. Derek was "filled with mental energy" and began writing his autobiography, with Jane typing. She referred to that project in the August 22 note to Mary Smith: "Did I tell you he was writing a book? It's coming on jolly well. First two chapters done, and I'm typing them. The publisher is very keen. Wants second consultation after reading these two chapters. It gives D. something to do, so he doesn't fret about inactivity. D. himself is very keen too! It all helps in these difficult days." They listened to classical music together. They prayed together. They visited with other patients, including Hephzibah Menuhin and her husband, Richard Hauser. ("Richard and Hephzibah believed in life after death, and in reincarnation," Jane writes in *Reason for Hope*. "We discussed these things in such a matter-of-fact way that Derek began to accept that they were true.") And they visited with each other. Talking for hours at a stretch, Jane and Derek became once again "very close in this strange new world, together almost every hour of every day."

But Derek's pain became increasingly hard to bear, and they both recognized that death was approaching. Jane hardly slept. She began spending her nights at the Krankenhaus, curled up in the chair next to Derek's bed or dozing in an empty bed nearby. At the end Derek could endure his pain only with the help of morphine, and then he slowly drifted, semi-comatose and still hurting. His last words were "I didn't know such pain was possible." He slipped away during the early-morning hours of October 11. Jane listened to his "rasping breathing," and then she heard "the death rattle, and knew he was, at last, free of pain and in peace." She climbed into his bed and clung to her life's great love, to his now emptied physical self, for the last time.

38

Picking Up the Pieces

1980–1986

DEREK HAD ASKED to be cremated, and Jane returned to Dar es Salaam that November with his remains inside a wooden box.

The ceremony began with Jane, Derek's son, Ian, and Derek's good friend Chief Adam Sapi Mkwawa huddling together against the rain with other mourners inside a small building near the quay, where a solemn appreciation written by members of the Kinondoni constituency was read in Swahili. Then three boats set off for one of Jane and Derek's favorite spots, an island amid Indian Ocean coral reefs, where they had not so long ago passed bright times swimming and snorkeling together. As Jane wrote home, the whole process was "helped along by <u>everything</u> going wrong." First, it "POURED with rain," and the rain made it impossible for anyone to see quite where they were or where they were going. Next, the three boats did not have enough gas to get to the island, so they stopped short, floating in rough seas over the reef. It took "ages" to unscrew the top of Derek's box. Jane cast a silver net of ashes into the air, onto the water—but after she thought to sink the box and a wreath by weighting them down with a stone, no one could find a rope to tie the stone to the box. Nor did anyone have a knife to cut the nonexistent rope. It was a comedy of oversights, she thought, and "I'm sure Derek was laughing."

That was the easy part. It was followed by a slow and wrenching habituation to life in Dar es Salaam alone, as a bereaved widow. "Oh dear— coming back to the house is even <u>worse</u> than I dreaded," she added.

She spent a few nights at the home of some good friends, American ambassador Richard Viets and his wife, Marina, returning during the day to the house she and Derek had shared on the beach: to work, to sort things out, to pick up the pieces of her life. But the Vietses' house soon seemed "too Ambassadorial—always dinners. They feel they have to invite me—& I feel I have to accept!" So she began sleeping at the home of some other friends, the MacMahons. The husband was on leave; the wife, Sigy, was happy for company, and they had a sweet dog, Boxer. But the MacMahon house was too chilly and noisy as a result of air conditioning, and within a few more days Jane moved back to her own place. "I have been sleeping in the house for the past 3 nights," she wrote to Grub around the end of the month. "It's not as bad as I feared. I sit up in your room, reading or working until it's very late, and then fall asleep."

As she prepared to return to England for Christmas with Grub and the rest of the family, Jane wrote to Mary Smith at the Geographic that she was "still feeling lost and alone and have spells when I don't see how I can bear all the thoughts of those last weeks." The pain Derek had endured, his sudden and early death, just seemed "so <u>unfair</u>," she went on. "Wouldn't you have thought Derek had already had enough to bear in one life time? However, I just plough on and hope that, with the passing of time, I shall be able to spend more time remembering the happy days."

Jane's mother, Vanne, was very ill that winter, and in January 1981 she underwent major surgery to replace a faulty heart valve with a newer and better one taken from a pig. Jane avoided visiting her in the hospital, apologizing that "I half wanted to be with you and half not. My associations with cut open people recently have been so horrid that even though your op is—thank <u>heavens</u>—quite different—I might have allowed some of the bad feelings to creep into you & that would have been no good. You are supposed to be more susceptible to telepathic communications when you are doped!"

Fortunately, the surgery was a complete success, and with the new valve in place, Vanne felt better than she had for some time. Jane, meanwhile, was inspired by the thought of the pig who had died so her mother could live, and she began compiling a book of pig pictures, concepts, facts, and stories, which she intended to present to Vanne the following Christmas. That January, while still in Bournemouth, she labored mightily to catch up on the translations, analyses, and typing of the daily Gombe reports and nearly finished with the August pile. But the pig book provided an extra activity once she returned to Dar es Salaam at the end of the month, something entertaining to do during the evenings, after she had worked on chimp and Gombe business all day long.

There was also the old fundraising problem, of course—and now the new problem of raising a fund. About six months before Derek became ill, he had been named chairman of the Tanzania Food and Nutrition Centre.

After he died, the board and staff of the center made a sympathetic gift of six thousand shillings (around $700) to his widow and son, Ian. Jane and Ian agreed to use that donation as seed money for the Derek Bryceson Scholarship in Food and Nutrition, for the training of Tanzanian students overseas, mainly at Cornell University in the United States, and so Jane began soliciting donations for that.

Meanwhile, the desk work in Dar was punctuated by visits to Gombe and by a trip in late March to see the family in England, followed by the spring lecture tour in the States (mid-April to mid-May), followed by a few days in Switzerland. Jane was back in Dar by May 22, and by the twenty-sixth she had tackled the most pressing of her correspondence and could report home rather positively that "I have settled into the routine here—early up, breakfast on the veranda, typing, rushing into town (to see all kinds of people, none of whom were there! and couldn't be rung ahead of time because of there being no phone), more typing, translating, blowing up [at] Heta, boiling water (they've run out of chemicals for the water so we have to boil it for 10 minutes to be sure it's safe!), supper in my little room away from the mosquitos, writing or reading until bed time."

Settling into a routine must have been a comfort, except that it never seemed to last very long. She set off for Gombe near the end of May and came back to Dar a couple of weeks later, only to be, as she soon wrote to Mary Smith, "laid low with one of the 4 worst <u>ever</u> bouts of malaria. I thought I would die!!" The malaria produced a couple of weeks' worth of high fevers, chills, sweating, headache, nausea—complete prostration—but by the first or second week of July she was recovering: "It is <u>fabulous</u> to feel well again—but I'm weak as a kitten!" Still, she was at least strong enough to solicit a pig favor from Smith in the same letter. "You know Mum has a pig valve in her heart? Well, I am making for Christmas a pig anthology. It's very fascinating—even here in Dar I've been able to do a lot of research. Various people are helping. Anyway, could you possibly spare me an extra copy of your super pig article—September 1978." She continued, "Oddly, I've <u>always</u> loved pigs. When I was 8 my ambition was to own 6 Tamworth pigs & join a Circus!!"

And by July 10 she could report to Joanne Hess at the Geographic that in spite of the "ghastly malaria," which had made her even more "frantic, disorganized & behind-hand than usual," she had finally "<u>FINISHED</u> my huge pop. dynamics paper. <u>Years</u> of work in it. I just hope someone will publish it now!"

In such a fashion Jane's ordinary routine in Dar es Salaam resumed, and it may have contributed in its own mysterious way to the healing of grief, a picking up of pieces. If a second hole of loss had been opened by the sudden deaths of beloved Spider and Wagga a year earlier, that was now being filled by a small pack of local mutts with whom Jane made daily excursions up and down the beach. Then, one day in July, she noticed a frightened, furtive, almost feral stray lurking around the vegetation near where Milton Obote had lived. This pathetic canine was, she soon realized, actually one of Obote's dogs, abandoned when he had left for Uganda a year earlier.

Jane named the dog Cinderella. According to a July 22 letter home, she was "the <u>exact</u> colour of Spider, with Wagga's floppy ears and skinny tail. About Wagga size. She has been beaten and ill used, and if you approach she retreats—into the sea if she is near the sea. She spends most of the time lying in the shrubs at the edge of the sand." But Jane soon "conceived the crazy idea of trying to reclaim her," and thus

> every morning and evening, I am "habituating" her! Really—just as though she's a wild animal. I'm afraid it may be a hopeless case. She is SO sad. But I have twice managed to throw her a cheese rind! And yesterday, as I sat there with Pip, Boxer and Patch (the last 2 are the MacMahon dogs, very boisterous, so I was hanging onto Boxer, the roughest) Cinderella actually came onto the beach and played a bit with Patch, and tried to play with Pip. The most discouraging thing is that she won't look at me! And there is not the tiniest weeniest suggestion of a tail wag—except with the other dogs, so at least I know she can wag!

The case turned out to be not at all hopeless, and by the middle of August, the dog had begun moving in. "Well," Jane reported home, "—Cinderella is <u>FANTASTIC</u>. She came home on Sunday—allowed me to give her a flea/tick bath (VERY necessary!) on Monday, <u>and</u> annoint her ears! This evening Prashant came to coffee. I was making it—Grub came in with the wishbone for me to pull. Prashant arrived with the news that Cinda was sitting at the table helping herself to the bones!!!" But, Jane went on, Cinderella was "super when we eat," as well as "very aristocratic when she moves —& <u>so</u> like Spider, in colouring."

Cinderella became a sweet and stalwart companion, a flea-bitten therapist bounding on the beach or curled up and dozing serenely on the floor in Dar es Salaam. But it was among the chimpanzees and in the forests of Gombe that Jane found her fullest healing. As she wrote in *Reason for Hope*,

> Time spent in the forests, following and watching and simply being with the chimpanzees, has always sustained the inner core of my being. And it did not fail me then. In the forest, death is not hidden—or only acciden-

tally, by the fallen leaves. It is all around you all the time, a part of the endless cycle of life. Chimpanzees are born, they grow older, they get sick, and they die. And always there are the young ones to carry on the life of the species. These things brought a sense of perspective back into my life, and with it peace. Gradually, my sense of loss was purged of bitterness, and the futile railing against fate was stilled.

She made a trip to Gombe soon after the funeral ceremony, in late November or early December 1980, but that was, she declared tersely to Mary Smith on December 10, "just the worst—'cos I met Derek there." Her second visit after Derek's death, in February 1981, was better. After a day of following chimps and a late-afternoon swim in the lake, she wrote to Vanne and Olly in a February 15 letter that the weather had been "<u>very</u> wet, but we were quite lucky today as the rain wasn't too <u>hard</u>. In fact, the forest was cool, greens blending with each other, all through to the yellows, oranges & browns. With splashes of red. Restful to the mind. Not such an awful trip as the last one, though still very sad."

On June 5, 1981, she sent an aerogram to Mary Smith, referring to what was so far "in lots of ways a lousy trip to Gombe—as far as the <u>chimps</u> go. The place itself is as beautiful and peaceful as ever. But the chimps are far away, and in nearly 2 weeks have seen <u>very</u> few. <u>No</u> Fifi yet. And only 3½ more days."

The timeless beauty of the forest had a deeply calming effect, but perhaps it was the chimpanzees, those emotional, calculating creatures half-hidden in a parallel universe, who made Gombe such an affirmative and anchoring experience. In August, Jane went to Gombe with Grub and Hugo, who had come with his latest girlfriend to do some photography. Jane wrote to the family on August 29 that Hugo seemed "quite amenable about everything, though it was awful how long it took him to get set up for photography. Luckily it didn't matter because Fifi was around so much—but she might not have been."

Fifi had recently given birth to little Fanni and was now being "a marvellous mother." And in fact "all the chimps were around," and Jane was able to follow and observe most of the mother-infant groups.

Then there was the drama of Pom, the once cannibalistic female now distracted by being a mother for two-year-old Pan. The first day Jane was there was "very, very cold and windy." She began by following Figan and Evered, and she watched those two males greet Pom, sitting high up in a palm tree with baby Pan. "I couldn't see them up there, 40 feet up, just occasionally a face looked round, or Pan moved from one frond to another. Suddenly—and it was like a nightmare and I couldn't believe it—I saw a tiny body, on its back, spreadeagled, coming down through the air. There was a sickening thud, then total silence exept for the wind in the trees." With "shaking legs," Jane moved toward the spot on the ground where the infant had landed. "I heard a tiny, high pitched squeak, long drawn out. Then another. Then silence. I saw the little body, still spreadeagled on its back, absolutely motionless." After about a minute, Pom climbed down the palm tree and approached little Pan slowly, "picked up what I thought was a dead body, and to my amazement he gripped with hands and feet. For the next three hours, he stayed curled up beside her (she rested a lot of the time, or ate on the ground) and then he opened his eyes." Pan was seen two days later, "clinging to her tummy, not moving about," but four days after that he had disappeared. "Poor little Pan," Jane concluded. Pom seemed herself very ill, "like a skeleton," and Jane thought she would soon die as well, which could "virtually eliminate the risk of cannibalism being perpetuated."

She survived, in fact, but her mother, Passion, was declining from some mysterious "wasting disease" and had only a few more months left. Jane last saw the old female during a "super week" at Gombe at the start of February 1982. "I know Passion is foul & all that," Jane wrote home at that time, "but it is PATHETIC to see her now. And after all, she didn't KNOW what she was doing. She is only skin & bone, can't climb tall trees—suddenly crouches down as though in pain. Moves VERY slowly. And has something obviously causing intense pain in one eye. She moves her eyes very, very slowly, as you do when something hurts, and each time she moves them, she touches the bad one with her hand. Sometimes she gently rubs the closed eye with one finger."

Passion died soon after that observation, with the year 1982 thus marking the beginning of the end for Kasekela's cannibal family. Passion's two older offspring, Pom and Prof, together cared for their helpless and otherwise doomed four-year-old brother, Pax.

For Jane, though, 1982 marked a full return to all of her old pleasures in Gombe. "Well, I really did have a lovely time at Gombe," she wrote to the family on May 15. "The weather was fabulous, for one thing. Sunny but cool, with one day of rain so that the ground was not too dry and skiddy. I spent a lot of time wandering in my old haunts, the Peak, and along my old tracks to Linda, and so on. Quite delicious, and I felt about 25 again! I found I was very fit, despite no mountains for so long!"

And a month later, on June 13, after another trip to Gombe, she repeated the same themes of return, rejuvenation, and reinvigoration more emphatically to Mary Smith. "The weather at Gombe was absolutely perfect for following—bright and sunny with cool winds. I was expecting a June greenhouse—but no, not at all. I had some of the most lovely days out in the forest." It was hard to admit, possibly, but "in a strange way," she continued, "I felt free as I have not felt free since Hugo arrived to film in 1963." Hugo's presence, as welcome as it must have been, was simultaneously a distraction; and then "for many years I didn't follow at all because of Grub (not enough time to do all the administration, and be a good mother AND follow chimps), and then, when I was there with Derek after the kidnapping, when Grub was in England I felt really guilty if I stayed out too long, when poor Derek was virtually a prisoner in camp." After Derek died, for the first few visits "I hated it. I really felt miserable, and bitter about everything. But quite suddenly, this last time, there was the incredible sense of freedom—wandering about and feeling 23 again!"

Jane's "incredible sense of freedom" that summer was more than a physical liberation, more than "wandering about and feeling 23 again" at Gombe. It was simultaneously a much broader sense of emotional and social liberation. The ordeal of Derek's illness had brought back the intimacy of their early years together, and his death had of course been devastating. But now, on the other side of that loss, Jane was returning to her old creative optimism and youthful sociability.

Several former Gombeites showed up during this period, becoming guests in Dar and sometimes at Gombe—David Bygott and his wife, Jeanette; Tony Collins; Hank Klein and his wife, Judy; Bill McGrew; Ann Pierce; Anne Pusey and Craig Packer. "I got Anne and Craig off to Gombe this morning," she wrote to the family in late February 1982. "I must say, Anne was a delight, and though it interfered with my work a bit having her, nevertheless it is really very nice indeed to be able to discuss chimps, papers, people etc with someone like Anne. She is so nice! She said she had a chimp grant (from Leakey foundation, actually) and so she should contribute to my well being, because she wouldn't be here, or have got the grant, but for me! So I am well stocked up indeed, with everything!"

Meanwhile, Jane's old friends from the diplomatic corps in Dar es Salaam were leaving for jobs or postings elsewhere, and their impermanence brought her to think about deliberately expanding her circle of Tanzanian friends. "I made a big decision," she wrote home in July 1982. "I was sitting here thinking about all my 'friends' going from Dar—all the diplomats. I thought I really should WORK at getting to know the Tanzanians. There are such fabulous ones about." Indeed, she hoped that Vanne would be able to meet a few of them next time she came out to Dar. She should meet "Chief Adam, of course, Timothy and his wife, Mary Bandu, Chris Liundi (who really IS a good friend—I don't know what I'd do without him, actually) and his wife—who I don't see much 'cos she's in Dodoma—and now

Chris's sister, or sister in law (it all gets muddled!) who is going to do work for me. Not because she particularly wants to—but because Chris thinks I'm working too hard and need some extra help. He came round with her this morning for coffee."

Friendship exists in an invisible barter economy, sometimes merely the exchange of entertaining conversation or sympathetic propinquity, but in Tanzania during this time, friendship's barter economy was often literal and particular, since the regular economy was falling apart. Derek's old political comrade Zuberi Mnyekeya ("no education, no English, salt of the earth," as Jane described him in a July 1981 letter home) came to the house one day that summer "like Father Christmas," hauling in a big load of fruit, vegetables, and sugar and declaring that he knew Derek wanted him to look after Jane, as a brother. If there was anything else she needed, from food to soap to train tickets, he would get it. Mnyekeya soon helped her navigate through the local bureaucracy to get a cesspit-cleaning work order signed, so that the cesspit workers would fix the bottom end of her plumbing system (worse than ever since President Nyerere had built an underground bomb shelter next door). The minister for water also that summer volunteered to find Jane whatever she needed. From him came a package of five hundred airmail envelopes, unavailable in Tanzania, delivered by his brother from Kenya. And Chief Adam Sapi Mkwawa ("such a super person, he renews one's faith in Tanzania") around the same time visited Jane in Dar and then at Gombe and supplemented dwindling supplies of paraffin for the Gombe lamps.

Around the start of 1982, Cinderella was joined by another adopted stray, Baggins—but food, including dog food, was getting expensive. Fortunately, by the start of 1983, Jane had made friends with Dimitri Mantheakis, a "charming Greek" (as she wrote home on January 24) "who has a meat business. And will drop by with food for the dogs! A great weight is lifted from my shoulders." Also, Mollie Miller, the wife of the new American ambassador, David Miller, agreed to contribute dry dog food from time to time. And, in the meantime, Jane's old friend Ramji Dharsi, a shopkeeper who formerly lived in Kigoma, had started bringing over the occasional bag of *sembe* (cornmeal) for her housekeeper and cook, Zeno Ng'anga, since that important item was in short supply as well.

On a plane flight that January, Jane happened to meet a passenger who, as a pilot, had taken Derek on his first ever trip to Gombe. Now working for Swiss Air, the man promised he would look into the possibility of cheap plane tickets for future Bryceson scholars or for visiting scientists. Then Jane's car needed repairs. Spare parts were sent into the country via the American diplomatic pouch, thanks to Ambassador Miller, while a U.S. Marine named Roger Taylor, a talented mechanic, agreed to do the work. Fish for Jane's fish tank in Dar were being supplied courtesy of friends Kirit and Jayant Vaitha, who exported tropical fish from Kigoma, while Tony Collins, coming to Dar after a short visit to Gombe, might be counted on to carry along sand and weeds to go with the fish.

"Tanzania certainly is in a bad state," Jane wrote to Mary Smith in mid-June 1983. "Mostly what is being done is all for the good—the short term effects are terrible, because all the people who kept the economy going have got nervous and simply don't work anymore. Also some injustices were, for sure, perpetrated. And victims still languish in prison. However, the worst problem is food. And that doesn't really affect me. Just finding food for one is not too difficult, and I have good friends who help with the dogs and with my servant Zeno."

Nevertheless, her house had been broken into the year before, with thieves hauling away her best camera, a typewriter, binoculars, clothes, watches meant for Gombe; and at the end of 1982 the two outboard motors at Gombe were stolen, including (as she wrote to Mary Smith at that time) "the lovely new little one that I adored and have only used 4 times. DAMN!" Jane was by then providing extra food for all the Gombe employees, and that additional expense combined with inflation and a bad exchange rate to take the estimated budget for Gombe up suddenly to $33,000 per year.

As the costs of maintaining the operation at Gombe rose, the institutional support from the United States—from the Grant Foundation and the National Geographic—fell, and Jane had largely given up applying for any more professional grants. She was still making her annual spring lecture tour in the States, giving an average of ten big lectures per year, raising approximately $2,500 per event. But that was no longer enough, and so, along with dog-food friends, car-repair friends, and fish-for-the-tank friends, she was now looking for money friends: generous donors to help out with the research and the chimps. In October 1983 she attended an embassy dinner party in Dar and sat next to Prince Bernhard of the Netherlands, whereupon, as she soon wrote home, she "'bent his ear' about money for Gombe." The conversation was "quite encouraging," and the prince asked her to send details. "I thought he'd forget, but he reminded me the last thing. Our farewells were rather funny. He and I shook hands formally. And he went off up the steps (we were on the veranda). Then his aide said goodbye with Dutch kisses on both cheeks. And PB actually came down the steps again, and said, 'I'd forgotten I dared to kiss you goodbye last year'! Wasn't it a hoot. He gaily calls me, 'Jane.' Isn't it funny how everyone does."

In the United States, many others also called her Jane and came to the rescue. Although the National Geographic Society no longer officially supported Gombe research, Melvin Payne arranged for a big-donor dinner in

Washington at the start of 1982, which raised, after expenses, $7,000 for Gombe. It was a simple act of friendship, which Jane soon acknowledged by naming Miff's fourth baby Mel.

Likewise, when Gremlin gave birth in June 1982, the baby was named Getty, in honor of Gordon Getty, the president of the Jane Goodall Institute since 1979, who had recently demonstrated his friendship with some big gifts supporting the Gombe research—and who by May 1983 pledged $250,000 as a matching-funds challenge grant meant to raise a half-million-dollar endowment for the institute.

The Jane Goodall Institute had existed as a legal entity ever since it had acquired tax-exempt status in the late 1970s, but Gordon Getty's earlier gifts and then his challenge grant for the endowment gave it a bank account and with that a measure of solidity and legitimacy. Until then the L.S.B. Leakey Foundation had arranged Jane's lectures and recycled the income as part of its larger grants for the Gombe work, but as of May 25, 1983, as Jane informed Deborah Spies, the foundation's acting director, "I intend to forgo all my United States income earned during this past lecture tour in favor of the Institute. This also concerns any moneys that may be donated to my work through the Leakey Foundation. I do hope this will be in order."

The endowment would, Jane hoped, eventually provide a steady income to ensure that Gombe's budget could be met even if she was unable to lecture for a season. It was unfortunate that whoever oversaw the fund put it into an account that earned only 2.5 percent annually and that the capital would be spent within a few years. But in any case, by late 1983 Jane was able to imagine the possibility of relief from "the hand to mouth way of living" (as she phrased it for Prince Bernhard) that had given her so many sleepless nights. And by the second half of 1984 there was the promise of at least enough of a surplus to launch a new project: ChimpanZoo.

For years Jane had been concerned about the treatment of apes in captivity. Her research had demonstrated that chimpanzees are intelligent, sensitive, social, emotional, surprisingly humanlike creatures, and yet they were still often being held in exhibits that resembled bad prisons, with steel bars, concrete floors, no one to socialize with, nothing to do. ChimpanZoo would attempt to improve zoo conditions for chimps by introducing something called "environmental enrichment," providing the apes with things to manipulate and think about, such as bedding and nesting materials, fresh tree branches, raisins embedded in logs, and artificial termite mounds. But if the project's ultimate goal was to engage the chimps, its more immediate goal was to engage people around the chimps. In short, ChimpanZoo would operate mainly as a research project whereby university professors and students could join zoo personnel to compare (using the ethological concepts and data collection techniques of Gombe) behaviors among zoo chimps and wild chimps at Gombe. ChimpanZoo would examine nature-versus-nurture issues, consider the effects of different child-rearing systems, look for evidence of chimp cultural traditions in zoo colonies, and so on.

In 1984, Ann Pierce, a former graduate researcher at Gombe, began searching for zoos and universities that might be interested in participating in ChimpanZoo. A North Carolina donor lent her a VW bus to travel about in, and Jane promised to cover her basic expenses. For three months Ann traveled around the country from zoo to zoo, and finally, near the start of 1985, she submitted a formal proposal for the project to the Jane Goodall Institute for a possible grant.

Ann had done an impressive job during those three months. Some twenty zookeepers and thirty-five university students were starting to collect data at six zoos around the country, with four more zoos about to join or at least expressing strong interest. Former Gombeite Jim Moore, now at the University of California at Davis, had agreed to sample data from each site and work on issues of compatibility, with the goal of establishing a central database; another former Gombeite, Larry Goldman, at George Mason University, agreed to participate as an adviser. But the proposal's estimated budget, including a year's salary for general coordinator, was $50,000. Jane was "absolutely horrified" by that figure, as she declared in a letter to Ann, since "that is more than it takes to run the whole of Gombe."

The proposal was finally submitted to the Jane Goodall Institute with a whittled-down budget of $18,500, and when the institute board still turned it down, Jane paid for ChimpanZoo's first year out of her own pocket. Within several months (by February 1, 1986), she was proudly describing to one new friend and potential supporter the exciting results:

> I must tell you that it is working, despite what everyone thought, most fabulously. I think the best tribute to Ann is the fact that on 8 February there is a very big ChimpanZoo workshop in Colorado Springs (where the college already teaches a course in conjunction with the program) WITHOUT MY BEING THERE!!! I'm sad to miss it, so are they, but they are coming anyway. 45 people signed up, 22 more wanting to join in. I think it's 13 zoos involved already. It is very exciting. So far it has cost nothing above Ann's salary and expenses because, as originally planned by me, the various zoos themselves provide us on the spot funding. Or the local colleges.

• • •

As Jane picked up the pieces of her emotional and financial life, she also began picking up the pieces of her professional life. She had periodically traded notes with her Japanese colleagues in the Mahale Mountains, south of Gombe, and occasionally she had conferred with them at conferences. In 1982 she was invited to give a paper at her first scientific conference in Japan, a symposium on parent-child bonding organized by two distinguished pioneers of ape studies, Junichiro Itani and Toshisada Nishida. Jane had a "FABULOUS time" there, she wrote to Joanne Hess at the Geographic on December 1, and she "learnt a lot and had some good new ideas." She tried some interesting new foods—among them raw sea cucumber, raw fish, and raw venison—and went to a wonderful inn in the mountains. But the best part was getting to know Dr. Itani: "He is the kindest, gentlest and most sensitive person, with a super wife, and a dear old mother in an old style kimono."

Beginning in 1981, meanwhile, Jane also regularly stopped in Switzerland to give lectures and confer with the ethologist Hans Kummer at the University of Zurich, who was becoming a good friend and increasingly a valued colleague. She began developing a professional friendship with two of Kummer's students, Christophe and Hedwige Boesch, who were then starting chimpanzee research in West Africa, doing "a MOST difficult chimp study in the Ivory Coast," according to a May 21 letter home. "The chimps there open nuts with hammer stones or hammers made of wood in the most FASCINATING way." Jane generously invited all of these scientists out to Gombe.

But getting to and staying at Gombe was not always easy. For one thing, the malaria seemed to be getting more aggressive and persistent. For another, starting in the second half of 1984, transportation became less reliable. The Kigoma airport fire engine broke down, which meant that no planes were allowed to land, and soon the train from Dar to Kigoma was booked two months in advance. The fire engine was eventually fixed, but a year later it was broken again, grounding planes again, and for a while the train stopped altogether because of a derailment that may have been deliberate sabotage by thieves.

Still, in spite of these and other obstacles, a few of Jane's colleagues made the trip. Christophe Boesch spent a couple of months at Gombe. Hans Kummer briefly visited her in Dar and at Gombe in October 1982. And for a few weeks each year, from 1984 through most of the decade, the linguistically oriented anthropologist Christopher Boehm from Northern Kentucky University carried out his chimpanzee vocalization research at Gombe.

"Chris was fortunate in seeing lots of things near camp—even a hunt! (Not successful.) But he saw meat eating—Goblin with the carcass of a monkey

Sparrow killed the day before," Jane commented in an August 1985 letter home. "Anyway, it was <u>really</u> good for the monograph that he came. We have discussed it endlessly and he has had some excellent comments."

The "monograph," originally conceived as a slim and simple update of her 1968 scientific monograph, *The Behaviour of Free-living Chimpanzees in the Gombe Stream Reserve,* was the project Jane had begun during her years with Derek. But the updated version had taken on a life of its own, until it was starting to look like a two-volume encyclopedia summarizing her life's work to date, with the date forever moving forward.

As with all her writing, Jane strove for simplicity and comprehensibility. She had made a vow right from the beginning of her scientific career, when she first went to Cambridge, to write in a language that most people could understand. Instead of describing the hair-raised state of excited, fearful, or enraged chimps as *piloerection,* for instance, why not call it *hair erection* or *bristling?* Using a fancy word when a simpler one would do always seemed pompous to Jane, and, worse, it excluded many people, created small barriers against ordinary understanding. In that regard, she made a second vow. If she had to read anyone else's sentence three times, she would put the book away. "I think I'm reasonably intelligent," Jane once told me, "and if I have to read something three times to understand what it means, why should I waste my time?" Having reached that conclusion about other people's writing, she developed the practice of reading her own work aloud, testing it for ease of comprehension. And of course in the monograph she continued her usual practice of giving chimps and other complex nonhumans the respect of ordinary personal pronouns: *he* and *she* and *who,* not *it* and *which.*

Jane returned to her work on the monograph by the end of 1981, and by early 1982 she had found an American publisher for it, Harvard University Press. But she could never count on extended blocks of time for work, and so the writing was squeezed in wherever it would fit: a few hours here, perhaps a lucky full day there. She was looking forward to one such day in October 1982, she wrote to Vanne, just as soon as she made a mince pie in the early morning to feed some expected guests, including Hans Kummer, whereupon she would return to her battle with a chapter on feeding. "<u>Nearly</u> done. But it's a <u>real</u> struggle. Real discipline to <u>make</u> myself bash on at the typewriter. I'm bored with it all. Oh well—I must get into the next chapter. What shall it be? Either <u>aggression</u> or <u>communication</u> or <u>friendly behaviour</u> (which may be part of communication) or ♀ social structure, or <u>SEX</u>."

When Hans Kummer did show up in Dar, Jane found it very reassuring to have a friend there, especially since Cinderella had recently gotten into a bad fight and needed emergency surgery. Jane wrote home to Vanne, "It was super for me to have Hans with me—to hold <u>my</u> hand as <u>I</u> held Cinderella's <u>paw</u>!" More significantly, the Swiss ethologist assured Jane that he would help with the monograph, and she realized that he could take the place of Robert Hinde as a distinguished colleague and mentor. "He is going to read each chapter of the Monograph & criticize it for me. It will mean a lot of extra work & probably <u>not</u> meeting the deadline—but just <u>so</u> worth while. It is what I have been needing for <u>ages</u>—being so cut off & isolated. As you remember," she continued, "I was wondering <u>who</u> could do it for me, & had given up. Now—an answer to prayer."

Jane also had a loyal handful of paid assistants and typists. The reliable Heta had been living with her husband, Prashant Pandit, in the guesthouse, but as their marriage disintegrated in 1981, she became less reliable and finally moved back to her family's home in India. Prashant quickly remarried, and his new wife, Trusha, took over where Heta had left off. "Trusha has worked like a trojan!" Jane wrote home in January 1983. And "I am already well into my next chapter."

By February 6, according to a note to one friend at the Geographic, Jane was "in the midst of a chapter on Aggression. Fascinating, but difficult." By June 17, as she wrote to another, she was "not getting on too fast with the Monograph"—but only because "I am going through the initial labour process, which is absolutely inevitable and absolutely hideous. Everything I have read and thought goes grinding and crashing about in my head, and I sit all day and end up with one page and tear up 100's more. But in the long run the chapter gets born! Right now it's 'Social structure'—which is unbelievably complex, and all too easy to oversimplify in a glib way. That is what most people seem to do. And if you don't oversimplify, then it is really difficult to write."

She took the dogs for walks on the beach to relax from writing late at night, or to relax before starting in the predawn morning, as she loved to watch the first faint light seep in at the horizon; and she began carrying along a small Dictaphone, just in case any monograph thoughts occurred while she was walking. If she was in a lyrical sort of mood, the Dictaphone could capture lines of poetry that might also come into her head. And in December 1983, she announced that "I have been OBSESSED with the Monograph" and "the END is in SIGHT!!!" She continued: "Mary—I've ended up doing <u>MAMMOTH</u> research into the MIND of the chimp. The evolution of intelligence, love, & <u>warfare</u>. It has become 2 or 3 times bigger than I originally planned. Worth it in the long run, but oh dear."

The end may have been in sight by then, but it still took almost a year before it was in hand. On October 6, 1984, Jane reported to the Geographic's Neva Folk that "I have to all intents and purposes got the book DONE.

Just typing the chapter that has hung over my head almost since I began the book — way back in the distant past." Finally, on October 28, she wrote to a pair of American friends that the book was really and truly and actually "FINISHED!!!!!!"

But there was still more to do, and the director of Harvard University Press decided to send one of its senior manuscript editors out to Africa to fight the editorial fight. The tall and elegant Vivian Wheeler dusted off her passport, began swallowing her antimalaria pills, and got her shots for cholera, typhoid, and yellow fever. She packed her green pens and summer clothing and a supply of fresh cheese that Jane had requested, and then she set off, flying Swiss Air and planning to rendezvous with Jane in Geneva for a Monday, February 11, connection that would take them together to Dar es Salaam. Unfortunately, a big snowstorm — "La Neige du Siècle," as the editor read in the newspaper headlines — interrupted everything. The plane for Dar had been diverted from Geneva to Zurich. Wheeler squeezed herself at the last second on a shuttle to Zurich and then boarded the Dar es Salaam plane with ten minutes to spare. Jane, however, coming by train from another direction, missed it, and so the editor anxiously buckled herself into a machine that was headed (as she later phrased it) "to a continent where I knew absolutely no one."

Vivian Wheeler went to Africa with a long list of questions and issues that she thought might be seriously debatable, but after Jane arrived two days later, she found that they agreed on everything. They were joined by Trusha Pandit, and the three of them descended on a big stack of pictures and charts and graphs and typed-upon sheets of flimsy blue tissue paper. After the initial panic of missed connections in Switzerland, Vivian thought, the novelties and vagaries of life in Dar — power blackouts, broken-down car, useless telephone, armed soldiers guarding Nyerere's house next door — all seemed "quite routine." They had a very good time, in fact, and so they soon decided to extend the editorial process for a couple of weeks and expand it out to Gombe.

At Gombe they cooked breakfast over a fire on the beach every morning at dawn, then pulled out whatever chapter was under consideration and headed "upstairs" to the provisioning camp, where they read and marked until the chimps showed up. Vivian and Trusha might watch and take photos of the chimps while Jane disappeared into the woods. After a light lunch, editor and assistant would return to their labors in camp until the end of the afternoon, whereupon they would go down to the beach and wait for Jane to show up. They would have a refreshing swim in the lake and then build the fire for their dinner, which was a stew, the same one — chunks of beef, beans, rice, tomatoes — every night. After dark, Vivian and Trusha would crawl into their beds, where they might lie awake and listen to the animals all around, while, as Vivian remembers, "Jane would light her candle and write up her follows or review the chapters I'd worked on during the day. What stamina."

When it came time to leave, the three women climbed with their supplies into Gombe's rubber dinghy. But the lake was dark and rough, and a huge storm was approaching. Jane was unable to get the little outboard to work. They began drifting. The lake got rougher, the sky increasingly ominous. Finally one of the staff members on shore saw what was wrong, swam out to the boat, and started the motor. Away they went. And then, as they slowly worked their way across the scalloped water toward one after another of the protective headlands stretching out from the shore, Jane would say, "All right, when we get around there, everybody gets an M&M."

That was the start of the editorial process, and it was followed during the next several months by the full titration: a complicated back-and-forthing of papers, scribbled notes, long typed letters, and static-filled phone calls. By early November, Jane had finally, as she wrote to some American friends, "sent off the very last re-writes, omissions, alterations, reorderings, lost bibliography references, etc, of my book. This was the galley proof stage. Phew! It's practically DONE."

And by the end of February 1986 she informed other friends that "my book is now in page proof, and I have been through every page — 700 of them!!!! The first copies come off the press in May or June. It is very exciting. But it is not due on the market until the fall. (It simply took longer than we hoped, being such a complicated book.)"

In mid-April she began her usual spring lecture tour in the States, stopping in Cambridge, Massachusetts, on May 17 for book publicity and an evening book party with members of the Harvard University Press editorial staff. She received an honorary doctorate at nearby Tufts University in the morning of the eighteenth, delivered an afternoon commencement address at Tufts Veterinary School, and was whirled away by helicopter to Connecticut for a late-afternoon fundraising dinner for the Bryceson Scholarship Fund. She was back in England by the start of June, talking about chimps to Grub's boarding school on the sixth, then flying to Switzerland for visits with Hans Kummer and the Boesches before returning to Dar es Salaam.

"Dar is quite cool during all but the hottest part of the day," she reported to Neva Folk in a June 15, 1986, note, "but there are millions of mosquitoes and I gather the malaria problem is even worse. But most of us hardened Tanzanians just shrug our shoulders, take as many sensible precautions as possible, and hope for the best!" Still, in spite of Jane's inclinations toward a shoulder-shrugging kind of optimism, her next trip to Gombe brought the "awful, bad, horrible news" (as she put it in a July 7 letter home) that four-year-old Getty was dead. "Why, of all the chimps, should it be Getty. His body was found after he had been missing 7 days — without a head. We cannot think it can be anything but witchcraft. And we have learned so much about witchcraft. There are 60 witchdoctors in Mwamgongo, with 6 all-powerful leaders. The talk is now open. At present the government has recently sent some white witchdoctors to purge them — but they fear they may be defeated."

Better news came later that summer, and it was threefold. First, Pom, who had disappeared about one and a half years earlier, was sighted in the territory of the northern community carrying a young baby. In other words, she had successfully emigrated from Kasekela and was starting a new life. Also, several members of the field staff had begun using portable video cameras, thus supplementing their daily written reports with an entirely new kind of record that documented subtle events and styles (such as individual differences in maternal behavior) and captured incidents never before put on film (males on territorial patrol, coordinated reactions to dangerous snakes, responses to the death of others, and so on).

Finally, around August 14, Jane returned to Dar from Gombe to find a package containing eight copies of the book. "It is SUPER. What a book! I actually had stopped believing in it," Jane immediately wrote to Vivian Wheeler and everyone else at Harvard Press. "Then, last night after a weary day getting back, THERE it lay! I gaze & gaze at the finished product." It was the realization of "the dream that I believed would come to me one day — that kept me going through the worst times."

Two or three or four times the weight of an ordinary book, it was long and wide and thick, with color-coded (black and green) print on more than 650 pages, each holding perhaps twice the information of ordinary pages. The cloth cover was forest green with richly embossed gold letters on the front and on the spine, announcing *The Chimpanzees of Gombe: Patterns of Behavior*. The book opened onto a frontispiece: a black-and-white scene of a half-dozen chimps walking down a trail, the farthest one pausing to look back over his shoulder. And the dedication named Jane's most important and beloved associates:

> *For my mother, Vanne,*
> *for the chimpanzees of Gombe themselves,*
> *and in memory of Louis Leakey*

Vanne loved the book, she told her daughter. The only problem: it was too big and heavy to read in bed.

Jane Goodall had demonstrated that it was possible to live and walk freely among wild chimpanzees, and that a person—even a bare-legged, pony-tailed, young female one—could over time and with great effort construct a critical understanding of what wild apes do, how they live, and who they are. She was the first scientist to discover and document that chimpanzees eat meat and that they use tools. She was among the first scientists to admit that chimpanzees and other large animals can have personalities, and her example as a scientist helped to make that once revolutionary perspective commonplace. She introduced the idea of chimpanzees as actors in their own drama, as individuals operating with complex intent, and thus she helped establish the scientific appreciation of animal will and intelligence. She propagated the idea that wild chimpanzees have emotions similar to those of humans, and that their emotional inheritance, their ordinary map of desire, helps account for the many ways in which chimpanzee behavior echoes and elucidates human behavior: patriarchal politics, for example, and male-driven intercommunity warfare. And she was the first or among the first proponents of the idea that chimpanzee behavior exists in a cultural context, that some patterns vary from region to region, community to community, and are passed down through the generations by learning and perhaps active teaching.

Jane Goodall practiced and taught a science that combined the cold purity of traditional European ethology with her own warm embrace of intuitive and ethical ways of thinking, and her work remains absolutely central, and seminal, to the larger achievement of twentieth- and twenty-first-century primatology. Through her remarkable personal generosity, her opening up of a place and a style and method, she also contributed powerfully to the community of her scientific peers, while helping to launch a significant portion of primatology's next generation. And if her science was part of a larger Western cultural method for rendering order out of chaos, of beating the unbearable buzz of existence into some aesthetic and utilitarian form, then so was her book a rendering of the rendering: giving bound construction to the chaos of twenty-five years' worth of data taken from a small but immensely rich bit of flickering forest at the edge of Lake Tanganyika. *The Chimpanzees of Gombe: Patterns of Behavior,* in sum, might serve as the index to or primary summation of a brilliant scientific career.

PART III

The Activist

39

Well-Being in a Cage

1986–1991

"OH—DID YOU HEAR about the conference they are putting on in Chicago to 'celebrate' the publication of the HUP book?" Jane wrote to Mary Smith at the National Geographic. "A full 3 days, sponsored by the Chicago Academy of Sciences—with chimp people from all over the world. Japanese, West African people—sign language and, of course, Chimp Zoo people. Exciting. I'm supposed to be organizing it, but they do all the arrangements including funds."

The big conference, "Understanding Chimpanzees," took place on November 7, 8, and 9, 1986. Jane was the queen bee at this event, of course, and her twenty-five years of research at Gombe served as a logical axis for the conference, since it had indeed been timed to celebrate the publication of her big book. For Jane, though, the Chicago conference marked the end of her active career as a scientist—a few years later she would describe her experience there as fundamentally transformative: "When I arrived in Chicago I was a research scientist, planning the second volume of The Chimpanzees of Gombe. When I left I was already, in my heart, committed to conservation and education. Somehow I knew that Volume 2 would probably never be written—certainly not while I was still active and filled with energy."

During the final hours of the Chicago conference, about thirty top chimpanzee experts agreed to form a new organization that would lobby on behalf of the chimps. Geza Teleki, the former Gombeite and current anthropologist at George Washington University, was elected its first chairman. Someone suggested the name Committee for Conservation and Care of Chimpanzees, which could be remembered through its stuttering acronym, CCCC. Jane would serve as the CCCC's celebrity public representative and (via the Jane Goodall Institute) significant financial backer. And during the

next four or five years, she would rely on Geza and the CCCC for intellectual and logistical support while using the CCCC offices, located in Geza's
home in suburban Washington, D.C., as her pied-à-terre in the nation's
capital.

Until recently an international trade in live animals had routinely raided
the forests of West Africa to harvest—by shotgun, at an estimated ratio of
ten dead for every one exported—baby chimps for research. This trade had
a major impact on some wild populations in West Africa, and it concentrated
on the offerings of two dealers, both exporting from Freetown, Sierra Leone. One of the Freetown dealers was a native Sierra Leonean, Suleiman
Mansaray, but U.S. laboratories preferred to buy their chimps from the second, supposedly more reputable dealer, an ex-convict and ex-Nazi known as
Dr. Franz Sitter. An international treaty and a national law (the Endangered
Species Act) had combined in 1975 to inhibit that trade into the United
States, but during the 1980s the leaders of the U.S. National Institutes of
Health (NIH) had begun trying in a number of imaginative ways to recon-
nect with live chimps harvested in Africa.

Thus, Jane's (and the CCCC's) first task was to improve the protection
offered to chimpanzees by U.S. law. She persuaded Senator John Melcher
of Montana to insert an amendment into a 1988 NIH appropriations bill
specifying that "no funds . . . shall be used by the National Institutes of
Health . . . on any project that entails the capture or procurement of chimpanzees obtained from the wild." Coordinating efforts with the Humane
Society of the United States and the World Wildlife Fund, she successfully
petitioned to upgrade the official status of chimpanzees as defined in the Endangered Species Act. And finally, as the top decision-makers at the National Institutes of Health continued to discuss and promote ways in which
they might overcome restrictions (for instance, by establishing partnerships
or setting up their own projects in Africa), Jane went right to the top: to
U.S. Secretary of State James A. Baker III.

Her first meeting with Secretary Baker took place on March 12, 1990,
when she and Geza were invited for a private luncheon in his office. After
Baker opened their lunchtime conversation by recollecting a visit to a zoo in
Australia where he had seen chimps, the talk turned to matters of chimpanzee conservation and the NIH's recent attempts to gather support in the
State Department for research on chimps in Africa. Baker was, according to
Geza's recollection, "clearly disturbed by that information." Moreover, "unlike some Washington VIPs, whose eyes swiftly glaze over after the oblig-
atory small talk of introductions, Baker impressed us with his focus on
chimpanzee issues." They talked about conservation in Africa. Baker offered support from his office for projects Jane was planning there. And at

the end of the hour, as he stood up from the table, the secretary of state declared emphatically that (according to Geza's paraphrase) "so long as he occupied the office . . . no federal agency is going to get [the U.S. Department of State's] help to breach American policy against exploitation of chimpanzees."

Jane communicated some of her sense of achievement in a subsequent letter to a friend. "I do think we are making progress," she wrote in the spring of 1990. "The lunch with James Baker was terrifically useful. Having US State Department behind me in Africa is really wonderful. And I had a long chat with Barbara Bush yesterday!!!"

Jane's second task was to improve conditions for chimpanzees already inside laboratory cages, and the campaign on that front began two days after Christmas 1986—a month and a half after the Chicago conference—when she sat down with the rest of the family in their Bournemouth living room to watch a videotape secretly made inside an American biomedical research laboratory known as Sema, Inc.

Sema was located inside an ordinary-looking, single-story building veiled by curtains behind plate glass windows and situated innocuously between a suburban bank and a steak eatery in Rockville, Maryland. Although the business inside was supported entirely by U.S. taxpayers ($1.5 million yearly through the National Institutes of Health), its workings were entirely closed to the taxpaying public. In early December 1986, however, members of an underground animal rights group broke into the facility after hours; stole some records, two cages, and four chimps; and produced a long videotape. The records and videotape were handed over to an aboveground animal rights group, People for the Ethical Treatment of Animals (PETA). Members of PETA edited the tape, entitled it *Breaking Barriers,* and mailed copies, along with a summary of their own investigation, to a number of potentially interested parties, including Jane Goodall.

Sema used around five hundred primates—chimpanzees and various monkey species—as experimental subjects, and the laboratory's own records revealed a high death rate for its primates: seventy-eight deaths over five years. Some were merely the consequence of accidents, such as the steaming to death of twenty-six monkeys on a bad-plumbing day. Other casualties, including the deaths of four chimpanzees, may have been the result of inadequate management and veterinary care. But the true horror of this laboratory was much simpler and more banal. Sema had for years been keeping many of its research subjects inside small, hermetically sealed boxes called "isolettes." The isolettes (40 inches high, 31 inches deep, 26 inches wide) superficially resembled microwave ovens, and they completely enclosed and isolated the animals inside. Supposed to limit the spread of airborne viruses, these boxes circulated air through a centralized filtration system that ran twenty-four hours a day, producing for any animal inside the endless sensation of rushing air and whirring fans. At that time Sema used 325 isolettes, with 32 reserved for their young chimpanzees. The chimps came from a large NIH breeding facility. Removed from their mothers at birth, bottle fed, and raised artificially in a nursery for eighteen months, they were then packed off to the suburban Maryland laboratory in pairs. At Sema the baby pairs were stored inside cages so small—2 feet in height, less in the other dimensions—they had barely enough room to turn around. Around the age of two, they were placed individually inside the hermetically sealed isolettes and kept there, deprived of sight, smell, taste, hearing, or even touch, hardly aware of any other creature in the universe for the remainder of the research protocol, which usually lasted from thirty to thirty-six months.

"We all sat watching the tape," Jane later wrote about her Christmas holiday viewing of *Breaking Barriers* with the family, "and we all were shattered. Afterward, we couldn't speak for a while."

Jane returned to Dar es Salaam by early January 1987. The weather, ordinarily oppressive at that time of year, was (she wrote home) "much cooler than usual with a lovely breeze—nay, often wind—almost all the time. Good for working. Just as well. Have not even done the newsletter yet." She was trying to produce a semiannual newsletter for the Jane Goodall Institute membership, working on a new book for children, and writing a sequel to *In the Shadow of Man,* as well as coping with various surprise visitors. She was trying to catch up on the backlog of Gombe data. And she was expecting her friend Ramji Dharsi to arrive soon with a whole new stack of mail from Kigoma.

Those were ordinary reconfigurations of the same old problems and tasks Jane had wrestled with for years. Now, however, she was also preoccupied with some new issues. For one, what to eat. She had finally read Peter Singer's book *Animal Liberation,* which introduced her to the horrors of factory farming; as a result, she decided to go vegetarian, or at least eschew the flesh of mammals and forgo eggs from chickens raised in small cages. She mentioned some of these matters in a January 29 letter to Sue Engel, the new director of the Jane Goodall Institute, who was trying to schedule her spring fundraising tour: "Sue, when you're talking with people I'm going to be staying with, or who are organizing my visits, could you please announce that I utterly will not eat animals' flesh or battery chicken eggs. Absolutely not. It'll have to be fish, and eggs from free-ranging chickens.

OK?" Eating fish was tricky because of Grub, who was so devoted to catching them and so convincing in his justifications. "I'll have to go on hoping, for a while, that it's not as bad for them. They have a free life first. And, as Grub is always saying, they eat each other alive, and if he didn't get a fish, a bigger fish, or shark would. And is it worse to be suffocated or digested!! So I'll eat fish."

Jane was also sending out copies of *Breaking Barriers* to every potentially sympathetic friend and colleague she could think of. She appended letters to the tapes—such as the January 18 one sent to the primatologist Alison Jolly, which described conditions inside Sema as "this horrifying inhumanity practised in the name of science." At the same time she prepared a professional assessment of the conditions at Sema and sent it off to her contacts at PETA, who planned to circulate it to the American media.

Having done these many things, she left on February 2 for a three-week stay at Gombe. In the United States, meanwhile, Jane's notarized statement assessing conditions inside the Sema laboratory, based on the PETA videotape, were released to the public—and so the battle of words began. Since Jane was by then recognized as the world's foremost authority on wild chimpanzees, her comments (such as "the stark, barren conditions are highly psychologically damaging to the apes, and inevitably cause profound stress leading to despair") provoked a defensive response from the unfortunate man who had just taken over as CEO of Sema, John Landon. "We are a superb facility," he told reporters, and people had to understand that Sema was a serious, working research laboratory. Landon was truly surprised that a thoughtful scientist like Dr. Goodall would base her criticisms on second-hand information, including stolen documents, without actually coming to see things for herself.

That was close to an invitation, and by the time Jane arrived for her spring tour in the United States, at the end of March, it had become one —for both her and Roger Fouts of Central Washington University, who was becoming an ally in the campaign. Having taught American Sign Language to chimps since the late 1960s, Roger brought not only years of expertise gained by working daily with chimps in his own laboratory but an additional perspective acquired by years of communicating with them. He and Jane were driven to suburban Maryland by a National Institutes of Health official, greeted at the Sema laboratory by John Landon, and given a tour.

After the tour Jane and Roger sat down for a brief discussion with the director, the head veterinarian, and several other scientists and staff members at the lab. As Roger later wrote, Jane opened the conversation by describing what she knew of chimpanzees in their natural state: the extended bonds between mothers and offspring, the elaborate social systems, the many indications that chimpanzees possess rich emotional lives. She spoke of chimpanzees laughing in amusing circumstances, mourning the death of a loved one, exhibiting signs of depression that come from social isolation. And she raised the critical issue of Sema's practice of confining individual youngsters by themselves inside small boxes for months at a time. How could any compassionate person subject a sentient and emotionally alive animal, a creature with the same needs for companionship as any human child, to such total isolation as part of an experimental protocol?

Scientists at the meeting objected that the isolettes were necessary to protect workers against infection from HIV or hepatitis.

Jane and Roger countered that there were probably workers at the lab infected with HIV or hepatitis, yet no one was placing them in isolettes. Why not put the chimps together in pairs or small groups, so that they could keep each other company during an experiment?

"That's inefficient," someone responded. "With two infected chimps in a cage we'll have only one 'data point' to study. It's a waste of a chimp."

Jane and Roger Fouts were driven back to Washington by the same NIH executive who had taken them out earlier in the day. The man must have imagined that the tour went well. "Jane," he said, talking over his shoulder to his passenger in the back seat, "at least you will agree that these chimpanzees are well cared for. I'm sure you'll have no problem writing a letter stating that this lab is up to USDA regs and that there are no violations." After wiping the tears from her face, Jane responded softly but emphatically: "By no means will I write you any such letter."

The spring tour unfolded over the next seven weeks: a transcontinental zig and zag to fourteen cities and six zoos where Jane gave twelve big lectures, seven press conferences, seven network television interviews, five dinner talks, and two seminars. Sitting down at a portable typewriter during occasional peaceful moments, she also wrote "A Plea for the Chimps," which was published in the *New York Times Magazine* on May 17, 1987.

The article began with a quick statement of the essential dilemma. That chimpanzees are almost 99 percent genetically identical to humans in biochemistry and physiology makes them attractive as lab animals. That they are also psychologically and emotionally so similar to humans raises the ethical question, "Are we justified in using an animal so close to us . . . as a human substitute in medical experimentation?" But because many respectable scientists were insisting on the critical need for chimpanzees in research, Jane would for the moment set aside the larger ethical issue and concentrate instead on a smaller one, which was our treatment of chimpanzees inside cages while they were being experimentally injected with harmful viruses.

Case in point: the Sema laboratory she had toured in late March. "It was a visit I shall never forget. Room after room was lined with small, bare cages, stacked one above the other, in which monkeys circled round and round and chimpanzees sat huddled, far gone in depression and despair." She saw young chimpanzees "crammed together" in the tiny storage cages, not yet part of any experiment; and she saw the experimental chimpanzees inside their isolation boxes, forced into "conditions of severe sensory deprivation" and responding, over time, in the way that any sentient and emotional being with powerful social needs would respond. "A juvenile female rocked from side to side, sealed off from the outside world behind the glass doors of her isolation chamber. She was in semidarkness. All she could hear was the incessant roar of air rushing through vents into her prison." Intending, perhaps, to demonstrate how well the chimps were cared for, a laboratory caretaker opened one of the boxes. The chimp inside did not respond. "She sat, unmoving." The caretaker reached inside, but the chimp did not greet him, nor he her. "As if drugged, she allowed him to take her out. She sat motionless in his arms. He did not speak to her, she did not look at him. He touched her lips briefly. She did not respond. He returned her to her cage. She sat again on the bars of the floor. The door closed."

Such total passivity and lack of affect were absolutely uncharacteristic of normal chimpanzees, Jane wrote, and it indicated deep depression. "Have you ever looked into the eyes of a person who, stressed beyond endurance, has given up, succumbed utterly to the crippling helplessness of despair? I once saw a little African boy, whose whole family had been killed during the fighting in Burundi. He too looked out at the world, unseeing, from dull, blank eyes."

Directly after her late-March visit to Sema, Jane spent an evening talking informally with a handful of top NIH nabobs, and she found them (as she put it in a thank-you note to the NIH's deputy director, William F. Raub) reassuringly "receptive to new ideas." They had defended conditions at Sema and spoken of economic constraints, but they also seemed sensitive to Jane's point of view. Jane was certain they could help the young chimps at Sema, and in the letter to Raub she listed some simple ways the lab might improve conditions quickly. Even better, she noted, her new friends at the NIH appeared ready to "begin a dialogue" on the well-being of chimpanzees in laboratories. Jane reminded Raub that they had even made plans to hold an international scientific conference in December that would place members of the biomedical research industry—researchers, administrators, veterinarians, and caretakers—under the same roof with field biologists, chimp behavioral experts, and others interested in animal welfare. The Jane Goodall Institute, working with the Humane Society of the United States and the World Wildlife Fund, would organize it, inviting around sixty-five carefully selected leaders from both sides of the debate. The NIH would pay for it.

In an April 28 letter to Thomas Wolfle, another of the NIH executives she had spoken with that evening, Jane elaborated on the value of such a conference. It was clear, she wrote, that the "central issue," the need for better treatment of laboratory chimps, was "<u>not</u> controversial." Therefore, assuming that all the conference attendees were "reasonable, honest, and caring people," such a meeting of diverse perspectives ought to achieve a great deal in terms of determining what changes were both desirable and possible. Perhaps they could arrive at a consensus, a fair summary of the legitimate needs of research scientists that also respected the psychological needs of chimpanzees.

As Jane and everyone at the NIH knew very well, though, openly philosophizing about the "psychological needs" of chimpanzees could have significant legal and financial consequences. Two years earlier, Senator John Melcher, the single member of Congress trained as a veterinarian, had stepped inside a regulation-sized cage for laboratory apes and noticed how cruelly small it was: five by five feet in area, no matter what size the chimp. Senator Melcher observed that chimpanzees in laboratories ought to have "space, exercise and things to make life interesting," and he inserted as a 1985 amendment to the Animal Welfare Act the dictum that any laboratory receiving federal funding would be required to provide a "physical environment adequate to promote the psychological well-being of primates."

That was a good idea, but what did it mean? The U.S. Department of Agriculture (USDA), charged with enforcing the Animal Welfare Act, hoped to translate those ten words into a blueprint for specific physical environments and in March 1987 published its proposed regulations and solicited public comment. So Jane's public attacks on Sema, her late-March meetings with the NIH executives, and their joint planning for a high-profile conference to be held in December were, in essence, part of a larger discussion about the legal definition of how U.S. laboratories would be required to promote the psychological well-being of their caged primates.

Jane ended her letter of April 28 to Thomas Wolfle on a personal note: "Tom—I hope this can be worked out. I had closed my eyes for too long with regard to the issue of chimpanzees in the laboratory. Now they have been opened so widely that it is hard for me to sleep at night."

She had entered the arena on behalf of laboratory chimps guided by her own ethical intuition, and she was motivated by compassion combined with the intellectual conviction that chimpanzees are emotional and sentient beings. She may have assumed that other people were similarly guided, motivated, and convinced. The NIH may have been run by intelligent and well-meaning people, including William F. Raub and Thomas Wolfle, but it was more than the sum of its parts, more than the many good individuals who worked there. It was also a huge bureaucracy and the biggest funder of biomedical research in the world, providing some $3.5 billion of the approximately $9 billion spent yearly on such research in the United States. The NIH was certainly in a position to improve the psychological well-being of primates in cages, but why should it? The welfare of animals was not part of its mission. The NIH stood at the center of an industry dedicated to improving human welfare at the lowest dollar cost per unit improvement, while the costs to promote the well-being of chimps could prove substantial. Bigger cages? Access to the outdoors? More caretakers? With some 1,800 chimps in U.S. labs, such changes could become very expensive. And what if laboratories were required to upgrade conditions for all primates in laboratory cages? Chimps were the only ape species in U.S. laboratories, but there were also approximately 23,000 monkeys of several species to think about. And did an accountant at NIH even want to think about upgrading conditions for the 100,000 cats, the 250,000 dogs, and the 60 million mice and rats in U.S. labs?

Jane, Roger Fouts, and volunteers at the Jane Goodall Institute spent the summer of 1987 organizing the great December dialogue between laboratory scientists and field scientists. But during a four-day visit to the United States in September, Jane learned that the NIH was withdrawing its support — and since the lateness of the change made it impossible to find alternative financing, she saw a calculated betrayal. "I should at least tell you," she wrote to an associate on September 22, "that the big NIH conference planned for December is off. They withdrew funding at the last minute — clearly so there would be no time to reorganize. The final federal regulations regarding the new Animal Welfare Bill are coming up early in 1988 — this is why NIH doesn't want a December conference."

In the end, Jane and the Jane Goodall Institute, in a partnership with the Humane Society of the United States, organized their own smaller event for about fifteen people. Held from December 1 to December 3 in Washington, D.C., the workshop assembled a cross-section of experts from biomedical research, veterinary care, fieldwork, and zoo administration, as well as people offering conservation and animal welfare points of view. During their three days together, this diverse group agreed that chimpanzees, given their evolutionary closeness to humans, deserved special treatment in laboratories and other captive situations. They articulated the ethical obligations of experimenters using chimpanzees. And they listed a series of basic requirements for the psychological well-being of chimpanzees: "space for vigorous activities such as running, climbing, and swinging to allow adequate exercise; material for making comfortable beds as substitutes for tree nests; frequent social contact with other chimpanzees and human caregivers; opportunity to establish close social bonds in groups of mixed age and sex; variety in basic routine, including diet, social interaction, and object manipulation; and presence of intellectual stimulation and challenge." Everything recommended was standard practice in one laboratory or another, so that Jane could declare on December 8, as she passed on a copy of the consensus statement to Senator John Melcher, that "the recommendations are therefore not based simply on humanitarian ideals."

Senator Melcher sent the statement on to his own contacts at the U.S. Department of Agriculture, urging that it become part of the discussion on how to promote primate psychological well-being as required by his amendment to the Animal Welfare Act.

Unfortunately, however, that useful statement quickly disappeared without a trace. The psychological well-being amendment to the 1985 Animal Welfare Act remained, in theory, the law of the land, but in practice it continued to languish in bureaucratic limbo during 1988, 1989, and 1990, with the regulations still not defined by Congress—while the NIH leadership and its allies continued to fight against change of any sort. As Jane described the situation to one correspondent on March 21, 1988, "We are . . . meeting incredible resistance. In fact it seems that the entire biomedical community is launching itself into a massive attack to prevent the new legislation going through in accordance with its spirit—I'm referring to the animal welfare act amendment passed by Congress in December 1985 but still not enacted upon in any way."

Meanwhile, Jane Goodall and Roger Fouts became convenient targets. As Roger later wrote, they were both "branded as heretics and animal rights extremists by NIH spokespersons. According to them, anyone who wanted to improve the welfare of animals was out to abolish biomedical research and ought to be excommunicated." One laboratory director tagged Jane as "a rabid antivivisectionist." Others, such as John Landon, the director of Sema, complained that she simply did not possess the expertise to fathom laboratory needs, such as the requirement for keeping hepatitis-infected chimps locked inside hermetically sealed little boxes because of the potential for cross-infections: a health risk to experimenters and a data risk to the experiment.

By then Jane had toured other laboratories, such as the TNO Primate Center in Holland and the Southwest Foundation for Biomedical Research in San Antonio, Texas, where conditions were very different from those in Sema and where she and her expertise were warmly received. She visited TNO first, in the spring of 1987, and found chimps kept in big cages and allowed to remain for the most part in groups. Naturally, the place was "not perfect" (as she soon wrote in an institute newsletter), but compared to what she had recently seen at the notorious Immuno laboratory in Austria and Sema in the United States, the conditions at the Dutch laboratory were "palatial." In addition, her own suggestions for improvement, such as enriching the physical environment with things for the caged apes to consider and manipulate, were taken seriously.

Scientists from both the TNO Center and the Southwest Foundation were using chimpanzees for research on blood-borne diseases such as hepatitis and AIDS, and yet they agreed that the psychological need of chimpanzees for companionship overrode any logistical need of researchers to keep them in isolation. They were joined in that opinion by virologist Alfred Prince of the New York Blood Center and lab director Betsy Brotman of the Liberian Institute for Biomedical Research. And so, during the latter part of 1987 and into 1988, Jane was busy collaborating with her new allies in the laboratory world on a properly staid and scientific article entitled "Appropriate Conditions for Maintenance of Chimpanzees in Studies with Blood-borne Viruses: An Epidemiologic and Psychological Perspective." Published in 1989, the article concluded that chimps infected with hepatitis and HIV could and should be kept in pairs or small groups, and that the "solid-walled isolator boxes" used by certain laboratories—such as Sema, Inc.—were "unnecessary for virologically adequate isolation" while they induced in the apes "sensory and psychological deprivation, which contravenes their psychological well-being."

Jane was also developing a relationship with two people from a big chimpanzee lab in Tuxedo, New York, the Laboratory for Experimental Medicine and Surgery in Primates (LEMSIP). James Mahoney, the Irish-born chief veterinarian, was a softhearted idealist who, by his own account, was left sleepless by the choices he made for his animals. Jan Moor-Jankowski, the Polish-born director, was a hard-minded realist with a stubborn independence and genuine integrity—enough that he always kept his laboratory open to journalists and other members of the inquisitive classes, while he usually kept his mind at least partly open to the unpleasant intrusions of other perspectives.

At the same time, though, LEMSIP's physical environment was very grim. The cages were of minimum legal size (5 feet wide and 5 deep), constructed out of aluminum bars, and suspended for sanitation purposes a few inches off the floor by hooks at the ceiling. The suspended cages looked like enormous birdcages, and the chimps inside were forced to spend their lives a few inches above the actual floor, stepping on a corrugated, half-open surface. Unlike the chimps at Sema, those at LEMSIP were able to see one another and call out to their fellow inmates, but except for the occasional cage interconnection arranged by laboratory staff, they could have no physical contact. They had no outdoor exercise runs—indeed, no way to see the outdoors or experience daylight, since the cages were arranged side by side, five in a row, inside windowless barns.

As it happened, Roger Fouts had already experienced a secondhand contact with Jan Moor-Jankowski, Jim Mahoney, and LEMSIP. In 1970, Roger had earned a Ph.D. in psychology from the University of Nevada based on his progress in teaching American Sign Language to a chimpanzee named Washoe. Washoe became famous as a sign-language-using chimp, and after Roger finished graduate school the celebrity ape and her best teacher went to Norman, Oklahoma, where he became a visiting professor at the University of Oklahoma and an associate of the Institute for Primate Studies, which was directed by a man named William Lemmon. By the end of the decade, the institute had approximately thirty chimpanzees, all of them able to communicate to some degree in sign language. At the same time, however, federal funding for language studies with great apes was starting to dry up. That funding reduction then combined with an unfortunate event. Washoe had bitten people several times, as had other chimps at the institute. But when Karl Pribram, an experimental surgeon from Stanford University, visited Washoe, she bit his finger so badly it had to be partially amputated. Afterward the chimpanzee was very apologetic. "Sorry! Sorry! Sorry!" Washoe signed again and again. But Pribram initiated a multimillion-dollar lawsuit against Roger Fouts, William Lemmon, and the University of Oklahoma, which had provided the institute with an academic imprimatur.

Although Pribram finally dropped his lawsuit, the University of Oklahoma terminated its association with Lemmon's Institute for Primate Studies, and Lemmon in turn decided to sell his chimps. Roger Fouts legally owned Washoe and two other chimps, and so, together with Roger's wife and partner, Debbi, they left Oklahoma and settled into a far better situation at Central Washington University in Washington State. But the remaining chimpanzees under Lemmon's control were trucked out to LEMSIP in Tuxedo, New York, in 1982, destined to become guinea pigs in the testing of hepatitis B vaccines.

Those chimps were by then friends of both Roger and Washoe. They were sweet, sometimes crafty creatures with names like Ally, Booee, Bruno, Cindy, Manny, Nim, and Thelma, and they arrived at LEMSIP communicating in sign language—surprised, conceivably, to find no one signing back. Jim Mahoney once told me that the first time he met Booee, the big male was sitting inside a cage on top of a large truck tire, and as Mahoney moved closer, Booee began making signs, obviously asking for something. The vet thought the chimp was requesting food, and so he announced, in spoken English, that he had no more food. Booee understood some spoken English, but he kept signing, going on and on with those abstruse gestures, so food was not the subject. Mahoney remembered that he had a camera around his neck. He pointed to the camera. "Is this what you want?" And Booee, apparently enraged at having to deal with such an ignoramus, picked up the truck tire as if it were a toy and slammed it down. After the dust settled, the chimp settled back into communication mode, trying once more to get his important message across. The veterinarian then looked down and saw that he had some cigarettes sticking out of his shirt pocket, so he drew one out. "Is this what you want?" And Booee became, as Mahoney put it, "just like a lamb," eagerly nodding his head again and again in the affirmative. The veterinarian gave him the cigarette, lit it, and then man and chimp calmly shared it, passing the cigarette back and forth between the bars like old pals, taking turns as they puffed away.

Jane entered the LEMSIP picture in late 1987, after Jan Moor-Jankowski and James Mahoney had participated in the December workshop in Washington, D.C., and the three of them began exchanging ideas on how to improve conditions at their lab. The easy part was changing the setup for very young chimps, who were comparatively manageable and still not being used for research. Jim Mahoney developed a special nursery department for the little ones, which he called "Little Africa," and Roger Fouts arranged to send a graduate student out to LEMSIP to consider what sort of environmental enrichment might be done for the older denizens. Jane and Moor-Jankowski, meanwhile, talked about how he might engineer outdoor runs for the adult chimps and in what other ways they might find relief from boredom.

In January 1988, after a couple of weeks at Gombe, Jane made a quick trip to Washington, D.C., for what by then had become a routine round of lobbying on Capitol Hill. But it was very cold in Washington just then, and the weather led to a chest cold and an unpleasant cough. She went to Sweden next, giving a lecture at the Grand Hotel in Stockholm, followed by dinner with Queen Silvia and King Carl XVI Gustaf of Sweden. The hotel ballroom had been transformed into an imitation tropical forest, but the reality outdoors was severely antitropical, with driving snow and a bitter wind, and as she continued on to Austria to visit with her friend Konrad Lorenz, Jane's coughy cold turned into walking pneumonia. She went to Holland, presented a paper at the TNO Primate Center for its own workshop on laboratory primate well-being, and then returned to England in order to see a doctor and start a course of antibiotics.

She was still coughing and swallowing pills for the pneumonia when the American lecture tour began in early April. After proceeding through about a dozen venues, she was in New York City by May 9 to receive an award from the American Society for the Prevention of Cruelty to Animals. New York City was not far from Tuxedo, New York, and so, after a morning of media interviews, a lunch, and a lecture, followed by forty-five minutes in a car, she was shown the interior of LEMSIP for the first time.

She suited up in protective gown, booties, and face mask, and then Jim Mahoney took her to the new nursery that he was so proud of. For the better part of an hour Jane relaxed on the carpeted floor, playing with a half-dozen diapered babies and toddlers. For as long as their infancy and early childhood lasted, these little chimps had plenty of toys to play with, a jungle gym to climb over, windows leading into the kitchenette to look through, lots of bustling activity in the corridor outside to consider, and human caretakers to give them the maternal comfort they so desperately needed. Jane was enchanted.

Then Dr. Mahoney showed her the rest of the lab, where the chimps went after two or three years of innocent existence in the nursery: the dungeon for grownups. "I got just inside the door," she wrote to her institute membership. "For the first five minutes or so the noise was deafening. The chimps, the appalling monotony of the day broken at an unexpected moment, were excited to see Jim, their friend. They called out and shook the bars of their prisons and beat on the floors and walls." But gradually, as the veterinarian talked to them, they quieted down, and then he introduced Jane to the first chimp on the right, one of his favorites, a real friend, a male named Spike. The veterinarian said, "He's very gentle; he won't hurt you," and she crouched down to look into the ape's sad, puzzled eyes and talk.

But Jane was exhausted from a very long day and now deeply saddened — by the dungeon, the apes in their giant birdcages, Spike's quiet gaze — and instead of talking she began quietly crying, the tears trickling down behind her mask. Spike reached through his bars and touched her cheek, wet with tears, and then inquisitively sniffed his wet finger and licked it. Mahoney, who had wandered off, returned and said something. Jane was unable to respond. He looked down, saw the tears, and sat down to put his arms around her, protesting gently, "Don't do that, Jane. I have to face this every morning of my life." After a while he stood up again, visibly upset himself by then, walked away . . . and was it now a case of overwrought emotion and failed communication, of a sensitive ape mistakenly deducing that this strange new woman had somehow hurt his longtime friend? In an instant Spike grabbed and roughly bit the tip of Jane's right thumb, severely mangling it.

Shocked, bleeding, and in pain, Jane stood up. With a cloth hastily wrapped around her thumb, she was rushed out of the lab and driven to a doctor's office for an examination, followed by the amputation of the tip of her thumb.

It was painful and would remain so for weeks, but it was also surprisingly debilitating. "I am still amazed by the extent to which I was incapacitated as a result of losing such a small piece of my anatomy," she wrote in the institute newsletter, "—although really, I suppose, it was the surgery and the antibiotics and the fact that it hurt that were incapacitating. Even so, it did surprise me to discover how much one depends on one's thumb, especially the right one." Still, she immediately stepped back into the lecture series—on to Buffalo by May 12—and when the thumb felt a little better, she took to wrapping it in a cloth that approximated the color of whatever dress she was wearing.

After finishing the lecture tour, she headed back to Washington to knock on more doors of more senators and representatives. "Make no mistake about it," Jane later wrote, "—they were grueling days, most of them. It is fine early in the morning talking to the first few appointments on the list. By midday one feels jaded and one's message stale—yet it is vital to appear as crisp, coherent and fresh as one was in the morning."

Around the end of May she flew home to Bournemouth to spend time with Grub and the family and get additional medical attention for the thumb. Her recuperation period was interrupted by a mad four-day dash out to Dar es Salaam in order to participate in a June 11 raffle and dance fundraiser for the construction of ranger posts at Gombe. And then, after returning to England for a few days, she flew back to Washington to resume politicking. She had help from an adviser who was accustomed to the ways and means of Washington and who helped guide her through the physical labyrinth linking government buildings. At the same time, though, Jane was navigating a more abstract maze, with perhaps an unseen enemy at the center and all around the sensation of inertia and intrigue—or was it indifference? What was the resistance to defining regulations in order to enforce an already established law?

On her way back from the last lobbying event of the last day, she settled into the back of a taxi and released an enormous sigh, and the taxi driver in front asked what the problem was. She said she was exhausted from a day of lobbying.

"Oh — what you lobbying about?"

She told him, and he turned around in his cab to look at her, whereupon his round face opened into a grin of amazement: "My God! You're Jane Goodall in my cab!"

The driver was African American, a nature lover, and he wanted to talk to his hero, driving with his head turned around so much that Jane was afraid he would crash. She made him stop so she could climb in the front seat, and they had a long and happy conversation about chimps and wildlife. "He is so nice," Jane wrote in a brief note to her National Geographic friend Neva Folk. "So interested. Wants for his kids to be interested." In the end the driver charged her only half fare, and she promised to find him some wildlife videotapes. Perhaps Neva could locate something at the Geographic offices, Jane thought, and she concluded with an uplifting idea: "The world has such wonderful people. It is NOT all bad."

She was back in Dar es Salaam by the first week of July, catching up again. Her thumb was still swollen and tender, but she typed away with nine digits at the keyboard of a new word processor, a little Toshiba 1000 donated by the Texas billionaire Ed Bass. Among many other things, she was sending dot-matrix missives out to a new friend, Franklin Loew, the dean of the Tufts University School of Veterinary Medicine. Loew was offering the Tufts vet school as the site of another, bigger workshop on the psychological well-being of laboratory primates, and Jane was very eager to pursue that offer. Or, as she put it in a July 28 letter to Loew, "Now, close to my heart is the Workshop."

She thought they could invite some of those who had come to the previous workshop, but she still hoped to break through the communication barrier with the NIH: "We MUST involve the NIH stronghold types on this next round. Senator Hatch said that he could arrange that for me."

The workshop would take place the following spring, and it could build on the progress already made at the Washington one in December 1987 and the February TNO symposium in Holland. Now that they had established some concepts and general recommendations for improving primate well-being, this third assembly of experts would concentrate on the particulars: a dollars-and-cents, inches-and-feet, steel-and-Plexiglas discussion. "Let us bring together a group of experts each of whom brings with him some concrete information," Jane wrote. "The BEST features of his lab. We do not gather to pull individuals or labs to pieces. We come thinking that EVERYONE will have at least one positive contribution. Something that has been used at one lab or other—and WORKS. That is the key. Something good, already tried and tested. (Even the infamous IMMUNO in Vienna has one good thing. Though I very much doubt that SEMA could contribute anything.)"

By August her thumb was hurting less, and she spent a busy and sad two or three weeks at Gombe. Busy because she was accompanied for some of that time by Chris Boehm, a photographer friend from Germany named Michael Neugebauer, Grub and three of his friends, and Tony Collins. Sad because her old friend Rashidi Kikwale had recently died from malaria. Rashidi had been with her from the day she arrived at Gombe twenty-eight years before. He was a dignified man with a subtle sense of humor, some twenty or thirty years her senior and intensely loyal—the one who, during the 1975 kidnapping, was badly beaten for refusing to give up the keys to the storehouse. As Jane wrote to the family, "It will never be the same without him. It's very hard to believe it's true. All those years. Everyone is shattered. Hilali & co say that it is terrible—they have no one, now, to keep an eye on the young men, to give wise council, to mediate the various factions here. Isn't it AWFUL."

The Tufts University workshop took place on May 10 and May 11, 1989, chaired by Dean Frank Loew and attended by some twenty top experts, including professionals in chimpanzee field research, a representative from the NIH, another from the National Academy of Sciences, and senior staff members from seven major primate facilities collectively holding almost nine hundred chimpanzees. "The mood on the first day was tense," according to Geza Teleki's report, "as both sides had been primed with negative opinions, including a false exaggeration of Goodall's alleged anti-research stance, but interactions loosened up considerably by the second day." The conference achieved a final consensus on one point: that the Sema-style isolettes were both scientifically unnecessary and ethically wrong. Consensus on other basic issues remained elusive, although after the NIH and National Academy of Sciences representatives left early, a last-minute compromise proposal on cage size (400 square feet of floor space) provoked strong positive interest. But instead of issuing a unanimous position statement from the May conference, Jane and her associates were able only to produce a generalized summary of results from all three of the psychological well-being workshops, which were then submitted to the U.S. Department of Agriculture.

That year Jane made seven different trips to Washington, visiting the secretary of agriculture and vigorously petitioning a number of other senior government officials as well as some thirty members of Congress. But another year passed . . . and another . . . until finally, in 1991, proposed regulations supposed to implement the 1985 Animal Welfare Act were sent to the White House Office of Management and Budget (OMB) for a final review.

The principal lobbying organization for the U.S. biomedical research industry, an entity known as the National Association for Biomedical Research, then communicated its dissatisfaction with the proposed regulations: that they "paint a very detailed picture of laboratory animal care. They tell you point by point—and that's what we object to." That objection was placed on the desks of the reviewing group at the OMB by James Wyngaarden, until recently the director of the NIH but now the adviser on science and technology for the White House. With Wyngaarden's canny guidance, the OMB then proceeded to gut the Department of Agriculture regulations, successfully arguing that the enforcement of the 1985 Animal Welfare Act could legitimately focus on self-reported "performance" standards rather than officially defined "engineering" ones. The resulting corpse of supposed regulations had nothing to say about increasing cage size or any of the other changes that Jane, Roger Fouts, the Jane Goodall Institute, the Humane Society of the United States, and so many other people and organizations had worked for so long to promote.

That was an enormous disappointment, counterbalanced to some degree by a nice surprise. In December 1991, Jane once again came in contact with the CEO of Sema, Inc., John Landon, who warmly invited her for a return visit to see how improved his laboratory was and how well the chimpanzees were. "He even thanked me," Jane later wrote, "for the part I had played in making it possible for him to instigate those improvements." Under Landon's oversight, and in a direct response to Jane's attacks, the Rockville lab had been altered from top to bottom, starting with the name. Sema had become Diagnon, and when I visited the place, several months after Jane did, its refrigerator-like isolettes had been replaced by two dozen spacious and partly open Plexiglas cubicles that included play and sleeping areas. The young chimps had space to move around, were able to see and hear one another, and were allowed at many points during their experimental protocol to live in groups and have physical contact with each other, while human caretakers were routinely scheduled to play with and comfort them. "When they moved into their new enclosures," Landon has said, "their personalities changed. I could see it."

40

Orphans, Children, and Sanctuaries

1986–1995

JANE'S MOST AMBITIOUS PROJECT following the 1986 Chicago conference was to promote the conservation of wild chimpanzees. Her colleague
Toshisada Nishida, the director of the Mahale Mountains Research Project,
agreed to work with the rest of the CCCC membership in formulating an
official conservation action plan, the general idea of which was simple: to
create a series of chimp reserves across Africa. Where and how were the
hard parts. Well, they could sponsor surveys to identify where the best areas
of chimp habitat to preserve were. The how would require persuading African governments to participate, sending in researchers and setting up research sites for medium-term stability, and somehow—through ecotourism,
perhaps—making these sites economically viable for the long haul.

In the spring of 1987, pneumonia swept through the study community at
Gombe, killing nine chimps and leaving two youngsters motherless. The
two orphans, both around three and a half years old, were Mel (son of Miff)
and Darbee (daughter of Little Bee). Infants and youngsters can survive the
loss of a mother if they are adopted by an older sibling. Darbee's older
brother might have taken on that role, but the two siblings were never very
close. As for Mel, his older siblings were all dead, so there was no one.

Jane learned of the epidemic during her spring lecture tour in North
America. Mel had been ill before, and now, with his mother gone, he was
wandering aimlessly around. He was tolerated by the others, but none of
them were particularly responsive. As she soon wrote, Jane "never expected
to see Mel again."

Then she received a telegram: "Mel adopted by spindle."

Spindle? Spindle was not a sibling. Spindle was a twelve-year-old male
with no obvious blood relationship to little Mel. But Spindle had lost his

own mother in the same epidemic, so perhaps he needed companionship. Whatever the motivation, he became a "wonderful caretaker. He shared his night nest with Mel, and he shared his food. He did his best to protect the infant, hurrying to retrieve him when the big males became socially aroused. When Mel whimpered during travel, Spindle waited and allowed him to clamber onto his back or even, if it was raining and cold, to cling on in the ventral position." Spindle, though, was reaching adolescence, and he liked to join the adult males in their social activities, which meant he was sometimes patrolling the territorial borders of Kasekela, other times traveling long distances with an enthusiastic party in search of delicious *mbula* fruit. Eager to keep up with the older males, he moved fast and hard, and while he often carried his adopted orphan, he sometimes expected Mel to proceed on his own.

Around the end of July the two became separated, and once again little Mel was observed wandering around weakly by himself. The older males were surprisingly gentle with the pathetic orphan. He could beg for food from any of them, even scrambling to get a bit of meat after a predation. But without a mother or a protector—without Spindle—he was unable to provide or care for himself.

Jane arrived at Gombe in the first week of August, and as she reported home on August 11, "Little orphans Mel and Darbie are doing OK. The super thing is that Mel, who was first carried for a month by the adolescent male Spindle . . . is now being cared for by little Pax!"

Pax was then around ten years old and small for his age, surely because he too had been an orphan. After his mother, Passion, had died when he was four, Pax had been mothered by his older sister, Pom, and older brother, Prof. Pom finally left Kasekela, emigrating to the community to the north, and Prof then became Pax's steady guardian. Even before the death of their mother, Jane later recalled, Prof was always a sensitive and very attentive older sibling. "I remember once when Pax, suffering from a wet-season cold, sneezed loudly and messily. Prof hastened over and gazed intently at Pax's runny nose—then picked a handful of leaves and carefully wiped the snot away." Pax and Prof, still moving together as a pair in August 1987, now adopted Mel, and Jane spent several days following the two brothers and their little adoptee. Prof usually led them in their travels, while Pax followed, carting baby Mel piggyback-style. As Spindle had before him, Pax shared his food with Mel, and they slept together each night in the same nest. The older Prof occasionally shared his food with both younger males.

They made a stable trio, but after a few weeks Spindle showed up, whereupon Mel left Pax and Prof and returned to his first caretaker.

The second orphan of 1987, Darbee, was adopted by a male named

Beethoven, but in later months Darbee began preferring the company of the childless female Gigi. Mel too eventually moved away from the protection of Spindle and found an adoptive mother in Gigi. In that way, the childless old female at last took on a pair of motherless children. "Gigi shows them little overt attention," Jane later summarized, "and their friendly interactions are, for the most part, confined to occasional grooming. But she provides the support they need in an often unfriendly world. Woe betide any boisterous juvenile or adolescent whose rough behaviour causes one of her small wards to scream—they have Gigi to contend with. When the orphans are with her they can, to some extent, relax, knowing that she will make all decisions regarding travel routes, sleeping places, and so on."

During the summer of 1987, Jane was working on her new book, *Through a Window: My Thirty Years with the Chimpanzees of Gombe*, and the story of Mel and Darbee and their surrogate parents found its way into the rough draft. But by the summer of 1988 the orphans part had to be revised. A mother named Winkle died, leaving three-year-old Wolfi alone. Fortunately, Wolfi had a close relationship with his older sister, nine-year-old Wunda. Wunda had always been fascinated by her tiny sibling. She had often played with, comforted, and cared for him. And now, when their mother suddenly vanished, Wunda took over the whole spectrum of maternal duties, including, apparently, nursing. Wunda was still two or three years too young to have her own baby, so the "nursing" was astonishing. Yet little Wolfi suckled so eagerly and convincingly that even Jane believed—wrongly, as she later realized—that Wunda was actually producing milk. As she wrote to a friend on August 13, "Amazing to relate, 10 year old Wunda has not only adopted [Wolfi] in that she carries, protects, waits for, and shares food and rest with him—she has also begun to LACTATE. This is truly amazing. . . . I only saw her the first day—and lost her when I fell on my wretched thumb."

Jane was still laboring over *Through a Window* in 1989. "I want to write another chapter to the sequel to Shadow," she mentioned in a March 7 letter to an associate in the United States, "but oh dear there is so much to do." The Jane Goodall Institute in the United Kingdom would officially open to public membership on May 25, but she was already at work on a JGI (UK) special project in the East African country of Burundi: "In Burundi I have to try to persuade the President and his ministers etc that the money obtained from the sale of illegal ivory and rhino horn should not only go to wildlife in general . . . but for chimps in particular. There are about 300 chimp lives at stake, so obviously I have to TRY."

Like Tanzania, Burundi is at the far eastern edge of chimpanzees' historic distribution across Africa, and by 1989 the chimp population was fragmented and declining as a result of forest-clearing for agriculture. About half the wild chimps left were located in Kibira National Park, in the north, and the remainder lived in scattered, isolated groups in central Burundi and the southwest, including the Rumonge Forest Reserve. In March, Jane toured Kibira and Rumonge and spoke with the president and several other government officials. Within a short while the JGI (UK) had permission to introduce a chimpanzee research and tourism project in the southern part of the country—starting with a three-month pilot study run by Charlotte Uhlenbroek, a recent zoology graduate from the University of Bristol.

Aside from the Burundi chimpanzees, though, there were Congolese ones to consider. Jane had learned about that sad situation earlier, while she was in England. She had been approached by Ian Redmond, a zoologist and writer for *BBC Wildlife* magazine, who showed her photographs of an emaciated chimpanzee inhabiting a putative zoo in the southwestern port city of Pointe-Noire in the People's Republic of Congo. The zoo held seven adults and two babies in tiny concrete-and-iron cages, Redmond said, and they were dying because the keepers seldom fed them or even gave them water. Within ten days Jane and the JGI (UK) had sent an English volunteer named Karen Pack out to Pointe-Noire on a rescue mission. But by the end of June, while Jane was in Washington on another of her lobbying expeditions on behalf of the U.S. laboratory chimps, Pack had telephoned to ask (as Jane soon recalled in a letter to a friend), "Jane, will JGI accept responsibility for the up to 20 infant chimps that are presently pets, and likely to be needing homes within the next couple of years?"

After arriving at The Birches around one o'clock in the morning of December 24, 1989, Jane celebrated Christmas with her family. Then, turning to the final pieces of *Through a Window*, she worked in a frenzied rush and completed it by the first days of the new year. The book had been "three years in the working," she wrote to Neva Folk at the Geographic on January 8, 1990, while in flight to Miami, "(though as I only ever got two weeks or so at a time it was actually much less)." However, she continued, "it's really only NOW—sitting on PA 009 to Miami and writing to you—that it has dawned on me—it is FINISHED!! Actually, I have been frantically doing the ACKNOWLEDGEMENTS and TWO appendices. And I only finished the last of those yesterday. And I have been selecting photos—and I am still doing that now! BUT ALL writing is DONE!!" She was so relieved to be entertaining the strange new concept of a finished book that she decided to press the overhead button, order a glass of good French wine from the flight attendant, and toast the great event: "So—CHEERS!"

Through a Window: My Thirty Years with the Chimpanzees of Gombe was in the bookstores by early autumn 1990, and like Jane's earlier bestseller, *In the Shadow of Man*, it took her readers once again into the world of the Gombe chimpanzees, with its once secret histories of sex and savagery, war and peace, prey and predators, princes and pretenders. But *Through a Window* also for the first time directly examined the distressing, even tragic relationship between the sibling species *Pan troglodytes* and *Homo sapiens*, and it detailed the dual concerns—of care and conservation—that had become so central to Jane's life since the Chicago conference.

For the past three years, in fact, Jane had done everything she could to increase public awareness about those concerns. She had given hundreds of media interviews, and she was ready to give hundreds more. She had been instrumental in the development of six national television productions in Europe and North America and had been a guest on several network television shows. She had encouraged the National Geographic to produce two separate films for cable television. She and Geza were working on a big article for the glossy German natural history magazine *Geo*. They had also persuaded *National Geographic* to plan a pair of articles on the great apes, now in process. And finally, by January 1990, Jane had already signed the contract for yet another major book, one that would focus almost entirely on the issues of care and conservation for chimpanzees.

It is possible to imagine, then, that Jane's cheerful toast made on PA 009 to Miami, acknowledging the completion of *Through a Window*—a glass of wine raised in quiet ceremony, then tipped and sipped—was followed by a second, less lightly considered drink. So much more to do! Yet another book! Still, the next book might be less of a burden, since she had agreed to work with a coauthor, someone Geza had found, who promised to devote his full attention to the project and could take advantage of Geza's expertise, not to mention his CCCC filing cabinets in Washington crammed with articles, clippings, documents, letters, logs, reports, and transcripts. Jane had so far coauthored only one book, *Innocent Killers*, and that had been a lot of work. But perhaps it was now a relief to consider that someone else would be responsible for much of the word processing and organizing, research and legwork, and even, possibly, some of the brainwork. So she was willing to take the risk, even though her new coauthor—his name was Dale Peterson—knew nothing about chimpanzees.

In southern Burundi, meanwhile, Charlotte Uhlenbroek's three-month pilot study was expanded to six months, and by February 1990 she was settled into a tiny brick house in a small village called Kirungu on top of a high hill. That hill was part of a wavy sea of high hills where people had replaced the original forests with cultivated plots and grassland wherever the sun shone long enough to make agriculture possible. But between those steep hills, within stream-cut valleys and precipitous ravines, it was not merely too dark but too steep for farming; and so those interstices endured as a cool and restful honeycomb of shadows and whistling birds, murmuring rust-colored streams, ferns, wildflowers, moss, and snaking forest galleries with baboons and chimpanzees lurking inside somewhere. Charlotte had hired five local men—short men with strong legs—to help her find the elusive apes. Over time the men were also supposed to help habituate them for research and tourism, but for now she was still just trying to find the chimps.

While Charlotte was doing her pilot study in the southern hills, though, Jane's interest in Burundi as a place with chimpanzees had caused a recipro-cal interest among Burundians. When I visited Charlotte at her little brick house in Kirungu that spring, she told me, "Actually, it's so exciting when you think it was only March last year when Jane Goodall first came to Bu-rundi. So much has happened since then, and already in Bujumbura, et cet-era, there's a growing awareness of chimpanzees. I mean, people in the taxi: 'Oh, you're the person who is studying the chimpanzees. When can we go and see the chimpanzees?'"

Only a few years earlier, almost no one had realized there were any wild chimpanzees in Burundi at all. But with this new awareness of their wild chimps, many Burundians were also becoming newly aware of the problem of chimp orphans. These were mainly accidental byproducts of the so-called bush-meat business, chimpanzees orphaned when a professional hunter shot a mother and discovered a live baby crawling around the dead tangle of flesh. Most of the orphans in Burundi had been imported from elsewhere, sold by hunters from Zaire, for example, and were sometimes kept as pets. Baby chimps are not so different from baby humans, and they therefore seem like attractive pets. But once that cute little creature reaches a certain age and size, he or she is much stronger than any human owner. In any case, the Burundi government was planning to confiscate them all—just as soon as there was a place to keep the confiscated apes.

Mimi O'Brien, an employee of the American embassy when I visited the capital city, Bujumbura, around this time, told me more. Around twenty or-phans were kept illegally as pets just in that city alone, she said, and in fact Jane and the Jane Goodall Institute were already negotiating with the gov-ernment to build a small sanctuary to care for the confiscated chimps: a fenced, protected area at the edge of Lake Tanganyika that the government had set aside by the spring of 1990. The previous American ambassador and his wife, Dan and Lucie Phillips, had been instrumental in the negotiations, she declared, and had even raised the money to build a first holding cage.

During her lunch hour, Mimi took me to her own house, where two young chimps, Poco and Socrates, were sharing that big cage in the back yard and waiting for bigger and better quarters to be built. Then she drove me to an electronics and electrical supply shop where, in a paved courtyard out back, there were cages containing a pair of African gray parrots, three yapping dogs, and a female orphaned chimp. The chimp, named Jojo, was very quiet, very gentle, and she reached through the bars, took my hand, pulled it to her face, and kissed it. With her other hand, she grasped Mimi's hand. And with our unoccupied hands, Mimi and I both reached through the bars and gently stroked Jojo's arms. Jojo's creamy, mildly freckly face had a distant and lost expression. "These people definitely want to get rid of her," Mimi said. "The man tells me, 'We're Muslim. My wife doesn't like these animals.'" Like Poco and Socrates, Jojo was also waiting for the new quarters.

After the visit with Jojo, we drove to a cinderblock-walled compound identified by a sign as the Atelier de Construction Métallique, where the owner showed us a concrete cell—a converted toilet—where his pet chimp now lived. The chimp, attached by a thick steel collar and a heavy steel chain to a steel post in the middle of his cell, was curled up in the corner and possibly asleep.

Mimi called out, "Whiskey! Whiskey!" The chimp turned to look at us and then lethargically dragged himself and his clanking chain in our direction. Mimi handed him a banana. He took a few bites and tossed the rest back to us. Standing upright, he turned his back to us, leaned forward, braced himself with his hands on the steel post in the middle of the room, and, looking back over his shoulder, reached back, ballerina-style, with a single outstretched leg in our direction, whereupon Mimi placed a second banana within the grasp of his foot. He took that second banana, turned around, sat down, ate some, and tossed us the remainder of that offering as well.

Whiskey's owner told us that sometimes he dressed the chimp up in women's clothing and took him out for an evening's drive, telling people that Whiskey was his bride. Whiskey was also waiting for a new home.

Jane had gone to Burundi on a straightforward mission: to create new chimp reserves that would sustain themselves through research and tourism. But as she expanded her mission in Africa and began to travel more widely on the continent, she gradually discovered the troubling and complicating problem of orphans.

In early March 1990 she made her first trip to the People's Republic of Congo, where Karen Pack was working to improve conditions at that small zoo in Pointe-Noire. She had organized a regular routine of cleaning, feeding, watering, and so on. The chimps' cages there were small steel-and-concrete cells, but it was possible to open some of the contiguous cages so the inmates could visit one another. One cage was left open all day long—escape was not a concern, since the old lady inside, La Vieille, was so frightened of the bright world outside that she remained neurotically huddled in a corner.

In a telephone call the previous June, Karen had told Jane that as many as twenty infant chimps in the area would soon need homes, and now, in Pointe-Noire, Jane was introduced to Aliette Jamart, a thin, frenetic Belgian woman who had opened her home to a burgeoning population of orphans. I met Aliette Jamart about a year later, when her house was still overflowing with little chimps (diapered infants tottering around inside and a gang of older youngsters running around in the yard outside, bouncing boomingly on the tin roof, hanging from the eaves and looking through the windows, clambering over the window grilles, crowding up at the front door and banging with their little fists on the glass), and perhaps her story then, told (for my benefit) in good French occasionally summarized in bad English, was similar to what Jane heard during her March 1990 visit.

An old neighbor of hers had died, she told me, leaving a pet chimp named Cuckoo. Cuckoo was taken to the Pointe-Noire zoo, escaped, and was probably killed. But by then Aliette Jamart had visited the zoo and seen how bad it was, and she began taking food to the zoo chimps. Then one day she noticed a new young female: a bush-meat orphan, kept in a village, given to a missionary, deposited at the zoo. But the chimp, Jeanette, was starving to death, and Madame Jamart and her husband took her home and began raising her themselves. "We very like Jeanette," she said. "She's my first baby."

Soon another orphan turned up, a male named Yombe who had been caught in a hunter's snare and had a gangrenous leg that finally was amputated. Yombe also went to live in the Jamarts' house. "He is a good boy, but he is the chief, and when a new person arrives in the home he has to prove he's the chief of all the chimps." That explained the three-legged chimp I could see banging so assertively on the glass at the front door.

But after the Jamarts had taken in Jeanette and Yombe, the local authorities began confiscating illegally kept pets. At the same time other chimps were being dropped off at the doorstep. Nkola was taken from an army officer. Toube arrived with a green face and a bad buckshot wound. Matalila appeared inside a metal box. Emmanuelle came in a bag, handed over to Madame Jamart by two white men, one of whom said, "Mrs. Jamart, I cannot love this chimp."

Then it was Sophie. Then Agatha. Then Marble. And so on.

• • •

By mid-August 1990, Jane was flying back from Washington, D.C., to the People's Republic of Congo. It was a free ride on a private jet, courtesy of the Texas-based oil company Conoco, accompanied by Max Pitcher, executive vice president for exploration and production. The company, prospecting for oil along Congo's Atlantic coast, had a headquarters in Pointe-Noire; soon after they arrived, Pitcher and Roger Simpson, president of the Congo operation, flew Jane over Conoco's seismic test operations to show her how they had brought in all the necessary equipment for exploration by helicopter rather than bulldozing a road through the forest. For comparison purposes, they showed her the messes their direct competitors were making. All the big oil companies were claiming to be green, but Pitcher did persuade Jane that, as he put it, "We walk where our talk is."

Conoco had anchored a couple of interconnected barges in the middle of the Kouilou River, flowing into the Atlantic Ocean a couple of hours north of Pointe-Noire, and from that steel platform a few dozen men ran an enormous rig that was clawing a hole about 2 miles down into the river bottom. Conoco had not yet found any oil in that test bore or others, but because it had so much economic potential to offer the people of Congo, the company still had political capital to spare for Jane's purposes. Conoco would help with the orphan chimps. Max Pitcher and Roger Simpson had already found a deserted island in the middle of the river where a chimp sanctuary might be built. They had already agreed to plan, finance, and construct such a sanctuary. Now they only needed permission from the government to do it all. Jane was thus flown in the company jet to the capital city of Brazzaville to meet with President Denis Sassou-Nguesso and explain to him the practical benefits a sanctuary for orphaned chimpanzees could bring: a boost to local economies, local employment, education, conservation, tourism.

She also found some time to visit the Brazzaville city zoo, a place where some of the animals were starving to death, since, as she was informed, the zoo director found it cheaper to buy new ones from hunters than to feed the old ones. . . . Still, as she could read on the sign over his cage, one of the chimpanzees, Grégoire, had been living there since 1944. When Jane looked through the iron bars into the wood-floored cage, she was astonished, and outraged, at the sight of this "strange being," with his "pale, almost hairless skin . . . stretched tightly over his emaciated body so that every bone could be seen." But he was still alive. How had Grégoire managed to survive for the past forty-six years? As she stood there looking at this gaunt, ghostly creature, a group of schoolchildren approached, and one girl, around ten years old, held up a banana and called out, "Danse! Grégoire—danse!" The pale apparition in the cage began to dance. With strange, graceless movements, he stood upright and turned around three times. Then he drummed his hands on a wooden shelf. He turned upside down and stood on his hands, his feet up and gripping the bars near the young girl with the banana. Finally the old ape turned back to an upright position and accepted his reward.

It was early September by the time Jane met with President Sassou-Nguesso to promote the idea of a chimp sanctuary in Congo, and after that she took a boat across the swirling Zaire River to Kinshasa, the capital of Zaire, where she had an appointment (arranged by her new friend the U.S. secretary of state) to meet with President Mobutu. She had hoped to speak with Mobutu about chimpanzee hunting and the illegal trade in ape orphans, but the president, distracted by discordant notes emerging from the orchestra of his government, was unable to follow through on that appointment.

While she was in town, though, passing through Kinshasa's main tourist market, Jane caught sight of a baby chimpanzee sitting out in the hot sun on top of a small box, tied with a string around his waist. Several monkeys were also for sale, tied to their cages, and some African gray parrots were stuffed inside tiny wire cages—all for sale. She was traveling with photographer Nick Nichols, and "when we approached the chimpanzee," Jane later wrote, "he sat up and looked at us with glazed and almost hopeless eyes. But when I crouched beside him and made small sounds of greeting, he put one arm around my neck. A noisy crowd had surrounded the captive, but when Nick began to take pictures they faded away. Only the seller, angry and demanding, remained." When they returned later in the afternoon, the chimp was lying down. "The thin shade of some acacias did little to lessen the scorching heat, and his face shone with sweat. Yet when we offered him a drink, he turned his face away. I didn't see how this infant could survive for long."

That market was located directly across from the American Cultural Center, where Jane gave a brief talk that evening. After the talk she was driven past the live-animal stalls again. This time the place was dark and nearly empty, but the little orphan was still there, "a tiny and solitary figure in the headlights," who "sat up as we slowed down and, as we drove past reached toward the car with one small arm. That did it! None of us would be able to sleep unless we first worked out some way of rescuing the infant." Little Jay, she called him.

The American ambassador asked Zaire's minister of the environment, conservation, and tourism to arrange for a confiscation, and the next day Jane and Nick Nichols returned to the marketplace and met with a gendarme who had already been stationed there. Jane cut the string binding Little Jay to his cage, whereupon the baby clambered into her arms and wrapped his arms around her neck. A woman living in Kinshasa named

Graziella Cotman, who had experience raising orphaned chimps, agreed to care for Little Jay.

Over the next several months Jane's supporters at the American embassy in Zaire engineered the official seizure of another half-dozen young chimps in the Kinshasa markets. In honor of Secretary of State Jim Baker, the first of these was named Little Jim B. The second was named Little Jane.

After an autumn spent promoting *Through a Window*, followed by lectures in Canada and meetings with the newly formed JGI in Canada, a late October trip to Japan to receive that nation's most prestigious award for scientific achievement (the Kyoto Prize), then Christmas at home in England, Jane returned to Brazzaville and Kinshasa once again, in January 1991. The institute had sent a volunteer to Brazzaville, who helped organize things at the zoo and hired a resourceful and dedicated Congolese man, Jean Mabotot, as head keeper for the chimps. The American ambassador and his wife, Dan and Lucie Phillips (recently rotated from the ambassadorship in Burundi), had arranged for a local hotel to deliver discarded food to the zoo animals, while a couple of British animal welfare organizations had made emergency donations. Grégoire was looking healthier.

In Kinshasa, meanwhile, a group from the American School had started a Friends of the Chimps club and were now traveling out to the city's N'Sele Zoo with food for the chimpanzees there. In addition, Jane's interest in the chimpanzee situation in Zaire, especially the problems of professional bushmeat hunting and orphans, had sparked a "strong conservation movement," as she later phrased it, "that included a number of enthusiastic Zaireans." And so Jane and the Jane Goodall Institute became tentatively involved in planning, in addition to the two proposed sanctuaries in Burundi and Congo, a third in Zaire, which might also, in its own small way, begin to improve the lives of a few of the many hundreds or even thousands of ape orphans still routinely emerging from the forests of east, west, and central equatorial Africa.

For some time Jane had also wanted to focus on the education of children and young people. She had hoped that the entertainer Michael Jackson would help. Jackson had asked her to his California ranch, Neverland, to advise him on caring for his own pet chimp, Bubbles. She had shown him the videotape of baby chimpanzees at the Sema laboratory. He kept the painful images in mind as he worked on his song "Heal the World," and he promised to contribute a percentage of the earnings to her cause. And they discussed how they could combine their different kinds of celebrity to reach and educate children.

"Are we going to make a book of your song?" Jane gently reminded

Jackson in a July 8, 1989, letter. "I have just finished 8 books for small children, on different animal families," she continued, with "superb colour photos, and plenty of them," which would be "marketed through things like chain stores and gas stations for about a dollar. That is a project I'm very excited about, as I think it will carry the message 'animals matter too' to thousands of children. If you and I did one together, it would reach millions, because of you, and convey a different sort of message than you alone, because of me. It could make a difference."

But soon it was 1990. Jackson developed other interests. And Jane became involved in the big plans for a Gombe thirtieth anniversary celebration, a three-day event to take place that October in Dar es Salaam. There would be cocktail parties, dinners, meetings and lectures, parades and dancing and films. For schoolchildren, Jane was planning a Tanzania-wide essay contest and an art contest. As the basic idea became more elaborate, though, it took longer to realize, until Gombe 30 Wildlife Week was finally scheduled for February 1991. The invasion of Kuwait by Saddam Hussein's Iraqi army and the subsequent U.S.-led Gulf War at the start of 1991 then made the celebration plans less elaborate, since the American embassy pulled most of its staff out of Tanzania and Americans were officially advised not to travel into that part of the world. Other foreigners seemed suddenly reluctant to travel there as well. Still, as Jane wrote home, "Dar is fine. No panic." It was sad that the event had lost some of its international character, but by the same token, it would become more Tanzanian, and more African, in character. "It will not be quite as planned," but it would still be "GOOD. Good for Tanzania."

The celebrations started on February 11 with a reception at the National Museum of Tanzania, hosted by the American ambassador, honored by the presence of Mwalimu Julius Nyerere, and featuring a display of the winners of the children's art contest, photographs by leading wildlife photographers, a video show, and chimpanzee tools from across Africa. During the rest of the week, five radio programs about chimpanzee behavior were aired, one each evening. The Dar es Salaam drive-in cinema showed a different wildlife film each night of the week. And Jane and Tony Collins lectured at several secondary schools in Dar es Salaam. They took sticks, branches, and leaves and showed how chimpanzees made and used tools. Jane demonstrated with gestures and postures and vocalizations how chimpanzees communicate, and Tony imitated male charging displays. And on February 15, the final evening of celebrations, the country's president, Ali Hassan Mwinyi, hosted a big formal dinner.

As Jane and Tony were touring the schools, they announced that any students interested in asking further questions should leave their names, and at the end of the week there was a long list of students. A couple of weeks later fourteen of them met on the veranda of Jane's house and sat down facing the Indian Ocean. They had come with questions based on Jane's school presentations, and so she talked more about the chimps and their personalities. It was, she said, the same with elephants and mongooses, who also had individuality and personalities. She also talked about the erosion of the coastline because of dynamite fishing, and the students eventually said, as Jane later recalled, "We don't learn things like that."

But local wildlife clubs sometimes went into the schools. What did they talk about?

"They talk about elephant poaching and shooting of giraffes."

"How many of you have seen elephants and giraffes?"

Only two. And so Jane decided to talk about chickens. "You've all seen hens? You've all seen them being carried by their wings? Or by their legs and upside down, and they're struggling to put their heads up?" Everybody had seen that, and so, based on what people had witnessed, it was possible to wonder whether hens felt pain and whether carrying them in such ways, or leaving them out in the hot sun at market time, was inflicting unnecessary discomfort or needless pain.

By the end of that morning the students had agreed to found their own young people's club dedicated to conserving the natural world, improving conditions for wild and domestic animals, and improving the human world. The club would be called Roots & Shoots.

As Jane explained in a first brief newsletter for the club, roots creep underground everywhere, where they provide even the greatest trees with a strong foundation. Shoots may seem frail and insignificant at first, but in moving toward the light they can break through concrete barriers and brick walls. Children and young people are like roots and shoots, while concrete and brick represent the problems that people have inflicted on the planet. Roots & Shoots would harness the power of young people's energy and idealism through collective action, and yet it would also emphasize the importance of individuals: "Every individual matters, whether human or animal. Every individual can make a difference."

Meanwhile, the proposed chimpanzee sanctuary in Pointe-Noire, Congo, had recently been placed on hold. For one thing, the Kouilou River island once considered a good location turned out to be inundated in the rainy season. For another, the Congolese government was falling apart, with multiple powers vying to dominate what had been a socialist, single-party system. So far no blood had been shed, but neither did anyone in the government feel bold enough to make serious decisions. Finally, Conoco's exploration wells had all come up dry and the company was starting to pull out of the country. Would it also pull out of its commitments to the chimps?

During Jane's spring 1991 fundraising tour in the States, she visited Conoco headquarters in Houston, Texas, to learn the answer to that question. Mary Lewis, an energetic Englishwoman who was an executive secretary at Conoco, remembers Jane's appearance at the headquarters. "It was a room of about two hundred fifty people, largely men. All Conoco. And she came in to meet Max Pitcher, our CEO. I was standing talking to him, and Jane came bouncing up. She was wearing yellow, and she looked absolutely marvelous. She was just shining. She just swept in and shone."

In spite of the dry wells, Conoco remained entirely committed to the project, Jane was assured — and Mary Lewis was invited to join a small Conoco group headed for the Gombe 30 celebration and fundraiser in Los Angeles, planned for May 6 at the Beverly Hilton Hotel.

Jane's profile in the movie capital had been raised recently by her attendance at the Academy Awards, where the HBO film *Chimps, So Like Us* had been nominated for an Oscar. At the same time two of her celebrity friends, Michael Jackson and Jack Lemmon, had been helping to promote the Gombe 30 gala, and by the evening of May 6 the grand ballroom of the Beverly Hilton had been turned into an African rain forest, more or less, with dinner tables festooned in moss, ferns, toadstools, and orchids. Amid the serving of dishes and clinking of silverware, video sequences covered thirty years at Gombe, an African group drummed and stilt-danced, the Los Angeles Children's Choir sang, and the Los Angeles Chamber String Quartet played Mozart. After a fundraising auction, the evening ended, as Jane put it in a letter to a friend, with "20 minutes of me. I doubt I've ever been more terrified! But the adrenalin flowed and, in my own reckoning, I got A+! Magic."

Flying back to Africa at the start of June, she stopped first in Brazzaville to check on the project for feeding the animals at the city zoo. The new keeper, Jean Mabotot, was, she wrote to a contact at the RSPCA, "truly wonderful. He has a terrific relationship with the chimps, monkeys and many of the other animals. Talks to them." While some of the chimps had recently died of a strange disease (never identified), the remaining five were in good shape. "<u>BUT</u> are all in solitary confinement. They need an expert to get them in <u>groups</u>." Old man Grégoire was vastly improved and "looks like a real chimp now! His hair has grown back everywhere & is glossy & black. His eyes are bright." All the other zoo animals — the birds, civets, monkeys, and mongooses, as well as the jackal and the pig — were also doing well. However, there was enough money to last only until the middle of

July, and so she could only "DESPERATELY HOPE THE RSPCA may grant at least <u>some</u> additional funds NOW."

After recovering from a debilitating bout of malaria near the end of June, Jane started work on another educational project, to promote Wildlife Awareness Weeks in various African countries, and to that end she began hauling around a portable chimpanzee museum. The museum was packed in suitcases and included videotapes, graphics, interpretive texts in French, English, and Swahili, and objects used by chimps as tools in different parts of Africa.

Conoco funded the portable museum and its portation, and Jane gradually toured Africa with it. She explained in a July 11 letter to her American friend Frank Loew: "I go with it, head of state (or closest we can get!) opens it, & we have a week of conservation awareness—kids bused in, radio & T.V. seminars, talks at schools—etc, etc. <u>Terrific</u>." Moving at a pace of about one country and capital city per week, she planned to visit four or five countries per year, starting in the summer of 1991 with Burundi, Zaire, Angola, and Congo. The next year she hoped to do Uganda, Mali, and Ivory Coast, as well as possibly Cameroon. "So," she summarized, "that's keeping me busy!"

By the third week of September 1991 she had returned to Brazzaville, taking along the suitcases and the chimpanzee museum and intending to inaugurate an official Wildlife Awareness Week there. First, though, she crossed the river to Zaire to meet with friends in Kinshasa and find out how seven recently confiscated chimp orphans were doing. She stayed in the apartment of Ruth and Cedric Dumas while visiting the two orphaned baby chimps they were taking care of, Chris and Calamity Jane. But on the night of September 22, Mobutu's Presidential Guard, unhappy over an inflation rate that made their wages nearly worthless, rebelled and thereby provoked looting and riots. The next day French paratroopers arrived in the city and fought their way to the center. A soldier was shot opposite the Dumases' balcony. A bullet shattered explosively through the bedroom window; fortunately, no one was hurt.

The following day was quiet, although Jane was still unable to leave the city or cross the river back to Brazzaville, where the Wildlife Awareness Week had started in her absence. Then Graziella Cotman, the Belgian woman working with chimpanzee orphans in Kinshasa, arrived at the Dumases' apartment traumatized, having been robbed of everything she had, including all her furniture and even the plumbing fixtures in her apartment.

The day after that Jane and Ruth Dumas were evacuated under military protection to Brazzaville—followed, a week later, by Graziella and seven young chimpanzees she had just rescued from the N'Sele Zoo. The seven orphans were placed in temporary quarters at the Brazzaville Zoo, with the idea that eventually they might move into the Congo sanctuary planned by JGI and Conoco near Pointe-Noire—but that, of course, was the end of the proposed sanctuary in Zaire.

Back in East Africa, meanwhile, life and politics may have seemed refreshingly stable. In Burundi, the Jane Goodall Institute had two full-time employees caring for thirteen orphan chimps in what was called a half-way house in Bujumbura, awaiting the construction of the sanctuary in the south. Alley, one of the chimps in the halfway house, loved to paint. Uruhara, who had arrived almost pathetically anxious and hairless, with a restraining leather strap half grown into his flesh, had turned into an eager, energetic little ball of black hair and muscle. Whiskey, the chimp once kept on a chain in an automotive repair shop lavatory, was also living in the half-way house now. He had another chimp to play with, volunteers were bringing in branches and forest fruit, and he seemed to enjoy making his own nest with the branches.

At the same time, the plans for a permanent sanctuary in Burundi were unfolding promisingly, with a site already selected (to the south and overlooking Lake Tanganyika), first-draft architectural drawings available, a budget already calculated.

By the summer of 1992, Conoco had located an alternative site for the Jane Goodall Institute chimpanzee sanctuary in Congo: about ninety minutes north of Pointe-Noire, in the Tchimpounga Valley. The full site amounted to about fifty acres of land with a beautiful view, a varied terrain, and an interesting mixture of woodland, marsh, and open savanna. The enclosed sanctuary within that site would include living quarters for any people involved and living quarters for the chimps: an open stretch of forest surrounded by an electric fence. The operation would require a generator to produce voltage for the fence, a well for water, some system for waste removal, a small grove of fruit trees and a vegetable garden for chimp and human food, a couple of four-wheel-drive vehicles for transportation, and possibly a big reintroduction cage that would double as entrance and exit to the fenced enclosure.

In December, the sanctuary, named Tchimpounga, was ready, and twenty-five young orphans, ill-treated ex-pets, and former zoo exhibits were welcomed to their new residence, complete with fresh air, trees, grass, and lots of room to romp.

Running a sanctuary in Congo proved surprisingly expensive, however.

Many things, such as steel and baby formula, had to be bought in Europe and imported at great expense. The initial construction cost Conoco around $660,000, and the Jane Goodall Institute took over responsibility for most of the $100,000-a-year operating budget. But the costs of operating Tchimpounga soon grew onerous—especially as 1993 became a time of recession and shrinking contributions to charities in the United States. Jane was staying at Gombe during the latter part of July that year, and she emerged from isolation at the end of the month to the unwelcome news that her institute in the United States was broke. "My problem is that I have no functioning office in USA," she explained to an acquaintance in a July 27 letter. Another acquaintance received the frank news, in a note of July 29, that "our finances are at ROCK BOTTOM."

The resigning executive director had just informed her by fax that the endowment was gone and the general account could support only another three months of operation before bankruptcy. In response, Jane transferred $50,000 from the previous year's Kyoto Prize—most of her personal savings—to the endowment account and got from one stalwart supporter a commitment for $75,000 to cover November expenses. Then she flew to Los Angeles for a second Hollywood fundraising extravaganza. The event was very successful, she informed her friend Mark Maglio in an August 13 letter, adding that "I THINK we have a fabulous person coming in to take over JGI."

Don Buford became the new executive director of JGI (US), and by October 1, 1993, he had moved the headquarters from Arizona to Connecticut. Buford was soon educating himself in the depth and complexity of Jane's work while trying to pull the institute out of its financial hole. Jane had telephoned and written to all her friends and supporters, declaring that the institute was surviving, that she was alive, that things were fine, and so on. She was also lecturing and networking and fundraising, a whirlwind of activity described in an October 22 note to Neva Folk, written during a Swiss Air flight from Zurich to Dar es Salaam. Jane planned to spend a week in Dar, she wrote, catching up with correspondence before returning to North America. "I shall be very busy," she continued, since she was bound for a "HUGE" event in Toronto that "could lead to very major benefits." From there she would head to Montreal for lunch with members of Canada's second wealthiest family, followed by Washington, D.C., for a November 8 lunch to honor former Soviet premier Mikhail Gorbachev, followed by meetings in Connecticut, then to New York, to Bournemouth. . . .

Yes, Jane was chalking up the miles again. At the moment, however, suspended in the cold, thin air a mile and a half above the bright, beautiful place known as Africa, she paused in her letter writing to reflect on the sobering news she had just read in the morning's paper: a short piece confirming that Burundi's president, Melchior Ndadaye, had been assassinated.

President Ndadaye had been a Hutu. His assassins, a radical cabal of Tutsi soliders, next killed a number of other high-ranking government officials and soon controlled the government and the army—whereupon Hutus around the nation took up their most handy weapons and during the next three months slaughtered between one and two hundred thousand Tutsis.

By the time Jane returned to East Africa, in late January 1994, the situation in Burundi was relatively stable, and she had reason to hope that with blue-helmeted United Nations peacekeepers in position, life at the northern end of Lake Tanganyika was returning to some semblance of a peaceful normalcy. She returned to the house in Dar es Salaam, where there were holes in the roof, rats, no water, and mounds of sand out front left over from a recent cesspit excavation. Normal. Grub, all grown up now and planning to start a sport-fishing business, discovered that his new boat for the business was stuck in customs, awaiting the requisite bribe. Also normal. Jane made a brief visit to Gombe, after which she left for Europe and the States for the normal round of business and lectures and fundraising.

But then, on April 6, 1994, after a plane carrying Rwanda's president and Burundi's interim president was shot down by unidentified men firing from the ground at Rwanda's Kigali airport, the already grim state of normal life in Burundi became grimmer, as crudely armed Hutu mobs in neighboring Rwanda massacred a half-million people, mostly Tutsis.

Jane was back in Africa by early June, taking along Don Buford and the longtime director of the UK institute, Dilys Vass, for a quick tour of the African projects, which by then included two more fledgling sanctuaries: one planned for Uganda and a second, nearly complete, in Kenya. The Kenyan sanctuary, Sweetwaters, was a two-hundred-acre, electric-fenced enclosure within an existing game reserve near the town of Nanyuki and was designed to be fully self-supporting as a tourist attraction. Jane thought conditions "very luxurious" at Sweetwaters, as she wrote home on June 8, "and quite spoiling for Don. He is going to find things so different in the rest of his trip. No more luxury!"

They traveled to Dar and from there to Gombe, which was "SUPER," as Jane put it in a July 12 letter to Neva Folk. But from Gombe they went on to Burundi. Jane's ambitious plans for the chimpanzees in Burundi—conservation, research, tourism, a sanctuary—had by then collapsed along with the country's infrastructure, and it seemed necessary now to close even the Bujumbura Halfway House. Its group of twenty orphans would eventually be transferred to Sweetwaters, but meanwhile, the people she met in Burundi, Jane added in the same letter, were living "in real <u>fear</u>." Although it was supposedly impossible to get visas, she had managed to get two for two little girls, who would soon be going to school in England. "Their parents were in tears every night — ½ at the thought that something might happen in Burundi, ½ at the thought of letting them go."

From Burundi, Jane and her pair of executive directors flew cross-continent to Pointe-Noire and drove north over rough roads to see Tchimpounga. By that time the Congolese sanctuary, built for twenty-five chimps, was holding significantly more — although Graziella Cotman, who by then had become the sanctuary manager, was, Jane reported home, "amazing" and doing a "<u>SUPER</u> job."

Then they flew back to Brazzaville, where Don Buford and Dilys Vass caught their return flight to England while Jane stayed on for another day, since she and the American ambassador had an appointment to confer with the Congolese president. The president was on that same day negotiating a ceasefire with leaders of the opposition, so both sides in the nation's latest conflict were showing force. As Jane traveled with Graziella in her pickup truck, crossing town to fetch the American ambassador, the vehicle was halted at a roadblock, the doors were yanked open, and both women were pulled out at gunpoint. The men were opposition forces, a machine-gun-waggling gang without uniforms, and it eventually became apparent that one of them had decided to take the pickup for his own use — nothing more serious. But Graziella absolutely refused to give up the keys, and the men holding the guns became increasingly hostile and threatening. Luckily, a Congolese man in another car joined in the argument and eventually managed to change the would-be carjacker's mind, whereupon Jane and Graziella were both pushed back into the vehicle at gunpoint and sent on their way.

When Jane visited the Tchimpounga sanctuary in July 1995, it was caring for around forty orphans. She wrote some of her impressions in a letter to two American friends: "To see 10 young chimps follow 2 Congolese men in blue uniforms onto the open plain, bordering the forest, all stop, each one be given a red cup of milk from a big blue bucket — except 2 that have bottles. Give back empty cup for refill. Then return when finished. Then all troop off into the forest for the morning. <u>Amazing</u>."

The ten young chimps were soon followed by twenty-six older ones, who came into the clearing from their indoor quarters. Each took a blue plastic cup filled with milk. And in the same fashion as the younger group, each drank the milk and then handed back the mug for a refill—except for one chimp, who habitually kept a spare piece of bread tucked beneath an arm, preferring to drink his milk while sopping the bread. When all the chimps had finished their milk, another caretaker arrived with a big sack full of bread, broken pieces of French loaves. "Each chimp gets one, some get 2. And then, on their own now, they go off to the forest for the day. Only the alpha—8 year old Maxillo, likes to patrol the boundary fence with a human. Well—with me! And in the evening, similar but in their sleeping quarters. And instead of bread, big plates of fruit & at the end, before milk, big sticky balls of rice!"

By the summer of 1996, Tchimpounga was holding well over fifty chimps. The old female La Vieille, who had once been so terrified of the world that she spent all her time huddled in a far corner of her cage, now spent several hours a day interacting with young chimp visitors who went inside her cage. Then one day she became confident enough to wander outside for the first time, and to edge very nervously along a concrete strip (intensely careful not to step on the grass) in order to visit a friend outside. The world, she was beginning to see, was not quite as bad as she had once thought.

41

Circumnavigations

1996–2000

JANE WAS BY NOW traveling 300 days a year in the service of a very exacting itinerary. In one typical seven-week stretch in North America, for example, she made 31 plane flights to 27 cities, giving 170 media interviews and lecturing at 71 different venues for a collective audience of around 33,000, while keeping up with her usual articles and books and correspondence (5 to 20 or more letters and notes a day), not to mention attending business meetings and meals.

She had, and has, help. Institute staff members and volunteers coordinate and logisticate, arranging flights, rides, meals, and hotels, while her personal assistant, Mary Lewis, remains, as much as anyone can, by her side.

When Jane travels, she carries, nestled in the crook of an arm or inside a small cloth bag, Mr. H, her stuffed toy monkey mascot. And she draws along at least one rolling, rackety suitcase — "the coffin," she and Mary call it — heavy because of all the books and papers, but also holding a few personal essentials, including a couple of simple dresses, a couple of easily pressed skirt-and-blouse combinations, a change of turtlenecks, a pair of moccasins, two pairs of more formal shoes, and several belts very neatly rolled up, along with a single-cup electrical heating element, an emergency supply of fruit or chocolates, and a small jar of Marmite.

Life on the road is kept relatively simple in part by the simplicity of Jane's needs. She dresses modestly, with minimal variety. She never seems to sweat. She sleeps or naps when and where she can, tolerates illogical changes in time and time zone. She can survive gracefully with very little food. A half slice of toast, a smear of butter, and perhaps a cup of coffee, with or without milk, will do for breakfast. Regular bread can be turned into toast on a hot clothes iron in the hotel room.

Mary, triangulating by schedule, cell phone, and Internet, navigates. A plane, a car, an escort, a hotel check-in; empty the coffin and hang up the clothes, then do business and make essential phone calls. Jane and Mary are then picked up and driven to the evening's lecture hall. Security guards escort them through a maze of doors and corridors. Mary (or Mouse, as Jane calls her affectionately) leads her to an empty room somewhere, and Jane sits down cross-legged in a corner. She scribbles a few notes on a small piece of paper, asking, "Who are our friends?" Jane will be sure to mention in her talk any friends and supporters likely to show up.

They consider the symbols to be used this time. Mary, opening the special bag containing a dozen inspirational objects, asks, "Do you want the Berlin Wall? Nelson Mandela?"

Jane has in her hand a small piece of herb. "Do we have any matches?" "No. You'll just have to sniff it." And she sniffs the herb, part of a Native American healing and mind-clearing exercise provided by her Karuk medicine-man friend Chictus. The next half-hour is quiet time, to jot a few more notes and consider the lecture this time around.

"People . . . are always asking where I find my energy," Jane has written.

> They also comment on how peaceful I seem. How can I be so peaceful? they ask. Do I meditate? Am I religious? Do I pray? Most of all, they ask how I can be so optimistic in the face of so much environmental destruction and human suffering; in the face of overpopulation and overconsumption, pollution, deforestation, desertification, poverty, famine, cruelty, hatred, greed, violence, and war. Does she really believe what she says? they seem to be wondering. What does she really think, deep down? What is her philosophy of life? What is the secret ingredient for her optimism, her hope?

In the early 1980s, Phillip Berman, a writer interested in comparative religion, assembled a collection of short essays by thirty-three prominent men and women, including Joan Baez, Rita Mae Brown, Robert Coles, Mario Cuomo, Hugh Downs, Jane Goodall, Tenzin Gyatso (the Dalai Lama), Billy Graham, Jim Henson, Elliot Richardson, Benjamin Spock, Edward Teller, Lech Walesa, Irving Wallace, Edward O. Wilson, and Michael York, on the subject of what they believed and how they had put those beliefs into action. The book, *The Courage of Conviction,* was a success, and Jane was quietly pleased with her own short essay in that collection. So when Berman asked her in 1995 to collaborate on a book about her spiritual philosophy, an expansion of the ideas she had explored in the essay, she agreed. It would be a small, simple book, she believed. Since she had no extra time, Berman agreed to do most of the work. The results—an ethologist's ideas filtered through the mind of a religion expert—might be interesting. He would ask the questions. She would edit her replies.

So he began to interview—in Bournemouth, in Dar es Salaam, at Gombe—and he went away with his tapes. Then one day in 1996 Jane received from the literary agent a bouquet of white flowers and a note: "Congratulations!" The note went on to say that the book proposal had been sold for an advance of $1 million. A one-hour film for public television, which would echo the contents of the book, repeat its title, and accompany its launch, was also under consideration.

Jane was shocked. The first problem was all that money, which meant that the book was not going to be the small, simple production she had imagined. The second was the implication of the working title, *Reverence for Life: The Spiritual Autobiography of Jane Goodall*. As she later told me, "I didn't imagine that this was going to be a 'spiritual autobiography.' If I had intended to do that, I would have planned to write it myself." It became, in her mind, "that bloody book." Still, she liked and trusted Phillip Berman. And the money, divided equally between the two of them, would come in handy. Jane was then raising around $2 million a year in donations and lectures and other activities, but that kept the institutes and projects functioning. Money had little meaning for her personally, and she lived frugally, like the rest of her family. Just then, for instance, the roof of the family home in Bournemouth was leaking badly whenever it rained. The house needed a new roof. The advance for the book would pay for that and also, Jane thought, for a simple stairway elevator to alleviate the increasingly difficult trek up the stairs at night for Olly (turning ninety-four that September) and Vanne (already ninety years old).

During the next several months Berman continued to interview Jane about her life, religious training, personal philosophy, spiritual thinking, and so on, and by 1998 he had produced a rough draft. Given the intimacy and complexity of the subject, it was perhaps predictable that Jane would not be entirely comfortable with that first pass . . . and finally she decided to take over the entire project. Using the structure her collaborator had provided from the interview transcripts, she sat down to write a book that she could be happy with. The process was unpleasant and surprisingly difficult. "Had I known," she later wrote, "how much time the writing would take, the sometimes painful searching of my soul that would be involved, I think I would not have accepted the challenge." It required all the time she usually reserved for family visits in Bournemouth, which now became thinking and word-processing marathons, causing her to wake up early in the morning and stay up late at night. Even then, it took much longer than she had expected.

The book, at last entitled *Reason for Hope: A Spiritual Journey,* was released in September 1999. Jane dreaded the first reviews. "I was convinced," she told me, "that people were going to say, 'Well, why should she think she has something to say on this subject?'" But the reviews were generally terrific. Initial sales soon took it onto the *New York Times* bestseller list, and subsequent sales have remained strong and steady.

The book opens with a moment in the spring of 1974, when Jane visited the cathedral of Notre Dame in Paris. The arching interior of the cathedral was unusually still, and Jane paused to gaze "in silent awe" at the great Rose Window, illuminated by the morning sun. Suddenly the whole cathedral was "filled with a huge volume of sound: an organ playing magnificently for a wedding taking place in a distant corner. Bach's Toccata and Fugue in D Minor. I had always loved the opening theme; but in the cathedral, filling the entire vastness, it seemed to enter and possess my whole self. It was as though the music itself was alive." This was a time of great turmoil in Jane's personal life, with her marriage to Hugo coming undone and her recently drifting affections attaching themselves so passionately to Derek. And that intensely aesthetic and emotional moment in the cathedral brought a new or renewed sense of self and time. It was "a suddenly captured moment of eternity . . . perhaps the closest I have ever come to experiencing ecstasy, the ecstasy of the mystic."

Jane grew up exposed to the gentle, noncoercive Christianity practiced by her family, especially her grandmother Danny. Her early, sometimes passionate and literalist beliefs were over time modified by experience and education—including personal talks with Louis Leakey, her acceptance of the validity of scientific method, and her formal scientific education at Cambridge. As a mature thinker, Jane finally came to see Christianity as a grand metaphor, a code for a complex truth that lies beyond rigid literalism— poetry, not prose. It was the poetry she grew up with and found comforting, but to take its figurative imagery as prosaic truth would be an imaginative failure that missed the grandeur of the tradition and excluded other ways of knowing. She had come to believe in "the spiritual power that, as a Christian, I called God. But as I grew older and learned about different faiths I came to believe that there was, after all, but One God with different names: Allah, Tao, the Creator, and so on. God, for me, was the Great Spirit in Whom 'we live and move and have our being.'"

Other life experiences affected her assessment of the childhood faith. She had gone to Gombe with a pragmatic goal, to study chimpanzees, but being there was at the same time a contemplative experience that "had a major impact on my thinking." As she came closer to nature and animals, she came closer to herself and "in tune with the spiritual power that I felt all around." She increasingly identified with the natural world and found herself absorbed in an aesthetic harmony and psychological unity with the forests and wilderness. She was also slowly becoming familiar with the wild apes. At that time most scientists and theologians were in agreement on at least one idea: the unexamined bias that "only humans had minds, only humans were capable of rational thought." Based on her earlier experiences with animals, Jane had intuitively known that they had emotions, personalities, minds, and so she found it easy to ascribe those qualities to chimpanzees. But with the chimpanzees especially, she could look into their eyes and powerfully sense a thinking and planning being who looked right back.

Jane found some strongly evocative parallels between human aggressive behavior and that of chimpanzees, who, like us, live in patriarchal communities separated by barriers (erected in the emotions and mind and enforced by the body) between *us* and *them*. Humans, she came to believe, have a "dark and evil side" profoundly connected to our evolutionary past, a "strong disposition to act aggressively in certain kinds of contexts," which are, in fact, the very contexts that produce aggression among chimpanzees. Chimpanzees and humans both are inheritors of territorially aggressive inclinations, a powerful psychology of xenophobia that readily fractures the species into mutually hostile communities. But because a larger brain and complex language bring, or can bring, greater understanding, these aspects of human nature make human aggression unique and uniquely troubling.

Contrasting with both species' obvious capacity for destruction, cruelty, and evil are many hopeful examples of the capacity for love, affection, caring, and altruism. Jane believes in the idea of moral evolution—that humans can over time learn to become "increasingly less aggressive and war-like and more caring and compassionate." Yet thinking about moral evolution is at best a long-term glimpse into a faraway land; and aside from the evil of hatred and human aggression against other humans, there is the reality of human aggression against the environment—overuse of water, destruction of the air, depletion of the soils, elimination of wilderness, extinction of species—caused by rapid population growth around the world combined with consumerist economics and the materialist lifestyles promoted in the West. Human aggression against the planet is a second sort of evil and a second compelling reason for alarm.

With ever more people in the world consuming ever more resources, where will it end? And what is the hope for the future? Jane's faith in the meaning of her life and the reality of a spiritual power, or possibly a Spiritual Power, gives her a quiet sense of personal logic and stability. But her more immediate reasons for hope, as described in the book, do not depend upon a personal deity, the sort of Being who might, after vigorous pleading or prayers, be persuaded to meddle in human affairs. She argues instead that humans must meddle in their own affairs, and so she finds her real reasons for hope at last in human potential and action. Her reasons for hope are precise and limited. There are four. First, the tremendous potential of the human brain. Second, the surprising resilience of nature. Third, the great creative energy possessed by young people. Fourth, what she calls "the indomitable human spirit."

Following the publication of *Reason for Hope,* Jane's lectures began increasingly to echo the book. Lectures that had at one time been in large part slide shows concentrating on chimpanzees and conservation were now expanded into the larger story of a spiritual quest and an appeal to values and action. Jane would open with autobiographical anecdotes covering her childhood and early years in Africa, describe her experiences of living among wild chimpanzees, draw from those experiences insights into human nature, refer to the desperate state of the environment in Africa and elsewhere, and conclude by identifying her four reasons for hope.

Her first reason for hope, the potential of the human brain, reminds us that humans are intellectually flexible and amazingly innovative. We can invent electric cars and other forms of power production that will reduce air pollution. Personal and industrial recycling can reduce waste pollution. Ecobricks, invented by her friend Gary Zeller, lock industrial wastes into a form that both solves the waste disposal problem and provides a strong yet inexpensive building material.

Her second reason for hope, the resilience of nature, reminds us that nature, given the chance or even prodded a bit, can recover from the human onslaught. She considers success stories from around the world, such as the return of clean water and fish and breeding birds to the Thames River ecosystem after a concerted cleanup operation. She may tell of the cleaning up of toxic waste around a nickel mine in Canada and the return, after forty years, of peregrine falcons. She usually describes her visit to Nagasaki, the city obliterated by an atomic bomb at the end of World War II. Scientists had declared ground zero in that city to be a desert where nothing would grow for at least thirty years—and yet small plants quickly began shooting up. One young sapling had somehow remained alive and intact through the blast. It was a great old tree by the time Jane saw it, twisted and cracked and yet still producing new leaves each spring. She was given one of the leaves from that tree, which she now — in the lecture — holds up for the audience to see. It is a symbol of hope.

She speaks of the return of species brought to the edge of extinction, such as the spotted Formosan deer: gone from the wild, bred into a viable herd from a small zoo population, placed back in the wild. An antler shed by one of those deer was given to Jane, and she shows it now. It is another symbol of hope. Or perhaps she describes the California condor project. That giant bird had been virtually extinguished, and yet through captive breeding the numbers were increased, then individuals were released, and the birds are now once again soaring majestically and musically (as wind ripples through their giant wing feathers) over the hills and valleys of California. Someone gave her a condor feather. She holds that remarkable object in the light: one more symbol of hope.

Jane's third reason for hope, the creative energy of young people, allows her to talk about her own young people's program, the Roots & Shoots clubs, which by April 1999 had grown to include around two thousand groups located in over forty countries around the world.

And her fourth reason for hope, the indomitable human spirit, calls on examples from among Jane's own personal heroes, friends and acquaintances who have overcome great adversity with courage and grace. Perhaps she mentions her friend Mikhail Gorbachev, who challenged the totalitarian ways of his own government and enabled freedom to prevail in Eastern Europe. Possibly she displays a piece of the Berlin Wall, retrieved just after it fell. She probably recalls meeting Nelson Mandela, the charismatic leader who emerged from thirty years of hard labor on Robben Island without bitterness or recrimination against his captors, who broke through the criminal regime of apartheid without bloodshed. And she holds up, now, another symbol of hope: a rock from Robben Island.

There are other indomitable human heroes, other symbols of hope. She might mention her friend Jon Stocking, who, while employed as a cook on a tuna fishing boat, jumped into the water to free a trapped mother and baby dolphin from the nets; he risked his life and lost his job, but he went on to create the Endangered Species Chocolate Company, which makes chocolate bars as a way to raise money to help endangered species. And she will certainly speak about her friend Gary Haun, a U.S. Marine who lost his eyesight in a helicopter crash but nonetheless became a skilled magician — the Amazing Haundini — as well as a scuba diver, skydiver, martial arts expert, and cross-country skier. In April 1994, Gary gave Jane a toy stuffed animal. He thought it was a chimp. Then Jane guided his hand to the tail, explaining that monkeys have tails but apes do not. That was Mr. H, as Jane named him. Mr. H is another symbol of hope.

Mr. H also provides tactile comfort on the road, and he does other things. "I tell people," Jane writes in *Reason for Hope*, "that they will never be quite the same again once they have touched him, for something of the indomitable spirit of Gary Haun will rub off on them. He has now been touched, patted, or kissed by well over 200,000 people—no wonder his once fluffy hair is matted, his once white face grubby-looking (despite repeated shampoos), and his body even more misshapen."

I recall one time riding in a crowded public boat, a water taxi, on Lake Tanganyika in the company of Jane and Mr. H and a dozen African schoolchildren, among many other passengers. Jane passed Mr. H around for everyone to hug and stroke, and the children broke into bright smiles and excited giggles and seemed perfectly ecstatic. Mr. H is Jane's personal icebreaker.

Breaking through the ego-ice that surrounds people is a skill she has cultivated, and she credits her many years in Africa with encouraging such cultivation. In Africa a person would never walk into a room without first establishing a private, personal connection and confirming a sense of friendship with people, even when friends are not actually present. One smiles profoundly, shakes hands warmly, inquires sincerely about the health of the other and the other's spouse, children, parents, and so on. Greetings and exchanges of that sort are formalized but at the same time meaningful enough to penetrate ordinary reserve. The African way has served Jane well, especially, for example, during the early 1990s, when she was lobbying in Washington, D.C. She would never enter a congressperson's office and start by referring to the business at hand. She would always first establish a personal connection.

Living with the chimpanzees has also helped. One time I accompanied Jane to the Federal Correctional Institute in Danbury, Connecticut, where a group of women prisoners had started a Roots & Shoots chapter. Arriving on a drizzly, misty morning, we were searched, fingerprinted, and otherwise processed into the lockup by a pair of guards, one of whom may not have had his morning coffee yet. He was big, burly, and businesslike—tough-looking, stony-faced—until Jane greeted him with a chimpanzee pant-hoot, which instantly shattered the stone of his demeanor. The other guard said, "That's the first time he's smiled in history. I've got to write that one down."

While in Los Angeles during a campaign to set up Roots & Shoots in the schools of South Central, Jane was invited to speak to the top ranks of the city police. It was a last-minute invitation, with no time to prepare, and a deputy chief took her upstairs into a room filled with all the top brass. She was told that she had ten minutes and that most of them probably would not be very interested in anything she had to say. The chief of police introduced her, and only two from the crowd of faces actually looked up. Jane was scared, she told me—"filled with adrenaline" and "not knowing what on earth to talk about" in that intimidating situation. So she opened with ex-actly what came to mind. She said, "If I were a female chimpanzee going into a room of very high-ranking males, like the ones I see here now, I'd be stupid if I didn't begin with a greeting of submission." She gave a female submissive greeting—and immediately had everyone's absolute attention.

In November 1998, Jane went to mainland China for the first time, lec-turing in Shanghai, then traveling to Beijing, where she was summoned to explain herself before the Chinese vice minister for the environment. The required meeting took place in a hotel room crowded with observers, bu-reaucrats, and security officers, as well as television crews pushing around lights, microphones, and cameras. Again Jane was given only ten minutes to speak, and of course the conversation would be inhibited by the necessary back-and-forth interpretations.

She and the vice minister were seated in chairs next to each other, and he seemed very formal, very stiff. What could she say to break through that formality and describe her mission in ten minutes? She decided to try the LAPD approach, describing their situation in chimpanzee terms: a lone fe-male meets a very high-ranking male in the forest. She made the proper sub-missive vocalization, then added, "And if you, the very high-ranking male, should approve of me and my expressions of submission, you would reach out"—she took his hand, felt the stiff resistance, heard the gasps emitted by some anxious members of the audience, pulled against the resisting hand and arm—"and pat me reassuringly on the head, just like this." And she leaned over and gently patted his hand on the top of her head.

The alarmed expression on the official's face turned into an astonished one, and then he leaned back and roared with laughter. Everyone else, at first unnerved by this brazen act but now reassured, joined in. The sched-uled ten minutes turned into an hour and a half, and so Jane was given the chance to describe her young naturalists' club to a television audience of 50 million people, after which the vice minister for the environment asked her to bring Roots & Shoots into the schools of China.

Circles have centers, and circumnavigations a port of departure and return, a place to rest and shift from public to private, a home. Being on the road more than three hundred days of the year means that Jane has fewer than sixty-five days each year to enjoy life at home. But where exactly is home? An acquaintance of mine once asked her that question and received the short answer. Jane pointed up to the sky and said, "Up there. In an airplane." The longer answer is that by the late 1990s she had three homes, in Bournemouth, Dar es Salaam, and Gombe.

The family residence in Bournemouth, The Birches at 10 Durley Chine Road South, was in many ways the same place Jane had known as a young girl: red-brick Victorian with slate roof and arched windows. Upstairs the old bookcases still contained all the old books: the Tarzan series, the Doctor Dolittle series, the squidgy poets, and so on. Jane's favorite childhood toy, a stuffed chimpanzee named Jubilee, was up there as well, though now hairless, stiff, and with a disintegrating left toe from which the cotton stuffing was slowly spilling out. Down in the kitchen, the sinks and cabinets were the same. The clothes-drying rack above the water heater, an elaborate construction of dowels and cords and ceiling-mounted pulleys that could be lowered into use or raised out of the way, was still there. Jane had watched, many years ago, as Mr. Upshall, the gardener and handyman, with a wooden leg, made it.

Now, though, only Olly and Vanne were living in the house, both of them well into their ninth decade, whittled down by time. When I first met Olly, in 1996, she was charming, delightful, sometimes wickedly funny, but she had become increasingly vague—or was it hard of hearing? Vanne was tiny, with laughing brown eyes, her hair brownish and billowy with white edges. She was also bright and ironic and witty, a penetrating intelligence caught in a shrinking body. Even the dog, Whiskey, or Wiskey-Biskey, was by then getting old and stiff and quiet.

In Dar es Salaam, the house Jane had once shared with Derek now served as her home—one of them—in Africa. And by the late 1990s it, like the family residence in Bournemouth, presented a mild and relaxed decrepitude. It was a brown stucco house, a little worn on the outside, with the Indian Ocean rising and falling before it on a sandy beach. Inside, a couple of dogs would be dozing on a cool concrete floor, and during the day light flickered through lace curtains drifting at the windows.

Dar was where Jane spent time with Grub and his wife, Maria Chilala, and their children, Merlin and Angel. Grub, having experimented with places and careers—anthropology for a semester at Oxford Polytechnic in England, animal photography for a year with his father in the Serengeti—by the second half of the 1990s had settled on his own passion and into Jane's guesthouse, where he ran a fishing business.

Jane's third home and third family, her chimpanzee family, were at Gombe. Gombe too was in many ways the same as it had always been.

There was that simple, airy cabin situated next to a great, lapping lake at the edge of a small but noisy forest. Jane continued as scientific director at Gombe, but now, of course, she relied on others to run things. Tony Collins managed the baboon study. The chimpanzee study, by the fall of 1997, was directed by Shadrack Kamenya, a soft-spoken native of Kigoma who had recently acquired his doctorate in anthropology at the University of Colorado. Still, Jane found there were often staff issues to sort out whenever she visited. There were typically guests and new researchers, all of whom required attention. And usually there would be social or medical problems among the chimps or baboons to worry about: respiratory ailments, for instance, or the sudden appearance of poachers' snares, which cost a young mother, Loretta, her hand in 1996 and caught three of the baboons in 1997.

That was home in three parts, and after a short visit to one place or another, or to two or all three in sequence, Jane would soon be buckled into an enormous flying machine somewhere, spinning out into orbit once more, starting the circumnavigations all over again: returning thus from an increasingly fragmented private life as Jane, daughter and mother and friend, and entering once more the ever-expanding public sphere of Dr. Jane Goodall.

For Roots & Shoots purposes, she was, more simply, Dr. Jane.

It has always been a source of pleasure and pride for her to note how Roots & Shoots caught on in Tanzania. In the Kigoma region alone there were some twenty-four different clubs by the year 2000, all working on projects to improve the well-being of animals, the environment, and the human community. The groups organized drawing and writing competitions, picked up trash at a local market, showed environmental movies, visited Gombe, planted thousands of trees. In Dar es Salaam, the many Roots & Shoots clubs were planting trees and cleaning up trash as well—also recycling paper, visiting hospital patients, giving concerts to raise environmental awareness, participating in peace marches and environmental lectures and debates. So the Tanzanian Roots & Shoots was spreading as Jane had hoped, and through the mails and the Internet and personal exchange programs, they were also forging partnerships with Roots & Shoots chapters in other countries and on other continents.

By the end of 2000, Roots & Shoots existed as more than three thousand groups active in sixty-seven countries around the world. Chapters were organized in elementary and secondary schools, colleges and universities, prisons and senior citizen homes and neighborhoods. Roots & Shoots groups in South Africa were working with children in a cancer ward. Roots & Shoots in Dar es Salaam organized the first annual National Sports Day for the Disabled. Two groups in Canada established a partnership to help Haitian students whose school had been bombed. Roots & Shoots in Germany sent fifty pairs of jeans to the Sahrawi refugees in Algeria. German groups were adopting local wetlands, working to improve the treatment of captive animals, developing environmental education programs. Taiwanese Roots & Shoots were recycling paper, cleaning up a local pond, raising money for the Save the Tiger Fund. A group in China was working to enrich the environment for chimpanzees in the Shanghai Zoo. The Waldo Middle School chapter in Oregon participated in a remote sensing project to study forest biodiversity. The Wilmington Middle School chapter in Ohio researched various local tree species and made a native forest quilt, with tree leaves printed on each square of the quilt by a special photographic process—and then sent the quilt to their partners in Tanzania, Roots & Shoots at the Mlimani Primary School of Dar es Salaam, along with a kit and equipment for the Mlimani chapter to make their own forest quilt.

Jane's circumnavigations have always been stimulated by the need for financing, and every year in the late 1990s brought a new schedule of lectures and other methods of raising money. But aside from the continuous fundraising lectures and events, she regularly attended national and international Roots & Shoots summits, and she always liked to lecture at the annual ChimpanZoo conferences. She also routinely participated in such high-profile affairs as the annual State of the World Forum. She twice gave the St. Francis Day sermon and oversaw the Blessing of the Animals woof-and-meow event held in San Francisco's Grace Cathedral. She maintained her professorship in zoology at the University of Dar es Salaam and at the same time continued with academic affiliations and obligations at four American universities. Between 1996 and 2000 she accepted honorary degrees from seven additional colleges and universities. She had already been elevated by Queen Elizabeth II to Commander of the British Empire in 1995. That distinction was supplemented in 1996 by the Zoological Society of London's Silver Medal, the Tanzanian Kilimanjaro Medal, the Primate Society of Great Britain's Conservation Award, the Caring Institute Award, the Polar Bear Award, and the William Proctor Prize for Scientific Achievement. In 1997 it was the John and Alice Tyler Prize for Environmental Achievement, the David S. Ingells Jr. Award for Excellence, the Common Wealth Award for Public Service, the Field Museum's Award of Merit, and the Royal Geographical Society/Discovery Channel's Award for a Lifetime of Discovery. In 1998, Jane became Disney's Animal Kingdom Eco-Hero and was presented with the National Science Board Public Service Award, the Orion Society's John Hay Award, and the Kristiansands Dyrepark's Julius Award; and in 1999 she accepted the International Peace Award and the Botanical

Research Institute of Texas International's Award for Excellence in Conservation. . . . And so, in that busy and very productive manner, Jane entered a new year, a new century, and a new millennium. But all three may have seemed at first a lot like the old ones, with a blur of airports and taxis and hotels, with the rotating wheel of business lunches and social dinners, of meetings and interviews, of lectures and then more lectures.

42

Messages

2000–2003

EARLY IN THE YEAR 2000, Jane spoke to a thousand religious delegates, all dressed in their traditional habiliments and colorful regalia, who had come from a hundred different countries to the United Nations' Millennium Peace Summit of Religious and Spiritual Leaders. Some of the leaders in that great assembly, Jane noticed, talked of human reconciliation and unity as a species. Others came with the opposite message. Aside from Jane and one Hindu leader, no one spoke on behalf of nonhuman animals. And no one referred to humanity's spiritual or ethical obligations to the environment—except for Angaangaq Lyberth, an Eskimo-Kalaallit elder, who said, "My brothers and sisters, I bring you a message from your brothers and sisters up in the north. Every day what you do in the south we are aware of. Up in the north the ice is melting." He paused before repeating the phrase and completing the idea: "Up in the north the ice is melting. What will it take to melt the ice in the human heart?"

That was the message Jane remembered best from those four days in New York City at the start of a new millennium. Meanwhile, Vanne had quietly witnessed the new millennium in a weakened state from her bed. The pig's heart valve that had been fitted into her heart twenty years earlier was supposed to last only ten years. Jane's sister, Judy, had returned home to The Birches to care for Vanne—and Olly, who was not well either—with some assistance from a visiting nurse. Jane telephoned often, and she spoke to her ninety-four-year-old mother on April 12, 2000, from a hotel room in St. Paul, Minnesota, with Judy relaying Vanne's whispered words. Vanne died later that day. "To the very end her mind was sharp and clear, though her body was giving up a little more each day," Jane wrote in a Roots & Shoots newsletter, adding, "No one can ever have had a better, more supportive mother."

As Jane liked to say, somewhat whimsically, Vanne had joined "the Cloud Contingent"—meaning that she had settled in with Danny, Uncle Eric, and Audrey and was drifting on a beautiful white cloud and looking down serenely at the rest of us.

July 14, 2000, was the fortieth anniversary of the day mother and daughter had first gone to Gombe, and Jane went back to celebrate. She spent much of the day wandering about and reminiscing, in part aloud and for the benefit of the video photographer Bill Wallauer. Other than herself, she recalled, only two creatures present at Gombe forty years before were still alive now. One was the staff member and *mzee* (distinguished elder) Jumanne Kikwale, who, as a little boy on the beach, had witnessed the strange spectacle of two white women appearing in a boat, coming ashore, and setting up canvas tents. The other was the chimpanzee matriarch Fifi, who forty years before had been a tiny baby protected in the cradle of Flo's arms.

Gombe was second only to a study of macaques in Japan as the longest-running animal behavior research project in history, and Jane used the fortieth anniversary year as a cause for celebration interspersed with old-fashioned fundraising—and a new-fashioned endowment campaign. A financial plan conceived on behalf of the Jane Goodall Institute had concluded that Jane's global mission would soon require around $5 million per year to sustain, and it optimistically suggested that an endowment of $50 million would produce that much through interest income. That large sum became the official goal, and at the time the robust state of the U.S. economy made it seem reasonable.

In 2001 a fundraising consultant asked if Jane might ring the opening bell on Wall Street one morning during the first week of January. According to a brief article in the *New York Times*, the consultant had said to her, "You speak the language of the jungle. We should get you down to the New York Stock Exchange." The article was premature, unfortunately, and the administrative powers at the exchange, possibly put off by its casual presumption, lost interest in the gesture. By then, however, the market itself was losing interest. High-tech stocks had fallen 40 percent during the previous several months, while altogether U.S. stocks had lost more than $2.5 trillion in value. During the early months of his election campaign, George W. Bush had promised not only to pay down the national debt by $2 trillion but simultaneously to pass out $1.6 trillion in tax cuts over the next ten years, based on the vision of vast government surpluses and unprecedented economic prosperity. Lately, though, with the market in trouble and signs that the economy was slowing down, the new president was describing his promised tax cut not as a deserved return to wealthy taxpayers but as an eco-

nomic stimulus package: an "insurance policy" to head off "potential economic downturn."

The state of the U.S. economy concerned Jane and members of her institute board, but of more immediate interest to Jane, at least, were the incom-
ing president's interests and assumptions on the environmental front. While
it was true that President Bush had been an oil man and was clearly pro-
business, he had talked positively about such green issues as cleaning up
toxic waste sites and increasing the funding for national parks. During his
campaign, moreover, he had pledged to reduce carbon dioxide emissions
from coal- and oil-burning power plants in the United States as an essential
first response to the threat of global warming.

A decade earlier, reasonable people could consider global warming a theory still under debate, but by the start of 2001 a comprehensive international
scientific study indicated that carbon dioxide levels in the atmosphere had
increased 30 percent beyond preindustrial levels, while average global temperatures had already risen by more than 1° Fahrenheit during the previous
century, with the last ten years the hottest decade on record. Global temperatures were rising at an accelerated rate; by the end of the twenty-first century, the average worldwide increase was predicted to range between 2.5° F
and 10.4° F. But rising temperatures, even seemingly small ones, were already having major effects. During the previous two decades, the annual
melting season in Antarctica had expanded by three weeks, and the Antarc-
tic icecap was getting thinner every year. One consequence of melting gla-
ciers and polar icecaps would be rising sea levels, which could result in
devastating floods, and warmer seas could stimulate increasingly violent
weather—severe hurricanes, for example. Combined with the possibility of
radically shifting agricultural production and large-scale extinctions, such
changes meant that global warming probably ranked as the most serious environmental issue of the century. Global warming was a challenge to international stability comparable to nuclear war, according to Paul O'Neill, the
new secretary of the Treasury.

The single international response to global warming, the 1997 Kyoto
Protocol, was an agreement among developed nations to begin limiting
their emissions of carbon dioxide and other greenhouse gases. The United
States had agreed to reduce its own emissions by 7 percent in fifteen years.
At the start of 2001, however, signatories of the protocol were still debating
the details, and then, in March, President Bush announced not only that he
would back away from his campaign pledge to curb power plant emissions
of carbon dioxide in the United States but that he was withdrawing from the
Kyoto Protocol.

The United States was by far the biggest source of atmospheric pollution, with 4 percent of the world's population delivering through its smoke-stacks and tailpipes 25 percent of the world's greenhouse gases—which meant that President Bush's precipitous withdrawal was simultaneously arrogant and dangerous. But the new president described himself as more worried about the immediate price of U.S. gasoline than about the longer-term global cost of melting polar ice. "Our economy has slowed down," he explained. "We also have an energy crisis, and the idea of placing caps on CO_2 does not make economic sense."

Still, he was new to the presidency. Undoubtedly he would mature in office. And perhaps he could be persuaded that the Kyoto Protocol should be shaped rather than scrapped. Based on that kind of optimistic thinking, Jane signed her name—alongside the signatures of Jimmy Carter, Walter Cronkite, Harrison Ford, John Glenn, Mikhail Gorbachev, George Soros, J. Craig Venter, and Edward O. Wilson and the fingerprint of Stephen Hawking—on a message to President Bush, which was published as a brief "essay" on the back page of the April 9, 2001, issue of *Time*.

Dear Mr. President,
    No challenge we face is more momentous than the threat of global climate change. The current provisions of the Kyoto Protocol are a matter of legitimate debate. But the situation is becoming more urgent, and it is time for consensus and action. There are many strategies for curbing greenhouse gas emissions without slowing economic growth. In fact, the spread of advanced, cleaner technology is more of an economic opportunity than a peril. We urge you to develop a plan to reduce U.S. production of greenhouse gases. The future of our children—and their children—depends on the resolve that you and other world leaders show.

Jane's father, Mortimer Morris-Goodall, who had been frail and who was taken to the hospital in early May 2001, died at the age of ninety-four on May 15. Jane, stopping in England on the way from Paris to Los Angeles, attended his funeral service in Brighton.

By July 2 she was back in Tanzania to spend some private time with Grub, Maria, and the grandchildren in Dar es Salaam. Hugo van Lawick was also there, having been forced by emphysema to leave his tented camp in the Serengeti, and was living with Grub and his family in the guesthouse. The Dar visit was followed by more time with the other side of the family, namely Judy and her children and grandchildren, in Bournemouth.

By September 7, Jane was headed back to the States. The weather on the eastern seaboard was stunningly beautiful: early autumn, bright skies, crisp air, restfully cool evenings. Accompanied by her assistant, Mary Lewis, Jane gave a lecture in Rhinebeck, New York, on September 8, followed by another in Vermont on September 9 for an Earth Charter event. The latter was a rural celebration wrapped in the grand pastoral mode, incorporating a silent barefoot walk through sun-brightened grass with one hundred fellow walkers and a shining Clydesdale mare named Lucy, an avenue of trees with white-gowned dancers elegantly performing from the branches, the haunting far-off sounds of Paul Winters playing saxophone, and a barn packed with two thousand people eagerly waiting for Jane to arrive.

Jane and Mary returned to New York City on the tenth and checked in at their favorite hotel, the Roger Smith, at 501 Lexington Avenue, where they received a faxed copy of a message from U.S. Secretary of State Colin Powell, regretfully declining an invitation to attend one of Jane's upcoming public events but adding that he would be "pleased to add my voice to those of your friends and colleagues in recognizing you as one of the world's outstanding citizens."

That evening Jane appeared on *The Charlie Rose Show* to promote her latest children's book. She woke up early, as usual, on September 11, and began preparing for more book promotion and a meeting with Fred Thompson, the new CEO for JGI (US), and Nona Gandelman, the vice president for communications. Fred was coming to the city by train. Nona was flying in. But around the time that Nona's plane was supposed to land, Mary Lewis came rushing into Jane's room at the hotel, saying, "Turn on your television. You've got to look." Jane never watched television if she could avoid it, but she did turn it on now, and she saw that a plane had crashed into one of the towers of the World Trade Center and the tower was now burning.

Nona, meanwhile, had arrived at the airport and was heading into the city in a taxi. The skyline came into view, but part of it, she saw, was marred by a billowing, ugly column of black smoke. She asked the driver what was going on. The driver said, "That's smoke. That's the World Trade Center."

The cab radio was on low. Nona failed to understand the words, but a voice was speaking with some urgency, and she asked the driver to turn it up—and soon deduced that a small plane had accidentally struck one of the twin towers. Nona, with some experience in piloting a small plane herself, had trouble imagining how it was possible to crash accidentally into such a massive landmark. But as she was puzzling over that, she saw a large passenger jet flying low over the city. And then she saw, within the churning column of inky smoke, a great flash of light. She said, "Oh, my God! We're under attack."

Back at the Roger Smith, meanwhile, Jane and Mary watched the news reports on television. None of the telephones seemed to work, although

later in the day Mary was able to send brief e-mail messages to several people on her list, including me.

> dear dale
> we are in nyc. what a terrible day. phones virtually impossible. . . . tried
> to have a meeting this A.M. but we were all in tears. empty streets except
> for ambulances and police cars. we are feeling very mortal. . . .
>
> love,
> m

They could smell and see the bitter smoke, and the city had gone eerily
quiet, with only the sounds of emergency vehicles. When Mary and Nona
finally went outside, into the smoke and the quiet, they entered a strangely
different, very un–New York atmosphere. People were civil and solicitous.
The enormous feeling of shock mixed with grief was shared by everyone,
and it spilled over into a sense of mutual sympathy and personal fragility, as
if the mask of the world had been set aside for a moment, as if the normal
rushing pushing honking business of the city had so casually shivered and
lifted, like a lace curtain in a warm breeze, to reveal the tender business of
life.

Seeing a woman walking a small dog, Mary and Nona ran after her and
asked if they could hug the dog. Then they were on their knees, embracing
the animal, giving hugs and getting kisses in return.

The airport was closed until the seventh day after the attacks, and Jane
and Mary left the day after that, flying to Portland, Oregon, to pick up the
pieces of an interrupted tour. After they had been in the air for about an
hour, though, Jane noticed that she was feeling peculiar, sick to her stomach
perhaps. It took a while before she recognized that her stomach was churning from fear. But fear of what? What was she afraid of? Not flying. Not
the possibility of yet another plane hijacking. No, she eventually realized,
she was afraid because she had no idea what to say on the morning of the
next day, when she was scheduled to address a group of eight hundred high
school students. It was to be a "Reason for Hope" lecture, but what was
there to be hopeful about?

That evening Jane attended a Roots & Shoots festival in Portland. All
the children had come with exhibits illustrating the wonderful projects they
had done, and of course they were very excited and full of life—while
Jane, looking around at all the young and enthusiastic members of Roots &
Shoots clubs at the festival, was thinking, *You don't understand. The world's
changed*. Then she returned to the obsessive question: What was she going
to say to those high school students tomorrow morning?

She arrived at the auditorium the next day, was introduced, and began her talk. She felt remarkably calm, even though she still had no clue where her words would lead. The opening part was easy enough, as she recounted the latest news on Goblin, Patti, Fifi and her family, Gremlin and the twins. She pointed out all the threats to wild chimpanzees in Africa, and she talked about how humans had already damaged so much of the natural environment. She enumerated her four reasons for hope. . . . Then she observed that in New York, on a single day, they had witnessed the worst possible human evil—using innocents to kill innocents—and, as the rescue workers risked and often gave their lives to free people trapped in the wreckage, the best in human courage and altruism. She spoke also of the great courage displayed by the rescue dogs, working to exhaustion day after day in the dangerously unstable and extremely toxic ruins of the collapsed towers.

She next placed the September 11 attacks in context. Yes, they had been utterly traumatic and unbelievably destructive, killing thousands of ordinary human beings in New York City, Washington, and Pennsylvania, as well as an American innocence about the human potential for evil and the dangers of the world. The physical and emotional landscape of New York would never be the same, and it was essential to acknowledge the devastating seriousness of the attacks. Yet it was also important to remember that terrorism had been going on for a long time. People in Europe had actually become used to terrorist bombs intended to kill innocent people. She herself had had a close experience in London when a large bomb was found in one of the meeting rooms at the Royal Overseas League, lodged inside what was to be a speaker's podium for a conference on IRA terrorism. Jane was evacuated from her room in the club, three floors directly above the device, at six o'clock one morning. Three times she had been evacuated from airports following bomb threats, and two other times she had been removed from train stations under similar circumstances. One adjusts. After all, tens of thousands of people are killed and seriously injured each year in traffic accidents, an ongoing carnage far worse than anything done by a mere terrorist, and yet even though people recognize the great danger cars present statistically, they are still not paralyzed by a fear of them.

She spoke of the horrors of World War II, most of which she experienced as a very young observer. She had a strong memory of hearing on the radio that England had declared war against Germany, and although she had been too young to comprehend the logic of what was being said, she had understood very well the anxiety and fear of the adults around her. Her father's brother, Rex, was killed in the war. Her second husband, Derek, was severely crippled in a plane crash. It was total war that swirled around the globe, and millions were killed or maimed as combatants or as unarmed civilian bystanders, while millions more were methodically starved and shot and gassed in the death factories organized by Hitler and the Nazis. It was a time when good people were afraid, and yet ultimately they triumphed, through action sustained by courage and directed by a sense of moral right. World War II was the end for the many people who lost their lives, but it was not the end of life on earth, or of civilization or even Western democracy. Likewise, the September 11 attacks, as terrible as they were, did not mark the end, and Americans would emerge whole from the crisis, not by giving in to fear but by rising to courage.

Jane received four new honorary academic degrees and five other significant awards during 2001, but the honor she valued most was the Gandhi/King Award for Nonviolence, conferred by the World Movement for Nonviolence on October 30 at the United Nations.

In the morning of October 30, before receiving that award, she spoke at a Roots & Shoots assembly at a school in the Bronx. After she finished talking, a New York Police Department officer, Steve Smaldon, came onstage with his German shepherd rescue dog, Hansan. Sergeant Smaldon spoke about the tremendous stresses of his work at Ground Zero, which involved coordinating with Hansan in searching for human remains inside a great toxic pit. They had worked there since September 11, he told Jane and the gathered schoolchildren, and they were putting in fifteen-hour shifts, with a single day off every two weeks. Hansan had cut his paw in the first week, however, and had been forced to work wearing a special little bootie, which Smaldon now presented to Jane.

Later that day she held up the paw bootie in the Trusteeship Council Chamber of the United Nations, displaying it during her address at the Gandhi/King Award event as a symbolic message of hope from a brave dog and his heroic human partner. She also spoke warmly of her own dog from childhood, Rusty, who had taught her so much about the true nature of animals. And, continuing on the theme of distinguished canines, she introduced Kessler, a Seeing Eye dog who was sitting in the audience alongside his nonseeing partner, Al Golabek, the blind ski-jumping world champion. Kessler must have been the first dog ever introduced in the United Nations, and he responded to all the attention by slobbering kisses onto Jane's face.

So the importance of animals in the lives of humans was a fundamental theme of her address that day. But were animals and animal lovers now relevant? The famous pair for whom the award was named, Martin Luther King and Mahatma Gandhi, and the previous two recipients, Kofi Annan and Nelson Mandela, were all inspired leaders who used nonviolent tools of negotiation and moral persuasion to make peaceful transformations in the human political scene.

UN Secretary-General Kofi Annan, in preparation for the World Summit on Sustainable Development (to be held in September 2002), had a few months earlier appointed Jane to an advisory panel of thirteen "eminent persons." The thirteen later assembled for a preliminary meeting at the United Nations, and after Annan asked them to summarize what they would do for sustainable development, Jane decided to say something about Roots & Shoots. She described how her children's program, with thousands of chapters in dozens of nations, was breaking down the barriers erected between people of different cultures and countries and religions. "We are truly sowing the seeds of global peace," she declared. After everyone had finished, Secretary-General Annan summed up—and Roots & Shoots seemed to be the only thing he wanted to talk about. He declared that he loved what Jane Goodall had said, that youth is the future, and he loved her idea about Roots & Shoots. They adjourned for a group lunch, and although Jane and Annan talked on the way to the lunchroom, they were seated at opposite sides of a big table, too far apart to continue their conversation—so he rearranged the seating in order to continue talking about Roots & Shoots.

Partly as a consequence of that conversation, Annan appointed Jane to the position of "United Nations messenger of peace," an honorary role that became official during a small ceremony in the secretary-general's private conference room on the thirty-eighth floor of the United Nations building on April 16, 2002. There the secretary-general cited Dr. Goodall for her "dedication to what is good in mankind" and stuck to her lapel a silver dove of peace designed by the artist Leni Fuhrman. Jane was the tenth messenger, joining, among others, Muhammad Ali, Magic Johnson, Wynton Marsalis, Luciano Pavarotti, and Elie Wiesel and agreeing to lend her energy and charisma to the United Nations' mission. She declared that she was "very honored" to be handed such a responsibility at such a time, "when the world desperately needs messages of peace and hope," and she pledged "to carry the message that to achieve global peace, we must not only stop fighting each other but also stop destroying the natural world."

Among the many who sent their congratulations to Jane was the former CBS television newscaster Walter Cronkite, who expressed his own urgent message of peace and hope: "If you can just awaken the world, and particularly the United States, to the foolishness of spending the treasure we do on devising and building new methods to more efficiently kill the maximum number of human beings we will be miles ahead of our present position on a useless treadmill."

U.S. Secretary of State Colin Powell also took a moment out from his increasingly hectic schedule to send a personal message, declaring in a handwritten note that he was "so pleased to hear from you again," and that "your 'Message of Peace' is needed more than ever."

So Dr. Jane Goodall had grown, or was in the process of growing, from her first incarnation as a distinguished scientist and the world's most famous expert on chimpanzees, to an activist on behalf of chimpanzees and other nonhumans, to a renowned authority on human spirituality and psychological well-being, to an eminent world citizen and spokesperson on matters of politics and peace.

That same month she gave one of her grand chimpanzee lectures, wearing the hat of a National Geographic explorer-in-residence and hooting wild chimpanzee calls for a wildly enthusiastic audience in Constitution Hall in Washington, D.C. That was followed, on May 6, by an appearance at the Ontario Science Center for the premiere of the giant-screen IMAX documentary *Jane Goodall's Wild Chimpanzees*. She also quietly donned her spirituality hat during this period, first for a "Service of Hope" at Sage Chapel on the campus of Cornell University on April 17 and then for a sermon on "Caring for Creation" at Grace Cathedral in San Francisco on May 12. Finally, she was practicing her new role as inspired political commentator and globe-trotting peace messenger, beginning in mid-January with a visit to Costa Rica and private conversations with President Miguel Rodriguez and former president Oscar Arias. In mid-February she attended a Haverford, Pennsylvania, symposium on "Global Responsibility." On April 16 she presented the Alan Cranston Peace Award to Jayantha Dhanapala, the UN under-secretary-general for disarmament affairs. In May she was the keynote speaker for Environmentally and Socially Sustainable Development Week at the World Bank. On May 14 she addressed a quietly exclusive bioterrorism conference in McLean, Virginia, on the subject of finding clues to human destructive behavior in the behavior of chimpanzees.

In Dar es Salaam, meanwhile, sixty-five-year-old Hugo van Lawick had gone to bed with the flu. Severely debilitated by emphysema, he was admitted to the hospital on May 5, released, then readmitted in a declining state. On Sunday, June 2, at seven o'clock in the morning, in the presence of Grub, Maria, and Tony Collins, Hugo slipped away.

Various powers in the Tanzanian government determined that he should have a state funeral with full honors in recognition of lifetime service to Serengeti conservation and tourism, and so his body was dressed in field clothes, garnished with flowers, and placed under the cooling protection of a great mango tree in Dar, where a large gathering assembled to deliver messages of grief, tribute, and farewell. The next day the body was flown out to the Serengeti and driven past the lions and hyenas, ostriches and zebras and other Serengeti denizens to Ndutu Lodge. Then, accompanied by a crowd of around two hundred mourners from Europe, America, Gombe, Dar es Salaam, and elsewhere in Tanzania, Hugo was carried to the site where his camp used to be. There was an emotional recitation by Tanzania's minister of tourism, the Honorable Zakia Meghji, followed by the memories and comments of several others. Once everyone had filed past the coffin for a final farewell, a group of park rangers carried it to a grave dug beneath a wavering high parasol formed by acacia trees. The box was lowered, earth was shoveled onto it, and guests and family members, including all the children present, cast bouquets of flowers over the earth. Then the mourning crowd returned to Ndutu Lodge for lunch.

Tony Collins e-mailed Jane that Hugo's grave was located in "a beautiful spot and very peaceful, and exactly the right place for him to be, where giraffes will come and browse overhead, beautiful herds of impala will drift by, and lions and hyaenas will call at night."

Jane returned to Africa by the middle of June, and by mid-July she had traveled to the forested northeast of Congo to join an expedition, led by a crew of Bangombé Pygmies, into the heart of one of the most difficult and remote places on the continent. The Goualougo Triangle, lodged within the intersection of Congo's Ndoki and Goualougo Rivers, was difficult as a result of extensive swamps and swarming insects, lurking elephants and unpredictable gorillas, and a confusing mess of vegetation vermiculated by elephant trails. Such discouragements had historically kept hunters out, which meant the place was so remote that the chimpanzees there had never learned to fear humans. Instead of disappearing at the first rustle and stink of their predatory two-legged cousins, these apes were known to circle in and hang out, hooting, screaming, and gawking.

Jane had gone to the Goualougo Triangle, as *National Geographic* reported in April 2003, because "conservationist Mike Fay said he needed Jane Goodall's help." About a dozen years earlier, J. Michael Fay had been conducting elephant surveys for the Wildlife Conservation Society when he and a Congolese colleague, Marcellin Agnagna, had wandered into the area and seen the naive chimps. Fay had successfully lobbied the Congolese government to create Nouabalé-Ndoki National Park, which protected some 1,621 square miles of pristine forest from logging—though not, because of political complications, the critical piece known as the Goualougo Triangle. In 2001, however, the park's southern edge had been extended to include 100 square miles of the Triangle, and now, in the summer of 2002,

Fay was hoping the government would protect a final 37 square miles. After their weeklong expedition was over, he and Jane were to return to Brazzaville and meet with the president of Congo to lobby for the protection of that last bit.

After penetrating the Ndoki swamps, they walked ten miles to their base camp in the Triangle, arriving after nightfall, wallowing cautiously through a final passage of thigh-deep swamp. The tents were erected and a late supper of beans and rice was prepared, and Jane finally had time to relax and feel quietly pleased to be there. It was her first real exploration in a long time and her first deep-forest experience in that part of Africa. Unfortunately, her feet were badly blistered, and for the next five days she had to bandage them with duct tape.

The only other flaw in the experience was an absence of solitude and privacy. Aside from Mike Fay and the trackers, the group included a couple of eager young chimp researchers and two people from *National Geographic*, David Quammen, the writer, and Nick Nichols, the photographer. In addition, a film crew from the society's TV division, complete with boom microphones and bodybuilder cameras, had joined them and were now all set to sop up any extra photons and vibrations: "hungry," in Quammen's words, "to record every word and glance." And thus "the forest itself became a TV stage," with Jane remaining, as ever, "patient and professional, hitting her mark in every scene, repeating this or that comment when another take was called for, using the television attention as she uses all such burdens and opportunities of fame—to get her message out." According to the writer's paraphrase, that message was that "every individual counts, both among nonhuman animals and among humans, so if you renounce callous anthropocentrism and cruelty, your personal actions will make Earth a better place."

Jane had taken along as the expedition's mascot her toy stuffed monkey, Mr. H, and as a final image for the article, Nichols posed an artistically blurred shot of her receding into the forest with Mr. H in her backpack. The hopeful message of Mr. H, she told the photographer, was "If a blind man can do magic, you can conquer the world."

It had become the nature of her existence by then to be looked upon as an oracle, a larger-than-life messenger: the silver-haired wise woman responsive to all those people eager for guidance, orientation, and hope. Of course, this new measure of her growing fame was simultaneously negative and positive. True, she was captive to it, a creature of others' interests and expectations, trapped and exposed in the amber of her public persona, lacking privacy and the freedom of anonymity. But she had discovered an almost magical power to open doors, to capture people's attention, to change minds, and thereby to do good things. It would be perverse to ignore such a power.

For *Time*'s August 26 special issue on the environment, meant to coincide with the opening of the World Summit on Sustainable Development, the magazine provided Jane with a full page to display, in the form of an essay, her message about the damaged global environment and how to fix it. And by the time that message had appeared on newsstands, Jane was in Johannesburg, attending the summit and delivering other messages.

The summit in Johannesburg was authorized by the United Nations General Assembly as a tenth anniversary sequel to the 1992 Earth Summit in Rio de Janeiro. The Rio summit had assembled environmentalists from around the planet, hopeful men and women who expressed the urge to reverse humanity's assault on the environment and lessen human poverty. Ten years later the environment was still declining and the human condition was getting worse. There were, in fact, simply more people—some three quarters of a billion human beings had been added to the planet during the decade. That meant more people to go hungry in some places, more to gain weight and waste resources in others. At the same time, much of the nonhuman world, including chimpanzees and the other great apes, was threatened by that astonishing spike in human numbers. The Johannesburg summit was convened over ten days, from August 26 to September 4, to respond to such trends and to replace the airy hopes of the Rio summit with a practical vision and concrete solutions.

Jane was, of course, one of the "eminent persons" who had helped shape and publicize it, and she gave as many as four talks a day during the event. She also took time off for a brief excursion, in the company of Kofi Annan and his wife and South African president Thabo Mbeki and his wife, to descend into the caves of Sterkfontein, where they examined the most fully intact *Australopithecus* skeleton ever found, still in situ. That was a remarkable look at humanity's ancient past. Later on Jane and the Annans ascended to the top of the Soweto Mountain of Hope to consider humanity's present and possible future.

The Soweto Mountain of Hope was a rocky knob, a *kopje,* located in the middle of Soweto Township. During the worst days of apartheid, it had been a bleak little heap of despair, a garbage dump and the dark site of some gruesome political executions. But a young man from Soweto who had survived those days, Mandla Mentoor, began cleaning it up. First he was helped by members of his family, but soon they were joined by others, until Mentoor had established a business enterprise, Amandla Waste Creations, that created new jobs through recycling waste. At the same time Mentoor and his family and associates cleaned up, terraced, and planted flower gardens across Soweto's heap of despair, thus transforming it into the Soweto Mountain of Hope. Mandla Mentoor was "a small, wiry man filled with enormous energy," Jane later wrote, with "a brilliant smile, the warmest of eyes, and he radiates love and caring." He had created "an oasis of peace and hope in the middle of an area still rife with crime."

At Jane's urging, the Children's Earth Summit, some 150 children and young people from around the world (including several Roots & Shoots members, meeting concurrently with the grownups' Sustainable Development Summit), assembled at the Soweto Mountain of Hope for their opening and closing ceremonies. Jane and Kofi and Nane Annan attended the closing ceremony, standing beside their leaders: fourteen-year-old Analiz Vergara, from Ecuador; eleven-year-old Liao Mingyu, from China; and eleven-year-old Justin Friesen, from Canada. Before a jumble of microphones and cameras erected by the global media, they declared, "Most world leaders do not listen. We are disappointed because too many adults are more interested in money than in the environment." And "Think of your children, your nieces, your grandchildren . . . what kind of world do you want to leave them?" And "Is it so hard to punish and imprison people who harm the environment?"

Secretary-General Annan was handed a five-page declaration, followed by a thousand origami peace cranes, folded by hand and made from newspapers representing all the languages spoken by the children's delegates. Inside each crane, a child had written down one individual promise he or she made to the world. Finally, Jane joined Kofi and Nane Annan in the dirt-and-shovel gesture of planting a tree for peace on the Mountain of Hope.

Jane was back in the United States by the middle of September, following the usual trail of obligations, which now led her from Connecticut to New York to California.

In New York, Secretary-General Annan prepared to celebrate United Nations Peace Day, September 21. This celebration was designed to encourage people around the world to think about and strive for peace—and Jane added her own thoughts on the topic, waking up before dawn in Sacramento, California, to provide a live television interview for CNN. At ten o'clock that morning, inside the UN building, Secretary-General Annan rang the big Peace Bell. Later he sent Jane a thank-you note that included a lighthearted apology for waking her up so early for the interview. "I am convinced," he declared, "that your own sacrifice of sleep will help shore up the commitment to peace felt by people around the world."

Within the context of that time and place, though, it is fair to ask whether such a sacrifice leading to such a possible commitment would in truth make much actual difference at all. Certainly the capacity to send symbolic messages—ringing a bell, planting a tree, standing on a mountain, giving a speech—and have them magnified and ricocheted around the globe is an enviable thing. Jane had been appointed a UN messenger of peace precisely because very large numbers of people would pay attention to whatever she said or did. But in the end, can sending symbolic messages really accomplish very much? Perhaps a greater power to change the world lies in the ability to send simpler but more tangible messages—the kind conveyed by a gun fired or a rocket launched.

Following the murderous attacks on the World Trade Center and the Pentagon of September 11, President Bush had sent the U.S. military into a war that was intended to restore Americans' security, or their sense of it, by killing or capturing the planner of the crime, Osama bin Laden, and by neutralizing his Afghanistan-based organization, al-Qaeda. By the fall of 2002, given some impressive military success in Afghanistan and the patriotic consensus that still powerfully sustained him back home, President Bush was promoting a new strategy for transforming the Middle East, starting with the problem of Iraq. Although Iraq's president, Saddam Hussein, had never supported the terrorists who attacked the World Trade Center, he supported other terrorists elsewhere, and his regime, as an excrescence of tyranny in the middle of the Middle East, threatened world stability. Most important, Bush argued, Saddam Hussein's regime was actively developing a deadly arsenal of chemical, biological, and nuclear devices capable of producing inconceivable devastation.

While debate over this possible new direction in American foreign policy was filling the newspapers, Jane was traveling—to the Far East and back to Europe and then to England by December 17 for Christmas with Judy and her children and grandchild in Bournemouth. During the year Jane had kept up a sporadic correspondence with Secretary of State Colin Powell, and she wrote to him again around this time, possibly from Bournemouth during her Christmas break. Meanwhile, President Bush, seeking international support for the invasion of Iraq, had enlisted the help of his distinguished secretary of state. After five days of intensive briefing on the subject with CIA director George Tenet, Secretary Powell traveled to New York on Wednesday, February 5, 2003, and presented the administration's case for war to the United Nations Security Council: mainly, that Saddam Hussein had illegally assembled an arsenal of weapons of mass destruction.

On February 14, Colin Powell returned to the Security Council for a debate on the matter. After entering a room packed with four hundred tense, expectant observers, he was seated at the Security Council's gleaming horseshoe-shaped table, facing the fifteen Security Council representatives, with Secretary-General Annan at the head.

French foreign minister Dominique de Villepin began the exchange, arguing against an invasion and in favor of more inspections, discussions, and time. Soon other members of the Security Council joined in, with three of the five permanent members—from France, Russia, and China— powerfully expressing the virtues of restraint and with Germany, a nonpermanent member also aligned against Powell and the U.S. position.

When it came his turn to speak, Secretary Powell placed his palms together for a moment, as if in prayer, then pressed them emphatically onto the tabletop and, with barely a glance at his notes, made his plea. It was certainly an impassioned and forceful one, but it did not produce any spontaneous applause or obviously change minds around the table. And, as became clear several months later, the secretary of state had been given seriously flawed intelligence. The argument that Saddam Hussein was assembling an arsenal of mass-destructive weapons was contradicted by the facts, or lack of them, on the ground. Powell eventually described his presentation to the United Nations that February as a permanent "blot" on his record. It felt "painful" and "terrible" and was indeed "devastating," he admitted, to realize that some of the experts at the CIA had failed to inform him that some of their sources were unreliable. But that was later.

Immediately after the debate at the Security Council, Powell may have felt relief that the most significant public task of his tenure as secretary of state was over. Perhaps he was also disappointed at his failure to generate agreement or a formal sanction for war from the Security Council, and he may also have felt dread. As the only member of the U.S. administration who had ever actually risked his own life for his country on the battlefield, Powell was in a distinctive position to consider the fire, blood, and treachery that lay ahead. It is possible to imagine him secluded at home that weekend, wearily catching up with his personal correspondence, including a response he owed Jane:

Dear Jane,

Thank you for your beautiful letter. I can sense and feel the inner peace you speak of. I'd love to visit Gombe one day.

These are difficult days as we seek peaceful solutions to the problems we face. Keep us in your thoughts.

I hope to see you again soon.

All the best,
C

Perhaps Powell's short note, with its reference to "peaceful solutions," could be taken as a tiny message of hope from someone hovering at the center of power. But the truth was getting less hopeful as each day passed, and on March 8, Jane sent a final message to someone she might in other circumstances have learned to regard as a good friend.

> Dear Colin—
> In such frightening times we must be Colin & Jane, not Goodall & Powell, doctor, general.
> My thoughts are indeed with you. I am praying for some kind of Divine intervention in the days ahead. I feel so fearful of the repercussions of an attack on Baghdad. Not only am I English, & UK & USA are lumped together, but my face is the wrong colour. In so many of the places where I spend time around the world, I fear the anger against our two countries will erupt. And a world with even more terrorism & hatred is horrible to contemplate.
> I just wish someone could reassure me that the worst scenario will not happen.
> I continue to be hopeful. I continue to pray. For the decision makers, for the people of the world, for the environment, for the future.
> Know that my thoughts are with you more than ever.
>
> Yours ever
> Jane

Saddam Hussein had been given the March 18 deadline of 8 P.M. EST to leave Iraq. On that day Jane was scheduled to lecture in Denver, Colorado, but because of severe snowstorms the Denver airport was closed, which enabled her to extend a Nebraska respite from the spring lecture marathon. She was spending time with a friend, the wildlife photographer Tom Mangelson, and two of his nephews. Mangelson's father had built a cabin on the Platte River, and Jane had gone there to watch the annual migration of sandhill cranes and snow geese, as they roosted, resting and feeding, on the banks of the river before continuing north to their summer breeding lands in Alaska and Siberia. It was a chance to withdraw from the pressures of traveling and socializing and speechmaking and consider a more peaceful natural world during the very moment when war in the human world was imminent.

On the evening of March 17, Jane and Tom watched as an endless carpet of geese and cranes passed overhead, the majestic birds traveling in huge flocks or drawn out into fragile, elegant skeins. Other groups were flying in from other directions, and they looked in the distance like softly undulating clouds. Even as the sun set and the sky turned yellow and then dark, they came. Then it was dark, and Jane and Tom and his nephews went inside the cabin and lit a fire for warmth and a candle for peace.

It was rainy and gusting with an icy wind at dawn on March 18, and they were all persuaded to stay inside the cabin. But at around ten o'clock, a flock of sandhill cranes spiraled overhead and then dropped into the stubbly remnants of a cornfield outside their windows. Soon the flock had grown to around two thousand birds, both cranes and snow geese, who were milling around the cabin.

Then Jane watched the birds dance. As she wrote in a Roots & Shoots newsletter, "For nearly two hours, first one group, and then another danced, leaping up again and again with outstretched wings, picking up bits of straw and clods of earth and throwing them into the air." They were like feathered ballerinas, like fragile long-legged white ghosts, like the most graceful of all possible messengers of peace. She watched this spectacular moving phenomenon, entranced: two thousand dancing cranes. Suddenly she was seized by a strong personal sense that the cranes possessed a special significance or idea on that cold and gray day—that they had brought a hopeful message: "I believe they were sent to tell us that, however dark these days may seem, there will be peace at the end. I had watched their Dance of Peace."

43

Woman Leaping Forward

2003–2004

FOR SOME TIME the Roots & Shoots festivals that Jane attended in the United States had been enlivened by lurching giant puppets, cheerful golems constructed and animated by a volunteer group of artisan puppeteers from the Puppet Farm of Ashland, Wisconsin. In April 2002, after Kofi Annan decorated Jane's lapel with the peace dove pin and named her a UN messenger of peace, three Puppet Farm members designed a giant peace dove puppet to commemorate the occasion.

The first giant peace dove was constructed out of recycled materials: bedsheets sewn together and given shape with a center of chicken wire. With a 5-foot-long conical white head (and no body), an eye painted black, a pointy beak painted yellow, a green cloth olive branch dangling from the beak, and serrated white wings spanning more than 20 feet from tip to tip, the puppet was both impressively big and reassuringly beneficent. And it could fly, in a puppety fashion, with the help of three human animators walking underneath and floating it above their heads with bamboo poles. One of the poles, 8 feet long, supported the great head, while two 12-foot poles at the wingtips spread the great wings and made them flap.

The Puppet Farm artisans flew their prototype in Duluth, Minnesota, where it flapped its great white wings during a chilly October 2002 peace rally. The full assemblage was surprisingly dramatic and beautiful, and Jane thought it should be adopted by Roots & Shoots as a symbol of peace, perhaps especially to call attention to the UN's International Peace Day. By February 2003 eight giant doves were flapping in a peace demonstration in Washington, D.C.—but eight was not the number Jane had in mind. It was more like ten thousand, she announced one day—enough giant birds to form a spectacle that could be seen from outer space. "One of the most important aspects of Roots & Shoots right now is our Peace Initiative: learn-

ing about people of different religions, cultures, and countries," she wrote
in a Roots & Shoots newsletter that year. She was particularly excited by the
giant peace dove puppets and hoped that each group would try to make at
least one. "Soon, we will plan a day when every R & S group flies at least
one giant dove—then we shall be seen from a satellite in space!" By 2003
some six thousand Roots & Shoots clubs had taken root and were sending
out shoots while working on at least six thousand different projects—for the
environment, for animals, for the human community. But what if each of
the chapters also took time for the extra project of constructing, from a few
simple scraps of used and recycled materials, a giant peace dove?

Jane and her sister threw a peace dove–making party that August, joining with family and friends in the garden at Bournemouth, and on September 21, International Peace Day, Judy and others held their dove aloft while
joining four more doves and hundreds of people for a grand procession
through Bournemouth. On the other side of the Atlantic, Jane joined Kofi
Annan at the United Nations in New York for the ten o'clock ringing of the
Peace Bell. After that, thirty Roots & Shoots members gathered with a thousand of their peers for an international student assembly, while on the lawn
of UN headquarters the giant peace dove puppets flew, with Jane joining
Kofi and Nane Annan to fly their own.

In fact, hundreds of the big birds were gnawing on olive branches and
taking flight in the United States and more than thirty other countries. And
as Jane listened to the sonorously ringing Peace Bell that morning in New
York, she was inspired by a vision, or audition, of ubiquitous tintinnabula-
tion. The international celebration ought to include ringing bells everywhere, she thought. She mentioned the idea to Secretary-General Annan,
who enthusiastically agreed. And so, as she wrote to the Roots & Shoots
membership that autumn:

> Next year, I hope there will be between 5,000 and 10,000 doves "flying"
> worldwide. Imagine—10.00 A.M. September 21, 2004 the bells ring out
> "Peace! Peace! Peace!," and the doves start to fly. The sound of the bells
> and the white wings of the doves will gradually move around the globe.
> Between now and then, keep track of all that you do for peace—in your
> own lives, your families, your schools, and your communities—and be-
> tween cultures, religions and nations. Next year we will "fly" our doves
> to celebrate our contribution towards world peace.

Meanwhile, the other war—the war against animals—continued unabated,
and for the great apes of Central Africa, it had recently turned ominous.
During the past two decades, European and Asian logging companies had

appeared in the heart of Africa and were now extracting well over 15 million cubic yards per year of African hardwood for European and Asian consumers. Central African loggers sometimes described themselves as practitioners of "sustainable development," cutting selectively, pulling out a few commercially valuable species. But while they were not clear-cutting huge swaths of forest, they had—by bulldozing a vast network of new roads—opened up those forests to a small army of professional hunters, who were now sending somewhere between 1 and 5 million tons of bush meat each year to urban markets.

The African bush-meat trade offered meat from every kind of forest animal—rats and bats, anteaters and antelopes, monkeys and apes—to city consumers as high-priced, exotic luxury fare. And thus a practice rooted in tradition and village life (where meat from the bush remained an important and relatively cheap source of protein) had by the end of the twentieth century become a $350-million-per-year industry generating significant cash income for rural hunters teamed with urban marketers. The explosion in commercial bush-meat hunting threatened the existence of several wild animal species, but it disproportionately devastated the great apes. Although only about 1 percent of the total bush-meat trade involves ape meat, apes are very slow reproducers. Slow reproduction means high vulnerability, and in fact apes are often the first group of animals eliminated by hunters entering a new forest. The great apes were being hunted into oblivion, with their carcasses showing up in pieces on tables in big-city markets across Central Africa.

In the 1990s a few scientists had begun studying the problem. In the summer of 1994, for example, one young researcher spent several weeks quietly waiting for the ancient meat truck that pulled in twice a week to the center of Ouesso, a logging boomtown in northern Congo. As the truck offloaded meat, he noted species, estimated weights, and eventually calculated that some 12,500 pounds of bush meat were sold there each week. For the town's population of 11,000, that amounted to more than a pound per week per person. The meat came from thirty-nine species, including bats, bush pigs, chevrotains, civets, crocodiles, eagles, elephants, genets, golden cats, leopards, mongooses, pangolins, porcupines, snakes, and eight different species of antelope, seven of monkey, and two of ape (chimps and gorillas).

By the end of the decade, apes were also disappearing over wide stretches of Central Africa as a result of an epidemic caused by the Ebola virus. Perhaps this new epidemic, soon spreading into ape communities across hundreds of thousands of square miles, was another consequence of logging in the region, since logging altered forest ecosystems in unanticipated ways and may have changed conditions for whatever species provided the virus's ultimate reservoir. No one knew. But now commercial hunting combined with the developing Ebola epidemic to wipe out large numbers of apes over very large areas.

It was one of the worst ecological crises anyone could have imagined. For the wild bonobos, chimpanzees, and gorillas of Africa, it looked like the start of a fast downward spiral. "Hopeless" was how Jane once privately described the situation, and certainly it was so for many thousands or tens of thousands of individual chimpanzees, caught between the chain saws and the shotguns. In the 2003 *National Geographic* article about Jane's trek into the Goualougo Triangle, she elaborated on her perspective: "When I'm thinking about some forest being logged, and the bush meat trade, it isn't just a population of chimps that's going. It's individuals. . . . I can't separate the loss of a population from the harm to individuals."

Jane continued her often lonely and sometimes stressful campaign for peace — for both the human and the animal world. To be sure, the loneliness and stress were mitigated by the logistical services of an official staff, paid and volunteer, from eighteen different Jane Goodall Institute offices around the world. And she was less officially sustained by a less disciplined army of friends and supporters and well-wishers, a complicated crew sometimes imperfectly categorized into Base Camps, FOJs (Friends of Jane), and Brothers (close male friends).

Base Camps were local groups who, thinking of Jane's peregrinations as a very long camping trip, maintained the metaphorical tents and fires in New York, Los Angeles, San Francisco, Houston, Boulder, and so on. Thus, for example, when Jane and Mary Lewis arrived in Los Angeles on January 5, 2004, they were picked up and dusted off by the LA Base Camp. The occasion was the Television Critics Association's preview of two new films for the Discovery channel, *Return to Gombe* and *The State of the Great Apes*. The event required three days of media interviews as well as a three-hour endurance contest by satellite with twenty-two television presenters, one by one, around the country. It was exhausting, but the evenings were fun and restful, spent as they were mainly in Jane's hotel room, eating Chinese takeout while chatting and brainstorming with members of the Base Camp.

Los Angeles was followed by New York: more media interviews, a Roots & Shoots gathering, a meeting with Kofi Annan, a board meeting for JGI (US). And representatives of the New York Base Camp blended seamlessly with a couple dozen FOJs at a late-evening party in Jane's suite at the Roger Smith Hotel.

New York was followed by London, where instead of Base Camps and FOJs there was family. Judy met Jane at Heathrow, having brought a suitcase packed with Jane's African clothes. After a period of resting and catching up in Mary's London apartment, they shopped for gifts for Jane's grandchildren. London was followed, on January 21, by Dar es Salaam, where the airport greeting party was a platoon of family, staff, and friends: Grub and the grandchildren, JGI (Tanzania) workers, a Peace Corps volunteer with Roots & Shoots, and so on.

Jane flew to Kigoma on January 24 to meet with an important group of government officials working on the Parks Management Plan for Gombe. On the morning of the first day of meetings, January 25, the case for continuing scientific work at Gombe was placed before the government officials. Anne Pusey, now overseeing Gombe's scientific research, chaired the meeting, while others discussed the latest research work, recent projects with satellite sensing and other technologies used to map forest fragments outside the park, and so on. Having heard what Gombe thought of itself, the government delegation next wanted to hear what the neighbors thought of Gombe. Each area village had sent five representatives to the meeting, and their spokespeople were asked to describe as frankly as they wished how the proximity to Gombe National Park had affected their lives—for better or worse. Those discussions were, as Jane later commented, "remarkably harmonious," adding that "certainly the activities of TACARE have greatly influenced the attitude of the villagers."

TACARE, the Lake Tanganyika Catchment Reforestation and Education project, was established in 1994 by the Jane Goodall Institute to promote agroforestry in the villages around Gombe, which by then had become an island of forest surrounded by a sea of bare earth and hardscrabble subsistence gardens. TACARE was a way for the Gombe community to reach out to neighboring communities—but nothing was imposed on anyone. Villagers voted to use or not to use the services. And other than smiles, songs, ideas, training, and initial services, nothing was given as charity. People earned the right to take advantage of TACARE. They bought seedlings, either with their own labor or with cash. They then learned to grow their own seedlings and to establish their own nurseries.

By 2004 thirty-two area villages had chosen the TACARE option and planted more than a million trees, hardy and fast-growing species to be used for firewood and building poles. Villagers had established more than sixty forest reserves for their own use and were running more than a hundred tree nurseries, distributing seedlings for continuing reforestation. But TACARE by then had expanded far beyond its original mission. It offered a hybridization project for high-yield oil palm seedlings, so palm oil became a significant cash crop; training in methods of sustainable agriculture for other cash crops, such as coffee, coconuts, and mushrooms; savings and credit programs offering small loans to help individuals start or expand small businesses; and village development funds for infrastructure projects, such as spring protection or school construction. It ran a scholarship program that by 2004 had provided nearly 150 local girls from the poorest families the chance to advance through secondary school and into college. TACARE also promoted the use of fuel-efficient stoves that reduced the need for firewood by two thirds. And in seventeen project villages, TACARE had introduced reproductive health and family planning services, training more than eighty local people to work as peer educators and providers. TACARE had created a successful alliance between the conservation-minded scientists who ran Gombe and the subsistence agriculturalists who surrounded it.

After the big National Parks meeting was over, several board members of the Jane Goodall Institute arrived at the Kigoma airport, headed for Gombe. But first they wished to learn more about TACARE, and so the next day, January 28, they all set off in an early-morning convoy to a village where, after the usual ceremonial greetings by senior community members, they were given a general description of a TACARE agroforestry project. The village managed nurseries, planted seedlings, and had set aside a large stand of forest to be used only for sustainable firewood harvesting. They also maintained a production plot of *Vetiveria*, a grass genus particularly useful in anchoring soil and undoing erosion.

Next, several villagers described how the TACARE project had helped them personally. Several women referred to the microcredit program, which had enabled them to start small businesses: fish processing, for example, or marketing. People in the microcredit group were given training in business and bookkeeping, and with their extra income they could buy extra food for their children or provide tuition for school. One girl described how her life had improved since receiving a TACARE scholarship for girls, which had enabled her to continue into secondary school. She planned to become a teacher.

Someone else explained the women's health and HIV/AIDS education programs and the family planning service. One woman stepped forward and announced that because of family planning and a microloan, she and her two children were not condemned to poverty. She had had one child, and she had managed her own small business and taken care of the child until he was six. Then she chose to have a second child, and she intended to limit herself to those two. "My children will be well educated, they will be well fed, and they will be well clothed," she said. "I want to thank TACARE for giving me my life." For a woman even to feel comfortable talking about such things in front of her village was a sign of change.

They also visited a farmer who had used TACARE services to reclaim soil that had been previously infertile owing to erosion and overuse. Now the soil supported a small farm, which was both productive and a model training center for other farmers interested in learning about sustainable agriculture. The guests ate their lunch in the shade offered by some newly planted trees, and they finished off with fresh pineapple, proudly presented by the farmer, who had grown it organically.

TACARE had become allied with Roots & Shoots, which meant that children in TACARE villages could form Roots & Shoots clubs; and on their last destination of the day, Jane and the delegation from America reached a place on the road where they were greeted by sixty children, smiling brightly, waving branches, and singing songs of welcome that included the words "Janey," "TACARE," and "Roots and Shootsy." The guests were escorted off the road and over to a school, where they were received warmly by the headmaster, the Roots & Shoots patron, and village elders and parents. The usual ceremonies proceeded through the usual speeches and reached a moment when someone handed Jane some scissors and directed her to cut a red ribbon into which flowers had been woven.

The children were very excited. The red ribbon was stretched across a door, and once it was cut, someone drew open the door so Jane could look inside. It was a new latrine, she saw, a VIP (ventilated improved pit) latrine, and she was peering into the girls' section. There were three holes, each with its own privacy cubicle and locking door, and the section was separated by a solid wall from the three-hole part for the boys. It was a Roots & Shoots latrine, the sign outside proclaimed, funded from New Zealand.

After more speeches, Jane took the occasion to note the significance of that Roots & Shoots sign. "Everyone will use this place at least once a day," she said. "You will always be reminded of us!"

But "how poignant," she later wrote, "to realize why the children were so excited—they didn't have a proper latrine before. There were no cubicles, no doors. There was dirt and a terrible smell and thousands of disease carrying flies." Moreover, she was told, one important reason that girls were not finishing school was the lack of privacy in the old rickety latrine shack, an overwhelming cause for embarrassment when they reached puberty. The VIP latrine had cost only $700 to build, money earned by a Roots & Shoots group in New Zealand and provided as part of a gift exchange with their Roots & Shoots partners in Tanzania.

The success of TACARE in East Africa suggested an interesting potential response to the problems in Central Africa, where many of the same dynamics operated—although instead of deforestation the biggest issues were professional hunting and the urban bush-meat commerce.

Jane had been going to Central Africa since the early 1990s, when the institute, in partnership with Conoco oil, built the Tchimpounga chimp sanctuary to care for zoo casualties and orphans created by hunters. Originally meant to hold around two dozen apes, Tchimpounga by 2004 contained 116 on a sixty-five-acre site, making it the largest chimpanzee sanctuary in Africa. By that time the Congolese government had decided to protect 18,000 acres of forest and savanna around Tchimpounga as a wildlife reserve, provided that the Jane Goodall Institute would maintain it.

Tchimpounga was always an ambitious thing, and in 2003 the institute brought a TACARE program to that part of Congo to help. This was a new chip off the old project, and one problem was the name, an acronym attached to Lake Tanganyika—easily solved by a simple shift of the tongue, so that something sounding vaguely French became clearly English, as in TakeCare. The harder parts are still being worked on, and they include constructing one village school, renovating a second, erecting a medical dispensary, introducing a teacher and new educational administrators, developing land-use plans and resource management agreements, hiring local guards to protect the reserve from poachers, and so on.

Starting in 2000, the Jane Goodall Institute also began to focus more deliberately on the Central African bush-meat trade, establishing what was called the Congo Basin Project, which at first consisted mainly of sending an ebullient Canadian named Christina Ellis to Cameroon for reconnoitering. By 2003, though, Christina and the institute were taking a TACARE-style community development project into villages within Cameroon's 250,000-acre Mengamé Reserve. And by 2005 the institute (now supported by a $1 million grant from USAID) had joined forces with the Dian Fossey Gorilla Fund International to establish another incarnation of TACARE for villages in a 7.4-million-acre conservation corridor in eastern Democratic Republic of Congo.

After the TACARE village visit in Tanzania and the ribbon-cutting for a new latrine, Jane enjoyed a couple of days at Gombe, including a few hours in the woods with her favorite living chimpanzee, Gremlin, and her family. She then flew to Nairobi for a board meeting of the newly formed JGI (Kenya). Then she returned to London and took the train to Bournemouth, hoping to work on her next book, on vegetarianism. She also made a quick excursion back to London and Buckingham Palace, where Prince Charles dubbed her a Dame of the British Empire—the country's highest civilian honor, a knighthood—and so she was now Dame Jane.

But her eyes were going bad. She flew to Washington, D.C., to attend another preview showing of *Return to Gombe*, where she noticed a slight irritation in one eye. She had often experienced that sort of thing. Not serious. But then, during four days back in Bournemouth before heading to Paris, the eye got worse and the irritation spread to the other eye. It felt as if, she later wrote, "insects were scratching about trying to get out of my eyeballs!" The whites turned red from the irritation, making her look, she thought, like Dracula. The family doctor gave her medicine for a bacterial infection. When that failed and the flesh surrounding her eyes became swollen, she tried an ointment for a viral infection, which also failed.

She left for Paris to receive the Jules Verne Award at the Jules Verne Film Festival. *Return to Gombe* was shown, after which Jane gave a brief talk from behind sunglasses. It was, she liked to say, her new "Hollywood look." Still, a brisk and dapper French doctor went to her hotel room to scribble a new scrip, and she hoped that the distressed orbs would soon be on the mend.

She was still weepy and red-eyed, however, and kept the Hollywood look in Johannesburg, where she attended a Roots & Shoots picnic, gathered with more Roots & Shoots students at someone's house, attended a breakfast fundraiser and press conference, and spoke after drinks and dinner at a big donors' Golf Day. There were other pleasurable events in other South African locations, more fundraisers, and an appointment with another ophthalmologist, who prescribed a new dribble of drops. Then, in Grahamstown, South Africa, Jane was chauffeured around by a young man who had been treated by a first-rate ophthalmologist after his own eye injury. On her way to the airport one Saturday, Jane met with that specialist, who, having specially opened his office, took time to peer deeply into her eyes. He conducted some new tests, gave more medications, and, as the previous expert had done, refused payment for services rendered.

Bleary and teary behind her shades, Jane advanced to North America and on March 24 commenced her spring lecture tour. She received an honorary degree from Occidental University in Santa Barbara, another from Haverford College in Philadelphia. The Scripps Institute of Oceanography in La Jolla presented her with the Nierenberg Prize for Science in the Public Interest. Columbia University Teachers College awarded her its medal for distinguished service. Chief Phil Lane, at a ceremony memorializing his late father, Phil Lane, Sr., a direct descendant of Chief Crazy Horse, honored Jane with a Dakota name that had come to his father in a dream: *Makoce Waji Yampi*, loosely translated as Woman Standing Up and Leaping Forward with Courage and Determination on Behalf of the Natural World.

On Saturday, April 3, her seventieth birthday, Jane leaped forward to Huntington Gardens in Pasadena, California, for a Roots & Shoots festival. More than fifty Roots & Shoots groups from the Los Angeles area had set up as many displays of their projects, and Jane (looking at once frail and vital, wearing a ruby turtleneck sweater and quilted jacket, carrying Mr. H and a recently manufactured, smaller version of him, Mr. H Jr.) paused to examine each exhibit and then to have her picture taken with each group.

Someone asked, "What's the secret of your youth?"

Her reply: "There's so much to do."

After posing for fifty-odd group portraits, shaking a few hundred outstretched little hands, gently smiling and offering small encouragements, she walked down to a grand open lawn where a few thousand people had settled onto the recently mown grass. Some Native Americans gave a welcome dance and song and then ceremonially bathed Jane with smoke. But after the dancing and smoke, the sky turned cloudy, and then the clouds began to spit, then sprinkle. A few umbrellas were raised and pressed open. Some sheets of plastic were held up. The president of Huntington Gardens gave a short speech as the sprinkle turned into rain. Finally it was time for Jane to talk, but just as she stood up, there emerged from a small woods behind the crowd a sound of bells and the white fluttering vision of a giant peace dove puppet, raised high and swaying gracefully, transported by three young Roots & Shootsers, each holding a pole, with a fourth child skipping along and ringing the bell. The crowd began to applaud.

Then a second giant peace dove appeared. Then a third, a fourth, a fifth . . . until forty-five giant white birds, each accompanied by its own bell ringer, flipped and flapped and flopped across the great lawn before finally assembling into a milling aviary behind the speaker's platform. The crowd applauded enthusiastically. Jane joined in, and then she prepared once again to give her talk. By then, however, the rain had turned into a small deluge, and she had begun wondering whether to postpone and reconvene. But just as she reached the microphone, the rain stopped, the clouds parted, the sun shone, and so she smiled and began to speak.

At the event's conclusion, she was escorted by three big security men through a reluctantly parting crowd, as people thrust things in her direction: gift, letter, scrap of paper, book to sign, hand or face or arm to touch or be touched. And then, with the long day finally over, she gathered in her hotel room with Mary Lewis and four Brothers: a soft-spoken UN diplomat, a mustachioed L.A. police detective, a hearty wildlife photographer, and a bearded writer. After Chinese takeout, they closed the day with a birthday celebration. A cake to cut and consume. Cards to open and notes to read. A few simple presents to unwrap and examine. That was the personal birthday, a quiet affair with a few close friends. The next morning, a Sunday, the same group, Mary and the four Brothers, returned to Jane's hotel room and, after coffee, joined in the postbirthday business, sorting through all the other gifts that had recently been handed on or slipped through the mails, writing down essential information for thank-you notes.

One of those gifts had come wrapped in plastic bubble wrap, the sort that children sometimes like to pop. Inspired, Jane tossed her bubble wrap onto the floor and started jumping on it: pop, pop, pop. Soon she was joined by the gang of five, all laughing, holding hands and bouncing up and down heavily like the overgrown children they actually were: pop, pop, pop, pop, pop, pop, pop, pop. Even a Woman Standing Up and Leaping Forward with Courage on Behalf of the Natural World needs to have fun once in a while.

But she was also the Woman of the Crawly Eyes and thus continued with the Hollywood look through her spring lecture tour, taking the opportunity, while in the States, to consult a couple of alternative healers and three regular physicians. The latter agreed that the problem was viral and the solution was rest. If only she would stop moving for a few days—take a holiday from the plane flights, the squinting at computer screens, the staring into glaring spotlights and flashing cameras. "The virus loves you," one of the doctors concluded, and the most direct way to terminate that unrequited association was rest and rejuvenation. She ignored the advice, kept the shades, and around May 19 left for Italy, then for Switzerland, Holland, Germany, Ireland, UK, Tanzania, Spain, and the USA once again. Soon it was nearly the end of July, and although her eyes were as irritated as ever, she had another important birthday party to attend and made the leap from New York to Paris to Brazzaville to Pointe-Noire and from there north to Tchimpounga.

Jane loved visiting Tchimpounga, and she tried to do it twice yearly, to catch up with the sanctuary staff and her chimpanzee friends, including two prominent senior citizens, old man Grégoire and old lady La Vieille. And in the same year that Jane celebrated her seventieth birthday, 2004, Grégoire was having his sixtieth, with the festivities scheduled to take place on Monday, July 26.

Someone had baked a cake for the superannuated ape, decorated with fruit slices, fruit jelly, black currants, and—his favorite—lantana leaves. But Grégoire was unimpressed, and he tossed away the leaves one by one. So the cake was presented to his elderly cage-mate, La Vieille, who likewise failed to appreciate it, picking at the black currants on top and dropping them onto the ground. The cake was still in its box. Jane thought she would pass it over to an onlooking crowd of juveniles, but La Vieille was now picking up all the black currants, now filthy, and, as if to fix what she had just broken, pressing them back onto the cake. The juveniles loved it anyway.

Sixteen schoolchildren were visiting the sanctuary that day, and when the children and their teachers arrived, the party moved into full swing. Grégoire was handed his big present, one orange and one passion fruit packed in a cardboard box and wrapped in fine cloth, with a lantana leaf bouquet on top. He took the box, examined it, plucked off the lantana leaves, and began picking at the cloth. He scratched open a hole and widened it until he could peer through with his one good eye. What he saw must have been a delightful vision, since he broke into a huge grin of delight, displaying the full shipwreck of his ancient teeth, then screamed with excitement. He pulled out the orange, settled down at a spot opposite the schoolchildren, and, squeaking with the pleasure of it all, began to eat.

With Jane joining in, everyone sang "Happy Birthday" to Grégoire in English, French, and Lingala. After that, four children addressed the old fellow and described their birthday wishes for him. The first three expressed predictable wishes for several more happy years. The fourth child said, "Grégoire, I wish you a happy birthday. And I wish that you will be very nice and kind to this woman"—referring to La Vieille—"who is living with you."

Meanwhile, Goblin was dying. Born on September 6, 1964, he was now Gombe's oldest living male chimpanzee. A month before his fortieth birthday, on August 7, 2004, a member of the field staff spotted him moving very slowly. He was obviously unwell and apparently not eating anything, and the staff took him food laced with antibiotics. During the nights when he was too weak to climb into a tree to weave his nest, they maintained all-night vigils against a possible leopard attack.

Then Gombe caught fire. The dry season had been harsh that year, and on the afternoon of August 18 a wavering wall of flame and smoke appeared at the high eastern edge of the park. Staff from Gombe and the Parks Department responded, beating down the flames with leafy branches, clearing breaks with ax, shovel, and hoe. But the fire moved quickly, stimulated by strong and gusty afternoon winds, and soon it was feeding fiercely on the trees and undergrowth within Gombe's dozen valleys. Reinforced by recruitments from the local villages, the firefighting continued day and night.

By then Goblin had built his final night nest. He remained there until, at a few minutes after midnight on Tuesday morning, August 24, his heart stopped beating and his eyes glazed over.

Goblin had been an ambitious and determined chimpanzee who began his rise in the male hierarchy at a surprisingly young age. From toddlerhood, moreover, he had liked to pester humans, and by the age of four he had turned into an impressive nuisance. He would scamper up to Jane or one of the female students, grab her wrist, and hang on mightily, an act that seriously inhibited note-taking. Jane and the students began carrying tins of secondhand motor oil or margarine, anything greasy, and whenever the little chimp appeared they slimed up their hands and wrists. Since Goblin disliked dirtying his hands, he gave up.

Then he reached adolescence. Like other males ambitious for social power, he began his long journey by challenging each of the females in turn, performing swaggering displays that were first irritating, then provocative. By the age of thirteen, Goblin had challenged and finally intimidated the toughest female, Gigi, whereupon he turned to the males and began testing their mettle. He astutely formed an alliance with the powerful Figan, who sponsored him in his rise to power. In addition, the young male's determination and persistence were coupled with a grasp of basic psychology. He understood, for instance, the advantage of hiding in the thickets and bursting out in a frightening charge when others approached, and of rising before dawn and displaying ferociously above his rivals while they were still groggy and curled up in their night nests. It was a long struggle, punctuated by some serious fights and many quiet contests of nerve, but by the time he was seventeen, Goblin was the undisputed alpha male of Kasekela, and for the next decade he retained that elevated status, which gave him superior access to the most important things: food and sex.

In 1989 he was unseated in a vigorous election process that left him severely wounded. The field staff found the deposed alpha in his hiding place and took him enough food and antibiotics for him to recover and return to society. Although Goblin never again reached the top, his political skills continued to serve him well. He would make friends with whoever the alpha male happened to be, expressing allegiance with grooming and supportive charging displays, and in that fashion he continued as a chimp of influence. He was survived by his siblings, Gremlin and Gimble; his daughters, Fanni and Tanga; and his grandsons, Fudge, Fundi, and Tom.

The fire was extinguished at last on August 25—but now where was Fifi? Fifi was the community's oldest member, the one remaining chimp who had been alive when Jane arrived in 1960. She had seemed in good health when she was last spotted (along with her youngest offspring, two-year-old Furuaha, and six-year-old Flirt) that August, but during the fire the B Record staff had been unable to follow her. She was seen once after the fire, but then she and her offspring vanished. At first her absence was hardly noticed, since Fifi had recently made herself scarce by ranging in the far-off northern valleys of Linda and Rutanga. But on September 17 researchers discovered Flirt wandering in the forest alone, atypical behavior for a female that young. Researchers and field staff searched methodically for Fifi and Furuaha during October but found neither, and mother and infant were presumed dead. A daughter of the great matriarch Flo, Fifi had become for her generation Kasekela's matriarch and most fertile female, having produced nine offspring, two of whom, Freud and Frodo, became alpha. Her daughters Fannie and Flossi and her son Frodo had given her at least ten grandchildren.

That same year saw the retirement of six of Gombe's senior staff: Yahaya Almas, Hilali Matama, Yahaya Matama, Hamisi Mkono, Eslom Mpongo, and Apollinaire Sindimwo. Altogether, those important experts had contributed some 130 years' worth of chimpanzee and baboon observations, and as a retirement gift (donated by Jane and Gombe alumni), Gombe's codirector of field research Shadrack Kamenya took them on a 3,000-mile safari, a grand tour to see the cities and national parks of Tanzania.

The fire of August, the worst anyone could remember, had charred about half the area of the park, killing many trees and threatening the chimpanzees' food supply. But by November the normal rains were sweeping in, and they turned the grasses green and stimulated many of the gnarled and blackened trees to sprout new shoots and leaves. There would be enough food for the chimps. And though the loss of Goblin and Fifi and Fifi's little Furuaha was sad, the six deaths in Kasekela that year were counterbalanced by six births and the successful immigration of one new adolescent female. Kasekela, with nearly sixty individuals at the start of 2005, would endure—at least for a while. And the loss of six distinguished elders from the Tanzanian staff, although it represented a serious diminution of authority and expertise, also made room for advancement among a staff that included nearly forty full-time members.

In short, the Gombe Stream Research Centre continued to function as the second longest continuous study of animal behavior in history and to prosper as one of the world's most productive tropical research stations. The program was as strong as ever, combining the work of a half-dozen senior scientists with that of a dozen associates and doctoral candidates from universities and other institutions in England, the United States, and Tanzania to produce thirteen scientific publications in 2004: a book chapter, two Ph.D. dissertations, ten journal articles. The work at Gombe that year was represented by a dozen formal presentations at international conferences.

Dr. Jane Goodall's campaign for peace in the human and animal worlds continued. On September 21, International Peace Day, she was in New York for the ringing of the Peace Bell and the flying of the Roots & Shoots giant peace dove puppets—several flapping in New York City among the three thousand flying brightly in Australia, Bahrain, Bosnia-Herzegovina, Canada, China, Costa Rica, Finland, Germany, Haiti, India, Iran, Israel, Italy,

Japan, Kenya, Lebanon, Mongolia, Nepal, the Netherlands, Pakistan, the Philippines, Russia, Saudi Arabia, Sierra Leone, Spain, South Africa, Syria, Tanzania, Uganda, the United Kingdom, and elsewhere in the United States.

By the start of October she was on her way to Germany, and from there to Austria and the Czech Republic. By the start of November she had leaped forward to Ottawa and Vancouver and then to Los Angeles, followed by Tulsa, Oklahoma. She flew to South Korea, and by November 11 she was in Japan. She visited with Gen Itani, the son of her first Japanese friend and colleague, Junichiro Itani; gave a long filmed interview; spoke at a primatology conference; lectured at the University of Tokyo; attended a party for JGI (Japan) volunteers; and took a train to the airport for a flight to Beijing in order to enter North Korea on November 16.

It was Jane's first trip to that country, and she stayed in a guesthouse in Pyongyang. A complete absence of streetlights made the evenings reminiscent of blackout evenings in wartime England so many years before. Still, riding in a car back to her room after a restaurant dinner, she could discern occasional lights burning faintly behind the windows of a few houses and appreciate the lovely bluish sheen cast by a quarter moon drifting overhead — and then she noted the moving dark shapes and shadows of a large and organized assembly of young men carrying guns, blocking the road for some time as they marched and turned this way and that in response to loudly barked-out commands.

The following day opened with a sunny morning's drive to Kim Il Sung University and a guided and translated tour through rooms lined with photos of the Great Leader along with glass cases displaying many of his letters and books. Jane met with seven professors and two students from the university, who told her about North Korean wildlife and conservation efforts while she spoke about her work with chimpanzees and the Roots & Shoots program.

On her last day there, November 19, she visited the Pyongyang Central Zoo. Before seeing any of the animals, though, she conferred with the zoo director, the head keeper, and the main chimpanzee caretaker. It was, Jane later recalled, a "strange meeting," which began with the men requesting help in getting more chimpanzees for the zoo, since theirs kept dying. She was asked about an appropriate diet for the apes. Finally she was taken out to see the exhibit: a stark enclosure entirely devoid of vegetation or even furniture, except for a strange pole-and-cable erection. Two 20-foot-long metal poles were stuck in the ground about 12 feet apart. The two poles were stabilized by angled wires, strengthened near their base by a crossbar parallel to the ground and some 5 feet above it, and connected at the top with a fully stretched tight wire. Jane also noticed a bicycle on the ground.

Soon the young caretaker appeared, leading by their hands two thin, obviously underfed chimpanzees, male and female, both awkwardly walking upright. With a commanding gesture, the caretaker sent the emaciated female climbing up one of the angled wires, grasping it with her curled feet and toes. Slowly, slowly, slowly she climbed up, making it halfway to the top before, as the angled wire began oscillating wildly, she lost her nerve and backed down. The caretaker gestured again, and this time the female climbed foot over foot to the very top. Then came the real challenge, a tightwire walk from pole to pole, 20 feet above the ground. But she succeeded in reaching the other side, slid down the pole, and scrambled back to her master's side.

Now it was the male's turn. Although Jane was told that he was an adult, this pathetic creature looked even more like a scarecrow than the female. The caretaker handed him half an apple to hold, uneaten, in his mouth, and the chimp then picked up the bicycle, climbed into the seat, and began pedaling. "He was so weak," Jane concluded, "he hardly had the strength to pedal. The bike wobbled. Desperately he moved on and at last made the circle of the enclosure. Even then he dared not eat the apple until he was ordered to."

Next the male chimp was instructed to do one-handed pull-ups on the metal crossbar, but he seemed to have hurt one arm. He stretched out the arm in a pleading gesture to the caretaker, again and again, but the caretaker repeated his severe gestured command. And so, slowly, apparently in pain, the emaciated chimp pulled himself up until his chin rested on the bar. With excruciating labor, he did it a second time. Then a third. Finally the caretaker gestured a command to the chimp that it was time to say goodbye, and so the chimp raised his arm and waved farewell to Jane.

Jane, whose eyes were still, after all those months, seriously infected and irritated, was wearing her Hollywood shades, and thus perhaps the dark lenses obscured the sight of her tears. But after a while the tears were gone, and she departed from the Pyongyang Central Zoo quietly determined to help those two sad creatures. She had already left some books about chimpanzees, and she would soon mail the zoo administration some printed information on chimpanzee diets. Possibly the director and head keeper would be allowed to visit the Beijing Zoo to observe how apes were cared for there. Certainly the nascent North Korean Roots & Shoots clubs should become involved . . . but oh, there was still so much, so very much, yet to do.

Notes

1. DADDY'S MACHINE, NANNY'S GARDEN (1930–1939)

Unpublished sources (primarily interviews and letters, as well as a partially completed biography of Jane Goodall written by her mother) are typically referenced in the text—with the exception, in this chapter, of an in-progress family history, very generously lent to me by Michael H. Goodall and the source for most of my material on the early Goodall family history. A second source on the Goodall playing-card business is Thorpe, 1980. Much of the background history on the Aston Martin is from Borgeson and Jaderquist, 1980, pp. 30–37. The story of Mortimer Morris-Goodall's first encounter with A. C. Bertelli is taken from Feather and Joscelyne, 1973. The material on Charles B. Cochran comes from Cochran, 1929, and Graves, n.d. The tale of the 1933 Le Mans Grand Prix d'Endurance is based on Hunter and Archer, 1992, and Feather and Joscelyne, 1973.

The curriculum at Norland Nursing School in Notting Hill Gate is according to Gathorne-Hardy, 1973, p. 176. The pram ride into Hyde Park is partly based on Bridget Tisdall's memoirs, as quoted in Gathorne-Hardy, p. 198. The same source (pp. 55, 56) references a study of physical punishment done at a slightly later (early 1950s) period. The birth of Jubilee at the London Zoo is described in "Chimpanzee Born," 1935. Source material on Brooklands comes from *Brooklands*, 1985, and Boddy, 1995. Some of the information on the Manor House and Westernhanger Castle comes from Michael and Jenny Mannon, who owned the house between 1987 and 1996; also from "Historical Notes" provided by G. Force, Ltd., Civil Engineering. Jane Goodall's recollections of the romantic Manor House, finding eggs, and riding on Painstaker come from Goodall, 1988, pp. 9–11.

2. WAR AND A DISAPPEARING FATHER (1939–1951)

The story of Hitler's "rough theater" and the subsequent invasion of Poland is based on Wernick, 1977, pp. 18–21. Ziegler, 1995, p. 44, describes some of the English preparations for war. Other sources for this section include *Spirit*, 1995, and Ferrell, 1984, pp. 216–17. The description of early preparations for an invasion in Bournemouth is from Forty, 1994. The view from inside the henhouse is quoted from Goodall, 1988, pp. 1, 2.

3. A CHILD'S PEACE (1940–1945)

This chapter, particularly the sections on family history and background, relies a good deal on Vanne Goodall's unpublished biography of her daughter. The quoted comment about Jane Goodall's never being told she was limited by her sex comes from a lecture at the Simmons College Conference on Women in Management, April 2003. The quoted descriptions of Danny and the household are from Goodall and Berman, 1999, pp. 8, 9. Government rationing is described in *Spirit*, 1995, p. 12. The first attack on Bournemouth is mentioned in Forty, 1994, p. 46. The quotation "not much affected by the war" is from Goodall, 1988, p. 13, and the quotations and references to the death camp photographs are from Goodall and Berman, 1999, p. 20.

4. CHILD IN THE TREES (1940–1951)

The quotations on Rusty's "lessons I have remembered" and "sense of justice" are from Goodall, 1988, pp. 22, 23. The quotation on attitudes toward school and V.J.'s preference for books is from Goodall and Berman, 1999, p. 11, and the quotation describing V.J.'s first reading of *The Story of Doctor Dolittle* is from Goodall, 1988, p. 14. The Doctor Dolittle quotation is from Lofting, 1988 (1920), p. 4.

5. CHILDHOOD'S END (1951–1952)

The quoted summary of Vanne's advice on careers ("My mother always used to say"), similar to published comments elsewhere, is from a lecture given at the October 1996 World Forum conference in San Francisco. On Jane's response to Trevor, the story about "the second mile" is from Goodall and Berman, 1999, p. 23.

6. DREAM DEFERRED (1952–1956)

Jane Goodall's quoted remarks about the Cologne cathedral appearing amid postwar ruins are from Goodall and Berman, 1999, p. 31, and Vanne's idealistic motivations for her daughter's trip to Germany are mentioned in that same source, p. 30. Information about Queen's Secretarial College is from Letts, n.d.; Lewis, 1994; and Murray, 1994.

7. DREAM RETURNED (1956–1957)

On the cost of a trip to Kenya: In a letter to Sally Cary written in May 1956, Goodall said she needed £90 for a ticket; that may have been her estimate for a one-way passage, but Goodall, 1988, p. 32, indicates she paid for a round-trip ticket. She had also planned to take a shorter route via Suez, which then was closed. According to the Union-Castle passenger fare schedule, as of March 1, 1957, the least expensive one-way ticket via Africa's west coast was £131. A roundtrip ticket would be calculated by doubling that number and then subtracting 10 percent. The quotation about counting her earnings one evening is from Goodall, 1988, p. 32. The relationship with Hans is characterized as "close to . . . an affair" in Goodall and Berman, 1999, p. 34. Details about the *Kenya Castle* are from Harris and Ingpen, 1994, and from a publicity press release from the Union-Castle Line dated February 27, 1952.

8. AFRICA! (1957)

Fire Fly's height is according to Goodall and Berman, 1999, p. 43. Biographical background on Louis Leakey is from Cole, 1975; Morrell, 1995; and Leakey, 1966 (1937). The first three Leakey quotations are from Leakey 1966 (1937), pp. 69, 70, 85. The Sonia Cole descriptions are from Cole, 1975, p. 20. "Jane's later account" is found in Goodall, 1988, p. 35. The quoted first exchange between Goodall and Leakey is according to Morrell, 1995, p. 238. The quotation about women coming to Louis Leakey "like moths to a flame" is from the same source, p. 73, while the discussion of problems regarding Leakey's previous secretary, his family, and a possible divorce, including quotations, are taken from pp. 243–46.

9. OLDUVAI (1957)

The story of Kattwinkel and Reck is based on material in Cole, 1975; Morrell, 1995; and Leakey, 1966 (1937). The quoted description of Reck is from Cole, 1975, p. 82. Morrell, 1995, pp. 60, 61, provides good background for the discussion on Olduvai as a quiet theater of time. The quoted remarks made by Louis Leakey on his first meeting with Reck, and the later remarks made to Reck at Olduvai, are from Leakey, 1966 (1937), pp. 177, 292. Morrell, 1995, pp. 62, 63, adds to the picture of that 1931 Leakey and Reck expedition; and the quoted comments of Leakey ("veritable paradise," etc.) are from Leakey, 1966 (1937), p. 295. The first hominid discoveries at Olduvai in 1955 come from Cole, 1975, p. 228, and Morrell, 1995, p. 179. Jane Goodall's comment made "more than forty years later" is in Goodall and Berman, 1999, p. 49. The reconstructed and paraphrased conversation with Leakey around the fire at Olduvai is based on Goodall and Berman, 1999, pp. 48–51. The subsequent conversation between Goodall and Leakey is recalled in Goodall and Berman, 1999, pp. 52–55. Morrell, 1995, provides the background information on Louis's early interest in the Gombe Stream Chimpanzee Reserve; Morrell's quoted comment comes from p. 239 of that source, as does the remark ("failed utterly") of Louis Leakey. The story of Walter Baumgartel and his Travellers Rest hotel is told in Baumgartel, 1976; the several quotations come from pp. 19, 36, 37, 38, 40, and 86. Morrell, 1995, p. 239, clarifies that Louis Leakey was corresponding with Geoffrey Browning in late 1956; and the same source, on p. 240, provides some text of the letter that Leakey wrote to Washburn. In a letter of February 12, 1959, to Leighton Wilkie, Leakey declares that Washburn never replied to the letter. The contemporary who described Louis's belief in the threatening effect of male observers was Leighton Wilkie, according to Morrell, 1995, p. 241. The quoted remark from Jane Goodall on Leakey looking for an "uncluttered" and "unbiased" mind comes from Goodall, 1971, p. 6.

10. LOVE AND OTHER COMPLICATIONS (1957–1958)

Jane Goodall's first look at the museum's ornithological collection is based on Goodall and Beckoff, 2002, p. 113. Goodall writes about Brian Herne in Goodall and Berman, 1999, and the quotation ("first real love") is from p. 54 of that source. White hunters David Ommanney and Derrick Dunn are nicely introduced in Herne, 1999, p. 381; some of the background details of Carr Hartley and his ranch are derived from the same source, pp. 310–13.

11. THE MENAGERIE (1958)

In *My Life with the Chimpanzees* (Goodall, 1988, p. 41), Jane Goodall misidentifies Kombo as Kobi and his "wife" as Lettuce; the letters clarify that her vervet monkey was named Kombo. The arrival of Thimble is never mentioned, but in a late letter to Sally Cary, written a few days before she left Africa, Goodall refers to a group of wild vervet monkeys as "scores of Kombos and Thimbles." The "Teddy Bear Picnics" are also described in Goodall, 1988, p. 43, where we can read that the hedgehog and the rat were never taken along and the cat stayed inside the car. The Olorgesailie Prehistoric Site and its discovery are described in Morrell, 1995, pp. 125, 126.

12. LONDON INTERLUDE (1959–1960)

Much of the background material on Leighton Wilkie and his first associations with Louis Leakey and Raymond Dart, including relevant quotations, is taken from Cole, 1975, pp. 212–15; see also "Africa Cradled," 1955, for details on the Wilkie journey to Rhodesia in 1955. Some details of Wilkie Foundation support are from unpublished sources, including a five-year report (1953–1957) of the Wilkie Foundation and private correspondence between Louis Leakey and Leighton Wilkie. Mary Leakey's quoted recollection of finding Zinj on July 17,

1959, is taken from Leakey, 1984, p. 121. Louis Leakey's quoted remarks on Zinj are from Leakey, 1959, p. 493. Mary Leakey's quoted comment on Tobias's reaction is from Leakey, 1984, p. 125. Cole, 1975, p. 233, describes the reception of Nutcracker Man in England and is the source of the quoted words of an attending newspaper reporter; see also Weiner, 1959. Leakey's quoted remarks at the University of Chicago come from Leakey, 1960, p. 17. Cole, 1975, pp. 234–36, provides background on his further travels in the United States. Danny's diary entry regarding Robert Young is quoted in Vanne's unpublished biography. For the early captive studies, see Köhler, 1925; Yerkes, 1916 (quotes from pp. 233, 234, 232); Yerkes, 1925 (quote from pp. 173, 174); and Kellogg and Kellogg, 1967 (1933). The first three twentieth-century field studies, all sponsored by Yerkes, are reported in Bingham, 1932; Nissen, 1931; and Carpenter, 1934. The Nissen quotations can be found in Nissen, 1931, pp. 13–15 (for all the "time-honored modes"), p. 25 ("nomadic"), p. 73 ("group size"), and p. 72 (urine versus feces).

13. LOLUI ISLAND AND THE ROAD TO GOMBE (1960)

The first Jane Goodall quotation ("trouble among the African fishermen") is from Goodall, 1971, pp. 7, 8. About Hassan Salimu: Mary Leakey's comment is from Leakey, 1984, p. 101. Morrell, 1995, p. 156, provides some of the background regarding the *Miocene Lady*. Richard Burton's early description is from Burton, 1995 (1860), p. 307. Discussion of the early problems of Congolese independence leading to chaos and an exodus of refugees is based on material in Reader, 1998, pp. 649–59. Jane Goodall's later recollection about Spam in Kigoma is from Goodall, 1971, p. 10, and the quote regarding her early "sense of detachment" upon seeing the shores of Gombe is from the same source, pp. 14, 15.

14. SUMMER IN PARADISE (1960)

The postprandial conversation with Jane Goodall is quoted from Peterson, 2003 (1995), p. 83. Some descriptions of the Gombe ecology and wildlife are based on Goodall, 1986, pp. 45–51; Gerald Rilling (personal communication) has given more detail on the wildlife, especially snakes. Wagner, 1996, provides background on Waha cultural attitudes, including a likely response to the Gombe terrain and wilderness. The quoted comment on Jane's "illogical fear" of leopards is from Goodall, 1971, p. 31. The selection of hired assistants and the quotations, including comments about Htwale, are from Goodall, 1971, p. 17. My account of Vanne's clinic combines material in her letters with commentary and the quotation ("good relations with our new neighbors") in Goodall, 1971, p. 40.

15. DAVID'S GIFT (1960)

The quotations and discussion of Jane Goodall's solo excursions after her malaria was over during the final week of August are from Goodall, 1971, p. 25. Herne, 1999, p. 376, is the source for some background on Derrick Dunn. Jane's "later writing" about Wilbert is in Goodall, 1971, p. 23. On the comparison between Goodall's early fieldwork and that of Henry Nissen: September 15 was Jane's sixty-fourth day at Gombe, but she had taken a few days off for camp errands, journeys to Kigoma, and so on; Nissen had spent seventy-eight days in "the bush," with sixty-four in "active field work" (Nissen, 1931, p. 16). The three quoted laws of chimp behavior in this part are from Nissen, 1931, pp. 18, 25, 30. George Schaller's self-described reactions on receiving the early reports of Rosalie Osborn and Jill Donisthorpe are from Schaller, 1964, pp. 9, 10, and the three quotes regarding gorilla personalities are from the same source, pp. 115, 116. Earlier written accounts of chimpanzee tool use are found in Beatty, 1951, and Merfield and Miller, p. 63. Schaller refers to those accounts in Schaller, 1964, pp. 224–27. The discussion of termites and termite fishing at Gombe comes from Goodall, 1986, pp. 248–51, 536–38; and the final two quotes regarding David Greybeard are from the same source, p. 61.

16. PRIMATES AND PARADIGMS (1960–1962)

Louis Leakey's response to the news of tool use at Gombe is cited in Goodall, 1971, p. 37, and Goodall, 1990, p. 19. Louis Leakey lecturing at Constitution Hall is described in Morrell, 1995, pp. 210, 211; the Grosvenor quotation is from Cole, 1975, p. 242. Adriaan Kortlandt's *Scientific American* article is Kortlandt, 1962; the first three quotations are from that source, p. 128. His recollection of the time sequence, described in two different sources, is mildly contradictory. In Kortlandt, 1999, p. 5, he states that "this work [at Beni] was all achieved in the period April–June 1960. It included three weeks of hide building and seven weeks of observation," which would suggest a total of three months, or perhaps two and a half months. In Kortlandt, 1991, p. 6, we learn that "I travelled around . . . for two months" and found the Beni site with "only four months left." In both accounts Kortlandt recalls a total of fifty-four successful observation sessions. Kortlandt describes his five blinds in Kortlandt, 1962; the first quotation regarding the blinds ("but then I was there") is from Kortlandt, 1991, p. 7; the second and third (about being in the high nest) are from Kortland, 1962, p. 129. Quoted descriptions of tense moments when a male chimp would try to peer inside the lower blinds are from Kortlandt, 1999, p. 4; the lifetime claim is in Kortlandt, 1986. My very brief sketch of Kortlandt's professional background is based on van Hooff, 2000, p. 121. The story of Watson and behaviorism is based on Sparks, 1982, pp. 155–66. Harry Harlow's story is based on Blum, 2002, with the two quotations from pp. 78 and 170. Sussman, 2002, p. 89, points out the early importance of Kroeber and Hooton. Rowell, 2002, p. 63, is my inspiration for thinking about the practical changes opening the way to primate field studies, and Sussman, 2002, pp. 85–103, is my source for the theory that the demise of a large-brain-first paradigm directly encouraged primate field studies. Strum and Fedigan, 2002, provides much of the background material for the Washburn story, including the idea of his overly optimistic hope for finding a primate pattern. On Japanese primatology: I am very grateful to Michael Huffmann and Takayoshi Kano (personal communications) for much of the material in this section, and to Toshisada Nishida; I have also relied on material in Takasaki, 2002; Nishida, 1989; and Nishida, 1990. Imanishi's letter to Walter Baumgartel was originally quoted in Baumgartel, 1976, p. 94. Nishida, 1989, and Nishida, 1990, describe the extended process leading to a provisioning-based research center in the Mahale Mountains; those written accounts have been supplemented by an interview with Nishida. The 1970s project in Zaire is described in Kano, 1992. George Schaller's description of being surrounded by screaming apes in the Budongo Forest is from Schaller, 1964, p. 222. The story of Vernon and Frances Reynolds in the Budongo is based on Reynolds, 1965, with the quotation from p. 51; also Reynolds and Reynolds, 1965. Kortlandt's criticisms of Jane's work and quotations are from Kortlandt, 1991, pp. 3, 7. The comparisons (and quotations) of his and Jane's work are from Kortlandt, 1986, p. 2. On experimentation: The quotation about "ethically sound and harmless experimentation" and reference to the leopard experiment are from Kortlandt, 1998, p. 3; other experiments ("egg-laden nests," etc.) are mentioned in Kortlandt, 1999; and the "St. Francis of Assisi" comment is from Kortlandt, 1998, p. 3. The quoted researcher's responses when a male chimpanzee approached one of the blinds is from Kortlandt, 1993, p. 141, and the claim about chimps having a "natural vegetable diet" and curiosity about why they failed to make tools are both from Kortlandt, 1962, p. 133.

17. THE MAGICAL AND THE MUNDANE (1960–1961)

The first brief pair of quotations from *Reason for Hope* are from Goodall and Berman, 1999, p. 71; the second, extended quotation is from the same source, p. 73.

18. A PHOTOGRAPHIC FAILURE (1961)

The quoted comments of a staff member regarding the character of Melville Bell Grosvenor are from Bryan, 1994 (1987), p. 334. The brief exchange between Louis Leakey and twenty-seven-year-old Mary Griswold is taken from a recollection in Smith, 1993. Bryan, 1994 (1987), p. 379, provides the quoted assessment of Ted Vosburgh's character, and Goodall, 1971, p. 67, gives the text for Louis Leakey's telegram to Vanne of early December 1961.

19. A DIFFERENT LANGUAGE (1961–1962)

The opening part of my introduction to ethology, including material on Heinroth and von Frisch, is largely based on Sparks, 1982, pp. 180–89; the quotations from von Frisch come from that source, p. 185. The brief summary of von Frisch's bee studies relies on von Frisch, 1967, pp. 109–14, and the conclusions about how remarkable bee orientation is refers especially to material on p. vi. On imprinting as a discovery and coinage of Heinroth, see Sparks, 1982, pp. 192, 193. Sparks, 1982, pp. 193–96, provides some of the Lorenz biographical background; the Lorenz quotation ("suddenly felt a longing to cram") is from Nisbett, 1976, p. 28. The brief biographical sketch of Tinbergen is largely paraphrased from Baerens, 1991. The quoted "one commentator" is Baerens, 1991, p. 12, and the idea of ethology as focused on "automatic, predictable, and characteristic" behavior derives from the same source, p. 9. Nisbett, 1976, p. xiii, provides the "we clicked immediately" quotation, and the observations of the complementing and contrasting personalities of Lorenz and Tinbergen, including relevant quotations, are from Baerens, 1991, p. 13. Biographical and background material on Thorpe is from Sparks, 1982, pp. 168–71, but Hinde, 1982, p. 82, provides the quoted description of a chaffinch song. Recollections of John Krebs are from Krebs, 1991, pp. 60, 61; the quote "objective scientific methods" is from Baerens, 1991, p. 9. And the discussion of Tinbergen's "Four Whys" is taken, with extended paraphrase, from Hinde, 1982, pp. 19–131; see also Lorenz, 1982 (1981). Lack's work on robins is based on Sparks, 1982, p. 202. Tinbergen's recollection of the young Robert Hinde is from Tinbergen, 1991, p. 463; Hinde's youthful recollection of Tinbergen is from Hinde, 1991, p. 31; and the possible distress caused by broad speculations by Desmond Morris is mentioned in the same source, p. 32. Hinde's establishment of a rhesus macaque colony at Madingley is described in Hinde, 2000. Jane Goodall's quoted descriptions of her reactions to Robert Hinde (starting with "terribly in awe") are from Goodall, 1991. Quotations from "her first scientific writing done at Cambridge" are from Goodall, 1963a, p. 39, and Goodall, 1962. The comments about "when I first got to Cambridge" and the reference to Rusty as a "marvelous teacher" are all from Goodall and Bekoff, 2002, p. 20.

20. FIRST SCIENTIFIC CONFERENCES (1962)

Regarding Sherwood Washburn and the development of a "new physical anthropology": The first quotations describing Washburn's physical appearance and his "vision" are from Grand, 1999, p. 229; the "contagious enthusiasm" quote belongs to Hamburg, 1999, p. xiii. Washburn himself is quoted from Washburn 1999a, p. 7, and Washburn, 1999b, p. 5; the colleague who reports the content of his letter is Zihlman, 1999, p. 182. DeVore, 1965, p. viii, summarizes the state of primatology at the start of the 1960s. Osborn, 1963, p. 36, is the source of the Rosalie Osborn quotation at the London conference, and Goodall, 1963a, p. 45, is the source of the Jane Goodall quotation there. The description of DeVore's filmed baboons in Kenya, shown at the conference, is paraphrased from Jolly, 2000, p. 74. I have based Zuckerman's biographical sketch mainly on Zuckerman, 1978; also Peyton, 2001; but the descriptions and assessments of Monkey Hill come from Sparks, 1982, p. 233, and Zuckerman, 1981 (1932), pp. 218–19. Zuckerman's quoted remarks from "years later" can be found in Zuckerman, 1978, p. 71. His original conclusion that a harem system was likely true for all primate societies can be found in Zuckerman, 1981 (1932), p. 209: "So far as can be judged from the accounts of monkeys and apes discussed in the two preceding chapters, the harem forms an essential element in the social lives of wild sub-human primates." Finally, all quotations from Solly Zuckerman at the London conference of 1962 are taken from Zuckerman, 1963. Historical assessments of "modern primate studies" (after 1960) are based on comments in Strum and Fedigan, 2000, especially pp. 15–17; also Jolly, 2000, 80–82.

21. A PHOTOGRAPHIC SUCCESS (1962)

The story of Hugo van Lawick's first picture-taking experience "creeping" up to small animals in Holland is from an interview I conducted in February 1997; a variant of that story (wild sheep instead of small animals) can be found in Goodall, 1967, p. 41. Mary Griswold's quoted assessment of Goodall on June 28, 1962, is from Smith, 1993, p. 30.

22. INTIMATE ENCOUNTERS (1963)

The quoted comments of Leonard Carmichael are from Carmichael, 1963. Jane Goodall's "radical assertion" is from Goodall, 1963b, pp. 296, 297. The society's mission is stated in Bryan, 1994 (1987), p. 24, and I have calculated the height of the 1963 release (15 miles) based on an assertion made in the same source, p. 49, that 5 million copies would produce a 25-mile stack.

23. LOVE AND ROMANCE, PASSION AND MARRIAGE (1963–1964)

The quotations from *Beyond the Rain Forest* can be found in Morris-Goodall, 1967, p. 35. The quoted remark ("most significant") regarding Goodall's October 11, 1963, reassuring touch from David Greybeard is from Addley, 2003. Jane Goodall's quoted comments about being in love with Hugo van Lawick, the text of his exciting telegram to Bournemouth, and the final comments about enjoying the wedding are all from Goodall, 1971, p. 90.

24. BABIES AND BANANAS (1964)

Dominic Bandora's note and its translation are taken from Goodall, 1965, p. 802. MacDonald, 1969, pp. 231, 232, is the background source for the brief sketch of Malcolm MacDonald; Lapping, 1985, p. 441, provides additional background, including the quoted assessment. The problems of the old Banana Club and the development of a more methodical system for provisioning are described in Goodall, 1971, pp. 92–98, which is a partial source for my description; my account of the move up to the Ridge Camp includes reference to the extended description in Goodall, 1967, pp. 77, 78. Goodall describes the concrete boxes in *Shadow* (Goodall, 1971, pp. 92, 93) and indicates, mistakenly, that they were first used by Kris Pirozynsky in December 1963; the letters clarify that van Lawick first ordered the steel boxes in February 1964, and that Hassan Salimu built the concrete box substitutes later, probably starting in June.

25. A PERMANENT RESEARCH CENTER (1964–1965)

On the "standard daily records, begun as early as 1963 when Flo first appeared," see Goodall, 1986, p. 598. Leonard Carmichael's encounter with an urban mugger is told in Galdikas, 1995, p. 59.

26. GOMBE FROM AFAR (1965)

On Dominic Bandora's possible retirement to Kigoma, see Goodall, 1967, p. 107. The book assembled and edited by Desmond Morris is Morris, 1967. The comments of Lyn Newman are quoted in Green, 1970, p. 189.

27. A PERIPATETIC DR. VAN LAWICK AND THE PALEOLITHIC VULTURE (1966–1967)

The reporter for the *Evening Star* is Schaden, 1966. The publication in *Nature* on tool use among the Gombe chimps is Goodall, 1964; the *Nature* account of tool use among the Serengeti Egyptian vultures is van Lawick-Goodall and van Lawick, 1966; and the *National Geographic* version is van Lawick-Goodall, 1968.

28. EPIDEMIC (1966–1967)

Some of the background information on Mr. McGregor, including the origin of his name, is taken from Goodall, 1971, pp. 32, 33; the speculation that McGregor and Humphrey may have been brothers is from the same source, pp. 222, 223. Morrell 1995, pp. 269, 270, provides the exchange between Mary Leakey and Dian Fossey, and Fossey's reaction to it, and Fossey, 1983, provides further background, including the quotation, on Fossey's brief association with Jane Goodall.

29. GRUBLIN (1967)

For more on Jane Goodall's thoughts about mothering based on chimpanzee principles, see "Chimps," 1970. Goodall's quoted comment about the Egyptian vultures' premature throwing of stones is from van Lawick, 1968, p. 638. A brief and seemingly expurgated version of Dian Fossey's trouble in Zaire is presented in Fossey, 1983, pp. 15–18. Morrell, 1995, p. 327, gives a fuller, more convincing, and far more disturbing version, and Leakey's summary as written to Melvin Payne is quoted in the same source, p. 327. On the experiments with vultures and various kinds of eggs: Hugo van Lawick describes some of their experimental work in a late-January letter to Joanne Hess at the National Geographic Society; my summary combines his description with Goodall's later one in the 1968 *National Geographic* article (van Lawick-Goodall, 1968).

30. PROMISE AND LOSS (1968–1969)

Some of the information on Count Samuel Teleki von Szek is taken from Heaton, 1989, pp. 6, 7.

31. HUGO'S BOOK (1967–1970)

The quoted remarks about the "innocent" if "horrifying" killing styles of the East African carnivores are from van Lawick-Goodall and van Lawick-Goodall, 1971, pp. 13, 14; the account of descending into the Ngorongoro Crater is paraphrased and quoted from the same source, pp. 30, 31. The practical aspects of van Lawick's approach to photography are described in Green, 1970, pp. 172–77, while the paraphrased and quoted impressions of Green on meeting the van Lawicks for the first time come from the same source, p. 160. All my comments on the social systems of spotted hyenas are derived from Kruuk, 1968. Some of Goodall's quoted impressions (as she "later wrote") of their camp at the edge of Lake Legaja come from van Lawick-Goodall and van Lawick-Goodall, 1971, pp. 38, 39; van Lawick's quoted words regarding the problem of finding and photographing wild dogs and life in the Genghis pack are from the same book but different chapters (pp. 40, 41, 50, 51, 54). The remarks of "one visitor to Ndutu camp" about George Dove's whiskers are from Rhodes, 1973, p. 232.

32. REGIME CHANGES (1970–1972)

Goodall, 1986, is my main source for the tale of clever Mike's rise to power, with the quotation from p. 426. Grub's problems in adjusting to English life, such as learning that cows moo and ducks quack, were originally described in "Chimps Instead of Spock," 1970, and the sad news in England of 1970 regarding Leakey's heart attack is based on material in Morrell, 1995, pp. 331, 332. The story of Figan's rise is paraphrased from Goodall, 1990, with the short quotations taken from pp. 43, 44. Humphrey's rise to power is recounted in Goodall, 1990, with the several quotations from pp. 46, 47.

33. ABUNDANCE, ESTRANGEMENT, AND DEATH (1972)

The remarks about human biology at Stanford are Donald Kennedy's, as quoted in Billings, 1997/1998. The information about Stanford students' preparations for Gombe was contributed by attendees at the Gombe Reunion in Minneapolis, Minnesota, October 2002. Packer, 1994, pp. 157, 158, gives information on evenings at the Mess; the same source, p. 29, provides the quoted description of Maulidi Yango. My discussion of the relationship between Figan and Humphrey and the conflict between Figan and Evered is based on material in Goodall, 1990, pp. 47, 48. Flo's reaction to Figan's fall and injury, including the quotes, is from the same source, p. 48, as is Flo's interaction with Crease (p. 30) and some of the details, including quotations, related to the discovery of her body (p. 31). Flo's obituary is "Old Flo," 1972. The story of Louis Leakey's final years, decline, and death is in large part based on material in Morrell, 1995, pp. 372–84, and Cole, 1975, pp. 274–398. The first Leakey quotation ("a swarm of bees") is in Morrell, 1995, p. 270, the second ("I do need the money") on pp. 370, 371. The quoted brief description of *Quest for Man* is from Vanne Goodall, 1975, p. 7. The description of Louis Leakey's death is based on Morrell, 1995, p. 402, and Cole, 1975, p. 405. The "intimate" comment is from Morrell, 1995, p. 250; the words of Charles Njonjo are from the same source, p. 403.

34. FRIENDS, ALLIES, AND LOVERS (1973)

The story of Figan's alliance with Faben and the defeat of Humphrey and Evered is based on material in Goodall, 1990, pp. 48–52, with the quotation from p. 49. Packer, 1994, is my source for the story of Craig Packer's embedded thorn and its excision (pp. 168, 169). Goodall's quoted comments about Bryceson's "sense of humor" and "forceful character" are from Goodall and Berman, 1999, p. 97. Biographical information on Julius Nyerere, including the quotes attributed to him, comes from "Julius K. Nyerere," 2004 (1994).

35. THINGS FALL DOWN — AND SOMETIMES APART (1974)

Background material on chimpanzee sexual behavior and consortships is taken mainly from Goodall, 1986, pp. 450–53. The story of the fallen whisky bottle is based largely on an account given by Julie Johnson at the Gombe Reunion in Minneapolis, Minnesota, October 2002. The story of the plane crash at Ruaha is based on a letter home written by Goodall and a later account in *Reason for*

Hope (Goodall and Berman, 1999, pp. 98–101), with most of the quotations taken from the letter. The fifty-day follow of Figan was finally reported in Riss and Busse, 1977.

36. DOMESTICITY AND DISASTER (1975)

A few details about the kidnapping are from a secondary account, Aaronstam, 1998, but my story is predominantly based on interviews with Carrie Hunter, Etha Lohay, and Emilie Riss, as well as a very thorough summary of events compiled by one of the students on the day after. Quoted references to Venas Garaba are from Packer, 1994, p. 183. The account of a brief postkidnap meeting between Goodall and Barbara Smuts, including quotations, is from "Kidnap Girl," 1975. The Reuters news report describing the positions of the U.S. embassy and the Tanzanian government was dated May 28. The quotation attributed to Ambassador Carter is from "Humane Diplomat," 1975. The *Los Angeles Times* account describing Mr. Hunter as "furious" comes from "Zaire Patrol," 1975. My source for Kissinger's reassignment of Ambassador Carter is Shannon, 1975.

37. A NEW NORMAL (1975–1980)

Packer, 1994, is the source for Craig Packer's quoted comments about Hilali Matama (p. 166) and Apollinaire Sindimwo (p. 158). My extended descriptions of the field staff's composition, training, and responsibilities, including the occasional quotations, are from Goodall, 1986, pp. 601–8. The quotation about Honey Bee's response to her dying mother is from Goodall and Berman, 1999, p. 118. The additional quotations ("kidnapping and its aftermath" and "dark side") are from Goodall and Berman, 1999, p. 117. Goodall's "written recollection" of the fall semester at Stanford can be found in Goodall and Berman, 1999, with the quotations from pp. 104 and 106. The Stanford alumni magazine article is Aaronstam, 1998, with the quotation from p. 78. The fourth *National Geographic* article is Goodall, 1979. Background information on Obote and Amin is from "Idi Amin" and "Uganda's Milton Obote." The story of Derek Bryceson's final months relies on Goodall's letters combined with the account in *Reason for Hope* (Goodall and Berman, 1999). The physician's exact words ("Take a taxi") are recalled in the latter, p. 156; other quotations from *Reason* can be found on pp. 158 and 159.

38. PICKING UP THE PIECES (1980–1986)

The population dynamics article was Goodall, 1983. The quotation from *Reason for Hope* (Goodall and Berman, 1999) is on p. 169.

39. WELL-BEING IN A CAGE (1986–1991)

Much of this chapter, including quotations, is based on chapters 10 and 11 of Peterson and Goodall, 1993, especially pp. 215–29 and 262–83. Other sources include Jane Goodall Institute newsletters during this period as well as progress reports prepared by Geza Teleki for the CCCC. Roger Fouts's account of his and Goodall's visit to Sema, including the quotations, is from Fouts and Mills, 1997, pp. 318–20. Quotations in the *New York Times Magazine* article are from Goodall, 1987, pp. 108, 109. Figures for annual funding for animal research in the U.S. are from Rowan, 1984, p. 21. The estimated number of chimps in U.S. labs (1,800) is based on my own research; see Peterson and Goodall, 1993, p. 250; estimates for other animal groups are from Rowan, 1984, p. 71. The conclusions of the December 1987 workshop are paraphrased and quoted from an appendix statement in Goodall and Peterson, 1993, pp. 314–19. Fouts and Mills, 1997, p. 324, is my source for Fouts's comment about being "branded." The article "Appropriate Conditions for Maintenance of Chimpanzees" is Prince et al., 1989. Both James Mahoney and Jan Moor-Jankowski submitted to interviews for an earlier book (Peterson and Goodall, 1993) that were useful for this one, but Mahoney's account has been supplemented by reference to Mahoney, 1998. The account of Jane Goodall's ill-fated visit to LEMSIP on May 9, 1988, is summarized from several sources, including newsletters, personal letters, and interviews. Goodall's final quoted comments about John Landon are taken from Goodall and Peterson, 1993, p. 277; John Landon's final quoted comments about his new laboratory are from Miller, 1995, p. 127.

40. ORPHANS, CHILDREN, AND SANCTUARIES (1986–1995)

Much of the material for this chapter comes from newsletters privately produced for JGI (US) and JGI (UK) memberships. The story of Spindle's adoption of little Mel also includes material, taken in paraphrase and quotes, from Goodall, 1990, p. 202. The quotation referring to Prof's special care of Pax is from Goodall, 1990, p. 198, and the quotation referring to Gigi is from the same source, p. 204. The story of Charlotte Uhlenbroek in Burundi, including quotations, relies on Peterson, 2003 (1995), pp. 97, 98; and the story of orphans in Bujumbura and the quoted comments of Mimi O'Brien are from the same source, pp. 94, 95. Madame Jamart's story, told in Pointe-Noire, also comes from that source, pp. 222–30. The quoted remark of Max Pitcher is from Peterson and Goodall, 1993, p. 305, as are Goodall's quoted comments about the Brazzaville city zoo and the story of Grégoire (pp. 294, 295) and the story of Little Jay found in the Kinshasa market (pp. 73, 74). The account of the founding of Roots & Shoots comes from a review of several sources, including early Roots & Shoots newsletters and a 2005 interview with Jane Goodall.

41. CIRCUMNAVIGATIONS (1996–2000)

The opening summary description of a "typical seven-week stretch in North America," is paraphrased from Goodall and Berman, 1999, p. xiii. That source is also the origin of several quotations in this chapter, including "People . . . are always asking" (pp. xiv, xv); "Had I known" (p. 280); on the interior of Notre Dame (p. xi); "How could I believe" and "the spiritual power" (pp. xi, xii); "major impact," "in tune with," "only humans had minds," "dark," and "strong disposition" (pp. 72–76); "Thus while it seemed" (134); "increasingly less aggressive" (p. 187); "indomitable human spirit" (p. 233); and, regarding Mr. H, "I tell people" (p. 249).

42. MESSAGES (2000–2003)

This chapter uses material appearing in several JGI and Roots & Shoots newsletters as well as the following. Goodall's bid to ring the opening bell on Wall Street is from "Did She Say," 2001. The summary of a declining U.S. economy is from Kadlec, 2001, and Lacayo, 2001, with the quotations from the latter, p. 26. The discussion of climate change and the U.S. withdrawal from Kyoto refers to material in Lemonick, 2001; Thompson, 2001; and Kluger, 2001. Quammen, 2003, provides the story, including quotations, of Goodall's trip to the Goualougo. Annan, 2002, summarizes the plan for the Johannesburg summit, while "Give Environment," 2002, provides the quoted remarks of the children's summit leaders. The description of Colin Powell's presentation and debate, including quotations, relies on Barringer, 2003; and Powell's retrospective assessment, quoted, is from "Powell Calls," 2005.

43. WOMAN LEAPING FORWARD (2003–2004)

JGI and Roots & Shoots newsletters and other comparable JGI publications provide much of the background, but the brief discussion of the Central African bush-meat crisis is largely based on Peterson, 2003, with the quotations from pp. 130–32. The Goodall quotation regarding the bush-meat crisis and the Ebola epidemic comes from Quammen, 2003, p. 103.

Works Cited

Aaronstam, Brian C. 1998. "Out of Africa." *Stanford Magazine* (July/Aug.): 76–80.

Addley, Esther. 2003. "The Ascent of One Woman." *Manchester Guardian*, Apr. 3.

"Africa Cradled Birth of Western Civilisation, Say U.S. Visitors." 1955. *Sunday Mail*, July 10.

Annan, Kofi. 2002. "Beyond the Horizon." *Time* (Aug. 26): A18–A19.

Baerends, Gerard P. 1991. "Early Ethology: Growing from Dutch Roots." In *The Tinbergen Legacy*. Ed. by M. S. Dawkins, T. R. Halliday, and R. Dawkins. London: Chapman and Hall: 1–17.

Barringer, Felicity. 2003. "Envoys Abandon Scripts on Iraq and Bring Emotion to U.N. Floor." *New York Times*, Feb. 15: A1, A9.

Baumgartel, Walter. 1976. *Up Among the Mountain Gorillas*. New York: Hawthorne.

Beatty, Harry. 1951. "A Note on the Behavior of the Chimpanzee." *Journal of Mammalogy* 32, 1: 118.

Beck, Benjamin B., et al., eds. 2001. *Great Apes and Humans: The Ethics of Coexistence*. Washington, D.C.: Smithsonian Institution.

Billings, Molly. 1997/1998. "Donald Kennedy and the Evolution of Human Biology." *Human Biology Newsletter* 5, 3: 1ff.

Bingham, Harold C. 1932. *Gorillas in a Native Habitat*. Washington, D.C.: Carnegie Institution.

Blum, Deborah. 2002. *Love at Goon Park: Harry Harlow and the Science of Affection*. Cambridge, Mass.: Perseus.

Boddy, Bill. 1995. *Brooklands Giants: Brave Men and Their Great Cars*. Sparkford, Eng.: Haynes.

Borgeson, Griffith, and Eugene Jaderquist. 1955. *Sports and Classic Cars*. New York: Bonanza.

Brooklands. 1985. Weybridge, Eng.: Brooklands Museum.

Bryan, C.D.B. 1994 (1987). *The National Geographic Society: 100 Years of Adventure and Discovery*. New York: Harry N. Abrams.

Burton, Richard F. 1995 (1860). *The Lake Regions of Central Africa*. New York: Dover.

Carmichael, Leonard. 1963. "Unique Scientific Record, Says Smithsonian's Secretary." *National Geographic* (Aug.): 274.

Carpenter, Clarence R. 1934. "A Field Study of the Behavior and Social Relations of Howling Monkeys (*Alouatta palliata*)." *Comparative Psychology Monographs* 10, 48: 1–168.

"Chimpanzee Born at the Zoo." 1935. *Times*, Feb. 16: 12.

"Chimps Instead of Spock." 1970. *Time* (Nov. 30): 51.

Cochran, Charles B. 1929. *The Secrets of a Showman*. London: Heinemann.

Cole, Sonia. 1975. *Leakey's Luck: The Life of Louis Seymour Bazett Leakey, 1903–1972*. New York: Harcourt Brace Jovanovich.

DeVore, Irven. 1965. "Preface." In *Primate Behavior: Field Studies of Monkeys and Apes*. Ed. by Irven DeVore. New York: Holt, Rinehart and Winston: vii–x.

"Did She Say Primate or Prime Rate?" 2001. *New York Times*, Feb. 4: sec. 3, p. 2.

Dunlop, Becky Norton. 1989. "Endangered and Threatened Wildlife and Plants, Proposed Endangered Status for Chimpanzee and Pygmy Chimpanzee, Proposed Rule." *Federal Register*, Feb. 24: 8152–57.

Feather, Adrian, and Brian Joscelyne. 1973. "The Memoirs of Mort Goodall: Part I, The Pre-War Years." *AM Magazine*: 35–43.

Ferrell, Robert H., ed. 1984. *The Twentieth Century: An Almanac*. New York: World Almanac.

Forty, George. 1994. *Frontline Dorset: A County at War, 1939–45*. Tiverton, Eng.: Dorset.

Fossey, Dian. 1983. *Gorillas in the Mist*. Boston: Houghton Mifflin.

Fouts, Roger, and Stephen Tukel Mills. 1997. *Next of Kin: What Chimpanzees Have Taught Me About Who We Are*. New York: William Morrow.

Galdikas, Biruté M. F. 1995. *Reflections of Eden: My Years with the Orangutans of Borneo*. Boston: Little, Brown.

Gathorne-Hardy, Jonathan. 1973. *The Unnatural History of the Nanny*. New York: Dial.

"Give Environment a Chance, Children Tell World Leaders." 2002. *Times*, Sept. 3: 12.

Goodall, Jane. 1991. "Robert Hinde in Africa." In *The Development and Integration of Behaviour: Essays in Honour of Robert Hinde*. Ed. by Patrick Bateson. Cambridge, Eng.: Cambridge University Press: 467–70.

———. 1990. *Through a Window: My Thirty Years with the Chimpanzees of Gombe*. Boston: Houghton Mifflin.

———. 1988. *My Life with the Chimpanzees.* New York: Simon and Schuster.

———. 1987. "A Plea for the Chimps." *New York Times Magazine,* May 17: 108ff.

———. 1986. *The Chimpanzees of Gombe: Patterns of Behavior.* Cambridge, Mass.: Harvard/Belknap.

———. 1983. "Population Dynamics During a 15-Year Period in One Community of Free-living Chimpanzees in the Gombe National Park, Tanzania." *Zeitschrift fuer Tierpsychologie* 61, 1: 1–60.

———. 1979. "Life and Death at Gombe." *National Geographic* (May): 593–621.

———. 1971. *In the Shadow of Man.* Boston: Houghton Mifflin.

———. 1967. *My Friends the Wild Chimpanzees.* Washington, D.C.: National Geographic Society.

———. 1965. "New Discoveries Among Africa's Chimpanzees." *National Geographic* (Dec.): 802–31.

———. 1964. "Tool-Using and Aimed Throwing in a Community of Free-living Chimpanzees." *Nature* 201: 1264–66.

———. 1963a. "Feeding Behaviour of Wild Chimpanzees: A Preliminary Report." In *The Primates. Symposia of the Zoological Society of London* 10 (Aug.): 39–47.

———. 1963b. "My Life Among Wild Chimpanzees." *National Geographic* (Aug.): 272–308.

———. 1962. "Nest Building Behavior in the Free-Ranging Chimpanzee." In *Annals of the New York Academy of Sciences* 102, 2: 455–67.

Goodall, Jane, and Marc Bekoff. 2002. *The Ten Trusts: What We Must Do to Care for the Animals We Love.* New York: Harper.

Goodall, Jane, and Phillip Berman. 1999. *Reason for Hope: A Spiritual Journey.* New York: Warner.

Goodall, Vanne, 1975. "Introduction." In *The Quest for Man.* Ed. by Vanne Goodall. New York: Praeger: 7–9.

Grand, Theodore I. 1999. "Sherry Washburn and the Revolution in Functional Anatomy. In *The New Physical Anthropology: Science, Humanism, and Critical Reflection.* Ed. by Shirley C. Strum, Donald G. Linburg, and David Hamburg. Upper Saddle River, N.J.: Prentice Hall: 228–36.

Graves, Charles. n.d. *The Cochran Story.* London: W. H. Allen.

Green, Timothy. 1970. *The Adventurers: Four Profiles of Contemporary Travelers.* London: Michael Joseph.

Hamburg, David A. 1999. "Introduction." In *The New Physical Anthropology: Science, Humanism, and Critical Reflection.* Ed. by Shirley C. Strum, Donald G. Linburg, and David Hamburg. Upper Saddle River, N.J.: Prentice Hall: xiii–xiv.

Harris, C. J., and Brian D. Ingpen. 1994. *Mailships of the Union-Castle Line.* Cape Town, S.A.: Fernwood.

Heaton, Tom. 1989. *In Teleki's Footsteps: A Walk Across East Africa.* London: Macmillan.

Herne, Brian. 1999. *White Hunters: The Golden Age of African Safaris.* New York: Henry Holt.

Hinde, Robert A. 2000. "Some Reflections on Primatology at Cambridge and the Science Studies Debate." In *Primate Encounters: Models of Science, Gender, and Society.* Ed. by Shirley C. Strum and Linda Marie Fedigan. Chicago: University of Chicago Press: 104–15.

———. 1991. "From Animals to Humans." In *The Tinbergen Legacy.* Ed. by M. S. Dawkins, T. R. Halliday, and R. Dawkins. London: Chapman and Hall: 31–39.

———. 1982. *Ethology: Its Nature and Relations with Other Sciences.* Oxford, Eng.: Oxford University Press.

"Humane Diplomat." 1975. *New York Times,* Aug. 14: 30.

Hunter, Inman, and Alan Archer. 1992. *Aston Martin, 1913–1947.* London: Osprey.

"Idi Amin." n.d. Heroes and Killers of the 20th Century. www.moreorless. au.com/killers.amin.html.

Inskipp, Tim, and Sue Wells. 1979. *International Trade in Wildlife.* London: Earthscan.

Jolly, Alison. 2000. "The Bad Old Days of Primatology?" In *Primate Encounters: Models of Science, Gender, and Society.* Ed. by Shirley C. Strum and Linda Marie Fedigan. Chicago: University of Chicago Press: 71–84.

"Julius K. Nyerere." 2004 (1994). Historic World Leaders; Gale Research. Reproduced in Biography Resource Center, Farmington Hills, Mich.: Thompson Gale. galenet.galegroup.com/servlet/BioRC.

Kadlec, Daniel. 2001. "How to Navigate the Storm." *Time,* Jan. 8: 23–25.

Kano, Takayoshi. 1992. *The Last Ape: Pygmy Chimpanzee Behavior and Ecology.* Stanford, Calif.: Stanford University Press.

Kellogg, Winthrop N., and Luella A. Kellogg. 1967 (1933). *The Ape and the Child: A Study of Environmental Influence upon Early Behavior.* New York: Hafner.

"Kidnap Girl Brings '$1 Million Ransom Demand.'" 1975. *Times,* May 26: 1.

Kluger, Jeffrey. 2001. "A Climate of Despair." *Time* (Apr. 9): 30–38.

Köhler, Wolfgang. 1925. *The Mentality of Apes.* London: Routledge and Kegan Paul.

Kortlandt, Adriaan. 1999. "An Ecosystem Approach to Ape and Human Evolution (and Some Truisms for Primatologists)." Circulated lecture text.

———. 1998. "Some Comments on American Teaching Programs in Primatology and Evolutionary Anthropology." Circulated preliminary draft. Mar. 10.

———. 1994. "The True History of the Rift Hypothesis of African Ape-Hominid Divergence." Circulated letter.

————. 1993. "Spirits Dressed in Furs?" In *The Great Ape Project: Equality Beyond Humanity*. Ed. by Paola Cavalieri and Peter Singer. New York: St. Martin's Press: 137–44.

————. 1991. "Open Letter to All Field Workers in Chimpanzee Research." Circulated letter.

————. 1986. "Statement." Circulated letter.

————. 1962. "Chimpanzees in the Wild." *Scientific American* 206, 5: 128–38.

Krebs, John R. 1991. "Animal Communication: Ideas Derived from Tinbergen's Activities." In *The Tinbergen Legacy*. Ed. by M. S. Dawkins, T. R. Halliday, and R. Dawkins. London: Chapman and Hall: 60–74.

Kruuk, Hans. 1968. "Hyenas: The Hunters Nobody Knows." *National Geographic* (July): 44–57.

Lacayo, Richard. 2001. "Is a Tax Cut the Right Remedy?" *Time* (Jan. 8): 26, 27.

Lapping, Brian. 1985. *End of Empire*. New York: St. Martin's.

Leakey, L.S.B. 1966 (1937). *White African: An Early Autobiography*. Cambridge, Mass.: Schenkman.

————. 1960. "The Origin of the Genus Homo." In *Evolution After Darwin*, vol. 2: *The Evolution of Man*. Ed. by Sol Tax. Chicago: University of Chicago Press: 17–32.

————. 1959. "A New Fossil Skull from Olduvai." *Nature* (Aug. 15): 419–93.

Leakey, Mary. 1984. *Disclosing the Past*. London: Weidenfeld and Nicolson.

Lemonick, Michael D. 2001. "Life in the Greenhouse." *Time* (Apr. 9): 24–29.

Letts, Quentin. n.d. *Daily Telegraph*.

Lewis, Julia. 1994. "The Queen's Secretarial College." *Jobs and Careers Weekly*, Aug. 5.

Lofting, Hugh. 1988 (1920). *The Story of Doctor Dolittle*. New York: Bantam Doubleday Dell.

Lorenz, Konrad. 1982 (1981). *The Foundations of Ethology: The Principal Ideas and Discoveries in Animal Behavior*. New York: Simon and Schuster.

MacDonald, Malcolm. 1969. *People and Places: Random Reminiscences of the Rt. Hon. Malcolm MacDonald*. London: Collins.

Mack, David, and Ardith Eudey. 1984. "A Review of the U.S. Primate Trade." In *The International Primate Trade*, vol. 1. Ed. by David Mack and Russell Mittermeier. Washington, D.C.: TRAFFIC (U.S.A.): 91–136.

Mahoney, James. 1998. *Saving Molly: A Research Veterinarian's Choices*. Chapel Hill, N.C.: Algonquin.

Merfield, Fred, and Harry Miller. 1956. *Gorillas Were My Neighbours*. London: Longmans, Green.

Miller, Peter. 1995. "Jane Goodall." *National Geographic* (Dec.): 102–28.

Morrell, Virginia. 1995. *Ancestral Passions: The Leakey Family and the Quest for Humankind's Beginnings*. New York: Simon and Schuster.

Morris, Desmond, ed. 1967. *Primate Ethology*. Chicago: Aldine.

Morris-Goodall, Vanne. 1967. *Beyond the Rain Forest*. London: Collins.

Murray, Iain. 1994. "Fergie's Former Ladies College Helps to Find Jobs for the Boys." *Daily Express*, Aug. 9.

Nisbett, Alec. 1976. *Konrad Lorenz*. New York: Harcourt Brace Jovanovich.

Nishida, Toshisada. 1990. "A Quarter Century of Research in the Mahale Mountains: An Overview." In *The Chimpanzees of the Mahale Mountains: Sexual and Life History Strategies*. Toyko: University of Tokyo Press: 3–35.

———. 1989. "Research at Mahale." In *Understanding Chimpanzees*. Ed. by Linda A. Marquardt and Paul G. Heltne. Cambridge, Mass.: Harvard University Press: 66–67.

Nissen, Henry W. 1931. "A Field Study of the Chimpanzee." *Comparative Psychology Monographs* 8, 1–121.

"Old Flo, the Matriarch of Gombe, Is Dead." 1972. *Sunday Times*, Oct. 1: 9.

Osborn, Rosalie M. 1963. "Observations on the Behaviour of the Mountain Gorilla." In *The Primates. Symposia of the Zoological Society of London* 10 (Aug.): 29–37.

Packer, Craig. 1994. *Into Africa*. Chicago: University of Chicago Press.

Peterson, Dale. 2003 (1995). *Chimpanzee Travels: On and Off the Road in Africa*. Athens: University of Georgia Press.

———. 2003. *Eating Apes*. Berkeley: University of California Press.

Peyton, John. 2001. *Solly Zuckerman: A Scientist Out of the Ordinary*. London: John Murray.

"Powell Calls His U.N. Speech a Lasting Blot on His Record." 2005. *New York Times*, Sept. 9: A10.

Prince, Alfred M., et al. 1988. "Chimpanzees and AIDS Research." *Nature* (June 9): 513.

———. 1987. "Appropriate Conditions for Maintenance of Chimpanzees in Studies with Blood-Borne Viruses: An Epidemiologic and Psychological Perspective." *Journal of Medical Primatology* 18: 27–42.

Quammen, David. 2003. "New Hope in Goualougo, Congo." *National Geographic* (Apr.): 90–103.

Reader, John. 1988. *Africa: A Biography of the Continent*. New York: Knopf.

Reynolds, Vernon. 1965. *Budongo: An African Forest and Its Chimpanzees*. Garden City, N.Y.: Natural History Press.

Reynolds, Vernon, and Frances Reynolds. 1965. "Chimpanzees of the Budongo Forest." In *Primate Behavior: Field Studies of Monkeys and Apes*. Ed. by Irven DeVore. New York: Holt, Rinehart and Winston: 368–424.

Rhodes, Richard, 1973. "Goodbye to Darkest Africa." *Playboy* (Nov.): 142ff.

Riss, David, and Curt Busse. 1977. "Fifty Day Observation of a Free-ranging Adult Male Chimpanzee." *Folia Primatologica* 28: 283–97.

Rowan, Andrew N. 1984. *Of Mice, Models, and Men: A Critical Evaluation of Animal Research*. Albany: SUNY Press.

Rowell, Thelma. 2000. "A Few Peculiar Primates." In *Primate Encounters: Mod-*

els of Science, Gender, and Society. Ed. by Shirley C. Strum and Linda Marie Fedigan. Chicago: University of Chicago Press: 57–70.

Schaden, Herman. 1966. "Baroness to Tell Chimp Story." *Evening Star,* Feb. 17: B2ff.

Schaller, George B. 1964. *The Year of the Gorilla.* Chicago: University of Chicago Press.

Shannon, Don. 1975. "Kissinger Fires Envoy Who Dealt with Zaire Kidnappers." *Los Angeles Times,* Aug. 16.

Smith, Mary G. 1993. "A History of Research." In *The Great Apes: Between Two Worlds.* Washington, D.C.: National Geographic Society: 22–41.

Sparks, John. 1982. *The Discovery of Animal Behavior.* Boston: Little, Brown.

The Spirit of Wartime: Memories of the Way We Were. 1995. London: Orbis.

Strum, Shirley C., and Linda M. Fedigan. 2000. "Changing Views of Primate Society: A Situated North American View." In *Primate Encounters: Models of Science, Gender, and Society.* Ed. by Shirley C. Strum and Linda Marie Fedigan. Chicago: University of Chicago Press: 3–49.

Sussman, Robert L. 2000. "Piltdown Man: The Father of American Field Primatology." In *Primate Encounters: Models of Science, Gender, and Society.* Ed. by Shirley C. Strum and Linda Marie Fedigan. Chicago: University of Chicago Press: 85–103.

Takasaki, Hiroyuki. 2000. "Traditions in the Kyoto School of Field Primatology in Japan." In *Primate Encounters: Models of Science, Gender, and Society.* Ed. by Shirley C. Strum and Linda Marie Fedigan. Chicago: University of Chicago Press: 151–64.

Taylor, A.J.P. 1975. *The Second World War: An Illustrated History.* London: Penguin.

Thompson, Dick. 2001. "Will Bush Turn Green?" *Time* (Mar. 12): 7.

Thorpe, John G. 1980. *The Playing Cards of the Worshipful Company of Makers of Playing Cards.* 5th ed. London: Stanley Gibbons.

Tinbergen, Nikolaas. 1991. "Some Personal Remarks." In *The Development and Integration of Behaviour: Essays in Honour of Robert Hinde.* Ed. by Patrick Bateson. Cambridge, Eng.: Cambridge University Press: 463–64.

"Uganda's Milton Obote." n.d. wiwi.essortment.com/ugandamiltonob_rhiw.htm.

Van Hooff, Jan A.R.A.M. 2000. "Primate Ethology and Socioecology in the Netherlands." In *Primate Encounters: Models of Science, Gender, and Society.* Ed. by Shirley C. Strum and Linda Marie Fedigan. Chicago: University of Chicago Press: 116–37.

van Lawick-Goodall, Hugo, and Jane van Lawick-Goodall. 1971. *Innocent Killers.* Boston: Houghton Mifflin.

van Lawick-Goodall, Jane. 1968. "Tool-using Bird: Egpytian Vulture Opens Ostrich Eggs." *National Geographic* (May): 630–41.

van Lawick-Goodall, Jane, and Hugo van Lawick. 1966. "Use of Tools by the Egyptian Vulture, *Neophron percnopterus." Nature* 212 (Dec. 24): 1468–69.

von Frisch, Karl. 1967. *The Dance Language and Orientation of Bees*. Cambridge, Mass.: Harvard/Belknap.

Wagner, Michele. 1996. "Nature in the Mind in Nineteenth- and Early Twentieth-Century Buha, Tanzania." In *Custodians of the Land: Ecology and Culture in the History of Tanzania*. Ed. by Gregory Maddox, James L. Giblin, and Isaria N. Kimambo. Athens: Ohio University Press: 175–99.

Washburn, Sherwood L. 1999a (1951). "The Analysis of Primate Evolution with Particular Reference to the Origin of Man." In *The New Physical Anthropology: Science, Humanism, and Critical Reflection*. Ed. by Shirley C. Strum, Donald G. Linburg, and David Hamburg. Upper Saddle River, N.J.: Prentice Hall: 7–17.

———. 1999b (1951). "The New Physical Anthropology." In *The New Physical Anthropology: Science, Humanism, and Critical Reflection*. Ed. by Shirley C. Strum, Donald G. Linburg, and David Hamburg. Upper Saddle River, N.J.: Prentice Hall: 1–5.

Weiner, J. S. 1959. "The Toolmaker's Skull from Olduvai." Sunday *Times*, Oct. 11.

Wernick, Robert. 1977. *Blitzkrieg*. Chicago: Time-Life.

Wilson, Michael L., and Richard W. Wrangham. 2003. "Intergroup Relations in Chimpanzees." *Annual Review of Anthropology* 32: 363–92.

Yerkes, Robert M. 1925. *Almost Human*. New York: Century.

———. 1916. "Provisions for the Study of Monkeys and Apes." *Science* 43, 1193: 231–34.

"Zaire Patrol Boat Blocks Rescue of 3 Students." 1975. *Los Angeles Times*, June 26: 17.

Ziegler, Philip. 1995. *London at War, 1939–1945*. London: Sinclair-Stevenson.

Zihlman, Adrienne. 1999. "Fashions and Models in Human Evolution: Contributions of Sherwood Washburn." In *The New Physical Anthropology: Science, Humanism, and Critical Reflection*. Ed. by Shirley C. Strum, Donald G. Linburg, and David Hamburg. Upper Saddle River, N.J.: Prentice Hall: 151–61.

Zuckerman, Solly. 1981 (1932). *The Social Life of Monkeys and Apes*. London: Routledge and Kegan Paul.

———. 1978. *From Apes to Warlords*. New York: Harper and Row.

———. 1962. "Concluding Remarks." In *The Primates. Symposia of the Zoological Society of London* 10 (Aug.): 119–23.

Acknowledgments

I was very fortunate, ten years ago, to begin writing a biography about a living person who is remarkably generous and unmanipulative, and thus I will start by acknowledging my deep gratitude to Jane Goodall, who always gave unquestioning access and perfect license. Her family as well—especially Olwen (Olly) Joseph, Margaret Myfanwe (Vanne) Joseph Goodall, and Judith Goodall Waters—were a biographer's dream. They welcomed me whenever I hoped, answered all questions, and asked none in return. The aunt cheered me up with whisky and funny stories. The mother supplied what seemed like an endless discovery, more and more and more letters from her daughter. The sister consented to inconvenient interviews and odd requests and gave me the keys to several filing cabinets. I am also grateful to several other family members—including Jane Goodall's son, Hugo (Grub) van Lawick-Goodall; her father, Mortimer Morris-Goodall; her first husband, Baron Hugo van Lawick; and her nieces, Emma and Pip Waters—for consenting kindly to the prodding and prying of interviews. My thanks go as well to Michael Goodall, a member of the larger Goodall clan, who generously lent me his work in progress on the family history.

Jane Goodall's nanny, Nancy Sowden Rillstone, and her childhood best friend, Sally Cary Pugh, should both be considered virtual family members, and I thank them too for their many hours spent remembering the past. Sally, with amazing generosity, gave up her personal cache of letters, a two-decade correspondence with Red Admiral that started in the mid-1940s.

Three other good friends of Jane Goodall's from the earlier years have honored that friendship by contributing written and spoken remembrances, and I must express deep appreciation to Margaret Arthur McCloy, Marie-Claude Mange Erskine, and Brian Herne. I am also particularly indebted to Jean Nitzsche, the sister of Ruth Davis, for allowing me to make use of Ruth's letters home and their mother's journal; and to David Riss and Emilie Bergmann-Riss for their special openness and the gift of personal memories, letters, and photographs.

Thanks in addition go to Anthony Collins, Carrie Hunter, Marietha Kibasa-Lohay, Mark Leighton, Patrick McGinnis, Anne Pusey, Gerald Rilling, Geza Teleki, Bill Wallauer, and Richard Wrangham for significant impressions of life in the old days at the Gombe Stream Research Centre—and a second thanks to Gerald Rilling, who also donated his herpetological expertise and access to books on East African culture and history via his important and very useful East African history and ecology book service, eafricbk@ix.netcom.com.

I am grateful to David Hamburg and Robert Hinde for helping fill in background about the scientific dimensions of the Gombe work; and likewise I acknowledge Irven DeVore, Biruté Galdikas, Michael Huffmann, Alison Jolly, Takayoshi Kano, Adriaan Kortlandt, Desmond Morris, Toshisada Nishida, George Schaller, and Richard Wrangham for offering further information about Goodall, Gombe, and primatology's anthropological, ethological, psychological, and zoological roots. Information about the status of chimpanzees in laboratories and other forms of captivity is significantly based on the information offered by several other experts, including Milton April, Jorg Eichberg, Roger Fouts, John Landon, James Mahoney, Shirley McGreal, Jan Moor-Jankowski, Alfred Prince, and Duane Rumbaugh. Mary Griswold Smith and Neva Folk, formerly of the National Geographic Society, both contributed information, memories, and letters; Neva also opened up the Jane Goodall and Hugo van Lawick files kept in that organization's archives. Other professional and archival contributions are thanks to Gideon Matwale and Mohemed Isahakia of the National Museums of Kenya and Joan Travis of the L.S.B. Leakey Foundation—and to James Whyman of the Aston Martin Owners Club, Richard Hermann of DoAll and the Wilkie Foundation, Mary Margetts of the Motor Cycling Club, Anne Tomson of Newnham College at Cambridge University, and Corinne Bickford, Lucy Napper, and Sara Wareing of the Queen's Business and Secretarial College.

Several members of the Jane Goodall Institute staff, both paid and volunteer, periodically fulfilled my often irritating requests for just one more document. In this context, Mary Lewis deserves a multipage appreciation all to herself, since she has served during the past several years as my single most reliable (and cheerful) contact with the institute and its resources and with Jane Goodall herself. Other JGI staff members who deserve special acknowledgment include Christina Ellis, Nona Gandelman, Jennifer

Gresham, Dilys MacKinnon, and Mary Paris. My researcher in London, Rachel Kennedy, proved to be exceptionally skilled in tracking down obscure facts and details, and Valerie Rohy did the same in the United States.

Additional information, altogether a wealth of essential facts and details, came from a host of volunteer informants, including Petal Allen, Karl and Kathy Ammann, David Anstey, Rick Asselta, Selena Bush, Teresa Caldwell, Janis Carter, Susan Cary Featherstone, Timothy Green, Richard Hermann, Cathryn Hilker, Aliette Jamart, Mrisho Mpambije Kagoha, Dennis Kane, Paul Kase, Jumanne Kikwale, Michael Latham, Jonathan Leakey, Richard Leakey, Franklin Loew, Kenneth Love, Mark Maglio, Michael and Jenny Mannion, Maureen Marshall, Eve Mitchell, Michael Neugebauer, Betty Pitman, Richard Rhodes, Kay Schaller, John Scherlis, David and Sheila Siddle, Kay Turner, Charlotte Uhlenbroek, Joy Upton, Fiona Vernon, Vivian Wheeler, Robert Young, and Philip Ziegler.

All that information still required some assembly, of course, and for that my editors, agent, friends, and family were critical. My editor, Harry Foster, showed exceptional patience, as did manuscript editors Liz Duvall and Peg Anderson. I am grateful as well for the support and wise counsel of my agent, Peter Matson, of Sterling Lord Literistic. For their important and regular contributions to my mental health during the writing, I should thank my friends David and Martha Reier. But finally, for their logistical and emotional support, I must acknowledge and thank the three people who are really at the center of any book I might imagine I could write: Wyn Kelley and Britt and Bayne Peterson.

Index

IN THE SHADOW OF MAN

"One of history's most impressive field studies" — *Time*

IN THIS GROUNDBREAKING BESTSELLER, Goodall recounts the remarkable discoveries she made in her first ten years of studying chimpanzees at Gombe Stream Reserve. With an introduction by Stephen Jay Gould and a postscript by Goodall. ISBN 978-0-618-05676-7

THROUGH A WINDOW

My Thirty Years with the Chimpanzees of Gombe

"A humbling and exalting book." — *Washington Post*

PERHAPS THE BEST BOOK EVER WRITTEN about animal behavior, *Through a Window* is the dramatic account of three decades in the life of a community, of birth and death, sex and love, power and war. ISBN 978-0-618-05677-4

AFRICA IN MY BLOOD

An Autobiography in Letters, The Early Years

"A fitting tribute to the woman who first made science friendly." — *Biography*

THIS EXTRAORDINARY SELF-PORTRAIT in letters and commentary, edited by Dale Peterson, tells the story of how a girl who loved animals became one of the greatest scientists of the twentieth century. ISBN 978-0-618-12735-1

BEYOND INNOCENCE

An Autobiography in Letters, The Later Years

"[Goodall] has become one of the most famous people on earth." — *USA Today*

THE SECOND VOLUME of Goodall's autobiography in letters tells of some of her greatest triumphs, her deepest tragedies, and the events that changed her from a rather private observer to a public crusader. Edited by Dale Peterson. ISBN 978-0-618-25734-8